7th EDITION
DAILY CELEBRITY ALMANAC
BY BOB BARRY

B&B PUBLISHING

B&B PUBLISHING, INC.
P.O. Box 96
Walworth, WI 53184

Researcher
   Bob Barry

Assistant Researcher
   Nancy McLaughlan

Editors
   Lisa Turner
   Katy O'Shea

Photo Researcher
   Margie Benson

Production Manager
   Katy O'Shea

Computer specialist
   Brian Bork

Production Assistant
   Kim VanVoorhees

Cover art
   Jay Martin

Contributing Writer
   Mike Alley

This book is dedicated to:
   Nancy, Rob, Heidi, and Mom for their love and support. They knew what it took to complete this book!

Special thanks to:
   the dedicated Radio-TV personalities, trivia buffs, and friends for encouragement.

Published by: B&B Publishing, Inc.
                     P.O. Box 96
                     Walworth, WI 53184

ISBN 1-880190-51-6

ISSN 1041-9616

7TH EDITION
DAILY CELEBRITY ALMANAC

TABLE OF CONTENTS

Michael Jackson • Janet Jackson • Wynonna Judd
Jon Bon Jovi • Tony Bennett • The Seinfeld Cast
Willem Dafoe • Marilyn Monroe • Jason Priestly
Luke Perry • David Letterman • Jane Pauley
Shaquille O'Neal • Stone Phillips

1995 at a Glance

JANUARY

Sun	Mon	Tue	Wed	Thu	Fri	Sat
1	2	3	4	5	6	7
8	9	10	11	12	13	14
15	16	17	18	19	20	21
22	23	24	25	26	27	28
29	30	31				

FEBRUARY

Sun	Mon	Tue	Wed	Thu	Fri	Sat
			1	2	3	4
5	6	7	8	9	10	11
12	13	14	15	16	17	18
19	20	21	22	23	24	25
26	27	28				

MARCH

Sun	Mon	Tue	Wed	Thu	Fri	Sat
			1	2	3	4
5	6	7	8	9	10	11
12	13	14	15	16	17	18
19	20	21	22	23	24	25
26	27	28	29	30	31	

APRIL

Sun	Mon	Tue	Wed	Thu	Fri	Sat
						1
2	3	4	5	6	7	8
9	10	11	12	13	14	15
16	17	18	19	20	21	22
23	24	25	26	27	28	29
30						

MAY

Sun	Mon	Tue	Wed	Thu	Fri	Sat
	1	2	3	4	5	6
7	8	9	10	11	12	13
14	15	16	17	18	19	20
21	22	23	24	25	26	27
28	29	30	31			

JUNE

Sun	Mon	Tue	Wed	Thu	Fri	Sat
				1	2	3
4	5	6	7	8	9	10
11	12	13	14	15	16	17
18	19	20	21	22	23	24
25	26	27	28	29	30	

JULY

Sun	Mon	Tue	Wed	Thu	Fri	Sat
						1
2	3	4	5	6	7	8
9	10	11	12	13	14	15
16	17	18	19	20	21	22
23	24	25	26	27	28	29
30	31					

AUGUST

Sun	Mon	Tue	Wed	Thu	Fri	Sat
		1	2	3	4	5
6	7	8	9	10	11	12
13	14	15	16	17	18	19
20	21	22	23	24	25	26
27	28	29	30	31		

SEPTEMBER

Sun	Mon	Tue	Wed	Thu	Fri	Sat
					1	2
3	4	5	6	7	8	9
10	11	12	13	14	15	16
17	18	19	20	21	22	23
24	25	26	27	28	29	30

OCTOBER

Sun	Mon	Tue	Wed	Thu	Fri	Sat
1	2	3	4	5	6	7
8	9	10	11	12	13	14
15	16	17	18	19	20	21
22	23	24	25	26	27	28
29	30	31				

NOVEMBER

Sun	Mon	Tue	Wed	Thu	Fri	Sat
			1	2	3	4
5	6	7	8	9	10	11
12	13	14	15	16	17	18
19	20	21	22	23	24	25
26	27	28	29	30		

DECEMBER

Sun	Mon	Tue	Wed	Thu	Fri	Sat
					1	2
3	4	5	6	7	8	9
10	11	12	13	14	15	16
17	18	19	20	21	22	23
24	25	26	27	28	29	30
31						

1996 at a Glance

JANUARY

Sun	Mon	Tue	Wed	Thu	Fri	Sat
	1	2	3	4	5	6
7	8	9	10	11	12	13
14	15	16	17	18	19	20
21	22	23	24	25	26	27
28	29	30	31			

FEBRUARY

Sun	Mon	Tue	Wed	Thu	Fri	Sat
				1	2	3
4	5	6	7	8	9	10
11	12	13	14	15	16	17
18	19	20	21	22	23	24
25	26	27	28	29		

MARCH

Sun	Mon	Tue	Wed	Thu	Fri	Sat
					1	2
3	4	5	6	7	8	9
10	11	12	13	14	15	16
17	18	19	20	21	22	23
24	25	26	27	28	29	30
31						

APRIL

Sun	Mon	Tue	Wed	Thu	Fri	Sat
	1	2	3	4	5	6
7	8	9	10	11	12	13
14	15	16	17	18	19	20
21	22	23	24	25	26	27
28	29	30				

MAY

Sun	Mon	Tue	Wed	Thu	Fri	Sat
			1	2	3	4
5	6	7	8	9	10	11
12	13	14	15	16	17	18
19	20	21	22	23	24	25
26	27	28	29	30	31	

JUNE

Sun	Mon	Tue	Wed	Thu	Fri	Sat
						1
2	3	4	5	6	7	8
9	10	11	12	13	14	15
16	17	18	19	20	21	22
23	24	25	26	27	28	29
30						

JULY

Sun	Mon	Tue	Wed	Thu	Fri	Sat
	1	2	3	4	5	6
7	8	9	10	11	12	13
14	15	16	17	18	19	20
21	22	23	24	25	26	27
28	29	30	31			

AUGUST

Sun	Mon	Tue	Wed	Thu	Fri	Sat
				1	2	3
4	5	6	7	8	9	10
11	12	13	14	15	16	17
18	19	20	21	22	23	24
25	26	27	28	29	30	31

SEPTEMBER

Sun	Mon	Tue	Wed	Thu	Fri	Sat
1	2	3	4	5	6	7
8	9	10	11	12	13	14
15	16	17	18	19	20	21
22	23	24	25	26	27	28
29	30					

OCTOBER

Sun	Mon	Tue	Wed	Thu	Fri	Sat
		1	2	3	4	5
6	7	8	9	10	11	12
13	14	15	16	17	18	19
20	21	22	23	24	25	26
27	28	29	30	31		

NOVEMBER

Sun	Mon	Tue	Wed	Thu	Fri	Sat
					1	2
3	4	5	6	7	8	9
10	11	12	13	14	15	16
17	18	19	20	21	22	23
24	25	26	27	28	29	30

DECEMBER

Sun	Mon	Tue	Wed	Thu	Fri	Sat
1	2	3	4	5	6	7
8	9	10	11	12	13	14
15	16	17	18	19	20	21
22	23	24	25	26	27	28
29	30	31				

1997 at a Glance

JANUARY

Sun	Mon	Tue	Wed	Thu	Fri	Sat
			1	2	3	4
5	6	7	8	9	10	11
12	13	14	15	16	17	18
19	20	21	22	23	24	25
26	27	28	29	30	31	

FEBRUARY

Sun	Mon	Tue	Wed	Thu	Fri	Sat
						1
2	3	4	5	6	7	8
9	10	11	12	13	14	15
16	17	18	19	20	21	22
23	24	25	26	27	28	

MARCH

Sun	Mon	Tue	Wed	Thu	Fri	Sat
						1
2	3	4	5	6	7	8
9	10	11	12	13	14	15
16	17	18	19	20	21	22
23	24	25	26	27	28	29
30	31					

APRIL

Sun	Mon	Tue	Wed	Thu	Fri	Sat
		1	2	3	4	5
6	7	8	9	10	11	12
13	14	15	16	17	18	19
20	21	22	23	24	25	26
27	28	29	30			

MAY

Sun	Mon	Tue	Wed	Thu	Fri	Sat
				1	2	3
4	5	6	7	8	9	10
11	12	13	14	15	16	17
18	19	20	21	22	23	24
25	26	27	28	29	30	31

JUNE

Sun	Mon	Tue	Wed	Thu	Fri	Sat
1	2	3	4	5	6	7
8	9	10	11	12	13	14
15	16	17	18	19	20	21
22	23	24	25	26	27	28
29	30					

JULY

Sun	Mon	Tue	Wed	Thu	Fri	Sat
		1	2	3	4	5
6	7	8	9	10	11	12
13	14	15	16	17	18	19
20	21	22	23	24	25	26
27	28	29	30	31		

AUGUST

Sun	Mon	Tue	Wed	Thu	Fri	Sat
					1	2
3	4	5	6	7	8	9
10	11	12	13	14	15	16
17	18	19	20	21	22	23
24	25	26	27	28	29	30
31						

SEPTEMBER

Sun	Mon	Tue	Wed	Thu	Fri	Sat
	1	2	3	4	5	6
7	8	9	10	11	12	13
14	15	16	17	18	19	20
21	22	23	24	25	26	27
28	29	30				

OCTOBER

Sun	Mon	Tue	Wed	Thu	Fri	Sat
			1	2	3	4
5	6	7	8	9	10	11
12	13	14	15	16	17	18
19	20	21	22	23	24	25
26	27	28	29	30	31	

NOVEMBER

Sun	Mon	Tue	Wed	Thu	Fri	Sat
						1
2	3	4	5	6	7	8
9	10	11	12	13	14	15
16	17	18	19	20	21	22
23	24	25	26	27	28	29
30						

DECEMBER

Sun	Mon	Tue	Wed	Thu	Fri	Sat
	1	2	3	4	5	6
7	8	9	10	11	12	13
14	15	16	17	18	19	20
21	22	23	24	25	26	27
28	29	30	31			

JANUARY MEMORIES

10 YEARS AGO

1985

POPULAR SONGS
"Like a Virgin" by Madonna

"I Want To Know What Love Is"
by Foreigner

MOVIES
Back To the Future
starring Michael J. Fox and Christopher Lloyd. A teen travels back in time to 1955.

Cocoon
starring Don Ameche, Maureen Stapleton, Brian Dennehy, and Gwen Verdon. Sci-fi comedy directed by Ron Howard.

TV SHOWS
"Code Name: Foxfire"
starring Joanna Cassidy as Elizabeth "Foxfire" Towne, a former CIA agent.

"Sara"
starring Brenda Vaccaro as a young schoolteacher in Independence, CO.

BOOKS
The Accidental Tourist by Anne Tyler

1986

POPULAR SONGS
"Say You Say Me" by Lionel Richie

"That's What Friends Are For" by Dionne Warwick and Friends

MOVIES
Little Shop of Horrors
starring Rick Moranis, Ellen Greene, Steve Martin, Vincent Gardenia, John Candy, and Bill Murray. Remake of 1960 classic.

The Morning After
starring Jane Fonda as an actress on the descent. Co-stars, Jeff Bridges and Raul Julia.

TV SHOWS
"You Again?"
comedy with Jack Klugman and John Stamos as father and son.

"Sidekicks"
police drama starring Gil Gerard and his grandson, Ernie Reyes, Jr.

BOOKS
A Perfect Spy by John le Carre

1987

POPULAR SONGS
"Shake You Down" by Gregory Abbott

"At This Moment" by Billy Vera & The Beaters

MOVIES
Moonstruck
starring Cher, Nicholas Cage, Danny Aiello and Olympia Dukakis. A woman falls in love with her fiance's brother.

Broadcast News
starring William Hurt and Holly Hunter. A behind the scenes look at TV network news.

TV SHOWS
"21 Jump Street"
starring Johnny Depp, Peter DeLuise, and Holly Robinson as young police officers.

"The Slap Maxwell Story"
starring Dabney Coleman as a sportwriter for a second-rate newspaper.

BOOKS
Presumed Innocent by Scott Turow

SPECIAL DAYS

JANUARY	1995	1996	1997
National Pizza Week	Jan. 8-14	Jan. 14-20	Jan. 12-18
Man Watchers Week	Jan. 8-14	Jan. 14-20	Jan. 12-18
Ice Box Days *(International Falls, MN)*	Jan. 20-29	Jan. 20-29	Jan. 20-29
Clean Off Your Desk Day	Jan. 9	Jan. 8	Jan. 13
Martin Luther King Day	Jan. 16	Jan. 15	Jan. 20
Super Bowl *(Miami, FL)*	Jan. 29		
Super Bowl *(Phoenix, AZ)*		Jan. 28	
Super Bowl *(New Orleans, LA)*			Jan. 26
Full Moon	Jan. 16	Jan. 5	Jan. 23
Blame Someone Else Day	Jan. 13		

25 YEARS AGO

1970

POPULAR SONGS
"Raindrops Keep Falling On My Head" by B.J. Thomas

"I Want You Back" by The Jackson 5

MOVIES
Ryan's Daughter
starring Sara Miles, Robert Mitchum, John Mills, and Christoper Jones. Story of a married woman's desire for a soldier.

I Never Sang For My Father
Gene Hackman and Melvyn Douglas received Oscas nominations for this movie.

TV SHOWS
"Tim Conway Show"
Tim played the head pilot and only pilot for Anywhere, Anytime Airline in this sitcom.

"Nanny and the Professor"
Juliet Mills stars as a nanny from England.

BOOKS
Present at the Creation: My Years in the State Department by Dean Acheson

1971

POPULAR SONGS
"Knock Three Times" by Tony Orlando & Dawn

"Mama's Pearl" by The Jackson 5

MOVIES
Sometimes A Great Notion
Paul Newman, Henry Fonda, Lee Remick, and Michael Sarrazin star in this story about an Oregon logging family.

The Gang That Couldn't Shoot Straight
starring Robert DeNiro in this comeday about a dimwit Mafia family.

TV SHOWS
"All In The Family"
a controversial sitcom with Carroll O'Connor, Jean Stapleton, Sally Struthers, and Rob Reiner.

"The Smith Family"
police drama starring Henry Fonda.

BOOKS   *The Winds of War* by Herman Wouk

1972

POPULAR SONGS
"American Pie Parts I & II" by Don McLean

"Bang A Gong (Get It On)" by T. Rex

MOVIES
Deliverance
starring Burt Reynolds, John Voight, Ned Beatty, and Ronny Cox. Four men take a canoe trip that turns into a nightmare.

Images
Susannah York and Rene Auberjonois star in this film about schizophrenia.

TV SHOWS
"Sanford and Son"
A Norman Lear sitcom starring Redd Foxx and Demond Wilson as Los Angeles junk dealers.

"The Sixth Sense"
Gary Collins stars as a parapsychologist exploring ESP, telepathy, etc.

BOOKS   *The Winds of War* by Herman Wouk

50 YEARS AGO

1945

POPULAR SONGS
"Don't Fence Me In" by Bing Crosby & The Andrew Sisters

"Ac-Cent-Tchu-Ate The Positive" by Johnny Mercer

MOVIES
A Tree Grows In Brooklyn
starring Joan Blondell, Dorothy McGuire, James Dunn, and Lloyd Nolan. The story is based on Betsy Smith's novel.

Anchors Aweigh
Frank Sinatra, Gene Kelly, and Kathryn Grayson in this musical comedy about two sailors on leave.

TV SHOWS
CBS transmitted the first color TV broadcast in history.

BOOKS
Unfinished Business by Stephen Bonsal

1946

POPULAR SONGS
"I Can't Begin To Tell You" by Bing Crosby & Carmen Cavallaro

"Let It Snow! Let It Snow!" by Vaughn Monroe

MOVIES
The Green Years
starring Hume Cronyn, Charles Coburn, Thomas Drake, and Dean Stockwell. An Irish boy goes to live with his grandparents in Scotland.

Henry V
Shakespeare's great story, directed and portrayed by Laurence Olivier.

TV SHOWS
No regularly scheduled TV shows until May of 1946.

BOOKS
Arch of Triumph by Erich Maria Remarque

1947

POPULAR SONGS
"White Christmas" by Bing Crosby

"Huggin'and Chalkin'" by Hoagy Carmichael

MOVIES
Great Expectations
John Mills, Valerie Hobson, Alec Guiness and Jean Simmons star in the Dicken's classic.

Odd Man Out
remake of *The Lost Man* starring James Mason, Robert Newton, and Kathleen Ryan.

TV SHOWS
"The World In Your Home"
weekly documentary.

BOOKS
The Wayward Bus by John Steinbeck

Rock and Roll Hall of Fame

1986
Non Performers
Alan Freed
Sam Phillips
Early Influences
Robert Johnson
Jimmie Rodgers
Jimmy Yancey
Artists
Chuck Berry
James Brown
Ray Charles
Sam Cooke
Fats Domino
The Everly Brothers
Buddy Holly
Jerry Lee Lewis
Elvis Presley
Little Richard
Lifetime Achievement Awards
John Hammond

1987
Non Performers
Leonard Chess
Ahmet Ertegun
Jerry Leiber & Mike Stoller
Jerry Wexler
Early Influences
Louis Jordan
T-Bone Walker
Hank Williams
Artists
The Coasters
Eddie Cochran
Bo Diddley
Aretha Franklin
Marvin Gaye
Bill Haley
B.B. King
Clyde McPhatter
Ricky Nelson
Roy Orbison
Carl Perkins
Smokey Robinson
Big Joe Turner
Muddy Waters
Jackie Wilson

1988
Non Performers
Berry Gordy, Jr.
Early Influences
Woody Guthrie
Leadbelly

Les Paul
Artists
The Beach Boys
The Beatles
The Drifters
Bob Dylan
The Supremes

1989
Non Performers
Phil Spector
Early Influences
The Ink Spots
Bessie Smith
The Soul Stirrers
Artists
Dion
Otis Redding
The Rolling Stones
The Temptations
Stevie Wonder

1990
Non Performers
Gerry Goffin & Carole King
Lamont Dozier, Brian
    Holland & Eddie Holland
Early Influences
Louis Armstrong
Charlie Christian
Ma Rainey
Artists
Hank Ballard
Bobby Darin
The Four Seasons
The Four Tops
The Who
The Kinks
The Platters
Simon & Garfunkel

1991
Non Performers
Dave Bartholomew
Ralph Bass
Early Influences
Howlin' Wolf
Artists
LaVern Baker
The Byrds
John Lee Hooker
The Impressions
Wilson Pickett
Jimmy Reed
Ike and Tina Turner

Lifetime Achievement Awards
Nesuhi Ertegun

1992
Non Performers
Leo Fender
Doc Pomus
Bill Graham
Early Influences
Elmore James
Professor Longhair
Artists
Bobby "Blue" Bland
Booker T. & the MG's
Johnny Cash
The Jimi Hendrix
    Experience
The Isley Brothers
Sam and Dave
The Yardbirds

1993
Non Performers
Dick Clark
Milt Gabler
Early Influences
Dinah Washington
Artists
Ruth Brown
Cream
Creedence Clearwater
    Revival
The Doors
Etta James
Frankie Lymon & the
    Teenagers
Van Morrison
Sly and the Family Stone

1994
Non-Performers
Johnny Otis
Early Influences
Willie Dixon
Artists
The Animals
The Band
Duane Eddy
The Grateful Dead
Elton John
John Lennon
Bob Marley
Rod Stewart

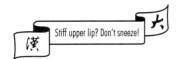

Stiff upper lip? Don't sneeze!

JANUARY 1

New Year's Day

BIRTHDAYS

- **GRANDMASTER FLASH** Rapper. Year/Age: 1995/**37** 1996/**38** 1997/**39**
- **DON NOVELLO** Comedian/actor. (Ashtabula, OH) Best known for his portrayal of Father Guido Sarducci on "Saturday Night Live." In *Godfather III.* Year/Age: 1995/**52** 1996/**53** 1997/**54**
- **BARRY GOLDWATER** Senator. (Phoenix, AZ) (R/AZ) He retired from politics in 1987. Year/Age: 1995/**86** 1996/**87** 1997/**88**
- **J.D. (Jerome David) SALINGER** Novelist. (NYC) Author of *Catcher in the Rye.* Year/Age: 1995/**76** 1996/**77** 1997/**78**
- **COUNTRY JOE McDONALD**. (El Monte, CA) Played at the Monterey Pop Festival in 1967 and Woodstock in 1969. Year/Age: 1995/**53** 1996/**54** 1997/**55**
- **FRANK LANGELLA** Actor. (Bayonne, NJ) Starred in *Dracula* on the stage and the film. In the movie *Dave.* Year/Age: 1995/**55** 1996/**56** 1997/**57**
- **IDI AMIN DADA** Ugandan Leader. Overthrew Milton Obote in 1971. Fled in 1979. Year/Age: 1995/**69** 1996/**70** 1997/**71**
- **ERNEST HOLLINGS** Senator. (Charleston, SC) (D/SC) Year/Age: 1995/**73** 1996/**74** 1997/**75**
- **LAMARR HOYT** Baseball. (Columbia, SC) Year/Age: 1995/**40** 1996/**41** 1997/**42**
- **HANK GREENBERG** Baseball In his 12 years of play, he hit 331 home runs, 1,276 RBI and had a career batting average of .313 Year/Age: 1995/**84** 1996/**85** 1997/**86**
- **E.M. FORSTER** Author. (1879-1970 – England) Wrote *Where Angels Fear to Tread*, *The Longest Journey*, and *A Passage to India.* (Died 7-7-70)
- **CAROLE LANDIS** Actress. (1919-1948 – Fairchild, WI) Film *Four Jills and a Jeep* in 1944 is about her days as a WWII pin-up and troop entertainer. (Died 7-5-48)
- **ELLIOT JANEWAY** Financial writer. (1913-1993 – NYC) He was nicknamed "Calamity Janeway" for his gloomy stock market predictions. (Died 2-8-93)
- **BETSY ROSS** (1752-1836 – Philadelphia, PA) American flagmaker. (Died 1-30-1836)
- **J. EDGAR HOOVER** (1895-1972 – DC) "J" stands for "John." Was director of the F.B.I. from 1924 until his death on 5-2-72.
- **KING KONG** (Hollywood, CA, in 1931) Famous for the *King Kong* movie in 1933 as well as remakes. "King" had romances with Fay Wray and Jessica Lange. In the 1976 remake of the film, two tons of Argentine horse tails were used to make the 40-foot-high, 61/2-ton beast look real. Other famous animals and birds "born" on this day were: WOODY WOODPECKER in 1941 and FRANCIS, THE TALKING MULE in 1950. He was the star of the movie series bearing his name with Donald O'Connor. Chill Wills did his voice. Also MITZI, THE DOLPHIN (1949-1971), star of the Flipper film and TV series, beginning in 1963.
- **PAUL REVERE** (1735-1818 – Boston, MA) American patriot and silversmith, famous for his "midnight ride" on April 18, 1775. He was once court-martialed for cowardice. He commanded a losing effort against the British and lost some ships in the encounter. (Died 5-10-1818)
- **XAVIER CUGAT** Musician. (1900-1990 – Born Francisco De Asia Javier Cugat Mingall de Bru Y Deulofeo in Spain) A band leader who introduced the rumba to millions of Americans. "Coogie" was featured in several movies including Neptune's Daughter with Esther Williams and Red Skelton. He was married and divorced 5 times. His wives included Brooklyn-born Abbe Lane and Spaniard Charo Balza. (Died 10-27-90)
- **ELLEN DeGENERES** Actress/comic (New Orleans, LA) Films include, Coneheads, Wisecrackers and TV series These Friends of Mine. Year/Age: 1995/**37** 1996/**38** 1997/**39**

FACTS FROM THE PAST

1863 **PRESIDENT ABRAHAM LINCOLN** signed the **EMANCIPATION PROCLAMATION** declaring all slaves in southern states were free!

1902 In the **FIRST ROSE BOWL**, the teams were so unevenly matched that the losers conceded in the middle of the fourth quarter. Michigan's Wolverines were ahead 49-0 when the Stanford Indians simply quit.

1960 At San Quentin prison, **JOHNNY CASH** played the first of many free jailhouse shows. **MERLE HAGGARD** was in the audience.

1962 The **BEATLES** were turned away after their first audition for Decca Records. The **TREMELOES** were signed instead.

1968 Daredevil **EVEL KNIEVEL** attempted a motorcycle jump over the fountains at Caesar's Palace in Las Vegas. After hitting the ramp at 100 mph, he went 30 ft. in the air and over the fountains, a leap of 150 ft. He wound up in the hospital after losing control on the down ramp.

1975 H.R. Haldeman, John Ehrlichman, John Mitchell, and Robert Mardian were convicted in the **WATERGATE COVERUP TRIAL.**

1977 Nurse **JACQUELINE MEANS** became the first woman to be ordained a priest in the Episcopal Church at an Indianapolis ceremony.

1992 The Soviet Union died. **MIKHAIL GORBACHEV** and the Russian President **BORIS YELTSIN** announced plans to transfer power to the Commonwealth of Independent States.

1994 Freshman **SCOTT BENTLEY** kicked a 22-yard field goal with 21 seconds remaining to give Florida State an Orange Bowl win over Nebraska and their first national championship.

JANUARY 2

Don't be put off by procrastinators.

BIRTHDAYS

• **ANNA LEE** Actress. TV's "General Hospital." Films include 1937 British version of *King Solomon's Mines* and *In Like Flint*. Year/Age: 1995/**81** 1996/**82** 1997/**83**

• **SIR MICHAEL TIPPETT** Composer. (England) Opera: *The Knot Garden*. Year/Age: 1995/**90** 1996/**91** 1997/**92**

• **VERA ZORINA** Actress. (Germany) Films include *The Goldwyn Follies*. Year/Age: 1995/**78** 1996/**79** 1997/**80**

• **JIM BAKKER** [bay' kur] Troubled TV evangelist (Muskegan, MI) Former leader of the PTL TV Ministry. Resigned after a sex scandal with Jessica Hahn. Sentenced to eight in prison in Jessup, GA. for bilking PTL followers of over $158 million. His thirty year marriage to Tammy Faye ended in a March, 1992 divorce. Currently he is out of prison, living in a halfway house. Year/Age: 1995/**56** 1996/**57** 1997/**58**

• **TIA CARRERE** Actress. Films: *True Lies, Waynes World, and Rising Sun*. Year/Age: 1995/**28** 1996/**29** 1997/**30**

• **DAVID LYNCH** Film director. (Missoula, MT) Directed *The Elephant Man*, *Blue Velvet* and the TV series "Twin Peaks." Year/Age: 1995/**49** 1996/**50** 1997/**51**

• **DANIEL ROSTENKOWSKI** Congressman. (Chicago, IL) (D/IL) Chairman of Ways and Means Committee. Accused of financial improprieties in 1993. Year/Age: 1995/**67** 1996/**68** 1997/**69**

• **JOANNA PACULA** Actress. TV's "General Hospital." Year/Age: 1995/**38** 1996/**39** 1997/**40**

• **JULIUS LaROSA** Singer. (Brooklyn, NY) His biggest hit was "Eh Campari" in 1953. Year/Age: 1995/**65** 1996/**66** 1997/**67**

• **ISAAC ASIMOV** Author. (1920-1992 – Russia) He's called the father of modern science fiction. He wrote more than 300 books. His story *Caves of Steel* was adapted for TV, created ABC's "Probe." (Died 4-6-92)

• **ROGER MILLER** Singer/songwriter (1936-1992 – Ft. Worth, TX) His biggest hit: "King of the Road" in 1965. Roger won eleven Grammy awards in two years, a feat that has not been equaled. Early in his career he fiddled for Minnie Pearl. At one time he was a fireman in Amarillo, TX until he slept through an alarm and was consequently fired. (Died 10-25-92)

FACTS FROM THE PAST

1865 HUGH O'NEILL, a 200-pound street fighter, fought professional boxer Con Orem to a draw, in 185 rounds of bare-knuckle boxing.

1890 ALICE SANGER became the first female on the White House staff, working for President Rutherford B. Hayes.

1900 A company set up by EMILE VERLINGER, the inventor of the Gramophone, began manufacturing seven-inch, single-sided records in Montreal.

1935 BRUNO HAUPTMANN went on trial in Flemington, NJ, on charges of kidnapping and murdering the baby son of aviator Charles Lindbergh. Hauptmann was found guilty and executed.

1936 Against the wishes of its advertising agency, BURMA SHAVE put up roadside signs offering: "Free! Free! A Trip to Mars For 900 Empty Jars." A supermarket manager, Arliss French, collected 900 jars and demanded he get the trip! After months of negotiations, Burma Shave settled with Arliss. They put him in a space suit and bubble helmet and sent him to Moers (pronounced "mars"), a small town near Dusseldorf, Germany.

1939 *Time* Magazine named German Chancellor ADOLF HITLER its Man of the Year.

1960 SENATOR JOHN F. KENNEDY (D/MA) announced he was seeking the Democratic nomination for President.

1965 The New York Jets signed University of Alabama quarterback JOE NAMATH for $400,000. At the time, he was the highest paid player in pro football.

1973 When ROBERT PLANT's car broke down, he and JIMMY PAGE were forced to hitchhike in the rain to that night's show in Sheffield, England.

1974 President RICHARD NIXON signed a bill requiring states to limit highway speeds to 55 mph or lose federal highway funds.

1980 QUEEN ELIZABETH made CLIFF RICHARD a member of the Order of the British Empire.

1980 BERT PARKS lost his job as host of the Miss America Pageant.

1983 The Broadway musical ANNIE closed after 2,377 performances.

1983 Cartoonist GARRY TRUDEAU took a 20-month break and the comic strip "Doonesbury" was gone from newspapers for a while.

1984 Philadelphia's first black mayor, W. WILSON GOODE, was sworn in.

1988 President RONALD REAGAN and Canadian Prime Minister BRIAN MULRONEY [muhl-roo'-nee] signed an agreement to lift trade restrictions between their countries.

1989 Over 200,000 baseball card packs were recalled. An obscenity was discovered painted on Baltimore Orioles' BILL RIPKIN'S bat handle.

1994 DIXY LEE RAY died at the age of 79. She was a controversial spokesperson for nuclear power and Washington state's only woman governor.

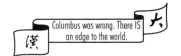

JANUARY 3

BIRTHDAYS

- **DANICA MAE McKELLAR** Actress. (La Jolla, CA) Winnie Cooper on TV's "The Wonder Years." Year/**Age**: 1995/**20** 1996/**21** 1997/**22**
- **MEL GIBSON** Actor. (Peerskill, NY) In the movies *The Road Warrior, Mad Max Beyond Thunderdome* with Tina Turner, *Tequila Sunrise, Brave Heart, Hamlet, Forever Young*, the *Lethal Weapon* films, Air America, *The Man Without a Face* and *Maverick*. He and his family moved to Australia when he was young. He is married to Robyn Moore. Year/**Age**: 1995/**39** 1996/**40** 1997/**41**
- **BETTY FURNESS** (1916-1994) Former actress/consumer reporter. (Born Elizabeth Mary Furness in NYC) She was one of the early female TV spokespersons for Westinghouse, and did live network commercials. (Died 4-2-94)
- **VICTOR BORGE** Pianist/comedian. (Born Borge Rosenbaum, Denmark) He learned to speak English by attending movies. Year/**Age**: 1995/**86** 1996/**87** 1997/**88**
- **STEPHEN STILLS** Singer with Crosby, Stills & Nash and Buffalo Springfield, (Dallas, TX) Biggest hit was "Love the One You're With" in 1971. Year/**Age**: 1995/**50** 1996/**51** 1997/**52**
- **CARLA HILLS** Cabinet member. (Los Angeles, CA) Secretary of HUD from 1975-77. U.S. Trade Representative in the George Bush cabinet. Year/**Age**: 1995/**61** 1996/**62** 1997/**63**
- **MAXINE ANDREWS** Singer. (Minneapolis, MN) One of the Andrews Sisters. Their biggest hit: "Rum and Coca-Cola" in 1945 and "Boogie Woogie Bugle Boy from Company B." Year/**Age**: 1995/**77** 1996/**78** 1997/**79**
- **BOBBY HULL** Hockey star. (Canada) He was an NHL all-star ten times. Year/**Age**: 1995/**56** 1996/**57** 1997/**58**
- **HANK STRAM** Football. He was coach of the K.C. Chiefs and now is a pro football announcer. Year/**Age**: 1995/**72** 1996/**73** 1997/**74**
- **BETTY ROLLIN** Journalist/author. (NYC) Wrote *First You Cry* in 1976. Year/**Age**: 1995/**59** 1996/**60** 1997/**61**

- **EDDIE EGAN** Actor. He's a former NY cop who played Sgt. Bernie Vincent on the TV show "Joe Forrester." Year/**Age**: 1995/**65** 1996/**66** 1997/**67**
- **JOHN STURGES** Film Director. Among his credits are *Bad Day at Black Rock, Gunfight at the OK Corral, The Magnificent Seven* and *The Great Escape*. Year/**Age**: 1995/**85** 1996/**86** 1997/**87**
- **JOHN PAUL JONES** Bassist. (England) His biggest record with LED ZEPPELIN "Whole Lotta Love" in 1969. Year/**Age**: 1995/**49** 1996/**50** 1997/**51**
- **VICTORIA PRINCIPAL** Actress. (Japan) She appeared as Pam on the TV soap "Dallas" and also does hair-care and healthclub commercials. She sued Joan Rivers for giving out her phone number on TV. Year/**Age**: 1995/**51** 1996/**52** 1997/**53**
- **DABNEY COLEMAN** Actor. (Austin, TX) He was in "That Girl" with Marlo Thomas, "Slap Maxwell," the *Beverly Hillbillies* film and *Clifford*. He's remembered for his ruthless boss role in the film *9 to 5* with Dolly Parton. Year/**Age**: 1995/**63** 1996/**64** 1997/**65**
- **ROBERT LOGGIA** Actor. (Staten Island, NY) In 1957 he had the starring role in Walt Disney's *Nine Lives of Elfego Baca* and appeared on the daytime Soap "Secret Storm" until 1974. Year/**Age**: 1995/**65** 1996/**66** 1997/**67**
- **GEORGE MARTIN** Record producer. (England) Producer and recording manager of the BEATLES. His technical knowledge played a part in the development of their recording sounds. He made the arrangements for their first recording audition June 6, 1962, for EMI, Abbey Road Studios, London. Year/**Age**: 1995/**69** 1996/**70** 1997/**71**
- **LEON McAULIFFE** Guitarist. (1917-1988 – Houston, TX) He was one of the first country musicians to use an electric steel guitar. (Died 8-20-88)

FACTS FROM THE PAST

1847 The city of Yerba Buena, CA, changed its name to **SAN FRANCISCO**. (Lucky for **TONY BENNETT**…"I Left My Heart in Yerba Buena" doesn't seem to have the right ring to it.)

1871 **HENRY W. BRADLEY** of Binghamton, NY received a patent for **OLEOMARGARINE**.

1947 **AL HERPIN** died at age 94. He never slept in his entire life. He lived in a shanty outside Trenton, NJ, and many doctors paraded to his home spending days with him trying to catch him asleep and expose him as a fraud. He said his **INSOMNIA** was caused by an injury his mother suffered days before he was born.

1969 30,000 copies of **JOHN LENNON** and **YOKO ONO**'s *Two Virgins* album were confiscated by police at Newark Airport in New Jersey. They said the nude cover photo of John and Yoko was "pornographic."

1970 The **BEATLES** recorded their **LAST SONG** together: "I Me Mine."

1973 **GEORGE STEINBRENNER**, a Florida shipbuilding tycoon, bought the New York Yankees from CBS for $10 million.

1989 The "**ARSENIO HALL SHOW**" premiered. He celebrated his 1,000th show May 14, 1993.

1990 Deposed Panamanian dictator **GENERAL MANUEL ANTONIO NORIEGA** surrendered to U.S. military authorities in Panama.

1993 The **BUFFALO BILLS** pulled off a wild comeback. No team had ever rallied from a 32-point deficit. The Bills, behind by 32 points, came back for an overtime victory over the **HOUSTON OILERS**, 41-38.

1994 **STEVEN SPIELBERG** (*Schindler's List*) won the National Society of Film Critics award in New York City.

JANUARY 4

Remember Rubik's Cube? Why?

BIRTHDAYS

- **DAVID GLASPER** Musician. (England) With BREATHE. Biggest Hit: "Hands To Heaven" in 1988. Year/**Age**: 1995/**29** 1996/**30** 1997/**31**

- **ARTHUR CONLEY** Singer. (Atlanta, GA) Biggest hit: "Sweet Soul Music." The song was originally called "Yeah Man" written by Sam Cooke. Otis Redding discovered Conley in 1965. Year/**Age**: 1995/**49** 1996/**50** 1997/**51**

- **MICHAEL STIPE** Singer. (Decatur, GA) With R.E.M. Hit "Stand" in 1989. Year/**Age**: 1995/**35** 1996/**36** 1997/**37**

- **JANE WYMAN** Actress. (Born Sarah Jane Fulks in St. Joseph, MO) She married then-actor Ronald Reagan in 1940, and they were divorced in 1948. Jane won an Oscar for best actress in *Johnny Belinda* in 1948 and was nominated in 1954 for *Magnificient Obsession* with Rock Hudson. She starred as the vindictive Angela Channing on TV's "Falcon Crest." Year/**Age**: 1995/**81** 1996/**82** 1997/**83**

- **DYAN CANNON** Actress. (Born Samille Diane "Frosty" Friesen in Tacoma, WA) She received an Oscar nomination for supporting actress in *Bob & Carol, Ted & Alice* in 1969 and *Heaven Can Wait* in 1978. She was one of Cary Grant's wives. They had a daughter, Jennifer, the only child of all of his marriages. Year/**Age**: 1995/**58** 1996/**59** 1997/**60**

- **DON SHULA** Stonefaced football coach. (Born Donald Francis Shula in Grand River, OH) He was once with the Baltimore Colts and later Miami Dolphins. With over 300 victories he became the winningest coach in the NFL in 1993. Year/**Age**: 1995/**65** 1996/**66** 1997/**67**

- **PATTY LOVELESS** C&W singer. (Pikesville, KY) Biggest hit: "A Little Bit in Love" in 1988. Year/**Age**: 1995/**38** 1996/**39** 1997/**40**

- **FLOYD PATTERSON** Boxer. (Waco, NC) He was twice heavyweight champion. Year/**Age**: 1995/**60** 1996/**61** 1997/**62**

- **WILLIAM COLBY** Former CIA Director. (St. Paul, MN) Year/**Age**: 1995/**75** 1996/**76** 1997/**77**

- **JEREMY LICHT** Actor. Year/**Age**: 1995/**24** 1996/**25** 1997/**26**

- **BARBARA RUSH** Actress. (Denver, CO) She was married to actor Jeffrey Hunter from 1950-1954, and their son Christopher was born in 1952. She has appeared in movies and on TV. Rush Street and Rush Medical College in Chicago were named for her grandfather, Dr. Benjamin Rush. Year/**Age**: 1995/**68** 1996/**69** 1997/**70**

- **MAUREEN REAGAN** Author. She is the daughter of Jane Wyman & Ronald Reagan. She was 7 years old when her parents separated. She co-wrote a book in 1989 with Dorothy Herrman, *First Father, First Daughter: A Memoir.* Year/**Age**: 1995/**54** 1996/**55** 1997/**56**

- **STERLING HOLLOWAY** Actor. (1905-1992 – Cedartown, GA) Voice of many Disney animals including Winnie the Pooh, and the snake in *The Jungle Book.* Among his films *Gold Diggers of 1933* and *Alice in Wonderland.* (Died 11-22-92)

- **LOUIS BRAILLE** Inventor. (1809-1852 – France) He invented the Braille system for the blind in 1829. He was blind from the age of 3. (Died 3-28-1852)

- **CHARLES SHERWOOD STRATTON** Entertainer. (1838-1883 – known as "Tom Thumb") Born weighing 9 pounds, he grew normally until he was 6 months old. At 5 years he was the same weight and only 2 feet, 1 inch tall. He was a true midget. In 1842, P.T. Barnum signed up the 5-year-old for $3.00 a week, billed him as "General Tom Thumb" and he became an internationally-known entertainer. (Died 7-15-1883)

FACTS FROM THE PAST

1493 **CHRISTOPHER COLUMBUS** returned to Europe with 6 native Americans he believed were Indians. He was under the false impression that he had sailed around the world to India.

1790 **GEORGE WASHINGTON** delivered the first annual presidential message to the nation.

1885 **DR. WILLIAM GRANT** of Davenport, Iowa, performed the first appendectomy operation. The patient was 22-year-old Mary Gartside. She died in 1919 of a different illness.

1887 The **FIRST AROUND-THE-WORLD BICYCLE TRIP** was completed in San Francisco, CA. Two years, 8^1/$_2$ months earlier, Thomas Stevens had left San Francisco and rode his bike to Boston, where he boarded a ship for Europe. He then pedaled across England, France, Germany, Austria—ending in Japan—where he boarded a ship back home. In all he bicycled 13,500 miles.

1954 **ELVIS** recorded a **10-MINUTE DEMO** at Sun Records in Memphis, TN. He paid $4 to record 2 songs for his mother: "My Happiness" and "That's When Your Heartaches Begin."

1957 **GRACE KELLY**'s picture appeared on the cover of the last edition of *Collier's* magazine. She recorded a #1 record in 1956 with Bing Crosby called "True Love" and won a best actress Oscar for *Country Girl* in 1954.

1969 **GEORGE JONES** and **DOLLY PARTON** joined the Grand Ol' Opry.

1974 **PRESIDENT NIXON** refused to turn over audio tape and documents subpoenaed by the Senate Watergate Committee.

1975 **DAVE FORBES**, Boston Bruins HNHL hockey star, cut up North Stars player **HENRY BOUCHA** with his hockey stick. Forbes was arrested and charged with aggravated assault. A possible $5,000 fine and 5 years in jail. He got off when the trial ended in a hung jury.

1982 **BRYANT GUMBEL** and **CHRIS WALLACE** replaced Tom Brokaw on the "Today Show."

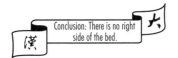

Conclusion: There is no right side of the bed.

JANUARY 5

BIRTHDAYS

- **GEORGE "FUNKY" BROWN** Drummer. (Jersey City, NJ) Best known hit with COOL AND THE GANG, "Celebration" in 1980. Year/**Age:** 1995/**46** 1996/**47** 1997/**48**

- **JEANE DIXON** Astrologer & clairvoyant. (Born Jeane Pinckert, Medford, WI) Year/**Age:** 1995/**77** 1996/**78** 1997/**79**

- **RAISA GORBACHEV** (Russia) Wife of former Soviet leader. Year/**Age:** 1995/**63** 1996/**64** 1997/**65**

- **JOHN Z. DELOREAN** Car maker. (Detroit, MI) Founded DeLorean Motors in 1975. Wrote *On a Clear Day You Can See General Motors.* Year/**Age:** 1995/**70** 1996/**71** 1997/**72**

- **ROBERT DUVALL** Actor. (San Diego, CA) His first film was *To Kill a Mockingbird* in 1963. He has appeared in *True Grit*, *M*A*S*H*, *Godfather I & II*, *The Great Santini*, *Falling Down* and *Geronomo*. He won an Oscar for *Tender Mercies* in 1983 for best actor. Year/**Age:** 1995/**77** 1996/**78** 1997/**79**

- **CHUCK NOLL** Played for the Cleveland Browns. Led the Steelers to four Super Bowl wins. In Football Hall of Fame Year/**Age:** 1995/**63** 1996/**64** 1997/**65**

- **WALTER "FRITZ" MONDALE** Former Vice President. (Born Walter Frederick Mondale in Ceylon, MN) He was the 42nd U.S. Vice President and unsuccessful Democratic presidential candidate in the 1984 election. Named Ambassador to Japan in 1993. Year/**Age:** 1995/**67** 1996/**68** 1997/**69**

- **DIANE KEATON** Actress. (Born Dianne Hall in Los Angeles, CA) She won an Oscar in 1977 for *Annie Hall*. In film *Manhattan Murder Mystery*. She directed the Disney film *Unstrung Heroes*. Year/**Age:** 1995/**49** 1996/**50** 1997/**51**

- **ERNEST GAINES** Author. (Oscar, LA) Known for *The Autobiography of Miss Jane Pittman*, which became an Emmy winning TV film in 1974. Also wrote *In My Father's House*, *A Gathering of Old Men*, and *A Lesson Before Dying*. Year/**Age:** 1995/**62** 1996/**63** 1997/**64**

- **CHRIS STEIN** Guitarist. (Brooklyn, NY) Hits with BLONDIE include: "Rapture," "The Tide Is High," "Call Me," and "Heart of Glass." Year/**Age:** 1995/**45** 1996/**46** 1997/**47**

- **PAMELA SUE MARTIN** Actress. (Westport, CT) She was in the "Nancy Drew Mysteries" and played Blake's devious and outspoken daughter, Fallon Carrington, on the "Dynasty" TV series. Year/**Age:** 1995/**42** 1996/**43** 1997/**44**

- **W.D. (William DeWitt) SNODGRASS** Poet. (Wilkinsburg, PA) Pulitzer Prize winner for *Hearts Needle*. Year/**Age:** 1995/**69** 1996/**70** 1997/**71**

- **ZEBULON PIKE** Mountain Climber. (1779-1813) He discovered Pike's Peak in Colorado.

- **JEANETTE PICCARD** Balloonist (1895-1981 – Chicago, IL) She was one of the first American women to qualify as a free balloon pilot in 1934 and one of the first women to be ordained as an Episcopal priest. (Died 5-17-81)

- **HUGH BRANNUM** Actor. (1910-1987 – Sandwich, IL) For 30 years he played Mr. Green Jeans, a friendly farmer, handyman and unsuccessful inventor on "Captain Kangaroo." (Died 4-19-87)

- **ALVIN AILEY** Dancer/choreographer. (1931-1989 – Rogers, TX) Dance group founder. (Died 12-1-89)

FACTS FROM THE PAST

1914   Henry Ford announced the adoption of a **MINIMUM WAGE** of **$5.00 A DAY**, an 8-hour workday and profit sharing.

1949   In his State of the Union address, **PRESIDENT HARRY S. TRUMAN** labeled his administration the Fair Deal.

1956   **ELVIS PRESLEY** recorded "Heartbreak Hotel" and 4 months later he had a No. 1 hit. The song was written by Mae Axton (Hoyt's mother) and was based on a true story.

1959   Carol Records released the **LAST BUDDY HOLLY RECORD**, "It Doesn't Matter Anymore," before his death. It was written by Paul Anka.

1968   A Boston Federal Grand Jury indicted **DR. BENJAMIN SPOCK** for conspiracy to abet, aid and counsel violators of the draft law.

1970   **JOSEPH YABLONSKI**, an unsuccessful reform candidate for the presidency of the United Mine Workers, was found murdered along with his wife and daughter at their home in Clarksville, PA. Union officials were later convicted for conspiring to have him murdered.

1970   **"ALL MY CHILDREN"** began on ABC. It tackles such touchy topics as wife beating, teen prostitution and alcoholism, gambling, legal abortion, drug abuse, AIDS and interracial couples. One of the stars, Ruth Warrick, the irrepressible Phoebe, played the wife of *Citizen Kane* in the 1941 film.

1972   **PRESIDENT RICHARD NIXON** signed a $5.5 billion-dollar bill to create the Space Shuttle.

1975   **"THE WIZ"** opens on Broadway with an all Black cast.

1981   British police arrested **PETER SUTCLIFFE**, a truck driver later convicted of the **YORKSHIRE RIPPER** killings of 13 women.

1983   President Reagan nominated **ELIZABETH DOLE** to succeed Drew Lewis as secretary of transportation, making her the first woman to head the Transportation Department.

1987   President **RONALD REAGAN** produced the first trillion-dollar budget in U.S. history.

1991   Basketball's **KEVIN BRADSHAW** scored 72 points, breaking Pete Marovich's 69-point record against Alabama on Feb. 7, 1970.

1993   **WESTLEY ALLAN DODD**, admitted child sex killer, was executed in the state of Washington. This was the first legal hanging in the U.S. since 1965.

JANUARY 6
Twelfth Day or Epiphany

Social Ill of the Day: parenthoodlum.

BIRTHDAYS

- **KIM WILSON** Lead singer. (Texas) FABULOUS THUNDER-BIRDS. Biggest hit: "Tuff Enuff" in 1986. Year/Age: 1995/43 1996/44 1997/45

- **MALCOM YOUNG** Musician. (Australia) Plays guitar with AC/DC, a hard rock band. Year/Age: 1995/41 1996/42 1997/43

- **LOUIS LEO HOLTZ** Notre Dame football coach. (East Liverpool, OH) Lou graduated 234th in a class of 278 in high school. His first job was selling cemetery plots. Year/Age: 1995/58 1996/59 1997/60

- **LOU HARRIS** Pollster. (New Haven, CT) Year/Age: 1995/74 1996/75 1997/76

- **JOEY ADAMS** Comedian. (Born Joseph Abramowitz in NYC) He has written a number of books on comedy. Had his own TV show in the '50s. Year/Age: 1995/84 1996/85 1997/86

- **BONNIE FRANKLIN** Actress. (Santa Monica, CA) Star of TV's "One Day at a Time." Appeared on Broadway in *Applause.* Year/Age: 1995/51 1996/52 1997/53

- **EARL SCRUGGS** Bluegrass banjo legend. (Flint Hill, NC) He had a 21-year association with Lester Flatt. They were known as THE FOGGY MOUNTAIN BOYS and best known for their hit, "Foggy Mountain Breakdown" which was played in the movie *Bonnie & Clyde* and was the theme of the "Beverly Hillbillies" TV series. Year/Age: 1995/71 1996/72 1997/73

- **DANNY PINTAURO** Actor. TV's "Who's The Boss." Year/Age: 1995/18 1996/19 1997/20

- **NANCY LOPEZ** Pro golfer. (Torrance, CA) Started her pro career in 1977, and is in the LPGA Hall of Fame. Year/Age: 1995/38 1996/39 1997/40

- **CHARLES HALEY** Football. (Gladys, VA) With the Dallas Cowboys. Year/Age: 1995/31 1996/32 1997/33

- **LOUIS FREEH** FBI director. (Jersey City, NJ) President Clinton selected Freeh on 7-20-93 – one day after he fired William Sessions as the agency's leader. Year/Age: 1995/44 1996/45 1997/46

- **EDGAR DOCTOROW** Novelist. (NYC) Wrote *Ragtime* in 1975. Year/Age: 1995/64 1996/65 1997/66

- **CARY MIDDLECOFF** Pro golfer. (Halls, TX) Year/Age: 1995/74 1996/75 1997/76

- **HOWIE LONG** Football. (Somerville, MA) With the L.A. Raiders. Year/Age: 1995/35 1996/36 1997/37

- **TOM MIX** Cowboy actor. (1880-1940 – Born in Mix Run, PA) Made his first western film in 1910 called *The Feud.* Starred in over 400 westerns. His horse's name was Tony. (Died 10-12-40)

- **VIC TAYBACK** Actor. (1930-1990) He played Mel on the "Alice" TV series. Played supporting roles in films *Bullitt* and *Papillon.* (Died 5-25-90)

- **DANNY THOMAS** Entertainer. (1914-1991 – Born Amos Jacobs in Deerfield, MI) The star of "Make Room for Daddy" from 1953-1964. He was Marlo Thomas's father and Phil Donahue's father-in-law. He founded the St. Jude Children's Hospital in Memphis, TN, and appeared in the movie, *The Jazz Singer* in 1953. (Died 2-6-91)

- **CAPUCINE** [kap-u-seen] Actress. (1933-1990 – Born Germaine Lefebvre in Toulon, France) Starred in *The Pink Panther,* *What's New Pussycat?,* and *A Walk On The Wild Side.* Actor William Holden bequeathed her $50,000. Her death was listed as a suicide jump from her eighth-floor apartment in Switzerland. (Died 3-17-90)

- **JOAN OF ARC** French heroine and saint. (1412-1431)

- **CARL SANDBURG** Poet/author/historian. (1878-1967 – Galesburg, IL) Three-time Pulitzer winner. He died at Flat Rock, NC, on 7-22-67 but is buried under Remembrance Rock in Galesburg.

- **SHERLOCK HOLMES** Fictional detective. ("Born" in 1854 at the farmstead of Mycroft in the North Riding of Yorkshire) Holmes, created by Sir Arthur Conan Doyle, was nearly named Sherrinford.

- **RICHARD II** King of England. (1367-1400) Handsome, blond 6-foot son of the Black Prince. He succeeded to the throne when he was 10 years old. He spent a vast amount of money on clothes and invented the handkerchief.

- **VAN McCOY** Writer/producer/arranger. (1944-1979 – Washington, DC) Biggest hit: "The Hustle" in 1975. He produced the DRIFTERS, SHIRELLES, GLADYS KNIGHT, and the STYLISTICS. (Died 7-6-79)

FACTS FROM THE PAST

1838 SAMUEL MORSE publicly demonstrated his telegraph for the first time in Morristown, NJ.

1945 GEORGE HERBERT WALKER BUSH married Barbara Pierce in Rye, N.Y.

1964 The ROLLING STONES began their first tour with top billing. They opened in London, sharing the stage with the Ronettes and Marty Wilde.

1969 GEORGIA GOVERNOR JIMMY CARTER and members of the Lions Club in Leary, Georgia, saw what they claimed was a UFO. The future president said he would never again make fun of people who say they've seen unidentified objects in the sky.

1975 TED TURNER bought the Atlanta Braves. He paid $11 million.

1982 RUSSELL MCBRIDE was arrested for making barking noises at Sarge, a Sonora, CA, POLICE DOG. The city has an ordinance making it a misdemeanor to tease an on-duty police dog.

1994 NANCY KERRIGAN was attacked in Detroit after practice and hit on her right leg by a man with an iron bar. The assailent was directly linked to Tonya Harding, Nancy's teammate and Olympic rival.

Silence: an imploded roar.

JANUARY 7

BIRTHDAYS

- **KATIE COURIC** NBC Anchorwoman on the "Today Show" and "Now" with Tom Brokow. Year/**Age**: 1995/**38** 1996/**39** 1997/**40**
- **KATHY VALENTINE** Bass player. (Los Angeles, CA) GO-GO's. Biggest hit: "We Got The Beat" in 1982. Year/**Age**: 1995/**36** 1996/**37** 1997/**38**
- **DONNA RICE** Model. Involved with Senator Gary Hart during the 1988 Presidential race. Year/**Age**: 1995/**37** 1996/**38** 1997/**39**
- **JACK GREENE** C&W. (Maryville, TN) Biggest hit: "There Goes My Everything" in 1966. Year/**Age**: 1995/**65** 1996/**66** 1997/**67**
- **NICOLAS CAGE** Actor. (Long Beach, CA) Appeared in films *It Could Happen To You, Raising Arizona, Moonstruck, Wild at Heart, Honeymoon in Vegas, Amos & Andrew*, and *Guarding Tess*. Year/**Age**: 1995/**31** 1996/**32** 1997/**33**
- **KENNY LOGGINS** Singer/songwriter. (Everett, WA) He wrote and performed the title songs to the hit films *Top Gun* and *Footloose*. Biggest hits: "Whenever I Call You Friend" with Stevie Nicks in 1978 and with Jim Messina, "Your Mama Don't Dance" in 1972. At one time he was with BUFFALO SPRINGFIELD and POCO. Year/**Age**: 1995/**47** 1996/**48** 1997/**49**
- **JEAN-PIERRE RAMPAL** Flutist. (France) Year/**Age**: 1995/**73** 1996/**74** 1997/**75**
- **WILLIAM PETER BLATTY** Author. (NYC) He wrote the *Exorcist,* best seller in 1971 with 10 million copies. Year/**Age**: 1995/**67** 1996/**68** 1997/**69**
- **JANN WENNER** *Rolling Stone* publisher. (NYC) Year/**Age**: 1995/**49** 1996/**50** 1997/**51**

- **DANNY WILLIAMS** Singer. (South Africa) Biggest hit in 1964: "White on White." Year/**Age**: 1995/**53** 1996/**54** 1997/**55**
- **PAUL REVERE** Keyboardist of PAUL REVERE AND THE RAIDERS. (Boise, ID) Biggest hit: "Indian Reservation" in 1971. Year/**Age**: 1995/**53** 1996/**54** 1997/**55**
- **ALVIN DARK** Baseball great. (Comanche, OK) He was "Rookie of the Year" with the Braves in 1948. He was traded with Eddie Stanky to the Giants after the 1949 season, and he was shortstop for the Giants in 1951. Year/**Age**: 1995/**73** 1996/**74** 1997/**75**
- **BUTTERFLY McQUEEN** American character actress. (Born Thelma McQueen in Tampa, FL) She appeared in *Gone With the Wind* as the weeping maid, *Cabin in the Sky, Duel in the Sun*, and others. Year/**Age**: 1995/**84** 1996/**85** 1997/**86**
- **VINCENT GARDENIA** Actor. (1922-1992 – Naples, Italy) He was Archie Bunker's neighbor Frank Lorenzo on TV's "All in the Family" and Oscar nominee as Cher's father in *Moonstruck*. (Died 12-9-92)
- **TONY CONIGLIARO** Baseball player. (1945-1990 – Revere, MA) A Boston Red Sox outfielder in the 1960's, he was the youngest player to hit 100 home runs.
- **MILLARD FILLMORE** Former U.S. President. (1800-1874 – Cayuga County, NY) The 13th U.S. President. He succeeded to the presidency upon the death of Zachary Taylor, but did not get the party nomination in 1852. He ran for President in 1856 as a candidate of the "Know-Nothing Party," whose platform demanded that every government employee should be a native-born citizen. (Died 3-8-1874)

FACTS FROM THE PAST

1714 The world's **FIRST TYPEWRITER** was patented by Englishman Henry Mill, who described his invention as "An Artificial Machine or Method for the Impressing or Transcribing of Letters Singly or Progressively one after another, as in Writing, whereby all whatever may be Engrossed in Paper or Parchment so Neat and Exact as not to be distinguished from Print." That machine was never manufactured.

1785 **DR. JOHN JEFFRIES**, a Boston physician, and **JEAN-PIERRE BLANCHARD**, a French aeronaut, crossed the English Channel from Dover to Calais in their balloon. To avoid coming down in the icy waters of the English Channel, the men were forced to throw out all of their ballast, equipment and even their clothing. They finally landed safely in France, stark naked and freezing.

1789 The first presidential election was held in the U.S. Americans voted for electors, who a month later voted to make **GEORGE WASHINGTON** the nation's first president.

1913 **WILLIAM M. BURTON** of Chicago was given a patent on the manufacture of gasoline. His method was used by Standard Oil.

1927 The **GLOBETROTTERS** played their first game in Hinckley, IL.

1953 **PRESIDENT HARRY TRUMAN** announced in his "State of the Union" address that the U.S. had developed a hydrogen bomb.

1962 "The Twist" by **CHUBBY CHECKER** set a record by reaching #1 for the second time (for 21 weeks). Previously, it was #1 on September 13, 1960, for 7 weeks.

1970 Neighboring farmers sued **MAX YASGUR** for $35,000 in damages caused by a little shindig he hosted called **WOODSTOCK.**

1992 Pitchers **ROLLIE FINGERS** and **TOM SEAVER** were elected to the Baseball Hall of Fame. When Reggie Jackson was asked how fast Seaver's pitches were, he said, "Blind people came to the game just to listen to his fastball."

1994 **PRESIDENT CLINTON** prepared to leave for an eight-day tour of Europe a day after his mother Virginia Kelley died at age 70 in Hot Springs, AK.

JANUARY 8

BIRTHDAYS

• **CRISTY LANE** C&W. (Born Eleanor Johnston in Peoria, IL) Biggest hit: "One Day At a Time" in 1980. Year/**Age**: 1995/**55** 1996/**56** 1997/**57**

• **RON MOODY** Actor. (London, England) Fagin in film musical version of *Oliver*. Year/**Age**: 1995/**71** 1996/**72** 1997/**73**

• **YVETTE MIMIEUX** Actress. (Hollywood, CA) She was in the movie *Joy in the Morning* with Richard Chamberlain, and *The Black Hole* in 1979. Year/**Age**: 1995/**54** 1996/**55** 1997/**56**

• **SHIRLEY BASSEY** Singer. (Cardiff, Wales) Her biggest record: "Goldfinger" in 1965 from the James Bond movie of the same name. Year/**Age**: 1995/**58** 1996/**59** 1997/**60**

• **DAVID BOWIE** Singer. (Born David Robert Jones in London, England) Biggest hit: "Fame" in 1975. He married model Iman in 1992, his second marriage. In film *The Man Who Fell to Earth* in 1976. Did "Elephant Man" on Broadway. Year/**Age**: 1995/**48** 1996/**49** 1997/**50**

• **LITTLE ANTHONY** Singer. (Born Anthony Gourdine in Hollywood, CA) Of the IMPERIALS. Their biggest hit: "Tears on My Pillow" in 1958. Year/**Age**: 1995/**54** 1996/**55** 1997/**56**

• **SANDER VANOCUR** CBS newsman. (Cleveland, OH) He's noted for the way he writes. He does mostly radio and some TV. Year/**Age**: 1995/**67** 1996/**68** 1997/**69**

• **EVELYN WOOD** Reading teacher. Year/**Age**: 1995/**86** 1996/**87** 1997/**88**

• **ROBBIE KRIEGER** Rock guitarist. (Los Angeles, CA) He was with The DOORS – popular in the late 1960's. Their biggest hit: "Light My Fire" in 1967. The DOORS got their name from a passage that Jim Morrison read by English poet Aldous Huxley from his 1952 *Doors of Perception*: "There are things that are known and things that are unknown. In between are the doors." Year/**Age**: 1995/**50** 1996/**51** 1997/**52**

• **CHARLES OSGOOD** CBS newsman. (Born Charles Wood in NYC) At one time he worked as an announcer for Bob & Ray. His books include: *Nothing Could Be Finer Than a Crisis That is Minor in the Morning* and TV's CBS "Sunday Morning." Also, radio's "The Osgood File." Year/**Age**: 1995/**62** 1996/**63** 1997/**64**

• **NOLAN MILLER** Designer. (Burkburnett, TX) Famous as a costume designer for "Dynasty" and has outfitted Joan Collins, Liz Taylor, Marlo Thomas, and many others. Year/**Age**: 1995/**60** 1996/**61** 1997/**62**

• **JOSÉ FERRER** Actor. (1912-1992 – Born José Vincente Ferrery Otero y Cintron in Santurce, Puerto Rico) He and Rosemary Clooney were married in 1953 and later divorced. Their son, Gabriel, is married to singer Debby Boone. José won an Oscar in 1950 for best actor in *Cyrano do Bergerac*. (Died 1-27-92)

• **BILL GRAHAM** Rock producer. (1931-1991 – Born Wolfgang Grajonca in Berlin, Germany) He was responsible for the success of many rock acts during the psychedelic era, and promoted many popular concerts at the Fillmore Auditorium in San Francisco and New York. Produced Live Aid Concert in 1986. He was killed in a helicopter crash near Vallejo, CA. (10-25-91)

• **ELVIS PRESLEY** Singer; "King of Rock-n-Roll" (1935-1977 – Tupelo, MS) His first record was on the "Sun" label in 1954: "That's Alright Mama" and "Blue Moon of Kentucky." His two biggest hits: "Don't Be Cruel" in 1956 and "All Shook Up" in 1957. He had 26 top-ten hits. He starred in 33 movies from 1956 to 1972. His Memphis home, Graceland, is a shrine for his many fans. (Died 8-16-77)

FACTS FROM THE PAST

1642 **ASTRONOMER GALILEO** died in Arcetri, Italy.

1815 **GENERAL ANDREW JACKSON** took a little trip down the mighty "Mississip" to defeat the British at the Battle of New Orleans. He hadn't heard that a peace treaty had been signed two weeks earlier. (Johnny Horton had a #1 record of the "Battle of New Orleans" in 1959.)

1959 **CHARLES DE GAULLE** was inaugurated as president of France's Fifth Republic.

1962 **JACK NICKLAUS,** 21 years old, placed 50th in the Los Angeles Open, his first pro appearance, winning $33.33.

1975 **JUDGE JOHN J. SIRICA** ordered the release of Watergate figures John W. Dean III, Herbert W. Kalmbach and Jeb Stuart Magruder from prison.

1985 **REVEREND LAWRENCE JENCO** was kidnapped in Lebanon. He was released after 19 months in captivity.

1988 Arizona **GOVERNOR EVAN MECHAM**, already facing impeachment, was indicted on charges he lied under oath about campaign contributions; he was convicted and removed from office.

1989 **"42ND STREET,"** the second-longest-running musical in Broadway history, closed. Its 3,486 performances were seen by 10 million people in eight years.

1992 **PRESIDENT BUSH** collapsed and vomited while seated at the state dinner at Prime Minister Kiichi Miyazawa's official residence. The president's press secretary called it a normal case of the flu.

1993 **ELVIS PRESLEY STAMPS** went on sale at post offices across the U.S. on what would have been the King's 58th birthday.

1994 **NANCY KERRIGAN** looked on as Tonya Harding skated to her second National Championship. Nancy Kerrigan was unable to compete as a result of the brutal attack on her knee on January 6.

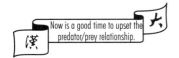

Now is a good time to upset the predator/prey relationship.

JANUARY 9

BIRTHDAYS

- **JIMMY BOYD** Singer. (McComb, MS) Biggest hit: "I Saw Mommy Kissing Santa Claus" in 1952. Year/**Age**: 1995/**55** 1996/**56** 1997/**57**

- **BUSTER POINDEXTER** Singer. (Born David Johansen) The dead taxi-driver in *Scrooged* starring Bill Murray. Year/**Age**: 1995/**45** 1996/**46** 1997/**47**

- **RICHARD MILHOUS NIXON** Former U.S. President. (Born into a Quaker family in Yorba Linda, CA in 1913) In 1952 the California Senator became V.P. for President Eisenhower. In 1968 he was elected the 37th President of the U.S. He eventually negotiated a cease-fire agreement with Vietnam and pulled out the U.S. troops. He visited Moscow and reopened contact with Mainland China. Following the Watergate Scandal he became the first president to resign – on Aug. 9, 1974. (Died 4-22-94.)

- **CRYSTAL GAYLE** Singer. (Born Brenda Gayle Webb in Paintsville, KY) Biggest hit: "Don't It Make My Brown Eyes Blue" in 1977. Her older sister, Loretta Lynn, nicknamed her "Crystal" from the Krystal Hamburger chain in the South. Year/**Age**: 1995/**44** 1996/**45** 1997/**46**

- **JOAN BAEZ** Singer and political activist at Boston University. (Staten Island, NY) Biggest record: "The Night They Drove Old Dixie Down" in 1971. Her autobiography was published in 1987. Year/**Age**: 1995/**54** 1996/**55** 1997/**56**

- **JIMMY PAGE** Lead guitarist. (England) Guitarist for LED ZEPPELIN. Their biggest hit: "Whole Lotta Love" in 1969. Year/**Age**: 1995/**50** 1996/**51** 1997/**52**

- **CARRIE LANE CHAPMAN CATT** Women's rights leader (1859-1947 – Ripon, WI) Founder of the National League of Women Voters in 1919. (Died 3-9-47)

- **BART STARR** Football Hall of Famer. (Montgomery, AL) His full name is Bryan Bartlett Starr. As quarterback, he led the Packers to 5 NFL titles and 2 Super Bowl victories. He is also an ex-Green Bay Packer coach. His son Bret died from a drug overdose in 1988. Year/**Age**: 1995/**61** 1996/**62** 1997/**63**

- **JUDITH KRANTZ** Author. (NYC) Wrote *Scruples, Princess Daisy,* and *Lovers.* Year/**Age**: 1995/**67** 1996/**68** 1997/**69**

- **DICK ENBERG** Sports announcer. (Mt. Clemens, MI) Year/**Age**: 1995/**60** 1996/**61** 1997/**62**

- **BOB DENVER** Actor. (NYC) He co-starred as beatnik Maynard G. Krebs in the TV series "Dobie Gillis" from 1959-1963. From 1964-1967 he starred as the well-meaning but inept "Willy Gilligan" on TV's "Gilligan's Island." Year/**Age**: 1995/**60** 1996/**61** 1997/**62**

- **LEE VAN CLEEF** Actor. (1925-1989 – Somerville, NJ) An American character actor, he appeared in *High Noon, The Man Who Shot Liberty Valance,* and *Chameleon, The Good, The Bad and The Ugly.* (Died 12-18-89.)

- **FERNANDO LAMAS** Actor. (1915-1982 – Argentina) He appeared in musical and comedy films in Hollywood including *Rose Marie, The Girl Who Had Everything* and others. Billy Crystal is now famous for the parody he did of Lamas on "Saturday Night Live"—his famous line: "You look mahhhavolous." Was married to Esther Williams and Arlene Dahl. (Died 10-8-82)

- **GEORGE BALANCHINE** Ballet star. (1904-1983 – Russia) He was considered by many to be the greatest choreographer of the 20th century. His most famous work was in 1936: a musical play called *On Your Toes.* In 1946 he founded the New York City Ballet. (Died 4-30-83.)

FACTS FROM THE PAST

1793 The first successful balloon flight in the U.S. was made by **JEAN-PIERRE-FRANCOIS BLANCHARD** over Philadelphia, PA. The event was watched by President George Washington and other high government officials. The balloon rose to a height of about 5,800 feet and traveled some 15 miles, landing 46 minutes later.

1972 Reclusive billionaire **HOWARD HUGHES** broke his public silence. He talked by telephone from the Bahamas to reporters in Hollywood, exposing a purported autobiography of him by Clifford Irving as a fraud.

1972 **KAREEM ABDUL-JABBAR** scored 39 points as the Milwaukee Bucks ended the Los Angeles Lakers' 33-game winning streak, 120-104.

1973 The **ROLLING STONES** were refused Japanese visas because of a drug bust in 1969. The whole tour was canceled.

1976 C.W. **McCALL**'s recording of "Convoy" hit number one on the country music charts.

1977 **EMMYLOU HARRIS** married **BRIAN AHERN.**

1979 K-Mart Department stores pulled **STEVE MARTIN**'s comedy album *Let's Get Small* off record shelves for being in "bad taste."

1979 **FRANK SINATRA** was paid a million dollars for a single performance to help launch a new resort on Australia's Gold Coast. It was his first performance in that country in 14 years. He had been banned by Australian unions after calling female reporters "hookers" and male reporters "drunks."

1988 V.P. **GEORGE BUSH** denied charges of involvement in the Iran-Contra affair made by rival presidential candidate Robert Dole. Said Bush, "I sensed that we were sending arms, and I sensed that we were trying to get hostages out, but *not* arms for hostages."

1991 Secretary of State **JAMES BAKER** met with Iraq's Foreign Minister, Tariq Aziz, for six hours in an attempt to head off the Mid-East War. The talks in Geneva failed.

1994 **PRESIDENT CLINTON** spoke to the NATO leaders in Brussels, Belgium and was given a saxophone from Dinant, the hometown of creator Adophe Sax.

JANUARY 10

Chainsaws make beautiful music—to a developer.

BIRTHDAYS

• **ROD STEWART** Singer. (Born Roderick David Stewart in London, England) His early influences included Sam Cooke and Bobby Darin. He is a very versatile performer with a disco hit, "Do You Think I'm Sexy?" – the title song to "Legal Eagles," and his biggest hit: "Tonight's the Night" from 1976. He played pro soccer when he was 16. He lasted three weeks. Year/**Age**: 1995/**50** 1996/**51** 1997/**52**

• **FRANK SINATRA JR.** Singer. (Jersey City, NJ) He was the victim of a controversial kidnapping in 1963. Year/**Age**: 1995/**51** 1996/**52** 1997/**53**

• **GISELE MacKENZIE** Singer. (Winnipeg, Canada) Biggest hit: "Hard to Get" in 1955. She was one of the stars of TV's "Your Hit Parade." Year/**Age**: 1995/**68** 1996/**69** 1997/**70**

• **DAVID HOROWITZ** Consumer advocate. Host of "Fight Back" on TV. Year/**Age**: 1995/**56** 1996/**57** 1997/**58**

• **PAT BENATAR** Singer. (Born Patricia Andrzejewski in Long Island, NY) Biggest hit: "Love is a Battlefield" in 1983. Year/**Age**: 1995/**42** 1996/**43** 1997/**44**

• **DONALD FAGEN** Singer. (Passaic, NJ) He was a member of the group STEELY DAN. Their biggest hit: "Rikki Don't Lose That Number" in 1974. Year/**Age**: 1995/**47** 1996/**48** 1997/**49**

• **MARLENE SANDERS** CBS news correspondent. (Cleveland, Ohio) Year/**Age**: 1995/**64** 1996/**65** 1997/**66**

• **WILLIE McCOVEY** Baseball player. (Mobile, AL) One of the few players in the history of baseball to hit over 500 home runs. Year/**Age**: 1995/**57** 1996/**58** 1997/**59**

• **RON GALELLA** Celebrity photographer. (NYC) At one time he was ordered to stay away from Jackie Onassis. Year/**Age**: 1995/**63** 1996/**64** 1997/**65**

• **SHERRILL MILNES** Baritone. (Downers Grove, IL) Debuted in *Faust*, 1965. Year/**Age**: 1995/**60** 1996/**61** 1997/**62**

• **DADDY MACK** Rap singer. (Born Chris Smith in Atlanta, GA) Of the rap duo KRIS KROSS. First hit "Jump" in 1992. Their first album *Totally Krossed Out* sold over 3 million copies. Year/**Age**: 1995/**16** 1996/**17** 1997/**18**

• **WILLIAM TOONEY** Decathlon Champion. (Philadelphia, PA) Year/**Age**: 1995/**56** 1996/**57** 1997/**58**

• **ETHAN ALLEN** Revolutionary War hero. (1738-1789 – Litchfield, CT) (Died 2-11-1789)

• **GEORGE FOREMAN** Fighter. (Marshall, TX) He won the heavyweight championship in 1973 when he kayoed Joe Frazier in the 2nd round in Kingston, Jamaica. He held the title until Oct. 1974, when Ali knocked him out in the 8th round. He retired in 1993 after losing a decision to Tommy Morrison. He was the first lone male cover boy in *Penthouse* magazine's 27-year history. His four sons are all named George. TV sitcom "George." Year/**Age**: 1995/**46** 1996/**47** 1997/**48**

• **BOBBY RAHAL** Race car driver. (Medina, OH) He won the Indy 500 in 1986. Career earnings exceed $12 million. Year/**Age**: 1995/**42** 1996/**43** 1997/**44**

• **PAUL HENREID** Actor. (1908-1992 – Italy) He appeared in *Casablanca* as the Nazi-fighting Resistance leader, Victor Lazlo. Also, lit two cigarettes at once when he comforted Bette Davis in a scene from *Now Voyager* in 1942. His Hollywood film career was hurt by the anti-communist blacklist. (Died 3-21-92)

• **JOHNNIE RAY** Singer. (1927-1990 – Dallas, OR) He's best known for his hit, "Cry" in 1951, which has sold more than 25 million copies since its original release, and the flip side, "Little White Cloud That Cried." Nicknamed "The Prince of Wails," his raw and emotional style was controversial for the early 1950's. He appeared in the 1954 film, *There's No Business Like Show Business*. He wore a hearing aid since he was 14 years old. (Died 2-24-90)

• **RAY BOLGER** Dancer/singer. (1904-1987 – Dorchester, MA) The rubber-legged scarecrow in *The Wizard of Oz*. (Died 1-15-87)

• **JIM CROCE** Singer. (1943-1973 – Philadelphia, PA) His biggest hit was "Bad, Bad, LeRoy Brown" in 1973. He died in a plane crash in Natchitoches [nah'kitosh], LA. The crash occurred while he was flying to a concert in Sherman, TX. His son A.J. is now recording. (Died 9-2-73)

• **SAL MINEO** Actor. (1939-1976 – NYC) He received an Academy Award nomination for supporting actor in *Rebel Without a Cause* in 1955, and in 1964 for *Exodus*. He had one hit record: "Start Movin" in 1957. His last film was *Escape from the Planet of the Apes*. Sal was murdered Feb. 12, 1976, in Los Angeles.

FACTS FROM THE PAST

1870 **JOHN D. ROCKEFELLER** incorporated Standard Oil.

1956 **ELVIS PRESLEY** began his first recording session in Nashville. Among the songs he recorded were "Heartbreak Hotel" and "I Was The One."

1958 "Great Balls of Fire" by **JERRY LEE LEWIS** became the number one song.

1981 The Gilbert & Sullivan Opera **PIRATES OF PENZANCE**, starring **LINDA RONSTADT** and **REX SMITH**, moved to Broadway.

1991 British diplomats pulled out of Iraq and the United Nations evacuated hundreds of employees and their families from Israel as fear of **WAR HEIGHTENED IN THE MIDDLE EAST** after the failed meeting in Geneva the previous day.

1991 **JUDY SWEET** became the first woman to be elected **NCAA** president.

1992 **DENNIS GREEN** was hired by the Minnesota Vikings, becoming the NFL's second black head coach.

1994 **LORENA BOBBITT** went on trial in Manassas, VA. She was accused of cutting off her husband's penis with a kitchen knife.

How would you look with no hair?

JANUARY 11

BIRTHDAYS

- **DARYL DAWKINS** Basketball. (Orlando, FL) He was known for breaking the glass backboards with his overpowering slam-dunks. Year/**Age:** 1995/**38** 1996/**39** 1997/**40**
- **DAVID L. WOLPER** Producer. The mini-series "Roots" in 1976. Year/**Age:** 1995/**67** 1996/**68** 1997/**69**
- **GRANT TINKER** TV Producer. (Stamford, CT) Former NBC Chairman of the Board. Former husband of Mary Tyler Moore. Year/**Age:** 1995/**69** 1996/**70** 1997/**71**
- **ROD TAYLOR** Actor. (Sydney, Australia) He was a middleweight boxer until the 1950's when he switched to acting and came to the U.S. to star in westerns and on TV. Starred in *The Birds* in 1963. Year/**Age:** 1995/**66** 1996/**67** 1997/**68**
- **DON CHERRY** Singing golfer. His biggest hit: "Band of Gold" in 1955. Year/**Age:** 1995/**71** 1996/**72** 1997/**73**
- **JUANITA KREPS** Former Commerce Secretary. (Harlan County, KY) Year/**Age:** 1995/**75** 1996/**76** 1997/**77**
- **NAOMI JUDD** Country singer. (Born Diana Ellen Judd in Ashland, KY) She took her name from the Bible. She and her daughter Wynonna (born Christina) were The JUDDS. They were in the movie *American Graffiti*. Biggest hits: "Why Not Me" and "Have Mercy." Year/**Age:** 1995/**49** 1996/**50** 1997/**51**
- **CLARENCE CLEMONS** Sax player. (Norfolk, VA) Member of BRUCE SPRINGSTEEN'S E STREET BAND. Toured in 1989 with Ringo Starr as part of the ALL-STARR BAND. Year/**Age:** 1995/**53** 1996/**54** 1997/**55**
- **EVA LeGALLIENNE** Actress/director (1899-1991 – London) Appeared in *Prince of Players* in 1954; *The Devil's Disciple* in 1959. (Died 6-3-91)

- **TRACY CAULKINS** Swimmer. (Winona, MN) Won three gold medals in '84 Olympics. Year/**Age:** 1995/**32** 1996/**33** 1997/**34**
- **DENNY GREENE** Entertainer. Of SHA NA NA. Year/**Age:** 1995/**46** 1996/**47** 1997/**48**
- **BEN CRENSHAW** Pro golfer. (Austin, TX) After missing a shot in the 1986 PGA Championship, he threw his club, hitting himself in the head, requiring hospital treatment. Year/**Age:** 1995/**43** 1996/**44** 1997/**45**
- **VICKI PETERSON** Guitarist. (Los Angeles, CA) Lead guitar player for a female quartet, The BANGLES, originally called The BANGS. Biggest hit: "Walk Like An Egyptian" in 1986. Year/**Age:** 1995/**37** 1996/**38** 1997/**39**
- **ALICE PAUL** Activist (1885-1977 – Moorestown, NJ) She founded the Women's Rights Party in 1913. (Died 7-10-77)
- **JOHN MacDONALD** Politician. (1815-1891 – Scotland) First Prime Minister of Canada. (Died 6-6-1891)
- **ALEXANDER HAMILTON** First Sec. of Treasury. (1757-1804 – British West Indies) He helped draft the U.S. Constitution and had been George Washington's Chief of Staff when he was only 20 years old. He was U.S. Treasury Secretary and lent money to a woman because her husband had run off and left her. That's when Alexander and Marie Reynolds began their affair. Her husband returned and blackmailed Hamilton. He died following a duel with Aaron Burr. (Died 7-12-1804)
- **TEX RITTER** Singer. (1907-1975 – Born Woodward Maurice Ritter in Murvaul, TX) He was best known as a country singer, but he appeared in 4 movies and recorded the title song for *High Noon* in 1952. Biggest hit: "I Dreamed Of A Hillbilly Heaven" in 1961. Actor John Ritter is his son. (Died 1-2-75)

FACTS FROM THE PAST

1935   Pioneer aviatrix **AMELIA EARHART** became the first woman to pilot solo from Hawaii to Mainland U.S. She took off from Honolulu, reaching Oakland, CA, in 18¼ hours.

1957   **LLOYD BRIDGES** began his stint as Mike Nelson in the TV series "Sea Hunt."

1963   The forerunner of the "discotheques," the **WHISKEY A-GO-GO** club, opened on Sunset Strip in Los Angeles, CA. The then-unknown **JOHNNY RIVERS** recorded his first hit there live: "Memphis."

1964   **DR. LUTHER TERRY**, the **U.S. SURGEON GENERAL**, issued the first government report saying that smoking was hazardous to one's health.

1984   Owner George Steinbrenner introduced **BILLY MARTIN** for the 3rd time as manager of the N.Y. Yankees, proclaiming the start of a new era. Martin was later fired, hired and fired again!

1984   The **SUPREME COURT** ruled that states have the power to award damages when there are nuclear safety violations, as in the case involving **KAREN SILKWOOD**, the worker who was contaminated with plutonium at a Kerr-McGee plant in Oklahoma.

1984   **MICHAEL JACKSON'S** *Thriller* became the best-selling album of all time, topping the 10-million-copy mark. It broke the previous record set by *Saturday Night Fever*. On the same day, Jackson was nominated for 12 Grammy Awards.

1984   U.S. Army pilot, **CHIEF WARRANT OFFICER JEFFRY SCHWAB**, was killed by the Sandinistas when his helicopter was shot down at the Nicaraguan Honduran boarder.

1989   Surgeon General **C. EVERETT KOOP** said that deaths from smoking were rising, and lung cancer, not breast cancer, had become the leading cause of cancer deaths among women.

1989   **PRESIDENT REAGAN** bade the nation farewell in a nationally broadcast address from the Oval Office.

1994   **MR. BLACKWELL** put Glenn Close at the top of his worst-dressed list. Others on the list were Diana Ross (whom he called "a Martian meter maid, starring in a cancan review"), Julia Roberts, Tanya Tucker and Daryl Hannah.

JANUARY 12

Is there a correct way to belch in public?

BIRTHDAYS

- **TOMMY PUETT** Actor. (Born Ralph T. Puett III) TV's "Life Goes On" and "America's Top Ten." Year/**Age**: 1995/**24** 1996/**25** 1997/**26**

- **DOMINIQUE WILKINS** Basketball. (Paris, France) Atlanta Hawks. Year/**Age**: 1995/**35** 1996/**36** 1997/**37**

- **BOBBY COLOMBY** Drummer. Hits with BLOOD SWEAT & TEARS included: "Spinning Wheel." Year/**Age**: 1995/**51** 1996/**52** 1997/**53**

- **WILLIAM LEE GOLDEN** Country singer. (Brewton, AL) Formerly of the OAK RIDGE BOYS. Year/**Age**: 1995/**56** 1996/**57** 1997/**58**

- **RUSH LIMBAUGH** Talk show host. (Kansas City, KS) Best Sellers *The Way Thigs Ought to Be* and *See I told You So*. He married for the third time of 5/17/94 to a women he met through CompuServe, Marta Fitzgerald. Year/**Age**: 1995/**44** 1996/**45** 1997/**46**

- **HOWARD STERN** Radio shock jock. Year/**Age**: 1995/**41** 1996/**42** 1997/**43**

- **RAY PRICE** Singer. (Perryville, TX) Biggest hit: "For the Good Times" in 1970, which sold over 11 million copies. He still tours and lives on a large ranch in Texarkana, TX. Year/**Age**: 1995/**69** 1996/**70** 1997/**71**

- **BILL MADLOCK** Baseball player for the Cubs and Pirates. (Memphis, TN) He was National League batting leader 3 times. Year/**Age**: 1995/**44** 1996/**45** 1997/**46**

- **RICKY VAN SHELTON** C&W singer. (Grit, VA) Year/**Age**: 1995/**43** 1996/**44** 1997/**45**

- **JAMES FARMER** Civil Rights leader. (Marshall, TX) Year/**Age**: 1995/**75** 1996/**76** 1997/**77**

- **THE AMAZING KRESKIN**. (Born George Kresge in Montclair, NJ) Psychic and magician. He wrote *Use Your Head to Get Ahead*. Year/**Age**: 1995/**60** 1996/**61** 1997/**62**

- **KIRSTIE ALLEY** Actress. (Wichita, KS) Rebecca Howe of "Cheers." She made her film debut in *Star Trek II* as the half-vulcan Lt. Saavic. Married to actor Parker Stevenson. In films *Look Who's Talking* and *Look Who's Talking Now*." Year/**Age**: 1995/**40** 1996/**41** 1997/**42**

- **LUISE RAINER** Actress. (Austria) She won Academy Awards for *The Great Ziegfeld* and *The Good Earth*. Year/**Age**: 1995/**83** 1996/**84** 1997/**85**

- **JOE FRAZIER** Fighter. (Beaufort, SC) Heavyweight champion from 1970-1973. Year/**Age**: 1995/**51** 1996/**52** 1997/**53**

- **PATSY KELLY** Actress. (1910-1981 – Brooklyn, NY) Tony Award winner for *No No Nanette*. (Died 9-24-81)

- **JACK LONDON** American author. (1876-1916 – San Francisco, CA) He gave us such works as *Call of the Wild* and *The Sea Wolf*. (Died 11-22-16)

- **CHARLES PERRAULT** Author. (1628-1703 – Paris, France) The first person to write down some of the most famous folk stories and fairy tales, including *Cinderella*. In the original story Cinderella's slippers were made of fur, but when the story was translated into English, the translator made a mistake. That's how in the English-language version Cinderella came to wear glass slippers. (Died 5-15-1703)

FACTS FROM THE PAST

1910   A couple from China became the **YOUNGEST PARENTS** in history. The dad was 9 and mom was 8 years old.

1932   **HATTIE CARAWAY** was the first woman elected to the U.S. Senate. She was appointed in 1931 to fill the Arkansas seat left vacant by the death of her husband, and then elected in 1932 and re-elected in 1938.

1942   Faithful dog Shep's 5½ year vigil came to an end when he was killed by a train at Fort Benton, MT. Shep began his long wait when the coffin of his master was put on a train at the station and taken away. From then on, Shep watched every train pull in and out and inspected the passengers, hoping to see his master again. His loyalty brought him nationwide fame. Great Northern received a huge amount of mail for Shep, and he became the **FIRST DOG** to have a full-time **PRIVATE SECRETARY**.

1943   Americans gave up hot dogs for "**VICTORY SAUSAGES**" until the end of World War II. They contained a little bit of meat, but mostly consisted of soybean meal. Most Americans agreed they weren't very appetizing.

1966   The TV hit "**BATMAN**" premiered on NBC. It starred **ADAM WEST** and **BURT WARD** with guest appearances by Cesar Romero, Frank Gorshin, and Burgess Meredith.

1971   The situation comedy, "All in the Family," starring **CARROLL O'CONNOR** and **JEAN STAPLETON**, premiered on CBS-TV.

1975   The **PITTSBURGH STEELERS** defeated the Minnesota Vikings 16-6 in **SUPER BOWL IX** to win their first NFL championship.

1981   The TV show "**DYNASTY**" premiered on ABC.

1986   The **SPACE SHUTTLE COLUMBIA** finally blasted off at Cape Canaveral after a record 26 days and 7 delays. Crew members, including the first Hispanic-American in space, Dr. Franklin Chang-Diaz, and U.S. Rep. Bill Nelson of Florida, packed lucky charms and one wore a Groucho Marx mask. (This was the last mission before the *Challenger* tragedy January 28, 1986.)

1987   Anglican Church envoy **TERRY WAITE** arrived in Lebanon on his latest mission to win the release of the hostages. It turned out to be a journey that resulted in his own disappearance.

1989   President-elect Bush named retired Admiral James Watkins Secretary of Energy and former Education Secretary William Bennett to be the first U.S. "Drug Czar."

He who hesitates...um...er...

JANUARY 13

BIRTHDAYS

• **RICHARD MOLL** Actor. (Pasadena, CA) Played Bull on "Night Court," canceled in 1992. Year/**Age:** 1995/**52** 1996/**53** 1997/**54**

• **RIP TAYLOR** Comedian. (Milwaukee, WI)One of the voices in *Tom & Jerry, the Movie*. In *Indecent Proposal*. Year/**Age:** 1995/**61** 1996/**62** 1997/**63**

• **ROBERT STACK** Actor. (Los Angeles, CA) He's probably best known for his portrayal of Eliot Ness in "The Untouchables" TV series from 1959-1963. Nominated for an Oscar in 1956 for *Written on the Wind*. TV series "Unsolved Mysteries." Year/**Age:** 1995/**76** 1996/**77** 1997/**78**

• **PENELOPE ANN MILLER** Actress. She starred in *Carlito's Way* and *The Gun in Betty Lou's Handbag*. Year/**Age:** 1995/**31** 1996/**32** 1997/**33**

• **FRANCES STERNHAGEN** Soap opera actress. On "Love of Life" and "The Secret Storm." She won a Tony award. Year/**Age:** 1995/**65** 1996/**66** 1997/**67**

• **CHARLES NELSON REILLY** Actor. (New York, NY) Actor/game show regular. He directed *The Nerd* and won a Tony for *How to Succeed in Business Without Really Trying*. Year/**Age:** 1995/**64** 1996/**65** 1997/**66**

• **JULIA LOUIS DREYFUS** Actress. Best known as Elaine on *Seinfeld*. Year/**Age:** 1995/**34** 1996/**35** 1997/**36**

• **GWEN VERDON** Actress/dancer. (Los Angeles, CA) Former wife of Bob Fosse. In the film *Cocoon*. She won 4 Tonys including *Damn Yankees* and *Can Can*. Year/**Age:** 1995/**70** 1996/**71** 1997/**72**

• **BRANDON TARTIKOFF** Former NBC-TV Chief. (Long Island, NY) Year/**Age:** 1995/**46** 1996/**47** 1997/**48**

• **FRANK GALLO** Artist. (Toledo, OH) Year/**Age:** 1995/**62** 1996/**63** 1997/**64**

• **ALFRED CARL FULLER** Businessman. (1885-1973 – Nova Scotia) He founded the Fuller Brush Company in 1906 and went into business on his own working on a bench between the furnace and coal bin in his sister's basement. In 1910 he recruited other salesmen. (Died 12-4-73)

• **HORATIO ALGER** Author. (1834-1899 – Revere, MA) The most successful boys-story-writer ever. He wrote one novel in two weeks and wrote a total of 119 books. (Died 7-18-1899)

• **SOPHIE TUCKER** Entertainer. (1884-1966 – Born Sonia Kalish in Russia) Was known as the "last of the red-hot mamas." (Died 2-9-66)

FACTS FROM THE PAST

1863 As a follow-up to another of his inventions, **THOMAS CRAPPER** pioneered the one-piece pedestal flushing toilet. He created the world's first self-raising seat, which worked on a system of counter weights, that left men free to concentrate on the job at hand.

1906 The **FIRST ADVERTISEMENT** for a **RADIO RECEIVER** appeared in *Scientific American*. The Electro Importing Company offered a radio set for $7.50, saying it would work up to one mile.

1929 **WYATT EARP** died at age 80. He survived the famous Gunfight at the OK Corral in Tombstone, AZ, when he was 33 years old. He wrote a book about it that made him a hero.

1957 The Wham-O Company developed the **FIRST FRISBEE.** Truck drivers for Frisbie's Pie Company of Connecticut had shown some Yale students how to toss the pie tins in the air. A representative of the Wham-O Company saw this and came up with the idea of mass-producing the plastic discs.

1966 Robert Weaver became the **FIRST BLACK CABINET MEMBER** when he was appointed secretary of Housing & Urban Development by President Lyndon Johnson.

1979 The **YMCA** filed a libel suit against **VILLAGE PEOPLE** for their "YMCA" single. The suit was later dropped.

1982 An **AIR FLORIDA 737**, taking off in a snowstorm, crashed into the 14th Street bridge in Washington, DC, and fell into the Potomac River, killing 78 people. Many died on impact, others drowned in the freezing water. Five survived. Seven motorists, stuck in traffic on the bridge, also were killed.

1982 Major League home-run leader **HANK AARON** was elected to the Baseball Hall of Fame. He played with the Milwaukee Braves from 1954-1965 and the Milwaukee Brewers from 1975-76. In between, he was with the Atlanta Braves.

1985 **OTTO BUCHER**, at 99 years old, became the oldest person to score a hole-in-one (130 yards) at a golf club in Spain.

1988 Plans to erect a 12-foot-tall statue of **MADONNA** in a bikini in the Italian village of her grandparents were dropped after the local mayor objected.

1989 Warner Bros. released "There's a Tear in My Beer," remixed with **HANK WILLIAMS, JR.**'s vocals for a "duet" with his late father.

1992 The 12-year relationship of **WOODY ALLEN** and **MIA FARROW** came to an end when Farrow found nude pictures of her adopted daughter Soon-Yi on Allen's Fifth Avenue apartment mantel. She was awarded custody of the children in June 1993.

1994 **TONYA HARDING'S BODYGUARD**, Shawn Eric Eckardt and Derrick Brian Smith were arrested and charged with conspiracy in the attack on skater Nancy Kerrigan.

JANUARY 14

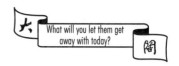

What will you let them get away with today?

BIRTHDAYS

- **FAYE DUNAWAY** Actress. (Born Dorothy Dunaway in Bascom, FL) One of her first films was *Hurry Sundown* in 1967. She won an Oscar in 1976 for *Network*. Starred opposite Warren Beatty in *Bonnie & Clyde*. Portrayed Joan Crawford in *Mommie Dearest*. Appeared in the film *The Temp*. TV's "It Had to Be You." Year/**Age**: 1995/**54** 1996/**55** 1997/**56**

- **JACK JONES** Singer/actor. (Hollywood, CA) His biggest hit was "Wives and Lovers" in 1966 and he also sang the theme song for "Love Boat." Year/**Age**: 1995/**57** 1996/**58** 1997/**59**

- **BILLY WALKER** C&W. (Ralls, TX) His hits include: "Charlie's Shoes" and "Funny How Time Slips Away." Year/**Age**: 1995/**66** 1996/**67** 1997/**68**

- **BILLY JO SPEARS** C&W. (Beaumont, TX) Her hits include: "Blanket On the Ground" and "Mr. Walker It's All Over." Year/**Age**: 1995/**57** 1996/**58** 1997/**59**

- **JULIAN BOND** Georgia Legislator. (Nashville, TN) He once hosted "Saturday Night Live." Year/**Age**: 1995/**55** 1996/**56** 1997/**57**

- **ANDY ROONEY** Humorist/author/TV personality. (Albany, NY) He appears at the end of "60 Minutes" on CBS. Year/**Age**: 1995/**76** 1996/**77** 1997/**78**

- **DAN SCHNEIDER** Actor. TV series "Head of the Class" and "Home Free." Year/**Age**: 1995/**29** 1996/**30** 1997/**31**

- **L.L. COOL J**.Singer/Actor. (Born James Todd Smith in Queens, NY) His stage name is the abbreviation for Ladies Love Cool James. Hits include "I Need Love" in 1987. In the film *Krush Groove*. and *Toys*. Year/**Age**: 1995/**26** 1996/**27** 1997/**28**

- **JASON BATEMAN** Actor. (Rye, NY) TV – "The Hogan Family." Brother of actress Justine Bateman. Year/**Age**: 1995/**26** 1996/**27** 1997/**28**

- **LAWRENCE KASDAN** Screenwriter. (Miami Beach, FL) *The Big Chill* and *The Empire Strikes Back*. Year/**Age**: 1995/**46** 1996/**47** 1997/**48**

- **HAL ROACH, SR.** Silent film producer. (1892-1992 – Elmira, NY) He was associated with "gag" comedies, teaming up with Harold Lloyd in 1916. He later made *Our Gang* and *Laurel & Hardy* films. He produced *Topper* starring Cary Grant and won an Academy Award for *The Music Box*. (Died 11-2-92)

- **TOM TRYON** Actor/author. (1926-1991 – Hartford, CT) Appeared in films: *The Cardinal* and *In Harms Way*. Wrote several bestsellers including *The Other*.

- **GUY WILLIAMS** Actor. (1924-1989 – Born Armand Catalano in NYC) He played Don Diego in *Zorro* in the late 1950's and Professor John Robinson in "Lost in Space" from 1965-1968.

- **WILLIAM BENDIX** Actor. (1906-1964 – NYC) He received an Oscar nomination for supporting actor in 1942 for *Wake Island* and in 1944 for *Lifeboat*. He portrayed The Babe in *The Babe Ruth Story* in 1948 and is probably best known by many for his TV series, "Life of Riley."

- **ALBERT SCHWEITZER** Humanitarian. (1875-1965 – Upper Alsace) He was the son of a Lutheran pastor. An organist, theologian, missionary and philosopher who won the 1952 Nobel Peace Prize. (Died 9-4-65)

- **BENEDICT ARNOLD** Traitor. (1741-1801 – Norwich, CT) On Sept. 25, 1780, he became a revolutionary traitor. For over a year he had been providing the enemy with military intelligence. Only the capture of their go-between, the unfortunate Major Andre, prevented Arnold from delivering West Point to the enemy. (Died 6-14-1801)

FACTS FROM THE PAST

1794 The first successful caesarean section operation was performed by **DR. JESSE BENNETT** of Edom, VA, on his wife. He used no anesthesia during the procedure.

1878 The first private phone call in Europe was made by **QUEEN VICTORIA** from her residence at Osborne House on the Isle of Wight. She could have shouted out the window. The call went next door.

1952 The "Today Show" premiered on NBC. **DAVE GARROWAY** was the host, with newscaster **FRANK BLAIR** assisted by Betsy Palmer. Barbara Walters and Jane Pauley have hosted the "Today" Show the longest – 12 years. The show's first theme song was "Sentimental Journey." Mr. Kokomo replaced the chimp, J. Fred Muggs.

1954 **MARILYN MONROE** married **JOE DIMAGGIO** at San Francisco's City Hall. The marriage lasted for 9 months.

1964 In her first public statement since the assassination of her husband, **JACQUELINE KENNEDY** appeared on television to thank the 800,000 people who had sent her messages of sympathy.

1984 **MADONNA** got her first taste of national exposure singing "Holiday" on American Bandstand.

1989 **PAUL McCARTNEY**'s *Back In The USSR* album was released exclusively in Russia. Bootleg copies sold for as much as $1,000 in the States.

1990 A somber **MARION S. BARRY, JR.**, his political career in smoke, prepared to be arraigned on a federal narcotics charge and then surrendered the day-to-day duties of D.C.'s mayor to the city's chief administrator, Carol B. Thompson.

1993 **DAVID LETTERMAN** left NBC after 11 years and signed a $16 million deal with CBS. Letterman was upset because NBC refused to put him on the "Tonight Show" instead of **JAY LENO**.

1994 As part of **PRESIDENT CLINTON'S** European tour, he delivered a speech to Russian citizens on a broadcast station showing support for Boris Yeltson. The people were disgusted and claimed Clinton did not understand what was going on in their country.

Grandmotherly types are usually bank robbers.

JANUARY 15
Quarterly Estimated Income Tax Due

BIRTHDAYS

- **CHAD LOWE** Actor. (Dayton, OH) Appeared on TV's "Life Goes On." He is the brother of Rob. Film *Nobody's Perfect.* Year/**Age:** 1995/**26** 1996/**27** 1997/**28**

- **LISA LISA** Singer. (Born Lisa Velez in Harlem, NY) With LISA LISA & CULT JAM, hits include "Lost in Emotion" and "Head To Toe." Year/**Age:** 1995/**28** 1996/**29** 1997/**30**

- **MARGARET O'BRIEN** Actress. (Born Angela Maxine O'Brien in Los Angeles, CA) She won a special Oscar in 1944, an honorary miniature statue for "Outstanding Child Actress." Gained fame in *Meet Me In St. Louis.* Year/**Age:** 1995/**58** 1996/**59** 1997/**60**

- **LLOYD BRIDGES** Actor. (San Leandro, CA.) Probably best known for his TV role as skin-diving Mike Nelson on "Sea Hunt." He also appeared in both of the *Airplane* movies, *Blown Away,* and *Honey, I Blew Up the Kid.* Father of actors Jeff and Beau Bridges. In TV's "Heart of the West" with son Beau and movie *Blown Away* with son Jeff. Year/**Age:** 1995/**82** 1996/**83** 1997/**84**

- **EDWARD TELLER** Physicist. (Budapest, Hungary) Father of the Atomic Bomb. Year/**Age:** 1995/**87** 1996/**88** 1997/**89**

- **CHARO** Actress/singer. (Spain) Her full name is Maria Rosana Pilar Martinez Molina Baeza. She supposedly had her age legally changed in 1977 subtracting 10 years. So she should be 10 years older. Year/**Age:** 1995/**44** 1996/**45** 1997/**46**

- **RONNIE VAN ZANT** Lead singer. (1949-1977 – Jacksonville, FL) He was the leader of the group LYNYRD SKYNYRD – Biggest hit: "Sweet Home Alabama." Ronnie was killed, along with members Steve and his sister Cassie Gaines, when their rented single-engine plane crashed in the swamps of Gillsburg, MS. (10-2-77)

- **CARDINAL JOHN O'CONNOR** Archbishop of New York. Year/**Age:** 1995/**74** 1996/**75** 1997/**76**

- **RANDY WHITE** Football Hall of Famer. Played for the Dallas Cowboys from 1975-88. 1104 tackles and 111 sacks. Year/**Age:** 1995/**42** 1996/**43** 1997/**44**.

- **ARISTOTLE ONASSIS** Tycoon. (1906-1975 – Turkey) Greek shipping magnate and husband of Jacqueline Kennedy Onassis. (Died 3-15-75)

- **DR. MARTIN LUTHER KING, JR.** Civil Rights leader. (1929-1968 – Atlanta, GA) King organized the boycott of the Montgomery, Alabama, Transit Co, the Washington March in 1963, and brought about the Civil Rights Act and Voting Rights Act in 1965. He won the Nobel Peace Prize in 1964 and was assassinated in Memphis, Tennessee, in 1968. The third Monday in January is a legal holiday in his honor. He once said "That old law about an eye for an eye leaves everybody blind." (Died 4-4-68)

- **HAL MASON** Advertising Executive. (1917-1986) He created the Pillsbury Dough Boy, Mr. Clean, the Hamm's Bear, and other animated characters. (Died 10-10-86.)

- **GENE KRUPA** Jazz drummer. (1909-1973 – Chicago, IL) Rivaled only by Buddy Rich as the most acclaimed drummer of the Big Band Era. Krupa achieved national fame with Benny Goodman, climaxed by the band's historic Carnegie Hall concert. (Died 10-16-73)

- **GOODMAN ACE** Radio/TV writer/actor/columnist. (1899-1982) He and his wife Jane appeared in, and created, "Easy Aces" on radio from 1928 to 1945. He asked that his tombstone be inscribed, "No flowers, please, I'm allergic." (Died 3-25-82)

FACTS FROM THE PAST

1870 The **DONKEY**, which became the symbol for the **DEMOCRATIC PARTY**, was seen for the first time. It was drawn by cartoonist **THOMAS NAST** in *Harper's Weekly.*

1896 The official photographer for the Union side in the Civil War died in poverty at Presbyterian Hospital in NYC. **MATTHEW BRADY** took 3,500 photos at a cost of $400,000. He was accused of frightening the soldiers with his mysterious machine. He also snapped 21 U.S. presidents.

1967 The **GREEN BAY PACKERS** defeated the Kansas City Chiefs 35-10 in the first Super Bowl. The game was played at Memorial Coliseum in Los Angeles. Max McGee caught seven passes from MVP Bart Starr for 138 yards and two touchdowns. Ray Scott and Jack Whitaker were the announcers for CBS. Curt Gowdy did play-by-play for NBC.

1974 "Happy Days" premiered, starring **RON HOWARD, ANSON WILLIAMS** and **HENRY WINKLER.** Bill Haley's "Rock Around the Clock" was the first theme for the show and was later replaced by the original "Happy Days" composition. You'll find Fonzie's leather jacket in the Smithsonian Institution. The final episode aired 7-12-84.

1976 **SARA JANE MOORE** was sentenced to life in prison for her attempt to shoot President Gerald R. Ford in San Francisco.

1983 Thom Syles of Van Nuys, CA, set a **WORLD RECORD** by keeping a single Life Saver candy intact in his mouth for seven hours and ten minutes.

1986 Singer **JIMMY DEAN** was ordered to pay his brother, Don, half a million dollars for causing him mental anguish in a feud over the family sausage business.

1988 **JIMMY** "The Greek" **SNYDER** was fired by CBS for racist remarks about black athletes.

1993 **PRESIDENT BILL CLINTON,** on his second day in office, wiped out many Republican abortion/family planning restrictions.

1994 **RICKY WATERS** scored the most touchdowns in any post-season game (5). San Francisco defeated the Giants 44-3.

JANUARY 16

BIRTHDAYS

• **DEBBIE ALLEN** Actress/dancer/choreographer. (Houston, TX) TV: "Fame" and "Roots." Films: *Jo Jo Dancer* and *Ragtime.* Year/**Age**: 1995/**45** 1996/**46** 1997/**47**

• **SADE** [shah' day] Singer. Former waitress/bicycle messenger. (Born Helen Folasade Adu in Nigeria) Moved to London at age 4. Biggest record: "Smooth Operator" in 1985. Grammy award in '86 for best newcomer. Year/**Age**: 1995/**36** 1996/**37** 1997/**38**

• **KATY JURADO** [ha-rod'-o] Actress. (Born Maria Garcia in Guadalajara, Mexico) Nominated for an Academy Award as supporting actress in *Broken Lance* in 1954. She was in *High Noon* and *Trapeze* and was married to actor Ernest Borgnine. Year/**Age**: 1995/**68** 1996/**69** 1997/**70**

• **A. J. FOYT** 4-time INDY 500 winner. (Houston, TX) He was the youngest driver in the "500" field for 3 years and, on his 4th try in 1961, he won. A.J. won his 4th Indy 500 when he was 42 years old. He was a millionaire by the time he was 30 years old. In 1990, he suffered the most severe crash of his career at Road America in Elkhart Lake, WI. He retired from racing Indy-cars in 1993. Year/**Age**: 1995/**60** 1996/**61** 1997/**62**

• **MARILYN HORNE** Opera singer. (Bradford, PA) Her voice is heard in the film *Carmen Jones* in 1954, singing for actress Dorothy Dandridge. Year/**Age**: 1995/**61** 1996/**62** 1997/**63**

• **DIZZY DEAN** Baseball great. (1911-1974 – Born Jay Hanna Dean in Lukas, AR) Pitcher for the St. Louis Cardinals, Hall of Fame member and later a radio/TV sports announcer and commentator. He became famous for his innovative delivery, for example: "He slud into third." Dean explained that he and brother Paul "Daffy" Dean didn't get much education. (Died 7-17-74)

• **JOHN CARPENTER** Horror film director. (Carthage, NY) One of his big successes was *Halloween* in 1978, making over $75 million dollars on a budget of $300,000. Married actress Adrienne Barbeau. Year/**Age**: 1995/**47** 1996/**48** 1997/**49**

• **WILLIAM KENNEDY** Author. Year/**Age**: 1995/**67** 1996/**68** 1997/**69**

• **FRANCESCO SCAVULLO** Photographer. (Staten Island, NY) Many of his photographs of celebrities and models appear in popular magazines. Year/**Age**: 1995/**66** 1996/**67** 1997/**68**

• **RONNIE MILSAP** Singer. (Robbinsville, NC) With his musical talent Ronnie did well in school. However, he would often get into trouble for playing rock and roll, and country in a classical music school. After his teachers realized they were not going to change him, he was allowed to form a band with other blind musicians called APPARITIONS. His biggest hit: "There's No Gettin' Over Me" in 1981. He has been sightless all of his life. Year/**Age**: 1995/**51** 1996/**52** 1997/**53**

• **ANDRÉ MICHELIN** French industrialist. (1853-1931 – Paris, France) Along with his brother Edward, he started the Michelin Tire Company in 1888, manufacturing bicycle tires. (Died 4-4-31)

• **ROBERT WILLIAM SERVICE** Poet. (1874-1958 – England) Lived in Canada. Best remembered for ballads, "The Shooting of Dan McGrew" and "The Cremation of Sam McGee." (Died 9-11-58)

• **ETHEL MERMAN** Entertainer. (1909-1984 – Born Ethel Zimmerman in Astoria, NY) Her voice was so loud that Irving Berlin said, "You'd better not write a bad song for Merman, because everyone in the audience will hear it." On Broadway in *Annie Get Your Gun* and *Hello Dolly.* (Died 2-15-84)

FACTS FROM THE PAST

1935   **MA BARKER DIED** in a four hour shootout with the FBI in Florida. Her real name was ARIZONA CLARK BARKER. She was never charged with a crime, though legend portrays her as the leader of the gang that included her four sons.

1938   **BENNY GOODMAN** took his band to **NEW YORK'S CARNEGIE HALL** for perhaps the most famous jazz concert ever.

1942   Actress **CAROLE LOMBARD**, her mother, and about 20 other people were killed when their plane crashed near Las Vegas, NV. She was married to Clark Gable at the time of her death.

1973   Little Joe, Hoss, Adam, and Ben Cartright rode into the sunset as **"BONANZA'S"** last show was aired.

1974   For the first time two teammates—**WHITEY FORD** and **MICKEY MANTLE**—were elected to the Baseball Hall of Fame at the same time.

1978   NASA named 35 candidates to fly on the space shuttle, including **SALLY K. RIDE,** who became America's first woman in space, and **GUION S. BLUFORD, JR.,** America's first Black Astronaut.

1979   The **DIVORCE OF GREGG AND CHER ALLMAN** was finalized. Cher had filed for divorce 9 days after the wedding.

1980   Former Beatle **PAUL MCCARTNEY** and his wife, Linda, were arrested in Tokyo after customs agents found marijuana in his luggage. On the same date four years later they were arrested for marijuana possession in Barbados.

1981   Protestant gunmen of Northern Ireland shot and wounded Irish nationalist leader **BERNADETTE DEVLIN MCALISKEY** and her husband.

1987   The **BEASTIE BOYS** were censored on "American Bandstand." A first for the popular TV show.

1991   U.S. and Allied Forces launched an attack on **IRAQ AND KUWAIT.**

1994   Rock-n-Roll star **BRYAN ADAMS** became the first Western entertainer to play in Vietnam since the end of the war.

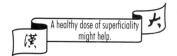

A healthy dose of superficiality might help.

JANUARY 17

BIRTHDAYS

• **PAUL YOUNG** Singer. (England) Biggest hit: "Everytime You Go Away" in 1985 written by Daryl Hall of HALL AND OATS. Year/**Age**: 1995/**39** 1996/**40** 1997/**41**

• **DON "Popeye" ZIMMER** Baseball. (Cincinnati, OH) Former manager of the Chicago Cubs. Coach of Colorado Rockies. Year/**Age**: 1995/**64** 1996/**65** 1997/**66**

• **JAMES EARL JONES** Actor. (Arabutla, MS) He received an Academy Award nomination for best actor in *The Great White Hope* in 1969. He played Captain Woodrow "Woody" Paris in the crime show "Paris" on TV. He was also the voice of Darth Vader in *Star Wars* movies. In *Pros and Cons* and *Sommersby*. The voice of King Mufasa (the Lion King's father) in Disney's *The Lion King*. Year/**Age**: 1995/**64** 1996/**65** 1997/**66**

• **JIM CARREY** Actor. Star of *Ace Ventura-Pet Detective*, *The Mask*, and will play the Riddler in the third Batman movie. Year/**Age**: 1995/**33** 1996/**34** 1997/**35**

• **MUHAMMAD ALI** "I'm The Greatest" Former heavyweight champion. (Born Cassius Marcellus Clay in Louisville, KY) He won the Olympic gold medal in 1960, was stripped of his WBA heavyweight title in 1967 for refusing military draft, and was reinstated in 1971. He was the first fighter to hold the heavyweight title three times. He was on the cover of *Sports Illustrated* more than any other sports figure. He was less known for recording the song "Stand By Me." Year/**Age**: 1995/**53** 1996/**54** 1997/**55**

• **BETTY WHITE** Actress. (Oak Park, IL) She played the lead in the TV comedy "Life With Elizabeth" in 1953 and was Sue Ann Nivens on the "Mary Tyler Moore Show." She was a semi-regular on the "Jack Paar Show" from 1959-62 and a star on the "Golden Girls." She was married to the late TV game-show host Allen Ludden. Year/**Age**: 1995/**73** 1996/**74** 1997/**75**

• **PETE LaCOCK** Baseball player. Son of Peter Marshall of "Hollywood Squares." Year/**Age**: 1995/**43** 1996/**44** 1997/**45**

• **MOIRA SHEARER** Ballerina/actress. (Scotland) Year/**Age**: 1995/**69** 1996/**70** 1997/**71**

• **MAURY POVICH** Talk show host. (DC) Married to CBS news celebrated anchor Connie Chung. Year/**Age**: 1995/**56** 1996/**57** 1997/**58**

• **DARREL PORTER** Major league catcher. (Joplin, MO) Played with Brewers, Royals, Cardinals and is currently with the Texas Rangers. Year/**Age**: 1995/**43** 1996/**44** 1997/**45**

• **SHARI LEWIS** Puppeteer. (Born Shari Hurwitz in NYC) She received an Emmy Award for the show "A Picture of Us" on NBC Children's Theater. Star of PBS show "Lamb Chop's Play-Along." Year/**Age**: 1995/**61** 1996/**62** 1997/**63**

• **SUSANNAH HOFFS** Vocalist. (Los Angeles, CA) Member of the BANGLES, their biggest hit was "Walk Like an Egyptian" in 1986. Year/**Age**: 1995/**38** 1996/**39** 1997/**40**

• **VIDAL SASSOON** Hair stylist. (London, England) Year/**Age**: 1995/**67** 1996/**68** 1997/**69**

• **MICK TAYLOR** Rock guitarist. (England) ROLLING STONES. He replaced Brian Jones in 1969. His first record with the Stones was "Honky Tonk Woman." Year/**Age**: 1995/**47** 1996/**48** 1997/**49**

• **ANDY KAUFMAN** Actor/comedian. (1949-1984 – NYC) He portrayed Latka on the "Taxi" TV series. (Died 5-16-84)

• **AL CAPONE** Racketeer. (1899-1947 – Born Alphonse in Naples, Italy) He was nicknamed "Scarface." He ordered the St. Valentine Day Massacre in Chicago. (Died 1-25-47)

• **BENJAMIN FRANKLIN** Inventor. (1706-1790 – Boston, MA) He was the oldest signer of the Declaration of Independence and the Constitution. He invented the lightning rod, the Franklin stove, bifocal glasses, and the platform rocking chair. He also created the first efficient postal system in America. He long suffered from gout and thought it was caused by not enjoying more sex. He had a reputation as a womanizer. (Died 4-17-1790)

FACTS FROM THE PAST

1871   **ANDREW S. HALLIDIE** received a patent for a cable car system that began service in San Francisco in 1873.

1874   **CHANG** and **ENG** died at age 63. Born of Chinese parents in Siam (hence the name "Siamese Twins"). They were joined at the breastbone, but otherwise fully developed, independent beings. They toured with P.T. Barnum's circus before becoming farmers in North Carolina. They spent three days of each week with one wife and three days with the other and between them produced 22 children. When one twin died, the other lived for only two more hours.

1910   **THOMAS CRAPPER**, developer of the flush toilet mechanism, died. He was a plumber in Victorian England. He and his partners founded Thomas Crapper & Co., and were responsible for many plumbing inventions.

1977   Convicted murderer **GARY GILMORE** got his wish to be shot by a firing squad at the Utah State Prison, becoming the first person to be executed in the United States in a decade.

1983   The *L.A. Times* reported on a fund-raising letter being mailed by evangelist **ORAL ROBERTS**, in which Roberts said he had a 7-hour conversation with Jesus, who told him to ask each of his followers to send Roberts $240 so he could complete his Tower of Faith research center in Tulsa, OK. Roberts said the center would find a cure for cancer, explaining, "I have become keenly aware of how Satan is trying to take control of the cells and cause them to multiply out of their divinely placed order."

1986   **ALDO GUCCI**, famous fashion leader, pleaded guilty to a $7 million dollar tax fraud.

1990   The Who, Simon & Garfunkel, the Four Seasons, the Four Tops, Hank Ballard, the Platters, and the Kinks were **INDUCTED INTO THE ROCK AND ROLL HALL OF FAME.** Ray Davies commented, "Rock and roll has become respectable. What a bummer."

1994   A major earthquake measuring 6.6 on the Richter scale struck just north of Los Angeles, killing 55 people.

JANUARY 18

Why talk with dolphins?
Seafood recommendations?

BIRTHDAYS

• **BOB ROSENBERG** Musician. (Florida) From the group WILL TO POWER. Biggest hit: "Baby I Love Your Ways" in 1988. Year/Age: 1995/**36** 1996/**37** 1997/**38**

• **RAY DOLBY** Inventor. Invented the Dolby Sound System for clearer sounding recordings. Year/**Age:** 1995/**62** 1996/**63** 1997/**64**

• **LAURIE LONDON** Singer. (England) His only hit was at age 13, "He's Got the Whole World in His Hands" in 1958. Year/Age: 1995/**51** 1996/**52** 1997/**53**

• **JOHN BOORMAN** Movie director. (England) Films: *Deliverance* and *Exorcist II*. Year/Age: 1995/**62** 1996/**63** 1997/**64**

• **TOM BAILEY** Singer. (England) Lead singer for the group THOMPSON TWINS. Biggest hit: "Hold Me Now" in 1984. Year/Age: 1995/**39** 1996/**40** 1997/**41**

• **KEVIN MICHAEL COSTNER** Actor. (Lynwood, CA) *Bull Durham, Robin Hood: Prince of Thieves, The Untouchables, Field of Dreams, JFK, The Bodyguard, Dances With Wolves, A Perfect World*, and *Wyatt Earp*. He was the body at the beginning of the film *The Big Chill*. He thought that would be his break in movies but all we saw was his hairline. Year/**Age:** 1995/**40** 1996/**41** 1997/**42**

• **BOBBY GOLDSBORO** Singer. (Marianne, FL) Biggest hit: "Honey" in 1968. He played guitar for Roy Orbison's band from 1962-1964. Year/Age: 1995/**54** 1996/**55** 1997/**56**

• **CURT FLOOD** Baseball. (Houston, TX) The St. Louis Cardinal's outfielder who hit over .300 six times. Year/**Age:** 1995/**57** 1996/**58** 1997/**59**

• **A. A. MILNE** Author. (1882-1956 – England) He created *Winnie the Pooh*. (Died 1-31-56)

• **BILL McGOWAN** Umpire. (1896-1954 – Wilmington, DL) The most colorful umpire of his time. He worked 8 World Series and 4 All-Star games. In 1925 he worked every inning of over 2,500 AL games. (Died 12-9-54)

• **OLIVER HARDY** Comedian. (1892-1957 – Atlanta, GA) Half of the comedy duo "Laurel and Hardy," with Stan Laurel. He entered show business at the age of 8, singing in a minstrel show. In 1913 he appeared in his first movie. His last movie was *The Fighting Kentuckian* in 1949. (Died 8-7-57)

• **DAVID RUFFIN** Singer. (1941-1991 – Meridian, MS) Original member of the TEMPTATIONS. He sang lead on "My Girl," "Beauty's Only Skin Deep" and "Ain't Too Proud To Beg." "My Girl" sold over a million copies and made the TEMPTATIONS the 1st male Motown group to have a #1 hit. Ruffin died from an accidental overdose of cocaine (6-1-91).

• **DANNY KAYE** Entertainer. (1913-1987 – Born David Kaminsky in Brooklyn, NY) His first film was *Up In Arms* with Dinah Shore, and he appeared in *Hans Christian Andersen, The Secret Life of Walter Mitty* and *White Christmas*. (Died 3-3-87)

• **CARY GRANT** Actor. (1904-1986 – Born Archibald Alexander Leach in Bristol, England) Among his 72 films, most notable include: *Bringing Up Baby* in 1938, *The Philadelphia Story* in 1940, *To Catch A Thief* in 1955, and *North by Northwest* in 1955. (Died 11-29-86)

• **PETER MARK ROGET** [ro-jhay] Author. (1779-1869 – London, England) Graduated from medical school at 19 years and became a famous physician. He helped establish the University of London and invented the economic chess board. He wrote a paper which sowed the seed for the invention of the movie camera and started the *Thesaurus* when he was 71 years old. (Died 9-12-1869)

FACTS FROM THE PAST

1778 **CAPTAIN JAMES COOK**, English explorer, discovered the Hawaiian Islands, which he dubbed the "Sandwich Islands." A year later he was killed at Kealakekua Bay by natives. His navigator was **WILLIAM BLIGH**; later to become captain of the *Bounty*.

1911 The first landing of an aircraft onto a ship took place as pilot **EUGENE B. ELY** brought his Curtiss bi-plane in for a safe landing on the deck of the U.S.S. *Pennsylvania*, a U.S. Navy cruiser in San Francisco, CA.

1912 **EXPLORER ROBERT SCOTT** had a bad day. He and his expedition reached the South Pole only to discover that Roald Amundsen had beaten them to it. To make matters worse, Scott and his party died on the return trip.

1956 The *Rock Around The Clock* Album by **BILL HALEY & HIS COMETS** hit national charts. It was the first rock LP to do so.

1968 Entertainer **EARTHA KITT** caused problems at the White House when she told **LADY BIRD JOHNSON** that the American youth were rebelling against the war in Vietnam.

1969 **PETE BEST** won his defamation suit against the Beatles, but was awarded considerably less than the $8 million he sought.

1973 **PINK FLOYD** began recording *Dark Side of the Moon*, which would become the longest-charting album in *Billboard* history. It was on the album chart for more than 14 years, until the middle of 1988. It sold more than 5 million copies.

1974 Paul Rodgers and Simon Kirke of **FREE**, Mick Ralphs of **MOTT THE HOOPLE** and Boz Burrell of **KING CRIMSON** formed **BAD COMPANY**. Biggest hit: "Can't Get Enough" in 1974.

1976 The **PITTSBURGH STEELERS** defeated the Dallas Cowboys 21-17 in **SUPER BOWL X** in Miami.

1990 Washington, D.C. **MAYOR MARION BARRY** was arrested in a FBI "sting" operation on drug-possession charges. He was later convicted of a misdemeanor. He spent six months in federal prison. Released 4-23-92.

1994 Lawrence Walsh's 566-page document revealed that both **RONALD REAGAN** and **GEORGE BUSH** had full knowledge and participation in the Iran Contra illegalities.

Time doesn't fit inside a bottle.

JANUARY 19

BIRTHDAYS

• **ANN COMPTON** ABC newswoman. (Chicago, IL) White House Correspondent. Year/Age: 1995/**48** 1996/**49** 1997/**50**

• **MICHAEL CRAWFORD** Actor. (England) Films include *Hello Dolly*, *How I Won The War* with John Lennon. On stage *The Phantom of the Opera*. Character voice in *Once upon a Forest*. Year/Age: 1995/**53** 1996/**54** 1997/**55**

• **ROBERT MacNEIL** PBS newsman. (Montreal, Quebec, Canada) "MacNeil-Lehrer Report." Year/Age: 1995/**64** 1996/**65** 1997/**66**

• **DOLLY PARTON** Entertainer. (Born Dolly Rebecca Parton in Sevierville, TN) Her biggest records were "Here You Come Again" in 1978, "Nine to Five," in 1980 from the movie of the same name. She also appeared in *Steel Magnolias* and *Best Little Whorehouse in Texas*. Songs: "I Will Always Love You" and "Romeo." Owns "Dollywood" Park in Pigeon Forge, TN. Year/Age: 1995/**49** 1996/**50** 1997/**51**

• **RICHARD LESTER** Producer/director. (Philadelphia, PA) Directed 2 Beatle films: *A Hard Day's Night* in 1964 and *Help!* in 1965. He signed John Lennon for his solo film debut as Private Gripweed in the 1967 film *How I Won The War*. Other movie credits: *Petulia*, *Juggernaut*, *The Three Musketeers* and *Superman II*. Year/Age: 1995/**63** 1996/**64** 1997/**65**

• **DESI ARNAZ, JR.** Actor. (Los Angeles, CA) The son of Lucille Ball and Desi Arnaz, Sr. His birth was a major media event in 1953, pushing the Eisenhower inauguration off the front pages. In the film *The Mambo Kings*, appeared as his dad, Desi Arnaz, Sr. Year/Age: 1995/**42** 1996/**43** 1997/**44**

• **STEFAN EDBERG** Tennis champ. Year/Age: 1995/**29** 1996/**30** 1997/**31**

• **JEAN STAPLETON** Actress. (Born Jeanne Murray in NYC) Probably best known for her role as Edith Bunker in "All in the Family." Year/Age: 1995/**72** 1996/**73** 1997/**74**

• **TIPPI HEDREN** Actress. (Born Natalie Kay in New Ulm, MN) Starred in *The Birds* and sequel. Mother of actress Melanie Griffith. Year/Age: 1995/**59** 1996/**60** 1997/**61**

• **ROBERT PALMER** Singer. (England) Biggest hits: "Addicted to Love" in 1985 and "Simply Irresistible." Year/Age: 1995/**46** 1996/**47** 1997/**48**

• **JODIE SWEETEN** Actress. On the poular T.V. series *Full House*. Year/Age: 1995/**13** 1996/**14** 1997/**15**

• **MARTHA DAVIS** Entertainer. (Los Angeles, CA) MOTELS. Biggest hit: "Only The Lonely" in 1982. Year/Age: 1995/**44** 1996/**45** 1997/**46**

• **SHELLEY FABARES** Actress. (Santa Monica, CA) Biggest hit: "Johnny Angel" came from TV's "Donna Reed Show," on which she played Mary Stone. A script was tailored around the song in 1962. She co-starred on the popular TV series "One Day At A Time." Now in "Coach." She co-starred with Elvis Presley in 3 movies. Married to Mike Farrell of "M*A*S*H." Year/Age: 1995/**51** 1996/**52** 1997/**53**

• **PHIL EVERLY** Singer of the EVERLY BROTHERS. (Chicago, IL) He and brother Don (see Feb. 1) have charted 38 records, including their biggest sellers: "Wake Up Little Suzie," "All I Have To Do Is Dream" and "Cathy's Clown." They split up in 1973 and reunited in 1983. They are in the Rock & Roll Hall of Fame. Year/Age: 1995/**56** 1996/**57** 1997/**58**

• **JANIS JOPLIN** Singer. (1943-1970 – Port Arthur, TX) Biggest hit: "Me & Bobby McGee." She died of a heroin overdose in her room at the Landmark Hotel in Hollywood. She had just finished recording her album *Pearl*. There is a monument of her in Port Arthur, TX, dedicated in 1987 under protest from some townsfolk. (Died 10-4-70)

• **ROBERT E. LEE** Military leader. (1807-1870 – Born Robert Edward Lee in Stratford, VA) Greatest military leader of the Confederacy. Lee's mother had a terrifying experience: She suffered a seizure, was declared dead and placed in a casket. She woke up screaming and clawing at the lid, which was hastily opened. (Died 10-12-1870)

• **EDGAR ALLEN POE** Poet. (1809-1849 – Boston, MA) American poet and story writer who gave us *The Raven* and *The Pit & the Pendulum*. He was secretly married to his 13-year-old cousin, so, Jerry Lee Lewis was not the first celebrity to do so. Often he would do his writing with a black cat on his shoulder. (Died 10-7-1849)

• **JAMES WATT** Inventor. (1736-1819 – Scotland) He invented the steam engine. (Died 8-19-1819)

FACTS FROM THE PAST

1825 **EZRA DAGGETT** and his nephew, **THOMAS KENSETT**, got a patent for their process of storing food in tin cans.

1840 Antarctica was discovered by **CHARLES WILKES.**

1853 Verdi's opera **IL TROVATORE** premiered in Rome.

1937 **HOWARD HUGHES** established a transcontinental air record when he flew across the U.S. in 7 hours, 28 minutes and 25 seconds.

1953 **LUCY** gave birth to Desi Arnaz, Jr., during the regularly scheduled show of "I Love Lucy." The scriptwriters had gambled—writing the script accordingly—that Lucille Ball would have a boy. Two-thirds of the country's viewers saw that show.

1955 A presidential news conference was filmed for TV for the first time, with the permission of **PRESIDENT DWIGHT D. EISENHOWER.**

1979 Former Atty. Gen. **JOHN MITCHELL** was released from prison after serving 19 months for his Watergate conviction. He told reporters: "Henceforth, don't call me, I'll call you."

1986 **BRUCE SPRINGSTEEN** made an unannounced appearance at an Asbury Park, NJ, benefit for Freehold 3M plant workers. Laid-off workers had adopted Springsteen's "My Hometown" as their anthem.

1994 **TONYA HARDING'S EX**, Jeff Gillooly, charged with the planning of the attack on Nancy Kerrigan.

JANUARY 20
Astrological Sign of Aquarius

Whatever happened to tube tops?

BIRTHDAYS

- **RAY ANTHONY** Band leader. (Born Raymond Antonini in Bentleyville, PA) He played lead trumput with Glen Miller at age 18. "Bunny Hop" in 1952. Year/Age: 1995/**73** 1996/**74** 1997/**75**
- **GEORGE BURNS** Entertainer. (Born Nathan Birnbaum in NYC) He won an Academy Award for best supporting actor in 1975 for *Sunshine Boys* and played God in the *Oh, God* movies. 100th birthday bash at Caesar's Palace already sold out! Year/Age: 1995/**99** 1996/**100** 1997/**101**
- **PATRICIA NEAL** Actress. (Packard, KY) She won an Academy Award for best actress in 1963 for *Hud* with Paul Newman. In her book, *Patricia Neal: As I Am*, she tells how she cried after deciding to abort a child she and Gary Cooper conceived out of wedlock while he was living with his wife and daughter. Their affair began during the filming of the movie *The Fountainhead*. She had a stroke, but had such drive she totally recovered. Year/Age: 1995/**69** 1996/**70** 1997/**71**
- **LORENZO LAMAS** Actor. (Los Angeles, CA) He appeared in the "Falcon Crest" TV series. Son of late actors Fernando Lamas and Arlene Dahl. In "Grease." Year/Age: 1995/**37** 1996/**38** 1997/**39**
- **EDWIN "BUZZ" ALDRIN** Astronaut. (Montclair, NJ) He set foot on the moon July 20, 1969 as only the second man to do so. Year/Age: 1995/**65** 1996/**66** 1997/**67**
- **PAUL STANLEY** Guitarist of KISS. (Born Paul Eisen in NYC) Their biggest hit: "Beth" in 1976. Year/Age: 1995/**45** 1996/**46** 1997/**47**

- **ARTE JOHNSON** Actor/comedian. (Chicago, IL) He was a big star in the "Laugh-In" TV series for which he won an Emmy in the 1968-1969 season. He made the most appearances by a male in TV's "Love Boat." Year/Age: 1995/**61** 1996/**62** 1997/**63**
- **DEFOREST KELLEY** Actor. (Atlanta, GA) He played Dr. Leonard "Bones" McCoy on the "Star Trek" TV series from 1966 to 1969. Year/Age: 1995/**75** 1996/**76** 1997/**77**
- **SLIM WHITMAN** C&W. (Born Otis Dewey Whitman in Tampa, FL) He has sold over 50 million records and has been named one of the most popular recording artists in Great Britain. In 1955, Slim became the first country singer to play the London Palladium. Year/Age: 1995/**71** 1996/**72** 1997/**73**
- **FEDERICO FELLINI** Italian film director. (Italy) At one time he was a cartoonist. He directed *La Dolce Vita* starring Anita Ekberg and Marcello Mastroianni. He won Best Foreign Film Oscars for *8½*, *La Strada*, *Le Nottidi Cabiria*, and *Amarcord*. Most famous for *La Dolce Vita*. (Died 10-31-93)
- **JOHN NABER** Swimmer. (Evanston, IL) Won 4 gold medals and 1 silver in the 1976 Olympics. Year/Age: 1995/**39** 1996/**40** 1997/**41**
- **MARIO LANZA** Singer. (1921-1959 – Philadelphia, PA) His biggest hit: "Be My Love" in 1950. (Died 10-7-59)
- **LEON AMES** Actor. (1902-1993) Films include *The Postman Always Rings Twice*, *Tora! Tora! Tora!*, and *Peggy Sue Got Married*. (Died 10-12-93)

FACTS FROM THE PAST

1885 A patent for the roller coaster was received by **L. A. THOMPSON** of Coney Island, NY.

1892 The **FIRST OFFICIALLY RECOGNIZED BASKETBALL GAME** was held at a YMCA training school in Springfield, MA. The game was invented by Canadian Dr. James Naismith. The players, after looking for some boxes, ended up using peach baskets (without cutting out the bottom) and every time a score was made, the game stopped while someone climbed a ladder to get the ball.

1937 **PRESIDENT FRANKLIN D. ROOSEVELT** became the first chief executive to be inaugurated on Jan. 20 instead of March 4. The 20th Amendment to the Constitution changed the inaugural date. He was also the first to be elected for a third and fourth term in 1941 and 1945, respectively.

1952 The first female professional bullfighter debuted in Mexico. **PATRICIA McCORMICK** of Big Spring, TX, defeated two bulls.

1961 **JOHN F. KENNEDY** was inaugurated as the nation's 35th President. As part of his brief address, he said, "Ask not what your country can do for you, ask what you can do for your country."

1973 The "Grand Ol' Opry" asked **JERRY LEE LEWIS** to make his first appearance there on two conditions: that he perform only country songs and not use profanity. He agreed, but violated both requests.

1973 1,976 musicians performed in the second inaugural parade for **PRESIDENT NIXON**. This was the largest marching band ever assembled in the U.S.

1977 **JIMMY CARTER** was sworn in as the 39th President of the United States.

1982 In Des Moines, IA, **OZZY OSBOURNE** tore the head off of a bat with his teeth during a concert performance.

1988 **BEACH BOY MIKE LOVE** insulted Paul McCartney, Diana Ross, Bruce Springsteen, and Mick Jagger while being inducted into the Rock and Roll Hall Of Fame.

1989 **GEORGE BUSH** was sworn in as the 41st president of the United States and **DAN QUAYLE** was sworn in as vice president.

1993 **WILLIAM JEFFERSON CLINTON**, 46-year-old ex-governor from Hope, Arkansas, became the 42nd President of the United States.

1994 **SHANNON FAULKNER,** on her 19th birthday, became the first woman to attend day classes with the all-male corps of cadets at The Citadel.

Have you hugged your VCR today?

JANUARY 21
Hat Day

BIRTHDAYS

- **GEENA DAVIS** Actress. (Wareham, MA) She's divorced from her co-star in *The Fly*, Jeff Goldblum. Nominated as best actress for *Thelma and Louise*. Appeared in *Tootsie, A League of Their Own*, The Long Kiss *Goodnight, Speechless, Hero,* and *Angie*. Year/**Age:** 1995/**38** 1996/**39** 1997/**40**

- **ROBBY BENSON** Actor. (Born Robert Segal in Dallas, TX) He moved toward stardom in the movie *The Ode to Billy Joe* and also appeared with Paul Newman in *Harry & Son*. Voice of the Beast in Disney's *Beauty and the Beast*. He replaced Rex Smith on Broadway in *The Pirates of Penzance*. Year/**Age:** 1995/**39** 1996/**40** 1997/**41**

- **MAC DAVIS** Singer/songwriter. (Lubbock, TX) Biggest hit: "Baby Don't Get Hooked On Me" in 1972. He wrote "In the Ghetto," a hit for Elvis; and "Something's Burning" by Kenny Rogers and the FIRST EDITION. He was in the movie *North Dallas Forty* in 1979 and appeared in *Will Rogers Follies* on Broadway. Year/**Age:** 1995/**53** 1996/**54** 1997/**55**

- **RICHIE HAVENS** Singer/guitarist. (Brooklyn, NY) Hit: "Here Comes the Sun" in 1971. Year/**Age:** 1995/**54** 1996/**55** 1997/**56**

- **JILL EIKENBERRY** Actress. (New Haven, CT) Starred in "L.A. Law." Married to actor Michael Tucker who was also in "L.A. Law." Year/**Age:** 1995/**48** 1996/**49** 1997/**50**

- **HAKEEM "The Dream" OLAJUWON** Basketball. (Lagos, Nigeria) Center for the Houston Rockets. He became the only player to be named regular season MVP, defensive player of the year and finals MVP. Year/**Age:** 1995/**32** 1996/**33** 1997/**34**

- **PLACIDO DOMINGO** Opera tenor. (Madrid, Spain) Biggest hit: "Perhaps Love" with John Denver in 1981. Year/**Age:** 1995/**54** 1996/**55** 1997/**56**

- **JACK NICKLAUS** Pro golfer. (Columbus, OH) He won the Ohio Open at age 16 and was a leading money winner eight times. Named PGA "player of the year" five times. Winner of 70 tournaments including 20 majors. Known as the Golden Bear. Year/**Age:** 1995/**55** 1996/**56** 1997/**57**

- **STEVE REEVES** Former Mr. World/Mr. Universe. (Glasgow, MT) Starred in *Hercules*. The "Arnold Schwarzenegger" of the 50's and he still works out. Wrote *Power Walking*. Year/**Age:** 1995/**69** 1996/**70** 1997/**71**

- **TELLY SAVALAS** Actor. (1923-1994 Born Aristoteles Savalas in Garden City, NY) He is probably best known for his role as Kojak in the TV series of the same name. His famous line: "Who loves ya baby?" Films include *Dirty Dozen,* and *Kelly's Heroes*. He shaved his head for two films: *Greatest Story Ever Told* and *Genghis Khan*. His baldness became a trademark. (Died 1-22-94 of bladder cancer.)

- **WOLFMAN JACK** DJ. (Born Bob Smith in Brooklyn, NY) His gravelly voice and howling made him a radio legend in the early 1960's. For much of the last decade, he was a fixture on NBC-TV's "Midnight Special." He was in the film *American Graffiti* and had a hit song, "Clap for the Wolfman," by the GUESS WHO. Year/**Age:** 1995/**57** 1996/**58** 1997/**59**

- **BILLY OCEAN** Singer. (Born Leslie Sebastian Charles in Trinidad.) Biggest hit: "Caribbean Queen" in 1984. Year/**Age:** 1995/**45** 1996/**46** 1997/**47**

- **CHARLOTTE ROSS** Actress. (Winetka, Il.) TV's "Days of Our Lives" as Eve and the sitcom "The Five Mrs. Buchanans." In the film *Foreign Student*. Year/**Age:** 1995/**27** 1996/**28** 1997/**29**

- **BENNY HILL** English comedian. (1925-1992 – Born Alfred Hawthorn Hill) Star of the bawdy British comedy show that began in 1969. The American version of his show was edited down. The British version contained much more nudity. In the film *Chitty Chitty Bang Bang* in 1968. (Died 4-20-92)

- **THOMAS "STONEWALL" JACKSON** General. (1824-1863 – Clarksburg, VA) A Civil War Confederate general, he earned his nickname by stopping attacks as effectively as a stone wall. Jackson died of gun shot wounds fired by his own troops in a battle near Chancellorsville, VA. (5-1-1863)

FACTS FROM THE PAST

1789 The first novel ever published in the U.S., written by **WILLIAM HILL BROWN**, went on sale. *The Power of Sympathy* was promoted as a lurid tale of romance and sex.

1950 **ALGER HISS** was convicted of perjury for his denial of espionage charges against the U.S. Richard Nixon was a leading prosecutor.

1957 **PATSY CLINE** appeared on "Arthur Godfrey's Talent Scouts."

1977 As one of his first acts as President, **JIMMY CARTER** pardoned American Vietnam War-era **DRAFT EVADERS**.

1979 The **PITTSBURGH STEELERS** became the first team to win three Super Bowls as they defeated the Dallas Cowboys in Super Bowl XIII by a score of 35 to 31.

1985 **PRESIDENT REAGAN** became the only President to take the oath of office in the Capitol Rotunda. Outdoor public inauguration ceremonies for the second term of 73-year-old Ronald Reagan (oldest man ever elected President) were canceled because of an Arctic cold wave. 10,000 young musicians representing 57 bands were disappointed.

1987 **JACKIE WILSON** was inducted into the Rock and Roll Hall of Fame on the anniversary of his death, along with Aretha Franklin, Bo Diddley, Rick Nelson, Bill Haley, Roy Orbison, Smokey Robinson, Marvin Gaye, Carl Perkins, B.B. King, and others.

1989 Former **KU KLUX KLAN LEADER** David Duke advanced to a run-off election for a seat in the Louisiana state House.

1990 **JOHN McENROE** was the first player kicked out of the Australian Open for misconduct in its 85-year history. McEnroe threw his racket and a tantrum and was defaulted by the umpire, which led to $6,500 in fines.

1994 A jury in Manassas, VA found **LORENA BOBBITT** not guilty by reason of insanity for cutting off her husband's penis.

JANUARY 22

BIRTHDAYS

- **MICHAEL HUTCHENCE** Singer. (Sydney, Australia) INXS. One of their biggest hits: "Need You Tonight" in 1987. Year/Age: 1995/**35** 1996/**36** 1997/**37**
- **TEDDY GENTRY** Musician. (Ft. Payne, AL) With the C&W group ALABAMA, they had many hits, including: "Love in the First Degree" in 1981. Randy Owen and Jeff Cook from the group are Teddy's cousins. Year/Age: 1995/**43** 1996/**44** 1997/**45**
- **PIPER LAURIE** Actress. (Born Rosetta Jacobs in Detroit, MI) Leading lady of the 1950's, she made her debut in a film called *Louise* in 1949. Appeared in the film *Rich In Love* and *Wrestling Earnest Hemingway.* Was on TV's "Twin Peaks." Year/Age: 1995/**63** 1996/**64** 1997/**65**
- **ANN SOTHERN** Actress. (Born Harriet Lake in Valley City, ND) She was one of MGM's great and shining stars as well as one of TV's early stars in "Private Secretary" and "The Ann Sothern Show." Appeared in the *Whales of August.* Year/Age: 1995/**86** 1996/**87** 1997/**88**
- **LINDA BLAIR** Actress. (St. Louis, MO) She was nominated for best supporting actress in 1973 for her role in *The Exorcist.* Year/Age: 1995/**36** 1996/**37** 1997/**38**
- **JOHN HURT** Actor. (England) He appeared in *A Man For All Seasons* in 1966 and won an Oscar for best actor in 1980 for *The Elephant Man.* Appeared in film *Even Cowgirls Get the Blues.* Year/Age: 1995/**55** 1996/**56** 1997/**57**
- **STEVE PERRY** Singer. (Hanford, CA) From the rock group JOURNEY. Their biggest hit: "Open Arms" in 1982. His biggest hit: "Oh Sherrie" in 1984. Year/Age: 1995/**46** 1996/**47** 1997/**48**
- **JAZZY JEFF** Rapper DJ. With Fresh Prince "Summertime." Year/Age: 1995/**30** 1996/**31** 1997/**32**

- **JOSEPH WAMBAUGH** Author. (Pittsburgh, PA) He wrote *The New Centurians, The Blue Knight, The Choir Boys, The Onion Field,* and *Finnegan's Week.* He was an ex-cop who writes books about law enforcement. Some became movies. Year/Age: 1995/**58** 1996/**59** 1997/**60**
- **OLIVIA D'ABO** Actress. She played Karen on TV's "The Wonder Years." Year/Age: 1995/**26** 1996/**27** 1997/**28**
- **MIKE BOSSY** Hockey player. (Canada) He is in the Hockey Hall of Fame. Year/Age: 1995/**38** 1996/**39** 1997/**40**
- **BILL BIXBY** Actor. (1934-1993 – San Francisco, CA) He played David Banner in "The Incredible Hulk," and Tom Corbett on TV's "The Courtship of Eddie's Father." Tragedy struck Bill when his 9-year-old son died of a virus and his wife committed suicide shortly after the boy's death. In films *Speedway* with Elvis and *My favorite Martian.* Directs TV's *Blossom.* (Died 11-21-93).
- **AUGUST STRINDBERG** Playwright. (1849-1912 – Sweden) Wrote *Miss Julie* and *The Ghost Sonata.* (Died 5-14-12)
- **SAM COOKE** Singer. (1935-1964 – Clarksdale, MS) His biggest hit: "You Send Me" in 1957. Before that, he was lead singer of the SOUL STIRRERS, a gospel group. He's a member of the Rock and Roll Hall of Fame. He was shot to death in a hotel room (Died 12-11-64).
- **D. W. (DAVID WARK) GRIFFITH** Film director. (1875-1948 – LaGrange, KY) Famous for film *Birth of a Nation* in 1915. (Died 7-23-48)
- **LORD GEORGE BYRON** Poet. (1788-1824) English poet, whose two major pursuits were poetry and women. He had an affair with his sister and was said to have fallen on chambermaids like a thunderbolt. (Died 4-19-1824)

FACTS FROM THE PAST

1901   Everybody in England loosened up as the Victorian Era ended with the death of The Black Widow, **QUEEN VICTORIA**, at age 82. She got that name when Prince Albert died and she went into mourning for a long time. She was on the throne for 63 years, the longest reign in history.

1917   **PRESIDENT WOODROW WILSON** pleaded for an end to the war in Europe, saying there had to be "Peace Without Victory." (By April, however, America was also at war.)

1968   The revolutionary NBC comedy "**ROWAN AND MARTIN'S LAUGH-IN**" premiered and started the careers of Goldie Hawn and Arte Johnson, among others.

1969   **GLEN CAMPBELL**'s "Wichita Lineman" becomes his first gold record.

1973   **GEORGE FOREMAN** knocked out **JOE FRAZIER** in the second round in Kingston, Jamaica, to win the world heavyweight title.

1980   The Soviet Union accused Nobel Laureate **ANDREI SAKHAROV** of subversive work and sent him and his wife, Yelena Bonner, into internal exile in the industrial city of Gorky.

1988   **MIKE TYSON** knocked out **LARRY HOLMES** in the fourth round at Atlantic City to retain the world heavyweight title.

1989   Football's **NORB DECKER** got his 7th Super Bowl Ring, as administrator for the San Francisco 49ers, winners of Super Bowl XXIII. He got his rings with the Rams, as player in 1951, Packers assistant coach '61, '62 and '65, and 49ers in '81 and '85 as assistant.

1989   The **SAN FRANCISCO 49ERS** won **SUPERBOWL XXIII** in a 20-16 victory over Cincinnati in the last 34 seconds when Joe Montana hit John Taylor with a 10-yard touchdown pass.

1990   A jury in Syracuse, NY, convicted graduate student Robert T. Morris of **FEDERAL COMPUTER TAMPERING** charges for unleashing a "worm" that crippled a computer network.

1994   **LONI ANDERSON** settles for $2 million and a vacation house as she and Burt Reynolds divorce.

JANUARY 23

BIRTHDAYS

• **JOHNNY RUSSELL** Country singer. (Sunflower County, MS.) He wrote "Act Naturally," a hit for Ringo and the BEATLES. Russell's biggest hit: "Red Necks, White Sox and Blue Ribbon Beer" in 1973. Year/**Age**: 1995/**55** 1996/**56** 1997/**57**

• **GIL GERARD** Actor. (Little Rock, AR) Starred in "Buck Rogers in the 25th Century" and "Code 3." Year/**Age**: 1995/**52** 1996/**53** 1997/**54**

• **RICHARD DEAN ANDERSON** Actor. (Minneapolis, MN) TV's "Mac Gyver," for seven seasons. Year/**Age**: 1995/**45** 1996/**46** 1997/**47**

• **JEANNE MOREAU** Actress. (Paris, France) Won a Cesar (French Academy Award). Year/**Age**: 1995/**67** 1996/**68** 1997/**69**

• **ROBIN ZANDER** Singer. (Rockford, IL) Vocalist with the rock quartet CHEAP TRICK. Their biggest hit: "I Want You to Want Me" in 1979. Year/**Age**: 1995/**42** 1996/**43** 1997/**44**

• **TIFFANI-AMBER THIESSEN** Actress. (Orange County, CA) Plays Valerie Malone on *Beverly Hills 90210*. Also starred in TV's *Saved By the Bell*. Year/**Age**: 1995/**21** 1996/**22** 1997/**23**

• **JERRY KRAMER** Former football star. (Jordan, MT) A Green Bay Packer star and one of the first football players to write a book – *Instant Replay* and later *Distant Replay*. Year/**Age**: 1995/**59** 1996/**60** 1997/**61**

• **PRINCESS CAROLINE OF MONACO** (Monte Carlo, Monaco) Daughter of the late Grace Kelly and Prince Rainier. Her 2nd husband, Stefano Cusiraghi, died in a speedboat race in 1990. Year/**Age**: 1995/**38** 1996/**39** 1997/**40**

• **ANITA POINTER** Singer. (Oakland, CA) POINTER SISTERS. Their biggest hit: "Slow Hand" in 1981. Year/**Age**: 1995/**47** 1996/**48** 1997/**49**

• **PATRICK SIMMONS** Singer/guitarist. (Aberdeen, WA) With the DOOBIE BROTHERS. He wrote their hit "Black Water" in 1974. Year/**Age**: 1995/**45** 1996/**46** 1997/**47**

• **CHITA RIVERA** Actress. (Washington, DC) She appeared in the movie *Sweet Charity* and on the "Dick Van Dyke Show" in the 1970's. In 1993 she won a Tony for *Kiss of the Spider Woman*. Year/**Age**: 1995/**62** 1996/**63** 1997/**64**

• **RUTGER HAUER** Actor. (The Netherlands) Appeared in many films including *Inside the Third Reich, Blindside, Blade Runner,* and *Surviving the Game*. Year/**Age**: 1995/**51** 1996/**52** 1997/**53**

• **RANDOLPH SCOTT** Actor. (1898-1987 – Born George Randolph Scott in Orange County, VA) He was a Hollywood producer's answer to Gary Cooper. The turning point in his career came at age 43 in 1946, when the movie *Badman's Territory* was a box office hit. Reportedly he was worth $50 to $100 million dollars. He made his last film in 1962: *Ride the High Country*. In all, he made about 100 pictures. The STATLER BROTHERS recorded a song about him: "Whatever Happened to Randolph Scott." (Died 3-2-87)

• **HUMPHREY BOGART** Actor. (1899-1957 – NYC) Nominated for best actor in 1943 for *Casablanca* and won an Oscar in 1951 for *The African Queen*. He was also nominated in 1954 for *Caine Mutiny*. In 1941, he starred in the *Maltese Falcon* as Sam Spade. He had a raspy lisp and limited use of his facial expressions due to a wound he suffered when his troop ship was shelled in the war. Many film historians list his birthdate as Dec. 25, 1900, which was done to make him appear less menacing. He smoked 5 packs of cigarettes a day, and if you watch any of his old movies, you'll notice he's either got a cigarette in his mouth, or is lighting one up. (Died of cancer at age 57 on 1-14-57.)

• **ERNIE KOVACS** Actor/comedian. (1919-1962 – Trenton, NJ) He was the host of the first early-morning TV show, a live 7-9 a.m. program from Philadelphia in 1950 – "3 to Get Ready." He was married to actress/singer Edie Adams. He died in a traffic accident in Hollywood, CA. (1-13-62)

• **JOHN HANCOCK** Statesman. (1737-1793 – Braintree, MA) Signed the Declaration of Independence. (Died 10-8-1793)

FACTS FROM THE PAST

1849 **DR. ELIZABETH BLACKWELL** became the first woman to receive an M.D. Degree. She was born in Bristol, England, and got the degree from the Medical Institute in Geneva, NY.

1943 The Academy Award-winning film **CASABLANCA** premiered. It starred Humphrey Bogart, Ingrid Bergman, and character actors Peter Lorre, Claude Rains, and Sidney Greenstreet. It nearly starred Ronald Reagan and Ann Sheridan.

1968 During a routine electronic intelligence mission, the **U.S. SHIP PUEBLO** and its 83-man crew commanded by Lloyd Bucher were seized by North Koreans who claimed the ship had intruded within their 12-mile limit. The North Koreans insisted on an apology, which they got December 22 from U.S. General Woodward, and the American crew was released. One crew member was killed.

1970 **JUDY COLLINS** was denied permission to sing her testimony at the Chicago Seven trial.

1973 **NEIL YOUNG** stopped to make an announcement in the middle of his concert in New York and brought the house down when he told of the U.S. reaching an accord in the **VIETNAM WAR.** The crowd cheered and cried.

1978 **TERRY KATH** of the group CHICAGO accidentally shot himself in the head with a pistol at age 32.

1986 **CHUCK BERRY, ELVIS PRESLEY**, and **FATS DOMINO** were among the first inductees into the Rock and Roll Hall of Fame.

1992 A tabloid report claimed that **GENNIFER FLOWERS**, a former singer and TV reporter, had a 12-year affair with **BILL CLINTON** and had tape recordings of phone conversations with Clinton.

1994 **DALLAS COWBOYS** defeat the 49ers as Jimmy Johnson predicted in the NFC Championship Game. Quarterback Troy Aikman suffers a head injury and can't recall where the Superbowl is being held. They won anyway and enjoyed another victory.

JANUARY 24

Touch-and-go

BIRTHDAYS

- **ROB DIBBLE** Baseball. (Bridgeport, CT) Cincinnati Reds star. He throws a 100 m.p.h. fastball. Year/**Age**: 1995/**31** 1996/**32** 1997/**33**

- **MARIA TALLCHIEF** Ballerina. (Fairfax, OK) In the movie *Million Dollar Mermaid*. Year/**Age**: 1995/**70** 1996/**71** 1997/**72**

- **BECKY HOBBS** C&W. (Bartlesville, OK) One of her hits, recorded with Moe Bandy, was "Let's Get Over Them Together." Year/**Age**: 1995/**45** 1996/**46** 1997/**47**

- **NEIL DIAMOND** Entertainer. (Brooklyn, NY) Biggest hits: "You Don't Bring Me Flowers" with Barbra Streisand in 1978, and "Cracklin' Rosie" in 1970. All together, he's racked up over 14 gold albums. At age 15, he decided to become a singer after seeing folk singer Pete Seeger perform. He has written songs for others, including "I'm a Believer" for the Monkees, and "Red Red Wine" for UB40. Year/**Age**: 1995/**54** 1996/**55** 1997/**56**

- **MARY LOU RETTON** Gymnast. (Fairmont, WV) In 1984 she was the first American woman to win an Olympic gold metal in gymnastics, and the first female athlete to do a Wheaties "Breakfast of Champions" TV commercial. Appeared in *Naked Gun 33 1/3*. Year/**Age**: 1995/**27** 1996/**28** 1997/**29**

- **MATTHEW WILDER** Singer/songwriter. (Manhattan, NY) Was a session singer for Bette Midler and Rickie Lee Jones. His biggest hit: "Break My Stride" in 1983. Year/**Age**: 1995/**42** 1996/**43** 1997/**44**

- **RAY STEVENS** Singer. (Born Ray Ragsdale in Clarksdale, GA) Biggest hits: "The Streak" in 1974, "Ahab the Arab" in 1962, and "Everything is Beautiful" in 1970. Year/**Age**: 1995/**54** 1996/**55** 1997/**56**

- **DOUG KERSHAW** Ragin' Cajun fiddler. (Telridge, LA) "Louisiana Man." Year/**Age**: 1995/**59** 1996/**60** 1997/**61**

- **ERNEST BORGNINE** Actor. (Born Ermes Effron Borgnine in Hamden, CT) Won an Oscar for best actor in 1955 for *Marty*. He was a co-star in the "Air Wolf" TV series. His hobby is appearing as a clown for charity events. He and his wife are often grand marshals for the famous Milwaukee Circus Parade. Year/**Age**: 1995/**78** 1996/**79** 1997/**80**

- **ANITA BAKER** Singer. (Toledo, OH) One of her biggest hits: "Sweet Love" from the album *Rapture* which catapulted her to the top of the charts in 1986. Year/**Age**: 1995/**37** 1996/**38** 1997/**39**

- **YAKOV SMIRNOFF** Comedian. (Odessa, USSR) Appears in ads for Best Western. Year/**Age**: 1995/**44** 1996/**45** 1997/**46**

- **ORAL ROBERTS** Evangelist. (Tulsa, OK) He began his preaching career in 1935. He once said he would be "called back to God" if he did not raise $8 million before the end of the fiscal year. He failed, but he didn't die. Year/**Age**: 1995/**77** 1996/**78** 1997/**79**

- **NASTASSIA KINSKI** Actress. (Germany) She starred in "Cat People," and with Dudley Moore in *Unfaithfully Yours*. Year/**Age**: 1995/**35** 1996/**36** 1997/**37**

- **MARK GOODSON** TV game-show producer.(1915-1992) One of his earliest and most successful game shows was "Beat the Clock," with Bud Collyer as host in 1950. He created "Family Feud" and "The Price Is Right." (Died 10-18-92)

- **JACK BRICKHOUSE** Former Chicago sportscaster. (Peoria, IL) He is in the Baseball Hall of Fame. Year/**Age**: 1995/**79** 1996/**80** 1997/**81**

- **AARON NEVILLE** Singer. (New Orleans, LA) Biggest hits: "Tell It Like It Is" in 1966 and "Don't Know Much" with Linda Ronstadt in 1989. Year/**Age**: 1995/**54** 1996/**55** 1997/**56**

- **GIOGIO CHINAGLIA** Soccer player. (Italy) Year/**Age**: 1995/**48** 1996/**49** 1997/**50**

- **JOHN BELUSHI** Actor. (1949-1982 – Wheaton, IL) One of the original stars of "Saturday Night Live" ("Not-Ready-For-Prime-Time-Players") from 1975-1979. He also starred in the popular *Blues Brothers* film with Dan Aykroyd, *National Lampoon's Animal House* and the romantic comedy *Continental Divide*. His much publicized fatal drug overdose was the subject of the bestseller and 1987 film release, *Wired*. (Died 3-5-82)

- **SHARON TATE** Actress. (1943-1969 – Dallas, TX) Married to film producer Roman Polanski. In the film *Valley of the Dolls* in 1967. She was murdered by Charles Manson's followers. (8-9-69)

FACTS FROM THE PAST

1848 The **CALIFORNIA GOLD RUSH** began when James Marshall discovered a bonanza near Colona, CA.

1899 Rubber heels were patented by **HUMPHREY O'SULLIVAN** of Lowell, MA. Unlike leather, they didn't slip on wet surfaces.

1922 **CHRISTIAN K. NELSON** of Onawa, Iowa, patented the Eskimo Pie.

1970 **ANDREW MOOG** introduced the Moog Synthesizer. The American Federation of Musicians considered banning the invention, fearing it would put live musicians out of work.

1982 The most-watched sporting event of all time took place at the Pontiac Silverdome, Pontiac, MI. San Francisco beat Cincinnati 26-21 in Super Bowl XVI. A Super Bowl record was set by Cincinnati's **DON ROSS**, who caught 11 passes for 104 yards. The MVP was **JOE MONTANA**, who completed 14 of 22 passes for 157 yards.

1989 Confessed serial killer **THEODORE BUNDY** was put to death in Florida's electric chair for the 1978 kidnap-murder of one of his victims, 12-year-old Kimberly Leach.

1989 **JAMES BROWN** pleaded guilty to drug possession and assault charges. He was sentenced to six years in jail.

1994 **SENATOR PACKWOOD** lost his suit to keep his diaries private while being investigated for sexual misconduct.

JANUARY 25

BIRTHDAYS

- **ETTA JAMES**. Singer. (Los Angeles, CA) Biggest hit: "Tell Mama" in 1967. Kicked the heroin habit in 1975. Year/**Age:** 1995/**57** 1996/**58** 1997/**59**
- **ERNIE HARWELL** Baseball. (Atlanta, GA) He's in the Baseball Hall of Fame. Broadcast the Detroit Tiger games on WJR 1960-1991, 1993. Year/**Age:** 1995/**77** 1996/**78** 1997/**79**
- **ANDY COX** Guitarist. (England) Hits with the FINE YOUNG CANNIBALS: "She Drives Me Crazy" and "Good Thing." Year/**Age:** 1995/**35** 1996/**36** 1997/**37**
- **EDWIN NEWMAN** TV newsman/author. (NYC) NBC newsman for many years and moderator on "Meet the Press." Year/**Age:** 1995/**76** 1996/**77** 1997/**78**
- **DEAN JONES** Actor. (Decatur, AL) He's been in movies since 1956 and probably his most popular was *The Love Bug* for Walt Disney in 1969. Also appeared in *Beethoven.* Year/**Age:** 1995/**64** 1996/**65** 1997/**66**
- **LOU GROZA** Football. (Martin's Ferry, OH) He played for the Cleveland Browns from 1946 to 1967. Year/**Age:** 1995/**71** 1996/**72** 1997/**73**
- **EDUARD SHEVARDNADZE** Diplomat. (Russia) Former Minister of Foreign Affairs replacing Andrei Gromyko in 1985. Controversial resignation in 1990. Year/**Age:** 1995/**67** 1996/**68** 1997/**69**
- **ELIZABETH ALLEN** Actress. (Born Elizabeth Gillease in Jersey City, NJ) Appeared in *Diamond Head, Donovan's Reef,* and other films. Year/**Age:** 1995/**61** 1996/**62** 1997/**63**

- **MARK "Super" DUPER** Football. (Pineville, LA) Miami wide receiver. Year/**Age:** 1995/**36** 1996/**37** 1997/**38**
- **GREG PALMER** Actor. (San Francisco, CA) Year/**Age:** 1995/**68** 1996/**69** 1997/**70**
- **HEIDI WOLFGRAMM** Musician. (Minneapolis, MN) Member of the JETS, a brothers and sisters group. Year/**Age:** 1995/**26** 1996/**27** 1997/**28**
- **LEIGH TAYLOR-YOUNG** Actress. Rachael Wells on TV's "Peyton Place." Year/**Age:** 1995/**50** 1996/**51** 1997/**52**
- **CORAZON (CORY) AQUINO** Former President of the Philippines. (Born Corazon Cojuangco) Her husband, Benigno Aquino, was assassinated in 1983 as he returned from exile in the United States. Year/**Age:** 1995/**62** 1996/**63** 1997/**64**
- **VIRGINIA WOOLF** English writer. (1882-1941 – London, England) She wrote *Jacob's Room* and *To the Lighthouse.* She committed suicide by drowning in Sussex, England. (3-28-41)
- **MILDRED DUNNOCK** Actress. (1901-1991 – Baltimore, MD) Nominated for an Academy Award for her role as the saleman's wife in *Death of a Salesman* in 1951. This character actress appeared in *The Jazz Singer* in 1953, *Love Me Tender* and *Peyton Place.* (Died 7-5-91)
- **SOMERSET MAUGHAM** Writer. (1874-1965 – France) One of his great works was *Of Human Bondage.* (Died 12-16-65)
- **ROBERT BURNS** Scottish Poet. (1759-1796 – Scotland) Among his works: *Auld Lang Syne, Red, Red Rose,* and *Comin' Through the Rye.* (Died 1-21-1796)

FACTS FROM THE PAST

1858 MENDELSSOHN'S "Wedding March" was composed for a royal wedding – the marriage of Queen Victoria's daughter.

1890 Reporter **"NELLIE BLY"** (Elizabeth Cochrane) of the *New York World* received a tumultuous welcome home after she completed a round-the-world journey in 72 days, six hours and eleven minutes.

1915 **ALEXANDER GRAHAM BELL** inaugurated transcontinental phone service in the United States. In New York, Bell repeated his famous words from 1876: "Mr. Watson, come here, I want you" to his assistant in San Francisco.

1945 **FIRST LT. AUDIE MURPHY** earned the Congressional Medal of Honor for ordering his men to retreat, jumping into a blazing tank destroyer, holding off the Germans singlehandedly with a machine gun and ordering an artillery strike on his own position. They only awarded 7 catagories of medals for heroism in WWII and he won 5 of them.

1947 Gangster **AL CAPONE** , broke and close to insanity, died of neurosyphilis. The church refused to have a funeral mass for him.

1961 The first presidential news conference was televised and broadcast on radio live from Washington, DC. **PRESIDENT KENNEDY** answered 31 questions in 38 minutes.

1969 **CREEDENCE CLEARWATER REVIVAL** released the polular LP "Proud Mary."

1971 **GRACE SLICK** gave birth to a girl. She and **PAUL KANTNER** originally wanted to name their daughter God, but decided on China. The couple were not married.

1971 **CHARLES MANSON** and 3 young women followers were convicted in Los Angeles of the 1969 **TATE-LABIANCA, MURDERS.** Manson said his murder spree was inspired by "secret messages" he heard on the Beatles *White Album.*

1980 **PAUL McCARTNEY**, charged with smuggling marijuana into the country, was released from a Japanese jail and deported.

1981 The **52 AMERICANS HELD HOSTAGE** by Iran for 444 days arrived back in the United States.

1993 President Clinton named **HILLARY RODHAM CLINTON** to lead the task force on health-care reform. He became the first President to give his wife a formal role in making domestic policy.

1994 **MICHAEL JACKSON** pacified both the courts and a 14-year-old boy who charged him with sexual molestation with $10-$24 million. He pleads not guilty.

JANUARY 26
Spouse's Day

It's hard to be humble when you're a hero

BIRTHDAYS

- **TOM KEIFER** Musician. (Pennsylvania) From the heavy metal group CINDERELLA. Biggest hit: "Don't Know What You Got," in 1988. Year/**Age**: 1995/**34** 1996/**35** 1997/**36**

- **JULES FEIFFER** Cartoonist/screenwriter. (NYC) Wrote *Carnal Knowledge* screenplay. Year/**Age**: 1995/**66** 1996/**67** 1997/**68**

- **PAUL NEWMAN** Actor. (Cleveland, OH) Nominated for 7 Academy Awards, Best Actor for *The Color of Money*. He's also involved in auto racing. Manufactures salad dressing, spaghetti sauce, and popcorn under his label. Proceeds go to charity. He and Joanne Woodward have 3 daughters. He was disqualified from Navy pilot school during WWII because he is color blind. Year/**Age**: 1995/**70** 1996/**71** 1997/**72**

- **EARTHA KITT** Singer. (North, SC) Grateful for a good harvest, her sharecropper father named her after the soil. Two hits in 1953: "C'est Si Bon" and "Santa Baby." She played the Catwoman on the "Batman" TV show. Appeared in the film *Boomerang* in 1992. Year/**Age**: 1995/**67** 1996/**68** 1997/**69**

- **ANNE JEFFRIES** Actress. (Goldsboro, NC) Leading lady of the 1940's. She was formerly in opera. Appeared in *Dillinger*, *Boys Night Out*, and "Topper" on TV. Year/**Age**: 1995/**72** 1996/**73** 1997/**74**

- **BOB UECKER** Sports announcer. (Milwaukee, WI) The radio voice of the Milwaukee Brewers, on the TV sitcom "Mr. Belvidere." Announcer in *Major League*. In 1963, when he was a Milwaukee Braves rookie catcher with one home run, his roommate was slugger Eddie Matthews. Uecker said, "Between me and my roomy, we've hit 400 home runs." Year/**Age**: 1995/**60** 1996/**61** 1997/**62**

- **ROGER VADIM** Film director. (Born Roger Vadim Piemiannikow in Paris, France) He wrote and directed *And God Created Woman*, and directed *Barbarella* and *Pretty Maids All in a Row*. Was married to Jane Fonda. Year/**Age**: 1995/**67** 1996/**68** 1997/**69**

- **GENE SISKEL** Movie critic. (Chicago, IL) "Siskel & Ebert." (He's the thin one.) Year/**Age**: 1995/**49** 1996/**50** 1997/**51**

- **ANGELA DAVIS** Political activist. (Birmingham, AL) In 1971 she was on FBI most wanted list for her membership in the Black Panther Party. Active in prison reform and women's suffrage. Year/**Age**: 1995/**51** 1996/**52** 1997/**53**

- **HUEY "PIANO" SMITH** Musician. (New Orleans, LA) Biggest hit: "Don't You Just Know It" in 1958. He played piano on "Sea Cruise" – a hit for Frankie Ford. Year/**Age**: 1995/**61** 1996/**62** 1997/**63**

- **WAYNE GRETZKY** Hockey star. (Canada) "The Great One" with the Los Angeles Kings. In 1989, he became the leading scorer in NHL history with 1,851 points. $25.5 million contract in '93; 8-time MVP. Year/**Age**: 1995/**34** 1996/**35** 1997/**36**

- **ANDREW RIDGELY** Guitarist. (England) He was part of duo WHAM. Biggest hit: "Wake Me Up Before You Go-Go" in 1984. Year/**Age**: 1995/**32** 1996/**33** 1997/**34**

- **EDDIE VAN HALEN** Guitarist. (Nijmegen, The Netherlands) VAN HALEN (the band) formed in Pasadena, CA, in 1974. Big hits: "Jump" in 1984, and "Right Now" in 1992. Married Valerie Bertinelli. Year/**Age**: 1995/**38** 1996/**39** 1997/**40**

- **JIMMY VAN HEUSEN** Composer. (1913-1990 – Born Edward Chester Babcock in Syracuse, NY) He took his professional name from the shirt company. His four Academy Award winners were "High Hopes," "Call Me Irresponsible," "All The Way," and "Swinging On A Star." (Died 2-7-90.)

- **MARIA VON TRAPP** Author. (1905-1987) Her life story was portrayed in the movie and on stage in *The Sound of Music*, starring Julie Andrews. (Died 3-28-87)

- **DOUGLAS MACARTHUR** General. (1880-1964 – Little Rock, AR) An American general, war hero, and Commander of the Allied Forces in Southwest Pacific during WWII. President Harry Truman relieved him of his command in April, 1951. (Died 4-5-64)

FACTS FROM THE PAST

1695 The notorious pirate, **CAPTAIN WILLIAM KIDD**, offered a kind of workmen's compensation to his crew: "If any man should lose an arm or leg in ye said service, he shall receive 600 pieces-of-eight or six able slaves."

1784 **BENJAMIN FRANKLIN** wrote a letter to his daughter supporting the turkey as America's national symbol, complaining that the eagle was a bird of bad moral character and the turkey was a more respectable bird.

1939 Principal photography began for **DAVID O. SELZNICK'S** movie version of *Gone With The Wind.*

1956 **BUDDY HOLLY** made his first recordings for DECCA in Nashville, with the Three Tunes country group. Exactly two years later he and the Crickets appeared on "The Ed Sullivan Show."

1977 The first lead guitarist for FLEETWOOD MAC, **PETER GREEN**, was committed to a mental hospital in England after he fired a gun at a delivery boy who was bringing a check to Green for royalties on the group's record sales.

1988 **ANDREW LLOYD WEBBER'S** *Phantom of the Opera* opened on Broadway.

1992 **WASHINGTON BEAT BUFFALO** 37-24 in Super Bowl XXVI. The Redskins' quarterback and MVP, Mark Rypien, threw for 292 yards and two touchdowns.

1992 Following the Super Bowl, **BILL CLINTON** appeared with his wife Hillary on "Sixty Minutes," denying an affair with Gennifer Flowers as reported in a tabloid. In defending her husband on the program, **HILLARY CLINTON** made **TAMMY WYNETTE** very upset when she said, "I'm not some little woman, standing by my man like Tammy Wynette."

1994 **PRINCE CHARLES** was making a speech in Sydney, Australia, when a 23-year-old man ran out of the crowd and fired two blanks at him from a starter pistol. The man was upset with the Prince for his treatment of the Cambodian boat people.

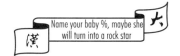

JANUARY 27

BIRTHDAYS

- **SETH JUSTMAN** Keyboardist. (Washington, DC) 1982 hit: "Centerfold" with J. GEILS BAND. Year/**Age:** 1995/**44** 1996/**45** 1997/**46**
- **TROY DONAHUE** Actor. (Born Merle Johnson in NYC) He appeared on TV in "Surfside 6" and "Hawaiian Eye." The movie *A Summer Place* was the beginning of his short in which he played Sandra Dee's boyfriend. Other films include *Godfather II.* Year/**Age:** 1995/**59** 1996/**60** 1997/**61**
- **SKITCH HENDERSON** Musician. (Born Lyle Henderson in Halstad, MN) His orchestra played on the "Today Show," "Garroway at Large," "Steve Allen Show," and the "Tonight Show" from 1962-1966. Year/**Age:** 1995/**77** 1996/**78** 1997/**79**
- **BRIDGET FONDA** Actress. In *Point of No Return,* a remake of the French film, *La Femme Nikita* and *It Could Happen To You.* Year/**Age:** 1995/**31** 1996/**32** 1997/**33**
- **MIKHAIL BARYSHNIKOV** Ballet star. (Riga, Latvia) He defected in 1974, and starred in the film *White Nights.* Currently with White Oak Dance Project, a modern dance company. Year/**Age:** 1995/**47** 1996/**48** 1997/**49**
- **BRIAN GOTTFRIED** Tennis pro. (Baltimore, MD) All-American, attended Trinity University in San Antonio, TX. Year/**Age:** 1995/**43** 1996/**44** 1997/**45**
- **MORDECAI RICHLER** Author. (Canada) He wrote *The Apprenticeship of Duddy Kravitz* in 1959. Year/**Age:** 1995/**64** 1996/**65** 1997/**66**
- **NICK MASON** Musician. (England) Drummer with PINK FLOYD, a progressive British rock band formed in 1965. Biggest hit: "Another Brick in The Wall (Part II)" in 1980. Year/**Age:** 1995/**50** 1996/**51** 1997/**52**
- **SAMUEL GOMPERS** Labor Leader. (1850-1924 – London, England) He was a labor leader and the first AFL president. (Died 12-13-24)

- **LEWIS CARROLL** English author. (1832-1898 – England) (Pseudonym of Charles Dodgson) Author of *Alice's Adventures in Wonderland.* (Died 1-14-1898)
- **DAVID SEVILLE** Musician (1919-1972 – Born Ross Bagdasarian in Fresno, CA) Creator of the CHIPMUNKS. Biggest hit: "The Chipmunk Song" in 1958. Seville had a hit called "Witch Doctor." He had small roles in *Rear Window* and *Stalag 17.* David's son still produces some Chipmunk records. The Chipmunks were named for Liberty Record Co. executives Alvin, Theodore, and Simon. (Died 1-16-72)
- **WOLFGANG AMADEUS MOZART** [am-uh day'-us] Composer. (1756-1791 – Salzburg, Austria) A member of a gifted musical family, he began playing at the age of 3, composing by age 5, and by age 13 had written concertos, sonatas, symphonies and a German operetta. Among his most famous works: the opera *Don Giovanni, Eine Kleine Nachtmusik, The Magic Flute,* and his last work, Symphony No. 41 "The Jupiter," which he wrote in less than sixteen days. He only lived to age 35. His life was the subject of the award-winning play-turned-motion picture, *Amadeus.* (Died 12-5-1791)
- **DONNA REED** Actress. (1921-1986 – Born Donna Belle Mullenger in Denison, IA) She won an Oscar for best supporting actress in 1953 for *From Here To Eternity.* For a short time, played the role of Miss Ellie on "Dallas." Best known for her starring role on "The Donna Reed Show," 1958-1966. (Died 1-14-86)
- **WILLIAM RANDOLPH HEARST JR.** Journalist .(1908-1993 – NYC) Pulitzer winner led the Hearst Newspaper empire. (Died 7-9-86)
- **JEROME KERN** Composer .(1885-1945 – NYC) He composed many memorable songs, including "Smoke Gets In Your Eyes," "Ol' Man River," and "The Last Time I Saw Paris." (Died 11-11-45)

FACTS FROM THE PAST

1926 The first demonstration of television was given by **JOHN BAIRD**, a Russian engineer who immigrated to the U.S. in 1919. He invented the Iconoscope in 1923. This was the first element necessary in the development of an all-electronic TV system. It was Valdimir Zworykin who was responsible for the invention of television, and John Baird for the development.

1958 Rock music pioneer **LITTLE RICHARD** (Richard Penniman) abandoned his career and enrolled in Oakwood Bible College in Huntsville, AL. He was inspired by a near-death experience: While on tour, the plane caught fire as they flew over the Philippines. His prayer to survive was answered.

1967 Three men died on the launch pad at Cape Kennedy (now Cape Canaveral). A flash fire trapped **ED WHITE, VIRGIL GRISSOM** and **ROGER CHAFFEE** inside the command module, and they could not rush out the escape hatch because it required special tools and 3 minutes time. Later the hatch was redesigned to open in 10 seconds.

1968 **OTIS REDDING**'s first hit "Dock of the Bay" was released posthumously. He and four members of his band, the BAR-KAYS, were killed in a plane crash on December 10, 1967. He had also written many hits including "Respect" for **ARETHA FRANKLIN** and "Sweet Soul Music" for **ARTHUR CONLEY.**

1973 The Vietnam Peace Treaty was signed by **HENRY KISSINGER** and **LE DUC THO** of North Vietnam. It ended the longest war in American history.

1984 Singer **MICHAEL JACKSON** suffered burns to his scalp when, by accident, a special-effects explosion during the filming of a TV Pepsi commercial set his hair on fire. Brother Tito Jackson put out the fire.

1993 American sumo wrestler **CHAD ROWAN** was awarded the Japanese sport's highest rank, becoming the first foreign "Yokozuna."

1994 Former National Security aide **OLIVER NORTH** announced that he was seeking the Republican nomination for the U.S. Senate seat held by Charles Robb (D-Va).

JANUARY 28

What's the uniform for chess?

BIRTHDAYS

- **ALAN ALDA** Actor/producer. (Born Alfonso Roberto D'Abruzzo in NYC) He is the son of actor Robert Alda. He played Hawkeye Pierce on the "M*A*S*H" TV series which is still going in reruns. His major films include: *Same Time Next Year* in 1978, *Seduction of Joe Tynan* in 1979, and *The Four Seasons* in 1981. Appeared in *Canadian Bacon* and *Whispers in the Dark* in 1992 with Jill Clayburgh. Year/**Age**: 1995/**59** 1996/**60** 1997/**61**

- **BARBI BENTON** Actress/Singer. (Born Barbara Klein in Sacramento, CA) She married the wealthy George Gradow in 1979 and they have one child. Year/**Age**: 1995/**45** 1996/**46** 1997/**47**

- **ACKER BILK** Clarinet player/composer. (Born Bernard Stanley Bilk in England) Biggest hit: "Stranger on The Shore" in 1962. Year/**Age**: 1995/**66** 1996/**67** 1997/**68**

- **SUSAN SONTAG** Contemporary writer. (NYC) Wrote *Death Kit* and *Benefactor*. Year/**Age**: 1995/**62** 1996/**63** 1997/**64**

- **SUSAN HOWARD** Actress. (Born Jeri Lynn Mooney in Marshall, TX) Played Donna Krebs on "Dallas" TV series. Year/**Age**: 1995/**52** 1996/**53** 1997/**54**

- **NICHOLAS PRICE** Golfer. (South Africa) He won the 74th PGA Championship in 1992 and received a check for $280,000. Year/**Age**: 1995/**38** 1996/**39** 1997/**40**

- **RICK ALLEN** Organist. (Memphis, TN) With the BOX TOPS. Biggest hit: "The Letter" in 1967. Year/**Age**: 1995/**49** 1996/**50** 1997/**51**

- **CLAES OLDENBURG** Sculptor/painter. (Sweden) Year/**Age**: 1995/**66** 1996/**67** 1997/**68**

- **JOHN BECK** Actor. (Chicago, IL) Appeared in "Dallas" and "Flamingo Road." Year/**Age**: 1995/**49** 1996/**50** 1997/**51**

- **SIR FRANCIS DRAKE** British admiral/explorer. (1540-1597) First Englishman to sail around the world from 1577 to 1580. (Died 1-28-1597)

- **ARTHUR RUBINSTEIN** Pianist. (1887-1982 – Poland) He became an American citizen in 1937. In 1961, he gave 10 recitals at Carnegie Hall, in four weeks time, all for different charities. Actor John Rubinstein is his son. (Died 12-2-82)

- **AUGUSTE PICCARD & JEAN FELIX PICCARD** – Twin brothers. Sky and ocean explorers. (Born in Switzerland in 1884) They made record-setting balloon ascents into the stratosphere and ocean-depth descents and explorations. They invented enclosed balloon gondolas for high-altitude flight and the bathyscape for ocean-deep diving. Jean died 1-28-63 and Auguste 3-24-62.

- **HENRY MORTON STANLEY** Explorer. (1841-1904 – Wales) He was an explorer who was the leader of the African expedition to find the missing missionary/explorer Stanley Livingstone. He found him at Ujiji, near Lake Tanganyika, on Nov. 10, 1871, and his first words were: "Dr. Livingstone, I presume?" (Died 5-10-04)

- **ELIJAH WOOD** Actor. Year/**Age**: 1995/**14** 1996/**15** 1997/**16**

FACTS FROM THE PAST

1547 England's **KING HENRY VIII** died. He was succeeded by his 9-year-old son, Edward VI, who couldn't do any worse. Henry's huge 6-foot, 10-inch, lead coffin was transported on a three-day journey from London to Windsor.

1878 The **FIRST COMMERCIAL TELEPHONE SWITCHBOARD** began operating during the day in New Haven, CT. They had 21 subscribers and one operator, George Coy. He answered saying: "Ahoy, Ahoy."

1904 The first college sports letters were given out. Seniors who played on the **UNIVERSITY OF CHICAGO**'s football team were awarded blankets with the letter "C" on them.

1948 Television's first **EMMY AWARDS** were given.

1951 The **FIRST X-RATED FILM** opened in London, England. The French film, *La Vie Commence Demain* (Life Begins Tomorrow), featured a sequence that dealt with artificial insemination.

1956 **ELVIS PRESLEY** appeared on his first network TV show, the summer replacement show for Jackie Gleason, with Tommy and Jimmy Dorsey. He caused a sensation singing "Heartbreak Hotel."

1958 Brooklyn Dodger catcher **ROY CAMPANELLA** severed his spinal cord in an auto accident, ending his major league career at age 36. He lived in a wheel chair until his death in 1993.

1960 Club owners voted to bring the **DALLAS COWBOYS** (and Cowgirl cheerleaders) into the **NFL.**

1978 **TED NUGENT** carves his name with a knife into a fan's arm in response to that fan's request

1985 The hit song "**WE ARE THE WORLD**" was recorded following the American Music Awards. The song was the collaboration of Michael Jackson, Lionel Richie, and Quincy Jones, with some of the biggest names in contemporary music including Bruce Springsteen, Stevie Wonder, Diana Ross, Kenny Rogers, and Bob Dylan. They raised millions for starving people in Ethiopia.

1986 The **SPACE SHUTTLE CHALLENGER EXPLODED** 73 seconds after lift-off from Cape Canaveral, FL. All seven crew members were killed: Flight commander Francis Scobee, pilot Michael Smith, Ronald McNair, Ellison Onizuka, Judith Resnik, Gregory Jarvis and New Hampshire schoolteacher Christa McAuliffe. In wake of the disaster, many radio stations pulled Billy Joe Royal's "Burned Like a Rocket."

1994 Jury returns deadlocked for the second time in the murder trial of the **MENENDEZ BROTHERS** accused of killing their parents.

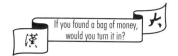
If you found a bag of money, would you turn it in?

JANUARY 29

BIRTHDAYS

- **IRLENE MANDRELL** C&W. (Houston, TX) The Mandrell sisters, Barbara, Louise and Irlene, had their own TV show from 1980-1982. Year/**Age**: 1995/**38** 1996/**39** 1997/**40**

- **JOHN FORSYTHE** Actor. (Born John Lincoln Freund in Penns Grove, NJ) America's favorite TV tycoon, Blake Carrington of the "Dynasty" clan. He was the unseen voice of Charlie Townsend on "Charlie's Angels." He wanted to be a baseball player and sports announcer, but couldn't make it, so he became an actor. Starred from 1957-1962 in TV's "Bachelor Father." Year/**Age**: 1995/**77** 1996/**78** 1997/**79**

- **TOM SELLECK** Actor. (Detroit, MI) Many called him an overnight success when he shot to fame on "Magnum P.I." Actually, he had struggled for years as a model and actor before landing the title role in the series. A guest appearance on "The Rockford Files" brought him recognition. He turned down the lead in *Raiders of the Lost Ark*. He starred in *Three Men and a Baby* in 1987. He played a major league ball player in *Mr. Baseball* and also appeared in *Christopher Columbus: The Discovery* in 1992. Year/**Age**: 1995/**50** 1996/**51** 1997/**52**

- **ANN JILLIAN** Actress. (Born Ann Jura Nauseda in Cambridge, MA) She played Millie on the TV series "Hazel" in the early 1960's. On Broadway in *Sugar Babies*. Year/**Age**: 1995/**44** 1996/**45** 1997/**46**

- **JUDY NORTON TAYLOR** Actress. (Santa Monica, CA) "The Waltons." Year/**Age**: 1995/**37** 1996/**38** 1997/**39**

- **GERMAINE GREER** Feminist/author. (Melbourne, Australia.) Wrote *The Female Eunuch* and *Sex and Destiny*. Year/**Age**: 1995/**56** 1996/**57** 1997/**58**

- **STEVE SAX** Baseball. (Sacramento, CA) With the Chicago White Sox. Year/**Age**: 1995/**35** 1996/**36** 1997/**37**

- **GREG LOUGANIS** [loo-gay'-nihs] Olympic gold medal diver in 1984 and 1988. Represents Speedo America swimwear. (San Diego, CA) Year/**Age**: 1995/**35** 1996/**36** 1997/**37**

- **KATHARINE ROSS** Actress. (Los Angeles, CA) Nominated in 1967 for supporting actress Oscar in *The Graduate*. In *Butch Cassidy and the Sundance Kid* in 1969. She's married to actor Sam Elliott. Appeared on TV's "Colbys." Year/**Age**: 1995/**52** 1996/**53** 1997/**54**

- **CLAUDINE LONGET** Singer. (Paris, France) A singer who was married to Andy Williams. In a jealous rage, she shot and killed skier Spider Savich. Year/**Age**: 1995/**52** 1996/**53** 1997/**54**

- **DONNA MARIE CAPONI** Pro golfer. (Detroit, MI) She has earned over a million dollars since turning pro in 1965. Year/**Age**: 1995/**50** 1996/**51** 1997/**52**

- **SARA GILBERT** Actress. Darlene on "Roseanne." She is the sister of actress Melissa Gilbert. Year/**Age**: 1995/**20** 1996/**21** 1997/**22**

- **OPRAH WINFREY** TV talk show hostess. (Kosciusko, MS) In 1984, Oprah went to Chicago to take over an ailing morning TV talk show and quickly became more popular there than Phil Donahue. In 1986, the "Oprah Winfrey Show" debuted nationally. She was one of the outstanding stars in the film *The Color Purple*. She used a liquid protein diet, Optifast, to lose 67 pounds and slim down to a size 10. Autobiography *Oprah*. Year/**Age**: 1995/**41** 1996/**42** 1997/**43**

- **THOMAS PAINE** Author. (1737-1809) (England) Wrote *Common Sense* and *Age of Reason*. (Died 6-8-1809)

- **WILLIAM McKINLEY** 25th U.S. President. (1843-1901 – Niles, OH.) A major in the army during the Civil War, also a lawyer, congressman and governor of Ohio before becoming President. He never allowed himself to be photographed unless he was perfectly dressed. He died in office at Buffalo, NY, as the result of a gunshot wound by an assassin while attending the Pan-American Exposition. (Died 9-14-01)

FACTS FROM THE PAST

1886   The first successful gasoline automobile was patented by **KARL BENZ**. He called it a Motor-wagon. It was a one-cylinder vehicle, weighing 560 pounds with three wheels, that could produce a top speed of 15 mph.

1936   The **BASEBALL HALL OF FAME** was established in Cooperstown, NY, with the naming of the first 5 members: Ty Cobb, Babe Ruth, Walter Johnson, Honus Wagner, and Christy Mathewson. The library contains a biography of every man ever to play even a half-inning of big league ball, along with the score of every game. (See page 251)

1971   **ALLEN KLEIN,** who once controlled the finances of the Beatles and the Rolling Stones, was found guilty of tax evasion. Klein's failure to rescue their financially ailing company, Apple Corps, is cited as one reason for the Beatles' breakup.

1979   **BRENDA SPENCER**, a San Diego teenager, shot and killed two people at school. When asked why she did it, she said, "I don't like Mondays." The Irish band Boomtown Rats later made a hit record using her answer as the title.

1984   **CHRISTIE'S GALLERY** auctioned off a dinner with two of America's best-known feminists, Gloria Steinem and Marlo Thomas, as part of the Variety Club's charity fund-raiser. The highest bid was submitted by Al Goldstein, publisher of one of the Women's Movement's least-favorite publications, *Screw* magazine, which features sexually explicit articles and photographs. Goldstein's phone-in bid of $3,000 was later invalidated because he had not submitted the bid in writing.

1990   Former *Exxon Valdez* skipper **JOSEPH HAZELWOOD** went on trial in Anchorage, Alaska, on charges stemming from the nation's worst oil spill. (Hazelwood was acquitted of the major charges and convicted of a misdemeanor.)

1993   President Clinton announced the abandonment of the ban on **HOMOSEXUALS IN THE MILITARY** effective as of July 15th.

1994   **MARY WISON,** former **SUPREME**, was injured and her son, age 14, was killed. The Jeep she was driving overturned.

JANUARY 30

A better way: go for the aorta.

BIRTHDAYS

- **JEANNE PRUETT** C&W singer. (Pell City, AL) Biggest hit record: "Satin Sheets" in 1973. Year/**Age**: 1995/**58** 1996/**59** 1997/**60**
- **JODY WATLEY** Singer. (Chicago, IL) She was a dancer on TV's "Soul Train." Jackie Wilson was her godfather. Biggest hit: "Looking For a New Love" in 1987. She won a Grammy for Best New Artist. Year/**Age**: 1995/**34** 1996/**35** 1997/**37**
- **CURTIS STRANGE** Golfer. (Norfolk, VA) The first player in history to win more than $1 million in a year. Year/**Age**: 1995/**40** 1996/**41** 1997/**42**
- **LOUIS RUKEYSER** Financial commentator. (NYC) PBS "Wall Street Week." Year/**Age**: 1995/**61** 1996/**62** 1997/**63**
- **VANESSA REDGRAVE** Actress. (London, England) Won an Academy Award for best supporting actress in the 1977 film *Julia*. Other films include *The House of Spirits Orpheus Descending* and *Howard's End*. Year/**Age**: 1995/**58** 1996/**59** 1997/**60**
- **DICK MARTIN** Comedian. (Detroit, MI) Co-starred with Dan Rowan on the "Laugh-In" show which premiered on Jan. 22, 1968. Year/**Age**: 1995/**73** 1996/**74** 1997/**75**
- **TAMMY GRIMES** Actress/singer. (Lynn, MA) She appeared on TV's "Love, American Style" and played Tammy Ward on the "Tammy Grimes Show" which lasted about a month on TV. Year/**Age**: 1995/**61** 1996/**62** 1997/**63**
- **MARTY BALIN** Singer. (Cincinnati, OH) Co-founder of JEFFERSON AIRPLANE/STARSHIP. His biggest hit: "Hearts" in 1981. Year/**Age**: 1995/**53** 1996/**54** 1997/**55**
- **DAVID WAYNE** Actor. (Born Wayne McKeekan in Traverse City, MI) A wiry character actor who appeared in *Adam's Rib*, *The Tender Trap*, and *The Last Angry Man*. Appeared on TV's "House Calls." Year/**Age**: 1995/**81** 1996/**82** 1997/**83**

- **HAROLD PRINCE** Producer/director. (NYC) His productions have included *Fiddler on the Roof, Phantom of the Opera, West Side Story,* and *42nd Street*. Year/**Age**: 1995/**67** 1996/**68** 1997/**69**
- **DICK CHENEY** [chay'-nee] Former Defense Secretary. (Lincoln, NE) Bush administration. Year/**Age**: 1995/**55** 1996/**56** 1997/**57**
- **GENE HACKMAN** Actor. (Born Eugene Alden Hackman in San Bernadino, CA) He won an Oscar in 1971 for best actor in *The French Connection*, and for supporting actor in *Unforgiven*, Oscar's best picture of 1992. Other films include *Mississippi Burning, Class Action, The Firm,* and *Geronimo.* Year/**Age**: 1995/**65** 1996/**66** 1997/**67**
- **WILLIAM KING** Musician. (Tuskegee, AL) With the COMMODORES. Their biggest hits: "Three Times a Lady" and "Still." Year/**Age**: 1995/**46** 1996/**47** 1997/**48**
- **BORIS SPASSKY** Chess master and journalist. (Leningrad, USSR) He lost to Bobby Fischer in 1972 and lost again in a rematch with Fischer in 1992. The winner received $3.35 million and the loser $1.65 million. Year/**Age**: 1995/**58** 1996/**59** 1997/**60**
- **JOHN IRELAND** Actor. (1915 - 1992 – Canada) He received an Oscar nomination for *All the King's Men*, in which he played a reporter. On TV, he was in the "Rawhide" series. (Died 3-21-92)
- **FRANKLIN DELANO ROOSEVELT** President. (1882-1945 – Hyde Park, NY) The 32nd U.S. President was the only President elected to four terms. When he had scarlet fever as a boy, his mother visited him by ladder outside his room to avoid going into quarantine. He was the first President to appear on TV and he coined the following terms: "bottleneck," "brain trust," "good-neighbor policy." (Died 4-12-45)

FACTS FROM THE PAST

1798 A brawl broke out in the House of Representatives in Philadelphia when **MATTHEW LYON** of Vermont spat in the face of Roger Griswold of Connecticut.

1835 The first assassination attempt against a U.S. President took place when painter **RICHARD LAWRENCE** took two shots at Andrew Jackson and missed.

1933 The first **"LONE RANGER"** radio program was broadcast. The Lone Ranger was played by George Seaton and Tonto was played by John Todd. The program debuted on WXYZ in Detroit and was narrated by Fred Foy. "Silver" was the Lone Ranger's horse, but Tonto's was first named "White Feller," and then "Paint," before becoming "Scout."

1948 Indian political and spiritual leader **MOHANDAS GANDHI** was **ASSASSINATED** in his garden in New Delhi by a Hindu fanatic who approached him, gave him the traditional salute of the faithful, and then shot him three times. Before dying, Gandhi blessed his assassin. Gandhi led his country to independence from British rule through his philosophy of non-violent confrontation.

1962 Two members of the **FLYING WALLENDAS** high-wire act were killed when their seven-person pyramid collapsed during a performance in Detroit.

1969 The **BEATLES** gave their **LAST PUBLIC PERFORMANCE** – a concert on the roof of their Apple Corps Headquarters, which is included in the film *Let It Be*. The police shut them down because nearby businesses complained about the noise.

1974 Musician **GREG LAKE** of Emerson, Lake & Palmer went skinny dipping in a hotel swimming pool in Salt Lake City. The only problem: the pool was in full view of people on the street.

1994 The Dallas Cowboys defeated the Buffalo Bills for the second time, 30-13, in **Super Bowl XXVIII**.

How many crackers can you eat at once?

JANUARY 31

BIRTHDAYS

- **ADRIAN VANDENBERG** Guitarist. (England) With the group WHITESNAKE. Biggest hit: "Here I Go Again," 1987. Year/**Age**: 1995/**37** 1996/**38** 1997/**39**

- **SUZANNE PLESHETTE** Actress. (NYC) Co-star of "The Bob Newhart Show" on TV. She also appeared in the movie *The Birds* in 1963 and TV series "Nightingales." Year/**Age**: 1995/**58** 1996/**59** 1997/**60**

- **CAROL CHANNING** Entertainer. (Seattle, WA) Best known for *Hello Dolly*. Year/**Age**: 1995/**72** 1996/**73** 1997/**74**

- **NORMAN MAILER** Author. (Long Branch, NJ) Wrote *The Executioner's Song* and *Harlot's Ghost*. Year/**Age**: 1995/**72** 1996/**73** 1997/**74**

- **JEAN SIMMONS** Actress. (London, England) She was nominated twice for Oscar, 1948 for *Hamlet* and 1969 for *The Happy Ending*. Also in *David Copperfield*. Year/**Age**: 1995/**66** 1996/**67** 1997/**68**

- **GARRY MOORE** TV host. (1915-1993 Born Thomas Garrison Morfit in Baltimore, MD) He had his own variety series, which ran successfully for 6 seasons in the late 1950's and early 1960's. One of his discoveries was Carol Burnett. Hosted "To Tell the Truth" and "I've Got A Secret." (Died 11-28-93)

- **ERNIE "MR. CUB" BANKS** Former baseball star. (Dallas, TX) Hall of Fame member. Now VP of New World Van Lines in California. In 1955, he hit 44 home runs, setting a major-league record for home runs in a season by a shortstop. Year/**Age**: 1995/**64** 1996/**65** 1997/**66**

- **NOLAN RYAN** Baseball pitcher. (Refugio, TX) He pitched a record 7 no-hitters, struck out a record 5,714 batters and compiled a record of 324-292 in 27 seasons. Fastball=100.8 mph. Year/**Age**: 1995/**48** 1996/**49** 1997/**50**

- **PHIL COLLINS** Singer. (England) The only performer to appear on both the English and American stages for the Live Aid Concert. His biggest hit was Oscar nominated "Against All Odds" in 1984. He starred in the film *Buster*. He was also an extra in the film *Chitty Chitty Bang Bang*. Year/**Age**: 1995/**44** 1996/**45** 1997/**46**

- **JERSEY JOE WALCOTT** Boxer. (1914-1994 Born Arnold Cream in New Jersey) Heavyweight champion in '51 & '52. Oldest to win the title (Died 2-25-94)

- **HENRY CASEY** Singer. (Hialeah, FL) Of K.C. AND THE SUNSHINE BAND. Biggest hit: "That's the Way I Like It" in 1975. Year/**Age**: 1995/**44** 1996/**45** 1997/**46**

- **RICHARD GEPHARDT** House Majority Leader. (St. Louis, MO) D/MO Year/**Age**: 1995/**54** 1996/**55** 1997/**56**

- **JOHNNY ROTTEN LYDON** Comtemporary rock muscian. Year/**Age**: 1995/**39** 1996/**40** 1997/**41**

- **JESSICA WALTER** Actress. (NYC) In the film *Play Misty for Me*. She won an Emmy for "Amy Prentiss." Year/**Age**: 1995/**51** 1996/**52** 1997/**53**

- **PHILIP GLASS** Composer. (Baltimore, MD) "Columbus Discovery" celebration for the NY Mets. Year/**Age**: 1995/**58** 1996/**59** 1997/**60**

- **TERRY KUTH** Singer. (1946-1978 – Chicago) Vocalist and guitarist for group CHICAGO. He died playing Russian Roulette. (1-23-78)

- **JACKIE ROBINSON** Baseball's (1919-1972 – Cairo, GA) The first man to break baseball's color barrier. He was elected to the Baseball Hall of Fame in 1962. He played for the Brooklyn Dodgers and was MVP in 1949. (Died 10-24-72)

- **EDDIE CANTOR** Entertainer. (1892-1964 – Born Edward Iskowitz in NYC) He started out as a singing waiter, and appeared frequently on "The Colgate Comedy Hour" and in 1955 "The Eddie Cantor Comedy Theater." (Died 10-1-64)

- **TALLULAH BANKHEAD** Actress. (1903-1968 – Huntsville, AL) Her last movie was *Fanatic* in 1965. (Died 12-12-68)

- **ZANE GREY** American author. (1875-1939 – Zanesville, OH) A dentist who later became a writer. He wrote much about the western frontier, selling more than 10 million books. One of his best was *Riders of the Purple Sage*. (Died 10-23-39)

- **FRANZ SCHUBERT** Composer. (1797-1828 – Austria) He finished *Unfinished Symphony* in 1822. Per his request, he was buried near the grave of Beethoven. (Died 11-19-1828)

FACTS FROM THE PAST

1851 **GAIL BORDEN** of Brooklyn, NY, announced the invention of evaporated milk. His idea was sparked by the problems of children who took ocean voyages and didn't have access to fresh milk.

1874 **JESSE JAMES** pulled off a robbery near Gadshill, MO. After he and his gang cleaned out the train's safe, James handed the engineer a prepared press release describing the robbery and instructing the victims to forward the information to the newspapers.

1949 The **FIRST TELEVISION DAYTIME SOAP OPERA,** "These Are My Children," was broadcast from the NBC station in Chicago. The program was created by **IRNA PHILLIPS** who later produced "As the World Turns" and "The Guiding Light."

1950 **PRESIDENT HARRY TRUMAN** announced that he ordered development of the hydrogen bomb by the Atomic Energy Commission.

1986 **MARY LUND** (age 40) of Kensington, MN, became the first female recipient of an artificial heart.

1989 A *Playboy* nude photo spread, featuring **LA TOYA JACKSON** posing with snakes, hit the newsstands.

1992 **HOWARD COSELL**, after 39 years on his radio show, "Speaking of Sports," retired from broadcasting.

1994 **SERGEI KRIKALEV** was among the crew launched in spaceshuttle Discovery for an 8-day NASA scientific mission. He was the first Russian to be a part of a U.S. space mission in 21 years.

FEBRUARY MEMORIES

YEARS AGO

1985

POPULAR SONGS
"Careless Whisper" by George Michael

"Easy Lover" by Phillip Bailey with Phil Collins

MOVIES
Mask
starring Cher in a drama about a teenage boy who suffers from a rare disease.

Witness
starring Harrison Ford as a detective investigating a murder witnessed by an Amish boy.

TV SHOWS
"Mr. Belvedere"
TV sitcom starring Bob Uecker, and Christopher Hewett as Mr. Belvedere.

"Off the Rack"
starring Ed Asner as a garment factory owner in L.A.

BOOKS
The House of the Spirits by Isabel Allende

1986

POPULAR SONGS
"How Will I Know" by Whitney Houston

"Kyrie" by Mr. Mister

MOVIES
Top Gun
starring Tom Cruise as a cocky Navy pilot. Co-stars Kelly McGillis, Anthony Edwards, Tom Skerritt, and Val Kilmer.

Pirates
starring Walter Matthau as Captain Red. A Roman Polanski film.

TV SHOWS
"Jack and Mike"
comedy/drama with Shelley Hack and Toni Mason. She works for a newspaper, he owns a restaurant.

"Together We Stand"
starring Elliott Gould as a sporting goods store owner with Dee Wallace Stone as his wife.

BOOKS
Prince of Tides by Pat Conroy

1987

POPULAR SONGS
"Open Your Heart" by Madonna

"Livin' On A Prayer" by Bon Jovi

MOVIES
Innerspace
starring Meg Ryan, Dennis Quaid, and Martin Short. A man is reduced in size.

Down and Out In Beverly Hills
comedy about a bum who lives with a wealthy family. Stars Bette Midler, Nick Nolte, and Richard Dreyfus.

TV SHOWS
"Buck James"
medical drama starring Dennis Weaver as Dr. James in a Texas University hospital.

"The Law and Harry McGraw"
Boston private eye, Jerry Orbach, and his attorney friend, Barbara Babcock.

BOOKS
Time Flies by Bill Cosby

SPECIAL DAYS

FEBRUARY	1995	1996	1997
World Marriage Day	Feb. 12	Feb. 11	Feb. 10
Shrove Tuesday (*New Orleans, LA*)	Feb. 28	Feb. 20	Feb. 11
Ash Wednesday	Mar. 1	Feb. 21	Feb. 12
President's Day	Feb. 20	Feb. 19	Feb. 18
Full Moon	Feb. 15	Feb. 4	Feb. 22

25 YEARS AGO

1970

POPULAR SONGS
"Venus" by The Shocking Blue

"Thank You (Falettinme Be Mice Elf Agin)" by Sly & The Family Stone

MOVIES
Patton
George C. Scott earned an Oscar for his portrayal of a tough W.W. II general.

Five Easy Pieces
a story about middle class America starring Jack Nicholson, Susan Anspach, Fannie Flagg, and Karen Black.

TV SHOWS
"The Engelbert Humperdinck Show"
A copy of the Tom Jones show.

"Dan August"
Burt Reynolds and Norman Fell star in this police drama.

BOOKS
No Place To Be Somebody by Charles Gordone

1971

POPULAR SONGS
"One Bad Apple" by The Osmonds

"What's Going On" by Marvin Gaye

MOVIES
Who Is Harry Kellerman and Why Is He Saying Those Terrible Things About Me?
Dustin Hoffman plays a pop composer.

The Andromeda Strain
Starring James Olson, Arthur Hill, and Kate Reid in a movie based on Micheal Crichton's sci-fi novel.

TV SHOWS
"Alias Smith and Jones"
western drama with Peter Deuel, Roger Davis, Ben Murphy, and Sally Field.

"The New Dick Van Dyke Show"
Van Dyke stars as a talk show host, Hope Lang plays his wife.

BOOKS
I'm O.K., You're O.K. by Thomas Harris

1972

POPULAR SONGS
"Let's Stay Together" by Al Green

"Without You" by Nilsson

MOVIES
Lady Sings the Blues
starring Diana Ross, Billy Dee Williams, and Richard Pryor in an imaginary story of singer Billy Holiday.

The Hot Rock
comedy/suspense about clumsy burglars, with George Segal and Robert Redford.

TV SHOWS
"Emergency"
drama about paramedics.

"Assignment Vienna," "Delphi Bureau," and "Jigsaw" rotate in one time slot called "The Men." One star was Robert Conrad.

BOOKS
The Peter Prescription by Laurence J. Peter

50 YEARS AGO

1945

POPULAR SONGS
"Rum And Coca-Cola" by Andrew Sisters

"Saturday Night (Is the Loneliest Night Of The Week)" by Frank Sinatra

MOVIES
Love Letters
love story drama featuring Joseph Cotton and Jennifer Jones.

The Picture of Dorian Gray
based on an Oscar Wilde novel. Angela Lansbury plays a singer. Co-stars George Sanders, Peter Lawford, and Donna Reed.

TV SHOWS
No regularly scheduled TV shows until May of 1946.

BOOKS
The Thurber Carnival by James Thurber

1946

POPULAR SONGS
"Doctor, Lawyer, Indian Chief" by Betty Hutton

"Personality" by Johnny Mercer

MOVIES
To Each His Own
starring Olivia de Havilland and John Lund in a story about a mother and her illegitimate son.

The Killers
a hit man seeks answers about why victims were killed. Stars John Cassavetes, Lee Marvin, Ronald Reagan, and Angie Dickinson.

TV SHOWS
No regularly scheduled TV shows until May of 1946.

BOOKS
The Egg and I by Betty Mac Donald

1947

POPULAR SONGS
"Managua Nicaragua" by Freddy Martin

"Open the Door Richard" by Count Basie

MOVIES
The Ghost and Mrs. Muir
comedy about the ghost of a sea captain and his widow. Stars Rex Harrison and Gene Tierney.

Mourning Become Electra
starring Rosalind Russell, Michael Redgrave, and Kirk Douglas in a Civil War era drama.

TV SHOWS
"Bristol-Myers Tele-Varieties"
variety show with features and interviews.

BOOKS
Speaking Frankly by James F. Byrnes

GRAMMY WINNERS

1958
Record: Domenico Modugno, "Nel Blu Dipinto Di Blu (Volare)"
Album: Henry Mancini, *The Music from Peter Gun*
Song: Domenico Modugno, "Nel Blu Dipinto Di Blu (Volare)"
Female Vocal: Ella Fitzgerald, *Ella Fitzgerald Sings the Irving Berlin Song Book*
Male Vocal: Perry Como, "Catch a Falling Star"

1959
Record: Bobby Darin, "Mack the Knife"
Album: Frank Sinatra, *Come Dance With Me*
Song: Jimmy Driftwood, "The Battle of New Orleans"
Female Vocal: Ella Fitzgerald, "But Not For Me"
Male Vocal: Frank Sinatra, "Come Dance With Me"

1960
Record: Percy Faith, "Theme from *A Summer Place*"
Album: Bob Newhart, *Button Down Mind*
Song: Ernest Gold, "Theme from *Exodus*"
New Artist: Bob Newhart
Female Vocal: Ella Fitzgerald, "Mack the Knife"
Male Vocal: Ray Charles, "Georgia on My Mind"

1961
Record: Henry Mancini, "Moon River"
Album: Judy Garland, *Judy at Carnegie Hall*
Song: Henry Mancini and Johnny Mercer, "Moon River"
New Artist: Peter Nero
Female Vocal: Judy Garland, *Judy at Carnegie Hall*
Male Vocal: Jack Jones, "Lollipops and Roses"

1962
Record: Tony Bennett, "I Left My Heart in San Francisco"

Album: Vaughn Meader, *The First Family*
Song: Leslie Bricusse and Anthony Newley, "What Kind of Fool Am I"
Female Vocal: Ella Fitzgerald, *Ella Swings Brightly with Nelson Riddle*
Male Vocal: Tony Bennett, "I Left My Heart in San Francisco"

1963
Record: Henry Mancini, "The Days of Wine and Roses"
Album: Barbra Streisand, *The Barbra Streisand Album*
Song: Henry Mancini and Johnny Mercer, "The Days of Wine and Roses"
New Artist: Swingle Sisters
Female Vocal: Barbra Streisand, *The Barbra Streisand Album*
Male Vocal: Jack Jones, "Wives and Lovers"

1964
Record: Stan Getz and Astrud Gilberto, "The Girl From Ipanema"
Album: Stan Getz and Joao Gilberto, *Getz/Gilberto*
Song: Jerry Herman, "Hello, Dolly!"
New Artist: The Beatles
Female Vocal: Barbra Streisand, "People"
Male Vocal: Louis Armstrong, "Hello, Dolly!"

1965
Record: Herb Alpert & the Tijuana Brass, "A Taste Of Honey"
Album: Frank Sinatra, *September of My Years*
Song: Paul Francis Webster and Johnny Mandel, "The Shadow of Your Smile" (Love Theme from *The Sandpiper*)
New Artist: Tom Jones

Female Vocal: Barbra Streisand, *My Name is Barbra*
Male Vocal: Frank Sinatra, "It Was a Very Good Year"

1966
Record: Frank Sinatra, "Strangers in the Night"
Album: Frank Sinatra, *Sinatra A Man and His Music*
Song: John Lennon, Paul McCartney, "Michelle"
Female Vocal: Eydie Gorme, "If He Walked into My Life"
Male Vocal: Frank Sinatra, "Strangers in the Night"

1967
Record: 5th Dimension, "Up, Up and Away"
Album: The Beatles, *Sgt. Pepper's Lonely Hearts Club Band*
Song: Jim Webb, "Up, Up and Away"
New Artist: Bobbie Gentry
Female Vocal: Bobbie Gentry, "Ode to Billie Joe"
Male Vocal: Glen Campbell, "By the Time I Get to Phoenix"

1968
Record: Simon & Garfunkel, "Mrs. Robinson"
Album: Glen Campbell, *By the Time I Get to Phoenix*
Song: Bobby Russell, "Little Green Apples"
New Artist: Jose Feliciano
Female Pop Vocal: Dionne Warwick, "Do You Know the Way to San Jose"
Male Pop Vocal: Jose Feliciano, "Light My Fire"

1969
Record: 5th Dimension, "Aquarius/Let the Sunshine In"
Album: Blood, Sweat and Tears, *Blood, Sweat and Tears*
Song: Joe South, "Games People Play"
New Artist: Crosby, Stills & Nash
Female Pop Vocal: Peggy Lee, "Is That All There Is"
Male Pop Vocal: Harry Nilsson, "Everybody's Talkin'"

GRAMMY WINNERS

1970

Record: Simon & Garfunkel, "Bridge Over Troubled Water"
Album: Simon & Garfunkel, *Bridge Over Troubled Water*
Song: Paul Simon, "Bridge Over Troubled Water"
New Artist: The Carpenters
Female Pop Vocal: Dionne Warwick, "I'll Never Fall in Love Again"
Male Pop Vocal: Ray Stevens, "Everything is Beautiful"

1971

Record: Carole King, "It's Too Late"
Album: Carole King, *Tapestry*
Song: Carole King, "You've Got a Friend"
New Artist: Carly Simon
Female Pop Vocal: Carole King, *Tapestry*
Male Pop Vocal: James Taylor, "You've Got a Friend"

1972

Record: Roberta Flack, "The First Time Ever I Saw Your Face"
Album: *The Concert for Bangla Desh*
Song: Ewan MacColl, "The First Time Ever I Saw Your Face"
New Artist: America
Female Pop Vocal: Helen Reddy, "I Am Woman"
Male Pop Vocal: Nilsson, "Without You"

1973

Record: Roberta Flack, "Killing Me Softly with His Song"
Album: Stevie Wonder, *Innervisions*
Song: Norman Gimbel, Charles Fox, "Killing Me Softly with His Song"
New Artist: Bette Midler
Female Pop Vocal: Roberta Flack, "Killing Me Softly with His Song"
Male Pop Vocal: Stevie Wonder, "You Are the Sunshine of My Life"

1974

Record: Olivia Newton-John, "I Honestly Love You"
Album: Stevie Wonder, *Fulfullingness' First Finale*
Song: Marilyn & Alan Bergman, Marvin Hamlisch, "The Way We Were"
New Artist: Marvin Hamlisch
Female Pop Vocal: Olivia Newton-John, "I Honestly Love You"
Male Pop Vocal: Stevie Wonder, *Fulfullingness' First Finale*

1975

Record: Captain & Tennille, "Love Will Keep Us Together"
Album: Paul Simon, *Still Crazy After All These Years*
Song: Stephen Sondheim, "Send in the Clowns"
New Artist: Natalie Cole
Female Pop Vocal: Janis Ian, "At Seventeen"
Male Pop Vocal: Paul Simon, *Still Crazy After All These Years*

1976

Record: George Benson, "This Masquerade"
Album: Stevie Wonder, *Songs in the Key of Life*
Song: Bruce Johnston, "I Write the Songs"
New Artist: Starland Vocal Band
Female Pop Vocal: Linda Ronstadt, *Hasten Down the Wind*
Male Pop Vocal: Stevie Wonder, *Songs in the Key of Life*

1977

Record: Eagles, "Hotel California"
Album: Fleetwood Mac, *Rumours*
Song: Barbra Streisand & Paul Williams, "Love Theme from *A Star is Born*" tied with Joe Brooks, "You Light Up My Life"
New Artist: Debby Boone
Female Pop Vocal: Barbra Streisand, "Love Theme from *A Star is Born*"
Male Pop Vocal: James Taylor, "Handy Man"

1978

Record: Billy Joel, "Just the Way You Are"
Album: Bee Gees, *Saturday Night Fever*
Song: Billy Joel, "Just the Way You Are"
New Artist: A Taste of Honey
Female Pop Vocal: Anne Murray, "You Needed Me"
Male Pop Vocal: Barry Manilow, "Copacabana (At the Copa)"

1979

Record: The Doobie Brothers, "What a Fool Believes"
Album: Billy Joel, *52nd Street*
Song: Kenny Loggins, Michael McDonald, "What a Fool Believes"
New Artist: Rickie Lee Jones
Female Pop Vocal: Dionne Warwick, "I'll Never Love This Way Again"
Male Pop Vocal: Billy Joel, *52nd Street*

1980

Record: Christopher Cross, "Sailing"
Album: Christopher Cross, *Christopher Cross*
Song: Christopher Cross, "Sailing"
New Artist: Christopher Cross
Female Pop Vocal: Bette Midler, "The Rose"
Male Pop Vocal: Kenny Loggins, "This Is It"

1981

Record: Kim Carnes, "Bette Davis Eyes"
Album: John Lennon, Yoko Ono, *Double Fantasy*
Song: Donna Weiss & Jackie DeShannon, "Bette Davis Eyes"
New Artist: Sheena Easton
Female Pop Vocal: Lena Horne, *Lena Horne: The Lady and Her Music Live on Broadway*

GRAMMY WINNERS

Male Pop Vocal: Al Jarreau, *Breakin Away*

1982
Record: Toto, "Rosanna"
Album: Toto, *Toto IV*
Song: Johnny Christopher, Mark James & Wayne Carson, "Always on My Mind"
New Artist: Men at Work
Female Pop Vocal: Melissa Manchester, "You Should Hear How She Talks About You"
Male Pop Vocal: Lionel Richie, "Truly"

1983
Record: Michael Jackson, "Beat It"
Album: Michael Jackson, *Thriller*
Song: Sting, "Every Breath You Take"
New Artist: Culture Club
Female Pop Vocal: Irene Cara, "Flashdance What A Feeling"
Male Pop Vocal: Michael Jackson, *Thriller*

1984
Record: Tina Turner, "What's Love Got to Do With It"
Album: Lionel Richie, *Can't Slow Down*
Song: Graham Lyle and Terry Britten, "What's Love Got to Do With It"
New Artist: Cyndi Lauper
Female Pop Vocal: Tina Turner, "What's Love Got to Do With It"
Male Pop Vocal: Phil Collins, "Against All Odds (Take a Look at Me Now)"

1985
Record: USA for Africa, "We Are the World"
Album: Phil Collins, *No Jacket Required*
Song: Michael Jackson & Lionel Richie, "We Are the World"
New Artist: Sade
Female Pop Vocal: Whitney Houston, "Saving All My Love for You"
Male Pop Vocal: Phil Collins, *No Jacket Required*

1986
Record: Steve Winwood, "Higher Love"
Album: Paul Simon, *Graceland*
Song: Burt Bacharach & Carole Bayer Sager, "That's What Friends Are For"
New Artist: Bruce Hornsby and The Range
Female Pop Vocal: Barbra Streisand, *The Broadway Album*
Male Pop Vocal: Steven Winwood, "Higher Love"

1987
Record: Paul Simon, "Graceland"
Album: U2, *Joshua Tree*
Song: James Horner, Barry Mann, Cynthia Weil, "Somewhere Out There"
New Artist: Jody Watley
Female Pop Vocal: Whitney Houston, "I Wanna Dance With Somebody (Who Loves Me)"
Male Pop Vocal: Sting, *Bring on the Night*

1988
Record: Bobby McFerrin, "Don't Worry Be Happy"
Album: George Michael, Faith
Song: Bobby McFerrin, "Don't Worry, Be Happy"
New Artist: Tracy Chapman
Female Pop Vocal: Tracy Chapman, "Fast Car"
Male Pop Vocal: Bobby McFerrin, "Don't Worry Be Happy"

1989
Record: Bette Midler, "Wind Beneath My Wings"
Album: Bonnie Raitt, *Nick of Time*
Song: Larry Henley & Jeff Silbar, "Wind Beneath My Wings"
New Artist: (No Award)
Female Pop Vocal: Bonnie Raitt, "Nick of Time"

Male Pop Vocal: Michael Bolton, "How Am I Supposed to Live Without You"

1990
Record: Phil Collins, "Another Day in Paradise"
Album: Quincy Jones, *Back on the Block*
Song: Julie Gold, "From a Distance"
New Artist: Mariah Carey
Female Pop Vocal: Mariah Carey, "Vision of Love"
Male Pop Vocal: Roy Orbison, "Oh Pretty Woman"

1991
Record: Natalie Cole, with Nat "King" Cole, "Unforgettable"
Album: Natalie Cole, with Nat "King" Cole, *Unforgettable*
Song: Irving Gordon, "Unforgettable"
New Artist: Marc Cohn
Female Pop Vocal: Bonnie Raitt, "Something to Talk About"
Male Pop Vocal: Michael Bolton, "When a Man Loves a Woman"

1992
Record: Eric Clapton, "Tears In Heaven"
Album: Eric Clapton, *Unplugged*
Song: Eric Clapton, "Tears In Heaven"
New Artist: Arrested Development
Female Pop Vocal: K.D. Lang, "Constant Craving"
Male Pop Vocal: Eric Clapton, "Tears In Heaven"

1993
Record: Whitney Houston, "I Will Always Love You"
Album: Whitney Houston, "The Bodyguard"
Song: Alan Menken & Tim Rice, "A Whole New World"
New Artist: Toni Braxton
Female Pop Vocal: Whitney Houston, "I Will Always Love You"
Male Pop Vocal: Sting, "If I Ever Lose My Faith In You"

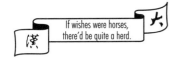

If wishes were horses, there'd be quite a herd.

FEBRUARY 1

BIRTHDAYS

- **LAURA DERN** Actress. (Hollywood, CA) *Wild At Heart, Ramblin' Rose, A Perfect World, Blue Velvet,* and *Jurassic Park*. Directed *The Gift*. Daughter of actor Bruce Dern and Diane Ladd. Mother and Daughter received Oscar nominations in the same year. Year/Age: 1995/**28** 1996/**29** 1997/**30**

- **RAY SAWYER** Musician/actor. (New Jersey) Better known as DR. HOOK, because of his eye patch. Biggest hit: "Sexy Eyes" in 1980. He was in the film *Who Is Harry Kellerman and Why Is He Saying Those Terrible Things About Me?* starring Dustin Hoffman. Year/Age: 1995/**58** 1996/**59** 1997/**60**

- **GARRETT MORRIS** Comedian/singer. (New Orleans, LA) Year/Age: 1995/**58** 1996/**59** 1997/**60**

- **DON EVERLY** Singer. (Born Isaac Donald Everly in Brownie, KY) The EVERLY BROTHERS. Biggest hit: "All I Have to Do is Dream" in 1958. Year/Age: 1995/**58** 1996/**59** 1997/**60**

- **BOB SHANE** Singer. (Hawaii) Member of the KINGSTON TRIO. Their biggest hit: "Tom Dooley" in 1958. Year/Age: 1995/**61** 1996/**62** 1997/**63**

- **SHERILYN FENN** Actress. Starred in TV's *Twin Peaks* and the movie *Boxing Helena*. Year/Age: 1995/**30** 1996/**31** 1997/**32**

- **PAULY SHORE** Actor/Comedienne Comic MTV host. Star of film *The Son-In-Law*; appeared in *Encino Man*. Year/Age: 1995/**25** 1996/**26** 1997/**27**

- **HILDEGARDE** Entertainer. (Born Hildegarde Loretta Sell in Adell, WI) She's known as The Incomparable Hildegarde – a title she was given while performing during WWII. Year/Age: 1995/**89** 1996/**90** 1997/**91**

- **PRINCESS STEPHANIE OF MONACO** She's the youngest of the royal family, and is now a model and singer. She was in the car with her mother, Princess Grace, when that fatal car accident killed her mother. Year/Age: 1995/**30** 1996/**31** 1997/**32**

- **BORIS YELTSIN** Russian President. Year/Age: 1995/**64** 1996/**65** 1997/**66**

- **LISA MARIE PRESLEY-KEOUGH** (Memphis, TN) Aspiring singer is the daughter of Priscilla and Elvis. She married Danny Keough in 1988, split in 1994. They have two children. Her name is on Elvis' plane on display at Graceland. Married Michael Jackson May 26, 1994. Year/Age: 1995/**27** 1996/**28** 1997/**29**

- **TERRY JONES** Director/writer. (Wales) Directed *Monty Python's Life of Brian* and wrote *Erik the Viking*. Year/Age: 1995/**53** 1996/**54** 1997/**55**

- **SHERMAN HEMSLEY** Actor. (Philadelphia, PA) Roles: The Deacon on "Amen" and George Jefferson on "The Jeffersons" TV sitcom, where his occupation was dry cleaning. He is B. P. Richfield's voice on "Dinosaurs" series. Year/Age: 1995/**57** 1996/**58** 1997/**59**

- **RICK JAMES** Singer. (Born James Johnson in Buffalo, NY) Punk/funk singer, songwriter and guitarist. Biggest hit: "You and I" in 1978. Year/Age: 1995/**43** 1996/**44** 1997/**45**

- **JOHN FORD** Film director. (1895-1973 – Cape Elizabeth, ME) He won an Academy Award for *The Quiet Man* in 1952; also nominated for *Mr. Roberts* in 1955. (Died 8-31-73)

- **CLARK GABLE** Actor. (1901-1960 – Born William Clark Gable in Cadiz, OH) He was one of America's best known leading men. He won an Oscar for his starring role in *It Happened One Night*, with Claudette Colbert. Some of his other films included: *Gone with the Wind*, as Rhett Butler; *Mutiny on the Bounty*; and his last film *The Misfits*, co-starring Marilyn Monroe. He won his screen test wearing a loin cloth and a rose behind his ear. (Died 11-16-60)

- **VICTOR HERBERT** Conductor/composer. (1859-1924 – Dublin, Ireland) He wrote *The Chocolate Soldier* and *Babes In Toyland* and was responsible for ASCAP. "ASCAP" stands for American Society of Composers and Publishers. (Died 5-27-24)

FACTS FROM THE PAST

1709 **ALEXANDER SELKIRK**, a Scottish sailor, was rescued from the uninhabited island he lived on for 5 years. His adventure was the basis for Daniel Defoe's book, *Robinson Crusoe*.

1862 The *Battle Hymn of the Republic*, a poem written by **JULIA WARD HOWE**, was published in the *Atlantic Monthly*.

1884 The *First Oxford Dictionary* was published by **SIR JAMES MURRAY** in Scotland. He sorted $2\frac{1}{2}$ million handwritten notes on slips of paper collected over 20 years to put it together.

1887 **HARVEY WILCOX** of Kansas subdivided 120 acres he owned in Southern California and started selling it off as a real estate development. His wife, Daeida, christened it Hollywood after the summer home of a woman she had met on a train.

1893 **THOMAS A. EDISON** completed work on the world's first motion picture studio in West Orange, NJ.

1898 Travelers Insurance Co. of Hartford, CT, issued the first auto insurance policy to a **DR. TRUMAN J. MARTIN** for $11.05.

1964 Indiana Governor declares "Louie, Louie" by the **KINGSMEN** a pornographic and suggestive song. It sold more copies than ever.

1979 **AYATOLLAH KHOMEINI** returned to Iran after 15 years in exile in France to direct a revolution against the Iranian government and overthrow the Shah.

1982 **LATE NIGHT WITH DAVID LETTERMAN** debuted on NBC-TV.

1986 Wearing a $12,000 gown, **DIANA ROSS** wed Arne Naess in a 900-year-old church in Geneva, Switzerland. She was 41 and he 46.

1994 **JEFF GILLOOLY** pleaded guilty for his part in the January 6th attack on Nancy Kerrigan.

FEBRUARY 2
Groundhog Day

Just think: you would have been out by now.

BIRTHDAYS

- **DEXTER MANLEY** Football lineman. (Houston, TX) With the Washington Redskins. Year/Age: 1995/37 1996/38 1997/39

- **LIZ SMITH** Gossip columnist. (Ft. Worth, TX) *New York Daily News*. Year/Age: 1995/72 1996/73 1997/74

- **HOWARD BELLAMY** Guitarist. (Darby, FL) He and his brother Dave head up the BELLAMY BROTHERS. Biggest hit: "Let Your Love Flow" in 1976. Year/Age: 1995/49 1996/50 1997/51

- **GARTH BROOKS** C&W singer. (Tulsa, OK) His number-one albums include *No Fences* and *Ropin' the Wind*. One of his singles that received a lot of airplay was "Friends in Low Places" in 1990. He earned a scholarship for javelin throwing at Oklahoma State University. Year/Age: 1995/33 1996/34 1997/35

- **BO HOPKINS** Actor. (Greenwood, SC) On TV's "Dynasty" and in the film *American Graffiti*. Year/Age: 1995/53 1996/54 1997/55

- **ROBERT MANDAN** Actor. (Clever, MO) Chester Tate on "Soap." Year/Age: 1995/63 1996/64 1997/65

- **CHRISTIE BRINKLEY** Model. (Monroe, MI) On Cover of Sports Illustrated Swimsuit Issue 3 times. Split with singer Billy Joel in 1994. Year/Age: 1995/42 1996/43 1997/44

- **FARRAH FAWCETT** Actress. (Born Mary Farrah Leni Fawcett in Corpus Christi, TX) She played Jill Monroe on "Charlie's Angels" and heralded in 1983 for film *The Burning Bed*. Year/Age: 1995/48 1996/49 1997/50

- **GALE GORDON** Actor. (NYC) He was the loud-mouthed banker, Mr. Mooney, on the old "Lucy" show and starred with Lucy on the short-lived comeback of Lucille Ball's series on TV in 1986. He also played Osgood Conklin in "Our Miss Brooks," and was on "Dennis the Menace." Year/Age: 1995/89 1996/90 1997/91

- **BRENT SPINER** Actor. Played Lt. Comdr. Data on *Star Trek: The Next Generation*." Year/Age: 1995/38 1996/39 1997/40

- **KIM ZIMMER** Actress. (Grand Rapids, MI) Emmy award winner as Reva Shane Lewis on soap "Guiding Light." Year/Age: 1995/40 1996/41 1997/42

- **HOLLY HUNTER** Actress. (Conyers, GA) *Raising Arizona, Broadcast News, Once Around, Mother's Son* and *The Firm*. She won Best Actress for her role in *The Piano*. Year/Age: 1995/37 1996/38 1997/39

- **CONRAD BAIN** Actor. (Canada) Has appeared on "Diff'rent Strokes" and the "Maude" TV series. Year/Age: 1995/72 1996/73 1997/74

- **RED SCHOENDIENST** Baseball. (Born Albert Schoendienst in Germantown, IL) He led the National League in stolen bases, with 26 as a St. Louis Cardinal rookie in 1945. Year/Age: 1995/72 1996/73 1997/74

- **BURTON LANE** Broadway composer. (NYC) Wrote the scores for *On A Clear Day* and *Finian's Rainbow*. Year/Age: 1995/83 1996/84 1997/85

- **TOMMY SMOTHERS** Comedian. (NYC) The SMOTHERS BROTHERS was a popular comedy team in the early 60's and had a number of successful off-beat comedy albums. They started on CBS-TV and, due to censors, moved to NBC where they sank into obscurity. They came back with a show in 1988. Year/Age: 1995/58 1996/59 1997/60

- **GRAHAM NASH** Guitarist. (England) Formerly of the HOLLIES and CROSBY, STILLS, NASH & YOUNG. The HOLLIES' biggest hit: "Long Cool Woman" in 1972, and the biggest for CSN&Y: "Woodstock" in 1970. Year/Age: 1995/53 1996/54 1997/55

- **STAN GETZ** Jazz saxophonist. (1927-1991 – Philadelphia, PA) Biggest hit: Grammy winner "Girl from Ipanema" in 1964 with Astrud Gilberto. They divorced after that hit. (Died 6-6-91)

- **FORREST TUCKER** Actor. (1919-1986 – Plainfield, IN) Star of TV series "F-Troop." He appeared in over 50 movies including *Sands of Iwo Jima* with close friend, John Wayne. (Died 10-25-86)

- **GEORGE HALAS** Football. (1895-1983) Founder/owner of the Chicago Bears. He was MVP in the 1919 Rose Bowl and he helped start the NFL. He retired as coach in 1968 with 8 NFL championships. During his 4 coaching stints with the Bears, he compiled a record of 326-151-31. (Died 10-31-83)

FACTS FROM THE PAST

1863 In Carson City, NV, a journalist sent a report into the *Virginia City Enterprise,* and for the first time he used the name that we would eventually know him by. His pseudonym came from an old Mississippi River pilot who died. It was the sound the boatman made for water two fathoms deep – **MARK TWAIN.**

1893 The **FIRST MOTION PICTURE CLOSE-UP** was filmed at the Edison Studio in West Orange, NJ. Cameraman **WILLIAM DICKSON** photographed comedian Fred Ott sneezing.

1915 An Alaskan Husky named **BALTO** led a dogsled team across 600 miles of ice and snow to **DELIVER DIPHTHERIA SERUM TO NOME,** where an epidemic was underway. The man driving the sled became snow-blind, so the dog led the team all by himself with the wind blowing 80 mph and the temperature 50 degrees below zero. The route became the Iditarod Trail International Sled Dog Race. Libby Riddles became the first woman to win, in 1985.

1940 **FRANK SINATRA** made his singing debut in Indianapolis with the Tommy Dorsey Orchestra.

1979 Sex Pistol **SID VICIOUS** died of a heroin overdose "escaping" legal charges against him for the murder of his girlfriend.

1983 US Marine Capt. Charles Johnson climbed aboard an Israeli tank in Beirut armed only with a pistol. He ordered an Israeli officer to take his three tanks out of the US-patrolled area, and told him they would pass the Marine line only "over my dead body." The Israelis left the area immediately.

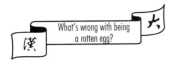

What's wrong with being a rotten egg?

FEBRUARY 3

BIRTHDAYS

- **BLYTHE DANNER** Actress. (Philadelphia, PA) *Future World II*, *Prince of Tides*, and *Mr. and Mrs. Bridge*. Year/**Age**: 1995/**52** 1996/**53** 1997/**54**

- **JOEY BISHOP** Entertainer. (Born Joseph Abraham Gottlieb in Bronx, NY) The "Joey Bishop Show" was a sitcom from 1961-1965. The "Joey Bishop Talk Show" (1967-1969) was one of several attempts by ABC to lure some of Johnny Carson's audience away. Year/**Age**: 1995/**77** 1996/**78** 1997/**79**

- **SHELLEY BERMAN** Comedian. (Chicago, IL) Record collectors will remember his comedy routines on the telephone. Year/**Age**: 1995/**69** 1996/**70** 1997/**71**

- **JAMES A. MICHENER** Author. (NYC) He told his war-time adventures in *Tales of the South Pacific*, for which he won a Pulitzer Prize for fiction. It later became a popular musical. He wrote *Bridges of Toko-Ri* and *The Source*. Year/**Age**: 1995/**88** 1996/**89** 1997/**90**

- **MELANIE** Singer. (Born Melanie Safka in Queens, NY) Biggest hit: "Brand New Key" in 1971. She was so scared at Woodstock that when it was time for her to take the stage, she got the dry heaves. She won an Emmy for writing the theme to TVs "Beauty and the Beast." Year/**Age**: 1995/**48** 1996/**49** 1997/**50**

- **FRAN TARKENTON** Former Minnesota Q.B. (Richmond, VA) He holds the career passing records for touchdown completions and yardage. Year/**Age**: 1995/**55** 1996/**56** 1997/**57**

- **DR. HENRY HEIMLICH** Invented the Heimlich Maneuver. Year/**Age**: 1995/**75** 1996/**76** 1997/**77**

- **DAVE DAVIES**. Guitarist and vocalist. (London, England) With the KINKS. Biggest hits: "You Really Got Me" and "All Day and All of the Night." Year/**Age**: 1995/**48** 1996/**49** 1997/**50**

- **MORGAN FAIRCHILD** Actress. (Born Patsy Ann McClenny in Dallas, TX) Formerly appeared on the daytime soap "Search for Tomorrow," "Falcon Crest," and occasionally on "Roseanne." Year/**Age**: 1995/**45** 1996/**46** 1997/**47**

- **BOB GRIESE** Former football quarterback. (Evansville, IN) With the Miami Dolphins and later a sports announcer. Year/**Age**: 1995/**50** 1996/**51** 1997/**52**

- **FRED LYNN** Baseball. (Chicago, IL) MVP winner. Hard-hitting American league outfielder. In 1983, at old Comisky Park in Chicago, Fred, then California Angel, got the first-ever grandslam home run hit in an All-Star game. Year/**Age**: 1995/**43** 1996/**44** 1997/**45**

- **VICTOR BUONO** Actor. (1938-1982 – Apple Valley, CA) Nominated for an Academy Award for *Whatever Happened to Baby Jane?* (Died 1-1-82)

- **GERTRUDE STEIN** Author. (1874-1946 – Allegheny, PA) American writer who wrote "A rose, is a rose, is a rose." (Died 7-29-46)

- **NORMAN ROCKWELL** Artist. (1894-1978 – NYC) Best known for his realistic and homey magazine cover art. He painted 317 covers for the *Saturday Evening Post*. His favorite subjects were children and animals. (Died 11-8-78.)

- **CHARLES CORRELL** Actor. (1890-1972 – Peoria, IL) He was Andy on the "Amos & Andy" radio program.

- **HORACE GREELEY** Journalist. (1811-1872 – Amherst, NH) Journalist and politician who did not coin the phrase "Go west, young man." It was first said by John Soule, editor of the *Terre Haute Express*, in 1851. Greeley simply heard the statement and popularized it in his own paper, the *New York Tribune*. It caught on, and Greeley was given credit for it. (Died 11-29-1872)

FACTS FROM THE PAST

1865 A conference aimed at ending the Civil War that included **PRESIDENT ABRAHAM LINCOLN** and Confederate Vice President **ALEXANDER H. STEPHENS** took place on the vessel *River Queen* off Virginia.

1876 **ALBERT SPALDING** and his brother took their $800 savings and started a sporting goods company. They manufactured the first official baseball, tennis ball, basketball, golf ball, and football.

1956 **ELVIS PRESLEY, JERRY LEE LEWIS, CARL PERKINS**, and **JOHNNY CASH**, recorded a two-and-a-half hour session in the Sun Studios.

1959 Entertainers **BUDDY HOLLY, RICHIE VALENS** and the **BIG BOPPER** died in a plane crash in Mason City, IA. On the 30th anniversary of their deaths, Clear Lake, IA, held its Annual Anniversary Concert at the Surf Ballroom where they gave their final performances. Holly's band, The Crickets, and Bobby Vee performed in Fargo, ND, the tour's next scheduled stop. Don McLean was 13 years old at the time of the crash, living in New Rochelle, NY. He never forgot Holly and in 1971 wrote a song that included the lyrics "the day the music died." That song, "American Pie," became a #1 hit for Don.

1969 Despite Paul McCartney's objections, the Beatles hired business manager **ALLEN KLEIN** to try to straighten out the tangled financial affairs of their company, Apple Corps Limited. The company's mismanagement was one of the main reasons the Beatles broke up a year later.

1973 The **ENDANGERED SPECIES ACT** was signed into law by President Nixon.

1986 **PRESIDENT REAGAN** appointed a 12-member commission to investigate the explosion that destroyed the space shuttle *Challenger* 73 seconds after liftoff, killing the seven crew members aboard.

1987 Members of the San Diego Yacht Club celebrated the victory of skipper **DENNIS CONNER** and the *Stars and Stripes* over Australia's *Kookaburra III*, sweeping them 4-0 at the **AMERICA'S CUP** series in Fremantle, Australia.

FEBRUARY 4

BIRTHDAYS

- **LAWRENCE TAYLOR** Football linebacker. (Williamsburg, VA) New York Giants. Wears #56. Year/Age: 1995/36 1996/37 1997/38
- **DAN QUAYLE** Former Vice-President. (Indianapolis, IN) The 44th U.S. vice-president. Wrote *Standing Firm*. Year/Age: 1995/48 1996/49 1997/50
- **ALICE COOPER** Rock star. (Born Vincent Daman Furneir in Detroit, MI) Biggest hit: "School's Out" in 1972. Appeared in *Wayne's World*. His name is derived from a 16th century witch. Year/Age: 1995/47 1996/48 1997/49
- **IDA LUPINO** Actress. (England) She appeared in many movies and was married to actor Howard Duff at one time. Year/Age: 1995/77 1996/78 1997/79
- **DAVID BRENNER** Comedian. (Philadelphia, PA) He has made over 150 appearances on the "Tonight Show" as host and/or guest. Year/Age: 1995/50 1996/51 1997/52
- **BETTY FRIEDAN** Author/feminist. (Born Betty Naomi Goldstein in Peoria, IL) Founder and first president of National Organization for Women (NOW). She wrote the best seller *The Feminine Mystique* in 1963 and *The Fountain of Age* in 1994. Year/Age: 1995/74 1996/75 1997/76
- **FLORENCE LaRUE** Singer. (Glenside, PA) Member of the 5th DIMENSION. Their biggest hit: "Aquarius" from the musical *Hair*. Year/Age: 1995/52 1996/53 1997/54

- **CLINT BLACK** C&W singer. (Katy, TX) His 1989 debut album *Killin' Time* turned out a record five consecutive #1 songs on the C&W charts. He married actress Lisa Hartman on October 20, 1991. Year/Age: 1995/33 1996/34 1997/35
- **ERICH LEINSDORF** Conductor. (Vienna) With the Boston Symphony 1962-69 and the NY Mets 1957-62. Year/Age: 1995/83 1996/84 1997/85
- **ROSA PARKS** Civil rights activist. (Tuskegee, AL) She became the symbol of the Civil Rights Movement in 1955 by refusing to give her seat on a bus to a white man. This triggered the year-long Montgomery, AL, bus boycott led by Martin Luther King, Jr. It resulted in desegregation of the bus system. Year/Age: 1995/82 1996/83 1997/84
- **MARK HOPKINS** Author. (1802-1887 – Stockbridge, MA) Educator, author and president of Williams College in Williamstown, MA.
- **CHARLES LINDBERGH** Aviator. (1902-1974 – Detroit, MI) First person to make a solo flight across the Atlantic Ocean on May 20, 1927 – New York to Paris in 33$\frac{1}{2}$ hours. Between 1927 and 1935, more than 250 songs were written to honor Lindbergh. One of the most popular was "Lucky Lindy." (Died 8-27-74)

FACTS FROM THE PAST

1789 GEORGE WASHINGTON was unanimously **ELECTED U.S. PRESIDENT** when all 690 presidential electors voted for him.

1858 In a heated filibuster over admitting Kansas to the Union, a **FIST FIGHT BROKE OUT IN THE US HOUSE** at 1:30 a.m. **LAWRENCE KEITT** of South Carolina called **GALUSHA GROW** "a black Republican puppy." Grow knocked Keitt down and when William Barksdale of Mississippi tried to stop Grow, Cadwallader Washburn of Wisconsin grabbed Barksdale by the hair, preparing to deck him. But Bill's wig came off in his hand, causing the entire group of politicians to laugh, and ending the fight.

1912 The first movie stuntman, **FREDERICK LAW**, jumped with a parachute from the torch of the Statue of Liberty.

1926 **JOHN GILA** of New York City danced the Charleston for 22$\frac{1}{2}$ hours. At this time in history, the Charleston was the favorite dance of "flappers" everywhere.

1945 President **FRANKLIN D. ROOSEVELT**, British Prime Minister **WINSTON CHURCHILL**, and Soviet leader **JOSEPH STALIN** met at a wartime conference at YALTA.

1951 **SUGAR RAY ROBINSON** won the World Middleweight Boxing title, beating Jake LaMotta.

1963 **RALPH FLORES'** monoplane crashed in a forest in the Yukon Territory of Canada. His jaw and ribs were broken in the crash, and his passenger, Helen Klaben, sprained her ankle and broke her arm. They had no survival kit and only the airplane's carpets to cover themselves with when temperatures dropped to 40 degrees below zero. Although they ran out of food, they survived another 40 days by eating snow and toothpaste. Ralph stamped out a huge SOS in the snow, which finally led to their rescue.

1971 The **OSMONDS** received their first gold record for "One Bad Apple." Lead vocalist Donny Osmond was 13 years old at the time.

1974 Newspaper heiress, 19-year-old **PATTY HEARST,** was kidnapped from her Berkeley, CA, apartment by 3 members of the Symbionese Liberation Army. She was brainwashed and took part in terrorist activities, including bank robbery. After 19 months she was captured by the FBI and sentenced to 7 years in prison, but President Jimmy Carter gave her a pardon in November of 1976. The story is told in the movie *The Patty Hearst Story*.

1993 The Boston Celtics retired **LARRY BIRD**'s famous number 16 during a sold-out ceremony at Boston Garden.

1993 Cincinnati Reds owner **MARGE SCHOTT** was suspended for one year and fined $25,000 for "racially and ethnically offensive" language.

1994 **LES ASPIN** officially left the office of Secretary of Defense, a day after William Perry was confirmed for the position by the Senate.

Few things are as dangerous as a loaded pun.

FEBRUARY 5
Weatherman's Day

BIRTHDAYS

• **BARRETT STRONG** Singer/songwriter. (Jackson, MS) Co-wrote "Cloud Nine," "Ball of Confusion" and "Just My Imagination" for the TEMPTATIONS. His biggest hit: "Money" in 1960. Year/Age: 1995/**54** 1996/**55** 1997/**56**

• **BOBBY BROWN** Singer/dancer. (Boston, MA) Hits include: "My Prerogative," "On Our Own," and "Every Little Step," for which he won a 1989 Grammy Award as best R&B male vocal. His LP "Don't Be Cruel" sold over 8 million copies. He married singer Whitney Houston July 18, 1992. They have a daughter. Year/Age: 1995/**26** 1996/**27** 1997/**28**

• **STUART DAMON** Actor. (Brooklyn, NY) Plays Dr. Alan Quartermain on TV's "General Hospital." Year/Age: 1995/**58** 1996/**59** 1997/**60**

• **HENRY "HANK" AARON** Baseball. (Mobile, AL) All-time home run king. He hit more home runs (755) than any other player in baseball history and had 6,856 total bases, 1,722 more than 2nd place, Stan Musial. He played in 24 All-Star games, a record he shares with Stan Musial and Willie Mays. He was elected to the Baseball Hall of Fame in 1982. Year/Age: 1995/**61** 1996/**62** 1997/**63**

• **RED BUTTONS** Actor/comedian. (Born Aaron Chwatt in NYC) He won an Oscar for supporting actor in *Sayonara* in 1957. He started his show biz career singing for pennies in Manhattan's Lower East Side. He was in some episodes of "Knots Landing" and the movie *18 Again* with George Burns. Year/Age: 1995/**76** 1996/**77** 1997/**78**

• **CLAUDE KING** C&W. (Shreveport, LA) Biggest hit: "Woverton Mountain" in 1969. Woverton Mountain is a real place in Arkansas where Clifton Clowers lived. King was in the TV mini-series "The Blue and the Gray" and the movie *Swamp Girl*. Year/Age: 1995/**62** 1996/**63** 1997/**64**

• **CHRISTOPHER GUEST** Writer/comic. (NYC) Wrote *A Few Good Men*. Year/Age: 1995/**47** 1996/**48** 1997/**49**

• **NIGEL OLSSON** Musician. He was a drummer with ELTON JOHN's band. His biggest hit: "Dancin' Shoes" in 1978. Year/Age: 1995/**46** 1996/**47** 1997/**48**

• **ROGER STAUBACH** Former Dallas Quarterback. (Cincinnati, OH) Leading NFC passer 5 times and graduate of the U.S. Naval Academy. For many years he did "Rolaids" TV commercials. Year/Age: 1995/**53** 1996/**54** 1997/**55**

• **CORY WELLS** Singer. (Los Angeles, CA) With THREE DOG NIGHT. Biggest hit: "Joy to the World" in 1971. Year/Age: 1995/**53** 1996/**54** 1997/**55**

• **DARRELL WALTRIP** Stock car driver. (Owensboro, KY) Year/Age: 1995/**47** 1996/**48** 1997/**49**

• **JANE BRYANT QUINN** Financial expert. (Niagara Falls, NY) Writer and TV correspondent. Wrote *Everyone's Money Book*. Mother of veejay Martha Quinn. Year/Age: 1995/**56** 1996/**57** 1997/**58**

• **AL KOOPER** Blues rock musician. (Brooklyn, NY) He played a big part in the success of BLOOD, SWEAT & TEARS, discovered LYNYRD SKYNYRD and the TUBES. Year/Age: 1995/**51** 1996/**52** 1997/**53**

• **BARBARA HERSHEY** Actress. (Born Barbara Hertzstein in Los Angeles, CA) She appeared in *The Last Temptation of Christ, Beaches, Hoosiers, Falling Down, A Dangerous Woman, Public Eye,* and *Splitting Heirs*. Year/Age: 1995/**47** 1996/**48** 1997/**49**

• **CHARLOTTE RAMPLING** Actress. (England) Leading lady who appeared in *Georgy Girl* and *The Damned*. Year/Age: 1995/**49** 1996/**50** 1997/**51**

• **JOHN JEFFRIES** Weatherman. (1744-1819 – Boston, MA) The physician kept detailed weather records and is known as America's first weatherman. (Died 9-16-1819)

• **JOHN CARRADINE** Actor. (1906-1988 – Born Richmond Reed Carradine in NYC) He was the father of all the Carradine boys who are actors. Appeared in *The Invisible Man, The Ten Commandments,* and *Of Human Bondage*. (Died 11-27-88)

• **ADLAI EWING STEVENSON** Politician. (1900-1965 – Los Angeles, CA) Governor of Illinois and Democratic candidate for U.S. President in 1952 and 1956. (Died 7-14-65)

FACTS FROM THE PAST

1850 The **FIRST ADDING MACHINE** was patented by Frank Baldwin. It weighed ten pounds and was 20 inches high.

1861 The first peep show viewer was patented by **SAMUAL GOODALE** of Cinncinati, Ohio. He called it a "mutoscope." The faster the mutoscope was cranked, the faster the images were presented, giving the semblance of continuous motion.

1937 The first **CHARLIE CHAPLIN** talkie, *Modern Times,* was released. The satire on dehumanizing conditions in an industrial plant was Chaplin's last appearance as the *Little Tramp*.

1945 U.S. troops, under **GENERAL DOUGLAS MACARTHUR,** entered Manila in the Philippines in World War II.

1971 Apollo XIV astronauts, **ALAN SHEPARD, JR.,** and **EDGAR MITCHELL,** landed on the moon.

1972 **PAUL SIMON** released his first solo single following his breakup with Art Garfunkel: "Mother and Child Reunion." It got up to number 4 on the charts.

1973 Funeral services were held for **LT. COL. WILLIAM NOLDE,** the last American killed before the Vietnam cease-fire.

1988 **GOVERNOR EVAN MECHAM** impeached by the Arizona House.

1994 Transport planes fly to **SARAJEVO** to evacuate those wounded by a mortar shell that hit the main marketplace in the city. Over 60 died.

FEBRUARY 6
Succession of Queen Elizabeth II

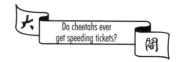
Do cheetahs ever get speeding tickets?

BIRTHDAYS

• **MICHAEL TUCKER** Actor. (Baltimore, MD) "L.A. Law." Married to Jill Eikenberry. Year/**Age**: 1995/**51** 1996/**52** 1997/**53**

• **W. AXL ROSE** Musician/lead singer. (Born Bill Bailey in Lafayette, IN) GUNS 'N ROSES. Big hit: "Sweet Child O' Mine" written for Don Everly's daughter whom he married on April 27, 1990; they divorced three weeks later. Year/**Age**: 1995/**33** 1996/**34** 1997/**35**

• **ROBERT TOWNSEND** Actor. (Detroit, MI) Appeared in *The Five Heart Beats*. Year/**Age**: 1995/**38** 1996/**39** 1997/**40**

• **RONALD WILSON REAGAN** Former President. (Tampico, IL) The oldest US President ever. He has made 53 movies. An excellent swimmer, he saved over 70 lives while working as a lifeguard when he was a teen. When he was a student at Eureka College in 1928, he led a student strike against the administration. In 1940, the University of Southern California's Division of Fine Arts selected him as having "the most nearly perfect male figure." He was the first president to be divorced. He was married to actress Jane Wyman from 1940-1948 and has been married to Nancy Davis Reagan since 1952. Year/**Age**: 1995/**84** 1996/**85** 1997/**86**

• **ZSA ZSA GABOR** Actress. (Born Sari Bagor in Budapest, Hungary) Some say she was born in 1923, which would have made her 13 years old when she was selected "Miss Hungary" in 1936. Some say she was born in 1917 which would make her 75. Cameo appearance in *Naked Gun 2¹/₂*. "It's Simple, Darling" workout tapes. Year/**Age**: 1995/**76** 1996/**77** 1997/**78**

• **MAMIE VAN DOREN** Actress. (Born Joan Lucille Olander in Rowena, SD) She was called the blond bombshell of the second feature in Hollywood in 1954. Probably best known for her role in *Teacher's Pet* with Clark Gable and Doris Day. Year/**Age**: 1995/**62** 1996/**64** 1997/**65**

• **RIP TORN** Actor. (Born Elmore Torn, Jr., in Temple, TX) Widower of actress Geraldine Page. Actress Sissy Spacek is his cousin. Appeared in *City Heat*, *Defending Your Life*, and *Robo Cop 3*. Year/**Age**: 1995/**64** 1996/**65** 1997/**66**

• **TOM BROKAW** NBC-TV anchor. (Yankton, SD) A high school athlete who married a former Miss South Dakota. He has been the NBC News anchor since 1981. "Prime Story" news magazine show with Katie Couric. Year/**Age**: 1995/**55** 1996/**56** 1997/**57**

• **RICK ASTLEY** Singer. (England) His hits include: "Never Gonna Give You Up" and "Together Forever." Year/**Age**: 1995/**29** 1996/**30** 1997/**31**

• **BRIAN TRAVERS** Musician. (England) From the group UB40. They got their name from a British unemployment benefit form. No. 1 hit in 1988: "Red Red Wine." Year/**Age**: 1995/**36** 1996/**37** 1997/**38**

• **MIKE FARRELL** Actor. (St. Paul, MN) He played B.J. Hunnicutt on TV's "M*A*S*H" series and appeared on "National Geographic." Married to Shelley Fabares of TV's "Coach." Year/**Age**: 1995/**56** 1996/**57** 1997/**58**

• **FABIAN** Former teen singing idol. (Born Fabian Anthony Forte in Philadelphia, PA) Biggest hit: "Tiger" in 1959. He was only 14 years old when a record company executive approached him outside his Philadelphia home where he was waiting for an ambulance to take his father to the hospital. He told him to "go to hell." His dad recovered from the heart attack and Fabian called the exec to accept the job. Year/**Age**: 1995/**52** 1996/**53** 1997/**54**

• **NATALIE COLE** Singer. (Los Angeles, CA) Daughter of the late Nat "King" Cole, she made her professional singing debut at age 11. Biggest records: "I've Got Love On My Mind" in 1977 and a 1991 duet with dad, "Unforgettable." Year/**Age**: 1995/**45** 1996/**46** 1997/**47**

• **GAYLE HUNNICUTT** Actress. (Ft. Worth, TX) Appeared on "Masterpiece Theater" and "The Martian Chronicles," a science-fiction mini-series, in 1980 with Rock Hudson. Year/**Age**: 1995/**52** 1996/**53** 1997/**54**

• **BOB MARLEY** Singer. (1945-1981 – Jamaica) The master of reggae. Bob wrote Eric Clapton's hit: "I Shot the Sheriff." (Died 5-11-81)

• **RAMON NAVARRO** Actor. (1899-1968 – Born Ramon Samaniegos) The romantic Latin lover appeared in *Ben Hur* and *Mata Hari*.

• **BABE RUTH** Baseball great. (1895-1948 – Born George Herman Ruth in Baltimore, MD) A New York Yankee outfielder, he had 60 home runs in 1927; 714 in his lifetime. He led the American League 11 times in homers. He played in 10 World Series and his team won 7 of those championships. (Died 8-16-48)

FACTS FROM THE PAST

1911 The **ROLLS ROYCE HOOD ORNAMENT** was cast for the first time. The model for the ornament was Lord Montagu's secretary.

1952 **KING GEORGE VI** died. He was found dead in bed by a servant delivering the morning tea. Princess Elizabeth Alexandra Mary became Queen Elizabeth II upon the death of her father. She was crowned June 2, 1953, in London's Westminster Abbey.

1955 **ELVIS PRESLEY**'s first live performance was held at the Memphis, TN, auditorium.

1971 The **U.S. APOLLO IV** astronauts prepared to head back to Earth after a 33-hour stay on the moon. Alan Shepard **PLAYED GOLF** on the moon before leaving, using a 6-iron.

1978 **MURIEL HUMPHREY** took the oath of office as a U.S. senator from Minnesota, filling the seat of her late husband, former Vice President Hubert Humphrey.

1990 **BILLY IDOL** ran a stop sign and rode his motorcycle into a car. He suffered a broken left arm and multiple breaks in his right leg. Ironically, he had just finished recording the *Charmed Life* album.

1994 Whoopi Goldberg succeeded Billy Crystal as host of the 1994 Oscar Telecast. She is the first black star to host the show solo.

Name five hits by Gary Puckett & the Union Gap.

FEBRUARY 7

BIRTHDAYS

- **GARTH BROOKS** C&W Singer. (Born Troyal Garth Brooks in Yukon, OK) His number-one albums include No Fences and Ropin' the Wind. One of his more popular singles was "Friends in Low Places" in 1990. He earned a scholarship for javelin throwing at Oklahoma State University. Year/**Age:** 1995/**33** 1996/**34** 1997/**35**
- **BURT HOOTEN** Baseball. Dodger pitcher. Year/**Age:** 1995/**45** 1996/**46** 1997/**47**
- **JASON MICHALE GEDRICK** Actor. (Chicago, IL) Plays David on "Class of '96." Year/**Age:** 1995/**30** 1996/**31** 1997/**32**
- **EDDIE BRACKEN** Actor. (NYC) Films included *Sweater Girl*, *Duffy's Tavern* and *National Lampoon's Vacation*, and *Home Alone II*. Year/**Age:** 1995/**75** 1996/**76** 1997/**77**
- **ROLF BEHIRSCHKE** Daytime host. "Wheel of Fortune" and former pro football kicker. Year/**Age:** 1995/**40** 1996/**41** 1997/**42**
- **JUAN PIZARRO** Baseball. Was a fastball pitcher on seven different teams in both major leagues. Year/**Age:** 1995/**58** 1996/**59** 1997/**60**
- **MARILYN COCHRAN** Skier. (Burlington, VT) Year/**Age:** 1995/**45** 1996/**46** 1997/**47**
- **CYNTHIA WOODHEAD** Swimmer. (Riverside, CA) Year/**Age:** 1995/**31** 1996/**32** 1997/**33**
- **SINCLAIR LEWIS** Author. (1885-1951 – Sauk Center, MN) He was the first American to win the Nobel Prize for Literature. His most popular book *Main Street* in 1947. (Died 1-1-51)
- **JOHN DEERE** Innovator (1804-1886 – Rutland, VT) He marketed the first steel plow. (Died 5-17-1886)

- **JOCK MAHONEY** Actor. (1919-1989) Perhaps Hollywood's most famous stuntman-turned-actor, famed for his TV roles as Tarzan, Yancy Derringer, and Range Rider. Stepfather to Sally Field. (Died 12-14-89)
- **CHRIS ROCK** Comedian on "Saturday Night Live." Year/**Age:** 1995/**29** 1996/**30** 1997/**31**
- **CHARLES DICKENS** Author. (1812-1870 – England) Best known for *A Christmas Carol*, *Tale of Two Cities*, *David Copperfield*, and *Oliver Twist*. (Died 6-9-1870)
- **KING CURTIS** Musician. (1934-1971 – Born Curtis Ousley in Ft. Worth, TX) Biggest hit: "Soul Twist" in 1962. His tenor sax can be heard on the Coasters' 1957 hit "Yakety Yak." He was stabbed to death in a quarrel outside his New York City apartment. (Died 8-13-71)
- **BUSTER CRABBE** Actor. (1908-1983 – Born Clarence Linden Crabbe in Oakland, CA) He won an Olympic gold medal in 1933 for swimming, and, as an actor, created *Buck Rogers* and *Flash Gordon*. (Died 4-23-83)
- **EUBIE BLAKE** Composer. (1883-1983 – Baltimore, MD) His life inspired *Eubie* on Broadway. He composed over 1,000 songs, among them "The Charleston Rag" and "I'm Just Wild About Harry." (Died 2-12-83)
- **SIR THOMAS MORE** Lawyer/scholar/author. (1478-1535 – London) As Lord Chancellor of England, he refused to recognize Henry the VIII's divorce from Queen Catherine. Known as the "Man for All Seasons," he was found guilty of treason and imprisoned in the Tower of London. He was beheaded and his head displayed from the Tower Bridge. He was canonized a saint in 1935. (Died 7-6-1535)

FACTS FROM THE PAST

1948   **DWIGHT EISENHOWER** (later President) resigned as Army Chief of Staff and was succeeded by General Omar Bradley.

1961   **JANE FONDA** made her TV acting debut in a drama called "A String of Beads" on NBC. She was 23 years old.

1964   The **BEATLES'** invasion of the U.S. began as thousands of screaming fans welcomed them at NY Kennedy Airport. The number-one song that day was "I Want To Hold Your Hand."

1969   Beatle **GEORGE HARRISON** was admitted to a London hospital with an infected back molar which infected his tonsils. The next day his tonsils were removed and he destroyed them so they could not be sold.

1976   Hockey's **DARRYL SITTLER** of the Toronto Maple Leafs scored six goals and four assists against the Boston Bruins.

1979   **STEPHEN STILLS** records on digital equipment at Plant Studio in L.A. but the material was never released; therefore, **RAY COODER** has the official title of being the first to employ the new technology.

1980   The **PINK FLOYD** "Wall" tour began in the United States.

1983   **ELIZABETH H. DOLE** was sworn in as the first female Secretary of Transportation by the first woman to sit on the U.S. Supreme Court, Justice Sandra Day O'Connor.

1984   Space shuttle astronauts **BRUCE McCANDLESS II** and **ROBERT L. STEWART** went on the first untethered space walk.

1984   **DAVID**, a 12-year old boy born without immunity to disease, touched his mother for the first time after he was removed from a germ-free bubble at Texas Children's Hospital in Houston.

1985   **BRUCE MORRIS**, playing for Huntington, WV, Marshall University against Appalachian, **SCORED AN 89-FOOT 10-INCH BASKET** to end the first half. It was the longest field goal in college basketball history. His team won the game 93-82.

1993   Orlando rookie player **SHAQUILLE O'NEAL** slamdunked a basketball so hard that he broke the support that holds up the backboard and delayed the game with the Phoenix Suns for 35 minutes.

1994   Former Chicago Bulls star **MICHAEL JORDON** signed a contract with the White Sox to play baseball.

FEBRUARY 8

Can you erase a tattoo?

BIRTHDAYS

- **AUDREY MEADOWS** Actress. (China) "Uncle Buck." Alice Kramden on the "Honeymooners" with Jackie Gleason. Year/**Age**: 1995/**71** 1996/**72** 1997/**73**
- **VINCE NEAL WHARTON** Singer. (Los Angeles, CA) With Hard Rock group, MOTLEY CRUE. Biggest hit: "Dr. Feelgood" in 1989. Year/**Age**: 1995/**34** 1996/**35** 1997/**36**
- **DAN SEALS** Singer. (Texas) Half of England Dan and John Ford Coley duo. Their biggest hit: "I'd Really Love To See You Tonight" in 1976. Year/**Age**: 1995/**45** 1996/**46** 1997/**47**
- **JACK LEMMON** Oscar-winning actor. (Born John Uhler Lemmon in Boston, MA, in an elevator. His dad missed getting mom to the hospital by a couple of minutes.) He won an Oscar for best-supporting actor as Ensign Pulver in *Mr. Roberts*. Other films include *The Apartment, Glengarry Glen Ross,* and *Grumpy Old Men*. Year/**Age**: 1995/**70** 1996/**71** 1997/**72**
- **GARY COLEMAN** Actor. (Zion, IL) "Diff'rent Strokes." Gary was born with a kidney problem that affected his growth. The California Superior Court awarded him $1.28 million in 1993 when it ruled on a four-year-old lawsuit Coleman had brought against his parents and former manager. The three had taken excessive salaries and fees for their services between 1983 and 1987. Year/**Age**: 1995/**27** 1996/**28** 1997/**29**
- **LANA TURNER** Screen legend. (Born Julia Jean Mildred Frances Turner in Wallace, ID) The "Sweater Girl" was married 7 times and was nominated for an Oscar in 1957 for best actress in *Peyton Place*. Was in *The Postman Always Rings Twice* in 1946. She made a few guest appearances on TV's "Falcon Crest." Year/**Age**: 1995/**75** 1996/**76** 1997/**77**
- **BUDDY MORROW** Bandleader. (Born Muni Zudekoff in New Haven CT) "Night Train" was one of his hits. Year/**Age**: 1995/**76** 1996/**77** 1997/**78**

- **JOHN GRISHAM** Author. (Southaven, MS) His books include: *A Time to Kill, The Firm, The Pelican Brief, The Client* and *The Chamber* He has a law degree and served in the Mississippi House from 1984 to 1990. Year/**Age**: 1995/**39** 1996/**40** 1997/**41**
- **TED KOPPEL** ABC newsman. (Lancashire, England) "Nightline. Year/**Age**: 1995/**55** 1996/**56** 1997/**57**
- **ROBERT KLEIN** Comedian. (NYC) He appeared with Lucie Arnaz on Broadway in Neil Simon's *They're Playing Our Song* in 1979. Year/**Age**: 1995/**53** 1996/**54** 1997/**55**
- **NICK NOLTE** Actor. (Omaha, NE) *48 Hours, Down and Out in Beverly Hills, Prince of Tides, Cape Fear, Lorenzo's Oil, I Love Trouble, I'll Do Anything,* and *Blue Chips*. He was convicted in the 60's for selling fake draft cards. Year/**Age**: 1995/**54** 1996/**55** 1997/**56**
- **MARY STEENBURGEN** Actress. (Little Rock, AK) Won an Oscar in 1981 for *Melvin & Howard*. Films include *Philadelphia, Clifford, Whats Eating Gillbert Grape,* and *Pontiac Moon*. She is a close friend of Bill and Hillary Clinton. Year/**Age**: 1995/**42** 1996/**43** 1997/**44**
- **JOHN WILLIAMS** Conductor. (NYC) He composed music for *Indiana Jones, Jaws, E.T., Superman, Star Wars, Jurassic Park, Schindler's List*, and the "NBC Nightly News" theme. Year/**Age**: 1995/**63** 1996/**64** 1997/**65**
- **JAMES DEAN** Actor. (1931-1955 – Marion, IN) Famous for his roles in *Rebel Without a Cause, Giant*, and *East of Eden*. He died in a car accident at age 24. He still has a cult following. (Died 9-30-55)
- **JULES VERNE** Author. (1828-1905 – France) Known as the father of science fiction. He was the French author of *Around the World in Eighty Days* and *Twenty Thousand Leagues Under the Sea*. (Died 3-24-05)

FACTS FROM THE PAST

1587 MARY, QUEEN OF SCOTS, was **BEHEADED** after being accused of plotting the murder of England's Queen Elizabeth I.

1915 The motion picture **THE BIRTH OF A NATION,** directed by **D.W. GRIFFITH,** premiered in Los Angeles, CA. It had a cast of 18,000 plus 3,000 horses. It was the first movie ever shown at the White House. Eighteen actors were killed filming the violent epic.

1924 The first execution by lethal gas took place in Carson City, NV, at Nevada State Prison. **JON GEE,** a Chinese-American convicted of murder, took six minutes to die.

1942 Congress advised **PRESIDENT ROOSEVELT** that, in light of the attack on Pearl Harbor two months earlier, Americans of Japanese descent should be locked up enmasse so they couldn't oppose the U.S. war effort. Within months, over 100,000 Japanese-Americans were placed in remote prison camps, and some remained behind barbed wire for three years.

1960 Congressional hearings on payola opened in Washington. Those accused of accepting payment for broadcasting records were disc jockeys **DICK CLARK** and **ALAN FREED**. Clark escaped the inquiry with his reputation intact; Freed did not. He ended up pleading guilty to two counts of commercial bribery and never worked in radio again. He died a broken man in January 1965.

1964 A speech by U.S. Representative **MARTHA GRIFFITHS** in Congress on sex discrimination resulted in civil rights protection for women being added to the the 1964 Civil Rights Act.

1969 **BLIND FAITH** was formed by Steve Winwood of TRAFFIC, Eric Clapton and Ginger Baker of CREAM, and Rick Grech of FAMILY.

1974 Three Skylab astronauts (**LT. CARR, DR. BISON** and **LT. POGUE**) returned to Earth after setting a record of 84 days in orbit.

1990 "60 Minutes" commentator **ANDY ROONEY** was suspended by CBS for racial remarks attributed to him by a gay magazine. Rooney was quoted as saying that blacks had watered down their genes. Bowing to public pressure and internal dissent, CBS News lifted its suspension with an essay on Rooney's predicament March 4, 1990.

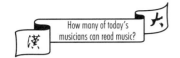
How many of today's musicians can read music?

FEBRUARY 9

BIRTHDAYS

• **HOLLY JOHNSON** Singer. (England) Formerly of FRANKIE GOES TO HOLLYWOOD. Name came from a headline about Frank Sinatra's movie career. Year/**Age**: 1995/**45** 1996/**46** 1997/**47**

• **MIA FARROW** Actress. (Born Maria de Lourdes Villers Farrow in Los Angeles, CA) She was married to Frank Sinatra from 1966-1968. She had a baby with Woody Allen. When the very first issue of *People* magazine appeared on the newsstands in March of 1974, Mia was pictured on the cover. Appeared in the film *Husbands and Wives* with Woody Allen in 1992, about problem relationships, released about the same time Mia and Woody were airing their differences. In 1993 she gained custody of their children. Year/**Age**: 1995/**50** 1996/**51** 1997/**52**

• **KATHRYN GRAYSON** Actress/singer. (Born Zelma Hedrick in Winston-Salem, NC) She appeared in *Show Boat, Kiss Me Kate, The Kissing Bandit,* and *The Vagabond King.* Year/**Age**: 1995/**73** 1996/**74** 1997/**75**

• **JOE PESCI** Actor. (Newark, NJ) His films include: *Home Alone, Lethal Weapon 3,* and *My Cousin Vinny.* He won the Best Supporting Actor Oscar for *Good Fellas.* Other films-- *With Honors* and *Jimmy Hollywood.* Before his acting days he was a member of the group JOEY DEE & THE STARLITERS. They had a number one hit in 1961, "Peppermint Twist." Year/**Age**: 1995/**52** 1996/**53** 1997/**54**

• **CAROLE KING** Singer/songwriter. (Born Carole Klein in Brooklyn, NY) She and her husband, Gerry Goffin, composed many hit songs including: "Will You Still Love Me Tomorrow" by the SHIRELLES and LITTLE EVA's "Locomotion. Her album *Tapestry* sold 11 million copies, and her biggest hit, "It's Too Late," came from the LP. Year/**Age**: 1995/**54** 1996/**55** 1997/**56**

• **JOHN KRUK** Baseball. (Charleston, WV) Philadelphia Phillies slugger. He was diagnosed with cancer in 1994. Year/**Age**: 1995/**24** 1996/**25** 1997/**26**

• **TRAVIS TRITT** C & W singer. (Marietta, GA) Hits include: "Here's a Quarter, Call Someone Who Cares" and Country Club." Autobiography *10 Feet Tall and Bulletproof.* Year/**Age**: 1995/**32** 1996/**33** 1997/**34**

• **ROGER MUDD** TV journalist. (Washington, DC) Year/**Age**: 1995/**67** 1996/**68** 1997/**69**

• **JUDITH LIGHT** Actress. (Trenton, NJ) TV's "Who's The Boss" as Angela. While on soap "One Life To Live" she married her boss Robert Desiderio, and won 2 Emmys for her role of Karen Woleck. Year/**Age**: 1995/**47** 1996/**48** 1997/**49**

• **CARMEN MIRANDA** Singer/dancer. (1913-1955 – Born Maria do Carmo da Cunha in Lisbon) Her trademark was huge hats with lots of fruit and flowers on top. (Died 8-5-55)

• **BILL VEECK** Former baseball owner and Chicago favorite. (1914-1986 – Hinsdale, IL) He owned three major league teams – St. Louis Browns, Cleveland Indians and Chicago White Sox twice. Among his many innovations were offering morning baseball to night shift workers during the war years, sending a midget up to the plate to pinch-hit, and exploding scoreboards. (Died 1-2-86)

• **ERNEST TUBB** C&W (1914-1984 – Crisp, TX) He was the sixth member elected to the Country Music Hall of Fame and sold about 30 million records and recorded more than 250 songs. He helped establish the honky-tonk sound with songs like "I'm Walking The Floor Over You." (Died 9-6-84.)

• **GYPSY ROSE LEE** Entertainer. (1914-1970 – Born Rose Louise Hovick in Seattle, WA) Her autobiography, *Gypsy,* was made into a Broadway musical and a motion picture. (Died 4-26-70)

• **WILLIAM HENRY HARRISON** 9th U.S. President. (1773-1841 – Berkeley, VA) He fathered 10 children who, in turn, produced 48, one of whom became the 23rd president, Benjamin Harrison. William's term of office was the shortest in our nation's history – 32 days. He gave the longest inaugural speech ever – 2 hours. (Died 4-4-1841)

FACTS FROM THE PAST

1861 **JEFFERSON DAVIS** was elected president of the Confederacy.

1950 **JOSEPH McCARTHY** (R/WI) charged in a speech at Wheeling, WV, that the State Department was riddled with Communists.

1964 The **BEATLES** appeared on TV's "Ed Sullivan Show" and earned $2,400. 73 million watched on television. 50,000 requests came in for 728 available seats.

1972 **PAUL MCCARTNEY** debuted his new band WINGS with a show at England's Nottingham University.

1975 **CHER** made her solo debut with her own TV show. Guests included Bette Midler, Elton John and Flip Wilson.

1980 The **IRANIAN MILITANTS** holding the American hostages said during a hastily called news conference they would obey orders only from the **AYATOLLAH KHOMEINI**.

1987 Former National Security adviser **ROBERT MCFARLANE**, who was facing tough questioning about his role in the Iran-contra affair, unsuccessfully **ATTEMPTED SUICIDE** by swallowing Valium.

1989 **PRESIDENT BUSH**, in his first major speech to Congress, **PROPOSED A $1.16 TRILLION "COMMON SENSE" BUDGET** for fiscal 1990.

1992 **MAGIC JOHNSON** played in the NBA All Star Game, his first competitive basketball game since retiring on November 7, 1991, after testing positive for the virus that causes **AIDS**. He scored 25 points and had 9 assists as his Western Conference team beat the East 153-115. He was the MVP.

FEBRUARY 10

Can-can: official dance of the Dept. of Redundancy Dept.

BIRTHDAYS

• **ROBERT WAGNER** Actor. (Detroit, MI) He was married to actress Natalie Wood twice, the second time from 1972 until her drowning accident in 1981. He appeared in the films *The Longest Day*, *Harper*, and *Notorious*. He starred with Stefanie Powers on TV's "Hart to Hart." Year/Age: 1995/**65** 1996/**66** 1997/**67**

• **ROBERTA FLACK** Singer. (Black Mountain, NC) Biggest hits: "First Time Ever I Saw Your Face" in 1972 and "Killing Me Softly With His Song" in 1973. Both won a Grammy for Record and Song of the Year. "The First Time Ever" was recorded on an album in 1969 and the song was in the film *Play Misty For Me*. Year/Age: 1995/**56** 1996/**57** 1997/**58**

• **GREG NORMAN** Golfer. (Australia) He turned professional golfer in 1976 and joined the Professional Golfers' Association in 1983. Up to 1993 he had won $2,547,904 in his career. His nickname is The White Shark. Year/Age: 1995/**40** 1996/**41** 1997/**42**

• **BOBBY BORIS PICKETT** Singer. (Sommerville, MA) His biggest hit: "Monster Mash" in 1962 and again in 1973. Year/Age: 1995/**55** 1996/**56** 1997/**57**

• **LEONTYNE PRICE** Opera singer. (Laurel, MS) Soprano. 1952-54 in *Porgy & Bess*, now retired. Year/Age: 1995/**68** 1996/**69** 1997/**70**

• **ROXANNE PULITZER** Socialite/novelist. Well known for her divorce from Peter Pulitzer in 1982. Year/Age: 1995/**43** 1996/**44** 1997/**45**

• **LENNY DYKSTRA** Baseball. (Santa Ana, CA) Philadelphia Phillies centerfielder. He came to bat more times in one season than anyone in history (773 times!) Year/Age: 1995/**32** 1996/**33** 1997/**34**

• **ALEX COMFORT** Author. Wrote *Joy of Sex*. Year/Age: 1995/**75** 1996/**76** 1997/**77**

• **GEORGE STEPHANOPOULOS** White House official. Received an Oscar nomination for his documentary *The War Room*. Year/Age: 1995/**34** 1996/**35** 1997/**36**

• **MARK SPITZ** Olympic swimmer. (Modesto, CA) His dad encouraged him to train for the Olympics. He won 7 Olympic gold medals in the 1972 Olympics. Most victorious athlete in Olympic history. He reaped $5 million in endorsements and sold over a million posters. His 1992 comeback attempt failed. Year/Age: 1995/**45** 1996/**46** 1997/**47**

• **DAME JUDITH ANDERSON** Actress. (1898 - 1992 – Born Frances Margaret Anderson in Australia) Probably best known for her role as Mrs. Danvers, a sinister housekeeper, in the movie *Rebecca*. (Died 1-3-92)

• **PETER ALLEN** Singer/songwriter. (1944-1992 – Australia) He wrote the song, "I Honestly Love You," OLIVIA NEWTON-JOHN's first big hit, and "Arthur's Theme" by CHRISTOPHER CROSS which won an Oscar. Judy Garland discovered him in Hong Kong. (Died 6-19-92)

• **JIMMY DURANTE** Entertainer. (1893-1980 – NYC) The long-nosed comedian (his nose was insured at Lloyds of London for $1 million) was famous for his signoff on TV: "Goodnight, Mrs. Calabash, wherever you are." Mrs. Calabash was his affectionate name for his wife. One of the Schnozzola's trademarks was the song "Inka Dinka Doo." *Sleepless in Seattle* featured his version of "As Time Goes By." (Died 1-29-80)

• **BORIS PASTERNAK** Russian poet/novelist. (1890-1960 – Moscow.) He wrote *Dr. Zhivago*. (Died 5-29-60)

FACTS FROM THE PAST

1840 **PRINCE ALBERT** married **QUEEN VICTORIA.** The English people were upset and said that he was after their fat queen and her fatter purse.

1863 Showman **P.T. BARNUM** staged the wedding of General Tom Thumb and Mercy Warren (both midgets) in New York. They had to stand on a piano to greet their guests. The best man was 29 inches tall and weighed 24 pounds.

1942 The first Gold Record was awarded for sales of over one million copies. It was Glenn Miller's "Chattanooga Choo Choo" on RCA, from the movie *Sun Valley Serenade*.

1949 **ARTHUR MILLER**'s play, *Death of a Salesman*, opened at Broadway's Morosco Theater with **LEE J. COBB** in the role of Willy Loman and **MILDRED DUNNOCK** as his wife, Linda.

1956 **ELVIS PRESLEY** made his first recording in Nashville. "Heartbreak Hotel" was the A-side; "I Was The One" was the B-side.

1987 Surgeon General **DR. EVERETT KOOP** told a House panel that he would advocate condoms on national TV because of a national health threat from AIDS.

1992 **MIKE TYSON** was convicted of rape and deviant sexual behavior by an Indianapolis jury.

1992 **BONNIE BLAIR** became the first U.S. medal winner at the Winter Olympics in Albertville in the women's 500-meter speed skating.

1993 In **OPRAH WINFREY**'s 90-minute live TV interview with **MICHAEL JACKSON**, he dispelled "godawful rumors including bleaching my skin." He said his light skin was caused by a disorder that destroys pigmentation of his skin called Vitiligo. He also admitted that he had minor plastic surgery to his nose. The program became the fourth most-watched show, excluding Super Bowls, in TV history with 90 million American viewers.

1994 **LT. PAULA COUGLIN,** the Navy helicopter pilot who caused the Tailhook investigation resigned. She gave her reason as continuing psychological abuse.

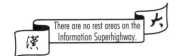

There are no rest areas on the Information Superhighway.

FEBRUARY 11

BIRTHDAYS

- **GERRY GOFFIN** Songwriter. (Brooklyn, NY) Married to singer Carole King 1958-1968. They co-wrote "Go Away Little Girl," "Will You Love Me Tomorrow," and "Locomotion." Year/**Age:** 1995/**56** 1996/**57** 1997/**58**

- **BURT REYNOLDS** Actor. (Waycross, GA) He was a football player with the NY Giants before he hit stardom twice in 1972 in two different medias: In the movie, *Deliverance* and as a nude centerfold in *Cosmopolitan* Magazine (which was when his career really took off). Star of the TV series "Evening Shade." In films *The Man from Left Field* and *Cop and a Half.* His wives included Judy Cannes and Loni Anderson (later separated – 6-10-93). Year/**Age:** 1995/**59** 1996/**60** 1997/**61**

- **EVA GABOR** Actress. (Budapest, Hungary) Married five times, her third husband was Dr. John Williams, a well-known plastic surgeon. Sister of Zsa Zsa, she was in the TV series, "Green Acres" from 1965-1968, and in the movie, *GiGi.* Year/**Age:** 1995/**74** 1996/**75** 1997/**76**

- **SERGIO MENDES** Entertainer. (Brazil) Biggest hit: "The Look of Love" with BRAZIL 66. Year/**Age:** 1995/**54** 1996/**55** 1997/**56**

- **SIDNEY SHELDON** Writer. (Chicago) *The Other Side of Midnight* and *Nothing Lasts Forever.* Year/**Age:** 1995/**78** 1996/**79** 1997/**80**

- **LESLIE NIELSEN** Actor/TV spokesman. (Canada) He was in the films *The Naked Gun, The Naked Gun 2¹/₂: The Smell Of Fear, Is This Some Kind of Bust? Naked Gun 4* as Lt. Frank Drebin, *Airplane,* and *Surf Ninjas.* His pseudoautobiography is "The Naked Truth." Year/**Age:** 1995/**73** 1996/**74** 1997/**75**

- **VIRGINIA JOHNSON-MASTERS** Sex therapist. (Springfield, MO) Year/**Age:** 1995/**70** 1996/**71** 1997/**72**

- **TINA LOUISE** Actress. (NYC) She made several films, including *God's Little Acre* and played movie star Ginger Grant on "Gilligan's Island" on TV. Year/**Age:** 1995/**61** 1996/**62** 1997/**63**

- **KIM STANLEY** Actress. (Born Patricia Reid in Tularose, NM) She won an Emmy for her TV appearance on a "Ben Casey" episode called "A Cardinal Act of Mercy" in the 1960's. Also in the films *Seance on a Wet Afternoon* and *The Right Stuff.* Year/**Age:** 1995/**70** 1996/**71** 1997/**72**

- **JOSEPH MANKIEWICZ** Director/film write.r (1909-1993 – Wilkes-Barre, PA) He won Oscars for writing and directing *A Letter to Three Wives* and *All About Eve.* In the latter, he was credited with the line spoken by Bette Davis: "Fasten your seatbelts, it's going to be a bumpy night." His other films include *The Philadelphia Story* and *Cleopatra.* (Died 2-5-93)

- **THOMAS ALVA EDISON** Inventor. (1847-1931 – Milan, [mi'-lin] OH) One of the greatest inventors of all time, he is credited with over 1,300 patents including the phonograph, electric lighting, motion picture camera, dictating machine and first practical typewriter. When he was a boy, his teachers told him he was too stupid to learn anything. (Died 10-18-31)

- **GENE VINCENT** Singer/songwriter/guitarist. (1935-1971 – Norfolk, VA) He died from an ulcer hemorrhage. He was injured in a car accident that killed Eddie Cochran in England in 1960. Vincent's biggest hit in 1956: "Be-Bop-A-Lula," about the comic strip character "Little Lulu." (Died 10-12-71)

FACTS FROM THE PAST

1927 The casket of **KING "TUT" TUTANKHAMEN** was opened. The Egyptian Pharaoh reigned around 1350 B.C. His tomb was discovered in Thebes with its treasures intact.

1960 **JACK PAAR** got up and **WALKED OFF THE "TONIGHT SHOW"** in front of millions of people who were watching live from the East Coast, after NBC censored 5 minutes worth of one of his anecdotes. He returned March 7, but two years later he left the $250,000 job for good, leaving it in the hands of a young Johnny Carson.

1964 The **BEATLES** performed their **FIRST CONCERT IN THE U.S.** at the Coliseum in Washington, DC.

1975 **MARGARET THATCHER** was elected leader of the Conservative Party of Great Britain, becoming the first woman to head that office.

1986 **BOY GEORGE** appeared on **"THE A-TEAM"** as a singer mistakenly booked into a country dance hall.

1987 After **LIBERACE**'s death and funeral, the *London Daily Mirror* asked for their $53,000 back. Liberace had sued them and won for what they printed. They called him "a fruit-flavored mincing ice-covered heap of mother love."

1989 **REV. BARBARA HARRIS** became the first woman bishop in the Episcopal Church during liturgy held in Boston.

1990 **DONALD TRUMP** informed the press that he was leaving his wife, **IVANA.**

1990 Marking what many herald as a new era in South African politics, **NELSON R. MANDELA** walked through a prison gate to freedom, setting off joyous celebrations and violent clashes as blacks nationwide welcomed their leader back from 27 years in prison for alleged sabotage and conspiracy to overthrow the government.

1990 **JAMES "BUSTER" DOUGLAS** knocked heavyweight champ **MIKE TYSON** down and out in 1 minute, 23 seconds into the tenth round. It was the first time Tyson was knocked out in his pro career.

1993 Miami prosecutor **JANET RENO** became the first female attorney general.

1994 **PAULA JONES**, former Arkansas state clerical worker, accused Bill Clinton of making unwanted and improper sexual advances during a brief encounter in a Little Rock hotel room in 1991.

FEBRUARY 12

70% of all U.S. brandy is consumed in Wisconsin.

BIRTHDAYS

- **JOANNA KERNS** Actress. (San Francisco, CA) Played the mother, Maggie, on the TV sitcom "Growing Pains." Films: *Coming To America* and *Harlem Nights.* Year/**Age**: 1995/**42** 1996/**43** 1997/**44**

- **FRANCO ZEFFERELLI** Film director. (Florence, Italy) His films include: *The Taming of the Shrew, Romeo & Juliet* (casting two unknown teenagers), *Endless Love, The Champ,* and *Hamlet.* Year/**Age**: 1995/**72** 1996/**73** 1997/**74**

- **JOE DON BAKER** Actor. (Groesbeck, TX) TV series "Eischied." Films include: *Walking Tall* and *Living Daylights.* Year/**Age**: 1995/**59** 1996/**60** 1997/**61**

- **RAY MANZAREK** [man-za'-rehk] Rock keyboardist. (Los Angeles, CA) With the DOORS. Their biggest hit: "Light My Fire" in 1967. Year/**Age**: 1995/**60** 1996/**61** 1997/**62**

- **TEX BENEKE** Bandleader/singer. (Born Gordon Beneke in Fort Worth, TX) One of his biggest hits was "Give Me Five Minutes More" in 1946, which he sang with the Glenn Miller Band. Year/**Age**: 1995/**81** 1996/**82** 1997/**83**

- **BILL RUSSELL** Basketball Hall of Famer. (Monroe, LA) He was the first black player to become the manager of a major sports team in 1966. He played with and later managed the Boston Celtics. He was MVP 5 times. Year/**Age**: 1995/**61** 1996/**62** 1997/**63**

- **JOE GARAGIOLA** Sportscaster. (St. Louis, MO) Former pro baseball catcher. "Today Show." Year/**Age**: 1995/**69** 1996/**70** 1997/**71**

- **STEVE HACKETT** Guitarist. (England) GENESIS guitar player till 1977. Biggest hit for the group: "Invisible Touch" in 1986. Year/**Age**: 1995/**45** 1996/**46** 1997/**47**

- **ARSENIO HALL** Actor/TV host.(Cleveland, OH) His last show aired 5-27-94. Year/**Age**: 1995/**40** 1996/**41** 1997/**42**

- **SCOTT TUROW** Author. (Chicago, IL) Wrote *Burden of Proof.* Year/**Age**: 1995/**46** 1996/**47** 1997/**48**

- **MOE BANDY** C&W. (Meridian, MS) He's nicknamed The King of Honky Tonk. His first hit was called: "I Just Started Hatin' Cheatin' Songs." Year/**Age**: 1995/**51** 1996/**52** 1997/**53**

- **JUDY BLUME** Children's writer. (Elizabeth, NJ) Wrote *Are You There, God? It's Me, Margaret.* Her best-selling "Fudge" books were turned into a TV series. Year/**Age**: 1995/**57** 1996/**58** 1997/**59**

- **MAUDE ADAMS** Actress. (Sweden) She appeared in the Bond films *Octopussy* and *Man with the Golden Gun.* Year/**Age**: 1995/**50** 1996/**51** 1997/**52**

- **DOM DIMAGGIO** Baseball. (Martinez, CA) His brothers Joe & Vince were also baseball players. Year/**Age**: 1995/**78** 1996/**79** 1997/**80**

- **CHYNNA PHILLIPS** Singer. (Los Angeles, CA) With the group WILSON PHILLIPS. Number 1 hits: "Hold On," and "The Dream is Still Alive." Her dad is John Phillips, of the MAMAS AND PAPAS. Year/**Age**: 1995/**27** 1996/**28** 1997/**29**

- **LORNE GREENE** Actor. (1915-1987 – Canada) Played the firm but gentle Ben Cartwright on TVs "Bonanza," which ran for 14 years. Later he was in *Battlestar Galactica* and *Code Red.* In 1964, he had a #1 hit, "Ringo," in which he talked rather than sang to the music. He did Alpo Dog Food commercials. (Died 9-11-87)

- **ABRAHAM LINCOLN** President. (1809-1865 – Hardin Cty., KY) He became a lawyer, but never attended law school. He was an Illinois state representative and was elected as the 16th U.S. President in 1861. He was the tallest president at six feet, four inches and the first to have his picture on a coin. He was shot in Washington, on April 14, 1865, while watching a performance of *Our American Cousin* at Ford's Theater. He died the next day.

- **CHARLES DARWIN** Scientist. (1809-1882 – England) Evolution theory. (Died 4-19-1882)

FACTS FROM THE PAST

1554 The 9-day reign of **LADY JANE GREY** as Queen of England came to an abrupt end when she was beheaded for treason.

1872 A toothpick making machine was patented by **SILAS NOBLE** and **JAMES P. COOLEY** of Granville, Massachusetts. It converted a block of wood into toothpicks. 7.5 million toothpicks can be made from one cord of wood.

1908 The first round-the-world automobile race began in New York and ended in Paris the following August. The winner, **GEORGE SCHUSTER** from the U.S., traveled 13,341 miles in 169 days driving a Thomas Flyer.

1957 A man lifted the heaviest weight ever. **PAUL "THE DIXIE DERRICK" ANDERSON** put 6,270 pounds on his back (the equivalent of two large cars or combined weight of all the players on two football teams). Paul weighed 364 pounds. He died 8-15-94.

1963 The premiere of a *Cleopatra* took place on this day: **LIZ TAYLOR** earned $1,500,000 plus a percentage. The film was the box office champion of the year, grossing $15,700,000.

1967 A famous **DRUG BUST** took place at the home of **KEITH RICHARDS** of the ROLLING STONES. The police found heroin, hashish, pills, and a naked lady (who turned out to be Mick Jagger's girlfriend, Marianne Faithful).

1974 The Philadelphia Mint struck the first **SUSAN B. ANTHONY DOLLARS.**

1978 San Antonio basketball star **GEORGE GERVIN** out-scored the entire Golden State Warrior team in the 4th quarter 23-22. But Golden State beat "the Ice Man" and the Spurs in overtime.

1979 The ratings came in from shows aired the night before and the "**ELVIS SPECIAL**" beat prime movies *One Flew Over the Cuckoo's Nest* and *Gone with the Wind.*

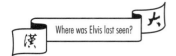
Where was Elvis last seen?

FEBRUARY 13

BIRTHDAYS

- **PETER HOOK** Musician. (England) NEW ORDER. Year/**Age**: 1995/**39** 1996/**40** 1997/**41**
- **CHUCK YEAGER** Pilot. (Myra, WV) America's most famous test pilot and the first man to fly faster than the speed of sound. Year/**Age**: 1995/**72** 1996/**73** 1997/**74**
- **DAVID NAUGHTON** Singer, dancer and actor. Star of TV's "Makin' It" (he had a hit record of the same name used in the movie *Meatballs* in 1979) and the film *An American Werewolf in London*. Year/**Age**: 1995/**45** 1996/**46** 1997/**47**
- **SAL BANDO** Baseball. (Cleveland, OH) Former Milwaukee Brewer and Oakland A's player, now general manager. Year/**Age**: 1995/**51** 1996/**52** 1997/**53**
- **EILEEN FARRELL** Opera singer. (Willimantic, CT) Grammy-winning soprano. Year/**Age**: 1995/**75** 1996/**76** 1997/**77**
- **PATTY BERG** Pro golfer. (Minneapolis, MN) In LPGA Hall of Fame. All-time women's leader in major championships. Year/**Age**: 1995/**77** 1996/**78** 1997/**79**
- **GEORGE SEGAL** Actor. (Great Neck, NY) He received an Academy Award nomination for supporting actor in *Who's Afraid of Virginia Woolf?* in 1966. Appeared in *Look Who's Talking*. Year/**Age**: 1995/**61** 1996/**62** 1997/**63**
- **PETER TORK** Musician. (Washington, DC) He was the first to leave the group in the late 60's, but returned when they got back together. The MONKEES' biggest record: "I'm a Believer" in 1967, written by Neil Diamond. Year/**Age**: 1995/**51** 1996/**52** 1997/**53**

- **CAROL LYNLEY** Former model/actress. (Born Carol Ann Jones in NYC) In *The Poseidon Adventure* and *Under the Yum Yum Tree*. Year/**Age**: 1995/**53** 1996/**54** 1997/**55**
- **OLIVER REED** Actor. (England) He appeared in the films: *The Damned, Oliver, The Jokers, The Three Musketeers*, and *Hamlet*. Year/**Age**: 1995/**57** 1996/**58** 1997/**59**
- **KIM NOVAK** Actress. (Born Marilyn Pauline Novak in Chicago, IL) She appeared in *Picnic* with William Holden and Alfred Hitchcock's *Vertigo*. For the 1956 film *Man with the Golden Arm*, she was paid $100 per week. Year/**Age**: 1995/**62** 1996/**63** 1997/**64**
- **STOCKARD CHANNING** Actress. (Born Susan Stockard in NYC) She appeared on TV in "Just Friends" in 1979, "The Stockard Channing Show" in 1980, *Six Degrees of Separation* and *Married to It*. Year/**Age**: 1995/**51** 1996/**52** 1997/**53**
- **TENNESSEE ERNIE FORD** Entertainer. (1919-1991 – Bristol, TN) His biggest hit: "Sixteen Tons" in 1955. It sold 4 million records. (Died 10-17-91)
- **BOUDLEAUX BRYANT** Songwriter. (1921-1987 – Shellman, GA) He and his wife, Felice, wrote over 400 songs including "All I Have to Do Is Dream" (which they wrote in 15 minutes), "Bye Bye Love," "Bird Dog" and "Wake Up Little Suzie," all by the EVERLY BROTHERS. (Died 6-27-87)
- **BESS TRUMAN** Former First Lady. (1885-1982 – Independence, MO) Wife of the 33rd U.S. President Harry S. Truman. (Died 10-18-82)

FACTS FROM THE PAST

1542 The fifth wife of England's King Henry VIII, **CATHERINE HOWARD**, was executed after being accused of adultery.

1633 Italian astronomer **GALILEO** arrived in Rome for trial for professing the belief that the earth revolves around the sun.

1741 **ANDREW BRADFORD** of Pennsylvania published the first magazine in the U.S, titled *The American Magazine*.

1867 "The Blue Danube" was first performed in public in Vienna. It was conducted by its composer, **JOHANN STRAUSS**. The science fiction movie, *2001: A Space Odyssey*, prominently featured this song.

1914 ASCAP, the American Society of Composers, Authors and Publishers, was formed as the first organization to protect the work of songwriters. Composer **VICTOR HERBERT** started it.

1935 **BRUNO RICHARD HAUPTMANN** was found guilty by a jury in Flemington, NJ, of first-degree murder in the kidnapping death of the baby of aviator Charles Lindbergh. The verdict carried an automatic death sentence.

1961 One of the industry's **FIRST CUSTOM LABELS** began when Frank Sinatra left Capitol Records to form Reprise Records. The first singers were Bing Crosby, Dean Martin and Sammy Davis, Jr., Frank sold the label to Warner Brothers in 1963. Frank's first song on the label was "Second Time Around."

1966 The **ROLLING STONES** made their first appearance on American television on "The Ed Sullivan Show."

1972 The Broadway show **GREASE** opened in NYC and went on to become one of the longest-running shows in history. Original cast members included Barry Bostwick and Adrienne Barbeau.

1984 It was reported in the *Washington Post* that Jesse Jackson referred to Jews as "Hymies" and to New York City as "Hymietown" in a private conversation, causing great controversy. On February 26, he apologized for those remarks.

1989 The judge in the **IRAN-CONTRA TRIAL OF OLIVER NORTH** sent the jury home amid a continuing disagreement between the prosecution and defense over protecting classified materials.

1992 Baseball slugger **JOSE CANSECO** was charged with aggravated battery in Miami after an argument with his wife. At 4 a.m. he deliberately rammed his Porsche into her BMW twice, running her off the road.

1994 **TOMMY MOE**, an American skier not favored to win a medal, won the men's downhill gold. It was the first time an American had won the gold in that event since 1984.

FEBRUARY 14
Saint Valentine's Day

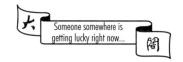

Someone somewhere is getting lucky right now...

BIRTHDAYS

- **CARL BERNSTEIN** Journalist. (Washington, DC) One of the reporters who uncovered the Watergate scandal, of Woodward & Bernstein. Year/**Age:** 1995/**50** 1996/**51** 1997/**52**

- **FLORENCE HENDERSON** Entertainer. (Dale, IN) She played Carol 'Mom' Brady on the "Brady Bunch" TV series and appeared on "Country Kitchen" on TNN. Year/**Age:** 1995/**61** 1996/**62** 1997/**63**

- **HUGH DOWNS** TV host. (Akron, OH) He began his career as a network announcer in Chicago and became Jack Paar's sidekick on the "Tonight Show." He hosted the "Today Show" from 1962-1971 and is currently the co-host, with Barbara Walters, on TV's "20/20" series. Year/**Age:** 1995/**74** 1996/**75** 1997/**76**

- **MEG TILLY** Actress. *Agnes of God, Body Snatchers, The Big Chill* and *Two Jakes*. She wrote the book *Singing Songs*. Year/**Age:** 1995/**35** 1996/**36** 1997/**37**

- **MEL ALLEN** Baseball Hall of Fame sportscaster. (Born Melvin Israel in Birmingham, AL) He was in New York planning to go to law school, and on a dare he went to CBS, took an announcing audition, and got the job. Year/**Age:** 1995/**82** 1996/**83** 1997/**84**

- **GREGORY HINES** Dancer/actor. (NYC) Appeared in the film *Taps* and also *The Cotton Club*. Year/**Age:** 1995/**49** 1996/**50** 1997/**51**

- **PETER GIMBEL** Explorer. (NYC) He was the first to photograph the sunken ship *Andrea Doria*. Risked his life filming a movie about sharks, *Blue Water, White Death,* in 1971. Year/**Age:** 1995/**67** 1996/**68** 1997/**69**

- **PAT O'BRIEN** CBS sports announcer. Also semi-regular on TV's "Entertainment Tonight." Co-host of TV's "How'd They Do That?" Year/**Age:** 1995/**47** 1996/**48** 1997/**49**

- **FRAGNIERE MANUELA MaLEEVA** Tennis star. (Sofia, Bulgaria) Year/**Age:** 1995/**28** 1996/**29** 1997/**30**

- **JIM KELLEY** Football. Buffalo Bills quarterback. Year/**Age:** 1995/**35** 1996/**36** 1997/**37**

- **JIMMY HOFFA** Labor leader. (1913 – Brazil, IN) Disappeared from a Detroit area restaurant July 30, 1975, and was officially declared dead in 1982. His body was never found.

- **GEORGE WASHINGTON FERRIS** Inventor. (1859-1896 – Galesburg, IL) Invented the Ferris Wheel for the World's Columbian Exposition at Chicago in 1893. It turned out to be the biggest attraction at the fair. (Died 11-22-1896)

- **WOODY HAYES** Former Ohio State football coach. (1913-1987 – Born Wayne Woodrow Hayes in Clifton, OH) He compiled a record of 238-72-10. He was fired a few hours after the '78 Gator Bowl when, in full view of national TV, he struck Charlie Bauman after the Clemson nose guard intercepted an Ohio State pass in the closing minutes of a 17-15 setback. (Died 3-12-87)

- **JACK BENNY** Entertainer. (1894-1974 – Born Benjamin "Benny" Kubelsky in Waukegan, IL) Jack was one of the great comedians who made the transition from radio to TV in the 50's. He had a weekly series on CBS-TV from 1950 through 1965. His automobile, often mentioned on the show, was a 1924 Maxwell. (Died 12-26-74)

- **EDMUND GEORGE LOVE** Author. (1912) (Flushing, MI) Said to be the only Love born on Valentine's Day. He wrote *Subways are for Sleeping* and *War is a Private Affair*.

- **VIC MORROW** Actor. (1932-1982) He was killed when a helicopter crashed during the filming of the movie *Twilight Zone*. Director John Landis and four associates were acquitted of manslaughter charges in the deaths. (Died 7-23-82)

FACTS FROM THE PAST

1876   Inventors **ALEXANDER GRAHAM BELL** and **ELISHA GRAY** applied separately for patents related to the telephone. The U.S. Supreme Court eventually ruled Bell the rightful inventor.

1884   **VALENTINE'S DAY** turned out to be a tragic day for **THEODORE ROOSEVELT.** Typhoid fever killed his mother in the morning and his wife died shortly after giving birth to a daughter that afternoon.

1929   What came to be known as the **ST. VALENTINE'S DAY MASSACRE** occurred when some of Al Capone's gangsters (some dressed as policemen) walked into the S.M.C. Cartage Co. Warehouse (owned by Bugs Moran) at 2122 N. Clark St. in Chicago. They shoved 7 members of a rival gang up against a brick wall and Tommy gunned them to death.

1958   **WALTER CRONKITE**, CBS TV newsman, reports that the Iranian government banned rock and roll. Iran said that rock music is against the concepts of Islam and a health hazard, charging that "Extreme gyrations of rock and roll dances are injurious to the hips."

1962   **FIRST LADY JACKIE KENNEDY** conducted a one-hour televised **TOUR OF THE WHITE HOUSE.** The first public peek into the presidential back rooms and bedrooms drew a record audience of 80,000,000.

1974   The **CAPTAIN (DARYL DRAGON)** married **TONI TENNILLE** in California.

1977   **JANIS IAN** received 461 Valentine's Day cards in resonse to the lack of them in her song "At Seventeen."

1980   CBS announced that **DAN RATHER** had been chosen to succeed **WALTER CRONKITE** as anchorman and managing editor of "The CBS Evening News" the following year.

1981   GENERATION X, the London punk band led by **BILLY IDOL**, broke up. Idol left for a solo career in the U.S.

1986   **FRANK ZAPPA** appeared on "Miami Vice" as a crime boss named Mr. Frankie.

1989   Iran's Ayatollah called on Moslems to kill **SALMAN RUSHDIE**, author of the novel *The Satanic Verses*, condemned as blasphemous throughout the Islamic world. Khomeini offered a $1 million reward for his death.

Many lakes shown on old maps no longer exist.

FEBRUARY 15

BIRTHDAYS

• **MATT GROENING** Cartoonist. (Portland, OR) He created the *Simpsons*. Matt named the characters after family members, his parents Homer and Marge, sisters Lisa and Maggie and Bart was an anagram of "brat." Year/**Age**: 1995/**41** 1996/**42** 1997/**43**

• **BRIAN HOLLAND** Songwriter. (Detroit, MI) Part of the successful songwriting team Dozier and Holland. They wrote many of Motown's biggest hits. Year/**Age**: 1995/**54** 1996/**55** 1997/**56**

• **ALI CAMPBELL** Singer. (England) Lead vocalist and rhythm guitarist with UB40. U.S. hit: "Red Red Wine." Year/**Age**: 1995/**36** 1996/**37** 1997/**38**

• **MELISSA MANCHESTER** Singer. (Bronx, NY) She got her start in the early '70's with a group that backed Bette Midler. Her biggest hit: "You Should Hear How She Talks About You" in 1982. Sang theme for *Rosie O'Neill*. She made a rare acting appearance on the 1993 TV series "Blossom." Year/**Age**: 1995/**44** 1996/**45** 1997/**46**

• **RON CEY** Baseball. (Tacoma, WA) Dodger and later Cub 3rd baseman. Year/**Age**: 1995/**47** 1996/**48** 1997/**49**

• **JANE SEYMOUR** Actress. (England) She appeared in the TV miniseries "East of Eden" and "War and Remembrance." Stars in the TV series "Dr. Quinn: Medicine Woman." Year/**Age**: 1995/**44** 1996/**45** 1997/**46**

• **HARVEY KORMAN** TV funnyman. (Chicago, IL) He was a regular on the "Danny Kaye Show" in the 1960's and won 4 Emmy Awards for his appearances on the "Carol Burnett Show." Appeared in *Blazing Saddles* in 1974. Year/**Age**: 1995/**68** 1996/**69** 1997/**70**

• **HANK LOCKLIN** C&W. (Born Lawrence Hankins Locklin in McLellan, FL) Biggest hit: "Please Help Me I'm Falling" on charts twice in 1960 and 1970. Year/**Age**: 1995/**77** 1996/**78** 1997/**79**

• **MARISA BERENSON** Actress/model. (NYC) Year/**Age**: 1995/**47** 1996/**48** 1997/**49**

• **KEVIN McCARTHY** Actor. (Seattle, WA) Appeared in *Death of a Salesman*, *The Prize* and a 1956 cult classic, *Invasion of the Body Snatchers*. Year/**Age**: 1995/**81** 1996/**82** 1997/**83**

• **MICK AVORY** Drummer. (England) Of the KINKS – Their biggest hit: "Tired of Waiting for You" in 1965. Year/**Age**: 1995/**51** 1996/**52** 1997/**53**

• **MIKEY CRAIG** Musician. (England) Bass player for CULTURE CLUB. Biggest hit: "Karma Chameleon" in 1983. Year/**Age**: 1995/**35** 1996/**36** 1997/**37**

• **CESAR ROMERO** Actor. (1907-1994, NYC) Handsome Latin leading man, former dancer and Broadway actor, seen on TV's "Falcon Crest." "Joker" on the Batman TV show.

• **CLAIRE BLOOM** Actress. (England) Appeared in *The Haunting, The Spy Who Came in From the Cold,* and others. Year/**Age**: 1995/**64** 1996/**65** 1997/**66**

• **KEN ANDERSON** Football quarterback. (Batavia, IL) Year/**Age**: 1995/**46** 1996/**47** 1997/**48**

• **HAROLD ARLEN** Songwriter. (1905-1986 – Born Hyman Arlur in Buffalo, NY) Wrote Academy Award winner "Over the Rainbow." (Died 4-23-86)

• **JOHN BARRYMORE** Actor. (1882-1942 – Philadelphia, PA) Appeared in *Grand Hotel, Rasputin,* and *Dr. Jekyll and Mr. Hyde*. Drew's grandfather. (Died 5-29-42)

• **HENRY STEINWAY** Piano maker. (Born this day in 1797)

• **SUSAN B. (BROWNWELL) ANTHONY** Feminist. (1820-1906 – Adams, MA) A militant advocate of women's suffrage and the first American woman to have her likeness on coinage ($1.00 coin). (Died 3-13-06)

• **GALILEO** Italian astronomer. (1564-1642 – Born Galileo Galilei) He studied for a medical career at the University of Pisa but changed to science. (Died 1-8-1642)

• **CHARLES TIFFANY** Jeweler. (1812-1902 – Killingly, CT) American jeweler whose name became synonymous with high standards of quality. (Died 2-18-02)

FACTS FROM THE PAST

1879 **PRESIDENT RUTHERFORD HAYES** signed a bill to allow women attorneys to argue cases before the U.S. Supreme Court.

1933 President-elect **FRANKLIN D. ROOSEVELT** escaped an assassination attempt in Miami, FL. Instead, the bullet killed Chicago Mayor Anton Cermak. Joseph Zangara, the assassin, was captured, convicted and put to death less than a month later.

1978 **LEON SPINKS** shocked the boxing world by beating **MUHAMMAD ALI** in a 15-round split decision, to capture the heavyweight title in Las Vegas…one of boxing's greatest upsets.

1980 Speed skater **ERIC HEIDEN** [hy'-dun] won the first of five gold medals at the Winter Olympic Games in Lake Placid, New York. That same day, U.S. figure skaters Tai [ty] Babilonia and Randy Gardner were forced to withdraw from the Olympics due to an injury suffered by Gardner.

1985 **POPE JOHN PAUL** met with leaders of the American Jewish Committee and issued a statement condemning anti-Semitism as "incompatible with Christ's teaching."

1986 The Philippines National Assembly proclaimed **FERDINAND E. MARCOS** president for another six years, capping an election marked by charges of fraud.

1989 **MIKHAIL GORBACHEV** withdrew the last of the Soviet troops from Afghanistan.

1992 **JEFFREY DAHMER**, confessed serial killer, was found sane when he killed 15 young men in Milwaukee County, Wisconsin, and destroyed their bodies. Dahmer had admitted to having sex with the corpses, boiling the skulls and eating body parts. He was sentenced to life in prison without parole.

FEBRUARY 16

BIRTHDAYS

- **WILLIAM KATT** Actor. (Los Angeles, CA) *Top of the Hill.* Year/**Age**: 1995/**40** 1996/**41** 1997/**42**

- **JAMES INGRAM** Singer/songwriter. (Akron, OH) Number 1 hit in 1982 with Patti Austin: "Baby Come To Me." Year/**Age**: 1995/**39** 1996/**40** 1997/**41**

- **JOHN McENROE, JR.** Tennis star. (West Germany) Divorced from actress Tatum O'Neal. His hobby is music. Year/**Age**: 1995/**36** 1996/**37** 1997/**38**

- **PATTY ANDREWS** Singer. With the ANDREWS SISTERS. Their biggest hit was "Rum 'n' Coca-Cola" in 1945. Year/**Age**: 1995/**75** 1996/**76** 1997/**77**

- **JIMMY WAKELEY** C&W. (Meneola, AR) Along with Margaret Whiting, their biggest hit was "Slippin' Around" in 1949. #1 on the C&W chart for 17 weeks. Year/**Age**: 1995/**80** 1996/**81** 1997/**82**

- **MARK PRICE** Basketball. He plays for the Washington Bullets. Year/**Age**: 1995/**31** 1996/**32** 1997/**33**.

- **JEROME BETTIS** Football. Year/**Age**: 1995/**23** 1996/**24** 1997/**25**

- **BILL DOGGETT** Organist. (Philadelphia) In 1956, his recording of "Honky Tonk" became one of the smash hits of the decade. It sold over 5 million copies, stayed on the charts for over 7 months and lost out only to Elvis Presley's "Heartbreak Hotel." The song was written on the spur of the moment in a Lima, Ohio, nightclub. Year/**Age**: 1995/**79** 1996/**80** 1997/**81**

- **JOHN SCHLESINGER** Film director. (England) Directed *Midnight Cowboy* in 1969. Year/**Age**: 1995/**69** 1996/**70** 1997/**71**

- **ANDY TAYLOR** Guitarist of DURAN DURAN. (Birmingham, England) He answered an ad in the paper looking for a live-wire guitarist. One of the group's biggest hits: "A View to a Kill" in 1985 from the James Bond film. They took their name from a character called Duran Duran, played by actor Milo O'Shea in the 1968 science-fiction film *Barbarella* starring Jane Fonda. Biggest hit: "The Reflex" in 1984. Year/**Age**: 1995/**34** 1996/**35** 1997/**36**

- **LeVAR BURTON** Actor. (Germany) He was a college student appearing in his first TV role as Kunta Kinte in "Roots." Starred in "Star Trek: The Next Generation" and PBS "Reading Rainbow." Year/**Age**: 1995/**38** 1996/**39** 1997/**40**

- **SONNY BONO** Entertainer. (Born Salvatore Bono in Detroit, MI) His biggest hit with Cher: "I Got You, Babe" in 1965. Sonny runs a restaurant and was mayor of Palm Springs, CA. Sonny was once quoted as saying: "The biggest mistake a performer can make is to try to stay a teenager." Year/**Age**: 1995/**60** 1996/**61** 1997/**62**

- **EDGAR BERGEN** Ventriloquist. (1903-1978 – Born Edgar John Bergren in Chicago) He was the voice of Charley McCarthy, Effie Klinker & Mortimer Snerd. He starred in the "Chase and Sanborn Hour" on radio with W. C. Fields, who made fun of Charley for being made out of wood and Charley would make fun of Fields for being a lush. An excellent book *Knock Wood* was written about Bergen by his daughter, Candice. (Died 9-3-78)

- **WAYNE KING** Bandleader. (1901-1985 – Savannah, IL) Known as "The Waltz King" His theme song: "The Waltz You Saved For Me." (Died 7-16-85)

FACTS FROM THE PAST

1937 **DR. WALLACE H. CAROTHERS** received a patent for nylon. Nylon is a strong, elastic, synthetic material made from coal, water and air. It quickly became called the "poor people's silk."

1941 **DUKE ELLINGTON** recorded "Take the A Train."

1950 "What's My Line" premiered on CBS-TV, with moderator **JOHN CHARLES DALY**. First panelists were: Dorothy Kilgallen, former New Jersey governor Harold Hoffman, Louis Untermeyer and psychiatrist Dr. Richard Hoffman. Arlene Francis made her appearance on the second show. It ran until Sept. 3, 1967.

1959 **FIDEL CASTRO** appointed himself as Premier of Cuba after the overthrow of Batista.

1963 The **BEATLES** got their first #1 British hit single: "Please Please Me."

1970 **ELVIS PRESLEY** recorded his show at the International Hotel in Las Vegas for a live album *On Stage, February, 1970.*

1978 The book *The Ends of Power* was published by former White House chief-of-staff **H.R. HALDEMAN** in which he accused his former employer, President Richard Nixon, of initiating the Watergate break-in.

1980 At the Winter Olympic Games in Lake Placid, New York, American speed skater **ERIC HEIDEN** [hy'-dun] captured the second of five gold medals, while the U.S. Hockey team defeated Norway 5-1.

1985 **MURRAY P. HAYDON**, a retired auto worker, became the third person to receive a permanent artificial heart as doctors at Humana Hospital Audubon in Louisville, KY, implanted the device. (Haydon lived 488 days with the heart.)

1989 **JAMES BOND**, an ornithologist whose name was adopted for the fictional British agent 007 in Ian Fleming's novels, died.

1989 Bookstores across the U.S. reported brisk sales of *The Satanic Verses*, a novel by **SALMAN RUSHDIE**, who became the target of death threats from Moslem fundamentalists who called the book blasphemous.

1994 TV's **DIANE SAWYER** signs for $7 million a year with ABC.

Turning the tables: Indian casinos.

FEBRUARY 17

BIRTHDAYS

• **LOU DIAMOND PHILLIPS** Actor. (Phillipines) Films *LaBamba, Stand & Deliver, The First Power, Young Guns, Sioux City,* and *Shadow of the Wolf.* Year/**Age**: 1995/**33** 1996/**34** 1997/**35**

• **ALAN BATES** English actor. He was the sexy artist who wooed divorcee Jill Clayburgh in *An Unmarried Woman* in 1970, played Bette Midler's manager in *The Rose* and appeared in *Duet for One* with Julie Andrews. Year/**Age**: 1995/**61** 1996/**62** 1997/**63**

• **HAL HOLBROOK** Actor. (Born Harold Rowe Holbrook, Jr. in Cleveland, OH) A movie, stage and TV actor, well known for his Mark Twain impersonation. Married to actress Dixie Carter. Appears on TV's "Designing Women" and "Evening Shade." In film *The Firm.* Year/**Age**: 1995/**70** 1996/**71** 1997/**72**

• **GENE PITNEY** Singer. (Hartford, CT) Pop singer of the 60's, his biggest hit: "Only Love Can Break a Heart." He wrote "He's a Rebel" for the CRYSTALS. Appeared in the films *Hairspray* and *Look Who's Talking.* Year/**Age**: 1995/**54** 1996/**55** 1997/**56**

• **MICHAEL JORDAN** Basketball Superstar. (Born Michael Jeffrrey Jordan in Brooklyn, NY) On the 1982 North Carolin NCAA basketball championship team. In the NBA he lead the Chicago Bulls to 3 consecutive championships. Seven-time lead-scorer, 21,541 career pts., and exceeded 50 pts.in a game 34 times. The baseball-wanna-be retired from basketball 10-6-93. Year/**Age**: 1995/**32** 1996/**33** 1997/**34**

• **MARGARET TRUMAN** Author. (Independence, MO) The daughter of 33rd U.S. President Harry Truman, now a successful author, including *Murder In The White House.* Married to *New York Times* editor Clifton Daniel, Jr. Year/**Age**: 1995/**71** 1996/**72** 1997/**73**

• **RICHARD KARN** Actor. TV's "Home Improvement." At one time he was an apartment building manager.

• **MARY ANN MOBLEY** Former Miss America. (Brandon, MS) Married to talk show host Gary Collins. Year/**Age**: 1995/**56** 1996/**57** 1997/**58**

• **JIM BROWN** Former football pro/turned actor. (St. Simon Island, GA) He was a Cleveland Brown fullback from 1957-65 who ran for a record 12,312 career yards. He was MVP 3 times and never missed a game. The Hall of Famer now heads the anti-gang Amer-I-Can program. Year/**Age**: 1995/**58** 1996/**59** 1997/**60**

• **MARIAN ANDERSON** Contralto. (1902-1993 – Philadelphia, PA) She was the first black artist to entertain at the White House and the NY Met. (Died 4-8-93)

• **RED BARBER** Sportscaster. (1907-1992 – Born Walter Lanier Barber in Columbus, MS) Began play-by-play for the Cincinnati Reds games, then voice of the Brooklyn Dodgers and New York Yankees. He was fired by the Yankees for mentioning the small crowd at a game. (Died 10-22-92)

• **ARTHUR KENNEDY** Actor. (1914-1990 – Worcester, MA) Films include *The Glass Menagerie* and *Lawrence of Arabia.* Character actor who was nominated for Academy Awards five times and who won a Tony Award for his stage portrayal of Biff in *Death of a Salesman.* (Died 1-5-90)

• **HUEY NEWTON** Activist. (1942-1989 – New Orleans, LA) Co-founder of the radical Black Panther Party who spent time as a fugitive in Cuba. He was gunned down in Oakland, CA. (8-22-89)

• **RENE LAENNEC** Inventor. (1781-1826) A French physician/author. He invented the stethoscope, which was the result of an inspiration while watching children play. The kids were playing with long sticks, tapping at one end and listening at the other. (Died 8-13-1826)

• **MONTGOMERY WARD** Tycoon. (1844-1913 – Chatham, NJ) Invented the mail-order catalog. (Died 12-7-13)

FACTS FROM THE PAST

1801 The U.S. House of Representatives broke an electoral tie and named **THOMAS JEFFERSON** the **THIRD U.S. PRESIDENT** and Aaron Burr, Vice President.

1897 **PATTY HEARST**'s great-grandmother co-founded the National Congress of Mothers in Washington, D.C. In 1924, it became the National Congress of Parents and Teachers (the **PTA**).

1904 **PUCCINI'S** opera *Madame Butterfly* premiered at La Scala in Milan, Italy. The audience booed the performers off the stage. Puccini said, "It is I who am right, you shall see," and he rewrote the opera, obtaining rave reviews.

1909 One of the most famous Indian leaders, **GERONIMO**, got drunk and fell off his horse. While he was lying outside all night he caught pneumonia and died at age 80 in Fort Sill, OK.

1960 **ELVIS PRESLEY** received his **FIRST GOLD LP** for *Elvis.*

1972 **PINK FLOYD** premiered "Dark Side of the Moon" during a concert at London's Rainbow Theater. The album by that name was released a year later and became the longest-charting Rock LP in *Billboard's* history. It was on the charts for 303 weeks.

1987 Texan **MICHELLE RENEE ROYER** was crowned Miss USA. Hours before the pageant, Bob Barker threatened to resign as host over an "animal rights" dispute.

1988 A 12-year-old **FAN OF MOTLEY CRUE** set his legs on fire while trying to imitate a stunt shown in the group's "Live Wire" video. The band offered condolences to the boy, saying their stunts should not be tried at home.

1994 Former U.S. **TREASURER CATALINA VILLALPANDO** was found guilty for evading over $47,000 in federal taxes.

FEBRUARY 18

Can anyone claim to be smaller than life?

BIRTHDAYS

- **DENNIS DE YOUNG** Singer/keyboardist. (Chicago, IL) STYX. Year/Age: 1995/**48** 1996/**49** 1997/**50**

- **ROBBIE BACHMAN** Drummer. (Canada) BACHMAN-TURNER OVERDRIVE. Their biggest hit: "You Ain't Seen Nothing Yet" in 1974. Year/Age: 1995/**42** 1996/**43** 1997/**44**

- **GEORGE KENNEDY** Actor. (NYC) He won an Oscar for supporting actor in *Cool Hand Luke* in 1967. Appeared in the films *Airport* and *Naked Gun 2¹/₂*. Year/Age: 1995/**70** 1996/**71** 1997/**72**

- **JACK PALANCE** Actor. (Born John Palahnuik, Jr., in Lattimer Mines, PA) Received an Oscar nomination for supporting actor in 1952 for *Sudden Fear* and in 1953 for *Shane*. In 1992 at the Academy Awards, Palance proceeded to do a series of one-armed push-ups to show he was still in shape. He received the best supporting Oscar for *City Slickers*. Recently in film *Tombstone*. Year/Age: 1995/**75** 1996/**76** 1997/**77**

- **MOLLY RINGWALD** Actress. (Roseville, CA) *The Breakfast Club*, *Pretty In Pink* and *Betsy's Wedding*. Year/Age: 1995/**27** 1996/**28** 1997/**29**

- **HELEN GURLEY BROWN** Editor. (Green Forest, AR) Author and Editor-in-Chief of *Cosmopolitan* magazine. She wrote books *Sex and the Single Girl* and *The Late Show*. She was first to feature a nude centerfold of Burt Reynolds. Year/Age: 1995/**73** 1996/**74** 1997/**75**

- **MANNY MOTA** Baseball. Power hitter with a record 150 lifetime pinch hits. Year/Age: 1995/**57** 1996/**58** 1997/**59**

- **MATT DILLON** Actor. (Westchester, NY) He appeared in *Flamingo Kid*, *Drugstore Cowboy*, *Singles*, *Mr. Wonderful*, *The Saint of Fort Washington* and *Golden Gate*. Year/Age: 1995/**31** 1996/**32** 1997/**33**

- **JOHN TRAVOLTA** Actor. (Englewood, NJ) He received an Oscar nomination for best actor in *Saturday Night Fever* in 1977 and played Vinnie Barbarino on "Welcome Back, Kotter" on TV. Other films include *Pulp Fictions*, *Look Who's Talking I* and *II* and *Look Who's Talking Now*. Year/Age: 1995/**41** 1996/**42** 1997/**43**

- **DICK STOCKTON** Tennis player. (NYC) Year/Age: 1995/**44** 1996/**45** 1997/**46**

- **CYBILL SHEPHERD** Actress. (Memphis, TN) In 1971 she made the first of several movies, *The Last Picture Show* in which she had a nude scene. Then she went home to Memphis and stayed several years before making her big TV comeback as Maddie Hayes in "Moonlighting." In the film *Married to It*. This former model has recorded several albums. Year/Age: 1995/**45** 1996/**46** 1997/**47**

- **JUICE NEWTON** Singer. (Born Judy Cohen in Virginia Beach, VA) Biggest record: "Queen of Hearts" in 1981. Also "Angel of the Morning." Year/Age: 1995/**43** 1996/**44** 1997/**45**

- **YOKO ONO** Artist/singer. (Tokyo, Japan) Her name means "ocean child" in Japanese. She was married to John Lennon from 1969 until his death on Dec. 8, 1980. Lennon wrote a song for her shortly before his death, "Woman," which became a hit in 1981. She is listed as one of the ten richest women in the world. Year/Age: 1995/**62** 1996/**63** 1997/**64**

- **MILOS** [mee'-lohsh] **FORMAN** Movie director. (Casla, Czechoslovakia) *Amadeus* and *One Flew Over The Cuckoo's Nest*. Year/Age: 1995/**63** 1996/**64** 1997/**65**

- **VANNA WHITE** Hostess. (Born Vanna Marie Rosich in Conway, SC – Her stepfather's name is White.) "Wheel of Fortune." She is the niece of late actor Christopher George. She was the second turner on "Wheel;" Susan Stafford was the first. Vanna married L.A. restaurant owner George Pietro in 1991. Year/Age: 1995/**38** 1996/**39** 1997/**40**

- **JUDY RANKIN** Pro golfer. (St. Louis, MO) Year/Age: 1995/**50** 1996/**51** 1997/**52**

- **BILL CULLEN** Radio/TV game-show host. (1920-1990 – Born William Lawrence Cullen in Pittsburgh, PA) His game-show resume included "The Price is Right," "$25,000 Pyramid," "To Tell The Truth," "I've Got A Secret," and "The Joker's Wild." (Died 7-7-90)

- **ANDRES SEGOVIA** Guitarist. (1893-1987 – Spain) Acclaimed as the world's premier classical guitarist. He was one of the few classical guitarists to have earned a gold record. (Died 6-2-87)

- **GEORGE GIPP** Football. (1905-1930) Notre Dame University, All-American running back portrayed by Ronald Reagan in *Knute Rockne*, died of pneumonia at age 25.

FACTS FROM THE PAST

1861   **JEFFERSON DAVIS** was inaugurated as President of the Confederate States. They played "Dixie" for him by mistake. "Dixie" was neither old nor Southern. It was written by a Northerner for a Broadway minstrel show in 1859.

1885   **MARK TWAIN** (Samuel Clemens) published *The Adventures of Huckleberry Finn*.

1930   The planet Pluto was discovered by **CLYDE TOMBAUGH** [tom'-bo], working at Lowell Observatory in Flagstaff, AZ. Pluto means "god of the dead and outer darkness."

1953   **LUCILLE BALL** and **DESI ARNEZ** signed the most lucrative contract of the day, $8 million, to continue the TV series "I Love Lucy" through 1955.

1953   The first 3-D movie opened at Loew's State Theater in NYC. It was *Bwana Devil* starring **ROBERT STACK** and **NIGEL BRUCE.**

1972   The **CALIFORNIA SUPREME COURT** declared an end to capital punishment, calling it "cruel and unusual punishment." Among those spared by the ruling were assassins Sirhan Sirhan and Charles Manson.

1972   **RANDY SMITH**, Buffalo guard, started his streak of playing 906 games in a row over 11 years in the NBA.

1994   **DAN JANSEN** finally won his gold medal in the 1,000 meter speed skating competition in a world record time of 1 minute 12.43 seconds.

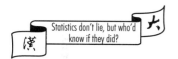

Statistics don't lie, but who'd know if they did?

FEBRUARY 19

BIRTHDAYS

- **WILLIAM "SMOKEY" ROBINSON** Singer/songwriter. (Detroit, MI) Biggest hit: "Tears of a Clown" with the MIRACLES in 1970. He formed the group while attending Detroit's Northern High School in 1957. Biggest hit: "Being With You" in 1981. Year/**Age**: 1995/**55** 1996/**56** 1997/**57**

- **LOU CHRISTIE** Singer. (Born Lugee Gene Sacco in Willard, PA) Biggest hit: "Lightnin' Strikes" in 1966. Year/**Age**: 1995/**52** 1996/**53** 1997/**54**

- **EDDIE ARCARO** Racehorse jockey. (Cincinnati, OH) He rode 5 Kentucky Derby winners, also 6 Preakness and Belmont Stakes champs. Year/**Age**: 1995/**79** 1996/**80** 1997/**81**

- **PRINCE ANDREW OF BRITAIN** He is seperated from Fergie. After Prince Charles's children, he is next in line to the British throne. Year/**Age**: 1995/**35** 1996/**36** 1997/**37**

- **HANA MANDLIKOVA** Tennis star. (Czechoslovakia) She upset Martina Navratilova in 1984, ending a 55-win streak, and again in 1987, stopping Martina after 58 straight match victories. Year/**Age**: 1995/**33** 1996/**34** 1997/**35**

- **PAUL DEAN** Lead guitar player. (Canada) He started the group LOVERBOY. Their biggest hit: "Lovin' Every Minute of It" in 1985. Year/**Age**: 1995/**49** 1996/**50** 1997/**51**

- **JUSTINE BATEMAN** Actress. (Rye, NY) Mallory on "Family Ties." Films: *Satisfaction* and *The Night We Never Met.* Year/**Age**: 1995/**29** 1996/**30** 1997/**31**

- **JEFF DANIELS** Actor. (Atlanta, GA) In films *Terms of Endearment, Speed, Dumb and Dumber,* and *Ragtime.* Year/**Age**: 1995/**40** 1996/**41** 1997/**42**

- **ANDREW SHUE** Actor. TV's "Melrose Place." Year/**Age**: 1995/**28** 1996/**29** 1997/**30**

- **MERLE OBERON** Actress. (1911-1979 – Born Estelle Merle O'Brien in India) She appeared in *A Song to Remember, Desiree,* and *The Oscar.*

- **GEORGE ROSE** Actor. (1920-1988 – England) He was on stage with Sandy Duncan in *Peter Pan* and Linda Ronstadt in *Pirates of Penzance.* He won a Tony for *My Fair Lady.* His films included: *A Night to Remember* and *Jack the Ripper.* He was killed in a car accident in the Northern Dominican Republic. (Died 5-5-88)

- **KAREN SILKWOOD** Technician. (1946-1974) She was a union activist at the Kerr-McGee Cimarron Plutonium plant near Crescent, OK, and was upset with the security and safety violations at the plant. Merryl Streep played her in the film *Silkwood.* (Died 11-13-74)

- **LEE MARVIN** Actor. (1924-1987 – NYC) He won an Oscar for best actor in 1965 for *Cat Ballou.* He was in "M-Squad" on TV and was a party in a historic palimony suit. He did a song called: "I Was Born Under a Wandering Star." (Died 8-29-87)

- **"MAMA" CASS ELLIOTT** Singer. (1941-1974) Born Ellen Cohen in Baltimore, MD) Biggest hit with the MAMAS & PAPAS: "Monday Monday" in 1966 and, on her own: "Dream a Little Dream of Me" in 1968. Died of a heart attack in the London flat of Harry Nilsson. (7-29-74)

- **NICOLAUS COPERNICUS** Astronomer. (1473-1543 – Poland) He set out to prove that the sun, not the earth, was the "center of our universe." He wrote about it in a book, but was afraid to publish it. Disciples of his were burned at the stake for their belief in his theory. But, he finally published his findings and dedicated his work to the Pope. (Died 5-25-1543)

FACTS FROM THE PAST

1807 Former **VICE PRESIDENT AARON BURR** was arrested in what was to become the State of Alabama. He subsequently was tried for treason and found "not guilty."

1878 **THOMAS EDISON** was granted a patent for the cylinder phonograph, which he called the "speaking machine." He never thought it would have much to do with music. The first words ever recorded in the history of man: "Mary had a little lamb."

1958 The **MIRACLES** released their first single, "Got A Job," in response to the Silhouettes' "Get A Job."

1964 A half-ton of **BEATLE WIGS** were flown to the U.S. from the U.K. to meet demands of the fans.

1976 **PATTY HEARST** invoked the Fifth Amendment nineteen times at her bank-robbery trial in San Francisco.

1977 **FLEETWOOD MAC'S** *Rumours* was released. It became one of the biggest-selling albums ever, selling over 15 million. copies

1981 Price-Waterhouse CPA **GLENN KANNRY** pleaded guilty to repeatedly taking cash from **DIANA ROSS**'s bank account.

1981 **GEORGE HARRISON** was found guilty of plagiarism and ordered to pay the owners of the song "She's So Fine" $587,000. They claimed similarities with his hit "My Sweet Lord."

1984 American twin brothers, **PHIL AND STEVE MAHRE**, won the gold and silver medals in the men's slalom on the final day of the Olympic Games in Sarajevo, Yugoslavia.

1989 Iran's **AYATOLLAH KHOMEINI** rejected the apology of *Satanic Verses* author Salman Rushdie [roosh'-dee], exhorting Moslems around the world to send him to hell for committing blasphemy.

1993 Miss Michigan, 22-year-old **KENYA** (named for the country) **MOORE** was crowned the new Miss U.S.A. She was the second black woman to win the title in the 42-year pageant history. The first black Miss USA was Carol Gist, crowned in 1990. On this day it was also revealed that the singers on the pageant broadcast lip-synced and all of the music was pre-recorded.

1994 American speedskater **BONNIE BLAIR** won her third straight Olympic championship in the 500-meter in a record time of 39.25 seconds.

FEBRUARY 20
Astrological sign of Pisces

Fat chance: very good, if you're on a diet.

BIRTHDAYS

- **CHARLES "BREAD TRUCK" BARKLEY** Basketball. (Leeds, AL) 6'6" Star forward. Six-time All Star. Plays for the Phoenix Suns and was a member of the 1992 U.S. Olympic Dream Team. In Nike's commercials. Year/**Age**: 1995/**32** 1996/**33** 1997/**34**

- **KELSEY GRAMMER** Actor. (St. Thomas, Virgin Islands) Played Dr. Frasier Crane on "Cheers." He took that character into his own NBC sitcom, "Frasier." Year/**Age**: 1995/**41** 1996/**42** 1997/**43**

- **SIDNEY POITIER** Actor. (Miami, FL) Won an Academy Award in 1963 for *Lilies of the Field*, becoming the first black actor to win an Oscar for best actor. Also appeared in *The Blackboard Jungle*, *To Sir With Love*, and *Sneakers*. Year/**Age**: 1995/**71** 1996/**72** 1997/**73**

- **SANDY DUNCAN** Actress/dancer. (Henderson, TX) She appeared in *Peter Pan*, *The Star-Spangled Girl* in 1971 and the TV series "Funny Face." Year/**Age**: 1995/**49** 1996/**50** 1997/**51**

- **CINDY CRAWFORD** Model. (DeKalb, IL) "Shape Your Body Workout" video and host of MTV's "House of Style" fashion show. She's married to actor Richard Gere. Year/**Age**: 1995/**29** 1996/**30** 1997/**31**

- **RANDY CALIFORNIA** Guitarist. (Los Angeles, CA) With SPIRIT. Year/**Age**: 1995/**44** 1996/**45** 1997/**46**

- **JENNIFER O'NEILL** Actress. (Rio de Janeiro, Brazil) She appeared in *The Summer of '42* and *Cover Up*. Year/**Age**: 1995/**47** 1996/**48** 1997/**49**

- **GLORIA VANDERBILT** Fashion designer/socialite. (NYC) Designer-brand jeans and perfume. She has written several books and several have been written about her. Year/**Age**: 1995/**71** 1996/**72** 1997/**73**

- **BUFFY SAINTE-MARIE** Singer/song writer. (Born Beverly Sainte-Marie in Canada) Co-writer of "Up Where We Belong" by Joe Cocker and Jennifer Warnes, #1 in 1982. Year/**Age**: 1995/**54** 1996/**55** 1997/**56**

- **PHIL ESPOSITO** Hockey star. (Canada) NHL scoring leader 5 times. Year/**Age**: 1995/**53** 1996/**54** 1997/**55**

- **PATRICIA HEARST SHAW** Newspaper heiress. Films *Cry-baby* and *Serial Mom* (San Francisco, CA) A.K.A. Tanya. Year/**Age**: 1995/**41** 1996/**42** 1997/**43**

- **BOBBY UNSER** Racecar driver. (Albuquerque, NM) 3-time Indy 500 winner and twice U.S. Auto Club national champion. Year/**Age**: 1995/**61** 1996/**62** 1997/**63**

- **ROBERT ALTMAN** Motion picture director. (Kansas City, MO) Some of his films include: *M*A*S*H*, *Nashville*, *The James Dean Story*, *Betsy's Wedding*, *Pret-a-Porter* and *The Player*. Year/**Age**: 1995/**70** 1996/**71** 1997/**72**

- **WALTER BECKER** Musician. (Los Angeles, CA) He played bass and sang with STEELY DAN. Name came from William Burrough's *Naked Lunch*. Biggest hit: "Rikki Don't Lose That Number" in 1974. Year/**Age**: 1995/**47** 1996/**48** 1997/**49**

- **MURIEL HUMPHREY** Politician. (Huron, SD) She was the wife of Minnesota Senator/U.S. Vice President Hubert Humphrey. Filled her husband's Senate seat and later remarried. Year/**Age**: 1995/**83** 1996/**84** 1997/**85**

- **WILLIAM PRESCOTT** Soldier. (1726-1795 – Groton MA) In the American Revolution, during the Battle of Bunker Hill, he said, "Don't fire until you see the whites of their eyes." (Died 10-13-1795)

- **JOHN CHARLES DALY** TV host/analyst. (1914-1991 – South Africa) He hosted TV's "What's My Line?" He was the last mystery guest when the show left the air Sept. 3. 1967. He introduced guests saying, "Sign in please." He was the newsman who announced that Pearl Harbor had been attacked. (Died 2-24-91)

- **AMANDA BLAKE** Actress. (1929-1989 – Born Beverly Louise Neill in Buffalo, NY) Played Miss Kitty, owner of the Longbranch Saloon, for 19 years on TV's "Gunsmoke." Her death was first reported as cancer-related, but one of her doctors said later that cause of death was AIDS. (Died 8-16-89)

FACTS FROM THE PAST

1792 **GEORGE WASHINGTON** signed the Postal Act, creating the Federal Postal System with a per-mile rate structure. The farther a letter went, the more it cost: 6 cents for 30 miles; 12 cents for 150 miles; etc.

1952 On this day in 1952, **CAROLYN CUMMINS** gave birth to the first of her five babies. The second was born in 1953, third in 1956, fourth in 1961 and the fifth in 1966. All five children have the same birthday.

1962 Astronaut **JOHN GLENN** became the first American to orbit the earth. He made 3 trips around the earth in his Mercury-Atlas spacecraft *Friendship 7* in just under 5 hours.

1965 The **SUPREMES'** "Stop! In The Name of Love" was released. It became their fourth number-one hit.

1974 **CHER** filed for separation from her husband, **SONNY BONO**, after ten years of marriage.

1982 Singer **PAT BENATAR** married guitarist **NEIL GERALDO**.

1987 Soviet authorities released Jewish activist **JOSEF BEGUN**, who spent three years in prison for teaching Hebrew.

1988 U.S. figure skater **BRIAN BOITANO** won a gold medal in the Winter Olympic Games in Calgary, Canada.

1989 **TONE LOC'S** [lohkz] "Wild Thing" became only the second single to be certified double-platinum.

1991 **BETTE MIDLER** won Song of the Year for the 2nd year in a row at the 33rd Annual Grammy Awards for "From A Distance."

1992 **ROSS PEROT** told **LARRY KING** that he would run for president if his supporters got his name on the ballot in all 50 states.

Try something new: live a dream today.

FEBRUARY 21

BIRTHDAYS

- **RUE McCLANAHAN** Actress. (Healdton, OK) TV's soap "Another World," and series "Maude," "Golden Girls," and "Golden Palace." Year/Age: 1995/59 1996/60 1997/61
- **TYNE DALY** Actress. (Madison, WI) She has received numerous awards for her role on TV's "Cagney & Lacey" as Mary Beth Lacey. On Broadway in *Gypsy*. Year/Age: 1995/48 1996/49 1997/50
- **JERRY HARRISON** Keyboardist/guitarist. (Milwaukee, WI) With the TALKING HEADS, New York City-based "new wave" quartet. Biggest hit: "Burning Down the House" in 1983 and "Risky Business" for the Tom Cruise movie. Year/Age: 1995/46 1996/47 1997/48
- **BARBARA JORDON** Texas lawyer/politician/teacher. (Houston, TX) A former member of Congress from Texas and an excellent speaker. Year/Age: 1995/59 1996/60 1997/61
- **HUBERT de GIVENCHY** Fashion designer. (France) Started his business in 1952. His designs were popularized by Audrey Hepburn. Year/Age: 1995/68 1996/69 1997/70
- **TRICIA NIXON COX**. (Yorba Linda, CA) The eldest daughter of the late President and Mrs. Nixon. Year/Age: 1995/49 1996/50 1997/51
- **ALAN TRAMMEL** Baseball. (Garden Grove, CA) With the Detroit Tigers. Year/Age: 1995/37 1996/38 1997/39
- **NINA SIMONE** Singer. (Born Eunice Kathleen Wayman in Tryon, NC) A singer and pianist with her biggest record in 1959: "I Loves You, Porgy" from the film *Porgy and Bess*. Year/Age: 1995/62 1996/63 1997/64
- **ERMA BOMBECK** Columnist/humorist/author. (Dayton, OH.) *Motherhood, The Second Oldest Profession*. Year/Age: 1995/68 1996/69 1997/70
- **CHRISTOPHER ATKINS** Actor. (Rye, NY) He never acted before appearing with Brooke Shields in *Blue Lagoon*. He was a lifeguard when he beat out hundreds of actors for the job. He was on TV in "Dallas" for a short time. Year/Age: 1995/34 1996/35 1997/36
- **SAM PECKINPAH** Film director. (1925-1984 – Fresno, CA) American director of tough westerns, including *Ride to the High Country* and *Wild Bunch*. (Died 12-28-84)
- **ANN SHERIDAN** Actress. (1915-1967 – Born Clara Lou Sheridan in Denton, TX) Appeared in many films including: *Kings Row*, *They Drive By Night*, *The Man Who Came to Dinner* and *I Was a Male War Bride*. (Died 1-21-67)
- **PRINCE MICHAEL ROMANOFF** (1890-1971 – Born Harry Geguzonoff in Lithuania) He appeared in 4 movies, but is probably best know for his Romanoff Restaurants in Beverly Hills and Palm Springs, CA.

FACTS FROM THE PAST

1846 SARAH G. BAGLEY became the first female telegrapher when she took charge at the new telegraph office in Lowell, MA.

1858 E. T. HOLMES of Boston installed the first burglar alarm in the U.S.

1866 LUCY B. HOBBS became the first woman to graduate from a dental school, the Ohio College of Dental Surgery in Cincinnati.

1882 JAMES SAUNDERS ran 120 miles in less than 24 hours in one of the most unusual competitions ever held in America. 14 competitors started the race and after 23 hours only 7 remained. (Sponsored by the Williamsburg Athletic Club in NYC, who paid Saunders $100 in cash.) A crowd of 800 fans cheered his feat.

1885 The WASHINGTON MONUMENT was dedicated by President Chester Arthur in Washington, DC. It took 102 years to finish, beginning in 1783 when Congress proposed it, but no money was available. Work was stopped several times because of financial problems. It is 555 feet, $5\frac{1}{8}$ inches tall. It was the largest man-made structure in the world at the time.

1934 Nicaraguan guerrilla leader CESAR SANDINO was killed by US Marines in Managua. The present-day Sandinistas were named for him.

1947 Inventor EDWIN H. LAND demonstrated his Polaroid Land Camera, which used self-developing film and produced a black and white photograph in 60 seconds.

1965 Black activist MALCOLM X was shot to death by assassins identified as Black Muslims as he was about to address a rally of several hundred followers in New York.

1972 Richard Nixon became the FIRST U.S. PRESIDENT to visit a country not diplomatically recognized by the U.S. when he went to the PEOPLE'S REPUBLIC OF CHINA.

1986 RYAN WHITE, 14-year-old AIDS victim, returned to public school in Kokomo, IN, after a lengthy court battle to allow him back. On this same day he received a temporary restraining order banning him from school again.

1988 TV evangelist JIMMY SWAGGART tearfully confessed in public that he was guilty of an unspecified sin, and said he was leaving the pulpit temporarily.

1990 BETTE MIDLER's "Wind Beneath My Wings" won song and RECORD OF THE YEAR at the 32nd Annual Grammy Awards.

1992 KRISTI YAMAGUCHI of the U.S. won an Olympic gold medal in figure skating, MIDORI ITO of Japan got the silver and NANCY KERRIGAN of the U.S. the bronze.

1994 Russian couple OKSANA GRTSCHUK AND EVGENY PLATOV take gold in ice dance finals.

FEBRUARY 22

If reincarnated, who or what would you come back as?

BIRTHDAYS

- **DREW BARRYMORE** Actress. (Los Angeles, CA) She was 7 years old when she played Gertie, the little sister in the film *E.T.* Also in *Firestarter, Irreconcilable Differences, Poison Ivy, The Amy Fisher Story, Bad Girls,* and *Wayne's World II.* Year/**Age**: 1995/**20** 1996/**21** 1997/**22**
- **MICHAEL CHANG** Tennis. Year/**Age**: 1995/**23** 1996/**24** 1997/**25**
- **NICKI LAUDA** Grand Prix driver. (Austria) Year/**Age**: 1995/**46** 1996/**47** 1997/**48**
- **KYLE MACLACHLAN** Actor. Agent Dale Cooper on TV's "Twin Peaks" and in the movie *Blue Velvet.* Year/**Age**: 1995/**36** 1996/**37** 1997/**38**
- **EDWARD MOORE "TED" KENNEDY** Senator. (Boston, MA) D/MA Year/**Age**: 1995/**63** 1996/**64** 1997/**65**
- **ROBERT YOUNG** Actor. (Chicago, IL) Starred on TV in "Father Knows Best," beginning in 1954 and "Marcus Welby, M.D." which began in 1969. He has a history of depression and alcoholism, and attempted suicide in 1991. Year/**Age**: 1995/**88** 1996/**89** 1997/**90**
- **ERNIE K-DOE** Singer. (Born Ernest Kador, Jr. in New Orleans, LA) Biggest hit: "Mother-In-Law" in 1966. Year/**Age**: 1995/**59** 1996/**60** 1997/**61**
- **JOHN MILLS** Actor. (England) He won an Oscar for best supporting actor in 1970 in *Ryan's Daughter.* He's the father of actresses Hayley and Juliet Mills. Year/**Age**: 1995/**87** 1996/**88** 1997/**89**
- **DON PARDO** Radio/TV announcer. Year/**Age**: 1995/**77** 1996/**78** 1997/**79**

- **SHELDON LEONARD** Actor/producer. (Born Sheldon Bershad in NYC) He played tough-guy roles in the movies and produced "The Danny Thomas Show" and "I Spy" with Bill Cosby. He played the gangster on the "Jack Benny Program." Year/**Age**: 1995/**88** 1996/**89** 1997/**90**
- **CHARLIE O. FINLEY** Baseball. (Birmingham, AL) Baseball owner. He had a big "A" Oakland insignia on the roof of his barn in South Bend, IN, and has had a business office in Chicago for years. Year/**Age**: 1995/**77** 1996/**78** 1997/**79**
- **JULIUS "DR. J" ERVING** Basketball star. (Roosevelt, NY) In 1975, he scored 63 points for his N.Y. Nets, beating San Diego, 176-166. Also with the Philadelphia 76ers. Year/**Age**: 1995/**45** 1996/**46** 1997/**47**
- **GEORGE LEE "SPARKY" ANDERSON** Baseball. (Bridgewater, SD) At the age of 35, in 1970, he became the youngest manager in the Major Leagues when he signed with the Cincinnati Reds. As manager, he won over 2,000 games. Year/**Age**: 1995/**61** 1996/**62** 1997/**63**
- **ROBERT BADEN-POWELL** Officer. (1857-1941 – England) British army officer who founded the Boy Scouts. (Died 10-8-41)
- **GEORGE WASHINGTON** President. (1732-1799 – Fredericksburg, VA) He was the first U.S. President – from 1789 to 1797. His salary was $25,000. He has 31 counties named for him in the U.S. He gave the shortest inaugural speech – 90 seconds on March 4, 1793. (Died 12-14-1799)
- **FREDERICK CHOPIN** Musician. (1810-1849) One of Poland's most famous pianists/composers. (Died 10-17-1849)

FACTS FROM THE PAST

1860 SHOEMAKERS in Lynn, MA, went on strike for higher wages. They chose George Washington's birthday as a symbol of their "demand for freedom." They were protesting the hiring of children to work new machinery, which was cutting the regular workers' salaries down to $3 per week.

1879 The F.W. WOOLWORTH CHAIN started in Utica, NY. It was the first store to arrange items according to price. It was also the first "dime store" to go broke after just a few months in business. Woolworth first tried the idea in Liverpool, England. His second store there almost caused a riot. They had to put up barriers to prevent the crowd from wrecking the place, it was so popular.

1902 A fist fight broke out on the Senate floor. Senator **McLAURIN** gave Senator **BENJAMIN TILLMAN** a bloody nose after Tillman accused McLaurin of bias on a tariff issue.

1924 CALVIN COOLIDGE delivered the first presidential radio broadcast speech from the White House.

1956 ELVIS PRESLEY hit #1 with "Heartbreak Hotel" written by Mae Boren Axton – a true story about a suicide in a hotel room.

1972 PRESIDENT RICHARD NIXON met with Chinese Premier Chou En-Lai in Peking, China. His historic Peking visit lasted through February 28th.

1983 Congressman **HAROLD WASHINGTON** defeated Mayor Jane Byrne and Cook County Attorney Richard Daley in the Democratic primary, on his way to becoming Chicago's first black mayor.

1989 JETHRO TULL won the first heavy metal Grammy. It became the first Accapella Record to hit #1 on the charts.

1990 Former **PRESIDENT RONALD REAGAN**'s videotaped testimony was released in Washington. In his deposition, Reagan said he never had "any inkling" his aides were secretly arming the Nicaraguan Contras.

1991 PRESIDENT GEORGE BUSH delivered a point-blank ultimatum to Iraq, giving Saddam Hussein until noon the next day to "begin his immediate and unconditional withdrawal from Kuwait" or face a decisive ground assault.

1994 ALDRICH AMES and his wife Maria del Rosario Casas Ames were arrested by the FBI on charges of spying for the Soviet Union since 1985.

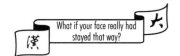
What if your face really had stayed that way?

FEBRUARY 23

BIRTHDAYS

- **RUSTY YOUNG** Steel guitarist. (Los Angeles, CA) With POCO. Biggest hit: "Crazy Love" in 1979. Year/**Age**: 1995/**49** 1996/**50** 1997/**51**

- **MARC PRICE** Actor. (Bedford, MA) Skippy on TV's "Family Ties" and host of the Disney Channel's "Teen Win, Lose or Draw." Year/**Age**: 1995/**27** 1996/**28** 1997/**29**

- **HELENA SUKOVA** Tennis pro. (Prague, Czechoslovakia) Year/**Age**: 1995/**30** 1996/**31** 1997/**32**

- **PETER FONDA** Actor. (NYC) His most-noted film appearance was in *Easy Rider* in 1969, the film that made Jack Nicholson a star. Peter is Jane Fonda's brother and the late Henry Fonda's son. Year/**Age**: 1995/**56** 1996/**57** 1997/**58**

- **GEORGE SCOTT** Baseball. First baseman for the Red Sox and Milwaukee Brewers. Year/**Age**: 1995/**51** 1996/**52** 1997/**53**

- **BRAD WHITFORD** Rhythm guitarist. (Sunapee, NH) Member of AEROSMITH. Their hits are "Angel" in 1988 and "Janie's Got A Gun" in 1989. Year/**Age**: 1995/**42** 1996/**43** 1997/**44**

- **HOWARD JONES** Singer. (England) Singer, songwriter and synthesizer wizard. He used to work for a cellophane wrap company. Biggest hit: "No One to Blame." in 1986. Year/**Age**: 1995/**40** 1996/**41** 1997/**42**

- **SYLVIA CHASE** ABC news correspondent. (Northfield, MN) She left the ABC "20/20" show to anchor a local newscast in San Francisco. Year/**Age**: 1995/**57** 1996/**58** 1997/**59**

- **WILLIAM L. SHIRER** Historian/journalist/author. (Chicago) *The Rise and Fall of the Third Reich*. First best-seller was *Berlin Diary*. Year/**Age**: 1995/**91** 1996/**92** 1997/**93**

- **BOBBY BONILLA** Baseball. (NYC) He signed a 5-year, $29-million contract in 1991with the New York Mets, the highest in baseball history at that time. Year/**Age**: 1995/**32** 1996/**33** 1997/**34**

- **REV. ALAAN BOESAK** South African anti-apartheid activist. Year/**Age**: 1995/**50** 1996/**51** 1997/**52**

- **JOHNNY WINTER** Blues-rock guitarist/vocalist. (Born John Dawson III in Leland, MS) Johnny and Edgar are albino brothers. Edgar was more successful, with a giant hit called "Frankenstein" in 1973. Year/**Age**: 1995/**51** 1996/**52** 1997/**53**

- **ED "TOO TALL" JONES** Football star. (Jackson, TN) He used so much deodorant powder that he set off the smoke alarm in the locker room numerous times. The defensive end for the Dallas Cowboys set records for games and seasons played. He never missed a game except in the 1979 season when he boxed as a heavyweight. He won six fights and then returned to the Cowboys. He played in 245 games and was on three Super Bowl teams. Year/**Age**: 1995/**44** 1996/**45** 1997/**46**

- **DIANE VARSI** Actress. (1938-1992 – San Francisco, CA) Nominated for supporting actress in *Peyton Place* in 1957. She played Allison MacKenzie, Lana Turner's troubled daughter. (Died 11-19-92)

- **GEORGE FREDERICK HANDEL** Composer. (1685-1759 – English composer born in Germany) His oratorio, *The Messiah*, was first heard in 1742. (Died 4-14-1759)

- **WILLIAM E. B. DuBOIS** Educator. (1868-1963 – Great Barrington, MA) American educator and leader of the movement for black people which later became the NAACP. (Died 8-27-63)

FACTS FROM THE PAST

1885 In England, officials attempted to hang murderer **JOHN LEE**. Everytime they tried to release the trap door, it failed. When they tested it without him, it opened. After several attempts, they gave up and changed his sentence to life in prison.

1861 President-elect **ABRAHAM LINCOLN** arrived secretly in Washington to take office after an **ASSASSINATION PLOT WAS STOPPED** in Baltimore.

1874 **MAJOR WALTER WINGFIELD** of Pimlico, England, patented the game of lawn tennis. Two years later, the All-England Croquet Club at Wimbleton decided to sponsor the first tennis championships. The first Wimbleton champ was Spencer Gore.

1905 A Chicago lawyer, **PAUL HARRIS,** and 3 friends founded the Rotary Club. Harris noticed that visitors to cities are often treated like strangers. The name comes from members rotating through various duties.

1927 **PRESIDENT CALVIN COOLIDGE** signed a bill creating the Federal Radio Commission – an action recognizing the fact that radio is an industry. The name was changed to Federal Communications Commission on July 1, 1934.

1945 The most memorable photo of World War II was taken by **JOE ROSENTHAL** of members of the 5th Division of the U.S. Marines planting an American flag atop Mt. Suribachi on Iwo Jima. In the 1949 John Wayne movie, *Sands of Iwo Jima*, the U.S. Marines who raised the flag were Rene Gagnon, Ira Hayes and John Bradley, who portrayed themselves.

1954 The first mass inoculation of children with the Salk **ANTI-POLIO VACCINE** began in Pittsburgh, PA. Dr. Jonas Salk developed it.

1983 **HERSCHEL WALKER** signed with the New Jersey Generals, becoming the first Heisman Trophy winner to be signed by the sort-lived U.S. Football League. He was paid about $6 million, a record at the time.

1988 **MICHAEL JACKSON** kicked off his first solo U.S. tour in Kansas City, MO.

1989 The Senate Armed Services Committee voted to reject the nomination of **JOHN G. TOWER** to be defense secretary and to recommend the full Senate do so as well.

1994 Fifth Olympic gold for **BONNIE BLAIR**; a silver for Nancy Kerrigan.

FEBRUARY 24

Kids really do jump for joy.

BIRTHDAYS

- **JAMES FARENTINO** Actor. (Brooklyn, NY) He appeared on the TV series "Blue Thunder" and in the TV film, "Sins" with Joan Collins. Pleaded no contest to accusations that he was stalking girlfriend Tina Sinatra. Year/**Age:** 1995/**57** 1996/**58** 1997/**59**

- **ABE VIGODA** Actor. (NYC) He played Fish on the "Barney Miller" TV series and a spinoff of that series called "Fish." Was a Mafia member in *Godfather* and appeared in "Look Who's Talking." Year/**Age:** 1995/**74** 1996/**75** 1997/**76**

- **EDWARD JAMES OLMOS** Actor. (Los Angeles, CA) Oscar nominee for best actor in *Stand and Deliver*. Appeared in *Triumph of the Spirit*. Year/**Age:** 1995/**48** 1996/**49** 1997/**50**

- **MICHEL LEGRAND** Composer. (France) He won an Oscar nomination for the music in *Summer of 42* and did music for *Yentl*. Year/**Age:** 1995/**63** 1996/**64** 1997/**65**

- **PAUL JONES** Singer. A former pop singer from England, with the group MANFRED MANN. Their biggest hit: "Do-Wah-Diddy-Do" in 1964. Year/**Age:** 1995/**51** 1996/**52** 1997/**53**

- **NICKY HOPKINS** Pianist. He played background piano on some of the BEATLES' recordings and with ROD STEWART and JEFFERSON AIRPLANE. The song "Session Man" was written in his honor by THE KINKS. Year/**Age:** 1995/**51** 1996/**52** 1997/**53**

- **BARRY BOSTWICK** Actor. (San Mateo, CA) He appeared on TV as George Washington and was in "Scruples." Also starred in *Rocky Horror Picture Show* and *Between Love and Hate*. Year/**Age:** 1995/**50** 1996/**51** 1997/**52**

- **JOHN VERNON** Actor. (Canada) Starred in *National Lampoon's Animal House* and *Dirty Harry*. Year/**Age:** 1995/**63** 1996/**64** 1997/**65**

- **PAULA ZAHN** TV hostess. Appears on "CBS This Morning." Year/**Age:** 1995/**39** 1996/**40** 1997/**41**

- **OSCAR DE LA HOYA** Fighter. (Los Angeles, CA) 1991 World Lightweight Champion. He won a gold medal at the 1992 Olympics. Year/**Age:** 1995/**22** 1996/**23** 1997/**24**

- **BARBARA LAWRENCE** Actress. An American wisecracking comedy actress in films *Margie* and *Oklahoma*. Year/**Age:** 1995/**65** 1996/**66** 1997/**67**

- **SALLY JESSY RAPHAEL** Talk-show host. (Easton, PA) Year/**Age:** 1995/**52** 1996/**53** 1997/**54**

- **RENATTA SCOTTO** Opera Singer. Year/**Age:** 1995/**60** 1996/**61** 1997/**62**.

- **HONUS WAGNER** American baseball great. (1874-1955 – Carnegie, PA) Known as "The Flying Dutchman." He was among the first five players elected to the Baseball Hall of Fame. Played with Pittsburgh from 1897-1917. (Died 12-6-55)

- **JOHN PHILLIP HOLLAND** Inventor. (1840-1914) He invented the submarine. The first one was built in 1875. (Died 8-12-14)

- **WILHELM CARL GRIMM** Author. (1786-1859 – Germany) He and his brother, Jacob, are remembered for *Grimm's Fairy Tales* in 1815, which include *Snow White*, *Sleeping Beauty*, *Goldilocks*, and *Little Red Riding Hood*. (Died 12-16-1859)

FACTS FROM THE PAST

1868 Congress began impeachment proceedings against **PRESIDENT ANDREW JOHNSON** who was charged with removing Secretary of War Edwin Stanton without notifying the Senate. He was tried 3 months later and acquitted by one vote.

1886 **THOMAS ALVA EDISON** married **MINA MILLER**, Akron, OH. The famous inventor had wooed the 19-year-old woman via Morse code. After he'd taught her the code, they spent many romantic hours together tapping out messages on each other's hands. After a year of this, Edison finally summoned up the courage to tap out the words, "Will you marry me?" Mina replied, "Yes" – in Morse code.

1920 A fledgling German political party that became known as the Nazi Party held its first meeting of importance in Munich. Its chief spokesman was **ADOLF HITLER.**

1922 **BLUEBEARD WAS EXECUTED** in France. His real name was **HENRI LANDRU**, a con man who charmed women, got their money and then murdered them. He defrauded over 300 woman. He was convicted of murdering ten women and one boy.

1937 Famous New York Yankee baseball star, **LOU GEHRIG**, was given a screen test for the role of Tarzan.

1968 **PETE SEEGER** was allowed to sing all six verses of his song "Waist Deep in the Big Muddy" on the "Smothers Brothers Comedy Hour." It was previously censored because it was critical of **PRESIDENT JOHNSON**'s Vietnam policy. A month later, Johnson decided not to run for office again. Seeger claimed his song influenced that decision.

1971 **JANIS JOPLIN** was awarded a gold record for the album *Pearl*, which contained the hit "Me & Bobby McGee."

1976 The **EAGLES** *Greatest Hits* became the first album in the U.S. to be certified platinum for selling two million copies.

1981 A jury in White Plains, NY, found former school headmistress **JEAN HARRIS** guilty of second-degree murder in the fatal shooting of Scarsdale Diet doctor, **HERMAN TARNOVER**. She is now serving 15 years to life in prison.

1989 The largest gathering of world leaders (162 nations) in modern times joined Japan in funeral ceremony for **EMPEROR HIROHITO** at the Shinjuku Imperial Garden. Despised 4 decades ago, he was honored in death.

1992 **GERALDO RIVERA**, while on the air, had fat cells from his derriere implanted into his wrinkled forehead.

1994 Comedian **GARRETT MORRISS**, "Saturday Night Live," was shot and critically wounded during a robbery attempt in Los Angeles. He recovered.

Does a plant feel pain?

FEBRUARY 25

BIRTHDAYS

- **FARON YOUNG** C&W Singer. (Shreveport, LA) Biggest hit: "Hello Walls." #1 on the C&W chart for 9 weeks. Year/**Age:** 1995/**63** 1996/**64** 1997/**65**
- **CARL HARRISON "STUMP" MERRILL** Baseball manager. Year/**Age:** 1995/**52** 1996/**53** 1997/**54**
- **RON SANTO** Baseball. Chicago Cubs 3rd baseman who hit 342 home runs. Lifetime average .277. Year/**Age:** 1995/**55** 1996/**56** 1997/**57**
- **GEORGE HARRISON** Musician/composer/singer. (Liverpool, England) Biggest hit with the BEATLES was "Hey Jude" in 1968. His biggest singles: "My Sweet Lord" and "Got My Mind Set On You." Member of the Grammy-winning best group in 1989, the TRAVELING WILBURYS. Year/**Age:** 1995/**52** 1996/**53** 1997/**54**
- **STUART "WOODY" WOOD** Musician. (Scotland) Member of the group THE BAY CITY ROLLERS. They chose their name by sticking a pin at random in a map of the U.S. The pin stuck on Bay City, MI. Biggest hit: "Saturday Night." Year/**Age:** 1995/**38** 1996/**39** 1997/**40**
- **TOM COURTENAY** British actor. (England) He was nominated for an Academy Award for both *Dr. Zhivago* and *The Dresser.* Year/**Age:** 1995/**58** 1996/**59** 1997/**60**
- **BOBBY RIGGS** Former tennis star (and hustler). (Los Angeles, CA) He still plays exhibition matches. He's the one who lost the match to Billie Jean King on Sept. 20, 1973. Year/**Age:** 1995/**77** 1996/**78** 1997/**79**
- **ANTHONY BURGESS** Author. (Manchester, England) Wrote over 50 novels including *Clockwork Orange* which led to the movie. Year/**Age:** 1995/**77** 1996/**78** 1997/**79**
- **KAREN GRASSLE** Actress. (Berkeley, CA) She was the mother on "Little House on the Prairie" Year/**Age:** 1995/**51** 1996/**52** 1997/**53**

- **LARRY GELBART** Writer/producer. (Chicago, IL) Creator of "M*A*S*H." He got his start at age 16 when he wrote some jokes for Danny Thomas. Larry's dad was Danny's barber. Year/**Age:** 1995/**67** 1996/**68** 1997/**69**
- **DIANE BAKER** Actress. (Hollywood, CA) She appeared in the films: *The Diary of Ann Frank, Strait Jacket, The Prize,* and *Silence of the Lambs.* Year/**Age:** 1995/**57** 1996/**58** 1997/**59**
- **SEAN AUSTIN** Actor. Year/**Age:** 1995/**24** 1996/**25** 1997/**26**
- **LISA KIRK** Actress/singer. (1925-1990 – Charleroi, PA) She appeared in *The Taming of the Shrew* with Charlton Heston. The brassy performer sang "The Gentleman Is a Dope" in *Allegro* and "Why Can't You Behave?" in *Kiss Me Kate.* (Died 11-11-90)
- **JIM BACKUS** Actor. (1913-1989 – Cleveland, OH) He was the voice of "Mr. Magoo" and appeared on the TV series "Gilligan's Island" as Thurston Howell III. He also played Judge Bradley Stevens on " I Married Joan" in the '50s. (Died 7-3-89)
- **ENRICO CARUSO** Singer. (1873-1921 – Born in the slums of Naples, Italy) This great tenor almost didn't make it as an opera singer. His music teacher tried to get him to give up singing, because every time he'd hit a high note, his voice would crack. He was the first artist to sell a million records. (Died 8-2-21)
- **ZEPPO MARX** Comedian. (1901-1979 – Born Herbert Marx in NYC) A member of the "Marx Brothers" comedy team with Groucho (Julius), Harpo (Arthur), Chico (Leonard), and Gummo (Milton). (Died 11-3-79)
- **PIERRE-AUGUSTE RENOIR** Artist. (1841-1919 – France) His subjects included nudes, social scenes, and flowers. (Died 12-17-19)
- **DAVEY ALLISON** Racecar driver. (1961-1993 – Hueytown, AL) 19 career victories including three Winston 500 titles. Died in a helicopter crash at the Talladega (AL) Superspeedway. (Died 7-12-93)

FACTS FROM THE PAST

1836 Inventor **SAMUEL COLT** patented his revolver.

1870 **HIRAM REVELS** from Mississippi became the first African-American U.S. Senator.

1957 **BUDDY HOLLY AND THE CRICKETS** recorded "That'll Be The Day" in Clovis, NM. It became Buddy's first hit.

1961 **ELVIS PRESLEY** played his first concert after being discharged from the army almost a year earlier.

1964 **CASSIUS CLAY** won the World Heavyweight Boxing Championship by beating **SONNY LISTON** at the Miami Convention Hall. Cassius shouted, "I am the greatest" and the next day announced his Muslim faith and changed his name to Muhammad Ali. He held the title off and on for 15 years. He said, "I'm better and prettier than Chubby Checker." Clay's "I Am The Greatest" album was in demand.

1985 **PETER BOGDANOVICH** sued Universal Pictures for $19 million to get Bruce Springsteen's songs back into the movie *Mask*. Universal didn't want to pay it, so Bob Seger wrote the score.

1986 A defeated **FERDINAND MARCOS** resigned as President of the Philippines and slipped away in the Manila night, setting off an explosion of joyous celebration among his countrymen.

1986 Under the new NBA drug rules **MICHAEL "SUGAR RAY" RICHARDSON**, New Jersey guard, became the first player to be banned from the league for life.

1990 In June of 1990, **GEORGE STEINBRENNER** made his 19th managerial change in 17 years as New York Yankees owner when he fired Bucky Dent and named Carl "Stump" Merrill to guide the last-place team.

1994 **CHUCK JONES** was convicted in New York for stealing footwear and undergarments from his ex-client Marla (Maples) Trump. He admitted he was sexually fascinated by her shoes.

FEBRUARY 26

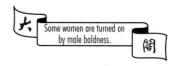
Some women are turned on by male baldness.

BIRTHDAYS

• **JOHNNY CASH** Entertainer. (Kingsland, AR) Biggest hit: "A Boy Named Sue" in 1969. It was recorded at San Quentin Prison in California; a South Dakota judge, Sue Hicks, was the inspiration for the song. His very first hit was "I Walk the Line," which he still uses to open his concerts. He is a member of the Country Music Hall of Fame. The combination of singing alone and with others has produced about 150 charted C&W records for him. Year/**Age**: 1995/**63** 1996/**64** 1997/**65**

• **JENNY THOMPSON** Swimmer. (Danvers, MA) She won two gold and one silver medal at the 1992 Olympics. Year/**Age**: 1995/**22** 1996/**23** 1997/**24**

• **FATS DOMINO** Singer. (Born Antoine Domino in New Orleans, LA) Biggest hit: "Blueberry Hill" in 1956. He got his nickname "Fats" from a song he recorded in 1949, "The Fat Man." Some say it was the first rock and roll record ever. He's had many hits, but never a #1 record. Year/**Age**: 1995/**67** 1996/**68** 1997/**69**

• **MITCH RYDER** Singer. (Born William Levise, Jr. in Detroit, MI) Leader of the DETROIT WHEELS. Biggest hit: "Devil With a Blue Dress On" in 1966. Year/**Age**: 1995/**50** 1996/**51** 1997/**52**

• **MASON ADAMS** Actor. (NYC) He was on "Lou Grant" and does many commercials. Film *The Son-In-Law*. Year/**Age**: 1995/**76** 1996/**77** 1997/**78**

• **JENNIFER GRANT** Actress. The daughter of Dyan Cannon and the late Cary Grant who was 62 when she was born. Appears in "Beverly Hills 90210." Year/**Age**: 1995/**29** 1996/**30** 1997/**31**

• **TONY RANDALL** Actor. (Born Leonard Rosenberg in Tulsa, OK.) Probably best known for his role as Felix Unger on the "Odd Couple" TV series. Year/**Age**: 1995/**75** 1996/**76** 1997/**77**

• **JONATHAN CAIN** Keyboardist. (San Francisco, CA) Played for JOURNEY. Biggest hit: "Open Arms" in 1982. Year/**Age**: 1995/**45** 1996/**46** 1997/**47**

• **BETTY HUTTON** Actress/singer. (Born Elizabeth Thornburg in Battle Creek, MI) Appeared in *Annie Get Your Gun* and *The Greatest Show on Earth* in 1952. Number one hit, "Doctor, Lawyer, Indian Chief" in 1945 from the movie *Stork Club*. Year/**Age**: 1995/**74** 1996/**75** 1997/**76**

• **JACKIE GLEASON** Entertainer. (1916-1987 – Born Herbert John Gleason in Brooklyn, NY) He starred on "The Honeymooners" as Ralph Kramden and "The Jackie Gleason Show," where he created the Poor Soul, Reggie van Gleason III and Joe the Bartender. In 1954, he was the top male TV comedian of the day and signed a series of contracts worth $16 million with CBS. In 1961, he got an Oscar nomination as a pool shark in *The Hustler*. He smoked 6 packs of cigarettes a day and died of cancer. (Died 6-24-87)

• **ROBERT ALDA** Actor. (1914-1986 – Born Alphonso d'Abruzzo in NYC) He portrayed George Gershwin in *Rhapsody in Blue* in 1945 and was in the original *Guys and Dolls* on Broadway. He was the father of actor Alan Alda. (Died 5-3-86)

• **DR. JOHN KELLOGG** Inventor. (1852-1943 – Tyrone, MI) He ran a sanitarium in Battle Creek, MI, and his brother, Will, was the bookkeeper. One day, seeking to develop a more digestible bread for the patients, they inadvertently found the principle of "tempering grains." Thereby were born corn, rice and wheat flakes.

• **WILLIAM F. "BUFFALO BILL" CODY** Sharpshooter. (1846-1917 – Scott County, IA) American frontiersman, Army scout, and professional actor, who claimed to have killed more than 4,000 bison. The animals were used to feed the Kansas-Pacific Rail Road construction crews. He is entombed in solid rock near Denver, CO, at the top of Lookout Mountain. (Died 1-10-17)

• **VICTOR HUGO** Writer. (1802-1885 – Besancon [buhz-an-sohn']) A great figure of French literature. He wrote *Les Miserables*. (Died 5-22-1885)

FACTS FROM THE PAST

1815 **NAPOLEON BONAPARTE** escaped from the island of Elba and began his second conquest of France.

1925 Billiards ace **JOE SCHAEFER** ran off 400 consecutive balls in 70 minutes for a 400-0 win over Erica Hagenlacher who never got to touch a cue stick.

1934 **PRESIDENT FRANKLIN ROOSEVELT** ordered the creation of a Communications Commission, which brought about the Federal Communications Commission.

1952 **PRIME MINISTER WINSTON CHURCHILL** announced that Britain had produced its own atomic bomb.

1970 The **BEATLES** released *Hey Jude*. It was made up of singles previously unavailable on LP.

1970 Twin boys were born to **MIA FARROW** and **ANDRE PREVIN**, named Mathew Phineas and Sacha Villiers.

1987 The Tower Commission, which probed the **IRAN-CONTRA AFFAIR**, issued its report, which rebuked President Ronald Reagan for failing to control his national security staff.

1987 The first four **BEATLES COMPACT DISCS** went on sale with $17 million in advance orders.

1993 A tremendous blast ripped apart the **WORLD TRADE CENTER** garage, causing death and injury and displacing 50,000 workers. Secretary of State **WARREN CHRISTOPHER** called it a terrorist attack. Arrests were made by the FBI within days.

1994 11 Branch **DAVIDIANS ARE ACQUITTED** on murder charges. 7 other followers of David Koresh were convicted on lesser charges.

 Why join hands at a seance?

FEBRUARY 27

BIRTHDAYS

- **MICHAEL BOLTON** Singer. (Born Michael Bolotin in New Haven, CT) Hits include "How Am I Supposed to Live Without You" #1 in 1989. Year/**Age**: 1995/**41** 1996/**42** 1997/**43**

- **GRANT SHOW** Actor. TV's *Melrose Place* and the police drama *True Blue*. Year/**Age**: 1995/**33** 1996/**34** 1997/**35**

- **CHELSEA CLINTON** First daughter. (Little Rock, AK) Daughter of President Bill and Hillary Clinton. Year/**Age**: 1995/**15** 1996/**16** 1997/**17**

- **RODERICK CLARK** Singer. (Waco, TX) #1 hit with HI-FIVE, "I Like The Way (The Kissing Game)." Year/**Age**: 1995/**22** 1996/**23** 1997/**24**

- **JOHNNY VAN ZANT** Singer. (Jacksonville, FL) LYNYRD SKYNYRD TRIBUTE BAND. (The band was named for a high school gym teacher, Leonard Skinner.) Year/**Age**: 1995/**36** 1996/**37** 1997/**38**

- **ADAM BALDWIN** Actor. Year/**Age**: 1995/**33** 1996/**34** 1997/**35**

- **JAMES WORTHY** Basketball player. (Gastonia, NC) With the LA Lakers. Year/**Age**: 1995/**34** 1996/**35** 1997/**36**

- **ELIZABETH TAYLOR** Actress. (London, England) She won two Oscars for best actress: in 1960 for *Butterfield 8* and in 1966 for *Who's Afraid of Virginia Woolf?* She is *Life* magazine's champion cover girl, appearing 11 times in 25 years. She has had 8 marriages; twice to Richard Burton. Her perfumes are "Passion" and "White Diamonds." Recently in the *Flintstones* movie. Year/**Age**: 1995/**63** 1996/**64** 1997/**65**

- **JOANNE WOODWARD** Actress. (Born Joanne Giognilliat in Thomasville, GA) She started out in school class plays, and in 1952 got her first professional job where she met Paul Newman. After he got a Mexican divorce, they were married on Jan. 29, 1958, in Las Vegas. They have 3 daughters. She won an Oscar for best actress in *Three Faces of Eve* in 1957. In *Philadelphia*. Year/**Age**: 1995/**65** 1996/**66** 1997/**67**

- **HOWARD HESSEMAN** Actor. (Salem, OR) He worked as a DJ at one time in San Francisco playing acid rock. Played Dr. Johnny Fever on "WKRP In Cincinnati" and a teacher on "Head of the Class." Year/**Age**: 1995/**55** 1996/**56** 1997/**57**

- **MARY FRANN** Actress. (Born Mary Luecke in St. Louis, MO) Joanna on "Newhart." Year/**Age**: 1995/**52** 1996/**53** 1997/**54**

- **RALPH NADER** Consumer advocate. (Winsted, CT) An American attorney/consumer advocate/author, he was the first guest on the Phil Donahue show in 1970. Year/**Age**: 1995/**61** 1996/**62** 1997/**63**

- **GENE SARAZEN** Golf legend. (Harrison, NY) He was the first player to win each of the four major championships in men's golf. He started with the 1922 U.S. Open and ended with the 1935 Master Tournament. Year/**Age**: 1995/**93** 1996/**94** 1997/**95**

- **JOAN BENNETT** Actress. (1910-1990 – Palisades, NJ) One of the most attractive stars of her time, sister of Barbara and Constance Bennett. In films *Little Women* and *Father of the Bride*. (Died 12-7-90.)

- **JOHN STEINBECK** Writer. (1902-1968 – Salinas, CA) He wrote *Of Mice and Men* and *East of Eden*. Churchmen called his *The Grapes of Wrath* obscene. Won the 1962 Nobel Prize for Literature. (Died 12-2-68.)

- **DEXTER GORDON** Jazz saxaphonist. (1922-1990) Nominated for an Oscar in 1987 for *Round Midnight*. He helped define bebop in the 1940's. (Died 4-25-90.)

- **HENRY WADSWORTH LONGFELLOW** American poet .(1807-1882 – Portland, ME.) He had a terrible nervous disorder. His poems include *Song of Hiawatha* and *Midnight Ride of Paul Revere*. (Died 3-24-1882.)

- **FRANCHOT TONE** Actor. (1905-1968 – Born Stanislaus Pascal Tone in Niagara Falls, NY) He received an Oscar nomination for best actor in 1935 for *Mutiny on the Bounty*. On TV's "Ben Casey," he played Dr. David Niles. (Died 9-18-68.)

FACTS FROM THE PAST

1883 The first practical **CIGAR-ROLLING MACHINE** was patented by Impressario **OSCAR HAMMERSTEIN**, grandfather of Broadway librettist Oscar Hammerstein II.

1959 The **BOSTON CELTICS** pounded the **MINNEAPOLIS LAKERS**, 179-139, as seven National Basketball Association records fell in the highest score ever recorded in basketball history. The Celtics set four records: most points (179), most points in a half (90), most points in a quarter (52) and most field goals (72). Boston's Tom Heinsohn led all scorers with 43 points and Bob Cousy added 31 while setting an NBA record with 28 assists.

1963 **MICKEY MANTLE** signed a $100,000 contract with the New York Yankees. It was the biggest contract in baseball at that time.

1977 **KEITH RICHARDS** of the ROLLING STONES was arrested at a Toronto hotel on heroin-possession charges. He was found guilty and the Stones were ordered to play two concerts for the blind.

1982 **WAYNE B. WILLIAMS** was found guilty of murdering two of the 28 young blacks whose bodies were found in the Atlanta area over a 22-month period.

1991 Soul singer **JAMES BROWN** was granted parole after serving two years of a six year sentence. The charges included assault with intent to murder.

1991 **PRESIDENT BUSH** declared that "Kuwait is liberated, Iraq's army is defeated." Offensive combat operations ended at midnight, after only 4 days in operation.

1992 16-year-old **TIGER WOODS** became the youngest golfer to play in a PGA Tour event in 35 years when he teed off at the Los Angeles Open.

FEBRUARY 28

Why are golf, fishing and bowling considered sports?

BIRTHDAYS

- **STEPHANIE BEACHAM** Actress. (England) TV's "Sister Kate." Year/**Age**: 1995/**48** 1996/**49** 1997/**50**

- **BERNADETTE PETERS** Actress. (Born Bernadette Lazarra in NYC) At age 11 she appeared on Broadway in *Most Happy Fella* and with Martin Short in *The Goodbye Girl* in 1993. In adult musicals like *George M* and *Dames at Sea*. In film *The Jerk*. Year/**Age**: 1995/**47** 1996/**48** 1997/**49**

- **GAVIN MacLEOD** Actor. (Mt. Kisco, NY) He played Captain Merrill Stubing on TV's "Love Boat" and played Murray Slaughter on "The Mary Tyler Moore Show." Year/**Age**: 1995/**65** 1996/**66** 1997/**67**

- **FRANK MALZONE** Baseball. Boston and California 3rd baseman with a lifetime average of .274. Year/**Age**: 1995/**65** 1996/**66** 1997/**67**

- **CHARLES DURNING** Actor. (Highland Falls, NY) "Another World" soap opera and many dramatic TV appearances throughout his career. He appears on TV's "Evening Shade." Year/**Age**: 1995/**72** 1996/**73** 1997/**74**

- **JOE SOUTH** Singer/guitarist/composer. (Born Joe Souter in Atlanta, GA.) He wrote "Rose Garden" and "Down in the Boondocks." Year/**Age**: 1995/**55** 1996/**56** 1997/**57**

- **MARIO ANDRETTI** Racecar driver. (Italy) Started racing in 1964 and won 52 Indy races. Won the Indy 500 in 1969 and retired in 1994. His son is also a driver. Year/**Age**: 1995/**56** 1996/**57** 1997/**58**

- **PAUL COTTON** Entertainer. (Los Angeles, CA) Member of the group POCO. Biggest hit: "Crazy Love" in 1979. Year/**Age**: 1995/**52** 1996/**53** 1997/**54**

- **BUBBA SMITH** Football player/actor. (Born Charles Aaron Smith in Orange, TX) His baby brother tried to call him brother and it came out "bubba." He appeared in the "Police Academy" movies. Year/**Age**: 1995/**50** 1996/**51** 1997/**52**

- **GRETA SCACCHI** Actress. Year/**Age**: 1995/**34** 1996/**35** 1997/**36**

- **TOMMY TUNE** Dancer/choreographer. (Wichita Falls, TX) One of his Tony award performances was in *My One and Only*. Year/**Age**: 1995/**56** 1996/**57** 1997/**58**

- **FRANK BONNER** Actor. (Little Rock, AR) He played Herb Tarlek, on "WKRP in Cincinnati," and the priest on "Just the Ten of Us." Year/**Age**: 1995/**53** 1996/**54** 1997/**55**

- **BENJAMIN "BUGSY" SIEGEL** Gangster. (1906-1947 – Beverly Hills, CA) Started syndicate gambling in Las Vegas, NV. The movie of his life, *Bugsy*, starred Warren Beatty. (Died 6-2-47.)

- **CHARLES BLONDIN** Daredevil. (Born Jean Francois Gravelet in France, 1824) He made the 1,100-foot trip across Niagara Falls, 160 feet above the raging waters on a bicycle, blindfolded, pushing a wheelbarrow in total darkness.

- **VINCENTE MINNELLI** Film director. (1913-1986 – Chicago, IL) Director and producer of Hollywood musicals, including *An American In Paris*. He won an Oscar for *GiGi* in 1958. Liza Minnelli is his daughter, from his marriage to Judy Garland. (Died 7-25-86)

- **BRIAN JONES** Guitarist. (1942-1968 – England) With the Rolling Stones. In 1968 he bought Cotchford Farms in Sussex, England, where A.A. Milne wrote *Winnie the Pooh*. There are Pooh character statues on the grounds. A month after he split from the group, he drowned in a swimming pool. (Died 7-3-69)

- **ZERO MOSTEL** Actor. (1915-1977 – Born Samuel Joel Mostel in Brooklyn, NY) He appeared in *A Funny Thing Happened on the Way to the Forum* in 1966. He also appeared as Tevya in *Fiddler on the Roof*. His son is Josh Mostel. (Died 9-8-77)

FACTS FROM THE PAST

1933 Francis Perkins was appointed Secretary of Labor by President Roosevelt. She was the first female cabinet member in U.S. history.

1844 Secretary of State Abel P. Upshur, Navy Secretary Thomas W. Gilmer, and several other people were killed when a 12-inch gun aboard the *USS Princeton* exploded.

1854 50 people opposed to slavery met at a schoolhouse in Ripon, WI, to call for a new political organization. The organization became known as the **REPUBLICAN PARTY**. Abraham Lincoln was elected in 1860 as the first Republican president.

1966 Liverpool's **CAVERN CLUB**, an early BEATLE stomping ground, closed when its owners went bankrupt.

1970 **JEFFERSON AIRPLANE** was fined $1,000 for singing the "F word" onstage during a concert in Oklahoma City.

1979 **MR. ED** died. He was the talking horse on the TV show of the same name. Allan Lane, a former western star, was the voice of Mr. Ed. Wilbur Post, played by Alan Young, talked to the horse.

1983 The last episode of "M*A*S*H" aired. It had the biggest TV audience ever: over 120 million!! (Premiered on Sept. 17, 1972.)

1984 **MICHAEL JACKSON** swept the Grammy Awards, all due to his album, *Thriller*.

1986 **WHAM!** announced it was breaking up. George Michael went on to a hugely successful solo career.

1987 Basketball announcer **CHICK HEARN** broadcast the 2,000th consecutive Laker game of his career. L.A. lost to Utah 107-100.

1989 Miss Texas, **GRETCHEN POLHEMUS**, 23, a cattle broker, was crowned Miss U.S.A. This marked the fifth consecutive victory for a Texan.

1993 Four federal agents and six branch davidians were killed at a compound near Waco, TX. after agents tried to serve warrants to **DAVID KORESH** and his followers. The standoff lasted 51 days.

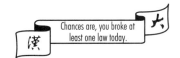

Chances are, you broke at least one law today.

FEBRUARY 29
Occurs 1996

BIRTHDAYS

- **HENRI RICHARD** Ex-hockey star. Year/**Age**: 1995/**37** 1996/**38** 1997/**39**

- **MICHELE MORGAN** Actress. (Born Simone Fousse in France.) Appeared in films: *Benjamin, The Fallen Idol* and *The Seven Deadly Sins.* Year/**Age**: 1995/**75** 1996/**76** 1997/**77**

- **JACK LOUSMA** Astronaut. (Grand Rapids, MI.) Year/**Age**: 1995/**59** 1996/**60** 1997/**61**

- **ARTHUR FRANZ** Actor. (Perth Amboy, NJ) American leading man; later a character actor. He appeared in *Sands of Iwo Jima, The Caine Mutiny* and *Abbott & Costello Meet The Invisible Man.* Year/**Age**: 1995/**74** 1996/**75** 1997/**76**

- **JOSS ACKLAND** Actor. (England) He appeared in *The House That Dripped Blood.* Year/**Age**: 1995/**67** 1996/**68** 1997/**69**

- **AL ROSEN** Baseball. Former Cleveland Indians third baseman and now San Francisco Giants general manager. Year/**Age**: 1995/**71** 1996/**72** 1997/**73**

- **WILLIE DONNELL SMITH** Designer. (Philadelphia, PA) He won the coveted Coty Award in 1983. Year/**Age**: 1995/**47** 1996/**48** 1997/**49**

- **JOHN NILAND** Ex-football pro. Year/**Age**: 1995/**51** 1996/**52** 1997/**53**

- **JOHN "PEPPER" MARTIN** Ex-baseball star. Outfielder for the St. Louis Cardinals in the 1930's. Year/**Age**: 1995/**92** 1996/**93** 1997/**94**

- **JIMMY DORSEY** Big band leader. (1904-1957 – Shenandoah, PA) Biggest hit "So Rare" in 1957 with Jimmy on sax.

- **GEOACCHINO ANTONIO ROSSINI** Italian operatic composer (1868-1972)

- **CHARLES PRITCHARD** British astronomer. (1808)

- **ANN LEE** Religous Leader. (1736-1784 – England) Founder of the Shakers in America. She claimed she had visions and revelations, spoke in tongues, preached against marriage and sex and was regarded by many followers as the second coming of Christ. Ann came to America in 1774 on instruction from a vision. She was arrested and imprisoned for conduct contrary to religious conventions.

FACTS FROM THE PAST

46 B.C. The **FIRST LEAP YEAR** occurred in 46 B.C. when the Romans added an extra day to make their calendar agree with the earth's orbital period.

1288 Before the dawn of sexual equality, **LEAP YEAR DAY** was traditionally the one day that a woman could propose to a man. This was the year that Scotland passed a law making it a crime for a man to refuse to marry a woman who made the proposal.

1504 **CHRISTOPHER COLUMBUS** was stranded on Jamaica Island with a sick and mutinous crew and was having trouble getting the natives to continue trading trinkets for food and supplies. He consulted an almanac, then warned the Jamaicans that he was going to cause the moon to disappear. That night there was a full lunar eclipse. The next day the natives resumed trading.

1704 The **TOWN OF DEERFIELD, MA** was burned to the ground by a French and Indian raiding party. 47 citizens were killed and 120 taken prisoners. A church bell was the cause of all this. The people of Deerfield had purchased the bell in Boston, not knowing that it had been pirated from a French ship bound for an Indian Village in Canada. The bell still hangs in that village today.

1804 Orders were given to build the **FIRST LIGHTHOUSE** on the Great Lakes.

1904 A man with the longest name was born in Germany. He had a Christian name for every letter in the alphabet. When he moved to Pennsylvania, he shortened it to **"MR. WOLFE PLUS 585, SR."**

1960 **MOROCCO** was hit by an earthquake, tidal wave and a fire, all on the same day.

1964 **FRANK RUGANI** sent his birdie flying a distance of 79 feet, $8\frac{1}{2}$ inches for the longest recorded drive of a badminton shuttlecock.

1972 **TOKYO** was rocked by an earthquake.

1972 **HANK AARON** signed baseball's first $200,000 contract with the Atlanta Braves.

1980 Hockey star **GORDIE HOWE**, at age 51, scored his 800th goal, playing for Hartford after many years with the Detroit Red Wings.

MARCH MEMORIES

10 YEARS AGO

1985

POPULAR SONGS
"Can't Fight This Feeling" by REO Speedwagon

"One More Night" by Phil Collins

MOVIES
Kiss of the Spider Woman
starring William Hurt and Raul Julia as a politial prisoner and a homosexual in jail.

The Purple Rose of Cairo
starring Jeff Daniels, Danny Aiello, Dianne Wiest, and Mia Farrow. This depression era film was directed by Woody Allen.

TV SHOWS
"Moonlighting"
starring Bruce Willis and Cybill Shepherd in a detective comedy.

"The Lucie Arnaz Show"
starring Lucie Arnaz and Tony Roberts.

BOOKS
Lonesome Dove by Larry McMurtry

1986

POPULAR SONGS
"Sara" by Starship

"These Dreams" by Heart

MOVIES
Platoon
starring Charlie Sheen, Johnny Depp, Tom Berenger, Willem DaFoe, and Kevin Dillon. Oliver Stone's story of the Vietnam war.

Stand By Me
starring River Phoenix, Jerry O'Connell, Corey Feldman, and Kiefer Sutherland. Four young boys find a corpse.

TV SHOWS
"Valerie"
sitcom stars Valerie Harper and Josh Taylor.

"Perfect Strangers"
two cousins, Mark Linn-Baker and Bronson Pinchot chase jobs and women.

BOOKS
You're Only Old Once by Dr. Seuss

1987

POPULAR SONGS
"Jacob's Ladder" by Huey Lewis & The NEWS

"Lean On Me" by Club Nouveau

MOVIES
The Untouchables
Mafia film starring Kevin Costner, Andy Garcia, Robert DeNiro, and Sean Connery.

Discreet Charm of the Bourgeoisie
starring Fernando Rey in a comedy about South American diplomats.

TV SHOWS
"Houston Knights"
starring Michael Pare as Sgt. Joey LaFiamma in a police drama.

"Max Headroom"
the story of a computer-generated character played by Matt Frewer.

BOOKS
Patriot Games by Tom Clancy

SPECIAL DAYS

MARCH	1995	1996	1997
Most Boring Films Of The Year	Mar. 13	Mar. 11	Mar. 10
Easter Sunday	Apr. 16	Apr. 7	Mar. 30
Girl Scouts Week	Mar. 5-11	Mar. 3-9	Mar. 2-8
Poison Prevention Week	Mar. 19-25	Mar. 17-23	Mar. 16-22
Full Moon	Mar. 17	Mar. 5	Mar. 24
Palm Sunday	Apr. 9	Mar. 31	Mar. 23
Ash Wednesday	Mar. 1		
Good Friday	Apr. 14	Apr. 5	Mar. 28

25 YEARS AGO

1970

POPULAR SONGS

"Bridge Over Toubled Waters" by Simon and Garfunkel

"Travelin' Band" by Creedence Clearwater Revival

MOVIES

The Great White Hope
starring James Earl Jones in the story of the first black heavy weight boxing champ.

The Landlord
starring Lee Grant, Lou Gossett, Beau Bridges, and Pearl Bailey. A landlord runs into trouble with his tenants.

TV SHOWS

"Arnie"
sitcom starring Herschel Bernardi

"The Young Lawyers"
starring Lee J. Cobb as lawyer David Barrett.

BOOKS

*Everything You Always Wanted To Know About Sex…*by Dr. David Reuben

1971

POPULAR SONGS

"Me and Bobby McGee" by Janis Joplin

"Just My Imagination (Running Away With Me)" by The Temptations

MOVIES

A Clockwork Orange
story about a violent antihero, played by Malcolm McDowell, and his gang.

Straw Dogs
starring Dustin Hoffman, Susan George, and David Warner. A man's wife is assualted.

TV SHOWS

"The D.A."
drama series starring Robert Conrad as Deputy District Attorney Paul Ryan.

"Getting Together"
sitcom starring teen idol Bobby Sherman as a struggling songwriter.

BOOKS

The Exorcist by William P. Blatty

1972

POPULAR SONGS

"Heart of Gold" by Neil Young

"A Horse With No Name" by America

MOVIES

Poseidon Adventure
passengers aboard an ocean liner struggle to survive when the boat begins to sink. Stars Gene Hackman, Ernest Borgnine, Shelley Winters, Red Buttons, and others.

Fat City
starring Stacy Keach, Susan Tyrrell, and Jeff Bridges in a story of an ex-boxer.

TV SHOWS

"Search"
three security agents protect the world. Hugh O'Brian and Burgess Meredith star.

"Ghost Story"
host Sebastian Cabot indtrouces stories of the supernatural.

BOOKS   *Jonathan Livingston Seagull* by Richard Bach

50 YEARS AGO

1945

POPULAR SONGS

"Candy" by Johnny Mercer, Jo Stafford, and The Pied Pipers.

"My Dreams Are Getting Better All The Time" by Les Brown

MOVIES

Objective Burma
paratroopers try to take out a Japanese radar station. Stars Errol Flynn.

Billy Rose's Diamond Horseshoe
starrring Betty Grable, Phil Silvers, and Dick Haymes. Grable portrays a nightclub singer in this comedy/drama.

TV SHOWS

regularly scheduled TV programming did not begin until May of 1946.

BOOKS

Unfinished Business by Stephen Bonsal

1946

POPULAR SONGS

"Oh! What It Seemed To Be" by Frank Sinatra

"Hey! Ba-Ba-Re-Bop" by Lionel Hampton Orchestra with Herbie Fields

MOVIES

Vacation From Marriage
starring Robert Donat, Deborah Kerr, and Glynis Johns. A British couple undergo personality changes when they enter the military.

Notorious
romantic Alfred Hitchcock thriller starring Cary Grant, Ingrid Bergman, and Claude Rains.

TV SHOWS

regularly scheduled TV programming did not begin until May of 1946.

BOOKS

The Snake Pit by Mary Jane Ward

1947

POPULAR SONGS

"Open the Door Richard!" by Three Flames

"Heartaches" by Elmo Tanner whistling with Ted Weems Orchestra

MOVIES

Green Dolphin Street
starring Lana Turner, Van Heflin, Donna Reed, and Frank Morgan. The story of a lady who travels to New Zealand to marry her sister's intended.

Gentleman's Agreement
a magazine writer sets out to prove discrimination. Stars Gregory Peck, John Grarfield, Celeste Holm, and Dorothy McGuire.

TV SHOWS

"Small Fry Club"
Bob Emery hosts kindergartners and presents their letters and pictures.

BOOKS

Gentleman's Agreement by Laura Z. Hobson

ACADEMY AWARD WINNERS

1927
Actor: Emil Jannings, *The Way of All Flesh*
Actress: Janet Gaynor, *Seventh Heaven*
Director: Frank Borzage, *Seventh Heaven*; Lewis Milestone, *Two Arabian Knights*
Picture: *Wings*, Paramount

1928-29
Actor: Warner Baxter, *In Old Arizona*
Actress: Mary Pickford, *Coquette*
Director: Frank Lloyd, *The Divine Lady*
Picture: *Broadway Melody*, MGM

1929-30
Actor: George Arliss, *Disraeli*
Actress: Norma Shearer, *The Divorcee*
Director: Lewis Milestone, *All Quiet on the Western Front*
Picture: *All Quiet on the Western Front*

1930-31
Actor: Lionel Barrymore, *Free Soul*
Actress: Marie Dressler, *Min and Bill*
Director: Norman Taurog, *Skippy*
Picture: *Cimarron*, RKO.

1931-32
Actor: Fredric March: *Dr. Jekyll and Mr. Hyde*
Wallace Beery, *The Champ* (tie)
Actress: Helen Hayes, *Sin of Madelon Claudet*
Director: Frank Borzage, *Bad Girl*
Picture: *Grand Hotel*, MGM
Special: Walt Disney, *Mickey Mouse*

1932-33
Actor: Charles Laughton, *Private Life of Henry VIII*
Actress: Katharine Hepburn, *Morning Glory*
Director: Frank Lloyd, *Cavalcade*
Picture: *Cavalcade*, Fox

1934
Actor: Clark Gable, *It Happened One Night*
Actress: Claudette Colbert, *It Happened One Night*
Director: Frank Capra, *It Happened One Night*
Picture: *It Happened One Night*, Columbia

1935
Actor: Victor McLaglen, *The Informer*
Actress: Bette Davis, *Dangerous*
Director: John Ford, *The Informer*
Picture: *Mutiny on the Bounty*, MGM

1936
Actor: Paul Muni, *Story of Louis Pasteur*
Actress: Luise Rainer, *The Great Ziegfeld*
Supporting Actor: Walter Brennan, *Come and Get It*
Supporting Actress: Gale Sondergaard, *Anthony Adverse*
Director: Frank Capra, *Mr. Deeds Goes to Town*
Picture: *The Great Ziegfeld*, MGM

1937
Actor: Spencer Tracy, *Captains Courageous*
Actress: Luise Rainer, *The Good Earth*
Supporting Actor: Joseph Schildkraut, *Life of Emile Zola*
Supporting Actress: Alice Brady, *In Old Chicago*
Director: Leo McCarey, *The Awful Truth*
Picture: *Life of Emile Zola*, Warner

1938
Actor: Spencer Tracy, *Boys Town*
Actress: Bette Davis, *Jezebel*
Supporting Actor: Walter Brennan, *Kentucky*
Supporting Actress: Fay Bainter, *Jezebel*
Director: Frank Capra, *You Can't Take It With You*
Picture: *You Can't Take It With You*, Columbia

1939
Actor: Robert Donat, *Goodbye Mr. Chips*
Actress: Vivien Leigh, *Gone With the Wind*
Supporting Actor: Thomas Mitchell, *Stage Coach*
Supporting Actress: Hattie McDaniel, *Gone With the Wind*
Director: Victor Fleming, *Gone With the Wind*
Picture: *Gone With the Wind*, Selznick International

1940
Actor: James Stewart, *The Philadelphia Story*
Actress: Ginger Rogers, *Kitty Foyle*
Supporting Actor: Walter Brennan, *The Westerner*
Supporting Actress: Jane Darwell, *The Grapes of Wrath*
Director: John Ford, *The Grapes of Wrath*
Picture: *Rebecca*, Selznick International

1941
Actor: Gary Cooper, *Sergeant York*
Actress: Joan Fontaine, *Suspicion*
Supporting Actor: Donald Crisp, *How Green Was My Valley*
Supporting Actress: Mary Astor, *The Great Lie*
Director: John Ford, *How Green Was My Valley*
Picture: *How Green Was My Valley*, 20th Century Fox.

1942
Actor: James Cagney, *Yankee Doodle Dandy*
Actress: Greer Garson, *Mrs. Miniver*
Supporting Actor: Van Heflin, *Johnny Eager*
Supporting Actress: Teresa Wright, *Mrs. Miniver*
Director: William Wyler, *Mrs. Miniver*
Picture: *Mrs. Miniver*, MGM

1943
Actor: Paul Lukas, Watch on the Rhine
Actress: Jennifer Jones, *The Song of Bernadette*
Supporting Actor: Charles Coburn, *The More the Merrier*
Supporting Actress: Katina Paxinou, *For Whom the Bell Tolls*
Director: Michael Curtiz, *Casablanca*
Picture: *Casablanca*, Warner

1944
Actor: Bing Crosby, *Going My Way*
Actress: Ingrid Bergman, *Gaslight*
Supporting Actor: Barry Fitzgerald, *Going My Way*
Supporting Actress: Ethel Barrymore, *None But the Lonely Heart*
Director: Leo McCarey, *Going My Way*
Picture: *Going My Way*, Paramount

1945
Actor: Ray Milland, *The Lost Weekend*
Actress: Joan Crawford, *Mildred Pierce*
Supporting Actor: James Dunn, *A Tree Grows in Brooklyn*

ACADEMY AWARD WINNERS CONTINUED

Supporting Actress: Anne Revere, *National Velvet*
Director: Billy Wilder, *The Lost Weekend*
Picture: *The Lost Weekend*, Paramount

1946
Actor: Fredric March, *Best Years of Our Lives*
Actress: Olivia de Havilland, *To Each His Own*
Supporting Actor: Harold Russell, *The Best Years of Our Lives*
Supporting Actress: Ann Baxter, *The Razor's Edge*
Director: William Wyler, *The Best Years of Our Lives*
Picture: *The Best Years of Our Lives*, Goldwyn, RKO

1947
Actor: Ronald Colman, *A Double Life*
Actress: Loretta Young, *The Farmer's Daughter*
Supporting Actor: Edmund Gwenn, *Miracle on 34th Street*
Supporting Actress: Celeste Holm, *Gentleman's Agreement*
Director: Elia Kazan, *Gentleman's Agreement*
Picture: *Gentleman's Agreement*, 20th Century Fox.

1948
Actor: Laurence Olivier, *Hamlet*
Actress: Jayne Wyman, *Johnny Belinda*
Supporting Actor: Walter Houston, *Treasure of Sierra Madre*
Supporting Actress: Claire Trevor, *Key Largo*
Director: John Huston, *Treasure of Sierra Madre*
Picture: *Hamlet*, Two Cities Film: Universal International

1949
Actor: Broderick Crawford, *All the King's Men*
Actress: Olivia de Havilland, *The Heiress*
Supporting Actor: Dean Jagger, *Twelve O'Clock High*
Supporting Actress: Mercedes McCambridge, *All the King's Men*
Director: Joseph L. Mankiewicz, *Letter to Three Wives*
Picture: *All the King's Men*, Columbia

1950
Actor: Jose Ferrer, *Cyrano de Bergerac*
Actress: Judy Holliday, *Born Yesterday*
Supporting Actor: George Sanders, *All About Eve*
Supporting Actress: Josephine Hull, *Harvey*
Director: Joseph L. Mankiewicz, *All About Eve*
Picture: *All About Eve*, 20th Century-Fox

1951
Actor: Humphrey Bogart, *The African Queen*
Actress: Vivien Leigh, *A Streetcar Named Desire*
Supporting Actor: Karl Malden, *A Streetcar Named Desire*
Supporting Actress: Kim Hunter, *A Streetcar Named Desire*
Director: G. Stevens, *A Place in the Sun*
Picture: *An American in Paris*, MGM

1952
Actor: Gary Cooper, *High Noon*
Actress: Shirley Booth, *Come Back, Little Sheba*
Supporting Actor: Anthony Quinn, *Viva Zapata!*
Supporting Actress: Gloria Grahame, *The Bad and the Beautiful*
Director: John Ford, *The Quiet Man*
Picture: *Greatest Show on Earth*, C.B. DeMille, Paramount

1953
Actor: William Holden, *Stalag 17*
Actress: Audrey Hepburn, *Roman Holiday*
Supporting Actor: Frank Sinatra, *From Here to Eternity*
Supporting Actress: Donna Reed, *From Here to Eternity*
Director: Fred Zinneman, *From Here to Eternity*
Picture: *From Here to Eternity*, Columbia

1954
Actor: Marlon Brando, *On the Waterfront*
Actress: Grace Kelly, *The Country Girl*
Supporting Actor: Edmond O'Brien, *The Barefoot Contessa*
Supporting Actress: Eva Marie Saint, *On the Waterfront*
Director: Elia Kazan, *On the Waterfront*
Picture: *On the Waterfront*, Horizon-American, Columbia

1955
Actor: Ernest Borgnine, *Marty*
Actress: Anna Magnani, *The Rose Tattoo*
Supporting Actor: Jack Lemmon, *Mister Roberts*

Supporting Actress: Jo Van Fleet, *East of Eden*
Director: Delbert Mann, *Marty*
Picture: *Marty*, Hecht and Lancaster's Steven Prods. U.A.

1956
Actor: Yul Brynner, *The King and I*
Actress: Ingrid Bergman, *Anastasia*
Supporting Actor: Anthony Quinn, *Lust for Life*
Sup. Actress: Dorothy Malone, *Written on the Wind*
Director: George Stevens, *Giant*
Picture: *Around the World in 80 Days*, Michael Todd, U.A.

1957
Actor: Alec Guinness, *The Bridge on the River Kwai*
Actress: Joanne Woodward, *The Three Faces of Eve*
Supporting Actor: Red Buttons, *Sayonara*
Supporting Actress: Miyoshi Umeki, *Sayonara*
Director: David Lean, *The Bridge on the River Kwai*
Picture: *The Bridge on the River Kwai*, Columbia

1958
Actor: David Niven, *Separate Tables*
Actress: Susan Hayward, *I Want to Live*
Supporting Actor: Burl Ives, *The Big Country*
Supporting Actress: Wendy Hiller, *Separate Tables*
Director: Vincente Minnelli, *Gigi*
Picture: *Gigi*, Arthur Freed Production, MGM

1959
Actor: Charlton Heston, *Ben-Hur*
Actress: Simone Signoret, *Room at the Top*
Supporting Actor: Hugh Griffith, *Ben-Hur*
Supporting Actress: Shelley Winters, *Diary of Anne Frank*
Director: William Wyler, *Ben-Hur*
Picture: *Ben-Hur*, MGM

1960
Actor: Burt Lancaster, *Elmer Gantry*
Actress: Elizabeth Taylor, *Butterfield 8*
Supporting Actor: Peter Ustinov, *Spartacus*
Supporting Actress: Shirley Jones, *Elmer Gantry*
Director: Billy Wilder, *The Apartment*
Picture: *The Apartment*, Mirisch Co., United Artists

1961
Actor: Maximilian Schell, *Judgment at Nuremberg*

ACADEMY AWARD WINNERS CONTINUED

Actress: Sophia Loren, *Two Women*
Supporting Actor: George Chakiris, *West Side Story*
Supporting Actress: Rita Moreno, *West Side Story*
Director: Jerome Robbins, Robert Wise, *West Side Story*
Picture: *West Side Story*, United Artists

1962
Actor: Gregory Peck, *To Kill a Mockingbird*
Actress: Anne Bancroft, *The Miracle Worker*
Supporting Actor: Ed Begley, *Sweet Bird of Youth*
Supporting Actress: Patty Duke, *The Miracle Worker*
Director: David Lean, *Lawrence of Arabia*
Picture: *Lawrence of Arabia*, Columbia

1963
Actor: Sidney Poitier, *Lilies of the Field*
Actress: Patricia Neal, *Hud*
Supporting Actor: Melvyn Douglas, *Hud*
Supporting Actress: Margaret Rutherford, *The V.I.P.s.*
Director: Tony Richardson, *Tom Jones*
Picture: *Tom Jones*, Woodfall Prod., United Artists-Lopert Pictures

1964
Actor: Rex Harrison, *My Fair Lady*
Actress: Julie Andrews, *Mary Poppins*
Supporting Actor: Peter Ustinov, *Topkapi*
Supporting Actress: Lila Kedrova, *Zorba the Greek*
Director: George Cukor, *My Fair Lady*
Picture: *My Fair Lady*, Warner Bros.

1965
Actor: Lee Marvin, *Cat Ballou*
Actress: Julie Christie, *Darling*
Supporting Actor: Martin Balsam, *A Thousand Clowns*
Supporting Actress: Shelly Winters, *A Patch of Blue*
Director: Robert Wise, *The Sound of Music*
Picture: *The Sound of Music*, 20th Century-Fox

1966
Actor: Paul Scofield, *A Man for All Seasons*
Actress: Elizabeth Taylor, *Who's Afraid of Virginia Woolf?*
Supporting Actor: Walter Matthau, *The Fortune Cookie*
Supporting Actress: Sandy Dennis, *Who's Afraid of Virginia Woolf?*

Director: Fred Zinnemann, *A Man for All Seasons*
Picture: *A Man for All Seasons*, Columbia

1967
Actor: Rod Steiger, *In the Heat of the Night*
Actress: Katharine Hepburn, *Guess Who's Coming to Dinner*
Supporting Actor: George Kennedy, *Cool Hand Luke*
Supporting Actress: Estelle Parsons, *Bonnie and Clyde*
Director: Mike Nichols, *The Graduate*
Picture: *In the Heat of the Night*

1968
Actor: Cliff Robertson, *Charly*
Actress: Katharine Hepburn, *The Lion in Winter* and
Barbra Streisand, *Funny Girl* (tie)
Supporting Actor: Jack Albertson, *The Subject Was Roses*
Supporting Actress: Ruth Gordon, *Rosemary's Baby*
Director: Sir Carol Reed, *Oliver!*
Picture: *Oliver!*

1969
Actor: John Wayne, *True Grit*
Actress: Maggie Smith, *The Prime of Miss Jean Brodie*
Supporting Actor: Gig Young, *They Shoot Horses, Don't They?*
Supporting Actress: Goldie Hawn, *Cactus Flower*
Director: John Schlesinger, *Midnight Cowboy*
Picture: *Midnight Cowboy*

1970
Actor: George C. Scott, *Patton* (refused)
Actress: Glenda Jackson, *Women in Love*
Supporting Actor: John Mills, *Ryan's Daughter*
Supporting Actress: Helen Hayes, *Airport*
Director: Franklin Schaffner, *Patton*
Picture: *Patton*

1971
Actor: Gene Hackman, *The French Connection*
Actress: Jane Fonda, *Klute*
Supporting Actor: Ben Johnson, *The Last Picture Show*
Supporting Actress: Cloris Leachman,

The Last Picture Show
Director: William Friedkin, *The French Connection*
Picture: *The French Connection*

1972
Actor: Marlon Brando, *The Godfather* (refused)
Actress: Liza Minnelli, *Cabaret*
Supporting Actor: Joel Grey, *Cabaret*
Supporting Actress: Eileen Heckart, *Butterflies are Free*
Director: Bob Fosse, *Cabaret*
Picture: *The Godfather*

1973
Actor: Jack Lemmon, *Save the Tiger*
Actress: Glenda Jackson, *A Touch of Class*
Supporting Actor: John Houseman, *The Paper Chase*
Supporting Actress: Tatum O'Neal, *Paper Moon*
Director: George Roy Hill, *The Sting*
Picture: *The Sting*

1974
Actor: Art Carney, *Harry and Tonto*
Actress: Ellen Burstyn, *Alice Doesn't Live Here Anymore*
Supporting Actor: Robert DeNiro, *The Godfather: Part II*
Supporting Actress: Ingrid Bergman, *Murder On the Orient Express*
Director: Francis Ford Coppola, *The Godfather: Part II*
Picture: *The Godfather: Part II*

1975
Actor: Jack Nicholson, *One Flew Over the Cuckoo's Nest*
Actress: Louise Fletcher, *One Flew Over the Cuckoo's Nest*
Supporting Actor: George Burns, *The Sunshine Boys*
Supporting Actress: Lee Grant, *Shampoo*

Director: Milos Forman, *One Flew Over the Cuckoo's Nest*
Picture: *One Flew Over the Cuckoo's Nest*

1976
Actor: Peter Finch, *Network*
Actress: Faye Dunaway, *Network*
Supporting Actor: Jason Robards, *All the President's Men*
Supporting Actress: Beatrice Straight, *Network*
Director: John G. Avildsen, *Rocky*
Picture: *Rocky*

1977
Actor: Richard Dreyfuss, *The Goodbye Girl*
Actress: Diane Keaton, *Annie Hall*

ACADEMY AWARD WINNERS CONTINUED

Supporting Actor: Jason Robards, *Julia*
Supporting Actress: Vanessa Redgrave, *Julia*
Director: Woody Allen, *Annie Hall*
Picture: *Annie Hall*

1978
Actor: John Voight, *Coming Home*
Actress: Jane Fonda, *Coming Home*
Supporting Actor: Christopher Walken, *The Deer Hunter*
Supporting Actress: Maggie Smith, *California Suite*
Director: Michael Cimino, *The Deer Hunter*
Picture: *The Deer Hunter*

1979
Actor: Dustin Hoffman, *Kramer vs. Kramer*
Actress: Sally Field, *Norma Rae*
Supporting Actor: Melvyn Douglas, *Being There*
Supporting Actress: Meryl Streep, *Kramer vs. Kramer*
Director: Robert Benton, *Kramer vs. Kramer*
Picture: *Kramer vs. Kramer*

1980
Actor: Robert DeNiro, *Raging Bull*
Actress: Sissy Spacek, *Coal Miner's Daughter*
Supporting Actor: Timothy Hutton, *Ordinary People*
Supporting Actress: Mary Steenburgen, *Melvin & Howard*
Director: Robert Redford, *Ordinary People*
Picture: *Ordinary People*

1981
Actor: Henry Fonda, *On Golden Pond*
Actress: Katharine Hepburn, *On Golden Pond*
Supporting Actor: John Gielgud, *Arthur*
Supporting Actress: Maureen Stapleton, *Reds*
Director: Warren Beatty, *Reds*
Picture: *Chariots of Fire*

1982
Actor: Ben Kingsley, *Gandhi*
Actress: Meryl Streep, *Sophie's Choice*
Supporting Actor: Louis Gosset, Jr., *An Officer and a Gentleman*
Supporting Actress: Jessica Lang, *Tootsie*
Director: Richard Attenborough, *Gandhi*
Picture: *Gandhi*

1983
Actor: Robert Duval, *Tender Mercies*
Actress: Shirley MacLaine, *Terms of Endearment*
Supporting Actor: Jack Nicholson, *Terms of Endearment*
Supporting Actress: Linda Hunt, *The Year of Living Dangerously*
Director: James L. Brooks, *Terms of Endearment*
Picture: *Terms of Endearment*

1984
Actor: F. Murray Abraham, *Amadeus*
Actress: Sally Field, *Places in the Heart*
Supporting Actor: Haing S. Ngor, *The Killing Fields*
Supporting Actress: Peggy Ashcroft, *A Passage to India*
Director: Milos Forman, *Amadeus*
Picture: *Amadeus*

1985
Actor: William Hurt, *Kiss of the Spider Woman*
Actress: Geraldine Page, *The Trip to Bountiful*
Supporting Actor: Don Ameche, *Cocoon*
Supporting Actress: Anjelica Huston, *Prizzi's Honor*
Director: Sydney Pollack, *Out of Africa*
Picture: *Out of Africa*

1986
Actor: Paul Newman, *The Color of Money*
Actress: Marlec Matlin, *Children of a Lesser God*
Supporting Actor: Michael Caine, *Hannah and Her Sisters*
Supporting Actress: Dianne Wiest, *Hannah and Her Sisters*
Director: Oliver Stone, *Platoon*
Picture: *Platoon*

1987
Actor: Michael Douglas, *Wall Street*
Actress: Cher, *Moonstruck*
Supporting Actor: Sean Connery, *The Untouchables*
Supporting Actress: Olivia Dukakis, *Moonstruck*

Director: Bernardo Bertolucci, *The Last Emperor*
Picture: *The Last Emperor*

1988

Actor: Dustin Hoffman, *Rain Man*
Actress: Jodie Foster, *The Accused*
Supporting Actor: Kevin Kline, *A Fish Called Wanda*
Supporting Actress: Geena Davis, *The Accidental Tourist*
Director: Barry Levinson, *Rain Man*
Picture: *Rain Man*

1989
Actor: Daniel Day-Lewis, *My Left Foot*
Actress: Jessica Tandy, *Driving Miss Daisy*
Supporting Actor: Denzel Washington, *Glory*
Supporting Actress: Brenda Fricker, *My Left Foot*
Director: Oliver Stone, *Born on the Fourth of July*
Picture: *Driving Miss Daisy*

1990
Actor: Jeremy Irons, *Reversal of Fortune*
Actress: Kathy Bates, *Misery*
Supporting Actor: Joe Pesci, *Goodfellas*
Supporting Actress: Whoopie Goldberg, *Ghost*
Director: Kevin Costner, *Dances With Wolves*
Picture: *Dances With Wolves*

1991
Actor: Anthony Hopkins, *The Silence of the Lambs*
Actress: Jodie Foster, *The Silence of the Lambs*
Supporting Actor: Jack Palance, *City Slickers*
Supporting Actress: Mercedes Ruehl, *The Fisher King*
Director: Jonathan Demme, *The Silence of the Lambs*
Picture: *The Silence of the Lambs*

1992
Actor: Al Pacino, *Scent of a Woman*
Actress: Emma Thompson, *Howards End*
Supporting Actor: Gene Hackman, *Unforgiven*
Supporting Actress: Marisa Tomei, *My Cousin Vinny*
Director: Clint Eastwood, *Unforgiven*
Picture: *Unforgiven*

1993
Actor: Tom Hanks, *Philadelphia*
Actress: Holly Hunter, *The Piano*
Supporting Actor: Tommy Lee Jones, *The Fugitive*
Supporting Actress: Anna Paquin, *The Piano*
Director: Steven Spielberg, *Schindler's List*
Picture: *Schindler's List*

MARCH 1
National Pig Day

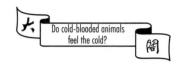
Do cold-blooded animals feel the cold?

BIRTHDAYS

- **MARK-PAUL GOSSELAAR** Actor. TV show "Saved by the Bell." Year/**Age**: 1995/**21** 1996/**22** 1997/**23**

- **RON HOWARD** Actor/producer. (Duncan, OK) Played Opie on the "Andy Griffith Show" as a child and was the star of the popular TV series "Happy Days." Produced *Backdraft*, *The Paper*, and *Far & Away*. His wife, Cheryl, and brother Clint have appeared in all of his films. He says they're his good-luck charms. Year/**Age**: 1995/**41** 1996/**42** 1997/**43**

- **HARRY BELAFONTE** Singer. (NYC) Biggest hit: "Banana Boat Song" in 1957. Popularized Calypso music. His music was used in *Beetlejuice*. Father of actress Shari. Year/**Age**: 1995/**68** 1996/**69** 1997/**70**

- **ROBERT CONRAD** Actor. (Born Conrad Robert Falk in Chicago, IL) He was in "Hawaiian Eye," "Wild Wild West," "Baa Baa Black Sheep" and the adventure series "High Mountain Rangers," later retitled "Jesse Hawkes," with his two sons, Shane and Christian. He made a record in 1961, "Bye Bye Baby." Year/**Age**: 1995/**60** 1996/**61** 1997/**62**

- **PETE ROZELLE** Former NFL Commissioner. (South Gate, CA) From 1960-1989. Year/**Age**: 1995/**69** 1996/**70** 1997/**71**

- **HARRY CARAY** Chicago Cub announcer. (St. Louis, MO) Baseball Hall of Famer who shouts "Holy Cow" after a good play. His two sons are announcers as well. Year/**Age**: 1995/**76** 1996/**77** 1997/**78**

- **TIM DALEY** Actor. TV's "Wings." Year/**Age**: 1995/**39** 1996/**40** 1997/**41**

- **ALAN THICKE** Actor. (Kirkland Lake, Ontario) Played dad Jason, on "Growing Pains." His occupation was a psychiatrist. Had TV talk show, "Thicke of the Night." He co-hosts the Rose Bowl Parade. Year/**Age**: 1995/**48** 1996/**49** 1997/**50**

- **DIRK BENEDICT** Actor. (Helena, MT) He played Starbuck in "Battlestar Galactica" on TV. Appeared in TV's "The A-Team." Year/**Age**: 1995/**50** 1996/**51** 1997/**52**

- **ROGER DALTRY** Musician. (London, England) Lead singer for THE WHO. Biggest hit: "I Can See for Miles" in 1967. In 1970, they became the first rock group to perform at the Metropolitan Opera House in New York City. Year/**Age**: 1995/**51** 1996/**52** 1997/**53**

- **DINAH SHORE** Entertainer. (1917-1994, Born Frances Rose Shore in Winchester, TN) She had two #1 hits: "I'll Walk Alone" in 1944 and "Buttons and Bows" in 1948. She was the first celebrity to entertain troops overseas in WWII. Her "Dinah Shore Show" won 8 Emmy Awards. (Died 2-24-94.)

- **DONALD "DEKE" SLAYTON** Astronaut. (1924-1993 – Sparta, WI) He was one of the original 7 U.S. astronauts. He had a heart murmur which kept him on the ground for a while, but he finally made it into outer space as part of the historic U.S.-Soviet space mission in 1975. (Died 6-13-93.)

- **DAVID NIVEN** Actor. (1910-1983 – Born James David Graham Niven in Scotland) Won an Oscar in 1958 for *Separate Tables*. He appeared in films including *Around the World in Eighty Days*, *Casino Royale*, and *The Pink Panther*. (Died 7-29-83.)

- **WILLIAM GAINES** *Mad Magazine* founder. (1922-1992) Also published *Tales From the Crypt*, later a cable TV series. (Died 6-3-92.)

- **EDMUND FITZGERALD** Ship.(1895-1986) Milwaukee civic leader whose name became a household word after the ship bearing his name sank in Lake Superior in a storm in 1975. It became the subject of a ballad by singer GORDON LIGHTFOOT.

- **GLENN MILLER** Bandleader (1904-1944 – Born Alton Glenn Miller in Clarinda, IA) He was very popular before and during WWII. His hit recordings included "In the Mood," "Moonlight Serenade," and "String of Pearls." Major Miller (at that time leader of the US Army Air Force Band) disappeared Dec. 15, 1944, over the English Channel on a flight to Paris for a show.

FACTS FROM THE PAST

1969 JIM MORRISON of THE DOORS was charged with lewd and lascivious behavior, indecent exposure, open profanity and public drunkenness after a concert in Miami. He was found guilty on the exposure and profanity charges and was sentenced to eight months hard labor and a $500 fine. His sentence was on appeal when Morrison died in Paris in 1971.

1972 Country star **MERLE HAGGARD** was pardoned by California Governor Ronald Reagan. Haggard had served time in San Quentin in the late 1950's for attempted burglary. Biggest hit: "If We Make It Through December" in 1973.

1977 SARA LOWNDES DYLAN filed for divorce from her husband of eleven years, **BOB DYLAN**. In the divorce, final in June, Sara retained legal custody of their children and million-dollar home in Santa Monica, CA. She had been the subject of Dylan songs "Sara" and "Lay Lady Lay."

1981 IRA MEMBER BOBBY SANDS began a hunger strike at Maze Prison in Northern Ireland that ended 65 days later with his death.

1988 For the fourth consecutive year a Texas woman won the Miss U.S.A. Pageant. **COURTNEY GIBBS** of Fort Worth took the crown. **BOB BARKER** ended his 21-year reign as host to protest the awarding of furs to the winner and use of furs during the show.

1989 JOHN TOWER told the National Press Club that rumors of his womanizing were true. "I have broken wedding vows," he said. Despite Tower's candor, his nomination to be Secretary of Defense was rejected March 9 by the Senate.

1993 A police badge was substituted for a stick of dynamite in the hand of a 75-foot balloon advertising Arnold Schwarzenegger's new film *The Last Action Hero*. Mayor David Dinkins said its appearance came too close to the World Trade Center bombing on February 26, 1993. Also, it was announced that Columbia Pictures would pay $500,000 to advertise the movie on a U.S. space vehicle, a first.

1994 FRANK SINATRA made his first appearance at the Grammys to accept a special Legends Award. Irish rocker Bono presented the award and said, "Frank is living proof that God is a Catholic."

MARCH 2

BIRTHDAYS

- **JOHN CULLUM** Actor. (Knoxville, TN) TV series "Northern Exposure." He was a Tony-winning Broadway singer. Year/**Age**: 1995/**65** 1996/**66** 1997/**67**

- **JENNIFER JONES** Actress. (Born Phyllis Isley in Tulsa, OK) She won an Oscar for best actress in 1943 for *Song of Bernadette.* Year/**Age**: 1995/**76** 1996/**77** 1997/**78**

- **MIKHAIL SERGEYVICH GORBACHEV** Former Soviet President. (Russia) He won the Nobel Peace Prize in 1990. Year/**Age**: 1995/**64** 1996/**65** 1997/**66**

- **LARAINE NEWMAN** Comic actress. (Los Angeles, CA) TV's Connie Conehead on the original "Saturday Night Live" and movie *Coneheads.* Year/**Age**: 1995/**43** 1996/**44** 1997/**45**

- **RON GRANT** Baseball. Year/**Age**: 1995/**30** 1996/**31** 1997/**32**

- **JON BON JOVI** Singer. (Born Jon Bongiovi in Sayreville, NJ) Lead vocalist for the rock quintet. Biggest hit: "You Give Love a Bad Name" in 1986. Solo 1990 hit: "Blaze of Glory." He gave away his house on MTV. BON JOVI's 1987 album, *Slippery When Wet,* sold more than 13 million copies. Year/**Age**: 1995/**33** 1996/**34** 1997/**35**

- **EDDIE MONEY** Singer. (Born Edward Mahoney in Brooklyn, NY) At one time he was a police officer. Biggest hit: "Take Me Home Tonight" in 1986 with Ronnie Spector singing the lead line from "Be My Baby." Year/**Age**: 1995/**46** 1996/**47** 1997/**48**

- **JOHN IRVING** Author. (Exeter, NH) Wrote *The World According to Garp, A Prayer for Owen Meany,* and *Cider House Rules.* Year/**Age**: 1995/**53** 1996/**54** 1997/**55**

- **TOM WOLFE** Author and journalist. (Born in Richmond, VA) He wrote: *The Right Stuff, The Electric Kool-Aid Acid Test,* and *Bonfire of the Vanities.* Year/**Age**: 1995/**64** 1996/**65** 1997/**66**

- **JAY OSMOND** Singer of the OSMOND BROTHERS. (Salt Lake City, UT) Biggest hit: "One Bad Apple" in 1971. Year/**Age**: 1995/**40** 1996/**41** 1997/**42**

- **RORY GALLAGHER** Irish rock guitarist. Year/**Age**: 1995/**46** 1996/**47** 1997/**48**

- **LOU REED** Singer/songwriter. (Born Louis Firbank in NYC) Biggest hit: "Walk On the Wild Side," produced by David Bowie in 1973. Year/**Age**: 1995/**53** 1996/**54** 1997/**55**

- **GORDON THOMSON** Actor. (Canada) Adam Carrington on TV's "Dynasty." Year/**Age**: 1995/**50** 1996/**51** 1997/**52**

- **DOC WATSON** C&W. (Born Arthel Watson) Won two Grammys with his son Merle in the 1970's. Year/**Age**: 1995/**72** 1996/**73** 1997/**74**

- **MARTIN RITT** Movie director. (1920-1990 – NYC) *HUD, Long Hot Summer,* and *Norma Rae.* (Died 12-8-90.)

- **KAREN CARPENTER** Entertainer. (1950-1983 – New Haven, CT) Biggest hit, with her brother Richard, "Close to You" in 1970. They were a successful duo, second only to the Everly Bros. Karen died of heart failure at age 32. For years she was affected by anorexia nervosa, an eating disorder. (Died 2-4-83.)

- **SAM HOUSTON** Politician. (1793-1863 – Born in Rockbridge Country, VA) An American soldier best remembered for his role in Texas history for avenging the Alamo massacre by defeating Santa Anna's troops. He was the only person ever elected governor for two different states, Tennessee and Texas. The city of Houston is named after him. (Died 7-26-1863.)

- **DESI ARNAZ, SR.** Actor. (1917-1986 – Cuba) He co-starred on the "I Love Lucy" TV series as Ricky Ricardo with then-wife Lucille Ball. Before that he was a bandleader. (Died 12-2-86.)

- **THEODOR "DR. SEUSS" GEISEL** Children's author. (1904-1991 – Born Theodore S. "Seuss" Geisel [guy-zul] in Springfield, MA) He got his pen name by adding "Dr." to his middle name. His first book was turned down by 27 publishers. The creator of the Christmas-stealing *Grinch* and *The Cat in the Hat.* He created the "Beginner Books" industry starting with *Horton Hears a Who* in 1954. (Died 9-24-91.)

FACTS FROM THE PAST

1927 After 13 years in pro baseball, **BABE RUTH** signed a history-making $70,000 contract with the New York Yankees. That year, the average working man was making $1,300 and baseball legend Lou Gehrig made $8,000. In his 24-year career, Babe's total earnings were about $967,000.

1962 Philadelphia Warriors' **WILT CHAMBERLAIN** scored an NBA record 100 points as Philly beat the New York Knicks 169-147. Wilt had 36 field goals and 28 free throws.

1964 The **BEATLES** began filming their first movie, *A Hard Day's Night.* While filming, George Harrison met his first wife, Pattie Boyd.

1974 **STEVIE WONDER** takes home 5 Grammies. Among them is "Album of the Year" for his LP "Innerventions."

1983 **SONY, PHILIPS AND POLYGRAM** introduced their compact-disc systems.

1984 Hollywood's Gold Star Recording Studios, where the **BEACH BOYS** and **PHIL SPECTOR** made most of their famous recordings, was closed. The building was eventually torn down to make room for a shopping mall.

1992 **RYNE SANDBERG** became baseball's highest-paid player, singing a five-year contract with the Chicago Cubs, worth $30.5 million.

1993 **MICHAEL GARTNER**, NBC News president, resigned less than a month after "Dateline NBC" admitted on the air that it had rigged a crash test involving GM pickup trucks.

1994 Six senior White House officials appeared in court regarding Clinton's involvement in an Arkansas land deal. Controversy is known as "The **WHITEWATER** Scandal."

MARCH 3

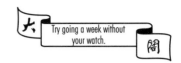
Try going a week without your watch.

BIRTHDAYS

- **DAVID FAUSTINO** Actor Bud Bundy on TV's "Married With Children." Year/**Age:** 1995/**21** 1996/**22** 1997/**23**
- **MARY PAGE KELLER** Actress. "Baby Talk," "Duet," "Open House," and "Life Goes On." Year/**Age:** 1995/**34** 1996/**35** 1997/**36**
- **MIKE PENDER** Guitarist. (Born Mike Prendergast, Liverpool, England) Member of the SEARCHERS (named after a John Wayne movie). Their hits include: "Love Potion Number Nine" and "Needles And Pins" in 1964. Year/**Age:** 1995/**53** 1996/**54** 1997/**55**
- **LEE RADZIWILL** Socialite. (Born Caroline Lee Bouvier in NYC) Sister of Jackie Onassis. She was married to Polish nobleman Stanislas Radziwell from 1959 to 1974. Year/**Age:** 1995/**62** 1996/**63** 1997/**64**
- **JAMES DOOHAN** Actor. (Canada) Scotty on "Star Trek." In the film *Loaded Weapon I.* Year/**Age:** 1995/**75** 1996/**76** 1997/**77**
- **TIM KAZARINSKY** Actor/director. (Johnstown, PA) In the *Police Academy* films. Year/**Age:** 1995/**45** 1996/**46** 1997/**47**
- **ED MARINARO** Actor. (NYC) In "Hill Street Blues" and "Sisters." At one time a Minnesota Vikings running back. Year/**Age:** 1995/**45** 1996/**46** 1997/**47**
- **HERSCHEL WALKER** Football. (Wrightsville, GA) Heisman Trophy Winner with Georgia in 1982. He had a great year with the Dallas Cowboys in 1987. Year/**Age:** 1995/**33** 1996/**34** 1997/**35**
- **ENZO STUARTI** Singer. (Rome, Italy) Year/**Age:** 1995/**70** 1996/**71** 1997/**72**

- **JACKIE JOYNER-KERSEE** Olympic champion. (East St. Louis, IL) She won gold medals in track at the 1988 and 1992 Olympics. Married Bob Kersee (woman's track coach) in 1986. Year/**Age:** 1995/**33** 1996/**34** 1997/**35**
- **GIA SCALA** Actress. (1936-1972; Born Giovanna Scoglio in Italy) Appeared in *Don't Go Near the Water* and *The Guns of Navarone.* (Died 4-30-72.)
- **JULIUS BOROS** Pro golfer. (1920-1994; Fairfield, CT) He won the U.S. Open in 1952 and 1963 and was the PGA champ in 1968. (Died 5-28-94.)
- **MATTHEW B. RIDGWAY** General. (1895-1993 – Fort Monroe, VA) He commanded the Army's first major airborne campaign, was the leader of the 82nd Airborne Division on D-Day and succeeded Gen. Douglas MacArthur during the Korean War. (Died 7-26-93.)
- **JEAN HARLOW** Actress. (1911-1937 – Born Harlean Carpentier in Kansas City, MO) American leading lady and most sensational star of the early 1930's. Called the "Blonde Bombshell." In film *Hells Angels* in 1930. (Died 6-7-37.)
- **ALEXANDER GRAHAM BELL** Inventor. (1847-1922 – Scotland) He invented the telephone, inspired by his association with so many people who were deaf. His mother was deaf, and both his father and grandfather dedicated their lives to teaching deaf people to speak. Bell married Mabel Hubbard who also was deaf. (Died 8-2-22.)
- **GEORGE PULLMAN** Inventor. (1831-1897 – Brocton, NY) He originated the railway sleeping car called the Pullman. (Died 10-19-1897.)

FACTS FROM THE PAST

1875   **GEORGES BIZET**'s opera *Carmen* premiered in Paris. The audience hated it and jeered Bizet as he fled the theatre.

1879   **BELVA ANN BENNETT LOCKWOOD** became the first woman admitted to practice before the U.S. Supreme Court.

1931   The **"STAR-SPANGLED BANNER"** became the official national anthem of the U.S., 117 years after the words were written by Francis Scott Key during the War of 1812.

1931   **CAB CALLOWAY** recorded "Minnie The Moocher." It became the first Jazz album ever to sell a million.

1939   At the Harvard Union, **LOTHROP WITHINGTON, JR.,** won a five-dollar bet for swallowing goldfish. The record for goldfish swallowing was set in 1967 by college student **ROBERT AUVE**, who swallowed 199 of them.

1955   **ELVIS** appeared on "Louisiana Hayride." It was his TV debut.

1957   **CARDINAL STRITCH** of Chicago, the largest archdiocese in the world, banned rock and roll from Catholic schools in his districts.

1966   **JOHN LENNON** was quoted in the *London Evening Standard* as saying the Beatles were more popular than Jesus Christ. The comment touched off international protest many months later.

1978   The remains of comedian **CHARLIE CHAPLIN** were stolen by extortionists from his grave in Cosier-sur-Vevey, Switzerland. The body was found near Lake Geneva 11 weeks later.

1982   **WAYNE GRETZKY** shattered the NHL record of goals scored in one season when he made his 77th goal. In the last two minutes of the game, Wayne scored #78 and #79.

1984   **PETER V. UEBERROTH** was named commissioner of baseball by the 26 major-league owners.

1988   The record for curtain calls – 165 – was set by **LUCIANO PAVAROTTI** in West Berlin with a standing ovation of 67 minutes.

1989   Madonna's "Like A Prayer" clip causes controversy and TV reps refuse to air it. Pepsi swallows its million-dollar investment.

1991   Los Angeles police were videotaped beating **RODNEY KING** by **GEORGE HOLLIDAY**.

1994   Apparently it's a trend to assault figure skaters. **TONYA HARDING** told police she was attacked in a city park. She suffered minor scrapes and a sprained wrist.

Unlike Smith and Baker, few last names have traceable roots

MARCH 4

BIRTHDAYS

- **JOANNE "Big Mama" CARNER** Pro golfer. (Kirkland, WA) Year/Age: 1995/**56** 1996/**57** 1997/**58**

- **CATHERINE O'HARA** Actress. (Canada) In the films *Beatlejuice*, *Home Alone I and II*, and *Nightmare Before Christmas*. Year/Age: 1995/**41** 1996/**42** 1997/**43**

- **KEVIN JOHNSON** Basketball. With the Phoenix Suns. Year/Age: 1995/**29** 1996/**30** 1997/**31**

- **EMILIO ESTEFAN** [eh-steh'-fahn] Percussionist. (Cuba) MIAMI SOUND MACHINE. Husband of Gloria. "Anything For You" in 1988. Year/Age: 1995/**42** 1996/**43** 1997/**44**

- **BARBARA McNAIR** Actress/singer. (Racine, WI) She was on Mitch Miller's program with Leslie Uggams and Diana Trask back in the 1960's and had a variety hour with little talk and lots of music in 1969-1970. Year/Age: 1995/**56** 1996/**57** 1997/**58**

- **CHASTITY BONO** (Los Angeles, CA) The daughter of Sonny and Cher. She has her own band, CEREMONY. The title of their first album was "Hang Out Your Poetry." *Chastity* was the title of a 1969 movie written by Sonny, in which Cher starred (her first solo film). Year/Age: 1995/**26** 1996/**27** 1997/**28**

- **MIRIAM MAKEBA** Singer. (Johannesburg, South Africa) South African singer. Biggest hit: "Pata Pata" in 1967. She was married to South African trumpeter Hugh Masekela before she returned to Africa as the wife of American black nationalist Stokely Carmichael. Year/Age: 1995/**63** 1996/**64** 1997/**65**

- **RAY "BOOM BOOM" MANCINI** Fighter. WBA lightweight champ in the '80s. Year/Age: 1995/**34** 1996/**35** 1997/**36**

- **JANE GOODALL** Anthropologist. (London, England) Famous for her work with chimps. Year/Age: 1995/**61** 1996/**62** 1997/**63**

- **EUGENE FODOR** Violinist. (Denver, CO) Year/Age: 1995/**44** 1996/**45** 1997/**46**

- **BOBBY FISCHER** First U.S. World Chess Champion. (Chicago, IL) He became champ in 1972. He was surrounded by 200 bodyguards when he played a 1992 rematch with Boris Spassky in Yugoslavia, only 50 miles from the Bosnia War zone. He won that match too. Year/Age: 1995/**51** 1996/**52** 1997/**53**

- **CHRIS SQUIRE** Guitarist. (England) With the group YES. Their biggest hit: "Owner of a Lonely Heart" in 1983. Year/Age: 1995/**47** 1996/**48** 1997/**49**

- **BOBBY WOMACK** Singer. (Cleveland, OH) A soul vocalist, guitarist and songwriter. He toured as SAM COOKE'S guitarist and played backup on sessions for WILSON PICKETT, BOX TOPS, JANIS JOPLIN and others. He was married for a time to Sam Cooke's widow. His biggest hit: "Lookin' For a Love" in 1974. Year/Age: 1995/**51** 1996/**52** 1997/**53**

- **KNUTE ROCKNE** Former Notre Dame football coach. (1888-1931 – Norway) Tired of being the lone Norwegian Protestant, he joined the Catholic Church and surprised his son by converting in time for them to celebrate their First Communions together. He was immortalized in the film *Knute Rockne,* with Pat O'Brien and then-actor former president Ronald Reagan as George "The Gipper" Gipp. Rockne died in a plane crash (3-31-31).

FACTS FROM THE PAST

1829   **ANDREW "Old Hickory" JACKSON** held the first inauguration outdoors on the East Front of the Capitol Building and invited his supporters to join him for punch and ice cream after the ceremony. 20,000 people showed up, consuming all the food and liquor they could, and then caused extensive damage in the all-night celebration. Jackson escaped and stayed at Badsby's Hotel.

1849   **DAVID RICE ATCHISON** served as President of the U.S. for one day. President-elect Zachary Taylor was supposed to assume office that day, but decided to wait until the next day—Monday—to be inaugurated. So the presidency passed from former President Polk to Atchison, who was President Pro Tem of the Senate.

1877   The microphone was invented by **EMILE BERLINER** and the Bell system later produced it, saving the company from financial ruin.

1881   **JAMES GARFIELD** became the first president to move his mother into the White House.

1917   **JEANNETTE RANKIN**, a Republican from Montana, took her seat as a member of Congress. She was the first woman to be elected to the House of Representatives.

1925   The first radio broadcast of a presidential inauguration took place when 30th U.S. President **CALVIN COOLIDGE** took office.

1933   **FRANKLIN DELANO ROOSEVELT** was inaugurated as the 32nd President. Part of his New Deal inauguration speech contained the famous quote: "The only thing we have to fear is fear itself." Roosevelt became the last U.S. President inaugurated on March 4th.

1950   **WALT DISNEY'S** *Cinderella* was released. In the original story the slipper was made of fur. In the movie it was glass.

1990   Loyola Marymount University basketball star **HANK GATHERS** died after collapsing on the court during a West Coast Conference post-season tournament game. He had begun easing the heart medication dosages because he said the medication was sapping his strength. He became the second player to lead Division I in scoring (32.7), rebounding (13.7) and was WCC's all-time leading scorer.

1993   **MOHAMMED A. SALAMEH** was charged in the Feb. 26, 1993, bombing of the New York Trade Center. More arrests followed.

1994   White House Counsel **BERNARD NUSSBAUM** informed Clinton of his resignation as a result of being subpoenaed by counsel investigating the Whitewater land deal.

MARCH 5

What else can hear a dog whistle?

BIRTHDAYS

• **SAMANTHA EGGAR** Actress. (Born Victoria Eggar in London, England) She received an Oscar nomination for best actress in 1965 for *The Collector*. She has also appeared in *Walk, Don't Run* and *Doctor Dolittle*. Year/**Age**: 1995/**55** 1996/**56** 1997/**57**

• **NIKKI TAYLOR** Model. Year/**Age**: 1995/**20** 1996/**21** 1997/**22**

• **DEAN STOCKWELL** Actor. (Hollywood, CA) American boy actor of the 1940's and later a leading man. He appeared in *The Green Years* and *The Boy With Green Hair* among others. Nominated for an Academy Award as best supporting actor in *Married to the Mob*. He played the son of Nick and Nora Charles in some of the *Thin Man* films. TV's "Quantum Leap." "Ben" in *Blue Velvet*. Year/**Age**: 1995/**59** 1996/**60** 1997/**61**

• **FRED WILLIAMSON** Football. (Gary, IN) Former defensive back – one-time announcer on "Monday Night Football" – and played the boyfriend on the TV series "Julia" starring Diahann Carroll. Year/**Age**: 1995/**57** 1996/**58** 1997/**59**

• **MICHAEL WARREN** Actor. (South Bend, IN) Played the level-headed officer, Bobby Hill, on "Hill Street Blues" and also was on the soap opera, "Days of our Lives." Year/**Age**: 1995/**49** 1996/**50** 1997/**51**

• **JAMES SIKKING** Actor. (Los Angeles, CA) Dr. James Hobart on TV's "General Hospital," Lt. Howard Hunter on "Hill Street Blues," and dad on "Doogie Howser." Year/**Age**: 1995/**62** 1996/**63** 1997/**64**

• **ROCKY BLEIER** Former Pittsburgh Steeler. (Appleton, WI) He played college ball at Notre Dame when the Fighting Irish won the National Championship in 1966. He was on four Steeler Super Bowl teams after he returned from duty in Vietnam with his leg damaged by an exploding grenade. Year/**Age**: 1995/**48** 1996/**49** 1997/**50**

• **EDDIE HODGES** Actor/singer. (Hattiesburg, MS) Hit: "I'm Gonna Knock on Your Door". Frank Sinatra's son in the film *Hole in the Head*. Year/**Age**: 1995/**48** 1996/**49** 1997/**50**

• **JAMES NOBLE** Actor. (Dallas, TX) In *A Tiger's Tale*. Year/**Age**: 1995/**73** 1996/**74** 1997/**75**

• **MICHAEL IRVIN** Football. (Fort Lauderdale, FL) With the Dallas Cowboys. Year/**Age**: 1995/**29** 1996/**30** 1997/**31**

• **PAUL SAND** Actor. (Born Paul Sanchez in Los Angeles, CA) He played Dr. Michael Ridley on "St. Elsewhere." Year/**Age**: 1995/**51** 1996/**52** 1997/**53**

• **MARSHA WARFIELD** Comedienne. Plays bailiff Roz Russell on TV's "Night Court." Year/**Age**: 1995/**41** 1996/**42** 1997/**43**

• **DEL CRANDALL** Former baseball catcher/manager. Now a TV announcer for Milwaukee Brewers. Year/**Age**: 1995/**65** 1996/**66** 1997/**67**

• **JACK CASSIDY** Actor. (1927-1976 – New York, NY) Tony winner for *She Loves Me*. He was married to Shirley Jones. (Died 12-12-76)

• **ANTOINE DE LA MOTHE CADILLAC** Settler. (1658-1730 – France) Founded the city of Detroit.

• **ANDY GIBB** Singer. (1958-1988 – Manchester, England) Younger brother of the BEE GEES (their name comes from the initials of a DJ and a promoter). His biggest hits: "Shadow Dancing" and "I Just Want to Be Your Everything." He sold more than 15 million records by the time he was 21. The two-time Grammy Award nominee died from a heart condition. In 1982, he became heavily involved in drugs after the breakup of his relationship with TV star Victoria Principal. (Died 3-1-88.)

• **EMMETT J. CULLIGAN** Tycoon. (1893-1970 – Yankton, SD) He started the water-treatment business in 1936, based on what he had learned when he softened wash water so his baby's diapers would come out fluffy. He eventually owned the world's largest water-treatment company. (Died 6-3-70.)

• **BOB WILLS** C&Wmusican. (1905-1975 – Born James Robert Wills in Kosse, TX) Formed the TEXAS PLAYBOYS in 1933. Their biggest hits: "San Antonio Rose" in 1940 and "New Spanish Two Step" in 1946 (#1 on the C&W charts for 16 weeks). (Died 3-13-75.)

• **SIR REX HARRISON** Actor. (1908-1990 – Born Reginald Carey Harrison in Huyton, England) He won an Oscar in 1964 for best actor as Professor Higgins in *My Fair Lady*. His first U.S. movie role was *Anna and the King of Siam* in 1946. He played the King. The plot of the film was adapted by Rodgers and Hammerstein as a musical, and filmed with great success in 1956 as *The King and I*. Also, *Doctor Dolittle*. (Died 6-2-90.)

FACTS FROM THE PAST

1766 Spaniard **DON ANTONIO DE ULLOA**, arrived in New Orleans to take possession of the Louisiana Territory from the French.

1924 **FRANK CARUANA,** from Buffalo, NY, bowled 29 straight strikes, for a three-game total of 847.

1946 At Westminster College in Fulton, MO, **WINSTON CHURCHILL** gave his famous speech about Stalin and Russia, calling the suppression of news in Russia "the Iron Curtain," using the term for the first time.

1953 *Science Digest* magazine hit the newsstands with an article entitled "Why Stalin May Live to Be 100." On that same day, **JOSEPH STALIN** died.

1960 Singer **ELVIS PRESLEY** was discharged from the army in one of the most-publicized returns of a soldier since General MacArthur.

1977 The first radio broadcast of a presidential phone-in took place nationwide on CBS. *Ask President Carter* featured the president and moderator **WALTER CRONKITE** from the White House oval office. The president fielded questions from 42 listeners in 26 states.

1982 Jake Blues, better known as **JOHN BELUSHI**, dies of a drug overdose.

1994 Former Jefferson Starship singer, **GRACE SLICK**, pointed a gun at police officers at her home and was charged with felony assault.

Why don't we feel radio waves?

MARCH 6

BIRTHDAYS

• **ROB REINER** Actor/director. (Bronx, NY) He won 2 Emmys for his role as the Meathead on "All in the Family." Son of Carl. He directed *Sleepless in Seattle* and *North.* Year/**Age:** 1995/**50** 1996/**51** 1997/**52**

• **SHAQUILLE "SHAQ" O'NEAL** Basketball. Plays for the Orlando Magic. 7-foot, 1-inch-tall, 300-pound NBA Rookie of the Year. He was in the film *Blue Chips*. Does Pepsi commercials. Discards size 20 shoes after 2 games (he doesn't like scuff marks). His biography is called *Shaq Attaq* and his rap CD is entitled *Shaq Diesel*. Year/**Age:** 1995/**22** 1996/**23** 1997/**24**

• **DAVID GILMOUR** Guitarist. (England) With PINK FLOYD. Biggest hit: "Another Brick in the Wall" in 1980. Toured in 1994. Year/**Age:** 1995/**48** 1996/**49** 1997/**50**

• **MARION S. BARRY, JR.** Former mayor of Washington, DC. (Itta Bena, MS) Year/**Age:** 1995/**59** 1996/**60** 1997/**61**

• **ED McMAHON** TV personality. (Detroit, MI) He began by selling pots and pans and vegetable slicers on the Boardwalk in Atlantic City. He broke into TV in 1954 as Johnny Carson's sidekick on a daytime quiz show, "Who Do You Trust?" and was on the "Tonight Show" from 1962 to 1992. He has also been involved with the TV shows "Star Search" and "Bloopers & Practical Jokes." Year/**Age:** 1995/**72** 1996/**73** 1997/**74**

• **TOM ARNOLD** Actor. The star of "The Jackie Thomas Show" and former husband of Roseanne Barr. Film *True Lies*. Year/**Age:** 1995/**36** 1996/**37** 1997/**38**

• **JOANNA MILES** Actress. Appeared on "All My Children." Won an Emmy in "The Glass Menagerie." Year/**Age:** 1995/**55** 1996/**56** 1997/**57**

• **KIKI DEE** Singer. (England) Her biggest hit with ELTON JOHN: "Don't Go Breaking My Heart" in 1976. Year/**Age:** 1995/**48** 1996/**49** 1997/**50**

• **BEN MURPHY** Actor. (Jonesboro, AR) He started his film career with a bit part in *The Graduate*. He appeared in "Name of the Game" and the "Winds of War" TV miniseries. He played Jed "Kid" Curry in "Alias Smith and Jones." Year/**Age:** 1995/**53** 1996/**54** 1997/**55**

• **LEROY GORDON COOPER** Astronaut. (Shawnee, OK) Of the original 7 astronauts. Year/**Age:** 1995/**68** 1996/**69** 1997/**70**

• **WILLIE STARGELL** Baseball. (Born Wilver Dornell in Earlsboro, OK) Pittsburgh Pirate slugger, chosen NL World Series MVP, 1979. In 1965, he hit a home run in the All-Star game and the ball landed inside a tuba in the area where the band was sitting. Year/**Age:** 1995/**54** 1996/**55** 1997/**56**

• **MARY WILSON** Singer. (Detroit, MI) One of the original SUPREMES. Before 1970, they had more consecutive number-one hits than any group in U.S. history. She has written a book about them. Their biggest hit: "Baby Love" in 1964. Year/**Age:** 1995/**51** 1996/**52** 1997/**53**

• **LOU COSTELLO** Actor. (1908-1959 – Paterson, NJ) The comedy team of Abbott and Costello was one of the best in the movies from 1941-51. Their most famous recording was "Who's On First?" for which they were inducted in the Baseball Hall of Fame. (Died 3-3-59.)

• **ELIZABETH BARRETT BROWNING** English poet. (1806-1861) She was addicted to opium because of a chronic spinal ailment. Her father was opposed to having his children marry so Elizabeth eloped with poet Robert Browning in 1846. She was 40 and he 33. (Died 6-29-1861.)

• **MICHELANGELO** Painter. (1475-1564 – Born Michelangelo di Lodovico Buonarroti-Simoni at Caprese, Tuscany) He spent $4^{1}/_{2}$ years single-handedly painting the ceiling of the Sistine Chapel in Rome. (Died 2-18-1564.)

FACTS FROM THE PAST

1836 The Alamo fell to a Mexican force when 5,000 Mexicans killed all 187 Texas revolutionaries in a 13-day siege. Among the dead were **DAVY CROCKETT** and the man who invented the Bowie knife, **JIM BOWIE.**

1853 VERDI'S opera *La Traviata* premiered in Venice, Italy.

1896 The first appearance of an automobile on the streets of Detroit occurred when **CHARLES BRADY KING** drove his horseless carriage down one of its main streets. When his auto broke down, spectators responded by telling him to "get a horse!"

1930 The first frozen food, developed by **CLARENCE BIRDSEYE**, was sold in grocery stores in Springfield, MA. Birdseye got his idea after seeing Canadians thawing and eating naturally frozen fish.

1933 A nationwide bank holiday declared by **PRESIDENT FRANKLIN D. ROOSEVELT** went into effect to help save the nation's faltering banking system. Most banks reopened after a 10-day "holiday."

1955 Comedienne **PHYLLIS DILLER** made her debut in San Francisco at the Purple Onion nightclub.

1967 The daughter of Joseph Stalin, **SVETLANA ALLILUYEVA,** appeared at the U.S. Embassy in India and announced her intention to defect to the West. She later returned to Russia.

1970 Notre Dame star **AUSTIN CARR** scored a playoff record 61 pts. as the Irish beat Ohio State 112-82 in an NCAA tournament game.

1972 **JOHN LENNON**'s temporary visa was revoked. The Department wanted Lennon deported because of a drug arrest and his involvement with the radical left. Lennon battled four years before being granted permanent-resident status in the U.S. in 1976.

1981 "CBS Evening News" anchorman **WALTER CRONKITE** retired after 19 years. His final words: "I'll be away on assignment, and Dan Rather will be sitting in for the next few years. Good night!"

1994 **FRANK SINATRA** collapsed on stage while performing in Richmond, VA. He was taken to the hospital, but was released within a couple of hours.

MARCH 7

Two burgers, a large fries—and a diet soft drink?

BIRTHDAYS

- **MATTHEW FISHER** Keyboardist. (England) With POCO HARUM, hits include: "Whiter Shade of Pale" in 1967. Their name comes from the pedigree papers of a drug dealer's Siamese cat, meaning "beyond these things." Year/**Age:** 1995/**49** 1996/**50** 1997/**51**

- **DANIEL TRAVANTI** Actor. (Kenosha, WI) His Emmy-winning performance as Capt. Frank Furillo on "Hill Street Blues" led to the role of John Walsh in "Adam," the TV docu-drama about missing children. In the movie *Millenium*. Year/**Age:** 1995/**55** 1996/**56** 1997/**57**

- **FRANCO HARRIS** Football running-back. (Fort Dix, NJ) He played for the Pittsburgh Steelers. Year/**Age:** 1995/**45** 1996/**46** 1997/**47**

- **LYNN SWANN** Football. (Alcoa, TN) Wide receiver for the Pittsburgh Steelers. 1975 Super Bowl MVP. Year/**Age:** 1995/**43** 1996/**44** 1997/**45**

- **JANET GUTHRIE** Racecar driver. (Iowa City, IA) She was the first woman to race in the Indy 500 in 1977. Year/**Age:** 1995/**57** 1996/**58** 1997/**59**

- **IVAN LENDL** Tennis star. (Czechoslovakia) One of the top players in the world. He spent 156 straight weeks as the number-one player in the world. Only Jimmy Connors has surpassed that record. He received his long-awaited U.S. citizenship in 1992. Year/**Age:** 1995/**35** 1996/**36** 1997/**37**

- **PETER WOLF** Singer. (Born Peter Blankfield in Boston, MA) With the J. GEILS BAND, biggest hit: "Centerfold" in 1981. Former Boston DJ, formerly married to actress Faye Dunaway. Year/**Age:** 1995/**49** 1996/**50** 1997/**51**

- **CHRIS WHITE** Bass guitarist. (England) With the ZOMBIES. Year/**Age:** 1995/**53** 1996/**54** 1997/**55**

- **JOE CARTER** Baseball. (Oklahoma City, OK) With the Toronto Blue Jays. '93 World Series star. Year/**Age:** 1995/**35** 1996/**36** 1997/**37**

- **MICHAEL EISNER** Chairman of Disney Corp. (Mt. Kisco, NY) Year/**Age:** 1995/**53** 1996/**54** 1997/**55**

- **WILLARD SCOTT** TV weatherman. (Alexandria, VA) Appears on the "Today Show." At one time he played "Bozo the Clown." Year/**Age:** 1995/**61** 1996/**62** 1997/**63**

- **LORD SNOWDON** Photographer. (Born Anthony Armstrong-Jones in London) He is England's most famous photographer. He was married and later divorced from Britain's Princess Margaret. Year/**Age:** 1995/**65** 1996/**66** 1997/**67**

- **KIM, THE KOREAN** Genius. Kim's I.Q. was measured at 210, the highest ever recorded. At age 5, he was writing poetry, speaking 4 languages and mastering calculus. Kim's parents were both university professors who were born the same day at exactly the same time. Year/**Age:** 1995/**32** 1996/**33** 1997/**34**

- **TAMMY FAYE BAKKER** TV evangelist. Jim Bakker's ex. Married Kansas developer Roe Messner in 1993. Year/**Age:** 1995/**53** 1996/**54** 1997/**55**

- **JOHN HEARD** Actor. (Washington, DC) He played Brother Timothy in *Heaven Help Us* and was Macaulay Culkin's dad in *Home Alone*. Also in *Big The Pelican Brief* and *Beaches*. Year/**Age:** 1995/**50** 1996/**51** 1997/**52**

- **JAMES BRODERICK** Actor (1927-1982 – Charlestown, NH) Played the husband in the TV series "Family." In the movie *Dog Day Afternoon*. (Died 11-1-82.)

- **MAURICE RAVEL** Composer. (1875-1937 – France) Composer of "Bolero," which was used as the theme in the movie *10*. (Died 12-28-37.)

FACTS FROM THE PAST

1530   **KING HENRY VIII'S** request for a divorce was turned down by the Pope. Henry then declared that he, not the Pope, was the supreme head of England's church.

1857   The **DRED SCOTT DECISION** was handed down by the Supreme Court. It said that black Americans were not full citizens, after an escaped slave named Scott filed a lawsuit to have himself declared free. His owner set him free anyway and Scott went on to become a hotel porter. Within a few years the slavery issue was resolved.

1876   **ALEXANDER GRAHAM BELL** patented the telephone, thinking he was creating a potential method of communicating with deaf people. (See March 3rd birthdays.) 50 years later, to the day, the first transatlantic call was made between New York and London.

1897   **DR. JOHN KELLOGG** served the world's first corn flakes to his patients at a mental hospital in Battle Creek, MI.

1936   **ADOLF HITLER** ordered his troops to march into the Rhineland, thereby breaking the Treaty of Versailles and the Locarno Pact.

1959   Melvin Garlow of Alexandria, VA, became the **FIRST PILOT** to log more than one **MILLION MILES** in a jet. It took him 4 years.

1969   The **WHO'S** "Pinball Wizard" was released in Britain. It was the first public airing of a selection from the rock opera *Tommy*, which would be played in its entirety later in the year.

1975   **JOHN EHRLICHMAN, CHARLES COLSON** and **G. GORDON LIDDY** were indicted for their part in the 1971 break-in at the office of Daniel Ellsberg's former psychiatrist, Dr. Louis Fielding. Ellsberg was the Pentagon's paper leaker.

1983   **PHIL MAHRE** won the Alpine World Cup Championship. He was the third person ever to win three consecutive titles.

1986   **THE VIOLENT FEMMES** are the first new wave group to play Carnegie Hall.

1990   Health and Human Services Secretary **LOUIS SULLIVAN** announced the government would propose a more informative food-labeling system that would require the disclosure of the fat, fiber and cholesterol content of nearly all packaged foods.

1994   Supreme Court rules **RAP RENDITION** of Roy Orbison's classic "Pretty Woman" by "2 Live Crew" legal.

If struck by lightning, you'll probably survive.

MARCH 8

BIRTHDAYS

- **MICKEY DOLENZ** Monkee. (Los Angeles, CA) Their biggest hit: "I'm a Believer" in 1967. Appeared in the TV series "Circus Boy" in 1956 as Mickey Braddock. Year/**Age**: 1995/**50** 1996/**51** 1997/**52**

- **PEGGY MARCH** Singer. (Born Margaret Battavio – Lansdale, PA.) At 15 years old, she became the youngest female artist to have a number-one record: "I Will Follow Him." Year/**Age**: 1995/**47** 1996/**48** 1997/**49**

- **CAROL BAYER SAGER** Lyricist. (NYC) Was married to composer Marvin Hamlisch and in 1982 married Burt Bacharach. Co-wrote: "Nobody Does It Better," "Midnight Blue." She also wrote "That's What Friends Are For." Year/**Age**: 1995/**49** 1996/**50** 1997/**51**

- **SUE ANN LANGDON** Actress. Appeared on the "Jackie Gleason Show" from 1962-1966. Year/**Age**: 1995/**59** 1996/**60** 1997/**61**

- **CLAIRE TREVOR** Actress. (Born Claire Wemlinger in NYC) She won an Oscar in 1948 for supporting actress in *Key Largo* with Humphrey Bogart. Year/**Age**: 1995/**86** 1996/**87** 1997/**88**

- **LYNN REDGRAVE** Actress. (London, England) Oscar nominee in 1966 for best actress in *Georgy Girl*. Sister of actress Vanessa, daughter of actor Sir Michael. She was fired from the TV series "House Calls" for breast-feeding her baby on the set. Year/**Age**: 1995/**52** 1996/**53** 1997/**54**

- **RANDY MEISNER** Bassist/vocalist. (Scottsbluff, NE) Formerly with The EAGLES. Biggest hit: "One of These Nights" in 1975. Also worked with POCO and Rick Nelson's STONE CANYON BAND. Year/**Age**: 1995/**49** 1996/**50** 1997/**51**

- **JIM RICE** Baseball player. (Anderson, SC) Boston Red Sox outfielder who led the AL in home runs in 1977-78 and was MVP in 1978. Year/**Age**: 1995/**42** 1996/**43** 1997/**44**

- **JIM BOUTON** Baseball player/sportscaster. (Newark, NJ) He wrote a controversial book, *Ball Four,* upsetting many players and their wives. Year/**Age**: 1995/**56** 1996/**57** 1997/**58**

- **MIKE LOWRY** Politician. Is Governor of Washington. Year/**Age**: 1995/**56** 1996/**57** 1997/**58**

- **RICHIE ALLEN** Baseball star. (Wampum, PA) He broke in with the Philadelphia Phillies in 1964, had 138 runs batted in and was rookie of the year. Year/**Age**: 1995/**53** 1996/**54** 1997/**55**

- **CYD CHARISSE** Dancer/actress. (Born Tula Finklea in Amarillo, TX) Last dancing partner of Fred Astaire. Appeared in *Brigadoon*. Year/**Age**: 1995/**74** 1996/**75** 1997/**76**

- **AIDAN QUINN** Actor. In Films *Avalon, Desperately Seeking Susan, Benny & Joon, Blink,* and *Legends of the Fall*. Year/**Age**: 1995/**36** 1996/**37** 1997/**38**

- **JAMIE LYN BAUR** Actress. (Chicago, IL) Soap opera star on "The Young & The Restless." Year/**Age**: 1995/**46** 1996/**47** 1997/**48**

- **JOHNNY DOLLAR** C&W singer (1933-1986 – Kilgore, TX) Biggest hit: "Stop the Start" in 1966.

- **ALAN HALE, JR.** Actor. (1918-1990 – Los Angeles, CA) Best known for playing the jovial skipper of a zany band of castaways on television's "Gilligan's Island." His father was a matinee idol in silent films, often a sidekick to Errol Flynn. He was cremated and his ashes scattered at sea. (Died 1-2-90.)

- **LEW DeWITT** C&W musician. (1938-1990 – Roanoke, VA) With STATLER BROTHERS. He wrote their biggest hit: "Flowers on the Wall" in 1966. He was the group's tenor and guitarist for 18 years before leaving in 1982. (Died 8-15-90.)

- **OLIVER WENDALL HOLMES, JR.** Justice. (1841–1935 – Boston, MA) On the U.S. Supreme Court from 1902-1932. (Died 3-6-35.)

- **SIMON CAMERON** Army Officer. (1808-1889 – Lancaster County, PA) Junior officer under Robert E. Lee. Later he became a high-ranking officer with the War Department in Washington. He was so vindictive that he confiscated General Robert E. Lee's house and made it into a military cemetery. His definition of an honest politician was "one who, when bought, stays bought." (Died 6-26-1889.)

- **SAM JAFFEE** Journalist. (1924-1985 – San Francisco, CA) ABC News correspondent who covered the Vietnam War from 1961-69. (Died 2-8-85.)

FACTS FROM THE PAST

1862 NAT GORDON, the last of the pirates, was hanged in NYC for stealing a cargo of about 1,000 slaves.

1930 Yankee slugger **BABE RUTH** signed an $80,000 per year contract. He was told he'd make more than President Hoover. Ruth said: "Why not, I had a better year than he did."

1950 **MARSHALL VOROSHILOV** announced that the Soviets had the A-Bomb.

1970 **DIANA ROSS** performed her first solo concert after leaving the Supremes. It was in Framingham, MA.

1971 Heavyweight champion **JOE FRAZIER** won a 15-round decision over **MUHAMMAD ALI** at Madison Square Garden in New York City. Ali was almost paralyzed from the fight. Frank Sinatra and Hugh Hefner had $250 ringside seats. Ali was previously undefeated.

1973 **PAUL McCARTNEY** was fined 100 pounds for growing marijuana on his Scotland farm.

1985 A new record entered the Guinness Book after **JOHN McPHERSON** from Newcastle, England, kissed 4,444 women in 8 hours.

1987 **BOB SEGER** announced during a concert in Detroit that his *Like a Rock* tour would be his last.

1992 Former Mousketeer and Beach Party movie star **ANNETTE FUNICELLO** revealed that she had multiple sclerosis.

MARCH 9

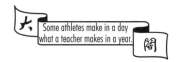
Some athletes make in a day what a teacher makes in a year.

BIRTHDAYS

- **ROBIN TROWER** Guitarist. (Essex, England) With POCO HARUM. Year/**Age**: 1995/**50** 1996/**51** 1997/**52**

- **RAUL JULIA** Actor. (Born Raul Rafael Carlos Julia Arcelay in San Juan, PR) *Kiss of the Spider Woman, Tequila Sunrise, and Adam Family Values.* Year/**Age**: 1995/**55** 1996/**56** 1997/**57**

- **TRISH VAN DEVERE** Actress. (Tenafly, NJ) American leading lady in the 1970's. She's married to George C. Scott. Appeared in *Islands in the Stream.* Year/**Age**: 1995/**52** 1996/**53** 1997/**54**

- **MICKEY SPILLANE** Mystery writer. (Born Frank Morrison in Brooklyn, NY) Before *Mike Hammer* detective books, Spillane was a comic book writer who helped create *Captain Marvel* and *Captain America.* Year/**Age**: 1995/**77** 1996/**78** 1997/**79**

- **EMMANUEL LEWIS** Actor. (Brooklyn, NY) From the TV series "Webster." Only 3 feet, 6 inches tall. Year/**Age**: 1995/**24** 1996/**25** 1997/**26**

- **KEELEY SMITH** Singer. (Norfolk, VA) With her husband, Louie Prima, biggest hit: "That Old Black Magic" in 1958. They divorced in 1962. Year/**Age**: 1995/**60** 1996/**61** 1997/**62**

- **NEIL ARMSTRONG** Former Chicago Bears coach. (Tishomingo, OK) Year/**Age**: 1995/**69** 1996/**70** 1997/**71**

- **JEFFREY OSBORNE** Singer. (Providence, RI) His hits include "You Should Be Mine" in 1986 and "On The Wings of Love" 1982. Year/**Age**: 1995/**47** 1996/**48** 1997/**49**

- **ANDY NORTH** Pro golfer. (WI) Year/**Age**: 1995/**45** 1996/**46** 1997/**47**

- **ANDRE COURREGES** Fashion designer. (Paris, France) Year/**Age**: 1995/**72** 1996/**73** 1997/**74**

- **MICKEY GILLEY** C&W. (Natchez, MS) Cousin to Jerry Lee Lewis and Evangelist Jimmy Swaggart. Biggest hit: "Stand By Me." He owned Gilley's Nightclub from 1971-89, the subject of the film *Urban Cowboy.* Year/**Age**: 1995/**59** 1996/**60** 1997/**61**

- **FAITH DANIELS** Talk-show hostess. TV's "A Closer Look." Year/**Age**: 1995/**38** 1996/**39** 1997/**40**

- **DANNY SULLIVAN** Racecar driver. (Louisville, KY) Won Indy 500 in 1985. Year/**Age**: 1995/**45** 1996/**46** 1997/**47**

- **JIMMIE FADDEN** Musician. (Long Beach, CA) With NITTY GRITTY DIRT BAND. Biggest hit: "Mr. Bojangles" in 1970. Year/**Age**: 1995/**47** 1996/**48** 1997/**49**

- **MARK LINDSAY** Singer. (Caldwell, ID) Former lead singer for PAUL REVERE AND THE RAIDERS. Biggest hits: "Arizona" and, with the Raiders, "Indian Reservation" in 1971. Year/**Age**: 1995/**52** 1996/**53** 1997/**54**

- **PAT LEAHY** Placekicker. (St. Louis, MO) Played 18 seasons with the New York Jets, the longest any kicker has lasted with one club. In 1992 he ranked third-highest scorer in NFL history, behind George Blanda and Jan Stenerud. Year/**Age**: 1995/**44** 1996/**45** 1997/**46**

- **FERNANDO BUJONES** Ballet dancer. (Miami, FL) Year/**Age**: 1995/**40** 1996/**41** 1997/**42**

- **BARBIE** Doll. Over 800 million dolls have sold since her birthday. Inventor Ruth Handler received complaints about her breasts. Year/**Age**: 1995/**36** 1996/**37** 1997/**38**

- **YURI GAGARIN** Cosmonaut. (1934-1968) The world's first spaceman; a Russian cosmonaut. At age 27 he made his famous 108-minute flight in a rocket-propelled five-ton space capsule, 187 miles above the earth's surface. In 1968, he was killed when his jet plane crashed on a routine training flight. After his death, his home town was renamed Gagarin; the Gagarin Museum was established in his boyhood home. (Died 3-27-68.)

- **AMERIGO VESPUCCI** [ves-pooch'-ee] Italian navigator. (1451-1512 – Florence, Italy) He sailed to the New World seven years after Columbus. In honor of his accomplishments, a mapmaker named Martin Waldseemueller published a book in 1507 that referred to the new land as America. (Died 2-22-1512.)

FACTS FROM THE PAST

1796 **NAPOLEON** married Josephine in Paris after he had arrived two hours late for the wedding. Both gave their ages as 28. In reality he was 27 and she 32. On their wedding night, her dog bit him on the leg.

1822 A patent for artificial teeth was granted to **CHARLES GRAHAM** of New York.

1832 **ABRAHAM LINCOLN** announced he was running for his first political office. He failed in his bid for a seat in the Illinois legislature. He was unsuccessful in four future tries for Congress and the Senate before becoming President of the U.S. in 1860.

1945 **NAPALM** was used on a large-scale basis for the first time in a raid over Tokyo, Japan, in World War II. **GENERAL CURTIS LEMAY** ordered more than 200 B-29 bombers to drop 1,900 tons of the burning gel. 80,000 were killed and a million left homeless.

1954 CBS newsman **EDWARD R. MURROW** critically reviewed Wisconsin Senator **JOSEPH R. McCARTHY'S** anti-communism campaign on the television program "See It Now."

1961 The first animal to return from space was a dog named **BLACKIE,** aboard the Soviet spacecraft Sputnik-9. A dog named Laika was orbited in Sputnik-2 but the Russians had no intention of bringing him back. He was killed following a radio command from Earth.

1969 The **SMOTHERS BROTHERS** TV show was canceled by CBS after they refused to censor a comment made by Joan Baez. She wanted to dedicate her song to her husband, David, who was about to go to jail for objecting to the draft.

1987 Paul McCartney, John Lennon, Carole King, Gerry Goffin, and Carole Bayer Sager were inducted into the **SONGWRITERS HALL OF FAME.**

1994 **BORIS YELTSON** refused to meet with Richard Nixon due to the former President's talks with the armed resistance against Yeltsen.

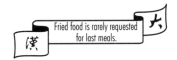

Fried food is rarely requested for last meals.

MARCH 10

BIRTHDAYS

- **CHUCK NORRIS** Actor. (Born Carlos Ray Norris in Ryan, OK) In films *Delta Force, Firewalker,* and *Sidekicks.* Year/Age: 1995/**55** 1996/**56** 1997/**57**
- **PRINCE EDWARD of BRITAIN** (London, England) His full name is Prince Edward Anthony Richard Louis. He is fifth in line for the Throne. Year/**Age:** 1995/**31** 1996/**32** 1997/**33**
- **SHARON STONE** Actress. (Pennsylvania) Appeared nude in *Basic Instinct* playing opposite Michael Douglas and in a *Playboy* layout in 1990. Films include: *Total Recall, Sliver, The Immortals, The Quick and the Dead,* and *Intersection.* Year/Age: 1995/**37** 1996/**38** 1997/**39**
- **PAMELA MASON** Actress. (Born Pamela Ostrer in Westgate, England) She was married to actor James Mason from 1940 to 1964, when they divorced. Year/Age: 1995/**77** 1996/**78** 1997/**79**
- **DEAN TORRENCE** Singer of JAN & DEAN. Their biggest hit: "Surf City" in 1963. Year/Age: 1995/**55** 1996/**56** 1997/**57**
- **KATHARINE HOUGHTON** Actress. (Los Angeles, CA) She played Joey, Sidney Poitier's fiancee in *Guess Who's Coming to Dinner* in 1967. She's the niece of Katharine Hepburn. Year/Age: 1995/**48** 1996/**49** 1997/**50**
- **TOM SCHOLZ** Musician. (Boston, MA) He formed the group BOSTON. He plays guitar and keyboards. Their biggest hit: "Amanda" in 1986. Year/Age: 1995/**48** 1996/**49** 1997/**50**
- **BOB GREENE** Newspaper columnist. (Columbus, OH) Wrote book *All Summer Long.* Year/**Age:** 1995/**48** 1996/**49** 1997/**50**
- **DAVID RABE** Playwright. (Dubuque, IA) Year/Age: 1995/**55** 1996/**56** 1997/**57**

- **SHANNON TWEED** Actress. TV's "Major Dad." One time Playboy Plammate of the Year. Year/Age: 1995/**38** 1996/**39** 1997/**40**
- **JASMINE GUY** Actress/singer. Plays Whitley Gilbert on "Different World." Appeared in the TV miniseries *Queen.* Year/Age: 1995/**31** 1996/**32** 1997/**33**
- **LINDA JEZEK** Swimmer. (Palo Alto, CA) Year/Age: 1995/**34** 1996/**35** 1997/**36**
- **EDIE BRICKELL** Singer Year/Age: 1995/**29** 1996/**30** 1997/**31**
- **BIX BEIDERBECKE** Jazz coronetist. (1903-1931 – Born Leon Beiderbecke in Davenport, IA) The first white musician to influence jazz. (Died 8-7-31.)
- **SAM JAFFE** Character actor. (1891-1984 – NYC) Appeared in *Gunga Din, Ben Hur, The Asphalt Jungle,* and on TV, he was Dr. David Zorba, chief of neurosurgery on the "Ben Casey" series. (Died 3-24-84.)
- **BARRY FITZGERALD** Actor. (1888-1961 – Born William Joseph Shields in Dublin, Ireland) He won an Oscar for supporting actor in 1944 in *Going My Way* with Bing Crosby, who won the Oscar for best actor. During WWII the Oscars were made of plaster, instead of metal. While Barry was practicing his golf swing at home, he decapitated his Oscar. (Died 1-4-61.)
- **KENNETH BURNS** Comic singer. (1923-1989 – Knoxville, TN) Jethro of HOMER and JETHRO, the original song parady duo. Biggest hit: "The Battle of Kookamonga" in 1959.

FACTS FROM THE PAST

1849 An Illinois attorney received a patent for an inflatable airbag to lift grounded boats off sandbars and shoals. The inventor, **ABE LINCOLN**, was too busy with politics to pursue the invention and it never got off the ground (or the water).

1863 The first royal wedding took place at Windsor Castle in St. George's chapel. **EDWARD, PRINCE OF WALES,** married **ALEXANDRA, PRINCESS OF DENMARK.** Victoria was Queen at the time.

1864 **ULYSSES S. GRANT** became commander of the Union armies in the Civil War.

1868 **HENRY WARD BEECHER**, pastor of the Plymouth Church in Brooklyn, NY, began selling printed copies of his sermons for 5 cents each. His sister was Harriet Beecher Stowe, the author of Uncle Tom's Cabin.

1876 While working, he spilled acid on his clothes and, in a panic, **ALEXANDER GRAHAM BELL** transmitted the first telephone message to his assistant in the next room: "Mr. Watson, come here, I want you." This happened at Cambridge, MA.

1933 The Great Long Beach Earthquake in Southern California was one of the quakes **DR. CHARLES RICHTER** studied in devising the "Richter Scale" of earthquake intensity. It was classed a 6.3.

1949 **MILDRED E. GILLARS**, who had made wartime broadcasts for the Nazis under the name Axis Sally, was convicted of treason in Washington. She served 12 years in prison.

1969 **JAMES EARL RAY** pleaded guilty in Memphis, TN, to the assassination of civil rights leader Martin Luther King, Jr. Ray later repudiated that plea. He was sentenced to 99 years in prison.

1980 **DR. HERMAN TARNOWER,** the famed diet doctor of Scarsdale, NY, was shot and killed in his home in Purchase, NY, and his long-time friend, Jean Harris, was charged with the murder. She was released from prison in ill health in 1992.

1980 The stage was set for the break-up of Ma Bell after investor **SAM WYLY** from Dallas won a $50 million lawsuit against AT&T.

1993 **DR. DAVID GUNN WAS SHOT** to death outside an abortion clinic in Pensacola, FL.

MARCH 11

Take a hike. Literally.

BIRTHDAYS

- **CHERYL LYNN** Singer. (Los Angeles, CA) She was discovered on "The Gong Show." Her biggest record: "Got to be Real" in 1978. Year/Age: 1995/**38** 1996/**39** 1997/**40**

- **SUSAN RICHARDSON** Actress. Susan Bradford on TV's "Eight Is Enough." Year/Age: 1995/**43** 1996/**44** 1997/**45**

- **SAM DONALDSON** ABC news correspondent. (El Paso, TX) "Prime Time Live." Year/**Age**: 1995/**61** 1996/**62** 1997/**63**

- **ANTONIN SCALIA** Supreme Court Justice. (Trenton, NJ) Reagan nominee, sworn in September 26, 1986. He's a conservative. Year/Age: 1995/**59** 1996/**60** 1997/**61**

- **MIKE HUGG** Drummer. With the British group MANFRED MANN. Their biggest hit: "Do Wah Diddy Diddy" in 1964. Year/Age: 1995/**55** 1996/**56** 1997/**57**

- **DOROTHY SCHIFF** Former *New York Post* publisher. (NYC) She was the first woman publisher in the U.S. Year/**Age**: 1995/**92** 1996/**93** 1997/**94**

- **RUPERT MURDOCH** Contemporary newspaper publisher. (Australia) *Times* of London, *NY Post* and *Boston Herald*. The *Post* suspended publication in 1993 after 192 years. Murdoch decided not to repurchase the paper. Year/**Age**: 1995/**64** 1996/**65** 1997/**66**

- **HAROLD WILSON** Former British Prime Minister. (Huddersfield, England) Held office twice. Year/Age: 1995/**79** 1996/**80** 1997/**81**

- **BOBBY McFERRIN** Singer. (New York, NY) Biggest hit: "Don't Worry, Be Happy" from the 1988 movie *Cocktail*. Year/**Age**: 1995/**45** 1996/**46** 1997/**47**

- **DOCK ELLIS** Baseball. He was with the Yankees in the 1970's. Year/Age: 1995/**49** 1996/**50** 1997/**51**

- **VALERIE FRENCH** Actress. (England) Year/Age: 1995/**63** 1996/**64** 1997/**65**

- **TROY RUTTMAN** Racecar driver. Year/Age: 1995/**65** 1996/**66** 1997/**67**

- **JERRY ZUCKER** Movie producer. (Whitefish Bay, WI) His films include: *Airplane, Ruthless People, Naked Gun, My Life,* and *Ghost.* Year/Age: 1995/**45** 1996/**46** 1997/**47**

- **LAWRENCE WELK** Bandleader. (1903 - 1992 – Strassburg, ND) He headed TV's most durable musical TV show, "The Lawrence Welk Show." It ran from 1951-1982, giving 1,542 performances, with "champagne" music. The theme was based on a letter from a fan who said the band's music sparkled and bubbled. A friend who had seen the Miller High Life billboard advertising the "champagne of bottled beer," suggested this would be a perfect tie-in. Welk's often imitated phrases included "Ah one, an' ah two." (Died 5-17-92.)

- **VANNEVAR BUSH** Engineer. (1890-1974 – Everett, MA) He constructed the world's first analog computer when he was 35 in 1925. It took up an entire 20 x 30 foot room. We can do the same job today with a computer that sits on our desk.

- **MALCOLM CAMPBELL** Racecar driver. (1885-1945 – England) The first man to travel 300 mph in an automobile.

- **DR. RALPH ABERNATHY** Civil Rights leader. (1926–1990 – Linden, AL) He was Martin Luther King, Jr.'s closest aide and best friend; together they organized the 1955 Montgomery bus boycott. (Died 4-17-90.)

FACTS FROM THE PAST

105   **TS'AI LUN** of China invented paper. He made it from bamboo, mulberry and other fibers, along with fish nets and rags.

1302   **ROMEO MONTEVECCIO** and **JULIET CAPPELLETO** were married in Citadela, Italy. Shakespeare based a play on their lives.

1619   **MARGARET AND PHILIPPA FLOWER** were burned at the stake for practicing witchcraft in Lincoln, England. Known as the Flower sisters, the two women, along with their mother, Joan, had cast spells upon various members of their employer's family. Joan didn't help things during the trial when she picked up a piece of bread and said, "May this choke me if I am guilty." Then she took a bite of the bread and dropped dead.

1810   Emperor **NAPOLEON BONAPARTE** married Marie Louise, the 18-year-old daughter of the Emperor of Austria. Marie had never seen Napoleon. She didn't even see him on the wedding day. He sent a stand-in to represent him in the marriage ceremony.

1930   **WILLIAM HOWARD TAFT** became the first president to be buried in Arlington National Cemetery. The portly president weighed more than 300 pounds at the time of his death.

1942   WWII **GENERAL DOUGLAS MACARTHUR** departed the Phillipines for Australia. Upon leaving, he said, "I shall return."

1954   The U.S. Army charged that Wisconsin **SENATOR JOSEPH MCCARTHY** and his subcommittee's chief counsel, Roy Cohn, had used pressure to obtain favored treatment for Private G. David Schine, a former consultant to the subcommittee.

1985   **MIKHAIL GORBACHEV** was named general secretary of the ruling **COMMUNIST PARTY**. At 54, he was the youngest ruler since Stalin. He took over the position one day after the death of Konstantin Chernenko.

1985   Labor Secretary **RAYMOND DONOVAN** resigned. He faced fraud charges in New York. He was the first sitting Cabinet member ever indicted.

1988   Saying "I got a fair hearing, and the people have decided," **GARY HART** withdrew a second time from the race for the 1988 Democratic presidential nomination.

1990   In Chile, **VICE PRESIDENT QUAYLE** sent a Secret Service agent into a shop to buy an anatomically correct Indian statuette.

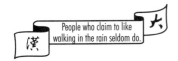
People who claim to like walking in the rain seldom do.

MARCH 12

BIRTHDAYS

- **EDWARD ALBEE** Broadway playwright. (Washington, D.C.) Wrote award winning play and movie, *Who's Afraid Of Virginia Woolf?*, *A Delicate Balance*, and *Fragment*. Year/**Age**: 1995/**67** 1996/**68** 1997/**69**

- **JERRY LEVINE** Actor. (New Brunswick, NJ) Appeared in *Born on the Fourth of July* and *Teen Wolf*. Year/**Age***:* 1995/**38** 1996/**39** 1997/**40**

- **LIZA MINNELLI** Entertainer. (Los Angeles, CA) She has won every major show-biz award: Emmy, Tony, Grammy and Oscar (for best actress in 1972 for *Cabaret*). Appeared in *Arthur II*. Liza is the daughter of Judy Garland and film director Vincente Minnelli. Year/**Age**: 1995/**49** 1996/**50** 1997/**51**

- **BARBARA FELDON** Actress. (Pittsburg, PA) She starred in the "Get Smart" TV series as Agent 99 from 1965-1969 on NBC with Don Adams. Year/**Age**: 1995/**54** 1996/**55** 1997/**56**

- **AL JARREAU** Soul/jazz vocalist. (Milwaukee, WI) He won four Grammys. His biggest hit "We're In This Love Together" in 1981. Year/**Age**: 1995/**55** 1996/**56** 1997/**57**

- **JOHNNY RUTHERFORD** Racecar driver. (Ft. Worth, TX) He has won the Indy 500 three times. Year/**Age**: 1995/**57** 1996/**58** 1997/**59**

- **JAMES TAYLOR** Singer. (Boston, MA) Biggest hit: "You've Got A Friend" in 1971. He had a popular album called *Sweet Baby James* in 1970. He was married to Carly Simon from 1972 to 1982. Year/**Age**: 1995/**47** 1996/**48** 1997/**49**

- **ANDREW YOUNG** Politician. (New Orleans, LA) Former Ambassador to the UN and ex-mayor of Atlanta, GA. Year/**Age**: 1995/**63** 1996/**64** 1997/**65**

- **WALLY SCHIRRA** Ex-astronaut. (Hackensack, NJ) Original Mercury VII astronaut who still does network commentary on the space program. Year/**Age**: 1995/**72** 1996/**73** 1997/**74**

- **LANE KIRKLAND** AFL-CIO President. (Camden, SC) Year/**Age**: 1995/**73** 1996/**74** 1997/**75**

- **DALE MURPHY** Baseball. (Portland, OR) His most productive years were with the Atlanta Braves. Later, the Philadelphia Phillies and Colorado Rockies. He retired in 1993. Year/**Age**: 1995/**39** 1996/**40** 1997/**41**

- **MARLON JACKSON** Singer. (Gary, IN) One of the JACKSON FIVE. Biggest hit: "I'll Be There" in 1970. Year/**Age**: 1995/**38** 1996/**39** 1997/**40**

- **PAUL KANTNER** Guitarist. (San Francisco, CA) With JEFFERSON AIRPLANE, formed in San Francisco by Paul and Marty Balin, and featuring lead singer Grace Slick. Their biggest hit: "Miracles" in 1975. Year/**Age**: 1995/**53** 1996/**54** 1997/**55**

- **DARRYL STRAWBERRY** Baseball. (Los Angeles, CA) Dodger outfielder, he signed a 20 million-dollar contract in 1990. Signed with the San Francisco Giants 6-19-94, six weeks after release from a drug treatment center. Year/**Age**: 1995/**33** 1996/**34** 1997/**35**

- **JON PROVOST** Actor. Timmy (1957-1964) on TV's "Lassie." Year/**Age**: 1995/**45** 1996/**46** 1997/**47**

- **CLEMENT STUDEBAKER** Manufacturer. (1831-1901 – near Gettysburg, PA) He was the largest producer of carriages and wagons in America.

- **EARL NIGHTINGALE** Radio commentator (1921-1989) He worked for WGN in Chicago and was the voice of the adventure character Sky King during the 1950's.

- **GORDON MacRAE** Actor/singer. (1921-1986 – East Orange, NJ) He starred in the movie musicals in the 1950's including *Oklahoma* and *Carousel*. (Died 1-24-86.)

- **CHARLES C. BOYCOTT** Land Owner. (1832-1897) He was a farm property manager in Ireland. When the crops failed and the farmers went broke, he unsympathetically gave them the choice of paying immediately or being evicted. The farmers retaliated and his staff quit. His family was isolated. This tactic gave us the word "boycott." (Died 6-19-1897.)

FACTS FROM THE PAST

1912   **JULIETTE GORDON LOW** founded an organization in Savannah, GA, called the Girl Guides, which later became the Girl Scouts of America, the world's largest organization for girls with more than 3 million members. This day ends Girl Scouts Week.

1933   **PRESIDENT FRANKLIN ROOSEVELT** became the first president to talk directly to Americans on radio.

1951   The comic strip "Dennis the Menace" by **HANK KETCHUM** debuted. Actor Jay North played Dennis on TV. Inspiration for the character was Ketchum's own son, Dennis.

1969   Beatle **PAUL McCARTNEY** married Linda Eastman in London. McCartney's brother Mike McGear was best man. No other Beatles attended.

1974   The TV show "Wonder Woman" premiered, starring **LYNDA CARTER.**

1980   A Chicago jury found birthday-party clown **JOHN WAYNE GACY** guilty of the murders of 33 men and boys. He was convicted of luring them to his home, where they were killed and buried beneath his house. He was executed by lethal injection 5-10-94.

1987   **WILLIAM LEE GOLDEN** was asked to leave the country group, the Oak Ridge Boys, after 22 years. He was replaced by Steve Sanders. Friction within the group had been rumored since Golden grew a beard and waist-length hair.

1992   **TAMMY FAYE BAKKER** announced that she was divorcing her husband, Jim, after 31 years of marriage. Jim Bakker got the news at the Federal Medical Center in Rochester, MN, where he is serving an 18-year sentence for swindling his PTL ministry followers.

1993   In the LPGA Tour, golfer **ANNE MARIE PALLI** was five under par in the ninth when her second shot hit a flying duck. Both the ball and the duck fell into the water. The dead duck cost her a penalty. She finished two under for the first 36 holes.

MARCH 13

BIRTHDAYS

- **ADAM CLAYTON** Bass guitarist. (Ireland) With U2. Hits include: "Desire" and "With or Without You." Year/**Age**: 1995/**35** 1996/**36** 1997/**37**
- **NEIL SEDAKA** Singer/songwriter. (Brooklyn, NY) While still in high school, he was selected by Arthur Rubenstein as NYC's young, outstanding classical pianist. At age 16, he thought the best way to make friends was to write "pop" music. He formed a songwriting team with lyricist Howard Greenfield while attending Lincoln High School, which lasted over 20 years. They wrote "Breaking Up is Hard to Do" and some songs for CONNIE FRANCIS. Neil's career revived in 1975 when he had his biggest hit with ELTON JOHN: "Bad Blood." Year/**Age**: 1995/**56** 1996/**57** 1997/**58**
- **WALTER ANNENBERG** Publisher. (Milwaukee, WI) He founded *TV Guide*. Former ambassador to Great Britain. Year/**Age**: 1995/**86** 1996/**87** 1997/**88**
- **ANDY BEAN** Golfer. (Lafayette, GA) He has earned well over $2 million since turning pro in 1975. Year/**Age**: 1995/**42** 1996/**43** 1997/**44**
- **DONALD DUCK** Disney Character. Year/**Age**: 1995/**61** 1996/**62** 1997/**63**
- **TESSIE O'SHEA** Actress. (Wales) British musical star. *The Russians Are Coming* and *Bedknobs & Broomsticks*. Year/**Age**: 1995/**77** 1996/**78** 1997/**79**
- **DANA DELANY** Actress. (New York, NY) She won an Emmy for TV series "China Beach." Was Hayley "As The World Turns." In films *Live Nude Girls, Housesitter, Tombstone, Exit to Eden,* and *Light Sleeper* in 1992. Year/**Age**: 1995/**39** 1996/**40** 1997/**41**
- **TRACY WELLS** Actress. (Encino, CA) Plays on TV's "Mr. Belvedere." Year/**Age**: 1995/**24** 1996/**25** 1997/**26**

- **WILL CLARK** Baseball. Year/**Age**: 1995/**31** 1996/**32** 1997/**33**
- **DEBORAH RAFFIN** Actress. (Los Angeles, CA) She appeared in *The Dove* in 1974 and *Haywire* as well as some TV roles. Year/**Age**: 1995/**42** 1996/**43** 1997/**44**
- **ROBIN DUKE** Actress. (Canada) Appeared on "Saturday Night Live" in 1984. Appears as Molly Earl on SCTV. Year/**Age**: 1995/**41** 1996/**42** 1997/**43**
- **DONNY YORK** Musician. Of SHA NA NA. Their biggest hit: "Just Like Romeo and Juliet" in 1975. Year/**Age**: 1995/**46** 1996/**47** 1997/**48**
- **LIZ ANDERSON** C&W singer. (Roseau, MN) Her first charted record was in 1964. Mother of C&W singer LYNN ANDERSON. Year/**Age**: 1995/**74** 1996/**75** 1997/**76**
- **PERCIVAL LOWELL** Astronomer. (1855-1916 – Boston) Founder of the Lowell Observatory at Flagstaff, AZ. He initiated the search that resulted in the discovery of the planet Pluto, announced 14 years after his death on this day in 1930. (Died 11-12-16.)
- **JOSEPH PRIESTLEY** English clergyman and scientist. (1733-1804) Discovered oxygen. (Died 2-6-1804.)
- **SAMMY KAYE** Bandleader. (1910-1987 – Born Samuel Zarnocay, Jr., in Lakewood, OH) Biggest hit: "Daddy" in 1941. Another of his hits was composed on the spur of the moment. On Dec. 7, 1941, his weekly "Sunday Serenade" radio show was interrupted by the news flash of the Japanese attack on Pearl Harbor. He was so affected by the news that he went home and wrote the song, "Remember Pearl Harbor." (Died 6-2-87.)
- **WILLIAM CASEY** Former CIA director. (1913-1987) He died at age 74, just when his testimony was wanted in the Iran-contra scandal. (Died 5-6-87.)

FACTS FROM THE PAST

1639 Harvard University was named for clergyman **JOHN HARVARD.**

1781 The planet Uranus was discovered by English astronomer **SIR WILLIAM HERSCHEL**. He first thought it was a comet.

1852 A tall, skinny old guy, wearing a beard and ridiculous red, white and blue clothes, made his debut as a cartoon character in the *New York Lantern.* "**UNCLE SAM**" became the symbol of the USA.

1868 The impeachment trial of **PRESIDENT ANDREW JOHNSON** began in the U.S. Senate.

1877 Teenager **CHESTER GREENWOOD** received a patent for earmuffs. He established a factory in his hometown of Farmington, ME.

1930 The 9th planet in the solar system, Pluto, was discovered by **CLYDE W. TOMBAUGH.** The planet is only one-tenth as large as Earth, has no atmosphere and is 4 billion miles away.

1934 **JOHN DILLINGER** and his gang robbed the First National Bank in Iowa. Baby Face Nelson waited outside in the getaway car. When a woman customer ran out of the bank and said, "They're robbing the bank," Nelson responded: "You're telling me."

1980 Ford Motor Chairman **HENRY FORD II** announced he was stepping down. That same day, a jury in Winamac, IN, found Ford Motor Company innocent of reckless homicide in the fiery deaths of three young women inside a Ford Pinto.

1986 The Philippine government confirmed it had discovered a bank account containing $800 million, in the name of exiled **PRESIDENT FERDINAND MARCOS** and within days, hundreds of millions more were discovered. When the presidential palace was opened to the public, the people saw many expensive possessions including hundreds of pairs of shoes owned by First Lady Imelda Marcos.

1987 "Heat of the Night" a hit by **BRYAN ADAMS** was first commercially released as a cassette single, marking the commencement of this new marketing technique.

1994 U.S. Troops pulled out of Somalia. General Jogn Shalikashvili told Marines to ignore those who called the mission a failure because, **"PEOPLE ARE ALIVE TODAY BECAUSE YOU ARE HERE."**

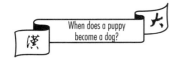

When does a puppy become a dog?

MARCH 14

BIRTHDAYS

- **HANK KETCHAM** Cartoonist. (Seattle, WA) Created cartoon strip "Dennis The Menace" in 1951. Year/**Age**: 1995/**74** 1996/**75** 1997/**76**
- **KATE MABERLY** Actress. *The Secret Garden.* Year/**Age**: 1995/**13** 1996/**14** 1997/**15**
- **J. FRED MUGGS** Chimpanzee. Former "Today Show" co-host. He worked with host, Dave Garroway, in 1953 at age 10 months. The 4¹/₂-foot chimp now weighs 162 pounds and lives with his owner, Buddy Mennella, in Tampa, FL. Year/**Age**: 1995/**42** 1996/**43** 1997/**44**
- **RICK DEES** TV/radio DJ. (Jacksonville, FL) Number one hit in 1976, "Disco Duck (Part I)." Talk show host, "Into The Night" and has a syndicated music radio show. Year/**Age**: 1995/**44** 1996/**45** 1997/**46**
- **LARRY JOHNSON** Basketball. Charlotte Hornets star who signed an $84 million contract in 1993. Year/**Age**: 1995/**26** 1996/**27** 1997/**28**
- **BILLY CRYSTAL** Entertainer. (Long Beach, NY) He played a gay on "Soap" and is well known for his Fernando Lamas routine on "Saturday Night Live." He starred with Danny DeVito in *Throw Mamma From the Train.* Also *City Slickers,* with daughter Lindsay and *Mr. Saturday Night.* Former MC of the Oscars. Year/**Age**: 1995/**48** 1996/**49** 1997/**50**
- **PHIL PHILLIPS** Singer. (Lake Charles, LA) He is a former DJ. His biggest hit: "Sea of Love" in 1959. It was used in the movie of the same name thirty years later. Year/**Age**: 1995/**63** 1996/**64** 1997/**65**
- **LES BROWN** Bandleader. (Reinerton, PA) Wrote "Sentimental Journey," recorded with Dinah Shore. Year/**Age**: 1995/**82** 1996/**83** 1997/**84**
- **MICHAEL CAINE** Actor. (Born Maurice Micklewhite in London, England.) He received Oscar nominations for best actor in *Alfie* in 1966, *Sleuth* in '72 and *Educating Rita* in 1984. He received an *Oscar for Hannah and Her Sisters* Year/**Age**: 1995/**61** 1996/**62** 1997/**63**
- **PRINCE ALBERT GRIMALDI of MONACO** Heir to the Monaco throne, son of Prince Rainier & Princess Grace of Monaco and brother of Princesses Caroline and Stephanie. Year/**Age**: 1995/**36** 1996/**37** 1997/**38**
- **WALTER PARAZAIDER** Saxophonist. (Chicago, IL) Hits with CHICAGO include: "Hard To Say I'm Sorry" and "If You Leave Me Now." Year/**Age**: 1995/**49** 1996/**50** 1997/**51**

- **FRANK BORMAN** Ex-astronaut. (Gary, IN) Retired Eastern Airlines President. Year/**Age**: 1995/**66** 1996/**67** 1997/**68**
- **KIRBY PUCKETT** Baseball. (Chicago, IL) Minnesota Twins heavy-hitting outfielder. Year/**Age**: 1995/**33** 1996/**34** 1997/**35**
- **EUGENE CERNAN** Former astronaut. (Chicago, IL) Year/**Age**: 1995/**60** 1996/**61** 1997/**62**
- **ADRIAN ZMED** Actor. (Chicago, IL) In the film *Grease II* and TV's "T.J. Hooker" series. Year/**Age**: 1995/**40** 1996/**41** 1997/**42**
- **WALTER PARAZAIDER** Saxophonist. (Chicago, IL) Hits with CHICAGO include: "Hard To Say I'm Sorry" and "If You Leave Me Now." Year/**Age**: 1995/**49** 1996/**50** 1997/**51**
- **QUINCY JONES** Musician. (Chicago, IL) At age 14, he met Ray Charles and worked the R&B clubs in Seattle with him. He was a jazz composer/arranger/bandleader in Europe by age 30. He produced Michael Jackson's *Thriller* album and is second in number of Grammy wins with 25. Sir Georg Solti is first with 30. Year/**Age**: 1995/**61** 1996/**62** 1997/**63**
- **JANN BROWNE** C&W singer. Her grandparents, Lillie Belle Moore and Foy Gene, were square dancers on the Grand Ole Opry. Year/**Age**: 1995/**40** 1996/**41** 1997/**42**
- **MAX SHULMAN** Novelist. (1919-1988 – St. Paul, MN) *The Many Loves of Dobie Gillis, Rally Round the Flag Boys,* and *The Tender Trap.* (Died 8-28-88.)
- **ALBERT EINSTEIN** Scientist. (1879-1955 – Germany) He was 27 years old when he originated the Theory of Relativity, making atomic weapons possible. Whenever he was confused he said, "I will go and do a little think." He failed a high school math class, and was so absentminded that he once used a $1,500 Rockefeller check as a bookmark – then lost the book. He was 4 years old before he could speak and 7 years old before he could read. (Died in Princeton, NJ, on 4-18-55.)
- **JOHN LUTHER "CASEY" JONES** Railroad engineer. (1864-1900 – Born near Cayce, KY) He died at age 36 in the wreck of the Cannonball Express in Mississippi. He became a hero for saving others lives in the crash and was celebrated in song and legend.
- **LUCY HOBBS TAYLOR** Dentist. (1833-1910 – New York State) The first woman in America to receive a degree in dentistry or to be admitted to membership in a state dental association. (Died 10-3-10.)

FACTS FROM THE PAST

1794   **ELI WHITNEY** received a patent on his cotton gin. The cotton gin separated cotton from its seed and revolutionized the South.

1923   **PRESIDENT WARREN G. HARDING** became the first chief executive to file an income tax report.

1940   The first motion picture featuring both **MAE WEST** and **W.C. FIELDS** was released: *My Little Chickadee.*

1964   A Dallas jury found tavern-owner **JACK RUBY** guilty of murdering Lee Harvey Oswald, the man accused of assassinating President Kennedy. Millions of people had seen Ruby shoot Oswald on live TV in 1963. Ruby died of cancer awaiting a new trial.

1972   California Governor **RONALD REAGAN** pardoned country star Merle Haggard, after he'd served three years in San Quentin.

1972   **BURT REYNOLDS** became the first nude centerfold when the April edition of *Cosmopolitan* magazine hit the newstands.

1990   The Soviet Congress elected **MIKHAIL S. GORBACHEV** to the country's presidency, one day after clearing the post.

MARCH 15
Buzzard's Day

What is your favorite
TV commercial?

BIRTHDAYS

• **FABIO** Male Model. (Born Fabio Lanzoni in Italy) Once the highest paid model in the world; named 1993 Sexiest Man of the Year by *Cosmopolitan* magazine. He models for covers of over 100 million copies of romance novels. Recorded album "Fabio After Dark" and appeared on TV's "Acupulco Heat." Year/**Age**: 1995/**34** 1996/**35** 1997/**36**

• **TERRY CUMMINGS** Basketball. (Chicago, IL) Milwaukee Bucks and Portland Trailblazers. Year/**Age**: 1995/**34** 1996/**35** 1997/**36**

• **TERENCE TRENT D'ARBY** Singer. (NYC) Number-one hit in 1988: "Wishing Well." Year/**Age**: 1995/**33** 1996/**34** 1997/**35**

• **JIMMY SWAGGART** Reverend. (Farriday, LA) In 1988, he admitted in a tearful confession that he had sinned. In 1991, he was stopped by police for a traffic violation with a prostitute in the car, who said he asked for sex. At one time, his TV ministry had millions of viewers. Year/**Age**: 1995/**60** 1996/**61** 1997/**62**

• **MacDONALD CAREY** Actor. (1913-1994 Sioux City, IA) Plays Dr. Tom Horton on the soap opera "Days of Our Lives," which premiered back in 1965. (Died 3-21-94.)

• **MIKE LOVE** Singer. (Los Angeles, CA) Biggest hit with the BEACH BOYS: "I Get Around" in 1964. Year/**Age**: 1995/**54** 1996/**55** 1997/**56**

• **SLY STONE** Singer. (Born Sylvester Stewart in Dallas, TX) With SLY & THE FAMILY STONE, their biggest record: "Everyday People." Year/**Age**: 1995/**51** 1996/**52** 1997/**53**

• **PHIL LESH** Bass guitarist. (San Francisco) With the psychedelic rock group, the GRATEFUL DEAD. Hit: "Touch of Grey" in 1987. Year/**Age**: 1995/**54** 1996/**55** 1997/**56**

• **PARK OVERALL** Actress. TV's "Empty Nest." Year/**Age**: 1995/**38** 1996/**39** 1997/**40**

• **RY COODER** Guitarist. Started as backup artist for Jackie DeShannon. He released the first digital rock album *Bop Till You Drop* in 1979. Year/**Age**: 1995/**48** 1996/**49** 1997/**50**

• **MARK GREEN** Columnist. (Brooklyn, NY) Seen on TV's "Crossfire." Year/**Age**: 1995/**50** 1996/**51** 1997/**52**

• **ALAN BEAN** Ex-astronaut. (Wheeler, TX) Year/**Age**: 1995/**63** 1996/**64** 1997/**65**

• **RUTH BADER GINSBURG** Judge. (Brooklyn, NY) Nominated to the Supreme Court by President Clinton to replace retiring Justice Byron White. Year/**Age**: 1995/**61** 1996/**62** 1997/**63**

• **CARL SMITH** C&W singer. (Maynardsville, TN) He sold over 16 million records in his career. Hit: "Let Old Mother Nature Have Her Way" in 1951. Year/**Age**: 1995/**67** 1996/**68** 1997/**69**

• **JUDD HIRSCH** Actor. (Bronx, NY) He played Alex Reiger, a career cabbie on "Taxi" and won 2 Emmys for the role. He was the psychiatrist in *Ordinary People*. Star of TV's "Dear John." Year/**Age**: 1995/**60** 1996/**61** 1997/**62**

• **DEE SNIDER** Singer. (Long Island, NY) TWISTED SISTER. "We're Not Gonna Take It," 1984. Year/**Age**: 1995/**40** 1996/**41** 1997/**42**

• **NORM VAN BROCKLIN** Football quarterback, (1926-1983 – Eagle Butte, MT) He was the quarterback of two NFL championship teams, later became a coach, and was inducted into the Pro Football Hall of Fame. (Died 5-2-83,)

• **HARRY JAMES** Trumpet player, (1916-1983 – Albany, GA) Some of his biggest hits include: "You Made Me Love You," "I Don't Want to Walk Without You," and "I've Heard That Song Before." He was married to Betty Grable. (Died 7-5-83,)

• **ANDREW JACKSON** 7th U.S. President, (1767-1845 – Born in Waxhaws, SC) Hero of the Battle of New Orleans. He was accused of marrying an adultress, kept race horses in the White House stable and spent most of his time gambling and dueling. Affectionately known as Old Hickory, he was wounded in a duel with Charlie Dickinson at Harrison's Mills, KY, on May 30, 1806. Charlie was killed in that duel. The bullet in Andy's chest was too close to his heart to be removed safely, so he carried it for the rest of his life. (Died 6-8-1845,)

FACTS FROM THE PAST

44 B.C. Emperor **JULIUS CAESAR** was assassinated in Rome. (Known as the Ides of March.)

1875 Roman Catholic Archbishop of New York **JOHN McCLOSKEY** was named the first American Cardinal by Pope Pius IX.

1892 The first escalator was patented by inventor **JESSE W. RENO** of New York City.

1913 **WOODROW WILSON** held the first presidential press conference after being in office for only 11 days. He insisted that questions be submitted in writing, and he chose which ones to answer. There were only newspapers at that time, no radio or TV!

1945 The **KING COLE TRIO** led by Nat King Cole had the first #1 LP on the first *Billboard* magazine top-selling record album chart.

1958 Entertainer **ELVIS PRESLEY** was drafted into the U.S. Army.

1962 Basketball star **WILT CHAMBERLAIN** scored his 4,000th point of the season, averaging 50.4 points per game.

1964 Actress **ELIZABETH TAYLOR** married **RICHARD BURTON** (for the first time) on the 8th floor of the Ritz-Carlton in Montreal.

1990 Pay-Per-View Cable TV broke all previous concert records with orders for the **NEW KIDS ON THE BLOCK** live in concert from Uniondale, NY. The concert was viewed in 13.7 million homes.

1994 **BURT REYNOLDS** was mugged as he left a book store. One of the attackers recognized him and ran. Burt said, "I guess with my divorce from Loni Anderson they realized I had no money."

Like scotch, opera is an acquired taste.

MARCH 16

BIRTHDAYS

• **LEO McKERN** Actor. (Australia) He appeared in *The Mouse That Roared*, the Beatles' film *Help!*, and *A Man For All Seasons*. In PBS TV series "Rumpole of the Bailey." Year/Age: 1995/75 1996/76 1997/77

• **JERRY LEWIS** Comic actor. (Born Josef Levitch in Newark, NJ) He's been chairman of the MD Association since 1950 and hosts the annual telethon. He had a successful film career with sidekick Dean Martin until 1958. He had a hit record in 1956: "Rock-a-Bye Your Baby with a Dixie Melody." Year/Age: 1995/69 1996/70 1997/71

• **BERNARDO BERTOLUCCI** Film director. (Italy) He directed *The Last Tango in Paris* and was charged with obscenity in Rome for the film. He was eventually cleared because of "changing morals." Bernardo directed *The Sheltering Sky* and won an Oscar in 1988 for *The Last Emperor*. Year/Age: 1995/55 1996/56 1997/57

• **WALTER CUNNINGHAM** Ex-astronaut. (Crescent, IA) Author of the book, *The All American Boys*. He was an astronaut for 8 years. Year/Age: 1995/53 1996/54 1997/55

• **HOLLIS STACY** Golfer. (Savannah, GA) On the pro golf circuit, she has earned over a million dollars. Year/Age: 1995/41 1996/42 1997/43

• **ERIK ESTRADA** Actor. (NYC) He appeared on the TV series "CHIPS." He appeared in National Lampoon's *Loaded Weapon I*, a Mexican soap opera and a Taco Bell commercial for which he was paid $150,000. Year/Age: 1995/46 1996/47 1997/48

• **JERRY JEFF WALKER** Singer/guitarist. (Born Ronald Crosby in Oreonta, NY) He wrote "Mr. Bojangles." Year/Age: 1995/53 1996/54 1997/55

• **HENNY YOUNGMAN** Comedian. (England) He had his own show with Rocky Graziano in 1955. It was designed to fill the rest of the hour, if and when ABC's Wednesday-night boxing matches were short. Year/Age: 1995/89 1996/90 1997/91

• **NANCY WILSON** Guitarist/singer. (Seattle, WA) HEART. Biggest hit: "Alone" 1987. Year/Age: 1995/41 1996/42 1997/43

• **DANIEL PATRICK MOYNIHAN** Senator. (Tulsa, OK) D/NY. He wrote the book *Maximum Feasible Misunderstanding*. Year/Age: 1995/68 1996/69 1997/70

• **KATE NELLIGAN** Actress. (Canada) Appeared on "Masterpiece Theater." Appeared in the films *Frankie & Johnny* and *Prince of Tides*. Year/Age: 1995/44 1996/45 1997/46

• **PAT NIXON** Former First Lady. (1911-1993 – Born Thelma Ryan in Ely, NV) Wife of the 37th U.S. President Richard Nixon. They were married for 53 years. Her dad nicknamed her Pat because she was born the day before St. Patrick's Day. (Died 6-22-93.)

• **JAMES MADISON** 4th U.S. President. (1751-1836 – Port Conway, VA) He graduated from Princeton, and drafted the "Virginia Plan" which became the basis of the U.S. Constitution. He was only 5 feet, 4 inches tall and weighed 100 pounds – the smallest U.S. president. He was the only president to face enemy gunfire while in office. (Died 6-28-1836.)

FACTS FROM THE PAST

1521 Portuguese navigator **FERDINAND MAGELLAN** reached the Philippines, where he was killed by natives the following month.

1850 *The Scarlet Letter*, written by **NATHANIEL HAWTHORNE**, was first published.

1926 **ROBERT GODDARD**, for whom a NASA space center is named, tested the first space-type liquid-fueled rocket. The rocket traveled for 2½ seconds, covering 184 feet at a speed of 60 miles per hour and attaining a maximum height of 41 feet.

1956 Former heavyweight champion **JOE LOUIS** made his debut as a pro wrestler. He knocked out 320-pound cowboy Rocky Lee. The referee was another former heavyweight champ, Jersey Joe Walcott.

1966 The **FIRST DOCKING IN ORBIT** was achieved by astronauts **NEIL ARMSTRONG** and **DAVID SCOTT** when **GEMINI VIII** docked with an Agena rocket. Soon afterward, the mission had to be discontinued when the spaceship began to spin violently.

1968 U.S. Marines attacked a village in Vietnam which they called Pinkville. They killed at least 347 civilians – possibly more than 500 – in the massacre at My Lai. Freelance reporter **RON RIDENHOUR** blew the whistle after a year of cover-ups and the war lost much support from middle-class Americans.

1970 Singer **TAMMI TERRELL** died at 24 following a sixth brain tumor operation. The tumor was discovered when she collapsed into Marvin Gaye's arms onstage in 1967. Her death moved Gaye toward writing more serious material.

1974 The first performance from the new Grand Ole Opry House at Opryland in Nashville, TN, took place. **PRESIDENT NIXON** helped open the new facility by playing three songs on the piano. He also played with a yo-yo on stage like opry star Roy Acuff.

1985 **TERRY ANDERSON**, chief Middle East correspondent for the Associated Press, was abducted by gunmen in Beirut. He was the longest-held American hostage in Lebanon. He was released Dec. 4, 1991.

1988 **JULIE CROTEAU** from St. Mary's College in Maryland became the **FIRST WOMAN TO PLAY ON A NCAA** men's baseball team.

1994 **TONYA HARDING AVOIDS JAIL** by pleading guilty to a felony charge associated with the Nancy Kerrigan attack.

MARCH 17
Saint Patrick's Day

Perhaps we should go back to the one-room school.

BIRTHDAYS

- **JIM WEATHERLY** C&W. (Pontotoc, MS) Wrote "The Best Thing That Ever Happened to Me" and "Midnight Train to Georgia," hits for GLADYS KNIGHT and the PIPS. His biggest hit: "I'll Still Love You" in 1975. Year/Age: 1995/**52** 1996/**53** 1997/**54**

- **SUSIE ALLANSON** C&W singer. (Minneapolis, MN) She was in the film *Jesus Christ Superstar*. Her biggest hits: "Maybe Baby" (a remake of Buddy Holly's 1958 hit) and "We Belong Together" in 1978. Year/Age: 1995/**43** 1996/**44** 1997/**45**

- **MERCEDES McCAMBRIDGE** Actress. (Joliet, IL) She won an Oscar for best supporting actress in *All the King's Men* in 1945. Year/Age: 1995/**77** 1996/**78** 1997/**79**

- **PATRICK DUFFY** Actor. (Townsend, MT) He made a strange return from Pam's dream on the "Dallas" TV series in 1987. Now on TV's "Step By Step." Year/Age: 1995/**46** 1996/**47** 1997/**48**

- **JOHN SEBASTIAN** Singer/composer. (NYC) He was a 1960's "rock" influence. When he was asked to compose the theme song for a new TV show called "kotter" the only title that seemed to work was "Welcome Back." The show's producers liked it and promptly changed the name of the show. He founded THE LOVIN' SPOONFUL. Biggest hit was "Summer in the City" in 1966. Year/Age: 1995/**51** 1996/**52** 1997/**53**

- **DANNY AINGE** Basketball. With the Phoenix Suns. Year/Age: 1995/**36** 1996/**37** 1997/**38**

- **HANK SAUER** Baseball. He was National League MVP with the Cubs in 1952, when he hit 37 homers and drove in 121 runs. He hit 30 or more home runs in six seasons. Year/Age: 1995/**76** 1996/**77** 1997/**78**

- **KURT RUSSELL** Actor. (Springfield, MA) Appeared as Elvis Presley on a made-for-TV movie in 1979 and in *Silkwood, Backdraft, Unlawful Entry, Stargate,* and played Wyatt Earp in the film *Tombstone*. Year/Age: 1995/**44** 1996/**45** 1997/**46**

- **HAROLD BROWN** Percussionist. (Long Beach, CA) From the group WAR. Their biggest hit: "The Cisco Kid" in 1973. Year/Age: 1995/**48** 1996/**49** 1997/**50**

- **TOM MATTINGLY** Ex-astronaut. (Chicago, IL) Year/Age: 1995/**59** 1996/**60** 1997/**61**

- **PAUL HORN** Musician. (NYC) Grammy award-winning flutist. Year/Age: 1995/**65** 1996/**66** 1997/**67**

- **LESLEY-ANNE DOWN** Actress. (London, England) Appeared on "Masterpiece Theater." In the film *Rough Cut*. Met Husband Don Fauntleroy on the set of "North and South." Year/Age: 1995/**41** 1996/**42** 1997/**43**

- **ROB LOWE** Actor. (Charlottesville, VA) Films include *St. Elmo's Fire, Masquerade, Bad Influence, Frank and Jesse,* and *Wayne's World*. His career suffered a major embarrassment when it was revealed he starred in a homemade porno video with an underaged girl. He married his Hollywood make-up artist, Sheryl Berkoff, in 1991. They met during the filming of *Bad Influence*. Year/Age: 1995/**31** 1996/**32** 1997/**33**

- **RUDOLPH NUREYEV** Ballet dancer. (1938-1993 – Irkutsk, Russia) Soviet defector who became a dance star in the West. (Died 1-6-93.)

- **JAMES IRWIN** Astronaut. (1929-1991 – Pittsburgh, PA) He combined his interests in science and evangelism by exploring the moon and later searching for Noah's Ark. He was the first of 12 men who walked on the moon to die. (Died 8-9-91.)

- **NAT "KING" COLE** Entertainer. (1919-1965 – Montgomery, AL) In 1956 he became the first major black entertainer to host his own TV series. He was a jazz pianist and didn't want to sing. Biggest hit: "Ramblin' Rose" in 1962. He had 78 hit singles between 1944 and 1964. (Died of lung cancer 2-15-65.)

- **BOBBY JONES** Pro golfer. (1902-1971 – Atlanta, GA) First to win the "Grand Slam" of golf, the four major American & British tournaments, in one year. (Died 12-18-71.)

FACTS FROM THE PAST

432 ST. PATRICK (a Bishop) was originally a pig farmer in England, carried off to Ireland as a slave. There he introduced Christianity to Ireland. Legend has it that he explained the Christian concept of the Holy Trinity by holding up a shamrock with its 3 leaves combined in a single plant. The date of St. Patrick's death is uncertain (either March 8th or 9th), so church officials compromised by adding the disputed dates, making St. Patrick's Day March 17th.

1755 The Transylvania Land Company bought what became the State of Kentucky for $50,000. They bought it from a Cherokee Indian Chief named GROUNDHOG SAUSAGE. The sale was opposed by another Indian leader, Chief Dragging Canoe.

1889 The submarine was invented by JOHN HOLLAND (who was born in Ireland in 1841). On this day, his Sub submerged off Staten Island, NY, for three hours. Holland's sub was not the first underwater boat, but is credited as the first practical one.

1912 The Camp Fire Girls organization was founded by MRS. LUTHER GULICK of Lake Sebago, ME. Their watchword is "wohelo," created from the first two letters of *work, health* and *love*. The organization has dropped the word "girls" from its name and is known now as Camp Fire. Headquarters are in Kansas City, MO.

1960 President EISENHOWER authorized secret training of Cuban exiles for an invasion of Cuba.

1969 A Milwaukee, Wisconsin, high school teacher, GOLDA MEIR, took office as Israel's fourth Prime Minister.

1976 Boxer REUBEN "Hurricane" CARTER was granted a second murder trial due to the Dylan classic "Hurricane."

1987 At a benefit in England, PRINCESS DIANA complimented BOY GEORGE on his black tights and white dress.

1989 DICK CHENEY is employed as Secretary of Defense.

1994 RONALD REAGAN accuses Oliver North of frabricating his evidence on the Iran-contra scandal.

Suddenly, everybody knows a few Jasons.

MARCH 18

BIRTHDAYS

- **BRAD DOURIF** Actor. (Huntington, West VA) Played mental patient Billy Bibbit in *One Flew Over The Cuckoo's Nest*. He also supplied the voice of Chucky, the killer doll, in *Child's Play* and its sequel. Year/Age: 1995/**45** 1996/**46** 1997/**47**

- **JAMIE WEST-ORAM** Guitarist. (England) 1983 hit with FIXX: "One Thing Leads To Another." Year/Age: 1995/**42** 1996/**43** 1997/**44**

- **VANESSA WILLIAMS** Former Miss America. (Tarrytown, NY) She was dethroned when they discovered she had posed nude for a magazine layout. She turned to singing and acting. Number 1 hit: "Save The Best For Last." Appeared in the film *Candyman* in 1992. She made her Broadway debut in *Kiss of the Spider Woman*. Year/Age: 1995/**32** 1996/**33** 1997/**34**

- **PETER GRAVES** Actor. (Born Peter Aurness in Minneapolis, MN.) He played a German spy in *Stalag 17* and appeared on the "Mission Impossible" TV series and the mini-series *Winds of War*. Brother of James Arness. Peter was a newscaster in the mid-forties in Minneapolis. He is the host of cable's A&E's "Biography." Year/Age: 1995/**69** 1996/**70** 1997/**71**

- **GEORGE PLIMPTON** Daredevil. (NYC) There seems to be nothing this "Walter Mitty" Plimpton won't try for the experience, to write about it afterwards. He fought Archie Moore, pitched for the NY Yankees for the film *Out of My League*, quarterbacked for the Detroit Lions in the film *Paper Lion* and golfed with Sam Snead. He said his most difficult feat was playing percussion for the New York Philharmonic under Leonard Bernstein. Appeared in the film *L.A. Story*. Year/Age: 1995/**68** 1996/**69** 1997/**70**

- **CHARLEY PRIDE** C&W. (Sledge, MS) Biggest hit: "Kiss An Angel Good Morning" in 1972. He was a minor league baseball pitcher in 1965 when RCA Records signed him to a recording contract. He was Nashville's first black country artist to have a #1 country record. He was discovered singing in a nightclub by Red Sovine. Year/Age: 1995/**57** 1996/**58** 1997/**59**

- **INGEMAR STENMARK** Alpine skier. (Sweden) Year/Age: 1995/**39** 1996/**40** 1997/**41**

- **IRENE CARA** Singer. (Bronx, NY) Her biggest hit was "Fame" in 1980 from the film of the same name. Year/Age: 1995/**36** 1996/**37** 1997/**38**

- **JOHN KANDER** Composer. (Kansas City, MO) Tony winner for *Cabaret*. He wrote *New York, New York*. Year/Age: 1995/**68** 1996/**69** 1997/**70**

- **ANDY GRANATELLI** Racecar owner and driver. Year/Age: 1995/**72** 1996/**73** 1997/**74**

- **WILSON PICKETT** Singer. (Prattville, AL) Biggest hit: "Land of a Thousand Dances" in 1966. Year/Age: 1995/**54** 1996/**55** 1997/**56**

- **JOHN UPDIKE** Novelist. (Shillington, PA) He wrote *The Witches of Eastwick*, *The Rabbit's Revenge* and *Rabbit At Rest*. Year/Age: 1995/**63** 1996/**64** 1997/**65**

- **KEVIN DOBSON** Actor. (NYC) Attorney M. Patrick MacKenzie who married Karen Fairgate on "Knots Landing," and Detective Bobby Crocker, Kojak's earnest right-hand man on "Kojak." Year/Age: 1995/**51** 1996/**52** 1997/**53**

- **BONNIE BLAIR** Olympic speedskater. (Cornwall, NY) Gold and bronze medalist in the 1988 and 1992 Olympics. Year/Age: 1995/**31** 1996/**32** 1997/**33**

- **ROBERT DONAT** Actor. (1905-1958 – England) He won the Academy Award for best actor in *Goodbye Mister Chips* in 1939. (Died 6-9-58.)

- **GROVER CLEVELAND** U.S. President. (1837-1908 – Caldwell, NJ) He was the 22nd and 24th President and was married in the White House in 1886. His daughter, Esther, was the first child of a president to be born in the White House. (Died 6-24-08.)

- **RUDOLF DIESEL** Inventor. (1858-1913 – Germany) He invented the diesel engine, an oil-burning engine that runs without sparkplugs. In 1913, on a trip across the English Channel to promote sales of the engine, he fell overboard and drowned at age 55. (Died 9-29-13.)

FACTS FROM THE PAST

1850 HENRY WELLS and WILLIAM FARGO began the American Express, and two years later they organized Wells Fargo, a coast-to-coast express business.

1902 ENRICO CARUSO became the first well-known performer to make a record. He sang ten songs for $500. The studio was a hotel room in Milan, Italy. Caruso didn't use a microphone, because they didn't exist.

1931 COLONEL JACOB SCHICK invented the first electric razor, which went on sale in Stamford, CT.

1940 MUSSOLINI agreed to join Hitler's forces in WWII.

1954 HOWARD HUGHES became the first individual to be the sole owner of a major motion picture studio.

1965 The first spacewalk took place as Soviet cosmonaut ALEKSEI LEONOV left his Voshkod II capsule and remained outside the spacecraft for 20 minutes, secured by a tether.

1982 In Philadelphia, entertainer TEDDY PENDERGRASS was paralyzed from the waist down when his Rolls Royce bounced off a divider and slammed into a tree.

1985 Baseball commissioner BOWIE KUHN reinstated Hall of Fame stars Mickey Mantle and Willie Mays. They had been banned from baseball after accepting PR jobs with gambling casinos.

1994 LT. ROBERT READINGER faced disciplinary action for giving an unauthorized ride to Billy Foel after the entertainer was involved in an accident. The singer was on his way to a concert thirty miles away.

MARCH 19
Swallows Return to Juan Capistrano

When's the last time you attended a rummage sale?

BIRTHDAYS

- **ROBIN LUKE** Singer. (Los Angeles, CA) Biggest hit: "Susie Darlin" in 1958. Year/Age: 1995/53 1996/54 1997/55
- **PAUL ATKINSON** Guitarist. (England) With the ZOMBIES. Year/Age: 1995/49 1996/50 1997/51
- **URSULA ANDRESS** Actress. (Bern, Switzerland) She appeared in *Dr. No* and *What's New Pussycat?* Year/Age: 1995/59 1996/60 1997/61
- **BRUCE WILLIS** Actor. (Penns Grove, NJ) Played David Addison on "Moonlighting." His films include: *The Color of Night, Pulp Fiction, Mortal Thoughts, Die Hard 1&2,* and *Death Becomes Her* with Meryl Streep and Goldie Hawn. He had a hit record in 1987: "Respect." He married actress Demi Moore, November 21, 1987. Year/Age: 1995/40 1996/41 1997/42
- **GLENN CLOSE** Actress. (Greenwich, CN) Five time Oscar nominee: *The World According to Garp, The Big Chill, The Natural, Fatal Attraction, Dangerous Liaisons, Skylark,* and *The Paper.* TV's "Sarah, Plain and Tall" and sequel. Year/Age: 1995/48 1996/49 1997/50
- **RUTH POINTER** Singer. (Oakland, CA) With the POINTER SISTERS, consisting of sisters Ruth, Anita, Bonnie and June. They did some back-up work for GRACE SLICK, BOZ SCAGGS and others. Biggest hit: "Slow Hand" in 1981. Year/Age: 1995/49 1996/50 1997/51
- **BARBARA FRANKLIN** Secretary of Commerce. (Lancaster, PA) She holds a masters degree from Harvard Business School. In 1990 she earned $315,000 working part-time as director of seven corporations. As commerce secretary, she is paid $143,800. Year/Age: 1995/55 1996/56 1997/57
- **PHYLLIS NEWMAN** Actress. (Jersey City, NJ) She appeared as a panelist on "To Tell the Truth" and in the movies *Picnic* and *Vagabond King.* Year/Age: 1995/60 1996/61 1997/62

- **ORNETTE COLEMAN** Sax player. (Ft. Worth, TX) Year/Age: 1995/65 1996/66 1997/67
- **PHILIP ROTH** Novelist. (Newark, NJ) Author of the 1969 best-seller *Portnoy's Complaint.* He won a National Book Award for *Goodbye Columbus.* He also wrote *Operation Shylock: A Confession* and *The Ghost Writer.* Year/Age: 1995/62 1996/63 1997/64
- **PATRICK McGOOHAN** Actor/director. (NYC) He played John Drake in the "Secret Agent" adventure series in the 1960's. The show's theme was "Secret Agent Man" by Johnny Rivers. Year/Age: 1995/67 1996/68 1997/69
- **TIGE ANDREWS** Actor. (Born Tiger Androwaous in Brooklyn, NY) Appeared in the film *Mr. Roberts* and on TV in "The Detectives" and "Mod Squad." Year/Age: 1995/72 1996/73 1997/74
- **RICHIE ASHBURN** Baseball. Played for the Phillies, Cubs and Mets before retiring in 1962. He led the NL in batting in 1955 with .338 and again in 1958 with .350. He hit over .300 nine times and .308 for his career. Year/Age: 1995/68 1996/69 1997/70
- **IRVING WALLACE** Author. (1916-1990 – Born Irving Wallechinsky in Chicago, IL) He quit college after two semesters because they wouldn't let him smoke in class. He intended to be a sports reporter but, after 1957, devoted all his time to books, including *People's Almanac, The Book of Lists, The Chapman Report* and *The Celestial Bed.* He wrote 33 books and some screenplays including *The West Point Story* and *Meet Me at the Fair.* (Died 6-29-90.)
- **WYATT EARP** U.S. frontiersman/lawman/gunfighter. (1848-1929 – Monmouth, IL) Portrayed by actor Hugh O'Brien on TV from 1955 to 1961. (Died 1-13-29.)

FACTS FROM THE PAST

1928 WMAQ in Chicago started airing the "Amos & Andy Show," starring (whites) **FREEMAN GOSDEN** and **CHARLES CORRELL** as (blacks) Amos Jones and Andrew H. Brown. Whey they left WGN, the station kept the names they had been using, Sam and Henry, so they changed their names to Amos and Andy for the new show.

1951 Herman Wouk's war novel *The Caine Mutiny* was published.

1953 The Academy Awards were telecast for the first time. Cecil B. DeMille's film, *The Greatest Show on Earth,* won the Best Picture of 1952. Gary Cooper was named best actor for *High Noon* and Shirley Booth, best actress in *Come Back, Little Sheba.*

1957 **ELVIS PRESLEY** bought the Graceland Estate in Memphis.

1958 **TOM & JERRY**, later known as Simon & Garfunkel, released their first single, "Our Song."

1974 **JEFFERSON AIRPLANE** began their first tour as Jefferson Starship.

1976 Buckingham Palace announced the separation of **PRINCESS MARGARET** and her husband, the **EARL OF SNOWDON**, after 16 years of marriage.

1982 Several members of **OZZY OSBOURNE**'s entourage were killed in a freak accident near Orlando, FL. Guitarist Randy Rhoads and two others were in a light plane which buzzed Osbourne's tour bus, clipped a wing and crashed into a house.

1985 **MEL SHARPLES** sold his diner on the TV show "Alice." This marked the end of the 10-year-old sitcom.

1987 Television evangelist **JIM BAKKER** resigned as chairman of his PTL ministry organization, saying he had been blackmailed by "treacherous former friends."

1988 **MICHAEL JACKSON** bought a ranch and built an amusement park and zoo on the grounds in Santa Ynez, CA.

1994 **SISKEL AND EBERT** refuse to appear on the "Arsenio Hall Show" because he allowed Louis Farrakhan to "spew hate unchallenged."

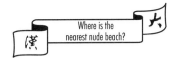
Where is the nearest nude beach?

MARCH 20

BIRTHDAYS

- **SPIKE LEE** Director/actor. (Born Shelton Jackson in Atlanta, GA) Directed *Do the Right Thing, School Daze, Crooklyn* and *Malcolm X* in 1992. Appears in many Nike commercials. Year/Age: 1995/**38** 1996/**39** 1997/**40**

- **PAT RILEY** Basketball. (Rome, NY) Former coach of the Lakers and known as the best-dressed man in basketball. He is the New York Knicks coach. Author of *The Winner Within: A Life Plan for Team Players.* Year/Age: 1995/**50** 1996/**51** 1997/**52**

- **JERRY REED** C&W singer. (Born Jerry Hubbard in Atlanta, GA) His biggest hit: "Amos Moses" in 1971. He's been in several films including *Smokey and the Bandit* with Burt Reynolds and Sally Field. Year/Age: 1995/**58** 1996/**59** 1997/**60**

- **CARL PALMER** Drummer. (Birmingham, England) With EMERSON, LAKE AND PALMER, "From The Beginning" in 1972. Year/Age: 1995/**48** 1996/**49** 1997/**50**

- **WILLIAM HURT** Actor. (Washington, DC) Star of *The Doctor, Broadcast News, Mr. Wonderful* and an Oscar nominee as best actor in *Children of a Lesser God.* He turned down the lead in *Jurassic Park.* Year/Age: 1995/**45** 1996/**46** 1997/**47**

- **JIMMIE VAUGHAN** Guitarist. (Austin, TX) THE FABULOUS THUNDERBIRDS. Brother of the late Stevie Ray. Biggest hit: "Tuff Enuff," 1986. Year/Age: 1995/**44** 1996/**45** 1997/**46**

- **HAL LINDEN** Actor. (Born Harold Lipshitz in Bronx, NY) Starred as Captain "Barney Miller" of the 12th Precinct in NYC from 1975-1982. Stars in TV's "Jack's Place." Year/Age: 1995/**64** 1996/**65** 1997/**66**

- **TED BESSELL** Actor. (Flushing, NY) Frankie Lombardi on "Gomer Pyle" in the 1960's. Also played Marlo Thomas's boyfriend on "That Girl." Year/Age: 1995/**59** 1996/**60** 1997/**61**

- **PAUL WITT** Producer. (NYC) TV's "Blossom" and "The Rookies." He won an Emmy for *Brian's Song.* Year/Age: 1995/**52** 1996/**53** 1997/**54**

- **FRED ROGERS** TV host. (Latrobe, PA) Star of the children's program "Mr. Rogers Neighborhood" on PBS. He has been doing the show since 1967, and it is PBS's longest-running children's program. Fred is a Presbyterian minister. Year/Age: 1995/**67** 1996/**68** 1997/**69**

- **CARL REINER** Author/actor/producer. (NYC) In *It's a Mad Mad, Mad, Mad World, The Russians are Coming,* and *Sibling Rivalry.* He recorded the LP "The 2000-Year-old Man" with Mel Brooks. Year/Age: 1995/**73** 1996/**74** 1997/**75**

- **BOBBY ORR** Hockey star. (Canada) He was the Boston Bruins defensive man and won the Norris trophy 8 times and led the NHL in scoring twice and assists 5 times. Year/Age: 1995/**47** 1996/**48** 1997/**49**

- **LARRY ELGART** Bandleader. (New London, CT) Bandleader of the 1940's who made a brief comeback in 1982 with "Hooked On Swing." Year/Age: 1995/**73** 1996/**74** 1997/**75**

- **RAY GOULDING** Comedian. (1922-1990 – Lowell, MA) Of the comedy team "Bob & Ray," he started in radio in the 1940's. Their skits parodied talk shows, soap operas, news programs and ads. Goulding and Ray Elliott met in 1946 at radio station WHDH in Boston, where Elliott was a disc jockey and Goulding was a newscaster. (Died 3-24-90.)

- **SIR MICHAEL REDGRAVE** Actor. (1908-1985 – Bristol, England) Nominated for an Academy Award for best actor in 1947 for *Mourning Becomes Electra.* Actresses Vanessa and Lynn are his daughters. (Died 3-21-85.)

- **OZZIE NELSON** Actor. (1907-1975 – Born Oswald Nelson in Jersey City, NJ) Bandleader-turned-actor who appeared in 5 movies and the popular "Ozzie & Harriet" TV series with wife, Harriet, and sons, David and Rick. Ozzie chose all of the songs that Rick turned into hits. (Died 6-3-75.)

- **JACK BARRY** Game show host. (1918-1984 – Lindenhurst, NJ) Host of "Joker's Wild." Jack and producer, Dan Enright, admitted that their show, "Twenty-One," hosted by Barry, gave participants questions and answers in advance. (Died 5-2-84.)

FACTS FROM THE PAST

1549 **SIR THOMAS SEYMOUR**, Lord High Admiral of the English navy, fell in love with a girl named Elizabeth. She happened to be Princess Elizabeth, later to become the Queen of England. She didn't reciprocate his love, yet Seymour kept pestering the girl. He became such a nuisance, he was charged with treason and beheaded on this day.

1865 A would-be-kidnapper was waiting for **PRESIDENT ABRAHAM LINCOLN** who was supposed to make a public appearance in Washington, DC. Because of a mix-up in the schedule, Lincoln did not show up. The man was **JOHN WILKES BOOTH**.

1899 **MARTHA M. PLACE** of Brooklyn, NY, became the first woman to be put to **DEATH BY ELECTROCUTION**. She was executed at Sing Sing for the murder of her stepdaughter.

1969 **JOHN LENNON** and **YOKO ONO ARE MARRIED** in a civil ceremony in Gibralter.

1985 **LIBBY RIDDLES** of Teller, AK, became the first woman to win the **IDITAROD TRAIL DOG SLED RACE**, covering 1,049 miles from Anchorage to Nome in nearly 18 days.

1990 **GLORIA ESTEFAN** suffered a broken back when her tour bus was hit by a skidding truck on an icy Pennsylvania highway.

1991 Eric Clapton's 4-year-old son **CONOR**, fell to his death from a 53rd floor window. Grieving dad wrote "Tears In Heaven" for his son.

MARCH 21
Astrological Sign of Aries/Bird Day in Iowa

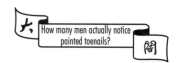

How many men actually notice painted toenails?

BIRTHDAYS

- **PATRICK LUCEY** Former Wisconsin Governor and ambassador. Year/**Age:** 1995/**77** 1996/**78** 1997/**79**
- **ROSIE O'DONNELL** Actress/comedienne. Films include *A League of Their Own*, *Flintstones*, and *Sleepless In Seattle*. Year/**Age:** 1995/**33** 1996/**34** 1997/**35**
- **SHAWON DUNSTON** Baseball. Chicago Cubs infielder. Year/**Age:** 1995/**32** 1996/**33** 1997/**34**
- **MATTHEW BRODERICK** Actor. (New York, NY) Appeared in *Ferris Bueller's Day Off*, *Glory*, *War Games*, *Biloxi Blues*, *Family Business*, *Out on a Limb*, *The Night We Never Met*, and *The Freshman*. In 1987 he was seriously injured in a two-car accident in Northern Ireland that killed two women. He was fined $175.00. Son of late actor James Broderick. Voice of adult Simba in *The Lion King*. Year/**Age:** 1995/**33** 1996/**34** 1997/**35**
- **AL FREEMAN, JR.** Actor. (San Antonio, TX) American leading man who appeared in *Finian's Rainbow*, *The Detective*, and *Malcolm X*. Appeared on the soap "One Life to Live." Year/**Age:** 1995/**61** 1996/**62** 1997/**63**
- **AYRTON SENNA** Race car driver. (1960-1994, Sao Paulo, Brazil) He won three Formula One races and 41 Grand Prix events. He crashed and died in the San Marino Grand Prix, Imola, Italy 5-1-94.
- **TOMMY DAVIS** Baseball star. NL batting champ in 1962 and 1963. He broke in with the LA Dodgers in 1959 and played for 10 clubs in an 18-year major-league career. Lifetime average: .294. Year/**Age:** 1995/**56** 1996/**57** 1997/**58**

- **TIMOTHY DALTON** Actor. (Wales) Appeared in *The Lion in Winter*, *Wuthering Heights*, *The Rocketeer*, and James Bond films. Year/**Age:** 1995/**49** 1996/**50** 1997/**51**
- **JULES BERGMAN** Newsman/science reporter. (1927-1987 – NYC) Wrote *Fire* and *Anyone Can Fly*. (Died 2-12-87.)
- **MANNY SANGUILLEN** Baseball catcher. In over 500 appearances he drew only 19 walks. Year/**Age:** 1995/**51** 1996/**52** 1997/**53**
- **ED BEGLEY** Actor. (1901-1970 – Hartford, CT) Won supporting actor Oscar in *Sweet Bird of Youth* in 1962. His son, Ed Begley, Jr., appeared on the TV series, "St. Elsewhere." (Died 4-28-70.)
- **JAMES COCO** Actor. (1929-1987 – NYC) Character/comic actor who appeared on Broadway in *Man of LaMancha*. Oscar nomination for *Only When I Laugh*. He wrote *The James Coco Diet*. Over the years he went from 95 to 305 pounds. (Died 2-25-87.)
- **JOHANN SEBASTIAN BACH** Composer. (1685-1750) German organist/composer who had 10 brothers; four were musicians. One of them wouldn't allow Johann to look at his scores, so he came down in the middle of the night and copied the scores by moonlight. This practice permanently impaired his vision. He fathered 20 children in two marriages. His gifted sons regarded him as a quaint practitioner of dead music, and they lost many of his scores after his death. For 80 years Bach was quite forgotten. Then in 1829, Felix Mendelssohn conducted a butchered version of the *St. Matthew Passion*, which awoke a new public to Bach's sounds. (Died 7-28-1750.)

FACTS FROM THE PAST

1790   **THOMAS JEFFERSON** reported to **PRESIDENT GEORGE WASHINGTON** in New York as the new Secretary of State.

1871   Journalist **HENRY M. STANLEY** began his famous expedition to Africa to locate the missing Scottish missionary, **DAVID LIVINGSTONE.**

1891   A marriage in Kentucky ended the feud between the **HATFIELDS AND McCOYS.** The last of the original feuding families died in 1984. The feud started with an accusation of pig-stealing and it lasted 20 years. No one but family members knew how many deaths had occurred, but outsiders were able to confirm at least a half-dozen vicious murders.

1952   **DJ ALAN FREED** hosted the first-ever rock-'n-roll concert at the Cleveland Arena. 25,000 people showed up, though only 10,000 seats were available.

1956   **CARL PERKINS** broke four ribs and his shoulder in a car accident that killed his brother, Jay, and his manager on their way to appear on "The Ed Sullivan Show." Perkins spent nine months in the hospital. By the time he recovered, Elvis Presley had covered his hit "Blue Suede Shoes" and his career was never the same again.

1963   **ALCATRAZ PRISON** closed in San Francisco Bay after 30 years by order of Attorney General Robert Kennedy. Reputed to be escape-proof, but 6 men swam for it and four were drowned, a fifth was never found. During the last escape in 1962, John Scott swam to shore, but was recaptured. The abandoned prison was a big tourist attraction, but it got too expensive hauling in water, etc., so they closed it down. Criminals housed there included "Machine Gun" Kelly, Al Capon, and "the Birdman" Robert Stroud.

1965   **DR. MARTIN LUTHER KING, JR.** led 3,000 Civil Rights demonstrators on a 54-mile walk from Selma to Montgomery, AL, demanding voting rights for blacks. By the end of the march, 25,000 had joined in.

1989   After 33 years, **DICK CLARK** announced he was stepping down as host of "American Bandstand." More than 65,000 records were played on the TV show. More than 10,000 musical guests have appeared on the show and over 600,000 teenagers have danced before the TV cameras. Clark was replaced by 26-year-old David Hirsh.

1989   **RANDALL DALE ADAMS,** whose 1977 conviction for killing a police officer was overturned after it was questioned in the documentary *The Thin Blue Line*, was released from a Texas prison.

1994   Former NBA star **MICHAEL JORDAN** was cut from the White Sox roster and sent to the minor league club.

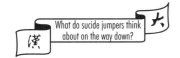

What do suicide jumpers think about on the way down?

MARCH 22
National Goof-Off Day

BIRTHDAYS

- **KARL MALDEN** Actor. (Born Mladen Sekulovich in Chicago) He starred in the TV series "Streets of San Francisco" from 1972-1977 with Michael Douglas. Karl has been spokesman on TV for American Express for years. He broke his nose twice playing football at Emerson High School in Gary, IN. Year/**Age:** 1995/**82** 1996/**83** 1997/**84**

- **WILLIAM SHATNER** Actor. (Montreal, Quebec, Canada) He plays the part of Captain Kirk in "Star Trek." The T in James T. Kirk stands for Tiberius. Also on the TV series "T.J. Hooker" and "Rescue 911." Appeared in the film *National Lampoon's Loaded Weapon 1.* His moonlighting business-hobby is showing horses. Year/**Age:** 1995/**64** 1996/**65** 1997/**66**

- **MARCEL MARCEAU** Famous mime. (Strasburg, France) Created "Bip" in 1947. Year/**Age:** 1995/**72** 1996/**73** 1997/**74**

- **STEPHEN SONDHEIM** Broadway lyricist. (NYC) He composed "Maria," "Tonight," and "Send in the Clowns," among others. Composed the music for the film *Dick Tracy.* Year/**Age:** 1995/**65** 1996/**66** 1997/**67**

- **SIR ANDREW LLOYD WEBBER** Composer. (England) Composed the music for *Jesus Christ Superstar, Cats, Phantom of the Opera, Aspects of Love,* and *Sunset Boulevard.* Year/**Age:** 1995/**65** 1996/**66** 1997/**67**

- **MATTHEW MODINE** Actor. *Gross Anatomy, Vision Quest,* and *Short Cuts.* Year/**Age:** 1995/**47** 1996/**48** 1997/**49**

- **GARY OLDHAM** Actor. Films include: *Romeo is Bleeding, Murder in the First, JFK,* and *Dracula.* Year/**Age:** 1995/**37** 1996/**38** 1997/**39**

- **ALLEN H. NEUHARTH** *USA Today* founder. Year/**Age:** 1995/**70** 1996/**71** 1997/**72**

- **JEREMY CLYDE** Singer. (England) Half of CHAD & JEREMY. Their biggest hit: "A Summer Song" in 1964. The duo had seven Top 40 hits during their career. Year/**Age:** 1995/**51** 1996/**52** 1997/**53**

- **WERNER KLEMPERER** Actor. (Germany) In the film *Ship of Fools,* and played Colonel Klink on TV's "Hogan's Heroes." Son of conductor Otto Klemperer. Year/**Age:** 1995/**75** 1996/**76** 1997/**77**

- **PAT ROBERTSON** TV Evangelist. (Lexington, VA) He founded the Christian Broadcasting Network with $70 in 1960. He was a presidential hopeful in 1988. Year/**Age:** 1995/**65** 1996/**66** 1997/**67**

- **STEPHANIE MILLS** Actress/singer. (Brooklyn, NY) She appeared in the Broadway show *Maggie Flynn* at age 7 and played the lead role of Dorothy in *The Wiz* at age 15. Her biggest record: "Never Knew Love Like This Before" in 1980. Year/**Age:** 1995/**39** 1996/**40** 1997/**41**

- **BOB COSTAS** Sports announcer. (Queens, NY) Made his pro debut on KMOX radio in St. Louis doing play-by-play basketball. Host of NBC's "NFL Live" since 1984. Also host of nationally syndicated radio talk show "Costas Coast-to-Coast." Cameo appearance in *The Paper.* Year/**Age:** 1995/**43** 1996/**44** 1997/**45**

- **CHICO MARX** Comedian. (1887-1961 – Born Leonard Marx in NYC) Oldest of the Marx Brothers. The Marx Brothers got their names from a comic strip called *Mager's Monks.* Some said Chico got his name from chasing chicks. Case in point: he was caught by his wife kissing a chorus girl and he explained that he wasn't kissing her, just "whispering in her mouth." (Died 11-11-61.)

FACTS FROM THE PAST

1687 French composer **JEAN BAPTISTE LULLY** died after conducting a rehearsal of his music. He got so carried away with his conducting that the cane he was beating time with came down hard on his toe. The toe became infected, and the infection spread above his foot. He died during the operation to amputate his foot.

1918 **ALEX WICKHAM** dove off a cliff from the height of 205 feet, 9 inches – as high as a 15-story building – and lived. The cliff overlooked the Yarra River near Melbourne, Australia. Halfway down, he lost consciousness, and he hit the water with such force that his bathing suit was ripped from his body. Fortunately, he regained consciousness upon impact.

1958 **HANK WILLIAMS, JR.,** made his stage debut when he was 8, at the urging of his mother.

1962 **BARBRA STREISAND,** 19 years old, opened on Broadway as Miss Marmelstein in *I Can Get It For You Wholesale.* A year later she married her co-star **ELLIOTT GOULD.**

1963 The **BEATLES'** first LP, *Please, Please Me,* was released in Britain. It included such hits as the title track, "Love Me Do," "I Saw Her Standing There," "Do You Want to know a Secret?," and "Twist and Shout."

1967 **MUHAMMAD ALI** kayoed Zora Foley in NY. This was his last fight before being stripped of his title for avoiding military draft.

1976 Presidential candidate **JIMMY CARTER** revealed that the GRATEFUL DEAD, LED ZEPPELIN and BOB DYLAN inspired him while he worked late nights at the Georgia governor's mansion. He quoted lines from Dylan's "Blowin' in the Wind" and "Yesterday" by the Beatles.

1989 **PETE ROZELLE,** who gave birth to the Super Bowl, stepped down as NFL Commissioner in his 30th year on the job.

1990 **GEORGE BUSH** said, "I do not like broccoli and I haven't liked it since I was a little kid and my mother made me eat it and I'm the President of the United States and I'm not going to eat any more broccoli."

1993 Two Cleveland Indian ballplayers were killed when their speeding boat crashed into a dock on a lake near Clermont, FL. Killed were **TIM CREWS,** the driver, who was legally drunk, and **STEVE OLIN.** A third player, **BOB OJEDA,** was injured.

MARCH 23

China and India harbor 40% of the world's population.

BIRTHDAYS

- **RICHARD GRIECO** Actor. Appears on TV's "21 Jump Street." Also appeared in *Mobsters* and *If Looks Could Kill.* Year/**Age:** 1995/**30** 1996/**31** 1997/**32**

- **MARTY ALLEN** Comedian. (Pittsburgh, PA) Half of the "Allen & Rossi" comedy team. He's the one with the wild hairdo. Year/**Age:** 1995/**73** 1996/**74** 1997/**75**

- **AKIRA KUROSAWA** Distinguished Japanese director. (Tokyo) His films include: *Rashomon, Seven Samurai,* and *Throne of Blood.* Year/**Age:** 1995/**85** 1996/**86** 1997/**87**

- **CRAIG BREEDLOVE** Racecar driver. (Los Angeles, CA) He set the record for the highest speed attained by a jet-engined car when he drove the 9,000-pound *Spirit of America* at 613.995 mph on Nov. 15, 1965. Eleven days earlier, his wife, Lee, became the fastest woman on wheels: 335 mph in the same car. Year/**Age:** 1995/**57** 1996/**58** 1997/**59**

- **CHAKA KHAN** Singer. (Born Yvette Marie Steven in Chicago, IL) Biggest hit: "I Feel For You" in 1984, written by PRINCE with STEVIE WONDER playing harmonica. Year/**Age:** 1995/**42** 1996/**43** 1997/**44**

- **LOUIE ANDERSON** Comedian. Year/**Age:** 1995/**42** 1996/**43** 1997/**44**

- **MONIQUE VAN VOOREN** Actress. (Rowera, SD) In film *Damn Yankees*, 1958. Year/**Age:** 1995/**62** 1996/**63** 1997/**64**

- **RIC OCASEK** Singer/guitarist. (Boston, MA) Formerly of the CARS. Biggest hit: "Drive" in 1984. Year/**Age:** 1995/**46** 1996/**47** 1997/**48**

- **MOSES MALONE** Pro basketball star. (Petersburg, VA) NBA center who was the MVP in 1979 and 1982. Played for the Atlanta Hawks and Mulwaukee Bucks. Year/**Age:** 1995/**40** 1996/**41** 1997/**42**

- **AMANDA PLUMMER** Actress. (New York, NY) Daughter of Christopher Plummer. In films *So I Married an Axe Murderer* and *Needful Things.* Year/**Age:** 1995/**38** 1996/**39** 1997/**40**

- **JOHNNY LOGAN** Baseball. Shortstop for the World Series champion Milwaukee Braves in 1957. Year/**Age:** 1995/**69** 1996/**70** 1997/**71**

- **MARTHA WRIGHT** Singer. (Seattle, WA) Nellie Forbush in *South Pacific* on Broadway in 1951. Year/**Age:** 1995/**68** 1996/**69** 1997/**70**

- **WERNER VON BRAUN** Rocket scientist. (1912-1977 – Germany) During WWII, he worked at a war plant, building rockets for Hitler. Eventually he was responsible for the American guided-missile program. After the war he handed all of his research over to the U.S. (Died 6-16-77.)

- **JOAN CRAWFORD** Actress. (1908-1977 – Born Lucille LeSueur in San Antonio, TX) She won an Oscar in 1945 for *Mildred Pierce.* Obsessed with hygiene, she used to wash her hands every hour on the hour. She would shower in a hotel room only after she personally scrubbed the bathroom floor. She mistreated her four adopted children. Her daughter Christina Crawford wrote a book about her, *Mommie Dearest*, which became a movie. (Died 5-10-77.)

FACTS FROM THE PAST

1743 The **FIRST STANDING OVATION** was recorded at the first performance of Handel's "Hallelujah Chorus" (from *Messiah*). King George was so inspired (or restless) that he jumped to his feet, and when the King did that, everyone else in the audience stood also.

1775 In a speech to the Virginia Provincial Convention, **PATRICK HENRY** made a plea for independence from Britain, saying, "I know not what course others might take, but as for me, give me liberty, or give me death." He was 38 years old.

1840 The most widely used Americanism "O.K." was first used in print in the NY publication *The New Era* by the Democratic OK Club. They got the name from Old Kinderhook, NY, where President **MARTIN VAN BUREN** was born. The Greeks say it comes from *ola kala* which means everything is good or all right.

1901 An Australian opera singer **HELEN MITCHELL** mentioned to reporters that she loved thin sliced bread. "I like to see through it and toasted to a crisp brown." Better known as **DAME NELLIE MELBA**, her idea caught on and the snack was named "Melba Toast."

1919 **BENITO MUSSOLINI** founded his fascist political movement in Milan, Italy.

1965 America's first two-person space flight began as Gemini Three—nicknamed the *Molly Brown*—blasted off from Cape Kennedy with astronauts **VIRGIL I. GRISSOM** and **JOHN W. YOUNG** on board.

1983 **PRESIDENT RONALD REAGAN** first proposed development of technology to intercept enemy missiles – a proposal that came to be known as the strategic defense initiative, or Star Wars.

1985 Billy Joe married model Christie Brinkley in NYC. They divorced in 1994.

1989 **FAWN HALL,** former secretary to one-time national security council aide Oliver North, completed two days of testimony at North's Iran-contra trial in Washington, DC.

1989 The **MOST EXPENSIVE WEDDING DRESS** in history was presented by **HELEN GAINVILLE** in Paris. It featured embroidered diamonds by Alexander Reza and was valued at over $7 million.

1991 L.A. Kings hockey center **WAYNE GRETZKY** and Kings owner **BRUCE MCNALL** bought a 1910 Honus Wagner baseball card at Sotheby's auction for $451,000, breaking a 1989 record: $115,000 for another Honus Wagner card.

1994 **LUIS DONALDO COLOSIAO**, the man expected to be the next president of Mexico, was assassinated during a campaign stop in Tijuana.

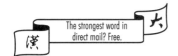

MARCH 24

BIRTHDAYS

- **LEE OSKAR** Harmonica player. (Long Beach, CA) With WAR. Biggest hit: "The Cisco Kid" in 1973. Year/**Age**: 1995/**49** 1996/**50** 1997/**51**

- **KELLY LEBROCK** Actress. The Lady in Red. Married to actor Steven Segal. Year/**Age**: 1995/**35** 1996/**36** 1997/**37**

- **DOUGGIE THOMPSON** Bass guitarist. (England) With SUPERTRAMP. Biggest hit: "The Logical Song" in 1979. Year/**Age**: 1995/**44** 1996/**45** 1997/**46**

- **PAT BRADLEY** Pro golfer. (Westfield, MA) The first woman in professional golf to pass $3 million in career earnings. The 12th inductee into the LPGA Hall of Fame. Year/**Age**: 1995/**44** 1996/**45** 1997/**46**

- **NORMAN FELL** Actor. (Philadelphia, PA) Appeared on "Three's Company" and "The Ropers" TV series. Year/**Age**: 1995/**70** 1996/**71** 1997/**72**

- **ROBERT CARRADINE** Actor. (Los Angeles, CA) Son of actor John Carradine. Year/**Age**: 1995/**41** 1996/**42** 1997/**43**

- **DENNY McLAIN** Baseball. (Chicago) His two best years were 1968 (31-6) and 1969 (24-9) Lifetime: 131-91. In 1971 Commissioner Bowie Kuhn suspended the Detroit ace for having become involved with gamblers. Supposedly, Denny had helped bankroll a bookmaking operation. He tried a comeback but his fastball didn't have it anymore. He ended the season with a 3-5 record and then was suspended again for throwing ice water at some sportswriters. Later was caught carrying a gun and his career was over. Year/**Age**: 1995/**51** 1996/**52** 1997/**53**

- **GENE NELSON** Actor/dancer. (Seattle, WA) In movies *Three Girls and a Sailor* and *Tea for Two.* Year/**Age**: 1995/**75** 1996/**76** 1997/**77**

- **BOB MACKIE** Hollywood costume/fashion designer. (Monterey, CA) Has designed clothes for Carol Burnett, Marie Osmond, Shirley MacLaine, and created some of the outrageous costumes that Cher wears. Year/**Age**: 1995/**55** 1996/**56** 1997/**57**

- **DONNA PESCOW** Actress. Co-starred with John Travolta in *Saturday Night Fever,* TV's "Angie," and "Out of This World." Year/**Age**: 1995/**41** 1996/**42** 1997/**43**

- **DR. ROGER BANNISTER** Distance runner. (England) He broke the 4-minute-mile barrier in 1954. Year/**Age**: 1995/**66** 1996/**67** 1997/**68**

- **BYRON JANIS** Concert pianist. (McKeesport, PA) He first appeared at Carnegie Hall when he was 20 years old. He has toured all over the world. He married Gary Cooper's daughter Maria in 1966. Year/**Age**: 1995/**67** 1996/**68** 1997/**69**

- **CLYDE BARROW** Bank robber. (1909-1934 – Telico, TX) Accused of killing 12 people. The 1967 movie, *Bonnie & Clyde* starring Warren Beatty and Faye Dunaway recounted the life story of the two minor desperadoes of the 1930's: Bonnie Parker & Clyde Barrow. (Died 5-23-34.)

- **BILLY STEWART** Singer. (1937-1970 – Washington, DC) Biggest hit: original version of "Summertime" from *Porgy and Bess* in 1966. He and three of his band members were killed when their car went out of control and plunged off a bridge into the River Neuse in North Carolina. (Died 1-17-70.)

- **STEVE McQUEEN** Actor. (1930-1980 – Born Terence Stephen McQueen in Indianapolis, IN) Nominated for best actor in 1966 for *The Sand Pebbles.* Also in *Bullitt* and *The Getaway.* TV's "Wanted: Dead or Alive." (Died 11-7-80.)

FACTS FROM THE PAST

1943 Rogers and Hammerstein's *Oklahoma* opened on Broadway. **ALFRED DRAKE** was the original Curly.

1955 The **TENNESSEE WILLIAMS'** play *Cat On a Hot Tin Roof* opened on Broadway with Barbara Bel Geddes as Maggie, Ben Gazarra as Brick and Burl Ives as Big Daddy.

1958 **ELVIS PRESLEY** was inducted into the Army in Memphis, TN. Thousands of fans wept the following day when his hair was cut by James Peterson at Ft. Chaffee, AK. Elvis, with his famed wry wit, quipped: "Hair today, gone tomorrow." Two years later, after his discarge, the singer became a movie star.

1962 Defending Welterweight Champion **BENNY "KID" PARET** lost consciousness when he was hammered 18 times on the ropes by Emile Griffith in the 12th round. He never regained consciousness and died nine days later.

1965 ROLLING STONE **BILL WYMAN** was knocked unconscious by a mike stand while performing in Denmark.

1973 An overzealous fan bit **LOU REED** on his butt. Afterward, Reed said, "America seems to breed real animals."

1986 **LIONEL RICHIE** won a Best Song Oscar for "Say You, Say Me" from the movie *White Nights.*

1989 The nation's second biggest oil spill occurred. **EXXON VALDEZ** rammed a charted reef about 25 miles from Port Valdez, Alaska. The tanker leaked 240,000 barrels of the 1.2 million on board. Captain **JOSEPH HAZELWOOD** was jailed, and acquitted in 1990. He was absolved of any criminal responsibility for the disaster in 1992 and he retained his sea license. The Valdez was renamed "Sea River Mediterranean."

1993 One of the wildest fights in NBA history cost the New York Knick's **GREG ANTHONY**, who came off the bench in street clothes, $85,500; **KEVIN JOHNSON** of Phoenix $60,000 and New York's **DOC RIVERS** $32,000. This was the league's largest ever monetary penalty.

1994 Convicted for the statuatory rape of Amy Fisher, **JOEY BUTTAFUOCO** was released 60 days before his 6 month sentence was up. Fisher is serving 5-15 years for shooting Buttafuoco's wife, Mary Jo.

MARCH 25

Do you believe in astrology?

BIRTHDAYS

- **DEBI THOMAS** Figure skater. (Poughkeepsie, NY) The first black World Champion figure skater. Year/**Age**: 1995/**28** 1996/**29** 1997/**30**

- **MARY GROSS** Comedienne. (Chicago, IL) Appeared on "Saturday Night Live" and in the film *Feds*. Year/**Age**: 1995/**42** 1996/**43** 1997/**44**

- **SARA JESSICA PARKER** Actress. Film *L.A. Story* with Steve Martin. Year/**Age**: 1995/**29** 1996/**30** 1997/**31**

- **NICK LOWE** Singer. (England) Biggest hit: "Cruel To Be Kind" in 1979. Married Carlene Carter in 1979. Year/**Age**: 1995/**46** 1996/**47** 1997/**48**

- **ELTON JOHN** Entertainer. (Born Reginald Kenneth Dwight in England) He earned a scholarship to the Royal Academy of Music at age 11. Elton John said he got his name from Elton Dean's and John Baldry's first names. Biggest hits: "Don't Go Breaking My Heart," recorded with Kiki Dee in 1976, and "Crocodile Rock." Year/**Age**: 1995/**48** 1996/**49** 1997/**50**

- **ARETHA FRANKLIN** Singer. (Memphis, TN) Biggest hit: "Respect" in 1967. The "Queen of Soul" was in the movie *The Blues Brothers* in 1980. Year/**Age**: 1995/**53** 1996/**54** 1997/**55**

- **ANITA BRYANT** Singer. (Barnsdall, OK) She had a hit in 1960, "Paper Roses." Year/**Age**: 1995/**55** 1996/**56** 1997/**57**

- **HOWARD COSELL** Sportscaster. (Born Howard William Cohen in Winston-Salem, NC) He holds a law degree. He worked "Monday Night Football" from 1970 - 1984. He announced his retirement from broadcasting January 31, 1992. Year/**Age**: 1995/**75** 1996/**76** 1997/**77**

- **HOYT AXTON** Singer/actor. (Duncan, OK) He had one song in the top 100 in 1974, "When Morning Comes." His mother, Mae Axton, composed "Heartbreak Hotel" for Elvis Presley. Films *Gremlins* and *The Black Stallion*. Year/**Age**: 1995/**57** 1996/**58** 1997/**59**

- **MARK BROOKS** Golfer. (Ft. Worth, TX) Year/**Age**: 1995/**34** 1996/**35** 1997/**36**

- **OLIVIA BURNETTE** Actress. Appeared in *Almost Home*. Year/**Age**: 1995/**18** 1996/**19** 1997/**20**

- **BONNIE BEDELIA** Actress. (NYC) Films include *They Shoot Horses, Don't They?* and *Presumed Innocent*. Year/**Age**: 1995/**48** 1996/**49** 1997/**50**

- **JOSEPH BARBERA** Animator. (NYC) Hanna Barbera cartoons, "Tom and Jerry," "The Smurfs," "Flintstones," and "Huckleberry Hound." Year/**Age**: 1995/**84** 1996/**85** 1997/**86**

- **PAUL MICHAEL GLASER** Actor. (Cambridge, MA) He appeared in the soap "Love of Life" and played Dave Starsky on "Starsky & Hutch" from 1975-1979. In the film *The Cutting Edge*. Year/**Age**: 1995/**52** 1996/**53** 1997/**54**

- **GLORIA STEINEM** Feminist. (Toledo, OH) Founder of *Ms Magazine*. Year/**Age**: 1995/**61** 1996/**62** 1997/**63**

- **EILEEN FORD** Model agency executive. (NYC) Year/**Age**: 1995/**73** 1996/**74** 1997/**75**

- **TOM MONAGHAN** Tycoon. (Ann Arbor, MI) Owner of the Detroit Tigers and head of Domino's Pizza restaurants. Year/**Age**: 1995/**58** 1996/**59** 1997/**60**

- **DAVID LEAN** Distinguished British director. (1908-1991 – Craydon, Engand) He won Oscars for *Bridge on the River Kwai* in 1957 and *Lawrence of Arabia* in 1962. He also directed *Dr. Zhivago* and *Ryan's Daughter*. (Died 4-16-91.)

- **GUTZON BORGLUM** American sculptor. (1867-1941 – Bear Lake, ID) He worked 14 years to create the huge sculpture of four American presidents on Mt. Rushmore. He died just before he finished his work. (Died 3-6-41.)

- **JOHNNY BURNETTE** Singer. (1934-1964 – Memphis, TN) His biggest hit: "You're Sixteen" in 1960. Along with his brother, Dorsey, he composed some songs for Rick Nelson. He died in a boating accident on Clear Lake in California at age 30. (8-14-64.)

- **ARTURO TOSCANINI** Music conductor. (1867 - 1957 – Italy) At first he was a cellist; later a good conductor, but the media made him a star. The maestro of abuse would throw his baton during rehearsals. He once said: "I kissed my first woman and smoked my first cigarette on the same day; I have never had time for tobacco since." (Died 1-16-57.)

FACTS FROM THE PAST

1937 The Quaker Oats Company announced that **BABE RUTH** was paid $25,000 for the use of his name in their ads.

1944 In a WWII raid over Germany, British Sergeant **NICK ALKEMADE**'s bomber was hit. His plane and parachute were on fire, so he jumped out without a parachute at 18,000 feet. He passed out during the fall and when he regained consciousness, he was in a snowbank in a forest. He was taken prisoner by the Germans who reported that other than having a few pine twigs stuck in him and some scratches and bruises, he was unhurt after falling over 3 miles.

1958 **SUGAR RAY ROBINSON** became the world's first boxing champion to win 5 times, beating Carmen Basilio in Chicago, IL.

1961 **ELVIS PRESLEY** played his last show for eight years at Hawaii's Block Arena. Elvis moved on to a booming movie career.

1965 **REV. MARTIN LUTHER KING, JR.** led 25,000 marchers to the state capitol in Montgomery, AL, to protest the denial of voting rights to blacks.

1990 In New York City, a man bounced from the Happy Land Social Club in the Bronx for quarreling with an ex-girlfriend returned with a jug of gasoline and set a fire that killed 87 people at the club, which had been ordered closed. **JULIO GONZALEZ**, 36, was charged with one count of arson and 87 counts of murder in the blaze.

1992 **COSMONAUT SERGEI KRIKALEV** returned to Moscow after spending 10 months in space. He was scheduled to stay in space for five months, but to cut costs, the Russians scrapped another flight and doubled his time. He was amazed upon returning that the Soviet Union no longer existed.

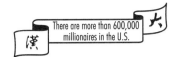

MARCH 26

BIRTHDAYS

- **MARCUS ALLEN** Football. (San Diego, CA) With the Kansas City Chiefs. Year/**Age**: 1995/**35** 1996/**36** 1997/**37**
- **JOHN STOCKTON** Basketball. (Spokane, WA) With Utah Jazz. Year/**Age**: 1995/**33** 1996/**34** 1997/**35**
- **TOM SULLIVAN** Singer/actor/composer. (Boston, MA) Sight-impaired entertainer who wrote *If You Could See What I Hear*, made into a film in 1982. Year/**Age**: 1995/**48** 1996/**49** 1997/**50**
- **GABRIELE KERNER** Singer. (Germany) As "Nena," hit in 1983: "99 Luftballons." Year/**Age**: 1995/**35** 1996/**36** 1997/**37**
- **JENNIFER GREY** Actress. (NYC) Daughter of actor Joel Grey. She was in the film *Wind*. She was in the car with Matthew Broderick when his car crashed, killing two women in Europe. Starred in *Dirty Dancing*. Year/**Age**: 1995/**35** 1996/**36** 1997/**37**
- **LEONARD NIMOY** Actor. (Boston, MA) Played Mr. Spock, in the science-fiction series "Star Trek," which premiered on TV on Sept. 8, 1966, and ran until March 1969, plus the feature films. He also portrayed Paris on the "Mission Impossible" TV series. Year/**Age**: 1995/**64** 1996/**65** 1997/**66**
- **ALAN ARKIN** Actor/director. (NYC) He received an Oscar nomination in 1966 for *The Russians are Coming*, and in 1968 for *The Heart is a Lonely Hunter*. Other films include *The In-Laws*, *Indian Summer*, and *Glengarry Glen Ross*. His son Adam is a comic actor. Year/**Age**: 1995/**61** 1996/**62** 1997/**63**
- **JAMES CAAN** Actor. (Bronx, NY) He received an Oscar nomination for supporting actor in *The Godfather* in 1972 and appeared on TV in *Brian's Song*. Other films were *Funny Lady*, *Dick Tracy*, *For The Boys*, *Flesh and Bone*, *Misery*, *A Bridge Too Far*, and *The Program*. He appeared in the film *Honeymoon in Vegas*. Year/**Age**: 1995/**56** 1996/**57** 1997/**58**
- **DIANA ROSS** Entertainer. (Detroit, MI) Biggest hits: "Endless Love" with Lionel Richie, "Upside Down," and with the SUPREMES, "Baby Love" in 1964. She was an Oscar nominee for the film *Lady Sings the Blues*, 1971. Year/**Age**: 1995/**51** 1996/**52** 1997/**53**
- **BOB WOODWARD** Watergate journalist. (Geneva, IL) He wrote *All The President's Men* and *Wired*, the story about John Belushi. Bob and John attended the same high school in Wheaton, IL. Year/**Age**: 1995/**51** 1996/**52** 1997/**53**
- **RONNIE McDOWELL** Country singer. (Fountain Head, TN) Biggest hit: "You're Gonna Ruin my Bad Reputation." Year/**Age**: 1995/**44** 1996/**45** 1997/**46**

- **CHARLEY McCLAIN** C&W. (Born Charlotte McClain in Jackson, TN) Biggest hit: "Radio Heart" in 1985. Year/**Age**: 1995/**39** 1996/**40** 1997/**41**
- **VICKI LAWRENCE** Talk-show hostess/actress. (Englewood, CA) She was chosen to be on the "Carol Burnett Show" because she looked like Carol. She had a hit in 1973: "The Night the Lights Went Out in Georgia." Has a TV show "Vicki" which was cancelled in 1994. Year/**Age**: 1995/**46** 1996/**47** 1997/**48**
- **STEVEN TYLER** Drummer. (NYC) Vocalist with AEROSMITH. Hit LP: *Toys in the Attic*. Year/**Age**: 1995/**47** 1996/**48** 1997/**49**
- **LEEZA GIBBONS** TV hostess. "Entertainment This Week" and "Entertainment Tonight." Year/**Age**: 1995/**38** 1996/**39** 1997/**40**
- **SANDRA DAY O'CONNOR** Supreme Court Justice. (El Paso, TX) First woman appointed to the U.S. Supreme Court. Before she was named a justice, she served as an Arizona state senator from 1969-1974. She was a Reagan nominee, sworn in September 25, 1981. She is a moderate conservative. Year/**Age**: 1995/**65** 1996/**66** 1997/**67**
- **TEDDY PENDERGRASS** Singer. (Philadelphia, PA) Before going out on his own, he was the lead singer of HAROLD MELVIN & THE BLUENOTES. Their biggest hit: "If You Don't Know Me By Now" in 1972. An auto accident in 1982 left him partially paralyzed. Year/**Age**: 1995/**45** 1996/**46** 1997/**47**
- **ERICA JONG** Author. (NYC) *Fear of Flying* and *How to Save Your Own Life*. Year/**Age**: 1995/**53** 1996/**54** 1997/**55**
- **MARTIN SHORT** Actor/comedian. (Hamilton, Ontario, Canada) *Three Amigos*, *Clifford* and "Saturday Night Live." In the Broadway musical *The Goodbye Girl* in 1993. Year/**Age**: 1995/**45** 1996/**46** 1997/**47**
- **TENNESSEE WILLIAMS** Playwright. (1911-1983 – Born Thomas Lanier Williams in Columbus, MS) His professional name came from an ancestor, the first senator of Tennessee. Williams was first published when he was 16, in a magazine called *Weird Tales*. He won two Pulitzer Prizes for *A Streetcar Named Desire* and *Cat on a Hot Tin Roof*. He died choking on a bottlecap in his New York hotel suite. (Died 2-25-83.)
- **ROBERT FROST** Poet. (1874-1963 – San Francisco, CA) Four-time Pulitzer Prize winner for poetry. Invited to read at the inauguration of President John F. Kennedy. (Died 1-29-63.)

FACTS FROM THE PAST

1966 The **BEATLES** posed with mutilated dolls and pieces of animal meat for the *Butcher* album photograph. The cover of the *Yesterday...and Today* album was released in the U.S. to much negative response. The original album is worth from $500 to $10,000.

1970 **PETER YARROW** of Peter, Paul and Mary found guilty of taking advantage of a 14-year-old girl. He spent 3 months in jail.

1979 The **CAMP DAVID PEACE TREATY** was signed by Israeli Prime Minister **MENACHEM BEGIN** (Men-ah'-kem Bay'-gihn) and Egyptian President **ANWAR SADAT** during a White House ceremony, with President **JIMMY CARTER** signing as a witness.

1992 **MIKE TYSON** was sentenced to six years in prison for raping a teenage beauty queen. A month later, the man who earned millions of dollars boxing began work in a prison recreation area in Plainfield, IN, for 65 cents a day.

1994 **PRESIDENT CLINTON** is his brother's best man at the marriage of Roger Clinton and Molly Martin.

MARCH 27

BIRTHDAYS

- **MARIAH CAREY** Singer. (Long Island, NY) Hits include: "Vision Of Love," "Someday," "I Don't Wanna Cry," and "I'll Be There." She is the only female artist to have eight consecutive Top 5 singles. Six of them made it to #1. She's married to Sony Music president, Tony Mottola. Year/Age: 1995/**25** 1996/**26** 1997/**27**

- **CLARK DATCHLER** Singer. (England) With the group JOHNNY HATES JAZZ. Biggest hit: "Scattered Dreams," 1988. Year/Age: 1995/**31** 1996/**32** 1997/**33**

- **MARIA SCHNEIDER** Actress. (Paris, France) Appeared with Marlon Brando in *Last Tango In Paris*. Year/Age: 1995/**43** 1996/**44** 1997/**45**

- **ANDREW FARRISS** Musician. (Sydney, Australia) Plays keyboard and guitar for INXS. Year/Age: 1995/**36** 1996/**37** 1997/**38**

- **TONY BANKS** Keyboardist. (England) With GENESIS, "Invisible Touch" in 1986. Year/Age: 1995/**45** 1996/**46** 1997/**47**

- **MICHAEL YORK** Actor. (Born Michael York-Johnson in Fulmer, England) He appeared in *The Taming of the Shrew*, *Romeo & Juliet, Cabaret,* and *Sword of Gideon*. Year/Age: 1995/**53** 1996/**54** 1997/**55**

- **CALE YARBOROUGH** Auto racer. (Born William Caleb Yarborough in Timmonsville, SC) Won Daytona 500 four times. In Motorsport's Hall of Fame. Year/Age: 1995/**56** 1996/**57** 1997/**58**

- **WES COVINGTON** Baseball. Hard-hitting outfielder for the Milwaukee Braves, who batted .330 in 1958. Year/Age: 1995/**63** 1996/**64** 1997/**65**

- **RANDY CUNNINGHAM** Football. (Santa Barbara, CA) Philadelphia Eagles quarterback. Year/Age: 1995/**32** 1996/**33** 1997/**34**

- **ARTHUR MITCHELL** Dance company director. (NYC) Dance Theater of Harlem, Inc. Year/Age: 1995/**61** 1996/**62** 1997/**63**

- **PATTY SMITH HILL** Composer. (1868-1946 – Anchorage, KY) Prominent kindergarten educator who wrote the most-sung song in the world, "Happy Birthday To You." (Died 5-25-46.)

- **DAVID JANSSEN** Actor. (1930-1980 – Born David Harold Meyer in Naponee, NE) He starred in the TV series "The Fugitive" from 1963-1967 and later, "Harry O." (Died 2-13-80.)

- **FRED ROYCE** Auto builder. (Born 1863 – England) In 1904, Royce built three experimental cars and talked car dealer C. S. Rolls into selling them. In 1906, Rolls and Royce merged to market the world's most luxurious cars.

- **SARAH VAUGHAN** Jazz singer. (1924-1990 – Newark, NJ) She was the first be-bop singer who sometimes would forget lyrics because she was concentrating on the notes and phrases. Her biggest hits: "Make Yourself Comfortable" in 1954 and "Broken Hearted Melody" in 1959. (Died 4-3-9.)

- **WILHELM ROENTGEN** [renk'-in] Scientist. (1845-1923 – Lennep, Prussia) German scientist who, at age 50, discovered the X-ray. He won the first Nobel Prize in physics. (Died 2-10-23.)

- **SNOOKY LANSON** Actor. (1914-1990 – Born Roy Landman in Memphis, TN) He was nicknamed Snooky at age 2 for the Irving Berlin song "Snooky-Ookums." He became best known as a star of TV's "Hit Parade" from 1952-1957. He had a hit record in 1949 called "The Old Master Painter." (Died 7-2-90.)

- **GLORIA SWANSON** Actress/businesswoman. (1899-1983 – Born Gloria May Josephine Svensson in Chicago, IL) She received 3 Oscar nominations, the last in 1950 for *Sunset Boulevard*. She was married 6 times, the first to actor Wallace Beery when she was 17. Her autobiography, *Swanson on Swanson*, was published in 1980. (Died 4-7-83.)

FACTS FROM THE PAST

1866 ANDREW RANKIN received a patent for the urinal.

1947 TOMMY RODGERS, a boxer with only one arm, knocked his opponent, Somersby Dowst, down twice in the 9th round to win the title fight in Cambridge, MA.

1955 STEVE McQUEEN made his network TV debut on a Goodyear Playhouse episode called *The Chivington Raid*.

1958 NIKITA KHRUSHCHEV became Soviet premier in addition to first secretary of the Communist Party.

1967 THE ROLLING STONES were pelted with bottles, chairs and even fireworks during a concert in Sweden. Police used dogs to help clear the unruly crowd.

1968 The world's first spaceman died. **SOVIET COSMONAUT YURI GAGARIN** became the first man in space in 1961. He died in a still-unexplained plane crash, when his jet nosed over and hit level ground in a pine forest outside Moscow. In Russia, there were many rumors that he was flying drunk, or flying carelessly. The Soviets never publicized the cause of the crash and used Gargarin's mother for PR appearances. She appeared dressed in black for dedications, etc.

1973 MARLON BRANDO turned down an Oscar for his performance in *The Godfather* as a gesture of support for the Indians occupying the Wounded Knee reservation in South Dakota.

1983 Former Hollywood stuntman, **STEVE WALLENDA**, got his name in the *Guinness Book of World Records* after crossing 4,166 feet on a highwire at an altitude of 31 feet.

1988 TINA TURNER gave what she called her **LAST LIVE PERFORMANCE** in Osaka, Japan. It included a surprise appearance by Mick Jagger who sang "Honky Tonk Woman" with her.

1994 "MAGIC" JOHNSON coached his first game for the LA Lakers who won 110-101 against the Milwaukee Bucks. He retired in April of

What's really inside "Hangar 18?"

MARCH 28

BIRTHDAYS

- **DIANNE WIEST** [weest] Actress. (Kansas City, MO) Won an Academy Award for best supporting actress in *Hannah & Her Sisters*, *Parenthood*, *Edward Scissorhands*, and *Little Man Tate*. Year/Age: 1995/**47** 1996/**48** 1997/**49**

- **KEN HOWARD** Actor. (El Centro, CA) In the TV series "White Shadow" and in the miniseries, "Thornbirds." He also appeared on "Dynasty" and "The Colbys." He was in the film *Rage of Angels*. He's married to Margo Coleman, daughter of Ann Landers. Year/Age: 1995/**51** 1996/**52** 1997/**53**

- **DIRK BOGARDE** Actor. (Born Derek Jules Gaspard Ulric Niven Van den Bogaerde) He's a British actor of Dutch descent. He appeared in *Tale of Two Cities*, *The Damned,* and *The Patricia Neal Story*. Year/Age: 1995/**74** 1996/**75** 1997/**76**

- **REBA McENTIRE** C&W singer. (Chockie, OK) Her dad was a world steer-roping champion and, while singing the National Anthem at a rodeo, Reba's career break came when Red Steagall heard her and was impressed enough to help her. She has won many country awards. Films *Tremors* and *North*. Year/Age: 1995/**41** 1996/**42** 1997/**43**

- **CHERL "SALT" JAMES** Rapper. (Queens, NY) Of the trio "Salt-n-Peppa." Hit in 1991, "Let's Talk About Sex." Year/Age: 1995/**26** 1996/**27** 1997/**28**

- **RICK BARRY** Pro basketball star. (Elizabeth, NJ) NBA rookie of the year in 1966, now a sportscaster and college coach. Very accurate freethrow shooter. His four sons play college and pro basketball. Year/Age: 1995/**51** 1996/**52** 1997/**53**

- **RUFUS THOMAS** Singer. (Cayce, MS) Hit: "Walking the Dog." He was a DJ at WDIA in Memphis. His daughter is Carla Thomas. Year/Age: 1995/**78** 1996/**79** 1997/**80**

- **JOHN EVANS** Keyboardist. (England) Biggest hits with JETHRO TULL: "Living in the Past" and "Bungle in the Jungle." Year/Age: 1995/**47** 1996/**48** 1997/**49**

- **MILAN WILLIAMS** Keyboardist. (Alabama) Hits with COMMODORES include: "Three Times a Lady," "Still," "Oh No," and "Easy." Year/Age: 1995/**47** 1996/**48** 1997/**49**

- **FREDDIE BARTHOLOMEW** Former child actor. 1924-1992 – England) He moved into advertising and was producer of "As The World Turns." He appeared in *David Copperfield* in 1935, *Little Lord Fauntleroy* in 1936, *Captains Courageous* in 1937 and *Swiss Family Robinson* in 1940. After Shirley Temple, he was the highest paid child star. (Died 1-23-92.)

- **AUGUST BUSCH, JR.** Brewer. (1899-1989) The last and biggest of the nation's old-time beer barons and president of the St. Louis Cardinals. In 1946, he took a small, troubled brewery started by his grandfather and turned it into the world's largest. Under August, the Cardinals became one of the most successful franchises in baseball, winning the World Series 3 times in 6 tries between 1964 and 1987. (Died 9-29-89.)

- **MARLIN PERKINS** Wildlife buff and zookeeper. (1905-1986) He was the host of "Wild Kingdom" on TV, but started in Chicago's Lincoln Park Zoo with a TV show called "Zoo Parade." (Died 6-14-86.)

FACTS FROM THE PAST

1384   CAT-EATING WAS CONDEMNED by England's Richard II. The peasants resented the King, whom they called "The Royal Cat," as he killed and ate thousands of cats. The expression "more than one way to skin a cat" came from this era when cats were cooked for dinner. A 1399 recipe book included a chapter on cat stews.

1834   The U.S. Senate voted to censure **PRESIDENT ANDREW JACKSON** for the removal of federal deposits from the Bank of the United States.

1915   **EMMA GOLDMAN** gave a speech to an audience in New York City. Her topic was shocking to that day's sedate society. The subject was contraception. She was arrested and given a choice of paying a $100 fine or going to jail for 15 days. She chose jail.

1969   Former **PRESIDENT DWIGHT EISENHOWER** died in Washington at the age of 78. Ike served as Supreme Commander of the Allied Troops in Europe during World War II and was the 34th U.S. President.

1970   **JANE BERINS** set a world record. The 16-year-old British girl **GO-GO DANCED FOR 18 HOURS.**

1973   Basketball's **WILT CHAMBERLAIN** played his last pro game. In 14 years, 1,045 games, he never once fouled out of a game.

1976   **GENESIS** opened its first North American tour with Phil Collins as lead vocalist after auditioning 400 singers.

1980   Former girls' school headmistress **JEAN S. HARRIS** pleaded innocent in White Plains, NY, to the shooting death of "Scarsdale Diet" doctor Herman Tarnower.

1983   **FRED JIPP** was sent to prison for 28 years in Phoenix, convicted of bigamy and fraud. He had married 104 women in 28 countries in 30 years.

1984   Without notice, **ROBERT IRSAY** moved the Baltimore Colts football team to Indianapolis in the middle of the night.

1989   **PRESIDENT BUSH** sent three high-ranking officials to Alaska to "take a hard look" at the *EXXON VALDEZ* OIL SPILL in Alaska's Prince William Sound.

1993   **RUSSIAN PRESIDENT BORIS YELTSIN** claimed victory after surviving attempts by the Russian Congress to expel them.

1994   Questions are raised as to the nature of **HILLARY CLINTON**'s business affairs as a report is released that her $1,000 land investment yielded $98,317 in profits over a time span of twenty-plus years.

MARCH 29

BIRTHDAYS

- **VANGELIS** Keyboardist/composer. (Born Evangelos Papathanassiou in Greece) Oscar-winning song: "Chariots of Fire." Year/Age: 1995/**52** 1996/**53** 1997/**54**
- **ELLE MacPHERSON** Actress/super model. She frequents Sports Illustrated Swimsuit Issues and appeared in the film *Sirens*. Year/Age: 1995/**31** 1996/**32** 1997/**33**
- **BUD CORT** Actor. (New Rochelle, NY) He was in "M*A*S*H" and *Harold & Maude*. Year/Age: 1995/**45** 1996/**46** 1997/**47**
- **ERIC IDLE** Actor/comedian. (Durham, England) Star of *Life of Brian*, *The Rutles*, *Splitting Heirs*, *Nuns on the Run*, and TV's "Nearly Departed." Year/Age: 1995/**52** 1996/**53** 1997/**54**
- **EARL CAMPBELL** Football pro. (Tyler, TX) Hall of Fame member. Played with Houston and New Orleans. Year/Age: 1995/**40** 1996/**41** 1997/**42**
- **KURT THOMAS** Olympic gymnast. (Terre Haute, IN) Year/Age: 1995/**39** 1996/**40** 1997/**41**
- **MARINA SIRTIS** Actress. Played Deanna Troi in the TV series "Star Trek: The Next Generation." Year/Age: 1995/**36** 1996/**37** 1997/**38**
- **WALT CLYDE FRAZIER** Basketball veteran. (Atlanta, GA) New York Knicks. Year/Age: 1995/**50** 1996/**51** 1997/**52**
- **BILLY VUKOVICH** Racecar driver. Raced Indy cars for 12 years. Indy 500 runner-up in 1973. Year/Age: 1995/**51** 1996/**52** 1997/**53**
- **EUGENE McCARTHY** Former Minnesota Senator. (Watkins, MN) 1968 presidential candidate. Year/Age: 1995/**79** 1996/**80** 1997/**81**
- **PHIL FOSTER** Actor/comedian. Played Frank DeFazio, Laverne's father, on "Laverne & Shirley". He also made a comedy record in the 1950's about a Brooklyn baseball fan. Year/Age: 1995/**82** 1996/**83** 1997/**84**
- **EILEEN HECKART** Actress. (Columbus, OH) Acted mainly on the stage, and appeared in the *The Bad Seed*. Year/Age: 1995/**76** 1996/**77** 1997/**78**
- **PEARL BAILEY** Entertainer. (1918-1990 – Newport News, VA) She received a Tony Award in 1968 for "Hello Dolly." She married drummer Louis Bellson in 1952 and was a government official. (Died 8-17-90.)
- **JENNIFER CAPRIATI** Former tennis star. (Saddlebrook, FL) She won the gold medal at the 1992 Olympics in Barcelona, Spain by beating Steffi Graf. She retired after being busted with marijuana twice Year/Age: 1995/**19** 1996/**20** 1997/**21**
- **SAM WALTON** (1918-1992 – Kingfisher, OK) Founded Wal-Mart Stores. Ranked among the world's most wealthy, building one store in 1962 into a $40 billion business. (Died 4-5-92.)
- **BILLY CARTER** Former "first brother". (1938-1988 – Plains, GA) He defined himself as a "beer-drinking good ol' boy." He put his name on a brand of beer that flopped and accepted money from Libya and was forced to sell some properties to pay his debt to the IRS. (Died 9-25-88.)
- **KAREN ANN QUINLAN** (1954-1985) At age 21, she lapsed into a coma at a birthday party which she remained in until her death at 31. Doctors said she was brain dead. Her parents went to the Supreme Court before getting permission to turn off her life-support system. The case touched off national debate over the right to die. Her parents used the profits from their book, *Karen Ann*, and a TV show (based on the book) to establish the Karen Ann Quinlan Center of Hope in 1980. (Died 6-11-85)
- **CY YOUNG** Baseball star. (1867-1955 – Born Denton True Young in Gilmore, OH) He was a $60-a-month baseball player when he was 23. He warmed up in the outfield by throwing the ball against a wooden fence and threw with such velocity that he splintered some of the boards.

FACTS FROM THE PAST

1812 The **FIRST WHITE HOUSE WEDDING** took place. Lucy Payne Washington, sister-in-law of President **JAMES MADISON**, married Supreme Court Justice Thomas Todd.

1886 The **FIRST BATCH OF COCA COLA** was brewed over a fire in a backyard in Atlanta, GA. John Pemberton created the concoction as a "hangover" cure and a stomach ache/headache remedy. He advertised it as a "brain tonic and intellectual beverage." Cocaine was an ingredient of Coke until 1904 when Congress banned it.

1932 A vaudeville comedian made his radio debut by saying: "Ladies and Gentlemen, this is **JACK BENNY** talking. There will be a slight pause while you say, "Who cares?"

1936 **ADOLF HITLER** got 98.8 percent of the vote in Germany's national elections.

1973 After protesting—in song—that they were never featured on the cover of *Rolling Stone* magazine, **DR. HOOK** got their wish. A week later, their single "Cover of the Rolling Stone" went gold.

1979 **ERIC CLAPTON** married **PATTIE BOYD**, the ex-wife of his friend, George Harrison.

1984 The *Wall Street Journal* reported columnist **R. FOSTER WINANS** was being investigated by the Securities and Exchange Commission for leaking inside information. (Winans was later convicted of securities fraud.)

1985 A wax figure of **MICHAEL JACKSON** was unveiled at Madame Tussaud's Museum in London.

1988 **MADONNA** made her stage debut in David Mamet's *Speed the Plow*, in New York.

1992 Presidential candidate **BILL CLINTON** admitted that he used marijuana but said he "didn't inhale."

1994 **DALLAS COWBOY COACH JIMMY JOHNSON** resigned after a long time feud with the owner. He led Dallas to two Superbowl victories.

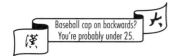

MARCH 30
Doctor's Day

BIRTHDAYS

• **HAMMER** Rapper. (Born Stanley Kirk Burrell in Oakland, CA) He was an Oakland A's batboy in the 1970s. A's slugger Pedro Garcia noticed that he resembled homerun champ Hank Aaron. Pedro started calling him Little Hammer and the name stuck with him. One of his hits: "U Can't Touch This" in 1990. He sold 8 million albums in 1990. Does ads for Kentucky Fried Chicken. Year/**Age**: 1995/**32** 1996/**33** 1997/**34**

• **PAUL REISER** Actor. TV's "My Two Dads" and "Mad About You." Year/**Age**: 1995/**38** 1996/**39** 1997/**40**

• **IAN ZIERING** Steve on "Beverly Hills 90210." Year/**Age**: 1995/**31** 1996/**32** 1997/**33**

• **WARREN BEATTY** Actor/producer. (Born Warren Beaty in Richmond, VA) He attended Northwestern University where he studied acting. He is the younger brother of Shirley MacLaine. Nominated for best actor in 1967 for *Bonnie & Clyde*. Won an Oscar for directing *Reds*. Starred as *Dick Tracy*. He was nominated for best actor for *Bugsy* and married his co-star, Annette Bening. Year/**Age**: 1995/**58** 1996/**59** 1997/**60**

• **CELINE DION** Singer. (Canada) Hits include: "If You Ask Me To" and "Where Does My Heart Beat Now." Year/**Age**: 1995/**27** 1996/**28** 1997/**29**

• **PETER MARSHALL** TV host. (Huntington, WVA) He won several Emmys for hosting "Hollywood Squares" on NBC-TV. The daytime version began in 1966. Year/**Age**: 1995/**65** 1996/**66** 1997/**67**

• **JOHN ASTIN** Actor. (Baltimore, MD) He appeared in *West Side Story* in 1961 and is the former husband of Patty Duke. Gomez on TV's "Addams Family." He is on TV's "Night Court." Year/**Age**: 1995/**65** 1996/**66** 1997/**67**

• **ERIC CLAPTON** Rock star. (Born Eric Patrick Clapp in England) Biggest hit: "I Shot the Sheriff" in 1974. He was a member of the YARDBIRDS in 1965 when they had their hit: "For Your Love." Ex-wife Pattie Boyd Harrison inspired Clapton to write "Layla," while she was still married to his buddy George Harrison. Year/**Age**: 1995/**50** 1996/**51** 1997/**52**

• **RANDY WANWARMER** Singer/guitarist/composer. (Indian Hills, CO) Hit in 1979, "Just When I Needed You." Year/**Age**: 1995/**40** 1996/**41** 1997/**42**

• **TRACY CHAPMAN** Singer. (Cleveland, OH) Won a Grammy for "Fast Car" in 1988. Year/**Age**: 1995/**31** 1996/**32** 1997**33**

• **FRANKIE LAINE** Singer. (Born Frank Paul LoVecchio in Chicago, IL) His biggest hit: "Lucky Old Sun" in 1949. Year/**Age**: 1995/**82** 1996/**83** 1997/**84**

• **JERRY LUCAS** Basketball's Hall of Fame star. With the L.A. Lakers. Year/**Age**: 1995/**55** 1996/**56** 1997/**57**

• **GRAEME EDGE** Drummer. (England) Biggest hit with MOODY BLUES, "Nights In White Satin." Year/**Age**: 1995/**53** 1996/**54** 1997/**55**

• **RICHARD DYSART** Actor. (Augusta, ME) "L.A. Law." Year/**Age**: 1995/**66** 1996/**67** 1997/**68**

• **SECRETARIAT** The greatest race horse ever. (1970-1989 – Meadows Stud Farm in Doswell, VA) He won the 1973 Triple Crown, becoming the only horse to break the 2-minute mark in the Kentucky Derby, and won at Belmont by an astonishing 31 lengths. He won 16 out of 21 races and $1,316,808 in two years. (Died 10-4-89 and is buried at Claiborne Farm in Paris, KY.)

• **SEAN O'CASEY** Playwright. (1880-1964 – Born John Casey in Ireland) He wrote comic-tragedy about violence in Irish history and about Ireland's revolutionary heroes. Most popular play: *Juno and the Paycock*. (Died 9-18-64.)

• **VINCENT VAN GOGH** Artist. (1853-1890) Dutch artist, best-known for his powerful use of color. He worked with the great Paul Gauguin for 2 months until their strained relationship ended. On Christmas Eve, 1888, the distraught Van Gogh cut off part of his own left ear and gave it to a prostitute. This mutilation was later to figure in his *Self-Portrait with Bandaged Ear*. In 1990 the American Medical Association said this was the result of a ear infection and not a mental disorder. (Died 7-29-1890.) [See 1987 below.]

FACTS FROM THE PAST

1842 In the days before painkillers, doctors would get a patient drunk in an attempt to lessen some of the pain. **DR. CRAWFORD LONG** of Jefferson, GA, placed an ether-soaked towel over the face of James Venable and removed a tumor from his neck. This was the **FIRST RECORDED USE OF ANESTHESIA.** Today is Doctor's Day in his honor.

1858 **HYMAN LIPMAN** of Philadelphia, PA, patented the **FIRST PENCIL WITH ERASER.** The average pencil can write a continuous line 35 miles long.

1867 **AMERICA BOUGHT ALASKA** from the Soviet Union due to pressure from Secretary of State William Seward. The critics called Alaska "Seward's Ice Box" and "Seward's Folly" and said we were paying an exorbitant price for land the nation didn't need. The price was $7.2 million or slightly more than 2 cents an acre.

1960 Congressman **TIP O'NEILL** demanded that the **FCC INVESTIGATE PAYOLA** and protect America's youth from rock and roll, which he called "a type of sensuous music unfit for impressionable minds."

1981 **PRESIDENT RONALD REAGAN** and three others were **SHOT AND WOUNDED** outside the Washington Hilton Hotel by John Hinckley, Jr., who wanted to impress actress Jodie Foster.

1987 An anonymous buyer paid over $39 million for **VINCENT VAN GOGH**'s *Sunflowers*. **DON McLEAN** wrote a song about him called "Vincent."

1991 Palm Beach police reported a woman's claim that she was raped at the Kennedy compound. **WILLIAM KENNEDY SMITH** was charged and eventually found innocent.

MARCH 31

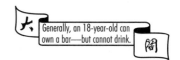
Generally, an 18-year-old can own a bar—but cannot drink.

BIRTHDAYS

- **LEO BUSCAGLIA** Author. (Los Angeles, CA) Educator and author who began the theory of hugging strangers and telling people one has never met, "I love you." Year/Age: 1995/**70** 1996/**71** 1997/**72**

- **ALBERT GORE, JR.** Vice-President (Washington, DC) Elected Vice President under Bill Clinton in the 1992 presidential election. His father, Albert Gore, Sr., was a Tennessee congressman and senator from 1938-1970. Year/Age: 1995/**47** 1996/**48** 1997/**49**

- **RICHARD CHAMBERLAIN** Actor. (Los Angeles, CA) He appeared on TV as "Dr. Kildare" in the early 1960's. In 1969, he played *Hamlet* on the British stage and won impressive reviews. He's called "king of the mini-series" for his roles in "Shogun," "Centennial," and as Father Ralph in "The Thornbirds." In 1989, he returned to TV as a doctor in the series "Island Son." Year/Age: 1995/**60** 1996/**61** 1997/**62**

- **SHIRLEY JONES** Entertainer. (Smithton, PA) She won an Oscar in 1960 as best supporting actress in *Elmer Gantry*. In *Oklahoma*, *Carousel*, and *Music Man*. Also the mother on the "Partridge Family." At age 17, she was Miss Pittsburgh in 1951. Year/Age: 1995/**61** 1996/**62** 1997/**63**

- **GABE KAPLAN** Actor/comedienne. (Born Gabriel Kaplan in Brooklyn, NY) He created the idea for TV's "Welcome Back, Kotter" which was based on his own Brooklyn childhood. Year/Age: 1995/**50** 1996/**51** 1997/**52**

- **CHRISTOPHER WALKEN** Actor. (NYC) He appeared in *Batman Returns*, *The Addiction*, *The Deer Hunter*, *Biloxi Blues*, *Wayne's World II*, and *True Romance* and was a guest aboard the yacht with Robert Wagner and Natalie Wood when Natalie drowned. Played the James Bond movie villain, Max Zorin. Year/Age: 1995/**52** 1996/**53** 1997/**54**

- **HERB ALPERT** Musician. (Los Angeles, CA) Biggest hit with the TIJUANA BRASS, "This Guy's in Love With You" in 1968. He had five #1 albums in the 1960's, and has won several Emmy Awards. Year/Age: 1995/**60** 1996/**61** 1997/**62**

- **LIZ CLAIBORNE** Fashion designer. (Belgium) Year/Age: 1995/**66** 1996/**67** 1997/**68**

- **SYDNEY CHAPLIN** Actor. (Beverly Hills, CA) In the film *Chaplin*. He is the son of Charley Chaplin. Year/Age: 1995/**69** 1996/**70** 1997/**71**

- **JOHN D. LOUDERMILK** C&W singer/songwriter. (Durham, NC) He wrote "Tobacco Road," "Indian Reservation," "Waterloo," and "Wonderful World" recorded by SAM COOKE. Year/Age: 1995/**61** 1996/**62** 1997/**63**

- **ANGUS YOUNG** Guitarist. (Australia) AC/DC. Year/Age: 1995/**36** 1996/**37** 1997/**38**

- **MICK RALPHS** Guitarist. (England) BAD COMPANY. Biggest hit: "Can't Get Enough" in 1974. Year/Age: 1995/**47** 1996/**48** 1997/**49**

- **RICHARD KILEY** Actor. (Chicago, IL) He appeared on Broadway in *Man of La Mancha*. He was the first to sing "The Impossible Dream." He appeared in *A Year in the Life*. Year/Age: 1995/**73** 1996/**74** 1997/**75**

- **HENRY MORGAN** Radio/TV personality. (1915-1994 NYC) Panelist on game shows such as "I've Got a Secret," and "What's My Line." He first worked on the radio at age 13.

- **WILLIAM DANIELS** Actor. (Brooklyn, NY) Played Dr. Craig on "St. Elsewhere." Year/Age: 1995/**68** 1996/**69** 1997/**70**

- **GORDIE HOWE** Hall-of Fame hockey star. (Canada) The hockey forward was the NHL "MVP" 6 times. He played 10 full hockey seasons following his 40th birthday. Year/Age: 1995/**67** 1996/**68** 1997/**69**

- **RHEA PERLMAN** Actress. (Brooklyn, NY) Wife of actor Danny DeVito. Emmy winning Carla on "Cheers." Year/Age: 1995/**47** 1996/**48** 1997/**49**

- **FRANZ JOSEPH HAYDN** Composer. (1732-1809 – Austria) He was called the "father of the symphony," composing over 100 symphonies, a dozen operas and hundreds of other musical works. Soon after Haydn's death and burial a prison warden who was an amateur phrenologist had grave robbers steal the head so he could examine it. The theft was not discovered until 1820 and it was not until 1954 that the body and skull were finally reunited. (Died 5-31-1809.)

FACTS FROM THE PAST

1870   **THOMAS PETERSON MUNDY** cast a ballot in a municipal election in Perth Amboy, NJ, becoming the **FIRST BLACK TO VOTE** after ratification of the 15th Amendment.

1889   French engineer **ALEXANDRE GUSTAVE EIFFEL** unfurled the French tricolor from atop the **EIFFEL TOWER** in Paris, officially marking its completion. The world's largest steel structure was built for a Paris exhibition.

1923   The **FIRST DANCE MARATHON** began at the Audubon Ballroom in NYC. **ALMA CUMMINGS** danced the fox trot, one-step and waltz for 27 hours and tired out six partners.

1967   At a Finsbury Park, UK, concert that included Engelbert Humperdinck and Cat Stevens, **JIMI HENDRIX** torched his guitar for the first time.

1987   A judge in Hackensack, NJ, awarded custody of **BABY M**, born to a surrogate mother, to her natural father and stripped mother Mary Beth Whitehead of all parental rights and upheld the $10,000 contract under which she agreed to give up the child.

1989   **WRESTLEMANIA-5** became the largest pay-per-view cable TV program in history. **HULK HOGAN** went up against Macho Man Savage.

1993   **BRANDON LEE**, 28, son of actor **BRUCE LEE**, died of abdominal wounds after being shot by a .44-caliber bullet from a gun supposedly rigged with blanks. He was filming a scene for the film *The Crow* in Wilmington, NC.

A pair of Jacksons: **JANET** to the right and **MICHAEL** above.

WYNONNA JUDD

JON BON JOVI

Clearly and presently **WILLEM DaFOE**

SEINFELD's cast

"Unplugged" **TONY BENNETT**

LUKE PERRY

Anchors of NBC's "Dateline" **JANE PAULEY & STONE PHILLIPS**

JASON PRIESTLEY

NBC's, CBS's, and the whole world's Mr. Late Night. . . **DAVID LETTERMAN**

"A candle in the wind" **MARILYN MONROE**

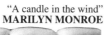

The Shaq attack **SHAQUILLE O'NEAL**

APRIL MEMORIES

YEARS AGO

1985

POPULAR SONGS
"We Are the World" by USA for Africa

"Rhythm of the Night" by DeBarge

MOVIES
Ran
starring Tasuya Nakadai and Satoshi Terao. This film retells Shakespeare's *King Lear*.

St. Elmo's Fire
starring Rob Lowe, Emilio Estevez, Ally Sheedy, and Demi Moore as young adults who struggle with growing up.

TV SHOWS
"Hail To the Chief"
starring Patty Duke as President Julia Mansfield in this comedy.

"Night Heat"
an action series about police detectives starring Alian Royal.

BOOKS
Lake Woebegone Days by Garrison Keller

1986

POPULAR SONGS
"Rock Me Amadeus" by Falco

"Kiss" by Prince & The Revolution

MOVIES
Peggy Sue Got Married
starring Kathleen Turner as a woman who goes back in time. Nicholas Cage co-stars.

Salvador
starring James Woods as Richard Boyle, a photographer sees the social injustice in El Salvador through the eye of his camera.

TV SHOWS
"Sledge Hammer!"
comedy with David Rasche as Detective Inspector Sledge Hammer.

"The Wizard"
starring David Rappaport as Simon McKay, who gets caught up in foreign intrigue.

BOOKS
It by Stephen King

1987

POPULAR SONGS
"Nothing's Gonna Stop Us Now" by Starship

"I Knew You Were Waiting (For Me)" by Aretha Franklin and George Michael

MOVIES
Cry Freedom
starring Kevin Kline and Denzel Washington. The story of newspaper editor in Africa.

Baby Boom
Diane Keaton unexpectedly inherits care of her cousin's baby.

TV SHOWS
"Married With Children"
comedy about the Bundy family. Stars Ed O'Neil, Katey Sagal, Christina Applegate, and David Faustino.

"The Tracy Ullman Show"
a variety comedy series.

BOOKS *The Great Depression of 1990* by Ravi Batra

SPECIAL DAYS

APRIL	1995	1996	1997
Good Friday	Apr. 14	Apr. 5	Mar. 28
Daylight Savings Time	Apr. 1	Apr. 6	Apr. 5
Easter Sunday	Apr. 16	Apr. 7	Mar. 30
Chicken Little Awards *(Maplewood, NJ)*	Apr. 3	Apr. 8	Apr. 7
Boston Marathon	Apr. 3	Apr. 1	Apr. 7
National Whistlers Convention	Apr. 28-30	Apr. 26-28	Apr. 25-27
Secretaries Week	Apr. 23-29	Apr. 21-27	Apr. 20-26
Full Moon	Apr. 15	Apr. 4	Apr. 22
National Typing Contest	Apr. 24-28	Apr. 22-26	Apr. 21-25
Secretary Day	Apr. 26	Apr. 24	Apr. 23
Passover	Apr. 15	Apr. 4	Apr. 22

YEARS AGO

1970

POPULAR SONGS
"Let It Be" by the Beatles

"ABC" by The Jackson 5

MOVIES
Lovers and Other Strangers
starring Gig Young, Richard Castellano, Bea Arthur, and Anne Meara. Story of two families together for a wedding.

Tora! Tora! Tora!
starring Joseph Cotton and Jason Robards, Jr. in a film about the bombing of Pearl Harbor.

TV SHOWS
"Nancy"
stitcom starring Renne Jarrett as the president's daughter. Celeste Holm plays her chaperone.

"Half Nelson"
starring Joe Pesci as a Beverly Hills detective. Co-stars Dick Butkus and Bubba Smith.

BOOKS
Sexual Politics by Katherine Murray

1971

POPULAR SONGS
"Joy To the World" by Three Dog Night

"Take Me Home, Country Roads" by John Denver

MOVIES
Klute
starring Jane Fonda, Donald Sutherland, and Roy Scheider. A policeman falls for a call girl.

The Boy Friend
starring Twiggy, Christopher Gable, and Tommy Tune. A musical comedy set in the 1920s.

TV SHOWS
"The Persuaders"
a story of two rich playboys starring Tony Curtis and Roger Moore.

"The Good Life"
sitcom starring Larry Hagman and Donna Mills, who work for a wealthy family.

BOOKS *The Betsy* by Harold Robbins

1972

POPULAR SONGS
"The First Time I Ever Saw Your Face" by Roberta Flack

"Rockin' Robin" by Michael Jackson

MOVIES
Sleuth
starring Laurence Olivier and Micheal Caine in a murder mystery.

Payday
Rip Torn portrays a struggling C&W singer.

TV SHOWS
"The Julie Andrews Hour"
a musical variety show with regulars Alice Ghostley and Rich Little.

"NBC Mystery Movie"
a rotating Wednesday night movie. Shows included, "Madigan" with Richard Widmark, "Cool Million" starring James Farentino, and "Banacek" featuring George Peppard.

BOOKS *Harry S. Truman* by Margaret Truman

YEARS AGO

1945

POPULAR SONGS
"I'm Beginning To See The Light" by Harry James

"Chloe" by Spike Jones & His City Slickers

MOVIES
The Story of G.I. Joe
starring Burgess Meredith as the famous war correspondent Ernie Pyle. Co-stars Robert Mitchum.

Wonder Man
comedy featuring Danny Kaye and Virginia Mayo. Kaye plays two roles in this story of a one-man show.

TV SHOWS
No regular TV programming until May of 1946.

BOOKS
The Animal Farm: A Fairy Story by George Orwell

1946

POPULAR SONGS
"Laughing On the Outside (Crying On the Inside)" by Teddy Walters

"Cement Mixer (Put-Ti, Put-Ti)" by Alvino Rey

MOVIES
The Razors Edge
starring Tyrone Power as a man seraching for faith. Co-stars Gene Tierney, Clifton Webb, and Anne Baxter.

Sister Kenny
starring Rosalind Russell in the title role of the story of a famous nurse.

TV SHOWS
No regular TV programming until May of 1946.

BOOKS
The Hucksters by Frederic Wakeman

1947

POPULAR SONGS
"Linda" by Buddy Clark with the Ray Noble Orchestra

"Mam'selle" by Frank Sinatra

MOVIES
The Bishop's Wife
starring Cary Grant as an angel who comes down to earth to help Loretta Young with her family.

The Perils of Pauline
starring Betty Hutton, John Lund, and Billy de Wolfe in a story of silent screen star Pearl White.

TV SHOWS
"Doorway To Fame"
a TV talent show with Johnny Olsen and the Ned Harvey Orchestra.

BOOKS
Prince of Foxes by Samuel Shellabarger

APRIL 1
April Fool's Day/Publicity Stunt Week

Were humans once as sharp-nosed as dogs?

BIRTHDAYS

- **ANNETTE O'TOOLE** Actress. (Houston, TX) In the film *Cross My Heart*. Year/Age: 1995/**43** 1996/**44** 1997/**45**

- **DEBBIE REYNOLDS** Actress. (Born Mary Frances Reynolds in El Paso, TX) She had a #1 hit in 1957: "Tammy" and was nominated for an Academy Award in 1964 for best actress in *The Unsinkable Molly Brown*. In film *Heaven and Earth*. Year/Age: 1995/**63** 1996/**64** 1997/**65**

- **BO SCHEMBECHLER** Football coach. (Barberton, OH) Retired from University of Michigan. Year/Age: 1995/**66** 1996/**67** 1997/**68**

- **ALI MacGRAW** Actress. (Pound Ridge, NY) She received an Oscar nomination for best actress for *Love Story* in 1970. She appeared on TV in "Winds of War" in 1983. Formerly married to the late Steve McQueen. Year/Age: 1995/**57** 1996/**58** 1997/**59**

- **MAGDALENA MALEEVA** Tennis star. Year/Age: 1995/**20** 1996/**21** 1997/**22**

- **JANE POWELL** Entertainer. (Born Suzanne Burce in Portland, OR) She appeared in *Small Town Girl* and *Three Sailors and a Girl*. Occasionally appeared in TV's "Growing Pains." Year/Age: 1995/**66** 1996/**67** 1997/**68**

- **MARK JACKSON** Basketball. Year/Age: 1995/**30** 1996/**31** 1997/**32**

- **GORDON JUMP** Actor. (Dayton, OH) "The Big Guy" Arthur Carlson, station manager on "WKRP in Cincinnati" and also played an editor on the "Lou Grant Show." TV's Maytag repairman. Year/Age: 1995/**63** 1996/**64** 1997/**65**

- **SCOTT STEVENS** Hockey. Year/Age: 1995/**31** 1996/**32** 1997/**33**

- **TOSHIRO MIFUNE** Actor. (Japan) Appeared in *Seven Samurai* and *Grand Prix*. Year/Age: 1995/**75** 1996/**76** 1997/**77**

- **DON HASTINGS** Actor. His first TV role, "Video Ranger," the Captain's main assistant on "Captain Video." He later went on to greater fame in "As the World Turns" and "Edge of Night" soap operas. Year/Age: 1995/**61** 1996/**62** 1997/**63**

- **PHIL NIEKRO** Baseball. (Lansing, OH) Atlanta Braves knuckleball pitcher. 275 wins and a no-hitter in his career. Year/Age: 1995/**56** 1996/**57** 1997/**58**

- **RUDOLPH ISLEY** Singer. (Cincinnati, OH) ISLEY BROS. Biggest hit: "It's Your Thing" in 1969. Their best known dance song, "Shout," did not even make the top 40. Year/Age: 1995/**56** 1996/**57** 1997/**58**

- **DAVID EISENHOWER** (West Point, NY) Grandson of former President Dwight Eisenhower, married to Julie Nixon, daughter of Richard Nixon. "Camp David" was named after him by his grandfather. Year/Age: 1995/**48** 1996/**49** 1997/**50**

- **ART LUND** Singer/actor. (1920-1990 – Salt Lake City, UT) Rose to fame with the Benny Goodman orchestra and later acted in such films as *The Molly McGuires* and TV shows like "Gunsmoke" and "Little House on the Prairie." (Died 5-31-90.)

- **SERGEI RACHMANINOFF** Composer. (1873-1943 – Russia) *Second Piano Concerto*. (Died 3-28-43.)

- **HANS CONRIED** Actor. (1915-1982 – Baltimore, MD) He began his career in radio appearing on "The Great Gildersleeve," "My Friend Irma," and "Life With Luigi." He's probably best known as "Uncle Tonoose" on the Danny Thomas "Make Room for Daddy" TV series. (Died 1-5-82.)

- **WALLACE BEERY** Actor. (1886-1949 – Kansas City, MO) He won an Oscar in 1931 for *The Champ* co-starring Jackie Cooper. He was the first husband of Gloria Swanson whom he married when she was 17 years old. (Died 4-15-49.)

- **EDGAR WALLACE** Writer. (1875-1932 – England) A human book factory, he wrote 10,000 words a day. He authored 173 books including *The Terror*, 23 plays, hundreds of articles and the screen play for *King Kong*. (Died 2-1-32.)

- **LON CHANEY** Actor. (1883-1930 – Colorado Springs, CO) Born to hearing-impaired parents, he starred in the classics: *The Phantom of the Opera* and *The Hunchback of Notre Dame*. Chaney, the "Man of a Thousand Faces," was played on film by James Cagney. (Died 8-26-30.)

FACTS FROM THE PAST

1929 The **YO YO WAS INTRODUCED** by Louie Marx purposely on April Fool's Day.

1930 Chicago Cubs baseball star **GABBY HARNETT** pulled off an April Fool's stunt, catching baseballs dropped from a Goodyear blimp hovering over Los Angeles.

1931 **JACKIE MITCHELL**, 19, became the first woman in history to be signed by an **ALL-MALE TEAM**. She pitched for a Chattanooga, TN, minor league team. She struck out quite a few batters.

1957 The **EVERLY BROTHERS'** second record was released, the first on the Cadence label. "Bye Bye Love," written by Boudleaux Bryant, was turned down by 30 acts before the Everlys decided to cut it.

1963 **"GENERAL HOSPITAL"** went on the air for the first time. The soap opera was one of daytime television's biggest success stories. The wedding of Luke and Laura in 1981, with guest star **LIZ TAYLOR**, attracted the largest audience ever to watch a daytime dramatic series.

1984 Singer **MARVIN GAYE** was shot to death by his father in LA. He pleaded guilty to voluntary manslaughter and was put on probation.

1993 President Clinton urges Americans to **HELP RUSSIA** in the interest of peace and prosperity, not charity.

1994 Model **CHRISTIE BRINKLEY** suffered minor injuries when a helicopter she was riding in with five other skiers crashed on a mountainside in Telluride, CO.

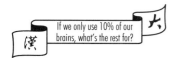

If we only use 10% of our brains, what's the rest for?

APRIL 2

BIRTHDAYS

- **LEON RUSSELL** Musician. (Lawton, OK) Hits include "Tight Rope" and "Lady Blue," and, with Willie Nelson, a #1 country hit, "Heartbreak Hotel." Year/Age: 1995/**54** 1996/**55** 1997/**56**
- **JOSEPH BERNARDIN** Archbishop of Chicago, Cardinal. Year/Age: 1995/**67** 1996/**68** 1997/**69**
- **SIR ALEC GUINNESS** Actor. (London, England) He played the driven British colonel in 1957 in *Bridge on the River Kwai* for which he won an Oscar. He also appeared in *Star Wars* as Obi-Wan-Kenobi and in *Passage to India*, a movie that received 11 Oscar nominations. Year/Age: 1995/**81** 1996/**82** 1997/**83**
- **EMMYLOU HARRIS** Singer. (Birmingham, AL) She's a laid-back country singer. Her biggest hit was "Mr. Sandman" in 1981. Part of Grammy-winning trio with Dolly Parton and Linda Ronstadt. Year/Age: 1995/**48** 1996/**49** 1997/**50**
- **RON PALILLO** Actor. (New Haven, CT) He played "Sweat Hog" Arnold Horshack on "Welcome Back, Kotter." Year/Age: 1995/**41** 1996/**42** 1997/**43**
- **BRIAN GOODELL** Swimmer. (Stockton, CA) Year/Age: 1995/**36** 1996/**37** 1997/**38**
- **BUDDY EBSEN** Actor. (Born Christian Rudolf Ebsen, Jr., in Belleville, IL) He was on the TV series "Beverly Hillbillies" as Jed Clampett, "Barnaby Jones" and "Matt Houston." He was originally cast in *The Wizard of Oz* as the Tin Man but he was allergic to the makeup. Wrote: *The Other Side of Oz*. Year/Age: 1995/**87** 1996/**88** 1997/**89**
- **LINDA HUNT** Actress. (Morristown, NJ) Won an Oscar in 1983, playing a man in the film *The Year of Living Dangerously*. Also in the film *Kindergarten Cop*. Year/Age: 1995/**50** 1996/**51** 1997/**52**
- **KEREN WOODWARD** Musician. (England) Member of the female trio BANANARAMA. Their biggest record: "Venus" in 1986. Year/Age: 1995/**34** 1996/**35** 1997/**36**
- **DON SUTTON** Baseball. (Clio, AL) Played most of his career pitching for the Oakland A's. Now a baseball announcer for the Atlanta Braves. Year/Age: 1995/**50** 1996/**51** 1997/**52**

- **WALTER CHRYSLER** Automaker. (1875-1940 – Wamego, KS) He quit GM in 1920 and eventually formed the Chrysler Corp. (Died 8-18-40.)
- **FREDERIC AUGUSTE BARTHOLDI** Sculptor. (1834-1904 – Colmar, France) Created the *Statue of Liberty* and gave it to America in 1886. (Died 10-4-04.)
- **HERBERT MILLS** Singer. (1912-1989 – Piqua, OH) The MILLS BROTHERS hold the record for the most hit records over the longest span of time. They scored their first of many hits in 1931 and were still hitting the charts in the late 1960's. Biggest hit: "Paper Doll" in 1943. They got their start on WLW radio in Cincinnati. (Died 4-12-89.)
- **JACK WEBB** Actor. (1920-1982 – Santa Monica, CA) Probably best known for his role as stonefaced Sgt. Joe Friday on the "Dragnet" series on radio and TV. The LA Police Dept. retired Jack Webb's badge, #714. He began his career as a radio announcer in San Francisco in 1945 on KGO. (Died 12-23-82.)
- **HANS CHRISTIAN ANDERSEN** Author. (1805-1875) Danish novelist and writer of children's fairy tales – 168, including *The Ugly Duckling* and *The Red Shoes*. He was a virgin, so his friends took him to a brothel one night where he and the lady of the night spent the entire night…talking! (Died 8-4-1875.)
- **MARVIN GAYE, JR.** Singer. (1939-1984 – Washington, DC) Biggest hit: "I Heard It Through The Grapevine." He won two Grammys for his million-selling "Sexual Healing" cut from his last album, *Midnight Love*. He was fatally shot (4-1-84) during a family argument. His 70-year-old father, Marvin Gaye, Sr. (an Apostolic minister), was charged with the shooting.
- **GIOVANNI CASANOVA** Writer/librarian/renowned lover. (1725-1798 – Venice, Italy) Factory worker, writer, gambler, church-goer. After preaching a sermon in church, the collection plate was filled with propositions from women. Once when he was turned down by a woman, he said he began to die. (Died 6-4-1798.)

FACTS FROM THE PAST

1513   Spanish explorer **PONCE DE LEON** landed in Florida searching for the **FOUNTAIN OF YOUTH**. It was the Easter Season, so he named the area Flowery Easter or Pascua Florida [pass'-ku-a flor-ree'-da].

1865   Confederate **PRESIDENT JEFFERSON DAVIS** and most of his cabinet fled the confederate capital of Richmond, Virginia.

1917   **PRESIDENT WOODROW WILSON** asked Congress to declare war saying, "The world must be made safe for democracy."

1932   Aviator **CHARLES LINDBERGH** and **DR. JOHN CONDON** turned over $50,000 to an unidentified man in a cemetery in Bronx, NY, as ransom for Lindbergh's kidnapped son, but he had already been murdered.

1974   The **BEST-REMEMBERED ACADEMY AWARD** surprise happened on this night. Actor **DAVID NIVEN** was finishing his presentation when he heard the audience roar and saw a figure dashing across the TV monitors. A man named **ROBERT OPEL** streaked across the stage naked. Niven didn't miss a beat and said, "Isn't it fascinating that probably the only laugh this man will ever get in life is by stripping off his clothes and showing his shortcomings?"

1980   Toshiaki Shirai and Yukiko Nagata of Tokyo set the **WORLD UNDERWATER KISSING RECORD** (2 minutes, 18 seconds).

1986   Alabama **GOVERNOR GEORGE C. WALLACE**, paralyzed 14 years before by a bullet, announced his retirement from public life.

1994   **VLADIMIR ZHIRLNOVSKY** threw a party conference and got himself declared leader of the Ultranationalist Liberal Democratic Party for 10 years. He declared he would win the presidency by 1996.

APRIL 3

If only coins could talk about where they've been...

BIRTHDAYS

• **JEFF BARRY** Songwriter. He wrote the song "Tell Her I Love Her." He and his wife Ellie Greenwich wrote many songs including "Hanky Panky," "Da Doo Ron Ron," and "Leader of the Pack." Year/Age: 1995/57 1996/58 1997/59

• **CARLOS SLINAS DE GORTARI** President of Mexico. Year/Age: 1995/47 1996/48 1997/49

• **DON GIBSON** C&W singer. (Shelby, NC) His biggest hit: "Oh Lonesome Me" which he wrote. He also wrote "I Can't Stop Loving You." Year/Age: 1995/67 1996/68 1997/69

• **EDDIE MURPHY** Actor/comedian. (Brooklyn, NY) He first became a star on "Saturday Night Live." Films include *Beverly Hills Cop*, *Boomerang*, *48 Hours*, and *The Distinguished Gentleman*. Biggest hit: "Party All the Time" in 1985. Married Nicole Mitchell March 18, 1993 at the Plaza Hotel in Manhattan. They have a young son and a daughter. His brother is "CB4" star Charlie Murphy. Year/Age: 1995/34 1996/35 1997/36

• **MELISSA ETHRIDGE** Singer. 1994 hit "Come To My Window." Year/Age: 1995/34 1996/35 1997/36

• **DORIS DAY** Entertainer. (Born Doris von Kapplehoff in Cincinnati, OH) She changed her name when a nightclub owner heard her singing "Day by Day." She received an Oscar nomination for best actress in 1959 for *Pillow Talk*, co-starring Rock Hudson. Her biggest hit was Oscar-winning "Que Sera Sera" in 1956, which she sang in an Alfred Hitchcock remake of *The Man Who Knew Too Much*. Year/Age: 1995/71 1996/72 1997/73

• **MARLON BRANDO** Actor. (Omaha, NE) He won an Oscar for best actor in 1954 for *On the Waterfront* and in 1972 for *The Godfather*. Expelled from the military academy, later he was voted Broadway's most promising actor. He made his film debut in 1950 in *The Men*. He was paid $5 million for his part in the 1992 film *Christopher Columbus: The Discovery*. Autobiography: *Brando*. Year/Age: 1995/71 1996/72 1997/73

• **WAYNE NEWTON** "Mr. Las Vegas." (Norfolk, VA) His break came in 1962 on the "Jackie Gleason Show." Bobby Darin produced his first charted single, "Danke Schoen." Biggest hit: "Daddy Don't You Walk so Fast" in 1972. Year/Age: 1995/53 1996/54 1997/55

• **MARSHA MASON** Actress. (St. Louis, MO) Nominated twice for an Academy Award for: *The Goodbye Girl* with Richard Dreyfuss and *Cinderella Liberty* with James Caan. Formerly married to Neil Simon. Year/Age: 1995/53 1996/54 1997/55

• **TONY ORLANDO** Entertainer. (Born Michael Anthony Cassavitis in Manhattan, NY) As leader of DAWN, Tony was one of pop music's most successful singers in the 1970's. Biggest hit: "Tie a Yellow Ribbon" in 1973, 2nd most recorded song of the rock era after the BEATLES "Yesterday." Year/Age: 1995/51 1996/52 1997/53

• **DONNY ANDERSON** Football player. (Brooklyn, NY) Year/Age: 1995/46 1996/47 1997/48

• **MIYOSHI UMEKI** Actress. Japanese leading lady who won an Academy Award for her performance in *Sayonara* in 1957. Also in *Flower Drum Song* and TV series "The Courtship of Eddie's Father." Year/Age: 1995/66 1996/67 1997/68

• **ALEC BALDWIN** Actor. (Massapequa, NY) With Kim Bassinger in *The Marrying Man* (they married in 1993) *Prelude to a Kiss*, *The Getaway*, *The Shadow*, *Malice*, and *Glengarry Glen Ross*. His brothers include actors Dan, Stephen, and Bill. Year/Age: 1995/37 1996/38 1997/39

• **LYLE ALZADO** Football star. (1949-1992 – Brooklyn, NY) NFL all-pro lineman. He played for the Los Angeles Raiders, Denver Broncos and Cleveland Browns. He blamed steroid use for his brain cancer. (Died 5-14-92.)

• **RICHARD MANUEL** Pianist. (1943-1986 – Canada) With the BAND. Hit: "Up On Cripple Creek" in 1969. (Died 3-4-86.)

• **LESLIE HOWARD** Actor. (1893-1943 – Born Leslie Stainer in England) Played Ashley in *Gone with the Wind*, co-starred with Norma Shearer in *Romeo & Juliet*. They had a rule in Hollywood at that time: if you made love you had to have both feet on the floor…and they did! He was killed when his civilian flight from Lisbon to London was shot down by Germans during WWII. (Died 6-1-43.)

• **SALLY RAND** Fan dancer. (1904-1979 – Born Helen Gould Beck at Hickory County, MO) American actress who created the "fan dance" which gained fame during the 1933 Chicago World's Fair. She still danced in her 70s. (Died 8-31-79.)

FACTS FROM THE PAST

1882 **JESSE JAMES** was shot in the back by his cousin, Robert Ford. When Robert went to get the $10,000 reward, he found that folks were upset that he shot the legend.

1920 It was wedding bells for **F. SCOTT FITZGERALD** and Zelda Sayre. Their honeymoon at the Biltmore Hotel in NYC became so boisterous that the management asked them to leave.

1936 **BRUNO HAUPTMANN** was electrocuted in Trenton, NJ, for the kidnap-murder of the Lindbergh infant.

1953 **TV GUIDE** was born. It sold for 15 cents a copy. Desi, Jr. (new baby of Lucille Ball and Desi Arnaz) appeared on the first cover.

1959 The **COASTERS' "CHARLIE BROWN"** was banned on England's BBC, because of the word "spitball."

1960 **ELVIS PRESLEY** recorded his first tracks since leaving the U.S. Army. One of the first recorded was "It's Now or Never."

1989 Nearly eleven million gallons of oil continued to spread from the **EXXON VALDEZ**, ten days after it went aground in Prince William Sound. The tanker was refloated April 5, the same day **CAPT. JOSEPH HAZELWOOD** was jailed in lieu of $1 million bail. He was released April 6 after another judge lowered the bail to $25,000 and in 1990 he was acquitted.

1994 Walt Disney's Frank Wells was killed in a helicopter crash in Nevada. Responsible for films *Aladdin*, *Sister Act*, and *Pretty Woman*.

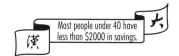

Most people under 40 have less than $2000 in savings.

APRIL 4

BIRTHDAYS

- **KITTY KELLEY** Author. (Hartford, CT) Wrote unauthorized biographies of Frank Sinatra and Nancy Reagan. Year/**Age**: 1995/**53** 1996/**54** 1997/**55**

- **STEVE GATLIN** Country music. (Brentwood, TN) GATLIN BROTHERS. Hit: "All the Gold." Year/**Age**: 1995/**44** 1996/**45** 1997/**46**

- **FRANCES LANGFORD** Entertainer. (Lakeland, FL) During World War II, she did many Christmas shows with Bob Hope and recorded "The Bickersons" albums with Don Ameche. Year/**Age**: 1995/**82** 1996/**83** 1997/**84**

- **KRIS JENSEN** Singer/guitarist. (New Haven, CT) Biggest hit: "Torture" in 1962. Year/**Age**: 1995/**53** 1996/**54** 1997/**55**

- **MAJOR LANCE** Soul singer. (Chicago, IL) In prison for selling cocaine from 1978-81. Biggest hit: "Um, Um, Um, Um, Um, Um," in 1964. Year/**Age**: 1995/**53** 1996/**54** 1997/**55**

- **HUGH MASEKELA** Trumpeter/bandleader/arranger. (South Africa) Formerly married to Miriam Makeba, formed his own band in 1964. Biggest hit: "Grazing in the Grass" in 1968. Year/**Age**: 1995/**56** 1996/**57** 1997/**58**

- **CHRISTINE LAHTI** Actress. (Detroit, MI) She received an Oscar nomination for *Swing Shift* in 1984. Also appeared in *Crazy From the Heart*, *The Doctor*, *Hideaway,* and *Leaving Normal*. Year/**Age**: 1995/**45** 1996/**46** 1997/**47**

- **NANCY McKEON** Actress. (Westbury, NY) "Facts of Life" TV series. Year/**Age**: 1995/**29** 1996/**30** 1997/**31**

- **MICHAEL PARKS** Actor. TV series "Bronson" and "Twin Peaks." Film: *The Bible*. Year/**Age**: 1995/**57** 1996/**58** 1997/**59**

- **RUSTY STAUB** Baseball player. (Born Daniel Staub in New Orleans, LA) First baseman. The first player to DH in all 162 games, in 1978 with the Detroit Tigers. Year/**Age**: 1995/**51** 1996/**52** 1997/**53**

- **ROBERT DOWNEY, Jr.** Actor. (NYC) In the films *Chaplin*, *Natural Born Killers*, *Short Cuts* and *Heart and Soul*. Son of Film producer Robert Downey, Sr. Year/**Age**: 1995/**30** 1996/**31** 1997/**32**

- **CRAIG T. NELSON** Actor. (Spokane, WA) "Coach." Year/**Age**: 1995/**48** 1996/**49** 1997/**50**

- **ELMER BERNSTEIN** Composer. (NYC) He won an Oscar for the score of *Thoroughly Modern Millie*. Year/**Age**: 1995/**73** 1996/**74** 1997/**75**

- **ERNIE TERRELL** Fighter. Year/**Age**: 1995/**56** 1996/**57** 1997/**58**

- **JOHN CAMERON SWAYZE** Newsman. (Wichita, KS) He was one of TV's first news anchors who began the popular 15-minute "Camel News Caravan" on NBC-TV from 1948-56. He was replaced by the "Huntley/Brinkley Report." Year/**Age**: 1995/**89** 1996/**90** 1997/**91**

- **JIM FREGOSI** Baseball. Shortstop who played for the Angels and was later traded to the Mets for Nolan Ryan. Batted 265 in his career. Year/**Age**: 1995/**53** 1996/**54** 1997/**55**

- **MAYA ANGELOU** Writer. (St. Louis, MO) *I Know Why the Caged Bird Sings.* Read her poem at Clinton's inauguration. Year/**Age**: 1995/**67** 1996/**68** 1997/**69**

- **ISOROKU YAMAMOTO** Naval leader. (1884-1943 – Japan) He planned the Pearl Harbor attack December 7, 1941. He was killed when his plane was shot down by U.S. aircraft (4-18-43.)

- **BERRY OAKLEY** Bassist. (1948-1972 – Macon, GA) Biggest hit with ALLMAN BROTHERS BAND: "Ramblin Man." He was killed in a motorcycle accident just 3 blocks from where Duane Allman's fatal accident happened a year earlier. (Died 11-11-72.)

- **ARTHUR MURRAY** Dance professional. (1895-1991 – Born Moses Teichman in NYC) He founded a string of 500 dance schools and hosted an 11-year TV show. (Died 3-3-91.)

- **A. BARTLETT GIAMATTI** [juh-mah'-tee] Baseball Commissioner. (1938-1989 – Boston, MA) He declared no one is above the game and kicked out Pete Rose. (Died 9-1-89.)

- **MUDDY WATERS** Blues guitarist. (1915-1983 – Born McKinley Morganfield in Rolling Fork, MS) There's a street named for him in Chicago. (Died 4-30-83.)

- **LINUS YALE** Painter/inventor. (1821-1868 – Salisbury, NY) Portrait painter and inventor who invented the Yale infallible bank lock and developed the cylinder lock. (Died 12-25-1868.)

FACTS FROM THE PAST

1887 Susanna Medora Salter became the **1ST WOMAN TO BE ELECTED MAYOR** of an American community; Argonia, KS.

1964 The **BEATLES** had the top five records on the *Billboard* magazine U.S. chart: "Can't Buy Me Love," "Twist and Shout," "She Loves You," "I Want to Hold Your Hand," and "Please Please Me."

1967 **JOHNNY CARSON** quit the "Tonight Show." He came back three weeks later after being offered a $30,000-a-week raise.

1968 Civil Rights leader **DR. MARTIN LUTHER KING, JR.,** was gunned down by a sniper as he stood on a motel balcony in Memphis, TN. James Brown appeared on national TV asking viewers to refrain from violence. Jimi Hendrix and B.B. King gathered musicians in a New York club and played blues all night, raising funds for King-sponsored organizations.

1969 Captain Kirk and his crew cut their 5-year mission short when **"STAR TREK"** was canceled by NBC, after a total of 79 episodes.

1974 **HANK AARON** of the Atlanta Braves tied **BABE RUTH**'s home-run record by hitting his 714th home run in Cincinnati.

1989 **RICHARD M. DALEY** was elected mayor of Chicago by a wide margin, capturing the office held by his father for 21 years.

1992 **JOHN TESH** of "Entertainment Tonight" married actress **CONNIE SELLACA** in Beverly Hills.

1993 **PRESIDENT CLINTON** and Russian leader **BORIS YELTSIN** concluded their summit with the president pledging $1.62 billion in aid to Russia.

APRIL 5

In reality, how many people can sleep in a 3-man tent?

BIRTHDAYS

- **AGNETHA FÄLTSKOG** Singer. (Stockholm, Sweden) With ABBA, biggest hit: "Dancing Queen" in 1977. Year/**Age**: 1995/**45** 1996/**46** 1997/**47**

- **JANE ASHER** Stage/screen/actress/author. (England) Best known as Paul McCartney's former fiancée. Sister of Peter, member of former PETER & GORDON. In film *Alfie*. Year/**Age**: 1995/**49** 1996/**50** 1997/**51**

- **TOMMY CASH** C&W. (Dyess, AK) Biggest hit: "Six White Horses" in 1969, a tribute to John & Robert Kennedy and Martin Luther King. Younger brother of Johnny Cash. Year/**Age**: 1995/**55** 1996/**56** 1997/**75**

- **GREGORY PECK** Actor. (Born Eldred Gregory Peck in LaJolla, CA) He won an Oscar in 1962 for best actor in *To Kill a Mockingbird*. Also in the film *The Portrait*. Year/**Age**: 1995/**79** 1996/**80** 1997/**81**

- **GALE STORM** Singer/actress. (Born Josephine Cottle in Bloomington, TX) She starred in "My Little Margie" on TV from 1952-1955. She had six top-ten hits during the 1950's including "I Hear You Knocking" and "Dark Moon." Year/**Age**: 1995/**73** 1996/**74** 1997/**75**

- **MICHAEL MORIARITY** Actor. (Detroit, MI) Won two Emmys: for supporting actor in *The Glass Menagerie* and for portraying an ambitious Nazi officer on *Holocaust* in 1978. Stars in TV's "Law & Order." Year/**Age**: 1995/**54** 1996/**55** 1997/**56**

- **ROGER CORMAN** Director. (Detroit, MI) Known for his horror films including *The Intruder, Tales of Terror, The St. Valentine's Day Massacre* and *The Pit and the Pendulum*. Year/**Age**: 1995/**69** 1996/**70** 1997/**71**

- **ARTHUR HAILEY** Author. (England) *Hotel, Airport,* and *Wheels*. Year/**Age**: 1995/**75** 1996/**76** 1997/**77**

- **MAX GAIL** Actor. (Detroit, MI) He played Sgt. Stan Wojehowicz "Wojo" on the "Barney Miller" TV show and was in "Normal Life." Year/**Age**: 1995/**52** 1996/**53** 1997/**54**

- **JOSEPH LISTER** Physcian. (1827-1912 – England) He was the founder of antiseptic surgery. (Died 2-10-12.)

- **COLIN POWELL** Retired military leader general. (New York, NY) First black chairman of the Joint Chiefs of Staff. Involved in Panama and Desert Storm conflicts. Year/**Age**: 1995/**58** 1996/**59** 1997/**60**

- **TONY WILLIAMS** Singer. (1928-1992 – Elizabeth, NJ) He was lead singer for the PLATTERS. Their biggest hit: "My Prayer" in 1956. While he was leader of the group, they had four #1 hits and 16 gold records. (Died 8-14-92)

- **WASHINGTON BURPEE** Botonist. (1858-1915 – Canada) Washington and his son David (born April 5, 1893) published the Burpee Seed Catalog and developed lima beans and many other hybrids.

- **BETTE DAVIS** Actress. (1908-1989 – Born Ruth Elizabeth Davis in Lowell, MA) Nominated for an Academy Award 10 times, won 2 Oscars: *Dangerous* in 1935 and *Jezebel* in 1938. She turned down the role of Scarlett in *Gone with the Wind*. (Died 10-6-89.)

- **JUDITH RESNIK** Teacher and Shuttle Passenger. (1949-1986 – Akron, OH) The second American woman in space. She was the mission specialist on the Space Shuttle Challenger when it exploded 1-28-86.

- **SPENCER TRACY** Actor. (1900-1967 – Milwaukee, WI) The 1930 film *Up the River* gave him his big break in the motion picture business. He won an Oscar for best actor in 1937 for *Captains Courageous*, in 1938 for *Boy's Town* and was nominated 7 more times, the last in 1967 for *Guess Who's Coming To Dinner* with Katharine Hepburn, his long-time companion. (Died 6-1-67.)

- **MELVYN DOUGLAS** Actor. (1905-1981 – Born Melvyn Hesselberg in Macon, GA) He won an Oscar in 1963 as supporting actor in *Hud*. At one time, his wife, Helen Gahagan, ran against Richard Nixon for a Congressional seat.

- **BOOKER T. WASHINGTON** Black leader. (1856-1915 – Franklin City, VA) His mother was a black slave. By age 9 he worked in a coal mine; then as a janitor, teacher and first Principal of Tuskegee Institute in Alabama. He founded self-help organizations for blacks. (Died 4-14-15.)

FACTS FROM THE PAST

1614 American Indian **PRINCESS POCAHONTAS**, daughter of Chief Powhatan, married Virginia colonist John Rolfe.

1887 Anne Sullivan made a breakthrough with blind/deaf student, **HELEN KELLER**, by conveying the meaning of the word "water."

1984 Basketball star **KAREEM ABDUL-JABBAR** of the LA Lakers became the highest-scoring player in NBA history. He reached 31,419 career points in a game against the Utah Jazz. The record was previously held by Wilt Chamberlain.

1985 Radio stations around the world dropped their usual programming for a simultaneous Good Friday broadcast of "**WE ARE THE WORLD.**" It was written by Michael Jackson and Lionel Richie and recorded by 46 U.S. artists for the Africa Relief Fund.

1990 **DONALD TRUMP'S** TAJ MAHAL, his Atlantic City hotel/casino, opened, hoping patrons would lose the necessary $1 million/day to keep the casino running.

1993 With 11 seconds left in the NCAA Championship game and North Carolina leading 73-71, Michigan's 20-year-old **CHRIS WEBBER** called timeout when there was none remaining, costing Michigan a technical foul. North Carolina went on to win 77-71.

1993 **SHERRY DAVIS** became the first woman to be a public address announcer for a major league baseball team. She won the audition for San Francisco Giants' P.A. announcer March 10, 1993 against 499 fellow auditioners.

1994 The longest serving member of congress, Rep. **JAMIE WHITTEN** (D/MS) announced his retirement. He was elected Nov. 4, 1941.

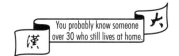

You probably know someone over 30 who still lives at home.

APRIL 6

BIRTHDAYS

- **JANET LYNN** Figure skater. (Rockford, IL) Year/**Age**: 1995/**42** 1996/**43** 1997/**44**

- **BILLY DEE WILLIAMS** Actor. (NYC) He played Diana Ross's lover in *Lady Sings the Blues* and was also in *Mahogany* with Ross. His big break came in 1980 in *The Empire Strikes Back* and in 1983, *The Return of the Jedi*. He also played Gale Sayers in the TV movie *Brian's Song*. He was in the TV film "The Jacksons: An American Dream." Year/**Age**: 1995/**58** 1996/**59** 1997/**60**

- **ANDRE PREVIN** Pianist/composer/conductor. (Berlin, Germany) His biggest hit: "Like Young" in 1958. He was married to actress Mia Farrow from 1970-1979. Year/**Age**: 1995/**66** 1996/**67** 1997/**68**

- **STERLING SHARP** Football. All pro Green Bay Packer wide receiver. Year/**Age**: 1995/**30** 1996/**31** 1997/**32**

- **IVAN DIXON** Actor. (NYC) "Hogan's Heroes." Year/**Age**: 1995/**65** 1996/**66** 1997/**67**

- **MICHELLE PHILLIPS** Actress/singer. (Long Beach, CA) She appeared in the soap "Search For Tomorrow," "Hotel," and "Knots Landing." She was with the MAMAS AND PAPAS when they released "Monday, Monday" on her birthday in 1966. Year/**Age**: 1995/**51** 1996/**52** 1997/**53**

- **MERLE HAGGARD** C&W. (Bakersfield, CA) Biggest hit: "If We Can Make It Through December" in 1974. At age 21 he was paroled from California's San Quentin Prison where he did a lot of rethinking in solitary. The first song he wrote, "Okie From Muskogee," became a phenomenon. Year/**Age**: 1995/**58** 1996/**59** 1997/**60**

- **JULIE ROGERS** Singer. (Born Julie Rolls in England) Biggest record: "The Wedding" in 1964. Year/**Age**: 1995/**51** 1996/**52** 1997/**53**

- **JASON HERVEY** Actor. TV's "The Wonder Years." Year/**Age**: 1995/**23** 1996/**24** 1997/**25**

- **BERT BLYLEVEN** Pitcher. Cleveland and Minnesota. He was released by the Twins in 1993, just 13 wins short of 300. Year/**Age**: 1995/**44** 1996/**45** 1997/**46**

- **CANDACE CAMERON** Actress..(LA, CA) Plays DJ Tanner on "Full House." She's the sister of "Growing Pains" star, Kirk Cameron. Year/**Age**: 1995/**19** 1996/**20** 1997/**21**

- **JOHN RATZENBERGER** Actor. (Bridgeport, CN) Played Cliff on "Cheers" until the last show May 20, 1993. Year/**Age**: 1995/**48** 1996/**49** 1997/**50**

- **ARI MEYERS** Actress. (San Juan, Puerto Rico) Kate's daughter Emma on "Kate & Allie." Year/**Age**: 1995/**26** 1996/**27** 1997/**28**

- **LOWELL THOMAS** Broadcaster/newsman. (1892-1981 – Woodington, OH) He was one of the first news people to broadcast from an airplane, a submarine and even from a coal mine. His radio sign off: "So long until tomorrow." The voice of "Movietone" movie news for nearly 20 years. (Died 8-29-81.)

- **HARRY HOUDINI** Magician. (1874-1926 – Born Ehrich Weiss in Appleton, WI) No locks, chains or manacles could hold this greatest of all escape artists. He was a great athlete and got out of strait jackets by contracting his muscles in such a way that he could slip one hand out of its bonds and then set the rest of his limbs free. Houdini left directions on how some of his stunts could be done, but everyone has failed. He died at Grace Hospital in Detroit, following a blow to his abdomen. He and his wife made a pact to contact each other from the hereafter, but the widow, who lived another 17 years, never received the message. (Died 10-31-26.)

FACTS FROM THE PAST

1868 **BRIGHAM YOUNG,** the Mormon Church leader, married his 27th and last wife.

1896 The **FIRST MODERN OLYMPIC GAMES** opened in Athens, Greece.

1909 Admiral Robert Peary and his black assistant Matthew Henson reached the **NORTH POLE**, the first expedition to get there. On this date in 1988 Henson was honored and his remains were reburied in Arlington National Cemetery.

1930 Bakery executive James Dewar invented a cream-filled sponge cake in order to use small baking pans that would otherwise remain in storage except for each year's brief strawberry shortcake season. **HOSTESS TWINKIES** became the original junkfood. About a billion Twinkies are consumed a year.

1935 **HAROLD "BUNNY" LEVITT** dunked 499 consecutive free throws. He missed on his 500th try. Then he threw in 371 more shots without a miss. The Harlem Globetrotters offered $1,000 to anyone who could beat his record. The closest anyone came was 86 out of 100 and the worst Levitt ever shot was 96. Why didn't he play college or pro ball? "Bunny" was only 5 feet 4 inches tall.

1947 The first **TONY AWARDS** were presented at a dinner in the Grand Ballroom of the Waldorf Astoria on Easter Sunday. The Tonys are named for **ANTOINETTE PERRY**, a stage actress very dedicated to the theatre.

1956 Paramount Pictures signed **ELVIS PRESLEY** to a three-picture contract five days after his first screen test.

1958 **ARNOLD PALMER** won the Masters Tournament, his first major pro golf victory.

1973 New York Yankee **RON BLOMBERG** became baseball's first designated hitter. He walked with the bases loaded against the Boston Red Sox' Luis Tiant. That year he hit .329 for 301 at-bats.

1992 **ELVIS PRESLEY** fans began to vote in the nation's first-ever election for postage stamp art. Over 1 million postcard ballots showed the younger Elvis winning over the older by a 3-1 margin. The stamp was issued in January 1993.

APRIL 7

From the Even-Keel Dept.:
Tiny Tim was just an act.

BIRTHDAYS

- **ALAN PAKULA** Movie producer/director. (NYC) Some of his credits include: *To Kill A Mockingbird, Love with the Proper Stranger,* and *Klute.* Year/**Age:** 1995/**67** 1996/**68** 1997/**69**

- **SPENCER DRYDEN** Drummer. (San Francisco, CA) JEFFERSON AIRPLANE. Left the group in 1970. Their biggest hit: "Somebody To Love," in 1967. Year/**Age:** 1995/**52** 1996/**53** 1997/**54**

- **JAMES GARNER** Actor. (Born James Baumgarner in Norman, OK) He first appeared on TV's "Maverick" then in the movie and also starred in "The Rockford Files" and the short-lived "Man of the People." He's seen often in TV commercials. James got an Oscar nomination for *Murphy's Romance* in 1986. In the film *Fire in the Sky.* Year/**Age:** 1995/**67** 1996/**68** 1997/**69**

- **TONY DORSETT** Heisman trophy-winning NFL football star. (Rochester, PA) 13-year veteran with the Dallas Cowboys and Denver Broncos, retired in 1990. In his career he rushed for 12,739 yards. He's in the Football Hall of Fame. Year/**Age:** 1995/**41** 1996/**42** 1997/**43**

- **JERRY BROWN** Former Governor of California. (San Francisco, CA) Unsuccessful Democratic presidential candidate in 1976, 1980, and 1992. Deputed his radio talk show in 1994. Year/**Age:** 1995/**57** 1996/**58** 1997/**59**

- **DAVID FROST** TV host/author. (England) He won a couple of Emmy awards for outstanding variety or musical series for the "David Frost Show." Year/**Age:** 1995/**56** 1996/**57** 1997/**58**

- **FRANCIS FORD COPPOLA** Writer/film director. (Detroit, MI) He started by making "nudie" movies. Won Oscars for *Patton,* and *Godfather I & II. Godfather II* is the only sequel to win best picture. Year/**Age:** 1995/**56** 1996/**57** 1997/**58**

- **JOHN OATES** Musician/singer. (NYC) Of HALL & OATES. Hit "Maneater," in 1982. Year/**Age:** 1995/**47** 1996/**48** 1997/**49**

- **BOBBY BARE** C&W. (Irontown, OH) Biggest hit: "All American Boy" in 1959, written by Bill Parsons, but Bobby Bare is the real vocalist on the song; a label error listed Parsons as the artist when it was released. Bare was in the Army, so Parsons toured lip synching to the record. Year/**Age:** 1995/**60** 1996/**61** 1997/**62**

- **HODDING CARTER** Media commentator. Year/**Age:** 1995/**60** 1996/**61** 1997/**62**

- **CAL SMITH** C&W. (Sallisaw, OK) One of his hits was "Country Bumpkin" in 1974. He and his wife Jennie own "The Bare Trap," featuring thousands of bear type gifts in Nashville, TN. Year/**Age:** 1995/**63** 1996/**64** 1997/**65**

- **SEYMOUR HERSH** Writer. (Chicago, IL) He won a Pulitzer Prize in 1970 for articles on the My Lai massacre. Year/**Age:** 1995/**58** 1996/**59** 1997/**60**

- **FRED EBB** Composer. (NYC) Wrote *New York, New York.* Won Tonys for *Woman of the Year* and *Cabaret.* In the Songwriters Hall of Fame. Year/**Age:** 1995/**62** 1996/**63** 1997/**64**

- **CHARLIE THOMAS** Tenor. One-time lead singer for the DRIFTERS. Their biggest hit: "Save the Last Dance for Me" in 1960. Year/**Age:** 1995/**58** 1996/**59** 1997/**60**

- **WAYNE ROGERS** Actor. (Birmingham, AL) Trapper John in TV series "M*A*S*H." Year/**Age:** 1995/**62** 1996/**63** 1997/**64**

- **RAVI SHANKAR** Sitar player. (India) He inspired George Harrison and a host of other musicians in the late 1960's with his Indian music. Year/**Age:** 1995/**75** 1996/**76** 1997/**77**

- **BILL KREUTZMANN** Drummer. (San Francisco, CA) GRATEFUL DEAD. Biggest hit: "Truckin'" in 1971. Year/**Age:** 1995/**49** 1996/**50** 1997/**51**

- **BILLIE HOLIDAY** Blues singer. (1915-1959 – Born Eleanora Fagan in Baltimore, MD) She sang with COUNT BASIE and ARTIE SHAW, and recorded with BENNY GOODMAN & PAUL WHITEMAN, among others. She had a hit song called "Them There Eyes." Died of a heroin overdose (7-17-59).

- **PERCY FAITH** Conductor/arranger. (1908-1976 – Toronto, Canada.) Worked with some of Columbia Records' leading artists in the 1950's. Biggest hit: "Theme from a Summer Place" which won a 1960 Grammy. The movie starred Sandra Dee, Dorothy McGuire and Troy Donahue. (Died 2-9-76.)

- **WALTER WINCHELL** Journalist. (1897-1972 – NYC) Controversial American journalist, gossip columnist and radio broadcaster who roused the ire of many prominent public figures. He also did some singing and acting and founded the Damon Runyon Cancer Fund in 1946. (Died 2-20-72.)

- **WILLIAM WORDSWORTH** Poet/philosopher. (1770-1850 – England) He said, "Poetry is the spontaneous overflow of powerful feelings: it takes its origin from emotion recollected in tranquillity." (Died 4-23-1850.)

FACTS FROM THE PAST

1920 **EDWARD, PRINCE OF WALES**, first met Lt. Winfield Spencer and his future wife, Wallis, at a reception in San Diego aboard the flagship *New Mexico.* 16 years later as King Edward VIII, he renounced his throne to marry Wallis, who was then twice-divorced.

1927 An audience in New York saw an image of Commerce Secretary Herbert Hoover transmitted from Washington in the **FIRST SUCCESSFUL LONG-DISTANCE DEMONSTRATION OF TELEVISION.**

1940 **BOOKER T. WASHINGTON** became the first African-American to be pictured on a U.S. postage stamp, a 10-cent stamp.

1949 The musical **SOUTH PACIFIC** opened on Broadway, based on the book *Tales of the South Pacific* by James Michener. It ran for 1925 performances. It starred Mary Martin and Ezio Pinza.

1970 **JOHN WAYNE** received his first Oscar for best actor, for his role in *True Grit.*

1994 Shannen Doherty of "90210" filed for **DIVORCE** with Ashley Hamilton citing irreconcilable differences after 5 months of marriage.

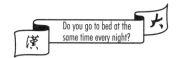

Do you go to bed at the same time every night?

APRIL 8

BIRTHDAYS

- **TERRY PORTER** Basketball. (Milwaukee, WI) With the Portland Trail Blazers Year/**Age**: 1995/**32** 1996/**33** 1997/**34**.
- **TARAN NOAH SMITH** Actor. On TV's "Home Improvement." Year/**Age**: 1995/**11** 1996/**12** 1997/**13**
- **J. J. JACKSON** Musician. (Born Jerome Jackson in Brooklyn, NY) Biggest hit: "But It's All Right" in 1966. Year/**Age**: 1995/**54** 1996/**55** 1997/**56**
- **MEL SCHAEHER** Bassis. (Flint, MI) Hits with GRAND FUNK RAILROAD include "We're An American Band" and "The Loco-Motion." Year/**Age**: 1995/**44** 1996/**45** 1997/**46**
- **BETTY FORD** Former First Lady. (Born Elizabeth Bloomer in Chicago, IL) Wife of the 38th U.S. President Gerald Ford. Founded the Betty Ford Clinic to treat addictions. Year/**Age**: 1995/**77** 1996/**78** 1997/**79**
- **JULIAN LENNON** Singer/musician. (Born John Charles Julian Lennon to John and Cynthia Lennon in Liverpool, England) First child born to BEATLE. Julian's biggest hit: "Too Late For Goodbyes" in 1985. Sean Lennon is John's son by second wife, Yoko Ono. Year/**Age**: 1995/**32** 1996/**33** 1997/**34**
- **PEGGY LENNON** Singer. (Los Angeles, CA) With the LENNON SISTERS. Their biggest hit, recorded with LAWRENCE WELK, was "Tonight You Belong to Me" in 1956. Year/**Age**: 1995/**54** 1996/**55** 1997/**56**
- **STEVE HOWE** Rock guitarist. (England) Started out with YES, then ASIA. Their biggest hit: "Heat of the Moment" in 1982. Year/**Age**: 1995/**48** 1996/**49** 1997/**50**
- **ADAM WOODS** Drummer. (England) With group FIXX. Biggest hit: "One Thing Leads to Another" in 1983. Year/**Age**: 1995/**42** 1996/**43** 1997/**44**
- **JOHN SCHNEIDER** Singer/actor. (Mt. Kisco, NY) Best known for his part in "Dukes of Hazzard." Year/**Age**: 1995/**41** 1996/**42** 1997/**43**
- **SHECKY GREENE** Comedian. (Born Sheldon Greenfield in Chicago, IL) In film *Tony Rome* in 1967. Year/**Age**: 1995/**70** 1996/**71** 1997/**72**
- **JOHN HAVLICEK** Basketball. (Martins Ferry, OH) Former star for the Boston Celtics. Scored over 26,000 NBA points during his career. Year/**Age**: 1995/**55** 1996/**56** 1997/**57**
- **JIM "CATFISH" HUNTER** Former Yankee baseball star. (Hertford, NC) He pitched a perfect game in 1968 and was a 20-game winner 5 times. Year/**Age**: 1995/**49** 1996/**50** 1997/**51**
- **MICHAEL BENNETT** Choreographer. (1943-1987 – Born Michael Bennett DiFiglia in Buffalo, NY) His credits include *Dreamgirls*, and he won two Tonys for *A Chorus Line*.
- **E.Y. "YIP" HARBURG** Songwriter. (1896-1981, NYC) His credits include: "Only A Paper Moon," "April in Paris," "Somewhere Over the Rainbow," from the *Wizard of Oz*, and *Finian's Rainbow*.
- **SONJA HENIE** Skater. (1913-1969 – Oslo, Norway) Olympic ice skating star; later a successful movie and ice show star. She won her first Olympic Gold Medal in 1928, when she was 15. She was the first female athlete to earn $1 million. (Died 10-12-69.)
- **MARY PICKFORD** Actress. (1893-1979 – Born Gladys Mary Smith in Toronto, Canada) Nicknamed "America's Sweetheart," she married Douglas Fairbanks, Sr., and Buddy Rogers. She won the 1929 Oscar for *Coquette*. (Died 5-29-79.)

FACTS FROM THE PAST

1941 Earles Graser was killed in an automobile accident near Detroit, MI. He was **RADIO'S FIRST LONE RANGER** and originator of the famous line, "Hi-yo Silver! Awa-ay!" The program claimed 15 million listeners.

1947 **FRANK SINATRA** punched out Lee Mortimer, amusement editor of the *New York Mirror*, at Ciro's restaurant in Hollywood after Mortimer suggested that Frank had been too friendly with gangsters in Havana. The blow cost Frank $25,000 in compensation and legal expenses. Sinatra said, "It was worth it."

1974 Baseball star **HANK AARON** of the Atlanta Braves broke **BABE RUTH**'s lifetime home run record, hitting his 715th in a game against the L.A. Dodgers. The record fell at 8:07 p.m. E.S.T. when Aaron drilled a 1-0 fastball from pitcher Al Downing in the Braves 7-4 victory.

1975 **FRANK ROBINSON**, Major League baseball's **FIRST BLACK MANAGER**, got off to a winning start as his team, the Cleveland Indians, defeated the New York Yankees, 5 to 3.

1986 Hollywood tough-guy **CLINT EASTWOOD** was elected mayor of Carmel-by-the-Sea, CA, by a landslide. He wanted to add a few stories to his building, where his bar "The Hogsbreath Inn" is located and the townsfolk turned him down. He said, "I'll show you" and became mayor. He then got the board to approve his project.

1987 **AL CAMPANIS**, Vice President of player personnel for the Los Angeles Dodgers, resigned in the wake of a controversy that began when he said on ABC's "Nightline" that blacks may lack some of the "necessities" to become baseball managers.

1988 The **REVEREND JIMMY SWAGGART** was defrocked as a minister of the Assemblies of God after he rejected an order from the church's national leaders to stop preaching for a year.

1990 **RYAN WHITE** lost his $5^{1}/_{2}$ year struggle with **AIDS**. Ryan, a hemophiliac, contracted the AIDS virus through a blood transfusion. His mother, his grandparents and Elton John were with him when he died. He became a household name in 1985 when he began his successful fight to attend the public school in Russiaville, IN, that had banned him amid a clamor from fearful parents.

1994 **KURT COBAIN**, lead singer of "grunge" band "Nirvanna" shot himself to death at his Seattle home.

APRIL 9

What's the difference between jam and preserves?

BIRTHDAYS

- **MARGO SMITH** C&W. (Dayton, OH) Her biggest record: "Don't Break the Heart That Loves You" in 1977, a hit for CONNIE FRANCIS in 1962. Year/**Age:** 1995/**53** 1996/**54** 1997/**55**

- **PAULINA PORIZKOVA** Actress/model. (Czechoslovakia) *Sports Illustrated* 1983 Swim Suit Issue. In film *Her Alibi* with Tom Selleck. Year/**Age:** 1995/**30** 1996/**31** 1997/**32**

- **MARSTON GLENN HEFNER**. (Los Angeles, CA) Son of *Playboy* magazine founder, Hugh Hefner. Year/**Age:** 1995/**5** 1996/**6** 1997/**7**

- **MICHAEL LEARNED** Actress. (Washington, DC) Played the mother on "The Waltons" TV series for which she won 3 Emmys. Year/**Age:** 1995/**56** 1996/**57** 1997/**58**

- **HUGH HEFNER** Publisher. (Chicago, IL) Founder of *Playboy* magazine which he originally wanted to call *Stag Party*. *Playboy's* first "playmate of the month" was Marilyn Monroe, but she was called the "sweetheart of the month" at that time. On his 64th birthday, Hugh and his wife, ex-playmate Kimberly, became parents of Marston Glenn Hefner. Year/**Age:** 1995/**69** 1996/**70** 1997/**71**

- **AVERY SCHREIBER** Comedian. (Chicago, IL) He was with "Second City." Years ago his first partner was George Carlin and later Jack Burns. Year/**Age:** 1995/**60** 1996/**61** 1997/**62**

- **BRAD DEXTER** Actor. American character actor often seen as a tough hoodlum. Appeared in *The Magnificent Seven* and *The Asphalt Jungle*. Year/**Age:** 1995/**78** 1996/**79** 1997/**80**

- **PHILIP WRIGHT** Lead singer/drummer. (Nottingham, England) With PAPER LACE made the hit "The Night Chicago Died." Year/**Age:** 1995/**45** 1996/**46** 1997/**47**

- **DENNIS QUAID** Actor. (Houston, TX) Appeared in *The Right Stuff*, *Big Easy*, and *Undercover Blues*. Played Jerry Lee Lewis in *Great Balls of Fire* in 1989. He and brother Randy appeared on Broadway together. Played Doc Holiday in the movie *Wyatt Earp*. In *D.O.A.* and *Flesh and Bone* with wife, Meg Ryan. Year/**Age:** 1995/**41** 1996/**42** 1997/**43**

- **CARL PERKINS** Singer. (Jackson, TN) Biggest hit: "Blue Suede Shoes" in 1956. Year/**Age:**1995/**63** 1996/**64** 1997/**659**

- **SEVE BALLESTEROS** Golfer. (Spain) Three-time British Open winner. Year/**Age:** 1995/**38** 1996/**39** 1997/**40**

- **KESHIA KNIGHT PULLIAM** Actress. (Newark, NJ) Rudy on the "Cosby Show." At 8 months, she made her first TV appearance in a diaper commercial; appeared in the movie *The Last Dragon*. Year/**Age:** 1995/**16** 1996/**17** 1997/**18**

- **GREGORY PINCUS** Medical researcher. (1903-1967 – Woodbine, NJ) He invented the birth control pill in 1955.

- **WARD BOND** Actor. (1903-1960 – Bendelman, NE) Appeared on the "Wagon Train" TV series. (Died 11-5-60.)

- **W. C. FIELDS** Actor. (1880-1946 – Born William Dunkenfield in Philadelphia, PA) He ran away from home at age 11 after an argument with his father and lived as a tramp for years. His self-imposed epitaph said, "On the whole, I'd rather be in Philadelphia." (Died 12-25-46.)

- **PAUL ROBESON** Actor. (1898-1976 – Princeton, NJ) African-American actor and singer; the son of ex-slaves. He was an All-American football player for Rutgers University and a preacher and lawyer. He made "Old Man River" a legendary ballad. Appeared in the films *King Solomon's Mines* and *The Proud Valley* and the stage play of *Showboat*. (Died 1-23-76.)

FACTS FROM THE PAST

1747 The **LAST BEHEADING** took place on **ENGLAND'S TOWER HILL**. The victim was **LORD LOVAT**, a leader of the Jacobite rebellion. He wanted to be hanged because his neck was short and he was obese. Shortly before the execution, the scaffold collapsed, killing 20 people.

1865 Confederate General **ROBERT E. LEE** surrendered to Gen. **U.S. GRANT** at Appomattox Court House, ending the Civil War. An estimated half a million men died during that war. Grant said he and Lee were so busy reminiscing, they almost forgot to sign the papers.

1874 **ALFERD PACKER** came out of the mountains of Colorado after five months, without his five partners. Searchers found the partially eaten bodies (murdered with an ax). Packer had a bad record of going out camping with people and coming back alone. The "Colorado Cannibal" was sentenced to 40 years and paroled after 17.

1878 The first egg rolling contest on the White House lawn was started by First Lady **LUCY HAYES**.

1913 **EBBETS FIELD** was opened in Brooklyn and the Philadelphia Phillies spoiled the inaugural by defeating the Dodgers, 1-0, before a crowd of 10,000. The stadium, which cost $750,000 to build, was named after **CHARLES EBBETS**, the Dodgers' principal owner.

1939 Black singer **MARIAN ANDERSON** performed a concert at the Lincoln Memorial in Washington after she was denied use of Constitution Hall by the Daughters of the American Revolution.

1959 NASA introduced the **FIRST 7 ASTRONAUTS TO THE U.S.:** John Glenn, Alan Shepard, Scott Carpenter, Gordon Cooper, Donald Slayton, Wally Shirra, and Virgil Grissom. The book *The Right Stuff* has some great background on the astronaut selection.

1985 **TOM SEAVER** of the Chicago White Sox broke Christy Mathewson's record of opening day starts with his 15th start on opening day. Seaver pitched $6\frac{2}{3}$ innings and was credited with the victory as the White Sox beat the Milwaukee Brewers 4-2.

1992 Ex-Panamanian leader, **MANUEL NORIEGA**, was convicted on drug and racketeering charges. He surrendered to U.S. invasion forces after a bloody Panama battle, January 1990.

1993 **THE COLORADO ROCKIES** played their first game and drew a Natl. League record crowd of 80,227 fans.

1994 **WAYNE NEWTON** married lawyer Kathleen McCrone. He had met her at one of his performances.

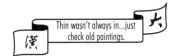
Thin wasn't always in...just check old paintings.

APRIL 10

BIRTHDAYS

- **BRIAN SETZER** Singer/guitarist. (Long Island, NY) With STRAY CATS. Biggest hit: "Stray Cat Strut" in 1982. Year/Age: 1995/**36** 1996/**37** 1997/**38**
- **SHELBY "Sheb" WOOLEY**. (Erick, OK) Biggest hit: "The Purple People Eater" in 1958. He also did parody songs as Ben Colder and wrote the "Hee Haw" theme song. He was Pete Nolan on TV's "Rawhide" and in the movies *Giant, High Noon*, and *Hoosiers*. Year/Age: 1995/**74** 1996/**75** 1997/**76**
- **STEVEN SEAGAL** Actor (Lansing, MI) Films include *On Deadly Ground, Above The Law, Hard to Kill, Out for Justice*, and, *Under Siege*. His first three films earned over $200 million. Year/Age: 1995/**43** 1996/**44** 1997/**45**
- **OMAR SHARIF** Actor. (Born Michael Shalhoub in Egypt) Nominated for an Oscar in 1962 for *Lawrence of Arabia*. He also starred in *Dr. Zhivago* and *Funny Girl*. He made millions of dollars in the movies, but lost most of it gambling. He is a bridge expert. Year/Age: 1995/**63** 1996/**64** 1997/**65**
- **HARRY MORGAN** Actor. (Born Harry Bratsburg in Detroit, MI) He was Col. Potter on the "M*A*S*H" TV series. In 1967 he starred with Jack Webb on "Dragnet." Year/Age: 1995/**80** 1996/**81** 1997/**82**
- **JOHN MADDEN** Sports announcer. (Austin, MN) He admits to being afraid of the dark and hates elevators, planes and trains. He does the Ace Hardware commercials. He signed a $30 million dollar contract with Fox network. Year/Age: 1995/**59** 1996/**60** 1997/**61**.
- **MAX VON SYDOW** Actor. (Born Carl Adolph von Sydow in Sweden) In *The Exorcist, Hawaii, Strange Brew, Pele*, and *Needful Things*. Year/Age: 1995/**66** 1996/**67** 1997/**68**

- **CATHY TURNER** Skater. Olympic gold-medal winner. Year/Age: 1995/**33** 1996/**34** 1997/**35**
- **DON MEREDITH** Football. (Mt. Vernon, TX) A former football star – Dallas Cowboys QB from 1960-1969. Later a sports announcer/commercial spokesman. Does the Lipton Iced Tea commercials. Year/Age: 1995/**57** 1996/**58** 1997/**59**
- **HARI RHODES** Actor. (Cincinnati, OH) D.A. William Washburn in TV series "The Bold Ones" and Mike, the African conservationist, in "Daktari." Year/Age: 1995/**62** 1996/**63** 1997/**64**
- **CHUCK CONNORS** Actor. (1921-1992 – Born Kevin Connors in Brooklyn, NY) Best known as the sharpshooting hero Lucas McCain on the "Rifleman" TV series from 1957-62. He was a pro basketball and baseball player before turning to acting. He played a lecherous slave owner in the 1977 miniseries *Roots*. (Died 11-10-92.)
- **CLARE BOOTHE LUCE** Former ambassador. (1903-1987 – NYC) Playwright, actress, politician, and diplomat. Wrote the play *The Women*. (Died 10-9-87.)
- **WILLIAM BOOTH** Salvation Army founder. (1829-1912 – England) He started the Christian Mission in London, which became the Salvation Army in 1878. (Died 8-20-12.)
- **JOSEPH PULITZER** Journalist. (1847-1911 – Hungary) American journalist and founder of the Pulitzer Prizes. (Died 10-29-11.)
- **FRANCES PERKINS** Cabinet member. (1880-1965 – NYC) First female member of the U.S. Presidential cabinet: Appointed Secretary of Labor by President Franklin Roosevelt in 1933 and served until 1945. (Died 5-14-65.)

FACTS FROM THE PAST

1781 A future president became a prisoner of war at age 14. **PRESIDENT ANDREW JACKSON** was held in a British prison camp in Camden, SC. He was severely scarred from a saber slash he received when he refused to clean a British officer's boots.

1866 The American Society for the Prevention of Cruelty to Animals was incorporated. **HENRY BERGH** saw a man beating his horse and got so angry, he called the police. He found out there was no law against animal abuse, so he founded the Society.

1877 The **FIRST HUMAN CANNONBALL ACT** was performed at West's Amphitheatre in London, England. A "beautiful lady" named Zazel was fired from a monstrous cannon and landed in a large safety net. Zazel did this five days a week for two years…and was paid according to how many times she hit the net!

1953 The **FIRST** feature-length **3-D MOVIE** in color premiered in New York City: *House of Wax* starring **VINCENT PRICE**.

1956 **NAT KING COLE** was beaten up by six anti-black vigilantes in Birmingham, Alabama. The white audience did not interfere.

1957 **RICK NELSON** made his first singing TV appearance on the family's show, "Ozzie & Harriet." The episode was called "Rickie the Drummer" and he sang "I'm Walkin'." He was 16 years old, and a year later he had his first #1 record, "Poor Little Fool."

1970 **JIM MORRISON** offered a Boston audience a peak at his genitals. A band member dragged him off stage before he was able to complete the action.

1970 Newspapers around the world carried **PAUL McCARTNEY**'s statement that the **BEATLES** would never work together again. He cited personal differences. It was later learned to stem from the disapproval of Yoko Ono, John Lennon's wife, and the Beatles' financial advisor, Allen Klein.

1976 **CHRIS CHAMBLISS**, Yankee first baseman, called time out just a split second before Milwaukee's **DON MONEY** hit a grand slam home run off **SPARKY LYLE**. The ump said no home run. Then Money hit a fly out and NY beat the Brewers 9-7.

1989 **ALABAMA** was named artist of the decade by the Academy of County Music.

1994 **CHARLES KURALT** hosted his last "Sunday Morning" show on CBS. He had joined CBS in 1967. Charles Osgood replaced him.

APRIL 11

BIRTHDAYS

- **ELLEN GOODMAN** Syndicated columinst. (Newton, MA) Writes syndicated column *At Large*. Pulitzer Prize winner in 1980. Year/Age: 1995/**47** 1996/**48** 1997/**49**
- **JOEL GREY** Entertainer. (Born Joel Katz in Cleveland, OH) He won an Oscar in 1972 for best supporting actor in *Cabaret*. His father was comedian Mickey Katz. His daughter is actress Jennifer. Year/Age: 1995/**63** 1996/**64** 1997/**65**
- **LOUISE LASSER** Actress. (NYC) She starred in the Norman Lear soap opera spoof, "Mary Hartman, Mary Hartman." Appeared in *It's a Living*. She was married to Woody Allen from 1966-70. Year/Age: 1995/**56** 1996/**57** 1997/**58**
- **JOHNNY SHEFFIELD** Actor. American boy actor of the 1930's, in the "Tarzan" and later the "Bomba" series. Year/Age: 1995/**64** 1996/**65** 1997/**66**
- **BILL IRWIN** Actor/choreographer. (Santa Monica, CA) *The Regard of Flight*, a big hit at the American Palace Theatre, and *Largely New York*. Year/Age: 1995/**45** 1996/**46** 1997/**47**
- **NICHOLAS BRADY** Former Treasury Secretary. (NYC) Year/Age: 1995/**65** 1996/**66** 1997/**67**
- **HOWARD KOCH** Former producer/director. His films included: *Frankenstein* in 1970, *Come Blow Your Horn*, *Airplane II*, and *The Odd Couple*. Year/Age: 1995/**79** 1996/**80** 1997/**81**
- **MICHAEL DEAVER** Former White House Chief of Staff. (Bakersfield, CA) Year/Age: 1995/**57** 1996/**58** 1997/**59**
- **STU ADAMSON** Singer. (Scotland) With BIG COUNTRY. Year/Age: 1995/**37** 1996/**38** 1997/**39**
- **PETER RIEGERT** Actor. Year/Age: 1995/**48** 1996/**49** 1997/**50**
- **OLEG CASSINI** Fashion designer. (Paris, France) He designed the clothes for the women on ABC TV's "Dynasty." Year/Age: 1995/**82** 1996/**83** 1997/**84**
- **HUGH CAREY** Former New York Governor. He was governor before Mario Cuomo. Year/Age: 1995/**75** 1996/**76** 1997/**77**
- **EDWARD EVERETT** American statesman/orator. (1794-1865 – Dorchester, MA) He delivered the main address at the dedication of the Gettysburg National Cemetery on Nov. 19, 1863. President Lincoln also spoke at the dedication, and his speech lasted less than 2 minutes.

FACTS FROM THE PAST

1814   **NAPOLEON BONAPARTE** abdicated as Emperor of France and was banished to the Island of Elba.

1831   The first **BUILDING-AND-LOAN MORTGAGE** was issued to a lamplighter named Comley Rich. The money came from rich home owners who pooled their cash and paid $3.00 a month into a fund until there was enough to build a house. Then the member who agreed to pay the most interest got the loan. Rich bid $10.00 to borrow $375.00 to build a house in Philadelphia, PA. That house is still there.

1865   Several days after the end of the Civil War, **PRESIDENT LINCOLN** made an optimistic speech about rebuilding the South and moving the nation forward. It turned out to be his last public speech. He was assassinated three days later.

1868   Future U.S. President **ULYSSES S. GRANT WAS STOPPED FOR SPEEDING**, while driving a horse and buggy. At the time, Grant was commander of the U.S. Army. A few months later, he was stopped again and fined $5. After he became U.S. President, a policeman again stopped him for speeding, but apologized when he realized whom he had stopped. Grant replied, "Officer, do your duty," and the officer complied by taking Grant to the police station.

1890   **JOHN MERRICK**, the **ELEPHANT MAN,** died at age 29. He was an Englishman with an enormous misshapen head with characteristics of an elephant. When he slept, he sat up in bed and on this night he apparently tried to put his head on the pillow, fell backward and dislocated his neck. His death was due to the desire that had dominated his life – to be like other people.

1921   Radio station **KDKA** in Pittsburgh broadcast the **FIRST RADIO SPORTS COMMENTARY** – a boxing match between Johnnie Ray and Johnny Dundee.

1947   **JACKIE ROBINSON** was signed to become the first black player to play for a major league team, joining the Brooklyn Dodgers in an exhibition game against the N.Y. Yankees. He retired in 1956; died in 1972 at age 53. He was the **FIRST AFRICAN-AMERICAN NAMED TO THE BASEBALL HALL OF FAME.**

1968   One week after the assassination of Dr. Martin Luther King, Jr., President Lyndon Johnson signed the **CIVIL RIGHTS ACT OF 1968**.

1970   Guitarist and vocalist Peter Green, one of the founders of **FLEETWOOD MAC**, announced he was leaving the group to follow his religious beliefs.

1979   Idi Amin was deposed as President of Uganda as rebels and exiles backed by **TANZANIAN** [tan-zuh-nee'-ahn] forces took control of the capital city of Kampala.

1981   **PRESIDENT REAGAN** returned to the White House from George Washington University Hospital, 12 days after he was wounded in an assassination attempt.

1985   Controversy erupted when it was announced that **PRESIDENT REAGAN** would be laying a wreath at a military cemetery during a visit to West Germany — even though some of the remains belonged to members of the notorious Waffen SS.

1994   Bill and Hillary **CLINTON** paid $14,615 in back taxes and interest due to profits on the first lady's land deal that had not been claimed.

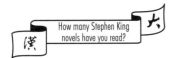

How many Stephen King novels have you read?

APRIL 12

BIRTHDAYS

- **ED O'NEILL** Actor. Al Bundy on TV's "Married...With Children." Year/**Age**: 1995/**49** 1996/**50** 1997/**51**

- **NED MILLER** C&W. (Born Henry Ned Miller in Raines, UT) Biggest hit: "From a Jack to a King" in 1962. Year/**Age**: 1995/**70** 1996/**71** 1997/**72**

- **DAVID LETTERMAN** TV host. (Indianapolis, IN) At one time he was a TV weatherman. "Late Night." Dave moved his show from NBC to CBS (the Ed Sullivan Theater in NY) on August 30, 1993. He made his film debut in *Cabin Boy*. Year/**Age**: 1995/**48** 1996/**49** 1997/**50**

- **TINY TIM**. (Born Herbert Khaury in NYC) Biggest hit: "Tiptoe through the Tulips" in 1968. Year/**Age**: 1995/**73** 1996/**74** 1997/**75**

- **VINCE GILL** C&W singer. (Norman, OK) Was with the group "Pure Prairie League" and had the 1990 Single of the Year, "When I Call Your Name," with Patty Loveless. Married to Janis Oliver. Year/**Age**: 1995/**38** 1996/**39** 1997/**40**

- **ANN MILLER** Long-legged actress/dancer. (Born Lucy Ann Collier in Cherino, TX) In films: *You Can't Take It With You*, *Kiss Me Kate*, and *Easter Parade*, and she toured with Mickey Rooney in *Sugar Babies*. Year/**Age**: 1995/**72** 1996/**73** 1997/**74**

- **DAVID CASSIDY** Entertainer. (NYC) Made his Broadway debut with half brother Shawn in "Blood Brothers" musical. Biggest hit: "Cherish" in 1971. He was lead vocalist for the PARTRIDGE FAMILY, popular TV series from 1972-74 which also starred his mother, Shirley Jones. He owns 18 gold records. He married his songwriting partner, Sue Shifrin. Autobiography: *C'mon Get Happy: Fear and Loathing on the Partridge Family Bus*. Year/**Age**: 1995/**45** 1996/**46** 1997/**47**

- **ANDY GARCIA** Actor. (Havana, Cuba) In the films *Godfather III*, *Hero*, *When a Man Loves a Woman*, and *Jennifer 8*. Year/**Age**: 1995/**39** 1996/**40** 1997/**41**

- **SHANNON DOHERTY** Actress. Appears on TV's "Our House," was Brenda Walsh on "Beverly Hills, 90210," and in the film *Blindfold*. She married Ashley Hamilton in 1993. It lasted 195 days. Year/**Age**: 1995/**24** 1996/**25** 1997/**26**

- **J. D. NICHOLAS** Entertainer. Biggest hits with COM-MODORES: "Still" and "Three Times a Lady." Year/**Age**: 1995/**43** 1996/**44** 1997/**45**

- **HERBIE HANCOCK** Jazz musician. (Chicago, IL) Modern jazz piano player, played a concert with the Chicago Symphony when he was 11 years old. Won a Grammy for "Rockit," did the sound track for Charles Bronson's *Death Wish* and composed, conducted and produced the music for *Round Midnight*. Year/**Age**: 1995/**55** 1996/**56** 1997/**57**

- **JOHN KAY** Singer. (Born Joachim Krauledat in East Germany) Vocalist/guitarist for STEPPENWOLF. Biggest hit: "Born to be Wild" in 1968. Year/**Age**: 1995/**51** 1996/**52** 1997/**39**

- **LIONEL HAMPTON** Bandleader. (Birmingham, AL) A vibraharpist, he was part of the famous concert in 1938 at Carnegie Hall with jazz greats Benny Goodman and Gene Krupa. A big hit for him in 1950 was "Rag Mop." Year/**Age**: 1995/**82** 1996/**83** 1997/**84**

- **BILLY VAUGHN** Composer/bandleader. (1919-1991 – Glasgow, KY) He began his career as a singer with the HILLTOPPPERS and later arranged songs for Pat Boone and the MILLS BROTHERS. Biggest hit: "Melody of Love" in 1954. (Died 9-26-91.)

FACTS FROM THE PAST

1814 **NAPOLEON BONAPARTE** attempted suicide following the downfall of Paris. He took poison, which caused a severe case of hiccups, causing him to vomit, ultimately foiling his plan.

1935 **"YOUR HIT PARADE"** program began on radio. It was a countdown show like many that are on the radio today, but the songs were sung by such stars as Frank Sinatra and Doris Day.

1945 **PRESIDENT FRANKLIN DELANO ROOSEVELT**, the 32nd President of the U.S. died of a cerebral hemorrhage in Warm Springs, GA, at age 63, just three months after beginning an unprecedented fourth term in office.

1954 **BILL HALEY AND THE COMETS** recorded two songs: "Thirteen Women" and "(We're Gonna) Rock Around The Clock" for DECCA records at the Pythian Temple Studio in New York City.

1961 Soviet Cosmonaut Yuri Gagarin took a one-orbit, 108-minute ride in a 10,395-lb. vehicle—Vostok I—to become the **FIRST MAN IN SPACE**. When he landed in his parachute, he was met by a terrified farm woman who threatened to attack him with a pitchfork.

1966 Jan Berry of **JAN & DEAN** was in a car/truck collision in Los Angeles. He escaped death but was totally paralyzed for over a year and suffered brain damage. Jan co-wrote the song "Dead Man's Curve" in 1964, which paralleled the crash.

1975 All three versions of **PETER TOWNSHEND**'s rock opera *Tommy* were on the charts simultaneously. They included Ken Russell's movie version, **THE WHO**'s original recording, and the classical rendition by the London Symphony Orchestra and an all-star cast.

1983 **HAROLD WASHINGTON** is elected the first black mayor of Chicago.

1985 **JAKE GARN** of Utah became **THE FIRST SENATOR TO FLY IN SPACE**, on board the shuttle *Discovery*, launched from Kennedy Space Center.

1988 **FRANK ROBINSON** became **BASEBALL'S FIRST BLACK MANAGER**. He replaced Cal Ripken of the Baltimore Orioles in a move made to rescue the club from its worst start in 33 years.

1992 Golfer **FRED COUPLES** won the Masters, his first major tournament victory.

1994 An exotic dancer, **"CHESTY LOVE"** leagally claims her surgical breast implants as a business expense.

APRIL 13

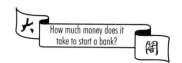
How much money does it take to start a bank?

BIRTHDAYS

• **JOSE RIJO** Baseball. (Dominican Republic) The Cincinnati Reds pitcher beat the Oakland A's twice and claimed the MVP award during the 1990 World Series. The Reds won the series in four straight games. Year/**Age:** 1995/**31** 1996/**32** 1997/**33**

• **WAYNE LEWIS** Singer. (White Plains, NY) ATLANTIC STARR. "Always," 1987. Year/**Age:** 1995/**39** 1996/**40** 1997/**41**

• **MAX WEINBERG** Drummer. (South Orange, NJ) The E STREET BAND and on "The Conen O'Brien Show." Year/**Age:** 1995/**44** 1996/**45** 1997/**46**

• **JACK CASADY** Bassist. (San Francisco, CA) JEFFERSON AIRPLANE. Year/**Age:** 1995/**51** 1996/**52** 1997/**53**

• **JIMMY DESTRI** Keyboardist. #1 hits with BLONDIE: "Heart Of Glass," "Call Me," "The Tide Is High," and "Rapture." Year/**Age:** 1995/**41** 1996/**42** 1997/**43**

• **EUDORA WELTY** Author. (Jackson, MO) Pulitzer Prize winner for *The Optimist's Daughter.* Year/**Age:** 1995/**86** 1996/**87** 1997/**88**

• **HOWARD KEEL** Actor/singer. (Gillespie, IL) Veteran of many musicals including *Kiss Me Kate,* and on "Dallas" as Clayton Farlow, Miss Ellie's husband. Year/**Age:** 1995/**76** 1996/**77** 1997/**78**

• **Al GREEN** Singer. (Forest City, AR) Biggest hit: "Let's Stay Together" in 1972. He was the #1 soul/pop singer in the early 1970's. More recently a gospel singer and a minister at the Full Tabernacle Church in Memphis, TN. Year/**Age:** 1995/**49** 1996/**50** 1997/**51**

• **RICK SCHRODER** Actor. (Staten Island, NY) Appeared in *The Champ* with Jon Voight, and on TV in "Silver Spoons" and miniseries *Lonesome Dove.* Year/**Age:** 1995/**25** 1996/**26** 1997/**27**

• **PEABO BRYSON** Singer. (Greenville, SC) Biggest hit: "If Ever You're in my Arms Again" in 1984. Year/**Age:** 1995/**44** 1996/**45** 1997/**46**

• **LYLE WAGGONER** Actor. (Kansas City, KS) On the "Carol Burnett Show" and as Major Steve Trevor on "Wonder Woman." Year/**Age:** 1995/**60** 1996/**61** 1997/**62**

• **RON PERLMAN** Actor. (NYC) *Beauty and the Beast.* Year/**Age:** 1995/**45** 1996/**46** 1997/**47**

• **BILL CONTI** Instrumentalist. (Providence, RI) His biggest hit: "Gonna Fly Now," the theme from *Rocky* in 1977. Wrote the theme for *Unmarried Woman* with Jill Clayburgh and has led the orchestra on Academy Award night. Year/**Age:** 1995/**53** 1996/**54** 1997/**55**

• **TONY DOW** Actor. (Hollywood, CA) Played Wally Cleaver on TV's "Leave it to Beaver." Year/**Age:** 1995/**50** 1996/**51** 1997/**52**

• **STANLEY DONEN** Director. (Columbia, SC) His films include: *Singin' in the Rain, The Pajama Game,* and *Charade.* Year/**Age:** 1995/**71** 1996/**72** 1997/**73**

• **EDWARD FOX** Actor. (England) He played the Jackal in *The Day of the Jackal.* Other films include: *A Bridge Too Far* and *The Dresser.* Year/**Age:** 1995/**58** 1996/**59** 1997/**60**

• **FRANK (F. W.) WOOLWORTH** Tycoon. (1852-1919 – Rodman, NY) Founder of the 5 & 10 cent stores. (Died 4-9-19.)

• **BUTCH CASSIDY** Outlaw. (Born George LeRoy Parker in 1866) He adopted his alias to honor Mike Cassidy, his original tutor in the arts of rustling and horse thievery. Subject of the film *Butch Cassidy & the Sundance Kid.*

• **THOMAS JEFFERSON** 3rd U.S. President. (1743-1826 – Shadwell, VA) He was the main author on the 5-man commission that drafted the Declaration of Independence, founded the University of Virginia, designed his own house in Monticello, invented the pedometer, the plow, and the perpetual clock. He went through about $10,000 worth of wine while at the White House. (Died 7-4-1826.)

• **SIR ROBERT WATSON-WATT** Inventor. (1892-1973 – Scotland) He was superintendent of the Radio Research Lab at Ditton Park, England, when he invented a new apparatus for the "detection and location of aircraft by radio methods." His "radar" turned out to be a major factor in the defeat of Germany in WWII. He was caught in one of the first radar speed traps and got a ticket. (Died 12-6-73.)

FACTS FROM THE PAST

1869   The **FIRST AIR BRAKES WERE PATENTED** by George Westinghouse.

1943   President Franklin D. Roosevelt dedicated the **JEFFERSON MEMORIAL** in Washington.

1964   Actor **SIDNEY POITIER** became the first African-American man to receive an Oscar as best actor, for *Lilies of the Field.*

1965   **ROGER MILLER** won five Grammy Awards, setting a record for C&W artists that still stands today.

1970   There was an explosion aboard the **APOLLO 13** spaceship on its way to the moon. Short of oxygen and flying a crippled ship, the crew of Lovell, Seigert & Haise aborted the moon landing and returned to earth under emergency conditions.

1983   Illinois congressman **HAROLD WASHINGTON** was declared the winner in Chicago's mayoral election, becoming the city's **FIRST BLACK CHIEF EXECUTIVE.** He died of a heart attack in his city hall office (11-25-87).

1984   **PETE ROSE** got his 4,000th hit. The only other player with more was **TY COBB** who had 4,191 hits during his 21-year career.

1992   The **LOOP IN CHICAGO WAS SHUT DOWN** after water flowed into a century-old underground tunnel system running beneath downtown and under the Chicago River. Estimated damage: over $200 million. Mayor Richard Daley fired the Acting Transportation Commissioner, John LaPlante, for not acting on an April 2 warning that the tunnel system was in need of $10,000 in repairs.

1994   **BILLY JOEL AND CHRISTIE BRINKLEY** announced their official separation.

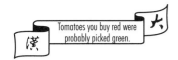

Tomatoes you buy red were probably picked green.

APRIL 14

BIRTHDAYS

- **EMMA THOMPSON** Actress. Academy Award for best actress in *Howards End*. Co-stars with director husband Kenneth Branagh in *Much Ado About Nothing*. Other films: *The Remains of the Day*, and *In the Name of the Father*. Year/**Age**: 1995/**36** 1996/**37** 1997/**38**

- **STEVE AVERY** Baseball. Pitcher for the Atlanta Braves. Year/**Age**: 1995/**25** 1996/**26** 1997/**27**

- **DAVID JUSTICE** Baseball. (Cincinnati, OH) Atlanta Braves outfielder. He's married to actress Halle Berry, of the *Queen* miniseries. Year/**Age**: 1995/**29** 1996/**30** 1997/**31**

- **GREG MADDUX** Baseball. (San Angelo, TX) Former Chicago Cub right-handed pitching ace, now with the Atlanta Braves. Year/**Age**: 1995/**29** 1996/**30** 1997/**31**

- **ANTHONY MICHAEL HALL** Actor. (Boston, MA) Films include: *Johnny B. Goode*, *16 Candles*, and *Edward Scissorhands*. Year/**Age**: 1995/**27** 1996/**28** 1997/**29**

- **ROD STEIGER** Actor. (Born Rodney Steiger in Westhampton, NY) He won an Oscar in 1967 as best actor in *Heat of the Night*. Other films include *Sword of Gideon* and *The Specialist*. Year/**Age**: 1995/**70** 1996/**71** 1997/**72**

- **SIR JOHN GIELGUD** [geel-good] Actor. (London) He won an Oscar for *Arthur*. Also in the film *Shining Through*. Year/**Age**: 1995/**91** 1996/**92** 1997/**93**

- **BRIAN FORESTER** Actor. Appeared as Chris in the "Partridge Family" TV series. Year/**Age**: 1995/**35** 1996/**36** 1997/**37**

- **FRANK SERPICO** Whistle-blowing cop. Year/**Age**: 1995/**59** 1996/**60** 1997/**61**

- **JULIE CHRISTIE** Actress. (India) She won an Oscar for best actress in *Darling* in 1965. Year/**Age**: 1995/**55** 1996/**56** 1997/**57**

- **RICHIE BLACKMORE** Guitarist. (England) With DEEP PURPLE. Biggest hit: "Smoke on the Water" in 1973. Year/**Age**: 1995/**50** 1996/**51** 1997/**52**

- **BOBBY NICHOLS** Golfer. In 1964, in the final rounds, he beat Arnold Palmer and Jack Nicklaus to win the PGA championship. Year/**Age**: 1995/**59** 1996/**60** 1997/**61**

- **LORETTA LYNN** C&W. (Butcher's Holler, KY) She had a successful book on her life which was on the *New York Times* bestseller list for 9 weeks and later became a hit movie, *Coalminer's Daughter*. Her sister Crystal Gayle and brother Jay Lee Webb are popular Country stars. She was a grandmother at age 29. She also does Crisco commercials. Year/**Age**: 1995/**60** 1996/**61** 1997/**62**

- **PETE ROSE** Former manager/player. (Cincinnati, OH) "Charley Hustle" holds the NL record for consecutive games batted in safely, 44 in 1978. [See 4-13] At age 45, he hit 5 for 5 in 1986, two years after beating Ty Cobb's all-time hit record. The Reds fired Pete when they found out that he placed bets on professional sports teams. Year/**Age**: 1995/**54** 1996/**55** 1997/**56**

- **ANTHONY (TONY) PERKINS** Actor. (1932-1992 – NYC) Oscar nominee for supporting actor in 1956 in *Friendly Persuasion*. He also portrayed Jimmy Piersall in *Fear Strikes Out* and is best known as Norman in the *Psycho* films. Less known for his recording of "Moonlight Swim." (Died 9-12-92.)

FACTS FROM THE PAST

1772 **ELIZABETH RUSSELL** of England died at the age of 104. Everyone who knew her thought she was a female. After her death it was discovered that "she" was a "he."

1865 **PRESIDENT ABRAHAM LINCOLN** was shot in the head by actor John Wilkes Booth at Ford's Theater in Washington, DC, and died the next morning at 7:22. The play that evening was *Our American Cousin*. Lincoln's bodyguard was out for a drink at the time of the shooting. Lincoln was holding his wife's hand when Mary asked the President what people would think of such a public display of affection. That's when the President said his last words: "They won't think anything about it."

1902 **J.C. PENNEY** opened his first store in Kemmerer, WY. The man's middle name was really "Cash!"

1910 **PRESIDENT WILLIAM HOWARD TAFT** (from Ohio) set a precedent by throwing out the first baseball at the opening of the baseball season. Washington's Walter Johnson held the A's to one hit, winning 3-0.

1912 The world's largest passenger ship, the **TITANIC**, struck an iceberg in the North Atlantic on its maiden voyage and began sinking. Because it had been publicized as being unsinkable, some people refused to abandon ship and some of the lifeboats departed only partially filled. Rescue ships picked up 706 survivors, while 1,517 went down with the *Titanic* at 2:20 a.m. the following morning. Tradition says at the time the ship went down, the band was playing the Sarah Adams hymn "Nearer My God to Thee" but according to the ship's wireless operator, Harold Bride, the band was playing "Autumn." In 1986 divers located the ship.

1940 Actress **HATTIE McDANIEL** became the **FIRST AFRICAN-AMERICAN TO WIN AN OSCAR**, as supporting actress in *Gone with the Wind*. She made 14 films before her death in 1952.

1976 **STEVIE WONDER** announced he signed a $13 million contract with Motown--the most lucrative in music history at the time.

1986 **U.S. PLANES ATTACKED LIBYA** with eighteen F-111s and fifteen A-6s. One plane with 2 pilots was lost by the U.S. The Libyans reported 15 dead including the 15-month-old adopted daughter of Libyan leader, Colonel Quaddafi.

1993 **DON CALHOUN**, an office supply salesman from Bloomington, IL, made a 79-foot basket at the Chicago Bulls-Miami Heat game collecting $1 million. He got his free ticket to the game from a friend. Don was chosen at random for the Bulls promotional gimmick, attracted by his bright yellow boots with rubber soles that wouldn't scuff the court.

APRIL 15
Income Tax Pay Day

How many countries now have nuclear weapons?

BIRTHDAYS

- **EVELYN ASHFORD** Track star. (Shreveport, LA) Olympic gold medalist in track. Year/**Age**: 1995/**38** 1996/**39** 1997/**40**

- **ELIZABETH MONTGOMERY** Actress. (Los Angeles, CA) Best known on the "Bewitched" TV series as Samantha from 1964-1972. Daughter of actor Robert Montgomery. Year/**Age**: 1995/**62** 1996/**63** 1997/**64**

- **CLAUDIA CARDINALE** Actress. (Tunisia) Her films included *The Pink Panther* and *Son of Pink Panther*. She did not manage to live up to the international star build-up she was given. Year/**Age**: 1995/**56** 1996/**57** 1997/**58**

- **ROY CLARK** C&W. (Meherrin, VA) He had a big hit in 1969: "Yesterday When I Was Young." He plays banjo, guitar and even classical guitar. He's been a side man for many groups and is one of the members of the "Hee-Haw" show. Autobiography: *My Life: in Spite of Myself.* Year/**Age**: 1995/**62** 1996/**63** 1997/**64**

- **HELOISE** Newspaper columnist of "Helpful Hints" fame. (Born Ponce Kiah Marchelle Heloise Cruse Evans in Waco, TX) She is the daughter of the original "Heloise." Year/**Age**: 1995/**43** 1996/**45** 1997/**46**

- **HARVEY LEMBECK** Actor. (1923-1982) Member of the "You'll Never Get Rich" cast, one of the favorite sitcoms of the 1950's, later called "The Phil Silvers Show," with the reruns titled "Sergeant Bilko." (Died 1-5-82.)

- **ROBERT WALKER, Jr.** Actor. Appeared in *Ensign Pulver* and *Easy Rider.* Year/**Age**: 1995/**56** 1996/**57** 1997/**58**

- **DAVE EDMUNDS** Singer. (Wales) Biggest hit: "I Hear You Knockin'," in 1970. The song was also a hit in 1955 by Gale Storm. Year/**Age**: 1995/**51** 1996/**52** 1997/**53**

- **SAMANTHA FOX** Singer. (England) She rose to stardom as a topless model for the U.K. *Daily Sun* newspaper. Her biggest record: "Touch Me" in 1986. Year/**Age**: 1995/**29** 1996/**30** 1997/**31**

- **MICHAEL ANSARA** Actor. (Lowell, MA) Played Cochise, Chief of the Apaches, on the TV western "Broken Arrow." Mike was less than thrilled with the role. In an interview he said, "Cochise could do one of two things, stand with his arms folded, looking noble; or stand with arms at his sides, looking noble." He was married to Barbara Eden. Year/**Age**: 1995/**73** 1996/**74** 1997/**75**

- **BOB LUMAN** Singer. (1937-1978 – Nacogdoches, TX) Biggest hit: "Let's Think About Living" in 1960. (Died 12-27-78.)

- **LEONARDO da VINCI** Painter. (1452-1519 – Vinci, Italy) Italian painter and sculptor, etc. He sold his *Mona Lisa* in Paris to King Francis I who paid $50,000 and hung it in the Louvre where it has been except from 1911-1913, when it was stolen. (Died 5-2-1519.)

FACTS FROM THE PAST

1865   **PRESIDENT LINCOLN** died at 7:22 a.m. in a Washington, DC, boarding house, across from Ford's Theater. Andrew Johnson was sworn in as the 17th President.

1878   Harley Procter developed **IVORY SOAP.** When one of his soap company workers went out to lunch one day and left the soap machine on, the mixture that developed made the finished bar of soap float. Harley named the product after Psalms 45:8: "All their garments smell of myrrh, and aloes, and cassia, out of the ivory palaces, whereby they have made thee glad." This unique soap made Procter and Gamble a multi-million dollar company.

1927   The first prints were left in cement at Grauman's Theatre, along the curb on Hollywood Boulevard, by actor **DOUGLAS FAIRBANKS** and actresses **MARY PICKFORD** and **NORMA TALMADGE**.

1947   **JACKIE ROBINSON** became the **FIRST AFRICAN-AMERICAN TO PLAY IN A MAJOR LEAGUE BASEBALL GAME,** as his Brooklyn Dodger teammates defeated the Boston Braves, 5-3. He got his first hit in his second game.

1955   The **GOLDEN ARCHES** appeared for the first time when the first **McDONALD**'s restaurant was opened in Des Plaines, IL. **RAY KROC** founded the company.

1957   "Whole Lotta Shakin" by **JERRY LEE LEWIS** was released by Sun Records. This was Jerry's first big hit.

1967   The **WHO** released "Happy Jack," which became the group's first U.S. hit.

1982   **BILLY JOEL** crashed his motorcycle on Long Island, NY. He had to undergo therapy on his hand.

1983   James L. Hardy, Jr., was awarded $25,000 **IN DAMAGES IN A LAWSUIT AGAINST DAYS INN** of America. Hardy had checked into a Days Inn in East Ridge, TN, but when he opened the door to the room he had been given, he discovered a "skimpily clad" woman in the room, and as he quickly turned to leave the room, he injured his neck.

1990   They called her the **BEAUTY QUEEN FROM HELL,** because Miss Norway, Mona Grudt [moo'-nah groot], 19, is from Hell, Norway. Grudt was crowned Miss Universe.

1992   Hotel queen, **LEONA HELMSLEY,** began serving a four-year prison term at the Federal Medical Center in Lexington, KY, for tax evasion. She was once quoted as saying: "Only the little people pay taxes." She reported to prison in her company's Boeing 727 jet. Her husband, Harry, had the lights in the Empire State Building, which they own, turned off in protest. She was released from prison 1-26-94.

1993   **SPARKY ANDERSON** won his 2,000th game as a manager He is the only manager to win more than 800 games with two teams.

1994   British figure skater **JOHN CURRY** died of AIDS at age 44. Known as "Nureyev On Ice," he won the gold at the 1976 Olympics.

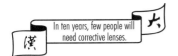

In ten years, few people will need corrective lenses.

APRIL 16

BIRTHDAYS

- **ELLEN BARKIN** Actress. (NYC) *Switch, Sea of Love, The Tool Shed, Into the West,* and *This Boy's Life.* Year/**Age**: 1995/**40** 1996/**41** 1997/**42**

- **MARTIN LAWRENCE** Actor/comedian. From TV's "Martin". Year/**Age**: 1995/**30** 1996/**31** 1997/**32**

- **HENRY MANCINI** Conductor/composer. (Cleveland, OH) He won 20 Grammys, 4 Oscars, and 6 gold albums. His hits included "Love Theme from Romeo and Juliet," "Moon River," "Days of Wine and Roses," and "Charade." He also composed the "Pink Panther" theme, TV's "Peter Gunn" theme, and his final work was the Broadway version of *Victor-Victoria.* (Died 6-14-94.)

- **BOBBY VINTON** Singer. (The "Polish Prince" was born Stanley Robert Vinton in Canonsburg, PA) His biggest hit: "Roses Are Red" in 1962. From 1962 to 1972 he sang more #1 hits than any male vocalist. He began his career as a clarinetist and bandleader. Year/**Age**: 1995/**60** 1996/**61** 1997/**62**

- **EDIE ADAMS** Actress/singer. (Born Edith Enke in Kingston, PA) She married comedian Ernie Kovacs in 1954 and was the "Muriel Cigar" girl for many years. Year/**Age**: 1995/**66** 1996/**67** 1997/**68**

- **SIR PETER USTINOV** Actor. (London, England) He won an Oscar for supporting actor in 1960 in *Spartacus* and in 1964 for *Topaki.* Other films include *Lorenzo's Oil.* Year/**Age**: 1995/**74** 1996/**75** 1997/**76**

- **JIMMY OSMOND** Singer. (Salt Lake City, UT) Youngest of the talented OSMONDS. Year/**Age**: 1995/**32** 1996/**33** 1997/**34**

- **DUSTY SPRINGFIELD** Singer. (Born Mary O'Brien in London, England) Biggest hit: "You Don't Have to Say You Love Me" in 1966. Year/**Age**: 1995/**56** 1996/**57** 1997/**58**

- **JON CRYER** Actor. Appears on TV's "Blossom" and "Gimme a Break." In movie *Hot Shots.* Year/**Age**: 1995/**30** 1996/**31** 1997/**32**

- **LUCAS HAAS** Actor. Starred in the 1991 film *Alan & Naomi.* Year/**Age**: 1995/**19** 1996/**20** 1997/**21**

- **GERARDO** Rapper. (Born Gerardo Mejia III in Ecuador) Biggest hit: "Rico Suave" in 1991, half Spanish, half English (Spanglish). In Movies *Colors* and *Can't Buy Me Love.* Year/**Age**: 1995/**28** 1996/**29** 1997/**30**

- **KAREEM ABDUL-JABBAR** Retired basketball star. (Born Ferdinand Lewis Alcindor, Jr., in NYC) He played in Milwaukee from 1969-75. The Bucks retired his #33 in 1993. He played for the L.A. Lakers. On April 4, 1984, he broke Wilt Chamberlain's all-time NBA regular season scoring record of 31,419 points, and early in 1985 he broke the record for most points scored in a professional basketball career. At age 40, he averaged 14.6 points a game. Year/**Age**: 1995/**48** 1996/**49** 1997/**50**

- **HERBIE MANN** Flutist. (NYC) He had several hit albums with his afro-jazz sextet. Year/**Age**: 1995/**65** 1996/**66** 1997/**67**

- **"NIGHT TRAIN" LANE** Former football great. Year/**Age**: 1995/**67** 1996/**68** 1997/**69**

- **ROY HAMILTON** Singer. (1929-1969 – Leesburg, GA) Biggest hit: "Unchained Melody" in 1955 from the movie *Unchained.* (Died 7-20-69.)

- **CHARLIE CHAPLIN** Actor/comedian. (1889-1977 – London, England) When he became a comic, he came to the U.S. Upset with his first film, he burned the original negative. His film classics included *City Lights, The Gold Rush,* and *The Tramp* . He wrote the song "This Is My Song," a hit later by Petula Clark from his film *A Countess of Hong Kong.* (Died 12-25-77.)

- **WILBUR WRIGHT** Aviation pioneer. (1867-1912 – Millville, IN) His brother, Orville, was the first man to fly an airplane, because on the day of the historic flight, they flipped a coin to see who would become the world's first pilot. (Died 5-30-12.)

FACTS FROM THE PAST

1935   The NBC radio classic comedy show, **"FIBBER McGEE & MOLLY,"** premiered and ran until 1957. It starred Jim and Marian Jordan. They resided at 79 Wistful Vista with the famous McGee closet.

1943   The first LSD trip took place. Swiss Chemist **ALBERT HOFFMAN** created lysergic acid diethylamide in his laboratory in 1938. On this day a tiny amount accidentally seeped through the skin on his finger.

1956   **EYEGLASSES WERE FIRST WORN BY AN UMPIRE** in a major league baseball game. Eddie Rommel had been an umpire for 18 years before admitting he needed some help with his vision.

1962   **WALTER CRONKITE** made his debut as anchorman of "The CBS Evening News" succeeding Douglas Edwards.

1972   **APOLLO XVI** astronauts were launched toward the moon: Astronauts Young, Duke & Mattingly set a new record of total exploration time on the moon – 20 hours, 14 minutes. The landing module was named *Orion.* This was the 5th successful moon landing. They splashed down in the Pacific April 27 with 214 pounds of moon rocks aboard.

1993   At Candlestick Park, San Francisco pitcher **ROD BECK** threw a strike, but no one was in the batter's box. Atlanta's **RON GANT** had walked away from the plate, angry over a call strike. Umpire **MARK HIRSCHBECK** told him to get back in the batter's box, when Gant refused, Hirschbeck instructed Beck to pitch. When Gant continued his at bat, he flew out to end the game. Giants won 1-0.

1993   Prsident Clinton received **GAY AND LESBIAN ACTIVISTS** in the Oval Office for a meeting.

1994   **WEDDING BELLS** rang for actor Dudley Moore and Nicole Rothschild, and singer/songwriter Harry Connick, Jr. married model/video diector Jill Goodacre.

APRIL 17

BIRTHDAYS

- **"BOOMER" ESIASON** Football quarterback. (Born Norman Esiason in West Islip, NY) Weighs 250 lbs. and stands 6'6". With the New York Jets. Year/Age: 1995/**34** 1996/**35** 1997/**36**

- **BILAL ABDUL-SAMAD** Singer. (Northridge, CA) BOYS. Hit: "Dial My Heart" in 1988. Year/Age: 1995/**17** 1996/**18** 1997/**19**

- **CHRIS BARBER** Bandleader/trombonist. (England) Biggest hit: "Petite Fleur" in 1959. Year/Age: 1995/**65** 1996/**66** 1997/**67**

- **JAN HAMMER** [yahn hah'-mur] Composer/musician. (Czechoslovakia) Music for "Miami Vice." Year/Age: 1995/**47** 1996/**48** 1997/**49**

- **GENEVIEVE** French entertainer and Jack Paar sidekick. Year/Age: 1995/**65** 1996/**66** 1997/**67**

- **LON McCALLISTER** Actor. (Los Angeles, CA) Appeared in *Babes in Arms*, *Stagedoor Canteen*, and *Home in Indiana* with Jeanne Crain. Year/Age: 1995/**72** 1996/**73** 1997/**74**

- **ANNE SHIRLEY** Actress. (Born Dawn Paris in NYC) She received an Oscar nomination for supporting actress in 1937 for *Stella Dallas*. As a child actress she was known as Dawn O'Day and retired at age 25. Year/Age: 1995/**77** 1996/**78** 1997/**79**

- **DON KIRSHNER** Rock concert promoter. (Bronx, NY) He owned a record company at one time and had a Saturday night TV show called "Rock Concert." Year/Age: 1995/**61** 1996/**62** 1997/**63**

- **HARRY REASONER** Newsman. (1923-1991 – Dakota City, IA) Three-time Emmy winner with "60 Minutes." The snowy-haired newsman was unhappily paired with Barbara Walters on the "ABC Evening News" in 1975, as network TV's first male-female evening anchor team. (Died 8-6-91.)

- **WILLIAM HOLDEN** Actor. (1918-1981 – Born William Franklin Beedle, Jr., O'Fallon, IL) His first role as a leading man was in *Golden Boy* in 1939, and his last was *S.O.B.* He won an Oscar for best actor in his role as a racketeer sergeant in *Stalag 17* in 1953. (Died 11-16-81.)

- **THORNTON WILDER** Writer. (1897-1975 – Madison, WI) Noted author of novels and plays, including *Our Town* and *The Skin of Our Teeth*. Three-time Pulitzer Prize winner. (Died 12-7-75.)

- **J. P. MORGAN** Financier. (1837-1913 – Hartford, CT) He built an industrial and financial empire in which he and his partners controlled 47 of the largest corporations, including U.S. Steel. (Died 3-31-13.)

- **NIKITA KHRUSHCHEV** Former Soviet Premier. (1894-1971 – Born in the Ukraine) Remembered by Americans for his show-down with President Kennedy in the Cuban Missile Crisis, and when he pounded his desk at the U.N. with his shoe. He told jokes—example: A Russian man was given a 25-year sentence for shouting "Khrushchev is a fool" and Nikita said, "Five years was for insulting the party secretary and 20 years for revealing a state secret." (Died 9-11-71.)

FACTS FROM THE PAST

1492 Queen Isabella and King Ferdinand of Spain agreed to finance **CHRISTOPHER COLUMBUS'S VOYAGE** of discovery to the **NEW WORLD**.

1912 The **FIRST "UNOFFICIAL" GOLD RECORD** was recorded. Al Jolson sang "Ragging the Baby to Sleep" for the Victor Talking Machine Company. The record sold a million copies in two years. (The **FIRST "OFFICIAL" GOLD RECORD** was Glenn Miller's "Chattanooga Choo Choo" in 1942.)

1929 **BABE RUTH** married Claire Hodgeson, a former member of the Ziegfeld Follies. They got married at 5:45 a.m. to avoid fans who were expecting the ceremony at 6:30 a.m. Asked where they were going for their honeymoon, Ruth said, "To the ballpark." He hit a home run for her that day. This was his second marriage.

1956 **WILLIE MOSCONI** of Philadelphia, matched against Jimmy Moore of Albuquerque, NM, in the world's pocket billiard tournament, ran the entire game (150 balls) in one inning. Moore played a safety on his first shot and never got another chance to play.

1961 The CIA launched the disastrous **BAY OF PIGS** invasion of Cuba using about 1,500 CIA-trained Cuban exiles. The attempt to overthrow the government of Fidel Castro failed. About 100 attackers were killed, 200 escaped, and the remaining 1,200 were captured and held for ransom.

1964 Geraldine Mock became the **FIRST WOMAN** to make a **SOLO FLIGHT AROUND THE WORLD** as she landed her plane in her hometown of Columbus, OH. She flew 23,000 miles in 29 days.

1969 **SIRHAN SIRHAN** was convicted of assassinating **SENATOR ROBERT F. KENNEDY**.

1970 **JOHNNY CASH** refused President Nixon's request to sing "Okie From Muskogee" and sang "A Boy Named Sue" instead.

1976 In one of the **WILDEST GAMES IN BASEBALL HISTORY**, Mike Schmidt belted 4 homers, as the Philadelphia Phillies wiped out an 11-run deficit, defeating the Chicago Cubs by a score of 18-16.

1993 Sgt. **STACEY KOON** and officer **LAURENCE POWELL** were found guilty of violating **RODNEY KING**'s civil rights in the video taped beating trial in Los Angeles, CA.

1994 Pink Floyd's **"DARK SIDE OF THE MOON"** became the 4th biggest selling album in U.S. music history. Released in 1973, it reached 13 million domestic sales and trailed only Michael Jackson's "Thriller," Fleetwood Mac's "Rumours," and the Eagles "Their Greatest Hits 1971-1975."

Scientists figure the universe is 15–20 billion years old.

APRIL 18
Pet Owner's Independance Day

BIRTHDAYS

- **ERIC ROBERTS** Actor. (Biloxi, MS) *The Coca Cola Kid,* and *The Specialist.* Year/Age: 1995/**39** 1996/**40** 1997/**41**

- **HAYLEY MILLS** Actress. (London, England) The daughter of actor John Mills and sister of actress Juliet Mills. She appeared in *Pollyanna* for which she received a special Oscar in 1960. She had a hit record called "Let's Get Together" from the movie *The Parent Trap* in 1961. Year/Age: 1995/**49** 1996/**50** 1997/**51**

- **JOHN JAMES** Actor. (Minneapolis, MN) On "Dynasty" and "The Colbys." Year/Age: 1995/**39** 1996/**40** 1997/**41**

- **MELODY THOMAS SCOTT** Actress. On the soap "Young and the Restless." Year/Age: 1995/**39** 1996/**40** 1997/**41**

- **CONAN O'BRIEN** Late night talk show host. At one time he was a writer for Saturday Night Live. Year/Age: 1995/**32** 1996/**33** 1997/**34**

- **LENNY BAKER** Musician. (NYC) Of SHA-NA-NA. Year/Age: 1995/**49** 1996/**50** 1997/**51**

- **JAMES WOODS** Actor. (Vernal, UT) Emmy award for *My Name is Bill W.* and *Promise.* He was nominated for best actor in *Salvador.* In the films *Chaplin, Diggstown, Straight Talk, The Getaway, Lorenzo's Oil,* and *The Specialist,* and with Michael J. Fox in *The Hard Way.* Year/Age: 1995/**48** 1996/**49** 1997/**50**

- **CLIVE REVILL** Actor. (New Zealand) Appeared in *Bunny Lake is Missing* and *Modesty Blaise.* Year/Age: 1995/**65** 1996/**66** 1997/**67**

- **DOROTHY LYMAN** Actress. (Minneapolis, MN) Emmy Award-winning soap opera actress: "All My Children," "Another World," "Edge of Night," and "Mama's Family." Year/Age: 1995/**48** 1996/**49** 1997/**50**

- **ROBERT HOOKS** Actor. (Washington, DC) He played Detective Jeff Ward on the "N.Y.P.D." TV series and was in the TV series "Shaft." Year/Age: 1995/**58** 1996/**59** 1997/**60**

- **BARBARA HALE** Actress. (DeKalb, IL) Best known as Della Street on the "Perry Mason" TV series. Year/Age: 1995/**73** 1996/**74** 1997/**75**

- **RICK MORANIS** Comedic actor. (Canada) He played Seymour, the guy who fed "Audrey II" in the remake of *Little Shop of Horrors.* Had the leading role in *Honey I Shrunk the Kids* and *Honey I Blew Up the Kid.* Co-starred in the *Ghostbusters* films, *Splitting Heirs,* and played Barney in *The Flintstones* movie. Year/Age: 1995/**42** 1996/**43** 1997/**44**

- **"TINY" NATE ARCHIBALD** Basketball star. (Bronx, NY) Barely 6 ft. tall, he topped everyone in the NBA, 1972-73, by scoring almost 35 points a game. Year/Age: 1995/**47** 1996/**48** 1997/**49**

- **WENDY BARRIE** Actress. (1912-1978 – Born Marguerite Wendy Jenkins in England) Films include *Hound of the Baskervilles* and *Private Life of Henry VIII.* (Died 2-2-78.)

- **SKIP STEPHENSON** Comedian. (1948-1992 – Omaha, NE) Original host of TV's "Real People." (Died 5-18-92.)

FACTS FROM THE PAST

1775 The **MIDNIGHT RIDE OF PAUL REVERE** began. As Bill Dawes and Sam Prescott took other routes, Revere rode from Boston to Concord in order to warn the colonists that the British were coming. Paul got all the glory, but was captured by the Redcoats before he got very far, and it was Dawes and Prescott who carried out most of the mission, becoming the unsung heroes of that historic evening.

1906 A devastating **EARTHQUAKE STRUCK SAN FRANCISCO,** followed by raging fires. It lasted 48 seconds and registered 8.25 on the Richter Scale, qualifying as America's worst ever earthquake. The city's downtown area burned for three days, destroying four square miles and killing 700 people. Publisher William Randolph Hearst advised a New York editor, "Don't overplay it. They often have earthquakes in California." Another powerful earthquake hit the area October 17, 1989.

1923 The **FIRST GAME** was played in **YANKEE STADIUM**, which later became known as the "House that Babe Ruth built." The Yankees defeated the Boston Red Sox, 4-1.

1934 The **FIRST LAUNDROMAT** was opened by J.F. Cantrell in Fort Wayne, IN. It was called a "washateria."

1942 General Jimmy Doolittle made history when he led 16 B-25 bombers on the **FIRST U.S. AIR RAID** against the Japanese mainland in WWII, four months after Pearl Harbor.

1955 Indonesia's President Sukarno made first use of the phrase **"THIRD WORLD"** in a speech about non-white and underdeveloped areas.

1956 Actress **GRACE KELLY** married **PRINCE RAINIER** [ray-neer'] of Monaco in a civil ceremony. (A church wedding took place the next day.)

1966 **BILL RUSSELL** was named player-coach of the Boston Celtics, the first African-American coach in the National Basketball Assn.

1981 The **LONGEST PROFESSIONAL BASEBALL GAME** began on this night at 8 p.m. Play spanned 3 days, 8 hours and 25 minutes. Umpires suspended play at 4:07 a.m. on April 23rd. with Pawtucket, RI, beating Rochester, NY, 3-2. Cal Ripken, Jr., played third base for Rochester. More than 1,000 pitches were thrown and 160 baseballs were used. 1,740 were in attendance for the first inning and 23 for the 32nd. A sellout crowd saw the final 33rd inning on April 23rd. As the fans left, Peggy Lee's "Is That All There Is" was played.

1993 **DAVID KORESH** and many of his followers were killed when the 51-day siege at trhe Branch Davidian compund near Waco, TX ended in fire after federal agents crashed their way in.

1994 **ROSEANNE ARNOLD** filed for divorce from Tom Arnold. They were married on January 20, 1990. Charges were dropped and she refiled on May 13.

APRIL 19

A googol is a one with a hundred zeroes behind it.

BIRTHDAYS

- **FRANK VIOLA** Baseball pitcher. (Hempstead, NY) New York Mets' Cy Young winner. Year/**Age**: 1995/**35** 1996/**36** 1997/**37**

- **ALAN PRICE** Singer/songwriter. (England) Organist with the original ANIMALS. Biggest hit: "House of the Rising Sun" in 1964; formed his own group in 1965 the ALAN PRICE SET. Year/**Age**: 1995/**53** 1996/**54** 1997/**55**

- **AL UNSER, JR.** Racecar driver. Won the Indy 500 in 1992 and 1994. His father had previously won 4 times. Year/**Age**: 1995/**33** 1996/**34** 1997/**35**

- **HUGH O'BRIAN** Actor. (Born Hugh Krampe in Rochester, NY) Best remembered for his TV portrayal of "Wyatt Earp." "The Life and Legend of Wyatt Earp" was the first of the adult westerns. Year/**Age**: 1995/**65** 1996/**66** 1997/**67**

- **JACK PARDEE** Football coach. Houston Oilers coach since 1990. Previously coached NFL Bears and Redskins. Year/**Age**: 1995/**59** 1996/**60** 1997/**61**

- **TIM CURRY** Actor. In the film *The Rocky Horror Show*, and *The Shadow*. Year/**Age**: 1995/**49** 1996/**50** 1997/**51**

- **DON BARBOUR** Singer. A member of the FOUR FRESHMEN, a popular 1950's group. Their biggest hit: "Graduation Day" in 1956. Year/**Age**: 1995/**66** 1996/**67** 1997/**68**

- **ELINOR DONAHUE** Actress. (Tacoma, WA) Daughter Betty on the "Father Knows Best" TV series with Robert Young and Miriam Welby, Felix's female friend, on "The Odd Couple." Year/**Age**: 1995/**58** 1996/**59** 1997/**60**

- **DON ADAMS** Actor/comedian. (NYC) Starred in TV's "Get Smart" from 1965-69. Year/**Age**: 1995/**68** 1996/**69** 1997/**70**

- **DUDLEY MOORE** Actor (London, England) He was a British cabaret pianist and comedian before his film career. He appeared in *10* with Bo Derek, *Arthur*, for which he received an Oscar nomination, and *Crazy People*. In the TV sitcom "Dudley." Year/**Age**: 1995/**60** 1996/**61** 1997/**62**

- **MARK VOLMAN** Singer. (Los Angeles, CA) Biggest hits with TURTLES: "Happy Together," "You Showed Me," and "It Ain't Me Babe." Year/**Age**: 1995/**51** 1996/**52** 1997/**53**

- **DICK SARGENT** Actor. (1930-1994, Carmel, CA) Samantha's husband, Darin, on TV's "Bewitched" from 1969-72, In film *A Touch of Mink* with Cary Grant. In 1991 he announced he was gay. (Died of prostate cancer 7-8-94.)

- **BOBBY RUSSELL** Composer/singer. (1940-1992 – Nashville, TN) He wrote "Honey," "Little Green Apples," and "The Night the Lights Went Out in Georgia." His biggest hit: "Saturday Morning Confusion" in 1971. (Died 11-19-92.)

- **JAYNE MANSFIELD** Actress/sex symbol. (1932-1967 – Born Jayne Palmer in Bryn Mawr, PA) Killed in an automobile accident. One of her husbands was Mickey Hargitay. Their daughter is Mariska Hargitay, Carly on "Falcon Crest." (Died 6-29-67.)

- **DICKIE GOODMAN** Entertainer. (1934-1989 – Hewlett, NY) He and partner Bill Buchanan originated the novelty "break-in" recordings featuring the original versions of Top 40 hits interwoven throughout the song. His last Top 10 record was "Mr. Jaws" in 1975. Television commentator John Cameron Swayze sued Goodman for using a character named John Cameron Cameron on "Flying Saucer Part I and II." Goodman shot and killed himself in Fayetteville, North Carolina. on 11-6-89)

FACTS FROM THE PAST

1897 The **BOSTON MARATHON** was held for the first time. The 26-mile, 385-yard race began in Hopkinton, MA, and ended at Exeter Street in Boston. John McDermott was the winner in 2 hours, 55 minutes and 10 seconds.

1951 **GENERAL DOUGLAS MacARTHUR** who had recently been relieved as Commander of the U.N. forces in Korea, appeared before Congress attacking the administration of Harry Truman. He delivered his "Old soldiers never die…they just fade away" speech and then went to work for the Rand Corporation. (He died April 5, 1964.)

1953 The longest recorded major league home run was hit by **MICKEY MANTLE**. It traveled 565 feet.

1956 Prince Rainier III of Monaco married actress Grace Kelly in what was called the **WEDDING OF THE YEAR**. She became the first American woman to marry a reigning prince. (They were actually married already in a private ceremony the previous day.) Princess Grace was the first actress to be depicted on a postage stamp which was issued in Monaco to commemorate their wedding. She had one hit record with Bing Crosby, "True Love" in 1956 from the film *High Society*.

1979 The L.A. Lakers won the coin toss in the first round of the college draft. They chose Michigan State guard **MAGIC JOHNSON**.

1982 **PAUL SIMON** and **ART GARFUNKEL** announced that they would stay together – as they put it – "As long as the fans want us." They had just finished their successful reunion concert in New York's Central Park. By the time the album they were working on came out 18 months later, all traces of Garfunkel's contributions had been electronically removed.

1982 Astronauts **SALLY K. RIDE** became the first woman and **GUION S. BLUFORD, JR.**, became the first African-American to be chosen for **U.S. SPACE MISSIONS.** Bluford retired in 1993 to work for an aerospace company.

1988 After the Baltimore Orioles lost their 11th straight game, WIYY/Baltimore **D.J. BOB RIVERS** vowed to stay on the air until they won. Eight games, two David Letterman calls, and 216 hours later, the O's won and Rivers finally got to sleep.

1993 Cult leader **DAVID KORESH** and possibly 86 of his followers died in a raging fire at the Branch Davidian headquarters in Waco, TX, after the FBI tried to drive them out with tear gas. President Clinton and Atty. Gen. Janet Reno approved the assault. The FBI called the deaths "a mass suicide."

1994 **RODNEY KING** was awarded $3.8 million from the city of Los Angeles for his 1991 beating by police.

Convenience factor: most folks still drink and drive.

APRIL 20
Astrological Sign of Taurus

BIRTHDAYS

- **JESSICA LANGE** Actress. (Cloquet, MN) King Kong's favorite handful and 5-time Oscar nominee. She won best-supporting actress Oscar for her role in *Tootsie*, and was nominated for *Country*, *Frances*, *Sweet Dreams*, and *Music Box*. In film *Night and the City*. Year/**Age**: 1995/**46** 1996/**47** 1997/**48**
- **TITO PUENTO** Bandleader. (NYC) Grammy winner in 1978 and 1983. Year/**Age**: 1995/**72** 1996/**73** 1997/**74**
- **JOEY LAWRENCE** Actor. TV's "Blossom" and "Gimme a Break." He had a hit song: "Nothin' My Love Can't Fix." He received 7,500 fan letters in one week in 1993. Year/**Age**: 1995/**19** 1996/**20** 1997/**21**
- **CRAIG FROST** Keyboardist. (Flint, MI) GRAND FUNK RAILROAD. Biggest hit: "The Locomotion" in 1974. Year/**Age**: 1995/**47** 1996/**48** 1997/**49**
- **DON MATTINGLY** Baseball. (Evansville, IN) New York Yankees first baseman. Named the American League's Most Valuable Player in 1985. Year/**Age**: 1995/**34** 1996/**35** 1997/**36**
- **JOHN PAUL STEVENS** Supreme Court Justice. (Chicago, IL) Nominated by President Ford December 19, 1975. He is an independent. Year/**Age**: 1995/**75** 1996/**76** 1997/**77**
- **GEORGE TAKEI** Actor. (San Francisco, CA) Sulu in "Star Trek." Year/**Age**: 1995/**55** 1996/**56** 1997/**57**
- **NINA FOCH** Actress. (Netherlands) Appeared in *Spartacus* and *An American in Paris*. Year/**Age**: 1995/**71** 1996/**72** 1997/**73**

- **JOHNNY TILLOTSON** Singer. (Jacksonville, FL) Biggest hit: "Poetry in Motion" in 1960. He was in the movie *Just for You*. Year/**Age**: 1995/**56** 1996/**57** 1997/**58**
- **LUTHER VANDROSS** Singer. (NYC) His biggest hit: "Stop to Love" in 1986. His voice is heard on many commercial jingles. Year/**Age**: 1995/**44** 1996/**45** 1997/**46**
- **RYAN O'NEAL** Actor. (Los Angeles, CA) With his lover Farrah Fawcett in *Good Sports*. Nominated for an Academy Award for best actor in *Love Story* in 1970. Year/**Age**: 1995/**54** 1996/**55** 1997/**56**
- **HAROLD LLOYD** Actor. (1893-1971 – Burchard, NE) Comedian who was a special Oscar winner in 1952. (Died 3-8-71.)
- **BRUCE CABOT** Actor (1904-1972 – Carlsbad, NM) Saved Fay Wray in the 1933 film *King Kong*. (Died 5-3-72.)
- **ADOLF HITLER** Dictator. (1889-1945 – Austria) The German dictator wrote *Mein Kampf* while serving a prison sentence. He was obsessed with superiority of the Aryan "race" and the evil of Marxism, which he saw as a Jewish plot. On April 30, 1945, facing certain defeat by the Allied Forces, Hitler shot himself in a Berlin bunker near the Brandenburg Gate.
- **JOHN MIRO** Artist. (1893-1983 – Barcelona, Spain) Surrealist and abstract artist with major works in building all over the world. (Died 12-25-83.)

FACTS FROM THE PAST

1812 GEORGE CLINTON, 4th Vice President of the U.S., died in Washington at age 73. He was the first V.P. to die while in office.

1902 Pierre and Marie Curie, a French husband-and-wife scientist team, completed the first successful atomic experiment isolating the radioactive element **RADIUM**. (Named radium because it radiates powerful invisible rays.) It was not known at that time that radiation was dangerous. Marie and their daughter, Irene, who had helped with some of the experiments, died of leukemia. The first commercial use of radium was to make wristwatches glow in the dark by painting phosphor and radium on the hands and numbers. They were big sellers for many years, but many people who painted them died.

1910 For the second time in his career, Cleveland pitcher **ADDIE JOSS** threw a no-hitter against the Chicago White Sox. The first time was in 1908. Both games ended with the score 1-0.

1932 Child actress **SHIRLEY TEMPLE**, 3$\frac{1}{2}$-years old, made her film debut with the release of *Stand Up and Cheer*.

1947 **FRED ALLEN'S NETWORK RADIO PROGRAM (USA)** was taken off the air after the comedian made a nasty crack about network vice presidents. The line, "On ships they call them barnacles; in radio they attach themselves to desks and are called vice presidents." NBC finally decided not to cancel the show when the incident drew lots of publicity.

1959 13-year-old **DOLLY PARTON** released her first single, "Puppy Love," on the Gold Band label.

1968 **PIERRE ELLIOTT TRUDEAU** was sworn in as Prime Minister of Canada.

1972 The lunar module of the **APOLLO XVI** landed on the moon with astronauts John Young and Charles Duke aboard. Thomas Mattingly remained in orbit around the moon aboard the command module. This was the third exploration of the moon.

1986 **VLADIMIR HOROWITZ** returned to the Soviet musical stage, giving a piano recital in Moscow that dazzled the audience and left many in tears. It was his first recital there since he left his homeland 61 years before. (He has won over 20 Grammys.)

1986 Ohio evangelist Jim Brown announced that the **MR. ED THEME SONG** included the hidden satanic messages "The source is Satan" and "Someone sung this song for Satan."

1990 **JANET JACKSON'S STAR STATUS** is symbolized on the Hollywood Walk of Fame.

1992 Denver Bronco wide receiver **VANCE JOHNSON** filed an invasion of privacy suit against HBO for showing him naked during a locker room celebration on the network's "Inside the NFL."

1994 **BARBRA STREISAND** launched her first consert tour in 27 years at London's Wembley Arena. Tickets cost $50 to $350.

APRIL 21

Is pizza one of the food goups?

BIRTHDAYS

- **ANTHONY QUINN** Actor. (Chihuahua, Mexico) Known best for *Zorba, the Greek*. He won an Oscar for supporting actor in 1952 for portraying Zapata's brother in *Viva, Zapata,* and in 1956 for *Lust for Life*. He played Auda Abu Tayi in *Lawrence of Arabia*. Co-starred in *Only the Lonely, The Mobsters*, and *Revenge*. Year/**Age**: 1995/**80** 1996/**81** 1997/**82**

- **CHARLES GRODIN** Actor. (Pittsburgh, PA) *Seems Like Old Times* with Goldie Hawn, *Heaven Can Wait, Midnight Run, Taking Care of Business, Beethoven, Clifford, Dave*, and *Heart and Souls*. Year/**Age**: 1995/**60** 1996/**61** 1997/**62**

- **IGGY POP** Punk rocker. (Born James Newell Osterberg in Ann Arbor, MI) His albums include *Brick by Brick* and *Choice Cuts*. Year/**Age**: 1995/**48** 1996/**49** 1997/**50**

- **PATTI LuPONE** Singer/actress. (Northport, NY) *Evita, Sunset Boulevard*, and TV's "Life Goes On." Year/**Age**: 1995/**46** 1996/**47** 1997/**48**

- **ELAINE MAY** Comic actress/writer. (Born Elaine Berlin in Philadelphia, PA) The comedy team of Nichols & May released some funny comedy albums. She directed the films *Ishtar* and *The Heartbreak Kid*. Year/**Age**: 1995/**63** 1996/**64** 1997/**65**

- **ROBERT SMITH** Lead Singer of THE CURE. Hits include "Kiss Me, Kiss Me, Kiss Me," "Love Cats," and "Pictures of You." Year/**Age**: 1995/**36** 1996/**37** 1997/**38**

- **DON CORNELL** Singer/guitarist. Biggest hit: "Hold My Hand" in 1954. Year/**Age**: 1995/**76** 1996/**77** 1997/**78**

- **ANDIE MACDOWELL** Actress. (Gaffney, SC) Films include *Green Card, Groundhog Day, The Player, St. Elmo's Fire, Bad Girls*, and *Four Weddings and a Funeral*. Year/**Age**: 1995/**37** 1996/**38** 1997/**39**

- **TONY DANZA** Actor. (Brooklyn, NY) Played the struggling boxer on the "Taxi" TV series and "Who's the Boss" for 8 seasons, ending in 1992. He's in the film *Angels in the Outfield*. Year/**Age**: 1995/**44** 1996/**45** 1997/**46**

- **PAUL DAVIS** Singer/songwriter. (Meridian, MS) Biggest hit: "I Go Crazy" in 1978. Year/**Age**: 1995/**46** 1996/**47** 1997/**48**

- **ERNIE MARESCA** Singer/songwriter. (Bronx, NY) His only hit, in 1962, was "Shout, Shout, Knock Yourself Out," but he wrote a couple of hits for DION: "Runaround Sue" and "The Wanderer." Year/**Age**: 1995/**56** 1996/**57** 1997/**58**

- **QUEEN ELIZABETH II** Britain. (Born Elizabeth Alexandra Mary in London) However, her birthday is always celebrated in June at the Trooping of the Colours. As soon as she gives up the throne (or dies), Prince Charles will be the King of England. Year/**Age**: 1995/**69** 1996/**70** 1997/**71**

- **SILVANA MANGANO** Italian actress. (1930-1989 – Rome, Italy) Former model, wife of producer Dino de Laurentiis. Her films included: *Tempest, Ulysses,* and *Five Branded Women*. (Died 12-16-89)

- **CHARLOTTE BRONTE** Author. (1816-1889 – England) She wrote the novel *Jane Eyre*, considered to be one of the great literary works of the 19th century. (Died 3-31-1889.)

FACTS FROM THE PAST

1509 **HENRY THE VIII** became King of England when his father, Henry the VII, died. Shortly afterward, he married his brother's widow, Catherine of Aragon, who had not consummated her marriage to Arthur.

1789 **JOHN ADAMS** was sworn in as the **FIRST VICE PRESIDENT** of the United States.

1836 An army of Texans led by **SAM HOUSTON** (yelling "Remember the Alamo") defeated General Santa Anna's Mexican Army in a mosquito-infested marsh at San Jacinto, assuring the **INDEPENDENCE OF TEXAS**. The 900 Texans caught the 1,200 Mexicans taking a siesta. The entire confrontation took only 18 minutes, took the lives of 600 Mexicans and 9 Texans. Santa Anna was captured.

1855 The **FIRST RAILROAD TRAIN CROSSED THE FIRST RAILROAD BRIDGE** over the Mississippi, between Rock Island, IL, and Davenport, IA. A river pilot damaged it two weeks later and **ABRAHAM LINCOLN** represented the railroad line.

1898 **BILL DUGGLEBY** of the Philadelphia Phillies hit a grand slam home run in his first major league at bat. A feat that still stands.

1913 The **ZIPPER WAS PATENTED** by Swedish engineer **GIDEON SUNDBACK**. He improved on an 1893 design of **WHITCOMB JUDSON** called a clasp-locker, which often jammed. Zippers were first used in World War I and appeared on civilian clothes in the 1920's.

1918 **BARON MANFRED VON RICHTHOFEN**, the German flying ace known as **THE RED BARON**, was shot down in his bright red Fokker triplane. With a bullet in his chest, the Red Baron made a perfect landing, then died. In WWI, he downed over 80 enemy planes.

1960 **DICK CLARK** told a Congressional Committee investigating "payola" that he had a financial interest in over a quarter of the records he had played on "American Bandstand" during the previous two years. He was ordered to sell off many of his holdings, but has survived it all with a net worth of over $100 million today!

1972 **APOLLO XVI** astronauts John Young and Charles Duke drove an electric car (LEM) on the surface of the moon. It's still up there along with expensive tools & some film they forgot.

1974 **DOLLY PARTON** and **PORTER WAGONER** quit performing together. Their feud lasted until 1988.

1992 **ROBERT ALTON HARRIS**, convicted murderer, died in the San Quentin gas chamber after four stays of execution. His execution was the first in California in 25 years.

1994 **EDDIE MURRAY**, of the Cleveland Indians, hit home runs from both sides of the plate for a record 11th time. Mickey Mantle held the record at 10.

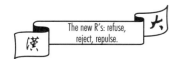

The new R's: refuse, reject, repulse.

APRIL 22

BIRTHDAYS

- **JACK NITZSCHE** Producer/composer/keyboardist. (Born Bernard Nitzsche in Chicago, IL) He scored films *An Officer and a Gentleman* and *One Flew Over the Cuckoo's Nest*. Wrote the song "Needles and Pins." Married Buffy Sainte-Marie. Year/**Age:** 1995/**58** 1996/**59** 1997/**60**

- **JACK NICHOLSON** Actor. (Neptune, NJ) He was once an errand boy at MGM Studio. He got his start in the 50's on TV's "Divorce Court." He won an Oscar for best actor in *One Flew Over the Cuckoo's Nest* in 1975. He played the "Joker" in *Batman*. Won the Oscar for best supporting actor in *Terms of Endearment* in 1983. In films *Man Trouble, Hoffa, A Few Good Men, The Crossing Guard,* and *Wolf*. Made his name in *Easy Rider*. Year/**Age:** 1995/**58** 1996/**59** 1997/**60**

- **EDDIE ALBERT** Actor. (Born Edward Albert Heimberger in Rock Island, IL) He was nominated for a supporting actor Oscar in 1953 for *Roman Holiday* with Audrey Hepburn, for which she won an Oscar. Eddie was also nominated in 1972 for supporting actor in *Heartbreak Kid* and he starred in the TV series "Green Acres." He was in the film *The Big Picture*. Actor Edward Albert is his son. Year/**Age:** 1995/**87** 1996/**88** 1997/**89**

- **CHARLOTTE RAE** Actress. (Born Charlotte Lubotsky in Milwaukee, WI) She appeared as Conrad Bain's maid on "Different Strokes" and the spinoff of that program, "Facts of Life." Also one of the voices in *Tom & Jerry: The Movie*. Year/**Age:** 1995/**69** 1996/**70** 1997/**71**

- **GLEN CAMPBELL** Singer. (Delight, AR) Biggest hit: "Rhinestone Cowboy" in 1975. In 1965, he toured briefly as guitarist with the BEACH BOYS. In 1969, he hosted the "Glen Campbell Goodtime Hour." He was in the film *True Grit*. Year/**Age:** 1995/**57** 1996/**58** 1997/**59**

- **PAUL CARRACK** Vocalist. (Sheffield, England) With MIKE & THE MECHANICS. Year/**Age:** 1995/**44** 1996/**45** 1997/**46**

- **JASON MILLER** Playwright. (Scranton, PA) Pulitzer and Tony Award winner for *That Championship Season* in 1973. Year/**Age:** 1995/**56** 1996/**57** 1997/**58**

- **DEANE BEMAN** Golfer. (Washington, DC) Commissioner of PGA Tournament since 1974. Year/**Age:** 1995/**57** 1996/**58** 1997/**59**

- **JOSEPH BOTTOMS** Actor. (Santa Barbara, CA) He appeared in the miniseries *Holocaust*. Year/**Age:** 1995/**41** 1996/**42** 1997/**43**

- **PETER FRAMPTON** Rock star. (Kent, England) He had nearly a decade of experience, first with The HERD, a teeny-bopper band, and then with blues rockers, HUMBLE PIE, before his big album *Frampton Comes Alive* in 1975. That album was recorded at San Francisco's Winterland and sold more than one million copies in a single week. Year/**Age:** 1995/**45** 1996/**46** 1997/**47**

- **MEL CARTER** Singer. (Cincinnati, OH) Biggest hit: "Hold Me, Thrill Me, Kiss Me" at the age of 22. He sang on local Cincinnati radio stations from the age of 4 and at 9 years, he was part of Lionel Hampton's stage revue. He is also an actor and has appeared on "Quincy," "Marcus Welby," and "Magnum, P.I." Year/**Age:** 1995/**52** 1996/**53** 1997/**54**

- **YEHUDI MENUHIN** Violinist. (NYC) At the age of 7 he debuted with the San Francisco Symphony. Year/**Age:** 1995/**79** 1996/**80** 1997/**81**

- **AARON SPELLING** TV producer. (Dallas, TX) Produced: "Fantasy Island," "Love Boat," "Starsky and Hutch," "Dynasty," "Melrose Place," and "Beverly Hills 90210." Year/**Age:** 1995/**70** 1996/**71** 1997/**72**

- **HENRY FIELDING** Writer. (1707-1754 – England) The "father of the English novel." He had a weakness for women and wrote about it in *Tom Jones*. (Died 10-8-1754.)

FACTS FROM THE PAST

1348 At a royal ball in England, the Countess of Salisbury was dancing with **KING EDWARD III** when her garter slipped down off her leg. The King chivalrously picked it up and placed it back where it belonged, and thus **BEGAN THE TRADITION OF BRITAIN'S KNIGHTS OF THE GARTER.**

1793 The **FIRST CIRCUS** in the U.S. was attended by President George Washington. It was called "Rickett's."

1937 **CLARK GABLE** was taken to court by Violet Wells Norton, who claimed he was the father of her 13-year-old daughter, Gwendoline. Violet lost the case. Gable never saw his only son because the actor died a few months before he was born in 1960.

1947 In the first pro basketball championship the **PHILADELPHIA WARRIORS** beat the **CHICAGO STAGS** 83-80 to win the series 4 games to 1. The Warriors' forward, **ART HILLHOUSE**, fouled out in all five games.

1964 President Lyndon B. Johnson opened the **NEW YORK WORLD'S FAIR.**

1976 **BARBARA WALTERS** accepted an offer to co-anchor the ABC Evening News with Harry Reasoner, becoming network television's **FIRST ANCHORWOMAN,** for a reported $1 million a year.

1983 The West German news magazine *Stern* announced the discovery of 60 volumes of personal diaries supposedly written by **ADOLF HITLER.** (The diaries, however, turned out to be a hoax.)

1990 **ROBERT POLHILL** was freed by pro-Iranian Shiite Moslem militants in Beirut after 1,182 days as a hostage. A former Beirut University College professor of business and accounting, he thanked the Syrian and U.S. governments for bringing him back "into the real world."

1994 Former President **RICHARD MILHOUS NIXON** died of a stroke at age 81. He was the only U.S. president to resign his office to avoid impeachment.

APRIL 23

Pop your pustule.

BIRTHDAYS

•**JANET BLAIR** Actress. (Altoona, PA) Films include: *Boys Night Out, The Fabulous Dorseys,* and *My Sister Eileen.* On TV in "The Smith Family." Year/**Age:** 1995/**74** 1996/**75** 1997/**76**

•**SHIRLEY TEMPLE BLACK** Actress/ambassador. (Santa Monica, CA) The child star of the 1930's grew up, married, had 3 children, and was named U.S. Ambassador to several different countries. She was the youngest person to accumulate an estate of $1 million dollars before she was 10 years old. Year/**Age:** 1995/**67** 1996/**68** 1997/**69**

•**JAN HOOKS** Actress. "Saturday Night Live" and "Designing Women." Film *A Dangerous Woman.* Year/**Age:** 1995/**38** 1996/**39** 1997/**40**

•**GAIL GOODRICH** Former basketball star. (Los Angeles, CA) Los Angeles Lakers. Year/**Age:** 1995/**52** 1996/**53** 1997/**54**

•**SANDRA DEE** Actress. (Born Alexandra Zuck in Bayonne, NJ) She was married to Bobby Darin from 1960-67. She was in the film *A Summer Place.* The film *Gidget* launched a brief superstar period for Sandra. Year/**Age:** 1995/**53** 1996/**54** 1997/**55**

•**JOYCE DeWITT** Actress. (Wheeling, WV) Appeared on the "Three's Company" TV series with John Ritter. Year/**Age:** 1995/**46** 1996/**47** 1997/**48**

•**VALERIE BERTINELLI** Actress. (Wilmington, DE) TV's "One Day at a Time" and "Sydney." In the film *What She Doesn't Know.* Married to rocker Eddie Van Halen. TV's "Cafe American." Year/**Age:** 1995/**35** 1996/**36** 1997/**37**

•**LEE MAJORS** Actor. (Wyandotte, MI) Starred in TV series "Six Million Dollar Man" and "Fall Guy." In film *Scrooged.* Year/**Age:** 1995/**55** 1996/**56** 1997/**57**

•**DAVID BIRNEY** Actor. (Washington, DC) Starred in *Bridget Loves Bernie* with co-star Meredith Baxter. They were married in real life and parents of twins before recent divorce. Appeared in the film *The Long Way Home.* Year/**Age:** 1995/**56** 1996/**57** 1997/**58**

•**RAY PETERSON** Singer. (Denton, TX) Biggest hit: "Tell Laura I Love Her" in 1960. Year/**Age:** 1995/**56** 1996/**57** 1997/**58**

•**SIMONE SIMONE** Actress. (France) Appeared in *Seventh Heaven* and *Cat People.* Year/**Age:** 1995/**81** 1996/**82** 1997/**83**

•**TONY ESPOSITO** Hockey star. (Canada) Year/**Age:** 1995/**52** 1996/**53** 1997/**54**

•**DON MASSENGALE** Golfer. Year/**Age:** 1995/**58** 1996/**59** 1997/**60**

•**WARREN SPAHN** Former Milwaukee Braves pitcher. He was one of the top left-handed pitchers in history and a member of the Baseball Hall of Fame. He won 363 games, was 20-game winner 13 times and got the Cy Young Award in 1957. Year/**Age:** 1995/**74** 1996/**75** 1997/**76**

•**HERVE VILLECHAIZE** Very small actor. (1943-1993, Paris, France) Formerly starred on "Fantasy Island" as Tattoo, filmed at the Coco Palms on the island of Kauai in Hawaii. Appeared in the film *Airplane II.* (He died of a self-inflicted gunshot wound 9-4-93.)

•**STEVE CLARK** Steamin' Guitarist. (1960-1991 – England) Guitarist for heavy metal group DEF LEPPARD. Their album *Hysteria* sold over 9.5 million copies. (Died 1-8-91.)

•**HALSTON** Fashion designer. (1932-1990 – Born Roy Halston Frowick in Des Moines, IA) An intensely private man. He created the pillbox hat made chic by Jacqueline Kennedy Onassis. (Died of AIDS 3-26-90.)

•**ROY ORBISON** Singer. (1936-1988 – Born in Wink, TX) Tragedy struck Roy three times. His wife Claudette was killed in a motorcycle accident which he witnessed June 5, 1966, and his two sons died in a fire in 1968. Roy wrote the song "Claudette" for his wife, recorded by the Everly Brothers. His biggest hit: "Pretty Woman" in 1964. He died of a massive heart attack (Died 12-6-88.)

•**WILLIAM SHAKESPEARE** Poet. (1564-1616 – Stratford-on-Avon, England) Author of at least 36 plays and 154 sonnets. He died on his 52nd birthday. (Died 4-23-1616.)

FACTS FROM THE PAST

1789 President-elect **GEORGE WASHINGTON AND WIFE MARTHA** moved into the first executive mansion, Franklin House in New York City. Construction of the **WHITE HOUSE** (known back then as the President's Palace) began about three years later and took seven years to complete, so the Washingtons were never able to live in it.

1915 The **FIRST PRODUCT ENDORSEMENT** given by a movie star: **FATTY ARBUCKLE** told the world how wonderful Murads – a brand of Egyptian cigarettes were.

1952 **HOYT WILHELM** of the Giants won his **FIRST MAJOR LEAGUE GAME** (in relief), but more dramatically, hit a home run at the Polo Grounds in his first major league at-bat. Although he pitched in 1,070 games in the majors, he never hit another homer.

1954 **HANK AARON** hit the first of his major league record 755 home runs against the Cardinals' Vic Rashi in the Milwaukee Braves' 7-5 win over St. Louis.

1956 **ELVIS PRESLEY** played Las Vegas for the first time and bombed. The middle-aged crowd at the new Frontier Hotel didn't like Elvis or his music. He was the warm-up act for comedian Shecky Greene. He didn't come back there until 1969.

1964 **KEN JOHNSON** of the Houston Colt 45's became the first pitcher to pitch a nine-inning no-hitter and lost when **PETE ROSE** scored an unearned run to give the Cincinnati Reds a 1-0 victory.

1969 **SIRHAN SIRHAN** was sentenced to death for the assassination of New York **SENATOR ROBERT F. KENNEDY.** (The sentence was later reduced to life imprisonment.)

1989 UCLA quarterback **TROY AIKMAN** bacame the first player chosen in the NFL draft when he was selected by the Dallas Cowboys.

Ready for a change, get a new coif.

APRIL 24

BIRTHDAYS

- **BARBRA STREISAND** Entertainer. (Brooklyn, NY) Biggest hit: "Evergreen" in 1976, from her movie *A Star is Born*. She was known primarily as an actress until an acting job gave her her first hit single, "People" in 1964 from *Funny Girl* on Broadway. In 1968 she tied with Katharine Hepburn for Best Actress Oscar in her film debut in *Funny Girl*. Directed and starred in *Yentl* and *Prince of Tides*. She signed a long-term film and recording contract with the Sony Corp., in 1992 for $60 million. Year/**Age**: 1995/**53** 1996/**54** 1997/**55**

- **SHIRLEY MacLAINE** Actress/dancer. (Born Shirley MacLean Beaty in Richmond, VA) She has been nominated for an Oscar 5 times for best actress, and won the award for *Terms of Endearment* in 1984. Other films: *Used People, Steal Magnolias,* and *Guarding Tess*. Warren Beatty is her brother. She has written several books about her personal spiritual guest. Year/**Age**: 1995/**61** 1996/**62** 1997/**63**

- **MICHAEL O'KEEFE** Actor. TV's "Against the Law" as Simon MacHeath. Year/**Age**: 1995/**40** 1996/**41** 1997/**42**

- **RICHARD STERBAN** Singer. (Oak Ridge, TN) With the OAK RIDGE BOYS. Biggest hit: "Elvira" in 1981. Year/**Age**: 1995/**48** 1996/**49** 1997/**50**

- **DOUG CLIFFORD** Drummer. (El Cerrito, CA) With CCR. Biggest hit: "Proud Mary" in 1969. Year/**Age**: 1995/**50** 1996/**51** 1997/**52**

- **J.D. CANNON** Actor. American character actor who appeared in *Cool Hand Luke, Cotton Comes to Harlem,* and the TV series, "McCloud," with Dennis Weaver. Year/**Age**: 1995/**73** 1996/**74** 1997/**75**

- **GLEN CORNICK** Bass guitarist. (England) With JETHRO TULL. Biggest hit: "Living in the Past" in 1972. Year/**Age**: 1995/**48** 1996/**49** 1997/**50**

- **FREDDY SCOTT** Singer. (Providence, RI) Attended Cooper High School in NYC. He recorded his first and only top ten hit, in 1963, "Hey Girl" while working as a songwriter for Columbia Music. Year/**Age**: 1995/**62** 1996/**63** 1997/**64**

- **RICHARD M. DALEY** Mayor of Chicago. (Chicago) He was inaugurated on his birthday in 1989. Year/**Age**: 1995/**53** 1996/**54** 1997/**55**

- **ERIC BOGOSIAN** Actor. (Boston, MA) Obie winner for a one-man show, "Drinking In America." In the film *Sex, Drugs and Rock & Roll*. Year/**Age**: 1995/**42** 1996/**43** 1997/**44**

- **ROBERT THOMAS** Publisher. (1766-1846 – Grafton, MA) Founded *Old Farmers Almanac*. (Died 5-19-1846.)

- **ROBERT PENN WARREN** Author. (1905-1989 – Guthrie, KY) Won Pulitzer Prize for *All The Kings Men*. (Died 9-15-89.)

- **ANTHONY TROLLOPE** Author. (1815-1882 – London, England) He used to start each day by writing 2,500 words before breakfast. Also, he invented the mailbox. (Died 12-6-1882.)

- **JILL IRELAND** Actress/author/producer. (1936-1990 – London, England) She divorced her first husband, actor David McCallum, co-star of "The Man From U.N.C.L.E.," in 1967 and married actor Charles Bronson in 1968. She wrote the best-seller *Life Wish*. She appeared in both *Death Wish* films with her husband and *Assassination*. (Died of cancer 5-18-90.)

FACTS FROM THE PAST

1061 HALLEY'S COMET heralded an invasion when it appeared over England. A monk spotted it and predicted the destruction of the country. The Battle of Hastings followed, killing thousands.

1792 The French national anthem, **"LA MARSEILLAISE"** [lah mahr-say-yehz'], was composed by **CLAUDE-JOSEPH ROUGET DE LISLE**. It was composed for the mayor of Strasbourg for a bottle of wine.

1897 William W. Price began work at the **WASHINGTON STAR** where he became the first regular White House reporter.

1898 British statesman **WINSTON CHURCHILL** was knighted by Queen Elizabeth II at Buckingham Palace.

1959 **THE DRIFTERS** released the first rock & roll record featuring a string section, "There Goes My Baby".

1961 **BOB DYLAN** made his recording debut (and $50) playing harmonica on the title track of Harry Belafonte's *Midnight Special* album.

1967 The Philadelphia 76ers, starring **WILT CHAMBERLAIN**, ended the Boston Celtics' 7-year reign of consecutive NBA crowns 125-122.

1967 Soviet cosmonaut **VLADMIR KOMAROV** was killed when parachute straps of his spacecraft became tangled during a landing attempt. He plunged 4 miles to earth. It was the **FIRST DEATH OF A HUMAN DURING A SPACE MISSION.** America had never lost an astronaut on a space mission until the **CHALLENGER** tragedy in 1986.

1970 **GRACE SLICK** and **ABBIE HOFFMAN** were turned away from Tricia Nixon's party even though they received invitations. They had promised to introduce Tricia to LSD-laced tea.

1974 **DAVID BOWIE**'s *Diamond Dogs* LP hit stores with a censored cover. The original art featured Bowie as a dog, with full genitalia.

1980 Following failed diplomatic initiatives, the **U.S. ATTEMPTED TO RESCUE THE AMERICANS HELD HOSTAGE** in the U.S. Embassy in Teheran. The commando mission was called off due to equipment failure. Eight soldiers were killed and 5 injured during the pull-out in a collision between a helicopter and a transport plane. U.S. would-be commander (if the mission had happened) Major **LOGAN FITCH**, said, "We would have been successful, had we been able to continue." He is now a stockbroker.

1994 The first player to be chosen in the 59th annual NFL draft was Ohio State defensive tackle Dan **"BIG DADDY"** Wilkinson. He went to the Cincinnati Bengals.

APRIL 25

You want to know why?
Just cuz...

BIRTHDAYS

- **AL PACINO** Actor. (Born Alfredo James Pacino in NYC) His career began as a theatre usher. Nominated for 8 Academy Awards. Films include, *Carlitos Way*, The *Godfather* films, *Dog Day Afternoon*, *And Justice for All*, *Sea of Love*, *Frankie & Johnny*, *Glengarry Glen Ross*, and the 1992 film *Scent of a Woman* that finally broke his Oscar losing streak. He won Best Actor. Year/Age: 1995/**55** 1996/**56** 1997/**57**

- **TALIA SHIRE** Actress. (Jamaica, NY) Won an Oscar for best supporting actress as Rocky's wife in the 1976 film *Rocky*. She was in The *Godfather* films. Her brother is director Francis Ford Coppola and her ex-husband, David Shire, is a musician who scores movies. Year/Age: 1995/**49** 1996/**50** 1997/**51**

- **ELLA FITZGERALD** Singer. (Newport News, VA) Her first hit was her biggest record ever: "Tisket-a Tasket" in 1938, with the Chick Webb Orchestra. It was number one for 10 weeks. She has won 12 Grammy Awards. She does Memorex commercials. Year/Age: 1995/**77** 1996/**78** 1997/**79**

- **MEADOWLARK LEMON** Basketball. (Lexington, SC) Talented "clown prince of basketball," he never played pro ball but played for the Harlem Globetrotters, a team that Abe Saperstein started in Chicago. Year/Age: 1995/**63** 1996/**64** 1997/**65**

- **STU COOK** Guitarist. (El Cerrito, CA.) Member of groups formed in high school, BLUE VELVETS, GOLLIWOGS, CREEDENCE CLEARWATER REVIVAL. Biggest hit with CCR: "Proud Mary" in 1969. Year/Age: 1995/**50** 1996/**51** 1997/**52**

- **BJÖEN ULVAEUS** Guitarist. (Stockholm, Sweden.) With ABBA. Biggest hits: "Dancing Queen" and "Take A Chance On Me." Year/Age: 1995/**50** 1996/**51** 1997/**52**

- **MICHAEL BROWN** Keyboardist.(NYC) With the LEFT BANKE. Biggest hit: "Walk Away Renee" in 1966. Year/**Age**: 1995/**46** 1996/**47** 1997/**48**

- **PAUL MAZURSKY** Director. (Brooklyn, NY) He co-wrote and directed *Bob & Carol, Ted & Alice,* and *Scenes from a Mall.* Year/Age: 1995/**65** 1996/**66** 1997/**67**

- **WILLIAM J. BRENNAN, JR.** Retired Supreme Court Justice. (Newark, NJ) Appointed by Pres. Dwight Eisenhower. He resigned July 20, 1990, after 33 years on the nation's highest court. Brennan has supported civil rights, freedom of speech and press, and the legality of abortion. Year/Age: 1995/**89** 1996/**90** 1997/**91**

- **EDWARD R. MURROW** News commentator. (1908-1965 – Born Egbert Roscoe Murrow in Greensboro, NC) He did the "Person to Person" TV series where he conducted "live" interviews from the guests' living rooms. In the 1950's, he was the first newsman to challenge the "witch hunting" tactics of Sen. Joseph McCarthy. He changed his first name to stop the teasing. (Died 4-27-65.)

- **GUGLIELMO MARCONI** Inventor. (1874-1937 – Bologna, Italy) He invented the wireless telegraph in 1895, today known as radio. The term "disc jockey" was coined the year Marconi died by *Variety* to describe radio announcers who stayed up all night "riding discs," or records. (Died 7-20-37.)

FACTS FROM THE PAST

1507 A book entitled *Cosmographiae Introductio* was published and in it mapmaker Martin Waldseemuller gave us the name **AMERIGO** or **AMERICA.** He believed navigator Amerigo Vespucci discovered the new land and didn't hear about Columbus until several years later.

1792 A French highwayman named Nicolas-Jacques Pellitier became the **FIRST HUMAN TO BE EXECUTED BY GUILLOTINE.** He fainted at the sight of the execution device and never regained consciousness...a great disappointment to the assembled crowd. The invention had previously been used only on sheep.

1876 Chicago's baseball team made their first appearance in the National League beating Louisville 4-0. **AL SPALDING** pitched the first of his 47 victories that season.

1898 **WILLIAM S. PORTER** entered the Ohio Penitentiary after being convicted of embezzlement. While in prison, he began writing short stories under the pseudonym "**O. HENRY.**"

1928 America's **FIRST GUIDE DOG** for the blind, a German Shepherd named "Buddy," was teamed up with its owner, **MORRIS FRANK.**

1956 **ELVIS PRESLEY** had the #1 hit on the charts called "Heartbreak Hotel," his first #1 record and his first million-seller. It was written by Hoyt Axton's mother, Mae Boren Axton.

1967 The governor of Colorado, **JOHN LOVE,** signed the first law legalizing abortion in the United States.

1974 Members Mike Love and Dennis Wilson of the **BEACH BOYS** appeared briefly onstage without briefs.

1983 Soviet Leader Yuri V. Andropov invited **SAMANTHA SMITH** to visit his country after receiving a letter from the Manchester, Maine, schoolgirl that had expressed fears about nuclear war.

1984 **DAVID KENNEDY,** 28-year-old son of the late Robert Kennedy was found dead in a hotel room in Palm Beach, FL.

1990 The Fender Statocaster that **JIMI HENDRIX** used to play the "Star Spangled Banner" at Woodstock was auctioned off in London for $295,000, a **WORLD RECORD FOR A GUITAR.**

1994 **MICHAEL BOLTON** lost a copyright suit with the Isley Brothers concerning Isley's song "Love Is a Wonderful Thing" from 1966.

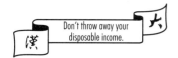

Don't throw away your disposable income.

APRIL 26

BIRTHDAYS

• **MICHAEL DAMIAN** Actor/singer. (Born Michael Damian Weir in San Diego, CA) "The Young & The Restless." Biggest hit: "Rock On." He toured as the star of "Joseph and the Amazing Technicolor Dreamcoat." Year/Age: 1995/**33** 1996/**34** 1997/**35**

• **CAROL BURNETT** Entertainer. (San Antonio, TX) She broke into TV on the "Garry Moore Show." Her first big show was the "Carol Burnett Show" from 1966-77. Every night at the end of the show she signalled her grandmother by pulling on her ear. The Emmy-winning show seldom dropped out of the top 20. In 1990 she returned with the weekly series "Carol and Company." Year/Age: 1995/**62** 1996/**63** 1997/**64**

• **DUANE EDDY** Guitarist. (Corning, NY) Biggest hits: "Because They're Young" in 1960 from the film of the same name and *Rebel Rouser* with the Rivingtons in 1958. Duane, with his twangy guitar and back-up group, the REBELS, is the all-time #1 rock 'n' roll instrumental artist worldwide. His music is still heard today on some commercials. He was married to singer Jessi Colter. Year/Age: 1995/**57** 1996/**58** 1997/**59**

• **BOBBY RYDELL** Singer. (Born Robert Louis Ridarelli in Philadelphia, PA) Biggest hit: "Wild One" in 1960. He achieved popularity on Dick Clark's "American Bandstand." He played Hugo in *Bye Bye Birdie* with Ann-Margret. Bobby and Frankie Avalon were in a group called ROCCO AND THE SAINTS in 1956. Year/Age: 1995/**53** 1996/**54** 1997/**55**

• **GARY WRIGHT** Singer/songwriter/keyboardist. (Englewood, NJ) Appeared in "Captain Video" TV series at age 7, in Broadway play *Fanny* and was co-leader of SPOOKY TOOTH. Biggest hit: "Dream Weaver" in 1976. Year/Age: 1995/**52** 1996/**53** 1997/**54**

• **ROGER TAYLOR** Drummer. (England) DURAN DURAN. Hits: "The Reflex," "Girls on Film," "Hungry Like The Wolf." in 1984. Year/Age: 1995/**35** 1996/**36** 1997/**37**

• **SAL MAGLIE** Former NY Giants righthander. (1917-1992) He was nicknamed "The Barber" for the close shaves he gave to the hitters. He was on the mound for the Dodgers when Yankee Don Larsen pitched a perfect game in the 1956 World Series. Maglie allowed only 5 hits in the 2-0 loss. He was the last of eight major leaguers to play for the New York Yankees, New York Giants and Brooklyn Dodgers. (Died 12-28-92.)

• **VIC PERRIN** Actor. (1916-1989 – Menomonee Falls, WI) On the "Outer Limits" TV show, Vic was the voice that opened the show with the warning: "There is nothing wrong with your television set. Do not attempt to adjust the picture. We are controlling transmission." He also appeared on "Dragnet," "Star Trek," and "Maverick." (Died 7-4-89.)

• **ANITA LOOS** Author. (1893-1981 – Sisson, CA) Best remembered for writing *Gentlemen Prefer Blondes*. She wrote a sequel, *But Gentlemen Marry Brunettes*. (Died 8-18-81.)

• **BERNARD MALAMUD** Author. (1914-1986 – NYC) Pulitzer Prize winner for *The Fixer*. Also wrote *The Natural* which later became a film with Robert Redford. (Died 3-18-86.)

• **CHARLES RICHTER** Geologist. (1900-1985 – Canada) Developed the Richter Scale for measuring earthquakes (the earthquake intensity scale.) Today is RICHTER SCALE DAY in his honor. (Died 9-30-85.)

• **JOHN JAMES AUDUBON** Painter. (1785-1851 – Haiti) After several failures, he came up with the idea of combining the talents of painting and birdwatching. He published several volumes of work that included nearly 500 paintings of North American birds. (Died 1-27-1851.)

• **RUDOLF HESS** Nazi. (1894-1987 – Alexandria, Egypt) Former deputy to Nazi dictator Adolf Hitler. Hess was convicted of war crimes at the Nuremberg trials after the war and sentenced to Spandau Allied Prison in Berlin where after 4 attempts, he succeeded in committing suicide (on 8-17-87).

FACTS FROM THE PAST

1607 **CAPTAIN JOHN SMITH** landed at Cape Henry, VA, to establish the first permanent English settlement in America.

1865 Abraham Lincoln's assassin, **JOHN WILKES BOOTH,** was found at Garrett's Tobacco Farm, near Port Royal, VA, 50 miles south of Washington. Federal troops were under orders to take him alive, but instead, set fire to the barn where he was hiding. When the flames lit up the interior, Booth could be seen and one of the soldiers shot him. The spot where he died is now on Hwy. 301.

1959 Cincinnati pitcher **WILLARD SCHMIDT** was hit by a pitch twice in the same game and later, while pitching to Milwaukee Braves shortstop Johnny Logan, he got hit by a line-drive and had to leave the game.

1978 **PAUL REVERE**'s expense account was auctioned off for $70,000. The account was for expenses incidental to his 2nd famous ride.

1978 **BERT LANCE**, a former aide to President Jimmy Carter, did not deny or admit to covering up questionable loans and overdrafts from two Georgia banks for himself and his relatives, but agreed to a consent order.

1982 Desiring more than an autograph, gunmen robbed **ROD STEWART** in broad daylight on Hollywood's Sunset Blvd.

1986 An explosion occurred at the Soviet Union's Chernobyl Atomic Power Station at Pripyat in the Ukraine. The resulting fire burned for days, sending radioactive material into the atmosphere which swept across several nations in Western Europe and eventually reached the U.S. It was the **WORLD'S WORST NUCLEAR REACTOR ACCIDENT**. The death toll was reported to be anywhere from several dozen to hundreds. Many more died later and the land is useless.

1994 **BLACKS VOTED** for the first time in South Africa and gave the power of government to the African National Congress and President Nelson Mandela.

APRIL 27

Digitize your dog.

BIRTHDAYS

- **ANOUK AIMEE** Actress. (France) *A Man and a Woman.* Year/Age: 1995/**63** 1996/**64** 1997/**65**

- **JACK KLUGMAN** Actor. (Philadelphia, PA) Half of "The Odd Couple" sitcom on TV from 1970-75, co-starring Tony Randall. Sportswriter Oscar's favorite romantic meal is red wine and fish sticks. He also appeared on TV's "Quincy" and Canon Copier ads. Year/Age: 1995/**73** 1996/**74** 1997/**759**

- **CASEY KASEM** Radio/TV host. (Detroit, MI) "Casey's Top 40" and TV's "American Top 40." He was inducted into the Radio Hall of Fame in 1992. Year/**Age**: 1995/**63** 1996/**64** 1997/**65**

- **CHUCK KNOX** Football. Only NFL coach to take 3 different teams to the playoffs: Buffalo, L.A. Rams and Seattle. Year/Age: 1995/**63** 1996/**64** 1997/**65**

- **JOHN SCALI** ABC news correspondent. (Canton, OH) U.S. Ambassador to the U.N. 1973-75. Year/**Age**: 1995/**77** 1996/**79** 81997/**79**

- **HAYLEY BARR** Actress. (Austria) Courtney Baxter on soap "As the World Turns." Year/Age: 1995/**24** 1996/**25** 1997/**269**

- **JUDY CARNE** Actress. (Born Joyce Botterill in England) She appeared on TV's "Laugh-in" from 1967-73 and was married to Burt Reynolds. Year/**Age**: 1995/**56** 1996/**57** 1997/**58**

- **PAUL "ACE" FREHLEY** Guitarist. (NYC) Lead guitar player for KISS. Biggest hit: "Beth" in 1976. Year/Age: 1995/**45** 1996/**46** 1997/**47**

- **SHEENA EASTON** Entertainer. (Born Sheena Shirley in Orr, Scotland) Her biggest record was her first: "Morning Train" in 1981. Rock star wife of Sonny Crocket on "Miami Vice" She's heard singing in the opening credits of the James Bond film *For Your Eyes Only.* Year/**Age**: 1995/**36** 1996/**37** 1997/**38**

- **GEORGE "THE ICEMAN" GERVIN** Basketball. (Detroit, MI) Leading NBA scorer from 1978-80 and in 1982. Year/**Age**: 1995/**43** 1996/**44** 1997/**45**

- **KATE PIERSON** Singer. (Athens, GA) With the B-52'S. Biggest hit: "Love Shack" in 1989. She can be heard on REM's "Out of Time." Year/**Age**: 1995/**47** 1996/**48** 1997/**49**

- **EARL ANTHONY** Pro bowler. (Kent, WA) Won PBA Championship 6 times. Year/Age: 1995/**57** 1996/**58** 1997/**59**.

- **WALTER LANTZ** Cartoonist. (Rochelle, NY) Created Woody Woodpecker when a woodpecker disrupted his honeymoon. His wife, Gracie, was the voice of that character for many years. She died in 1992. Year/**Age**: 1995/**95** 1996/**96** 1997/**97**

- **ENOS SLAUGHTER** Baseball. Played for the St. Louis Cardinals. He had 10 seasons of .300 and finished his 19 years with exactly that batting average. Year/**Age**: 1995/**79** 1996/**80** 1997/**81**

- **SANDY DENNIS** Actress. (1937-1992 – Hastings, NE) She won an Oscar for supporting actress as Honey in *Who's Afraid of Virginia Woolf?* in 1966. She made her acting debut in 1961, in *Splendor in the Grass.* (Died 3-2-92.)

- **PETE HAM** Singer. (1947-1975 – England) With BADFINGER, his hits include "Day After Day," "Come and Get It," and "No Matter What." He committed suicide by hanging himself in his London garage (5-1-75).

- **ULYSSES S. GRANT** 18th U.S. President. (1822-1885 – Point Pleasant, OH) He got many migraine headaches for which his wife, Julia, would go through a ritual of ministering to him in a dark room: a hot mustard footbath and pills until he fell asleep. For 2 days before the end of the Civil War, Grant rode toward Appomattox, suffering from a vicious migraine. The instant he read General Lee's note of surrender, his headache disappeared. (Died 7-23-1885.)

- **EDWARD GIBBON** Author. (1737-1794) English historian/author who wrote *Decline & Fall of the Roman Empire* which remains a model of literature and history. (Died 1-6-1794.)

- **SAMUEL F.B. MORSE** Inventor. (1791-1872 – Charlestown, MA) Invented the telegraph. He was better known as a portrait painter than as a scientist. His *Marquis de Lafayette* still hangs in New York's City Hall. He ran for Mayor of New York City, in 1836 and 1841, and lost both times. (Died 4-2-1872.)

FACTS FROM THE PAST

1950 The Boston Celtics hired **ARNOLD AUERBACH** to coach their losing team. In 16 seasons, he led them to 9 NBA championships

1964 **JOHN LENNON'S** book *In His Own Write* was published in the U.S. with a first printing of 90,000 copies. In 1988, this first edition in near mint condition was worth $60.00.

1967 **EXPO '67** was officially opened in Montreal by Canadian Prime Minister Lester B. Pearson.

1968 **SIMON AND GARFUNKEL's** "Mrs. Robinson" was released. It is widely associated with the film *The Graduate.*

1973 **FBI DIRECTOR L. PATRICK GRAY RESIGNED** in the midst of the Watergate scandal.

1981 **RINGO STARR**, former Beatle, married actress Barbara Bach. The two met during the filming of the movie *Cave Man.*

1982 **JOHN W. HINKLEY, JR**'s trial began for shooting 4 people including Ronald Reagan. He was acquitted by reason of insanity.

1983 **NOLAN RYAN** (Houston Astros) struck out the 3,509th batter of his career to pass Walter Johnson as all time strike out king.

1993 **JACK KEVORKIAN**, called "Dr. Death" for his practice of euthanasia, lost his California medical license.

1994 **EVANDER HOLYFIELD**, the richest fighter even at $102 million and former world heavyweight champion, retired.

1994 Police Officers **JOSEPH GABRISH** and **JOHN BALCERZAK** were reinstated with retroactive pay. They were fired for failing to arrest **JEFFREY DAHMER** during a confrontation in 1991.

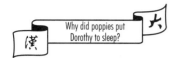

Why did poppies put Dorothy to sleep?

APRIL 28

BIRTHDAYS

- **NICKLAS LIDSTROM** Hockey. Year/Age: 1995/25 1996/26 1997/27
- **BARRY LARKIN** Baseball. (Cincinnati, OH) All-Star shortstop. Year/Age: 1995/31 1996/32 1997/33
- **SADDAM HUSSEIN** Iraqi President. He warned that the Gulf War would be the "Mother of all Battles." Instead, it became the "Mother of all Surrenders." Year/Age: 1995/60 1996/61 1997/62
- **JOHN DALY** Pro Golpher. Year/Age: 1995/29 1996/30 1997/31
- **ANN-MARGRET** Entertainer. (Born Ann-Margret Olsson in Stockholm, Sweden) She was nominated for best supporting actress in *Carnal Knowledge* and for best actress in *Tommy*. In the films *Newsies* and *Grumpy Old Men*. Married to ex-actor Roger Smith "77 Sunset Strip." Year/Age: 1995/54 1996/55 1997/56
- **ROBERT ANDERSON** Playwright. (NYC) Wrote *I Never Sang for My Father*. Year/Age: 1995/78 1996/79 1997/80
- **JAY LENO** TV host/comedian. (New Rochelle, NY) He is host of the "Tonight Show." He was rejected by Johnny Carson when he first auditioned for the show. Carson said: "You seem like a very funny man, but you're not right for the show. You don't have enough jokes." Leno took over in 1992. Year/Age: 1995/45 1996/46 1997/47
- **HARPER LEE** Author. (Born Nelle Harper in Monroeville, AL) Pulitzer Prize winner for *To Kill a Mockingbird*. Year/Age: 1995/69 1996/70 1997/71

- **TOM STURDIVANT** Former Yankee pitcher. Year/Age: 1995/65 1996/66 1997/67
- **MARCIA STRASSMAN** Actress. (NYC) She played Gabe Kaplan's wife on "Welcome Back Kotter." Appeared in the films *Honey I Shrunk the Kids* and *Honey I Blew Up the Kid*. Year/Age: 1995/47 1996/48 1997/49
- **LOUISE HOMER** Opera singer. (1871-1947 – Sewickley, PA) In *Samson et Dalila* with Enrico Caruso. (Died 5-6-47.)
- **CAROLYN JONES** Actress. (1933-1983 – Amarillo, TX) She appeared on TV's "Addams Family." Appeared with Elvis in *Jailhouse Rock*.
- **LIONEL BARRYMORE** Veteran American actor. (1878-1954 – Philadelphia, PA) He won an Oscar for best actor in *A Free Soul* in 1930 and annually portrayed Scrooge in *A Christmas Carol* on radio. (Died 11-15-54.)
- **JAMES MONROE** 5th U.S. President. (1758-1831 – Westmoreland County, VA) He served two terms, winning his second term by a huge landslide, capturing all but one vote in the electoral college. Monrovia, the capital city of Liberia, is named after him, as is the Monroe Doctrine, which he enunciated at Washington on Dec. 2, 1823. He was the last of 3 presidents to die on the 4th of July (7-4-1831)
- **RUSS MORGAN** Bandleader/trombonist. (1904-1969 – Scranton, PA) Biggest hits: "Cruising Down The River" in 1949 and "Dance with a Dolly with a Hole in Her Stocking." Also wrote "You're Nobody Till Somebody Loves You." (Died 8-7-69.)

FACTS FROM THE PAST

1789 First Mate **FLETCHER CHRISTIAN** masterminded the **MUTINY ON THE BOUNTY** and set **CAPTAIN BLIGH** and 18 sailors adrift in the South Pacific Ocean. Captain Bligh survived 41 days and navigated 3,600 miles to later become a Vice-Admiral in the British Navy and Governor of New South Wales, Australia. Two films were made about the incident and a replica of the *Bounty* built by MGM for one of the movies is a tourist attraction in St. Petersburg, FL.

1919 The **FIRST FREE-FALL PARACHUTE JUMP** was made by **LESLIE ERVIN** who broke his ankle on landing. Until then, it was believed people falling "free" would become unconscious, unable to pull the ripcord. Shortly after the jump, Ervin opened a parachute factory which eventually became the biggest in the world.

1945 **MUSSOLINI** and his mistress were executed by Italian partisans.

1947 A six-man expedition, led by **THOR HEYERDAHL**, sailed from Peru aboard a balsa-wood raft named the **KON-TIKI** on a 101-day journey that would take them across the Pacific Ocean to Polynesia.

1963 A former associate of Brian Epstein, 19-year-old Andrew Loog Oldham, saw the Rolling Stones first performance at the Crawdaddy Club in London. He became their manager the next day.

1967 Boxing champion **MUHAMMAD ALI** refused to be inducted into the army. He was stripped of his title by the WBC and WBA.

1968 The musical **HAIR** opened on Broadway at the Biltmore Theater for over 1,700 performances.

1985 New York Yankees owner **GEORGE STEINBRENNER** fired **YOGI BERRA** as manager and reinstated **BILLY MARTIN** . . . again. It was the 13th managerial change in 11 years for the Yankees and was Martin's 4th time back with the team. He was fired . . . brought back . . . and fired again before his death in a car accident on Christmas Day in 1989.

1988 The winless **BALTIMORE ORIOLES** set an American League record by losing their 21st straight game, 4-2, to the Minnesota Twins.

1988 An **ALOHA AIRLINES JETLINER** wobbled 25 miles to an emergency landing after an explosion blew away part of the forward passenger cabin. The Boeing 737, piloted by Captain **ROBERT SCHORNSTHEIMER**, landed at Kahului Airport on Maui Island with one of its two engines on fire and about 20 feet of its front cabin exposed. A flight attendant was killed and 61 persons were injured.

1990 *A Chorus Line*, the **LONGEST-RUNNING SHOW IN BROADWAY** history, closed due to dwindling ticket sales, closing after 6,137 performances, a Pulitzer Prize and nine Tony awards. It had opened on Broadway in July of 1975.

APRIL 29

BIRTHDAYS

• **MICHELLE PFEIFFER** Actress. (Santa Ana, CA) She was Miss Orange County, CA. Films include *Tequila Sunrise, Frankie & Johnny, The Age of Innocence,* and *Batman Returns.* Oscar nominations for *Dangerous Liaisons, Wolf, The Fabulous Baker Boys,* and *Love Field.* She turned down the role of Clarice in *Silence of the Lambs.* Year/Age: 1995/**38** 1996/**39** 1997/**40**

• **DANIEL DAY-LEWIS** Actor. (England) Won an Oscar for *My Left Foot* and played Hawkeye in *The Last of the Mohicans.* Also in films *Age of Innocence* and *In the Name of the Father.* Year/Age: 1995/**38** 1996/**39** 1997/**40**

• **EVE PLUMB** Actress. "The Brady Bunch." Year/Age: 1995/**37** 1996/**38** 1997/**39**

• **CELESTE HOLM** Actress. (NYC) She won an Oscar for supporting actress in 1947 for *Gentlemen's Agreement.* Also on "Falcon Crest." Year/Age: 1995/**76** 1996/**77** 1997/**78**

• **JERRY SEINFELD** Actor/comedian. "Frankie" on TV's "Benson." His own show "Seinfeld" premiered in 1990. Auto biography: *Sein Language.* Year/Age: 1995/**41** 1996/**42** 1997/**43**

• **JIM HART** Football. St. Louis Cardinals quarterback. Year/Age: 1995/**51** 1996/**52** 1997/**53**

• **JIM OTIS** Football. Year/Age: 1995/**47** 1996/**48** 1997/**49**

• **DANNY DAVIS** C&W. (Born George Nowlan in Dorchester, MA) A trumpet player. Biggest hit, with the Nashville Brass, "Night Life" featuring Willie Nelson. Year/Age: 1995/**65** 1996/**66** 1997/**67**

• **JOHNNY MILLER** Pro golfer. (San Francisco, CA.) He won the U.S. Open in 1973 and the British Open in 1976. Year/Age: 1995/**48** 1996/**49** 1997/**50**

• **FRED ZINNEMANN** Film director. (Austria) He directed *High Noon, From Here to Eternity,* and the Oscar-winning *A Man for All Seasons.* Year/Age: 1995/**88** 1996/**89** 1997/**90**

• **NORA DUNN** Actress. (Chicago, IL) "Saturday Night Live." Year/Age: 1995/**44** 1996/**45** 1997/**46**

• **DUANE ALLEN** Lead singer. (Taylortown, TX) Member of the OAK RIDGE BOYS, originally a gospel quartet during WWII and after many changes in personnel switched to country/pop in the 1970's. Biggest hit: "Elvira" in 1981. Year/Age: 1995/**52** 1996/**53** 1997/**54**

• **TOMMY JAMES** Singer. (Born Thomas Gregory Jackson in Dayton, OH) He had two #1 hits with the SHONDELLS: "Crimson & Clover" and "Hanky Panky." Biggest hit was "Draggin' the Line" in 1971. Year/Age: 1995/**48** 1996/**49** 1997/**50**

• **CARL GARDNER** Lead singer. (Los Angeles, CA) With the COASTERS. Biggest hit: "Yakety Yak" in 1958. Year/Age: 1995/**68** 1996/**69** 1997/**70**

• **ANDRE AGASSI** Tennis star. (Las Vegas, NV) Won the Grand Slam tennis title in 1992. Year/Age: 1995/**25** 1996/**26** 1997/**27**

• **CARNIE WILSON** Singer. (Los Angeles, CA) Member of the group WILSON PHILLIPS. Their first two records reached #1: "Hold On" and "Release Me." Her sister Wendy and Chynna Phillips make up the rest of the trio. Her dad is Beach Boy Brian Wilson. Year/Age: 1995/**27** 1996/**28** 1997/**29**

• **LUIS APARICIO** Baseball. (Venezuela) White Sox shortstop who led in fielding 8 straight seasons. Set a record by leading in stolen bases his first 9 years in the big leagues. Year/Age: 1995/**61** 1996/**62** 1997/**63**

• **KATE MULGREW** Actress. (Dubuque, IA) Mary Ryan on "Ryan's Hope" and Mrs. Columbo on "Kate Loves a Mystery." Year/Age: 1995/**40** 1996/**41** 1997/**42**

• **GEORGE ALLEN** Pro football coach. (1918-1990 – Detroit, MI) He coached the L.A. Rams and Washington Redskins in the NFL, and ranks as the winningest coach in team history for both of those teams. (Died 12-31-90.)

• **DUKE ELLINGTON** Jazz musician. (1899-1974 – Born Edward Kennedy Ellington in Washington, DC) Wrote "Take the A Train" and "Mood Indigo." (Died 5-24-74.)

FACTS FROM THE PAST

1932 "One Man's Family," radio's longest running serial, debuted on NBC. It starred Ellen Minetta as Fanny Barbour and J. Anthony Smythe as Henry Barbour. The program continued until 1960.

1939 Baseball's "iron horse," **LOU GEHRIG**, played in his 2,130th consecutive game, setting a major league record that still stands by not missing a game between June 1, 1925, and April 30, 1939. The Yankee slugger died in 1941 of a rare form of paralysis, known today as ALS or "Lou Gehrig's Disease."

1988 **ERIC CLAPTON** and his wife Pattie Boyd filed divorce papers in London. Boyd blamed Clapton's affair with an Italian TV personality, who bore Clapton's child. His child was killed in a fall out of window in New York City in 1991.

1988 **BURT REYNOLDS** and longtime companion, **LONI ANDERSON**, were married at his 160-acre horse ranch in Jupiter, FL. He filed for divorce 6-10-93.

1992 Four white Los Angeles police officers were acquitted in the video-taped beating of black motorist Rodney King, setting off days of rioting that left over 50 dead with more than $735 million in damages.

1992 Actor **EMILIO ESTEVEZ** married singer **PAULA ABDUL** in a Santa Monica courthouse.

1993 After a fire at Windsor Castle, **BUCKINGHAM PALACE** was opened to visitors for the first time to help raise money for repairs.

1994 Majel Barrett Roddenberry, widow of "**STAR TREK**" creator Gene Roddenberry, revealed that after her husband's death in 1991, his ashes were secretly carried into space aboard a space shuttle and returned to earth.

 A spoon left standing in cola will soon dissolve.

APRIL 30

BIRTHDAYS

• **JOHNNY GALECKI** Actor. Appears on TV's "Roseanne." Year/Age: 1995/**20** 1996/**21** 1997/**22**

• **JOEY RESTIVO** Percussionist. (NYC) With Lin-EAR. Hits include "Sending All My Love." Year/Age: 1995/**28** 1996/**29** 1997/**30**

• **CLORIS LEACHMAN** Actress. (Des Moines, IA) She won an Oscar for supporting actress in 1971 for *The Last Picture Show*. Mary's landlady on "The Mary Tyler Moore Show." In "The Nutt House" and "The Powers That Be." Film *Beverly Hillbillies*. Year/Age: 1995/**65** 1996/**66** 1997/**679**

• **AL TOON** Football player. (Newport News, VA) Pro football wide receiver for the New York Jets. Al is the only Jet elected his team's MVP 3 years in a row. He was the University of Wisconsin's all-time leading pass receiver. He retired from football in 1992 after suffering his ninth concussion in eight NFL seasons. Year/Age: 1995/**32** 1996/**33** 1997/**34**

• **WILLIE NELSON** Entertainer. (Abbott, TX) At one time he was a door-to-door salesman and a DJ. Biggest hits: "Always On My Mind" in 1982 and, with Julio Iglesias, "To All the Girls I've Loved Before" in 1984. His first hit didn't come until he was 42 years old. Patsy Cline recorded his song "Crazy." Faron Young then recorded "Hello Walls." In 1961 he wrote the classic "Funny How Time Slips Away," which would eventually be recorded by more than 80 artists. The next day his house burned down. He was inducted into the Country Music Hall of Fame in 1993. Willie was in the movies *Electric Horseman* and *Honeysuckle Rose*. Year/Age: 1995/**62** 1996/**63** 1997/**64**

• **JILL CLAYBURGH** Actress. (NYC) Appeared on TV's soap opera "Search for Tomorrow" before reaching Broadway in *The Rothschilds*. She has appeared in the films *Silver Streak*, *An Unmarried Woman*, *Starting Over*, *Whispers in the Dark*, *Semi-Tough* with Burt Reynolds, and *Shy People*. Year/Age: 1995/**51** 1996/**52** 1997/**53**

• **BOBBY VEE** Singer. (Born Robert Velline in Fargo, ND) Biggest hit: "Take Good Care of My Baby" in 1961. When he was 15, he was called upon to perform in front of a hometown crowd in Fargo because the star of the show had been killed in a plane crash, and Bobby knew the lyrics to the songs. The star was Buddy Holly. Year/Age: 1995/**52** 1996/**53** 1997/**54**

• **ISIAH THOMAS** Former basketball star. (Chicago, IL) Detroit Pistons. 2 NBA titles in 13 years. Year/Age: 1995/**34** 1996/**35** 1997/**36**

• **BOB HENDLEY** Former Chicago Cub. Pitcher. Year/Age: 1995/**56** 1996/**57** 1997/**58**

• **GARY COLLINS** TV host. (Boston, MA) Host of "Hour Magazine," married to former Miss America Mary Ann Mobley. Now host of "Home Show" on ABC-TV. Year/Age: 1995/**57** 1996/**58** 1997/**59**

• **BURT YOUNG** Actor. (NYC) He's the one with the horrible cackle in *The Choirboys*. He was an Oscar nominee in 1976 for *Rocky*. Year/Age: 1995/**55** 1996/**56** 1997/**57**

• **PERRY KING** Actor. (Alliance, OH) Played private eye Cody Allen on "Riptide" and the wicked Cutter Amberville in TV miniseries *I'll Take Manhattan*. Year/Age: 1995/**46** 1996/**47** 1997/**48**

• **AL LEWIS** Actor. Grandpa Munster on "The Munsters" TV series from 1964-1966. Year/Age: 1995/**72** 1996/**73** 1997/**74**

• **EVE ARDEN** Actress. (1912-1990 – Born Eunice Quedens in Mill Valley, CA) Nominated for supporting actress in 1945 for *Mildred Pierce*. Best remembered for "Our Miss Brooks," a successful CBS sitcom from 1952-57. She won an Emmy in 1953. She also appeared in the *Grease* films. (Died 11-12-90.)

• **JOHNNY HORTON** Singer. (1929-1960 – Tyler, TX) Biggest hit: "Battle of New Orleans" in 1959. He was killed in an auto accident near Austin. Ironically, Horton had just performed at the Skyline, where Hank Williams played his last show. Both men left the same widow, Billie Jean. (Died 11-5-60.)

FACTS FROM THE PAST

1789 **GEORGE WASHINGTON** took office in New York as the **FIRST PRESIDENT** of the United States.

1900 **JOHN LUTHER "CASEY" JONES** was the engineer on "Old 382" of the Illinois Central Railroad. At 4 a.m. near Vaughan, MS, he saw a stalled freight train and couldn't stop in time. "Casey" rode the engine into the collision. They found his mangled body with one hand on the whistle cord and the other on the brake. He was the only casualty of the wreck. His friend Wallace Sanders wrote a song about the tragedy, "The Ballad of Casey Jones." The tune immortalized Casey's name and made him a legendary folk figure. His nickname came from his birthplace, Caycee, KY.

1939 **FRANKLIN D. ROOSEVELT** became the **FIRST U.S. PRESIDENT TO APPEAR ON TV** when he spoke at the NY World's Fair to an estimated 30,000 American viewers about peace. (World War II was imminent.)

1945 **ADOLF HITLER AND WIFE EVA BRAUN** committed suicide as Russian troops apprached his Berlin bunker.

1945 **"ARTHUR GODFREY TIME"** made its debut on the CBS radio network.

1947 President **HARRY S. TRUMAN** signed a measure officially changing the name of **BOULDER DAM** to **HOOVER DAM**.

1973 **PRESIDENT NIXON** announced the **RESIGNATIONS OF HIS AIDES,** H. R. Haldeman and John Ehrlichman, along with Attorney General Richard G. Kleindienst and White House Counsel John Dean.

1992 After eight successful seasons on NBC, the final episode of **"THE COSBY SHOW"** was aired. It attracted over 44 million viewers.

1993 Tennis star **MONICA SELES** was stabbed in the back a match in Hamburg, Germany. The attacker was a fan of her 2nd ranked opponent **STEFFI GRAF**.

MAY MEMORIES

10 YEARS AGO

1985

POPULAR SONGS
"Crazy For You" by Madonna

"Don't You (Forget About Me)" by Simple Minds

MOVIES
Plenty
starring Meryl Streep, Tracey Ullman, and John Geilgud in a story of the greedy and bigoted side of England during WWII.

My Beautiful Laundrette
starring Daniel Day Lewis. A comedy/ drama about a London laundromat.

TV SHOWS
"Amazing Stories"
short fantasy stories by Steven Spielberg.

"Hometown"
starring Jane Kaczmarek and Franc Luz as Mary Newell Abbott and her husband, Ben Abbott.

BOOKS
Moonshine by Alex Wilkinson

1986

POPULAR SONGS
"West End Girls" by Pet Shop Boys

"Greatest Love of All" by Whitney Houston

MOVIES
Children Of a Lesser God
starring William Hurt and Marlee Matlin as a teacher and a deaf woman.

Heartbreak Ridge
starring Clint Eastwood, Marsha Mason, Mario Van Pebbles, Eileen Heckart, and Bo Svenson. A group of new U.S. Marines invade Grenada.

TV SHOWS
"Starman"
a Sci-Fi show starring Paul Forrester as "Starman."

"Easy Street"
sit-com featuring Loni Anderson as a showgirl from Las Vegas, turned rich widow.

BOOKS
Fatherhood by Bill Cosby

1987

POPULAR SONGS
"(I Just) Died In You Arms" by The Cutting Crew

"With Or Without You" by U2

MOVIES
Dirty Dancing
a young woman, Jennifer Gray, becomes attracted to a dance instructor, Patrick Swayze.

Tin Men
starring Danny DeVito and Richard Dreyfus in the story of two disillusioned salesmen.

TV SHOWS
"Duet"
starring Matthew Laurance, Mary Page Keller, Allison La Placa, and Chris Lem-mon. Comedy/drama about two romantic couples.

"The Oldest Rookie"
Paul Sorvino stars as Detective Ike Porter.

BOOKS *The Eyes of the Dragon* by Stephen King

SPECIAL DAYS

MAY	1995	1996	1997
Lobster Races *(Aiken, SC)*	May 5-7	May 3-5	May 2-4
Pun-Off World Championship *(Austin, TX)*	May 7	May 5	May 4
Kentucky Derby	May 6	May 4	May 3
Catfish Races *(Greenville, MS)*	May 12-14	May 10-12	May 9-11
Mother's Day	May 14	May 12	May 11
Receptionist Day	May 10	May 8	May 14
Ascension Day	May 26	May 17	May 9
The Preakness Stakes	May 13	May 11	May 10
Rhubarb Festival *(Intercourse, PA)*	Apr. 24-28	Apr. 22-26	Apr. 21-25
Armed Forces Day	May 20	May 18	May 17
Full Moon	May 14	May 3	May 22
Indianapolis 500	May 28	May 26	May 25
Memorial Day	May 29	May 27	May 26

25 YEARS AGO

1970

POPULAR SONGS

"American Woman" by the Guess Who

"Everything Is Beautiful" by Ray Stevens

MOVIES

Let It Be
starring the Beatles in their last feature film.

The Baby Maker
Barbara Hershey bears a child with the husband of a couple who are childless.

TV SHOWS

"Barefoot In the Park"
stitcom with an all black cast based on Neil Simon's play. Stars Thelma Carpenter and Nipsey Russell.

"The Interns"
starring Mike Farrell, Broderick Crawford, and Christopher Stone in this dramatic medical series.

BOOKS

The Great White Hope by Howard Sackler

1971

POPULAR SONGS

"Brown Sugar" by the Rolling Stones

"Rainy Days and Mondays" by The Carpenters

MOVIES

The Hospital
starring George C. Scott, Diana Rigg, and Richard Dysart. The story of a New York metropolitan hospital.

Shaft
starring Richard Roundtree, Moses Gun, and Charles Cioffi. A black super-cop takes on Harlem's mafia.

TV SHOWS

"Columbo"
Peter Falk plays Lt. Columbo, a police detective in Los Angeles. Show rotates with "McMillan and Wife" a police drama starring Rock Hudson and Susan St. James.

BOOKS *Bury Me At Wounded Knee* by Dee Brown

1972

POPULAR SONGS

"Oh Girl" by Chi-Lites

"I'll Take You There" by The Staple Singers

MOVIES

The Emigrants
starring Max von Sydow, Liv Ullmann, and Eddie Axberg. 19th century Swedish family comes to America.

Butterflies Are Free
starring Goldie Hawn, Edward Albert, and Eileen Heckart in the story of an actress and a blind boy.

TV SHOWS

"The Paul Lynde Show"
sitcom starring Paul Lynde with Elizabeth Allen as his wife.

"Banyon"
1930s private eye series starring Robert Forster and Joan Blondell.

BOOKS *The Odessa File* by Frederick Forsyth

50 YEARS AGO

1945

POPULAR SONGS

"Sentimental Journey" by Doris Day with Les Brown Orchestra

"Laura" by Dick Haymesl

MOVIES

Brewster's Millions
starring June Havoc and Dennis O'Keefe. A young man must spend a $1 million inheritance in two months.

State Fair
starring Dana Andrews, Jeanne Crain, Dick Haymes, and Vivian Blaine. Movie produced the popular songs "A Grand Night For Singing" and "It Might As Well Be Spring."

TV SHOWS

No regularly scheduled TV programming until May of 1946.

BOOKS

Commodore Hornblower by C.S. Forester

1946

POPULAR SONGS

"Prisoner of Love" by Perry Como

"The Gypsy" by Dinah Shore

MOVIES

The Jolson Story
Larry Parks portayed Al Jolson's life story.

Saratoga Trunk
starring Gary Cooper and Ingrid Bergman. The Edna Ferber story of a Texas millionaire and a creole beauty.

TV SHOWS

"Hourglass"
starring Helen Parrish and Eddie Mayehoff. One of the first TV shows with emcees. Talent for the show included ventriloquist Edgar Bergen, Peggy Lee, Evelyn Knight, Dennis Day, and Doodles Weaver.

BOOKS

The King's General by Daphne du Maurier

1947

POPULAR SONGS

"Mam'selle" by Art Lund

"Peg O' My Heart" by Harmonicats

MOVIES

T-Men
starring Alfred Ryder, Dennis O'Keefe, and June Lockart. Treasury agents catch a gang of counter-feiters.

Good News
starring Peter Lawford, June Allyson, Patricia Marshall, Mel Torme, and Joan McCracken in a nostalgic musical.

TV SHOWS

"Kraft Television Theatre"
starring top name actors in dramatic and comedy plays. Top-rated show.

BOOKS

Kingsblood Royal by Sinclair Lewis

Basketball Hall of Fame

PLAYERS

Chuck Hyatt – 1959
Angelo "Hank" Luisetti – 1959
George Mikan – 1959
John Schommer – 1959

Victor Hanson – 1960
Ed Macauley – 1960
Branch McCracken – 1960
Charles "Stretch" Murphy – 1960

Bennie Borgmann – 1961
Forrest DeBernardi – 1961
Bob Kurland – 1961
Andy Phillip – 1961
John S. Roosma – 1961
Christian Steinmetz – 1961
Edward Wachter – 1961

Jack McCracken – 1962
Harlan O. "Pat" Page – 1962
Barney Sedran – 1962
John "Cat" Thompson – 1962

Robert "Ace" Gruenig – 1963
Bobby McDermott – 1963

Harold "Bud" Foster – 1964
Nat Holman – 1964
John "Honey" Russell – 1964

Joe Lapchick – 1966

Henry "Dutch" Dehnert – 1968

Bob Davies – 1969

Bob Cousy – 1970
Bob Pettit – 1970

Paul Endacott – 1971
Max Friedman – 1971

John Beckman – 1972
Adolph Schayes – 1972

Ernest Schmidt – 1973

Joseph Brennan – 1974
Bill Russell – 1974
Fuzzy Vandivier – 1974

Tom Gola – 1975
Edward "Moose" Krause – 1975
Bill Sharman – 1975

Elgin Baylor – 1976
Charles Cooper – 1976
Lauren Gale – 1976
William Johnson – 1976

Paul Arizin – 1977
Joe Fulks – 1977
Cliff Hagan – 1977
Jim Pollard – 1977

Wilt Chamberlain – 1978

Jerry Lucas – 1979
Oscar Robertson – 1979
Jerry West – 1979

Thomas Barlow – 1980

Hal Greer – 1981
Slater Martin – 1981
Frank Ramsey – 1981
Willis Reed – 1981

Bill Bradley – 1982
Dave DeBusschere – 1982
Jack Twyman – 1982

John Havlicek – 1983
Sam Jones – 1983

Al Cervi – 1984
Nate Thurmond – 1984

Billy Cunningham – 1985-86
Tom Heinsohn – 1985-86

Rick Barry – 1986-87
Walt Frazier – 1986-87
Bob Houbregs – 1986-87
Pete Maravich – 1986-87
Bobby Wanzer – 1986-87

Clyde Lovellette – 1987-88
Wes Unseld – 1987-88

William "Pop" Gates – 1988-89
K.C. Jones – 1988-89
Lenny Wilkins – 1988-89

Dave Bing – 1989-90
Elvin Hayes – 1989-90
Neil Johnston – 1989-90
Earl Monroe – 1989-90

Nate Archibald – 1992
Sergei Belov – 1992
Dave Cowens – 1992
Harry Gallatin – 1992
Luisa Harris – 1992
Connie Hawkins – 1992
Bob Lanier –1992
Nera White – 1992
John Wooden – 1992

Walt Bellamy – 1993
Julius Erving – 1993
Richie Guerin – 1993
Dan Issel – 1993
Dick McGuire – 1993
Ann Meyers – 1993
Calvin Murphy – 1993
Juliana Semenova – 1993
Bill Walton – 1993

Carol Blazejowski -1994
Harry (Buddy) Jeannette - 1994

COACHES

Forrest C. Allen – 1959
Dr. H. C. Carlson – 1959
Dr. W. E. Meanwell – 1959

Ernest Blood – 1960
Frank Keaney – 1960
Ward Lambert – 1960

George Keogan – 1961
Leonard Sachs – 1961

Kenneth Loeffler – 1964
Howard Hobson – 1965

Everett Dean – 1966

Howard Cann – 1967
Amory "Slats" Gill – 1967
Alvin Julian – 1967

Red Auerbach – 1968
Hank Iba – 1968
Adolph Rupp – 1968

Ben Carnevale – 1969

Edgar Diddle – 1971

Bruce Drake – 1972
Arthur "Dutch" Lonborg – 1972

Harry Litwack – 1975

Al McGuire – 1976

Sam Barry – 1978
Edgar Hickey – 1978
John McLendon – 1978
Ray Meyer – 1978
Pete Newell – 1978

Everett Shelton – 1979

Arad McCutchan – 1980

Everett Case – 1981
Clarence Gaines – 1981

Dean Smith – 1982

Jack Gardner – 1983

W. Harold Anderson – 1984
Marv Harshman – 1984
Bertha Teague – 1984
Margaret Wade – 1984

Red Holzman – 1985-86
Fred Taylor – 1985-86
Stan Watts – 1985-86

Ralph Miller – 1987-88

Lou Camesecca – 1992
Bob Knight – 1992
Frank McGuire – 1992
Jack Ramsay – 1992
John Wooden – 1992
Phil Woolpert – 1992

Cesare Rubini - 1994
Denzil E. Crum - 1994
Cahrles J. Daly - 1994

REFEREES

Matthew Kennedy – 1959
George Hepbron – 1960

George Hoyt – 1961
Ernest Quigley – 1961

David Tobey – 1961
David Walsh – 1961

John Nucatola – 1977

James Enright – 1978

J. Dallas Shirley – 1979

Lloyd Leith – 1982

Red Mihalik – 1985-86

CONTRIBUTORS

Edward "Ned" Irish – 1942

Dr. L. H. Gulick – 1959
Edward Hickox – 1959
Ralph Morgan – 1959
Dr. James Naismith – 1959
Harold Olsen – 1959
Amos Alonzo Stagg – 1959
Oswald Tower – 1959

H. V. Porter – 1960

John O'Brien – 1961
Arthur Schabinger – 1961
Arthur Trester – 1961

Frank Morgenweck – 1962
Lynn St. John – 1962

William Reid – 1963

John Bunn – 1964
R. William Jones – 1964

Walter Brown – 1965
Paul Hinkle – 1965
Bill Mokray – 1965

Clair Bee – 1967

Chuck Taylor – 1968

Abe Saperstein – 1970

Bob Douglas – 1971
Edward Gottlieb – 1971
Clifford Wells – 1971

Elmer Ripley – 1972

Harry Fisher – 1973
Maurice Podoloff – 1973

Emil Liston – 1974

Lester Harrison – 1979

Dr. Ferenc Hepp – 1980
Walter Kennedy – 1980
Alva O. Duer – 1981
Lou Wilke – 1982
Cliff Fagan – 1983
Edward Steitz – 1983
Sendra B. Abbott – 1984
Joe Morgan – 1990
Phog Allen – 1992
Larry Fleisher – 1992
Larry O'Brien –1992

Where is heaven?

MAY 1
May Day/Lei Day

BIRTHDAYS

• **GLENN FORD** Actor. (Born Gwyllyn Samuel Newton Ford in Canada) He took his name from his father's birthplace, Glenford. He is a descendant of 8th U.S. President Martin Van Buren. He starred in *Blackboard Jungle* in 1955. BILL HALEY'S "Rock Around the Clock" was the theme song of the movie. He was also in *Superman*. Year/**Age**: 1995/**79** 1996/**80** 1997/**81**

• **JACK PAAR** TV host. (Canton, OH) Host of the "Tonight Show" from 1957 to 1962. His announcer was Hugh Downs, now of "20/20." Year/**Age**: 1995/**77** 1996/**78** 1997/**79**

• **JUDY COLLINS** Singer. (Seattle, WA) Biggest hit: "Both Sides Now" in 1968. STEPHEN STILLS wrote "Suite Judy Blue Eyes" for her. They were together when he wrote it. At age 14, she tried to take her life with an overdose of asprin and her only son, Clark, committed suicide in 1992. She sang at President Clinton's inauguration. Year/**Age**: 1995/**56** 1996/**57** 1997/**58**

• **RITA COOLIDGE** Singer. (Nashville, TN) Biggest hit: "Higher & Higher" in 1977. At one time she was married to Kris Kristofferson. Year/**Age**: 1995/**50** 1996/**51** 1997/**52**

• **MACK DADDY** Rap singer. (Born Chris Kelly in Atlanta, GA) Of the rap duo KRIS KROSS. First hit: "Jump" in 1992. Their first album *Totally Krossed Out* sold over 3 million copies. Year/**Age**: 1995/**17** 1996/**18** 1997/**19**

• **DAN O'HERLIHY** Actor. (Ireland.) Films included *Odd Man Out*, *Robinson Crusoe*, and *Robocop II*. Year/**Age**: 1995/**76** 1996/**77** 1997/**78**

• **JOHN BERADINO** Actor. (Los Angeles, CA) Former major league baseball star, turned actor on "General Hospital" as Steve Hardy and "One Life to Live." Year/**Age**: 1995/**78** 1996/**79** 1997/**80**

• **SONNY JAMES** Singer. (Born Jimmy Loden in Hackleburg, AL) Year/**Age**: 1995/**66** 1996/**67** 1997/**68**

• **SCOTT CARPENTER** Astronaut. (Boulder, CO) He was an original Mercury astronaut and the first to get a divorce. His wife, Rene, wrote a book about their problems. Year/**Age**: 1995/**70** 1996/**71** 1997/**72**

• **STEVE CAUTHEN** Racehorse jockey. (Covington, KY) He was a racing legend at age 18, the year he won the Triple Crown, astride Affirmed. He began jockey training at age 12. Year/**Age**: 1995/**35** 1996/**36** 1997/**37**

• **RAY PARKER, JR.** Singer. (Detroit, MI) Biggest hit: "Ghostbusters," theme from the 1984 movie. Year/**Age**: 1995/**41** 1996/**42** 1997/**43**

• **MAX ROBINSON** Newsman. (1939-1988 – Richmond, VA) First black network TV anchorman. (Died of AIDS 12-20-88.)

• **KATE SMITH** Singer. (1909-1986 – Born Kathryn Elizabeth Smith in Greenville, VA) A major radio star who made the transition to TV with 2 shows in the early '50s. Her rendition of "God Bless America," which Irving Berlin wrote for her, inspired $600 million dollars worth of WWII bond sales. When the Philadelphia Flyers Hockey Team substituted her recording of "God Bless America" for the national anthem, they were nearly unbeatable. (Died 6-17-86.)

FACTS FROM THE PAST

1868 **TOM DULA** was executed, a few days after writing the song about himself which says, "Hang down your head, Tom Dooley, poor boy, you're going to die." A North Carolina jury sentenced him to hang for the murder of an ex-girlfriend. Almost a century later, "Tom Dooley" became the **KINGSTON TRIO**'s only #1 hit (1958).

1898 **COMMODORE GEORGE DEWEY** gave the famous command, "You may fire when you are ready, Gridley," as an American naval force destroyed a Spanish fleet in Manila Bay.

1931 **KATE SMITH** began her long-running radio show on CBS on her 22nd birthday. She started out at $10 a week, but in a month her salary was $1,500 a week.

1941 Orson Welles's film classic, **CITIZEN KANE,** premiered in NY. It is considered by many to be the greatest movie of all time.

1961 The first ever airplane hijacking took place on board a National Airlines twin-engine Convair. The routine flight from Miami to Key West, FL, was hijacked by **ANTULIO RAMIREZ ORTIZ**, who held a knife to the throat of the captain and a gun on the co-pilot and demanded he be taken to Cuba. The lone flight attendant was Inez Harlow from Manitowoc, WI.

1963 **JAMES W. WHITTAKER** of Redmond, WA, became the **FIRST AMERICAN TO CONQUER MOUNT EVEREST** as he and a Sherpa guide reached the summit.

1967 **ELVIS PRESLEY** married Priscilla Beaulieu at the Aladdin Hotel in Las Vegas. They dropped the word "obey" from the traditional vows. The cake alone cost $3,500. They took a limo to their honeymoon retreat in Palm Springs, CA. Daughter Lisa Marie was born 9 months to the day after the ceremony. They separated in 1971 and Elvis filed for divorce in 1973.

1975 **HANK AARON**, then playing for the Milwaukee Brewers, drove in two runs, breaking Babe Ruth's lifetime RBI record of 2,209. He achieved a final record of 2,297.

1988 Billy Joel escaped punishment for defamation charges brough against him by Jack Powers whom he had labelled "a creep" during a Playboy interview. The Nevada judge cited First Amendment rights and dropped all charges.

1992 **PRESIDENT BUSH** ordered 4,000 Army troops and 1,000 federal officers into Los Angeles in an attempt to restore order. In the days of rioting, over 50 died, 200 were injured, with over $700 million in damages. More than 11,000 people were arrested.

1994 Race car champion **AYRTON SENNA** died of head injuries after his car hit a concrete wall going 185 mph during the San Marino Grand Prix in Imola, Italy.

MAY 2

It really could rain cats and dogs!

BIRTHDAYS

- **LESLEY GORE** Singer. (Tenafly, NJ) Her biggest record: "It's My Party" in 1963. She was discovered by Quincy Jones who has since produced Lionel Richie, Michael Jackson, etc. Year/**Age**: 1995/**49** 1996/**50** 1997/**51**

- **JENNA VON OY** Actress. Plays "Six" on TV's "Blossum." Year/**Age**: 1995/**18** 1996/**19** 1997/**20**

- **JAMAAL WILKES** Basketball. Year/**Age**: 1995/**42** 1996/**43** 1997/**44**

- **LARRY GATLIN** C&W. (Seminole, TX) GATLIN BROTHERS. He won a Grammy Award in 1966 for "Broken Lady." Year/**Age**: 1995/**47** 1996/**48** 1997/**49**

- **DR. BENJAMIN SPOCK** Pediatrician/author. (New Haven, CT) His book *Baby and Child Care* sold more than 30 million copies. In 1968, he ran for president as the Peoples Party candidate. Year/**Age**: 1995/**92** 1996/**93** 1997/**94**

- **THEODORE BIKEL** [bih-kehl'] Actor. (Vienna, Austria) Versatile actor capable of playing many nationalities. He appeared in *The African Queen*, *My Fair Lady*, *The Russians Are Coming*, and TV's "War and Remembrance." Year/**Age**: 1995/**71** 1996/**72** 1997/**73**

- **BIANCA JAGGER** Former wife of MICK JAGGER. (Managua, Nicaragua) Year/**Age**: 1995/**50** 1996/**51** 1997/**52**

- **LOU GRAMM** Singer. (Born Lou Grammatica in Rochester, NY) FOREIGNER'S. Hits include: "I Want to Know What Love Is," "Double Vision," and "Waiting For a Girl Like You." Year/**Age**: 1995/**45** 1996/**46** 1997/**47**

- **KEITH MORELAND** Baseball. Former outfielder for the Chicago Cubs. Year/**Age**: 1995/**42** 1996/**43** 1997/**44**

- **LINK WRAY** Guitarist. (Dunn, NC) Part American Indian, his band, LINK WRAY & HIS RAY MEN, had a top-40 hit: "Rumble" in 1958. He recorded until the late '70s. Year/**Age**: 1995/**60** 1996/**61** 1997/**62**

- **BING CROSBY** Singer. (1904-1977 – Born Harry Lillis Crosby, Jr., in Tacoma, WA) Biggest hit: "White Christmas," which he sang for the first time in a film called *Holiday Inn* with Fred Astaire. He won an Oscar for *Going My Way*. His last film was *King of Jazz* in 1966. He played an alcoholic doctor, a part originated by Thomas Mitchell in the original version of the film in 1930. He was spokesperson for Minute Maid orange juice. He died on a golf course near Madrid, Spain (10-14-77.)

- **MANFRED "THE RED BARON" RICHTHOFEN** German air ace. (1892-1918) He shot down 80 U.S. planes before being hit himself. The record hit, "Snoopy vs. The Red Baron" by the ROYAL GUARDSMEN was inspired by his battles. (Died 4-21-18.)

FACTS FROM THE PAST

1519 **LEONARDO DA VINCI** died at age 67. At one time, he dissected cadavers to make the first accurate and detailed anatomical drawings.

1536 England's **QUEEN ANNE BOLEYN** [boh-lin'] was sent to the **TOWER OF LONDON** and eventually beheaded at the order of Henry VIII. To this day, there are many stories of the chopping block and about the Tower of London being haunted.

1863 Confederate **GENERAL THOMAS "STONEWALL" JACKSON** was mistaken for a Yankee scout and fatally wounded by his own soldiers when he failed to give the password.

1902 The **FIRST SCIENCE FICTION FILM** was released: *A Trip To The Moon* created by French magician Georges Melies.

1923 **OAKLEY KELLY** and **JOHN MACREADY** flew from New York to California in a Fokker monoplane in 27 hours. It takes 5 hours today!

1932 **JACK BENNY**'s first radio show made its debut on the NBC Blue Network.

1939 **LOU GEHRIG**, New York Yankees first baseman, did not play against the Detroit Tigers, ending his streak of 2,130 consecutive games. Gehrig never played another game.

1954 **STAN MUSIAL** became the first major league ballplayer to hit 5 home runs in a double-header. After age 40 he still hit 46 home runs.

1980 South African authorities banned **PINK FLOYD**'s "Another Brick in the Wall," which had become the anthem of blacks involved in a strike against government schools.

1988 Cincinnati Reds baseball manager **PETE ROSE** was suspended for 30 days by National League President A. Bartlett Giamatti, two days after Rose shoved an umpire during a game won by the New York Mets, 6-5.

1989 A Simi Valley, CA, mall security guard followed a suspicious-looking man in false teeth, hair, glasses and moustache, wearing polyester clothing. After being questioned and unmasked, **MICHAEL JACKSON** signed autographs for the guard and his buddies.

1990 **BRENT MUSBURGER** wasn't out of work long. Fired by CBS April 1, the TV sportscaster signed on with ABC for $11 million over six years. Musburger remains TV sports' highest-paid announcer.

1992 Lil E. Tee, at 17-1, won the 118th running of the **KENTUCKY DERBY**. The horse beat the highly favored French entry, Arazi.

1993 The remains of cult leader **DAVID KORESH** were recovered by authorities from the burned out Branch Davidian compound near Waco, TX.

1994 A judge in L.A. dismissed criminal charges against actor **JACK NICHOLSON**, who on Feb. 8 shattered the windshield of a car with a golf club.

How do you explain crop circles?

MAY 3

BIRTHDAYS

- **PETER GABRIEL** Singer. He was the lead singer of "Genesis" before starting a solo career. Hits: "Sledgehammer" and "In Your Eyes." He wrote the music for the soundtrack to *The Last Temptation of Christ*. The album is called "Passion." Year/**Age**: 1995/**45** 1996/**46** 1997/**47**
- **CHRISTOPHER CROSS** Singer. (San Antonia, TX) Biggest hits: "Sailing" in 1980 and "Arthur's Theme (Best That You Can Do)" in 1981. Year/**Age**: 1995/**44** 1996/**45** 1997/**46**
- **PETER STAPLES** Bass guitarist. (England) With the TROGGS. Their biggest hit: "Wild Thing" in 1966. Year/**Age**: 1995/**51** 1996/**52** 1997/**53**
- **FRANKIE VALLI** Singer. (Born Francis Castelluccio in Newark, NJ) His biggest hits: "Grease" in 1978 and "My Eyes Adored You" in 1974. Biggest hit with the FOUR SEASONS: "Big Girls Don't Cry" in 1962. Year/**Age**: 1995/**58** 1996/**59** 1997/**60**
- **PETE SEEGER** Folk singer. (NYC) He was the leader of the WEAVERS, a folk/rock group in the '50s and ranks with WOODY GUTHRIE as the all-time great protest singer. His biggest hit was "Little Boxes" in 1964. He also wrote "If I Had a Hammer" for PETER, PAUL & MARY. Year/**Age**: 1995/**76** 1996/**77** 1997/**78**
- **GOOSE TATUM** Basketball. Played with the Harlem Globetrotters. Year/**Age**: 1995/**74** 1996/**75** 1997/**76**
- **ENGELBERT HUMPERDINCK** Singer. (Born Arnold Dorsey in Madras, India) His agent, Gordon Mills, tagged him "Engelbert Humperdinck" after a long-dead German composer. Biggest hit: "Release Me" in 1967. Year/**Age**: 1995/**59** 1996/**60** 1997/**61**
- **GREG GUMBEL** Sports announcer. Brother of Bryant "Today Show" Gumbel. Host for the 1994 Winter Olympics in Norway. Year/**Age**: 1995/**49** 1996/**50** 1997/**51**

- **JAMES BROWN** Mr. Dynamite. (Augusta, GA) Sang in a gospel group, then formed his own vocal group, the FAMOUS FLAMES. "The Godfather of Soul" made appearances in the films *Rocky IV* and *The Blues Brothers*. Biggest hit: "I Got You, I Feel Good" in 1965. Brown served time for aggravated assault and failing to stop for police during a chase across the Georgia-South Carolina border Sept. 26, 1988. Year/**Age**: 1995/**62** 1996/**63** 1997/**64**
- **MARY HOPKIN** Welsh pop singer. (Wales) Biggest record: "Those Were the Days" in 1968. Year/**Age**: 1995/**44** 1996/**45** 1997/**46**
- **DOUG HENNING** Magician. (Canada) He produced and starred in *The Magic Show*, a musical. Year/**Age**: 1995/**48** 1996/**49** 1997/**50**
- **JOE AMES** Singer. (Malden, MA) One of the AMES BROTHERS, who had the hit: "The Naughty Lady of Shady Lane" in 1954. Year/**Age**: 1995/**71** 1996/**72** 1997/**73**
- **DAVE DUDLEY** C&W singer. (Born David Pedruska in Spencer, WI) Biggest hit: "Six Days on the Road" in 1963. He played semi-pro baseball in Wausau, WI, and was a DJ. Year/**Age**: 1995/**67** 1996/**68** 1997/**69**
- **DAVEY LOPES** Baseball. Former L.A. Dodgers infielder. Year/**Age**: 1995/**49** 1996/**50** 1997/**51**
- **SUGAR RAY ROBINSON** Former boxing champion. (1921-1989 – Born Walter Smith in Detroit, MI) He was middleweight champion 5 times and also welterweight champ. Retired in 1965 with a record of 175-19-6 including 110 knockouts. (Died 4-12-89.)
- **MARY ASTOR** Actress. (1906-1987 – Born Lucille Langhanke in Quincy, IL) She won an Oscar for best supporting actress in *The Great Lie* in 1941. She played the treacherous temptress Brigid O'Shaughnessy in *The Maltese Falcon* and appeared in over 100 other films. (Died 9-25-87.)

FACTS FROM THE PAST

1936   JOE DIMAGGIO played in his first major league game. He got 3 hits in the Yankees' 14-5 win over St. Louis.

1937   MARGARET MITCHELL won a Pulitzer Prize for *Gone with the Wind.*

1968   The BEACH BOYS began a U.S. tour in New York that featured the Maharishi Mahesh Yogi speaking on spiritual regeneration. But audiences weren't exactly wild about the Maharishi, and half the tour dates were canceled.

1971   After ignoring the media since their inception three years earlier, GRAND FUNK RAILROAD finally agreed to talk to the press. Of the 150 reporters invited, only six showed up.

1976   PAUL McCARTNEY made his first American stage appearance in ten years, with his "Wings Over America" tour. It opened in Fort Worth, TX.

1979   Great Britain elected its FIRST WOMAN PRIME MINISTER, 53-year-old MARGARET THATCHER, Conservative Party Leader. She remained in office for 12 years.

1986   DOLLY PARTON opened her DOLLYWOOD AMUSEMENT PARK near Gatlinburg, Tennessee.

1987   The *Miami Herald* said its reporters had observed a young woman entering a Washington townhouse belonging to Democratic PRESIDENTIAL CANDIDATE, GARY HART.

1988   MADONNA debuted on Broadway in *Speed the Plow* by David Mamet. She received mixed reviews.

1989   CARLY SIMON opened New York's Riverrun art gallery, named after her Oscar-winning song, "Let The River Run."

1994   THE ROLLING STONES announced a world tour beginning August 1st. When Mick Jagger was asked if money was the incentive, he said, "all the beer you can drink, all the girls down in front...there are other things than money."

MAY 4

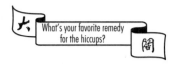

What's your favorite remedy for the hiccups?

BIRTHDAYS

• **TYRONE DAVIS** Singer. (Greenville, MS) He was Freddie King's (Blues guitarist) valet and chauffeur from 1959 to 1962. His biggest hits: "Can I Change My Mind" and "Turn Back the Hands of Time" in 1970. Year/**Age**: 1995/**57** 1996/**58** 1997/**59**

• **RANDY TRAVIS** C&W singer. (Born Randy Bruce Traywick in Marshville, NC) He was once a dishwasher at a night club. He first recorded as Randy Traywick and Randy Ray before adopting his stage name. One of his many hits was "Forever and Ever, Amen" on the country charts at #1 for 3 weeks in 1987. Year/**Age**: 1995/**36** 1996/**37** 1997/**38**

• **JACKIE JACKSON** Singer. (Born Sigmund Jackson in Gary, IN) He and his brothers were known as the JACKSON 5 from 1968-75. Biggest hit: "I'll Be There" in 1970. They re-grouped as the JACKSONS for 1984's highly publicized *Victory* album and tour. Year/**Age**: 1995/**44** 1996/**45** 1997/**46**

• **NICKOLAS ASHFORD** Singer. (Fairfield, SC) ASHFORD & SIMPSON. Biggest hit: "Solid" in 1984. Year/**Age**: 1995/**53** 1996/**54** 1997/**55**

• **PEGGY SANTIGLIA** Lead singer. (Orange, NJ) Biggest hit with the ANGELS, "My Boyfriend's Back" in 1963. Year/**Age**: 1995/**51** 1996/**52** 1997/**53**

• **MARK HERNDON** Singer. (Fort Payne, AL) Member of ALABAMA. Year/**Age**: 1995/**40** 1996/**41** 1997/**42**

• **ROBERTA PETERS** Opera star. (Born Roberta Peterman in NYC) A soprano, she made her NY Met debut when she was 20 years old. Year/**Age**: 1995/**65** 1996/**66** 1997/**67**

• **MAYNARD FERGUSON** Jazz trumpeter. (Canada) Formerly with the STAN KENTON Orchestra. Biggest hit with his own orchestra was "Gonna Fly Now," the theme from *Rocky*. Year/**Age**: 1995/**67** 1996/**68** 1997/**69**

• **EL CORDOBES** Matador. (Born Manuel Benitez Perez in Spain) He became a multimillionaire in 1965, when he fought 111 corridas, receiving over $15,000 for each half hour in the ring. In 1970, he received $1,800,000 for 121 fights. He was gored more than 20 times. If you total the length of his scars, they would be three times the length of his waist. Year/**Age**: 1995/**59** 1996/**60** 1997/**61**

• **PIA ZADORA** Actress/Singer. In the film *Naked Gun 33 1/3*. She was married to millionaire Meshulam Riklis for 16 years. Year/**Age**: 1995/**39** 1996/**40** 1997/**41**

• **RONNIE BOND** Drummer. (1944-1992 – England) With British rock group the TROGGS. Biggest hit: "Wild Thing" in 1966. (Died 11-13-92.)

• **HOWARD DA SILVA** Actor. (1909-1986 – Born Howard Silverblatt in Cleveland, OH) He appeared in *The Lost Weekend*, *The Sea Wolf*, and *The Great Gatsby*. (Died 2-16-86.)

• **AUDREY HEPBURN** Actress. (1930-1993 – Born Edda van Heemstra Hepburn-Ruston in Brussels, Belgium) She won an Academy Award for best actress in 1953 for *Roman Holiday*. Some of her 26 films include: *Breakfast at Tiffany's*, *The Nun's Story*, and *Charade*. Audrey was a UNICEF ambassador until her death. (Died 1-20-93.)

FACTS FROM THE PAST

1626 Peter Minuit, a Dutch colonist, landed on **MANHATTAN**. He later bought the island from the Indians for trinkets said to be worth $24.

1904 The U.S. took possession of the **PANAMA CANAL ZONE** and, during his term as U.S. President, Jimmy Carter gave it back.

1932 **AL CAPONE,** Chicago gang boss/racketeer, was convicted of income tax evasion and sent to Atlanta Penitentiary.

1957 Championship **JOCKEY WILLIE SHOEMAKER** misjudged the finish line. Shoemaker stood up in his stirrups while Iron Liege passed him up to win the Kentucky Derby.

1959 The winners of the **FIRST ANNUAL GRAMMY AWARDS** were: Domenico Modugno's "Volare," as record of the year. Henry Mancini's *Peter Gunn* won album of the year. The Champs' "Tequila" won best R&B performance. And the Kingston Trio was best C&W performance of the year, with "Tom Dooley." Most awards went to Ross (David Seville) Bagdasarian whose "Chipmunks" song won for "best recording for children," "best comedy," and "best engineered."

1964 The **MOODY BLUES** were formed in Birmingham, England. Members included Denny Laine, Mike Pinder, Ray Thomas, Graeme Edge, and Clint Warwick. The band was reorganized in 1967 when Justin Hayward became their new lead vocalist.

1970 **STUDENT REACTION TO U.S. OPERATIONS IN CAMBODIA** resulted in a confrontation between 100 National Guardsmen and 600 students at Kent State University in Ohio. Four students were killed and 11 wounded. **NEIL YOUNG** wrote the song "Ohio" as a response.

1973 A **WORLD RECORD FOR HAMBURGER EATING** was set by University of Rhode Island student **BOB MATERN**, who ate 83 of them in 2 1/2 hours.

1977 Former President **RICHARD NIXON** came out of seclusion to give his first of four TV interviews to talk show host David Frost.

1989 After 12 days of deliberation, a Federal Court jury convicted **OLIVER NORTH** on felony charges of altering and shredding documents, aiding and abetting an obstruction of Congress, and illegally accepting a gratuity, a $13,800 home security system. North was convicted of 3 of 12 charges in the Iran-Contra case.

1994 The Chicago Cubs ended their 12-game home losing streak (the worst home start in the National League this century) against the Cleveland Reds. **ERNIE BANKS** paraded a goat around Wrigley Field for good luck while fans had sent them a post card from St. Jude, patron saint of hopeless cases and a voodoo doll.

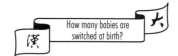

How many babies are switched at birth?

MAY 5

BIRTHDAYS

- **TINA YOTHERS** Actress. (Whittier, CA) Played Jennifer on "Family Ties." Film *Poison Ivy.* Year/Age: 1995/**22** 1996/**23** 1997/**24**

- **TAMMY WYNETTE** Singer. (Born Virginia Wynette Pugh on her grandfather's farm in Red Bay, AL) "Our property crossed the state line," she explains, "so I tell people my top half comes from Mississippi and my bottom half from Alabama, and if they're not happy, turn me around." "Stand By Your Man," a song she co-wrote with Billy Sherrill, became an anthem for all the women with hard-to-understand men, and Tammy became a sort of unofficial spokesperson for the wronged woman. Ironically, in that same year she married her idol, country star George Jones, a man whose drinking habits made him ultimately impossible to stand by. Year/Age: 1995/**53** 1996/**54** 1997/**55**

- **JOHN RHYS-DAVIES** Actor. TV's "Untouchables." Many miniseries including "Shogun." Year/Age: 1995/**51** 1996/**52** 1997/**53**

- **ALICE FAYE** Actress/singer. (Born Ann Leppert in NYC) She sang with Rudy Vallee's band and appeared in many movies. She came out of retirement in 1962 to make the film *State Fair* co-starring Ann-Margret, Pat Boone, and Bobby Darin. She was married to Tony Martin 1937-40 and married Phil Harris in 1941. Year/Age: 1995/**80** 1996/**81** 1997/**82**

- **ANN B. DAVIS** Actress. (Schenectady, NY) She played Alice Nelson, the harried housekeeper on "The Brady Bunch" TV series and Bob Cummings' girl Friday on the "Bob Cummings Show." Year/Age: 1995/**69** 1996/**70** 1997/**71**

- **HAROLD MINER** Basketball. Year/Age: 1995/**24** 1996/**25** 1997/**26**

- **MICHAEL MURPHY** Singer. (Austin, TX) Biggest hit: "Wildfire" in 1975. Year/Age: 1995/**57** 1996/**58** 1997/**59**

- **JOHNNIE TAYLOR** R&B. (Crawfordville, AR) In the 1950s, he replaced Sam Cooke in a gospel group, the SOUL STIRRERS. Biggest hit: "Disco Lady" in 1976. Year/Age: 1995/**58** 1996/**59** 1997/**60**

- **ROGER REES** Actor. (Wales) Tony award winner. Starred in *Nicholas Nickleby.* Year/Age: 1995/**51** 1996/**52** 1997/**53**

- **ACE CANNON** Saxophonist. (Granada, MS) Biggest hit: "Tuff" in 1962. Year/Age: 1995/**61** 1996/**62** 1997/**63**

- **ANNETTE BENING** Actress. (Topeka, KS) Appeared in *The Grifters* and *Bugsy.* At one time she was married to George Hamilton. Married her film co-star, Warren Beatty. Year/Age: 1995/**36** 1996/**37** 1997/**38**

- **PAT CARROLL** Actress/comedienne. (Shreveport, LA) She won an Emmy in 1956 for best supporting performance by an actress on "Caesar's Hour" on NBC. Sea witch Ursula's voice in *The Little Mermaid.* Year/Age: 1995/**68** 1996/**69** 1997/**70**

- **MICHAEL PALIN** Comedian/actor. (England) Appeared on "Monty Python's Flying Circus" produced for the BBC and aired in Great Britain from 1969-1971. Film *American Friends.* Year/Age: 1995/**52** 1996/**53** 1997/**54**

- **KARL MARX** Socialist. (1818-1883 – Germany) Founder and father of modern communism, author of *Das Kapital,* the *Communist Manifesto.* (Died 3-14-1883.)

FACTS FROM THE PAST

1821 **NAPOLEON BONAPARTE** died in exile on the island of St. Helena at age 51. A deal had to be worked out with the British to get his body back to France. Sixteen years later, when they opened the coffin, his body was perfectly embalmed. They say his doctors were feeding him arsenic to prolong his life, instead it shortened it. But that is why his body was so well preserved.

1891 **CARNEGIE HALL** (originally named "Music Hall") had its opening night in New York City, with a concert that included works conducted by Peter Ilich Tchaikovsky and Walter Damrosch.

1904 **CY YOUNG** of the Boston Americans pitched the American League's first perfect game, defeating Philadelphia, 3-0. He became the first pitcher to throw a no-hitter in each league.

1925 **JOHN SCOPES**, biology teacher in Dayton, TN, was arrested for teaching the theory of **EVOLUTION** in violation of state statute. His trial became the play and movie *Inherit the Wind.*

1926 **AUTHOR SINCLAIR LEWIS** turned down the Pulitzer Prize for his novel *Arrowsmith*, telling the committee in a letter that "All prizes, like all titles, are dangerous."

1961 Astronaut Alan B. Shepard, Jr., became America's **FIRST SPACE TRAVELER** when he made a 15-minute sub-orbital flight in a capsule launched from Cape Canaveral, Florida.

1968 Following a Long Beach, CA, gig, **BUFFALO SPRINGFIELD** broke up. Stephen Stills and Neil Young formed a group with Graham Nash and David Crosby.

1979 With lines at California service stations getting longer and **GASOLINE SHORTAGES** being reported nationwide, President Jimmy Carter said during a visit to Los Angeles that he'd ordered Energy Secretary James Schlesinger to look into the situation.

1984 **SWALE,** the offspring of 1977 Triple Crown winner **SEATTLE SLEW,** won the Kentucky Derby. Swale went on to lose the Preakness, won the Belmont Stakes, then died unexpectedly on June 17th. It was the first Derby win for jockey Laffit Pincay, Jr.

1988 **PEPSI-COLA** commercials featuring Michael Jackson aired in the USSR as the first non-Russian company to do so.

1994 American teen **MICHAEL FAY** received 4 lashes on his buttocks with a 4-foot long, $^1/_2$ inch split bamboo cane. He was punished for commiting several acts of vandalism in Singapore.

MAY 6

If there is nothing, does time exist?

BIRTHDAYS

- **WILLIE MAYS** Baseball legend. (Westfield, AL) National League Most Valuable Player twice. In 1954 he made one of the most spectacular catches in World Series history when he caught a 460-ft. line drive in centerfield with his back to the plate, which would have given the Cleveland Indians a first-game victory. Year/**Age**: 1995/**64** 1996/**65** 1997/**66**

- **BOB SEGER** Rock singer/guitarist/songwriter. (Ann Arbor, MI) First recorded in 1966, formed the SYSTEM in '68, attended college until '71 and formed his own back-up group the SILVER BULLET BAND in 1976. Hit: "Shame on the Moon" in 1982. His only #1 was "Shake Down" from *Beverly Hills Cop* Year/**Age**: 1995/**50** 1996/**51** 1997/**52**

- **WEEB EWBANK** Football. (Richmond, IN) The only coach in pro football history to win both the American and National Football League championships. Twice with the NFL Baltimore Colts and once with the AFL NY Jets. He guided that team, with Joe Namath, to a Super Bowl upset win. Year/**Age**: 1995/**88** 1996/**89** 1997/**90**

- **CARMEN CAVALLARO** Bandleader. (1913-1993, New York, NY) He led the orchestra that played the *Eddy Duchin Story* sound track in 1956. Year/**Age**: 1995/**82** 1996/**83** 1997/**84**

- **MARGUERITE PIAZZA** Operatic soprano. (New Orleans, LA) Year/**Age**: 1995/**69** 1996/**70** 1997/**71**

- **MARY MacGREGOR** Singer. (St. Paul, MN) Hit in 1976: "Torn Between Two Lovers." Year/**Age**: 1995/**46** 1996/**47** 1997/**48**

- **STEWART GRANGER** Actor. (1913-1993 – Born James Stewart in London, England) Because of the conflict of names with actor Jimmy Stewart, he changed his name. He appeared in many films including *King Solomon's Mines* and *The Great White Hunter,* and on TV's "The Hound of the Baskervilles" as Holmes. (Died 8-16-93.)

- **ORSON WELLES** Actor/director/producer/writer. (1915-1985 – Born George Orson Welles in Kenosha, WI) Nominated for two Academy Awards: in 1941, for best actor & director in *Citizen Kane* which was based on the life of William Randolph Hearst – one of the greatest movies of all time. He also panicked all of America in 1938 with a vivid radio broadcast of "War of the Worlds." (Died 10-10-85.)

- **RUDOLPH VALENTINO** Actor. (1895-1926 – Born Rodolfo Pietro Alfonzo Filiberto Raeffella Guglielemi di Valentina d'Antonguolla in Italy) Arrived in America with $1. His first job was gardener in Central Park. He became a star overnight in the film *The Four Horsemen of the Apocalypse* and was the screen lover of the day. (Died 8-23-26.)

- **SIGMUND FREUD** Physician/psychiatrist. (1856-1939 – Czechoslovakia) Founder of psychoanalysis. He was a neurotic, depressed most of the time, hated trains, was deathly afraid of open spaces and lived in terror of dying at the age of 51. He spent a half-hour every day analyzing himself and said he only worked well when he didn't feel good. His dog would escort his patients into his office and out.

FACTS FROM THE PAST

1891 Electrician Irwin H. Hoover began installing the **FIRST ELECTRICAL WIRING IN THE WHITE HOUSE.** President Benjamin Harrison and his wife, Caroline, refused to touch the newly installed electric light switches because they were afraid of being shocked.

1915 **BABE RUTH** 20 years old, hit his first major league home run while playing for the Boston Red Sox, against the New York Yankees' starting pitcher Jack Warhop in New York.

1947 The sheet music for "**WHITE CHRISTMAS**" by **IRVING BERLIN** was first published.

1953 **BOBO HOLLOMAN** of the St. Louis Browns pitched his very first major league baseball game. He won it, 6-0, pitching a **NO-HITTER**—the only person ever to do so in his very first game.

1954 Medical student **ROGER BANNISTER** broke the 4-minute mile during a track meet in Oxford, England. He ran the mile in 3:59:04. In 1993 Noureddine Morceli of Algeria ran the mile in 3:44:4.

1960 Britain's **PRINCESS MARGARET** married **ANTHONY ARMSTRONG-JONES**, a commoner, at Westminster Abbey. The marriage ended in divorce in 1978.

1962 In the first test of its kind, the submerged submarine **U.S.S.** *ETHAN ALLEN* fired a Polaris missile armed with a nuclear warhead that detonated above the Pacific Ocean.

1965 **KEITH RICHARDS** fell asleep while improvising on a new guitar. The next morning he struggled to remember a riff, noticed a tape recorder he left running, and played back "(I Can't Get No) Satisfaction."

1973 **PAUL SIMON** began his first solo tour in Boston, MA, three years after splitting up with Art Garfunkel.

1983 West German government experts announced that tests had proved the purported **HITLER DIARIES** to be "obvious fakes."

1984 **TINA TURNER'S** comeback hit, "What's Love Got To Do With It," was released. It went to number one. A movie by the same name, about her life, was released in 1993.

1989 Jockey **PATRICK VALENZUELA** rode **SUNDAY SILENCE** to victory in the 115th running of the Kentucky Derby.

1991 Philadelphia Phillies **CENTER FIELDER LENNY DYKSTRA** and catcher Darren Daulton were badly injured when Dykstra's car spun out of control and into two trees in a Philadelphia suburb. Dykstra was **CHARGED WITH DRUNKEN DRIVING.**

1994 A former Arkansas state worker **SUED PRESIDENT CLINTON** for $700,000 in Federal Court claiming that Clinton violated her civil rights by making unwanted sexual advances in 1991 when he was Governor.

Is a futures contract on cheese considered binding?

MAY 7

BIRTHDAYS

- **JIMMY RUFFIN** Singer. (Collinsville, MS) David Ruffin's brother. Biggest hit: "What Becomes of the Broken Hearted" in 1966. Year/**Age**: 1995/**56** 1996/**57** 1997/**58**

- **ROBIN STRASSER** Actress. (New York, NY) Portrayed Dorian Lord on soap "One Life To Live." Year/**Age**: 1995/**50** 1996/**51** 1997/**52**

- **DARREN McGAVIN** Actor. (Spokane, WA) Starred in the "Nightstalker" TV series. Year/**Age**: 1995/**73** 1996/**74** 1997/**75**

- **JIM LOWE** Singer. (Springfield, OH) He was a DJ who had one hit in 1956: "Green Door" which was on the charts for 6 months. He accompanied himself on the piano and was the only musician on that song which was recorded in an apartment. Year/**Age**: 1995/**68** 1996/**69** 1997/**70**

- **TERESA BREWER** Singer. (Toledo, OH) Her many hits include "Music, Music, Music," "Till I Waltz Again With You" in the early '50s, and "The Hula Hoop Song" in 1958. Year/**Age**: 1995/**64** 1996/**65** 1997/**66**

- **JOHNNY UNITAS** Football star. (Pittsburgh, PA) Quarterback for the Baltimore Colts, passed for over 40,000 yards, and he never played college football. He was cut by the Pittsburgh Steelers early in his career. Year/**Age**: 1995/**62** 1996/**63** 1997/**64**

- **DICK WILLIAMS** Baseball. (St. Louis, MO) As a rookie manager he took the Boston Red Sox from a 9th place finish to the A.L. pennant in 1967 and led the Oakland A's to World Championships in 1972 and 1973. Year/**Age**: 1995/**66** 1996/**67** 1997/**68**

- **BILL DANOFF** Singer/songwriter. (Springfield, MA) #1 hit "Afternoon Delight" with STARLAND VOCAL BAND in 1976. Year/**Age**: 1995/**49** 1996/**50** 1997/**51**

- **TRACI LORDS** Actress. (Born Nora Louise Kuzma in Steubenville, OH) Her X-rated career started when she was 15. By 18, she had made 70 adult films, was broke, weighed 90 pounds, was addicted to cocaine and in a hospital suicide ward. Films include *Skinner, Cry Baby,* and miniseries *Tommy Knockers.* She was in *Serial Mom* and TV's "Married With Children." Year/**Age**: 1995/**27** 1996/**28** 1997/**29**

- **DAVID TOMLINSON** Actor. (Scotland) In the film *Bedknobs and Broomsticks* and *Mary Poppins.* Year/**Age**: 1995/**78** 1996/**79** 1997/**80**

- **GEORGE "GABBY" HAYES** Actor. (1885-1969) Old-time Western star. (Died 2-9-69.)

- **ROBERT BROWNING** Poet. (1812-1889 – London) Wrote *Pippa Passes.* He married Elizabeth Barrett in 1846. (Died 12-12-1889.)

- **JOHANNES BRAHMS** Composer. (1833-1897 – Germany) His mentor was Robert Schumann. He was an avowed cat hater. He spent much time at the window trying to hit the neighborhood cats with a bow and arrow, a sport at which he became quite adept. (Died 4-3-1897.)

- **GARY COOPER** Actor. (1901-1961 – Born Frank James Cooper in Helena, MT) He started out as a cowboy extra at $5.00 a fall. He injured his hip [if you go back and look at the old Cooper movies, you'll never see him get on or off a horse due to that injury]. In 1939, he got $480,000 for making films . . . a lot of money at that time. Received best actor Oscars for *Sergeant York* in 1941 and *High Noon* in 1952. (Died 5-13-61.)

- **ANNE BAXTER** Actress. (1923-1985 – Michigan City, IN) She won an Oscar for supporting actress in *The Razor's Edge* in 1946 and appeared in "Hotel" on TV. Her grandfather was famous architect Frank Lloyd Wright. (Died 12-12-85.)

FACTS FROM THE PAST

1789 The **FIRST PRESIDENTIAL INAUGURAL BALL** was held in NYC in honor of President and Mrs. George Washington.

1824 **BEETHOVEN**'s *Ninth Symphony* premiered in Vienna.

1914 A number of U.S. Congressmen introduced a proposed **NATIONAL MOTHER'S DAY HOLIDAY** for the 2nd Sunday in May, and there was not a single "no" vote. **ANNA JARVIS** spent many years campaigning for this holiday and was pleased until it became too commercialized. She became a recluse, wishing she'd never started the campaign.

1929 "Scarface" **AL CAPONE** personally killed three of his own gunmen with a baseball bat after dinner at the Hawthorn Hotel in Cicero, IL. He considered them disloyal. Their corpses were dumped over the Indiana state line and when the coroner examined them he discovered that almost every one of their bones was broken.

1945 **WORLD WAR II** in Europe came to an end when Germany signed an unconditional surrender at General **DWIGHT D. EISENHOWER**'s headquarters in Rheims, France.

1957 **ELIOT NESS,** the government agent who hunted gangster Al Capone in the early 1930s, died. He was the inspiration for the TV show "The Untouchables."

1975 President **GERALD R. FORD** formally declared an **END TO THE VIETNAM ERA.** In Ho Chi Minh City – formerly Siagon – the Viet Cong staged a rally to celebrate their takeover.

1992 Jockey **ANGEL CORDERO, JR.,** retired at age 49, due to injuries suffered in a spill in January 1992. He was the second all-time money winner and third in races won.

1993 **18-YEAR-OLD SHERRY JOHNSON** said she was the sixth patient to contract AIDS from the late Dr. David Acer, her dentist.

1994 **GERALD MCCLELLAN** knocked out Julian Jackson in 1 minute, 23 seconds in the first round to reatin the World Boxing Council middleweight championship.

MAY 8

How do belly dancers do that?

BIRTHDAYS

- **JACK BLANCHARD** Singer. (Buffalo, NY) He and his wife, Misty Morgan, had a hit in 1970, "Tennessee Bird Walk." They met each other while working in Florida. Year/**Age:** 1995/**53** 1996/**54** 1997/**55**

- **CHRIS FRANTZ** Drummer. (New York, NY) With TALKING HEADS. Biggest hit: "Burning Down The House" in 1983. He formed the TOM TOM CLUB. Year/**Age:** 1995/**44** 1996/**45** 1997/**46**

- **DON RICKLES** Entertainer. (Long Island, NY) Don starred as CPO Sharkey in a service sitcom of the same name, in the mid-'70s. Also appeared in films, including *Kelly's Heroes* with Clint Eastwood. Insult comedian. TV's "Daddy Dearest." Year/**Age:** 1995/**69** 1996/**70** 1997/**71**

- **MELISSA GILBERT** Actress. (Los Angeles, CA) Played Laura Ingalls on TV's "Little House on the Prairie." Kid sister Sara appeared on "Roseanne." She is the older sister of actor Jonathan Gilbert. In *The Diary of Anne Frank* and "Sweet Justice" TV series. Previously married to actor Bo Brinkman. Currently engaged to Bruce Boxleiter ("Scarecrow and Mrs. King") Year/**Age:** 1995/**31** 1996/**32** 1997/**33**

- **PETER BENCHLEY** Author. (NYC) He wrote *Jaws* and had a small part in the movie as a TV reporter. *The Beast.* Year/**Age:** 1995/**55** 1996/**56** 1997/**57**

- **TONI TENNILLE** Singer. (Montgomery, AL) Biggest hit with CAPTAIN & TENNILLE was "Love Will Keep Us Together" in 1975, a Grammy winner, written by Neil Sedaka. Married Daryl Dragon – "The Captain" – in 1975. Year/**Age:** 1995/**52** 1996/**53** 1997/**54**

- **ANGEL CORDERO** Jockey. (Puerto Rico) He has ridden 3 Kentucky Derby winners. The last was Spend-a-Buck in 1985. The Hall of Famer has ridden more than 7,000 winners and his mounts have earned over $155 million. He retired in 1992. Year/**Age:** 1995/**53** 1996/**54** 1997/**55**

- **MIKE CUELLAR** Baseball lefty. Traded to Baltimore from Houston in 1969 and went on to four 20-game seasons for the Orioles before retiring in 1977 with lifetime record of 185-130. Year/**Age:** 1995/**58** 1996/**59** 1997/**60**

- **PAUL SAMWELL-SMITH** Bass/keyboard player. With the YARDBIRDS. Biggest hit: "For Your Love" in 1965. Year/**Age:** 1995/**52** 1996/**53** 1997/**54**

- **RONNIE LOTT** Football. (Albuquerque, NM) Los Angeles Raiders. Year/**Age:** 1995/**36** 1996/**37** 1997/**38**

- **ALEX VAN HALEN** Singer. (Holland) Hits include: "Jump" and "Oh, Pretty Woman." Year/**Age:** 1995/**40** 1996/**41** 1997/**42**

- **PHILIP BAILEY** Singer. (Denver, CO) Biggest hit: "Easy Lover" with Phil Collins in 1984. Was vocalist with EARTH, WIND & FIRE. Biggest hit: "Shining Star" in 1975. Year/**Age:** 1995/**44** 1996/**45** 1997/**46**

- **GARY GLITTER** Singer. (Born Paul Gadd in England) First recorded as Paul Raven in the early '60s, then as Paul Monday, then Gary Glitter in 1971. Biggest hit: "Rock and Roll Part 2" in 1972. Year/**Age:** 1995/**51** 1996/**52** 1997/**53**

- **SONNY LISTON** Boxer. (1932-1970 or 71) Heavyweight fighter who is in the record books as fighting in front of the smallest attendance for the world heavyweight title: 2,234 fans saw him fight Cassius Clay in Lewiston, ME, on May 25, 1965. He had been dead several days when his body was found on Jan. 5, 1971.

- **RICK NELSON** Actor/singer. (1940-1985 – Born Eric Hilliard Nelson in Teaneck, NJ) Made his fame as a TV actor with his family in "Ozzie & Harriet," then as a singer and songwriter. He became an instant teen idol when he sang "I'm Walkin'," on the show. His last hit was "Garden Party" in 1972. He had nine gold singles, and sold 35 million records. His marriage to Kris Harmon produced 4 children, including twin entertainers, Gunnar and Matthew, and an actress, Tracey. Rick died in a plane crash near DeKalb, TX, on New Year's Eve, 1985.

- **HARRY TRUMAN** U.S. President. (1884-1972 – Lamar, MO) He became the 33rd U.S. president on the death of Franklin D. Roosevelt on April 12, 1945, and served until Jan. 20, 1953. His full name is Harry S Truman, the S is not an abbreviation but a name in itself, and when properly written is not followed by a period. Using a single letter as a middle name was a common

FACTS FROM THE PAST

1541   Spanish explorer **HERNANDO DE SOTO** discovered the **MISSISSIPPI RIVER** at a point near the present city of Memphis, TN.

1846   The first major battle of the **MEXICAN WAR** was fought at Palo Alto, TX, resulting in victory for General Zachary Taylor's forces.

1886   **COCA-COLA WAS INTRODUCED** by pharmacist **DR. JOHN PEMBERTON** who had been working on a new patent medicine, a headache and hangover remedy. At first he used straight water, but the drugstore clerk used carbonated water, and that was the beginning of Coke as we know it today. In the world, over 12 million gallons are consumed daily.

1956   **ALFRED E. NEUMAN** ("What, me worry?") first appeared on the cover of *Mad* magazine. He even got some votes in the presidential election, which was won by Dwight Eisenhower in 1956. *Mad* magazine was founded by the late **WILLIAM GAINES**.

1958   In one of the six crises he later would write about, **VICE PRESIDENT RICHARD NIXON** was shoved, stoned, booed, and spat upon by anti-American protesters in Lima, Peru.

1972   Keyboard player/singer **BILLY PRESTON** became the first rock performer to headline at **RADIO CITY MUSIC HALL**.

1978   **DAVID R. BERKOWITZ** pleaded guilty in a Brooklyn courtroom to the six murder charges against him in the **SON OF SAM** .44-caliber shootings that had terrified New Yorkers.

1994   **PRO GOLFER JOHN DALY** won the BellSouth Classic in a way he said he had never won a tournament before–sober.

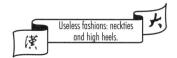

Useless fashions: neckties and high heels.

MAY 9

BIRTHDAYS

- **DAVE GAHAN** Singer. (England) With DEPECHE MODE which is French for "fast fashion." Year/Age: 1995/**33** 1996/**34** 1997/**35**
- **CANDICE BERGEN** Actress. (Beverly Hill, CA) Appeared in *Carnal Knowledge*, *Sand Pebbles,* and *The Group*. Ventriloquist Edgar Bergen (who died in 1978) was her dad. She wrote a book, *Knock on Wood*, about her life with her dad's "dummies." Emmy award-winning star of "Murphy Brown," made popular by VP Dan Quayle. She appears in SPRINT commercials. Year/Age: 1995/**49** 1996/**50** 1997/**51**
- **GLENDA JACKSON** Actress. (England) She won two Oscars: in 1970 for *Women in Love* and 1973 *A Touch of Class*. Year/Age: 1995/**58** 1996/**59** 1997/**60**
- **ALBERT FINNEY** Actor. (England) Nominated for best actor in 1963 for *Tom Jones*, 1974 for *Murder on the Orient Express,* and 1983 for *The Dresser*. Other films: *Used People*, and *The Browning Version*. Year/Age: 1995/**59** 1996/**60** 1997/**61**
- **TONY GWYNNE** Baseball. (Los Angeles, CA) San Diego Padres. Year/Age: 1995/**35** 1996/**36** 1997/**37**
- **BILLY JOEL** Entertainer. (Long Island, NY) Talented singer/composer who struggled for years in small bands and cocktail lounges. Wrote *Piano Man* about his experiences playing piano at the Executive Room, a sleazy lounge in the Wilshire district of L.A. Married Christie Brinkley in 1985. They divorced in 1994. Year/Age: 1995/**46** 1996/**47** 1997/**48**
- **STEVE YZERMAN** [I'-zer-man] Hockey center. (Canada) Year/Age: 1995/**29** 1996/**30** 1997/**31**
- **JAMES L. BROOKS** Director. (Brooklyn, NY) TVs "Mary Tyler Moore Show" and the film *Terms of Endearment*. Year/Age: 1995/**55** 1996/**56** 1997/**57**
- **STEVE KATZ** Guitarist. Biggest hits with BLOOD SWEAT AND TEARS: "Spinning Wheel," "You've Made Me So Very Happy," and "And When I Die," all in 1969. Year/Age: 1995/**50** 1996/**51** 1997/**52**
- **MIKE WALLACE** CBS correspondent/newsman (Born Myron Wallace in Brookline, MA) Appears on CBS "60 Minutes." His son, Chris, is a correspondent for NBC. Year/Age: 1995/**77** 1996/**78** 1997/**79**
- **HANK SNOW** C&W singer. (Born Clarence Snow in Liverpool, Nova Scotia) At one time he was a Fuller Brush salesman. He recorded for RCA, beginning in 1936. Biggest hit: "I'm Moving On" in 1950. It was number one for 21 weeks on the C&W chart. Year/Age: 1995/**81** 1996/**82** 1997/**83**
- **RICHARD ALONZO "PONCHO" GONZALEZ** Tennis player. (Los Angeles, CA) He won the Davis Cup for the U.S. in 1949. He is now a tennis coach at a California health spa. Year/Age: 1995/**67** 1996/**68** 1997/**69**
- **KEVIN PETER HALL** Actor. (1956-1991 – Pittsburgh, PA) The 7-foot, 2-inch star of the movie *Predator* and TV's "Harry and the Hendersons." (Died 4-10-91.)
- **TERRY DRINKWATER** CBS newsman. (1936-1989) His career at CBS started in 1963. He covered politics, space exploration, airline disasters, the Patty Hearst kidnapping and the eruption of Mount St. Helens. (Died 5-31-89.)

FACTS FROM THE PAST

1754 The **FIRST NEWSPAPER CARTOON** appeared in the colonies. The illustration in Ben Franklin's *Pennsylvania Gazette* depicted a dissected snake, with each part representing a colony. The caption read: "Join or die."

1864 During the Civil War, **UNION GENERAL JOHN SEDGEWICK** was killed by a Confederate sharpshooter at Spotsylvania, VA. His last words were: "They couldn't hit an elephant at this distance."

1926 Americans Richard Byrd and Floyd Bennett became the **FIRST MEN** to make an **AIRPLANE FLIGHT OVER THE NORTH POLE.**

1940 **VIVIEN LEIGH** made her American stage debut, starring with Laurence Olivier in *Romeo and Juliet.*

1944 **JIMMY DAVIS,** who wrote the song "You Are My Sunshine," became Governor of Louisiana.

1967 **MUHAMMAD ALI** was stripped of his heavyweight championship title by the board of the World Boxing Association. Ali had been indicted for refusing to be drafted into the Army.

1974 The House Judiciary Committee began hearings on whether to recommend the impeachment of **PRESIDENT RICHARD M. NIXON.**

1975 **BRIAN OLDFIELD** became the first person to shot put 75 feet, in El Paso, TX.

1984 The **CHICAGO WHITE SOX** and the **MILWAUKEE BREWERS** battled for 8 hours 6 minutes in the **LONGEST GAME EVER.** After playing 17 innings the previous day, the teams met again before playing a regularly scheduled game, thus making the total 34 innings in 2 days. Harold Baines hit a home run off Chuck Porter in the 25th inning. The Sox won 7-6 and **TOM SEAVER** was the winning pitcher in both games. In 1991, the Brewers beat the Sox in a 19-inning game.

1988 The book *For the Record: From Wall Street to Washington* by **DONALD REGAN** was released. It described the daily workings inside the White House, even detailed how former First Lady Nancy Reagan consulted astrologers.

1990 **SINEAD O'CONNOR** refused to appear with Andrew Dice Clay on "Saturday Night Live."

1992 **MIKE TYSON** was found guilty of threatening a guard and disorderly conduct at the Indiana Youth Center. His release date was set back from March 25, 1995 to April 9, 1995.

1994 C&W star **WILLIE NELSON** was arrested on a misdemenor drug charge after police in Hewitt, TX found the butt of a joint in his Mercedes-Benz ashtray.

MAY 10

Name the entire "Who's On First" ball team.

BIRTHDAYS

- **PHIL** and **STEVE MAHRE** Olympic medalist skiers. (White Pass, WA) Year/**Age**: 1995/**37** 1996/**38** 1997/**39**
- **PAT SUMMERALL** Announcer. Sports announcer and TV pitchman. He played pro football for the Chicago Cardinals and New York Giants. Year/**Age**: 1995/**65** 1996/**66** 1997/**67**
- **JULIUS WECHTER** Marimba player. (Chicago, IL) Leader of the Baja Marimba Band and earlier was a member of Herb Alperts Tijuana Bras. One of Wechter's hits: "Ghost Riders in the Sky." Year/**Age**: 1995/**60** 1996/**61** 1997/**62**
- **DAVE MASON** Vocalist/composer/guitarist. (England) Original member of TRAFFIC. Member of new "Fleetwood Mac." Biggest hit: "We Just Disagree." Year/**Age**: 1995/**49** 1996/**50** 1997/**51**
- **GRAHAM GOULDMAN** Bass guitarist. (England) With 10CC, later with duo WAX. Biggest hit for 10CC: "I'm Not In Love." Year/**Age**: 1995/**49** 1996/**50** 1997/**51**
- **PAUL "BONO" HEWSON** Lead Singer. (Ireland) Vocalist for U2. Year/**Age**: 1995/**35** 1996/**36** 1997/**37**
- **DONOVAN** Singer. (Born Donovan Leitch in Glasgow, Scotland) Biggest hits: "Sunshine Superman," and "Mellow Yellow," with Paul McCartney adding the whispering. Year/**Age**: 1995/**49** 1996/**50** 1997/**51**
- **PETER NEWMAN** Author. (Vienna, Austria) He was *MacLean's Magazine.* Year/**Age**: 1995/**66** 1996/**67** 1997/**68**
- **MEG FOSTER** Actress. Year/**Age**: 1995/**47** 1996/**48** 1997/**49**

- **LARRY WILLIAMS** Singer. (1935-1980 – New Orleans, LA) Biggest hits: "Short Fat Fannie" and "Bony Maronie." He committed suicide 1-7-80, despondent over his fading popularity.
- **NANCY WALKER** Comedienne. (1921-1992 – Born Anna Myrtle Swoyer in Philadelphia, PA) Among her many roles was Rhoda's mom, Mrs. Morgenstern, and the maid on Rock Hudson's TV series, "McMillan and Wife." Was seen on the Bounty Towels TV commercial. (Died 3-25-92.)
- **DANNY RAPP** Singer. (1941-1983 – Philadelphia, PA) He formed a group called the JUVENAIRS in high school which later became DANNY & THE JUNIORS. Biggest hit: "At the Hop" in 1957. Rapp committed suicide 4-8-83.
- **FRED ASTAIRE** Dancer/actor. (1899-1987 – Born Frederick Austerlitz in Omaha, NE) His most frequent dance partner was Ginger Rogers with whom he appeared in musicals of the 1930's and '40's, including *The Gay Divorcee* and *Top Hat.* He appeared in *The Towering Inferno* in 1974 for which he received an Oscar nomination. His first wife died in 1954 after 21 years of marriage and he remained unmarried until his surprise wedding June 28, 1980, to Robyn Smith, a jockey. (Died 5-22-87).
- **SIR THOMAS LIPTON** Tycoon. (1850-1931 – Scotland) When he was 26, he opened a grocery store in Glasgow and eventually created the world's first grocery chain with over 400 stores. He grew tea, which he packaged in small silk sacks. His Lipton Tea made him a multimillionaire by age 40. (Died 10-2-31.)

FACTS FROM THE PAST

1497 Italian navigator **AMERIGO VESPUCCI** sailed on his first voyage to the **NEW WORLD.** America was named for him.

1775 **ETHAN ALLEN AND HIS GREEN MOUNTAIN BOYS** captured the British-held fortress at Ticonderoga, New York.

1872 Victoria Woodhull became the **FIRST WOMAN NOMINATED FOR THE U.S. PRESIDENCY.** She was nominated by the National Equal Rights Party.

1908 The **FIRST MOTHER'S DAY** observance took place during church services in Grafton, West Virginia, and Philadelphia.

1913 **DONERAIL** won the Kentucky Derby—a **91-TO-1 LONGSHOT!**

1940 British Prime Minister Neville Chamberlain resigned, and **WINSTON CHURCHILL** formed a new government.

1941 Top **NAZI OFFICIAL RUDOLF HESS** landed by parachute in Scotland in a private effort to make peace in WWII. Hess was convicted of war crimes at the Nuremberg trials. He committed suicide at Spandau in 1987 at age 93.

1967 **MICK JAGGER** was formally charged with illegal possession of pep pills, and **KEITH RICHARDS** was charged with permitting cannabis to be smoked on his premises. As the case was going to court, police arrested fellow Stone, **BRIAN JONES**, at his London apartment and charged him with drug possession.

1975 **STEVIE WONDER** played before 125,000 people at the Washington Monument as part of Human Kindness Day.

1982 At **JOHN HINCKLEY, JR.**'s trial for shooting President Reagan and others, a psychiatrist who had treated him in Colorado said Hinckley never showed one symptom of mental illness. Six weeks later, Hinckley was found not guilty by reason of insanity.

1986 ABC interviewer **BARBARA WALTERS** and TV executive **MERV ADELSON** were married in Beverly Hills, CA.

1986 500 guests witnessed **MOTLEY CRUE'S TOMMY LEE** wed actress **HEATHER LOCKLEAR**.

1989 The government of Gerneral **MANUEL NORIEGA** announced it had nullified Panama's elections which the opposition said they had won by a 3-1 margin. May 9, 1994 millionaire businessman Ernesto Perez Balladares won Panama's first general election since the U.S. invaded in 1989.

1994 Serial killer John Wayne **GACY WAS EXECUTED** by lethal injection at Stateville penitentiary in Joliet, IL. He was convicted of killing 33 young men and boys during the 1970s.

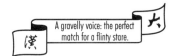

A gravelly voice: the perfect match for a flinty stare.

MAY 11

BIRTHDAYS

• **DOUG McCLURE** Actor. (Glendale, CA) In movies and TV's "Checkmate" from 1960-62 and "Out of this World." *Barbary Coast* with William Shatner and *Maverick*. Year/**Age**: 1995/**60** 1996/**61** 1997/**62**

• **MORT SAHL** Actor/comedian. (Born Morton Lyon Sahl in Canada) 1960s nightclub comic. Did a one-man show on Broadway in the fall of 1987. Year/**Age**: 1995/**68** 1996/**69** 1997/**70**

• **FOSTER BROOKS** Actor/comedian. (Louisville, KY) Best known for his drunk routines on "The Dean Martin Show." Year/**Age**: 1995/**83** 1996/**84** 1997/**85**

• **LOUIS FARRAKHAN** Muslim Activist. Year/**Age**: 1995/**62** 1996/**63** 1997/**64**

• **NATASHA RICHARDSON** Actress (London, England) Daughter of Vanessa Redgrave and Tony Richardson. Films include *Widow's Peak* and *The Comfort of Strangers*. She married actor Liam Neeson in 1994. Year/**Age**: 1995/**32** 1996/**33** 1997/**34**

• **ERIC BURDON** Singer. (England) Biggest hit with the ANIMALS: "House of the Rising Sun" in 1964 and with WAR, "Spill the Wine" in 1970. Year/**Age**: 1995/**54** 1996/**55** 1997/**56**

• **SALVADOR DALI** [dol'-lee] Surrealist artist. (1904-1989 – Spain) A nasty kid, he beat his sister, and once took a bite from a dead bat. He was so hated in his hometown, they stoned him in the streets. (Died 1-23-89.)

• **JACQUELINE COCHRAN (ODLUM)** Famous speed pilot. (1906-1980 – Pensacola, FL) Air Force colonel and cosmetics maker. First woman to fly faster than the speed of sound. Wrote her story in *Stars at Noon*. (Died 8-9-80.)

• **MARTHA QUINN** TV hostess. (Albany, NY) MTV Veejay. Year/**Age**: 1995/**36** 1996/**37** 1997/**38**

• **MARTHA GRAHAM** Dancer. (1894-1991 – Allegheny, PA) She was the primary influence on the development of the modern dance in America. (Died 4-1-91.)

• **PHIL SILVERS** Actor/comedian. (1912-1985 – Born Philip Silversmith in Brooklyn, NY) He attended school only until the age of 12, when he joined Gus Edwards' famous children's vaudeville troupe as a boy soprano. Probably best known for his character Sgt. Bilko. (Died 11-1-85.)

• **IRVING BERLIN** Composer. (1888-1989 – Born Israel Baline in Russia) "Mr. American Music." He wrote "God Bless America" for Kate Smith. He wrote *Smile and Show Your Dimple* in 1917, but it was not produced until 17 years later, then titled *Easter Parade*. In Hollywood, Berlin did the scores of *Holiday Inn* with Fred Astaire and Bing Crosby, including "Blue Skies," and "White Christmas" which he won an Oscar for. He had been presenting at the same time and opened the envelope and said, "The winner is me.." He wrote both words and music, but could only play in one key on the piano. He died at the age of 101 (9-22-89.)

• **CHANG** and **ENG BUNKER** Siamese twins. (1811-1874) They were brought to America by Robert Hunter. They were a showbiz success when they were exhibited around the world in the P.T. Barnum Circus. They married two sisters and between them sired 21 children. One drank a lot and the other stayed up late playing poker. Chang got hauled into court on an assault charge, but they couldn't send him to prison or the other would have to go, too. As they got older they fought and built separate homes. They spent 3 days of each week with one wife and 3 days with the other. What they did on the 7th day, no one knows!

FACTS FROM THE PAST

1921 In a prohibition prosecution in New York, the **POLICE DRANK THE EVIDENCE**. Saloon owner William Manning and his bartender John Riley were arrested for keeping a bottle behind the bar, containing, as it said in the police report, a reddish liquid with a whiskey smell. So the lieutenant seized the bottle as evidence. The judge said, "Let's see the whiskey." But it was gone. The lieutenant said "We all tasted it, so we'd have a good case." Case was dismissed!

1947 **B.F. GOODRICH CO.** of Akron, Ohio, announced the development of the **TUBELESS TIRE**.

1971 **STEVE DUNNING** of the Cleveland Indians became the last pitcher to hit a grand slam home run in the American League. When the designated hitter rule came to the American League, pitchers were not allowed to hit.

1973 Charges against Daniel Ellsberg for his role in the **PENTAGON PAPERS** case were dismissed by a judge who cited government misconduct.

1982 Advice columnist **ABIGAIL VAN BUREN** admitted she'd reused letters in her column without labeling them as such. The revelation followed a similar admission by Van Buren's twin sister, advice columnist Ann Landers.

1985 **CONTROVERSY** erupted when it was announced that **PRESIDENT RONALD REAGAN** would be laying a wreath at a German military cemetery during a visit to Europe.

1989 **PRESIDENT BUSH** ordered nearly 2,000 combat troops to go to Panama, saying the increase in U.S. military strength there was designed "to protect the lives of American citizens."

1992 Controversial Police Chief Daryl Gates, his officers and FBI agents arrested three men in the dramatic televised beating of truck driver, **REGINALD DENNY**. The man was nearly beaten to death during the **LOS ANGELES RIOTING**, April 29, 1992.

1992 **NERA WHITE** and **LUISA HARRIS (STEWART)** became the first women to be inducted into the Basketball Hall of Fame. (See page 148)

1994 Point Guard **ISIAH THOMAS** retired after leading the Detroit Pistons to two NBA titles during 13 years.

MAY 12

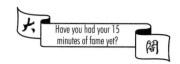

Have you had your 15 minutes of fame yet?

BIRTHDAYS

• **STEPHEN BALDWIN** Actor. (Massapequa, NY) Cody on TV's "The Young Riders." Films *Posse* and *Threesome*. Year/Age: 1995/**29** 1996/**30** 1997/**31**

• **GEORGE CARLIN** Comedian/satirist. (NYC) A former disc jockey, probably best known as the originator of the "Seven Dirty Words" routine. He was in the film *Prince of Tides*. Year/Age: 1995/**58** 1996/**59** 1997/**60**

• **STEVE WINWOOD** Singer. (England) Lead singer of THE SPENCER DAVIS GROUP, BLIND FAITH, and TRAFFIC. Recorded "Gimme Some Lovin" with Spencer Davis when he was 16. Year/Age: 1995/**47** 1996/**48** 1997/**49**

• **BRUCE BOXLEITNER** Actor. (Elgin, IL) He played Babe Ruth's teammate, Joe Dugan, in the 1992 film *The Babe*. TV series "The Scarecrow and Mrs. King" with Kate Jackson as Amanda King. He got his acting start with five lines on "The Mary Tyler Moore Show" in 1972. Year/Age: 1995/**45** 1996/**46** 1997/**47**

• **JAMES PURIFY** Singer. (Pensacola, FL) Of JAMES & BOBBY PURIFY. Biggest hit: "I'm Your Puppet" in 1966. Year/Age: 1995/**51** 1996/**52** 1997/**53**

• **FELIPE ALOU** Baseball. Oldest of the 3 Alou brothers, each of whom came up with the San Francisco Giants. Joined Montreal Expos in 1992. Year/Age: 1995/**60** 1996/**61** 1997/**62**

• **YOGI BERRA** Baseball Hall of Famer. (Born Lawrence Peter Berra in St. Louis, MO) Former NY Yankee catcher, manager, MVP 3 times, and he played in 14 World Series games. He hit the first pinch-hit home run in World Series history in 1947. Once he played 148 straight games without an error. Year/Age: 1995/**70** 1996/**71** 1997/**72**

• **KATHARINE HEPBURN** Actress. For decades, all publications have given her birthdate as Nov. 8, but in 1992 she announced that she had given the wrong date years ago and she was really born today. Year/Age: 1995/**88** 1996/**89** 1997/**90**

• **SUSAN HAMPSHIRE** Actress. (England) Won Emmys for *The Forsyte Saga*, *The First Churchills*, and *Vanity Fair*. Year/Age: 1995/**53** 1996/**54** 1997/**55**

• **KIM FIELDS** Actress. (Los Angeles, CA) Tootie on "The Facts of Life" and in "Living Single" TV sitcom, and "Slim Fast" commercials. Year/Age: 1995/**26** 1996/**27** 1997/**28**

• **BURT BACHARACH** Composer. (Kansas City, MO) With Hal David, he wrote "Raindrops Keep Falling on My Head," "Alfie," "That's What Friends Are For," and many others. He is responsible for many of DIONNE WARWICK's hit songs. Once was married to actress Angie Dickinson. Now married to Carole Bayer Sager. Year/Age: 1995/**66** 1996/**67** 1997/**68**

• **EMILIO ESTEVEZ** Actor. (New York, NY) Films include: *Men at Work*, *Young Guns*, *Freejack*, *Judgement Night*, *Stakeout*, *Another Stakeout*, and *Loaded Weapon 1*. Son of Martin Sheen, brother of Charlie. Married Paula Abdul in 1992. Year/Age: 1995/**33** 1996/**34** 1997/**35**

• **BILLY SWAN** C&W singer. (Cape Girardeau, MO) Biggest hit: "I Can Help" in 1974. He wrote a hit for CLYDE McPHATTER, "Lover Please." Year/Age: 1995/**53** 1996/**54** 1997/**55**

• **LOU WHITAKER** Baseball. (Brooklyn, NY) Detroit Tiger second baseman. He scored 6 runs in the 1984 World Series. Year/Age: 1995/**38** 1996/**39** 1997/**40**

• **WILFRED HYDE-WHITE** Actor. (1903-1991 – England) Portrayed Colonel Pickering in the 1964 musical film, *My Fair Lady*. and the movie *You Only Live Twice*. (Died 5-6-91.)

• **EDWARD LEAR** Poet. (1812-1888 – England) Best known for his limericks. This is LIMERICK DAY in his honor. A limerick has been described as the only "fixed verse form" indigenous to the English language. (Died 1-29-1888.)

• **SOCRATES** Philosopher. (470-399 B.C.) He was condemned to death by Athens for atheism. (Died 5-7-399 B.C.)

FACTS FROM THE PAST

1839 A Shawnee Indian uttered a curse on the **GREAT WHITE FATHER** for violating Indian treaties, beginning the curious cycle of American presidential deaths. Every Chief Exec. elected or re-elected at 20-year cycles has died in office from 1840-1960. When Nancy Reagan heard about this, she started consulting astrologers. Ronald Reagan survived his terms and the cycle was broken.

1937 Britain's **KING GEORGE VI** was crowned at Westminster Abbey in London, along with his consort, Queen Elizabeth. The coronation was the **FIRST RADIO BROADCAST HEARD ROUND-THE-WORLD**.

1955 Sam "Toothpick" Jones of the Chicago Cubs got a no-hit, no-run game the hard way. In the 9th inning against Pittsburgh, he walked the bases full and proceeded to strike out the next three batters for a 4-0 victory. It was the first no-hitter at Wrigley Field in 38 years.

1960 **FRANK SINATRA AND ELVIS PRESLEY** exchanged hits when they appeared on the same TV special. Sinatra sang "Love Me Tender" and Elvis sang "Witchcraft."

1963 **BOB DYLAN**, upset because he would not be allowed to perform "Talking John Birch Society" walked out on Ed Sullivan.

1964 **BARBRA STREISAND** won her first two Grammys for *The Barbra Streisand Album*. **QUINCY JONES** won his first, too.

1980 Maxie Anderson and his son, Chris, were the **FIRST** to make a **NON-STOP BALLOON FLIGHT** across North America in a 75-foot-high helium-filled balloon, *The Kitty Hawk*. They went from San Francisco to Quebec in 4 days, 2,200 miles.

1985 Accused-rapist **GARY DOTSON** was freed after 6 years in prison after **CATHLEEN CROWELL WEBB** admitted that she lied and he was innocent.

1994 **JOHN SMITH**, leader of Britain's Opposition's Labor Party died in London after suffering a heart attack.

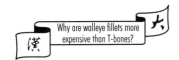

Why are walleye fillets more expensive than T-bones?

MAY 13

BIRTHDAYS

- **STEVIE WONDER** Composer/singer. (Born Steveland Morris Hardaway in Saginaw, MI) Blind from birth, he had his first hit at age 13 called "Fingertips Part 2." He received an Oscar in 1985 for "I Just Called to Say I Love You." Year/**Age:** 1995/**45** 1996/**46** 1997/**47**

- **BEATRICE "BEA" ARTHUR** Actress. (Born Bernice Frankel in NYC) "Maude" and "Golden Girls." Bea won a Tony Award for the play *Mame.* Year/**Age:** 1995/**69** 1996/**70** 1997/**71**

- **PETER GABRIEL**.Singer. (London, England) Lead singer of GENESIS from 1966-75. Phil Collins replaced him. Peter's biggest hit: "Sledgehammer" in 1986. He scored the film *Last Temptation of Christ.* Year/**Age:** 1995/**45** 1996/**46** 1997/**47**

- **DUSTY RHODES** Baseball. Hit .341 as a part-timer for the Giants in 1954; kept on hitting in the World Series. Year/**Age:** 1995/**68** 1996/**69** 1997/**70**

- **DANNY KLEIN** Bassist. (NYC) Member of the J. GEILS BAND. 1982 hit: "Centerfold." Year/**Age:** 1995/**49** 1996/**50** 1997/**51**

- **JULIANNE PHILLIPS** Actress. Frankie on TV's "Sisters." Once married to Bruce Springsteen. Year/**Age:** 1995/**33** 1996/**34** 1997/**35**

- **MARSHALL FIELD V** Tycoon. (Charlottesville, VA) The grandson of department store/publishing founder. In 1969 he became the youngest (28) major newspaper publisher in the United States when he took over the *Chicago Sun Times* and the *Daily News.* Year/**Age:** 1995/**54** 1996/**55** 1997/**56**

- **HARVEY KEITEL** Actor. (Brooklyn, NY) Films include *Alice Doesn't Live Here Anymore, Taxi Dirver, Bugsy,* and *The Piano.* Year/**Age:** 1995/**56** 1996/**57** 1997/**58**

- **DENNIS RODHAM** NBA star sometimes referred to as basketball's "Bad Boy." Year/**Age:** 1995/34 1996/**35** 1997/**36**

- **MARY WELLS** Singer. (1943-1992 – Detroit, MI) Biggest record: "My Guy" in 1964. Larynx cancer left her voiceless and without medical insurance. A group of recording stars raised money for her care. (Died 7-26-92.)

- **GOTTLIEB DAIMLER** Inventor. (1834-1900 – Germany) He invented the world's first motorcycle in 1884. His original single-cylinder, four-stroke motor bike was later developed into the Daimler motor car. A year later he launched the first gasoline-driven motorboat. Commercial production began in 1890. A car later created in the Daimler factory was named for his daughter, Mercedes. (Died 3-6-1900.)

- **RICHIE VALENS** Singer. (1941-1959 – Born Richard Valenzuela in Pacoima, CA) Latin rock singer, songwriter, guitarist was killed in a plane crash that also took the lives of Buddy Holly and the Big Bopper. Biggest hits: "Donna," about his high school sweetheart Donna Ludwig, and "La Bamba." *La Bamba* is the title of his film bio released in 1987. (Died 2-3-59.)

- **JOE LOUIS** Boxer. (1914-1981 – Born Joe Louis Barrow in Lafayette, AL) Heavyweight boxing champ from 1937-49. His knock-out of Max Schmeling at Yankee Stadium on June 22, 1938, is listed as one of the most dramatic sporting events in history. "The Brown Bomber" is buried at Arlington National Cemetery, by presidential waiver—the 39th exception ever to the rules for burial there. The first boxer honored with his own stamp. He retired undefeated (Died 4-12-81.)

- **SIR ARTHUR SULLIVAN** Composer. (1842-1900 – England) He wrote 14 operas and was Sir William Gilbert's partner. Their works included *The Pirates of Penzance.* (Died 11-22-1900.)

FACTS FROM THE PAST

1639 The **TABLE KNIFE WAS CREATED** by Cardinal Richelieu in France. Until this time, daggers were used to cut meat, as well as to pick one's teeth. Richelieu had the points rounded off all of the knives to be used at his table.

1917 Three peasant children near Fatima, Portugal, reported a **VISION OF THE VIRGIN MARY.**

1940 In his first speech as prime minister of Britain, **WINSTON CHURCHILL** told the House of Commons: "I have nothing to offer but blood, toil, tears, and sweat."

1954 President Dwight D. Eisenhower signed into law the **ST. LAWRENCE SEAWAY DEVELOPMENT ACT.**

1971 Grace Slick of **JEFFERSON AIRPLANE** smashed her car into a wall making a scheduled recording session impossible.

1981 **POPE JOHN PAUL II** was shot and seriously wounded in St. Peter's Square by Turkish assailant Mehmet Ali Agca [meh'-met ah'-lee ah'-juh]. The 24-year-old terrorist was arrested and convicted. He was a member of the Turkish "Gray Wolves" right-wing extremist group.

1985 Rock star **BRUCE SPRINGSTEEN** married actress Julianne Phillips at Lake Oswego, OR, in a secret ceremony at 12:15 a.m. on her birthday. He met her backstage at a Los Angeles concert six months earlier. They were divorced in 1988.

1988 Guglielmo Marconi, Benny Goodman, Edward R. Murrow, Orson Welles, Alan Freed, and 13 others were inducted into the newly created **RADIO HALL OF FAME.**

1991 **NOLAN RYAN** pitched his seventh no-hitter, a record, in a 3-0 win over Toronto. He struck out 16 batters.

1992 **ASTRONAUTS** Pierre Thuot, Tom Akers, and Richard Hieb made history when they **GRABBED A WAYWARD 4-TON SATELLITE.** Also, on board the shuttle *Endeavor* was the first mother to walk in space, **KATHY THORNTON.**

MAY 14

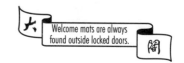
Welcome mats are always found outside locked doors.

BIRTHDAYS

- **FAB MORAN** Entertainer. (France) MILLI VANILLI with Rob Pilatus. Their biggest hit: "Blame It on the Rain." When it was discovered that they didn't sing on their records, their 1989 Grammy Award was taken away from them. Year/**Age**: 1995/**29** 1996/**30** 1997/**31**

- **GENE CORNISH** Singer. (Ottawa, Canada) With the YOUNG RASCALS. Their biggest hit: "People Gotta Be Free" in 1968. They were originally called the RASCALS but had to add "Young" to their name because the harmonica Rascals threatened to sue them. Their music has been heard in the films: *Platoon*, *Legal Eagles,* and *The Big Chill*. Year/**Age**: 1995/**51** 1996/**52** 1997/**53**

- **GEORGE LUCAS** Movie producer/director. (Modesto, CA) He directed *Star Wars* and *Indiana Jones*. TV's "Young Indiana Jones Chronicles." Year/**Age**: 1995/**51** 1996/**52** 1997/**53**

- **JACK BRUCE** Bass player. (Scotland) With the British supergroup CREAM. Biggest hit: "Sunshine of Your Love" in 1968. Year/**Age**: 1995/**52** 1996/**53** 1997/**54**

- **DAVID BYRNE** Rock artist. (Scotland) With group TALKING HEADS. Biggest hit: "Burning Down the House." Year/**Age**: 1995/**43** 1996/**44** 1997/**45**

- **SEASON HUBLEY** Actress. TV soap "Love of Life," ran for 28 years from 1951-1980. Year/**Age**: 1995/**44** 1996/**45** 1997/**46**

- **SHANICE WILSON** Singer. She had a #1 R&B hit: "I Love Your Smile." Year/**Age**: 1995/**22** 1996/**23** 1997/**24**

- **TONY PEREZ** Baseball. Part of the "Big Red Machine" who helped Cincinnati to a couple of pennants in the '70s. Fired as manager of Reds after only 44 games of the 1993 season. Year/**Age**: 1995/**53** 1996/**54** 1997/**55**

- **TROY SHONDELL** Singer. (Ft. Wayne, IN) Biggest hit: "This Time" in 1961. Year/**Age**: 1995/**51** 1996/**52** 1997/**53**

- **JOSE MARTINEZ** Baseball player. (Nicaragua) He pitched a perfect game for the Montreal Expos in 1991. Year/**Age**: 1995/**40** 1996/**41** 1997/**42**

- **DANIEL WILLIAM WOOD** Singer/dancer. (Boston, MA) NEW KIDS ON THE BLOCK hits include: "Hangin' Tough" and "This One's for the Children." Year/**Age**: 1995/**26** 1996/**27** 1997/**28**

- **BOBBY DARIN** Entertainer. (1936-1973 – Born Robert Cassotto in NYC) Became a teen idol in the late '50s and early '60s with hits: "Splish Splash" and "Mack the Knife." He was married to actress Sandra Dee. He was nominated for an Academy Award in the movie *Captain Newman, M.D.* (Died of heart failure, which occurred during his second open-heart surgery on 12-20-73.)

- **RICHARD DEACON** Character actor. (1920-1984) He played Mel Cooley on the "Dick Van Dyke Show," was Sheriff Masters on "B.J. and the Bear" and Lumpy's dad on "Leave it to Beaver."

- **GABRIEL FAHRENHEIT** Inventor. (1686-1736 – Germany) He invented the mercury thermometer. (Died 9-16-1736.)

FACTS FROM THE PAST

1607 Captains **JOHN SMITH** and **CHRISTOPHER NEWPORT** established the first permanent English settlement in the future United States, at Jamestown, VA.

1643 **LOUIS THE XIV** became the King of France at age 4 upon the death of his father, Louis the XIII.

1796 English physician **EDWARD JENNER** tested the first vaccination against **SMALLPOX**, injecting infected cells into an 8-year-old boy.

1829 **CHARLES CHARLESWORTH** died of old age at age 7. He appeared to be a happy and healthy child at birth but by age 4 he began growing whiskers and body hair and within the next 3 years his veins stood out like those of a man of 70 and he reached sexual maturity. His hair turned white, his skin wrinkled like a prune's and his posture became stooped. At age 7 he died.

1856 The **FIRST CAMELS** were imported commercially in the the U.S., arriving in Texas. Secretary of War Jefferson Davis wanted to test them as pack animals, but abandoned the idea because of their bad tempers and smell. Some escaped, turned wild, scaring the Indians.

1878 **VASELINE** became the registered trademark for petroleum jelly. It was developed by English-born chemist **ROBERT CHESEBROUGH** in Pennsylvania.

1904 The **OLYMPICS** were held in the U.S. for the first time at St. Louis, MO. They did not return to America for nearly 30 years. Eddie Tolan won the "gold" in 100 meters.

1970 **CROSBY, STILLS, NASH, AND YOUNG** announced their breakup. The band regrouped several times afterward without Neil Young.

1976 Ex-YARDBIRDS vocalist **KEITH RELF** was electrocuted in his London home while tuning his guitar in the bathtub.

1980 President Jimmy Carter inaugurated the **DEPARTMENT OF HEALTH AND HUMAN SERVICES**, the successor to the Department of Health, Education and Welfare, which was re-formed to create a separate education department.

1987 Captain Furillo (**DANIEL J. TRAVANTI**) turned in his gun and his badge after 146 episodes, of "**HILL STREET BLUES.**" The series ceased production with a program entitled "It Ain't Over Until It's Over."

1992 CEO **LEE IACOCCA** stepped down as head of the Chrysler Corporation.

1994 **PATTI DAVIS**, daughter of **RONALD AND NANCY REAGAN**, announced that she was proud of her nude shots in the upcoming July issue of "Playboy" magazine. she said, "At 41, I look better than I did at 21."

MAY 15

BIRTHDAYS

• **LENNY WELCH** Singer. (Asbury Park, NJ) Biggest hit: "Since I Fell For You" in 1963. Year/**Age**: 1995/**57** 1996/**58** 1997/**59**

• **TRINI LOPEZ** Entertainer. (Born Trinidad Lopez III in Dallas, TX) Biggest hit: "If I Had a Hammer" in 1963. Frank Sinatra saw him appearing at PJ's Nightclub in Los Angeles and signed him to his label to start his career. Year/**Age**: 1995/**58** 1996/**59** 1996/**60**

• **KEN VENTURI** Golfer. Year/**Age**: 1995/**64** 1996/**65** 1997/**66**

• **RICHARD AVEDON** Photographer. (NYC) Year/**Age**: 1995/**72** 1996/**73** 1997/**74**

• **JOSEPH COTTEN** Actor. (1905-1994, Petersburg, VA) He made his screen debut in *Citizen Kane*, and his broadway debut in *The PhiladelphiaStory*. Other films included *Duel in the Sun* and *Hush Hush Sweet Charlotte*. (Died 2-6-94.)

• **EDDY ARNOLD** C&W singer. (Born Richard Edward Arnold near Henderson, TN) The "Tennessee Plowboy" was elected to the Country Music Hall of Fame in 1966. He recorded over 145 charted country records. Biggest hit: "Make the World Go Away" in 1965. In addition to making records, Eddy helped develop the luxury Nashville suburb of Brentwood. Year/**Age**: 1995/**77** 1996/**78** 1997/**79**

• **LAINIE KAZAN** Entertainer/actress. (Born Lainie Levine in NYC) She was working at the famous Mr. Kelly's Nightclub in Chicago when it burned down. Appeared in *Moonstruck* with Cher and *Beaches*. Year/**Age**: 1995/**55** 1996/**56** 1997/**57**

• **BRIAN ENO** Singer/songwriter. Worked with David Bowie. Year/**Age**: 1995/**47** 1996/**48** 1997/**49**

• **DON NELSON** Basketball coach. (Muskegon, MI) Golden State Warriors. Year/**Age**: 1995/**55** 1996/**56** 1997/**57**

• **ANNA MARIE ALBERGHETTI** Actress/singer. (Italy) Starred in films as a teenager, appeared on the "Arthur Godfrey Show." She won a Tony in 1962 for *Carnival*, and had her own salad dressing. Year/**Age**: 1995/**59** 1996/**60** 1997/**61**

• **GEORGE BRETT** Baseball. (Glendale, WV) Kansas City Royals 3rd baseman, he led the American League in batting in 1976 and 1980 and was MVP in 1980. In 1992 he became the 18th player to get 3,000 hits, over 300 homers and 200 steals Retired 10-3-93. Year/**Age**: 1995/**42** 1996/**43** 1997/**44**

• **CONSTANCE CUMMINGS** Actress. (Born Constance Halverstadt in Seattle, WA) Appeared in *Blithe Spirit* and *Busman's Honeymoon*. Won a Tony award for *Wings*. Year/**Age**: 1995/**85** 1996/**86** 1997/**87**

• **LEE HORSLEY** Actor. (Muleshoe, TX) Star of "Matt Houston" TV crime show 1982-1985 and CBS series, "Bodies of Evidence" in 1992. He played "Ethan Allen Cord" in "Guns of Paradise" TV series, 1988-91. Year/**Age**: 1995/**40** 1996/**41** 1997/**42**

• **JAMES MASON** Actor. (1909-1984 – England) He received Oscar nominations in 1954 for *A Star is Born* and 1966 for *Georgy Girl* and *The Verdict* in 1982. (Died 7-27-84.)

FACTS FROM THE PAST

1536 Anne Boleyn and her brother, Lord Rochford, were found guilty of **ADULTERY AND INCEST IN ENGLAND.** Lord Rochford was executed May 17th and Anne was beheaded May 19th.

1602 **CAPE COD WAS DISCOVERED** by the English navigator **BARTHOLOMEW GOSNOLD.**

1800 **KING GEORGE III** escaped assassination twice. He was reviewing troops at London's Hyde Park and the man next to him was shot by a bullet meant for him. That evening George went to the theater and two bullets whizzed past his head and lodged in the woodwork. He was not shaken and told them to continue with the performance . . . but then he fell asleep.

1930 **ELLEN CHURCH,** the **FIRST AIRLINE STEWARDESS,** went on duty aboard a United Airlines flight between San Francisco and Cheyenne, WY. She served chicken, fruit salad, and rolls. After the flight, she swept out the plane, filled it with fuel and helped push it back out on the runway. With the plane short of seats, she sat on mailbags.

1941 **JOE DIMAGGIO** began his record 56-game hitting streak by singling off Chicago White Sox pitcher Ed Smith in a game played at Yankee Stadium. The Yankees lost, 13-1.

1970 In the early hours, **PHILLIP LAFAYETTE GIBBS** and **JAMES EARL GREEN,** two black students at Jackson State University in Mississippi, were killed when police opened fire during student protests near a women's dormitory.

1970 **PRESIDENT NIXON** appointed America's first two female generals: Colonels Elizabeth Hoisington and Anna Mae Mays.

1972 Democratic presidential candidate **GEORGE C. WALLACE** was shot and left paralyzed while campaigning in Laurel, Maryland. **ARTHUR BREMER** was convicted of the attempted assassination.

1974 Bass player Bill Wyman became the **FIRST ROLLING STONE** to have a **SOLO LP** with the release of "Monkey Grip."

1980 The West German Olympic Committee voted not to send a team to the **MOSCOW OLYMPICS,** in compliance with President Jimmy Carter's call for an international boycott.

1988 **MICHAEL JACKSON** moon-walked to the top of the New York Times best-sellers list with Autobiography *Moonwalker*.

1988 A musical version of **STEPHEN KING**'s novel, **CARRIE,** closed in New York after a short run. It lost about eight million dollars, making it one of the most expensive flops in Broadway history.

1994 British golfer **LAURA DAVIES** won the McDonald's LPGA Championship in Wilmington, DE. to capture her fourth victory of the year.

MAY 16

When a rock star dies, it's always the lead story.

BIRTHDAYS

- **LENNY KRAVITZ** Singer. Once married to Lisa Bonet. Year/Age: 1995/31 1996/32 1997/33

- **JOHN SALLEY** Basketball. Year/Age: 1995/31 1996/32 1997/33

- **THURMAN THOMAS** Football. Year/Age: 1995/29 1996/30 1997/31

- **GABRIELA SABATINI** Tennis pro. (Buenos Aires) Year/Age: 1995/25 1996/26 1997/27

- **RICHARD PAGE** Singer. (Los Angeles, CA) MR. MISTER. Biggest hit: "Broken Wings." Year/Age: 1995/40 1996/41 1997/42

- **DEBRA WINGER** Actress. (Cleveland, OH) Best actress Oscar nominations for *An Officer and a Gentleman* and *Terms of Endearment*. Also appeared in *Shadowlands, Dangerous Woman* (she took the part because she liked the wardrobe), and *Leap of Faith.* Year/Age: 1995/40 1996/41 1997/42

- **PIERCE BROSNAN** Actor. (Ireland) Co-star of "Remington Steele" as Steele in the crime show and the movies *The Lawn Mower Man* and *Mrs. Doubtfire*. In 1994 he was chosen to be the new James Bond. Year/Age: 1995/43 1996/44 1997/45

- **OLGA KORBUT** Olympic gymnast star. (Russia) Won 3 gold medals in 1972. She is suffering from radiation poisoning from the 1986 Chernobyl nuclear incident. Year/Age: 1995/40 1996/41 1997/42

- **TRACEY GOLD** Actress. (NYC) TV's "Growing Pains" as sister, Carol. She suffers from anorexia. Year/Age: 1995/26 1996/27 1997/28

- **YANNICK NOAH** Tennis star. (Sedan, France) Year/Age: 1995/34 1996/35 1997/36

- **TORI SPELLING** Actress. Appears on TV's "Beverly Hills 90210." as "Donna." Her father is film producer Aaron Spelling. She was in the film *The Last Action Hero*. Year/Age: 1995/22 1996/23 1997/24

- **MARE WINNINGHAM** Actress. (Phoenix, AZ) In the miniseries *The Thornbirds*. Films: *St. Elmo's Fire, Turner and Hooch*, and *Earp* Year/Age: 1995/36 1996/37 1997/38

- **RALPH TRESVANT** Singer. Formerly of NEW EDITION. Hits include: "Sensitivity." Year/Age: 1995/27 1996/28 1997/29

- **JANET JACKSON** Singer/Actress. (Gary, IN) Debuted at age 7 with her brothers. Played little Penny Gordon, a victim of child abuse on TV's "Good Times." Hits include: "That's The Way Love Goes," "Control," "Rhythm Nation," "Escapade," and "Miss You Much." In TV's "Different Strokes" as Charlene DuPrey and "Fame." Film *Poetic Justice*. Year/Age: 1995/29 1996/30 1997/31

- **BILLY MARTIN** Controversial baseball manager. (1928-1989 – Born Alfred Manual Pesano in Berkeley, CA) He led the NY Yankees to a World Series title in 1977.(Died in auto crash 12-25-89.)

- **LIBERACE** Entertainer. (1919-1987 – Born Wladziu Valentino Liberace in West Allis, WI) He was a flamboyant pianist known for extravagant showmanship, costumes, and giant candelabra. AIDS-related disease was blamed for his death. (Died 2-4-87.)

- **HENRY FONDA** Actor. (1905-1982 – Grand Island, MI) Won an Oscar for best actor in 1981 for On *Golden Pond*. The only other film he was ever nominated for was *Grapes of Wrath* in 1940, which was the year that Jimmy Stewart won the Oscar for *The Philadelphia Story*. (Died 8-12-82.)

FACTS FROM THE PAST

1770   It was wedding bells for 17-year-old **MARIE ANTOINETTE** and the future King of France, 15-year-old **LOUIS XVI**.

1903   **GEORGE WYMAN** of San Francisco became the **FIRST PERSON TO CROSS AMERICA IN A MOTORIZED VEHICLE**: a 1.5 h.p. California motorcycle. Most lawn mowers have more power than that.

1929   The **ACADEMY OF MOTION PICTURE ARTS & SCIENCES** awarded its first Oscars to Janet Gaynor, best actress in *Seventh Heaven* and Emil Jannings, best actor in *The Way of All Flesh*. The movie *Wings* won best picture.

1970   **MARTY BALIN** of the JEFFERSON AIRPLANE and two others were arrested for possession of marijuana and contributing to the delinquency of minors in Bloomington, MN. They were taken into custody after a party involving teenaged girls. Balin's sentence of a year's hard labor was reduced on appeal to a $100 fine.

1980   **DR. GEORGE NICKOPOULAS,** Elvis Presley's personal physician and close friend, was indicted by the Shelby Country Grand Jury in Memphis, TN, on 14 counts of **ILLEGALLY PRESCRIBING DRUGS** for Elvis, Jerry Lee Lewis, and nine others. He was reprimanded and barred from practice.

1986   Country singer **JOHNNY PAYCHECK** was found guilty of shooting and wounding a man after an argument in a bar in Hillsboro, OH. Sentenced to $9^{1}/_{2}$ years in prison, he was released in 1991.

1988   Surgeon General **C. EVERETT KOOP** released a report declaring that **NICOTINE** was addictive in ways similar to heroin and cocaine.

1989   During his visit to Beijing, **SOVIET PRESIDENT MIKHAIL S. GORBACHEV** met with Chinese leader **DENG XIAO PING**, formally ending a 30-year rift between the two communist powers.

1991   **QUEEN ELIZABETH** II became the first British monarch to address the U.S. Congress.

1994   Police in Coral Gables, FL arrested former tennis star **JENNIFER CAPRIATI** after finding a small bag of marijuana in her hotel room. A friend said she used a variety of drugs. Two days later she entered an addiction treatment center in Miami Beach.

Many country folk still don't lock their doors at night.

MAY 17

BIRTHDAYS

- **BILL BRUFORD** Drummer. (England) With YES. Biggest hit: "Owner of a Lonely Heart." Year/Age: 1995/45 1996/46 1997/47
- **JORDAN NATHANIEL MARCEL KNIGHT** Singer/dancer. (Worcester, MA) Hits with NEW KIDS ON THE BLOCK (now known as NKOTB) include: "You Got It (The Right Stuff)," "Step By Step," and "If You Go Away." Brother Jonathan is also a member of the group. Year/Age: 1995/25 1996/26 1997/27
- **DENNIS HOPPER** Actor. (Dodge City, KS) He appeared in *Easy Rider*, the film which helped make Jack Nicholson a star. He was nominated for best supporting actor in *Hoosiers* in 1987. Films *Flashback, Super Mario Bros., Speed, Blue Velvet,* and *True Romance.* Directed *Chasers.* Appears in Nike ads. Year/Age: 1995/59 1996/60 1997/61
- **MAUREEN O'SULLIVAN** Actress. (Ireland) Was Tarzan's most famous Jane, appeared in *Hannah and Her Sisters* with her daughter Mia Farrow. Year/Age: 1995/84 1996/85 1997/86
- **BILL PAXTON** Actor. Film *True Lies* with Arnold Schwartzenegger. Year/Age: 1995/40 1996/41 1997/42
- **SUGAR RAY LEONARD** Boxing champ. (Born Ray Charles Leonard in Wilmington, NC) Compiled 145-5 record as an amateur. Won Junior Welterweight gold medal in the 1976 Olympics. Diet Coke commercials. Year/Age: 1995/39 1996/40 1997/41

- **BOB SAGET** Actor. (Philadelphia, PA) Danny Tanner on TV sitcom "Full House" and host of "America's Funniest Home Videos." Year/Age: 1995/39 1996/40 1997/41
- **ENYA** Singer. Two hit albums: "Shepard's Moon" and "Watermark." Her sister also belongs to a new age group called "Clannad" Year/Age: 1995/34 1996/35 1997/36.
- **KATHLEEN SULLIVAN** TV journalist. (Pasadena, CA) Anchored "ABC World News This Morning." She was the first woman anchor hired by CNN. She reported the Sarajevo Olympics for ABC. Weight Watchers commercials. Year/Age: 1995/41 1996/42 1997/43
- **EARL MORRALL** Football vet. (Muskegon, MI) Year/Age: 1995/61 1996/62 1997/63
- **AYATOLLAH KHOMEINI** Iranian leader. (1900-1989 – Born Ruhollah Musawi in Persia) A long-time U.S. problem. He condoned the seizure of 52 U.S. Embassy hostages in Teheran, waged war on Iraq and blessed the executions of tens of thousands of Iranians. During his funeral procession, his body fell out of the casket. (Died 6-3-89.)
- **CAROLINE OF BRUNSWICK** Queen. (1768-1821) Strange Queen of England, married to King George IV, her cousin. Once she appeared topless at a ball in Geneva. At a hunting party, she wore a pumpkin on her head. The "mad princess" had a couple of illegitimate children. Her marriage to the king was dissolved. (Died 8-7-1821.)

FACTS FROM THE PAST

1875 The **FIRST KENTUCKY DERBY** was run at Louisville, KY. The winner, Aristides, covered the $1\frac{1}{4}$ mile in about 2.5 minutes and won $2,800. The race was created by Col. **M. LEWIS CLARK**, of Louisville, KY, who 3 years earlier had been impressed by watching the Epsom Downs Derby in England. With a group of friends, Clark acquired a parcel of land in Kentucky from the Churchill brothers, laid out the track, constructed a grandstand. He named it Churchill Downs.

1939 The **FIRST SPORTS EVENT WAS TELEVISED** by NBC – a college basketball game between Columbia and Princeton. **BILL STERN** was the announcer. They used only one camera on the program.

1946 President **HARRY S. TRUMAN** seized control of the nation's railroads, delaying a threatened strike by engineers and trainmen.

1954 The U.S. Supreme Court issued its landmark **BROWN VS. THE BOARD OF EDUCATION** of Topeka, Kansas, ruling. The court unanimously reversed its 1896 "Separate but Equal" **PLESSY VS. FERGUSON** decision, declaring that racially segregated public schools were inherently unequal. This was depicted in a 1991 TV movie starring **SIDNEY POITIER.**

1969 **CHICAGO** released the group's **FIRST ALBUM**: *Chicago Transit Authority.* The band was sued by the real Chicago Transit Authority and had to shorten their name to **CHICAGO.** They were the only group to make their record debut with a double album.

1973 The number one U.S. record dealt with public nudity in the **RAY STEVENS'** classic, "The Streak."

1975 **ELTON JOHN** was awarded a platinum record for sales of a million copies of his album, *Captain Fantastic and The Brown Dirt Cowboy.* It was the first album in recording history to sell a **MILLION COPIES ON ITS DAY OF RELEASE.**

1978 For the **FIRST TIME, WOMEN** were included in the White House Honor Guard as President **JIMMY CARTER** welcomed Zambian President Kenneth Kaunda.

1980 **KISS DRUMMER PETER CRISS**—the one who wore the catlike makeup—left the heavy-metal quartet for a solo career.

1984 A pitcher struck out 4 batters in one inning in a game against the Chicago Cubs. With two out, Cincinnati pitcher **MARIO SOTO** threw strike three, but the catcher missed the ball and the batter got on base, so Soto had to strike out another batter. Seventeen different pitchers share this record.

1987 President **SADDAM HUSSEIN** of Iraq apologized after two Iraqi missiles struck the *USS Stark* in the Persian Gulf, killing 37 sailors.

1994 Champion race car driver **AL UNSER, SR.** announced that he was retiring. He won the Indy 500 4 times, was a 3-time Indy Car National Champ and became the first driver to race against his son at Indianapolis in 1983.

MAY 18

Is a Cape Cod also a bungalow?

BIRTHDAYS

• **JOE BONSALL** Singer. (Philadelphia, PA) Sings tenor with the OAK RIDGE BOYS. Biggest hit: "Elvira" in 1981. Year/**Age:** 1995/**47** 1996/**48** 1997/**49**

• **MARTIKA** Singer/actress. (Born Marta Marrero in Whittier, CA) Biggest hit: "Toy Soldiers" in 1989. In the movie *Annie*. Year/**Age:** 1995/**26** 1996/**27** 1997/**28**

• **RODNEY DILLARD** Musician. (Ozarks, MO) Of the bluegrass group, the DILLARDS. Year/**Age:** 1995/**53** 1996/**54** 1997/**55**

• **PERRY COMO** Entertainer. (Born Pierino Roland Como in Canonsburg, PA) Biggest hit: "Round and Round" in 1957. In 1976, he received his 15th gold record for "And I Love You So." He and his childhood sweetheart, Roselle Belline, have been married since 1933. Year/**Age:** 1995/**83** 1996/**84** 1997/**85**

• **JAMES STEPHENS** Actor. (Mt. Kisco, NY) *Paper Chase*. On TV in "Father Dowling Mysteries." Year/**Age:** 1995/**44** 1996/**45** 1997/**46**

• **GEORGE STRAIT** C&W singer. (Pearsall, TX) He taught himself how to play guitar. One of his biggest hits: "Fool Hearted Memory" in 1982, from the film *The Soldier*. Year/**Age:** 1995/**43** 1996/**44** 1997/**45**

• **BILL MACY** Actor. (Revere, MA) He played Bea Arthur's husband, Walter, on the TV series "Maude." At one time, he was a cabdriver. In the film *Nothing In Common*. Year/**Age:** 1995/**73** 1996/**74** 1997/**75**

• **PERNELL ROBERTS** Actor. (Waycross, GA) Oldest son on the "Bonanza" TV series and Dr. John "Trapper" McIntyre on "Trapper John, M.D." Year/**Age:** 1995/**65** 1996/**66** 1997/**67**

• **ROBERT MORSE** Actor. (Newton, MA) Soap opera "Secret Storm." He won the Tony Award for *Tru* in 1990. Best known for *How to Succceed in Business Without Really Trying*. Year/**Age:** 1995/**64** 1996/**65** 1997/**66**

• **ENIGMA** Musician. (Born Michael Cretu in Romania) Biggest hit: "Sadeness Part 1" (pronounced "sadness") featuring his wife Sandra as vocalist. Year/**Age:** 1995/**38** 1996/**39** 1997/**40**

• **REGGIE JACKSON** Baseball. (Wyncote, PA) He led the American League in home runs 4 times, was MVP in 1973 and hit 5 World Series home runs in 1977. His greatest moment came in game 6 of the 1977 World Series when "Mr. October" hit 3 home runs on 3 first pitches from 3 different Dodger pitchers, the last one traveling 450 feet. Elected to the Baseball Hall of Fame in 1993. Year/**Age:** 1995/**49** 1996/**50** 1997/**51**

• **JACK WHITAKER** Sports announcer. Year/**Age:** 1995/**71** 1996/**72** 1997/**73**

• **RICK WAKEMAN** Keyboardist. (England) In the film *The Naked Gun*. With YES until 1980. Re-formed in 1983. Biggest hit: "Owner of a Lonely Heart" in 1983. Year/**Age:** 1995/**46** 1996/**47** 1997/**48**

• **BROOKS ROBINSON** Former Baltimore 3rd baseman. (Little Rock, AK) He played in 4 World Series and was MVP in 1964. Year/**Age:** 1995/**58** 1996/**59** 1997/**60**

• **POPE JOHN PAUL II** (Born Karol Wojtyla in Poland) The 264th Pope of the Roman Catholic Church, elected on Oct. 16, 1978. The first non-Italian to be elected Pope in 456 years, the first Polish Pope, and the first to write a book made into a movie: *The Jewelers Shop* with Olivia Hussey. He underwent colon surgery in 1992. Year/**Age:** 1995/**75** 1996/**76** 1997/**77**

• **DWAYNE HICKMAN** Actor is 60. (Los Angeles, CA) Played Dobie in TV series "The Many Loves of Dobie Gillis" from 1959-1963. Year/**Age:** 1995/**61** 1996/**62** 1997/**63**

• **RICHARD BROOKS** Writer/director. (1912-1992 – Philadelphia, PA) He directed *The Blackboard Jungle* and *In Cold Blood*, and he wrote *Key Largo*. Won an Academy Award for writing *Elmer Gantry*. He also wrote one of the best novels about Hollywood, *The Producer*. (Died 3-11-92.)

• **FRANK CAPRA** Movie director. (1897-1991 – Italy) He was the first to win 3 Oscars – for *It Happened One Night, Mr. Deeds Goes to Town*, and *You Can't Take It With You*. He also directed the classic *It's A Wonderful Life*. (Died 9-3-91.)

• **"BIG JOE" TURNER** R&B Singer. (1911-1985 – Kansas City, MO) Biggest hit: "Corrine Corrina" in 1956. (Died 11-24-85.)

FACTS FROM THE PAST

1831   Edwin Budding, the man who built the **FIRST LAWN MOWER**, placed his first advertisement which read: "Country gentlemen may find in this machine, an amusing and useful healthy exercise." Budding got the idea for a mower when he worked in a cloth factory in England. Much of the cloth turned out fuzzy and had to be trimmed. A little machine was developed for that purpose which consisted of revolving blades fixed between rollers. Ed made the connection between trimming cloth and trimming lawns.

1860   **ABRAHAM LINCOLN** was nominated as the Republican candidate for U.S. President at a convention in Chicago.

1912   After Detroit Tiger star outfielder **TY COBB** was suspended by the Baseball Commissioner for attacking a New York fan, the Tiger team staged the first walkout ever by baseball players.

1927   **GRAUMAN'S CHINESE THEATER OPENED** in Hollywood, CA, with the premiere of Cecil B. De Mille's *The King of Kings*, preceded by one of Grauman's live shows used to complement the feature film that followed.

1979   A federal jury in Oklahoma City awarded the three children of the late **KAREN SILKWOOD** $10.5 million dollars, finding that **KERR-McGEE CORPORATION** was negligent in its operation of a plant where Silkwood had worked. Kerr-McGee later settled the case by agreeing to pay **SILKWOOD'S HEIRS $1 MILLION** after an appeals court ordered a new trial.

1982   A jury in New York City convicted the **REVEREND SUN MYUNG MOON**, founder of the Unification Church, of tax evasion.

1989   Soviet President **MIKHAIL S. GORBACHEV** concluded his historic visit to China, which officially marked the end of a 30-year Sino-Soviet rift.

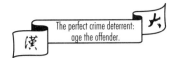

The perfect crime deterrent: age the offender.

MAY 19

BIRTHDAYS

- **BILL LAIMBEER** Basketball pro. (Boston, MA) With the Detroit Pistons. Year/**Age**: 1995/**38** 1996/**39** 1997/**40**
- **DUSTY HILL** Singer. (Houston, TX) ZZ TOP. Biggest hit: "Legs." Year/**Age**: 1995/**46** 1996/**47** 1997/**48**
- **JAMES FOX** Actor. (England) *The Russia House*. Year/**Age**: 1995/**56** 1996/**57** 1997/**58**
- **DAVID HARTMAN** Actor/TV host. (Pawtucket, RI) Former "Good Morning America" host and was featured on several primetime series: "Lucas Tanner" and "The Bold Ones." Year/**Age**: 1995/**60** 1996/**61** 1997/**62**
- **ARCHIE MANNING** Football. Year/**Age**: 1995/**46** 1996/**47** 1997/**48**
- **MICKEY NEWBURY** Singer. (Houston, TX) Biggest hit: "An American Trilogy" in 1971. Year/**Age**: 1995/**55** 1996/**56** 1997/**57**
- **PETER TOWNSHEND** Musician. (London, England) Youngest of THE WHO's original members. The group was first called HIGH NUMBERS but they though it sounded like a bingo game promotion. He was writer/composer/guitarist for the group and received rave reviews for his brilliant and ambitious rock opera, *Tommy*, which opened on Broadway April 22, 1993. Their biggest hit: "I Can See For Miles" in 1967. Year/**Age**: 1995/**50** 1996/**51** 1997/**52**
- **GRACE JONES** Singer/actress. (Jamaica) A striking, strange lady who appeared in *A View to Kill* as James Bond's menace and in *Conan the Destroyer*. Year/**Age**: 1995/**43** 1996/**44** 1997/**45**
- **RICK CERONE** Baseball. (Newark, NJ) Played with the New York Mets. Year/**Age**: 1995/**41** 1996/**42** 1997/**43**

- **TOM SCOTT** Musician/composer. He contributed to over 500 albums including ones by Michael Jackson, Paul McCartney, and Barbra Streisand. Year/**Age**: 1995/**47** 1996/**48** 1997/**49**
- **NORA EPHRON** Author. (NYC) A movie with Meryl Streep and Jack Nicholson was based on her book, a true story about her marriage to Carl Bernstein, called *Heartburn*. She is now writing magazine articles. Wrote *Sleepless In Seattle*. Year/**Age**: 1995/**54** 1996/**55** 1997/**56**
- **STEVEN FORD** Actor. Son of former President and Mrs. Gerald Ford, now a soap opera star. Films include *When Harry Met Sally*. Year/**Age**: 1995/**39** 1996/**40** 1997/**41**
- **JIM LEHRER** Broadcast journalist and novelist. (Wichita, KS) "MacNeil-Lehrer Report" on PBS. Wrote novel *Blue Hearts*. Year/**Age**: 1995/**61** 1996/**62** 1997/**63**
- **GIL McDOUGALD** Baseball. Played second, short and third for the NY Yankees from 1951-60. It was Gil's line drive that struck the great Cleveland lefty, Herb Score, in the eye. Year/**Age**: 1995/**67** 1996/**68** 1997/**69**
- **STEPHEN YOUNG** Actor. Played Ben Caldwell on *Judd for the Defense*. Year/**Age**: 1995/**56** 1996/**57** 1997/**58**
- **NELLIE MELBA** Opera singer. (1859-1931 – Australia) The "Peach Melba" dessert was created for her. (Died 2-23-31.)
- **FRANCIS "DICK" SCOBEE** Astronaut. (1939-1986 – Cle Elum, WA) Commander of the ill-fated Space Shuttle *Challenger*. He had been an astronaut since 1978 and piloted the *Challenger* in 1984. (Died 1-28-86.)
- **MALCOLM X** Civil Rights activist. (1925-1965 – Born Malcolm Little in Omaha, NE) He was assassinated as he spoke in a meeting at the Audubon Ballroom in NYC. (Died 2-21-65.)

FACTS FROM THE PAST

1536 **ANNE BOLEYN,** second wife of England's King Henry the VIII, was beheaded after being convicted of adultery and incest with her brother, Lord Rochford. Even her father testified against her. The King was upset because Anne did not produce a male heir for him. The charges were false, so just in case that failed, he was ready to have her charged with witchcraft. For one thing, she had six fingers on one hand. She had a fear of axes, so Henry brought in a great swordsman to do the job. He did, with a single blow. Henry married Jane Seymour the next day.

1911 The **FIRST AMERICAN** criminal conviction based on **FINGERPRINT EVIDENCE** happened in NYC when a small-time burglar named Crispey was sent up for 6 months because he had touched a store window. No exact fingerprint matches of two people have ever been found. Even identical twins don't have exact prints. In one case the FBI successfully lifted a print from an object 41 years after it was touched.

1926 **THOMAS EDISON** spoke on the radio for the first time. During the dinner of the National Electric Light Association in Atlantic City, NJ, he was confronted with the microphone and said, "I don't know what to say, this is the first time I ever spoke into one of these things . . . Good Night."

1974 The Philadelphia Flyers won the National Hockey League championship 4 games to 2 over Boston. They got help from Kate Smith, who sang the National Anthem at 66 games in 1974 of which the Flyers won 55 with 2 ties.

1987 The ill-fated movie *Ishtar* premiered starring **DUSTIN HOFFMAN** and **WARREN BEATTY.**

1992 **DAVE GAUDER,** 224 pounds, from England, pulled a 196-ton jumbo jet three inches across the runway at Heathrow Airport in London for the world record for pulling a heavy object.

1992 Vice President **DAN QUAYLE**, while campaigning in San Francisco, talked of the "poverty of values," referring to absent fathers and unwed mothers as the cause of the Los Angeles riots. He used the unwed fictional character of "Murphy Brown" to make his point. On TV the day before, she had given birth to a son, with 38 million people watching.

1992 **STEVE YOUNG** was named the NFL's MVP, the third time in four seasons a San Francisco quarterback received the honor. Joe Montana got the other two.

1994 **JACQUELINE KENNEDY ONASSIS** died of "non-Hodgkin's lymphomia" cancer at the age of 64.

MAY 20

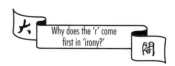

Why does the 'r' come first in 'irony?'

BIRTHDAYS

- **JANE WIEDLIN** [weed'-lyn] Guitarist. (Oconomowoc, WI) GO GO's. – Biggest hit: "Rush Hour" in 1988. Year/**Age**: 1995/**37** 1996/**38** 1997/**39**

- **MINDY COHN** Actress. (Los Angeles, CA) Played Natalie on "Facts of Life." Year/**Age**: 1995/**29** 1996/**30** 1997/**31**

- **DAVE THOMAS** Actor. "Second City" comedy writer and actor. He had his own short lived syndicated comedy show in 1990. Year/**Age**: 1995/**47** 1996/**48** 1997/**49**

- **CHER** Actress. (Born Cherilyn Sarkisian in El Centro, CA) Won an Oscar for best actress in *Moonstruck*. Biggest hit: "Half Breed" in 1973 and with Sonny Bono "I Got You Babe" in 1965. Cher was nominated for an Oscar in 1984 for her role in *Silkwood*. She was also in *The Player*. She has her own line of beauty products and exercise videos. Year/**Age**: 1995/**49** 1996/**50** 1997/**51**

- **JIMMY STEWART** Actor. (Indiana, PA) He won an Oscar in 1940 for *The Philadelphia Story* and was nominated four other times. In his 1946 film *It's a Wonderful Life* censors forced director Frank Capra to make these changes: Two uses of the word "impotent" and the word "jerk" were considered unacceptable. The phrase "I wish to God I'd never been born" changed "God" to "heaven." Year/**Age**: 1995/**87** 1996/**88** 1997/**89**

- **HAL NEWHOUSER** Baseball. (Detroit, MI) Left-handed pitcher with Detroit and Cleveland. Only pitcher in major league history to win back-to-back MVP awards. Year/**Age**: 1995/**74** 1996/**75** 1997/**76**

- **BUD GRANT** Football coach and Hall of Famer. (Superior, WI) Coached the Minnesota Vikings to 4 Super Bowls. Year/**Age**: 1995/**68** 1996/**69** 1997/**70**

- **JOE COCKER** British rock singer. (Born John Robert Cocker in England) Biggest hit: "You Are So Beautiful" in 1975. With Jennifer Warnes, his first #1 record in America: "Up Where You Belong" in 1982, theme from *An Officer and a Gentleman*. Year/**Age**: 1995/**51** 1996/**52** 1997/**53**

- **BOBBY MURCER** Retired New York Yankee. Now a broadcaster. Year/**Age**: 1995/**49** 1996/**50** 1997/**51**

- **RON REAGAN, JR.** Talk-show host. (Los Angeles, CA) The former president's wild actor-type son. Year/**Age**: 1995/**37** 1996/**38** 1997/**39**

- **STEVE GEORGE** Musician. (Los Angeles, CA) With the pop/rock quartet MR. MISTER. Biggest hit: "Broken Wings" in 1985. Year/**Age**: 1995/**40** 1996/**41** 1997/**42**

- **STAN MIKITA** Hockey star. (Czechoslovakia) He's also a golf pro and trains kids at hockey camps. Year/**Age**: 1995/**55** 1996/**56** 1997/**57**

- **BRONSON PINCHOT** Actor. (NYC) Balki on TV series "Perfect Strangers." He played a homosexual in *Beverly Hills Cop I and III* and appeared with Tom Cruise in *Risky Business*. TV's "The Trouble with Larry." Year/**Age**: 1995/**36** 1996/**37** 1997/**38**

- **GEORGE GOBEL** Comedian/actor. (1919-1991 – Chicago, IL) He appeared on the old "WLS Barn Dance" in Chicago and starred on the "George Gobel Show" 1954-1960. "Lonesome George" and "Old Alice" were the stars. Alice was played by the late Jeff Donnell. He was in the film *Harper Valley PTA*. (Died 2-25-91.)

- **VIC AMES** Singer. (1926-1978 – Malden, MA [family name Urick]) One of the AMES BROTHERS. They also had their own TV show in 1955.

FACTS FROM THE PAST

1506   **CHRISTOPHER COLUMBUS** died in poverty in Spain.

1862   President **ABRAHAM LINCOLN** signed the **HOMESTEAD ACT**, opening millions of acres of free land to settlers in the West.

1870   **JAMES SMITH** became the **FIRST BLACK CADET** at West Point.

1927   **CHARLES LINDBERGH** began his solo flight across the Atlantic to Paris, France, taking off from NY's Roosevelt Field in his monoplane, *The Spirit of St. Louis*. He landed at Le Bourget Airfield, winning a $25,000 prize and becoming the **FIRST PERSON TO FLY NONSTOP AND ALONE ACROSS THE ATLANTIC** – without a bathroom.

1932   Pilot **AMELIA EARHART** took off from Newfoundland for Ireland. When she landed at Londonderry less than 15 hours later, she became the first woman to fly the Atlantic Ocean solo.

1940   The **FIRST WORKING HELICOPTER** was publicly demonstrated by its inventor, Igor Sikorsky. Igor thought of the Vought-Sikorsky VS-300 primarily as a "rescue machine."

1954   **BILL HALEY**'s "Rock Around the Clock" was released. It didn't catch on until it appeared on the soundtrack of *Blackboard Jungle* the following year.

1958   Pianist **VAN CLIBURN** came home a winner from the Tchaikovsky Piano Competition in Moscow, and became the **FIRST MUSICIAN** ever to receive a **TICKER-TAPE PARADE** in New York.

1971   **PETER CETERA** of CHICAGO was beaten by three men at a Cubs game, apparently because they didn't like the length of his hair. Cetera lost four teeth and needed five hours of surgery.

1993   **JAY LENO** celebrated the **FINAL EPISODE OF "CHEERS"** with a live broadcast of the "Tonight Show" at the Bull and Finch, the bar that served as the model for "Cheers." Most of the cast was drunk.

1994   18-year-old **SUSHMITA SEN** was crowned Miss Universe in Manila, Philippines as the first Miss India to win.

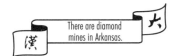

There are diamond mines in Arkansas.

MAY 21

BIRTHDAYS

- **RAYMOND BURR** Actor. (1917-1993, Born William Stacey Burr in British Columbia, Canada) He starred in two very successful TV series: "Perry Mason" and "Ironsides." He was in the film *Rear Window*. (Died 9-12-93.)

- **MR. T** Actor. (Born Lawrence Terro in Chicago, IL) At one time a bouncer at a nightclub in Chicago, he appeared on the "A-Team." On his 35th birthday, he wore a hard hat and cut down all the trees at his Lake Forest, IL, home with a chain saw, saying he was allergic to trees. Film *Freaked*. Year/**Age**: 1995/**43** 1996/**44** 1997/**45**

- **PEGGY CASS** Actress. (Brookline, MA) She was on the radio serial "The Doctors" and was a regular panelist on the syndicated version of "To Tell the Truth" and frequent guest on the "Jack Paar Tonight Show" mainly due to her gift of gab. In *Women in Prison*. Year/**Age**: 1995/**71** 1996/**72** 1997/**73**

- **DAVID GROH** Actor. (Brooklyn, NY) Played D.L. Brock on "General Hospital" and Joe Gerard, Rhoda's boyfriend and later husband on "Rhoda" with Valerie Harper. Year/**Age**: 1995/**56** 1996/**57** 1997/**58**

- **RONALD ISLEY** Singer. (Cincinnati, OH) With the R&B trio ISLEY BROTHERS, formed as a gospel group in the early '50s, later adding two more brothers and brother-in-law. Biggest hit: "It's Your Thing" in 1969. Year/**Age**: 1995/**54** 1996/**55** 1997/**56**

- **RICK JASON** Actor. TV's "Combat" from 1962-67. Year/**Age**: 1995/**69** 1996/**70** 1997/**71**

- **JUDGE REINHOLD** Actor. (Wilmington, DE) Films include: *Vice-Versa*, *Beverly Hills Cop*, *Beverly Hills Cop II*, *Daddy's Dyin'*, and *Zandalee*. Year/**Age**: 1995/**38** 1996/**39** 1997/**40**

- **HAROLD ROBBINS** Novelist. (Born Harold Rubin in NYC) He authored over 20 steamy novels, including *The Dream Merchants*, *The Carpetbaggers*, and *The Betsy*. Year/**Age**: 1995/**79** 1996/**80** 1997/**81**

- **JEFFREY L. DAHMER** Serial killer. He is serving 16 consecutive life sentences at the Columbia Correctional Institution in Portage, WI, for killing 17 young men over a period of 13 years, beginning in 1978. Year/**Age**: 1995/**34** 1996/**35** 1997/**36**

- **LEO SAYER** Singer. (Born Gerard Sayer in England) Biggest hit: "You Make Me Feel Like Dancing" in 1976. Year/**Age**: 1995/**47** 1996/**48** 1997/**49**

- **ROBERT MONTGOMERY** Actor/director/producer. (1904-1981 – Beacon, NY) He hosted "Robert Montgomery Presents" in 1956 on TV, the same year he joined the White House staff as vocal coach to President Eisenhower who felt uneasy before TV cameras. Father of actress Elizabeth of "Bewitched" (Died 9-27-81.)

- **ALEXANDER POPE** English poet. (1688-1744 – England) In 1727 he wrote: "A man should never be ashamed to own he has been in the wrong, which is but saying, in other words, that he is wiser today than he was yesterday." (Died 5-30-1744.)

- **ARMAND HAMMER** Manufacturer/financier. (1898-1990 – NYC) (Died 12-10-90.)

- **DENNIS DAY** Golden-voiced Irish singer. (1917-1988 – Born Eugene Denis McNulty in NYC) Biggest hit: "Mam'selle" in 1947. Also gained fame with "Danny Boy" and "Clancy Lowered the Boom." His best known line on the Jack Benny radio show was, "Gee, Mr. Benny!" (Died 6-22-88.)

FACTS FROM THE PAST

1922 ROLLIN KIRBY won the Pulitzer Prize for his cartoon "On the Road to Moscow," the first cartoon to receive the prize.

1924 14-year-old **BOBBY FRANKS** was murdered in a thrill-killing by two brilliant students from the University of Chicago: Nathan Leopold, Jr. and Richard Loeb. Clarence Darrow appeared in their defense.

1927 **CHARLES A. LINDBERGH** landed his *Spirit of St. Louis* near Paris, completing the **FIRST SOLO AIRPLANE FLIGHT ACROSS THE ATLANTIC OCEAN.** Lindbergh covered a distance of more than 3,600 miles in 33$\frac{1}{2}$ hours. He was awarded a $25,000 prize.

1945 **HUMPHREY BOGART** and **LAUREN BACALL** were married, and both cried during the ceremony, which took three minutes. It was one of Hollywood's most talked about marriages—likable tough guy and sultry leading lady. They were in many films together including *Key Largo*, *The Big Sleep,* and *To Have and Have Not.*

1959 The musical *Gypsy,* inspired by the life of stripper **GYPSY ROSE LEE**, opened on Broadway. **ETHEL MERMAN** played the role of Gypsy's mother, Rose.

1963 **STEVIE WONDER** recorded "Fingertips Part 2" live in Chicago at the Regal Theater during a "Motown Revue." The song became his first #1 hit at age 13.

1979 **ELTON JOHN** began a short tour of the **SOVIET UNION** in Leningrad. It was the first tour by a Western rock star allowed by the Soviets.

1980 **ENSIGN JEAN MARIE BUTLER** accepted her degree and commission from the Coast Guard Academy in New London, Connecticut, becoming the **FIRST WOMAN TO GRADUATE FROM A U.S. SERVICE ACADEMY.**

1985 **PATTI FRUSTACI** gave birth to six live babies, three of whom survived their first weeks.

1989 Yulia Sukhanova became the **FIRST MISS USSR** in a beauty pageant.

1991 The candidate for prime minister of India, **RAJIV GANDHI,** was **ASSASSINATED** in a bomb attack.

1994 Three years after serving a jail sentence for cocaine possession, **MARION BARRY** announced he would run for Mayor of D.C.

MAY 22

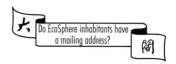
Do EcoSphere inhabitants have a mailing address?

BIRTHDAYS

- **SUSAN STRASBERG** Actress. (NYC) She made her film debut in *Picnic* in 1955. Her father, Lee Strasberg, founded the Actors Studio. Year/**Age:** 1995/**57** 1996/**58** 1997/**59**

- **BERNIE TAUPIN** Songwriter. (England) Wrote lyrics for most of Elton John's hits. Year/**Age:** 1995/**45** 1996/**46** 1997/**47**

- **RICHARD BENJAMIN** Actor/director. (NYC) His films include: *Goodbye Columbus*, *Portnoy's Complaint*, and *Sunshine Boys*. He directed *Mermaids* with Cher. He and Paula Prentiss have been married since 1960. Year/**Age:** 1995/**57** 1996/**58** 1997/**59**

- **PETER NERO** Pianist. (NYC) His biggest hit: "Theme from The Summer of '42" in 1971. Year/**Age:** 1995/**61** 1996/**62** 1997/**63**

- **MICHAEL SARRAZIN** Actor. (Canada) His films included: *The Flim Flam Man*, *They Shoot Horses, Don't They?*, and *Keeping Track*. Year/**Age:** 1995/**55** 1996/**56** 1997/**57**

- **FRANK CONVERSE** Actor. (St. Louis, MO) Played Detective Johnny Corso on "N.Y.P.D." Year/**Age:** 1995/**57** 1996/**58** 1997/**59**

- **MICHAEL CONSTANTINE** Actor. (Reading, PA) Greek/American character actor, appeared on the TV series "Room 222" for which he won an Emmy in 1970. Year/**Age:** 1995/**68** 1996/**69** 1997/**70**

- **BARBARA PARKINS** Actress. (Vancouver, BC, Canada) She was in both the original and the remake of *Peyton Place*. Year/**Age:** 1995/**53** 1996/**54** 1997/**55**

- **PAUL WINFIELD** Actor. (Los Angeles, CA) Nominated for an Oscar in *Sounder* with Cicely Tyson, for an Emmy in *Roots II* and played Judge Laren Lyttle in *Presumed Innocent*. TV's "Family Matters." Year/**Age:** 1995/**54** 1996/**55** 1997/**56**

- **LORD LAURENCE OLIVIER** Actor. (1907-1989 – England) He won an Oscar in 1948 for *Hamlet*. (the only actor to direct himself to an Oscar) Made his debut at age 15, as Katherine in *The Taming of the Shrew*. He had a stormy 21-year marriage to Vivien Leigh. Films include: *Spartacus*, *Wuthering Heights*, *Rebecca* and *Sleuth*. He played the Nazi who tortured Dustin Hoffman in *Marathon Man*. His last film was *War Requiem* in 1988. (Died 7-11-89.)

- **RICHARD WAGNER** Composer. (1813-1883 – Germany) His mother married a police clerk, but his real father was an actor who lodged with the family. Spent his early years running from creditors. He was loved by the Nazis for his anti-Semitic operas, which are very long. He wrote *Tristan*, *Isolde*, and *Lohengrin*. (Died 2-13-1883.)

- **SIR ARTHUR CONAN DOYLE** Writer. (1859-1930 – Scotland) Creator of *Sherlock Holmes*. One of Doyle's professors at the University of Edinburgh, Dr. Joseph Bell, was the model for his famous detective. Doyle was deeply interested in the subject of spiritualism. The Holmes character has been portrayed more times than any other on film, in 186 movies by 68 actors. The earliest was the 1903 film *Sherlock Holmes Baffled*. (Died 7-7-30.)

FACTS FROM THE PAST

1570 The **FIRST MODERN ATLAS**, containing 70 maps, was published in Belgium by Abraham Ortelius, a Flemish cartographer/map seller.

1807 Former **VICE PRESIDENT AARON BURR** was put on trial for treason in Richmond, VA, but was acquitted in August.

1891 The **FIRST PUBLIC MOTION PICTURE SHOW** was given. 147 members of the National Federation of Women's Clubs visiting Thomas Edison's lab viewed the film through a one-inch hole in a pine box. It showed a man bowling.

1892 A British dentist, **DR. SHEFFIELD**, invented the toothpaste tube.

1958 **JERRY LEE LEWIS** announced his marriage to his 13-year-old cousin, Myra. The resulting furor caused Lewis to be booed off stage and forced the cancellation of all but three of his concerts on his British tour. It took years for Lewis's career to recover.

1966 At age 16, **BRUCE SPRINGSTEEN** recorded his first song, "That's What You'll Get," with his band, the CASTILES.

1966 We saw the last original episode of the **"PERRY MASON" TV SERIES**, entitled "The Cast of the Final Fade-Out." It featured writer **ERLE STANLEY GARDNER**, the creator of Perry Mason, as the judge.

1967 **"MISTER ROGERS' NEIGHBORHOOD"** premiered on PBS – public television's **LONGEST-RUNNING CHILDREN'S PROGRAM.** Rogers is a Presbyterian minister from Pittsburgh.

1969 Astronauts **THOMAS STAFFORD**, **JOHN YOUNG**, and **EUGENE CERNAN**, aboard **APOLLO TEN** orbited the moon. The spacecraft's lunar module (nicknamed "Snoopy") separated from the command module (nicknamed "Charlie Brown") and flew to within nine miles of the lunar surface in a dress rehearsal for the first moon landing the following July.

1972 President **NIXON** became the **FIRST PRESIDENT TO VISIT RUSSIA**. His talks in Moscow with the Russian leaders led to the S.A.L.T. Agreement in 1977.

1977 **JANET GUTHRIE** became the first woman driver to qualify for the Indianapolis 500. She drove over 180 m.p.h.

1993 **JOHNNY CARSON**, **ED MCMAHON**, and **DOC SEVERINSEN** retired from the **"TONIGHT SHOW"** after 30 years. 55 million people watched the farewell program. He had no guests on the show, only flashbacks of previous programs.

1994 Just to prove he's not a feminist, **POPE JOHN PAUL II** issued a strong statement saying that the Roman Catholic Church won't ordain women as priests.

 Imagine life with Ann Landers...

MAY 23

BIRTHDAYS

• **JOAN COLLINS** Actress. (England) Alexis on TV soap "Dynasty." At age 46, she defied her age and played in sexually explicit scenes for the movie *The Stud* which was written by her sister, Jackie. At age 50, she appeared in the nude in *Playboy* magazine. She was married to Anthony Newley. Her autobiography is *Past Imperfect.* Year/Age: 1995/**62** 1996/**63** 1997/**64**

• **DAVID GRAHAM** Golfer. (Australia) Year/Age: 1995/**49** 1996/**50** 1997/**51**

• **MARVELOUS MARVIN HAGLER** Boxer. (Newark, NJ) Year/Age: 1995/**43** 1996/**44** 1997/**45**

• **SHELLEY WEST** C&W. (Cleveland) Daughter of singer Dottie West. Biggest hit: "Jose Cuervo." Year/Age: 1995/**37** 1996/**38** 1997/**39**

• **JOHN NEWCOMBE** Tennis legend. (Australia) Year/Age: 1995/**52** 1996/**53** 1997/**54**

• **ROBERT MOOG** Musician. (Flushing, NY) Built the first successful music synthesizer in the '60s. The first Moog album was *Switched On Bach* in 1968—best-selling classical album of all time. Year/Age: 1995/**61** 1996/**62** 1997/**63**

• **NIGEL DAVENPORT** Actor. (England) Appeared in the film *A Man for All Seasons.* Year/Age: 1995/**67** 1996/**68** 1997/**69**

• **ARTIE SHAW** Bandleader. (Born Arthur Arshawsky in NYC) His first hit was "Begin the Beguine" in 1938. Year/Age: 1995/**85** 1996/**86** 1997/**87**

• **ROSEMARY CLOONEY** Singer. (Maysville, KY) She had three #1 hits in the '50s: "Come-on-a-My-House," "Hey There," and "This Ole House." She was discovered by Mitch Miller while singing with the TONY PASTOR BAND. Her brother, Nick Clooney, is a TV anchorman in Cincinnati. Year/Age: 1995/**67** 1996/**68** 1997/**69**

• **BARBARA BARRIE** Actress. (Chicago, IL) Played Barney Miller's wife, Elizabeth, and Mamie Eisenhower in miniseries *Backstairs at the White House.* Year/Age: 1995/**64** 1996/**65** 1997/**66**

• **LAUREN CHAPIN** Actress. "Father Knows Best." She played the role of Kathy, "Kitten" to her father. Year/Age: 1995/**50** 1996/**51** 1997/**52**

• **BETTY GARRETT** Actress. (St. Joseph, MO) Neighbor Irene Lorenzo on "All in the Family." She was the landlady on "LaVerne & Shirley." Year/Age: 1995/**76** 1996/**77** 1997/**78**

• **HELEN O'CONNELL** Singer. (1920-1993 – Lima, OH) Featured vocalist with Jimmy Dorsey Orchestra. Sang duets with Bob Eberly, including: "Amapola," "Green Eyes," and "Tangerine." Worked with Dave Garroway on the "Today Show" and toured with "Four Girls Four" with Rose Marie, Rosemary Clooney, and Margaret Whiting. She was married to Band leader Frank DeVol. (Died 9-9-93.)

• **JOHN PAYNE** Actor. (1912-1989 – Roanoke, VA) Leading man who starred with Alice Faye and Betty Grable and appeared in dramas such as *Miracle on 34th Street.* (Died 12-5-89.)

FACTS FROM THE PAST

1553 The marriage of England's **KING HENRY VIII** to Catherine of Aragon was declared null and void.

1701 Captain **WILLIAM KIDD** was hanged in London after he was convicted of piracy and murder.

1785 **BENJAMIN FRANKLIN** wrote in a letter that he had invented bi-focals, making it unnecessary to carry two pairs of glasses.

1903 **NELSON JACKSON** set out on the first transcontinental automobile trip, driving his Winton from San Francisco to New York.

1934 Outlaws **BONNIE PARKER** and **CLYDE BARROW** were ambushed by lawmen and shot dead on a road outside Bienville Parish, LA. Bonnie was shot 50 times and Clyde 27 and their car had more than 250 bullet holes. Clyde was 25 years old and Bonnie 23. They had killed 14 people during their bank robberies. The movie *Bonnie and Clyde* in 1967 made stars of Warren Beatty and Faye Dunaway. A hit record, "Ballad of Bonnie and Clyde," in 1968 by Georgie Fame told the story.

1960 Israel disclosed that former Nazi **ADOLF EICHMANN** had been captured in Argentina and would be tried as a war criminal. He was executed May 31, 1962, by hanging, after an Israeli court rejected his appeal.

1970 The album *Let It Be* by the **BEATLES** set an advanced sales record in the U.S. with almost 4 million albums ordered before release.

1976 Ohio **CONGRESSMAN WAYNE HAYS** was exposed by the *Washington Post*. The newspaper reported that he was paying Elizabeth Ray, his secretary, $14,000 a year, considered a high wage at that time . . . and she couldn't type.

1983 **VLADIMIR DANCHEV**, an announcer on Radio Moscow, surprised everyone by praising Moslem rebels in Afghanistan and criticizing Soviet policy before he was taken off the air.

1984 **SURGEON GENERAL C. EVERETT KOOP** said smoking was costing the nation $40 billion a year in health expenses and lost productivity

1984 A **HOUSE SUBCOMMITTEE** released a report on the investigation into stolen campaign briefing materials from the Carter White House and how they were passed along to officials in the Reagan campaign.

1987 12 former members of the **DOOBIE BROTHERS** reunited for a charity concert at the Hollywood Bowl in Los Angeles. The show raised $360,000 for Vietnam veterans. The group then decided to make more appearances.

1994 **ROMAN HERZOG** was elected president of Germany, the first person chosen for the position since the country's unification in 1990. He is backed by Chancellor Helmut Kohl.

MAY 24

BIRTHDAYS

- **BOB DYLAN** Singer. (Born Robert Zimmerman in Duluth, MN) Musician/poet/figurehead of the '60s generation. Biggest hit: "Like A Rolling Stone" in 1965. One of the TRAVELING WILBURYS. Year/**Age:** 1995/**54** 1996/**55** 1997/**56**

- **PATTI LaBELLE** Singer. (Born Patricia Louise Holte in Philadelphia, PA) Biggest hit: "Lady Marmalade" in 1975. The song was in the movie *Soldier's Story*; a controversial record with French lyrics about a "lady of the night" in the New Orleans French Quarter. In 1986, she had a #1 song with Michael McDonald, "On My Own." Played Chelsea Paige in the NBC TV series "Out All Night." Of four sisters, she is the only one to see age 50. Year/**Age:** 1995/**51** 1996/**52** 1997/**53**

- **ROSEANNE CASH** Singer. (Memphis, TN) Daughter of Johnny Cash. Divorced from country artist and producer Rodney Crowell in 1991. The day after Roseanne graduated from high school, she joined her dad's band and began working in wardrobe, later singing back-up with her half-sister Rosie and eventually they opened the show for Johnny. Roseanne's biggest hit: "Seven Year Ache" in 1981. Year/**Age:** 1995/**40** 1996/**41** 1997/**42**

- **TOMMY CHONG** Comedian. (Canada) Half of Cheech and Chong, the comedy team who had top 10 hits, "Earache, My Eye" and "Far Out Man." Year/**Age:** 1995/**57** 1996/**58** 1997/**59**

- **FRANK OZ** Puppeteer/director. (Born Frank Oznowicz in England) *Dirty Rotten Scoundrels* and *What About Bob?* Most famous for his work with the Muppets. Is the voice of Miss Piggy. Year/**Age:** 1995/**51** 1996/**52** 1997/**53**

- **TONY VALENTINO** Guitarist. (Los Angeles, CA) Biggest hit with the STANDELLS: "Dirty Water." Year/**Age:** 1995/**54** 1996/**55** 1997/**56**

- **TOMMY PAGE** Singer. (Glenridge, NJ) His 1990 #1 hit: "I'll Be Your Everything" with backup vocals by 3 of the New Kids on the Block. Year/**Age:** 1995/**28** 1996/**29** 1997/**30**

- **GARY BURGHOFF** Actor. (Bristol, CT) Most famous for his role as Corporal Radar O'Reilly on the "M*A*S*H" TV series for 7 seasons. He was the only actor in the movie *M*A*S*H* to appear as a regular on the television version. Year/**Age:** 1995/**52** 1996/**53** 1997/**54**

- **PRISCILLA ANN BEAULIEU PRESLEY** Actress. (Brooklyn, NY) Appeared on the "Dallas" TV series. Wrote *Elvis and Me*—turned into a made-for-TV movie. She married Elvis in 1967, they had Lisa Marie in 1968, and divorced in 1973, four years before Presley died. Films include *The Naked Gun, The Naked Gun 2^1/$_2$*, and *The Naked Gun 33^1/$_3$: For the Record*. She has a perfume named "Moments." Year/**Age:** 1995/**50** 1996/**51** 1997/**52**

- **WILBUR MILLS** Policitian. (1909-1992 – Kensatt, AR) The powerful Arkansas Democrat, head of the House Ways and Means Committee, saw his career ruined in 1974 when he was stopped for drunken driving. His passenger, stripper Fanne Foxe, jumped into Washington's Tidal Basin. (Died 5-2-92.)

- **LILLI PALMER** Stage/screen/TV actress. (1914-1986 – Born Lilli Peiser in Germany) She also painted and wrote several novels and an autobiography. (Died 1-27-86.)

FACTS FROM THE PAST

1626 PETER MINUIT of the Dutch West India Trading Company bought the **ISLAND OF MANHATTAN** from the Carnarsee Indians, reportedly for blankets, cattle and various trinkets valued in all at $24.

1844 SAMUEL F.B. MORSE transmitted the words, "What hath God wrought," from Washington to Baltimore as he formally opened America's **FIRST TELEGRAPH LINE.**

1935 The first major league baseball game played at night took place at Crosley Field in Cincinnati, as the Reds beat the Phillies, 2 - 1. President **FRANKLIN ROOSEVELT** threw the switch on the floodlights from Washington, DC, by remote.

1962 Astronaut **SCOTT CARPENTER** became the **SECOND AMERICAN TO ORBIT** the earth as he circled the globe three times aboard *Friendship 7.*

1968 MICK JAGGER of the ROLLING STONES and his girlfried, Marianne Faithful, were arrested for marijuana possession.

1980 PHIL COLLINS, MIKE RUTHERFORD, and TONY BANKS of GENESIS surprised their fans by showing up in person at the box office of the Roxy Nightclub in Los Angeles, CA. They sold tickets to their benefit for local hospitals the following night.

1982 Mrs. Christina Samane of South Africa gave birth to the **HEAVIEST BABY EVER BORN**—a 22-pound, 8-ounce son.

1984 Detroit pitcher **JACK MORRIS** led the Tigers to their 17th straight victory on the road, setting an **AMERICAN LEAGUE RECORD.** Morris allowed only 4 hits as the Tigers beat the California Angels 5-1.

1988 JOHN MOSCHITTA set the Guinness World Record for fast talking: 586 words per minute.

1990 AXL ROSE AND ERIN EVERLY (Don's daughter) filed for divorce. They were married for 27 days.

1992 AL UNSER, JR., WON THE INDIANAPOLIS 500 in the closest finish ever. He beat out **SCOTT GOODYEAR** by .043 seconds. Thirteen drivers were forced out of the race and **LYN ST. JAMES** became the only one of seven rookie drivers who started the race to be at the finish.

1993 The Senate confirmed **ROBERTA ACHTEN BERG**, an acknowledged lesbian, to be a top housing official.

1994 White House aides used **TWO MILITARY HELICOPTERS** for a golf outing. Officials said taxpayers would be reimbersed for the costs.

Does anybody have gold teeth anymore?

MAY 25

BIRTHDAYS

- **KAREN VALENTINE** Actress. (Santa Rosa, CA) She played schoolteacher Alice Johnson on TV's "Room 222." Year/**Age**: 1995/**48** 1996/**49** 1997/**50**

- **LESLIE UGGAMS** Singer/actress. (NYC) Appeared on "Sing Along with Mitch" TV show in the early '60s. She played Kizzy in *Roots*. Year/**Age**: 1995/**52** 1996/**53** 1997/**54**

- **CONNIE SELLECCA** Actress. (NYC) Christine Francis, the assistant manager on "Hotel" and attorney Pam Davidson on "The Great American Hero." Married to *E.T.'s* John Tesh. Year/**Age**: 1995/**40** 1996/**41** 1997/**42**

- **DIXIE CARTER** Actress. (McLemoresville, TN) Joined the "Different Strokes" cast in 1984 as Maggie McKinney. Co-star on "Designing Women" which was cancelled in 1993. Married to actor Hal Holbrook. Year/**Age**: 1995/**56** 1996/**57** 1997/**58**

- **KITTY KALLEN** Singer. (Philadelphia, PA) Biggest hit: "Little Things Mean a Lot" in 1954. Year/**Age**: 1995/**69** 1996/**70** 1997/**71**

- **TOM T. HALL** C&W singer/composer. (Olive Hill, KY) Biggest hit: "The Year That Clayton Delaney Died" in 1971. He only made about $90,000 on "Harper Valley PTA" which he wrote. It sold in the millions for Jeannie C. Riley. Year/**Age**: 1995/**59** 1996/**60** 1997/**61**

- **JEANNE CRAIN** Actress. (Barstow, CA) She was nominated for best actress in *Pinky*. Began acting in 1944. Year/**Age**: 1995/**70** 1996/**71** 1997/**72**

- **K.C. JONES** Basketball. Year/**Age**: 1995/**63** 1996/**64** 1997/**65**

- **ROBERT LUDLUM** Author. (NYC) He wrote *The Gemini Contenders* in 1976. Year/**Age**: 1995/**68** 1996/**69** 1997/**70**

- **RON NESSEN** Broadcast news executive. Year/**Age**: 1995/**61** 1996/**62** 1997/**63**

- **HAL DAVID** Songwriter. (NYC) He and Burt Bacharach wrote dozens of hits together. Year/**Age**: 1995/**74** 1996/**75** 1997/**76**

- **BEVERLY SILLS** Retired opera star, now opera director. (Born Belle Silverman in Brooklyn, NY) Chairperson of the Lincoln Center. Year/**Age**: 1995/**66** 1996/**67** 1997/**68**

- **JESSI COLTER** C&W. (Born Miriam Johnson in Phoenix, AZ) Biggest record: "I'm Not Lisa" in 1975. She was married to Duane Eddy from 1962-1968, then married Waylon Jennings in 1969. Year/**Age**: 1995/**52** 1996/**53** 1997/**54**

- **CLAUDE AKINS** Actor. (1918-1994, Nelson, GA) Polygrip commercials. He was TV's "Sheriff Lobo" on "B.J. and the Bear" and had a movie role in 1953, *From Here to Eternity*. and *The Cain Mutiny*. (Died 1-27-94)

- **MILES DAVIS** Jazz trumpeter. (1926-1991 – Alton, IL) He created "cool jazz." Biggest LP: "Bitches Brew." He was married and divorced 3 times, including actress Cicely Tyson. (Died 9-28-91.)

- **RALPH WALDO EMERSON** American essayist and poet. (1803-1882 – Boston, MA) Was pastor of the Second Unitarian Church in Boston, resigned over heterodox views. (Died 4-27-1882.)

- **GENE TUNNEY** Boxer. (1898-1978 – Born James Joseph Tunney in NYC) Became world heavyweight boxing champ in 1926 by beating Jack Dempsey in a 1927 rematch in Chicago, won again after a controversial "long count" (see 9-22). (Died 11-7-78.)

FACTS FROM THE PAST

1721 John Copsen became the **FIRST INSURANCE AGENT** in the U.S. when he advertised coverage for "vessels and other goods."

1935 At the Big Ten conference championships held in Ann Arbor, MI, **JESSE OWENS**, who had been sick the previous day, ran the 100-yard dash in 9.4 seconds to tie the world's record. Ten minutes later he leaped 26 feet, 8.25 inches to set a new world's record. Nine minutes later, running in the 220-yard dash, Jesse sped down the course in 20.3 seconds to smash another world's record. And just about 45 minutes after he had participated in the first event, he negotiated the 220-yard hurdles in 22.6 seconds, shattering still another world's record.

1935 Baseball's great **BABE RUTH** hit the 714th and **FINAL HOME RUN** of his career for the Boston Braves, in a game against the Pittsburgh Pirates at Forbes Field. This record survived 39 years until it was broken by Hank Aaron in 1974.

1961 **PRESIDENT JOHN F. KENNEDY** asked the nation to work toward putting a **MAN ON THE MOON** by the end of the decade. The first man landed on the moon on July 20, 1969, accomplishing Kennedy's dream.

1973 **CAROLE KING's** concert in New York City's Central Park attracted 100,000 people.

1976 **U.S. REPRESENTATIVE WAYNE L. HAYS** (Democrat, Ohio) admitted to a "personal relationship" with **ELIZABETH RAY,** a committee secretary who claimed she'd received her job in order to be Hays's mistress.

1981 **MARIO ANDRETTI** was awarded the victory at the **INDY 500** the day after the race, when **BOBBY UNSER**, whose car finished first, was penalized one lap and dropped from 1st to 2nd for passing illegally under a yellow caution flag. Unser appealed and the panel agreed that the penalty was too severe and restored the victory to him. Unser ended up paying a $4,000 fine.

1986 An estimated 7 million Americans participated in **HANDS ACROSS AMERICA**, forming a line across the country to raise money for the nation's hungry and homeless.

1992 **JAY LENO** replaced Johnny Carson on the **"TONIGHT SHOW."** His first guest was Billy Crystal. After he was given an audience ovation, he said: "Let's see how you feel in 30 years."

1992 **DAN BIASONE** died at age 83. He was the **FATHER OF THE NBA 24-SECOND SHOT CLOCK.**

1994 A parole board denied **JAMES EARL RAY**'s petition to be released from his 99-year sentence for assassinating Reverend Martin King, Jr. in 1968.

MAY 26

BIRTHDAYS

• **DR. SALLY KRISTEN RIDE** Astronaut/astrophysicist. (Encino, CA) The first American woman in space, on board Space Shuttle *Challenger* June 18-24, 1983. She left the astronaut corps to take a position as scientist for her alma mater, Stanford University. She and astronaut Steve Hawley have divorced after a 5-year marriage. Year/**Age**: 1995/**44** 1996/**45** 1997/**46**

• **JAMES ARNESS** Actor. (Born James Aurness in Minneapolis, MN) A lumberjack, he was badly wounded in WWII. He played Matt Dillon on "Gunsmoke." John Wayne was offered the part, turned it down and recommended Arness. He began his career as a radio newscaster in Minneapolis. His brother is actor Peter Graves from "Mission Impossible." Year/**Age**: 1995/**72** 1996/**73** 1997/**74**

• **PHILIP MICHAEL THOMAS** Actor. (Los Angeles, CA) "Miami Vice." Year/**Age**: 1995/**46** 1996/**47** 1997/**48**

• **HANK WILLIAMS, JR.** C&W singer/songwriter. (Shreveport, LA) Son of country music's first superstar, Hank Williams, Sr. Following in dad's footsteps, at age 11 he sang "Lovesick Blues" on the Grand Ole Opry and his career was launched. Year/**Age**: 1995/**46** 1996/**47** 1997/**48**

• **GENIE FRANCIS** Actress. (Englewood, NJ) She played Laura on TV's "General Hospital" and was in the top-rated segment, "The Wedding of Luke and Laura." She left "General Hospital" in 1981 because she was on the verge of an emotional breakdown. She'd sit in her car, sobbing at the end of the day, too embarrassed to admit she was having problems. While filming TV's "North and South" she met her husband Jonathan Frakes. Year/**Age**: 1995/**33** 1996/**34** 1997/**35**

• **BRENT MUSBURGER** ABC sports announcer. (Portland, OR) Year/**Age**: 1995/**56** 1996/**57** 1997/**58**

• **TERESA STRATAS** Opera singer. (Canada) Grammy and Tony winning soprano. Year/**Age**: 1995/**57** 1996/**58** 1997/**59**

• **DARRELL EVANS** Baseball. (Pasadena, CA) With the Atlanta Braves. Was the 1985 home run leader with Detroit. He hit 40. Year/**Age**: 1995/**48** 1996/**49** 1997/**50**

• **DAN PASTORINI** Football. Year/**Age**: 1995/**46** 1996/**47** 1997/**48**

• **BOBCAT GOLDTHWAIT** Comedian. Films include *Police Academy*. Year/**Age**: 1995/**33** 1996/**34** 1997/**35**

• **STEVIE NICKS** Singer. (California) With FLEETWOOD MAC. Their biggest hit: "Dreams" in 1977. Years ago she had liposuction. Year/**Age**: 1995/**47** 1996/**48** 1997/**49**

• **PEGGY LEE** Singer. (Born Norma Engstrom in Jamestown, ND) Biggest record: "Fever" in 1958. In 1955 she was nominated for an Oscar in *Pete Kelly's Blues*. She sang with Benny Goodman's orchestra and married the band's guitarist Dave Barbour in 1943. Year/**Age**: 1995/**75** 1996/**76** 1997/**77**

• **LEVON HELM** Drummer. (New York) From the group THE BAND. Biggest hit: "Up on Cripple Creek," in 1969. Year/**Age**: 1995/**53** 1996/**54** 1997/**55**

• **JACQUES BERGERAC** Actor. (France) In the film *Gigi*. Year/**Age**: 1995/**68** 1996/**69** 1997/**70**

• **JAY SILVERHEELS** Actor. (1922-1980 – Canada) "Tonto" on TV series "The Lone Ranger." (Died 3-5-80)

• **ROBERT MORLEY** Actor (1908-1992 – England) He was nominated for best supporting actor in *Marie Antoinette* in 1938. He also appeared in *Around The World in 80 Days,* and *The African Queen.* TV's "War and Remembrance" and "U.S. Steel." (Died 6-3-92.)

• **JOHN WAYNE** Actor. (1907-1979 – Born Marion Michael Morrison in Winterset, IA) Tom Mix got "the Duke" – son of a druggist – his first job in movies in the 20th Century Fox property department. He got his break standing in for stunt men. There was only one year between 1949 and 1968 when Wayne wasn't in the box office top ten. He turned down the lead in *Dirty Harry*. He made over 200 films and won an Oscar in 1969 for best actor in *True Grit*. (Died 6-11-79.)

• **AL JOLSON** Singer/actor. (1886-1950 – Born Asa Yoelson in St. Petersburg, Russia) Star of *The Jazz Singer* in 1927, ushering in the age of sound motion pictures. His biggest record: "Sonny Boy" in 1928. (Died 10-23-50.)

FACTS FROM THE PAST

1868 President **ANDREW JOHNSON**, Abe Lincoln's successor, avoided being impeached for "high crimes" by a margin of one vote.

1896 The **DOW JONES INDUSTRIAL AVERAGE**, co-founded by **CHARLES DOW**, first appeared in the *Wall Street Journal*.

1959 Pittsburgh's **HARVEY HADDIX** hurled a perfect game for 12 innings, retiring all 36 Milwaukee batters to face him, in probably the single greatest pitching performance in baseball history.

1960 U.N. Ambassador **HENRY CABOT LODGE** accused the Soviets of hiding a microphone inside a wood carving of the Great Seal of the United States that had been given as a gift to the U.S. Embassy in Moscow.

1962 **WILLIE NELSON** charted his first country song, "Touch Me."

1977 The **HUMAN FLY, GEORGE WILLIG**, scaled the side of the NY World Trade Center. After climbing $3^1/_2$ hours, he was arrested at the top of the 110-story building for criminal trespass and reckless endangerment. He was fined $1.10, a penny for each story.

1993 Cleveland's **CARLOS MARTINEZ** hit a long fly ball that bounced off outfielder Jose Canseco's head and over the right field wall for a home run.

1993 **FIRST LADY CLINTON** denounced price gougers and profiteers in medicine before a crowd of union activists in Washington.

1994 Game show host **BOB BARKER** admitted to fooling around with "Price Is Right" model Diane Parkinson but denied her charge that he sexually harassed her.

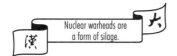

Nuclear warheads are a form of silage.

MAY 27

BIRTHDAYS

- **CHRISTOPHER LEE** Actor. (England) Has played many sinister and horrific roles, such as *Dracula* in 1958. He also starred in *The Far Pavilions*. Year/**Age**: 1995/**73** 1996/**74** 1997/**75**
- **LEE MERIWETHER** Actress. (Los Angeles, CA) The former "Miss America" appeared on the "Barnaby Jones" TV series. Also, on "Batman" for a while as Catwoman. Year/**Age**: 1995/**60** 1996/**61** 1997/**62**
- **LOU GOSSETT, JR.** Actor. (Brooklyn, NY) He won best supporting actor Oscar for his role in *An Officer and a Gentleman* in 1982. Also appeared in *Iron Eagle III* and *Diggstown*. Year/**Age**: 1995/**59** 1996/**60** 1997/**61**
- **TODD BRIDGES** Actor. (San Francisco, CA) "Diff'rent Strokes." Year/**Age**: 1995/**30** 1996/**31** 1997/**32**
- **HENRY KISSINGER** Former Secretary of State. (Germany) Won the Nobel Peace Prize in 1973. Year/**Age**: 1995/**72** 1996/**73** 1997/**74**
- **SAM SNEAD** Pro golfer. (Hot Springs, VA) He was PGA and Masters champ 3 times each. Year/**Age**: 1995/**83** 1996/**84** 1997/**85**
- **RAMSEY LEWIS** Jazz musician. (Chicago, IL.) Biggest hit: "The In Crowd" in 1965. Year/**Age**: 1995/**60** 1996/**61** 1997/**62**
- **DON WILLIAMS** C&W singer. (Floydada, TX) Had over 15 #1 hits. His biggest: "I Believe In You" in 1980. The one-time leader of the POZO-SECO SINGERS appeared in the film *Smokey and The Bandit II*. Year/**Age**: 1995/**56** 1996/**57** 1997/**58**
- **WILLIAM SESSIONS** Former FBI Director. (Ft. Smith, AK) "Unsolved Mysteries" appearances. Year/**Age**: 1995/**65** 1996/**66** 1997/**67**
- **DONDRE WHITFIELD** Actor. (Brooklyn, NY) Plays Terrence Frye on the soap, "All My Children." Year/**Age**: 1995/**26** 1996/**27** 1997/**28**

- **BRUCE WEITZ** Actor. (Norwalk, CT) On "Hill St. Blues" as scruffy Detective Mick Belker, who sometimes resorted to biting the felons he apprehended. Year/**Age**: 1995/**52** 1996/**53** 1997/**54**
- **LEFT EYE** Singer. (Born Lisa Lopes) With TLC. Hits include: "Ain't 2 Proud 2 Beg" and "Baby, Baby, Baby." Year/**Age**: 1995/**24** 1996/**25** 1997/**26**
- **CATHY SILVERS** Actress. Played Joanie's boy crazy girfriend Jenny Piccalo on "Happy Days." Cathy is the daughter of the late comedian Phil Silvers. Year/**Age**: 1995/**34** 1996/**35** 1997/**36**
- **FRANK THOMAS** Baseball. Chicago White Sox power hitter. Year/**Age**: 1995/**27** 1996/**28** 1997/**29**
- **CILLA BLACK** Singer/actress. (Born Priscilla White in Liverpool, England) Biggest hit: "You're My World' in 1964. Year/**Age**: 1995/**52** 1996/**53** 1997/**54**
- **PAT CASH** Tennis star. (Australia) Former U.S. Open winner. Year/**Age**: 1995/**30** 1996/**31** 1997/**32**
- **VINCENT PRICE** Actor. (1911-1993, St. Louis, MO.) Was also an artist/gourmet chef/author. Has acted in movies, on radio and TV and did TV commercials. A friend of Michael Jackson, he did the scary voice on his "Thriller" cut. He has written a couple of cookbooks. In the films *Edward Scissorhands*, *Laura*, *The Raven*, and *House of Wax*. (Died 10-25-93.)
- **"WILD BILL" HICKOK** Gunslinger. (1837-1876 – Born James Butler Hickok in Troy Grove, IL) He was shot to death while playing poker. In his hand, two aces and two eights, now called the "dead man's hand." (Died 8-2-1876.)
- **ISADORA DUNCAN** Dancer. (1878-1927 – San Francisco, CA) She had a unique style of dancing and wore revealing costumes and shocked audiences. One time she exposed her breasts while dancing in Boston and said, "This is beauty." (Died 9-14-27.)

FACTS FROM THE PAST

1790 The **LAZIEST MAN IN HISTORY** went to bed and stayed there for the next 70 years. England's **JEREMIAH CARLTON** was 19 years old and the heir to a large fortune when he climbed into bed. A team of more than 40 servants bathed and fed him in bed until his death 70 years later.

1931 **AUGUSTE PICCARD** and **CHARLES KNIPFER** took man's first trip into the stratosphere when they rode their balloon to an altitude of 51,793 feet.

1941 Amid rising world tensions, **PRESIDENT FRANKLIN D. ROOSEVELT** proclaimed an unlimited national emergency.

1949 **MARILYN MONROE**, at the time an unknown actress, posed nude for a calendar photo. Within a few months, she landed roles in two major movies. Photographer Tom Kelly took the picture which appeared in the first issue of *Playboy* magazine.

1950 **FRANK SINATRA** made his television debut with Bob Hope on NBC.

1955 President **HARRY TRUMAN**, appearing on Edward R. Murrow's "Person to Person" TV show, said that he heard **STRANGE SOUNDS IN THE WHITE HOUSE**. At 3 a.m. there was a rapping on his door. When he opened it, and no one was there. The president said it was no mortal knocking, but a visitation from the ghost of **ABRAHAM LINCOLN**.

1989 **CHICAGO** and **THE BEACH BOYS** toured together for the first time in 14 years. Brian Wilson joined them for three songs.

1993 **DALE MURPHY**, 17-year baseball veteran, retired only 2 home runs short of the 400 homer mark.

1994 After 20 years in exile, Nobel Prize-winning author **ALEXANDER SOLZHENITSYN** returned to Russia. He was expelled for charges of treason 2-13-74.

MAY 28

Do they still have public baths in Japan?

BIRTHDAYS

- **GLADYS KNIGHT** Singer. (Atlanta, GA) Biggest record: "Midnight Train to Georgia" in 1973. She and the PIPS' first hit was "Every Beat of My Heart" in 1961. The PIPS consist of her brother, sister, and two cousins, named for cousin, manager James "Pip" Woods. Year/**Age**: 1995/**51** 1996/**52** 1997/**53**

- **SONDRA LOCKE** Actress. (Shelbyville, TN) Clint Eastwood's ex-girlfriend, appeared in some of his films, including *Sudden Impact*. Year/**Age**: 1995/**48** 1996/**49** 1997/**50**

- **JEANNIE CARSON** Actress. A regular on the "Red Buttons Show" and star of sitcom "Hey, Jeannie" in the 1950s. Year/**Age**: 1995/**66** 1996/**67** 1997/**68**

- **BETH HOWLAND** Actress. (Boston, MA) Played Vera, a mousy, scatterbrained waitress in the TV series "Alice." Year/**Age**: 1995/**48** 1996/**49** 1997/**50**

- **BILLY VERA** Singer. (Riverside, CA) Formed the BEATERS, a 10-piece R&B band, in 1979. Biggest hit: "At This Moment," popularized through play on TV's "Family Ties." Year/**Age**: 1995/**51** 1996/**52** 1997/**53**

- **JOHN FOGERTY** Singer. (Berkeley, CA) Leader of CREEDENCE CLEARWATER REVIVAL and recorded entirely solo as the BLUE RIDGE RANGERS. Biggest hits: "The Old Man Down the Road" in 1984 and with CCR "Proud Mary" in 1969. Year/**Age**: 1995/**50** 1996/**51** 1997/**52**

- **CARROLL BAKER** Actress. (Johnstown, PA) Oscar nomination for best actress in *Baby Doll* in 1956. Also appeared in *Giant*, *Carpetbaggers*, and *Harlow*. Year/**Age**: 1995/**64** 1996/**65** 1997/**66**

- **KIRK GIBSON** Baseball player. (Pontiac, MI) He hit a game-winning home run in the 1989 World Series for the Los Angeles Dodgers. Year/**Age**: 1995/**38** 1996/**39** 1997/**40**

- **GARY STEWART** C&W singer. (Letcher County, KY) Biggest hit: "She's Acting Single" in 1975. Year/**Age**: 1995/**50** 1996/**51** 1997/**52**

- **JERRY WEST** Former basketball player/coach. (Cabin Creek, WV) Joined L.A. Lakers in 1960 and by the time he retired in 1974 he scored over 25,000 points. In playoff games, he averaged 29 points a game. Year/**Age**: 1995/**57** 1996/**58** 1997/**59**

- **KYLIE MINOGUE** Singer. (Melbourne, Australia.) Biggest hit: "Locomotion," a remake of Little Eva's hit. Appeared on Australian soap opera "Neighbours" for 3 years. Year/**Age**: 1995/**27** 1996/**28** 1997/**29**

- **JIM THORPE** Distinguished American Indian athlete, star of the 1912 Olympics, as well as a baseball and football star. (1888-1953 – Prague, OK) His Olympic gold medals for the pentathlon and decathlon were taken away from him when it was learned that he played semi-pro baseball. In 1982, the medals were reinstated posthumously. (Died 3-28-53.)

- **IAN FLEMING** Author. (1908-1964 – London, England) He created the James Bond character. He sold the right to *Casino Royale* to CBS for $1,000. They turned it into an episode of "Climax Mystery Theater" starring Barry Nelson as the first James Bond in 1954.

FACTS FROM THE PAST

1929 Warner Brothers released the **FIRST TALKING FILM** produced entirely **IN COLOR**: *On with the Show* with Ethel Waters, Joe E. Brown, and Betty Compton. The film premiered in New York.

1959 Two monkeys, Abel and Baker, were rocketed 300 miles into orbit from Cape Canaveral as part of an experiment leading to manned space flight. The **JUPITER ROCKET** was recovered $1^{1}/_{2}$ hours later, 1,700 miles from Cape Canaveral by U.S. frogmen.

1976 The **ALLMAN BROTHERS BAND** broke up after Gregg Allman testified against Scooter Herring, his personal road manager, who was charged with drug trafficking. Herring was later sentenced to 75 years in jail. The band reformed in 1978.

1977 A **FIRE** raged through the **BEVERLY HILLS SUPPER CLUB** in Southgate, KY, and 164 people died, 130 injured. Singer **JOHN DAVIDSON** escaped the blaze and assisted in helping the injured.

1978 **AL UNSER, SR.,** became the **FIFTH MAN TO WIN THE INDY 500 A THIRD TIME,** with an average speed of 161.363 mph. He won it a fourth time in 1987.

1983 The **U.S. FESTIVAL OPENED IN SAN BERNARDINO**, CA. Apple Computer's founder **STEVE WOZNIAK** [wuz'-nee-ak] lost millions on the festival, mainly because performers like David Bowie and Van Halen were paid fees of a million each.

1986 Viewers taking part in Dick Clark's "America Picks the Number-One Songs" chose **BILL HALEY'S** "Rock Around the Clock," **SIMON AND GARFUNKEL'S** "Bridge Over Troubled Water" and "All Night Long" by **LIONEL RICHIE** as the greatest hits of the rock era.

1987 **MATHIAS RUST** [rewst], a 19-year-old West German pilot, stunned the world as he landed a private plane in Moscow's Red Square, having evaded Soviet air defenses. Rust was sentenced to a labor camp for 4 years, but was released in 11 months. The Soviet Defense Minister and Chief on Air Defenses were fired.

1989 **EMERSON FITTIPALDI,** two-time Formula One champion, conquered the 73rd running of the Indianapolis 500. The 42-year-old driver picked off the richest and most coveted prize in auto racing by surviving a wheel-to-wheel confrontation with **AL UNSER, JR.,** on lap 199, winning the first million-dollar purse.

1994 The Clintons hosted the **FIRST WEDDING** at the White House in 23 years. The president's brother-in-law Tony Rodham married Nicole Boxer, the daughter of Senator Boxer (D/CA).

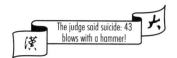

The judge said suicide: 43 blows with a hammer!

MAY 29

BIRTHDAYS

- **DANNY ELFMAN** Singer. (Los Angeles, CA) Composed soundtracks for *Batman* and *Beetlejuice*. A charter member of OINGO BOINGO, a new wave group. He scored "The Simpsons." Film *The Nightmare Before Christmas*. Year/**Age**: 1995/**42** 1996/**43** 1997/**44**

- **LATOYA JACKSON** Singer. (Gary, IN) Member of the Jackson family. Appeared nude in *Playboy* magazine. Wrote a controversial book. Year/**Age**: 1995/**38** 1996/**39** 1997/**40**

- **BOB HOPE** Comedian. (Born Leslie Townes Hope in Eltham, England) He never received an Oscar but has 4 special awards from the Academy. In his young days, he boxed. He and his wife, Dolores, have been married for over 60 years. He hosted the Oscars 17 times. Year/**Age**: 1995/**92** 1996/**93** 1997/**94**

- **REBBIE JACKSON** Singer. (Born Maureen Jackson in Gary, IN) Oldest of the Jackson family. One hit alone: "Centipede" in 1984, written by brother Michael. Year/**Age**: 1995/**45** 1996/**46** 1997/**47**

- **LISA WHELCHEL** Actress. (Littlefield, TX) She was the spoiled Blair on TV's "Facts of Life." Year/**Age**: 1995/**32** 1996/**33** 1997/**34**

- **ERIC DAVIS** Baseball. (Los Angeles, CA) He plays for the Dodgers. Year/**Age**: 1995/**33** 1996/**34** 1997/**35**

- **AL UNSER, SR.** Automobile race driver. (Albuquerque, NM) Won the INDY 500 two years in a row in 1970 and 71, and came in second in 1972. He also won the 500 in 1978 and 1987. Al has driven over 8,000 miles in 22 Indy races. Retired in 1994. Year/**Age**: 1995/**56** 1996/**57** 1997/**58**

- **FRANCIS T. (FAY) VINCENT, JR.** Lawyer. (Waterbury, CT) Commissioner of Major League Baseball, until forced to resign in September 1992. Year/**Age**: 1995/**57** 1996/**58** 1997/**59**

- **HELMUT BERGER** Actor. (Germany) Films include *The Damned* and *Dorian Gray*. Year/**Age**: 1995/**51** 1996/**52** 1997/**53**

- **ANTHONY GEARY** Soap opera star. (Coalville, UT) Appeared on "General Hospital" as Luke in the top-rated wedding scene with Laura, played by Genie Francis. Year/**Age**: 1995/**47** 1996/**48** 1997/**49**

- **GARY BROOKER** Singer. (England) Vocals and piano, formed the group PROCOL HARUM. Biggest hit: "Whiter Shade of Pale" in 1967. Year/**Age**: 1995/**46** 1996/**47** 1997/**48**

- **ROY CREWSDON** Guitar player. (England) With FREDDIE AND THE DREAMERS. Biggest hit: "I'm Telling You Now" in 1965. Year/**Age**: 1995/**54** 1996/**55** 1997/**56**

- **JOHN FITZGERALD KENNEDY** 35th U.S. President. (1917-1963 – Brookline, MA) Youngest man ever elected to the presidency, the first Roman Catholic and first president to have served in the U.S. Navy. He won a Pulitzer Prize for *Profiles in Courage* and was the first president to win a Purple Heart. Like all of his brothers and sisters, he inherited a million dollars when he was 21 years old. He was idolized by millions and when he succeeded President Eisenhower, one of Ike's aids said, "This administration will do for sex what the last one did for golf." John Kennedy was the 4th president to be assassinated and the second to be buried at Arlington National Cemetery; the first was William Howard Taft.

FACTS FROM THE PAST

1856 **ABRAHAM LINCOLN** gave a speech in Bloomington, IL, in which he proclaimed, "You can fool some of the people all of the time, and all of the people some of the time, but you can't fool all of the people all of the time."

1910 An **AIRPLANE RACED A TRAIN** from Albany, NY, to New York City. The airplane won and aviator **GLENN CURTISS** was awarded $10,000.

1912 *Ladies Home Journal* editor **EDWARD BOK** fired 15 women when he caught them dancing the Turkey Trot during their lunch hour.

1942 The biggest-selling single song, ever, was recorded by Bing Crosby on a warm day 50 years ago. **"WHITE CHRISTMAS,"** written by Irving Berlin, made the charts every Christmas season from 1942-62, except two. It has sold over 40 million copies.

1952 Country singer **HANK WILLIAMS** was divorced by his wife, Audrey Shepherd.

1953 **MT. EVEREST** was conquered as **EDMUND HILLARY** of New Zealand and **TENSING NORKAY** of Nepal became the first climbers to reach the summit of the 29,000-foot Himalayan mountain. When asked what their first thought was after reaching the top, the answer was: "How to get down." About 100 climbers have conquered Mt. Everest and 50 died trying.

1973 **TOM BRADLEY** was elected the **FIRST BLACK MAYOR OF LOS ANGELES**. He retired in 1993.

1977 **A.J. FOYT** won the INDY 500 for a record 4th time. The race featured the first appearance of the only woman to qualify at Indy, Janet Guthrie, forced to drop out with engine trouble.

1982 A 450-year-old schism between the Church of Rome and the Church of England came closer to an end as **POPE JOHN PAUL II** and the **ARCHBISHOP OF CANTERBURY, ROBERT RUNCIE**, prayed together in Canterbury Cathedral.

1987 A jury in Los Angeles found **TWILIGHT ZONE** movie director **JOHN LANDIS** and four associates innocent of involuntary manslaughter in the deaths of actor **VIC MORROW** and two children.

1988 **RICK MEARS** scored his third Indianapolis 500 victory in 11 starts as yellow flags appeared in record numbers for the 72nd race.

1988 **RONALD REAGAN** became the first American president in 14 years to visit Moscow.

1994 **AL UNSER, JR.** won his second Indy 500 race after his teammate hit the fence, pushing him from 2nd to 17th. Al Jr. said that winning was a great way to celebrate his Dad's birthday.

MAY 30

Why is the city of Ebla never mentioned in the Bible?

BIRTHDAYS

- **MARIE FREDRIKKSON** Singer. (Sweden) Lead singer of ROXETTE. Hits include: "The Look" and "It Must Have Been Love." Year/**Age:** 1995/**37** 1996/**38** 1997/**39**

- **RUTA LEE** Actress. TV's "Pantomime Quiz" regular. Year/**Age:** 1995/**59** 1996/**60** 1997/**61**

- **CLINT WALKER** Actor. (Hartford, IL) One of the stars of *The Dirty Dozen* in 1967. He was impaled some years ago by a ski pole just below the chest cavity and lived to tell about it. Best known as "Cheyenne" on the TV series from 1955-1963. Year/**Age:** 1995/**68** 1996/**69** 1997/**70**

- **WYNONNA JUDD** C&W singer. (Born Christina Ciminella in Ashland, KY) She and her mother, Naomi, born Diane, were the JUDDS. Two of their biggest records: "Why Not Me" and "Have Mercy." Naomi quit in 1992 for health reasons and Wynonna went on alone. Year/**Age:** 1995/**31** 1996/**32** 1997/**33**

- **MEREDITH MacRAE** Actress. Daughter of the late singer Gordon McRae. Appeared in TVs "Petticoat Junction." Year/**Age:** 1995/**50** 1996/**51** 1997/**52**

- **MICHAEL POLLARD** Actor. (Passaic, NJ) Pint-sized character actor who appeared in *Bonnie and Clyde*, and made a cameo appearance in *Dick Tracy*. Year/**Age:** 1995/**56** 1996/**57** 1997/**58**

- **FRANKLIN SCHAFFNER** Director. (1920-1989 – Tokyo, Japan) Won an Oscar for directing *Patton*. (Died 7-2-89.)

- **KEIR DULLEA** Actor. (Cleveland, OH) Played the lead in *2001: A Space Odyssey* in 1969. Year/**Age:** 1995/**59** 1996/**60** 1997/**61**

- **LYDELL MITCHELL** Football. Year/**Age:** 1995/**56** 1996/**57** 1997/**58**

- **GALE SAYERS** Former football star. (Wichita, KS) He scored 36 points for the Chicago Bears in a 61-20 win over the San Francisco 49ers in December, 1965. Year/**Age:** 1995/**52** 1996/**53** 1997/**54**

- **CHRISTINE JORGENSEN** Sex change pioneer. (1926-1989 – NYC) She was George Jorgensen before undergoing a series of sex change operations in Denmark in 1952. After her operation, she became a nightclub performer and lecturer. George was a bomber pilot in WWII before the operation. (Died 5-3-89.)

- **BENNY GOODMAN** The "King of Swing." (1909-1986 – Chicago, IL) Started with a 14-piece band in 1935 which included Gene Krupa on drums, Bunny Berigan on trumpet, and vocalist Helen Ward. His biggest hits include: "Jersey Bounce" and "Taking a Chance on Love." One of his best known arrangements was "Sing, Sing, Sing." His theme song was "Let's Dance." He was best known for taking jazz to Carnegie Hall in the 1930s. (Died 6-13-86.)

- **MEL BLANC** The man of a thousand voices. (1908-1989 – Born Melvin Jerome Blanc in San Francisco, CA) Musician/voice special effects recording star, he began doing Warner Bros. cartoons in 1937, and the "Flintstones" TV series in 1960. He was the voice of Porky Pig, Daffy Duck, Tweeti-Pie ["I taut I saw a puddy tat"], but his favorite was Bugs Bunny ["Ehhh, what's up, doc?"]. Warner Bros. produced about 800 "Looney Tune" cartoons from the mid-'30s to 1969. Mel created many characters for the Jack Benny radio show and did Daffy Duck in *Who Framed Roger Rabbit?* in 1988. Blanc's autobiography is titled *That's Not All, Folks*. Mel had "That's All, Folks" inscribed on his tombstone. (Died 7-10-89.)

FACTS FROM THE PAST

1431   **JOAN OF ARC**, the French heroine and martyr, was burned at the stake at the age of 19 in Rouen, France, after being convicted and found guilty of sorcery and heresy. She was declared a saint in 1920.

1783   **BENJAMIN TOWNER** of Philadelphia published the first daily newspaper in the United States, the *Pennsylvania Evening Post*.

1868   General **JOHN LOGAN** suggested a national Decoration Day (which became **MEMORIAL DAY**) after seeing women decorating graves of Civil War heroes. In 1972, the traditional date of May 30th was changed to the last Monday in May.

1904   Chicago Cubs first baseman **FRANK CHANCE** got hit by five pitches in a doubleheader against the Pittsburgh Pirates.

1911   The **FIRST INDIANAPOLIS 500** race was held. Ray Harroun was the winner with a speed averaging 74.4 mph. One driver was killed.

1922   The **ST. LOUIS CARDINALS** played the **CHICAGO CUBS** in a baseball doubleheader. In the first game, **CLIFF HEATHCOTE** played in the Cardinal outfield, while outfielder **MAX FLACK** played for the Cubs. Between games, the two players were traded—for each other. So, in the second game, Max Flack played for the Cardinals, while Cliff Heathcote played for the Cubs.

1967   At the Ascot Speedway in Gardena, CA, **EVEL KNIEVEL** gunned his Triumph motorcycle and jumped off a ramp at a speed of 80 mph. That allowed him to clear 16 automobiles standing in a row. To prove it was no fluke, within the next few months, he did it four more times.

1990   **MIDNIGHT OIL** gave a free concert on flatbed trucks outside of the Exxon Buiding as a response to the environmentally-careless spill in Alaska.

1993   Brazilian racecar driver **EMERSON FITTIPALDI** won the 77th **INDY 500**. This was his second Indianapolis victory, the first in 1989. The 46-year-old driver earned $1,155,304 from a record Indy Motor Speedway purse of $7,681,300. He beat second place Arie Luyendyk by 2.862 seconds.

1994   **ON MEMORIAL DAY** President Clinton payed homage to U.S. soldiers who died in action on D-Day at Normandy Beach.

Finally—hot dogs and buns both come in 8-packs.

MAY 31

BIRTHDAYS

• **CLINT EASTWOOD** Actor. (San Francisco, CA.) Powerful dramatic actor/producer/director. He began his career in the '50s with a series on TV, "Rawhide," which ran for 8 seasons. He reached his greatest fame beginning in 1971 as *Dirty Harry* and made his directing debut in 1969 in *Play Misty for Me* set in Carmel, CA, where he was the mayor for two years. He won producer and director Oscars for the 1992 film *Unforgiven*. Also in *In the Line of Fire*, *When the Stars Fell on Henrietta, The Bridges of Madison County*, and he directed *A Perfect World* in 1993. Year/**Age**: 1995/**65** 1996/**66** 1997/**67**

• **GREGORY HARRISON** Actor. (Avalon, CA) He was Gonzo on the "Trapper John, M.D." TV series. Also on "Family Man." Year/**Age**: 1995/**45** 1996/**46** 1997/**47**

• **DON AMECHE** Actor. (1908-1993, Born Dominic Felix Amici in Kenosha, WI) His comeback started with *Trading Places* and his last film was *Corrina, Corrina*. Don won an Oscar in 1986 for best supporting actor in *Cocoon*. He was inducted into the Radio Hall of Fame in 1992. He and Frances Langford did the funny "Bickersons" albums. His brother, Jim Ameche, was *Jack Armstrong, the All-American Boy,* on radio. (Died 12-6-93.)

• **JOE NAMATH** Former football star/actor. (Beaver Falls, PA) "Broadway Joe." Flexall 400 ointment commercials. Year/**Age**: 1995/**52** 1996/**53** 1997/**54**

• **CHRIS ELLIOTT** Writer/actor. Wrote for David Letterman. Stars on TV's "Get a Life." Films *Groundhog Day* and *Cabin Boy.* Year/**Age**: 1995/**35** 1996/**36** 1997/**37**

• **PETER YARROW** Singer. (NYC) With PETER, PAUL AND MARY, Biggest hit: "Leaving on a Jet Plane" in 1969. Year/**Age**: 1995/**57** 1996/**58** 1997/**59**

• **PRINCE RAINIER OF MONACO** He was married to Grace Kelly. Year/**Age**: 1995/**72** 1996/**73** 1997/**74**

• **TOM BERENGER** Actor. (Chicago, IL) *Platoon, At Play in the Fields of the Lord, Major League, Sliver, Bill Chill, Eddie and the Cruisers, Gettysburg,* and *Chasers.* Year/**Age**: 1995/**45** 1996/**46** 1997/**47**

• **SHIRLEY VERRETT** Soprano. (New Orleans, LA) Debuted with the N.Y. Met in 1968. Year/**Age**: 1995/**62** 1996/**63** 1997/**64**

• **JOHNNY PAYCHECK** C&W singer. (Born Don Lytle in Greenfield, OH) Biggest hit: "Take This Job and Shove It." He spent 2 years in prison after shooting a man in a Hillsboro, OH, bar in 1985. Year/**Age**: 1995/**54** 1996/**55** 1997/**56**

• **SHARON GLESS** Actress. (Los Angeles, CA) TV's "Cagney and Lacey" and "Trials of Rosie O'Neill." Year/**Age**: 1995/**52** 1996/**53** 1997/**54**

• **BROOKE SHIELDS** Actress. (Born Christa Brooke Camille Shields in NYC) Her first modeling job was at 11 months as the Ivory Snow baby. *Brenda Starr, The Seventh Floor,* and *Backstreet Dreams.* Year/**Age**: 1995/**30** 1996/**31** 1997/**32**

• **NORMAN VINCENT PEALE** Religious leader. (1898-1993, Bowersville, OH) He practiced his ministry on the radio. Best known for *The Power of Positive Thinking,* which sold over a million copies. (Died 12-24-1993.)

• **DENHOLM ELLIOTT** Actor. (1922-1992 – England) Oscar nominee for *A Room With a View.* Also appeared in *Alfie* and two *Indiana Jones* films.

• **WALT WHITMAN** Poet. (1819-1892 – West Hills, NY) Author of *Leaves of Grass,* he wrote "No really great song can ever attain full purport until long after the death of its singer . . . until it has accrued and incorporated the many passions, the many joys and sorrows, it has itself aroused." (Died 3-26-1892.)

FACTS FROM THE PAST

1836 **JOHN JACOB ASTOR**, a rich fur trader, opened the doors to his **ASTORIA HOTEL** in New York City. Years later, it became the Waldorf-Astoria.

1958 Sheb Wooley's **"PURPLE PEOPLE EATER"** began a six-week stay on top of the pop charts.

1961 **BERRYLAND AMUSEMENT PARK** opens outside St. Louis, MO. It is the creation of Chuck Berry.

1962 WWII Gestapo Chief, **ADOLF EICHMANN,** was hanged in Israel for his role in the Nazi holocaust. His body was cremated, and the ashes were scattered in the Mediterranean Sea the following day.

1964 The Giants **DEL CRANDALL** drove in the winning runs for a 8-6 victory over the New York Mets to end a 7-hour and 23-minute, 23 inning game. Including the first game of the doubleheader, the two teams played for a total of 10 hours, 16 minutes.

1976 The **WHO** made the *Guinness Book of World Records* by playing the loudest concert in history: a total output of 76,000 eardrum-splitting watts of power, 120 decibels. The record has since been broken.

1986 **BOBBY RAHAL** won the rain-delayed Indianapolis 500 with a record average speed of 170.722 mph.

1989 **ELVIS PRESLEY'S** daughter, Lisa Marie, gave birth to a girl named Danielle. Priscilla became a grandmother! And **MICHAEL J. FOX** and his wife, Tracy, became parents of a boy, Sam Michael Fox.

1989 The **FIRST INTERNATIONAL ROCK AWARDS** ceremony was held in NYC. *Volume One* by the Traveling Wilburys was named Album of the Year; Artist of the Year was **GUNS AND ROSES.** The band **LIVING COLOR** won as newcomer.

1989 House Speaker **JIM WRIGHT**, tired of questions about his ethics, announced he would resign. Tom Foley succeeded him.

1994 Rep. **DAN ROSTENKOWSKI** was indicted on 17 counts of felony alleging he took close to $700,000.00 from the government, used public funds for personal gain, handed out gifts to friends and paychecks were kicked back to his office by ghost employees.

JUNE MEMORIES

10 YEARS AGO

1985

POPULAR SONGS
"Everybody Wants To Rule the World" by Tears For Fears

"Heaven" by Bryan Adams

MOVIES
Rambo, First Blood Part II
Sylvester Stallone and Richard Crenna looking for MIA's in Vietnam.

The Color Purple
starring Oprah Winfrey, Whoopie Goldberg, and Danny Glover in this film based on Alice Walker's novel.

TV SHOWS
"Stick"
starring Burt Reynolds as an ex-con. With Candice Bergen and George Segal.

"Holywood Beat"
starring Jack Scalia as Detective Nick McCarren in this police show.

BOOKS
The Good War by Studs Terkel

1986

POPULAR SONGS
"Live To Tell" by Madonna

"On My Own" by Patti LaBelle and Michael McDonald

MOVIES
Crimes of the Heart
starring Diane Keaton, Jessica Lange, Sissy Spacek, and Tess Harper as sisters who come together for their grandfather.

Mona Lisa
a British film starring Bob Hoskins, Cathy Tyson, and Michael Caine.

TV SHOWS
"Prime-Time"
a news magazine show with Connie Chung and Roger Mudd.

"Downtown"
starring Michael Nouri, Blair Underwood, and Millicent Martin in this police drama.

BOOKS
Wanderlust by Danielle Steel

1987

POPULAR SONGS
"You Keep Me Hanging On" by Kim Wilde

"Always" by Atlantic Starr

MOVIES
Street Smart
starring Christopher Reeve, Kathy Baker, and Morgan Freeman. The show delves into journlistic corruption.

Full Metal Jacket
Adam Baldwin and Matthew Modine star in the story of Marines in Vietnam during the Tet offensive.

TV SHOWS
"J.J. Starbuck"
starring Dale Robertson as Texas billionaire Jerome Jeremiah Starbuck.

"Dolly"
starring country singer Dolly Parton in this musical variety show.

BOOKS *Windmills of the Gods* by Sidney Sheldon

SPECIAL DAYS

JUNE	1995	1996	1997
Belmont Stakes *(Belmont Park, NY)*	June 10	June 8	June 7
Superman Celebration *(Metropolis, IL)*	June 11-17	June 9-15	June 8-14
Blame Someone Else Day			June 13
Betty Picnic *(Grants Pass, OR)*	June 10	June 8	June 7
Children's Day	June 11	June 9	June 8
National Hollerin' Contest *(Spivey's Corner, NC)*	June 17	June 15	June 21
Father's Day	June 18	June 16	June 22
Summer Begins	June 21	June 20	June 21
Chicken Clucking Contest *(Baltimore, MD)*	June 21	June 19	June 18
Full Moon	June 13	June 1	June 20
Watermelon Thump *(Spivey's Corner, NC)*	June 22-24	June 27-29	June 26-28

25 YEARS AGO

1970

POPULAR SONGS
"The Long and Winding Road" by the Beatles

"The Love You Save" by The Jackson 5

MOVIES
The Tropic of Cancer
starring Rip Torn and James Callahan in this story of Paris, France in the late '60s.

Woodstock
footage of the four-day historical rock concert featuring Joe Cocker, Jimi Hendrix, etc.

TV SHOWS
"Kraft Music Hall Presents the Des O'Connor Show"
British variety show.

"Andy Williams Presents Ray Stevens"
starring Ray Stevens in this summer replacement for Andy Williams.

BOOKS
House Made of Dawn by N. Scott Momaday

1971

POPULAR SONGS
"Want Ads" by The Honey Cone

"It's Too Late" by Carole King

MOVIES
Kotch
starring Walter Matthau, Deborah Winters, and Felicia Farr in the story of a widower who turns into a do-gooder.

Summer of '42
starring Jennifer O'Neill, Gary Grimes, Jerry Houser, and Oliver Connant. A teenage boy falls for an older woman.

TV SHOWS
"The Chicago Teddy Bears"
sit-com about a 1920s speakeasy with Dean Jones and Jamie Farr.

"O'Hara, U.S. Treasury"
cop show with David Janssen as a Treasury Department special agent.

BOOKS *Wunnerful! Wunnerful!* by Lawrence Welk

1972

POPULAR SONGS
"The Candy Man" by Sammy Davis, Jr.

"Song Sung Blue" by Neil Diamond

MOVIES
The Heartbreak Kid
starring Eddie Albert, Cybil Shepherd, and Charles Grodin. Newlyweds have marriage trouble on the way to their honeymoon.

The Life and Times of Judge Roy Bean
starring Paul Newman, Anthony Perkins, Tab Hunter, and Ava Gardner in the story of a Texas judge during the 1880s.

TV SHOWS
"Temperatures Rising"
medical sitcom with Joan Van Ark, James Whitmore, and Cleavon Little.

"NBC Reports"
news documentary show featuring various subjects.

BOOKS *The Word* by Irving Wallace

50 YEARS AGO

1945

POPULAR SONGS
"There I've Said It Again" by Vaughn Moore

"Bell Bottom Trousers" by Guy Lombardo

MOVIES
A Bell For Adano
starring William Bendix, Harry Morgan, and Gene Tierney. The story of Americans who occupy Adano, a small town in Italy.

Enchanted Cottage
starring Dorothy McGuire and Robert Young in this romantic drama.

TV SHOWS
No regularly scheduled TV programming until May 1946.

BOOKS
Black Boy by Richard Wright

1946

POPULAR SONGS
"Hawaiian War Chant (Ta-Hu-Wa-Hu-Wai)" by Spike Jones & His City Slickers wtih the Wacky Wakakians

"The Gypsy" by Ink Spots

MOVIES
The Spiral Staircase
starring Dorothy McGuire, George Brent, and Elsa Lanchester in this mystery about a mute girl.

Brief Encounter
starring Trevor Howard in this Noel Coward drama about an extra-marital affair.

TV SHOWS
"Face To Face"
a cartoon game show featuring Eddie and Bill Dunn.

"Seving Through Science"
Dr. McClintock discusses films with guests.

BOOKS
Top Secret by Ralph Ingersoll

1947

POPULAR SONGS
"Chi-Baba, Chi-Baba, (My Bambino Go To Sleep)" by Perry Como

"Temptation (Tim-Tayshun)" by Red Ingle

MOVIES
Crossfire
featuring Robert Ryan, Robert Mitchum, Robert Young, and Gloria Grahame. Police pursue an anti-Semitic criminal.

Body and Soul
starring John Garfield, Lilli Palmer, and William Conrad in the story of a man trying to become a top prizefighter.

TV SHOWS
"Birthday Party"
show visits children's birthday parties, with host Bill Slater.

BOOKS
Inside U.S. A. by John Gunther

TONY WINNERS

1947

Actors (Dramatic)
José Ferrer, *Cyrano de Bergerac*
Fredric March, *Years Ago*
Actress (Dramatic)
Ingrid Bergman, *Joan of Lorraine*
Helen Hayes, *Happy Birthday*
Actress, Supporting or Featured (Dramatic)
Patricia Neal, *Another Part of the Forest*
Actor, Supporting or Featured (Musical)
David Wayne, *Finian's Rainbow*
Play
Cyrano de Bergerac

1948

Actors (Dramatic)
Henry Fonda, *Mister Roberts*
Actress (Dramatic)
Judith Anderson, *Medea*
Actor (Musical)
Paul Hartman, *Angel in the Wings*
Actress (Musical)
Grace Hartman, *Angel in the Wings*
Play
Mister Roberts

1949

Actor (Dramatic)
Rex Harrison, *Anne of the Thousand Days*
Actress (Dramatic)
Martita Hunt, *The Madwoman of Chaillot*
Actor, Supporting or Featured (Dramatic)
Arthur Kennedy, *Death of a Salesman*
Actress, Supporting or Featured (Dramatic)
Shirley Booth, *Goodbye, My Fancy*
Actor (Musical)
Ray Bolger, *Where's Charley?*
Actress (Musical)
Nanette Fabray, *Love Life*
Play
Death of a Salesman by Arthur Miller
Musical
Kiss Me Kate

1950

Actor (Dramatic)
Sidney Blackmer, *Come Back, Little Sheba*
Actress (Dramatic)
Shirley Booth, *Come Back, Little Sheba*
Actor (Musical)
Ezio Pinza, *South Pacific*
Actress (Musical)
Mary Martin, *South Pacific*
Actor, Supporting or Featured (Musical)
Myron McCormick, *South Pacific*
Actress, Supporting or Featured (Musical)
Juanita Hall, *South Pacific*
Play
The Cocktail Party
Musical
South Pacific

1951

Actor (Dramatic)
Claude Rains, *Darkness At Noon*
Actress (Dramatic)
Uta Hagen, *The Country Girl*
Actor, Supporting or Featured (Dramatic)
Eli Wallach, *The Rose Tattoo*
Actress, Supporting or Featured (Dramatic)
Maureen Stapleton, *The Rose Tattoo*
Actor (Musical)
Robert Alda, *Guys and Dolls*
Actress (Musical)
Ethel Merman, *Call Me Madam*
Actor, Supporting or Featured (Musical)
Russell Nype, *Call Me Madam*
Actress, Supporting or Featured (Musical)
Isabel Bigley, *Guys and Dolls*
Play
The Rose Tattoo
Musical
Guys and Dolls

1952

Actor (Dramatic)
José Ferrer, *The Shrike*
Actress (Dramatic)
Julie Harris, *I Am a Camera*
Actress (Musical)
Gertrude Lawrence, *The King & I*
Actor (Musical)
Phil Silvers, *Top Banana*
Actor, Supporting or Featured (Dramatic)
John Cromwell, *Point of No Return*
Actress, Supporting or Featured (Dramatic)
Marian Winters, *I Am a Camera*
Actor, Supporting or Featured (Musical)
Yul Brynner, *The King & I*
Actress, Supporting or Featured (Musical)
Helen Gallagher, *Pal Joey*
Play
The Fourposter
Musical
The King & I

1953

Actor (Dramatic)
Tom Ewell, *The Seven Year Itch*
Actress (Dramatic)
Shirley Booth, *Time of the Cuckoo*
Actor, Supporting or Featured (Dramatic)
John Williams, *Dial M for Murder*
Actress, Supporting or Featured (Dramatic)
Beatrice Straight, *The Crucible*
Actor (Musical)
Thomas Mitchell, *Hazel Flagg*
Actress (Musical)
Rosalind Russell, *Wonderful Town*
Actor, Supporting or Featured (Musical)
Hiram Sherman, *Two's Company*
Actress, Supporting or Featured (Musical)
Sheila Bond, *Wish You Were Here*

Play
The Crucible by Arthur Miller
Musical
Wonderful Town

1954

Actor (Dramatic)
David Wayne, *The Teahouse of the August Moon*
Actress (Dramatic)
Audrey Hepburn, *Ondine*
Actor, Supporting or Featured (Dramatic)
John Kerr, *Tea and Sympathy*
Actress, Supporting or Featured (Dramatic)
Jo Van Fleet, *The Trip to Bountiful*
Actor (Musical)
Alfred Drake, *Kismet*
Play
The Teahouse of the August Moon

1955

Actor (Dramatic)
Alfred Lunt, *Quadrille*
Actress (Dramatic)
Nancy Kelly, *The Bad Seed*
Actor, Supporting or Featured (Dramatic)
Francis L. Sullivan, *Witness for the Prosecution*
Actress, Supporting or Featured (Dramatic)
Patricia Jessel, *Witness for the Prosecution*
Actor (Musical)
Walter Slezak, *Fanny*
Actress (Musical)
Mary Martin, *Peter Pan*
Actor, Supporting or Featured (Musical)
Cyril Ritchard, *Peter Pan*
Actress, Supporting or Featured (Musical)
Carol Haney, *The Pajama Game*
Play
The Desperate Hours
Musical
The Pajama Game

1956

Actor
Paul Muni, *Inherit the Wind*
Actress (Dramatic)
Julie Harris, *The Lark*
Actor, Supporting or Featured (Dramatic)
Ed Begley, *Inherit the Wind*
Actress, Supporting or Featured (Dramatic)
Una Merkel, *The Ponder Heart*
Actor (Musical)
Ray Walston, *Damn Yankees*
Actress (Musical)
Gwen Verdon, *Damn Yankees*
Actor, Supporting or Featured (Musical)
Russ Brown, *Damn Yankees*
Actress, Supporting or Featured (Musical)
Lotte Lenya, *The Threepenny Opera*
Play
The Diary of Anne Frank
Musical
Damn Yankees

1957

Actor (Dramatic)
    Fredric March, *Long Day's Journey Into Night*
Actress (Dramatic)
    Margaret Leighton, *Separate Tables*
Actor, Supporting or Featured (Dramatic)
    Frank Conroy, *The Potting Shed*
Actress, Supporting or Featured (Dramatic)
    Peggy Cass, *Auntie Mame*
Actor (Musical)
    Rex Harrison, *My Fair Lady*
Actress (Musical)
    Judy Holiday, *Bells Are Ringing*
Actor, Supporting or Featured (Musical)
    Sydney Chaplin, *Bells Are Ringing*
Actress, Supporting or Featured (Musical)
    Edith Adams, *Lil'l Abner*
Play
    Long Day's Journey Into Night
Musical
    Bells Are Ringing

1958

Actor (Dramatic)
    Ralph Bellamy, *Sunrise At Campobello*
Actress (Dramatic)
    Helen Hayes, *Time Remembered*
Actor, Supporting or Featured (Dramatic)
    Henry Jones, *Sunrise At Campobello*
Actress, Supporting or Featured (Dramatic)
    Anne Bancroft, *Two For The Seesaw*
Actor (Musical)
    Robert Preston, *The Music Man*
Actress (Musical)
    Thelma Ritter, *New Girl In Town*
Actor, Supporting or Featured (Musical)
    David Burns, *The Music Man*
Actress, Supporting or Featured (Musical)
    Barbara Cook, *The Music Man*
Play
    Sunrise At Campobello
Musical
    The Music Man

1959

Actor (Dramatic)
    Jason Robards, Jr., *The Disenchanted*
Actress (Dramatic)
    Gertrude Berg, *A Majority of One*
Actor, Supporting or Featured (Dramatic)
    Charlie Ruggles, *The Pleasure of His Company*
Actress, Supporting or Featured (Dramatic)
    Julie Newmar, *The Marriage-Go-Round*
Actor (Musical)
    Richard Kiley, *Redhead*
Actress (Musical)
    Gwen Verdon, *Redhead*
Actor, Supporting or Featured (Musical)
    Russell Nype, *Goldilocks* and Cast of *La Plume de Ma Tante*
Actress, Supporting or Featured (Musical)
    Pat Stanley, *Goldilocks*
Play
    J.B.
Musical
    Flower Drum Song

1960

Actor (Dramatic)
    Melvyn Douglas, *The Best Man*
Actress (Dramatic)
    Anne Bancroft, *The Miracle Worker*
Actor, Supporting or Featured (Dramatic)
    Roddy McDowall, *The Fighting Cock*
Actress, Supporting or Featured (Dramatic)
    Anne Revere, *Toys in the Attic*
Actor (Musical)
    Jackie Gleason, *Take Me Along*
Actress (Musical)
    Mary Martin, *The Sound of Music*
Actor, Supporting or Featured (Musical)
    Tom Bosley, *Fiorello!*
Actress, Supporting or Featured (Musical)
    Patricia Neway, *The Sound of Music*
Play
    The Miracle Worker by William Gibson
Musical
    Fiorello!

1961

Actor (Dramatic)
    Zero Mostel, *Rhinoceros*
Actress (Dramatic)
    Joan Plowright, *A Taste of Honey*
Actor, Supporting or Featured (Dramatic)
    Martin Gabel, *Big Fish, Little Fish*
Actress, Supporting or Featured (Dramatic)
    Colleen Dewhurst, *All the Way Home*
Actor (Musical)
    Richard Burton, *Camelot*
Actress (Musical)
    Elizabeth Seal, *Irma la Douce*
Actor, Supporting or Featured (Musical)
    Dick Van Dyke, *Bye, Bye Birdie*
Actress, Supporting or Featured (Musical)
    Tammy Grimes, *The Unsinkable Molly Brown*
Play
    Becket
Musical
    Bye, Bye Birdie

1962

Actor (Dramatic)
    Paul Scofield, *A Man for All Seasons*
Actress (Dramatic)
    Margaret Leighton, *Night of the Iguana*
Actor, Supporting or Featured (Dramatic)
    Walter Matthau, *A Shot in the Dark*
Actress, Supporting or Featured (Dramatic)
    Elizabeth Ashley, *Take Her, She's Mine*
Actor (Musical)
    Robert Morse, *How to Succeed in Business Without Really Trying*
Actress (Musical)
    Anna Marie Alberghetti, *Carnival* and Diahann Carroll, *No Strings*
Actor, Supporting or Featured (Musical)
    Charles Nelson Reilly, *How to Succeed in Business Without Really Trying*
Actress, Supporting or Featured (Musical)
    Phyllis Newman, *Subways Are for Sleeping*
Play
    A Man for All Seasons
Musical
    How to Succeed in Business Without Really Trying

1963

Actor (Dramatic)
    Arthur Hill, *Who's Afraid of Virginia Woolf?*
Actress (Dramatic)
    Uta Hagen, *Who's Afraid of Virginia Woolf?*
Actor, Supporting or Featured (Dramatic)
    Alan Arkin, *Enter Laughing*
Actress, Supporting or Featured (Dramatic)
    Sandy Dennis, *A Thousand Clowns*
Actor (Musical)
    Zero Mostel, *A Funny Thing Happened on the Way to the Forum*
Actress (Musical)
    Vivien Leigh, *Tovarich*
Actor, Supporting or Featured (Musical)
    David Burns, *A Funny Thing Happened on the Way to the Forum*
Actress, Supporting or Featured (Musical)
    Anna Quayle, *Stop the World – I Want to Get Off*
Play
    Who's Afraid of Virginia Woolf?
Musical
    A Funny Thing Happened on the Way to the Forum

1964

Actor (Dramatic)
    Alec Guinness, *Dylan*
Actress (Dramatic)
    Sandy Dennis, *Any Wednesday*
Actor, Supporting or Featured (Dramatic)
    Hume Cronyn, *Hamlet*
Actress, Supporting or Featured (Dramatic)
    Barbara Loden, *After the Fall*
Actor (Musical)
    Bert Lahr, *Foxy*
Actress (Musical)
    Carol Channing, *Hello, Dolly!*
Actor, Supporting or Featured (Musical)
    Jack Cassidy, *She Loves Me*
Actress, Supporting or Featured (Musical)
    Tessie O'Shea, *The Girl Who Came to Supper*
Play,
    Luther
Musical,
    Hello, Dolly!

1965

Actor (Dramatic)
    Walter Matthau, *The Odd Couple*
Actress (Dramatic)
    Irene Worth, *Tiny Alice*
Actor, Supporting or Featured (Dramatic)
    Jack Albertson, *The Subject Was Roses*
Actress, Supporting or Featured (Dramatic)
    Alice Ghostley, *The Sign in Sidney Brustein's Window*
Actor (Musical)
    Zero Mostel, *Fiddler on the Roof*
Actress (Musical)
    Liza Minnelli, *Flora, The Red Menace*
Actor, Supporting or Featured (Musical)
    Victor Spinetti, *Oh, What A Lovely War*
Actress, Supporting or Featured (Musical)
    Maria Karnilova, *Fiddler on the Roof*
Play
    The Subject Was Roses
Musical
    Fiddler on the Roof

1966

Actor (Dramatic)
    Hal Holbrook, *Mark Twain Tonight!*
Actress (Dramatic)
    Rosemary Harris, *The Lion in Winter*
Actor, Supporting or Featured (Dramatic)
    Patrick Magee, *Marat/Sade*

Actress, Supporting or Featured (Dramatic
    Zoe Caldwell, *Slapstick Tragedy*
Actor (Musical)
    Richard Kiley, *Man of La Mancha*
Actress (Musical)
    Angela Lansbury, *Mame*
Actor, Supporting or Featured (Musical)
    Frankie Michaels, *Mame*
Actress, Supporting or Featured (Musical
    Beatrice Arthur, *Mame*
Play
    Marat/Sade
Musical
    Man of La Mancha

1967

Actor (Dramatic)
    Paul Rogers, *The Homecoming*
Actress (Dramatic)
    Beryl Reid, *The Killing of Sister
    George*
Actor, Supporting or Featured (Dramatic)
    Ian Holm, *The Homecoming*
Actress, Supporting or Featured (Dramatic)
    Marian Seldes, *A Delicate Balance*
Actor (Musical)
    Robert Preston, *I Do! I Do!*
Actress (Musical)
    Barbara Harris, *The Apple Tree*
Actor, Supporting or Featured (Musical)
    Joel Grey, *Cabaret*
Actress, Supporting or Featured (Musical)
    Peg Murray, *Cabaret*
Play
    The Homecoming
Musical
    Cabaret

1968

Actor (Dramatic)
    Martin Balsam, *You Know I Can't
    Hear You When the Water's Running*
Actress (Dramatic)
    Zoe Caldwell, *The Prime of Miss Jean
    Brodie*
Actor, Supporting or Featured (Dramatic)
    James Patterson, *The Birthday Party*
Actress, Supporting or Featured (Dramatic)
    Zena Walker, *Joe Egg*
Actor (Musical)
    Robert Goulet, *The Happy Time*
Actress (Musical)
    Patricia Routledge, *Darling of the Day*
    and Leslie Uggams, *Hallelujah, Baby!*
Actor, Supporting or Featured (Musical)
    Hiram Sherman, *How Now, Dow Jones*
Actress, Supporting or Featured (Musical)
    Lillian Hayman, *Hallelujah, Baby!*
Play
    *Rosencrantz and Guilderstern Are
    Dead*
Musical
    Hallelujah, Baby!

1969

Actor (Dramatic)
    James Earl Jones, *The Great White
    Hope*
Actress (Dramatic)
    Julie Harris, *Forty Carats*
Actor, Supporting or Featured (Dramatic)
    Al Pacino, *Does a Tiger Wear a
    Necktie?*
Actress, Supporting or Featured (Dramatic)
    Jane Alexander, *The Great White Hope*
Actor (Musical)

Jerry Orbach, *Promises, Promises*
Actress (Musical)
    Angela Lansbury, *Dear World*
Actor, Supporting or Featured (Musical
    Ronald Holgate, *1776*
Actress, Supporting or Featured (Musical)
    Marian Mercer, *Promises, Promises*
Play
    The Great White Hope
Musical
    1776

1970

Actor (Dramatic)
    Fritz Weaver, *Child's Play*
Actress (Dramatic)
    Tammy Grimes, *Private Lives*
    (Revival)
Actor, Supporting or Featured (Dramatic)
    Ken Howard, *Child's Play*
Actress, Supporting or Featured (Dramatic)
    Blythe Danner, *Butterflies Are Free*
Actor (Musical)
    Cleavon Little, *Purlie*
Actress (Musical)
    Lauren Bacall, *Applause*
Actor, Supporting or Featured (Musical)
    René Auberjonois, *Coco*
Actress, Supporting of Featured (Musical)
    Melba Moore, *Purlie*
Play
    Borstal Boy
Musical
    Applause

1971

Actor (Dramatic)
    Brian Bedford, *The School for Wives*
Actress (Dramatic)
    Maureen Stapleton, *Gingerbread Lady*
Actor, Supporting or Featured (Dramatic)
    Paul Sand, *Story Theatre*
Actress, Supporting or Featured (Dramatic)
    Rae Allen, *And Miss Reardon Drinks a
    Little*
Actor (Musical)
    Hal Linden, *The Rothschilds*
Actress (Musical)
    Helen Gallagher, *No, No, Nanette*
Actor, Supporting or Featured (Musical)
    Keene Curtis, *The Rothschilds*
Actress, Supporting or Featured (Musical)
    Patsy Kelly, *No, No, Nanette*
Play
    Sleuth
Musical
    Company

1972

Actor (Dramatic)
    Cliff Gorman, *Lenny*
Actress (Dramatic)
    Sada Thompson, *Twigs*
Actor, Supporting or Featured (Dramatic)
    Vincent Gardenia, *The Prisoner of
    Second Avenue*
Actress, Supporting or Featured (Dramatic)
    Elizabeth Wilson, *Sticks and Bones*
Actor (Musical)
    Phil Silvers, *A Funny Thing Happened
    on the Way to the Forum* (Revival)
Actress (Musical)
    Alexis Smith, *Follies*
Actor, Supporting or Featured (Musical)
    Larry Blyden, *A Funny Thing*

Happened on the Way to the Forum
    (Revival)
Actress, Supporting or Featured (Musical)
    Linda Hopkins, *Inner City*
Play
    Sticks and Bones
Musical
    Two Gentlemen of Verona

1973

Actor (Dramatic)
    Alan Bates, *Butley*
Actress (Dramatic)
    Julie Harris, *The Last of Mrs. Lincoln*
Actor, Supporting or Featured (Dramatic)
    John Lithgow, *The Changing Room*
Actress, Supporting or Featured (Dramatic)
    Leona Dana, *The Last of Mrs. Lincoln*
Actor (Musical)
    Ben Vereen, *Pippin*
Actress (Musical)
    Glynnis Johns, *A Little Night Music*
Actor, Supporting or Featured (Musical)
    George S. Irving, *Irene*
Actress, Supporting or Featured (Musical)
    Patricia Elliot, *A Little Night Music*
Play
    That Championship Season
Musical
    A Little Night Music

1974

Actor (Dramatic)
    Michael Moriarty, *Find Your Way
    Home*
Actress (Dramatic)
    Colleen Dewhurst, *A Moon for the
    Misbegotten*
Actor, Supporting or Featured (Dramatic)
    Ed Flanders, *A Moon for the
    Misbegotten*
Actress, Supporting or Featured (Dramatic)
    Frances Sternhagen, *The Good Doctor*
Actor (Musical)
    Christopher Plummer, *Cyrano*
Actress (Musical)
    Virginia Capers, *Raisin*
Actor, Supporting or Featured (Musical)
    Tommy Tune, *Seesaw*
Actress, Supporting or Featured (Musical)
    Janie Sell, *Over Here!*
Play
    The River Niger
Musical
    Raisin

1975

Actor (Dramatic)
    John Kani and Winston Ntshona,
    Swizwe Banzi is Dead and The Island
Actress (Dramatic)
    Ellen Burstyn, *Same Time, Next Year*
Actor, Supporting or Featured (Dramatic)
    Frank Langella, *Seascape*
Actress, Supporting or Featured (Dramatic
    Rita Moreno, *The Ritz*
Actor (Musical)
    John Cullum, *Shenandoah*
Actress (Musical)
    Angela Lansbury, *Gypsy*
Actor, Supporting or Featured (Musical)
    Ted Ross, *The Wiz*
Actress Supporting or Featured (Musical)
    Dee Dee Bridgewater, *The Wiz*

Play
Equus
Musical
The Wiz

1976

Actor (Play)
John Wood, *Travesties*
Actress (Play)
Irene Worth, *Sweet Bird of Youth*
Actor (Featured role - Play)
Edward Hermann, *Mrs. Warren's Profession*
Actress (Featured role - Play)
Shirley Knight, *Kennedy's Children*
Actor (Musical)
George Rose, *My Fair Lady*
Actress (Musical)
Donna McKechnie, *A Chorus Line*
Actor (Featured role - Musical)
Sammy Williams, *A Chorus Line*
Actress (Featured role - Musical)
Carole Bishop, *A Chorus Line*
Play
Travesties
Musical
A Chorus Line

1977

Actor (Play)
Al Pacino, *The Basic Training of Pavlo Hummel*
Actress (Play)
Julie Harris, *The Belle of Amherst*
Actor (Featured Role - Play)
Jonathan Pryce, *Comedians*
Actress (Featured Role - Play)
Trazana Beverly, *For Colored Girls Who Have Considered Suicide! When The Rainbow is Enuf*
Actor (Musical)
Barry Bostwick, *The Robber Bridegroom*
Actress (Musical)
Dorothy Loudon, *Annie*
Actor (Featured Role - Musical)
Lenny Baker, *I Love My Wife*
Actress (Featured Role - Musical)
Delores Hall, *Your Arm's Too Short To Box With God*
Play
The Shadow Box
Musical
Annie

1978

Actor (Play)
Barnard Hughes, *Da*
Actress (Play)
Jessica Tandy, *The Gin Game*
Actor (Featured Role - Play)
Lester Rawlins, *Da*
Actress (Featured Role - Play)
Ann Wedgeworth, *Chapter Two*
Actor (Musical)
John Cullum, *On the Twentieth Century*
Actress (Musical)
Liza Minnelli, *The Act*
Actor (Featured Role - Musical)
Kevin Kline, *On the Twentieth Century*
Actress (Featured Role - Musical)
Nell Carter, *Ain't Misbehavin'*
Play
Da

Musical
Ain't Misbehavin'

1979

Actor (Play)
Tom Conti, *Whose Life Is It Anyway?*
Actress (Play)
Constance Cummings, *Wings*
Carole Shelley, *The Elephant Man*
Actor (Featured Role - Play)
Michael Gough, *Bedroom Farce*
Actress (Featured Role - Play)
Joan Hickson, *Bedroom Farce*
Actor (Musical)
Len Cariou, *Sweeney Todd*
Actress (Musical)
Angela Lansbury, *Sweeney Todd*
Actor (Featured Role - Musical)
Henderson Forsythe, *The Best Little Whorehouse in Texas*
Actress (Featured Role - Musical)
Carlin Glynn, *The Best Little Whorehouse in Texas*
Play
The Elephant Man
Musical
Sweeney Todd

1980

Actor (Play)
John Rubinstein, *Children of a Lesser God*
Actress (Play)
Phyllis Frelich, *Children of a Lesser God*
Actor (Featured Role - Play)
David Rounds, *Morning's At Seven*
Actress (Featured Role - Play)
Dinah Manoff, *I Ought To Be In Pictures*
Actor (Musical)
Jim Dale, *Barnum*
Actress (Musical)
Patti LuPone, *Evita*
Actor (Featured Role - Musical)
Mandy Patinkin, *Evita*
Actress (Featured Role - Musical)
Priscilla Lopez, *A Day in Hollywood/A Night in the Ukraine*
Play
Children of a Lesser God
Musical
Evita

1981

Actor (Play)
Ian McKellen, *Amadeus*
Actress (Play)
Jane Lapotaire, *Piaf*
Actor (Featured Role - Play)
Brian Backer, *The Floating Light Bulb*
Actress (Featured Role - Play)
Swoosie Kurtz, *Fifth of July*
Actor (Musical)
Kevin Kline, *Pirates of Penzance*

Actress (Musical)
Lauren Bacall, *Woman of the Year*
Actor (Featured Role - Musical)
Hinton Battle, *Sophisticated Ladies*
Actress (Featured Role - Musical)
Marilyn Cooper, *Woman of the Year*
Play
Amadeus
Musical

42nd Street

1982

Actor (Play)
Roger Rees, *The Life and Adventures of Nicholas Nickleby*
Actress (Play)
Zoe Caldwell, *Medea*
Actor (Featured Role - Play)
Richard Kavanaugh, *The Hothouse*
Actress (Featured Role - Play)
Amanda Plummer, *Agnes of God*
Actor (Musical)
Ben Harney, *Dreamgirls*
Actress (Musical)
Jennifer Holliday, *Dreamgirls*
Actor (Featured Role - Musical)
Cleavant Derricks, *Dreamgirls*
Actress (Featured Role - Musical)
Liliane Montevecchi, *Nine*
Play
The Life and Adventures of Nicholas Nickleby
Musical
Nine

1983

Actor (Play)
Harvey Feirstein, *Torch Song Trilogy*
Actress (Play)
Jessica Tandy, *Foxfire*
Actor (Featured Role - Play)
Matthew Broderick, *Brighton Beach Memoirs*
Actress (Featured Role - Play)
Judith Ivey, *Steaming*
Actor (Musical)
Tommy Tune, *My One and Only*
Actress (Musical)
Natalia Makarova, *On Your Toes*
Actor (Featured Role - Musical)
Charles Honi Coles, *On Your Toes*
Actress (Featured Role - Musical)
Betty Buckley, *Cats*
Play
Torch Song Trilogy
Musical
Cats

1984

Actor (Play)
Jeremy Irons, *The Real Thing*
Actress (Play)
Glenn Close, *The Real Thing*
Actor (Featured Role - Play)
Joe Mantegna, *Glengarry Glen Ross*
Actress (Featured Role - Play)
Christine Baranski, *The Real Thing*
Actor (Musical)
George Hearn, *La Cage aux Folles*
Actress (Musical)
Chita Rivera, *The Rink*
Actor (Featured Role - Musical)
Hinton Battle, *The Tap Dance Kid*

Actress (Featured Role - Musical)
Lila Kedrova, *Zorba*
Play
The Real Thing
Musical
La Cage aux Folles

1985

Actor (Play)
  Derek Jacobi, *Much Ado About Nothing*
Actress (Play)
  Stockard Channing, *Joe Egg*
Actor (Featured Role - Play)
  Barry Miller, *Biloxi Blues*
Actress (Featured Role - Play)
  Judith Ivey, *Hurlyburly*
Actor (Musical)
  Ron Richardson, *Big River*
Actress (Musical)
  Leilani Jones, *Grind*
Play
  Biloxi Blues
Musical
  Big River

1986

Actor (Play)
  Judd Hirsch, *I'm Not Rappaport*
Actress (Play)
  Lily Tomlin, *The Search for Signs of Intelligent Life in the Universe*
Actor (Featured Role - Play)
  John Mahoney, *The House of Blue Leaves*
Actress (Featured Role - Play)
  Swoosie Kurtz, *The House of Blue Leaves*
Actor (Musical)
  George Rose, *The Mystery of Edwin Drood*
Actress (Musical)
  Bernadette Peters, *Song & Dance*
Actor (Featured Role - Musical)
  Michael Rupert, *Sweet Charity*
Actress (Featured Role - Musical)
  Bebe Neuwirth, *Sweet Charity*
Play
  I'm Not Rappaport
Musical
  The Mystery of Edwin Drood

1987

Actor (Play)
  James Earl Jones, *Fences*
Actress (Play)
  Linda Lavin, *Broadway Bound*
Actor (Featured Role - Play)
  Jason Randolph, *Broadway Bound*
Actress (Featured Role - Play)
  Mary Alice, *Fences*
Actor (Musical)
  Robert Lindsay, *Me and My Girl*
Actress (Musical)
  Maryann Plunkett, *Me and My Girl*
Actor (Featured Role - Musical)
  Michael Maguire, *Les Miserables*
Actress (Featured Role - Musical)
  Frances Ruffelle, *Les Miserables*
Play
  Fences
Musical
  Les Miserables

1988

Actor (Play)
  Ron Silver, *Speed-the-Plow*
Actress (Play)
  Joan Allen, *Burn This*
Actor (Featured Role - Play)
  B. D. Wong, *Madam Butterfly*
Actress (Featured Role - Play
Actor (Musical)
  Michael Crawford, *The Phantom of the Opera*

Actress (Musical)
  Joanna Gleason, *Into the Woods*
Actor (Featured Role - Musical)
  Bill McCutcheon, *Anything Goes*
Actress (Featured Role - Musical)
  Judy Kaye, *The Phantom of the Opera*
Play
  Madam Butterfly
Musical
  The Phantom of the Opera

1989

Actor (Play)
  Philip Bosco, *Lend Me a Tenor*
Actress (Play)
  Pauline Collins, *Shirley Valentine*
Actor (Featured Role - Play)
  Boyd Gaines, *The Heidi Chronicles*
Actress (Featured Role - Play
  Christine Baranski, *Rumore*
Actor (Musical)
  Jason Alexander, *Jerome Robbins's Broadway*
Actress (Musical)
  Ruth Brown, *Black and Blue*
Actor (Featured Role - Musical)
  Scott Wise, *Jerome Robbins's Broadway*
Actress (Featured Role - Musical)
  Debbie Shapiro, *Jerome Robbins's Broadway*
Play
  The Heidi Chronicles
Musical
  Jerome Robbins's Broadway

1990

Actor (Play)
  Robert Morse, *Tru*
Actress (Play)
  Maggie Smith, *Lettice and Lovage*
Actor (Featured Role - Play)
  Charles Durning, *Cat on a Hot Tin Roof*
Actress (Featured Role - Play)
  Margaret Tyzack, *Lettice and Lovage*
Actor (Musical)
  James Naughton, *City of Angels*
Actress (Musical)
  Tyne Daly, *Gypsy*
Actor (Featured Role - Musical)
  Michael Jeter, *Grand Hotel*
Actress (Featured Role - Musical)
  Randy Graff, *City of Angels*
Play
  The Grapes of Wrath
Musical
  City of Angels

1991

Actor (Play)
  Nigel Hawthorne, *Shadowlands*
Actress (Play)
  Mercedes Ruehl, *Lost in Yonkers*
Actor (Featured Role - Play)
  Kevin Spacey, *Lost in Yonkers*
Actress (Featured Role - Play)
  Irene Worth, *Lost in Yonkers*
Actor (Musical)
  Jonathan Pryce, *Miss Saigon*
Actress (Musical)
  Lea Salonga, *Miss Saigon*
Actor (Featured Role - Musical)
  Hinton Battle, *Miss Saigon*
Actress (Featured Role - Musical)
  Daisy Eagan, *The Secret Garden*
Play
  Lost in Yonkers

Musical
  The Will Rogers Follies

1992

Actor (Play)
  Judd Hirsch, *Conversations with My Father*
Actress (Play)
  Glenn Close, *Death and the Maiden*
Actor (Featured Role - Play)
  Larry Fishburne, *Two Trains Running*
Actress (Featured Role - Play)
  Brid Brennan, *Dancing at Lughnasa*
Actor (Musical)
  Gregory Hines, *Jelly's Last Jam*
Actress (Musical)
  Faith Prince, *Guys and Dolls*
Actor (Featured Role - Musical)
  Scott Waara, *The Most Happy Fella*
Actress (Featured Role - Musical)
  Tonya Pinkins, *Jelly's Last Jam*
Play
  Dancing at Lughnasa
Musical
  Crazy for You

1993

Actor (Play)
  Ron Leibman, *Angels in America: Millennium Approaches*
Actress (Play)
  Madeline Kahn, *The Sisters Rosensweig*
Actor (Featured Role - Play)
  Stephen Spinella, *Angels in America: Millennium Approaches*
Actress (Featured Role - Play)
  Debra Monk, *Redwood Curtain*
Actor (Musical)
  Brent Carver, *Kiss of the Spider Woman*
Actress (Musical)
  Chita Rivera, *Kiss of the Spider Woman*
Actor (Featured Role - Musical)
  Anthony Crivello, *Kiss of the Spider Woman*
Actress (Featured Role - Musical)
  Andrea Martin, *My Favorite Year*
Play
  Angels in America: Millennium Approaches
Musical
  Kiss of the Spider Woman

1994

Actor (Play)
  Steihpen Spinella, *Angels in America: Perestroika*
Actress (Play)
  Diana Rigg, *Medea*
Actor (Featured Role--Play)
  Jeffry Wright, *Angels in America: Perestroika*
Actress (Featured Role--Play)
  Jane Adams, *An Inspector Calls*
Actor (Musical)
  Boyd Gaines, *She Loves Me*
Actress (Musical)
  Donna Murphy, *Passion*
Actor (Featured Role--Musical)
  Jarrod Emick, *Damn Yankees*
Actress (Featured Role--Musical)
  Audra Ann McDonald, *Carousel*
Play
  Angels in America: Perestroika
Musical
  Passion

Show me a good farmer, and I'll show you a good mechanic.

JUNE 1

BIRTHDAYS

- **LISA HARTMAN** Actress. (Houston, TX) "Knots Landing." She married country singer Clint Black Oct. 20, 1991. Year/**Age**: 1995/**39** 1996/**40** 1997/**41**

- **POWERS BOOTHE** Actor. Film *Tombstone*. Year/**Age**: 1995/**46** 1996/**47** 1997/**48**

- **MORGAN FREEMAN** Actor. (Memphis, TN) He was on PBS with the "Electric Company" in the 70s. Oscar nomination for *Driving Miss Daisy*. Also in *Glory*, *Unforgiven*, and played Azem in *Robin Hood: Prince of Thieves*. TV's soap "Another World" and miniseries "Queen." He directed the film *Bopha*. Year/**Age**: 1995/**58** 1996/**59** 1997/**60**

- **RONNIE DUNN** C & W singer. (Coleman, TX) Biggest hit with Kix Brooks, "Boot Scootin' Boogie." Year/**Age**: 1995/**42** 1996/**43** 1997/**44**

- **ANDY GRIFFITH** Actor. (Mount Airy, NC) His "Andy Griffith Show" did well for 5 seasons in the 1960s. He's been an actor/singer/producer on TV and appeared in *A Face in the Crowd*, *No Time for Sergeants*, and "Matlock." Year/**Age**: 1995/**69** 1996/**70** 1997/**71**

- **PAT BOONE** Entertainer. (Born Charles Eugene Boone in Jacksonville, FL) A teen idol in the 1950s, he graduated *magna cum laude* from Columbia University. His biggest hit: "Love Letters in the Sand" in 1957. He's married to the former Shirley Foley, daughter of Red Foley, and they have 4 daughters. Year/**Age**: 1995/**61** 1996/**62** 1997/**63**

- **RON WOOD** Guitarist. (England) He replaced Mick Taylor in the ROLLING STONES in 1975. Year/**Age**: 1995/**48** 1996/**49** 1997/**50**

- **TOM SNEVA** Racecar driver. (Spokane, WA) He won the Indy 500 in 1983. Year/**Age**: 1995/**47** 1996/**48** 1997/**49**

- **EDWARD WOODWARD** Actor. (Croyden, England) TV's "The Equalizer." Year/**Age**: 1995/**65** 1996/**66** 1997/**67**

- **GRAHAM RUSSELL** Singer. (England) With AIR SUPPLY, biggest hit: "The One That You Love" in 1981. Year/**Age**: 1995/**45** 1996/**46** 1997/**47**

- **FRANK MORGAN** Actor. (1890-1949 – Born Francis Wuppermann in NYC) The Wizard in *The Wizard of Oz*. (Died 9-18-49.)

- **CLEAVON LITTLE** Actor/comedian & former football star. (1940-1992 – Chickasha, OK) Won a Tony award for the 1970 musical *Purlie* and an Emmy in 1989 for a guest appearance on the television series "Dear John." Most remembered for his performance as Bart the sheriff in the film *Blazing Saddles*. (Died 10-22-92.)

- **ALAN "THE HORSE" AMECHE** Football fullback. (1933-1988 - Kenosha, WI) An All-American fullback at the University of Wisconsin and the only Badger player to win the Heisman Trophy. He played pro with the Baltimore Colts and a multi-millionaire in the fast food business. (Died 8-24-88.)

- **NELSON RIDDLE** Bandleader. (1921-1985 – Hackensack, NJ) He did the arranging and conducting for Frank Sinatra and was credited with bringing the song "Mona Lisa" to Nat "King" Cole the first time they met at the Chicago Theater. He had a #1 hit in 1956: "Lisbon Antigua."

- **MARILYN MONROE** Actress. (1926-1962 – Born Norma Jean Baker in Los Angeles, CA) Marilyn was born out of wedlock to Gladys Baker, a studio worker, and Edward Mortenson, a baker, who disappeared before her birth. She was found dead in the bedroom of her home in LA. Her death at age 36 was ruled a "probable suicide" caused by an overdose of sleeping pills. Her films included: *Some Like It Hot*, *The Asphalt Jungle*, and *Gentlemen Prefer Blondes*. Her last film was *The Misfits* with Clark Gable. When asked what she wore to bed, her reply was, "Chanel Number Five." "Candle in the Wind," by Elton John is a tribute to Marilyn. (Died 8-5-62.)

FACTS FROM THE PAST

1813 The mortally wounded commander of the U.S. Frigate *Chesapeake*, Captain **JAMES LAWRENCE**, was heard to say, "**DON'T GIVE UP THE SHIP**" during a losing battle with the British frigate, *Shannon*.

1819 **MADAME ADOLPHE** of Paris performed at the Anthony Street Theatre in New York City. It was the **FIRST** North American performance by a **WOMAN TIGHTROPE ARTIST**.

1869 The **ELECTRIC VOTE RECORDER** was patented by Thomas Edison.

1927 **LIZZIE BORDEN**, accused of the ax murders of her stepmother and father in Fall River, MA, died at age 66.

1938 The Man of Steel, **SUPERMAN**, appeared in the first issue of *Action Comics*. The world's first superhero was created by **JERRY SIEGEL** after he dreamed about the Biblical story of Moses, whose parents abandoned him as a baby in order to save his life. This became the plot of the first Superman story.

1958 **CHARLES DE GAULLE** became the Premier of France.

1964 The **ROLLING STONES** arrived in New York to begin their first American tour. Their first date was at a high school stadium in Lynn, MA.

1967 The **BEATLES** released their now-classic album *Sergeant Pepper's Lonely Hearts Club Band*. It won 4 Grammys: best engineered, best album, best contemporary album, and best album cover. The LP was #1 for four months. (Capitol Records estimates the album's worldwide sales to date at over 15 million copies.)

1993 CBS-TV tried dual news anchors for the first time. **DAN RATHER** and **CONNIE CHUNG** began working together on "The CBS Evening News."

1994 **RODNEY KING** lost a request for millions of dollars in punitive damages in what the jury forewoman said was a compromise between jurors who thought King was brutalized and those who thought police were just doing their job.

JUNE 2

BIRTHDAYS

- **WILLIAM GUEST** Singer. (Atlanta, GA) One of the PIPS with Gladys Knight. Biggest hit: "Midnight Train to Georgia." Year/**Age:** 1995/**54** 1996/**55** 1997/**56**

- **DANA CARVEY** Actor. (Missoula, MT) TV's "Saturday Night Live," in films *Clean Slate, It Happened in Paradise,* and played Garth Algar in *Wayne's World I* and *II.* He said, "I was a nerd in high school. At my reunion no one would remember me. I'd have to go as Garth." Year/**Age:** 1995/**40** 1996/**41** 1997/**42**

- **SALLY KELLERMAN** Actress. (Long Beach, CA) She was nominated for an Oscar for supporting actress as the original "Hot Lips Houlihan" in the 1970 film *M*A*S*H* and also starred in *Boris and Natasha.* Year/**Age:** 1995/**58** 1996/**59** 1997/**60**

- **GARO YEPEMIAN** Football. Miami kicker. Year/**Age:** 1995/**51** 1996/**52** 1997/**53**

- **STACY KEACH** Actor. (Savannah, GA) Mickey Spillane's "Mike Hammer" on TV. He also played Ernest Hemingway in a made-for-TV film. Year/**Age:** 1995/**54** 1996/**55** 1997/**56**

- **MICHAEL STEELE** Bass guitarist. With the BANGLES; originally named the BANGS. Biggest hit: "Walk Like an Egyptian" in 1986. Year/**Age:** 1995/**41** 1996/**42** 1997/**43**

- **CARL BUTLER** C&W singer. (1927-1992, Knoxville, TN) Biggest hit: "Don't Let Me Cross Over" in 1962. (Died 9-4-92.)

- **CHARLES HAID** Actor. (San Francisco, CA) Played Officer Andy Renko on "Hill Street Blues." Year/**Age:** 1995/**52** 1996/**53** 1997/**54**

- **JERRY MATHERS** Actor. (Sioux City, IA) Played Theodore Cleaver, "The Beaver," on the "Leave it to Beaver" TV series in the late '50s, early '60s. Also "Still the Beaver." Year/**Age:** 1995/**47** 1996/**48** 1997/**49**

- **CHARLIE WATTS** Drummer. (England) With the ROLLING STONES. Biggest hits: "Satisfaction" and "Honky Tonk Women." Charlie always had a desire to play big band music and made a live recording with some of the best side men in England. Year/**Age:** 1995/**54** 1996/**55** 1997/**56**

- **DIANA CANOVA** Actress. (West Palm Beach, FL) *Throb* and TV sitcom "Home Free." Daughter of entertainer Judy Canova. Year/**Age:** 1995/**42** 1996/**43** 1997/**44**

- **BARRY LEVINSON** Director. (Baltimore, MD) Oscar winner in 1989 for *Rain Man.* Year/**Age:** 1995/**62** 1996/**63** 1997/**64**

- **MARVIN HAMLISCH** Songwriter. (NYC) In 1973, he won 3 Oscars: for best song, "The Way We Were;" best original dramatic score; and best scoring adaptation for *The Sting.* He's also well-known for writing *They're Playing Our Song* which starred Lucie Arnaz & Robert Klein on Broadway. He composed the music for "Good Morning America." Year/**Age:** 1995/**51** 1996/**52** 1997/**53**

- **JERRY LUMPE** Baseball. Most of his career he played for Kansas City and Detroit. .268 lifetime average. Year/**Age:** 1995/**62** 1996/**63** 1997/**64**

- **JOHNNY WEISSMULLER** Athlete/actor. (1904-1984 – Born John Peter Weissmuller in Chicago, IL) From 1932 he played Tarzan more often than anyone else. Prior to his movie career, he won 5 Olympic gold medals, and held 67 world records and 52 national swimming records. (Died 1-21-84.)

- **HEDDA HOPPER** Hollywood gossip columnist. (1890-1966 – Born Elda Furry in Hollidaysburg, PA) (Died 2-1-66.)

- **MARQUIS de SADE** (1740-1814 – Paris, France) He spent most of his life in prison for acts of violence and cruelty from which he received gratification. The word "sadism" is derived from his name. (Died 12-2-1814.)

FACTS FROM THE PAST

1835   **P.T. BARNUM** toured the first circus in the United States.

1886   At 49, **GROVER CLEVELAND** became the first president to be married in the White House. He wed Frances Folsom (22 years old.)

1895   Guglielmo Marconi received a **U.S. PATENT** for his invention – the **RADIO**.

1899   **BUTCH CASSIDY AND THE SUNDANCE KID** and their gang held up the Overland Express in Wyoming. While they were arguing with the conductor, they forgot about the explosives they had planted and the bridge blew up.

1925   Baseball great **LOU GEHRIG** played in his first game with the Yankees when he pinch-hit for the ailing first-baseman Wally Pipp. Gehrig continued playing for 15 years – 2,130 consecutive games. He died on this day in 1941.

1933   President **FRANKLIN D. ROOSEVELT** dedicated the first swimming pool in the White House.

1953   The **CORONATION OF QUEEN ELIZABETH** (the first coronation televised) took place in Westminster Abbey. She practiced the ceremony for months at Buckingham Palace wearing a big sheet she attached to her shoulders. Elizabeth had ascended to the British throne four months earlier upon the death of her father, King George.

1979   Pope John Paul II arrived in his native Poland for the **FIRST VISIT BY A POPE** to a Communist country.

1986   The first **TELEVISED PROCEEDINGS** of the **U.S. SENATE** took place as a six-week experiment of sessions began on TV.

1989   ROLLING STONES bassist **BILL WYMAN**, 48, married 19-year-old model Mandy Smith. They divorced in 1991.

1992   **ROD STEWART** and **RACHEL HUNTER** had a baby – Renee.

1993   **WINNIE MANDELA**'s conviction for kidnapping four young blacks was upheld by South Africa's Supreme Court. They determined, however, that she would not have to serve any of her 5-year prison term.

5'7" Spud Webb once won the NBA Slam Dunk competition.

JUNE 3

BIRTHDAYS

- **BOOTS RANDOLPH** Sax player. (Born Homer Randolph III in Paducah, KY) Biggest hit: "Yakety Sax" in 1963. Year/**Age:** 1995/**68** 1996/**69** 1997/**70**
- **TONY CURTIS** Actor. (Born Bernard Schwartz on the east side of New York) He appeared in *Naked in New York, The Great Imposter, Some Like It Hot,* and was nominated for an Oscar in 1958 as best actor in *The Defiant Ones.* In the 1992 cable TV film, *Christmas In Connecticut.* Year/**Age:** 1995/**70** 1996/**71** 1997/**72**
- **CHUCK BARRIS** TV producer. (Philadelphia, PA) He developed the "Dating Game," and "The Gong Show." He wrote "Palisades Park" a hit for Freddy Cannon in the 60s and the "Newlywed Game." Year/**Age:** 1995/**66** 1996/**67** 1997/**68**
- **CURTIS MAYFIELD** Soul singer/musician/songwriter. (Chicago, IL) He owned a Chicago record company called Curtom. He's a Grammy Award winner. Biggest hit: "Freddie's Dead" in 1972 from the film *Superfly.* He wrote many of the IMPRESSIONS', hits. Year/**Age:** 1995/**53** 1996/**54** 1997/**55**
- **DENIECE WILLIAMS** Singer. (Gary IN) She and Johnny Mathis had a #1 single on this day in 1978: "Too Much, Too Little, Too Late." Her biggest hit: "Let's Hear It For the Boy" from the film *Footloose* in 1984. She was backup singer for Stevie Wonder in the '70s. Year/**Age:** 1995/**44** 1996/**45** 1997/**46**
- **SUZI QUATRO** Singer. (Detroit, MI) Biggest hit with Chris Norman: "Stumblin' In" in 1979. On "Happy Days" she was Pinky Tuscadero, the singer with Richie's band. Year/**Age:** 1995/**45** 1996/**46** 1997/**47**
- **DAN HILL** Singer. (Canada) Biggest hit: "Sometimes When We Touch" in 1977. Year/**Age:** 1995/**41** 1996/**42** 1997/**43**
- **SCOTT VALENTINE** Actor. (Saratoga Springs, NY) Nick on "Family Ties." Year/**Age:** 1995/**37** 1996/**38** 1997/**39**
- **TRISTAN RODGERS** Actor. "General Hospital." Year/**Age:** 1995/**49** 1996/**50** 1997/**51**
- **ALAIN RESNAIS** Director. (France) Directed *Last Year at Marienbad.* Year/**Age:** 1995/**73** 1996/**74** 1997/**75**

- **HALE IRWIN** Golfer. (Joplin, MO) He turned pro in 1968. He won the U.S. Open three times. Year/**Age:** 1995/**50** 1996/**51** 1997/**52**
- **BILL CUNNINGHAM** Basketball coach. Year/**Age:** 1995/**52** 1996/**53** 1997/**54**
- **IAN HUNTER** Vocalist. (England) Leader of MOTT THE HOOPLE, British glitter rock group. Year/**Age:** 1995/**49** 1996/**50** 1997/**51**
- **MIKE CLARKE** Drummer. (1944-1993, Los Angeles, CA) Original member of The BYRDS. Biggest hits: "Mr. Tambourine Man" and "Turn! Turn! Turn!" (Died 12-20-93.)
- **JAN PEERCE** Tenor. (1904-1984 – Brooklyn, NY) Opera, recording and concert star. One hit record: "Bluebird of Happiness" in 1945. Played Tevye in *Fiddler on the Roof.*
- **COLLEEN DEWHURST** Actress. (1926-1991 – Canada, Raised in Milwaukee, WI) Associated with plays of Eugene O'Neill. Won Tony Awards for *All The Way Home* in 1961 and *A Moon for the Misbegotten* in 1974. In *Anne of Green Gables.* Won an Emmy playing Candice Bergen's mom on "Murphy Brown." In films *Annie Hall*, *Nun's Story*, and *Dying Young*, which also starred Campbell Scott, her son by ex-husband George C. Scott. (Died 8-22-91.)
- **PAULETTE GODDARD** Actress. (1911-1990 – Born Marion Levy in Great Neck, NY) She began her acting career in 1931 and was nominated for best supporting actress in *So Proudly We Hail.* Also, she was one of the top contenders for the role of Scarlett O'Hara in *Gone with the Wind.* Once married to actors Charlie Chaplin and Burgess Meredith. (Died 4-23-90.)
- **MAURICE EVANS** Actor. (1901-1989 – England) A Shakespearean and character actor, he appeared as an ape in *Planet of the Apes.* In the TV series "Bewitched," as Samantha's dad, and Maurice and The Puzzler on *Batman.* (Died 3-12-89.)
- **JEFFERSON DAVIS** President. (1808-1889 – Kentucky) The first and only president of the Confederacy, captain in the U.S. Army and engineering architect who helped design the project that reversed the flow of the Chicago River. (Died 10-6-1889.)

FACTS FROM THE PAST

1888   The poem **CASEY AT THE BAT**, by **ERNEST LAWRENCE THAYER**, was first published in the *San Francisco Daily Examiner.* He received $5.00.

1937   The **DUKE OF WINDSOR,** who abdicated the British throne, married divorcee Wallis Warfield Simpson in a civil ceremony at the Chateau de Cande in Monts, France.

1964   The **ROLLING STONES** made their U.S. TV debut on "Hollywood Palace" hosted by Dean Martin.

1965   Astronaut **EDWARD WHITE** became the first American to walk in space during the flight of the GEMINI IV. The Russians were first in the world with a spacewalk on March 18, 1965.

1969   **DIANA ROSS**'s two pet dogs were poisoned by rat bait in her dressing room in Philadelphia.

1970   **RAY DAVIES** of the KINKS traveled round trip from New York to London to change one word in the recording of "**LOLA.**" He changed "Coca-Cola" to "Cherry Cola" because the BBC banned commercial references in songs.

1987   The song "**I WANT YOUR SEX,**" by **GEORGE MICHAEL**, was banned by the BBC in England.

1992   Democratic presidential candidate **BILL CLINTON** played saxophone on TV's "Arsenio Hall." He wailed through "Heartbreak Hotel" and "God Bless the Child."

1994   Actor Don Johnson checked into the Betty Ford Clinic in Rancho Mirage, CA for treatment of alcohol and prescription drug abuse.

JUNE 4

There'll probably never be a Thirties Preservation Society.

BIRTHDAYS

- **DENNIS WEAVER** Actor. (Joplin, MO) He won an Emmy in 1960 for the TV series "Gunsmoke," in which he played Marshal Dillon's deputy, Chester Goode, for 9 years. It was one of the most popular TV shows of all time. He also appeared in "McCloud," "Gentle Ben," and many TV movies. Year/**Age**: 1995/**71** 1996/**72** 1997/**73**

- **GENE BARRY** Actor. (Born Eugene Klass in NYC) On broadway, *La Cage Aux Folles*. On the TV series "Bat Masterson" and "Burke's Law." Year/**Age**: 1995/**73** 1996/**74** 1997/**75**

- **PARKER STEVENSON** Actor. (Philadelphia, PA) He played Frank Hardy on "The Hardy Boys/Nancy Drew Mysteries." In "Baywatch." Married to actress Kirstie Alley. Year/**Age**: 1995/**43** 1996/**44** 1997/**45**

- **FREDDIE FENDER** Singer. (Born Baldemar Huerta in San Benito, TX) Biggest hit: "Before the Next Teardrop Falls" in 1975. He was in prison on a marijuana possession charge from 1960-1963. Year/**Age**: 1995/**58** 1996/**59** 1997/**60**

- **BRUCE DERN** Actor. (Chicago, IL) Appeared in *They Shoot Horses Don't They?*, *The Great Gatsby*, *Coming Home*, *The burbs*, and *Diggstown*. Father of actress Laura Dern. Year/**Age**: 1995/**59** 1996/**60** 1997/**61**

- **MICHELLE PHILLIPS** Actress/singer. (Born Holly Michelle Gilliam in Long Beach, CA) She appeared in the soaps "Search For Tomorrow," "Hotel," and "Knots Landing." She was with the MAMAS AND PAPAS when they released "Monday, Monday" on her birthday in 1966. Year/**Age**: 1995/**51** 1996/**52** 1997/**53**

- **ANDREA JAEGER** Tennis star. (Chicago, IL) Year/**Age**: 1995/**30** 1996/**31** 1997/**32**

- **ROSALIND RUSSELL** Actress. (1908-1976 – Waterbury, CT) She received four Oscar nominations for *My Sister Eileen*, *Sister Kenny*, *Auntie Mame*, and *Mourning Becomes Electra*.

- **ROBERT FULGHUM** Author. (Waco, TX) In 1989, he became the only author to have the No. 1 and No. 2 book on the NY best-seller list at the same time: "It Was on Fire When I Lay Down on It" and "All I Really Need to Know I Learned in Kindergarten." Year/**Age**: 1995/**58** 1996/**59** 1997/**60**

- **ELDRA DeBARGE** Singer. (Grand Rapids, MI) Lead singer of the family group DEBARGE. Biggest hit: "Who's Johnny" from movie *Short Circuit*. Year/**Age**: 1995/**34** 1996/**35** 1997/**36**

- **DANNY BROWN** Bass player. (England) With the group FIXX, biggest hit: "One Thing Leads to Another" in 1983. Year/**Age**: 1995/**44** 1996/**45** 1997/**46**

- **BRIAN O'NEIL** Singer. (Los Angeles, CA) With the sextet THE BUS BOYS. Appeared in the film *48 Hours* and did the song "Cleanin' Up the Town" in the film *Ghostbusters*. Year/**Age**: 1995/**39** 1996/**40** 1997/**41**

- **CHARLES COLLINGWOOD** CBS news correspondent (1917-1985 – Three Rivers, MI) Covered main events over four decades, including WWII and the Vietnam war. (Died 10-3-85)

- **ROBERT HUGHES** The world's heaviest man (1926-1958) Weighed 203 pounds at age 6; 378 lbs. at age 10; 693 lbs. at age 18; and 1,069 lbs. when he died.

FACTS FROM THE PAST

1784 Marie Thible of Lyons, France, accompanied by a pilot, became the **FIRST WOMAN IN HISTORY TO FLY IN A FREE BALLOON** which reached a height of 8,500 feet. The trip lasted about 45 minutes.

1800 The **WHITE HOUSE WAS COMPLETED** and its first occupants, President and Mrs. John Adams, moved in.

1896 **HENRY FORD** made a successful **TEST RUN** with his first car in a nighttime drive through the streets of Detroit. He had to wait an extra hour before he could test-drive it, though, because the car was too big to fit through the shed's door and workers had to knock away some of the brick framework to get it out.

1937 The **SHOPPING CART**, invented by **SYLVAN GOLDMAN**, made its debut in Oklahoma City. Goldman owned some grocery stores and wanted to make it easy for customers to buy more in one trip, but folks used to the hand baskets didn't immediately accept the carts.

1940 The Allied military **EVACUATION FROM DUNKIRK, FRANCE, ENDED.** British Prime Minister Winston Churchill told the House of Commons, "We shall fight on the beaches, we shall fight on the landing grounds, we shall fight in the fields and in the streets, we shall fight in the hills; we shall never surrender."

1942 **CAPITOL RECORDS OPENS** under the direction of Glenn Wallich who started the idea of sending new releases to influential DJs.

1967 **THE MONKEES** take home an Emmy for their **OUTSTANDING COMEDY SERIES.**

1968 Dodger right-handed pitcher **DON DRYSDALE** scored his 6th straight shutout, beating Pittsburgh 5-0. His 58 scoreless-inning streak ended in his next outing.

1972 African-American militant **ANGELA DAVIS** was acquitted of murder, kidnapping and criminal conspiracy charges stemming from a California courtroom shoot-out in which a judge and three others were killed.

1986 A former Navy intelligence analyst, **JONATHAN JAY POLLARD** pleaded guilty in Washington of spying for Israel. He was sentenced to life in prison.

1987 The congressional Iran-Contra committees voted to grant limited immunity to former national security council aid **OLIVER NORTH** following an appeal by independent counsel Lawrence Walsh to reject immunity.

1992 **MAGIC JOHNSON**'s wife, Cookie, gave birth to a 7-pound, 15-ounce, HIV-negative Earvin Johnson III.

Ichthyology: Sunday School for slimy fish.

JUNE 5

BIRTHDAYS

• **MARKY MARK** Rapper. (Born Mark Robert Wahlberg in Boston, MA) With MARKY MARK AND THE FUNKY BUNCH, number 1 hit: "Good Vibrations" in 1991. Brother of NKOTB Donnie. Calvin Klein commercials. He made his film debut in *Renaissance Man.* Year/Age: 1995/**24** 1996/**25** 1997/**26**

• **BILL HAYES** Entertainer. (Harvey, IL) He had a #1 hit in 1955: "The Ballad of Davy Crockett," and he starred with his wife, Susan Seaforth, in the soap opera "Days of Our Lives." Year/Age: 1995/**69** 1996/**70** 1997/**71**

• **ROBERT LANSING** Actor. (Born Robert Howell Brown in San Diego, CA) Appeared in some movies and the "Twelve O'Clock High," "87th Precinct," and "The Equalizer." TV series Year/Age: 1995/**66** 1996/**67** 1997/**68**.

• **FLOYD BUTLER** Singer. (San Diego, CA.) Started out with the HI FI'S, who were later called the FRIENDS OF DISTINCTION. Biggest hit: "Grazing in the Grass" in 1969. Year/Age: 1995/**54** 1996/**55** 1997/**56**

• **JOE CLARK** Former Canadian Prime Minister. (High River, Alberta) He was the youngest to ever hold that office. Year/Age: 1995/**56** 1996/**57** 1997/**58**.

• **DON REID** C&W singer. (Staunton, VA) STATLER BROTHERS. Biggest hit: "Flowers on the Wall" in 1966. He's their lead singer. Year/Age: 1995/**49** 1996/**50** 1997/**51**.

• **KENNY G** (Gorelick) Sax player. (Seattle, WA) Saxophonist who at the age of 17 played in Barry White's Love Unlimited Orchestra. Hit: "Songbird" in 1987. Year/Age: 1995/**39** 1996/**40** 1997/**41**

• **BILL MOYERS** TV journalist. (Hugo, OK.) At one time connected with the Johnson administration as press secretary, he also worked with Dan Rather on CBS before becoming PBS news commentator. Numerous Emmys. Best-selling book, *Healing and the Mind.* Year/Age: 1995/**61** 1996/**62** 1997/**63**.

• **FRED STONE** Entertainer. (Dallas, TX) SLY AND THE FAMILY STONE. Their biggest hit: "Everyday People" in 1968. Year/Age: 1995/**49** 1996/**50** 1997/**51**.

• **RONNIE DYSON** Singer/actor. (1950-1990 – Washington, DC) Biggest hit: "If You Let Me Make Love To You Then Why Can't I Touch You" in 1970. In *Hair* on Broadway and movie *Putney Swope.* (Died 11-10-90.)

• **WILLIAM BOYD** Actor. (1898-1972 – Cambridge, OH) American leading man in films from 1919 to 1948, internationally famous as cowboy hero "Hopalong Cassidy" in the 1930s and 1940s. (Died 9-12-72.)

• **TONY RICHARDSON** Movie director. (1928-1991 – England) Directed *Tom Jones* (got an Oscar) and *A Taste of Honey.* (Died 11-14-91.)

FACTS FROM THE PAST

1752 **BENJAMIN FRANKLIN FIRST FLEW A KITE** during a storm to demonstrate that lightning is a form of electricity. The Philadelphia cow pasture where he flew the kite is now the intersection of 4th and Vine.

1783 The first public demonstration of a **HOT AIR BALLOON** took place at Annonay, France, by brothers Joseph and Jacques Montgolfier. It rose 1,500 feet and traveled about $1^1/_2$ miles in ten minutes.

1884 Civil War hero **GENERAL WILLIAM T. SHERMAN** refused the Republican presidential nomination with the words, "I will not accept if nominated and will not serve if elected."

1933 President Franklin D. Roosevelt signed a bill taking the U.S. off the **GOLD STANDARD**.

1956 **ELVIS PRESLEY** went on the "Milton Berle TV Show" with his traditional hip-gyrating act. It caused so much controversy that from then on the cameras would only film him from the waist up.

1968 **NEW YORK SENATOR ROBERT KENNEDY** was shot and killed by assassin Sirhan Sirhan after claiming victory in the California primary. He died the next day at the age of 42. Sirhan was tried for murder and imprisoned in California serving a life term. Five others were wounded in the shooting at the Ambassador Hotel in Los Angeles. The ROLLING STONES inserted a reference to the killing in "Sympathy for the Devil," which was released the next day.

1974 **SLY STONE MARRIED KATHY SILVA** on stage during a SLY AND THE FAMILY STONE concert at Madison Square Garden in NY.

1977 **ALICE COOPER**'s pet boa constrictor was fatally bitten by a rat it was being fed.

1981 The **FIRST CASE OF AIDS WAS REPORTED**. In the ten years following, more than 174,000 U.S. AIDS cases were reported.

1982 Actress **SOPHIA LOREN** learned that crime bears bitter fruit. She became a "free" woman after serving a 17-day sentence in an Italian jail for tax evasion.

1989 **TORONTO'S SKY DOME OPENED**. The Milwaukee Brewers spoiled the party by beating the Blue Jays 5-3. The first pitch by Jimmy Key to Paul Molitor was a curve-ball strike. The ball was sent to the Baseball Hall of Fame.

1993 29-year-old **JULIE KRONE**, riding "Colonial Affair," became the first female jockey to win the Belmont Stakes in the 125-year history of the race.

1994 The White House refected a book, *The Agenda: The Clinton White House*, by Bob Woodward. Press secretary Dee Dee Myers dismissed the book as "all process."

JUNE 6
Yo-Yo Day

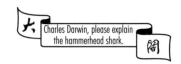

Charles Darwin, please explain the hammerhead shark.

BIRTHDAYS

- **PETER ALBIN** Bass player. (San Francisco, CA) BIG BROTHER AND THE HOLDING COMPANY. Year/**Age:** 1995/**51** 1996/**52** 1997/**53**

- **DAVID DUKES** Actor. He plays Dr. Wade Halsey on TV's "Sisters." Year/**Age:** 1995/**50** 1996/**51** 1997/**52**

- **BJORN BORG** Former tennis star. (Sweden) He retired Jan. 24, 1983, saying he did not have the same motivation he once had. He did return to tournament tennis in 1991. Year/**Age:** 1995/**39** 1996/**40** 1997/**41**

- **GARY "U.S." BONDS** Singer. (Born Gary Anderson in Jacksonville, FL) Biggest hit: "Quarter to Three" in 1961. Year/**Age:** 1995/**56** 1996/**57** 1997/**58**

- **ROY INNIS** Civil Rights Activist. Year/**Age:** 1995/**61** 1996/**62** 1997/**63**

- **BILLIE WHITELAW** Actress. (England) In Hitchcock's *Frenzy* and *The Dressmaker*. Year/**Age:** 1995/**63** 1996/**64** 1997/**65**

- **STEVE VAI** Musician. With the DAVID LEE ROTH BAND. Biggest hit: "California Girls." Year/**Age:** 1995/**35** 1996/**36** 1997/**37**

- **LUKAS HAAS** Actor. Appeared in the films *Witness* and *Leap of Faith,* and the TV movie "The Ryan White Story." Year/**Age:** 1995/**19** 1996/**20** 1997/**21**

- **JOE STAMPLEY** C&W singer. (Springhill, LA) Biggest hit: "Soul Song" in 1973. Year/**Age:** 1995/**52** 1996/**53** 1997/**54**

- **BILL DICKEY** Baseball Hall of Fame star. (1907-1993, Dastrop, LA) New York Yankee catcher. He played on 8 pennant-winning clubs and was in 11 All-Star games. (Died 11-13-93.)

- **ROBERT ENGLUND** Actor. (Glendale, CA) Razor-fingered Freddy in the *Nightmare* films. He also appeared in *A Star Is Born*, *Hustle*, and with Andrew Dice Clay in *The Adventures of Ford Fairlane*. Year/**Age:** 1995/**47** 1996/**48** 1997/**49**

- **AMANDA PAYS** Actress. (Australia) *The Flash*. She is married to Corben Bersen. Year/**Age:** 1995/**36** 1996/**37** 1997/**38**

- **SANDRA BERNHARD** Comedienne/actress. (Flint, MI) Films include *Truth or Dare*. Is a part-time actress on "Roseanne." Year/**Age:** 1995/**40** 1996/**41** 1997/**42**

- **DALAI LAMA** Leader. Tibet's spiritual leader and Nobel Peace Prize winner. Year/**Age:** 1995/**60** 1996/**61** 1997/**62**

- **ESTHER SHAPIRO** Writer/producer. (Born Esther Mayesh in NYC) She and her husband, Richard, produced "Dynasty." Year/**Age:** 1995/**61** 1996/**62** 1997/**63**

- **STACI KEANAN** Actress. TV's "My Two Dads," "Going Places," and "Step by Step." Year/**Age:** 1995/**20** 1996/**21** 1997/**22**

- **HARVEY FIERSTEIN** [fyr'-steen] Playwright/actor. (NYC) *Torch Song Trilogy* won him 2 Tony awards, best playwright and best actor. He also wrote *La Cage aux Folles*. Film *Mrs. Doubtfire*. Year/**Age:** 1995/**41** 1996/**42** 1997/**43**

FACTS FROM THE PAST

1896 **GEORGE HARBO** and **FRANK SAMUELSON** became the first people to cross the Atlantic Ocean by boat using only their own brawny arms for power. They left New York harbor in a 18-foot boat, with no sail, in a raging storm. They took 5 pairs of oars, 60 gallons of water and lots of canned goods. Each man rowed 18 hours a day. Five hours a day were allotted for rest, and one hour a day for eating. They kept to a schedule of 54 miles a day. 56 days and over 3,000 miles later they rowed onto the coast of the Isles of Scilly, England.

1936 The **1ST HELICOPTER** was tested in Berlin, Germany. Pilot Hanna Reitsch flew twin-roter "Focke-Wulf FW-61" inside a building.

1960 **TONY WILLIAMS**, the lead singer of the **PLATTERS**, left the group for a solo career.

1966 Black activist James Meredith was shot and wounded on a Mississippi highway while he was promting black voter registration. Martin Luther King later organized a march to continue his protest and hundreds of people walked that highway.

1968 At 1:44 a.m. Pacific Time, **SENATOR ROBERT F. KENNEDY DIED** at Good Samaritan Hospital in Los Angeles, 25$^1/_2$ hours after he was shot at the Ambassador Hotel by Sirhan Bishara Sirhan.

1968 Stock car driver Buddy Baker crashed his racer into the wall at Smokey Mountain Raceway. He was wisked off in an ambulance. As they pulled away, the back door opened and Baker fell out. He survived and continued racing.

1971 The **"ED SULLIVAN SHOW" WAS CANCELLED** after 23 years. It was TV's longest-running variety show. Ed was originally a newspaper columnist and hosted a couple of radio shows before trying TV in 1948. Sullivan couldn't sing or dance, but he knew who could, and signed them for his show. GLADYS KNIGHT & THE PIPS were Ed Sullivan's last musical guests.

1978 ABCs **"20/20"** TV interview program debuted with Harold Hayes and Robert Hughes. They were fired after the first show and replaced with **HUGH DOWNS** and later **BARBARA WALTERS** with one of the correspondents being Geraldo Rivera. The first celebrity interviewed was **FLIP WILSON**.

1990 A judge in Fort Lauderdale, FL, **JOSÉ GONZALES**, ruled that **2 LIVE CREW'S** *As Nasty As They Wanna Be* was obscene, making it **ILLEGAL TO SELL THE ALBUM**. The action set off a storm of controversy over First Amendment rights. Two days later, a Florida record store owner was jailed and later convicted for selling the LP.

1994 On the beaches of **NORMANDY** President Clinton and other world leaders honored the thousands of Allied troops who died in the "D-Day" invasion of Europe during WWII June 6, 1944.

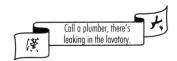

Call a plumber, there's leaking in the lavatory.

JUNE 7

BIRTHDAYS

- **JIMMY GREENSPOON** Keyboardist. (Los Angeles, CA) With THREE DOG NIGHT. Biggest hit: "Joy to the World." Year/**Age**: 1995/**47** 1996/**48** 1997/**49**

- **BILL KREUTZMAN** Drummer. (Palo Alto, CA) GRATEFUL DEAD. Hit: "Touch of Grey." Year/**Age**: 1995/**49** 1996/**50** 1997/**51**

- **TOM JONES** Singer. (Born Thomas Jones Woodward in Pontypridd, Wales) Biggest hit: "She's a Lady" in 1971. He started his career as TOMMY SCOTT AND THE SENATORS, then changed his name to Tom Jones in 1964 after the bawdy Albert Finney film of the same name. Year/**Age**: 1995/**55** 1996/**56** 1997/**57**

- **LIAM NEESON** Actor. Film *Schindler's List*. Year/**Age**: 1995/**43** 1996/**44** 1997/**45**

- **JESSICA TANDY** Actress. (England) In films: *The Birds*, *Forever Amber*, *Fried Green Tomatoes*, *Cocoon*, *Camilla*, and *Used People*. At age 80, she was the oldest person to win an Academy Award. She was named best actress for her role in *Driving Miss Daisy*, in which she played Daisy Werthan, an elderly southern Jewish lady who resented the needs of a chauffeur. Married to actor Hume Cronyn with whom she frequently appeared on the stage. Year/**Age**: 1995/**86** 1996/**87** 1997/**88**

- **JENNY JONES** Talk show hostess. Year/**Age**: 1995/**49** 1996/**50** 1997/**51**

- **KEN OSMOND** Actor. (Los Angeles, CA) Eddie Haskel on "Leave it to Beaver." Year/**Age**: 1995/**52** 1996/**53** 1997/**54**

- **NIKKI GIOVANNI** Poet. (Knoxville, TN) Wrote *The Women and the Men* and *My House*. Year/**Age**: 1995/**52** 1996/**53** 1997/**54**

- **PRINCE** Entertainer. (Born Prince Rogers Nelson in Minneapolis, MN) He's 5'3" tall. He starred in the film: *Purple Rain*. Biggest hit: "When Doves Cry." In 1993 he declared he wanted to be known as Victor. Months later he changed his name to an unpronounceable symbol. Year/**Age**: 1995/**37** 1996/**38** 1997/**39**

- **WYNN STEWART** C&W singer. (1934-1985 – Morrisville, MO) Biggest hit: "It's Such a Pretty World Today" in 1967. (Died 7-17-85.)

- **PAUL GAUGUIN** Post-impressionist painter. (1848-1903 – Paris, France. Brought up in Peru) Gaugin spent much of his most creative period in Tahiti. Rather than attempting to recreate an exact image on canvas, Gaugin used strong color in his art to express emotion in scenes. (Died 5-9-03.)

- **BEAU BRUMMELL** Fashion leader. (1778-1840 – Born George Bryan Brummell in London) He started by inheriting about $30,000. His lack of tact led him to poverty and disrepute. Brummell made long pants fashionable and popularized the custom of taking baths with soap and water, rather than trying to cover body odors with perfume. (Died 3-30-1840.)

- **THURMON MUNSON** Baseball. (1947-1979 – Akron, OH) He was a star NY Yankee catcher, killed when his private jet crashed while he was practicing takeoffs and landings at Akron Canton Regional Airport in Ohio.

FACTS FROM THE PAST

1769   **DANIEL BOONE** began his exploration of the Kentucky wilds. Boone died in Missouri at 86 and was buried there. Kentucky said he should be buried in the "Bluegrass State" and told Missouri to send his body there. Missouri did, but later decided they made a mistake and asked Kentucky to return it. Kentucky refused and that's when Missouri claimed they hadn't sent the real body but an imposter. So Kentucky says Boone is buried in Frankfort, KY, and Missouri says his body lies in Defiance, MO.

1776   **RICHARD HENRY LEE** of Virginia proposed to the Continental Congress a resolution calling for a **DECLARATION OF INDEPENDENCE**.

1864   **ABRAHAM LINCOLN** was renominated for President at his party's convention in Baltimore.

1955   **DWIGHT EISENHOWER** became the first U.S. President to appear on color TV when he gave an address at West Point.

1963   The **ROLLING STONES** released their first single, "Come On," and made their debut on British TV's "Thank Your Lucky Stars." It was the only time they ever appeared on TV wearing identical suits, plus white shirts and ties. The show's producer told the Stones' manager to "Get rid of that vile-looking singer with the tire-tred lips."

1966   Singer **ROY ORBISON'S FIRST WIFE**, Claudette, was killed in a motorcycle accident which Roy witnessed. The EVERLY BROTHERS recorded a song that Roy wrote for her, called "Claudette."

1969   The supergroup **BLIND FAITH** made their debut in a free concert attended by 100,000 fans in London's Hyde Park. BLIND FAITH consisted of Eric Clapton, Steve Winwood, Ginger Baker, and Rick Grech.

1969   **TOMMY,** The WHO'S rock opera, first entered the charts. Roger Daltrey said that many believed he was Tommy. A year later The WHO performed it at the Metropolitan Opera. It opened on Broadway in 1993.

1979   **CHUCK BERRY** was charged with three counts of income tax evasion. He eventually served 100 days in prison.

1993   **CHUCK BERRY, BILLY JOEL,** and **PETE TOWNSHEND** were among the celebrities attending the ground-breaking ceremonies for the **ROCK 'N ROLL HALL OF FAME** in Cleveland, OH. (See page 10)

1993   **WOODY ALLEN** lost his bitter custody battle with Mia Farrow.

1994   A 12-year-old sixth grader from Meadville, PA, **VICKI VAN METER**, became the yougest girl to pilot a plane to Europe. She took off from Augusta, ME and ended up at Glasgow, Scotland.

JUNE 8

Skate away today.

BIRTHDAYS

- **JOAN RIVERS** Comedienne/talk show host. (Brooklyn, NY) She got her first big break on the "Tonight" show. Her own show "Can We Talk" was cancelled in 1994. Year/Age: 1995/**62** 1996/**63** 1997/**64**

- **KATHY BAKER** Actress. (Midland, TX) TV's "Picket Fences" and films *Edward Scissorhands, Jennifer 8, and Mad Dog and Glory.* Year/Age: 1995/**45** 1996/**46** 1997/**47**

- **ROB PILATUS** Entertainer. (Germany) He and Fabrice Morvan fronted the MILLI VANILLI act. They lost their Grammy award when it was discovered they didn't sing on their album. Biggest hit: "Blame It on the Rain." Year/Age: 1995/**30** 1996/**31** 1997/**32**

- **DEL ENNIS** Baseball. Phillies power-hitter. Drove in over 100 runs in seven seasons. Year/Age: 1995/**70** 1996/**71** 1997/**72**

- **HERB ADDERLEY** Football. (Philadelphia, PA) Green Bay Packer great. Year/Age: 1995/**56** 1996/**57** 1997/**58**

- **KEENEN IVORY WAYANS** Actor. (New York, NY) "In Living Color." Year/Age: 1995/**37** 1996/**38** 1997/**39**

- **NANCY SINATRA** Singer. (Jersey City, NJ) Sang "Somethin' Stupid" in 1967 with her dad, Frank. Her biggest hit: "These Boots Were Made for Walkin'" in 1966. She also wrote a book about her dad. Year/Age: 1995/**55** 1996/**56** 1997/**57**

- **JAMES DARREN** Singer. (Born James Ercolani in Philadelphia, PA) Biggest hit: "Goodbye, Cruel World" in 1961. He recorded the theme song for the very first *Gidget* film in 1959. Was in the film *Guns of Navarone* and TV's "Time Tunnel" and as Officer Jim Corrigan on "T.J. Hooker." Year/Age: 1995/**59** 1996/**60** 1997/**61**

- **BARBARA BUSH** Former First Lady. (Rye, NY) Co-authored *Millie's Book*, along with the white house pooch. Year/Age: 1995/**70** 1996/**71** 1997/**72**

- **CHUCK NEGRON** Singer. (Los Angeles, CA) Singer with THREE DOG NIGHT. Biggest hit: "Joy to the World" in 1971. Year/Age: 1995/**52** 1996/**53** 1997/**54**

- **BOZ SCAGGS** Singer. (Dallas, TX) Biggest hit: "Lowdown" in 1976. Year/Age: 1995/**51** 1996/**52** 1997/**53**

- **GRIFFIN DUNNE** Actor/producer. (New York, NY) "Straight Talk." Year/Age: 1995/**40** 1996/**41** 1997/**42**

- **NICK RHODES** Guitar player. (England) With British quintet DURAN DURAN. Biggest hits: "The Reflex" in 1984 and "A View To a Kill" in 1985. Year/Age: 1995/**33** 1996/**34** 1997/**35**

- **BONNIE TYLER** Singer. (Wales) Her distinctive raspy vocals were caused by an operation to remove throat modules in 1976. Biggest record: "Total Eclipse of the Heart." Year/Age: 1995/**42** 1996/**43** 1997/**44**

- **DANA WYNTER** Actress. (England) Appeared in films: *Invasion of the Body Snatchers, Sink the Bismarck,* and *Airport.* Year/Age: 1995/**65** 1996/**66** 1997/**67**

- **JERRY STILLER** Actor/comedian. (Brooklyn, NY) Appears with his wife, Anne Meara, on TV and radio commercials. In film *Hairspray.* Year/Age: 1995/**66** 1996/**67** 1997/**68**

- **JOHNNY DEPP** Actor. (Los Angeles, CA) TV's "21 Jump Street." Films include: *Edward Scissorhands, What's Eating Gilbert Grape, Platoon, Benny and Joon,* and *Arizona Dreams.* Year/Age: 1995/**32** 1996/**33** 1997/**34**

- **ROBERT PRESTON** Actor. (1918-1987 – Born Robert Preston Meservey in Newton Highlands, MA) Portrayed "Prof. Howard Hill" on Broadway and in the 1962 film *Music Man.* Also in *Mame, How the West Was Won* and with Julie Andrews in *Victor Victoria.* (Died 3-21-87.)

- **FRANK LLOYD WRIGHT** Architect. (1867-1959 – Richland Center, WI) Descended from a long line of Welch preachers. His mother decided on his career long before he pursued it. She hung his bedroom walls full of engravings of cathedrals. He said that architecture should carefully relate to its setting. When asked how to improve Pittsburgh, he said, "Destroy it and start again." (Died 4-9-59.)

FACTS FROM THE PAST

1928 **SIR CHARLES KINGSFORD** flew from Oakland, CA, to Hawaii, Fiji, and arrived this day in Brisbane, Australia. It was the first flight ever from the United States to Australia.

1948 **MILTON BERLE'S** "Texaco Star Theater," which would become the season's top-rated TV show, premiered on NBC-TV, and Tuesday night became "Uncle Miltie Night." In 1954, NBC rewarded Milt with a 30-year contract, guaranteeing him $200,000 per year.

1959 **LIBERACE** defended himself successfully in a lawsuit against William Connor. Connor called him " a fruit-flavored, mince-covered heap of mother love, biggest sentimental vomit of all time and a calculating candy floss."

1968 The suspected assassin of Civil Rights leader Dr. Martin Luther King, Jr. **JAMES EARL RAY** was **CAPTURE IN LONDON.**

1969 **MICKEY MANTLE'S NUMBER (#7) WAS RETIRED** by the New York Yankees. The switch-hitting outfielder won the 1956 triple batting crown, leading the American League in average, RBI and home runs.

1978 A jury in Clark County, NV, ruled that the "Mormon Will," purportedly written by late billionaire **HOWARD HUGHES,** was a forgery.

1989 Chinese Premier **LI PENG** praised army soldiers for their role in crushing the student-led Tiananmen Square democracy movement.

1993 **CROWN PRINCE NARUHITO** married commoner Masako Owada in Tokyo, Japan, bringing a Westernized generation to the 1,500-year-old Chrysanthemum Throne.

1994 **MEG RYAN** publicly chastised actor Walter Matthau for pinching her during the shooting of the movie IX at Princeton's Institute of Advanced Studies. She said his hand work was beyond script demands.

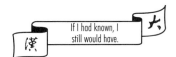

If I had known, I still would have.

JUNE 9

BIRTHDAYS

- **JACKIE MASON** Comedian. (Born Yacov Moshe Maza in Sheboygan, WI) He is also an ordained rabbi. Film *Chicken Soup*. Year/**Age**: 1995/**61** 1996/**62** 1997/**63**
- **MICHAEL J. FOX** Actor. (Canada) Played Alex Keaton on "Family Ties" TV series and star of films: *The Secret of My Success, Bright Lights, Big City, Back to the Future, Doc Hollywood, Life with Mikey, For Love or Money,* and *Homeward Bound: The Incredible Journey* as the voice of the American bulldog puppy. He gave his fans a nude rear view in the film *Greedy*. Married to actress Tracy Pollan. Year/**Age**: 1995/**34** 1996/**35** 1997/**36**
- **LES PAUL** Entertainer. (Born Lester Polfus in Waukesha, WI) Had two #1 hits with ex-wife Mary Ford: "How High the Moon" in 1951 and "Vaya Con Dios" in 1953. Their song "Sittin' on Top of the World" was played for the space shuttle *Endeavor* astronauts on 6-22-93. Les is responsible for developing over-dubbed vocals and the electric guitar. He was inducted into the Rock and Roll Hall of Fame in 1988. Mary Ford died in 1977 at age 51. Year/**Age**: 1995/**79** 1996/**80** 1997/**81**
- **MONA FREEMAN** Actress. American leading lady, at her peak as a troublesome teenager in the 1940s. In the films *National Velvet* with Liz Taylor, *Black Beauty,* and *Dear Ruth*. Year/**Age**: 1995/**69** 1996/**70** 1997/**71**
- **GEORGE AXELROD** Screenwriter. (NYC) Wrote *Seven Year Itch* and *Breakfast at Tiffany's*. Year/**Age**: 1995/**73** 1996/**74** 1997/**75**
- **MARVIN KALB** Former NBC news correspondent. He has written a few books and is a permanent panel member of "Meet The Press." Year/**Age**: 1995/**65** 1996/**66** 1997/**67**
- **ROY SMALLEY, SR.** Baseball. Shortstop for the Cubs, Milwaukee Braves and Phillies in the '40s and '50s. He is the brother-in-law of former major league manager Gene Mauch. Year/**Age**: 1995/**69** 1996/**70** 1997/**71**

- **ROBERT McNAMARA** Former Defense Secretary. (San Francisco, CA) Former World Bank president and Defense Secretary under President Kennedy. At one time, he was a Detroit automobile executive. Year/**Age**: 1995/**79** 1996/**80** 1997/**81**
- **DAVE PARKER** Baseball. (Jackson, MS) Former major league baseball star with over 2,500 career hits. Year/**Age**: 1995/**44** 1996/**45** 1997/**46**
- **JON LORD** Keyboardist. (England) With WHITESNAKE, hit: "Here I Go Again," and with DEEP PURPLE, hit: "Smoke on the Water." Year/**Age**: 1995/**53** 1996/**54** 1997/**55**
- **ROBERT CUMMINGS** Actor. (1910-1990 – Joplin, MO) Starred in the "Bob Cummings Show" on TV, portraying a fashion photographer. He appeared in numerous movies, and his grandfather was aviation pioneer Orville Wright. Won an Emmy for *Twelve Angry Men* in 1954. (Died 12-2-90.)
- **COLE PORTER** Composer. (1893-1964 – Peru, IN) His lyrics were some of the wittiest ever written for popular songs. His scores include the musicals *Anything Goes* and *Kiss Me Kate* and the film *High Society*. Porter was a happily married gay who wrote the song, "Always True to you, Darlin', in My Fashion" for an elevator operator. He had a tragic riding accident in the late '30s and broke both legs and they had to amputate one in 1958. He was in constant pain but continued to write those great scores. (Died 10-15-64.)
- **FRED WARING** Bandleader. (1900-1984 – Tyrone, PA) His PENNSYLVANIANS accompanied some of the biggest names in entertainment, including Sinatra, Crosby and Irving Berlin. It is said his greatest contribution is that he made choral music acceptable. He also invented the Waring blender.
- **JACKIE WILSON** Singer. (1934-1984 – Detroit, MI.) Biggest hit: "Night" in 1960. His goddaughter is Jody Watley. He collapsed into a coma on stage at New Jersey's Latin Casino, Sept. 25, 1975, and never recovered. (Died 1-21-84.)

FACTS FROM THE PAST

68 A.D. **ROMAN EMPEROR NERO** committed suicide at age 32. He had tried two or three times to kill himself. After being declared a public enemy by the Senate, the calvary was going to carry him off and beat him to death. So he ordered a grave dug and stuck a newly sharpened knife into his neck. His last words: "Dead, dead and so great an artist."

1534 French explorer **JACQUES CARTIER**, looking for gold and a northwest passage to the Orient, was the first to sail into the mouth of a river he named for **ST. LAWRENCE**.

1784 **JOHN CARROLL**, who would become the **FIRST ROMAN CATHOLIC BISHOP IN THE U.S.**, was appointed supervisor of Catholic missions in the U.S.

1790 The **FIRST AMERICAN BOOK TO BE COPYRIGHTED** was John Barry's *Philadelphia Spelling Book*.

1934 **DONALD DUCK** made his debut as a bit player in *The Little Wise Hen*.

1969 Brian Jones said he was leaving the **ROLLING STONES** because of differences with the other members of the band. He was replaced by Mick Taylor. Less than a month later, Jones was found dead in his swimming pool.

1970 Princeton awards **BOB DYLAN** an honorary doctorate of music.

1980 Actor/comedian **RICHARD PRYOR** suffered third degree burns on most of his upper body while "freebasing" cocaine. The mixture of alcohol and cocaine ignites and explodes. Pryor endured two months of painful skin-grafting operations and survived.

1984 Tennis star **MARTINA NAVRATILOVA** won a $1 million bonus by beating Chris Evert Lloyd 6-3, 6-1 at Wimbledon. She got the bonus for taking the French, the U.S. Open, and Wimbledon.

JUNE 10

Can a clock with no hands tell time?

BIRTHDAYS

- **F. (FRANCIS) LEE BAILEY** Attorney/author. (Waltham, MA) Some of his famous clients include: Albert DeSalvo (the Boston Strangler), Patty Hearst, Dr. Sam Sheppard, and Capt. Ernest Medina. Year/**Age**: 1995/**62** 1996/**63** 1997/**64**

- **MAURICE SENDAK** Children's book author. (Brooklyn, NY) He wrote and illustrated *Where The Wild Things Are.* Year/**Age**: 1995/**67** 1996/**68** 1997/**69**

- **SHIRLEY ALSTON** Singer. (Passaic, NJ) Lead singer of The SHIRELLES. Their biggest hits: "Soldier Boy" and "Will You Love Me Tomorrow," the first #1 song for writers Carole King and Gerry Goffin. She and 3 high school friends formed the group in 1958, originally called the POQUELLOS. Year/**Age**: 1995/**54** 1996/**55** 1997/**56**

- **ANDREW STEVENS** Actor. Son of actress Stella Stevens and at one time married to Kate Jackson. He was in the short-lived TV series "Code Red" with Lorne Greene. Year/**Age**: 1995/**40** 1996/**41** 1997/**42**

- **EARL HAMNER** Writer/producer. (Schuyler, VA) He created and wrote "The Waltons" based on his own childhood, with Richard Thomas as "John-Boy." Also, the executive producer of "Falcon Crest." Year/**Age**: 1995/**72** 1996/**73** 1997/**74**

- **JON McGLOCKLIN** Former Milwaukee Bucks star. He is now a sports announcer and financial advisor. Year/**Age**: 1995/**52** 1996/**53** 1997/**54**

- **BARRY MORSE** Actor. (England) Played Lt. Gerard on TV series "The Fugitive" from 1963-1967. Year/**Age**: 1995/**76** 1996/**77** 1997/**78**

- **JAMES McDIVITT** Former astronaut. (Chicago, IL) Year/**Age**: 1995/**65** 1996/**66** 1997/**67**

- **DAN FOUTS** Football. The San Diego quarterback passed for over 43,000 yards and 254 TDs. Year/**Age**: 1995/**44** 1996/**45** 1997/**46**

- **JEFF GREENFIELD** Media commentator. (NYC) ABC News analyst. Year/**Age**: 1995/**52** 1996/**53** 1997/**54**

- **JUNE HAVER** Actress. (Born June Stovenour in Rock Island, IL) Married Fred McMurray. Appeared in films: *The Dolly Sisters* and *Look for the Silver Lining.* Year/**Age**: 1995/**69** 1996/**70** 1997/**71**

- **FREDERICK LOEWE** Composer. (1901-1988 – Austria) He created tunes for Alan Lerner's lyrics in *My Fair Lady*, *Brigadoon*, and *Gigi.* They parted bitterly after *Camelot* in 1960. They reunited in 1973 and stayed friends. (Died 2-14-88.)

- **JUDY GARLAND** Singer. (1922-1969 – Born Frances Gumm in Grand Rapids, MN) There are a museum and street named for her in her hometown. George Jessel is credited with changing her name. Among her best known films: *The Wizard of Oz*, *Meet Me in St. Louis*, *A Star is Born*, and *Easter Parade.* When she was young to hide her snub nose she wore a latex bridge. Mother of Liza Minnelli and Lorna Luft. (Died 6-22-69.)

- **HATTIE McDANIEL** Actress. (1895-1952 – Wichita, KS) She was the first African-American actress to receive an Oscar—best supporting actress in *Gone With the Wind.* At one time she was a ladies room attendant at Ricks Club Madrid in Milwaukee, WI. (Died 10-26-52.)

FACTS FROM THE PAST

1692 **BRIDGET BISHOP, THE FIRST SALEM WITCH, WAS HANGED.** She was one of 150 citizens accused of witchcraft by a hysterical band of young girls.

1842 **BICYCLE INVENTOR KIRKPATRICK MacMILLAN** committed the **EARLIEST RECORDED BICYCLING OFFENSE** in Glasgow, England. The bicycle was a novelty in those days. People gathered to see the novelty—including a child, who got in the way and was hit by the bike. MacMillan was fined 5 shillings.

1902 The **WINDOW ENVELOPE WAS PATENTED** by A. F. Callahan of Chicago, IL. The inventor called it the "outlook envelope."

1935 **ALCOHOLICS ANONYMOUS WAS FOUNDED** in Akron, OH, by **WILLIAM G. WILSON** ("Bill") and **DR. ROBERT SMITH** ("Dr. Bob").

1943 The **BALLPOINT PEN WAS PATENTED** by **LASALO BIRO** of Budapest, Hungary. After fleeing Hungary to escape the Nazis, he was employed by the British Royal Air Force, making their pens. They needed a pen that would write under low atmospheric pressure at high altitudes.

1966 **JANIS JOPLIN** performed with **BIG BROTHER & THE HOLDING COMPANY** for the first time at the Avalon Ballroom in San Francisco.

1977 **JAMES EARL RAY**, the convicted assassin of Civil Rights leader Martin Luther King. Jr., escaped from Brushy Mountain State Prison in Tennessee with six other convicts. Ray was recaptured June 13th.

1978 "Affirmed," ridden by **STEVE CAUTHEN**, won the **BELMONT STAKES** and, with it, horse racing's triple crown.

1985 Socialite **CLAUS VON BULOW WAS ACQUITTED** by a jury in Providence, RI, in his retrial on charges he'd tried to murder his heiress wife, Martha "Sunny" Von Bulow.

1986 **NANCY LIEBERMAN-CLINE** became the **FIRST WOMAN TO PLAY IN A MEN'S PRO BASKETBALL LEAGUE.** She was a member of the Springfield, MA, Fame in the U.S. Basketball League.

1992 A Texas law enforcement agency heard the lyrics to **"COP KILLER"** by **ICE-T** and called for a nationwide boycott of the album and other Time Warner products. After that, sales skyrocketed. Ice-T is now in films, including *Surviving the Game.*

1994 Representative **DAN ROSTENKOWSKI** pleaded innocent to a 17-count federal corruption indictment and predicted that he would be vindicated.

Every hotdog has its day.

JUNE 11

BIRTHDAYS

- **GIOIA BRUNO** Musician. (New York, NY) EXPOSE hits include "Season's Change" in 1987. Year/**Age**: 1995/**30** 1996/**31** 1997/**32**
- **FRANK BEARD** Drummer. (Texas) ZZ TOP. He's the only group member without a beard. Hit: "Legs" in 1984. Year/**Age**: 1995/**46** 1996/**47** 1997/**48**
- **GENE WILDER** Actor. (Born Jerry Silberman in Milwaukee, WI) Appeared in *Bonnie and Clyde, Willy Wonka & the Chocolate Factory, Another You,* and *The Producers.* While filming *Lady in Red,* he met and married the late Gilda Radner. Year/**Age**: 1995/**61** 1996/**62** 1997/**63**
- **CHAD EVERETT** Actor. (Born Ray Lee Canton in South Bend, IN) He appeared on TV's "Medical Center" and the Energizer commercials. Year/**Age**: 1995/**59** 1996/**60** 1997/**61**
- **JACQUES COUSTEAU** [koo-stoh'] Marine explorer. (France) Oscar-winning film maker who also produces PBS TV shows. He was co-inventor of the aqualung in 1943, which made SCUBA (Self Contained Underwater Breathing Apparatus) diving possible. Year/**Age**: 1995/**85** 1996/**86** 1997/**87**
- **ADRIENNE BARBEAU** Actress. (Sacramento, CA) Played Carol Traynor, Maude's divorced daughter, on the TV series "Maude." Year/**Age**: 1995/**50** 1996/**51** 1997/**52**
- **JACKIE STEWART** Racecar driver. (Scotland) 3-time World Grand Prix champion, he scored 27 Grand Prix race wins. Now he's a color commentator on racing shows and does some TV commercials. Year/**Age**: 1995/**56** 1996/**57** 1997/**58**
- **RISE STEVENS** [ree'-zuh] Opera star. (NYC) Year/**Age**: 1995/**82** 1996/**83** 1997/**84**

- **JOEY DEE** Singer. (Born Joe DeNocola in Passaic, NJ) Biggest hit: "Peppermint Twist" in 1962. Year/**Age**: 1995/**55** 1996/**56** 1997/**57**
- **WILLIAM STYRON** Novelist. (Newport News, VA) Bestseller *The Confessions of Nat Turner* in 1967. Year/**Age**: 1995/**70** 1996/**71** 1997/**72**
- **RICHARD TODD** Actor. (Ireland) Academy Award nomination for *The Hasty Heart.* Year/**Age**: 1995/**76** 1996/**77** 1997/**78**
- **LUCIANA PALUZZI** Actor. (Italy) Films include: *Three Coins in the Fountain* and *Thunderball.* Year/**Age**: 1995/**56** 1996/**57** 1997/**58**
- **JOE MONTANA** Pro football quarterback. (New Eagle, PA) Set a Super Bowl record in 1989, passing for 357 yards. He led the San Francisco 49ers to four Super Bowl victories before going to Kansas City in 1993. Year/**Age**: 1995/**39** 1996/**40** 1997/**41**
- **LAWRENCE SPIVAK** Broadcast journalist. (1900-1994, Brooklyn, NY) Co-founder, producer and panel member of "Meet the Press." His first guest was the chairman of the Democratic National Committee James Farley and the last was President Gerald Ford. (Died 3-9-94.)
- **VINCE LOMBARDI** Former Green Bay Packer Coach. (1913-1970 – Brooklyn, NY) Pro Football Hall of Fame member, led the Packers to the first two Super Bowl Championships in 1967-1968. (Died 9-3-70.)
- **RICHARD STRAUSS** Composer. (1864-1949 – Germany) His most remembered works include: *Also Sprach Zarathustra* and *Don Quixote.* (Died 9-8-49.)

FACTS FROM THE PAST

1742 The **STOVE WAS INVENTED** by Benjamin Franklin.

1770 **CAPTAIN COOK** discovered the Great Barrier Reef, Australia, by grounding the *Endeavour* on it.

1928 *The Case of Jonathon Drew,* **ALFRED HITCHCOCK'S FIRST FILM,** was released in America.

1959 D. H. Lawrence's book, **LADY CHATTERLEY'S LOVER,** was banned by the Postmaster General. He said it was obscene.

1962 **PRESIDENT JOHN F. KENNEDY** accepted an honorary degree from Yale. His acceptance speech offered a classic example of the Kennedy wit when the President said he had the best of both worlds now, "a Harvard education and a Yale degree."

1963 **ALABAMA GOVERNOR GEORGE C. WALLACE,** who had defied a federal order to allow two African-Americans to enroll at the University of Alabama by standing at the schoolhouse door, relented after a confrontation with federal troops.

1978 **JOSEPH FREEMAN, JR.,** became the **FIRST AFRICAN-AMERICAN TO BE ORDAINED A PRIEST** in the Church of Jesus Christ of Latter-Day Saints.

1978 Christa Tybus of London set a **HULA-HOOP RECORD** by keeping her hula hoop hooping non-stop for $24^1/_2$ hours.

1979 **CHUCK BERRY** pleaded guilty to income tax evasion. He was sentenced to four months in prison.

1982 **LARRY HOLMES** retained his **WORLD BOXING HEAVYWEIGHT CHAMPIONSHIP** by defeating Gerry Cooney.

1982 Movie director **STEVEN SPIELBERG** released his science-fiction film, *ET, The Extra-Terrestrial.*

1987 Prime Minister **MARGARET THATCHER** won a third successive term. The last person to do that was Lord Liverpool in 1826.

1990 **NOLAN RYAN,** 43-year-old right-hander, pitched the sixth no-hitter of his career, extending his major-league record as the Texas Rangers beat the Oakland Athletics, 5-0. Ryan became the **FIRST MAN TO PITCH NO-HITTERS FOR THREE DIFFERENT TEAMS** and became the oldest to throw one.

1992 Major league baseball owners approved the **SALE OF THE SEATTLE MARINERS** to a Japanese group, led by Hiroshi Yamauchi, president of Japan's Nintendo Company.

1994 A California internist was chosen to be the **FIRST BLACK PRESIDENT** in the American Medical Association's 147-year history.

JUNE 12
Hug Day

BIRTHDAYS

- **PER GESSLE** Songwriter. (Sweden) With ROXETTE, hits include: "Dangerous," "The Look," and "Joyride." Year/Age: 1995/**36** 1996/**37** 1997/**38**

- **GEORGE BUSH** President. (Milton, MA) 41st U.S. President and 43rd Vice President. He was a Congressman from Texas, a fighter pilot in WWII and head of the CIA. He tried for the GOP presidential nomination in 1980, but ended up serving as V.P. He was president during the Persian Gulf War. Year/Age: 1995/**71** 1996/**72** 1997/**73**

- **RONA JAFFE** Author. (NYC) Wrote *The Last Chance* and *Class Reunion.* Year/Age: 1995/**63** 1996/**64** 1997/**65**

- **BUN E. CARLOS** Drummer. (Born Brad Carlson in Rockford, IL) CHEAP TRICK. Their biggest hit: "I Want You to Want Me." Year/Age: 1995/**44** 1996/**45** 1997/**46**

- **CHICK COREA** [koh-ree-uh] Jazz musician. (Chelsea, MS) Won four Grammies. Year/Age: 1995/**54** 1996/**55** 1997/**56**

- **UTA HAGEN** [oo'-tuh-hah'-guhn] Actress. (Germany) She was brought to Madison, WI, as a child and made her professional debut in the Eva LeGallienne Civic Repertory Co. in Dennis, MA, in 1937. Year/Age: 1995/**76** 1996/**77** 1997/**78**

- **JIM NABORS** Actor. (Sylacauga, AL) Had 3 TV series in the '60s: "Andy Griffith," "Gomer Pyle," and "The Jim Nabors Variety Hour." He now raises macadamia nuts in Maui, Hawaii, where he lives. "Return to Mayberry." Year/Age: 1995/**63** 1996/**64** 1997/**65**

- **VIC DAMONE** Singer. (Born Vito Farinola in Brooklyn, NY) Biggest hit: "On the Street Where You Live" in 1956. Year/Age: 1995/**67** 1996/**68** 1997/**69**

- **TIMOTHY BUSFIELD** Actor. (East Lansing, MI) Appeared on "thirtysomething." Films include *Little Big League* and *The Birds of Paradise.* Year/Age: 1995/**45** 1996/**46** 1997/**47**

- **BRAD DELP** Singer. (Boston) Lead vocalist with the group BOSTON. Biggest hit: "Amanda" in 1986. Year/Age: 1995/**44** 1996/**45** 1997/**46**

- **REG PRESLEY** Singer. (England) With the TROGGS. Their biggest hit: "Wild Thing," in 1966. Year/Age: 1995/**51** 1996/**52** 1997/**53**

- **IRWIN ALLEN** Disaster film producer. (1916-1991 – NYC) *Towering Inferno, Poseidon Adventure,* and *Voyage to the Bottom of the Sea.* (Died 11-2-91.)

FACTS FROM THE PAST

1767 **DR. JEAN BAPTISTE DENYS** administered the **FIRST HUMAN BLOOD TRANSFUSION**. The blood, taken from a lamb, was transfused into the neck of a boy. The patient recovered, but none of the doctor's future victims made it.

1825 **PRESIDENT JOHN QUINCY ADAMS** went skinny dipping in the Potomac river, as he often did. This early morning he almost drowned. He was quite embarrassed during the rescue.

1839 **ABNER DOUBLEDAY** "INVENTED" (set down rules for) **BASEBALL** in Cooperstown, NY. The U.S. Union general was also known as the first man to fire a Union gun in defense of Fort Sumter.

1923 Magician **HARRY HOUDINI** escaped from a strait jacket suspeded upside down 40 feet above the ground.

1935 Senator **HUEY LONG** of Louisiana spoke continually for $15^1/_2$ hour in the Senates. It was **THE LONGEST SPEECH ON RECORD**. His 150,000 words filled 100 pages in the "Congressional Record" and cost the Government $5,000 to print.

1939 The **BASEBALL HALL OF FAME** opened in Cooperstown, NY, where baseball had been devised by Abner Doubleday 100 years earlier. The first players chosen for membership were: Babe Ruth, Ty Cobb, Honus Wagner, Christy Mathewson, and Walter Johnson.

1963 The movie **CLEOPATRA** premiered at the Rivoli Theater in NYC. **JOE MANKIEWICZ**, who directed the film, said it was the toughest three pictures he ever made. He shot 96 hours of film during 2 years at a cost of $40 million dollars. Liz Taylor got $1.5 million, plus a percentage of the gross. A famous ad for the film showed Liz reclining seductively under the admiring gaze of co-star, Richard Burton. The body belonged to Lois Bennett who got $35.00 as a body stand-in for Taylor. It was Liz's face.

1963 Civil Rights leader and secretary of the NAACP, **MEDGAR EVERS,** was murdered by a sniper in Jackson, MS outside his home.

1965 Under protest, the **BEATLES** were made members of the "Most Excellent Order of the British Empire" (MBE). The Queen thought the Beatles' worldwide record sales had done a lot for the British economy. John Lennon returned his medal in 1969.

1979 Twenty-six-year-old cyclist **BRYAN ALLEN** flew the man-powered **GOSSAMER ALBATROSS** across the English Channel, 22 miles, in 2 hours, 49 minutes, winning a long-standing prize.

1982 750,000 attended a **RALLY FOR NUCLEAR DISARMAMENT** in NYC's Central Park, the largest assemblage ever to gather for a political rally. The stars included Linda Ronstadt, James Taylor, Bruce Springsteen, Jackson Browne, and Gary U.S. Bonds.

1988 Halftime at the LA. Lakers/Detroit Pistons was composed of a **SING-OFF** between The Beach Boys (who rooted for the former) and The Four Tops (singing for the Pistons).

1991 **BORIS YELTSIN** was elected president of the Russian Republic.

1994 **RYAN SANDBERG**, all-star second baseman for the Chicago Cubs, decided to retire. Saying his performance was poor, he left behind over $15 million in salary.

Beware of naked DJ's.

JUNE 13

BIRTHDAYS

• **RICHARD THOMAS** Actor. (NYC) John-Boy on the TV series "The Waltons." Also appeared in "Roots the Next Generation" on TV, and the Minute Maid commercials. He is the father of triplets. Year/**Age**: 1995/**44** 1996/**45** 1997/**46**

• **ALLY SHEEDY** Actress. (NYC) *The Breakfast Club, Man's Best Friend, Betsy's Wedding,* and *Only the Lonely.* Year/**Age**: 1995/**33** 1996/**34** 1997/**35**

• **SHIRL CONWAY** Actress. On TV's "Caesar's Hour" in the '50s; Nurse Liz Thorpe in "The Nurses" in the 1960s. Year/**Age**: 1995/**79** 1996/**80** 1997/**81**

• **BO DONALDSON** Singer. (Cincinnati, OH) His group the HEYWOODS were regulars on the Dick Clark "Action" TV show in the '70s. Their biggest hit: "Billy, Don't Be a Hero." Year/**Age**: 1995/**41** 1996/**42** 1997/**43**

• **MARY KATE** and **ASHLEY OLSEN** Actresses. The twin actresses are on "Full House." Year/**Age**: 1995/**7** 1996/**8** 1997/**9**

• **MALCOLM McDOWELL** Actor. (Leeds, England) His films include *Clockwork Orange, The Player,* and *Blue Thunder.* Year/**Age**: 1995/**52** 1996/**53** 1997/**54**

• **BOBBY FREEMAN** Singer. (San Francisco, CA) Biggest hit: "Do You Wanna Dance" in 1958. Year/**Age**: 1995/**55** 1996/**56** 1997/**57**

• **TIM ALLEN** Actor/comedian. (Denver, CO) TV's "Home Improvement." Year/**Age**: 1995/**41** 1996/**42** 1997/**43**

• **BETTINA BUNGE** Tennis player. (Switzerland) Year/**Age**: 1995/**32** 1996/**33** 1997/**34**

• **RALPH EDWARDS** TV producer/host. (Merino, CO) Host of TV series "This is Your Life" and "Truth or Consequences" in the '50s. The only person to ever substitute for Ralph, while he was in the hospital, was Ronald Reagan. Year/**Age**: 1995/**82** 1996/**83** 1997/**84**

• **CHRISTO** Artist. (Born Christo Javacheff in Bulgaria) Creates controversial outdoor art from cloth and plastic, like the big yellow umbrellas in California and Japan. Year/**Age**: 1995/**60** 1996/**61** 1997/**62**

• **DENNIS LOCORRIERE** Musician. (New Jersey) DR. HOOK. Biggest hits: "Sylvia's Mother" and "Sexy Eyes." Year/**Age**: 1995/**46** 1996/**47** 1997/**48**

• **RED GRANGE** Football. (1904-1991 – Born Harold Grange in Forksville, PA) He played for the Univ. of Illinois and the Chicago Bears. He was called the "Galloping Ghost" of football. (Died 1-28-91.)

• **BASIL RATHBONE** Actor. (1892-1967 – South Africa) Nominated for an Oscar for *Romeo & Juliet* and *If I Were King.* Best known for playing Sherlock Holmes. (Died 7-21-67.)

FACTS FROM THE PAST

1825 Walter Hunt of NYC **PATENTED AN INVENTION** so he could pay a $15 debt. It only took him 3 hours to make a sketch of his idea—the **SAFETY PIN**—to which he sold the rights for $400 dollars. Since then, billions of safety pins have been sold.

1912 The **FIRST SUCCESSFUL PARACHUTE JUMP** from an airplane was made by **CAPTAIN ALBERT BERRY** in Jefferson, MS.

1921 **BABE RUTH** hit his **LONGEST HOME RUN** of 460 feet at the polo grounds in New York.

1922 The **LONGEST ATTACK OF HICCUPS** began on this day. 98-year-old **CHARLIE OSBORNE** had hiccuped over 435 million times before it stopped. He died just 11 months after his hiccups stopped in 1991.

1925 Telecast of **OBJECTS IN MOTION WAS INVENTED** by Charles Jenkins. He called it "visions by radio."

1927 The first ticker tape parade ever in New York City. honored **CHARLES LINDBERGH** and his first-ever solo trans-Atlantic flight.

1937 Yankee outfielder **JOE DiMAGGIO** hit 3 for 3, had 3 putouts, scored 3 runs and drove in 3 runners. This was in the 3rd game of a 3-game series against St. Louis.

1951 Joe Louis knocked out Lee Savold in the **FIRST CLOSED-CIRCUIT TV BOXING MATCH.**

1966 The **SUPREME COURT "MIRANDA" RULING** granted suspects the right to remain silent, or to have an attorney present at questioning. **ERNESTO MIRANDA**, the 23-year-old whose name became nationally known, was retried after the Miranda Decision, convicted and sent back to prison. After his parole the "celebrity" sold autographed copies of the cards police carry to inform suspects of their rights. Miranda was stabbed to death in a card game dispute in Phoenix, AZ, in 1976.

1967 Solicitor-General **THURGOOD MARSHALL** was nominated to be the first African-American justice of the U.S. Supreme Court**.**

1969 Mick Taylor replaced Brian Jones as drummer of **THE ROLLING STONES.**

1971 *The N.Y. Times* began publishing **THE PENTAGON PAPERS**, a 2.5 million-word, top-secret history of American involvement in Indochina from 1945-1968, compiled by order of Secretary of Defense Robert McNamara, and leaked to the *Times* by Daniel Ellsberg, a former government researcher.

1989 **GEORGE BUSH** exercised his **FIRST PRESIDENTAL VETO** on a bill dealing with the minimum wage.

1992 **BILL CLINTON** upset **RAPPER SISTER SOULJAH** when he compared her post L.A. riot comments ("If black people kill black people every day, why not have a week and kill white people?") to something David Duke might say.

1993 Defense minister **KIM CAMPBELL** was chosen as **CANADA'S FIRST WOMAN PRIME MINISTER**. The lawyer from Vancouver was elected party leader at the Conservative Party convention succeeding Brian Mulroney.

JUNE 14
Flag Day

What year are you stuck in?

BIRTHDAYS

- **STEFFI GRAF** Tennis star. (Bruhl, Germany) She started playing at age 4 and won 17 professional singles titles before the age of 18. An Olympic gold medal winner, she also won the professional "Grand Slam." She attributes much of her success to her dad who ran a tennis school in West Germany. Year/Age: 1995/**26** 1996/**27** 1997/**28**

- **DONALD TRUMP** Tycoon. Real estate developer. Year/**Age:** 1995/**49** 1996/**50** 1997/**51**

- **BURL IVES** Entertainer. (Hunt, IL) Biggest hit: "A Little Bitty Tear" in 1962. Movie credits include: *Cat on a Hot Tin Roof* in 1957. He won an Oscar for supporting actor in *The Big Country*, 1958. Year/Age: 1995/**86** 1996/**87** 1997/**88**

- **DOROTHY McGUIRE** Actress. (Omaha, NE) She received an Oscar nomination in 1947 for *Gentlemen's Agreement*. Year/Age: 1995/**77** 1996/**78** 1997/**79**

- **SAM WANAMAKER** Actor/director. (1919-1993, Chicago, IL) His films include: *Guilty By Suspicion, Those Magnificent Men in Their Flying Machines, The Spy Who Came in from the Cold*, and *Baby Boom*. He was Goldie Hawn's dad in *Private Benjamin*.

- **MARLA GIBBS** Actress. (Chicago, IL) Maid on "The Jeffersons" TV series, and Mary on "227." In *The Meteor Man*. Year/Age: 1995/**64** 1996/**65** 1997/**66**

- **BOY GEORGE** Entertainer. (Born George O'Dowd in London, England) Biggest hit with CULTURE CLUB: "Karma Chameleon" in 1983. Sang the title song for the film *Crying Game*. Year/Age: 1995/**34** 1996/**35** 1997/**36**

- **CY COLEMAN** Pianist/composer. (NYC) Wrote "If My Friends Could See Me Now." Year/Age: 1995/**67** 1996/**68** 1997/**69**

- **LASH LaRUE** Cowboy star. Year/Age: 1995/**78** 1996/**79** 1997/**80**

- **EDDIE MEKKA** Actor. (Worcester, MA) Played the macho Carmine Ragusa on the "Laverne & Shirley" TV series. Appears on soap "Guiding Light" as Grady. Year/Age: 1995/**43** 1996/**44** 1997/**45**

- **ERIC HEIDEN** Olympic speed skater. (Madison, WI) He won 5 gold medals in the 1980 Olympics. Year/Age: 1995/**37** 1996/**38** 1997/**39**

- **MUFF WINWOOD** Bass guitarist. (England) Member of SPENCER DAVIS GROUP. "Gimme Some Lovin" in 1967. Year/Age: 1995/**52** 1996/**53** 1997/**54**

- **ROD ARGENT** Keyboardist. (England) With the ZOMBIES. Hits include: "She's Not There," "Time of the Season" and "Tell Her No." Year/Age: 1995/**50** 1996/**51** 1997/**52**

- **BEN DAVIDSON** Football player/actor. Year/**Age:** 1995/**55** 1996/**56** 1997/**57**

- **ALAN WHITE** Drummer. (England) With the group YES. Biggest hit: "Owner of a Lonely Heart" in 1983. Year/**Age:** 1995/**46** 1996/**47** 1997/**48**

- **HARRIET BEECHER STOWE** Author. (1811-1896 – Litchfield, CT) Author of *Uncle Tom's Cabin*, an anti-slavery novel that provoked a storm of protest. When President Lincoln met her he said, "So you're the little woman who wrote the book that made this great war." The last 10 years of her life she had what we now call Alzheimer's Disease. [See next entry] (Died 7-1-1896.)

- **ALOIS ALZHEIMER** Psychiatrist/pathologist. (1864-1915 – Germany) In 1907 he wrote an article describing the disease which was named for him. It was thought of as a kind of pre-senile problem, usually beginning at 40-60 years of age. (Died 12-19-15.)

FACTS FROM THE PAST

1777 The Continental Congress made the **STARS & STRIPES** the **FIRST NATIONAL FLAG**. No one knows who designed the first American flag. It is believed by some to have been an early military banner carried into battle during the American Revolution. The notion that Betsy Ross designed it has no historical basis.

1919 The first non-stop trans-Atlantic flight began. Captain **JOHN ALCOCK** and Lt. **ARTHUR BROWN** flew 1,900 miles non-stop from Newfoundland to Ireland. Despite their crash landing in an Irish peat bog, their flight inspired more interest in aviation and led to a lot of other flights.

1922 President **WARREN HARDING** became the first president to make a radio speech, which was broadcast over WEAR, Baltimore, at the dedication of a memorial to Francis Scott Key at Ft. McHenry.

1940 In German-occupied Poland, the Nazis opened their concentration camp at Auschwitz [owsh'-vitz], where an estimated three to four million people, many of them Jews, were exterminated as part of **ADOLF HITLER**'s "Final Solution."

1954 President Dwight D. Eisenhower signed an order adding the words "under God" to the "**PLEDGE OF ALLEGIANCE.**"

1970 Eric Clapton's band, **DEREK AND THE DOMINOES**, made their live debut in Britain. They were joined by Dave Mason, who played the guitar parts performed by Duane Allman on the studio version of "Layla."

1982 Argentine General **MARIO MENENDEZ** surrendered his army of one thousand to British Major General Jeremy Moore at Stanley in the short Falkland War.

1989 Actress **ZSA ZSA GABOR** was arrested for slapping a Beverly Hills motorcycle patrolman

1992 The Chicago Bulls won their second straight NBA basketball title, 4 games to 2, by beating the Portland Trail Blazers 97-93. **MICHAEL JORDAN** became the first player to win the MVP award for regular season and Finals two years in a row.

1994 The bloodied bodies of Nicole Brown Simpson and Ronald Goldman were found near Nicole Simpson's West Los Angeles condominium. Former husband of the victim, **OJ SIMPSON**, a main suspect was formally charged.

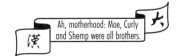

Ah, motherhood: Moe, Curly and Shemp were all brothers.

JUNE 15

BIRTHDAYS

- **NEIL PATRICK HARRIS** Actor. TV's "Doogie Howser." Film *Snowbound.* Year/**Age:** 1995/**22** 1996/**23** 1997/**24**

- **WADE BOGGS** New York Yankees star. (Omaha, NE) Played 3rd base 11 years for the Boston Red Sox. Year/**Age:** 1995/**37** 1996/**38** 1997/**39**

- **COURTENEY COX** Actress. (Birmingham, AL) "Family Ties." She was in the film *Ace Ventura Pet Detective* and danced with Bruce Springsteen in his "Dancing in the Dark" video. Year/**Age:** 1995/**31** 1996/**32** 1997/**33**

- **WAYLON JENNINGS** C&W singer. (Littlefield, TX) Biggest hit: "Luckenbach, Texas" with Willie Nelson, #1 on the C&W chart for 6 weeks in 1977. He was one of the CRICKETS with Buddy Holly. Also sang the theme and narrated the TV show, "The Dukes of Hazzard." "The Outlaw" married Jessi Colter in 1969. He was in the movie *Urban Cowboy.* Lives in Brentwood, TN. Year/**Age:** 1995/**58** 1996/**59** 1997/**60**

- **BRETT BUTLER** L.A. Dodgers outfielder. (Los Angeles, CA) Year/**Age:** 1995/**38** 1996/**39** 1997/**40**

- **HARRY NILSSON** Singer/songwriter. (1941-1994, Brooklyn, NY) His biggest hit: "Without You" in 1972 and he sang the title song, "Everybody's Talkin'," for the movie *Midnight Cowboy.* His Nilsson Schmilsson album sold over a million copies. He wrote "One" for Three Dog Night.

- **BILLY WILLIAMS** Former Chicago Cub. One of the toughest hitters in the NL from 1959-1974. From Sept. 1963 through Sept. 1970, he played in 1,117 consecutive games, setting a NL record. Year/**Age:** 1995/**57** 1996/**58** 1997/**59**

- **RUSS HITCHCOCK** Singer. (Australia) With AIR SUPPLY. Biggest hit: "The One That You Love" in 1981. Year/**Age:** 1995/**46** 1996/**47** 1997/**48**

- **TERRI GIBBS** C&W singer. (Augusta, GA) Blind since birth. Biggest record: "Somebody's Knockin'" in 1981. Year/**Age:** 1995/**51** 1996/**52** 1997/**53**

- **MORRIS UDALL** Former Congressman. D/AZ. Year/**Age:** 1995/**73** 1996/**74** 1997/**75**

- **MARIO CUOMO** [kwoh'-moh] Governor of New York. (Queens, NY) Year/**Age:** 1995/**63** 1996/**64** 1997/**65**

- **HELEN HUNT** Actress. (Los Angeles, CA) *Kiss of Death, My Life and Times,* and TV's "Mad About You." Year/**Age:** 1995/**32** 1996/**33** 1997/**34**

- **JIM VARNEY** Actor. (Lexington, KY) *Ernest Goes To Camp, Ernest Saves Christmas, Ernest Goes To Jail,* and *The Beverly Hillbillies.* Jim's famous line: "Know what I mean, Vern?" Year/**Age:** 1995/**46** 1996/**47** 1997/**48**

- **JIM BELUSHI** Comedian/actor. (Chicago, IL) *K-9, Principal,* and *Trading Places.* TV's "Saturday Night Live" and "Wild Palms." He is the younger brother of the late John Belushi. Year/**Age:** 1995/**41** 1996/**42** 1997/**43**

- **DAVID ROSE** Bandleader/composer. (1910-1990 – England) Biggest hit: "The Stripper" in 1962. He and Judy Garland were married from 1941 to 1944. Composed music for "Little House on the Prairie" and "Bonanza." His 65-year career was marked by four Emmys and 22 Grammys. He also composed background music and themes for 22 other TV series including "Sea Hunt" and "Highway Patrol." (Died 8-23-90.)

- **ERROLL GARNER** Jazz pianist. (1921-1977 – Pittsburgh, PA) "Misty" was his most famous composition which won an award from ASCAP in 1984 as one of the 11 most-performed standards of the last decade. (Died 1-2-77.)

FACTS FROM THE PAST

1520 Pope Leo X threatened to excommunicate **MARTIN LUTHER** if he did not recant his religious beliefs.

1752 In a dangerous experiment, **BENJAMIN FRANKLIN** and his son demonstrated the relationship between lightning and electricity by flying a kite in a thunderstorm with an iron key suspended from a string, which produced a little spark. He and his son could have been electrocuted if the spark had been bigger. The church condemned him for "interfering with God." He later showed his respect for lightning by creating the world's first lightning rods to prevent fires caused by lightning.

1785 Jean Pilatre de Rozier, the **FIRST HUMAN AVIATOR,** was taking a passenger across the English Channel when the balloon caught fire. The first man to fly died in the first fatal aviation accident.

1844 **CHARLES GOODYEAR** received a patent for his process to strengthen rubber. Goodyear failed to benefit from his invention, and died in poverty in 1860.

1864 Secretary of War **EDWIN M. STANTON** signed an order designating a site in Arlington, VA, as a **MILITARY CEMETERY**.

1869 A **PATENT FOR THE FIRST PLASTIC**, celluloid, was given to **WESLEY and ISAIAH HYATT**.

1938 Cincinnati Reds pitcher **JOHNNY VANDERMEER** hurled his 2nd straight no-hitter, the only man to ever do that. Leo Durocher, then a shortstop for the Dodgers, flew out to end the game. Vandermeer beat the Boston Braves on June 11th for his first no-hitter.

1965 **BOB DYLAN** recorded "Like A Rolling Stone."

1967 Singer/guitarist **PETER GREEN** left John Mayall's Blues Breakers to form **FLEETWOOD MAC** with Mick Fleetwood, John McVie, and Jeremy Spencer.

1978 **KING HUSSEIN** [hoo-sayn'] of Jordan married 26-year-old American Elizabeth (Lisa) Halaby, and proclaimed his bride Queen Noor Al-Hussein, Arabic for "Light of Hussein."

1992 Vice President **DAN QUAYLE** erroneously told a Trenton, NY elementary school student to spell potato with an "e" at the end.

1994 **DAVID LAWSON,** convicted murderer who was sentenced to death and wanted his execution televised on Donahue, screamed "I'm human, I'm human" just before he died.

JUNE 16

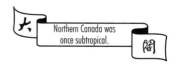
Northern Canada was
once subtropical.

BIRTHDAYS

- **JOAN VAN ARK** Actress. (NYC) Former "Knot's Landing" star. Year/**Age:** 1995/**52** 1996/**53** 1997/**54**

- **RON LeFLORE** Outfielder. (Detroit, MI) Stole 97 bases for Montreal in 1980. Year/**Age:** 1995/**43** 1996/**44** 1997/**45**

- **EDDIE LEVERT** Singer. (Canton, OH) Formed a group called the TRIUMPHS in 1958, later renamed by DJ Eddie O'Jay, THE O'JAYS. Biggest hit: "Love Train" in 1973. Year/**Age:** 1995/**53** 1996/**54** 1997/**55**

- **PEPPY CASTRO** Singer/guitarist. (Bronx, NY) Leader of the psychedelic rock quintet BLUES MAGOOS. Biggest hit: "We Ain't Got Nothin' Yet" in 1966. Year/**Age:** 1995/**46** 1996/**47** 1997/**48**

- **BILLY "CRASH" CRADDOCK** C&W singer. (Greensboro, NC) Got his nickname "Crash" during his high school football days. He had nine #1 country singles from 1971-1977, including a cross-over hit, "Rub It In" in 1974. Year/**Age:** 1995/**56** 1996/**57** 1997/**58**

- **LAMONT DOZIER** Songwriter. (Detroit, MI) He's responsible for some of the biggest Motown hits of the 1960s, including "Baby Love" by the SUPREMES and "I Can't Help Myself" by the FOUR TOPS with help from Eddie and Brian Holland. Year/**Age:** 1995/**54** 1996/**55** 1997/**56**

- **LAURIE METCALF** Actress. Emmy-award winner for "Roseanne." Year/**Age:** 1995/**40** 1996/**41** 1997/**42**

- **FREDERICK KOEHLER** Actor. Played Allie's son, Chip, on TV's "Kate & Allie." Year/**Age:** 1995/**20** 1996/**21** 1997/**22**

- **FAITH DOMERQUE** Actress. In films: *Vendetta* and *Legacy of Blood.* Year/**Age:** 1995/**70** 1996/**71** 1997/**72**

- **ERICH SEGAL** Novelist. (Brooklyn, NY.) Professor at Yale from 1965-73. Wrote *Oliver's Story* and *Love Story,* and is responsible for the line "love means never having to say you're sorry." Recent novel: *Act of Faith.* Year/**Age:** 1995/**58** 1996/**59** 1997/**60**

- **ROBERTO DURAN** Fighter. (Panama) World lightweight champion from 1972-1979, turned welterweight. One of his most famous fights was June 20, 1980, when he beat Sugar Ray Leonard in 15 rounds at Montreal, Canada. Year/**Age:** 1995/**44** 1996/**45** 1997/**46**

- **GINO VANNELLI** Singer. (Canada) Biggest hit: "I Just Want to Stop" in 1978. Year/**Age:** 1995/**43** 1996/**44** 1997/**45**

- **JACK ALBERTSON** Actor. (1910-1981 – Malden, MA) Won an Oscar for best supporting actor in *The Subject Was Roses* in 1968. He was one of the few actors to win an Oscar on the screen, a Tony on the stage and Emmys on TV. His last TV series was "Chico & the Man" with Freddie Prinze. He was in show biz for more than 50 years. (Died 11-25-81.)

- **STAN LAUREL** Actor. (1890-1965 – Born Arthur Stanley Jefferson in England) Of the comedy team "Laurel & Hardy." There's a museum in England that houses some of their memorabilia, donated by their wives. They made over 200 films between 1927-1945. (Died 2-23-65.)

- **JOHN HOWARD GRIFFIN** Author. (1920-1980 – Dallas, TX) Author & photographer concerned with racial problems in the U.S. He blackened his skin by the use of chemicals and ultraviolet light and traveled through the South, keeping a journal which resulted in the book *Black Like Me.* (Died 9-9-80.)

FACTS FROM THE PAST

1858 In a speech in Springfield, IL, Senate candidate **ABRAHAM LINCOLN** said the slavery issue had to be resolved, declaring, "A house divided against itself cannot stand."

1929 **OTTO E. FUNK**, 62 years old, ended a **MARATHON WALK** from New York City to San Francisco. He traveled 4,165 miles in 183 days, playing his violin all the way.

1946 Pro golfer **BYRON NELSON** lost the U.S. Open by one stroke when his caddy, Eddie Martin, accidentally kicked the ball as he tried to protect Nelson's lie from the moving crowd of fans.

1961 Soviet ballet dancer **RUDOLF NUREYEV** defected to the West while his troupe was in Paris.

1963 The world's **FIRST FEMALE SPACE TRAVELER,** 26-year-old **VALENTINA TERESHKOVA**, was launched into space from a base in the Soviet Union. She manually controlled VOSTOK-VI during the 70-hour flight through 48 orbits of the earth.

1965 **HERMAN'S HERMITS'** go gold with "Mrs. Brown, You've Got A Lovely Daughter."

1967 The **MONTEREY INTERNATIONAL POP FESTIVAL** opened in California. It was the first major rock festival. 50,000 fans attended over three days to see two dozen rock acts including **JANIS JOPLIN, JIMI HENDRIX, THE WHO**, and **The GRATEFUL DEAD**. Tickets cost from $3.50 to $6.50. The performers played for free.

1977 **SOVIET COMMUNIST PARTY GENERAL SECRETARY LEONID BREZHNEV** was named president, becoming the first person to hold both posts simultaneously.

1989 "Smoke, the most sensual woman's perfume," created by **SMOKEY ROBINSON** entered the perfume market.

1992 **CASPER WEINBERGER** became the highest-ranking official of the Reagan administration to be indicted in the Iran-Contra affair.

1992 **PRESIDENT BUSH** and **RUSSIAN PRESIDENT BORIS YELTSIN**, agreed to drastically cut the number of each nation's long-range nuclear warheads. Yeltsin also revealed that some U.S. soldiers reported missing in action could be in Russia.

1994 Bass player for **COURTNEY LOVE**'s band Hole was found dead in her bathtub. Drug paraphinalia surrounded her. Love's husband, Nirvana singer Kurt Cobain, shot himslf to death earlier in the year.

Thomas Crapper invented the flush toilet.

JUNE 17

BIRTHDAYS

• **JOE PISCOPO** Actor/comedian. (Passaic, NJ) In 1980 he joined the second generation of "Saturday Night Live" entertainers. He's into body-building. Film *Sidekicks*. Year/**Age**: 1995/**44** 1996/**45** 1997/**46**

• **BARRY MANILOW** Singer/composer. (Brooklyn, NY) His biggest hit: Grammy winner, "I Write the Songs" in 1975. Studied at Juilliard NY College of Music, did Dr. Pepper, Pepsi and McDonald's commercials. His music is featured in the film *Thumbelina*. He played accordion by age 7 and was given a piano for his bar mitzvah. Year/**Age**: 1995/**49** 1996/**50** 1997/**51**

• **DAN JANSEN** Olympic speed skater. (West Allis, WI) Finally got his gold medal in 1994 while setting a new world record for the 500 meter race.

• **MARK LINN-BAKER** Actor. (St. Louis, MO) Cousin Larry on TV's "Perfect Strangers." Year/**Age**: 1995/**42** 1996/**43** 1997/**44**

• **DAVE CONCEPCION** Shortstop. (Venezuela) Played for the Cincinnati Reds' "Big Red Machine" when they won the World Series in 1975. Year/**Age**: 1995/**47** 1996/**48** 1997/**49**

• **KEVIN THORNTON** Singer. (Oklahoma City, OK) With COLOR ME BADD. #1 hit: "I Wanna Sex You Up" from the film *New Jack City*. Year/**Age**: 1995/**26** 1996/**27** 1997/**28**

• **ELROY "CRAZY LEGS" HIRSCH** Football. (Wausau, WI) Former football star and athletic director at the Univ. of Wisconsin in Madison. He got his nickname because he moved so gracefully and was so hard to bring down, it looked like he was running with crazy legs. Year/**Age**: 1995/**72** 1996/**73** 1997/**74**

• **DEAN MARTIN** Entertainer. (Born Dino Crocetti in Steubenville, OH) Biggest hit: "Memories are Made of This" in 1956. The first film to star Dean Martin and his former partner, Jerry Lewis, was *My Friend Irma*. Year/**Age**: 1995/**78** 1996/**79** 1997/**80**

• **JOHN HERSEY** Author. (1917-1993 – China) He wrote *A Bell For Adano* and *Hiroshima*. (Died 3-24-93.)

• **RALPH BELLAMY** Actor. 1904-1991 – Chicago, IL) Nominated for an Oscar in 1937 for *The Awful Truth* with Cary Grant and Irene Dunne. Portrayed Franklin D. Roosevelt on the stage, in films and TV. (Died 11-29-91.)

• **IGOR STRAVINSKY** Composer/author. (1882-1971 – Born near Leningrad, Russia) He died in New York City. (Died 4-6-71.)

• **RED FOLEY** C&W singer. (1910-1968 – Born Clyde Julian Foley in Blue Lick, KY) His daughter, Shirley, is married to singer Pat Boone. One of Red's biggest hits was "Chattanooga Shoe Shine Boy" in 1950. (Died 9-19-68.)

FACTS FROM THE PAST

1775 The Revolutionary War **BATTLE OF BUNKER HILL** was fought when over 3,000 British troops launched an attack on more than 1,000 American soldiers near Boston. The Americans were led by **COLONEL WILLIAM PRESCOTT**, who told his troops, "Don't fire till you see the whites of their eyes." The British forces succeeded in taking the hill, but a third of their men were wiped out.

1862 **W.H. FANCHER** and **C.M. FRENCH** received a patent for a **COMBINED PLOW AND GUN.**

1928 **AMELIA EARHART** embarked on a trans-Atlantic flight from Newfoundland to Wales – the first ever by a woman.

1943 Boston Red Sox Manager **JOE CRONIN** became the only player in baseball history to hit two pinch-hit homeruns in the same day. As manager, he chose himself to pinch hit twice and hit 3-run homers each time at bat against Philadelphia.

1953 Supreme Court Justice **WILLIAM O. DOUGLAS** stayed the executions of **CONVICTED SPIES JULIUS AND ETHEL ROSENBERG,** scheduled for the next day. Douglas' intervention prevented the executions from taking place on the Rosenbergs' 14th wedding anniversary. They were executed on June 19 at Ossining, NY.

1972 Five men were arrested carrying electronic eavesdropping equipment in the **WATERGATE** office building headquarters of the Democratic Party National Committee. The arrest prompted an investigation and led to President **RICHARD NIXON**'s inner councils. Eventually Nixon resigned and White House staffers were convicted.

1982 **LEOPOLD GALTIERI**, the president of Argentina, resigned after his country lost to Britain in the Falkland Islands conflict.

1982 **PRESIDENT REAGAN ADDRESSED THE U.N. GENERAL ASSEMBLY** for the first time and accused the Soviet Union of world oppression.

1984 **SWALE,** the 3-year-old horse that won the Kentucky Derby and Belmont Stakes, died after a routine work-out. The cause of death was unknown. Almost $36 million dollars was lost in stud fees. He was the son of **SEATTLE SLEW,** 1977 Triple Crown Champ.

1986 **STEVIE WONDER** warned the critics covering his Seattle tour, "If you give me a bad review, I'll put you in my car and drive you home myself."

1989 **RINGO STARR** announced he would embark on his first concert tour in years. Joining him in the ALL STARR BAND were Clarence Clemons, Joe Walsh, Billy Preston, Dr. John, Nils Lofgren, Rick Danko, and Levon Helm.

1991 **PRESIDENT ZACHARY TAYLOR**'s remains were exhumed in Louisville, KY, because of persistent rumors that he had died of arsenic poisoning July 9, 1850. Tests proved that he died from natural causes, 141 years before.

1994 95 million Americans watched the eight hour police chase of **O.J. SIMPSON**. He threatened suicide and refused to leave the vehicle he was in upon arrival at his home.

JUNE 18

Why are atom smashers so huge?

BIRTHDAYS

• **PAUL McCARTNEY** Singer/musician/composer. (Born James Paul McCartney in Liverpool, England) Biggest hit, with the BEATLES: "Hey Jude" in 1968, and his biggest with WINGS: "Silly Love Songs" in 1976. Paul is one of the wealthiest performers in the world; worth over $700 million. Paul hit the top of the classical charts in 1991 with his *Liverpool Oratorio*. Year/**Age**: 1995/**53** 1996/**54** 1997/**55**

• **E.G. MARSHALL** Actor. (Born Edda Gunnar Marshall in Owatonna, MN) Emmys for "The Defenders." Year/**Age**: 1995/**85** 1996/**86** 1997/**87**

• **CAROL KANE** Actress. (Cleveland, OH) Played "Simka," Latka's wife on the "Taxi" TV series for which she won a couple of Emmys. She was in *Addams Family Values* and *Scrooged,* and was nominated for an Oscar for best actress in *Hester Street*. Year/**Age**: 1995/**43** 1996/**44** 1997/**45**

• **ROGER EBERT** Critic. (Urbana, IL) Chicago film critic who won a Pulitzer Prize in 1975. TV's "Siskel & Ebert." He's the short, heavier one with glasses. Year/**Age**: 1995/**53** 1996/**54** 1997/**55**

• **ISABELLA ROSSELLINI** Actress. (Italy) TV's "Twin Peaks." She is the daughter of Ingrid Bergman and director Roberto Rossellini. Films include *Fearless* and *Blue Velvet*. She has been on the cover of over 500 magazines and a cosmetic spokesperson. Year/**Age**: 1995/**43** 1996/**44** 1997/**45**

• **LOU BROCK** Baseball player. (El Dorado, AR) Former Chicago Cub and St. Louis Cardinal outfielder who stole a record 118 bases in 1974 [937 career]. He led the NL 8 times. Year/**Age**: 1995/**56** 1996/**57** 1997/**58**

• **EVA BARTOK** Actress. (Born Eva Martha Szoke in Hungry) Her autobiography is titled *Worth Living For*. Year/**Age**: 1995/**69** 1996/**70** 1997/**71**

• **ALISON MOYET** Singer. (Born Genevieve Alison Moyet in England) Year/**Age**: 1995/**34** 1996/**35** 1997/**36**

• **SAMMY CAHN** Composer. (Born Saumel Cohen 1913-1993 – NYC) The lyricist received four Oscars – "Call Me Irresponsible," "All the Way," "High Hopes," and "Three Coins in the Fountain." He won an Emmy for Frank Sinatra's rendition of "Love and Marriage," introduced in the 1955 TV musical "Our Town." It's the theme song for the TV series "Married With Children." (Died 1-15-93.)

• **SYLVIA PORTER** Financial reporter/author. (1913-1991 – Patchoque, NY) Her 1975 *Money Book* sold over a million copies. (Died 6-5-91.)

• **KEYE LUKE** Actor. (1904-1991 – Canton, China) In the 1930s he played Charlie Chan's #1 son and was in the TV series "Kung Fu" in 1972, playing Master Po. His last film was Woody Allen's *Alice*. (Died 1-12-91.)

• **RICHARD BOONE** Actor. (1917-1981 – Los Angeles, CA) Attended Stanford University before becoming an actor. Besides movies he starred in the TV series "Have Gun, Will Travel," as Paladin. (Died 1-1-81.)

• **GEORGE MALLORY** Explorer/mountain climber. (1886-1924 – England) Last seen climbing toward the summit of the highest mountain in the world, Mt. Everest, on the morning of June 8, 1924. He's best remembered for his answer when asked why he wanted to climb Mt. Everest – "Because it is there."

FACTS FROM THE PAST

1682 WILLIAM PENN founded the city of Philadelphia and gave it the name: "City of Brotherly Love."

1815 NAPOLEON BONAPARTE met his Waterloo as British and Prussian troups defeated the French forces in Belgium. He was sent to the Caribbean Island of St. Helena and never returned. (The story is told briefly in the song "Waterloo" by Stonewall Jackson.)

1873 SUFFRAGIST SUSAN B. ANTHONY was fined $100 for attempting to vote in the 1872 presidential election. She refused to pay the fine. Fourteen years after she died, women were given right to vote.

1880 JOHN SUTTER died. He was **ONE OF AMERICA'S RICHEST MEN**, but died a pauper in a cheap hotel in Washington. He owned the land in California where gold was first discovered in 1848.

1915 A.P. (Alvin) Carter and Sara Dougherty married in Virginia. Together with Maybelle Addington, who married A.P.'s brother, they formed the **CARTER FAMILY**, one of the most influential groups in country music. Alvin died 11-7-60.

1928 Aviator **AMELIA EARHART** completed a flight from Newfoundland to Wales in 21 hours, becomig the first woman to fly across the Atlantic Ocean.

1966 "River Deep and Mountain High" by **IKE AND TINA TURNER** entered the British charts. It got as high as #3. But the record did so poorly in the U.S. that producer Phil Spector temporarily retired in disgust. He didn't make another record for three years.

1975 SAUDI PRINCE Faisal Ibn Mussed Abdul Aziz was beheaded in Riyadh under Islamic law for the assassination of his uncle, the king.

1977 SEX PISTOLS members Paul Cook and Johnny Rotten were stabbed by men who found the group's "God Save The Queen." offensive.

1983 Astronaut **SALLY R. RIDE** became America's **FIRST WOMAN IN SPACE** as she and four colleagues blasted off aboard the space shuttle *Challenger*.

1984 ALAN BERG, a Denver radio talk show host, was **SHOT TO DEATH** outside his home. Two white supremacists were later convicted of civil rights violations in the slaying.

1987 A woman **SUED MOTLEY CRUE** for $5,000, claiming hearing loss due to the volume level of their concert.

1987 BRUCE SPRINGSTEEN officially separated from wife, Julianne. Photos of Springsteen with backup singer Patti Scialfa appeared on "Entertainment Tonight."

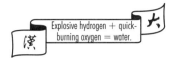

Explosive hydrogen + quick-burning oxygen = water.

JUNE 19

BIRTHDAYS

- **SALMAN RUSHDIE** Author. (Bombay, India) Iranian author who, because of his alleged anti-Islamic writings—*The Satanic Verses*—has a contract out on his life for five million dollars. Year/Age: 1995/**48** 1996/**49** 1997/**50**

- **PAULA ABDUL** Singer/dancer/choreographer. (Los Angeles, CA) A "Laker Girl" for four seasons. Hits include: "Straight Up," "Opposites Attract," "Forever Your Girl," and "Promise of a New Day." She married Emilio Estevez in 1992. The split in 1994. In Diet Coke commercials. Year/Age: 1995/**33** 1996/**34** 1997/**35**

- **PHYLICIA RASHAD** Actress. (Born Phylicia Ayers Allen in Houston, TX) America's favorite TV wife, Claire Huxtable on "The Cosby Show." She worked on Broadway and played Courtney Wright on the soap "One Life to Live." Cosby played Cupid for Phylicia and football commentator Ahmad Rashad, who proposed to her on live TV at halftime of an NFL game. She is choreographer Debbie Allen's sister. Year/Age: 1995/**47** 1996/**48** 1997/**49**.

- **GENA ROWLANDS** Actress. (Cambria, WI) Her dad was Wisconsin State Senator. Among her films: *Night on Earth* and *A Woman Under the Influence* in 1974 for which she received a best actress Oscar nomination. She was married to actor/director John Cassavetes. Year/Age: 1995/**59** 1996/**60** 1997/**61**

- **AL WILSON** singer/drummer. (Meridian, MS) Biggest hit: "Show and Tell" in 1973. Year/Age: 1995/**56** 1996/**57** 1997/**58**

- **ELAINE "SPANKY" McFARLANE** Singer. (Peoria, IL) Lead singer for folk/pop group SPANKY & OUR GANG. Biggest hit: "Sunday Will Never Be the Same" in 1967. She became the lead singer of the new MAMAS & THE PAPAS in the early 1980s. Year/Age: 1995/**53** 1996/**54** 1997/**55**

- **MARK DeBARGE** Trumpet/sax player. (Grand Rapids, MI) Member of family group DEBARGE. Top hit: "Rhythm of the Night" from the Berry Gordy film *The Last Dragon* in 1985. Year/Age: 1995/**36** 1996/**37** 1997/**38**

- **ALAN CRANSTON** Senator. (Palo Alto, CA) (D/CA) Year/Age: 1995/**81** 1996/**82** 1997/**83**

- **LOUIS JOURDAN** Actor. (Born Louis Gendre in France) His film career started in 1939. *Three Coins in a Fountain*, *Gigi*, and *The VIPs*. Year/Age: 1995/**75** 1996/**76** 1997/**77**

- **KATHLEEN TURNER** Actress. (Springfield, MO) Was "Nola Dancy" on soap "The Doctors." Films include: *Romancing the Stone*, *Peggy Sue Got Married*, *Accidental Tourist*, *The War of the Roses*, *Serial Mom*, *Naked in New York House of Cards*, *Undercover Blues*, and also the voice of Roger Rabbit's sexy girl friend, Jessica Rabbit. Year/Age: 1995/**41** 1996/**42** 1997/**43**

- **ANN WILSON** Singer. (San Diego, CA) Lead singer from the group HEART. Their debut album in 1976 was a big smash called *Dreamboat Annie*. Biggest single: "These Dreams" in 1986. Year/Age: 1995/**44** 1996/**45** 1997/**46**

- **MILDRED NATWICK** Actress. (Baltimore, MD) *The Snoop Sisters* and an Oscar nomination for *Barefoot in the Park*. Year/Age: 1995/**87** 1996/**88** 199789

- **MOE HOWARD** Actor. (1897-1975) Original member of "The Three Stooges."

- **LOU GEHRIG** Baseball great. (1903-1941 – NYC) He played the last of his 2,130 consecutive games on April 30, 1939. Gary Cooper starred in a movie based on his life. The tradition of retiring uniform numbers began with the Yankee's retiring Gehrig's #4 in 1939. (Died 6-2-41.)

- **GUY LOMBARDO** Bandleader. (1902-1977 – Canada) "The Third Man Theme" in 1950, #1 for 11 weeks. (Died 11-5-77.)

FACTS FROM THE PAST

1848   **ELIZABETH CADY STANTON** and **LUCRETIA MOTT** opened the **FIRST WOMEN'S RIGHTS CONVENTION** in the U.S. at Seneca Falls, NY.

1946   The first heavyweight boxing championship was televised by WNBT-TV in New York City. **JOE LOUIS** defended his title against Billy Conn. He knocked him out in the 8th round. Conn died in 1993.

1947   Mobster **BENJAMIN "BUGSY" SIEGEL** was shot to death at his girlfriend's Beverly Hills, CA, mansion. The mob was angry over the exorbitant amounts of money Siegel was spending on the Flamingo resort in Las Vegas, NV.

1952   The celebrity-panel game show **"I'VE GOT A SECRET"** made its debut on CBS TV with Garry Moore as host.

1960   "Honky Tonk Girl" became **LORETTA LYNN'**s first record to make the *Billboard* country chart.

1967   **KATHERINE MURPHY** set a record in Bonsall, CA, becoming the first female to play 150 straight holes of golf without stopping.

1973   The stage production of **"THE ROCKY HORROR SHOW"** opened in London. **TIM CURRY** later repeated his starring role in the 1975 movie version that still plays in some cities today. It was on TV for the first time in 1993.

1978   **GARFIELD**, the cartoon about America's favorite lasagna-loving cat, appeared for the first time. **JIM DAVIS** created the comic strip.

1986   University of Maryland basketball star **LEN BIAS**, a 22-year-old All-American forward and first-round draft pick of the Boston Celtics, suffered a fatal cocaine-induced seizure.

1992   *Batman Returns* – starring **MICHAEL KEATON, DANNY DEVITO**, and **MICHELLE PFEIFFER** – opened and pulled in a record-breaking $16.8 million its first day.

1994   **ERNESTO SAMPER** was elected president of Colombia. In the 1980s he was shot 11 times, an assassination attempt by the Medellin drug cartel.

JUNE 20

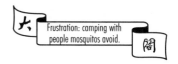

Frustration: camping with people mosquitos avoid.

BIRTHDAYS

- **DANNY AIELLO** Actor. (NYC) *Moonstruck, Do the Right Thing, Ruby, Mistress, Me and the Kid, The Cemetery Club,* and *The Pickle.* Year/**Age:** 1995/**62** 1996/**63** 1997/**64**

- **MICHAEL ANTHONY** Bass guitarist. (Chicago, IL) Hit with VAN HALEN: "Jump" in 1984. Year/**Age:** 1995/**40** 1996/**41** 1997/**42**

- **NICOLE KIDMAN** Actress. Films include *Batman Forever, Malice, Days of Thunder,* and *Far and Away.* She married her frequent co-star Tom Cruise. Year/**Age:** 1995/**28** 1996/**29** 1997/**30**

- **JOHN GOODMAN** Actor. (St. Louis, MO) TV sitcom "Roseanne." Films include *King Ralph, The Babe, Matinee,* and *Born Yesterday.* He played Fred in the movie *The Flintstones.*Year/**Age:** 1995/**43** 1996/**44** 1997/**45**

- **TINA SINATRA** Actress. Year/**Age:** 1995/**47** 1996/**48** 1997/**49**

- **LENNY DAWSON** Football. (Alliance, OH) The Kansas City Chief's quarterback once fumbled the ball 7 times in one game in 1964. In the Pro Football Hall of Fame. Year/**Age:** 1995/**60** 1996/**61** 1997/**62**

- **BRIAN WILSON** Entertainer. (Hawthorne, CA) Keyboards/ bass/composer for the BEACH BOYS. Biggest hit: "I Get Around" in 1964. Though he wrote many songs about surfing, he never rode a wave. Year/**Age:** 1995/**53** 1996/**54** 1997/**55**

- **ANNE MURRAY** Entertainer. (Nova Scotia) The former gym teacher burst on the North American pop/country scene in 1970 with "Snowbird." Her biggest hit: "You Needed Me" in 1978. Year/**Age:** 1995/**50** 1996/**51** 1997/**52**

- **CHET ATKINS** Nashville's top guitarist. (Luttrell, TN) Elected to the Country Music Hall of Fame in 1973. Has influenced a generation of guitarists ranging from George Harrison to Earl Klugh. In 36 years has made over 100 albums. He oversaw Elvis Presley's biggest records, including "Hound Dog" and "Heartbreak Hotel." Year/**Age:** 1995/**71** 1996/**72** 1997/**73**

- **LIONEL RICHIE** Entertainer. (Born Lionel Brockman Richie, Jr. in Tuskagee, AL) Lionel started with a group called the COMMODORES, originally named the JAYS. Appeared in the film *Thank God It's Friday.* Biggest hit: "All Night Long," which he sang to close the 1984 Olympics. He wrote "Three Times a Lady" for his mother, for his parents 25th wedding anniversary. Year/**Age:** 1995/**46** 1996/**47** 1997/**48**

- **CYNDI LAUPER** Entertainer. (Queens, NY) Biggest records: "Time after Time" and "True Colors." She lost her voice in 1977. Doctors said she would never sing again. Won a Grammy in 1984 for best new artist. She made her acting debut in TVs "Mad About You." Film *Life With Mikey.* For two years she managed Wendy Richter, the female world wrestling champion. Year/**Age:** 1995/**42** 1996/**43** 1997/**44**

- **MARTIN LANDAU** Actor. (Brooklyn, NY) Played Paris on "Mission Impossible." An Oscar nominee for best supporting actor in both *Crimes and Misdemeanors,* and *Tucker: The Man and His Dreams.* Appeared in *By Dawn's Early Light* and *Mistress.* Year/**Age:** 1995/**64** 1996/**65** 1997/**66**

- **JOHN TAYLOR** Bass guitarist. (England) Bass player for DURAN DURAN. Biggest hit: "The Reflex." Also recorded "A View To a Kill" and appeared in the James Bond film of the same name. Year/**Age:** 1995/**35** 1996/**36** 1997/**37**

- **OLYMPIA DUKAKIS** Actress. (Lowell, MA) Won Oscar for best supporting actress in *Moonstruck.* Cousin of 1988 presidential hopeful Michael Dukakis. She also appeared in *Working Girl, Jeffery, Look Who's Talking II,* and *The Cemetery Club.* Year/**Age:** 1995/**64** 1996/**65** 1997/**66**

- **ERROL FLYNN** Actor. (1909-1959 – Tasmania) Led an adventurous life on and off the screen. Films include: *Charge of the Light Brigade, The Adventures of Robin Hood,* and *Captain Blood.* Autobiography: *My Wicked, Wicked Ways.* (Died 10-14-59.)

FACTS FROM THE PAST

1782 The **GREAT SEAL OF THE U.S.** was adopted by Congress. **WILLIAM BARTON** designed the seal, which depicted an eagle clutching an olive branch in one talon and 13 arrows in the other, and in its beak, a ribbon bearing the motto "E PLURIBUS UNUM," meaning "one out of many." Benjamin Franklin thought the turkey would be a more appropriate symbol and wrote to his daughter from France: "The turkey, in comparison, is a much more respectable bird."

1837 **QUEEN VICTORIA** ascended the British throne after the death of her uncle, King William IV. At age 18, Victoria began a reign that lasted more than 63 years, ending with her death in 1901.

1893 The court in New Bedford, MA, acquitted **LIZZIE BORDEN** of killing her parents with an ax.

1901 Starting on this day, to August 9, 1906, **JACK TAYLOR** pitched 188 consecutive complete games, playing for the Chicago Cubs and St. Louis Cards. He pitched a total of 1,727 innings without relief.

1948 The TV variety show, "**TOAST OF THE TOWN,**" hosted by Ed Sullivan, premiered. Eventually, it was changed to the "Ed Sullivan Show." It was an important showcase for such rock stars as **ELVIS PRESLEY**, the **BEATLES**, and the **ROLLING STONES**. His first guests were Dean Martin and Jerry Lewis. The total budget was $375.

1967 Former heavyweight champion **MUHAMMAD ALI** was fined $10,000 and sentenced to 5 years in jail in a Houston court for draft evasion. It was later overturned.

1980 "It's Still Rock & Roll To Me" became **BILLY JOEL**'s first #1 hit.

1993 The **CHICAGO BULLS** won their **3RD STRAIGHT NBA CHAMPIONSHIP**, the first team to "3-peat" since the 1966 Boston Celtics. The sixth game that wrapped up the title was won on a three-point basket by John Paxson with four seconds remaining on the clock.

1994 South African, **ARNIE ELS** sank a 3-foot par putt on the 20th hole, defeating Loren Roberts to win the 94th U.S. Open.

Where do butterflies hide out in high winds?

JUNE 21

BIRTHDAYS

- **MEREDITH BAXTER** Actress. (Los Angeles, CA) Played the mother on "Family Ties" TV sitcom. Year/**Age:** 1995/**48** 1996/**49** 1997/**50**

- **MICHAEL GROSS** Actor. (Chicago, IL) Played the father on "Family Ties," President Reagan's favorite show. Year/**Age:** 1995/**48** 1996/**49** 1997/**50**

- **MAUREEN STAPLETON** Actress. (Troy, NY) Appeared in *A View from the Bridge* and *Bye, Bye Birdie.* Also, *Cocoon: The Return.* Year/**Age:** 1995/**70** 1996/**71** 1997/**72**

- **MARIETTE HARTLEY** Actress. (NYC) Has appeared in many TV films. Former co-host on the CBS-TV "Morning Program." "The Betty Broderick Story." Year/**Age:** 1995/**55** 1996/**56** 1997/**57**

- **ROBERT PASTORELLI** Actor. He plays Eldin Bernecky on TVs "Murphy Brown." Year/**Age:** 1995/**41** 1996/**42** 1997/**43**

- **JANE RUSSELL** Actress. (Born Ernestine Jane Geraldine Russell in Bemidji, MN) In the film *Paleface* with Bob Hope in 1948. She also appears in Playtex commercials. Year/**Age:** 1995/**74** 1996/**75** 1997/**76**

- **BERNIE KOPELL** Actor. (NYC) Appeared on "Love American Style" and played Adam Bricker, the ship's doctor on "Love Boat." Year/**Age:** 1995/**62** 1996/**63** 1997/**64**

- **JULIETTE LEWIS** Actress. Starred in *Cape Fear* and *Husbands and Wives.* She received an Oscar nomination for *Cape Fear.* She was also in *Natural Born Killers, Kalifornia* and *Romeo is Bleeding.* Year/**Age:** 1995/**22** 1996/**23** 1997/**24**

- **RON ELY** (e-lee) Actor. The first Tarzan on TV in 1966. Later host of the "Miss America" pageant. Year/**Age:** 1995/**57** 1996/**58** 1997/**59**

- **DERRICK COLEMAN** Basketball. Year/**Age:** 1995/**28** 1996/**29** 1997/**30**

- **WADE PHILLIPS** Denver Broncos head coach. (Orange, TX) Year/**Age:** 1995/**48** 1996/**49** 1997/**50**

- **DWAYNE THOMAS** Football star. Year/**Age:** 1995/**48** 1996/**49** 1997/**50**

- **JOEY KRAMER** Drummer. (Sunapee, NH) With AEROSMITH. Biggest hit: "Dream On" in 1976. Year/**Age:** 1995/**39** 1996/**40** 1997/**41**

- **O.C. SMITH** Singer. (Mansfield, LA) Biggest hit: "Little Green Apples" in 1972. At one time, he was a vocalist for the Count Basie Orchestra. Year/**Age:** 1995/**62** 1996/**63** 1997/**64**

- **RAY DAVIES** Singer/guitarist. (England) Vocalist for the KINKS. Biggest hit: "Tired of Waiting for You" in 1965. He composed most of their hits and was leader of the group. Year/**Age:** 1995/**51** 1996/**52** 1997/**53**

- **MERLE HARMON** Sportscaster. He also owns some sporting goods stores around the country called "Fan Fair." Year/**Age:** 1995/**68** 1996/**69** 1997/**70**

- **JOEY MOLLAND** Entertainer. With the group BADFINGER; originally the IVEYS. Hit: "Come and Get it," from the film *The Magic Christian* starring Ringo Starr. Year/**Age:** 1995/**47** 1996/**48** 1997/**49**

FACTS FROM THE PAST

1611 While searching for the fabled Northwest Passage, **EXPLORER HENRY HUDSON**'s crew mutinied and set him and his son adrift on a small boat. They were never seen again.

1879 **FRANK WOOLWORTH** opened the **FIRST 5 & 10 CENT** store in Lancaster, PA. He sold items for no more than a dime and went broke. He opened another store in a better location and went on to become one of America's richest men.

1932 **HEAVYWEIGHT MAX SCHMELING** lost a title fight by decision to Jack Sharkey, prompting Schmeling's manager, Joe Jacobs, to exclaim, "We was robbed!"

1940 **RICHARD NIXON** married Thelma "Pat" Nixon.

1948 **DR. PETER GOLDMARK** of CBS demonstrated his **LONG-PLAYING RECORD,** which revolutionized the recording industry. Before the LPs a record made 78 revolutions per minute. One of the first albums was the original cast of *South Pacific.*

1955 **JOHNNY CASH** released his first single, "Hey, Porter." It sold about 100,000 copies.

1958 **BOBBY DARIN** recorded his first hit, "Splish Splash" which took him 10 minutes to write.

1964 Civil Rights workers Michael H. Schwerner, Andrew Goodman, and James E. Chaney disappeared in Philadelphia, Mississippi. Their **BODIES WERE FOUND BURIED IN AN EARTH DAM** six weeks later. Seven men, including a chief deputy sheriff and a KKK leader, were convicted in 1967 of conspiracy in the killings. Inspired the film *Mississippi Burning.*

1966 The **ROLLING STONES** sued 14 New York Hotels that had banned them, saying it hurt their career.

1970 **PETE TOWNSHEND**'s use of the British **SLANG TERM "BOMB"** to describe the success of the WHO's rock opera, *Tommy,* caused him to be detained at the Memphis Airport. The FBI thought it was a bomb threat.

1973 **BREAD** performed for the last time in Salt Lake City, Utah. Their biggest hit: "Make It With You" in 1970.

1977 **ELVIS PRESLEY** made his last TV appearance. He died less than two months later.

1982 A jury in Washington, DC, found **JOHN HINCKLEY, JR.,** innocent by reason of insanity in the shootings of President Ronald Reagan and three others more than a year earlier.

1994 **GEORGE MICHAEL** lost his lawsuit against Sony. He claimed that his 15-year contract was "professional slavery" since Sony could refuse to release albums they thought to be un-commercial.

JUNE 22

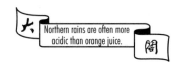

Northern rains are often more acidic than orange juice.

BIRTHDAYS

- **KLAUS MARIA BRANDAUER** Actor. (Austria) *Out of Africa.* Year/Age: 1995/**51** 1996/**52** 1997/**53**

- **TRACY POLLAN** Actress. "Family Ties." Her romance on the TV series led to her marriage to Michael J. Fox. Year/Age: 1995/**35** 1996/**36** 1997/**37**

- **MERYL STREEP** Actress. (Born Mary Louise Streep in Summit, NJ) She won an Oscar for *Sophie's Choice* and *Kramer vs. Kramer* and was nominated for many more. Starred in *House of Spirits, Bridges of Madison County, River Wild, Postcards From The Edge, Death Becomes Her* with Bruce Willis and Goldie Hawn, and *River Wild.* After winning the award for *Kramer vs. Kramer,* she realized that in all the excitement she had left her Oscar in the ladies room stall. Year/Age: 1995/**46** 1996/**47** 1997/**48**

- **BILLY WILDER** Movie director. (Austria) Won Oscars for *The Lost Weekend* and *The Apartment.* When he directed *Sunset Boulevard,* he told the cameraman, "Keep it out of focus, I want to win the foreign film award." Year/Age: 1995/**89** 1996/**90** 1997/**91**

- **RALPH WAITE** Actor. (White Plains, NY) Played the father on "The Waltons" TV series and played Slater in "Roots" in 1977. He also had a part in *Cliffhanger* and *The Bodyguard.* Year/Age: 1995/**67** 1996/**68** 1997/**69**

- **KRIS KRISTOFFERSON** Singer/actor. (Born Kristoffer Kristofferson in Brownsville, TX) Wrote "Help Me Make it Through the Night," "Me and Bobby McGee," and "For the Good Times." His biggest hit: "Why Me" in 1973. Co-starred with Barbra Streisand in *A Star is Born.* He was in a TV movie "Christmas In Connecticut." Married 3 times and has 6 children. He was named "father of the year" in 1988. Year/Age: 1995/**59** 1996/**60** 1997/**61**

- **BILL BLASS** Fashion designer. (Fort Wayne, IN) Famous for women's and men's clothes, furs, luggage, grooming products ,and chocolates. Year/Age: 1995/**73** 1996/**74** 1997/**75**

- **ALLEN OSMOND** Entertainer. (Ogden, UT) The OSMONDS biggest hit: "One Bad Apple" in 1970. Year/Age: 1995/**46** 1996/**47** 1997/**48**

- **CLYDE "THE GLIDE" DREXLER** Basketball player. (Houston, TX) Portland Trailblazers. Year/Age: 1995/**33** 1996/**34** 1997/**35**

- **PAULA IRVINE** Actress. Plays Lilly Blake on soap opera "Santa Barbara." Year/Age: 1995/**27** 1996/**28** 1997/**29**

- **LINDSAY WAGNER** Actress. (Los Angeles, CA) Appeared as the "Bionic Woman" on TV. "Fire in the Dark" and "Nurses on the Line." Year/Age: 1995/**46** 1996/**47** 1997/**48**

- **ED BRADLEY** Newsman. (Philadelphia, PA) CBS correspondent on "60 Minutes." He wears an earring, which is novel for someone his age. Host of "Street Stories." Year/Age: 1995/**54** 1996/**55** 1997/**56**

- **DIANE FEINSTEIN** Senator. (San Francisco, CA) D/CA. Ex-mayor of San Francisco. She and Barbara Boxer set a record for the first time a state has had two female senators. Year/Age: 1995/**62** 1996/**63** 1997/**64**

- **ROY DRUSKY** C&W singer. (Atlanta, GA) Hit: "Three Hearts in a Tangle" in 1961. Year/Age: 1995/**65** 1996/**66** 1997/**67**

- **TODD RUNDGREN** Singer/musician. (Upper Darby, PA) Biggest hit: "Hello It's Me" in 1973. The original version of that song was done by NAZZ in 1969 when Todd was the leader of that group. Year/Age: 1995/**46** 1996/**47** 1997/**48**

- **CHRIS LEMMON** Actor. (Los Angeles, CA) A roving reporter on TV's "Fantasy," an early-'80s game show hosted by Peter Marshall and Leslie Uggams. They surprised people by fullfilling their dreams. In a 1989 film *Dad,* he played his father, Jack Lemmon, as a younger man in a dream sequence. Year/Age: 1995/**41** 1996/**42** 1997/**43**

- **HOWARD KAYLON** Singer. Biggest hit with the TURTLES: "Happy Together" in 1967. He and Mark Volman are lead singers for the group. Year/Age: 1995/**48** 1996/**49** 1997/**50**

- **FREDDIE PRINZE** Actor. (1954-1977 – Born Frederick Carl Preutzel in NYC) With Jack Albertson in "Chico and the Man." (He committed suicide on 1-28-77 at age 22.)

- **JOHN DILLINGER** Gangster. (1903-1934 – Indianapolis, IN) Hated his dad who was a grocer. He robbed a grocer outside a church and was sent to prison for the first time. His girlfriend said he was just an ordinary guy who liked to hold up a few banks. (Died 7-22-34.)

- **CARL HUBBELL** Lefty pitcher. (1903-1988 – Carthage, MO) Led by "The Meal Ticket" (his nickname), the NY Giants won pennants in 1936 and 1937. Over 2 seasons he won 24 straight games and his lifetime record was 253-154.

FACTS FROM THE PAST

1938 JOE LOUIS began his reign as world heavyweight boxing champion by knocking out Jim Braddock in Chicago. A year later to the day, he knocked out Max Schmeling in the 1st round in NYC. He retained his title until he retired in 1949.

1968 The **JEFF BECK GROUP MADE ITS DEBUT** at the Fillmore East. Lead singer Rod Stewart was so shy, he hid behind speakers for the first few songs.

1969 JUDY GARLAND died after taking an overdose of drugs.

1970 PRESIDENT NIXON signed a bill lowering the voting age to 18.

1977 JOHN MITCHELL became the first former attorney general to go to prison. He was in a minimum security facility at Maxwell AFB near Montgomery, AL. He began serving his sentence for his role in the **WATERGATE** coverup and was released 19 months later.

1981 MARK DAVID CHAPMAN pleaded guilty to killing John Lennon outside the entertainer's NYC apartment building.

1990 BILLY JOEL became the first rock 'n' roll artist to perform at Yankee Stadium.

1994 MVP **HAKEEM OLAJUWON** led the Houston Rockets to the 1994 NBA championship by defeating the New York Knicks 90-84.

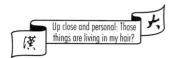

Up close and personal: Those things are living in my hair?

JUNE 23

BIRTHDAYS

• **JUNE CARTER CASH** Entertainer. (Maces Spring, VA) Biggest record with husband Johnny Cash, "If I Were a Carpenter" in 1970. She wrote the Cash hit, "Ring of Fire." Year/**Age**: 1995/**66** 1996/**67** 1997/**68**

• **TED SHAKELFORD** Actor. (Oklahoma City, OK) He played Gary Ewing on "Knots Landing." Year/**Age**: 1995/**49** 1996/**50** 1997/**51**

• **IRENE WORTH** Actress. (Nebraska) Did a lot of Tennessee Williams' plays. Tony Award winner for *Sweet Bird of Youth*. Film *Lost In Yonkers*. Year/**Age**: 1995/**79** 1996/**80** 1997/**81**

• **ROSETTA HIGHTOWER** Singer. (Philadelphia, PA) She was with the group, the ORLONS. Their biggest record: "The Wah Watusi" in 1962. Year/**Age**: 1995/**51** 1996/**52** 1997/**53**

• **JAMES LEVINE** Conductor. (Cincinnati, OH) Director of the Metropolitan Opera. Year/**Age**: 1995/**52** 1996/**53** 1997/**54**

• **CLARENCE THOMAS** Supreme Court Judge. (Pin Point, GA) He was the second African-American in history to be named to the high court. A lot of controversy preceded his confirmation. Bush nominee, sworn in October 23, 1991. He's a conservative. Year/**Age**: 1995/**47** 1996/**48** 1997/**49**

• **WILMA RUDOLPH** Runner. (Bethlehem, TN) Winner of 3 Olympic gold medals for track at the 1960 Rome games. An Olympic Hall of Fame member. Year/**Age**: 1995/**55** 1996/**56** 1997/**57**

• **DONN EISELE** Astronaut. (1930-1987 – Columbus, OH)

• **DIANA TRASK** C&W singer. Year/**Age**: 1995/**55** 1996/**56** 1997/**57**

• **ROBERT REICH** Labor Secretary. Year/**Age**: 1995/**49** 1996/**50** 1997/**51**

• **BRYAN BROWN** Actor. Year/**Age**: 1995/**47** 1996/48 1997/**49**

• **JEAN MARIE ANOUILH** Dramatist. (1910-1987 – France) His plays include *Becket* and *Antigone*. (Died 10-3-87.)

• **DR. ALFRED KINSEY** (1894-1956 – Hoboken, NJ) Famous for his sex books. When he was young he was an Eagle Scout. He was very quiet and never dated. He once wrote a scientific paper called: "What do Birds do When it Rains?" He married at age 27 and in 1948 wrote *The Sexual Behavior in the Human Male.*

• **BOB FOSSE** Choreographer/director. (1927-1987 – Chicago, IL) Won Tony Awards for *Pippin, Pajama Game, Dancin', Damn Yankees, Sweet Charity, Redhead,* and won an Academy Award for *Cabaret* in 1972. The 1979 movie he wrote and directed, *All That Jazz,* is based on his life. (Died 9-23-87.)

• **JOSEPHINE** Napoleon's wife. (1763-1814 – Martinique) They were married twice to each other. She was not very pretty and had bad teeth. She spent a lot of Napoleon's money and they eventually divorced when she failed to give Napoleon an heir. (Died 5-29-1814.)

• **IRVIN S. COBB** American writer/humorist. (1876-1944) (Died 3-10-44.)

FACTS FROM THE PAST

1683   William Penn signed a **FRIENDSHIP TREATY** with the Lenni Lenape Indians near what is now Philadelphia.

1931   Aviators **WILEY POST** and **HAROLD CATTY** took off from New York for a **FLIGHT AROUND THE WORLD.**

1846   The **SAXOPHONE WAS PATENTED** by Antoine Joseph Sax.

1868   **CHRISTOPHER LATHAM SHOLES,** Wisconsin journalist and Senator, received a **PATENT** for his **TYPEWRITER**. It only had capitol letters and took up as much room as a good-sized table. The typists didn't know if they were making errors because the paper could not be seen as it was being typed; it was inside the machine. He was born in Milwaukee, WI.

1917   In an **ALMOST PERFECT BASEBALL GAME,** two Boston Red Sox pitchers combined forces to pitch a no-hitter. The starting pitcher **BABE RUTH,** was a great hurler before he switched to full-time outfielder. He walked the first batter and then disputed the umpire's call of "ball four" to the point he was ejected from the game. The replacement pitcher, **ERNIE SHORE,** then took over. The base runner was thrown out during an attempted steal, and not a single Washington player reached first base for the rest of the game.

1947   The Senate joined the House of Representatives in overriding President Harry S. Truman's veto of the **TAFT-HARTLEY ACT**. The new law banned the closed shop, provided for a cooling-off period before strikes, required that union finances be made public, and prohibited unions from making donations to political campaigns.

1967   **PRESIDENT JOHNSON** and **RUSSIAN PREMIER KOSYGIN,** meeting at Glassboro State College in New Jersey, agreed not to let anything happen that would lead their two countries into nuclear war.

1972   President **RICHARD NIXON** and White House chief of staff **H. R. HALDEMAN** agreed on a plan to use the CIA to obstruct the FBI's Watergate investigation. A White House recording of this conversation led to Nixon's resignation in August 1974.

1987   **TIFFANY** began her famous "Shopping Mall Tour" at the Bergen mall in Paramus, NJ.

1987   **ALICE COOPER** broke six ribs after falling off the stage during a concert in Vancouver, resulting in several canceled concerts.

1989   The **NEW KIDS ON THE BLOCK** were almost tossed out of an Anaheim hotel when they were caught bombing guests with Kool-Aid-filled balloons.

1990   **GARY BUSEY**, who played lead in *The Buddy Holly Story*, paid **$242,000** for one of **HOLLY'S GUITARS** at a New York auction.

1992   **OPRAH WINFREY** won her second straight Daytime Emmy. "All My Children's" Susan Lucci lost for the 13th straight year, but received a standing ovation.

JUNE 24

Ultimate creativity: supermarket tabloids.

BIRTHDAYS

- **COLIN BLUNSTONE** Singer. (England) With ZOMBIES. Biggest hit: "She's Not There" in 1964. Year/**Age**: 1995/**50** 1996/**51** 1997/**52**

- **ARTHUR BROWN** Singer. (England) Biggest hit: "Fire" in 1968. Year/**Age**: 1995/**51** 1996/**52** 1997/**53**

- **MICHELE LEE** Actress. (Born Michele Dusick in Los Angeles, CA) Karen MacKenzie in TV's "Knots Landing." Also in films *The Love Bug* and *How to Succeed in Business.* Year/**Age**: 1995/**53** 1996/**54** 1997/**55**

- **GLENN MEDEIROS** Singer. (Hawaii) Hit with Bobby Brown: "She Ain't Worth It" in 1990. Year/**Age**: 1995/**25** 1996/**26** 1997/**27**

- **AL MOLINARO** Actor. (Kenosha, WI) Was Al DelVecchio, proprietor of Arnold's, on "Happy Days." He married Chachi's mother on "Joanie Loves Chachi." Year/**Age**: 1995/**76** 1996/**77** 1997/**78**

- **JEFF BECK** Guitarist. (England) Replaced Eric Clapton as lead guitar player with the YARDBIRDS and later formed the JEFF BECK GROUP in 1967, which included Rod Stewart and Ron Wood. Year/**Age**: 1995/**51** 1996/**52** 1997/**53**

- **PHIL HARRIS** Musician/comedian. (Linton, IN) He says his real first name is "Wonga," meaning "Swift Messenger" in Cherokee. His biggest hit was "The Thing" in 1950. He has been married to Alice Faye since 1941. He gained fame on the "Jack Benny Show" as the jazz-talking, hard-drinking musician with little education and a huge ego. Year/**Age**: 1995/**89** 1996/**90** 1997/**91**

- **JACK CARTER** Comedian. (NYC) He hosted the "Cavalcade of Stars" on the short-lived DuMont Network in 1949-50. Year/**Age**: 1995/**72** 1996/**73** 1997/**74**

- **CURT SMITH** Vocalist/bass player. (England) In the group TEARS FOR FEARS. Their biggest: "Shout." Year/**Age**: 1995/**34** 1996/**35** 1997/**36**

- **RON KRAMER** Football. Green Bay Packer great. Year/**Age**: 1995/**60** 1996/**61** 1997/**62**

- **MICK FLEETWOOD** Drummer. (England) From the group FLEETWOOD MAC, one of the most popular rock groups of the '70s. Their biggest hit: "Dreams" in 1977. Year/**Age**: 1995/**53** 1996/**54** 1997/**55**

- **BILLY CASPER** Pro golfer. (San Diego, CA) He won the U.S. Open Championships in 1959 and 1966 and was PGA Player of the Year in 1966, 1968, and 1970. Year/**Age**: 1995/**64** 1996/**65** 1997/**66**

- **NANCY ALLEN** Actress. (NYC) *Dressed to Kill, I Wanna Hold Your Hand*, and *Robo Cop III.* Year/**Age**: 1995/**45** 1996/**46** 1997/**47**

- **GEORGE STANFORD BROWN** Actor/director. Officer Terry Webster on "The Rookies" TV series. Ex-husband of Tyne Daly. Year/**Age**: 1995/**52** 1996/**53** 1997/**54**

- **NORMAN COUSINS** Magazine editor/publisher. (1912-1990 – Union Hill, NJ) He wrote *Anatomy of an Illness* in which he said, "Humor is the best therapy." (Died 11-30-90.)

- **CHRIS WOOD** Flute and sax player. (1944-1983) TRAFFIC. Biggest hit: "Gimme Some Lovin" in 1971.

- **JACK DEMPSEY** Former heavyweight boxing champ. (1895-1983 – Born William Harrison Dempsey in Manassa, CO) Known as the "Manassa Mauler," he was world heavyweight boxing champion from 1919-1926. He won the title in 1919 by beating Jess Willard. After his boxing career, he became a successful NY restauranteur. (Died 5-31-83.)

FACTS FROM THE PAST

1497 The first recorded discovery of the North American Continent took place as explorer **JOHN CABOT**, on a voyage for England, sighted land, probably in present-day Canada.

1509 **HENRY VIII** was crowned king of England.

1647 Margaret Brent, a niece of Lord Baltimore, **SHOCKED THE MARYLAND ASSEMBLY** by demanding a place and vote in that governing body. She was ejected from the room.

1892 **ROBERT FORD** was killed in his own bar in Creede, CO. He had been a **MEMBER OF THE JESSE JAMES GANG** and bought the tavern with the $10,000 reward that he collected for killing Jesse earlier that year.

1947 A search-and-rescue pilot, **KENNETH ARNOLD** of Boise, Idaho, reported 9 UFOs over Mount Rainier, WA. He estimated their speed at 1,700 mph and described their flight pattern as similar to a saucer skipping across water, inspiring a newspaper man to name them **FLYING SAUCERS**.

1948 At the Republican National Convention in Philadelphia, PA, Governor **THOMAS E. DEWEY (NY)** was nominated for president.

1967 The classics "White Rabbit": by **JEFFERSON AIRPLANE**, and "Whiter Shade of Pale" by **POCO HARUM** were released.

1973 Singer and keyboardist Al Kooper reunited the original **BLUES PROJECT** for a one-shot concert in New York's Central Park.

1978 The **OAK RIDGE BOYS** hit #1 on the Country Charts for the first time with "I'll Be True To You."

1988 **POPE JOHN PAUL II CONDEMNED NAZISM** while visiting the Mauthausen death camp in Austria.

1990 Donnie Wahlberg of **NEW KIDS ON THE BLOCK** accidentally fell nine feet through a stage trapdoor during their Magic Summer Concert Tour in Saratoga, NY. He suffered minor cuts and bruises. Treatment during the two-night hospital stay included nine stitches.

1994 **PRESIDENT CLINTON** complained that Rush Limbaugh and TV evangelist Jerry Falwell were feeding Americans unfair and negative reports about him.

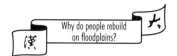

Why do people rebuild on floodplains?

JUNE 25

BIRTHDAYS

• **PHYLLIS GEORGE** Former Miss America. (Denton, TX) TV Co-anchor "NFL Today" and "CBS Morning News" Interview show on TNN. Married to former Governor John Brown of Kentucky. Year/**Age**: 1995/**46** 1996/**47** 1997/**48**

• **JIMMIE WALKER** Entertainer. (NYC) Jive-talking James "J.J." Evans, Jr. whose yell: "DY-NO-MITE" was remembered by all who watched the "Good Times" TV show, which was a spin-off of "All in the Family," "Maude," and "Bustin' Loose." Year/**Age**: 1995/**46** 1996/**47** 1997/**48**

• **EDDIE FLOYD** Singer. (Montgomery, AL.) His biggest songs: "Bring it Home to Me" and "Knock on Wood." He was a member of the FALCONS group in the 1950s. Their biggest hit: "You're So Fine" in 1959. Year/**Age**: 1995/**60** 1996/**61** 1997/**62**

• **GEORGE MICHAEL** Singer. (Born George Michael Panos in England) Part of the duo WHAM with Andrew Ridgely. Biggest hits: "Wake Me Up Before You Go-Go" in 1984 and "Careless Whisper" in 1985. They broke up in 1986. In 1987 his hit, "I Want Your Sex," was banned by one out of three U.S. radio stations. Michael's biggest hit: "Faith" in 1987. Year/**Age**: 1995/**32** 1996/**33** 1997/**34**

• **SIDNEY LUMET** [loo-meht'] Film director. (Philadelphia, PA) Directed *The Pawnbroker*, *Serpico*, *Dog Day Afternoon*, *Network*, *Family Business*, and over 200 "Playhouse 90" TV shows. Year/**Age**: 1995/**71** 1996/**72** 1997/**73**

• **DIKEMBE MUTUMBO** Basketball. Denver Nuggets. Year/**Age**: 1995/**29** 1996/**30** 1997/**31**

• **WILLIS REED** Basketball player. (Hico, LA) Center and captain of the New York Knicks, he helped to make them the best defensive team in the league during the 70s. Year/**Age**: 1995/**53** 1996/**54** 1997/**55**

• **JUNE LOCKHART** Actress. (NYC) She was Timmy's mother, Ruth Martin, on the "Lassie" TV series, Maureen Robinson in "Lost In Space," and Dr. Janet Craig on "Petticoat Junction." Year/**Age**: 1995/**70** 1996/**71** 1997/**72**

• **PETER LIND HAYES** Actor. (San Francisco, CA) He and his wife, Mary Healy, hosted two variety shows and co-starred in the sitcom "Peter Loves Mary." Year/**Age**: 1995/**80** 1996/**81** 1997/**82**

• **IAN McDONALD** Keyboardist/guitarist. (London, England) Hits with FOREIGNER include: "I Want To Know What Love Is," "Double Vision," and "Waiting For a Girl Like You." Year/**Age**: 1995/**49** 1996/**50** 1997/**51**

• **CARLY SIMON** Singer. (New York City, NY) She started a folk duo, The SIMON SISTERS, with her elder sister Lucy, then went on her own to record a number of hits including her biggest, "You're So Vain," in 1973. Her dad is co-founder of Simon and Schuster Publishing Co. Married singer/songwriter James Taylor in 1972; separated in 1982. She won an Academy Award for "Let The River Run" from *Working Girl*. She also writes children's books. Year/**Age**: 1995/**50** 1996/**51** 1997/**52**

• **GEORGE ORWELL** Author. (1903-1950 – Born Eric Arthur Blair in India) Satirist, author of *Animal Farm* and the controversial *1984*. (Died 1-21-50.)

FACTS FROM THE PAST

1630 Massachusetts Governor John Winthrop **INTRODUCED THE TABLE FORK TO AMERICA.**

1815 **NAPOLEON BONAPARTE** delivered a farewell address before being exiled to the Island of St. Helena.

1868 **PRESIDENT ANDREW JOHNSON**, instituted the first 8-hour work day for government workers.

1876 **GENERAL GEORGE CUSTER** and 265 men of the Seventh Cavalry were killed at the **BATTLE OF THE LITTLE BIG HORN** in Montana. The Sioux and Cheyenne Indians, led by Chief Crazy Horse and Chief Sitting Bull, wiped them out in less than 2 hours.

1906 A **LOVE TRIANGLE** came to a violent end on top of Madison Square Garden in NYC when architect Stanford White, the building's designer was shot to death by Harry Thaw, jealous husband of Evelyn Newbit.

1938 **THE WAGE AND HOURS ACT** was signed into law by President Franklin Roosevelt. It established a minimum wage of 25 cents an hour and a maximum 44-hour work week.

1951 The **FIRST COMMERCIAL COLOR TELECAST** took place as CBS transmitted a one-hour special from New York to four other cities. It starred Arthur Godfrey, Ed Sullivan, Faye Emerson, Garry Moore and Robert Alda.

1969 **MICK TAYLOR** made his first appearance with the **ROLLING STONES** at the coliseum in Rome. Taylor replaced Brian Jones on guitar. Jones was found dead in his swimming pool a week later.

1977 **LIGHTNING STRUCK ROY SULLIVAN.** It was the eighth time in his life he had been struck by lightning. He was on a fishing trip standing near his truck when a bolt hit him, knocking his shoes off. It burned his hat and the hair off his arms and legs. Most of the strikes came while he was a park ranger in the Blue Ridge mountains of Virginia. One of his scorched Smokey Bear hats is in a park museum with a big hole in it.

1982 Secretary of State **ALEXANDER HAIG** resigned over disagreement of foreign policy. President Reagan appointed George Schultz.

1984 In Cuba, **JESSE JACKSON** secured the release of 48 U.S. and Cuban prisoners after talking with President Fidel Castro.

1993 Vice President **AL GORE BROKE THE TIE VOTE**, giving President Clinton a victory for his massive budget-cutting package with tax increases on the wealthy and cuts in Medicare.

1994 Hall of Fame baseball announcer for the Chicago Cubs, **HARRY CARAY** was interviewed from a hospital rooom. It was his first air stint since he fell face-first on the steps at Joe Robbie Staduim in Miami June 23rd.

JUNE 26

If you're telekinetic, please raise my hand.

BIRTHDAYS

- **ELEANOR PARKER** Actress. (Cedarville, OH) She appeared in *Of Human Bondage* and as the countess in *Sound of Music*. She was nominated for an Oscar for best actress in *Caged*. Year/**Age**: 1995/**73** 1996/**74** 1997/**75**

- **MICK JONES** Guitarist. (England) Member of the New Wave rock group THE CLASH. Biggest hit: "Rock the Casbah" in 1982. They disbanded in 1986. Year/**Age**: 1995/**40** 1996/**41** 1997/**42**

- **TERRI NUNN** Vocalist. (Los Angeles, CA) Member of trio BERLIN. Biggest hit: "Take My Breath Away" in 1986, theme from *Top Gun* which won "Best Song of the Year." Year/**Age**: 1995/**34** 1996/**35** 1997/**36**

- **BILLY DAVIS, JR.** Singer. (Los Angeles, CA) Member of the 5TH DIMENSION. Biggest hit: "Aquarius/Let the Sunshine In" in 1969. He is married to another member of the group, Marilyn McCoo. They had a hit in 1976: "You Don't Have to Be a Star." Year/**Age**: 1995/**55** 1996/**56** 1997/**57**

- **PAMELA BELLWOOD** Actress. (NYC) Played Claudia Blaisdel on "Dynasty." Year/**Age**: 1995/**52** 1996/**53** 1997/**54**

- **PATTY SMYTH** Singer. (NYC) Lead singer with rock group SCANDAL. Hit: "The Warrior" in 1984. She had a hit with Don Henley in 1992 "Sometimes Love Just Ain't Enough." Year/**Age**: 1995/**38** 1996/**39** 1997/**40**

- **GEORGIE FAME** Singer. (Born Clive Powell in England) Biggest hit: "The Ballad of Bonnie and Clyde" in 1968. Year/**Age**: 1995/**52** 1996/**53** 1997/**54**

- **CHRIS O'DONNELL** Actor. In films *Three Musketeers*, *Dead Poets Society* and *Scent of a Woman*. Year/**Age**: 1995/**25** 1996/**26** 1997/**27**

- **DAVE GRUSIN** Movie score composer/keyboardist. (Littleton, CO) He received Academy Award nominations for scoring *On Golden Pond*, *Heaven Can Wait*, and *Tootsie*. Year/**Age**: 1995/**61** 1996/**62** 1997/**63**

- **LARRY TAYLOR** Bass player. CANNED HEAT. Their biggest hit was "Goin' Up the Country" in 1986. Year/**Age**: 1995/**53** 1996/**54** 1997/**55**

- **MILDRED "BABE" DIDRIKSON ZAHARIAS** Athlete. (1914-1956 – Port Arthur, TX) Olympic Gold medalist whose tombstone epitaph reads, "World's Greatest Woman Athlete." She excelled in basketball, track and field, golf, and several other sports. (Died 9-27-56.)

- **RICHARD MALTBY** Bandleader. (1914-1991 – Chicago, IL) Trumpet player. Had a hit in 1956: "Theme from *Man With the Golden Arm*" starring Frank Sinatra.

- **ABNER DOUBLEDAY** Baseball. (1819-1893 – Ballston Spa, NY) It is believed by some that he invented the game of baseball in 1839 in Cooperstown, NY. (Died 1-26-1893.)

- **PETER LORRE** Actor. (1904-1964 – Born Laszlo Loewenstein in Hungary) Short, horror film actor whose films included *The Maltese Falcon* with Humphrey Bogart. He played the first James Bond film villain, Le Chiffre. (Died 3-24-64.)

FACTS FROM THE PAST

1284 In **GRIMM'S FAIRY TALE**, today was the day that the **PIED PIPER** led the children out of Hamlin, Germany, never to be seen again. He did this after not being paid for piping the rats out of Hamlin.

1830 **ENGLAND'S FATTEST KING**, King George IV, died at age 67. For breakfast he would consume 2 pigeons, 3 beef steaks, a bottle of wine, a glass of champagne and one brandy. He had 500 wallets, a pile of love letters, ladies gloves, and dozens of locks of hair.

1918 The **BICYCLE WAS PATENTED** by **WILLIAM CLARKSON, JR.**, of New York. They were called "curricles," or "velocipedes."

1959 President Dwight D. Eisenhower joined Britain's Queen Elizabeth II in ceremonies opening the **ST. LAWRENCE SEAWAY.**

1963 **PRESIDENT JOHN F. KENNEDY** visited West Berlin, where he declared, "*Ich bin ein Berliner.*" ("I am a Berliner.") But because of a slight mispronunciation, some people in the crowd laughed, thinking he'd called himself a jelly donut.

1975 **SONNY AND CHER** divorced after 11 years of marriage; a year after their TV variety show ended its three-year run. Cher married Gregg Allman four days later and divorced him after 10 days. Sonny and Cher revived the program for the 1976-1977 season and worked together despite the divorce.

1976 In what was advertised as the World Heavyweight Martial Arts Championship, **MUHAMMAD ALI** and Japanese Wrestler **KANJI ANTONIO INOKI** fought 15 rounds to a draw.

1977 **ELVIS PRESLEY** made his last concert appearance at the Market Square Arena in Indianapolis, IN. His final song was "Can't Help Falling in Love." He died 7 weeks later.

1979 Heavyweight boxing champion **MUHAMMAD ALI** confirmed to reporters that he'd sent a letter to the World Boxing Association resigning his title, saying his third announced retirement was indeed final.

1989 A report showed that **PETE ROSE** bet on the Cincinnati Reds regularly from 1985-87 – sometimes wagering $2,000 a game.

1990 **PRESIDENT BUSH**, who had campaigned for office on a pledge of "**NO NEW TAXES,**" conceded that tax increases would have to be included in any deficit-reduction package worked out with Congressional negotiations.

1993 President **CLINTON ORDERED A U.S. TOMAHAWK MISSILE ATTACK** on Iraqi intelligence headquarters in Baghdad. The strike was in retaliation for a plot to assassinate former President Bush.

1994 **DRAG QUEEN RUPAUL** sang, "Ain't No Stoppin' Us Now" in Central Park and Gregory Hines and Liza Minelli performed as thousands of gays marched up Fifth Avenue in New York carrying signs and shouting slogans.

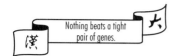

Nothing beats a tight pair of genes.

JUNE 27

BIRTHDAYS

- **CHARLES BRONFMAN** Canadian industrialist. (Canada) With Seagrams and the Montreal Expos. Year/**Age**: 1995/**64** 1996/**65** 1997/**66**

- **JULIA DUFFY** Actress. (St. Paul, MN) Maid Stephanie on TV's "Newhart," "Designing Women," and "The Mommies." Year/**Age**: 1995/**44** 1996/**45** 1997/**46**

- **FRANK MILLS** Pianist. Biggest hit: "Music Box Dancer" in 1978. Year/**Age**: 1995/**53** 1996/**54** 1997/**55**

- **DAVID SHALIKASHVILI** (Warsaw, Poland) He is the first foreign born chairman of the Joint Chiefs of Staff. He and his family fled to Germany from Poland in 1944. Year/**Age**: 1995/**59** 1996/**60** 1997/**61**

- **ISABELLE ADJANI** Actress. (France) She was nominated for an Academy Award for *The Story of Adele H* in 1975. Year/**Age**: 1995/**40** 1996/**41** 1997/**42**

- **BOB "CAPTAIN KANGAROO" KEESHAN**. (Lynbrook, NY) Clarabelle the Clown on the "Howdy Doody Show" from 1947-1952. Created "Captain Kangaroo" in 1955, ran for many years on CBS. Year/**Age**: 1995/**68** 1996/**69** 1997/**70**

- **ANNA MOFFO** Soprano. (Wayne, PA) Star of the Metropolitan Opera from 1959-1969. Year/**Age**: 1995/**61** 1996/**62** 1997/**63**

- **BRUCE BABBITT** Interior Secretary. (Los Angeles, CA) Year/**Age**: 1995/**57** 1996/**58** 1997/**59**

- **I. A. L. DIAMOND** Screenwriter. (1920-1988, Rumania) He's responsible for *Some Like it Hot*, *The Apartment*, and *Irma La Douce*.

- **GARY CROSBY**. Bing's oldest son. In "Adam-12." Year/**Age**: 1995/**62** 1996/**63** 1997/**64**

- **BRUCE JOHNSTON** Musician. With the BEACH BOYS. He wrote "I Write the Songs," a hit for Barry Manilow. He won a Grammy in 1976. Year/**Age**: 1995/**51** 1996/**52** 1997/**53**

- **WILLIE MOSCONI** Pocket-billiards player. (1913-1993, Philadelphia, PA) He was the world titleholder 15 times from 1940-57. At one time he pocketed 5226 consecutive balls in exhibition play. (Died 9-16-93)

- **ROSS PEROT** Billionaire computer tycoon. (Texarkana, TX) His estimated worth is over $2 billion. He had his eyes on the U.S. presidency in 1992. Year/**Age**: 1995/**65** 1996/**66** 1997/**67**

- **HELEN KELLER** (1880-1968 – Tuscumbia, AL) When she was 19 months old, she got a disease that left her totally blind and deaf, but she became one of the world's most respected figures by overcoming her handicaps. She was instrumental in changing the old policy of routinely dumping blind people into insane asylums. She learned to read and write in Braille and became a lecturer and an author. (Died 6-1-68.)

FACTS FROM THE PAST

1776   **THOMAS HICKEY**, one of George Washington's guards, went into the history books for all the wrong reasons. He was convicted of plotting to deliver George Washington to the British and became the first person to be executed by the army in the U.S.

1829   **JAMES SMITHSON** died at age 64. The illegitimate son of Hugh Smithson, Duke of Northumberland, and Elizabeth Hungerford Keats. His will bequeathing his great wealth to a nation he had never visited, and to found "at Washington, DC under the name of the **SMITHSONIAN INSTITUTION**, an establishment for the increase and diffusion of knowledge among men." Against strong opposition, Congress approved establishment of "the nation's attic," Aug. 10, 1846.

1844   In dispute over the **PRACTICE OF POLYGAMY**, an angry mob attacked a jail in Carthage, IL, killing Morman leaders Joseph & Hyrum Smith. Brigham Young then became the head of the church.

1859   Louisville school teacher Mildred J. Hill composed a tune for her students, and called it "Good Morning To All." Her sister Patty wrote the lyrics and later added a verse that began, "Happy birthday to you." The song became—and still is—the **WORLD'S MOST POPULAR SONG**.

1949   **"CAPTAIN VIDEO AND HIS VIDEO RANGERS" PREMIERED** on the Dumont Television Network. Captain Video battled bad guys all over the universe.

1950   **PRESIDENT HARRY S. TRUMAN** ordered the U.S. Air Force and Navy into the Korean conflict, following a call from the UN Security Council for member nations to help South Korea repel the invasion from the north. 54,000 U.S. troops died in the 3-year war.

1969   The American **HOMOSEXUAL-RIGHTS MOVEMENT WAS BORN** as patrons at the Stonewall Inn, a gay bar in New York's Greenwich Village, clashed with police who were attempting to raid the establishment.

1975   **LEE TREVINO, BOBBY NICHOLS**, and **JERRY HEARD** were struck by lightning during the second round of the Western Open in Chicago, IL. Before that disaster, the three had won a total of 34 tournaments, and for several years afterwards, only one of them won a tournament. The lightning appearently affected their nervous systems. Trevino says today that even a flashbulb will shake him up.

1988   21,785 fans at Atlantic City Convention Hall paid up to $1,500 to witness the fourth shortest heavyweight title fight in boxing history. **MIKE TYSON** KO'd **MICHAEL SPINKS** in 1:31 of the first round, with a solid right hand to the chin.

1989   President Bush critisized a Supreme Court decision upholding desecration of the **AMERICAN FLAG** as a form of political protest. He called for a constitutional amendment to protect the flag.

1993   Actress **JULIA ROBERTS** married singer **LYLE LOVETT**.

1993   NY Mets pitcher **ANTHONY YOUNG** broke an 82-year-old record held by Cliff Curis by losing his 24th game in a row.

JUNE 28

BIRTHDAYS

- **MARY STUART MASTERSON** Actress. (New York, NY) *Funny about Love, Bad Girls, Radioland Murders, Benny and Joon,* and *Married To It.* Year/**Age:** 1995/**29** 1996/**30** 1997/**31**

- **PAT MORITA** Actor. (Born Noriyuki Morita in Berkeley, CA) Arnold on TV series "Happy Days" and Mr. Miyagi, teacher of martial arts, in the *Karate Kid* movies. Year/**Age:** 1995/**65** 1996/**66** 1997/**67**

- **JOHN ELWAY** Quarterback. (Pt. Angeles, WA) With the Denver Broncos. In 1993 he signed a four-year contract for $20 million. Also does TV Diet Coke commercials. Year/**Age:** 1995/**35** 1996/**36** 1997/**37**

- **JOHN CUSACK** Actor. (Chicago) *Say Anything, Money for Nothing,* and *The Player.* Year/**Age:** 1995/**29** 1996/**30** 1997/**31**

- **MEL BROOKS** Actor/producer. (Born Melvin Kaminsky in NYC) He started out as a nightclub comedian. Later, he was one of the writers for Sid Caesar's "Show of Shows" for which he made $2,500 per week. Recorded an album with Carl Reiner in the 1960s: "The 2,000-Year-Old Man." He co-wrote "Get Smart" for TV. His best-known films include *Blazing Saddles, Young Frankenstein, Silent Movie, High Anxiety, Life Stinks,* and *Space Balls.* He's married to actress Anne Bancroft. Year/**Age:** 1995/**69** 1996/**70** 1997/**71**

- **DANIELLE BRISEBOIS** Actress. (NYC) Appeared in "All in the Family" at age 10 and at age 6 she was in the original Broadway musical production of *Annie.* Year/**Age:** 1995/**26** 1996/**27** 1997/**28**

- **RON LUCIANO** Former umpire/author. He wrote *The Umpire Strikes Back, Strike Two,* and *The Fall of the Roman Umpire.* Year/**Age:** 1995/**57** 1996/**58** 1997/**59**

- **DAVID KNIGHTS** Musician. Bass player with PROCOL HARUM. Biggest hit: "A Whiter Shade of Pale." Year/**Age:** 1995/**50** 1996/**51** 1997/**52**

- **MARK GRACE** Baseball. (Winston-Salem, NC) Chicago Cubs first baseman. Year/**Age:** 1995/**31** 1996/**32** 1997/**33**

- **DON BAYLOR** Baseball manager. (Austin, TX) Colorado Rockies. American League MVP in 1970 with the California Angels. Holds the record for most times hit by a pitch in a career with 255 and a single season total of 35. Year/**Age:** 1995/**45** 1996/**46** 1997/**47**

- **LAURA D'ANDREA TYSON** Chief economic advisor for President Clinton. Year/**Age:** 1995/**47** 1996/**48** 1997/**49**

- **KATHY BATES** Actress. (Memphis, TN) Won an Oscar for best actress in *Misery.* Also in *Home of Our Own, Fried Green Tomatoes, Fields of the Lord, Prelude to a Kiss,* and *Used People.* Year/**Age:** 1995/**47** 1996/**48** 1997/**49**

- **"PISTOL" PETE MARAVICH** (1948-1988) The former NBA legend died while playing in a half-court game at a church in Pasadena, CA. His last words before collapsing were, "I'm really feeling good." Greatest scorer in NCAA basketball history, averaging 44.2 pts. a game. Played pro in Atlanta, New Orleans, Salt Lake City and Boston. (Died 1-5-88.)

- **GILDA RADNER** Comedian/actress/writer. (1946-1989 – Detroit, MI) Emmy Award-winning "Saturday Night Live" star, married to actor/filmmaker Gene Wilder. They appeared together on screen in the 1986 comedy *Haunted Honeymoon!* Radner was best known for her characters Roseanne Roseannadanna and Miss Emily Litella. Shortly before her death she was preparing to have her second book, *It's Always Something,* published, an account of her struggle with cancer. (Died 5-2-89.)

- **RICHARD RODGERS** Songwriter. (1902-1979 – NYC) He wrote "It Might as Well be Spring" from *State Fair* for which he won an Oscar in 1945. With partners Hammerstein and Hart he scored *Sound of Music, South Pacific, Carousel,* and *Oklahoma.*

- **LESTER FLATT** C&W guitarist. (1914-1979 – Overton County, TN) Half of the bluegrass duo with Earl Scruggs. They had two hits: "Ballad of Jed Clampett" from "The Beverly Hillbillies" TV series and "Foggy Mountain Breakdown," theme from *Bonnie & Clyde.* (Died 5-11-79.)

FACTS FROM THE PAST

1838 Britain's **QUEEN VICTORIA** was crowned in Westminster Abby.

1911 W.A. BURPEE – the seed king – broke his eyeglasses just before his ship set sail for England. He sent them to be repaired. The store hired aviator **TOM SOPWITH** to fly out to Burpee's ship several miles out at sea to deliver them. Sopwith made the delivery by dropping the package on the ship's deck – the **FIRST CHARTER AIRCRAFT FLIGHT.**

1914 A 19-year-old Serbian terrorist, **GAVRILO PRINCIP,** assassinated **ARCHDUKE FRANZ FERDINAND** in Sarajevo (now Yugoslavia). This led to World War I.

1939 "Two-Ton Tony" Galenta (he really weighed only 234 pounds), the **"GREAT WHITE HOPE,"** attempted to take the heavyweight crown from Joe Louis at Yankee Stadium. He entered the ring with the immortal words: "I'll moida da bum." He floored Joe with a devastating left hook . . . Louis was startled. Next round Louis connected with 27 consecutive blows to Tony's head and body. The referee stopped the fight.

1969 The debut album by **CROSBY, STILLS, AND NASH** made the charts in the U.S. The first single, "Marrakesh Express," became a hit on both sides of the Atlantic. They added guitarist/singer Neil Young and began to tour.

1992 President Bush canceled his golf game and returned to the White House for briefings on the earthquake in the Mojave Desert, the **STRONGEST QUAKE TO HIT CALIFORNIA IN 40 YEARS.**

1994 In a TV documentary, **PRINCE CHARLES** admitted to cheating on his wife Diana, but only after their marriage was irretrievably broken.

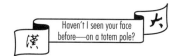

JUNE 29

BIRTHDAYS

- **GARY BUSEY** [bue'-see] Actor. (Goose Creek, TX) Star of *The Buddy Holly Story*. He did the singing, too. Films include *The Firm, Surviving the Game, Rookie of the Year,* and *Predator*. He had a near-fatal motorcycle accident. Year/**Age**: 1995/**51** 1996/**52** 1997/**53**

- **LITTLE EVA** Singer. (Born Eva Narcissus Boyd in Bellhaven, NC) She was a babysitter for Carole King and Gerry Goffin. They wrote her biggest hit: "The Loco-Motion" in 1962. Year/**Age**: 1995/**50** 1996/**51** 1997/**52**

- **IAN PAIGE** Drummer. (England) Member of hard-rock band DEEP PURPLE. Their biggest hit: "Smoke on the Water" in 1973. Year/**Age**: 1995/**47** 1996/**48** 1997/**49**

- **ROBERT EVANS** Actor/producer. (NYC) He was in *The Man of a Thousand Faces* and *The Sun Also Rises* in 1957. He directed *Chinatown* and *Love Story*. He was married to Ali MacGraw and Phyllis George. Year/**Age**: 1995/**65** 1996/**66** 1997/**67**

- **RUTH WARRICK** Actress. (St. Louis, MO.) Phoebe Tyler Wallingford on the daytime soap opera "All My Children." Year/**Age**: 1995/**80** 1996/**81** 1997/**82**

- **CARA WILLIAMS** Actress. Appeared in *The Defiant Ones* and *The Girl Next Door*. She had her own show on TV in 1964 and appeared in the TV series "Pete & Gladys." Year/**Age**: 1995/**70** 1996/**71** 1997/**72**

- **AMANDA DONOHOE** Actress. Appears in "L.A. Law." Year/**Age**: 1995/**33** 1996/**34** 1997/**35**

- **JOHN TOLAND** Author. (LaCrosse, WI) He wrote *The Rising Sun* for which he won a Pulitzer Prize in 1970. Year/**Age**: 1995/**83** 1996/**84** 1997/**85**

- **RICHARD LEWIS** Comedian. (New York, NY) Co-starred with Jamie Lee Curtis on TV's "Anything But Love" and "Daddy Dearest." He was in films *Robin Hood: Men in Tights* and *Wagon's East*. Year/**Age**: 1995/**48** 1996/**49** 1997/**50**

- **FRED GRANDY** Iowa Congressman. (Sioux City, IA) Former "Love Boat" star as "Gopher." Year/**Age**: 1995/**47** 1996/**48** 1997/**49**

- **DAN DIERDORF** Monday football. (Canton, OH) Year/**Age**: 1995/**46** 1996/**47** 1997/**48**

- **HARMON KILLEBREW** Former Minnesota Twins slugger. (Payette, ID) Led the American League in home runs for six years. Year/**Age**: 1995/**58** 1996/**59** 1997/**60**

- **SLIM PICKENS** Actor. (1919-1983 – Born Louis Bert Lindley, Jr., in Kingsberg, CA) He was in *Dr. Strangelove* in 1963 and *The Swarm* in 1978. Cowboy Hall of Fame. (Died 12-8-83.)

- **PETER PAUL RUBENS** Mass-production artist. (1577-1640 – Germany) He set up a factory of artists to mass produce paintings because he was swamped with commissions. It was hard to tell an original from a copy. *The Last Judgement* was said to be done by an apprentice. (Died 5-30-1640.)

- **NELSON EDDY** Singer. (1901-1967 – Providence, RI) Starred in many movie musicals in the 1930s and 1940s with Jeanette MacDonald. (Died 3-6-67.)

- **WILLIAM MAYO** Physician. (1861-1939 – LeSeuer, MN) Co-founder of the Mayo Clinic in Rochester, MN. (Died 7-28-39.)

- **GEORGE WASHINGTON GOETHALS** Engineer. (1858-1928 – Brooklyn, NY) Engineer and Army officer who was the chief engineer of the Panama Canal. (Died 1-21-28.)

FACTS FROM THE PAST

A.D. 68   **SAINT PETER THE APOSTLE**, the first Bishop of the Catholic Church, was crucified by Roman Emperor Nero and Saint Paul was beheaded. Peter was buried in a mass grave outside Nero's amphitheater. Later a small church was built in place of the amphitheater. The altar was placed over the site of Peter's grave. Here many popes and emperors, among them Charlemagne, were crowned. In 1506 Pope Julian II replaced it with a church large enough to house 80,000 people, at that time the entire population of Rome. Today, St. Peter's remains the greatest structure of the Vatican. It's a feast day in some Christian Churches today.

1613   **SHAKESPEARE'S GLOBE THEATER** caught fire during a performance of *Henry VIII* and burned to the ground.

1937   **RIP COLLINS**, first baseman for the Chicago Cubs, played a whole game without a put-out or an assist.

1940   In the spring issue of **BATMAN COMICS,** mobsters rubbed out a circus highwire team known as the Flying Graysons, leaving their son an orphan. Dick Grayson was then adopted by millionaire Bruce Wayne and became his sidekick, Robin.

1955   BILL HALEY & THE COMETS's **"ROCK AROUND THE CLOCK"** went #1. It stayed there for seven weeks.

1956   **ELVIS PRESLEY** appeared on Steve Allen's TV variety show. Dressed in tails, Elvis sang "Hound Dog" to a forlorn basset hound sitting on a stool. Allen has been disliked by rock fans ever since.

1956   High jumper **CHARLIE DUMAS** became the first person to jump 7 feet, clearing 7 feet, $^5/_8$ inches at the Los Angeles Olympic trials.

1956   **MARILYN MONROE** married playwright Arthur Miller at the home of Miller's literary agent in Katonak, KY.

1959   **DICK CLARK** announced his first "Caravan of Stars."

1963   **DEL SHANNON** hit the charts with "From Me to You." It was the first BEATLES cover tune on the U.S. charts.

1967   **MICK JAGGER** and **KEITH RICHARDS** were found guilty in London of drug possession. Jagger was sentenced to three months to a year and Richards to one year. The sentences were suspended on appeal.

1990   Oakland's Dave Stewart pitched the first of two no-hitters, beating Toronto 5-0 at the Skydome. L.A.'s Fernando Valenzuela threw a no-hitter against St. Louis winning 6-0. They set major league records for **TWO NO-HITTERS PITCHED** in both leagues on the same day and two pitchers with complete-game no-hitters on the same night.

JUNE 30

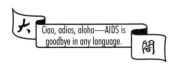
Ciao, adios, aloha—AIDS is goodbye in any language.

BIRTHDAYS

- **LENA HORNE** Entertainer. (Brooklyn, NY) Won a Tony Award for her one-woman Broadway show. She was the first African-American woman signed to a Hollywood movie contract. When her films, *Ziegfeld Follies, Stormy Weather,* and others, were shown in the Deep South, many of her parts were cut. She played the good witch in "The Wiz." Her biggest record: "Love Me or Leave Me" in 1955. Year/**Age**: 1995/**78** 1996/**79** 1997/**80**

- **ROBERT BALLARD** Scientist/Author (Wichita, KS) He discovered the sunken Titanic in 1985. He's written several best-sellers including "Discovery of the Titanic" and "Discovery of the Bismark." He is the Technical advisor of the TV series "Sea Quest DSV." Year/**Age**: 1995/**53** 1996/**54** 1997/**55**

- **MIKE TYSON** Former heavyweight champion. (Brooklyn, NY) Imprisoned in 1992 for rape. Year/**Age**: 1995/**29** 1996/**30** 1997/**31**

- **LARRY HALL** Singer. (Cincinnati) Had one hit in 1964 called "Sandy." Year/**Age**: 1995/**54** 1996/**55** 1997/**56**

- **NANCY DUSSAULT** [dus-so'] Actress. (Pensacola, FL) She was David Hartman's first co-host on "Good Morning America" and co-star of "Too Close For Comfort," playing Ted Knight's wife, Muriel. Year/**Age**: 1995/**59** 1996/**60** 1997/**61**

- **TONY MUSANTE** Actor. He played Lt. William Cawley in the TV special "Judgment" and was David Toma on the crime show "Toma." Year/**Age**: 1995/**59** 1996/**60** 1997/**61**

- **RON SWOBODA** Baseball. NY Mets outfielder. Year/**Age**: 1995/**51** 1996/**52** 1997/**53**

- **GLENN SHORROCK** Singer. (England) Former lead singer for the LITTLE RIVER BAND. Their biggest hit: "Reminiscing" in 1978. Year/**Age**: 1995/**52** 1996/**53** 1997/**54**

- **ADRIAN WRIGHT** Synthesizer. (England) Member of 6-piece electronic pop band the HUMAN LEAGUE. Biggest hit: "Don't You Want Me" in 1982. Year/**Age**: 1995/**29** 1996/**30** 1997/**31**

- **BRIAN BLOOM** Soap star. "As The World Turns." Year/**Age**: 1995/**25** 1996/**26** 1997/**27**

- **JUNE VALLI** Singer. (1930-1993 – Bronx, NY) Top 10 hit in 1953 "Crying in the Chapel." She was on TVs "Your Hit Parade" and "Stop the Music." She was at one time the voice of Chiquita Banana. (Died 3-12-93.)

- **FLORENCE BALLARD** Singer. (1943-1976 – Detroit, MI) One of the original SUPREMES. Biggest record: "Baby Love" in 1964. At one time a millionaire, she later lived on welfare in a Detroit housing project, unable to handle the fame and fortune. (Died 2-21-76.)

- **SUSAN HAYWARD** Actress. (1919-1975 – Born Edythe Marrener in Brooklyn, NY) She won an Oscar in 1958 for *I Want to Live*. (Died 3-14-75)

- **BUDDY RICH** Legendary drummer. (1917-1987 – Born Bernard Rich in Brooklyn, NY) He made his professional debut when he was 18 months old. By the time he was 15, his $1,000-a-week salary made him second only to Jackie Coogan as the highest-paid child performer. On his death bed, the nurse asked him: "Is there anything making you uncomfortable?" He opened one eye and said, "Yes, country music." (Died 4-2-87.)

FACTS FROM THE PAST

1859 A crowd of 5,000 watched **CHARLES BLONDIN**, a French acrobat and aerialist, walk across **NIAGARA FALLS** on a **TIGHTROPE**. It took only 5 minutes and, later, he crossed blindfolded on stilts, pushing a wheelbarrow, while carrying a man on his back.

1870 **ADA H. KEPLEY** of Effingham, IL, became America's **FIRST FEMALE LAW SCHOOL GRADUATE**. She graduated from Union College of Law in Chicago.

1899 **CHARLES "MILE-A-MINUTE" MURPHY** broke the 60 mph speed barrier on a bicycle. The Long Island Railroad built a wooden road between the rails and he kept up with the train for a mile.

1936 The novel **GONE WITH THE WIND** by **MARGARET MITCHELL** was published in New York.

1940 Artist **DALE** (real name Dalia) **MESSICK** introduced the comic strip "Brenda Starr," the red-headed "star reporter." Messick's autobiography is called *Still Stripping at 80*.

1948 Cleveland Indians' **BOB LEMON** pitched the first American League no-hitter at night, a 2-0 win over the Detroit Tigers.

1975 **CHER** and **GREGG ALLMAN** of the ALLMAN BROTHERS were married four days after Cher divorced Sonny Bono. Cher sued Allman for divorce nine days later.

1976 **NEIL DIAMOND**'s home was raided by police. They didn't find enough marijuana for an arrest, but left with some free albums.

1977 Avid comic fan **GENE SIMMONS** authorized the **FIRST KISS COMIC BOOK**. Marvel's inaugural issue sold 500,000 copies.

1983 The **EVERLY BROTHERS** patched up their differences and started to tour again.

1985 Entertainer **YUL BRYNNER** ended his reign as the King of Siam in **THE KING AND I** which brought him 2 Tony Awards, an Oscar and worldwide fame. He did the show on and off for 34 years, more than 4,500 performances.

1988 After three guards were suspended for off-duty cocaine use, President Reagan instituted **RANDOM DRUG TESTING** for all **WHITE HOUSE** employees.

1994 Stone Gossard and Jeff Ament of the rock group **PEARL JAM TESTIFIED** at a congressional hearing concerning rising concert ticket prices.

Football Hall of Fame

Sammy Baugh – 1963
Bert Bell – 1963
Joe Carr – 1963
Earl "Dutch" Clark – 1963
Harold "Red" Grange – 1963
George Halas – 1963
Mel Hein – 1963
Pete Henry – 1963
Cal Hubbard – 1963
Don Hutson – 1963
Earl "Curly" Lambeau – 1963
Tim Mara – 1963
George P. Marshall – 1963
John "Blood" McNally – 1963
Bronko Nagurski – 1963
Ernie Nevers – 1963
Jim Thorpe – 1963

Jim Conzelman – 1964
Ed Healey – 1964
Clarke Hinkle – 1964
W. R. "Link" Lyman – 1964
Mike Michalske – 1964
Art Rooney – 1964
George Trafton – 1964

Guy Chamberlin – 1965
John "Paddy" Driscoll – 1965
Dr. Daniel Fortmann – 1965
Otto Graham – 1965
Sid Luckman – 1965
Steve Van Buren – 1965
Bob Waterfield – 1965

Bill Dudley – 1966
Joe Guyon – 1966
Arnold Herber – 1966
Walt Kiesling – 1966
George McAfee – 1966
Steve Owen – 1966
Hugh "Shorty" Ray – 1966
Clyde "Bulldog" Turner – 1966

Chuck Bednarik – 1967
Charles W. Bidwell – 1967
Paul Brown – 1967
Bobby Layne – 1967
Dan Reeves – 1967
Ken Strong – 1967
Joe Stydahr – 1967
Emlen Tunnell – 1967

Cliff Battles – 1968
Art Donovan – 1968
Elroy "Crazy Legs" Hirsch – 1968
Wayne Milner – 1968
Marion Motley – 1968
Charlie Trippi – 1968
Alex Wojciechowicz – 1968

Turk Edwards – 1969
Earl "Greasy" Neale – 1969
Leo Nomellini – 1969
Joe Perry – 1969
Ernie Stautner – 1969

Jack Christiansen – 1970
Tom Fears – 1970
Hugh McElhenny – 1970
Pete Pihos – 1970

Jim Brown – 1971
Bill Hewitt – 1971
Frank (Bruiser) Kinard – 1971
Vince Lombardi – 1971
Andy Robustelli – 1971
Y.A. Tittle – 1971
Norm Van Brocklin – 1971

Gino Marchetti – 1972
Ollie Matson – 1972
Clarence "Ace" Parker – 1972

Raymond Berry – 1973
Jim Parker – 1973
Joe Schmidt – 1973

Tony Canadeo – 1974
Bill George – 1974
Lou Groza – 1974
Dick "Night Train" Lane – 1974

Roosevelt Brown – 1975
George Connor – 1975
Dante Lavelli – 1975
Leonard "Lenny" Moore – 1975

Ray Flaherty – 1976
Len Ford – 1976
Jim Taylor – 1976

Frank Gifford – 1977

Forrest Gregg – 1977
Gale Sayers – 1977
Bart Starr – 1977
Bill Willis – 1977

Lance Alworth – 1978
Weeb Ewbank – 1978
Alphonse "Tuffy" Leemans – 1978
Ray Nitschke – 1978
Larry Wilson – 1978

Dick Butkus – 1979
Yale Lary – 1979
Ron Mix – 1979
Johnny Unitas – 1979

Herb Adderley – 1980
David "Deacon" Jones – 1980
Bob Lilly – 1980
Jim Otto – 1980

Morris (Red) Badgro – 1981
George Blanda – 1981
Willie Davis – 1981
Jim Ringo – 1981

Doug Atkins – 1982
Sam Huff – 1982
George Musso – 1982
Merlin Olsen – 1982

Bobby Bell – 1983
Sid Gillman – 1983
Sonny Jurgensen – 1983
Bobby Mitchell – 1983
Paul Warfield – 1983

Willie Brown – 1984
Mike McCormack – 1984
Charlie Taylor – 1984
Arnie Weinmeister – 1984

Frank Gatski – 1985
Joe Namath – 1985
Pete Rozelle – 1985
O.J. Simpson – 1985
Roger Staubach – 1985

Paul Hornung – 1986
Ken Houston – 1986
Willie Lanier – 1986
Fran Tarkenton – 1986
Doak Walker – 1986

Larry Csonka – 1987
Len Dawson – 1987
"Mean Joe" Greene – 1987
John Henry Johnson – 1987
Jim Langer – 1987
Don Maynard – 1987
Gene Upshaw – 1987

Fred Biletnikoff – 1988
Mike Ditka – 1988
Jack Ham – 1988
Alan Page – 1988

Mel Blount – 1989
Terry Bradshaw – 1989
Art Shell – 1989
Willie Wood – 1989

Junious "Buck" Buchanan – 1990
Bob Griese – 1990
Franco Harris – 1990
Ted Hendricks – 1990
Jack Lambert – 1990
Tom Landry – 1990
Bob St. Clair – 1990

Earl Campbell – 1991
John Hannah – 1991
Stan Jones – 1991
Tex Schramm – 1991
Jan Stenerud – 1991

Lem Barney – 1992
Al Davis – 1992
Lamar Hunt – 1992
John Mackey – 1992
John Riggins – 1992

Dan Fouts – 1993
Chuck Noll – 1993
Larry Little – 1993
Walter Payton – 1993
Bill Walsh – 1993

Tony Dorsett - 1994
Bud Grant - 1994
Leroy Kelly - 1994
Jimmy Johnson - 1994
Jackie Smith - 1994
Randy White - 1994

JULY MEMORIES

YEARS AGO

1985

POPULAR SONGS
"A View To A Kill" by Duran Duran

"Everytime You Go Away" by Paul Young

MOVIES
Agnes of God
starring Meg Tilly, Jane Fonda and Anne Bancroft. A nun is accused of killing her new baby.

Jagged Edge
starring Jeff Bridges and Glenn Close in this suspense thriller.

TV SHOWS
"The New Leave It To Beaver"
rivival of the sitcom starring Jerry Mathers, Barbara Billingsley, and Ken Osmond.

"Lime Street"
the story of a Virginia inspector played by Robert Wagner.

BOOKS
World's Fair by E.L. Doctorow

1986

POPULAR SONGS
"There'll Be Sad Songs (To Make You Cry)" by Billy Ocean

"Holding Back the Years" by Simply Red

MOVIES
Ruthless People
Bette Midler is kidnapped in this comedy. Danny DeVito plays her husband.

Blue Velvet
David Lynch directs this cult film starring Dennis Hopper, Isabella Rosselini, Laura Dern, and Kyle MacLachlan.

TV SHOWS
"The Ellen Burstyn Show"
starring Ellen Burstyn as writer Ellen Brewer.

"Heart of the City"
starring Robert Desiderio as detective Wes Kennedy in this police drama.

BOOKS
Red Storm Rising by Tom Clancy

1987

POPULAR SONGS
"I wanna Dance With Somebody (Who Loves Me)" by Whitney Houston

"Shakedown" by Bob Seger

MOVIES
Fatal Attraction
a one night stand turns into a nightmare for Michael Douglas. Also stars Ann Archer and Glenn Close.

Ferris Bueller's Day Off
a teen plays hooky. Featuring Matthew Broderick, Cindy Pickett, Jennifer Gray, Mia Sara, and Charlie Sheen.

TV SHOWS
"Werewolf"
starring John J. York and Chuck Connors in the story of a man with a werewolf curse.

"A Year In The Life"
starring Richard Kiley and Wendy Phillips in this family drama.

BOOKS *Kaleidoscope* by Danielle Steel

SPECIAL DAYS

JULY	1995	1996	1997
Cherry Pit Spitting Championship *(Eau Claire, MI)*	July 1	July 6	July 5
Man Watchers Compliment Week	July 2-8	July 7-13	July 6-12
Moose Dropping Festival *(Talkeetna, AK)*	July 14-15	July 12-13	July 11-12
Hog Calling Championship *(Baltimore, MD)*	May 12-14	May 10-12	May 9-11
National Ice Cream Day *(Sundae Sunday)*	July 16	July 21	July 20
Full Moon	July 12	July 1	July 20
Garlic Festival *(Gilroy, CA)*	July 28-30	July 26-28	July 25-27
Great Texas Mosquito Festival	July 27-29	July 25-27	July 24-26

1970

POPULAR SONGS
"Mama Told Me (Not To Come)" by Three Dog Night

"(They Long To Be) Close To You" by The Carpenters

MOVIES
Diary of a Mad Housewife
starring Carrie Snodgrass and Richard Benjamin in this drama.

Women In Love
Glenda Jackson won an Oscar for her role.

TV SHOWS
"Johnny Cash Presents the Everly Brothers Show"
Don and Phil Everly fill in for Johnny Cash during summer.

"The Don Knotts Show"
comedy variety show also starring Gary Burghoff (later in "M*A*S*H").

BOOKS
Future Shock by Alvin Toffler

1971

POPULAR SONGS
"Indian Reservation" by Paul Revere and the Raiders

"You've Got A Friend" by James Taylor

MOVIES
Sunday, Bloody Sunday
starring Glenda Jackson and Peter Finch. Directed by John Schlesinger.

Diamonds Are Forever
starring Sean Connery as 007 in America's Southwest.

TV SHOWS
"Bearcats"
starring Rod Taylor and Dennis Cole. A Stutz Bearcat was featured in this short-lived series

"Nichols"
starring James Garner in this western. Co-stars Margot Kidder and Alice Ghostly.

BOOKS *The Sensuous Man* by "M." Lyle Stuart

1972

POPULAR SONGS
"Lean On Me" by Bill Withers

"Alone Again (Naturally)" by Gilbert O'Sullivan

MOVIES
1776
based on the Declaration of Independence, this musical features Ken Howard, Howard Da Silva, and Blythe Danner.

The Getaway
starring Steve McQueen and Ali MacGraw in this action adventure film.

TV SHOWS
"The Sandy Duncan Show"
Duncan plays Sandy Stockton who works in an advertsing agency.

"The Marty Feldman Comedy Machine"
a British comedy with Thelma Houston, Orson Welles, and Barbara Feldon.

BOOKS *Dr. Atkin's Diet Revolution* by Robert C. Atkins

1945

POPULAR SONGS
"On the Atchison, Topeka and Santa Fe" by Johnny Mercer

"Tampico" by Stan Kenton

MOVIES
Blood On the Sun
starring James Cagney in this suspense film about Japan before the war.

The Corn Is Green
the story of a school teacher, Bette Davis, in a Welsh minimg town.

TV SHOWS
No regularly scheduled TV programming until May 1946.

BOOKS
Cass Timberlane by Red Lewis

1946

POPULAR SONGS
"Give Me Five Minutes More" by Tex Beneke

"Stone Cold Dead In the Market (He Had It Coming)" by Ella Fitzgerald & Louis Jordan

MOVIES
Duel In the Sun
starring Jennifer Jones as a half-breed Indian. With Gregory Peck and Lionel Barrymore.

Centennial Summer
the story of a Philadelphia family during the Centennial Expo of 1876.

TV SHOWS
"Cash and Carry"
contestants play a grocery store quiz show with host Dennis James.

"Voice of Firestone Televues"
short documentary films on various topics including football, farming, etc.

BOOKS
I Chose Freedom by Victor Kravchenko

1947

POPULAR SONGS
"Smoke! Smoke! Smoke! (That Cigarette)" by Tex Williams

"Peg O' My Heart" by Three Suns

MOVIES
Kiss Of Death
starring Victor Mature, Mildred Dunnock, and Brian Donlevy. Richard Widmark debuts as a giggling killer.

Forever Amber
starring Linda Darnell, Cornel Wilde, George Sanders, and Jessica Tandy. A young woman in the Court of Charles II.

TV SHOWS
"Musical Merry-Go-Round"
this show features live entertainment and music with songs by Eve Young, Jack Kilty, and others.

BOOKS
The Moneyman by Thomas Costain

JULY 1
Canada Day

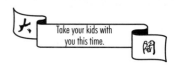
Take your kids with you this time.

BIRTHDAYS

- **DIANA PRINCESS OF WALES**. (Sandringham, England – Formerly Lady Diana Spencer) She married Prince Charles in July of 1981, and they were officially separated Dec. 9, 1992. She had been one of the most admired in royal history. Year/**Age**: 1995/**34** 1996/**35** 1997/**36**

- **OLIVIA de HAVILLAND** Actress. (Tokyo, Japan) Received an Oscar for best actress in 1946 for *To Each His Own* and in 1949 for *The Heiress*. She is the last surviving name star from *Gone with the Wind*. Her sister is Joan Fontaine. Year/**Age**: 1995/**79** 1996/**80** 1997/**81**

- **KAREN BLACK** Actress. (Born Karen Ziegler in Park Ridge, IL) She was in *Nashville, Portnoy's Complaint, The Great Gatsby*, and she received an Oscar nomination for *Five Easy Pieces* in 1970. Year/**Age**: 1995/**53** 1996/**54** 1997/**55**

- **LESLIE CARON** Actress/dancer. (France) Nominated for best actress in 1953 for *Lili* and in 1963 for *The L-Shaped Room*. She appeared in *Gigi* with Louis Jourdan. Year/**Age**: 1995/**64** 1996/**65** 1997/**66**

- **GENEVIEVE BUJOLD** Actress. (Montreal, Canada) Films include: *Anne of a Thousand Days, Coma*, and *Dead Ringers*. Year/**Age**: 1995/**53** 1996/**54** 1997/**55**

- **DAN AYKROYD** Actor. (Canada) "Saturday Night Live." Films include: *North, Exit to Eden, Chaplin, Sneakers, Coneheads, Blues Brothers* as Elwood Blues with John Belushi, and *Dragnet*, a remake of the old TV series. Nominated for best supporting actor in *Driving Miss Daisy*. He was also in *My Girl* and a TV sitcom, "C.C.P.D." He studied criminology at Carlton College in Ottaway. Year/**Age**: 1995/**43** 1996/**44** 1997/**45**

- **JAMIE FARR** Actor. (Born Jameel Farah in Toledo, OH) Klinger on the "M*A*S*H" TV series and in the film *Scrooged*. Year/**Age**: 1995/**61** 1996/**62** 1997/**63**

- **FRED SCHNEIDER** Singer. Hits with B52's include: "Love Shack." Year/**Age**: 1995/**44** 1996/**45** 1997/**46**

- **CARL LEWIS** Olympic track star. (Houston, TX) Gold medal winner several times. Year/**Age**: 1995/**34** 1996/**35** 1997/**36**

- **PAMELA ANDERSON** Actress. (Canada) C.J. on "Baywatch" and formerly on "Home Improvement." She was a *Playboy* cover girl in 1993. Year/**Age**: 1995/**27** 1996/**28** 1997/**29**

- **DEBORAH HARRY** Singer. (Miami, FL) At one time she was a Playboy Club waitress. Vocalist for BLONDIE, a group formed in NYC, from 1975-83. Biggest hit: "Call Me" from the 1980 film *American Gigolo*. Other hits include *Heart of Glass*, and *The Tide is High*. Year/**Age**: 1995/**50** 1996/**51** 1997/**52**

- **JEAN MARSH** Actress. (England) Appeared on PBS series "Upstairs/Downstairs" as Rose, the upstairs maid. Also in *The Jewel in the Crown*. Year/**Age**: 1995/**61** 1996/**62** 1997/**63**

- **DAVID DUKE** Politician. (Tulsa, OK) Former grand wizard of the Ku Klux Klan, ran three times for the Louisiana Legislature, winning in 1989. He also ran for president of the U.S. in 1988 as Populist Party candidate. Year/**Age**: 1995/**45** 1996/**46** 1997/**47**

- **EVELYN "CHAMPAGNE" KING** Singer. Biggest record: "Shame" in 1978. A producer discovered her singing while she was doing janitorial work at Philadelphia International Records. Year/**Age**: 1995/**35** 1996/**36** 1997/**37**

- **SYDNEY POLLACK** Movie director/actor. (South Bend, IN) His films include: *They Shoot Horses, Don't They, The Way We Were, Tootsie, Havana, Husbands and Wives, Used People*, and *The Firm*. Year/**Age**: 1995/**61** 1996/**62** 1997/**63**

- **BOBBY DAY** Singer. (1930-1990 – Born Robert James Byrd, Sr., in Fort Worth, TX) Biggest hit: "Rockin' Robin" in 1958. Formed a group, the HOLLYWOOD FLAMES, in the '50s; also part of the duo BOB & EARL. (Died 7-27-90.)

- **KEITH WHITLEY** C&W singer. (1955-1989 – Sandy Hook, KY) Biggest hit: "When You Say Nothing At All" in 1988. (Died of alcohol abuse 5-9-89.)

FACTS FROM THE PAST

1847   The **FIRST NATIONAL ADHESIVE POSTAGE STAMPS** in the U.S. were issued. They were 5-cent stamps bearing a likeness of **BENJAMIN FRANKLIN** and a 10-cent stamp with a picture featuring **GEORGE WASHINGTON**. At the time, the cost of mailing a letter was 5 cents an ounce, more than it was a century later.

1911   A Polish biochemist, **CASIMIR FUNK,** published a report using the word "**VITAMINS,**" meaning certain chemicals required for a healthy diet. ("Vitamins" is from the Latin word for life, "vita," and ammonia derivatives, "amine.")

1915   Movie-goers saw their **FIRST NUDE SCENE**. Australian actress Annette Kellerman stripped for the film *Daughter of the Gods*.

1956   **ELVIS PRESLEY** appeared on "The Steve Allen Show." Allen made Elvis look ridiculous, by making him wear tails and sing "Hound Dog" to a bassett hound. He was forbidden to dance. Teens protested the next day in front of NBC, saying they wanted the "real Elvis."

1969   Britain's **PRINCE CHARLES** was invested as the Prince of Wales in a ceremony at Caernarvon Castle seen in the U.S. via satellite.

1987   President Reagan nominated Federal appeals court judge **ROBERT BORK** to the Supreme Court. He was later rejected by the Senate.

1989   With a teary "I do," **HUGH HEFNER** relinquished his title as the world's most famous bachelor. The 63-year-old *Playboy* mogul wed Playmate-of-the-Year Kimberly Conrad, 26, in a traditional ceremony.

1991   President Bush nominated **CLARENCE THOMAS** to the U.S. Supreme Court.

1993   **DWIGHT GOODEN** hit his 7th career home run against the Florida Marlins, breaking the NY Mets team record for homers by a pitcher. He used a bat borrowed from a Marlins player, Garry Sheffield, his cousin.

1994   PLO Chairman **YASSER ARAFAT** visited the Gaza Strip for the first time in 27 years, since the beginning of Palestinian self-rule.

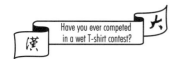

JULY 2

BIRTHDAYS

• **PETE BRIQUETTE** Musician. BOOMTOWN RATS. Year/Age: 1995/**41** 1996/**42** 1997/**43**

• **LEAPY LEE** Singer. (Born Lee Graham in England) Biggest hit: "Little Arrows." Year/Age: 1995/**47** 1996/**48** 1997/**49**

• **POLLY HOLLIDAY** Actress. (Jasper, AL) Played the wisecracking Flo on the "Alice" TV series. She left in 1980 to star in a spinoff called "Flo" and was also in the final episodes of "Private Benjamin" as Major Allen after Eileen Brennan was injured in an auto accident. Year/Age: 1995/**58** 1996/**59** 1997/**60**

• **AHMAD JAMAL** Jazz musician. (Pittsburgh, PA) His *But Not For Me* album was on the Top 10 chart for over 100 weeks. Year/Age: 1995/**65** 1996/**66** 1997/**67**

• **JIMMY McNICHOL** Actor. (Los Angeles, CA) Brother of actress Kristy McNichol, he played Jack on the TV show "The Fitzpatricks." Year/Age: 1995/**34** 1996/**35** 1997/**36**

• **MARVIN RAINWATER** Singer. (Born Marvin Perey in Wichita, KS) Had a hit in 1967: "Gonna Find Me a Bluebird." Year/Age: 1995/**70** 1996/**71** 1997/**72**

• **TOM SPRINGFIELD** Singer. (England) Folk trio the SPRINGFIELDS consisted of Tom, his sister Dusty and Tim Field. Biggest hit: "Silver Threads and Golden Needles" in 1962. Year/Age: 1995/**59** 1996/**60** 1997/**61**

• **JOE PUERTA** Singer. (Los Angeles, CA) With the group, AMBROSIA. Biggest hit: "How Much I Feel," closely followed by "The Biggest Part of Me." Year/Age: 1995/**44** 1996/**45** 1997/**46**

• **RON SILVER** Actor. (New York, NY) Films include: *Blue Steel, Reversal of Fortune,* and *Married To It.* Year/Age: 1995/**49** 1996/**50** 1997/**51**

• **CHERYL LADD** Actress (Born Cheryl Stoppelmoor in Huron, SD) In the movie *Poison Ivy.* She was married to David, son of actor Alan Ladd from 1978-79. Played Kris Monroe on "Charlie's Angels." Year/Age: 1995/**44** 1996/**45** 1997/**46**

• **BROCK PETERS** Actor. (NYC) Appeared in *The Pawnbroker* and *To Kill a Mockingbird.* Year/Age: 1995/**68** 1996/**69** 1997/**70**

• **IMELDA MARCOS** Former Philippine First Lady. She left behind 2,400 pairs of shoes (size $8^1/_2$) when she and hubby Ferdinand went into exile in 1986. Year/Age: 1995/**65** 1996/**66** 1997/**67**

• **RICHARD LEE PETTY** Racecar driver. (Level Cross, NC) Won the Daytona 500 seven times. He was stock car racing's first $1 million winner. Year/Age: 1995/**58** 1996/**59** 1997/**60**

• **JOSE CANSECO** Baseball. (Cuba) The popular player was voted into the All Star Game in 1989 even though he was out with injuries from the beginning of the season. Year/Age: 1995/**31** 1996/**32** 1997/**33**

• **THURGOOD MARSHALL** Former Supreme Court Justice. (1908-1993 – Baltimore, MD.) First black Justice, appointed in 1967 by President Lyndon Johnson. Retired in 1991. (Died 1-24-93.)

• **KEN CURTIS** Actor. (1916-1991 – Lamar, CO) He first made his mark as a singer, replacing Frank Sinatra in Tommy Dorsey's band, and later sang along with Roy Rogers in the group SONS OF THE PIONEERS. Played Festus on the "Gunsmoke" TV series, beginning in 1963. (Died 4-30-91.)

• **DAN ROWAN** Entertainer. (1922-1987 – Beggs, OK) Starred on the "Laugh-in" TV series, which premiered on Jan. 22, 1968. His partner was Dick Martin. (Died 9-22-87.)

FACTS FROM THE PAST

1881 **PRESIDENT JAMES GARFIELD WAS SHOT** by Charles Guiteau at the Washington railroad station. He used a British Bulldog revolver. The bullet landed in the president's pancreas and severed an artery. Guiteau claimed he was prime minister of England. The jury thought he was insane when he sang to them. Garfield died September 19th at age 49 and Guiteau was hanged.

1915 Philadelphia A's pitcher **BRUNO HAAS** set a **MAJOR LEAGUE RECORD** by walking 16 batters in one game.

1937 Aviator **AMELIA EARHART** and her navigator, Fred Noonan, disappeared over the Pacific Ocean while attempting to make the first around-the-world flight at the equator. It remains a mystery, though some aircraft remnants have been found.

1955 The "LAWRENCE WELK SHOW" premiered on ABC television.

1964 President Johnson signed the **CIVIL RIGHTS ACT** banning racial discrimination in employment, public accommodations and voting.

1969 Ralph Nader warned that loud rock music threatened to produce a **NATION OF HEARING-IMPAIRED PEOPLE.**

1970 **LYMAN DICKINSON BOWLED A 299 GAME** in Albany, NY, **WHILE STANDING ON TWO ARTIFICIAL LEGS.** His legs had been amputated a few years earlier and he had to learn to walk and play sports all over again.

1982 Using a lawn chair hoisted by 42 helium-filled weather balloons, **LARRY WALTERS** of North Hollywood, CA, took off from San Pedro and **ROSE TO A HEIGHT OF 16,000 FEET.**

1988 **MICHAEL JACKSON** became the **FIRST ARTIST TO HAVE FIVE NUMBER-ONE SINGLES FROM ONE ALBUM** when "Dirty Diana" went to number one on *Billboard*'s pop chart. The other four chart-toppers from *Bad* were the title track, "I Just Can't Stop Loving You," "The Way You Make Me Feel," and "Man in the Mirror."

1991 **JOEY BUTTAFUOCO** had sexual relations with 16-year-old Amy Fisher at the Freeport Motel in NY. Fisher was sentenced five to 15 years in prison for shooting his wife, Mary Joe in May 1992.

1994 **MARTINA NAVRITILOVA**, 37, announced her retirement from singles competition after her loss to Conchita Martinez, 22, at Wimbleton.

JULY 3

Imagine if animals kept you in a zoo...

BIRTHDAYS

• **JOHNNY LEE** C&W singer. (Born John Lee Ham in Texas City, TX) After working at Gilley's nightclub, he opened his own club down the road. He was married to actress Charlene Tilton from 1982-84. Biggest hit: "Lookin' For Love" in 1980 from the movie *Urban Cowboy.* Year/**Age:** 1995/**49** 1996/**50** 1997/**51**

• **TOM CRUISE** Actor. (Born Thomas Cruise Mapother IV in Syracuse, NY) Starred in *Top Gun, The Color of Money, Cocktail, Rain Man, Days of Thunder, A Few Good Men, Interview With a Vampire,* and *The Firm.* Enjoys race car driving. Has raced with co-star Paul Newman. Received an Oscar nomination for *Born on the 4th of July.* He married his *Days of Thunder* and *Far and Away* co-star, Nicole Kidman, on Dec. 24, 1990. He suffers from dyslexia. Year/**Age:** 1995/**33** 1996/**34** 1997/**35**

• **JAN SMITHERS** Actress. (North Hollywood, CA) She was secretary to the Program Director on "WKRP in Cincinnati." She's married to actor James Brolin. Year/**Age:** 1995/**46** 1996/**47** 1997/**48**

• **MICHAEL COLE** Actor. (Madison, WI) He appeared in the "Mod Squad" TV series. Year/**Age:** 1995/**50** 1996/**51** 1997/**52**

• **PETE FOUNTAIN** Jazz clarinetist. (New Orleans, LA) He got his start on Lawrence Welk's show in 1957. Owned a popular nightclub in New Orleans, LA. Year/**Age:** 1995/**65** 1996/**66** 1997/**67**

• **LAURA BRANIGAN** Singer. (Brewster, NY) Hits include "Gloria" and "How Am I Supposed To Live Without You." Year/**Age:** 1995/**38** 1996/**39** 1997/**40**

• **BETTY BUCKLEY** Actress. (Big Springs, TX) Played Abby Abbott on "Eight is Enough" and appeared in *Cats* on Broadway. Sang "Memories" on the *Cats* soundtrack LP. Year/**Age:** 1995/**48** 1996/**49** 1997/**50**

• **TAYLOR DAYNE** Singer. (Born Leslie Wonderman in Long Island, NY) One of her biggests hits: "Love Will Send You Back." She did the soundtrack for film *Shadow.* Year/**Age:** 1995/**32** 1996/**33** 1997/**34**

• **TOM STOPPARD** Playwright. (Czechoslovakia) *Empire of the Sun.* and *The Real Thing* Year/**Age:** 1995/**57** 1996/**58** 1997/**59**

• **FONTELLA BASS** Vocalist. (St. Louis, MO) Sang "Rescue Me" in 1965. Song used in an American Express commercial, sung by Fontella. Year/**Age:** 1995/**55** 1996/**56** 1997/**57**

• **FRANK TANANA** Baseball player. (Detroit, MI) Tiger pitcher. Year/**Age:** 1995/**42** 1996/**43** 1997/**44**

• **KEN RUSSELL** Director. (England) Expert in shock films. Directed *Women In Love* and *The Music Lovers.* Year/**Age:** 1995/**68** 1996/**69** 1997/**70**

• **GEORGE SANDERS** Actor. (1906-1972 - St. Petersburg, Russia) Snobbish character actor who won an Oscar for best supporting actor in 1950 in *All About Eve.* Was married to both Zsa Zsa and Magda Gabor. Committed suicide because he was bored with life. (Died 4-25-72.)

• **GEORGE M. COHAN** Composer/actor/dramatist. (1878-1942 – Providence, RI) He wrote "Yankee Doodle Dandy" and was portrayed on film in a memorable performance by James Cagney. (Died 11-5-42.)

FACTS FROM THE PAST

1608 The city of **QUEBEC** was founded by **SAMUEL DE CHAMPLAIN**.

1863 The 3-day Civil War **BATTLE OF GETTYSBURG** ended in a major victory for the North, with the retreat of the Confederate troops. Abraham Lincoln dedicated a national cemetery on the battlefield the following November.

1886 **KARL BENZ** test-drove the world's first automobile on the streets of Mannheim, Germany, reaching a top speed of ten miles per hour.

1929 **U.S. PRESIDENT HERBERT HOOVER** announced that due to a combination of hot weather and sore fingers, he would wait until September to resume shaking hands.

1940 **ABBOTT** and **COSTELLO** made their radio debut on NBC replacing **FRED ALLEN** for the remainder of the summer.

1965 **TRIGGER, ROY ROGERS' HORSE**, died at age 33. He was stuffed and remains at the Roy Rogers Museum in California.

1969 **BRIAN JONES** was found dead at the bottom of his swimming pool at his mansion in England. He had left the ROLLING STONES a few weeks earlier. At one of his drug trials, a psychiatrist told the court that Brian had suicidal tendencies.

1971 The DOORS' lead singer **JIM MORRISON** died of a heart attack in the bath of his Paris home at age 27. His death was not announced for six days. He was already buried. He quit music a few months earlier to become a poet. He is buried in a Paris cemetery with the epitaph "James Morrison, Poet."

1978 The **U.S. SUPREME COURT** ruled the Federal Communications Commission was within its authority to reprimand New York radio station WBAI-FM for broadcasting a **GEORGE CARLIN** comedy routine titled "Filthy Words."

1985 CBS bought back 21 percent of its own stock for nearly one billion dollars to stop a takeover bid by **TED TURNER**.

1986 President **RONALD REAGAN** presided over a ceremony in New York Harbor where the renovated **STATUE OF LIBERTY** was re-lit.

1987 **RICHARD BRANSON** and **PER LINDSTRAND** became the first hot-air balloon travelers to cross the Atlantic Ocean.

1988 **ROCKY KENOYER** set a record by making 403 parachute jumps within 24 hours; one jump every three minutes including the time it took for the airplane to reach an altitude of 1,200 feet. Rocky 's "staff" consisted of 50 parachute packers, seven airplanes and ten pilots.

1994 Another inmate attempted to cut **JEFFREY DAHMER**'s throat while the serial killer was attending a religious service in the chapel at Columbia Correctional Institution in Portage, WI.

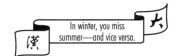

In winter, you miss summer—and vice versa.

JULY 4

Independence day/
Nude Recreation Week Begins

BIRTHDAYS

- **GERALDO RIVERA** TV talk-show host. (NYC) He'll never live down the opening of Al Capone's wall. Year/**Age**: 1995/**52** 1996/**53** 1997/**54**

- **LEONA HELMSLEY** Convicted hotel executive. (Brooklyn, NY) She served 17 months in a Connecticut prison and a short time in a halfway house in NYC for $1.7 million income tax evasion. Of taxes, she said, "only the little people pay them." Year/**Age**: 1995/**75** 1996/**76** 1997/**77**

- **ABIGAIL VAN BUREN** and **ANN LANDERS** Lovelorn columnist/twins. (Born Pauline Esther Friedman and Esther Pauline Friedman in Sioux City, IA) Their columns appear in over 1,000 newspapers around the U.S., claiming a readership of 70 million each. Year/**Age**: 1995/**77** 1996/**78** 1997/**79**

- **EVA MARIE SAINT** Actress. (East Orange, NJ) She won an Oscar for supporting actress in 1954 for *On the Waterfront* with Marlon Brando. Also in *A Year in the Life*. Year/**Age**: 1995/**71** 1996/**72** 1997/**73**

- **GINA LOLLOBRIGIDA** Actress/photographer. (Italy) In films since 1947 including: *Solomon & Sheba*, *Strange Bedfellows*, and *Come September*. Year/**Age**: 1995/**67** 1996/**68** 1997/**69**

- **NEIL SIMON** Comedy playwright. (Born Marvin Neal Simon in the Bronx, NY) His Broadway success has been remarkable with shows including: *The Odd Couple*, *The Sunshine Boys*, *The Goodbye Girl*, *Biloxi Blues*, *Brighton Beach Memoirs*, and *Lost in Yonkers*. Year/**Age**: 1995/**68** 1996/**69** 1997/**70**

- **AL DAVIS** Football general manager. (Brockton, MA) Led the Oakland/Los Angeles Raiders to three Super Bowl titles. Only one in pro football history to be a scout, assistant coach, head coach, GM, league commissioner and owner. Year/**Age**: 1995/**66** 1996/**67** 1997/**68**

- **HORACE JUNIOR GRANT** Basketball. (Augusta, GA) With the Chicago Bulls. Year/**Age**: 1995/**30** 1996/**31** 1997/**32**

- **GEORGE STEINBRENNER** NY Yankee owner. (Rocky River, OH) In 1990, he was punished for paying gambler Howard Spira for information to discredit former Yankee outfielder Dave Winfield. He returned to his duties as managing partner of the New York Yankees in 1993. Year/**Age**: 1995/**65** 1996/**66** 1997/**67**

- **PAM SHRIVER** Tennis star. (Baltimore, MD) Year/**Age**: 1995/**33** 1996/**34** 1997/**35**

- **JOHN WAITE** Singer. (England) Biggest hit: "Missing You" in 1984. Year/**Age**: 1995/**40** 1996/**41** 1997/**42**

- **BILL WITHERS** Singer. (Slab Fork, WV) Biggest hits: "Lean on Me," the original version, and "Ain't No Sunshine." Year/**Age**: 1995/**57** 1996/**58** 1997/**59**

- **TOKYO ROSE** (Born Iva Toguri d'Aquino in Los Angeles, CA) She was trapped in Japan at the time of Pearl Harbor and claimed the Japanese forced her to make broadcasts to servicemen during WWII. She was pardoned by President Gerald Ford and, at last report, lives and works in Chicago, IL. Year/**Age**: 1995/**79** 1996/**80** 1997/**81**

- **GEORGE MURPHY** Actor/politician. (1902-1992 – New Haven, CT) In films *This is the Army* with Ronald Reagan, *Little Miss Broadway* with Shirley Temple, and *For Me and My Gal* with Judy Garland. He became the first professional actor ever elected to the U.S. Senate in 1964. (Died 5-3-92.)

- **STEPHEN FOSTER** Composer. (1826-1864 – Pittsburgh, PA) Composed nearly 200 songs including: "Oh, Susannah," "Swanee River," "Camptown Races," and "Old Black Joe." He died in poverty at Bellevue Hospital in NYC. (Died 1-13-1864.)

- **CALVIN COOLIDGE** 30th U.S. President. (1872-1933 – Plymouth, VT) He was the first president to have his inaugural ceremonies broadcast over the radio. He was nicknamed "Silent Cal," who once said, "If you don't say anything, you won't be called on to repeat it." (Died 1-5-33.)

FACTS FROM THE PAST

1817 Gov. **DEWITT CLINTON** of New York broke ground for the Erie Canal.

1826 **JOHN ADAMS AND THOMAS JEFFERSON** – the second and third Presidents of the United States – both died, 50 years to the day after the Declaration of Independence was adopted.

1831 Baptist Minister Dr. **S.F. SMITH** composed "America" for Independence Day services. He wrote the words, borrowing the tune from an old German songbook. He didn't realize at the time, the British were using the same tune for their national anthem.

1862 English clergyman Charles L. Dodgson (better known as **LEWIS CARROLL**) began inventing the story of **ALICE IN WONDERLAND** for his friend Alice Pleasance Liddell [lih'-dulh] during a boating trip.

1939 In a farewell speech at New York's Yankee Stadium, baseball's "Iron Horse" **LOU GEHRIG,** called himself "The luckiest man on the face of the earth."

1946 President **HARRY TRUMAN** declared the Philippines independent after nearly 50 years of those islands being U.S. territory.

1970 "**AMERICAN TOP 40,**" hosted by **CASEY KASEM,** was heard for the first time on radio.

1987 **KLAUS BARBIE,** the former Gestapo Chief known as the "Butcher of Lyon," was convicted by a French court of crimes against humanity and sentenced to life in prison.

1993 In the first all-American Wimbledon final since Connors and McEnroe in 1984, **PETE SAMPRAS** beat **JIM COURIER** 7-6, (3-6), 7-6, (6-8), 6-3, 6-3.

1994 The Colorado Rockies and the Chicago cubs played two games covering 24 innings and 10 hours 10 minutes. Cubs catcher said, "It's the **LONGEST DOUBLE-HEADER** I've ever been involved in...we even ran out of food." Each team won one game.

JULY 5

The end of the vacation is always looming.

BIRTHDAYS

- **HUEY LEWIS** Entertainer. (Born Hugh Anthony Cregg III in NYC) Formed his San Francisco 6-man band, the NEWS, in 1980. Biggest hits: "The Power of Love" from the film *Back to the Future* and "Stuck with You." Film debut: *Shortcuts.* Year/**Age**: 1995/**45** 1996/**46** 1997/**47**

- **ROBBIE ROBERTSON** Guitarist. (Toronto, Canada) Played guitar for the BAND in the '60s and '70s. Their biggest hit: "Up on Cripple Creek" in 1969. The group backed Bob Dylan for a while. Robbie is in the movies now and toured with Ringo's ALL STARR BAND. Year/**Age**: 1995/**51** 1996/**52** 1997/**53**

- **KATHERINE HELMOND** Actress. (Galveston, TX) Played Jessica Tate on the prime-time TV serial "Soap" and the Mona on the TV series "Who's the Boss" for eight seasons. Year/**Age**: 1995/**61** 1996/**62** 1997/**63**

- **SHIRLEY KNIGHT** Actress. (Goessel, KS) Appeared in *Dark at the Top of the Stairs* and *The Group.* Year/**Age**: 1995/**59** 1996/**60** 1997/**61**

- **RICH "GOOSE" GOSSAGE** NY Yankee relief pitcher. (Colorado Springs, CO) Year/**Age**: 1995/**44** 1996/**45** 1997/**46**

- **WARREN OATES** Actor. (1928-1982 – Depoy, KY) He started out in the 50s testing stunts for "Beat the Clock." His supporting roles included some psychopathic heavies in the films: *Wild Bunch*, *In the Heat of the Night,* and the lead in *Dillinger.* The villain on "Have Gun Will Travel," "Gunsmoke," and "Rawhide" on TV. (Died 4-3-82.)

- **JAMES LOFTON** Football. (Fort Ord, CA) Buffalo Bills wide receiver. Year/**Age**: 1995/**39** 1996/**40** 1997/**41**

- **MILBURN STONE** Actor. (1904-1980) Played Doc Adams on "Gunsmoke" with James Arness. (Died 6-12-80.)

- **HENRY CABOT LODGE** Ex-ambassador to the UN and South Vietnam. (1902-1985 – Nahant, MA) A descendant of one of America's oldest families. (Died 2-27-85.)

- **CLARA ZETKIN** Women's activist. (1857-1933 – Germany) Initiated International Women's Day, observed on March 8th since 1910. (Died 6-20-33.)

- **JOHN BROUGHTON** Boxing champ. (1704-1789 – England) He was the "father of the sport of boxing," which originated in England in the 18th century. It replaced sword fighting. The very first boxing champion, Broughton held the title for 18 years. (Died 1-8-1789.)

- **PHINEAS TAYLOR (P.T.) BARNUM** Circus king. (1810-1891 – Bethel, CT) He may have been the most effective promoter and showiest showman America has ever produced. His most famous fraud was the "Fiji mermaid" which was actually the dried head and torso of a monkey sewed to the body of a fish. Hundreds of people paid 25 cents to see a horse with the head where the tail should be. He got a regular horse, backed it into a stall and tied the tail to a feed trough. His most famous quote was: "There's a sucker born every minute." Barnum put up signs inside his tents saying, "This way to the Egress." People following the signs found themselves outside of the grounds—"egress" means "exit." (Died 4-7-1891.)

FACTS FROM THE PAST

1841 **THOMAS COOK STARTED THE TRAVEL AGENCY** business. His first guided tour was a train trip in England for a temperance meeting.

1865 **WILLIAM BOOTH** founded the **SALVATION ARMY** in London, England. All Salvation Army officers are ordained ministers who have joined for life. The Army operates in over 80 countries.

1942 **IAN FLEMING** was the first graduate from "Special 25," **A TRAINING SCHOOL FOR SPIES** in Canada. This training proved to be invaluable to his future career: creating James Bond.

1946 Designer **LOUIS REARD** of France first presented his revealing creation, the **BIKINI,** at a Paris fashion show, four days after the American atomic detonation on Bikini Atoll. Reard coined "bikini" to reflect his concept of the "ultimate." The first bikini was worn by dancer Micheline Bernardi. Her photo, seen all over the world, brought fan mail from thousands of admirers.

1947 **LARRY DOBY** signed a contract with the Cleveland Indians, becoming the **FIRST BLACK PLAYER IN BASEBALL'S AMERICAN LEAGUE.** In his debut the same day, Doby struck out as a pinch-hitter against the White Sox in Chicago in a game the Indians lost, 6 to 5.

1950 Private **KENNETH SHADRICK** of Skin Fork, WV, became the **FIRST U.S. FATALITY IN THE KOREAN WAR.**

1964 "Liza Jane" was released, the debut record by David Jones and the King Bees. Jones became famous in the 1970's under a new name designed to avoid confusion with Davy Jones of the MONKEES, calling himself **DAVID BOWIE.**

1975 **ARTHUR ASHE** beat Jimmy Connors to become the first black man to win a Wimbleton singles title.

1986 The **STATUTE OF LIBERTY** was officially reopened in a ceremony led by First Lady **NANCY REAGAN.** The national shrine had been closed three years for restoration.

1989 Former National Security Council aide **OLIVER NORTH** received a $150,000 fine and a suspended prison term as a judge sentenced him for his conviction on Iran-Contra-related crimes.

1992 **ANDRE AGASSI WON HIS FIRST GRAND SLAM TENNIS TITLE** at Wimbledon and became the first American to win the prize since 1984. Agassi, the No. 12 seed, beat No. 8 Goran Ivanisevic of Croatia 6-7, (8-10), 6-4, 6-4, 1-6, 4-4.

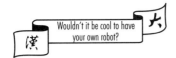

Wouldn't it be cool to have your own robot?

JULY 6

BIRTHDAYS

- **GRANT GOODEVE** Actor. (New Haven, CT) TV's "Eight is Enough" and "Northern Exposure." Year/**Age**: 1995/**43** 1996/**44** 1997/**45**

- **JEANNIE SEELY** C&W singer. (Titusville, PA) Biggest record: "Don't Touch Me" in 1966. Year/**Age**: 1995/**55** 1996/**56** 1997/**57**

- **NANCY REAGAN** Former First Lady. (Born Anne Frances Robbins in NYC) She was adopted by her stepfather, Dr. Loyal Davis, a Chicago neurosurgeon, in 1935. She graduated from Smith College in 1943 and married Ronald Reagan in 1952. Nancy made 11 movies between 1949 and 1956 including *Hellcats of the Navy*. Has a book, *My Turn.* Year/**Age**: 1995/**74** 1996/**75** 1997/**76**

- **JANET LEIGH** Actress. (Born Jeanette Morrison Reames in Merced, CA) Nominated for best supporting actress in 1960 for the famous shower scene in *Psycho.* Mother of actress Jamie Lee Curtis. Year/**Age**: 1995/**68** 1996/**69** 1997/**70**

- **SYLVESTER STALLONE** Actor. (NYC) He got his start with a bit part in a Woody Allen film *Bananas.* His first film was X rated. Sly received an Oscar nomination in 1976 for best actor in *Rocky.*– a script he wrote after rejecting 32 others. Also starred in the *Rambo* films, *The Specialist, Demoliton Man, Oscar, Stop! Or My Mom Will Shoot,* and *Cliffhanger.* Before his success, he cleaned cages at the NY Central Park Zoo to support himself, and was once a gym instructor at a girls' boarding school in Switzerland. He is co-owner of the "Planet Hollywood" restaurants. Year/**Age**: 1995/**49** 1996/**50** 1997/**51**

- **DELLA REESE** Singer. (Born Delloreese Patricia Early in Detroit, MI) Biggest: "Don't You Know" in 1959. She played Della Rogers on TV in "Chico and the Man" Also in the TV series "Royal Family." Year/**Age**: 1995/**63** 1996/**64** 1997/**65**

- **MERV GRIFFIN** TV host/producer. (San Mateo, CA) He appeared on many TV shows, including his own talk show and owns some game shows including "Wheel of Fortune" and "Jeopardy." He had a hit recording in 1949: "I've Got A Lovely Bunch of Coconuts" with Freddy Martin's Orchestra. Year/**Age**: 1995/**70** 1996/**71** 1997/**72**

- **BURT WARD** Actor. (Los Angeles, CA) Played Robin, the Boy Wonder in the "Batman" TV series. Year/**Age**: 1995/**49** 1996/**50** 1997/**51**

- **GENE CHANDLER** Singer. (Born Eugene Dixon in Chicago, IL) Biggest hit: "Duke of Earl" in 1962. Year/**Age**: 1995/**58** 1996/**59** 1997/**60**

- **NED BEATTY** Actor. (Louisville, KY) He starred in several special TV movies including *Friendly Fire* and *The Guyana Tragedy,* the story of Jim Jones. Also appeared in *Superman* films and *Rudy.* Year/**Age**: 1995/**58** 1996/**59** 1997/**60**

- **ALLYCE BEASLEY** Actress. (Born Allyce Tannenberg in Brooklyn, NY) She played Agnes Dipesto, the receptionist on TV's "Moonlighting" series and is married to character actor Vince Schiavelli. Year/**Age**: 1995/**41** 1996/**42** 1997/**43**

- **RON DUGUAY** Hockey. Year/**Age**: 1995/**38** 1996/**39** 1997/**40**

- **WILLIAM SCHALLERT** Actor. Dobie's English teacher on TV's "Dobie Gillis," Nancy's father on "The Hardy Boys/Nancy Drew Mysteries," Patty's father on "The Patty Duke Show." Year/**Age**: 1995/**73** 1996/**74** 1997/**75**

- **SHELLEY HACK** Actress. (Greenwich, CT) Played Tiffany Welles on "Charlie's Angels" after Kate Jackson left the show. Year/**Age**: 1995/**43** 1996/**44** 1997/**45**

- **OTTO GRAHAM** Football star. (Waukegan, IL) Cleveland Brown's quarterback, All Pro four times. Year/**Age**: 1995/**70** 1996/**71** 1997/**72**

- **FRED DRYER** Football player/actor. (Hawthorne, CA) Played defensive end for the NY Giants and LA Rams before acting. Star of TV's"Hunter." Was in the running for Sam Malone on "Cheers." Year/**Age**: 1995/**49** 1996/**50** 1997/**51**

- **BILL HALEY** Entertainer. (1927-1981 – Highland Park, MI) He's credited with starting the "rock 'n roll" era in 1955, with "Rock Around the Clock" which was later used in several films including *Blackboard Jungle* and was the first theme song for the TV series "Happy Days." (Died 2-9-81.)

- **SEBASTIAN CABOT** Actor. (1918-1977 – England) Appeared on the TV series "Family Affair" as Mr. French. (Died 8-23-77.)

FACTS FROM THE PAST

1535   **SIR THOMAS MORE** was executed in England for treason. He was sainted on May 19, 1935.

1885   French scientist **DR. LOUIS PASTEUR** successfully tested an **ANTI-RABIES TREATMENT** on a boy who had been bitten by an infected dog. The boy became director of the Pasteur Institute.

1933   The **FIRST ALL-STAR GAME** was held, and **BABE RUTH** hit a game-winning home run. The American League beat the National League, 4 to 2.

1955   **ELVIS PRESLEY** hit the *Billboard* country chart for the first time as "Baby Let's Play House" reached #10.

1957   **ALTHEA GIBSON** became the first black tennis player to win a Wimbledon singles title, defeating fellow American Darlene Hard 6-3, 6-2.

1964   The movie *A Hard Day's Night* with the **BEATLES** opened in London at the London Pavillion.

1965   Marty Balin and Paul Kantner formed a folk-rock group that would eventually become the **JEFFERSON AIRPLANE**. The Airplane made its debut the following month in San Francisco.

1983   **FRED LYNN** of the California Angels hit the first grand slam in an All-Star Game as the American League scored to a 13-to-3 victory over the National League in Chicago.

1991   **STEFFI GRAF** defeated **GABRIELA SABATINI** 6-4, 3-6, 8-6 to win the women's singles title at Wimbledon.

JULY 7

BIRTHDAYS

- **RINGO STARR** Drummer/singer/actor. (Born Richard Starkey in Liverpool, England) Met the Beatles at the Star Club in Hamburg, Germany, while playing with a group called Rory Storm and the Hurricanes. In August of 1962, he replaced Pete Best as the BEATLES' drummer. He is married to Barbara Bach and is a grandfather. His biggest hits were: "Photograph," written by George Harrison and Ringo, and "You're Sixteen." Ringo also sang lead on the Beatles' "Yellow Submarine." Received an Emmy nomination for *Shining Time Station*. Year/Age: 1995/**55** 1996/**56** 1997/**57**

- **PIERRE CARDIN** Fashion designer. (Italy) Designer of clothes, watches and cologne. Year/Age: 1995/**73** 1996/**74** 1997/**75**

- **MICHELLE KWAN** Figure Skater. Year/Age: 1995/**15** 1996/**16** 1997/**17**

- **WALLY PHILLIPS** Broadcasting legend for WGN radio. Year/Age: 1995/**69** 1996/**70** 1997/**71**

- **CHARLIE LOUVIN** C&W singer. (Born Charlie Loudermilk in TN) Hit: "I Don't Love You Anymore" in 1964. In film *Music City USA*. Year/Age: 1995/**68** 1996/**69** 1997/**70**

- **VINCE EDWARDS** Actor. (Brooklyn, NY) Appeared on the "Ben Casey" TV series for 5 seasons in the '60s. Year/Age: 1995/**66** 1996/**67** 1997/**68**

- **SHELLEY DUVALL** Actress. (Houston, TX) Played Olive Oyl in *Popeye*. Discovered by director Robert Altman, she also appeared in *Roxanne, Brewster McCloud, Nashville,* and *The Shining*. Year/Age: 1995/**46** 1996/**47** 1997/**48**

- **JOE SPANO** Actor. (San Francisco) Played hostage negotiator Lieutenant Goldblum in TV series "Hill Street Blues." Year/Age: 1995/**49** 1996/**50** 1997/**51**

- **CARL "DOC" SEVERINSEN** Bandleader. (Arlington, OR) On the "Tonight Show," 1967-1992. Before that, with Charlie Barnet and Tommy Dorsey's Orchestras. Year/Age: 1995/**68** 1996/**69** 1997/**70**

- **RALPH LEE SAMPSON** Basketball. (Harrisonburg, VA) Played college ball at Virginia. Year/Age: 1995/**35** 1996/**36** 1997/**37**

- **CREE SUMMER** Actress. (Canada) Appears on TV's "A Different World." She is the voice of Penny on "Inspector Gadget," Elmyra on "Tiny Toons," and also does voices on *Care Bear* movies. In the films *Wild Thing* and *The Return of Billy Jack*. Year/Age: 1995/**25** 1996/**26** 1997/**27**

- **MATT SUHEY** Football. (Bellefonte, PA) Played for the Indianapolis Colts. Year/Age: 1995/**37** 1996/**38** 1997/**39**

- **GIAN CARLO MENOTTI** Composer. (Italy) Pulitzer Prize winner for operas *The Consul* and *The Saint of Bleecker Street*. Year/Age: 1995/**84** 1996/**85** 1997/**86**

- **JESSICA HAHN** Model. (Massapeque, NY) Involved in the TV evangelist Jim Bakker scandal. Her "Celebrity Centerfold Video" was *Playboy's* fastest selling and highest charting video ever. Year/Age: 1995/**36** 1996/**37** 1997/**38**

- **GEORGE CUKOR** Movie director. (1899-1983 – NYC) His credits include: *My Fair Lady* and *A Star is Born*. He directed Katharine Hepburn and Marilyn Monroe, and (Died 1-24-83.)

- **EZZARD CHARLES** Boxer. (1921-1975 – Lawrenceville, GA) The only boxer, besides Muhammad Ali, to try to regain the heavyweight championship 3 times, and he lost all 3 times. (Died 5-28-75.)

- **MARY FORD** Singer. (1924-1977 – Born Iris Colleen Summer in Pasadena, CA) She and Les Paul had #1 hits with "How High the Moon" and "Vaya Con Dios" in 1953. (Died 9-3-77.)

- **LeROY "SATCHEL" PAIGE** Baseball. (1906-1982 – Mobile, AL) The only pitcher in the Baseball Hall of Fame with a major league losing record 28-31. He was the greatest pitcher in the history of the black leagues, but those victories didn't count. It was only in the big leagues in 1948, with Bill Veeck's Cleveland Indians, that his wins and losses were counted. One of his famous sayings was: "Don't look back, something might be gaining on you." (Died 6-8-82.)

FACTS FROM THE PAST

1865   **FOUR PEOPLE** convicted of conspiring with John Wilkes Booth to assassinate President Lincoln were hanged in Washinton , D.C.

1946   Italian-born Mother Frances Xavier Cabrini was canonized as the **FIRST AMERICAN SAINT.** She founded the Missionary Sisters of the Sacred Heart.

1949   The police drama "**DRAGNET**" starring **JACK WEBB** and Barton Yarborough premiered on NBC radio. It became a TV series in 1951 and again in 1967 and later was made into a movie with Tom Hanks and Dan Aykroyd.

1968   The **YARDBIRDS BROKE UP.** Guitarist Jimmy Page formed the **NEW YARDBIRDS** to fulfill concert obligations. The WHO drummer Keith Moon said, "It'll go over like a lead zeppelin." Inspired, Page renamed the group **LED ZEPPELIN.**

1975   **KEITH RICHARDS** was charged with possession of an offensive weapon and reckless driving in Arkansas. Hundreds of teenaged girls stormed the jail where Richards was being held. He was cleared of the charges in August.

1978   **MORRIS, THE CAT** (of TV fame) was rescued by trainer Bob Martwick from the welfare pound just a few minutes before he was to be put to sleep. Bob brought him to stardom in the "9 Lives" cat food commercials. The original MORRIS was 19 when he died of old age.

1981   The **FIRST WOMAN** was appointed to the **SUPREME COURT** when President Reagan nominated Arizona Judge **SANDRA DAY O'CONNOR.** She served as Arizona's Assistant Attorney General and as a State Senator before her appointment to the Supreme Court.

1987   **LT. COL. OLIVER NORTH** began testimony at the **IRAN-CONTRA HEARINGS** on Capitol Hill, telling House members that he "never carried out a single act, not one," without authorization.

JULY 8

BIRTHDAYS

- **PHIL GRAMM** Texas Senator. (Fort Benning, GA) Co-author of the Gramm-Rudman Act. Year/**Age:** 1995/**53** 1996/**54** 1997/**55**

- **ANJELICA HUSTON** Actress. (Los Angeles, CA) She played Morticia in *The Addams Family* movie. Year/**Age:** 1995/**44** 1996/**45** 1997/**46**

- **ANDY FLETCHER** Musician. DEPECHE MODE. "Enjoy The Silence." Year/**Age:** 1995/**34** 1996/**35** 1997/**36**

- **STEVE LAWRENCE** Entertainer. (Born Sidney Leibowitz in Brooklyn, NY) Biggest hit: "Go Away Little Girl" in 1957, written by Carole King & Gerry Goffin. He and Eydie Gorme have been married for 33 years and frequently appear together in concert. His father was a rabbi, and Steve started out as a cantor in a synagogue. Year/**Age:** 1995/**60** 1996/**61** 1997/**62**

- **KIM DARBY** Actress. (Born Deborah Zerby in Hollywood, CA) She appeared in *True Grit*. Year/**Age:** 1995/**47** 1996/**48** 1997/**49**

- **KEVIN BACON** Actor. Starred in *Footloose, Murder in the First, The Air Up There, A Few Good Men, The River Wild*, and soap opera "The Guiding Light" 1980-81. Year/**Age:** 1995/**37** 1996/**38** 1997/**39**

- **MARTY FELDMAN** Actor. (1934-1982) A pop-eyed British comic. Films included: *Young Frankenstein* as Eye-gore and *Silent Movie* as Marty Eggs. (Died 12-2-82.)

- **CYNTHIA GREGORY** Ballerina. (Los Angeles, CA) American Ballet Theatre dancer. Year/**Age:** 1995/**49** 1996/**50** 1997/**51**

- **JERRY VALE** Singer. (Bronx, NY) Biggest hit: "You Don't Know Me" in 1956. Year/**Age:** 1995/**64** 1996/**65** 1997/**66**

- **CRAIG STEVENS** Actor. TV's "Peter Gunn." Year/**Age:** 1995/**76** 1996/**77** 1997/**78**

- **BILLY ECKSTINE** Singer. (1914-1993 – Pittsburgh, PA) Biggest hits: "My Foolish Heart" and "I Apologize." His style was copied by Nat Cole, Tony Bennett, Sarah Vaughan, and Joe Williams. Signing with MGM in 1947, he became the first black singer to record for a major white label. (Died 3-8-93.)

- **LOUIE JORDAN** Singer. (1908-1975 – Brinkley, AK) Biggest hits: "Is You Or Is You Ain't My Baby" in 1944, from the movie *Follow the Boys*, "Open the Door, Richard," "G.I. Jive," and "Ain't Nobody Here But Us Chickens." (Died 2-4-75.)

- **NELSON ALDRICH ROCKEFELLER** Vice President. (1908-1979 – Bar Harbor, ME) 41st Vice President of the U.S. The second person to become V.P. without being elected. Gerald Ford was the first non-elected V.P. Rockefeller was Governor of New York state from 1958-1973. (Died 1-26-79.)

- **FAYE EMERSON** Actress (1917-1983 – Elizabeth, LA) Appeared in movies, on Broadway, and often guested on TV shows in the early 1950s, including the "Jack Benny Show." (Died 3-9-83.)

FACTS FROM THE PAST

1776   Colonel John Nixon read the **DECLARATION OF INDEPENDENCE** to assembled residents at Philadelphia's Independence Square. It was the first public reading of the document.

1800   **DR. BENJAMIN WATERHOUSE**, a Harvard professor, injected the first smallpox vaccination in America.

1835   The **LIBERTY BELL CRACKED** for the third time while being rung for the funeral of Supreme Court Justice John Marshall.

1881   A druggist, Edward Berner of Two Rivers, WI, **INVENTED THE ICE CREAM SUNDAE.** A customer asked the druggist/soda fountain owner to top a dish of ice cream with chocolate sauce; the sauce previously only used for ice cream sodas. Berner offered his "sundae" concoction only on Sundays.

1889   The **LAST BARE-KNUCKLE** world heavyweight boxing championship was fought. **JOHN L. SULLIVAN** retained his title in a marathon 75-round match at Richburg, MS, against Jake Kilrain. Bare-knuckle fighting was barred to cut down on broken hands.

1907   Florenz Ziegfeld staged his first **FOLLIES** on the roof of the New York Theater.

1911   **NAN ASPINWALL** arrived in New York City after riding horseback for 301 days, close to 4,500 miles. She left San Francisco September 10, 1910.

1950   General **DOUGLAS MACARTHUR** was named commander-in-chief of United Nations forces in Korea.

1959   Major Dale R. Buis of Imperial Beach, CA, and Master Sergeant Chester M. Ovnand of Copperas Cove, TX, became the **FIRST AMERICAN SOLDIERS TO BE KILLED DURING THE VIETNAM WAR.**

1976   Former President **RICHARD NIXON** was removed from the New York Bar Assn. His license to practice law there was revoked.

1983   **MA BELL** was about to hang up her monopoly. **AT&T'S DIVESTITURE PLAN** was given tentative approval.

1984   **JOHN MCENROE** defeated Jimmy Connors in straight sets to become the first American man in 46 years to win back-to-back Wimbledon titles.

1985   *Playboy* and *Penthouse* magazines raced to the newsstands, each displaying **NUDE PHOTOS OF MADONNA.**

1986   **KURT WALDHEIM** was inaugurated president of Austria over controversy of his alleged ties to Nazi war crimes.

1987   **KITTY DUKAKIS**, wife of democratic presidential candidate Michael Dukakis, revealed that she had been addicted to amphetamines for 26 years.

1994   North Korean dictator **KIM IL SUNG** died of a heart attack at age 82.

JULY 9

It's always so peaceful before a telemarketer calls.

BIRTHDAYS

• **JIMMY SMITS** Actor. (NYC) TV's "L.A. Law," "Birdland," and "NYPD Blue", Films include *Mi Familia, Cisco Kid.* Year/Age: 1995/**37** 1996/**38** 1997/**39**

• **BRIAN DENNEHY** Actor. (Bridgeport CT) *10, Presumed Innocent, F/X II*, and *Cocoon* films. Year/Age: 1995/**57** 1996/**58** 1997/**59**

• **TOM HANKS** Actor. (Concord, CA) Appeared in *Dragnet* with Dan Aykroyd, received Academy Award nomination for *Big*, a comic fantasy about a 12 year old who wishes to be big and suddenly finds he has grown into a 35 year old. Other films include: *Punchline, Turner and Hooch, Joe Versus The Volcano, Sleepless in Seattle, Forrest Gump, Philadelphia*, and *A League of Their Own* with Madonna. Year/Age: 1995/**39** 1996/**40** 1997/**41**

• **KELLY McGILLIS** Actress. She has appeared in *The Accused, Top Gun*, and *Witness*. Year/Age: 1995/**38** 1996/**39** 1997/**40**

• **JAMES HAMPTON** Actor. (Oklahoma City, OK) On the "Doris Day Show" and "Love American Style." TVs "Evening Shade" and "F Troop." Year/Age: 1995/**59** 1996/**60** 1997/**61**

• **JOHN TESH** TV host. (Garden City, NY) "Entertainment Tonight." Also a musician and composer. Was one of the 1992 Olympic commentators. Married to actress Connie Sellecca. Year/Age: 1995/**43** 1996/**44** 1997/**45**

• **O. J. SIMPSON** Football Hall of Famer/accused murderer. (Born Orenthal James Simpson in San Francisco, CA) Accused of killing his ex-wife Nicole and her friend Ronald Goldman in 1994. He is a former football star turned sportscaster/TV commercial pitchman, and actor. He won the Heisman Trophy in 1968 and set an NFL rushing record. Year/Age: 1995/**48** 1996/**49** 1997/**50**

• **ED AMES** Singer. (Malden, MA) He played "Mingo," a Cherokee Indian on the "Daniel Boone" TV series. Started out with the AMES BROTHERS and later on his own. His biggest hit was: "My Cup Runneth Over" from the musical *I Do, I Do.* Year/Age: 1995/**66** 1996/**67** 1997/**68**

• **LEE HAZELWOOD** Entertainer. (Manford, OK) He had a hit with Nancy Sinatra in 1967: "Jackson." He co-wrote most of Duane Eddy's material. Year/Age: 1995/**66** 1996/**67** 1997/**68**

• **DEBBIE SLEDGE** Singer. She and her sisters have a group called SISTERS SLEDGE. Their biggest record: "We Are Family" in 1979. The Pittsburgh Pirates have used it as their theme. Year/Age: 1995/**41** 1996/**42** 1997/**43**

• **MITCH MITCHELL** Drummer. Hit with JIMI HENDRIX EXPERIENCE, "All Along the Watchtower." Year/Age: 1995/**49** 1996/**50** 1997/**51**

• **FRED SAVAGE** Actor. (Highland Park, IL) Kevin Arnold on TV's Emmy Award winning series "The Wonder Years." Films include: *Princess Bride* and *Little Monsters*. Year/Age: 1995/**19** 1996/**20** 1997/**21**

• **JIM KERR** Singer. (Scotland) Lead singer for group SIMPLE MINDS. Biggest hit: "Don't You Forget About Me" from the movie *The Breakfast Club*. Year/Age: 1995/**36** 1996/**37** 1997/**38**

• **ELIAS HOWE** Inventor. (1819-1867 – Spencer, MA) He couldn't earn enough to support his family, and his wife took in sewing to make extra money. While watching her, Elias got the idea for a sewing machine. In 1845, Howe demonstrated his invention and easily beat five women who were sewing by hand. But sales were slow until the Civil War when thousands of uniforms had to be made quickly. (Died 10-3-1867.)

FACTS FROM THE PAST

1755 British **GENERAL EDWARD BRADDOCK** was mortally wounded as his troops suffered a **MAJOR DEFEAT** at the hands of the French, Canadian and Indian forces near present-day Pittsburgh. An aide to Braddock, Colonel George Washington, survived.

1792 At Columbia College in New York, Samuel Mitchell was named the **FIRST PROFESSOR OF AGRICULTURE IN AMERICA.**

1795 James Swan personally **PAID OFF THE ENTIRE U.S. NATIONAL DEBT** of $2,024,899.

1869 The **CORNCOB PIPE** was invented. The pipe is made from a special type of corn with smaller kernels on the cob. Famous corncob smokers included Presidents Gerald Ford and Dwight Eisenhower . . . and, of course, Popeye.

1942 **ANNE FRANK**, 13, went into hiding with her family and four other Jews in the warehouse behind her father's Amsterdam business.

1945 **MAYOR FIORELLO LAGUARDIA** read the funnies over radio station WNYC so the kids wouldn't miss them during the newspaper strike in NYC.

1947 Britain's **PRINCESS ELIZABETH**'s engagement to Lieutenant Philip Mountbatten was announced.

1955 "Rock Around the Clock" by **BILL HALEY AND THE COMETS** hit #1 on the *Billboard* charts.

1956 **DICK CLARK** made his debut as host of "Bandstand" on Philadelphia TV station WFIL. Later, ABC showed interest and the name was changed to **AMERICAN BANDSTAND.**

1982 Queen Elizabeth awoke to a stranger in her bedroom. **MICHAEL FAGAN** had broken into Buckingham Palace undetected by guards.

1987 During his third day of testimony, **LT. COL. OLIVER NORTH** told House members on Capitol Hill that he had **SHREDDED EVIDENCE** as part of a cover-up in the Iran-Contra affair.

1992 **BILL CLINTON** named Senator **AL GORE** as his Vice Presidential running mate.

1994 Sprinter **LEROY BURRELL** cut one-hundredth of a second off Carl Lewis' best time in the 100-m dash to recapture the world record at a meet in Lausanne, Switzerland. The time was 9.85 seconds.

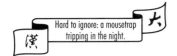

Hard to ignore: a mousetrap tripping in the night.

JULY 10

BIRTHDAYS

- **RON GLASS** Actor. (Evansville, IN) "227" and played Ron Harris on "Barney Miller." Year/Age: 1995/**50** 1996/**51** 1997/**52**

- **DAVE SMALLEY** Bassist. Bass player with the RASPBERRIES. Hit: "Go All The Way" in 1972. Year/Age: 1995/**47** 1996/**48** 1997/**49**

- **JEAN KERR** Author. (Scranton, PA) *Please Don't Eat the Daisies.* Year/Age: 1995/**72** 1996/**73** 1997/**74**

- **NEIL TENNANT** Singer. The PET SHOP BOYS. Biggest hit: "West End Girls" in 1986. Year/Age: 1995/**41** 1996/**42** 1997/**43**

- **DAVID BRINKLEY** News commentator. (Wilmington, NC) "Huntley-Brinkley Report" and "This Week" on ABC. Year/Age: 1995/**75** 1996/**76** 1997/**77**

- **JAKE LAMOTTA** Boxer. He was the *Raging Bull.* Year/Age: 1995/**74** 1996/**75** 1997/**76**

- **VIRGINIA WADE** Tennis player. (England) Wimbledon champion in 1977. Year/Age: 1995/**50** 1996/**51** 1997/**52**

- **ARLO GUTHRIE** Entertainer. (Brooklyn, NY) Son of Woody Guthrie, famous folksinger of the 1930s and 1940s. Arlo is best known for his 1967 hit, "Alice's Restaurant," but his biggest record was "City of New Orleans" in 1972. Year/Age: 1995/**48** 1996/**49** 1997/**50**

- **DAVID DINKINS** Mayor of New York. (Trenton, NJ) 1st African-American mayor of NYC. Year/Age: 1995/**68** 1996/**69** 1997/**70**

- **JERRY HERMAN** Broadway composer. (NYC) *Hello, Dolly!* Year/Age: 1995/**62** 1996/**63** 1997/**64**

- **ANDRÉ DAWSON** Baseball. (Miami, FL) Boston Red Sox outfielder. Year/Age: 1995/**41** 1996/**42** 1997/**43**

- **IAN WHITCOMB** Singer. "You Turn Me On" in 1965. Year/Age: 1995/**54** 1996/**55** 1997/**56**

- **ROGER CRAIG** Football. (Davenport, IA) Played for the Dallas Cowboys. Year/Age: 1995/**35** 1996/**36** 1997/**37**

- **FRED GWYNNE** Actor. (1926-1993 – NYC) Played Herman Munster in "The Munsters" and Officer Francis Muldoon in the TV series "Car 54, Where Are You?," *My Cousin Vinny*, *Fatal Attraction*, and the horror film *Pet Sematary* in 1989. (Died 7-2-93.)

- **ARTHUR ASHE** Tennis star. (1943-1993 – Richmond, VA) First African-American man to win a grand slam event and the only one to win the U.S. Open, 1968; Australian Open, 1970; and Wimbledon, 1975. Also first African-American inducted into the International Tennis Hall of Fame, 1985. Wrote the bestseller *Days of Grace*. His medical problems included quadruple bypass surgery in 1979, a second bypass in 1983. Tests after a 1988 surgery revealed he had the AIDS virus. Ashe held a news conference April 8, 1992, to admit he had become infected with the AIDS virus from a blood transfusion. (Died 2-6-93.)

- **JEFF DONNELL** Actress. (1921-1988 – Born Jean Marie Donnell in South Windham, ME) Played George Gobel's wife, Alice, on his 1950s TV series. Also in films *Gidget Goes Hawiian* and *Gidget Goes to Rome*. (Died 4-11-88.)

- **JOHN GILBERT** Actor. (1897-1936 – Born John Pringle in Logan, UT) He was a silent film star who worked his way from bit parts to romantic leads, but sound revealed his voice to be less dashing than his looks and his career ended overnight. He had been making as much as $250,000 a picture until then. He was romantically linked to Gretta Garbo. (Died 1-9-36.)

- **ADOLPHUS BUSCH** Brewer. (1842-1913 – Germany) He immigrated to St. Louis and built the world's largest brewery, creating Budweiser beer. It was the country's first nationally distributed brand, because they were able to pasteurize it and it could be shipped without spoiling. (Died 10-10-13.)

- **JAMES ABBOTT McNEILL WHISTLER** Artist. (1834-1903 – Lowell, MA) Best known for his painting *Arrangement in Grey and Black No. 1*, better known as *Whistler's Mother*. (Died 7-17-03.)

FACTS FROM THE PAST

1925 **CLARENCE DARROW** defended John Scopes in the **SCOPES "MONKEY" TRIAL** in Dayton, TN. Scopes was accused of teaching evolution in the public schools. Orator William Jennings Bryan spoke for the prosecution. Scopes was found guilty and fined $100.

1928 **COLOR MOTION PICTURES** were first demonstrated by inventor George Eastman.

1962 American frogman **FRED BALDASARE** swam the English Channel underwater, 42 miles in 18 hours.

1964 The **BEATLES** released the song and the film, *A Hard Day's Night*. They appeared at the premiere in their hometown of Liverpool, England, and 100,000 showed up for a parade through the city.

1967 **KENNY ROGERS** left the **NEW CHRISTY MINSTRELS** singing group. John Denver and John Davidson also sang with the group at one time. Rogers formed the **FIRST EDITION**, which had the hit "Just Dropped In."

1979 **CHUCK BERRY** was sentenced to four months in prison for income tax evasion. He underpaid $200,000 on his 1973 tax return.

1982 **ARCHBISHOP JOSEPH BERNARDIN** was named by Pope John Paul II to succeed the late Cardinal John Cody as head of the Chicago Archdiocese.

1992 **CAPTAIN JOSEPH HAZELWOOD** was cleared of criminal responsibility for environmental damage caused by the oil spill from the *Exxon Valdez*. The oil tanker ran aground, causing the worst oil spill in U.S. history, March 24, 1989, in Prince William Sound, Alaska.

1994 Russian President **BORIS YELTSIN** surprised many when he joined Western nations vowing to work for peace in Bosnia by putting pressure on the Serbs, traditionally the Soviet's allies.

JULY 11

What does humble pie taste like?

BIRTHDAYS

- **TAB HUNTER** Actor. (Born Arthur Gelian in NYC) He had a hit record in 1957: "Young Love." When they copied the lyrics to that song, they got them wrong. The line "feel that it's true" should have rhymed with "you" . . . instead they used "me." In *The Pleasure of His Company*, *Damn Yankees*, and *Operation Bikini*. Year/**Age**: 1995/**64** 1996/**65** 1997/**66**

- **SELA WARD** Actress. (Meridian, MS) TVs "Sisters." Also appeared in the film *The Fugitive*. Year/**Age**: 1995/**39** 1996/**40** 1997/**41**

- **MARK LESTER** Actor. (England) Played Oliver in the 1968 film of that name. He made over $500,000 on the movie and blew it all. He is now a medical student. Year/**Age**: 1995/**37** 1996/**38** 1997/**39**

- **RICHIE SAMBORA** Guitarist. (Passaic, NJ) With BON JOVI. One of their biggest hits: "Livin' On a Prayer" in 1986. Year/**Age**: 1995/**37** 1996/**38** 1997/**39**

- **BONNIE POINTER** Singer. (East Oakland, CA) With the POINTER SISTERS. "Slow Hand" was their biggest record. Year/**Age**: 1995/**44** 1996/**45** 1997/**46**

- **BOB ALLISON** Baseball. Power hitter with the Washington Senators and Minnesota Twins. His big year was 1963, when he hit 35 home runs. Year/**Age**: 1995/**61** 1996/**62** 1997/**63**

- **LEON SPINKS** Boxer. (St. Louis, MO) Heavyweight champ in 1981 and 1983. Year/**Age**: 1995/**42** 1996/**43** 1997/**44**

- **SUZANNE VEGA** Singer. (NYC) Biggest hit: "Luka" in 1987. Year/**Age**: 1995/**36** 1996/**37** 1997/**38**

- **JEFF HANNA** Singer/guitarist. (Long Beach, CA) With the NITTY GRITTY DIRT BAND. Hit: "Mr. Bojangles" in 1970. Year/**Age**: 1995/**48** 1996/**49** 1997/**50**

- **LARRY LAORETTI** Golfer. (Mahopac, NY) Won the U.S. Senior Open in 1992. Year/**Age**: 1995/**56** 1996/**57** 1997/**58**

- **MYRA GALE BROWN** Singer. (Memphis, TN) She married Jerry Lee Lewis and when word got out, Jerry's career went downhill. She was his 13-year-old cousin. Year/**Age**: 1995/**50** 1996/**51** 1997/**52**

- **DEBBIE DUNNING** Actress on TV's "Home Improvement." Year/**Age**: 1995/**29** 1996/**30** 1997/**31**

- **GENE EVANS** Actor. (Holbrook, AZ) Rob on '50s TV series "My Friend Flicka." He was in films *Walking Tall* and *Support Your Local Sheriff*. Year/**Age**: 1995/**71** 1996/**72** 1997/**73**

- **YUL BRYNNER** Actor. (1920-1985 – Russia) Won a Tony in 1951 and an Oscar for best actor in 1956 as the King in *The King & I* and set a record of 4,625 performances on stage in that musical. He died of lung cancer. Shortly before his death he appeared on "60 Minutes" proclaiming smoking to be suicide and taped some TV messages saying he would be alive today if he hadn't smoked. They were some of the most dramatic spots ever seen on TV. (Died 10-1-85.)

- **JOHN QUINCY ADAMS** Former president. (1767-1848 – Braintree, MA) Son of the 2nd President, John Adams, and the only president whose father had also been a U.S. president. He was also a published poet. (Died 2-23-1848.)

FACTS FROM THE PAST

1804 **AARON BURR**, upset over a negative comment made to the press, dueled with **ALEXANDER HAMILTON** on the bluffs of the Hudson River at Weehawken, NJ. Hamilton was shot and died the next day.

1864 **WASHINGTON, DC, WAS INVADED** by General **JUBAL EARLY**'s confederate troops.

1914 A Boston Red Sox rookie pitcher appeared in his first major league baseball game, after signing a contract paying him $2,900 for the season. His name was **GEORGE HERMAN "BABE" RUTH**, and for the next few years, he was one of the best pitchers in the American League before becoming a full-time outfielder for the Yankees.

1944 **PRESIDENT FRANKLIN ROOSEVELT** announced he was available for an unprecedented fourth term.

1952 The Republican National Convention nominated **DWIGHT EISENHOWER** for president and Richard Nixon for vice president.

1961 **STU MILLER** of the San Francisco Giants was pitching during the All-Star Game at Candlestick Park when one of the park's legendary winds came up — and blew him off the mound!

1964 After several years of trying, with no success, the **SUPREMES** released their first hit: "Where Did Our Love Go."

1969 A federal appeals court in Boston reversed the convictions of **DR. BENJAMIN SPOCK** and three others found guilty in 1968 of conspiring to counsel **EVASION OF THE MILITARY DRAFT.**

1971 Andrew Lloyd Webber's **JESUS CHRIST SUPERSTAR**, which began as an album, had its first stage performance in Pittsburgh.

1977 The Medal of Freedom was awarded posthumously to the **REV. MARTIN LUTHER KING, JR.**, in a White House ceremony.

1979 The **FIRST DIGITAL ROCK ALBUM**, *Bop Till You Drop*, by **RY COODER**, was released.

1980 Iran released U.S. hostage **RICHARD QUEEN** on the 250th day of captivity, when he was diagnosed as having multiple sclerosis.

1981 **NEVA ROCKEFELLER** became the first woman to be ordered by the court to pay alimony to her husband.

1985 **NOLAN RYAN** of the Houston Astros became the **FIRST PITCHER** in major league baseball to strike out 4,000 batters, fanning Danny Heep of the New York Mets.

1994 **DANTE CAPUTO**, special UN envoy for Haiti said the Ministry of Foreign Affairs gave the United Nations and the Organization of American States 48 hours to leave the Caribbean country.

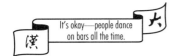

It's okay—people dance on bars all the time.

JULY 12

BIRTHDAYS

- **TRACIE SPENCER** Singer. "This House." Year/**Age**: 1995/**19** 1996/**20** 1997/**21**

- **BILL COSBY** Actor/comedian. (Philadelphia, PA) The "Cosby Show" aired from Sept. 20, 1984, through April 30, 1992. The show won six Emmys and 14 NAACP Image Awards. Recorded many popular comedy albums; hit single "Little Ole Man" in 1967. First black dramatic TV actor as Alexander Scott on "I Spy" with Robert Culp. Movies include *California Suite*, *The Meteor Man*, and *Ghost Dad*. He received a football scholarship at Temple University. Does Jello and Kodak commercials. Host of "You Bet Your Life," a short-lived 1992 TV game show. Year/**Age**: 1995/**58** 1996/**59** 1997/**60**

- **DENISE NICHOLAS** Actress. "Room 222." Film Ghost Dad and TVs "In the Heat of the Night." Year/**Age**: 1995/**51** 1996/**52** 1997/**53**

- **MILTON BERLE** TV's first superstar/comedian "Mr. Television." (Born Milton Berlinger, NYC) In 1948, Uncle Miltie's budget for the "Texaco Star Theater," the most popular one-hour show on TV, was $15,000 for the entire hour. Berle dressed in drag, was hit in the face with cream pies and was called the "thief of bad gags." He hosted the first telethon, for cancer research, raising over a million dollars. Year/**Age**: 1995/**87** 1996/**88** 1997/**89**

- **CHRISTIE McVIE** Singer. (England) With the popular English/American band FLEETWOOD MAC. Their biggest hit: "Dreams" in 1977. Her biggest record: "Got a Hold on Me" in 1984. Their song "Don't Stop Thinking About Tomorrow" got a boost when it was used as the Clinton campaign theme. Year/**Age**: 1995/**52** 1996/**53** 1997/**54**

- **JOHN WETTON** Bassist. (England) With the group ASIA. Biggest hit: "Heat of the Moment" in 1982. Year/**Age**: 1995/**46** 1996/**47** 1997/**48**

- **MARK HATFIELD** Former senator. (Dallas, OR) (R-OR) He wrote *Between a Rock and a Hard Place*. Year/**Age**: 1995/**73** 1996/**74** 1997/**75**

- **KRISTI YAMAGUCHI** Olympic figure skater. Gold Medal winner in 1992. She said she will not attempt to defend her title. Year/**Age**: 1995/**24** 1996/**25** 1997/**26**

- **ROGER SMITH** Former GM Chairman. (Columbus, OH) The subject of *Roger and Me*. Year/**Age**: 1995/**70** 1996/**71** 1997/**72**

- **ANDREW WYETH** Artist. (Chadds Ford, PA) He stunned the art world in 1986 with a multi-million-dollar sale of 246 works (many nudes) on the subject of "Helga" to art collector Leonard Andrews. "Helga" was a neighbor. Year/**Age**: 1995/**78** 1996/**79** 1997/**80**

- **RICHARD SIMMONS** Health and exercise guru. (New Orleans, LA) *Sweatin' To The Oldies* series on video. Year/**Age**: 1995/**47** 1996/**48** 1997/**49**

- **MEL HARRIS** Actress. TV's "Thirtysomething." Films include *Cameron's Closet*. Year/**Age**: 1995/**38** 1996/**39** 1997/**40**

- **ERIC CARR** Drummer. (1950-1991 – NYC) Replaced Peter Criss on the hard-rock band KISS in 1981. The group's biggest hit: "Beth" in 1976. (Died 11-25-91.)

- **HENRY DAVID THOREAU** American writer/philosopher (1817-1862 – Concord, MA) *On Walden Pond*. (Died 5-6-1862.)

- **JULIUS CAESAR** Roman statesman/general/dictator. (100-44 B.C.) He was so vain that he put up a statue to himself, inscribed "to the unconquerable god." He ordered the month of his birth to be named after him. He was very clean shaven; even plucked his beard out by the roots.

- **GEORGE EASTMAN** Industrialist/inventor. (1854-1932 – Waterville, NY) He created the world's first successful low-priced camera in 1888 and named it "Kodak" because he liked the letter "K" and believed "Kodak" could be easily pronounced in any language.

- **JOE DeRITA** Actor. (1909-1993 – Philadelphia, PA) The "Three Stooges." Joining the group in 1959, he replaced Joe Besser and became the second and last of the Shemp replacements. (Died 7-3-93.)

FACTS FROM THE PAST

1876 Signorina **MARIA SPELTERINA** walked across Niagara Falls on a tightrope – wearing peach baskets on her feet. It took the 23-year-old woman 11 minutes to cross and only 10 minutes to return, walking backward the entire way. A week later she walked across the tightrope blindfolded, and a few days later she did it again — this time with her wrists and ankles manacled.

1949 The **FIRST INTEGRATED BASEBALL ALL-STAR GAME** included players Jackie Robinson, Larry Doby, Roy Campanella, and Don Newcombe.

1957 President **DWIGHT EISENHOWER** became the first U.S. chief executive to ride in a helicopter during a top-level civil defense exercise simulating a nuclear attack on targets including the White House. Ike was flown away in a Huey (Bell UH13J) chopper.

1969 A record by **JOHN LENNON** and **YOKO ONO**, "The Ballad of John and Yoko," was banned by many Top Forty AM radio stations. They found the phrase "Christ, you know it ain't easy . . ." offensive and sacrilegious.

1977 **PRESIDENT JIMMY CARTER** defended the Supreme Court's decision limiting government payments for poor women's abortions, saying, "There are many things in life that are not fair."

1979 A Chicago disc jockey held a **DISCO DEMOLITION** between games of a baseball doubleheader at Comiskey Park. **STEVE DAHL** burned disco records brought by fans. Some fans started their own fires and a mini-riot followed. The White Sox were forced to forfeit the second game of the doubleheader.

1984 Political history was made when the then-likely presidential nominee, **WALTER MONDALE**, named Representative Geraldine Ferraro of New York as his choice for Vice President. She and Mondale were defeated in the fall elections by Reagan and Bush.

JULY 13

Is it hot hot
or spicy hot?

BIRTHDAYS

- **HARRISON FORD** Actor. (Chicago, IL) Appeared as the hot-rodder in *American Graffiti* and got the critics' attention in that film, then went on to play Han Solo in *Star Wars*, *The Empire Strikes Back* and *Return of the Jedi*. Also in all *Indiana Jones* films, *Regarding Henry*, *Patriot Games*, *Blade Runner*, *The Fugitive*, a remake of the classic TV series and *Clear and Present Danger*. Year/Age: 1995/**53** 1996/**54** 1997/**55**

- **ROGER McGUINN** Singer. (Born James McGuinn in Chicago) Founder of The BYRDS. Their biggest hit: "Turn, Turn, Turn" in 1965. The song had the oldest lyrics, taken from a biblical passage in the Book of Ecclesiastes. Early in his career he was with the Chad Mitchell Trio and Bobby Darin's band. Year/Age: 1995/**53** 1996/**54** 1997/**55**

- **ROBERT FORSTER** Actor. (Rochester, NY) Sardonic-looking American leading man who reminds many of actor John Garfield. In the film *Reflections of a Golden Eye* and TV series "Banyon." Year/Age: 1995/**54** 1996/**55** 1997/**56**

- **RICHARD "CHEECH" MARIN** Comedian. (Los Angeles, CA) Half of "Cheech and Chong" comedy team who had a top 10 hit in 1974: "Earache, My Eye." Films include *Rude Awakening*. In the TV series "Golden Palace." Film *Cisco Kid*. Year/Age: 1995/**49** 1996/**50** 1997/**51**

- **PATRICK STEWART** Actor. Plays Captain Jean Luc Piccard on TV's "STAR TREK: The Next Generation." A veteran of Britain's Royal Shakespeare Company. Films *Gunmen* and *Jeffery*. Year/Age: 1995/**55** 1996/**56** 1997/**57**

- **ANTHONY JEROME "SPUD" WEBB** Basketball. (Dallas, TX) With the Sacramento Kings. Year/Age: 1995/**32** 1996/**33** 1997/**34**

- **STEPHEN JO BLADD** Drummer. Biggest hit with J. GEILS BAND: "Centerfold" in 1982. Year/Age: 1995/**53** 1996/**54** 1997/**55**

- **LOUISE MANDRELL** C&W singer. (Corpus Christi, TX) One of the famous Mandrell Sisters. Year/Age: 1995/**41** 1996/**42** 1997/**43**

- **JACK KEMP** Politician. (Los Angeles, CA) Was a 1988 GOP presidential candidate. Former Secretary of Housing and Urban Development. Year/Age: 1995/**60** 1996/**61** 1997/**62**

- **CAMERON CROWE** Actor. Year/Age: 1995/**37** 1996/**38** 1997/**39**

- **SAM HANKS** Racecar driver. Year/Age: 1995/**81** 1996/**82** 1997/**83**

- **DANNY GAYOL** Entertainer. BO DEANS. Year/Age: 1995/**37** 1996/**38** 1997/**39**

- **ERNO RUBIK** Inventor. (Born in a hospital air raid shelter in Budapest) Made millions from the Rubik's Cube. Year/Age: 1995/**51** 1996/**52** 1997/**53**

- **BOB CRANE** Actor. (1928-1978) Star of "Hogan's Heroes" TV series, was found murdered June 29, 1978, in an apartment in Scottsdale, AZ. The murder is still one of Hollywood's unsolved mysteries.

- **DAVE GARROWAY** TV talk-show host. (1913-1982 – Schenectady, NY) He was a network page as a young man and a DJ. He became the first host of the "Today" show, which premiered Jan. 14, 1952. J. Fred Muggs, a chimp, was his partner on the show and Dave always signed off with "Peace." He took his own life on 7-21-82.

FACTS FROM THE PAST

1837 Queen Victoria became the **FIRST MONARCH TO OCCUPY BUCKINGHAM PALACE.** They put 50 lavatories in the palace, but most of them didn't work. Much of the royalty didn't like it there. Four miles of corridors took ten men working continuously to keep the 4,000 windows clean. One man works full time just cleaning clocks. George the V tried to sell it to a hotel chain. George the VI called it the "ice box." Queen Elizabeth said it's a house where you need a bicycle.

1925 The **ZIEGFELD FOLLIES** needed a last-minute replacement for W.C. Fields, who had gone home to attend his mother's funeral. They picked a struggling unknown comedian named **WILL ROGERS.**

1939 **FRANK SINATRA MADE HIS FIRST RECORD,** singing "From the Bottom of My Heart" and "Melancholy Mood" with the HARRY JAMES ORCHESTRA.

1954 Although he never threw a pitch, **DEAN STONE** got the victory in the All-Star Game. With two outs, Stone came in to pitch, but before he threw the ball, **RED SCHOENDIENST** attempted to steal home. Stone threw him out. The American League went ahead in the ninth and **VIRGIL TRUCKS** came in to pitch saving the win for Stone.

1960 Massachusetts Senator **JOHN F. KENNEDY** won the Democratic presidential nomination at his party's convention in Los Angeles.

1978 **LEE IACOCCA** was fired as president of Ford Motor Company by Chairman Henry Ford II.

1985 The **LIVE AID CONCERTS** to aid starving Africans took place on duel stages in London and Philadelphia. Boomstown Rats singer **BOB GELDOF** organized the concerts, viewed and listened to by over a billion people in 156 countries. Performers included Mick Jagger, Tina Turner, Madonna, Bob Dylan, and Paul McCartney, who suffered embarrassment when his microphone wouldn't work. They wanted to stage the U.S. portion of the concert at Shea Stadium in New York, but some of the seats were not safe and Mayor Koch would not guarantee police protection.

1985 **PRESIDENT REAGAN** underwent an operation to remove a cancerous polyp from his lower intestine.

1988 On golf courses 1,650 miles apart, twins **KYLE** and **KIM RICHARDSON** both made eagles at 2 p.m. Both shots were 160-yard 7-irons, hit on the ninth hole, both 410-yard par-4's. Kyle at Grand Lake, CO, golf course and Kim at Indian Springs Country Club, Silver Springs, MD.

Today, just go ahead.
Step on the grass.

JULY 14

BIRTHDAYS

- **GERALD FORD** 38th U.S. President. (Born Leslie Lynch King, Jr., in Omaha, NE) The first non-elected president and vice president. He became the 41st V.P. on Dec. 6, 1973, by appointment, following the resignation of Spiro Agnew and became president following the resignation of Richard Nixon. At one time, he was a male model. He was the only president to survive 2 assassination attempts. Year/Age: 1995/**82** 1996/**83** 1997/**84**

- **JOHN CHANCELLOR** Newsman. (Chicago, IL) Started his career at the *Chicago Sun Times* in 1947, then joined WMAQ in Chicago. Later he anchored the "Today" show," and then "NBC Nightly News" from 1972-1982. Retired in July 1993. Year/Age: 1995/**68** 1996/**69** 1997/**70**

- **INGMAR BERGMAN** Filmmaker. (Uppsala, Sweden) He won an Oscar for *Through a Glass Darkly* in 1961. *Wild Strawberries,* and *Fanny and Alexander.* Year/Age: 1995/**77** 1996/**78** 1997/**79**

- **POLLY BERGEN** Actress/singer. (Born Nellie Paulina Burgin in Knoxville, TN) "War and Remembrance" and "Baby Talk." Year/Age: 1995/**65** 1996/**66** 1997/**67**

- **NANCY OLSON** Actress In *Sunset Boulevard, The Absent-minded Professor* and *Son of Flubber.* Year/Age: 1995/**67** 1996/**68** 1997/**69**

- **DEL REEVES** C&W singer. (Born Franklin Delano Reeves in Sparta, NC) Biggest hit: "Girl on a Billboard." Year/Age: 1995/**62** 1996/**63** 1997/**64**

- **ARTHUR LAURENTS** Playwright. (NYC) Wrote *Home of the Brave* and *Summertime.* Co-wrote *West Side Story.* Year/Age: 1995/**77** 1996/**78** 1997/**79**

- **ROSEY GRIER** Former football star/turned actor. (Born Roosevelt Grier in Cuthbert, GA) Year/Age: 1995/**63** 1996/**64** 1997/**65**

- **MISSY GOLD** Actress. (Great Falls, MT) "Benson." Year/Age: 1995/**25** 1996/**26** 1997/**27**

- **STEVE STONE** Former Baltimore Oriole pitcher. He won the Cy Young Award in 1980. Year/Age: 1995/**48** 1996/**49** 1997/**50**

- **WILLIAM HANNA** Cartoonist (Melrose, NM) Half of Hanna-Barbera of cartoon fame, especially "Flintstones." Year/Age: 1995/**85** 1996/**86** 1997/**87**

- **DOUGLAS EDWARDS** CBS news commentator. (1917-1990 – Ada, OK) He was television's first evening news anchor, in 1948, for CBS. Did the first TV coverage of presidential nominating conventions. He covered the assassination attempt against President Truman and the sinking of the *Andrea Doria.* Walter Cronkite replaced Edwards in 1962. (Died 10-13-90.)

- **TERRY THOMAS** Actor. (1911-1990 – Born Thomas Terry Hoar Stevens in London, England) Portrayed the consummate upper-class rotter in dozens of film comedies including *It's A Mad Mad Mad Mad World* and *Those Magnificent Men in Their Flying Machines.* (Died 1-8-90.)

- **IRVING STONE** Author. (1903-1989 – Born Irving Tennenbaum in San Francisco, CA) He wrote fictionalized portraits of Vincent Van Gogh in *Lust for Life,* Abraham and Mary Lincoln in *Love is Eternal* and Michelangelo in *The Agony and the Ecstasy.* Five of his 25 books were made into movies. (Died 8-26-89.)

- **WOODY GUTHRIE** American folksinger. (1912-1967 – Born Woodrow Wilson Guthrie in Okemah, OK) Named after President Wilson. He wrote the song "This Land is Your Land" and was the father of Arlo Guthrie. (Died 10-3-67.)

- **KEN MURRAY** Actor. (1903-1988 – Born Don Court in NYC) Appeared in films: *Son of Flubber* and *The Man Who Shot Liberty Valance.*

FACTS FROM THE PAST

1789 A French mob stormed the Paris fortress, freed a handful of prisoners, killed some defenders, and stuck the Bastille governor's head up on a pitchfork. **BASTILLE DAY** is celebrated as the birth of freedom in France, a high point of the progress which eventually forced the king, Louis XVI, to sign a new constitution acknowledging certain human rights.

1865 The 14,690-ft. **MATTERHORN PEAK** was first conquered by **EDWARD WHYMPER** and party. Seven climbers reached the top, but during the descent, the rope broke, and 4 climbers fell 4,000 feet to their deaths.

1881 Outlaw William H. Bonney, Jr., alias **BILLY THE KID,** was shot and killed by Sheriff Pat Garrett in Fort Sumner, NM.

1946 **DR. BENJAMIN SPOCK**'s *The Common Sense Book of Baby and Child Care* was published. In the next 3 decades, it became one of the best-selling books in history.

1967 **THE WHO** played North America for the first time. On that tour, they were only the opening act. The star attraction was another British group, **HERMAN'S HERMITS.**

1973 The **EVERLY BROTHERS,** after deciding to quit their duo, performed their last show at Knotts' Berry Farm. The show was stopped by the entertainment director Bill Hollingshead because he claimed **DON EVERLY** was not performing well. This caused **PHIL EVERLY** to smash his guitar and rush off stage.

1992 Actress **DEMI MOORE** appeared on the cover of *Vanity Fair* in nothing but a painted-on birthday suit.

1993 **PRESIDENT CLINTON** took a helicopter ride over the Midwest's submerged homes and farms and unveiled a $2.48 billion federal flood relief program.

1994 **ECHOING DAN QUAYLE**'s comment, Health and Human Services Secretary Donna Shalala said that TV character Murphy Brown set a bad example by having a fictional baby out of wedlock.

JULY 15
St. Swithin's Day

A handful of soft grapes feels just like eyeballs.

BIRTHDAYS

• **LINDA RONSTADT** Entertainer. (Tucson, AZ) Started the STONE PONEYS in Los Angeles when she was 18 years old. They had a hit: "Different Drum" in 1967. Her biggest single: "You're No Good" in 1974. She was in the *Pirates of Penzance* operetta at the Uris Theatre in New York City in 1980 and also the film in 1983. Year/**Age**: 1995/**49** 1996/**50** 1997/**51**

• **IRIS MURDOCH** Writer. (Dublin, Ireland) She wrote *The Good Apprentice* in 1985 and *Black Prince*. Year/**Age**: 1995/**76** 1996/**77** 1997/**78**

• **ALEX KARRAS** Football star/actor. (Gary, IN) In the TV series "Webster" with his wife Susan Clark. He did the Lazy Boy TV commercials. Year/**Age**: 1995/**60** 1996/**61** 1997/**62**

• **JAN-MICHAEL VINCENT** Actor. (Denver, CO) In the TV series "Air Wolf" and miniseries "Winds of War." Year/**Age**: 1995/**51** 1996/**52** 1997/**53**

• **PHILIP CAREY** Actor. Played Custer in *The Great Sioux Massacre*, also on TV in "Philip Marlowe" and "Laredo," as well as soap opera "One Life To Live." Year/**Age**: 1995/**73** 1996/**74** 1997/**75**

• **DAVID PACK** Singer. With AMBROSIA. Biggest hit: "The Biggest Part of Me" in 1980. Year/**Age**: 1995/**42** 1996/**43** 1997/**44**

• **WILLIE AAMES** Actor. (Newport Beach, CA) He played Tommy on "Eight is Enough" and starred in "Charles in Charge." Year/**Age**: 1995/**35** 1996/**36** 1997/**37**

• **BRIAN AUSTIN GREEN** Actor. Appears on "Beverly Hills 90210" and "Knots Landing." Year/**Age**: 1995/**22** 1996/**23** 1997/**24**

• **MILLIE JACKSON** Singer. (Thompson, GA) Biggest record: "Hurts So Good" in 1973, from the movie *Cleopatra Jones*. Year/**Age**: 1995/**51** 1996/**52** 1997/**53**

• **CLIVE CUSSLER** Writer. Wrote *Raise the Titanic*, *Deep Six*, *Sahara*, and *Cyclops*. Year/**Age**: 1995/**64** 1996/**65** 1997/**66**

• **KEN KERCHEVAL** Actor. (Wolcottsville, IN) Played the obnoxious Cliff Barnes on TV's "Dallas" and also was in the soap opera "Search for Tomorrow." Year/**Age**: 1995/**60** 1996/**61** 1997/**62**

• **DONN CLENDENON** Baseball. Former Pittsburgh Pirate heavy hitter. Year/**Age**: 1995/**60** 1996/**61** 1997/**62**

• **FOREST WHITAKER** Actor. Appeared in *The Bodysnatchers*, *Downtown*, and *The Crying Game*. Year/**Age**: 1995/**34** 1996/**35** 1997/**36**

• **COWBOY COPAS** C&W singer. (1913-1963 – Muskego, OK) Biggest hit: "Alabam" in 1960. His last hit was "Goodbye Kisses." He died in a plane crash with Patsy Cline and Hawkshaw Hawkins March 5, 1963.

• **CLEMENT CLARKE MOORE** Author/teacher. (1779-1863 – NYC) Best remembered for *A Visit from St. Nicholas* or *Twas the Night Before Christmas*, which he wrote for his children. It was first published anonymously, and without Moore's knowledge, on December 23, 1823. (Died 7-10-1863.)

• **REMBRANDT HARMENSZOON VAN RIJN** Artist. (1606-1669 – Netherlands) Rembrandt established a studio at Amsterdam in 1630. Paintings of his early period were excellent and brought financial success, but later his works were mysterious and cost him his popularity and led to his bankruptcy.

FACTS FROM THE PAST

971 **BISHOP SWITHIN** of Winchester, England, died in 862. His remains were reinterred at Winchester Cathedral on this day. Legend says his spirit was angry with the move, causing a downpour of rain and it continued to rain for the next forty days. It is believed if it rains today – St. Swithin's Day – it will rain for the next forty days.

1876 **WASHINGTON BRADLEY** pitched baseball's first no-hitter, as St. Louis beat Hartford 2 to 0.

1933 Aviator **WILEY POST**, flying a Lockheed Vega called *Winnie Mae*, left New York for the **FIRST SOLO FLIGHT AROUND THE WORLD.** It took 7 days, 18 hours and 49$\frac{1}{2}$ minutes.

1954 The **TRENIERS**, a black vocal group, recorded "Say Hay (The Willie Mays Song)" in New York City. The song also featured the voice of NY Giants centerfielder Willie Mays himself. It was recorded under the direction of then 21-year-old Quincy Jones.

1971 **PRESIDENT RICHARD NIXON** announced in a nationally broadcast address that he would visit the People's Republic of China to seek a "normalization of relations." He went in February.

1979 **PRESIDENT JIMMY CARTER** delivered his now famous "malaise" speech. He lamented on what he called a "crisis of confidence" and scolded Americans for not having the spirit and self-discipline necessary to combat energy shortages and inflation.

1982 **GEORGE SHULTZ** was confirmed by the U.S. Senate as America's 60th secretary of state. The vote was 97-0.

1986 The aircraft Voyager set a new world record of 111 hours of continuous flight, covering 11,600 miles without refueling. The pilots, **RICHARD RUTAN** and **JEANA YEAGER** cruised at speeds of 80-100 miles an hour. The plane designed by Rutan's brother, Burt, is made of plastic, with a 111-foot wing span, weighing less than a ton without fuel.

1987 **JOHN POINDEXTER**, former National Security Advisor, testified at the Iran-Contra hearings that he never told President Reagan about using Iranian arms sales money for the Contras to protect him from political embarrassment.

1992 **POPE JOHN PAUL** underwent colon and gallbladder **SURGERY**. Doctors removed a 3-inch benign tumor.

1994 Professional wrestler and actor **HULK HOGAN** admitted under oath in a NY court room that he had indeed injected and swallowed steroids between the years of 1976 and 1989. He did it, he said, "…to get big."

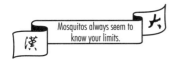

Mosquitos always seem to know your limits.

JULY 16

BIRTHDAYS

- **RAIN PRYOR** Actress. TV's "Head of the Class." Daughter of Richard Pryor. Year/**Age**: 1995/**26** 1996/**27** 1997/**28**

- **PHOEBE CATES** Actress. (NYC) *Gremlin* films and *Drop Dead Fred*. She was in the film *Princess Caraboo* with husband Kevin Kline. Year/**Age**: 1995/**32** 1996/**33** 1997/**34**

- **COREY SCOTT FELDMAN** Actor. Films include: *License to Drive, The Burbs, Dream a Little Dream* and *National Lampoon's Last Resort* with First Brother Roger Clinton (Clinton's first film). He was the voice of Donatello in *Teenage Mutant Ninja Turtles*. Year/**Age**: 1995/**24** 1996/**25** 1997/**26**

- **ORVILLE REDENBACHER** Popcorn tycoon. (Brazil, IN) Graduated from high school in 1924, third in a class of 99. Majored in agronomy and genetics at Purdue University, graduating in 1928. In 1987, his popcorn business passed the $1 billion sales mark. Year/**Age**: 1995/**88** 1996/**89** 1997/**90**

- **GINGER ROGERS** Entertainer. (Born Virginia Katherine McMath in Independence, MO) In 1940, she won an Oscar for *Kitty Foyle* and is remembered for her success as one of Fred Astaire's dancing partners. Year/**Age**: 1995/**84** 1996/**85** 1997/**86**

- **RUBEN BLADES** Actor. Year/**Age**: 1995/**46** 1996/**47** 1997/**48**

- **BARNARD HUGHES** Actor. (Bedford Hills, NY) Was on the soap "The Guiding Light" and won an Emmy for outstanding lead actor in a single appearance as a judge on the "Lou Grant Show." Was in *Prelude to a Kiss*. Year/**Age**: 1995/**80** 1996/**81** 1997/**82**

- **DESMOND DEKKER** Singer. (Born Desmond Dacris in Kingston, Jamaica) He was the pioneer of reggae music. His only hit: "Israelites" in 1969. Year/**Age**: 1995/**53** 1996/**54** 1997/**55**

- **JIMMY JOHNSON** Former Dallas coach. (Port Arthur, TX) He won the college football National championship, in 1987, coaching Miami. He won two straight Super Bowls, 1992-93 Year/**Age**: 1995/**52** 1996/**53** 1997/**54**

- **JIM RATHMANN** Race driver. Year/**Age**: 1995/**67** 1996/**68** 1997/**69**

- **BARRY SANDERS** Football. (Wichita, KS) With the Detroit Lions. He rushed over 1,000 yards in each of his first five seasons.Year/**Age**: 1995/**27** 1996/**28** 1997/**29**

- **STEWART COPELAND** Rock drummer and composer. (McLean, VA) With the trio POLICE from 1977. Biggest hit: "Every Breath You Take" in 1983. Year/**Age**: 1995/**43** 1996/**44** 1997/**45**

- **BARBARA STANWYCK** Actress (1907-1990 – Born Ruby Stevens in Brooklyn, NY) Affectionately known as Missy to her film crews. She brought life to more than 80 characters over her 66-year career. Nominated for best actress 4 times, including *Sorry, Wrong Number* in 1948. She won 3 Emmy awards including her appearance in "The Thornbirds," a TV miniseries. Starred in the TV soap "The Colbys" and on "The Big Valley." Once married to Robert Taylor. (Died 1-21-90)

FACTS FROM THE PAST

1769 The first of the California missions, the **MISSION SAN DIEGO de ALCALA,** was founded by Father Junipero Serra.

1912 **JIM THORPE** was given two medals in the **STOCKHOLM OLYMPICS.** When the King of Sweden gave him the medals, Thorpe said, "Hi, King." He later had the medals taken away.

1918 The Bolsheviks killed the Russian royal family, **NICHOLAS II**, his wife, their four daughters (though the skeletons of two were never found) and their sickly young son. They were taken into a filthy cellar where they were shot, bayoneted, and clubbed to death.

1947 **ROCKY GRAZIANO** won the world middle-weight boxing championship. He scored a TKO over Tony Zale in the 6th round.

1951 J.D. Salinger's **THE CATCHER IN THE RYE** was published.

1957 Marine Major **JOHN GLENN** set a **TRANSCONTINENTAL SPEED RECORD** when he flew a jet from California to New York in 3 hours, 23 minutes and 8 seconds.

1969 **APOLLO ELEVEN**, carrying astronauts **NEIL ARMSTRONG, EDWIN "BUZZ" ALDRIN**, and **MICHAEL COLLINS**, blasted off from Cape Kennedy on the first mission to the surface of the moon.

1972 **SMOKEY ROBINSON** gave his last concert with the Miracles in Washington, DC. Their biggest hit was "Tears of a Clown."

1973 At the **WATERGATE** Hearings in Washington, Alexander Butterfield, presidential appointments secretary, revealed that President Nixon's conversations in the White House had been taped.

1973 **ROGER ENGLISH** of La Jolla, California, stopped dancing the Twist after a record 102 hours 29 minutes.

1979 **SADDAM HUSSEIN** took over as president of Iraq.

1986 Dolly Parton's **DOLLYWOOD AMUSEMENT PARK** opened in Tennessee.

1989 Actress **REBECCA SCHAEFFER**, star of "My Sister Sam," was shot to death at her Los Angeles home by obsessed fan Robert Bardo, who was later sentenced to life in prison. She was 21-years-old.

1992 At a nationally televised news conference, Dallas billionaire, **ROSS PEROT** said he couldn't win in November and his candidacy would throw the election to the House of Representatives. He had decided to **END HIS BID FOR THE PRESIDENCY.**

1994 **LUCIANO PAVAROTTI, PLACIDO DOMINGO, AND JOSE CARRERAS** reunited the night before the World Cup soccer final for a concert that drew a estimated 1.3 billion TV viewers. 56,000 jammed Dodger Staduim in LA, paying $15 to $1,000 a ticket.

JULY 17

Just for fun,
try on a straitjacket.

BIRTHDAYS

- **TERRY "GEEZER" BUTLER** Musician. (England) Member of heavy metal group BLACK SABBATH. Year/Age: 1995/**46** 1996/**47** 1997/**48**

- **NELSON MANDELA** South African President. (South Africa) Had been jailed for 28 years before his release in 1990. He won the Nobel Peace Prize in 1993. Year/Age: 1995/**77** 1996/**78** 1997/**79**

- **DONALD SUTHERLAND** Actor. (Canada) Films: *The Dirty Dozen, M*A*S*H, Klute, 1969, Benefit of the Doubt, Six Degrees of Seperation,* and *Backdraft.* Year/Age: 1995/**61** 1996/**62** 1997/**63**

- **LUCIE ARNAZ** Actress. (Hollywood, CA) The late Lucille Ball's daughter. In "Here's Luci," on stage in *They're Playing Our Song,* and on CBS-TV on "The Lucie Arnaz Show." She's married to actor Lawrence Luckenbill. They named their first baby after Neil Simon, because they met while performing in Simon's plays. She was in *They're Playing Our Song* and he was in *Chapter Two.* Year/Age: 1995/**44** 1996/**45** 1997/**46**

- **PHOEBE SNOW** Singer. (NYC) Biggest hit: "Poetry Man" in 1975. Year/Age: 1995/**43** 1996/**44** 1997/**45**

- **PHYLLIS DILLER** Comedienne. (Born Phyllis Driver in Lima, OH) She was a housewife, discovered at the Purple Onion nightclub. She was the one who said: "Never go to bed mad. Stay up and fight." Year/Age: 1995/**78** 1996/**79** 1997/**80**

- **ART LINKLETTER** Radio/TV host. (Canada) Author of several books, including *Kids Say the Darndest Things.* He started out as a man-on-the-street interviewer in San Francisco. Year/Age: 1995/**83** 1996/**84** 1997/**85**

- **DIAHANN CARROLL** Entertainer. (Born Carol Diahann Johnson in Bronx, NY) Nominated for best actress in 1974 for *Claudine* and appeared on the "Dynasty" soap. She appeared in "Julia" on TV. Year/Age: 1995/**60** 1996/**61** 1997/**62**

- **SPENCER DAVIS** Singer/guitarist. Hit in 1967 called "Gimme Some Lovin'." Year/Age: 1995/**53** 1996/**54** 1997/**55**

- **ROBERT THIGPEN** Baseball. (Tallahassee, FL) Chicago White Sox relief pitcher. Year/Age: 1995/**32** 1996/**33** 1997/**34**

- **PAT McCORMICK** Comedian/writer. He was the comic and the show's head writer on the "Don Rickles Show." Year/Age: 1995/**61** 1996/**62** 1997/**63**

- **DAVID HASSELHOFF** Actor. (Baltimore, MD) He was a waiter in a L.A. resaurant when he was spotted by a casting director. "Knight Rider," "Bay Watch," and soap opera "The Young and the Restless." Year/Age: 1995/**43** 1996/**44** 1997/**45**

- **NICOLETTE LARSON** Singer. (Helena, MT) Former back-up harmony singer with Neil Young, Linda Ronstadt, and the DOOBIE BROTHERS. Her biggest hit: "Lotta Love" in 1978. Year/Age: 1995/**43** 1996/**44** 1997/**45**

- **DON KESSINGER** Baseball. Former Chicago Cub shortstop. Now is a securities broker in Memphis, TN. Year/Age: 1995/**53** 1996/**54** 1997/**55**

- **ROY McMILLAN** Baseball. Played over 2,000 games at shortstop for the Reds, Braves, and Mets from 1951-1966. Year/Age: 1995/**65** 1996/**66** 1997/**67**

- **DARYLE LAMONICA** Football. (Fresno, CA) Former Oakland quarterback. He led the Raiders to two touchdowns in 65 seconds to beat the Jets in the now-famous "Heidi" game. [See Nov. 17, 1968] Year/Age: 1995/**54** 1996/**55** 1997/**56**

- **RED SOVINE** C&W singer. (1918-1980 – Born Woodrow Wilson Sovine in Charleston, WV) Biggest hit: "Giddyup Go" in 1965. (Died 4-14-80.)

- **ERLE STANLEY GARDNER** Author. (1889-1970 – Malden, MA) Author of detective fiction, best remembered for his "Perry Mason" TV series. He also wrote novels under the pseudonym A. A. Fair. (Died 3-11-70.)

- **JAMES CAGNEY** Actor. (1899-1986 – Born James Francis Cagney, Jr., in NYC) Won an Oscar for best actor in *Yankee Doodle Dandy* in 1942, playing George M. Cohan. (Died 3-3-86.)

FACTS FROM THE PAST

1941 JOE DIMAGGIO batted 0-3 in Cleveland, ending his 56-game hitting streak.

1945 President **HARRY S. TRUMAN,** Soviet Premier **JOSEPH STALIN** and British Prime Minister **WINSTON S. CHURCHILL** began meeting at Potsdam in the **FINAL ALLIED SUMMIT OF WORLD WAR II.**

1961 The **SUPREMES'** first record, "Buttered Popcorn," was released and missed the charts by miles. Their first top 40 record came in 1963, "When the Lovelight Starts Shining Through His Eyes" hit #23.

1961 **JOHN CHANCELLOR REPLACED DAVE GARROWAY** on the "Today Show," but admitted he hated the job and wanted out after the first day. He was replaced by Hugh Downs on Sept. 10, 1962.

1967 In a most unusual pairing, the **JIMI HENDRIX EXPERIENCE** opened the show for the **MONKEES** at Forest Hills Stadium in New York.

1986 White House Chief of Staff **DONALD REGAN DREW CRITICISM** after he was identified as the official who had suggested in an interview that American women would not be prepared to "Give up all their jewelry" if the U.S. were to impose economic sanctions against South Africa.

1990 At Fenway Park in Boston, the **MINNESOTA TWINS** became the first team in major league history to pull off **TWO TRIPLE PLAYS IN ONE GAME.**

1992 Democratic candidates, **BILL CLINTON, AL GORE,** and their wives began a bus caravan from New York to St. Louis.

1994 After **120 MINUTES** of scoreless soccer, Brazil celebrated a 3-2 victory when Italy drove a penalty kick over the net.

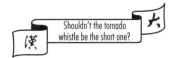

Shouldn't the tornado whistle be the short one?

JULY 18

BIRTHDAYS

- **"SCREAMIN" JAY HAWKINS** Rocker. (Cleveland, OH) Singer, pianist. LP in 1982, *Frenzy*. Year/**Age**: 1995/**66** 1996/**67** 1997/**68**

- **RED SKELTON** Entertainer. (Born Richard Bernard Skelton in Vincennes, IN) He had a record on the charts in 1969: "The Pledge of Allegiance" which he performed on the "Red Skelton Hour" on Jan. 14, 1969. He received such a tremendous response that Columbia Records released it as a single. He is also an artist who specializes in painting clowns. Year/**Age**: 1995/**82** 1996/**83** 1997/**84**

- **DION DiMUCCI** Singer. (Bronx, NY) Biggest hit: "Runaround Sue" in 1961. When he was with the BELMONTS, their biggest record: "Teenager in Love." Year/**Age**: 1995/**56** 1996/**57** 1997/**58**

- **HARRIET NELSON** Actress. (Born Harriet Hilliard in Des Moines, IA) Mother of Rick and David Nelson. Big band singer before the "Ozzie & Harriet" TV series. Her husband, Ozzie, died of cancer in 1975, and son Rick died in a plane crash on New Year's Eve, 1985. Her twin grandsons are now making it big. Year/**Age**: 1995/**81** 1996/**82** 1997/**83**

- **CALVIN PEETE** Pro golfer. (Detroit, MI) Year/**Age**: 1995/**52** 1996/**53** 1997/**54**

- **JOHN GLENN, JR.** Former astronaut/politician. (Cambridge, OH) First American to orbit the Earth, on Feb. 20, 1962. When he was a marine major, he appeared on the TV quiz show "Name That Tune" and won $15,000. Year/**Age**: 1995/**74** 1996/**75** 1997/**76**

- **JOE TORRE** Former baseball star/Atlanta Braves manager. (Brooklyn, NY) Year/**Age**: 1995/**55** 1996/**56** 1997/**57**

- **RICKY SKAGGS** C&W singer. (Cordell, KY) Bluegrass guitarist. One of country's big singers and instrumentalists, he appeared on TV with FLATT AND SCRUGGS when he was just 7 years old. In 1977 he took a job with the EMMYLOU HARRIS BAND. One of his biggest hits: "Crying My Heart Out Over You" in 1982. Year/**Age**: 1995/**41** 1996/**42** 1997/**43**

- **HUME CRONYN** Actor. (Canada) Appeared in many movies, and he and his wife, Jessica Tandy, appeared together on stage in such plays as *The Four Poster*, *Fox Fire,* and *The Gin Game*. Films: *Cocoon, The Return*. Year/**Age**: 1995/**84** 1996/**85** 1997/**86**

- **MARTHA REEVES** Singer. (Detroit, MI) Leader of one of soul music's most popular groups, MARTHA & THE VANDELLAS, whose biggest hit was "Dancing in the Street" in 1964. She was a secretary at Motown Records. One day when singer Mary Wells didn't show up for a session, Martha stood in and that was the start of her career. Year/**Age**: 1995/**54** 1996/**55** 1997/**56**

- **DICK BUTTON** Olympic skating champion. (Englewood, NJ) Now commentator. Year/**Age**: 1995/**66** 1996/**67** 1997/**68**

- **AUDREY LANDERS** Actress. (Philadelphia, PA) Soap opera actress in "Somerset" and "Dallas." Her sister is Judy. Year/**Age**: 1995/**36** 1996/**37** 1997/**38**

- **ELIZABETH McGOVERN** Actress (Evanston, IL) *The Bedroom Window*. Year/**Age**: 1995/**34** 1996/**35** 1997/**36**

- **JAMES BROLIN** Actor. (Born James Bruderlin in Los Angeles, CA) He appeared with Robert Young in "Marcus Welby, M.D." beginning in 1973, and on the "Hotel" TV series. TV's "Angel Falls." Year/**Age**: 1995/**55** 1996/**56** 1997/**57**

FACTS FROM THE PAST

1877   Thomas Edison had the inspiration for the **PHONOGRAPH**. He shouted "Mary had a little lamb" into the phonograph and heard the machine recite it back.

1927   **TY COBB** got the 4,000th hit of his career.

1938   **PILOT DOUGLAS** "Wrong Way" **CORRIGAN** arrived in Ireland 28 hours after leaving New York, after saying he was flying to Los Angeles, CA. Corrigan claims he misread his compass, but he had been refused a permit to fly across the Atlantic.

1940   The Democratic National Convention in Chicago nominated **PRESIDENT FRANKLIN D. ROOSEVELT** for an unprecedented third term in office.

1947   President **HARRY S. TRUMAN** signed the **PRESIDENTIAL SUCCESSION ACT**, which designated the Speaker of the House next in line to the Presidency after the Vice President, followed by the Senate President Pro Tem, then by members of the cabinet.

1951   **JERSEY JOE WALCOTT** won the **HEAVYWEIGHT BOXING** title at age 37. He knocked out Ezzard Charles in the 7th round at Forbes Field in Pittsburgh, becoming the oldest man ever to win the world's title.

1953   18-year-old **ELVIS PRESLEY** recorded "My Happiness" as a gift for his mother. The so-called vanity disc was his first recording.

1960   **HANK BALLARD** and the Midnighters released their record, **"THE TWIST."** Hank wrote the song, the B-side of his top ten "Finger Poppin' Time." The tune did nothing until Chubby Checker recorded it later that year.

1966   **BOBBY FULLER** of the Bobby Fuller Four group was found dead in his car in Los Angeles. The cause of death was not proven. Their biggest hit, "I Fought the Law" in 1966, was written by **SONNY CURTIS**, once a member of Buddy Holly and the Crickets.

1969   A car driven by Senator **EDWARD KENNEDY** plunged off a bridge at Chappaquiddick, Martha's Vineyard, MA. He escaped, but the drowned body of his companion, **MARY JO KOPECHNE**, was found in the car. He didn't report the accident until 10 hours later.

1976   **NADIA COMANECI**, [co-ma-neech'] a 14-year-old gymnast from Romania, scored the **FIRST PERFECT 10 IN OLYMPIC HISTORY**, and went on to win three gold medals. She fled her native country and came to America in 1989.

1994   **ALL STAR ALBERT BELLE** of the Cleveland Indians was found guilty of corking his bat and suspended for 10 days.

JULY 19

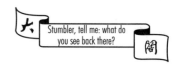

Stumbler, tell me: what do you see back there?

BIRTHDAYS

- **SHEILA BEGA** Singer. (NYC) SWEET SENSATION. Biggest hit: "If Wishes Came True" in 1990. Year/Age: 1995/**26** 1996/**27** 1997/**28**
- **LEROY WOLFGRAMM** Musician. (Minneapolis, MN) The JETS. Biggest hit: "You Got It All." Year/Age: 1995/**29** 1996/**30** 1997/**31**
- **NATALYA BESSMERTNOVA** Ballerina. (Moscow) Prima ballerina with the famous Bolshoi Ballet. Year/Age: 1995/**54** 1996/**55** 1997/**56**
- **VIKKI CARR** Singer. (Born Florencia Bisenta de Casellas Martinez Cardona in El Paso, TX) Biggest hit: "It Must Be Him" in 1967. Year/Age: 1995/**54** 1996/**55** 1997/**56**
- **ILIE NASTASE** Tennis star. (Bucharest, Romania) He was the first player from an Iron Curtain country to win the U.S. Open. Year/Age: 1995/**49** 1996/**50** 1997/**51**
- **GEORGE HAMILTON IV** Singer. (Winston-Salem, NC) Biggest hit: "A Rose & a Baby Ruth" in 1956. He also recorded a song with Paul Anka and Johnny Nash: "The Teen Commandments," sort of a Boy Scout oath for teens in 1958. George was the first C&W artist to perform behind the Iron Curtain. Year/Age: 1995/**58** 1996/**59** 1997/**60**
- **DENNIS COLE** Actor. "Young & the Restless" soap. Year/Age: 1995/**52** 1996/**53** 1997/**54**
- **BRIAN HAROLD MAY** Guitarist. (England) With QUEEN. Biggest hits: "Crazy Little Thing Called Love" and "Another One Bites the Dust." Year/Age: 1995/**48** 1996/**49** 1997/**50**
- **HELEN GALLAGHER** Actress. (NYC) "Ryan's Hope." Year/Age: 1995/**69** 1996/**70** 1997/**71**

- **PAT HINGLE** Actor. (Denver, CO) Films include: *On the Waterfront*, *Splendor in the Grass*, *Hang 'Em High*, *The Grifters*, and *Batman Returns*. Year/Age: 1995/**71** 1996/**72** 1997/**73**
- **PETER BARTON** Actor. Year/Age: 1995/**36** 1996/**37** 1997/**38**
- **PHILIP AGEE** Former CIA agent. (Tacoma Park, FL) Wrote *Inside the Company: CIA Diary* in 1975. Year/Age: 1995/**60** 1996/**61** 1997/**62**
- **GEORGE McGOVERN** Politician. (Avon, SD) Democratic senator from South Dakota. He lost the presidential election in a landslide to Richard Nixon in 1972. Year/Age: 1995/**73** 1996/**74** 1997/**75**
- **RICHARD JORDAN** Actor. (1937-1993, NYC) TV's "Captains and The Kings" and "The Bunker," about the last days of Adolf Hitler. Also the film *Hunt For Red October*. (Died 8-30-93.)
- **ALLAN GORRIE** Singer/guitarist. (Scotland) He founded the AVERAGE WHITE BAND. Their biggest hit: "Pick Up the Pieces" in 1974. Year/Age: 1995/**46** 1996/**47** 1997/**48**
- **KEITH GODCHAUX** Keyboardist. (1948-1980) GRATEFUL DEAD. (Died in car accident on 7-23-80.)
- **SAMUEL COLT** Inventor. (1814-1862) Invented the six-shooter and other firearms. (Died 1-10-1862.)
- **A. J. (ARCHIBALD JOHN) CRONIN** Author. (1896-1981 – Scotland) *The Citadel* and *Keys of the Kingdom*. (Died 1-6-81.)
- **CHARLES HORACE MAYO** Surgeon. (1865-1939 – Rochester, MN) One of the founders of the Mayo Clinic and Mayo Foundation. (Died 5-26-39.)

FACTS FROM THE PAST

1553 15-year-old **LADY JANE GREY WAS DEPOSED AS QUEEN OF ENGLAND** after claiming the crown for 9 days. King Henry the VIII's daughter Mary was proclaimed Queen.

1848 A pioneer **WOMEN'S RIGHTS CONVENTION** called by Elizabeth Cady Stanton and Lucretia Mott convened in Seneca Falls, NY. **BLOOMERS WERE INTRODUCED** at the convention for the first time, named in honor of Mrs. Amelia Bloomer.

1914 The **BOSTON BRAVES** were in last place in baseball's National League, but soon became known as **"THE MIRACLE TEAM"** because they started winning almost every game they played and ended up winning both the pennant and the World Series.

1940 The two-finger **V-FOR-VICTORY** hand signal was introduced by Sir Winston Churchill. Today that signal stands for "peace."

1962 50-year-old José Meiffret of France set a **WORLD BICYCLE SPEED RECORD** in Freiburg, West Germany. He pedalled at a top speed of 127.243 miles per hour.

1966 **FRANK SINATRA** married **MIA FARROW**. He was 51 and she was 21.

1969 **JOHN FAIRFAX** of Britain arrived at Hollywood Beach, FL, after **ROWING 180 DAYS ACROSS THE ATLANTIC OCEAN ALONE.** He shoved off from the Canary Islands in his 24-foot unsinkable rowboat, the *Britannia*, traveling 4,000 miles in all, becoming the first person to attempt such a feat.

1980 **DAVID BOWIE** made his stage debut in Denver in the starring role of *The Elephant Man*.

1986 **CAROLINE KENNEDY**, 28, and **EDWIN SCHLOSSBERG**, 42, were married at Hyannis Port, MA. Her uncle, Senator Edward "Ted" Kennedy, gave her away and her mother, Jackie Onassis, cried during the ceremony.

1989 112 people were killed when a **UNITED AIR LINES DC-10 WHICH HAD SUFFERED TOTAL HYDRAULIC FAILURE CRASHED** while attempting to make an emergency landing at Sioux City, Iowa. Another 184 people survived. The pilot, **ALFRED HAYES**, and his crew were credited with saving the lives of the survivors.

1990 Former Cincinnati Reds manager **PETE ROSE** was sentenced to 5 months in prison, 3 months in a halfway house, plus 1,000 hours community service and a $50,000 fine for cheating on his taxes.

Kids are a joy when they're someone else's.

JULY 20

BIRTHDAYS

- **"DINO" ESPOSITO** Singer. Hits include: "I Like It" and "Romeo." Year/Age: 1995/**32** 1996/**33** 1997/**34**

- **CHARLIE KORSMO** Actor. "Kid" in *Dick Tracy.* Year/Age: 1995/**17** 1996/**18** 1997/**19**

- **SIR EDMUND HILLARY** Explorer. New Zealand explorer and first man to conquer Mt. Everest, on May 29, 1953. Mt. Everest is the highest mountain in the world: 29,028 feet high. Year/Age: 1995/**76** 1996/**77** 1997/**78**

- **PETE HAMILTON** Racecar driver. Year/Age: 1995/**53** 1996/**54** 1997/**55**

- **DIANA RIGG** Actress. (England) "The Avengers" TV series, in the '60s. *In Trust* and *Follies* in London in 1987. Hosts "Mystery" on PBS. Year/Age: 1995/**57** 1996/**58** 1997/**59**

- **T. G. SHEPPARD** C&W singer. (Born Bill Browder in Humboldt, TN) Got his stage name from his neighbor's barking German shepherd. Elvis Presley was his friend and gave T. G. his touring bus. Biggest hit: "I Loved 'Em Every One" in 1981. Year/Age: 1995/**51** 1996/**52** 1997/**53**

- **CHUCK DALY** Basketball. (St. Mary's, PA) The New Jersey Nets coach. Year/Age: 1995/**62** 1996/**63** 1997/**64**

- **DONNA DIXON** Actress. Played Sonny on "Bosom Buddies" sitcom. She is the wife of actor Dan Aykroyd. Year/Age: 1995/**38** 1996/**39** 1997/**40**

- **TONY OLIVA** Baseball outfielder. (Born Pedro Oliva in Cuba) American League batting champion three times. Year/Age: 1995/**55** 1996/**56** 1997/**57**

- **CARLOS SANTANA** Musician. (Mexico) One of the original members of the group SANTANA, appeared at the 3-day music-fest, Woodstock. Biggest hits: "Black Magic Woman" in 1970. "Evil Ways" was a big record for him and Buddy Miles in 1972. Also rhythm guitarist with PAPERLACE. Their biggest hit: "The Night Chicago Died." Year/Age: 1995/**48** 1996/**49** 1997/**50**

- **HENSON CARGIL** C&W singer. (Oklahoma City, OK) Biggest hit: "Skip a Rope" in 1968. Year/Age: 1995/**60** 1996/**61** 1997/**62**

- **JOHN LODGE** Singer/guitarist. (England) With MOODY BLUES. Biggest hit: "Nights in White Satin" in 1972. Year/Age: 1995/**52** 1996/**53** 1997/**54**

- **KIM CARNES** Singer. (Hollywood, CA) She and Kenny Rogers were members of the NEW CHRISTY MINSTRELS. Her biggest hit, double Grammy winner in 1981 for song and record of the year: "Bette Davis Eyes," co-written by Jackie DeShannon. She and Kenny recorded "Don't Fall in Love with a Dreamer." Year/Age: 1995/**49** 1996/**50** 1997/**51**

- **NATALIE WOOD** Actress. (1938-1981 – Born Natasha Gurdin in San Francisco, CA) Nominated for 3 Academy Awards; married to Robert Wagner twice. While taking a break from filming *Brainstorm*, she drowned in the waters off Catalina Island where she and her husband, Robert Wagner, and actor Christopher Walken were spending the weekend aboard their 60-ft. yacht (11-29-81).

FACTS FROM THE PAST

1881   Sioux Indian leader **SITTING BULL** surrendered to federal troops. He had been a fugitive since the Battle of Little Big Horn.

1940   *Billboard* began publishing the **FIRST RECORD SALES CHART**. The top song was "I'll Never Smile Again" by Frank Sinatra and the Tommy Dorsey Orchestra. Frank was a newcomer to the biz at the time.

1944   **PRESIDENT FRANKLIN D. ROOSEVELT** was nominated for an unprecedented fourth term of office at the Democratic National Convention in Chicago.

1944   A bomb was placed under **ADOLPH HITLER**'s conference table by a top officer of the Whehrmacht in an attempt to overthrow the government. An oak support shielded Hitler, who survived. Thousands of officers were arrested, tortured and executed.

1965   **BOB DYLAN'S** single "Like a Rolling Stone" was released. It was Dylan's first major hit.

1968   Jane Asher announced on the BBC's #1 TV Show "Dee Time" that her engagement to **PAUL McCARTNEY** was off. McCartney, who was watching the program at a friend's house, was said to have been taken by surprise.

1969   APOLLO XI astronauts **NEIL ARMSTRONG** and **EDWIN "Buzz" ALDRIN** became the **FIRST MEN TO SET FOOT ON THE MOON.** Armstrong stepped on the lunar surface at 10:56 p.m. EDT and proclaimed, "That's one small step for man, one giant leap for mankind." He spent time on the trip to the moon thinking about what he would say. He said he really wanted to say, "One small step for *a* man," but goofed. The Apollo XI astronauts collected 48.5 pounds of "moon rocks" and stayed on the moon for over 21 hours. There were anxious moments when computers failed in the last minute of descent. Armstrong's pulse registered 160 beats a minute.

1974   **HANK AARON** broke **TY COBB**'s record, appearing in his 3,034 career game. Aaron was 40 years old, playing his 20th major league baseball season.

1984   **VANESSA WILLIAMS, MISS AMERICA** 1984, was asked by pageant officials to resign because of nude photographs of her that turned up in *Penthouse* magazine. (Williams relinquished her title three days later.)

1988   Iranian leader Ayatollah Khomeini accepted a truce with Iraq, but said it was like drinking poison.

1993   Deputy White House counsel **VINCE FOSTER** committed suicide. He was a former partner of Hillary Clinton at Rose Law Firm. Documents related to Whitewater were taken from his office and turned over to Clinton's lawyers.

1994   O.J. Simpson put up a **$500,000 REWARD** for the capture of his wife's "real killer." Simpson's legal advisers activated a toll-free number for leads.

JULY 21

Could you communicate with a deaf person?

BIRTHDAYS

- **JON LOVITZ** Actor. (Tarzana, CA) "Saturday Night Live." He played a baseball scout in the film *A League of Their Own*. He was also in the film *City Slickers: The Legend of Culy's Gold*. He's the voice of TVs "The Critic." Year/**Age:** 1995/**38** 1996/**39** 1997/**40**

- **ROBIN WILLIAMS** Actor. (Chicago, IL) Started as a street mime and then attended Julliard. Became famous as TV's favorite space alien, Mork from Ork, in "Mork & Mindy." The alien "Mork" first appeared in Richie Cunningham's dream on "Happy Days." Appeared in films: *Popeye, Good Morning Vietnam, Dead Poet's Society, Awakenings, The Fisher King, Toys, Mrs. Doubtfire*, and was the genie's voice in *Aladdin*. Year/**Age:** 1995/**43** 1996/**44** 1997/**45**

- **ISAAC STERN** Concert violinist. (Russia) He started playing when he was 11 years old. Responsible for the *Fiddler on the Roof* movie soundtrack. Year/**Age:** 1995/**75** 1996/**76** 1997/**77**

- **DON KNOTTS** Comedian. (Morgantown, WV) Won a couple of Emmys for his appearance as Deputy Barney Fife on the "Andy Griffith Show" and also played landlord Ralph Furley on "Three's Company." Year/**Age:** 1995/**71** 1996/**72** 1997/**73**

- **KAY STARR** Singer. (Born Kay Starks in Dougherty, OK) Her biggest hit was "Rock 'n Roll Waltz" in 1956. Year/**Age:** 1995/**73** 1996/**74** 1997/**75**

- **JANET RENO** Attorney General. Year/**Age:** 1995/**57** 1996/**58** 1997/**59**

- **NORMAN JEWISON** Movie director. (Canada) His films include: *The Russians Are Coming, Fiddler on the Roof, Jesus Christ Superstar,* and *Moonstruck*. Year/**Age:** 1995/**69** 1996/**70** 1997/**71**

- **GENE LITTLER** Pro golfer. (LaJolla, CA) Year/**Age:** 1995/**65** 1996/**66** 1997/**67**

- **LES ASPIN** Politician. (Milwaukee, WI) Former Democratic Congressman from Wisconsin and chairman of the House Armed Services. Former Clinton Defense Secretary. He resigned 12/15/93. Year/**Age:** 1995/**57** 1996/**58** 1997/**59**

- **CAT STEVENS** Singer/songwriter. (Born Steven Georgiou in England) A couple of years ago, he gave up all his worldly goods, guitars, etc., and joined the Moslem religion and changed his name to Yusuf Islam. Year/**Age:** 1995/**47** 1996/**48** 1997/**49**

- **EDWARD HERRMANN** Actor. (Washington, DC) He played President Franklin D. Roosevelt on TV. Also, he appeared in *Big Business*. Year/**Age:** 1995/**52** 1996/**53** 1997/**54**

- **ERNEST HEMINGWAY** Author. (1899-1961 – Oak Park, IL) Winner of both the Pulitzer and Nobel prizes. His mother dressed him in girls' clothes until he was 12 years old. He didn't have many kind things to say about mom in later life. He wanted to be macho. A critic one time said he had fake hair on his chest, so Hemingway beat him up. He shot himself to death (on 7-2-61).

FACTS FROM THE PAST

1861 The first major battle of the Civil War between the Union, led by Gen. McDowell, and the Confederate troops, led by Gen. Beauregard, took place about 35 miles southwest of Washington, DC. The **BATTLE OF BULL RUN CREEK** was won by the Confederates with the help of Gen. Thomas Jackson, who held the Union like a "stone wall" and Gen. E. Kirby Smith who turned the tide against the Union forces. 60,000 men fought for 10 hours, during which time many of the socialities, dressed in their finest, came to picnic and watch the encounter.

1873 Outlaw **JESSE JAMES** held up the Rock Island Express near Adair, IA, in his **FIRST TRAIN ROBBERY**. A loss of $6,000 was reported, but a gang insider said it was $65,000. The train company didn't want the public to know they carried that much money.

1884 During one of the dirtiest presidential campaigns in U.S. history, the *Buffalo Evening Telegraph* revealed that **GROVER CLEVELAND** had an illegitimate 10-year-old son. His opponent, James Blaine, involved in shady business practices, lost the election by a close vote. Cleveland was the only president to be elected to two non-consecutive terms.

1925 The so-called **MONKEY TRIAL** ended in Dayton, TN, with school teacher **JOHN T. SCOPES** found guilty and fined $100 for teaching Darwin's theory of evolution. The conviction was later overturned. Shown in the play and film: *Inherit The Wind*.

1969 Apollo XI astronauts **NEIL ARMSTRONG** and **EDWIN** "Buzz" **ALDRIN** blasted off from the moon after $21\frac{1}{2}$ hours on the surface and returned to the command module, piloted by **MICHAEL COLLINS**. The astronauts left behind the lunar module's lower section, on which is mounted a plaque reading, "Here men from the planet Earth first set foot upon the moon, July 1969 A.D. We came in peace for all mankind."

1971 **CAROLE KING** received a gold LP for *Tapestry*. The album was #1 in the U.S. for 15 weeks, and was on the LP chart for 292 weeks.

1972 Comedian **GEORGE CARLIN** discovered that the "7 WORDS" that performers are prohibited from saying on TV are also taboo on stage. The comedian was arrested and charged with disorderly conduct and profanity at Summerfest in Milwaukee, WI.

1975 **WILLIE NELSON** made his debut on the album charts with *Red Headed Stranger* containing the hit, "Blue Eyes Crying in the Rain."

1988 Massachusetts Governor **MICHAEL DUKAKIS** accepted the Democratic presidential nomination at the party's convention in Atlanta, declaring, "This election isn't about idealogy, it's about competence."

1992 Murder charges against **DR. JACK KEVORKIAN** were dropped in Pontiac, MI. He was accused of helping four chronically ill women to commit suicide with a machine that dispensed lethal gas and drugs.

1994 Florida's 12-member Citrus Commission said they would not renew talk show host **RUSH LIMBAUGH'S $1-MILLION CONTRACT**. They denied cancelling the contract was due to criticism of Limbaugh's conservative views.

Remember to cap your pen this time.

JULY 22

BIRTHDAYS

• **ORSON BEAN** Actor/comedian. (Born Dallas F. Burroughs in Burlington, VT) Regular panelist on "To Tell the Truth." He was a guest on the "Tonight Show" Feb. 11, 1960, when Jack Paar walked off the show in dispute with NBC and left Hugh Downs to finish the program. Appears as the shopkeeper Loren Bray on *Doctor Quinn, Medicine Woman.* He is married to actress Alley Mills of "The Wonder Years." He wrote a book for cats, *25 Ways to Cook a Mouse.* Year/**Age:** 1995/**67** 1996/**68** 1997/**69**

• **ALEX TREBEK** Game-show host. (Canada) Game shows, "Concentration" and "Jeopardy." Year/**Age:** 1995/**55** 1996/**56** 1997/**57**

• **ROBERT J. DOLE** Senator. (Russell, KS) Senate Minority Leader, husband of Elizabeth Dole, former Secretary of Transportation and now head of the American Red Cross. Year/**Age:** 1995/**72** 1996/**73** 1997/**74**

• **BOBBY SHERMAN** Singer. (Santa Monica, CA) Biggest hit: "Little Woman" in 1969. He played Jeremy Bolt on the "Here Comes the Brides" TV series. TV's "Shindig" in 1966. He is now a certified Emergency Medical Technician and founder of a paramedics group, TAC-5. Year/**Age:** 1995/**50** 1996/**51** 1997/**52**

• **TERENCE STAMP** Actor. (England) In *The Collector, Far From the Madding Crowd, Superman, The Real McCoy,* and *Wall Street.* Year/**Age:** 1995/**56** 1996/**57** 1997/**58**

• **DANNY GLOVER** Actor. (San Francisco, CA) Films *The Color Purple, Angels in the Outfield, The Saint of Fort Washington, Bopha!, Places in the Heart,* and the *Lethal Weapon* movies. Year/**Age:** 1995/**48** 1996/**49** 1997/**50**

• **DON HENLEY** Singer/drummer. (Linden, TX) Was Linda Ronstadt's drummer and later co-founded the EAGLES. Their biggest hit: "Hotel California" in 1977. He went solo in 1981 with hits: "Dirty Laundry" and "Boys of Summer." He reunited for the Eagles "Hell Freezes Over Tour" in 1994. Year/**Age:** 1995/**48** 1996/**49** 1997/**50**

• **ALVIN ROBERTSON** Milwaukee Bucks Guard. Year/**Age:** 1995/**33** 1996/**34** 1997/**35**

• **OSCAR de la RENTA** Fashion designer. (Dominican Republic) A long-time fashion leader, beginning in the '60s. Year/**Age:** 1995/**63** 1996/**64** 1997/**65**

• **ALBERT BROOKS** Actor. (Born Albert Einstein in Los Angeles, CA) Made a couple of comedy albums and was on the "Golddiggers Show," summer replacement for Dean Martin. In films *The Scout, I'll Do Anything, Defending Your Life* and *Broadcast News.* Year/**Age:** 1995/**48** 1996/**49** 1997/**50**

• **RICK DAVIES** Singer/keyboardist. (England) Formed the British rock quintet SUPERTRAMP in 1970. Their biggest hit: "The Logical Song" in 1979. Year/**Age:** 1995/**51** 1996/**52** 1997/**53**

• **SPARKY LYLE** Baseball relief pitcher.. Yankee hurler, winner of the Cy Young Award as best pitcher in the American League in 1977. Year/**Age:** 1995/**51** 1996/**52** 1997/**53**

• **WILLEM DAFOE** Actor. (Appleton, WI) *Mississippi Burning, Last Temptation of Christ, Born on the Fourth of July, Wild at Heart, Light Sleeper, Clear and Present Danger,* and *Flight of the Intruder.* Nominated for an Oscar for *Platoon.* Year/**Age:** 1995/**40** 1996/**41** 1997/**42**

FACTS FROM THE PAST

1284 The **PIED PIPER OF HAMELIN**, Germany, angry because city fathers decided not to pay him for ridding the town of rats, took up his pipes and tootled the town's tots into the side of the mountain, never to be seen again.

1867 After spending five years in Thailand teaching the royal children, **ANNA LEONOWENS** sailed home to England. Her memoirs inspired **THE KING AND I.**

1893 Katharine Lee bates, a professor at Wellesley College, wrote the original version of her poem "**AMERICA THE BEAUTIFUL**" in Colorado Springs, inspired by the view from Pikes Peak.

1922 Actress **GRETA GARBO** was fired as a hat sales clerk at Bergstrom's department store.

1933 American aviator Wiley Post completed the **FIRST SOLO FLIGHT AROUND THE WORLD** in 7 days, 18³/₄ hours.

1934 Public Enemy #1, **JOHN DILLINGER,** was shot to death by federal agents outside Chicago's Biograph Theater, where he had just seen the movie *Manhattan Melodrama* starring Clark Gable and Myrna Loy. He was betrayed by the "lady in red." The story was front-page news every day for a month.

1975 More than a century after his death, the House of Representatives and the Senate voted to restore the American citzenship of **CONFEDERATE GENERAL ROBERT E. LEE.**

1982 The **BIGGEST MASS WEDDING** in history was performed by the **REVEREND SUN MYUNG MOON.** He married 2,200 couples at Madison Square Garden in New York City.

1984 **ISAMA AGMED MOMTAZA** of Egypt set the men's world record for swimming the English Channel both ways non stop in 21 hours and 37 minutes. Irene van der Laan of the Netherlands holds the all-time record of 18 hours and 15 minutes.

1989 **THE YOUNGEST PILOT TO FLY AROUND THE WORLD:** 11-year old **TONY ALIENGENA** returned to John Wayne Airport in Orange County, California, nearly seven weeks and 21,567 miles after taking off in a Cessna 210 Centurion.

1991 **JEFFREY DAHMER WAS ARRESTED.** Milwaukee police found 11 skulls, 3 headless torsos sealed in a vat and other body parts in his apartment. Dahmer confessed to killing as many as 17 men, placing some of the remains in a filing cabinet, refrigerator, freezer and kettles. Others he dumped into the trash bin.

1994 O.J. Simpson pleaded "absolutely **100% NOT GUILTY**" to murder charges.

JULY 23
Astrological Sign of Leo

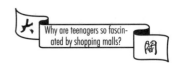

Why are teenagers so fascin-ated by shopping malls?

BIRTHDAYS

- **SAM WATTERS** Singer. (Oklahoma City, OK) Biggest hit with COLOR ME BAD: "I Wanna Sex You Up," from film, *New Jack City*. Year/**Age**: 1995/**25** 1996/**26** 1997/**27**

- **MARTIN GORE** Musician. (England) With DEPECHE MODE, 1990 hit: "Enjoy The Silence." Year/**Age**: 1995/**34** 1996/**35** 1997/**36**

- **TIM KELLET** Musician. (England) SIMPLY RED. Biggest hit: "Holding Back the Years" in 1986. Year/**Age**: 1995/**31** 1996/**32** 1997/**33**

- **GLORIA DeHAVEN** Actress. (Los Angeles, CA) Appeared in films since 1940, mostly light musicals such as *Three Little Words* and *Two Girls & a Sailor*. Year/**Age**: 1995/**70** 1996/**71** 1997/**72**

- **DAVID ESSEX** Singer/actor. (Born David Cook in England) Portrayed Christ in the London production of *Godspell*. opposite Jeremy Irons as Judas. He was also in the London production of *Evita*. Biggest hit: "Rock On" in 1973. Film *That'll Be the Day* with Ringo Starr. Year/**Age**: 1995/**48** 1996/**49** 1997/**50**

- **BELINDA MONTGOMERY** Actress. (Canada) TV series "A Man from Atlantis" and "Doogie Howser, M.D." Year/**Age**: 1995/**45** 1996/**46** 1997/**47**

- **ANTHONY M. KENNEDY** Supreme Court Justice. (Sacramento, CA) A Reagan nominee, sworn in February 18, 1988. He's a moderate conservative. Year/**Age**: 1995/**59** 1996/**60** 1997/**61**

- **PEEWEE REESE** Baseball. (Born Harold Reese in Ekron, KY) One of the all-time great shortstops, with the Dodgers. Year/**Age**: 1995/**76** 1996/**77** 1997/**78**

- **DINO DANELLI** Singer. (NYC) With the RASCALS. Biggest hit: "People Gotta Be Free" in 1968. Year/**Age**: 1995/**50** 1996/**51** 1997/**52**

- **GARY PAYTON** Basketball. (Oakland, CA) With the Seattle Supersonics. Year/**Age**: 1995/**27** 1996/**28** 1997/**29**

- **CALVERT DeFOREST** Actor. (Brooklyn, NY) Larry "Bud" Melman on "Late Night with Letterman." NBC would not allow him to take the Melman name to the CBS Letterman show. Year/**Age**: 1995/**74** 1996/**75** 1997/**76**

- **DON DRYSDALE** Hall of Famer and former Dodger. (1936-1993 – Van Nuys, CA) Cy Young Award winner in 1962. The sidearm pitcher, in 1968, had a string of 58 shutout innings. He wrote the book *Once a Bum, Always a Dodger*. His wife was UCLA Hall of Fame basketball player Ann Meyers. (Died 7-3-93.)

- **CLEVE DUNCAN** Singer. (Los Angeles, CA) He was the lead singer of The PENGUINS. Biggest hit: "Earth Angel" in 1955. Year/**Age**: 1995/**60** 1996/**61** 1997/**62**

- **EDIE McGLURGE** Actress. TV's "WKRP" and "The Hogan Family." Year/**Age**: 1995/**44** 1996/**45** 1997/**46**

- **WOODY HARRELSON** Actor. (Born Woodrow Tracy Harrelson in Midland, TX) Emmy supporting actor on "Cheers." He played Woody Boyd, his real nickname. Starred in the films *White Men Can't Jump*, *The Cowboy Way*, *Indecent Proposal*, and *Natural Born Killers*. Year/**Age**: 1995/**34** 1996/**35** 1997/**36**

- **CORAL BROWNE** Actress. (1913-1991 – Australia) Films included *Auntie Mame* and *The Killing of Sister George*. She was married to Vincent Price. (Died 5-29-91.)

- **BERT CONVY** Actor/singer. (1933-1991 – St. Louis, MO) Host of "Win, Lose or Draw." Appeared on the TV soap "Love of Life" and hosted the game show "Tattletales." In the mid-'50s, Convy was a singer in a rock 'n' roll band called the CHEERS. Biggest hit: "Black Leather Jacket and Motorcycle Boots." (Died 7-15-91.)

FACTS FROM THE PAST

1846 Philosopher/poet **HENRY DAVID THOREAU** protested the Mexican War and slavery and in showing his displeasure, he was jailed for refusing to pay a one-dollar poll tax.

1962 British record producer **JOE MEEK** was inspired when the communications satellite, Telstar, made the first transatlantic TV transmission. He wrote an instrumental called "Telstar," recorded by a group he formed, the TORNADOES. It was number one for three weeks in '62. (Meek committed suicide 2-3-67.)

1979 **AYATOLLAH KHOMEINI BANNED ROCK 'N ROLL MUSIC** following the revolution in Iran. He wanted to eliminate signs of Western civilization. Today a black market provides American music.

1982 Actor **VIC MORROW** and two child actors were killed when a helicopter crashed on top of them while they were filming a Vietnam War scene for *Twilight Zone: The Movie*. Director John Landis and four others were acquitted of charges in the deaths.

1984 **VANESSA WILLIAMS** became the **FIRST MISS AMERICA TO GIVE UP THE TITLE,** after it was discovered she had posed in explicit nude photos for *Penthouse* magazine. Suzette Charles succeeded her.

1986 His Royal Highness **PRINCE ANDREW** married **SARAH FERGUSON** in Westminster Abbey. The marriage fell apart in 1992.

1989 **RINGO STARR** kicked off his first tour since the breakup of the BEATLES. Starr's backup band at the concert in Dallas included Joe Walsh, Billy Preston, and Clarence Clemons.

1992 A federal judge blocked **BASEBALL COMMISSIONER, FAY VINCENT**'s order to move the Chicago Cubs to the National League West. The Cubs sued Vincent after he revealed his plans to realign the NL in 1993.

1993 **JAMES JORDAN**, father of basketball great Michael Jordan, was murdered along US 74 near Interstate 95 near Bennettsville, SC.

1994 **AMY OSMOND** was crowned Junior Miss. She is daughter of singing brother Wayne Osmond. Her aunt is Marie and her uncle in Donny. She played Marie in the TV movie "Side by Side."

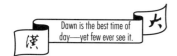

Dawn is the best time of day—yet few ever see it.

JULY 24

BIRTHDAYS

• **KEVIN BUTLER** Kicker. (Savannah, GA) Chicago Bear football star. Year/**Age**: 1995/**33** 1996/**34** 1997/**35**

• **ROBBIE GREY** Singer. (England) MODERN ENGLISH. Year/**Age**: 1995/**38** 1996/**39** 1997/**40**

• **LYNDA CARTER** Actress. (Phoenix, AZ) "Wonder Woman" and some TV movies. Married to a Washington DC, banker. Year/**Age**: 1995/**44** 1996/**45** 1997/**46**

• **ROBERT HAYS** Actor. (Bethesda, MD) *Airplane, Starman,* and *FM.* Year/**Age**: 1995/**48** 1996/**49** 1997/**50**

• **PAT OLIPHANT** Political cartoonist. Year/**Age**: 1995/**60** 1996/**61** 1997/**62**

• **RUTH BUZZI** Comedienne. (Westerly, RI) She received 3 Emmy nominations for the "Laugh-In" TV series. Ruth made her film debut in 1977 in *Freaky Friday.* She funs the thrift show "Finders Keepers" and appears on "Sesame Street." Year/**Age**: 1995/**59** 1996/**60** 1997/**61**

• **CHRIS SARANDON** Actor. (Berkley, WV) Was Tom Halverson on "The Guiding Light" soap. In the films *The Nightmare Before Christmas, Deadly Temptress, The Deer Hunter,* and *The Princess Bride.* Year/**Age**: 1995/**53** 1996/**54** 1997/**55**

• **PAM TILLIS** C & W. Her father is country star Mel Tillis. Year/**Age**: 1995/**36** 1996/**37** 1997/**38**

• **KADEEM HARDISON** Actor. Is Dwayne Wayne on "Different World." Year/**Age**: 1995/**30** 1996/**31** 1997/**32**

• **MICHAEL RICHARDS** Actor. TV's "Seinfeld." Film *Unstrung Heros.* Year/**Age**: 1995/**46** 1996/**47** 1997/**48**

• **BARBARA JEAN LOVE** Singer. (Los Angeles, CA) With the FRIENDS OF DISTINCTION. Their biggest hit: "Grazing in the Grass." Year/**Age**: 1995/**54** 1996/**55** 1997/**56**

• **KARL MALONE** Basketball. (Mt. Sinai, LA) Utah Jazz star. Year/**Age**: 1995/**32** 1996/**33** 1997/**34**

• **JOE BARRY CARROLL** Basketball. (Pine Bluff, AR) Played college ball at North Carolina. Year/**Age**: 1995/**37** 1996/**38** 1997/**39**

• **BARRY BONDS** Baseball. San Francisco Giants star outfielder. In three out of four years he was named National League MVP Year/**Age**: 1995/**31** 1996/**32** 1997/**33**

• **AMELIA EARHART** Aviatrix. (1898-1937 – Atchison, KS) First woman to fly across the Atlantic Ocean and was lost on a flight from New Guinea to Howland Island in the Pacific Ocean on July 2, 1937.

• **SIMON BOLIVAR** [see-mone' bo-lee-var'] Latin American patriot. (1783-1830 – Caracas, Venezuela) Raised by a slave after his parents died. He fought 300 battles in 15 years. Known as the "Great Liberator," he helped win independence from Spain for Venezuela, Colombia, Ecuador, Bolivia and Peru. Most of these South American countries celebrate today as a major holiday to honor Bolivar. He had 200 mistresses. Soldiers called him "old irontail." He died of syphilis. (Died 12-17-1830.)

• **ALEXANDRE DUMAS** French playwright/novelist. (1802-1870) Wrote more than 1,200 volumes, including *The Count of Monte Cristo* and *The Three Musketeers.* He may have fathered over 500 children. (Died 12-5-1870.)

FACTS FROM THE PAST

1847 BRIGHAM YOUNG and his Mormon followers entered Salt Lake Valley in Utah. Today, in Utah it's a state holiday.

1945 While the Potsdam Conference was going on, the Secretary of State wanted to get the **RESULTS OF THE A-BOMB TEST** to President Truman. The telegram read in code: "Doctor most enthusiastic that the little boy is as husky as his big brother." The clerk who typed the telegram thought that the 78 year old had just become a dad.

1952 HIGH NOON starring **GARY COOPER** and **GRACE KELLY** opened at theaters across the country. Cooper usually got over $250,000 per picture, but was so impressed with this film that he accepted $60,000 plus a percentage. He made the right decision. Cooper won an Oscar as best actor and ended up with a lot more money.

1959 During a visit to the Soviet Union, Vice President **RICHARD NIXON** got into a well-publicized debate with Soviet leader **NIKITA KHRUSHCHEV** on the merits of Communism versus Capitalism. The confrontation took place in a model kitchen at a U.S. Exhibition and became known as the **KITCHEN DEBATE.**

1967 French President **CHARLES DE GAULLE** caused controversy during a visit to Montreal, Canada, when he declared, *"Vive le Quebec libre!"* ("Long live free Quebec!")

1976 ELTON JOHN finally got a hit in England: "Don't Go Breaking My Heart" with Kiki Dee.

1979 LITTLE RICHARD spoke to a revival meeting in San Francisco about the dangers of rock 'n' roll.

1983 A 2-run homer by **GEORGE BRETT** of the Kansas City Royals was disallowed after New York Yankees manager **BILLY MARTIN** pointed out there was too much pine tar on Brett's bat. (However, American League president Lee MacPhail reinstated the home run.)

1987 91-year-old **HULDA CROOKS** from California became the oldest woman to climb Japan's highest peak, Mount Fuji.

1990 Parents of suicidal teens charged **JUDAS PRIEST** with implanting harmful, subliminal messages within their Stained Glass LP. They admitted that backwards messages had been put into the song "Love Bites" from a different LP but denied any other tampering with the music.

1993 Three people were injured outside Dodger Stadium in Los Angeles when New York Mets' **VINCE COLEMAN** threw an explosive device the equivalent of a quarter stick of dynamite into the crowd.

1994 GOLPHER PATTY SHEEHAN won the U.S. Women's Open for the second time in three years.

JULY 25

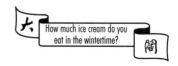

BIRTHDAYS

- **BARBARA HARRIS** Actress. (Evanston, IL) *Dirty Rotten Scoundrels.* Nominated for an Oscar in 1972 for *Who is Harry Kellerman and Why is He Saying Those Terrible Things About Me?* Year/**Age:** 1995/**60** 1996/**61** 1997/**62**

- **ESTELLE GETTY** Actress. (NYC) She played Sophia, the mother, on the "Golden Girls" and "Golden Palace" sitcoms. Also "Young at Heart Body Conditioning" workout tape. Year/**Age:** 1995/**72** 1996/**73** 1997/**74**

- **IMAN** Model/actress. Married to singer David Bowie. In film "Exit to Eden." Year/**Age:** 1995/**39** 1996/**40** 1997/**41**

- **VERDINE WHITE** Bass guitarist. Biggest hit with EARTH, WIND & FIRE: "Shining Star" in 1975. Year/**Age:** 1995/**44** 1996/**45** 1997/**46**

- **WALTER PAYTON** Football star. (Columbia, MS) In 1977, the Chicago Bears running back ran for a game record 275 yards against the Minnesota Vikings. He is the NFL's all-time rusher in 13 seasons, 16,726 yards, 110 touchdowns. Nicknamed "Sweetness," Year/**Age:** 1995/**41** 1996/**42** 1997/**43**

- **WHITEY LOCKMAN** Baseball. 1950s NY Giants first baseman. Year/**Age:** 1995/**69** 1996/**70** 1997/**71**

- **LOUISE BROWN** First test-tube baby. (Oldham, England) First documented birth of a baby conceived outside the body of a woman. She was delivered by Dr. Patrick Steptoe. Year/**Age:** 1995/**17** 1996/**18** 1997/**19**

- **MARK CLARKE** Musician. (England) URIAH HEEP. The name comes from a character in the Dickens book *Great Expectations.* Year/**Age:** 1995/**45** 1996/**46** 1997/**47**

- **JIM McCARTY** Drummer. (England) With the YARDBIRDS. Biggest hit: "For Your Love" in 1965. Two former members of that group were Jeff Beck and Eric Clapton. Jim later formed the group RENAISSANCE. Year/**Age:** 1995/**52** 1996/**53** 1997/**54**

- **GLYNN "SCOTTY" WOLFE**, World's most married man. The Blyth, CA, man married 27 times, is marrying Linda Lou Essex, the world's most married woman (22 times). Year/**Age:** 1995/**87** 1996/**88** 1997/**89**

- **STEVE PODBORSKI** Skier. (Canada) He is a former World Cup Ski Champion. Year/**Age:** 1995/**38** 1996/**39** 1997/**40**

- **ROGER CLINTON** Entertainer. (Hot Springs, AK) Brother of President Bill Clinton. Year/**Age:** 1995/**38** 1996/**39** 1997/**40**

- **NATE THURMOND** Basketball. (Akron, OH) Former 6'11" San Francisco center. Year/**Age:** 1995/**54** 1996/**55** 1997/**56**

- **WALTER BRENNAN** Actor/entertainer. (1894-1974 – Lynn, MA) Biggest hit: "Old River" in 1962. He was Grandpa on TV's "Real McCoys." He won three Oscars. (Died 9-22-74.)

- **JACK GILFORD** Actor. (1907-1990 – NYC) He received an Oscar nomination for *Save the Tiger.* He had movie roles in *Cocoon* and *Cocoon II, A Funny Thing Happened on the Way to the Forum, Enter Laughing,* and *Catch-22.* He was a longtime pitchman on TV for Cracker Jack snacks. (Died 6-4-90.)

- **JERRY PARIS** Actor. (1925-1986 – San Francisco, CA) Played the neighbor on the "Dick Van Dyke Show" and later directed "Happy Days" and the movie *Police Academy.* (Died 4-2-86.)

FACTS FROM THE PAST

1866 ULYSSES S. GRANT was named General of the Army, the first officer to hold that rank.

1871 WILLIAM SCHNEIDER of Davenport, IA, invented the MERRY-GO-ROUND.

1909 LOUIS BLERIOT from France accomplished the WORLD'S FIRST INTERNATIONAL OVERSEAS AIRPLANE FLIGHT, from France to England, flying a 28-hp monoplane with a 23-foot wingspan.

1946 DEAN MARTIN and JERRY LEWIS began their 10-year partnership as a nightclub song and comedy act, playing Club 500 in Atlantic City. They split up in 1956.

1956 BILL BUCHANAN and "DICKIE" GOODMAN put parts of popular records together to make the FIRST NOVELTY RECORD, "Flying Saucer." It became a hit on this day.

1965 BOB DYLAN was booed off the stage at the Newport Folk Festival when he started playing an electric guitar. He was backed by the Paul Butterfield Blues Band.

1969 NEIL YOUNG joined CROSBY, STILLS, AND NASH for the first time at a concert at New York's Fillmore East. Neil had been a member of BUFFALO SPRINGFIELD with Stephen Stills.

1979 PRESIDENT CARTER issued a letter absolving DR. SAMUEL MUDD, the physician who had treated the broken leg on John Wilkes Booth, of any role in the assassination of President Abraham Lincoln.

1984 Soviet Cosmonaut SVETLANA SAVITSKAYA [sah-veets'-kah-yah] became the FIRST WOMAN TO WALK IN SPACE as she carried out more than three hours of experiments outside the orbiting space station *Salyut Seven.*

1987 Secretary of Commerce MALCOLM BALDRIDGE was thrown from his horse and killed while practicing for a steer-roping contest in California.

1990 ROSEANNE BARR sang the National Anthem in San Diego, spit, then scratched herself. The crowd booed and she later apologized.

1992 The Summer Olympics got underway when ANTONIO REBOLLO, a bronze medalist archer from Madrid, SHOT A FLAMING ARROW into the cauldron touching off the flame that would burn during the 15-day games. He fired 700 arrows in practice, only missing two times. The 25th Olympics theme, "Friends for Life," was written by ANDREW LLOYD WEBBER.

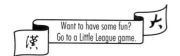

Want to have some fun?
Go to a Little League game.

JULY 26

BIRTHDAYS

- **DOBIE GRAY** Singer. (Born Leonard Ainsworth in Brookshire, TX) Biggest hit: "Drift Away" in 1973. Year/**Age**: 1995/**53** 1996/**54** 1997/**55**

- **BOBBY HEBB** Singer. (Nashville, TN) He was on the Grand Ole Opera at age 12. Biggest hit: "Sunny" in 1966. Year/**Age**: 1995/**54** 1996/**55** 1997/**56**

- **HELEN MIRREN** Actress. (London, England) Detective Jan Tennison on PBS "Prime Suspect" films include *Age of Consent, Hawk,* and *White Nights.* Year/**Age**: 1995/**49** 1996/**50** 1997/**51**

- **MICK JAGGER** Rock star. (Born Michael Philip Jagger in Dartford, England) With the ROLLING STONES. Their biggest hit: "Honky Tonk Woman" in 1969. Films include *Freejack, Ned Kelly,* and *Performance.* Married to Bianca Rose Perez Moreno de Macias and later to Jerry Hall. Year/**Age**: 1995/**52** 1996/**53** 1997/**54**

- **STANLEY KUBRICK** Movie writer/producer/director. (NYC) Best known for: *2001: A Space Odyssey, Dr. Strangelove, The Shining,* and a Vietnam film, *Full Metal Jacket.* Year/**Age**: 1995/**67** 1996/**68** 1997/**69**

- **BLAKE EDWARDS** Producer/director. (Born William Blake McEdwards in Tulsa, OK) Directed *Breakfast at Tiffany's, Days of Wine and Roses,* and *Switch.* He is married to actress Julie Andrews. Year/**Age**: 1995/**73** 1996/**74** 1997/**75**

- **KEEDY** Singer. (Born Kelly Keedy in Abilene, TX) Biggest hit: "Save Some Love" in 1991. She married her songwriter, Greg Gerard, leader of the group GERARD. Year/**Age**: 1995/**30** 1996/**31** 1997/**32**

- **SUSAN GEORGE** Actress. (England) She was in the musical version of "Dr. Jekyl & Mr. Hyde" on TV. With Dustin Hoffman in *Straw Dogs.* Year/**Age**: 1995/**45** 1996/**46** 1997/**47**

- **VITAS GERULAITIS** Tennis champ. (Brooklyn, NY) His first major victory was in 1975 when he won the Wimbledon doubles with Sandy Mayer. Year/**Age**: 1995/**41** 1996/**42** 1997/**42**

- **RICK MARTIN** Canadian hockey player. Year/**Age**: 1995/**44** 1996/**45** 1997/**46**

- **BOB LILLY** Former Dallas football star. Played 14 seasons for the Cowboys without missing a game. Year/**Age**: 1995/**56** 1996/**57** 1997/**58**

- **JASON ROBARDS, JR.** Actor. (Chicago, IL) Son of Jason Robards, Sr. He has appeared on the stage and in movies and portrayed Richard Nixon in a TV mini-series. In 1975 he and Don "Miami Vice" Johnson appeared in a science fiction film, *A Boy and His Dog.* Also in the films *The Adventures of Huck Finn* and *Philadelphia.* Year/**Age**: 1995/**73** 1996/**74** 1997/**75**

- **HOYT WILHELM** Former pitcher. Famous for his knuckleball. Year/**Age**: 1995/**72** 1996/**73** 1997/**74**

- **JENNIFER ASHE** Actress. "As the World Turns" TV soap star. Year/**Age**: 1995/**29** 1996/**30** 1997/**31**

- **KIEL MARTIN** Actor. (1944-1990) TV's "Hill Street Blues" and "L.A. Law." (Died 12-28-90.)

- **VIVIAN VANCE** Actress. (1912-1979 – Cherryville, KS) She played Lucy's TV pal, Ethel Mertz, on sitcom "I Love Lucy." (Died 8-17-79.)

- **GRACIE ALLEN** Actress. (1906-1964 – Born Gracie Ethel Cecile Rosalie Allen in San Francisco, CA) She and George Burns were married from 1926 until her death. (Died 8-27-64.)

- **GEORGE BERNARD SHAW** Playwright/essayist. (1856-1950 – Dublin, Ireland) The Broadway musical and movie *My Fair Lady* was adapted from his play *Pygmalion.* (Died 11-2-50.)

FACTS FROM THE PAST

1775 **BENJAMIN FRANKLIN** became the first American Postmaster General, at a salary of $1,000 a year.

1908 U.S. Attorney General **CHARLES J. BONAPARTE** issued an order creating an investigative agency within **THE DEPARTMENT OF JUSTICE** that was a forerunner of the FBI.

1945 **WINSTON CHURCHILL** resigned as Britain's prime minister after his conservatives were soundly defeated in elections by the Labor Party. Clement Atlee became the new prime minister.

1947 President **HARRY S. TRUMAN** signed the National Security Act, which created the Department of Defense, the National Security Council and the Joint Chiefs of Staff. The first Secretary of Defense was **JAMES FORRESTAL** and the first Chairman of the Joint Chiefs was General **OMAR BRADLEY**.

1953 The **"26TH OF JULY MOVEMENT"** was started by **FIDEL CASTRO**, a revolution against Cuba's dictator Batista.

1958 **QUEEN ELIZABETH II** proclaimed her son, **CHARLES**, to be **PRINCE OF WALES.**

1964 Teamsters President **JIMMY HOFFA** and six others were convicted of fraud and conspiracy in the handling of a union pension fund.

1969 **SHARON ADAMS** became the first woman to sail solo across the Pacific Ocean. The 31-year-old homemaker sailed her 31-foot ketch 5,618 miles from Yokohama, Japan, to San Diego in 74 days.

1986 **REVEREND LAWRENCE MARTIN JENCO**, kidnapped in Beirut, was released.

1989 **MARK WELLMAN**, a 29-year-old paraplegic, reached the summit of El Capitan in Yosemite National Park after hauling himself up the granite cliff six inches at a time over nine days.

1991 Paul Reubens, also known by his screen name of **PEE-WEE HERMAN**, was arrested inside a movie theater in Sarasota, FL. The arresting officer said that Reubens exposed himself twice while watching the movie *Tiger Shark.* CBS pulled reruns of "Pee-Wee's Playhouse" off the air.

JULY 27

BIRTHDAYS

- **NORMAN LEAR** TV producer. (New Haven, CT) His many television hits include "All in the Family." He created the Archie Bunker character like his own father, whom Lear says was a bigot. "Good Times," "Maude," "Sanford & Son," and "Powers That Be." Year/**Age:** 1995/**73** 1996/**74** 1997/**75**
- **PEGGY FLEMING** Olympic star. (San Jose, CA) 1968 Olympic gold medal champion. Has starred in the "Ice Follies" and her own TV specials. Her married name is Jenkins. Year/**Age:** 1995/**47** 1996/**48** 1997/**49**
- **BETTY THOMAS** Actress. (St. Louis, MO) Played Lucy Bates on "Hill Street Blues" and in *The Seventh Sign*. Year/**Age:** 1995/**47** 1996/**48** 1997/**49**
- **MAUREEN McGOVERN** Singer. (Youngstown, OH) Biggest record: "The Morning After" from the film *Poseidon Adventure*. She starred on Broadway in *The Pirates of Penzance*. Year/**Age:** 1995/**46** 1996/**47** 1997/**48**
- **BOBBIE GENTRY** Singer. (Born Roberta Lee Streeter in Chickasaw County, MS) Biggest hit: "Ode to Billy Joe" in 1967. Married Jim Stafford in 1978. Year/**Age:** 1995/**53** 1996/**54** 1997/**55**

- **NICK REYNOLDS** Guitarist/singer. (San Francisco, CA) KINGSTON TRIO. Biggest hit: "Tom Dooley" in 1958. Year/**Age:** 1995/**62** 1996/**63** 1997/**64**
- **RICHARD DENNIS RALSTON** Tennis player. (Bakersfield, CA) He was a Wimbledon finalist and ranked in the top ten in the world several times. Year/**Age:** 1995/**53** 1996/**54** 1997/**55**
- **MICHAEL VAUGHN** Guitarist. (Sheffeld, England) PAPERLACE. Biggest hit: "The Night Chicago Died." Year/**Age:** 1995/**45** 1996/**46** 1997/**47**
- **JERRY VAN DYKE** Actor. (Danville, IL) TV's "Coach" and brother of actor Dick Van Dyke. Turned down the lead role of Gilligan for TV's "Gilligan's Island." Year/**Age:** 1995/**64** 1996/**65** 1997/**66**
- **LEO DUROCHER** Former major league baseball manager. (1905-1991 – West Springfield, MA) He gained fame as the aggressive manager of the Dodgers and Giants in the '40s and '50s. (Died 10-7-91.)
- **KEENAN WYNN** Actor. (1916-1986 – Born Francis Xavier Aloysius Keenan Wynn in NYC) *Dr. Strangelove*, *Nashville*, *Finian's Rainbow*, and *Kiss Me Kate*. (Died 10-14-86.)

FACTS FROM THE PAST

1586   **TOBACCO** was first brought to England from Virginia by Sir Walter Raleigh.

1866   **CYRUS FIELD** succeeded in laying the **FIRST UNDERWATER TELEGRAPH CABLE** between North America and Europe.

1890   **VINCENT VAN GOGH** shot himself, dying two days later from the self-inflicted bullet wound. He was only 37 years old. During his lifetime, he sold only one of his paintings. Now they sell for top prices.

1909   **ORVILLE WRIGHT** tested the Army's first airplane, flying himself and a passenger for 1 hour and 12 minutes, a record at this time.

1910   **CHARLES ROLLS**, co-founder of the Rolls-Royce Company, died at age 33. He was at the controls of a Wright Brothers biplane, flying at 50 feet when something snapped and he crashed. He was the first to fly both ways across the English Channel and the first to die in a plane crash in England.

1921   **INSULIN WAS DISCOVERED** by Canadian **DOCTOR FREDERICK BANTING** and his assistant, Charles Best, at the University of Toronto Medical School. A 14-year-old boy became the first human to receive insulin a few months later. They came up with the discovery while experimenting on a dog. Millions of lives of diabetics have been saved by this discovery.

1940   The **FIRST "BUGS BUNNY" CARTOON**, "A wild hare," appeared. He was patterned after Clark Gable. His creator's inspiration came from the scene in *It Happened One Night* where Gable, munching a carrot, is sitting on a stoop with Claudette Colbert.

1960   **RICHARD NIXON** was nominated for president at the Republican National Convention in Chicago, IL.

1965   **PRESIDENT JOHNSON** signed the bill requiring cigarette packages and ads to display the U.S. Surgeon General's warning against the effect of smoking.

1974   The House Judiciary Committee voted 27 to 11 to recommend the impeachment of President **RICHARD NIXON** on charges that he had personally engaged in a course of conduct designed to obstruct justice in the **WATERGATE** case.

1976   **JOHN LENNON** was granted permanent residency in the United States.

1976   Air Force veteran **RAY BRENNAN** became the first person to die of so-called Legionnaire's Disease, following an outbreak at a Philadelphia hotel where an American Legion convention had taken place.

1984   The movie **PURPLE RAIN**, starring Prince, opened. It is supposedly autobiographical.

1984   **PETE ROSE** exceeded Ty Cobb's total for the most singles in a career with number 3,503.

1987   **JOHN DEMJANJUK**, retired Ohio autoworker, known as **"IVAN THE TERRIBLE,"** a sadistic Nazi guard, said at his trial in Jerusalem, "I am not the hangman you're after."

1993   The Boston Celtics star, **REGGIE LEWIS**, died at age 27, after collapsing on a Brandeis University basketball court during practice.

1994   **VANESSA WILLIAMS**, who lost her Miss America crown in 1984 after nude photos of her were published, replaced Chita Rivera in the Broadway musical *Kiss of the Spider Woman*.

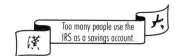

Too many people use the IRS as a savings account.

JULY 28

BIRTHDAYS

• **RICK WRIGHT** Keyboardist. (England) PINK FLOYD. Biggest hit: "Another Brick on the Wall" in 1980. Comeback album in 1994 was titled "The Division Bell." Year/Age: 1995/**50** 1996/**51** 1997/**52**

• **ELIZABETH BERKLEY** Actress. Year/Age: 1995/**23** 1996/**24** 1997/**25**

• **SIMON KIRKE** Drummer. Hits with FREE "All Right Now" in 1970 and with BAD COMPANY "Can't Get Enough" in 1974. Year/Age: 1995/**47** 1996/**48** 1997/**49**

• **FRANKIE YANKOVIC** Accordionist. (Davis, WV) Member of the Polka Hall of Fame, and the first polka artist to win a Grammy. Hits: "Just Because" and "Blue Skirt Waltz," with his band, the YANKS. Year/Age: 1995/**80** 1996/**81** 1997/**82**

• **JIM DAVIS** Cartoonist. (Marion, IN) He created "Garfield the Cat." Year/Age: 1995/**50** 1996/**51** 1997/**52**

• **SALLY STRUTHERS** Actress. (Portland, OR) Best known for Gloria, Archie Bunker's daughter on TV's "All in the Family," for which she won a couple of Emmys. She appeared in the film *Five Easy Pieces* and on Broadway in *The Odd Couple*. She promotes the Christian Children's Fund. Year/Age: 1995/**47** 1996/**48** 1997/**49**

• **GEORGIA ENGEL** Actress. (Washington, DC) Played Georgette Franklin, Ted Baxter's naive girlfriend and later wife on "The Mary Tyler Moore Show." On the TV series "Coach." Year/Age: 1995/**47** 1996/**48** 1997/**49**

• **DARRYL HICKMAN** Actor. (Los Angeles, CA) Played Dobie Gillis's brother Davey. His brother Dwayne played Dobie. Later he was executive producer of daytime soap "Love of Life." Year/Age: 1995/**64** 1996/**65** 1997/**66**

• **JACQUES d' AMBOISE** Ballet dancer. (Dedham, MA) Year/Age: 1995/**61** 1996/**62** 1997/**63**

• **PETER DOYLE** Singer. (Australia) With the NEW SEEKERS. Their biggest hit: "I'd Like to Teach the World to Sing" in 1971. Year/Age: 1995/**45** 1996/**46** 1997/**47**

• **LINDA KELSEY** Actress. (Minneapolis, MN) Played reporter Billie Newman on the "Lou Grant" TV series. Also in "Day by Day." Year/Age: 1995/**49** 1996/**50** 1997/**51**

• **BILL BRADLEY** Senator. (Crystal City, MO) Former NY Knicks basketball star. (D-NJ) Year/Age: 1995/**52** 1996/**53** 1997/**54**

• **VIDA BLUE** Baseball pitcher (Mansfield, LA) He won the Cy Young Award and was the league's MVP in 1971, pitching for the Oakland A's. Year/Age: 1995/**46** 1996/**47** 1997/**48**

• **JACKIE KENNEDY ONASSIS** Presidential wife. (1930-1994, Born Jacqueline Lee Bouvier in Southampton, NY) Widow of the 35th U.S. President John F. Kennedy and, later, Greek shipping magnate Aristotle Onassis. She was an editor at Doubleday Publishing Co. She died of cancer 5-19-94.

• **MIKE BLOOMFIELD** Guitarist. (1944-1981 – Chicago, IL) Played electric guitar on Bob Dylan's "Like a Rolling Stone." He died of a drug overdose on 2-15-81.

• **RUDY VALLEE** Entertainer. (1901-1986 – Born Hubert Prior Vallee in Island Pond, VT) His biggest hit was "My Time is Your Time" in 1929 which became his theme song. He grew up in Westbrook, ME, where his father was a pharmacist. He was the recipient of the first singing telegram, "Happy Birthday," on his 32nd birthday in 1933. He died while watching the Statue of Liberty Centennial ceremonies on TV. (Died 7-3-86.)

FACTS FROM THE PAST

1540 King Henry VIII's chief minister, **THOMAS CROMWELL**, was executed.

1866 A telegraph on the newly completed Atlantic cable brought greetings from **QUEEN VICTORIA** to **PRESIDENT ANDREW JOHNSON**.

1943 President **FRANKLIN D. ROOSEVELT** announced the end of coffee rationing in the U.S.

1952 The TV show "Up to Paar," starring **JACK PAAR,** made its debut, but it lasted only 3 months. Later, Jack hosted "The Tonight Show."

1957 **JERRY LEE LEWIS** appeared on "The Steve Allen Show." It was his TV debut.

1970 **MICK JAGGER** played the title role of the film *Ned Kelly*.

1973 The **BIGGEST ROCK FESTIVAL IN HISTORY** took place in New York state at Watkins Glen when 600,000 people watched the **GRATEFUL DEAD, THE ALLMAN BROTHERS,** and **THE BAND.**

1982 **PRESIDENT REAGAN** warned, in his 12th news conference as president, that America's recovery from the recession would be slow, and he expressed guarded optimism about a peaceful resolution to the crisis in Lebanon.

1986 NASA released a transcript of a restored intercom recording from the doomed space shuttle *CHALLENGER*. Pilot **MICHAEL SMITH** could be heard saying, "Uh-oh!" just as the spacecraft disintegrated.

1987 **ATTORNEY GENERAL EDWIN MEESE** told the Iran-Contra committee that President Reagan was "quite surprised" when he told him about diversion of Iran arms-sales profits for use by the Contra rebels.

1987 Lawyers for the **BEATLES** sued Nike and Capitol Records to halt the use of "Revolution" in shoe commercials.

1991 **DENNIS MARTINEZ** pitched the 15th perfect game in major league history as the Montreal Expos beat the L.A. Dodgers 2-0.

1993 New York Mets pitcher **ANTHONY YOUNG** won his first game after a 27-game losing streak. He broke an 82-year-old major league record on his 24th loss.

JULY 29

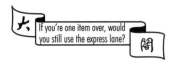
If you're one item over, would you still use the express lane?

BIRTHDAYS

- **PATTI SCIALFA** Back-up singer. (Deal, NJ) She is Mrs. Bruce Springsteen. Year/Age: 1995/**39** 1996/**40** 1997/**41**
- **MARILYN QUAYLE** Former Second Lady. (Indianapolis, IN) Wife of U.S. Vice-President Dan Quayle. Graduate of Indiana School of Law. Year/Age: 1995/**46** 1996/**47** 1997/**48**
- **ALEXANDRA PAUL** Actress. On TV's "Baywatch." Year/Age: 1995/**32** 1996/**33** 1997/**34**
- **PETER JENNINGS** ABC news anchor. (Toronto, Canada) Was an anchorman back in 1967, but gave it up to become a reporter. Then, after 15 years, he returned to the high-paying top job. His first job was hosting the Canadian equivalent of "American Bandstand" in 1959. Year/Age: 1995/**57** 1996/**58** 1997/**59**
- **LLOYD BOCHNER** Actor. (Canada) He was Cecil Colby on TV's "Dynasty." Year/Age: 1995/**71** 1996/**72** 1997/**73**
- **ROBERT HORTON** Actor. (Los Angeles, CA) Appeared on the TV series "Wagon Train" and in *A Man Called Shenandoah.* Year/Age: 1995/**71** 1996/**72** 1997/**73**
- **ROBERT FULLER** Actor. He was in the TV series "Laramie" "Wagon Train," and "Emergency." He was in the film *Maveric.* Year/Age: 1995/**61** 1996/**62** 1997/**63**
- **DAVID WARNER** Actor. (England) Played Blifil in *Tom Jones.* Also in *Time Bandits, Star Trek V: The Final Frontier,* and *Star Trek VI.* Year/Age: 1995/**54** 1996/**55** 1997/**56**
- **NEAL DOUGHTY** Keyboardist. (Champaign, IL) With REO SPEEDWAGON. Their biggest hits: "Keep On Loving You" and "Can't Fight This Feeling." Year/Age: 1995/**48** 1996/**49** 1997/**50**
- **ELIZABETH DOLE** (Born Elizabeth Hanford in Salsbury, NC) Former Secretary of Labor and married to Senate Majority Leader Robert Dole. Now President of the American Red Cross. Year/Age: 1995/**59** 1996/**60** 1997/**61**

- **DON CARTER** Bowler. (Miami, FL) In the '50s and '60s he was named Pro Bowler of the Year six times. Year/Age: 1995/**65** 1996/**66** 1997/**67**
- **GEDDY LEE** Singer/bassist. (Toronto, Canada) With the rock trio RUSH. Year/Age: 1995/**42** 1996/**43** 1997/**44**
- **KEN BURNS** Filmmaker. He specializes in documentaries. The "Civil War" series. Year/Age: 1995/**42** 1996/**43** 1997/**44**
- **NANCY KASSEBAUM** Senator. (Topeka, KS) (R/KS) She's the daughter of FDR opposition Alf Landon. Year/Age: 1995/**63** 1996/**64** 1997/**65**
- **RODNEY ALLEN RIPPY** Actor. Jack-in-the-Box hamburger chain TV commercials. Year/Age: 1995/**27** 1996/**28** 1997/**29**
- **WIL WHEATON** Actor. *Stand By Me* and *Toy Soldiers.* TV series "Star Trek: The Next Generation." Year/Age: 1995/**23** 1996/**24** 1997/**25**
- **HENRY "HOMER" HAYNES** Entertainer. (1917-1971 – Knoxville, TN) Of the country comedy duo HOMER AND JETHRO. Biggest hit: "The Battle of Kookamonga" in 1959, a parody of "The Battle of New Orleans."
- **RICHARD EGAN** Actor. (1923-1987 – San Francisco, CA) Rugged leading man in action and Western movies. His more than 30 films included *Love Me Tender, The Hunters,* and *A Summer Place.* (Died 7-2-87.)
- **BOOTH TARKINGTON** American novelist. (1869-1946 – Indianapolis, IN) Author and Pulitzer Prize winner for *Alice Adams* and *The Magnificent Ambersons.* (Died 5-16-46.)
- **BENITO MUSSOLINI** Italian dictator. (1883-1945) He governed Italy first as prime minister and, later, as absolute dictator. The military defeat of Italy in WWII was his downfall. Attempting to flee in disguise to Switzerland, he and his mistress were shot and killed by Italian partisans near Lake Como. (Died 4-28-45.)

FACTS FROM THE PAST

1771 An after-dinner drink, **AQUA TUFANIA**, was banned in England. It contained poison. It had arsenic in it for husbands who wanted to kill their wives, business enemies, etc. A woman in France, **MADAME TUFANIA**, started making the poison cocktails for royalty to use on their rivals. The drink was responsible for many deaths. Tufania was publicly strangled for her crimes.

1957 **JACK PAAR** made his debut as host of the **"THE TONIGHT SHOW."**

1958 President **DWIGHT EISENHOWER** signed the act creating the **NATIONAL AERONAUTICS & SPACE ADMINISTRATION** (NASA). Eisenhower called the legislation a "historic step" that would further equip the U.S. "for leadership in the Space Age."

1966 **BOB DYLAN** was injured in a "Triumph 55" motorcycle accident that kept him off the stage for months. It happened near his home in Woodstock, NY.

1968 **POPE PAUL VI** reaffirmed the Roman Catholic Church's stand against artificial birth control in his encyclical "Humanae Vitae."

1972 **"SCREAMING" LORD SUTCH** was arrested in London after a publicity stunt. He and four nude women jumped off a bus on Downing Street in front of the prime minister's residence attempting to promote a concert.

1981 Britain's **PRINCE CHARLES** married **LADY DIANA SPENCER** at St. Paul's Cathedral in London, with 2,500 guests attending, and watched by 700 million viewers around the world. They separated in 1993.

1982 **PRESIDENT REAGAN** reached an agreement with Indian prime minister **INDIRA GANDHI** under which India could obtain uranium fuel from France for a U.S.-built nuclear power plant near Bombay.

1991 **JACK NICKLAUS** joined **ARNOLD PALMER** as the only men to win the U.S. Amateur, the U.S. Open and the U.S. Sr. Open.

1994 A man with a shotgun killed abortion doctor **JOHN BRITTON** and his volunteer escort James Barrett and wounded Britton's wife June Barrett as they arrived at an abortion clinic in Pensacola, FL.

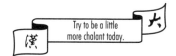

Try to be a little more chalant today.

JULY 30

BIRTHDAYS

- **PAUL ANKA** Singer/composer. (Canada) Hits: "Lonely Boy" in 1959, "You're Having My Baby" in 1974 with Odia Coates. Feminists wanted the song changed to "Having Our Baby." He wrote the "Tonight Show Theme," the lyrics for "My Way" and "She's a Lady." Paul was a millionaire by the time he was 19. Year/**Age**: 1995/**54** 1996/**55** 1997/**56**

- **ED "KOOKIE" BYRNES** Actor. (Los Angeles, CA) Gained fame on TV's "77 Sunset Strip." He was always combing his hair, which led to hit song: "Kookie, Kookie, Lend me Your Comb," recorded with Connie Stevens. He holds the record for appearing on more magazine covers in one month than any other person: 20 in October 1960. Year/**Age**: 1995/**62** 1996/**63** 1997/**64**

- **LARRY FISHBURNE** Actor. Won a tony in 1992 for "Two Trains Running." Year/**Age**: 1995/**34** 1996/**35** 1997/**36**

- **PETER BOGDANOVICH** Movie producer. (Kingston, NY) *Texasville*. Directed *The Last Picture Show* and *Paper Moon*. He wrote the controversial book *The Last Unicorn* about Playboy bunny Dorothy Stratton. He was involved with her when her other boyfriend killed her and himself. Year/**Age**: 1995/**56** 1996/**57** 1997/**58**

- **DAVID SANBORN** Muscian. Year/**Age**: 1995/**50** 1996/**51** 1997/**52**

- **DELTA BURKE** Actress. (Orlando, FL) In TV western series "The Chisholm" and spoof of Dallas called "Filthy Rich," Suzanne on "Designing Women," and "Delta." Married actor Gerald McRaney ("Major Dad") May 28, 1989. Year/**Age**: 1995/**39** 1996/**40** 1997/**41**

- **KATE BUSH** Singer/composer. (England) Hit: "Running Up That Hill" in 1985. Year/**Age**: 1995/**37** 1996/**38** 1997/**39**

- **ALLAN "BUD" SELIG** Baseball. (Milwaukee, WI) President and CEO of the Milwaukee Brewers baseball team. Named Major League Executive of the Year in 1978. Took over the duties of the Baseball Commissioner when Fay Vincent stepped down in 1992. Year/**Age**: 1995/**61** 1996/**62** 1997/**63**

- **BILL CARTWRIGHT** Basketball. (Lodi, CA) With the Chicago Bulls. Year/**Age**: 1995/**38** 1996/**39** 1997/**40**

- **KEN OLIN** Actor. (Chicago, IL) TV's "Thirtysome-thing." Married to actress Patricia Wettig. Year/**Age**: 1995/**41** 1996/**42** 1997/**43**

- **HILARY SWANK** Actress. (Portland, OR) TV's "Growing Pains" and "Evening Shade." In Film *The Next Karate Kid.* Year/**Age**: 1995/**21** 1996/**22** 1997/**23**

- **ANITA HILL** Law professor. (OK) She testified to the Senate Judiciary Committee, in a nationally televised broadcast, that Supreme Court nominee Clarence Thomas engaged in unwanted sexually explicit conversations on the job. Year/**Age**: 1995/**39** 1996/**40** 1997/**41**

- **JOE NUXHALL** Baseball. Signed with Cincinnati just out of high school, becoming the youngest player ever in the major leagues. He won 135 games. Year/**Age**: 1995/**67** 1996/**68** 1997/**69**

- **ARNOLD SCHWARZENEGGER** Body-building expert/actor. (Austria) He was Mr. Universe 5 times. Started in films with a documentary *Pumping Iron* and then starred in *The Terminator, Predator, Conan, Red Heat, Twins, Terminator II, Kindergarten Cop, The Last Action Hero, True Lies,* and *Total Recall.* Married to newswoman and Kennedy family member Maria Schriver. The one-time steroid user was named Chairman of the President's Council on Physical Fitness in 1990. He is co-owner of the "Planet Hollywood" Restaurants. Year/**Age**: 1995/**48** 1996/**49** 1997/**50**

- **CHRISTOPHER MULLIN** Basketball star. (NYC) He was on the Olympic "Dream Team" in 1992. Year/**Age**: 1995/**32** 1996/**33** 1997/**34**

- **CASEY STENGEL** Baseball. (1890-1975 – Kansas City, MO) Managed the NY Yankees to 10 pennants and 7 world championships: 1949-1960. (Died 9-29-75.)

- **HENRY FORD** Auto tycoon. (1863-1947 – Dearborn, MI) Developed assembly line production and introduced a $5.00-a-day wage for auto workers. The Tin Lizzy brought him most of his fortune. (Died 4-7-47.)

- **MARC BOLAN** Singer. (1948-1977 – Born Marc Feld in England) Lead singer for T. REX. The group's biggest hit: "Bang a Gong." He was killed when the car he was riding in, crashed into a tree in London. (Died 9-16-77.)

FACTS FROM THE PAST

1928 **GEORGE EASTMAN** demonstrated the first color movies. He invented almost everything we now take for granted, including roll film, cheap portable cameras, and even color movies. At the age of 77, he astonished his friends by shooting himself in the heart, leaving a note saying "To my friends: my work is done . . . why wait?"

1942 President **FRANKLIN D. ROOSEVELT** signed a bill creating a women's auxiliary agency in the Navy. The legislation was called **WOMEN ACCEPTED FOR VOLUNTEER EMERGENCY SERVICES**, or "Waves."

1965 The **MEDICARE BILL WAS SIGNED** by President Lyndon B. Johnson.

1974 It was recommended by the House Judiciary Committee that three articles of **IMPEACHMENT BE BROUGHT AGAINST PRESIDENT RICHARD NIXON** for his part in the Watergate cover-up.

1975 **JIMMY HOFFA**, the former Teamsters Union chief, was last seen outside a restaurant near Detroit, MI. The 62-year-old Hoffa had his 13-year federal prison sentence commuted by former President Nixon in 1971. An Oakland County judge declared Hoffa officially dead after 7 years and 131 days.

1987 **DONALD REGAN**, former White House Chief of Staff, told the Iran-Contra congressional committees that he had urged President Reagan to break-off arms sales to Iran.

1994 **POPE JOHN PAUL** was promised more than $6 million for the publishing rights to his book *Crossing the Threshold of Hope*.

JULY 31

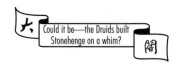

Could it be—the Druids built Stonehenge on a whim?

BIRTHDAYS

- **LOBO** Singer. (Born Roland Lavoie in Tallahassee, FL) Biggest hit: "I'd Love You To Want Me" in 1972. Year/**Age**: 1995/**52** 1996/**53** 1997/**54**

- **GERALDINE CHAPLIN** Actress. (Santa Monica, CA) Daughter of comedian Charlie Chaplin, she appeared in *Dr. Zhivago* in 1965, *Chaplin*, and *The Wedding*. She has a line of clothing at Sears. Year/**Age**: 1995/**51** 1996/**52** 1997/**53**

- **WESLEY SNIPES** Actor. (Orlando, FL) His films include *Jungle Fever, New Jack City, Major League, Rising Sun*, and *Demolition Man*. Year/**Age**: 1995/**33** 1996/**34** 1997/**35**

- **DEAN CAIN** Actor. (Mt. Clemens, MI) Clark Kent on TV's "Lois and Clark: The New Adventures of Superman." Year/**Age**: 1995/**29** 1996/**30** 1997/**31**

- **ROBERT SUTHERLAND TELFER** Actor (NYC) TV's "Saved By the Bell." Year/**Age**: 1995/**18** 1996/**19** 1997/**20**

- **MILTON FRIEDMAN** Economist/presidential advisor. (Brooklyn, NY) Won the Nobel Prize for Economics in 1976. Year/**Age**: 1995/**83** 1996/**84** 1997/**85**

- **SUSAN FLANNERY** Actress. (NYC) "Dallas." Year/**Age**: 1995/**52** 1996/**53** 1997/**54**

- **DON MURRAY** Actor. (Hollywood, CA) In many movies and in the TV series "The Outcasts" in 1968 and *Baby the Rain Must Fall*. Year/**Age**: 1995/**66** 1996/**67** 1997/**68**

- **KENNY BURRELL** Guitarist. Year/**Age**: 1995/**64** 1996/**65** 1997/**66**

- **BOB WELCH** Singer. (Los Angeles, CA) Started out as a guitarist/vocalist with FLEETWOOD MAC. His biggest hit: "Sentimental Lady" in 1977 with backup vocals by Christie McVie & Lindsey Buckingham. Year/**Age**: 1995/**49** 1996/**50** 1997/**51**

- **FRANCE NUYEN** [noy'-ehn] Actress. (France) Appeared in *South Pacific* and *Diamond Head*. On TV's "St. Elsewhere." Year/**Age**: 1995/**56** 1996/**57** 1997/**58**

- **GARY LEWIS** Singer. His biggest hit: "This Diamond Ring" in 1965, which was recorded as a surprise for his dad, Jerry Lewis, who knew nothing about it. Year/**Age**: 1995/**50** 1996/**52** 1997/**53**

- **EVONNE GOOLEGONG** Tennis star. (Australia) First aborigine in international sports. Year/**Age**: 1995/**44** 1996/**45** 1997/**46**

- **HANK BAUER** Former big league manager. While playing outfield for the Yankees in the 1958 World Series, he had 4 home runs against the Milwaukee Braves. Year/**Age**: 1995/**73** 1996/**74** 1997/**75**

- **SHERRY LANSING** Movie producer. (Chicago, IL) *The Accused* and *Fatal Attraction*. First woman to head a major studio. Year/**Age**: 1995/**51** 1996/**52** 1997/**53**

- **WILLIAM TODMAN** Game-show producer. (1913-1979 – NYC) "Beat the Clock," "Family Feud," "I've Got a Secret," .and "What's My Line." (Died 7-29-79)

FACTS FROM THE PAST

11485	Sir Thomas Malory published *Le Morte D'Arthur*, recounting those bygone chivalrous days of **KING ARTHUR** and the **KNIGHTS OF THE ROUND TABLE**.
1498	Trinidad was discovered by **CHRISTOPHER COLUMBUS** on his 3rd voyage.
1790	The U.S. Government issued its **FIRST PATENT** to **SAMUEL HOPKINS** for his process in making potash. He was from Vermont.
1928	**LEO, THE LION** roared for the first time at the beginning of MGM's first talking picture, *White Shadows in the South Seas*. The only word of dialogue in the entire film was "Hello."
1933	High school sweethearts **PERRY COMO** and his wife, Roselle, were married on this day.
1948	New York's International Airport at Idlewild Field was dedicated by President Harry S. Truman. It was later renamed **JOHN F. KENNEDY INTERNATIONAL AIRPORT**.
1954	**JOE ADCOCK** hit four homers and a double to give the Milwaukee Braves a 15-to-7 victory over Brooklyn.
1970	After 15 years on NBC "Nightly News," **CHET HUNTLEY** retired and said "Goodnight David" to David Brinkley for the last time.
1980	**"PAPA" JOHN PHILLIPS** was arrested for conspiracy to distribute narcotics at his summer home on Long Island, NY. He was sentenced to eight years in prison and fined $15,000. The sentence was later reduced to 30 days in jail.
1984	The U.S. men's gymnastics team won the team gold medal at the LA Summer Olympics in a major upset over the Chinese that included perfect 10 performances by **MITCH GAYLORD, BART CONNER,** and **TIM DAGGETT**.
1989	A Shiite Moslem group claimed that it had executed **LIEUTENANT COLONEL WILLIAM R. HIGGINS** and released a videotape purporting to show the U.S. Marine hanging from a makeshift gallows. The group said the execution was carried out in retaliation for Israel's kidnapping of a Moslem cleric July 28.
1990	**NOLAN RYAN** pitched the Texas Rangers to an 11-3 victory over the Milwaukee Brewers in Milwaukee to become the 20th pitcher in major league history to win 300 games in a career. He was 43 years old. **CY YOUNG** won the most games in a career with 511.
1991	The Strategic Arms Reduction Treaty was signed in Moscow by **PRESIDENT BUSH** and Soviet President **MIKHAIL GORBACHEV**. They used pens made of metal from nuclear missiles that were destroyed under the 1987 treaty.
1994	Haiti's de facto president Emile Jonassaint declared a national state of siege and said "**THE BATTLE OF HAITI** is under way." His announcement came after the UN cleared the way for a possible U.S. led invasion.

Baseball Hall of Fame

Ty Cobb – 1936
Walter Johnson – 1936
Christopher Mathewson – 1936
Babe Ruth – 1936
Honus Wagner – 1936

Morgan Bulkeley – 1937
Byron Johnson – 1937
Napoleon Lajoie – 1937
Connie Mack – 1937
John McGraw – 1937
Tristram Speaker – 1937
George Wright – 1937
Cy Young – 1937

Grover C. Alexander – 1938
Alexander Cartwright – 1938
Henry Chadwick – 1938

Cap Ansan – 1939
Eddie Collins – 1939
Charles Comiskey – 1939
Candy Cummings – 1939
Buck Ewing – 1939
Lou Gehrig – 1939
William Keeler – 1939
Charlie Radbourn – 1939
George Sisler – 1939
Albert Spalding – 1939

Rogers Hornsby – 1942

Kenesaw M. Landis – 1944

Roger Bresnahan – 1945
Dan Brouthers – 1945
Fred Clarke – 1945
James Collins – 1945
Ed Delahanty – 1945
Hugh Duffy – 1945
Hugh Jennings – 1945
King Kelly – 1945
James O'Rourke – 1945
Wilbert Robinson – 1945

Jesse C. Burkett – 1946
Frank Chance – 1946
Jack Chesbro – 1946
John Evers – 1946
Clark Griffith – 1946
Thomas McCarthy – 1946
Joe McGinnity – 1946
Ed Plank – 1946
Joe Tinker – 1946
Rube Waddell – 1946
Ed Walsh – 1946

Mickey Cochrane – 1947
Frank Frisch – 1947
Lefty Grove – 1947
Carl Hubbell – 1947

Herb Pennock – 1948
Pie Traynor – 1948

Mordecai Brown – 1949

Charles Gehringer – 1949
Kid Nichols – 1949

Jimmie Foxx – 1951
Mel Ott – 1951

Harry Heilmann – 1952
Paul Waner – 1952

Edward Barrow – 1953
Chief Bender – 1953
Thomas Connolly – 1953
Dizzy Dean – 1953
Bill Klem – 1953
Al Simmons – 1953
Bobby Wallace – 1953
Harry Wright – 1953

Bill Dickey – 1954
Rabbit Maranville – 1954
Bill Terry – 1954

Home Run Baker – 1955
Joe DiMaggio – 1955
Gabby Hartnett – 1955
Ted Lyons – 1955
Ray Schalk – 1955
Dazzy Vance – 1955

Joe Cronin – 1956
Hank Greenberg – 1956

Sam Crawford – 1957
Joe McCarthy – 1957

Zach Wheat – 1959

Max Carey – 1961
Bill Hamilton – 1961

Bill McKechnie – 1962
Bob Feller – 1962
Jackie Robinson – 1962

John Clarkson – 1963
Elmer H. Flick – 1963
Sam Rice – 1963

Luke Appling – 1964
Urban "Red" Faber – 1964
Burleigh Grimes – 1964
Miller Huggins – 1964
Timothy Keefe – 1964
Henry Manush – 1964
John Ward – 1964

Pud Galvin – 1965

Casey Stengel – 1966
Ted Williams – 1966

Branch Rickey – 1967
Red Ruffing – 1967
Lloyd Waner – 1967

Kiki Cuyler – 1968
Goose Goslin – 1968
Joe Medwick – 1968
Roy Campanella – 1969

Stan Coveleski – 1969
Waite Hoyt – 1969
Stan Musial – 1969

Lou Boudreau – 1970
Earle Combs – 1970
Ford Frick – 1970
Jesse Haines – 1970

Dave Bancroft – 1971
Jake Beckley – 1971
Chick Hafey – 1971
Harry Hooper – 1971
Joe Kelley – 1971
Rube Marquard – 1971
Satchel Paige – 1971
George Weiss – 1971

Yogi Berra – 1972
Josh Gibson – 1972
Lefty Gomez – 1972
Will Harridge – 1972
Sandy Koufax – 1972
Buck Leonard – 1972
Early Wynn – 1972
Ross Youngs – 1972

Roberto Clemente – 1973
Billy Evans – 1973
Monte Irvin – 1973
George Kelly – 1973
Warren Spahn – 1973
Mickey Welch – 1973

James "Cool Papa" Bell – 1974
Jim Bottomley – 1974
Jocko Conlan – 1974
Whitey Ford – 1974
Mickey Mantle – 1974
Sam Thompson – 1974

Earl Averill – 1975
Bucky Harris – 1975
Billy Herman – 1975
William "Judy" Johnson – 1975
Ralph Kiner – 1975

Oscar Charleston – 1976
Roger Connor – 1976
Cal Hubbard – 1976
Bob Lemon – 1976
Fred Lindstrom – 1976
Robin Roberts – 1976

Ernie Banks – 1977
Martin Dihigo – 1977
Pop Lloyd – 1977
Al Lopez – 1977
Amos Rusie – 1977
Joe Sewell – 1977

Addie Joss – 1978
Larry MacPhail – 1978
Eddie Matthews – 1978

Warren Giles – 1979

Willie Mays – 1979
Hack Wilson – 1979

Al Kaline – 1980
Chuck Klein – 1980
Duke Snider – 1980
Tom Yawkey – 1980

Andrew Foster – 1981
Bob Gibson – 1981
Johnny Mize – 1981

Hank Aaron – 1982
Happy Chandler – 1982
Travis Jackson – 1982
Frank Robinson – 1982

Walt Alston – 1983
George Kell – 1983
Juan Marichal – 1983
Brooks Robinson – 1983

Luis Aparicio – 1984
Don Drysdale – 1984
Rick Ferrell – 1984
Harmon Killebrew – 1984
Pee Wee Reese – 1984

Lou Brock – 1985
Enos Slaughter – 1985
Arky Vaughan – 1985
Hoyt Wilhelm – 1985

Bobby Doerr – 1986
Ernie Lombardi – 1986
Willie McCovey – 1986

Ray Dandridge – 1987
Catfish Hunter – 1987
Billy Williams – 1987

Willie Stargell – 1988

Al Barlick – 1989
Johnny Bench – 1989
Red Schoendienst – 1989
Carl Yastrzemski – 1989

Jim Palmer – 1990

Rod Carew – 1991
Ferguson Jenkins – 1991
Tony Lazzeri – 1991
Gaylord Perry – 1991
Bill Veeck – 1991

Rollie Fingers – 1992
Bill McGowan – 1992
Joe Morgan – 1992
Hal Newhouser – 1992
Uppa Rixey – 1992
Edd Roush – 1992
Tom Seaver – 1992

Reggie Jackson – 1993

Leo Durocher – 1994
Steve Carlton - 1994
Phil Rizzuto - 1994

AUGUST MEMORIES

YEARS AGO

1985

POPULAR SONGS

"Shout" by Tears for Fears

"The Power of Love" by Huey Lewis & The News

MOVIES

The Goonies
a Steven Spielberg adventure starring Corey Feldman, Josh Brolin, Martha Plimpton, and John Matuszak.

King David
a Biblical film featuring Richard Gere, Edward Woodward, and Alice Quilley.

TV SHOWS

"West 57th"
similar to "60 Minutes" with John Ferrugia, Bob Sirott, and others.

"MacGyver"
starring Richard Dean Anderson.

BOOKS

Her First American by Lore Segal

1986

POPULAR SONGS

"Papa Don't Preach" by Madonna

"Higher Love" by Steve Winwood

MOVIES

Crocodile Dundee
romantic comedy with Paul Hogan and Linda Kozlowsi. The story travels from Australia to New York city.

Round Midnight
starring Dexter Gordon, Gabrielle Haker, and Francois Cloyer. The story of a troubled American jazz musician.

TV SHOWS

"Our World"
hosts Linda Ellerbee and Ray Gandolf review various years in history.

"Amazing Stories"
Steven Spielberg's fantasy anthology with many famous guest stars.

BOOKS

His Way by Kitty Kelly

1987

POPULAR SONGS

"Who's That Girl" by Madonna

"LaBamba" by Los Lobos

MOVIES

Ironweed
stars Meryl Streep and Jack Nicholson in the story of the depression and two transients.

Back To School
a father, Rodney Dangerfield, goes to college with his son. Co-stars Sally Kellerman and Robert Downey, Jr.

TV SHOWS

"Frank's Place"
Tim Reid and real-life wife Daphne Maxwell Reid star in this sitcom.

"Beauty and the Beast"
this romantic drama takes place in New York with Linda Hamilton as the beauty and Ron Perlman as the beast.

BOOKS

Presumed Innocent by Scott Turow

SPECIAL DAYS

AUGUST	1995	1996	1997
National Smile Week	Aug. 7-13	Aug. 5-11	Aug. 4-10
Soap Box Derby Week	Aug. 7-13	Aug. 5-11	Aug. 4-10
World Whimmy Diddle Competion (*Asheville, NC*)	Aug. 12	Aug. 10	Aug. 9
Hobo Convention (*Britt, IA*)	Aug. 12	Aug. 10	Aug. 9
Friendship Week	Aug. 6-12	Aug. 4-10	Aug. 3-9
Twin's Day (*Twinsburg, OH*)	Aug. 4-6	Aug. 2-4	Aug. 1-3
Psychic Week	Aug. 6-12	Aug. 4-10	Aug. 3-9
Miss Crustacean (*Ocean City, NJ*)	Aug. 9	Aug. 14	Aug. 13
Full Moon	Aug. 10	Aug. 28	Aug. 18
Be Kind To Humankind Week	Aug. 20-26	Aug. 25-31	Aug. 24-30
Oatmeal Festival (*Bertram, TX*)	Sep. 1-2	Aug. 30-31	Aug. 29-30

1970

POPULAR SONGS
"Make It With You" by Bread

"War" by Edwin Starr

MOVIES
Cromwell
17th century civil war film with Alec Guiness, Richard Harris, Timothy Dalton, and Robert Morley.

Sunflower
starring Sophia Loren and Marcello Mastroianni in this film.

TV SHOWS
"McCloud"
starring Dennis Weaver as Deputy Marshall Sam McCloud in this police show.

"The Odd Couple"
starring Tony Randall and Jack Klugman as friends with opposite tastes who try to live together.

BOOKS *The Greening of America* by Professor Charles Reich

1971

POPULAR SONGS
"How Can You Mend a Broken Heart" by The Bee Gees

"Uncle Albert, Admiral Halsey" by Paul & Linda McCartney

MOVIES
The French Connection
starring Gene Hackman as a New York cop who busts an international drug ring.

Willy Wonka and the Chocolate Factory
starring Gene Wilder as a candy maker is this children's film.

TV SHOWS
"Sonny and Cher Comedy Hour"
the famous duo hosts a variety show.

"Sarge"
starring George Kennedy as a priest in San Diego. Before he became a priest he was a homicide detective.

BOOKS
Eleanor and Franklin by Joseph P. Lash

1972

POPULAR SONGS
"Brandy (You're a Fine Girl)" by Looking Glass

"Saturday in the Park" by Chicago

MOVIES
Ben (Sequel to Willard)
Michael Jackson sings the theme song and Lee Harcourt Montgomery stars.

Young Winston
starring Robert Shaw and Anne Bancroft as Winston Churchill's parents. Simon Ward portrays Winston.

TV SHOWS
"Anna and the King"
sitcom starring Yul Brynner as the King of Siam. Sammantha Eggar plays Anna Owens.

"The Rookies"
rookie officers hit the streets of southern California. Stars Kate Jackson.

BOOKS *Open Marriage* by Nena and George O'Neill

1945

POPULAR SONGS
"Paper Moon" by Benny Goodman

"Love Letters" by Dick Haymes

MOVIES
Isle of the Dead
horror film starring Boris Karloff. A man dies of the plague so a general and his crew are quarantined on an island.

A Song To Remember
starring Cornel Wilde, Paul Muni, and Merle Oberon. Chronicles the life of composer Chopin.

TV SHOWS
No regularly scheduled TV programming until May 1946.

BOOKS
Harvey by Mary Chase

1946

POPULAR SONGS
"To Each His Own" by Eddy Howard

"Surrender" by Perry Como

MOVIES
The Yearling
starring Gregory Peck, Jane Wyman, and Claude Jarman, Jr. in this film. A man breaks his son's heart when he destroys a fawn.

Anna and the King of Siam
the non-musical version of the *King and I* starring Irene Dunne, Linda Darnell, and Rex Harrison.

TV SHOWS
"I Love To Eat"
James Beard hosts this cooking show.

BOOKS
This Side of Innocence by Taylor Caldwell

1947

POPULAR SONGS
"Near You" by Francis Craig

"I Have But One Heart ("O Maninariello")" by Vic Damone

MOVIES
The Bachelor and the Bobby-Soxer
a teenager, Shirley Temple, has a big crush on Cary Grant. Also stars Myrna Loy and Rudy Vallee.

Boomerang
starring Dana Andrews, Jane Wyatt, and Lee J. Cobb in the story of a prosecuting lawyer.

TV SHOWS
"In The Kelvinator Kitchen"
Alma Kitchell hosts this cooking show.

BOOKS
The Vixens by Frank Yerby

AUGUST 1
Beauty QueenWeek/Clown Week Begins

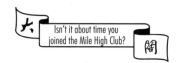
Isn't it about time you joined the Mile High Club?

BIRTHDAYS

- **ROBERT CRAY** Blues singer. (Columbus, GA) Grammy winner for albums *Showdown* and *Strong Persuader*. Year/**Age**: 1995/**42** 1996/**43** 1997/**44**

- **DOM DeLUISE** Entertainer. (Brooklyn, NY) He was one of the stars of the "Dean Martin Show" and hosted the variety hour summer replacement for the "Jackie Gleason Show." He's seen often on freezer bag commercials. Dom is a close friend of Burt Reynolds and appears in his movies. Films include *Loose Cannons*. He was host of the "New Candid Camera." Year/**Age**: 1995/**62** 1996/**63** 1997/**64**

- **ALFONSE D'AMATO** Senator. (Brooklyn, NY) (R/NY) Year/**Age**: 1995/**58** 1996/**59** 1997/**60**

- **RONALD BROWN** Democratic National Committee Chairman. (Washington, DC) Elected in 1989, he was the first African-American to head a major political party. Year/**Age**: 1995/**54** 1996/**55** 1997/**56**

- **JERRY GARCIA** Guitarist. (San Francisco, CA) Co-founder of the GRATEFUL DEAD. He got the name from a Funk and Wagnalls dictionary, opened to a page, with his eyes closed, and pointed to "grateful dead" (a type of Folk Ballad about death and reincarnation). The Ben & Jerry's ice cream "Cherry Garcia" was named for him. Year/**Age**: 1995/**53** 1996/**54** 1997/**55**

- **ARTHUR HILL** Actor. (Canada) Star of TV series "Owen Marshall, Counselor at Law." Among his films: *Harper*. Year/**Age**: 1995/**73** 1996/**74** 1997/**75**

- **TEMPEST BLEDSOE** Actress. (Chicago, IL) Vanessa on "The Cosby Show." Year/**Age**: 1995/**22** 1996/**23** 1997/**24**

- **JACK KRAMER** Former tennis star. Occasionally heard as TV commentator for tennis tournaments. Year/**Age**: 1995/**74** 1996/**75** 1997/**76**

- **GEOFFREY HOLDER** Actor/choreographer. (Trinidad) In the 1950's, he won $16,000 on the "$64,000 Question." He was the "Cola Nut" man on TV. Year/**Age**: 1995/**65** 1996/**66** 1997/**67**

- **YVES SAINT-LAURENT** French fashion designer. (Born Henry Donat Mathieu in Algeria) Produces the perfumes "Opium" and "Paris." Year/**Age**: 1995/**59** 1996/**60** 1997/**61**

- **JOE ELLIOT** Singer. (England) Lead singer for the heavy metal group DEF LEPPARD. Group was first to sell more than 5 million copies of 2 consecutive LPs in the U.S., including *Adrenalize* and #1 LP *Hysteria*. Year/**Age**: 1995/**36** 1996/**37** 1997/**38**

- **ROBERT TODD LINCOLN** Lawyer. (1843-1926 – Springfield, IL) The only son of President Abraham Lincoln to survive to manhood. He arrived at the scenes minutes after the assassination of three presidents: his dad, Garfield and McKinley. When he fell between two railroad cars in Jersey City, he was rescued by Edwin Booth, the brother of the man who killed his father. (Died 7-26-26.)

- **HERMAN MELVILLE** Author. (1819-1891 – NYC) Author of *Moby Dick*. (Died 9-28-1891.)

- **FRANCIS SCOTT KEY** Composer. (1779-1843 – Frederick County, MD) He was an American attorney, social worker, poet, and composer. While on a legal mission, he was detained on board a ship off Baltimore during the British bombardment of Fort McHenry on the night of Sept. 13, 1814. He wrote the "Star Spangled Banner" when he saw a flag flying over the fort at daybreak. It was set to the music of an old English tune, "Anachreon in Heaven," but did not become the official U.S. national anthem until 117 years later when President Herbert Hoover signed it into law. (Died 1-11-1843.)

FACTS FROM THE PAST

1774 British scientist **JOSEPH PRIESTLEY** discovered oxygen. He succeeded in isolating it.

1873 Andrew S. Hallidie successfully tested a **CABLE CAR** he had designed for the city of San Francisco, as a solution to the problem of providing mass transit up San Francisco's steep hills.

1936 The **OLYMPIC GAMES** opened in Berlin with a ceremony presided over by Adolf Hitler.

1960 **CHUBBY CHECKER** released "The Twist," which became the dance craze of the early 1960s and is still popular at sock hops.

1971 **TWO CONCERTS FOR BANGLADESH** were held at Madison Square Garden in New York City. George Harrison brought together Bob Dylan, Leon Russell, Ringo Starr, and Ravi Shankar for the benefit concerts. The shows and an album of the event raised nearly $11 million for the starving people of Bangladesh.

1978 **PETE ROSE** of the Cincinnati Reds, who had tied the National League record of hitting in 44 consecutive games, saw his streak end in a game against the Atlanta Braves.

1980 **GEORGE HARRISON** formed "Hand Made Films Productions Ltd." Some of his films include: *Life of Brian*, *Mona Lisa*, *Time Bandits*, *A Private Function*, and *Shanghai Surprise*.

1981 The rock music video channel, **MTV,** made its debut. The first video shown was called *Video Killed the Radio Star*, by the BUGGLES. The average number of videos shown per day is 200.

1986 Tennis star **JOHN McENROE** and actress **TATUM O'NEAL** were married in Oyster Bay, NY. Their son, Kevin, was born May 23, 1986. They are now divorced.

1992 At the Summer Olympics in Barcelona, U.S. light flyweight boxer **ERIC GRIFFIN** won on all five judges' score sheets but, because of the new computer scoring system, lost to **RAFAEL LOZANO** of Spain.

1994 The **ROLLING STONES** began a 43-city stadium tour in Washington, D.C. They declined an invitation to play at the White House.

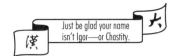

Just be glad your name isn't Igor—or Chastity.

AUGUST 2

BIRTHDAYS

- **DORIS KENNER** Singer. (Passaic, NJ) With THE SHIRELLES. Biggest hits: "Soldier Boy" and "Will You Love Me Tomorrow." Year/**Age**: 1995/**54** 1996/**55** 1997/**56**
- **PETER O'TOOLE** Actor. (Born Peter Seamus O'Toole in Ireland) He never won an Oscar, but has been nominated six times. He appeared in *Lawrence of Arabia, Becket, A Lion in Winter, The Last Emperor*, and *King Ralph*. Wrote his autobiography, *Loitering With Intent*. Year/**Age**: 1995/**63** 1996/**64** 1997/**65**
- **CARROLL O'CONNOR** Actor. (NYC) Appeared as Archie Bunker in "All in the Family." He has a college degree in English and speaks five languages. Won an Emmy award for lead actor in a drama: TV's "In the Heat of the Night." He auditioned for the part of Skipper on Gilligan's Island. Year/**Age**: 1995/**71** 1996/**72** 1997/**73**
- **LINDA FRATIANNE** Figure skater. (Los Angeles, CA) Year/**Age**: 1995/**35** 1996/**36** 1997/**37**
- **EDDIE FURLONG** Actor. In the movie *Terminator 2, Judgement Day, Brain Scan,* and *A Home of Our Own..* Year/**Age**: 1995/**18** 1996/**19** 1997/**20**
- **CYNTHIA STEVENSON** Actress. (Oakland, CA) In the films *The Player* and *The Gun in Betty Lou's Handbag*. On TV's "Bob." Year/**Age**: 1995/**32** 1996/**33** 1997/**34**

- **CEDRIC STEVENSON** Basketball. Year/**Age**: 1995/**26** 1996/**27** 1997/**28**
- **GARTH HUDSON** Keyboard player. (Woodstock, NY) With The BAND. Their biggest hit: "Up on Cripple Creek" in 1969. Year/**Age**: 1995/**58** 1996/**59** 1997/**60**
- **ANDREW GOLD** Singer. (Burbank, CA) Biggest hit: "Lonely Boy" in 1977. He's the son of soundtrack composer Ernest Gold and did session and arranging work for Linda Ronstadt since the early 1970s. Year/**Age**: 1995/**44** 1996/**45** 1997/**46**
- **JOANNA CASSIDY** Actress. On the "Buffalo Bill" TV show with Dabney Coleman and TV's "Hotel Malibu." In the films *Who Framed Roger Rabbit?* and thriller *The Package* in 1989. Year/**Age**: 1995/**51** 1996/**52** 1997/**53**
- **ANN DVORAK** Actress. (1912-1979 – New York, NY) Her films include *Scarface* in 1932. (Died 12-1-79.)
- **GARY MERRILL** Actor. (1915-1990 – Hartford, CT) He was married to Bette Davis at one time. He appeared in *Twelve O'Clock High* and *All About Eve*. (Died 3-5-90.)
- **MYRNA LOY** Actress. (1904-1993 - Born Myrna Williams in Helena, MT) Best known for her portrayal of Nora Charles in the *Thin Man* movies, with William Powell as Nick Charles. In TV's "Love Sidney." (Died 12/14/93.)

FACTS FROM THE PAST

1782   George Washington invented the **HONORARY BADGE OF DISTINCTION** in lieu of cash. It was a white stripe above the left cuff, and was to be the **FIRST HASH MARK** on a soldier's uniform.

1876   Frontiersman **WILD BILL HICKOK** was shot from behind and killed while playing poker at a saloon in Deadwood, South Dakota. The man who shot Hickok, Jack McCall, was later hanged. He never gave a motive for the shooting. When he died, Hickok was holding black aces and eights, which later became known as the **DEAD MAN'S HAND.**

1877   The famous stagecoach robber, **BLACK BART**, robbed his first coach. They later found the empty safe deposit box with a note, in poetic form, explaining his deed.

1892   The **FIRST PRACTICAL MOVING STAIRCASE**—the escalator—was patented by Charles A. Wheeler. It never was built, but some of its features were incorporated in the prototype built by the Otis Elevator Company in 1899.

1934   German President **PAUL VON HINDENBURG** died, paving the way for **ADOLF HITLER**'s complete takeover.

1938   Brooklyn Dodger General Manager **LARRY MacPHAIL** introduced a yellow baseball. It was the first time the traditional white ball was not used in a major league game. Brooklyn beat St. Louis 6-2 and Johnny Mize (who died in 1993) was the only player to hit a home run with the off-color ball.

1939   Scientist/refugee from Nazi Germany **ALBERT EINSTEIN** wrote an historic letter to President Franklin Roosevelt on the **ATOM BOMB**, which marked the start of atomic weaponry. He wrote in part: "A single bomb of this type, carried by boat and exploded in a port, might very well destroy the whole port together with some of the surrounding territory." Six years later, on August 6, 1945, **HIROSHIMA** was destroyed.

1943   Navy **LIEUTENANT JOHN F. KENNEDY** became a war hero by rescuing members of his crew when their PT boat was cut in two by a Japanese destroyer.

1969   **BOB DYLAN** showed up unexpectedly at his 10th year high school reunion at the Moose Lodge in Hibbing, MN. He and his wife, Sara, left an hour later after a drunk tried to pick a fight with him.

1975   A **CHAMPAGNE-CORK-POPPING RECORD** was set by Gary P. Mahan of La Habra Heights, CA. He popped the cork 103 feet.

1983   The U.S. House of Representatives voted to designate the third Monday in January a **FEDERAL HOLIDAY** in honor of civil rights leader **DR. MARTIN LUTHER KING, JR.**

1987   Fans at a **BILLY JOEL** concert in Leningrad jumped up and down on their seats, breaking about 200 chairs. Members of the audience carried Joel out on their shoulders at the end of his performance.

1990   Iraq's powerful army, led by President **SADDAM HUSSEIN**, overran Kuwait before dawn. Tank-led troops quickly seized the ruler's palace and other government buildings. The U.N. Security Council condemned the invasion and demanded that Iraq withdraw from Kuwait. Iraq refused and was attacked by U.S. and Allied Forces on January 16, 1991.

AUGUST 3

BIRTHDAYS

• **MARTIN SHEEN** Actor. (Born Ramon Estevez in Dayton, OH) In the films: *Gettysburg, Apocalypse Now, Gandhi, Wall Street, J.F.K.*, and *Hear No Evil*. Year/**Age**: 1995/**55** 1996/**56** 1997/**57**

• **TONY BENNETT** Entertainer. (Born Antonio Dominick Benedetto in Astoria, Long Island, NY) Bob Hope gave him his stage name in 1950 backstage at the Paramount Theater in NY. Hope told Bennett, "You can't be a big star with a name like Benedetto. It'll never fit on the marquee." Biggest hit: "I Left My Heart in San Francisco" in 1962. It was a big hit, but never got higher than #19 on the charts. He won a "Record of the Year" Grammy for the song. Year/**Age**: 1995/**69** 1996/**70** 1997/**71**

• **JAY NORTH** Actor. (Hollywood, CA) Played "Dennis, the Menace" on TV from 1959-63. He was 7 years old when the series started. Year/**Age**: 1995/**44** 1996/**45** 1997/**46**

• **VICTORIA JACKSON** Comedienne/actress. Appeared on "Saturday Night Live." In films *Casual Sex* and *The Pickup Artist*. Voice of Bamm Bamm on the "Flintstones." Year/**Age**: 1995/**36** 1996/**37** 1997/**38**

• **JOMARIE PAYTON** Actress. Appears on TV's "Perfect Strangers" and "Family Matters." Year/**Age**: 1995/**45** 1996/**46** 1997/**47**

• **MARTHA STEWART** Lifestyle advisor. She has a magazine and many books. Year/**Age**: 1995/**54** 1996/**55** 1997/**56**

• **MARCEL DIONNE** Hockey. (Canada) Year/**Age**: 1995/**44** 1996/**45** 1997/**46**

• **JOHN STENNIS** Former senator. (Kemper County, MS) (D/MS) Year/**Age**: 1995/**93** 1996/**94** 1997/**95**

• **JOHN GRAHAM** Guitarist. (Los Angeles, CA) With EARTH, WIND & FIRE. Biggest hit: "Shining Star" in 1975. Year/**Age**: 1995/**44** 1996/**45** 1997/**46**

• **ALEX CORD** Actor. Played Michael Archangel on the TV series "Airwolf." Year/**Age**: 1995/**64** 1996/**65** 1997/**66**

• **ELSA MARTINELLI** Actress. (Italy) Appeared in *Hatari, Candy*, and *The Boat Men*. Year/**Age**: 1995/**62** 1996/**63** 1997/**64**

• **RICHARD ADLER** Songwriter. (New York, NY) Tony winner for *Damn Yankees* and *Pajama Game*. He also did the musical film scores for these shows. Year/**Age**: 1995/**74** 1996/**75** 1997/**76**

• **JOHN LANDIS** Director. (Chicago, IL) *Twilight Zone*. He directed the "Thriller" video by Michael Jackson. Year/**Age**: 1995/**45** 1996/**46** 1997/**47**

• **LANCE ALWORTH** Football. (Houston, TX) Former San Diego Charger. Year/**Age**: 1995/**55** 1996/**56** 1997/**57**

• **MAGGIE KUHN** Reformer. (Buffalo, NY) Forced to retire when she turned 65, she got together with others in the same situation and they formed the Grey Panthers, an organization that helps seniors citizens fight problems that confront them in the work place and socially as they get older. Year/**Age**: 1995/**92** 1996/**93** 1997/**94**

• **DOLORES DEL RIO** Actress. (1905-1983 – Born Lolita Dolores Martinez Asunsolo Lopez Negrette in Durango, MX) During the Great Depression of the 1930s, she was earning $9,000 a week and was named the most beautiful woman in Hollywood. Films *Fugitive*, and *Journey Into Fear* and played Elvis's mom in *Flaming Star*. (Died 4-11-83.)

FACTS FROM THE PAST

1492 **CHRISTOPHER COLUMBUS** set sail from Palos, Spain, with 3 ships: *Nina, Pinta* and *Santa Maria*, on a voyage that would take him to the New World and the discovery of America. The expedition cost about $7,000 total: $3,000 for his three ships; his personal salary of $300 a year, and $2.50 per crew member per month.

1921 Baseball Commissioner **KENESAW LANDIS** refused to reinstate the former Chicago White Sox players implicated in the Black Sox Scandal, despite their acquittals in a jury trial.

1923 **CALVIN COOLIDGE** was sworn in as the 30th U.S. President, following the death of Warren Harding. He was sworn in by his dad, who was a notary public. After the swearing in, he said goodnight and went back to bed.

1943 During World War II, **GENERAL GEORGE PATTON** slapped a G.I. at an army hospital in Sicily, accusing him of cowardice. Patton later apologized for the incident, and for a second, similar episode.

1981 **U.S. AIR TRAFFIC CONTROLLERS** went on an illegal strike, causing suspension of half of the nation's nearly 15,000 daily flights. President Reagan took a tough stance on the walkout and ordered the 13,000 striking controllers to go back to work within 48 hours or risk being fired. Two days later, President Reagan dismissed all those who defied his order.

1981 Marine Corps Major **OLIVER NORTH** was assigned to the National Security Council.

1984 At the Los Angeles Olympics, **MARY LOU RETTON** won the gold medal in the individual all-around event in women's gymnastics.

1987 The **IRAN-CONTRA CONGRESSIONAL HEARINGS** ended, with none of the 29 witnesses tying President Reagan directly to the diversion of arms-sales profits to Nicaraguan rebels.

1988 **MATHIAS RUST** was released by the Russians. He spent 14 months in a Soviet prison for flying across 500 miles of Soviet airspace in a small plane and landing in Red Square.

1993 **DANIEL** and **CARA SCHMIDT**, the biological parents of "**JESSICA**," were given custody of the $2^1/_2$ year old by the U.S. Supreme Court and flew her to their home in Cedar Rapids, IA. The only people she had ever known were her adopted parents, **ROBERTA** and **JAN DeBOER** of Ann Arbor, MI.

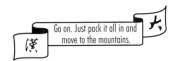

Go on. Just pack it all in and move to the mountains.

AUGUST 4

BIRTHDAYS

- **MAURICE RICHARD** [rih'-shard] Hockey player. (Canada) In 1957, became the first player to score 500 career goals. Year/**Age**: 1995/**72** 1996/**73** 1997/**74**

- **FRANKIE FORD** Singer. (Born Frank Guzzo in Gretna, LA) Biggest hit: "Sea Cruise" in 1959. Originally a Huey Piano Smith tune, Ford's voice was substituted and sped up. He was in the movie *American Hot Wax*. Year/**Age**: 1995/**55** 1996/**56** 1997/**57**

- **TIMI YURO** Singer. (Born Rosemarie Timothy Yufo in Chicago) Biggest hit: "Hurt" in 1961. She lost her voice in 1980 and underwent three throat operations. Year/**Age**: 1995/**54** 1996/**55** 1997/**56**

- **WESLEY ADDY** Actor. (Omaha, NE) In films: *Kiss Me Deadly*, and *What Ever Happened to Baby Jane*. Year/**Age**: 1995/**82** 1996/**83** 1997/**84**

- **RICHARD BELZER** Comedian/actor. In the film *Mad Dog and Glory* and in the TV series "Homicide: Life on the Street." Year/**Age**: 1995/**51** 1996/**52** 1997/**53**

- **WILLIAM SCHUMAN** Composer. (New York, NY) Year/**Age**: 1995/**85** 1996/**86** 1997/**87**

- **WESLEY SNIPES** Actor. Police officer in the film *Rising Sun* and played an airline security expert in *Passenger 57*. Also in *Drop Zone* and he was in drag for *To Wong Foo, Thanks For Everything, Julie Newmar*. He received a $7,000 fine after leading a trooper on a high speed chase. Year/**Age**: 1995/**33** 1996/**34** 1997/**35**

- **YASSER ARAFAT** PLO Leader. Chairman of the Palestine Liberation Organization. Year/**Age**: 1995/**66** 1996/**67** 1997/**68**

- **KENNETH DRYDEN** Hockey player. (Canada) Year/**Age**: 1995/**54** 1996/**55** 1997/**56**

- **HELEN THOMAS** Dean of the White House press corps. (Winchester, KY) Year/**Age**: 1995/**75** 1996/**76** 1997/**77**

- **MARY DECKER SLANY** Track star. Year/**Age**: 1995/**37** 1996/**38** 1997/**39**

- **ROGER CLEMENS** Baseball. (Dayton, OH) Boston star pitcher. The 3-time Cy Young Award winner led the league in ERA and shutouts three consecutive seasons. He said in 1993, "I'd like to play until the year 2000." Year/**Age**: 1995/**33** 1996/**34** 1997/**35**

- **JOHN RIGGINS** Football star. (Centralia, KS) This Pro Hall of Fame star broke Gale Sayers' rushing record at the University of Kansas. He was the Jets 1971 first-round draft pick. He later played for the Washington Redskins. Year/**Age**: 1995/**46** 1996/**47** 1997/**48**

- **LOUIS ARMSTRONG** Entertainer. (1900-1971 – Born Daniel Louis Armstrong in New Orleans, LA) Known as "Satchmo" (short for "satchelmouth"). Biggest hit: "Hello Dolly." His song "What a Wonderful World" was used in the film *Good Morning, Vietnam*. He always said his birthday was July 4, 1900, but his baptism certificate from Sacred Heart of Jesus Church in New Orleans shows he was baptized August 25, 1901, three weeks after his birth on August 4th. (Died 7-6-71.)

FACTS FROM THE PAST

1735 A jury acquitted New York publisher **JOHN PETER ZENGER** of libel, saying that "the truth is not libelous," thus establishing freedom of press in America.

1892 Sunday school teacher **LIZZIE BORDEN** was arrested in Fall River, Massachusetts, charged with the hatchet murders of her father and stepmother. (She was acquitted at the trial.)

1922 **EVERY TELEPHONE IN THE U.S. AND CANADA WENT DEAD**, as AT&T and the Bell Systems shut down all its switchboards and switching stations for one minute—in memory of **ALEXANDER GRAHAM BELL**, who had died two days earlier. During this one-time only historical event, none of the 13 million telephones in operation could be used.

1944 The Gestapo raided the secret annex of a house in Amsterdam where the Frank family had been hiding for two years to avoid extermination by the Nazis during WWII. They arrested 8 people, including 14-year-old **ANNE FRANK.** Her diary, kept while in hiding, gained international fame years after her death in a concentration camp.

1957 **THE EVERLY BROTHERS** appeared on the "Ed Sullivan Show" and sang their latest hit, "Wake Up Little Susie." At that time it was a controversial song and banned by many radio stations.

1962 **NELSON MANDELA** was captured by police. Mandela, a black South African leader, lawyer and political activist, in 1952 established the **FIRST AFRICAN-AMERICAN LAW PARTNERSHIP** in South Africa. Having been in conflict with the white government there much of his life, he was apprehended by security police, and sentenced to five years in prison. In 1963 he faced a new trial for sabotage, high treason and conspiracy to overthrow the government. In June 1964 he was sentenced to life in prison. He was released in 1990, 28 years after his capture.

1973 **STEVIE WONDER** was seriously hurt when the car he was riding in collided with a lumber truck in Salisbury, North Carolina.

1984 **CARL LEWIS** won the **GOLD MEDAL** in the 100-meter dash at the L.A. Summer Olympics; the first of 4 he would win altogether.

1992 Indictments were handed down charging officers Laurence Powell, Timothy Wind, and Theodore Briseno with aiding and abetting the videotaped kicking and baton beating of **RODNEY KING**, a African-American motorist.

1992 Actor **CHARLIE SHEEN** paid $93,500 for the baseball that **MOOKIE WILSON** bounced through Bill Buckner's legs, ending Game 6 of the 1986 World Series.

1993 Police officers **STACEY KOON** and **LAURENCE POWELL**, convicted of violating **RODNEY KING**'s civil rights, were sentenced to $2\frac{1}{2}$ years in prison.

AUGUST 5

You're not getting fatter—
the world's getting thinner.

BIRTHDAYS

- **VERN GOSDIN** C&W singer. (Woodland, AL) Biggest hit: "I Can Tell By the Way You Dance, You're Gonna Love Me Tonight" in 1984. Year/**Age**: 1995/**61** 1996/**62** 1997/**63**

- **JONATHAN SILVERMAN** Actor. TV's "Gimme A Break." In film *Weekend at Bernie's II.* Year/**Age**: 1995/**29** 1996/**30** 1997/**31**

- **NEIL ARMSTRONG** Former astronaut. (Wapakoneta, OH) He was the first man on the moon. The former Navy pilot and first civilian astronaut went into space as commander of Gemini 8 in 1966 and the moon shot as Commander of Apollo 11 in 1969. Year/**Age**: 1995/**65** 1996/**66** 1997/**67**

- **GORDON JOHNCOCK** Racecar driver. Year/**Age**: 1995/**59** 1996/**60** 1997/**61**

- **ROMAN GABRIEL** Football great. Rams and Oakland quarterback. Year/**Age**: 1995/**55** 1996/**56** 1997/**57**

- **LONI ANDERSON** Actress. (St. Paul, MN) Gained fame as secretary Jennifer Marlowe on the TV sitcom "WKRP in Cincinnati" and later on "Easy Street," "Necessity," and "Nurses." Was married to Burt Reynolds for 5 years until separation in 1993. They have an adopted son. Year/**Age**: 1995/**50** 1996/**51** 1997/**52**

- **SAMMI SMITH** C&W singer. (Orange, CA) Biggest hit: "Help Me Make it Through the Night," which sold over 2 million copies. Year/**Age**: 1995/**52** 1996/**53** 1997/**54**

- **TAWNY KITAEN** Actress. TV's "New WKRP in Cincinnati" and "America's Funniest People." Year/**Age**: 1995/**34** 1996/**35** 1997/**36**

- **ERIKA SLEZAK** Actress. (Los Angeles, CA) Emmy winner for role of Victoria Lord Buchanan in soap opera "One Life to Live." Year/**Age**: 1995/**49** 1996/**50** 1997/**51**

- **PATRICK EWING** Basketball star. (Kingston, Jamaica) Member of 1992 Olympic Dream Team. He led the U.S. team to a gold medal at the 1984 games. Named NBA Rookie of the year in 1986. Year/**Age**: 1995/**33** 1996/**34** 1997/**35**

- **RICK HUXLEY** Musician. (England) With the DAVE CLARK FIVE. Their biggest hit: "Over & Over" in 1965. Year/**Age**: 1995/**53** 1996/**54** 1997/**55**

- **JOHN SAXON** Actor. (NYC) A former model. In films including: *The Cardinal* and *Death of a Gunfighter.* He was also on TV in "The Bold Ones." Year/**Age**: 1995/**60** 1996/**61** 1997/**62**

- **SAMANTHA SANG** Singer. (Australia) Her biggest record in 1977: "Emotion." Barry Gibb did the back-up vocal. Year/**Age**: 1995/**42** 1996/**43** 1997/**44**

- **ROBERT TAYLOR** Actor. (1911-1969 – Born Spangler Arlington Brugh in Filley, NE) Classic leading man in the movies. Played Billy the Kid in his younger days. He signed with MGM for 26 years, and never argued about his films—he said they knew what they were doing. (Died 6-8-69.)

- **JOHN HUSTON** Producer/director/actor. (1906-1987 – Nevada, MO) Known for prize-winning movies including *The Maltese Falcon* and *The African Queen.* He won the Oscar in 1948 for best director of the film *Treasure of Sierra Madre* and directed his daughter Angelica in *Prizzi's Honor* for which she won an Academy Award. (Died 8-28-87.)

FACTS FROM THE PAST

1583 The first English colony in North America was established when English explorer **SIR HUMPHREY GILBERT,** sailing off the coast of Newfoundland, in his ship called *Squirrel*, claimed the harbor of St. Johns for the crown.

1861 Abraham Lincoln signed into law the **FIRST FEDERAL INCOME TAX**. It was a 3 percent tax levied on incomes over $800. It was an emergency Civil War-time tax only, and was rescinded in 1872.

1864 During the Civil War, Union Admiral **DAVID FARRAGUT** was said to have given his famous order, "Damn the torpedoes...full speed ahead," as he led his fleet against Mobile Bay, AL. Union forces disabled the Confederate ship *Tennessee* and secured the bay.

1921 **HAROLD ARLIN** of **KDKA RADIO** in Pittsburgh, PA, broadcast the first major league baseball game held at Forbes Field. The Pirates won over Philadelphia, 8 to 5. Arlin died on March 14, 1986. He was 90 years old.

1924 The comic strip **LITTLE ORPHAN ANNIE,** by **HAROLD GRAY**, made its debut, in the *New York Daily News.*

1954 24 boxers became the first inductees into the **BOXING HALL OF FAME**, including Henry Armstrong, Gentleman Jim Corbett, Jack Dempsey, Jack Johnson, Joe Louis, and John L. Sullivan.

1957 Dick Clark's **"AMERICAN BANDSTAND"** made its TV debut in Philadelphia, PA. The first guests were "The Chordettes," a female quartet from Sheboygan, WI, singing "Born to be with You." The first record played was "That'll Be the Day" by Buddy Holly. It was a local show at first and then was picked up by ABC-TV.

1962 Actress **MARILYN MONROE**'s nude, lifeless body was found by the housekeeper in the bedroom of her Los Angeles home. Her death was ruled a "possible suicide" caused by an acute barbiturate poisoning.

1975 **STEVIE WONDER** signed what at the time was the richest record deal ever — a $13 million deal with Motown.

1983 **DAVID CROSBY** was sentenced to 8 years in prison for drug and firearms possession after reportedly sleeping through most of the trial. He was paroled in 1986.

1986 It was revealed that artist **ANDREW WYETH** had, over a 15-year period, secretly created 240 drawings and paintings of a woman named Helga Testrof, a neighbor in Chadds Ford, PA.

1994 **BILL COSBY** had to pay damages of 20 cents for assaulting a photographer. The photographer had sued for $2 million.

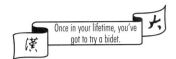

Once in your lifetime, you've got to try a bidet.

AUGUST 6

BIRTHDAYS

- **STEPFANIE KRAMER** Actress. Dee Dee McColl on TV's "Hunter." Year/**Age**: 1995/**39** 1996/**40** 1997/**41**

- **ROBERT MITCHUM** Actor. (Bridgeport, CT) Got his start in the Hopalong Cassidy films. He was nominated for best supporting actor in *G.I. Joe*, and appeared in the TV mini-series *Winds of War* and *War and Remembrance*. He played villian Max Cody in the original *Cape Fear*. Year/**Age**: 1995/**78** 1996/**79** 1997/**80**

- **PETER BONERZ** Actor/director. (Portsmouth, NH) Played orthodontist Jerry Robinson on the "Bob Newhart Show." Now a director for "Murphy Brown." Year/**Age**: 1995/**57** 1996/**58** 1997/**59**

- **RANDY DeBARGE** Bass player. (Grand Rapids, MI) Member of the family group DeBARGE. Biggest hit: "Rhythm of the Night" from the Berry Gordy film *The Last Dragon*. Year/**Age**: 1995/**37** 1996/**38** 1997/**39**

- **RAY BUKTENICA** Actor. (New York, NY) Appeared on "Rhoda" and "House Calls." Year/**Age**: 1995/**53** 1996/**54** 1997/**55**

- **DAVID ROBINSON** Pro basketball player. (Key West, FL) The San Antonia Spurs Center was named NBA Rookie of the Year in 1990. He played for the bronze-medal-winning U.S. team at the 1988 Olympics in Seoul and took home the gold with the 1992 Dream Team in Barcelona. Year/**Age**: 1995/**30** 1996/**31** 1997/**32**

- **ANDY MESSERSMITH** Baseball pitcher. (Toms River, NJ) One of the first players to go free agent. Year/**Age**: 1995/**50** 1996/**51** 1997/**52**

- **CATHERINE HICKS** Actress. (Scottsdale, AZ) Played Dr. Emily Rappant on "Bad News Bears," and was on the soap "Ryan's Hope." Her films include *She's Out of Control*. Year/**Age**: 1995/**44** 1996/**45** 1997/**46**

- **SOLEIL MOON FRYE** Actress. (Glendora, CA) TV's "Punky Brewster." Had a breast reduction at age 15. Year/**Age**: 1995/**19** 1996/**20** 1997/**21**

- **LUCILLE BALL** Actress. (1911-1989 – Celoron, a village near Jamestown, NY) She was told in drama school, at age 15, that she was too introverted to succeed in show business. Before she did "I Love Lucy" with husband Desi Arnaz, she appeared in over 70 movies including: *Yours, Mine and Ours* and, later, *Mame*. She won five Emmys for Best Comedienne, and "I Love Lucy" won over 200 awards. She was married to Desi from 1940-1960 and had been married to Gary Morton since 1961. (Died 4-26-89.)

- **ANDY WARHOL** Pop artist. (1928-1987 – Pittsburgh, PA) A dead-pan Peter Pan of Pop Art who turned images of soup cans and superstars into museum pieces, like his famous oil-on-canvas painting, *Campbell's Soup* in 1965. (Died 2-22-87.)

- **LOUELLA PARSONS** Hollywood gossip columnist. (1881-1972 – Born Louella Oettinger in Freeport, IL) (Died 12-9-72.)

FACTS FROM THE PAST

1890 The **ELECTRIC CHAIR WAS FIRST USED** in a prison in Auburn, NY, for the execution of convicted axe murderer **WILLIAM KEMMELER,** who killed his sweetheart in Buffalo, NY. There was a storm of controversy over whether the chair was a humane form of Execution. At the Florida State Corrections Dept., there's a waiting list for people who want to watch a "live" execution.

1890 **DENTON TRUE YOUNG** (better known as "Cy") pitched his first major league baseball game, for Cleveland (of the National League, not the American League, which hadn't been founded yet). The annual award for best pitcher was named for him. He gained the first of his 511 major league victories as he pitched Cleveland to a 6-1 win over Chicago. He won at least 20 games each season from 1891 through 1904. During his 22 years as a major leaguer, he set lifetime records for most complete games pitched (751), most innings pitched (7,377), most games won (507), and even most games lost (307).

1926 **HARRY HOUDINI** stayed underwater for 91 minutes, inside an airtight compartment that supposedly had enough air to keep a man alive for no more than 6 minutes.

1926 20-year-old **GERTRUDE EDERLE** from New York City was the **FIRST WOMAN TO SWIM THE ENGLISH CHANNEL,** covering 35 miles in 14 hours, 39 minutes, bettering the men's record by two hours.

1945 At 8:15 a.m. local time, an American B-29 Super Fortress, the **ENOLA GAY,** dropped an **ATOMIC BOMB,** code named "Little Boy," on Hiroshima, Japan. The 10-foot-long bomb killed an estimated 100,000 people, including the Japanese 2nd Army and many more who later died from radiation poisoning. Four square miles were wiped out. This was the **FIRST NUCLEAR WEAPON USED IN WARFARE.** A second A-bomb was dropped on Nagasaki three days later.

1952 47-year-old **SATCHEL PAIGE** became the oldest major league pitcher to complete a game or shutout when he beat Virgil Trucks and the Detroit Tigers, 1-0, in 12 innings.

1978 **POPE PAUL VI** died at age 80. He had a massive heart attack at 9:40 p.m. At the same moment, his alarm clock that was set for 6 a.m. started to ring, and minutes after his death a cloud-burst drenched the valley in northeastern Italy, causing the worst flooding there in 25 years. Pope Paul VI was responsible for dropping the law against eating meat on Friday and simplifying the liturgy. His successor, Pope John Paul I, died after 34 days in office, making 1978 the year that had 3 different popes on the throne of St. Peter's.

1992 The **FIRST OSCAR EVER SOLD** was auctioned off in New York for $60,500. It cost the Academy less than $500 to make the statuette of britannia metal and plated 24-karat gold. **HAROLD RUSSELL,** who won the award in 1947 for *The Best Years of Our Lives*, sold the Oscar against the Academy's wishes for reasons that included eye surgery for his wife.

1994 In Budapest, newlyweds **MICHAEL JACKSON** and **LISA MARIE PRESLEY** made their first public appearance together.

AUGUST 7

Eek. A mouse.

BIRTHDAYS

- **STAN FREBERG** Comedian/adman. (Pasadena, CA) One of the great creative geniuses in the radio commercial business. His first hit record was "St. George & the Dragonet" in 1953. His *U.S. of America* album is probably aired the most of all his recordings. Year/**Age:** 1995/**69** 1996/**70** 1997/**71**

- **B.J. (BILLY JOE) THOMAS** Singer. (Houston, TX) Hit: "Raindrops Keep Falling On My Head" in 1970, from the movie *Butch Cassidy & the Sundance Kid*. Wrote the TV theme for "Growing Pains." Year/**Age:** 1995/**53** 1996/**54** 1997/**55**

- **FELICE BRYANT** Composer. Along with her husband, Boudleaux Bryant (deceased), wrote "Only the Lonely," which was recorded by Roy Orbison, and a lot of the Everly Brothers hits, including: "All I Have to do is Dream," "Bye, Bye Love," and "Bird Dog." Year/**Age:** 1995/**70** 1996/**71** 1997/**72**

- **LANA CANTRELL** Singer. (Sydney, Australia) Grammy Award winner in 1967. Year/**Age:** 1995/**52** 1996/**53** 1997/**54**

- **ALBERTO SALAZAR** Marathon runner. (Havana, Cuba) Year/**Age:** 1995/**37** 1996/**38** 1997/**39**

- **GARRISON KEILLOR** Writer/producer. (Anoka, MN) The originator of *A Prairie Home Companion*. He created Lake Wobegone in 1978. Year/**Age:** 1995/**53** 1996/**54** 1997/**55**

- **ALAN PAGE** Football star. (OH) The Hall of Famer played for the Vikings from 1967-78 and the Bears 1978-81. He is Minnesota's first African-American Supreme Court Justice and the first African-American ever elected to state-wide office in Minnesota. Year/**Age:** 1995/**50** 1996/**51** 1997/**52**

- **RODNEY CROWELL** Songwriter. (Houston, TX) Wrote "Shame on the Moon" for Bob Seger. One of his biggest hits was with his former wife, Rosanne Cash, daughter of Johnny Cash: "It's Such A Small World" in 1988. Won his first Grammy in 1990 for best country song: "After All This Time." Year/**Age:** 1995/**45** 1996/**46** 1997/**47**

- **DON LARSEN** Former NY Yankee pitcher. In 1956, he became the first, and only, pitcher to hurl a perfect game in World Series play. The Yankees won the series over the old Brooklyn Dodgers, 4-3. Year/**Age:** 1995/**66** 1996/**67** 1997/**68**

- **EDWIN EDWARDS** Louisiana governor. (Avoyelles Parish, LA) Defeated former KKK officer David Duke in the 1992 election. Year/**Age:** 1995/**68** 1996/**69** 1997/**70**

- **RALPH JOHNSON BUNCHE** American statesman. (1904-1971 – Detroit, MI) UN official and Nobel Peace Prize recipient. (Died 12-9-71.)

FACTS FROM THE PAST

1782 George Washington established the **ORDER OF THE PURPLE HEART** at Newburgh, NY, when he was Commander-in-Chief of the Continental Army in the closing years of the Revolutionary War. The first recipients of the order were honored the following May.

1861 The **FIRST MAN TO FLY** professionally for the American military flew reconnaissance over rebel forces **IN A BALLOON. THADDEUS LOWE** was officially appointed to be the Union army's military aeronaut by President Lincoln.

1882 A little feud broke out between the **HATFIELD** family of southern West Virginia and the **McCOYS** of eastern Kentucky. By the time it ended, about 100 men, women, and children had been either killed or wounded.

1888 The **REVOLVING DOOR** was patented by Theophilus Van Kannel of Philadelphia.

1927 The **PEACE BRIDGE** between the United States and Canada was dedicated during ceremonies attended by the Prince of Wales and Vice President Charles Dawes.

1934 The U.S. Court of Appeals upheld a lower court ruling striking down the government's attempt to ban the controversial James Joyce novel, *Ulysses*.

1935 Seattle high school teacher **RALPH UPTON** died. He invented the phrase "Stop, Look and Listen," used to teach children how to cross streets and railroad tracks.

1948 **HANK WILLIAMS** made his first appearance on the "Louisiana Hayride" radio show over station KWKH in Shreveport.

1954 **ROGER BANNISTER**, from England, became the first person to run the mile in less than four minutes.

1963 The first "Beach Blanket" movie opened. *Beach Party* starred **ANNETTE FUNICELLO** and **FRANKIE AVALON**.

1964 Relying on fabricated intelligence information, Congress passed the **GULF OF TONKIN RESOLUTION**, giving President Johnson broad powers in dealing with North Vietnam. Johnson used the resolution as **A DECLARATION OF WAR.**

1970 **CHRISTINE McVIE** became the first female member of **FLEETWOOD MAC**. McVie was married to the group's bass player, John McVie.

1974 French stuntman **PHILIPPE PETIT** dodged security guards and walked on a **TIGHTROPE** strung between the twin towers of the **WORLD TRADE CENTER** in NYC, 1,350 feet above the street.

1984 The U.S. **WOMEN'S BASKETBALL TEAM** won the **GOLD MEDAL** at the Los Angeles Olympics, defeating the South Korean team, 85-55.

1986 Actor **TOM SELLECK** married **JILLIE MACK**.

1990 President Bush ordered U.S. air and ground forces to Saudi Arabia as the White House warned of a growing and "imminent" **IRAQI THREAT** to the oil-rich nation.

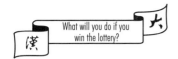

What will you do if you win the lottery?

AUGUST 8

Sneak a Zucchini onto Your Neighbor's Porch Day

BIRTHDAYS

• **DUSTIN HOFFMAN** Actor. (Los Angeles, CA) Named after a silent-movie cowboy, Dustin Farnum. Appeared in the soap "Search For Tomorrow." He won an Oscar in 1980 for *Kramer vs. Kramer* and in 1989 for *Rain Man*. Mike Nichols gave him his break when he cast him as Benjamin in *The Graduate* in 1967. Appeared in *Midnight Cowboy, Little Big Man, Ishtar, Hero* and portrayed "Mumbles" in *Dick Tracy*. He took ballet lessons for his role in the movie *Hook*. Year/**Age**: 1995/**58** 1996/**59** 1997/**60**

• **ESTHER WILLIAMS** Actress. (Los Angeles, CA) Starred in many of the swimming extravaganza movies of the 1940s, *Neptures Daughter* and *Million Dollar Mermaid*. She was married to Fernando Lamas until his death in 1983. Her stepson, Lorenzo Lamas of "Falcon Crest," credits her with much of his success. Year/**Age**: 1995/**72** 1996/**73** 1997/**74**

• **DONNY MOST** Actor. (NYC) He played the loud-mouthed redhead, Ralph Malph, on "Happy Days." Year/**Age**: 1995/**42** 1996/**43** 1997/**44**

• **DINO DeLAURENTIIS** Producer. (Born in Torre Annunziata, Italy) Credits include *The Bible, Barbarella, Jaws IV*, and the remake of *King Kong* in 1976 with Jessica Lange. Year/**Age**: 1995/**76** 1996/**77** 1997/**78**

• **KEITH CARRADINE** Actor/singer. (San Mateo, CA) Had a hit in 1976: "I'm Easy." He sang it to Lily Tomlin in a motel room in the film *Nashville*. Also in film "Andre." It won an Oscar for Best Song. Also appeared on Broadway in *Will Rogers Follies*. Year/**Age**: 1995/**45** 1996/**46** 1997/**47**

• **MICHAEL JOHNSON** Singer/guitarist. (Denver, CO) Once with CHAD MITCHELL TRIO. Mike's biggest hit: "Bluer Than Blue" in 1978. Year/**Age**: 1995/**51** 1996/**52** 1997/**53**

• **DAVID "The Edge" EVANS** Guitarist. (Ireland) With the group U2. Year/**Age**: 1995/**34** 1996/**35** 1997/**36**

• **DEBORAH NORVILLE** TV hostess. (Dalton, GA) Jane Pauley's replacement on the "Today Show" 1990-91. Year/**Age**: 1995/**37** 1996/**38** 1997/**39**

• **SYLVIA SIDNEY** Actress. (Born Sophia Kosow in New York City) Her many films include *You Only Live Once, Les Miserables, Love From a Stranger*, and *Thirty Something*. Year/**Age**: 1995/**85** 1996/**86** 1997/**87**

• **JERRY TARKANIAN** Basketball coach. (Euclid, OH) Controversial former basketball coach of the Nevada-Las Vegas Runnin' Rebels, and NBA's San Antonio Spurs. He was fired after coaching only 20 games for the San Antonio Spurs. Year/**Age**: 1995/**65** 1996/**66** 1997/**67**

• **MEL TILLIS** C&W singer. (Born Lonnie Melvin in Tampa, FL) He has written over 500 songs including: "Ruby Don't Take Your Love to Town" and "Detroit City." His biggest hits: "I Ain't Never" and "Good Woman Blues." His autobiography is titled *Stutterin' Boy*. He was in the movies *Smokey and the Bandit 2* and *W.W. & the Dixie Dance King*. His daughter Pam is also a country singer. Year/**Age**: 1995/**63** 1996/**64** 1997/**65**

• **PHIL BALSLEY** C&W singer. (Augusta County, VA) Sings baritone with the STATLER BROTHERS. Their biggest hit: "Flowers on the Wall." Year/**Age**: 1995/**56** 1996/**57** 1997/**58**

• **PETER WEIR** Movie director. (Sydney, Australia) *Dead Poets Society, Witness*, and *Green Card*. Year/**Age**: 1995/**51** 1996/**52** 1997/**53**

• **CONNIE STEVENS** Singer/actress. (Born Concetta Anne Ingolia in Brooklyn, NY) She starred in the TV series "Hawaiian Eye" as Cricket Blake from 1959 to 1963, and she had a hit record in 1960: "Sixteen Reasons." Has a line of "Forever Spring" cosmetics. Year/**Age**: 1995/**57** 1996/**58** 1997/**59**

• **WEBB PIERCE** C&W singer. (1926-1991 – West Monroe, LA) His first 28 releases hit Top 10 on C&W charts. He had 51 Top 10 C&W records. His biggest hit: "In the Jailhouse Now" in 1955 was #1 for 21 weeks. (Died 2-24-91.)

• **JOE TEX** Singer. (1933-1982 – Born Joseph Arrington, Jr., in Rogers, TX) Biggest hit: "I Gotcha" in 1972. Died of a heart attack on 8-13-82.

FACTS FROM THE PAST

1876 THOMAS A. EDISON received a patent for his **MIMEOGRAPH**, which he described as a "method of preparing autographic stencils for printing."

1940 Nazi warplanes began bombing Southeastern England in what would be remembered as **"THE BATTLE OF BRITAIN."**

1960 DECCA Records in Britain destroyed 25,000 copies of the song **"TELL LAURA I LOVE HER"** by Ray Peterson. The company refused to release the single, saying it was "too tasteless and vulgar for the English sensibility."

1963 A gang of 15 thieves made off with over $7 million in Britain's **GREAT TRAIN ROBBERY**. The men reportedly planned the caper for a year from a barn nearby the train station. The crime required the men to steal 2 $\frac{1}{2}$ tons of banks notes. All but three of the criminals were identified by the fingerprints which covered the barn.. One of the convicted men, Ronald Biggs, escaped shortly after sentancing, and is still at large. Only about $1 million of the stolen money was ever recovered.

1973 V.P. SPIRO T. AGNEW branded as "damned lies" reports he had taken kickbacks from government contracts in Maryland. He vowed never to resign. He resigned on Oct. 10, 1973.

1974 PRESIDENT RICHARD NIXON announced in a nationally broadcast address that he would resign his office at noon the following day. Nixon's decision followed new revelations of his direct involvement in the Watergate coverup.

1992 The **U.S. OLYMPIC DREAM TEAM** defeated Croatia 117-85 to win the gold medal. The team averaged 117.3 points a game, led 306 minutes 54 seconds out of a possible 320 minutes, and its largest lead was 66 points.

1994 Israeli Prime Minister **YITZHAK RABIN** and **CROWN PRINCE HASSAN OF JORDAN** cut the ceremonial ribbon opening The first border point between Irael and Jordan.

AUGUST 9

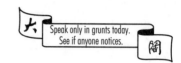
Speak only in grunts today.
See if anyone notices.

BIRTHDAYS

• **WHITNEY HOUSTON** Singer. (Newark, NJ) Her cousin is Dionne Warwick. One of her most popular songs, "Greatest Love of All," was originally released as the flip side of "You Give Good Love." Three of her albums have sold more than 40 million copies. She made her acting debut opposite Kevin Costner in *The Bodyguard*. She is married to Bobby Brown and had a baby in 1993. Year/**Age:** 1995/**32** 1996/**33** 1997/**34**

• **DAVID STEINBERG** Comedian/director. (Canada) Appears on TV commercials for Magnavox. Year/**Age:** 1995/**53** 1996/**54** 1997/**55**

• **MELANIE GRIFFITH** Actress. (NYC) Best actress Academy Award nominee for *Working Girl*. Also in *A Stranger Among Us* and *Born Yesterday*. Daughter of actress Tippi Hedren and wife of actor Don Johnson. Year/**Age:** 1995/**38** 1996/**39** 1997/**40**

• **DEION SANDERS** Athlete. Pro football player with the Atlanta Falcons and baseball with the Atlanta Braves. Year/**Age:** 1995/**28** 1996/**29** 1997/**30**

• **BARBARA MASON** Singer. (Philadelphia, PA) Biggest record: "Yes, I'm Ready" in 1965, which she wrote. Year/**Age:** 1995/**58** 1996/**59** 1997/**60**

• **BILLY HENDERSON** Singer. With the SPINNERS. Biggest hit: "Working My Way Back to You" in 1979. Year/**Age:** 1995/**56** 1996/**57** 1997/**58**

• **KURTIS BLOW** Rapper. (Harlem, NY) Known as the first successful "rap star." Year/**Age:** 1995/**35** 1996/**36** 1997/**37**

• **PAT PETERSON** Actor. "Knots Landing." Year/**Age:** 1995/**29** 1996/**30** 1997/**31**

• **ROD LAVER** Tennis champ. (Australia) He won Wimbledon, the French, Australian and U.S. Opens to complete a tennis grand slam in 1969. Year/**Age:** 1995/**57** 1996/**58** 1997/**59**

• **MERLE KILGORE** C&W singer. (Chickasha, OK) Wrote "Ring of Fire" for JOHNNY CASH in 1963 and "Wolverton Mountain," a #1 record for CLAUDE KING in 1962. He was in the movie *Five Card Stud*. Also manager for HANK WILLIAMS, JR. Biggest hit: "Love Has Made You Beautiful" in 1960. Year/**Age:** 1995/**61** 1996/**62** 1997/**63**

• **SAM ELLIOTT** Actor. (Sacramento, CA) Films include *Lonesome Dove, Gettsburg*, and *Mask* with Cher. Year/**Age:** 1995/**51** 1996/**52** 1997/**53**

• **RALPH HOUK** Former baseball manager. Year/**Age:** 1995/**76** 1996/**77** 1997/**78**

• **AMANDA BERSE** Actress. Marcy on TV's "Married With Children." Year/**Age:** 1995/**37** 1996/**38** 1997/**39**

• **BOB COUSY** Basketball Hall of Famer. (NYC) Boston Celtics guard. Wrote autobiography "The Killer Instinct." In the film *Blue Chips* as an athletic director opposite Nick Nolte. Year/**Age:** 1995/**66** 1996/**67** 1997/**68**

• **KEN NORTON** Boxer. (Jacksonville, FL) WBC heavyweight champ in 1978. He beat Mohammed Ali in 1963. In the boxing Hall of Fame. Year/**Age:** 1995/**50** 1996/**51** 1997/**52**

• **ELIZABETH VASSEY** Actress. (Raleigh, NC) Played Emily Ann Sago on "All My Children." Year/**Age:** 1995/**23** 1996/**24** 1997/**25**

• **DOUG WILLIAMS** Football. Quarterback for Washington Redskins. Year/**Age:** 1995/**40** 1996/**41** 1997/**42**

• **CHARLES FARRELL** Actor. (1901-1990 – Onset Bay, MA) Silent film and TV actor, best known as the widower father opposite Gale Storm on TV's "My Little Margie." He worked with Ralph Bellamy to develop posh Palm Springs Racquet Clubs, which became a mecca for Hollywood elite. (Died 5-11-90.)

FACTS FROM THE PAST

1638 Jonas Bronck bought the **BRONX** from the Indians. He paid 400 beads.

1848 The **FREE-SOIL PARTY** nominated Martin Van Buren for president at its convention in Buffalo, New York.

1854 **HENRY DAVID THOREAU** published *Walden,* in which he described his experiences while living in a small cabin near Walden Pond in Massachusetts. The area is now open to visitors.

1902 **EDWARD VII** was crowned King of Great Britain and Ireland. He is responsible for the practice of leaving the bottom button undone on the vest of a man's three-piece suit, because he was too fat to button his bottom button.

1930 The forerunner of the cartoon character **BETTY BOOP** first appeared in the animated short *Dizzy Dishes* by Max Fleischer.

1936 **JESSE OWENS** became the first person to win 4 gold medals at the Berlin Olympics as the U.S. took 1st place in the 400-meter relay.

1942 Britain arrested Indian nationalist **MOHANDAS K. GANDHI.** He was not released until 1944.

1944 **SMOKEY THE BEAR** was created by the Forest Service and Wartime Advertising Council to represent forest-fire prevention.

1969 Actress **SHARON TATE**, hair stylist **JAY SEBRING**, coffee heiress **ABIGAIL FOLGER**, movie director **VOITYCK FRYKOWSKI,** and high school graduate **STEVEN PARENT** were found brutally murdered in the Los Angeles home Tate shared with her husband, movie director Roman Polanski. Cult leader Charles Manson and a group of his young disciples were later convicted of the murders.

1974 V.P. Gerald Ford was sworn in as 38th U.S. President after **RICHARD NIXON** became the **FIRST AMERICAN PRESIDENT TO RESIGN** the office. Two V.P.s had resigned: John Calhoun in 1832 and Spiro Agnew, 1973.

1988 The Edmonton Oilers traded National Hockey League star **WAYNE GRETZKY** to the Los Angeles Kings. His wife, Janet, an actress, spent time in L.A. and Wayne wanted to be with her. The Kings gave up two players and $15 million for Gretzky.

1993 Charges were brought against Hollywood madam **HEIDI FLEISS** for running an exclusive call-girl operation in Los Angeles.

A primal scream will do you good.

AUGUST 10

BIRTHDAYS

- **RHONDA FLEMING** Actress. (Born Marilyn Louis in Los Angeles, CA) Redheaded beauty of 1940s films including *Little Egypt* and *Inferno*. She runs a women's cancer clinic in memory of her sister. Year/**Age**: 1995/**72** 1996/**73** 1997/**74**

- **BOBBY HATFIELD** Singer. (Beaver Dam, WI) He and Bill Medley made up the RIGHTEOUS BROTHERS. They first recorded under the name The Paramours, until a man in a nightclub yelled out, "That's righteous, brothers!" Bobby is the one with the high voice. Their biggest hit: "You've Lost That Lovin' Feeling" in 1964. Their "Unchained Melody" is heard in the film *Ghost*. Year/**Age**: 1995/**55** 1996/**56** 1997/**57**

- **RONNIE BENNETT SPECTOR** Singer. (Born Veronica Bennett in NYC) Ronnie, her sister, and cousin were discovered by Phil Spector, whom she later married. Their group was The RONETTES and their biggest record: "Be My Baby" in 1963. In the film: *Twist Around the Clock*. The Ronettes split up in 1966; Ronnie and Phil split in 1974. Year/**Age**: 1995/**52** 1996/**53** 1997/**54**

- **GINO TORRETTA** Football. (Pinole, CA) 1992 Heisman Trophy winner. He was a child actor sharing scenes with Clint Eastwood long before dreaming of being a quarterback with the Miami Hurricanes. Year/**Age**: 1995/**25** 1996/**26** 1997/**27**

- **NENEH CHERRY** Singer. (Stockholm, Sweden) Hits: "Buffalo Stance" and "Kisses on the Wind" in 1989. Year/**Age**: 1995/**31** 1996/**32** 1997/**33**

- **ROSANNA ARQUETTE** Actress. (NYC) In TV movie *The Executioner's Song* about convicted killer Gary Gilmore. Starred in *After Hours* and with Madonna in *Desperately Seeking Susan*. Year/**Age**: 1995/**36** 1996/**37** 1997/**38**

- **IAN ANDERSON** Singer. (England) He was the lead singer and flutist with JETHRO TULL. Their biggest hit: "Living in the Past" in 1972. Year/**Age**: 1995/**48** 1996/**49** 1997/**50**

- **JIMMY DEAN** Entertainer/sausage maker. (Born Seth Ward in Plainview, TX) His biggest hit: "Big Bad John," which he wrote in an hour and a half on an airplane flight heading to Nashville. It was on the charts 4 months and made it to #1 in late 1961. He was also responsible for the "Muppets" early success. Year/**Age**: 1995/**67** 1996/**68** 1997/**69**

- **EDDIE FISHER** Singer. (Born Edwin Jack Fisher in Philadelphia, PA) His biggest hit: "Oh! My Pa-Pa." He has been married to Elizabeth Taylor, Connie Stevens, and Debbie Reynolds. Debbie and Eddie are parents of Carrie Fisher, who was the princess in *Star Wars*. Year/**Age**: 1995/**67** 1996/**68** 1997/**69**

- **PATTI AUSTIN** Singer. (NYC) Made her debut when she was 3 years old at Harlem's Apollo Theater, singing "Teach Me, Tonight." Her first #1 hit didn't come until 1982, sung with James Ingram: "Baby, Come to Me." She had another big hit with Ingram: "How Do You Keep the Music Playing" in 1983 from the movie *Best Friends*. In the film *Tucker*. Year/**Age**: 1995/**47** 1996/**48** 1997/**49**

- **JACK HALEY** Actor. (1902-1979 – Born Jonathan Haley in Boston, MA) He was the tin man in *The Wizard of Oz*. (Died 6-6-79.)

- **HERBERT CLARK HOOVER** 31st U.S. President. (1874-1964 – West Branch, IA) First president to have a telephone on his desk, installed in 1929. (Died 10-20-64.)

FACTS FROM THE PAST

1846   Congress chartered the "Nation's Attic," the **SMITHSONIAN INSTITUTION**. It was named in honor of English scientist Joseph Smithson, whose bequest of $500,000 made it possible. The museum contains everything from the Wright Brothers airplane to Archie Bunker's chair.

1901   Chicago's **FRANK ISBELL** set an **AMERICAN LEAGUE RECORD** by stranding 11 teammates on the basepaths in one game.

1921   **FRANKLIN D. ROOSEVELT** was stricken with **POLIO** while at his summer home on the Canadian Island of Campobello.

1948   **CANDID CAMERA** debuted, created and hosted by Allen Funt. The idea originated when Funt was in the Army and recorded servicemen's gripes and broadcast them on Armed Forces Radio.

1959   The male members of the vocal group **THE PLATTERS**, including Tony Williams, were arrested in a room at the Sheraton Gibston Hotel in Cincinnati. The four African-American men with four 19-year-old women, three white and one African-American, were in various stages of undress.

1969   **LENO** and **ROSEMARY LaBIANCA** were murdered in their L.A. home by members of Charles Manson's cult, one day after actress Sharon Tate and four other people were slain.

1972   **PAUL** and **LINDA MCCARTNEY** were arrested for drug possession in Gothenburg, Sweden. They were fined $1,200. Paul said, "This will make good publicity for our concert tonight."

1981   **PETE ROSE**, playing for the Phillies, hit a single off St. Louis pitcher Mark Littal to break the **NATIONAL LEAGUE ALL-TIME HIT RECORD** of 3,630 held by Stan Musial.

1984   The women's 3,000-meter race at the 1984 Los Angeles Summer **OLYMPICS** ended abruptly for American runner **MARY DECKER** when she fell after colliding with Zola Budd, who was competing for Britain. Romanian Maricica Puica won the race.

1985   **MICHAEL JACKSON** paid $47.5 million for **ATV MUSIC**, the Northern Songs Catalogue of the **BEATLES'** copyrights, which includes 251 songs written by John Lennon and Paul McCartney.

1994   After talks between players and managers broke off, **DONALD FEHR**, the head of the Major League Baseball Players Assn. said the players were prepared for a long strike. The baseball strike officially began 8/11/94 after the last game was played that day.

AUGUST 11

BIRTHDAYS

- **JOHN CONLEE** C&W. (Versailles, KY) He was a mortician, and later a DJ at WLAC in Nashville. He wrote his first hit, "Rose Colored Glasses" with Glenn Barber. Year/Age: 1995/49 1996/50 1997/51

- **JOE JACKSON** Singer. (England) Biggest hit: "Steppin' Out" in 1982. He taught himself how to play the piano and later graduated from the Royal Academy of Music. Year/Age: 1995/40 1996/41 1997/42

- **ERIC CARMEN** Singer. (Cleveland, OH) Was lead singer with the RASPBERRIES from 1970-1974. Eric's biggest hit: "All By Myself" in 1975. He did the song "Hungry Eyes" in the film *Dirty Dancing*. Year/Age: 1995/46 1996/47 1997/48

- **CARL ROWAN** Newspaper columnist. (Ravenscraft, TN) He was the first African-American man on the National Security Council. Won the Scribes Book Award for *Dream Makers, Dream Breakers: The World of Justice Thurgood Marshall*. Year/Age: 1995/70 1996/71 1997/72

- **HULK HOGAN** Wrestler. (Born Terry Gene Bolle in Augusta, GA) He starred in the films *Suburban Commando* and *Mr. Nanny*. Year/Age: 1995/42 1996/43 1997/44

- **JERRY FALWELL** Clergyman. (Lynchburg, VA) Custodian of Jim and Tammy Bakker's scandal-stained PTL ministry. Year/Age: 1995/62 1996/63 1997/64

- **JEAN PARKER** Actress. (Born Mae Green in Butte, MT) Appeared in *Little Women* and *The Gunfighter*. Year/Age: 1995/83 1996/84 1997/85

- **GUY VALLARI** Singer. With the REGENTS. Biggest hit: "Barbara Ann" in 1961. Year/Age: 1995/52 1996/53 1997/54

- **ARLENE DAHL** Actress. (Minneapolis, MN) Red-haired leading lady, former model and author of 12 books about beauty. Appears on "One Life to Live." She is Lorenzo Lamas's mother. Year/Age: 1995/67 1996/68 1997/69

- **ANNA MASSEY** Actress. (England) Appeared in *Bunny Lake is Missing* and *Frenzy*. Year/Age: 1995/58 1996/59 1997/60

- **ALEX HALEY** Writer. (1921-1992 – Ithaca, NY) Author of *Roots*, for which he received the 1977 Pulitzer Prize. It sold 6 million copies. *Roots* was made into the most popular TV miniseries ever, with 130 million viewers. He wrote the best seller, *The Autobiography of Malcolm X* and *Queen*. (Died 2-10-92.)

- **CARRIE JACOBS BOND** Composer. (1892-1946 – Janesville, WI) Songs include "I Love You Truly." (Died 12-28-46.)

- **BUSTER BROWN** Singer. (1915-1976) Biggest hit: "Fannie Mae" in 1960.

- **LLOYD NOLAN** Actor. (1902-1985 – San Francisco, CA) Co-starred in *Peyton Place* in 1958 and *Airport* in 1969. (Died 9-27-85.)

- **DAVID ATCHISON** Politician. (1807-1886 – Frogtown, KY) He served as president pro tempore of the Senate a number of times and became President of the U.S. for one day on Sunday, March 4, 1849, pending the swearing in of President-elect Zachary Taylor. Atchison, KS, is named for him. (Died 1-26-1886.)

FACTS FROM THE PAST

1896 A patent was issued to Harvey Hubbell for the **ELECTRIC LIGHT BULB** socket with a pull-chain.

1919 Scottish-born steel magnate **ANDREW CARNEGIE** died at age 83. He wanted to leave this world poor, so he sold all of his interests 19 years before he died and spent the rest of his life trying to give his money away. He got rid of $308 million and had $22 million left when he died.

1941 President Roosevelt and British Prime Minister Winston Churchill signed the **ATLANTIC CHARTER** on a warship in the western Atlantic.

1944 Four members of the **JAMES MARVIN COSSON FAMILY** were killed when a U.S. Air Force plane, testing bombs, accidentally dropped three on their home in DeFuniak Springs, FL.

1951 The **FIRST BASEBALL GAME TELEVISED IN COLOR** was between the Boston Braves and the Brooklyn Dodgers, broadcast from Ebbets Field. The Dodger's won 8-1.

1961 Milwaukee Braves baseball pitcher **WARREN SPAHN** got his 300th victory, beating the Cubs 2-1. He's now a rancher in Oklahoma.

1972 **ELVIS** and **PRISCILLA PRESLEY** filed for divorce after less than five years of marriage.

1977 **DAVID "SON OF SAM" BERKOWITZ** was arrested. The psychotic murderer was caught when he got a parking ticket a couple of blocks from the scene of one of the killings.

1984 During a sound check for his weekly radio address, **PRESIDENT REAGAN** joked, "My fellow Americans, I am pleased to tell you that I just signed legislation that would outlaw Russia forever. We begin bombing in five minutes."

1986 The **MONKEES** first four LPs re-entered *Billboard's* top albums chart after almost 20 years.

1986 Baseball umpire **TOM GORMAN** died at the age of 67. He was buried in his umpire uniform with the ball-strike recorder in his hand, showing 3 balls and 2 strikes.

1987 **CLARA PELLER** died at age 86. She was the grandmother whose hamburger commercials had Johnny Carson, Walter Mondale and much of the U.S. asking, "Where's the beef?" Wendy's sales jumped 31 percent.

1994 **PRESIDENT CLINTON**'s presidency suffered a major defeat when his $33.2 billion crime bill lost a procedural vote in the House. 10 days later, after trimming $3 billion the House approved the bill.

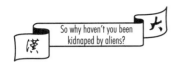

AUGUST 12

BIRTHDAYS

- **WILLIAM GOLDMAN** Author. (Chicago, IL) Wrote screen plays for *Princess Bride* and *Butch Cassidy and the Sundance Kid.* Year/Age: 1995/**64** 1996/**65** 1997/**66**
- **PETE SAMPRAS** Tennis star. (Potomac, MD) He became the youngest man to win the U.S. Open, in 1990, beating Andre Agassi in the final match. Year/Age: 1995/**24** 1996/**25** 1997/**26**
- **GEORGE HAMILTON** Actor. (Memphis, TN) Has portrayed Dracula, Zorro, and Evel Knievel. On TV in "Dynasty." Appeared in *Godfather III.* Year/Age: 1995/**56** 1996/**57** 1997/**58**
- **JOHN DEREK** Actor/producer/director. (Born Derek Harris in Hollywood, CA) Husband of Bo Derek, at one time married to Linda Evans and Ursula Andress. In *The Ten Command-ments, Tomahawk Gap, Ambush,* and *Exodus.* Directed *Bolero.* Year/Age: 1995/**69** 1996/**70** 1997/**71**
- **BUCK OWENS** C&W entertainer. (Born Alvis Edgar Owens, Jr, in Sherman, TX) Biggest hit: "I've Got a Tiger by the Tail" in 1965. From 1963-1972, Buck & his Buckaroos had 25 consecutive Top-10 hits on the C&W charts. He wrote "Crying Time" for Ray Charles. He co-hosted "Hee Haw" on TV from 1969-86. Biggest hit: "A Satisfied Mind" in 1955. Year/Age: 1995/**66** 1996/**67** 1997/**68**
- **MARK KNOPFLER** Singer/Guitarist. (England) Leader of the group DIRE STRAITS. Biggest hit: "Money for Nothing" written by Mark and Sting. Year/Age: 1995/**46** 1996/**47** 1997/**48**
- **JOE JONES** Singer. (New Orleans, LA) Biggest hit: "You Talk Too Much" in 1960. Early in his career he worked for B.B. King as valet and piano player. Year/Age: 1995/**69** 1996/**70** 1997/**71**
- **JANE WYATT** Actress. (Campgaw, NJ) Appeared in TV series "Father Knows Best" and "St. Elsewhere." Year/Age: 1995/**83** 1996/**84** 1997/**85**

- **DALE BUMPERS** Senator. (Charleston, AR) D/AK. Year/Age: 1995/**70** 1996/**71** 1997/**72**
- **PARNELLI JONES** Racecar driver. Year/Age: 1995/**62** 1996/**63** 1997/**64**
- **PORTER WAGONER** C&W singer. (West Plains, MO) Year/Age: 1995/**65** 1996/**66** 1997/**67**
- **ROY HAY** Guitarist. (London, England) With CULTURE CLUB. Hit: "Karma Chameleon." Year/Age: 1995/**34** 1996/**35** 1997/**36**
- **ABBOTT THAYER** American painter. (Born 1849) He created camouflage—a combination of colors for military uniforms that are hard to see in combat.
- **CANTINFLAS** Actor/comedian. (1911-1993 – Born Mario Moreno in Mexico) In *Pepe.* He was best-known for his role as David Niven's servant, Passepartout, in *Around the World in Eighty Days.* (Died 4-20-93.)
- **JOE BESSER** Actor. (1907-1988 – St. Louis, MO) Was one of the "Three Stooges" after Shemp died in 1955. (Died 3-1-88.)
- **PAUL WILLIAMS** Singer. (1942-1973 – Detroit, MI) With the TEMPTATIONS. Their biggest hit: "I Can't Get Next to You" in 1969. Paul shot and killed himself in Detroit after a show. (Died 8-17-73.)
- **CHRISTOPHER "CHRISTY" MATHEWSON** Baseball player. (1880-1925 – Factoryville, PA) He pitched 3 complete games during the 1905 World Series, without allowing opponents to score a run. In 17 years, he won 372 games, lost 188, and struck out 2,499 players. He was one of the first players to be named to the Baseball Hall of Fame. (Died 10-7-25.)
- **CECIL B. DeMILLE** Producer/director. (1881-1959 – Ashfield, MA) Received an Oscar nomination in 1952 for directing *The Greatest Show On Earth.* His early company evolved into Paramount Pictures, known for lavish screen spectaculars. (Died 1-21-59.)

FACTS FROM THE PAST

1827 After studying Louis Pasteur's theory that infections are caused by bacteria, **DR. JOSEPH LISTER** became the first surgeon to use disinfectant during an operation. From his name we get "Listerine."

1851 Isaac Singer patented his **SEWING MACHINE.** He opened for business in Boston, MA, with a $40 investment.

1856 The **FIRST U.S. PATENT** for an **ACCORDIAN** was issued to Anthony Fass.

1936 13-year-old diver American diver **MARJORIE GESTRING** became the youngest athlete to win a gold medal at the Olympics, winning the springboard event in Berlin, Germany.

1966 The **BEATLES** started their last North American tour at the International Amphitheater in Chicago. That was the same day that John Lennon apologized for saying the **BEATLES** were more popular than Jesus Christ. The *Catholic Herald* in London called his remark "arrogant" but added, "it's still probably true." This was their **LAST TOUR EVER!**

1984 The **23RD OLYMPICS** at Los Angeles ended with the U.S. winning 83 gold medals, 61 silver and 30 bronze medals, an **ALL-TIME RECORD FOR GOLD MEDALS** won by any country.

1988 The controversial film **THE LAST TEMPTATION OF CHRIST**, directed by Martin Scorsese opened despite objections by Christians who called the film sacrilegious.

1992 Producer for ABC's Sam Donaldson, **DAVID KAPLAN**, was killed by sniper fire in Yugoslavia, near the Sarajevo airport.

1993 **PRESIDENT CLINTON** signed a relief package for the heavily flooded Midwest.

1994 Three days before **SHANNON FAULKNER** was to break the 151 year all-male tradition at The Citadel, a federal appeals court ordered her back to civilian life.

AUGUST 13
National Left-Handers Day

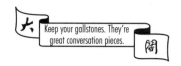

Keep your gallstones. They're great conversation pieces.

BIRTHDAYS

- **DANNY BONADUCE** Actor. (Philadelphia, PA) Played Danny on "The Partridge Family," a popular TV sitcom from 1970-1974. He has been a DJ in Phoenix, AZ, following two arrests for cocaine possession. Year/**Age**: 1995/**36** 1996/**37** 1997/**38**

- **DAN FOGELBERG** Singer. (Peoria, IL) Has worked with Van Morrison and toured with the EAGLES. Biggest hit: "Longer" in 1979. Year/**Age**: 1995/**44** 1996/**45** 1997/**46**

- **GRETCHEN CORBETT** Actress. Played defense attorney Beth Davenport on the "Rockford Files" with James Garner. Year/**Age**: 1995/**48** 1996/**49** 1997/**50**

- **PAT HARRINGTON, JR.** Comedian. (NYC) He played Dwayne Schneider on "One Day at a Time." Year/**Age**: 1995/**66** 1996/**67** 1997/**68**

- **BUDDY ROGERS** Actor. (Born Charles Rogers in Olathe, KS) Married to Mary Pickford and appeared in *Abie's Irish Rose* and *Varsity*. Year/**Age**: 1995/**91** 1996/**92** 1997/**93**

- **FIDEL CASTRO** Cuba's president. He demonstrated how strong-willed he was at an early age. When he was a boy, his parents didn't want to send him to school and he threatened to burn down their house if they didn't. He was voted Cuba's best all-around school athlete by age 18, and earned his law degree at age 24. Year/**Age**: 1995/**69** 1996/**70** 1997/**71**

- **QUINN CUMMINGS** Actress. (Los Angeles, CA) On TV series "Family." Year/**Age**: 1995/**28** 1996/**29** 1997/**30**

- **GEORGE SHEARING** Sightless jazz pianist. (England) He composed the song "Lullabye of Birdland." Year/**Age**: 1995/**76** 1996/**77** 1997/**78**

- **DON HO** Singer. (Kakaako, HI) Biggest hit: "Tiny Bubbles" in 1966. Entertainer at the Hilton Hawaiian Village. Year/**Age**: 1995/**65** 1996/**66** 1997/**67**

- **DAWNN LEWIS** Actress. (New York, NY) Appeared on TV's "Different World." Year/**Age**: 1995/**34** 1996/**35** 1997/**36**

- **BEN HOGAN** Pro golfer. (Dublin, TX) He won four U.S. Opens, two PGAs and two Masters tournaments. He won the British Golfer of the Year award four times. Year/**Age**: 1995/**83** 1996/**84** 1997/**85**

- **ANDRÉ THORNTON** Baseball slugger. Year/**Age**: 1995/**46** 1996/**47** 1997/**48**

- **CLIFF FISH** Bassist. (Ripley, England) With PAPERLACE. Biggest hit: "The Night Chicago Died." Year/**Age**: 1995/**46** 1996/**47** 1997/**48**

- **NEVILLE BRAND** Actor. (1921-1992 – Kewanee, IL) The 4th most-decorated soldier in the U.S. Army in WWII. In over 40 movies, including *Stalag 17* with William Holden and *Birdman of Alcatraz* with Burt Lancaster. He played a convict in *Riot in Cell Block II*, and appeared on the TV series "Laredo." (Died 4-16-92.)

- **ALFRED HITCHCOCK** Movie producer. (1899-1980) Son of a London, England grocer. Nominated 5 times for Oscars, including *Psycho* in 1960 for best director. A woman asked Hitchcock after she saw *Psycho*, "How will I ever take a shower again?" He told her, "Have you ever considered dry cleaning?" His motto was, "make the audience suffer." He did, with over 50 terrifying films. (Died 4-29-80.)

- **BERT LAHR** Actor/comedian. (1895-1967 – Born Irving Lahrheim in NYC) Played the "cowardly lion" in *The Wizard of Oz* in 1939. (Died 12-4-67.)

- **ANNIE OAKLEY** Sharpshooter. (1860-1926 – Darke County, OH) She was 15 years old when she married Frank Butler, a professional marksman. They met in Cincinnati, where she beat him in a shooting match. (Died 11-2-26.)

FACTS FROM THE PAST

1914 Carl Wickman couldn't sell his gray car, so he began using it as a taxi to haul miners from their shacks to huge open-pit mines in Minnesota. The big 7-passenger Hupmobile was sometimes jammed with 20 people. When business prospered, he bought more Hupmobiles and eventually his business became the **GREYHOUND CORPORATION** in honor of that old car that nobody would buy.

1924 "The Prisoner's Song" by **VERNON DALHART** sold a million copies being the first country record to do so.

1930 The long-distance airspeed record was set. **CAPTAIN FRANK HAWKES** flew from Los Angeles to New York in 12 hours, 25 minutes.

1935 20,000 fans at Chicago Stadium attended the **FIRST ROLLER DERBY**, invented by promoter Les Seltzer.

1952 The careers of songwriters and producers **JERRY LEIBER** and **MIKE STOLLER** were launched when **BIG MAMA THORNTON** recorded their song "Hound Dog." It topped the R-and-B chart for seven weeks the following year. **ELVIS** took it to number one in 1956. Some of Leiber and Stoller's other hits include: "Love Me Tender," "Charlie Brown," and "Yakety Yak."

1980 Four men in masks took some valuable items after tying up **TODD RUNDGREN**, his girlfriend and houseguests at his home in Woodstock, NY. One of the thieves hummed Rundgren's hit "I Saw the Light" during the robbery.

1991 Former Secretary of Defense (under Johnson) **CLARK CLIFFORD** resigned as chairman of First American Bankshares Inc., a Washington-based bank holding company. The government said it had been illegally acquired by the Bank of Credit and Commerce International. He was later indicted.

1992 President Bush chose long-time friend, Secretary of State **JIM BAKER**, to be his White House chief of staff, replacing Sam Skinner. Baker was to help Bush with his re-election campaign. Deputy Secretary of State Lawrence Eagleburger served as acting secretary of state.

1992 Actor/director **WOODY ALLEN** began legal action against Mia Farrow to get custody of their three children. He later lost the battle.

1994 Rwanda's Interior Minister **SETH SENDASHONGA** told large fleeing crowds fearing death that "It's wonderful to be in one's home. Don't be afraid, the United Nations is here. Stay."

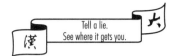

Tell a lie.
See where it gets you.

AUGUST 14

BIRTHDAYS

• **SUSAN ST. JAMES** Actress. (Born Sue Miller in Long Beach, CA) She appeared with Rock Hudson in "MacMillan & Wife" and with Jane Curtin in "Kate & Allie." Year/**Age:** 1995/**49** 1996/**50** 1997/**51**

• **LARRY GRAHAM** Singer. (Beaumont, TX) In the early 70s, he played bass guitar for SLY AND THE FAMILY STONE. Hit in : "One in a Million You." Year/**Age:** 1995/**49** 1996/**50** 1997/**51**

• **STEVE MARTIN** Actor/comedian. (Waco, TX) Films include *Parenthood*, *A Simple Twist of Fate*, *Leap of Faith*, *Father of the Bride* and *House- Sitter* with Goldie Hawn. Appeared in *L.A. Story* with his wife, Victoria Tennant. Worked 8 years at Disneyland selling Mouseketeer ears and Davy Crockett coonskin hats. Hosted Saturday Night Live the most times (12) as of 1993. Year/**Age:** 1995/**50** 1996/**51** 1997/**52**

• **DASH CROFTS** Singer. (Cisco, TX) Of SEALS AND CROFTS. Their biggest hits: "Summer Breeze," "Diamond Girl," and "Get Closer," featuring Carolyn Willis. Year/**Age:** 1995/**55** 1996/**56** 1997/**57**

• **DAVID CROSBY** Singer. (Los Angeles, CA) Of CROSBY, STILLS, NASH & YOUNG. Their biggest hit: "Woodstock" in 1970. They reunited in 1985 for the "Live Aid" concert. Earlier in David's career, he founded the BYRDS. Year/**Age:** 1995/**54** 1996/**55** 1997/**56**

• **ALICE GHOSTLEY** Actress. (Eve, MO) Played Esmeralda, a witch, on "Bewitched" 1968-1970. Also appeared on "Mayberry, R.F.D" and "Designing Women." Year/**Age:** 1995/**69** 1996/**70** 1997/**71**

• **GARY LARSON** Cartoonist. (Tacoma, WA) "The Far Side." Year/**Age:** 1995/**45** 1996/**46** 1997/**47**

• **CONNIE SMITH** C&W singer. (Born Constance Meadows in Elkhart, IN) Her biggest hit: "Once A Day" in 1964. Bill Anderson discovered her. Year/**Age:** 1995/**54** 1996/**55** 1997/**56**

• **DANIELLE STEEL** Romance novelist. (New York, NY) *Daddy.* Year/**Age:** 1995/**48** 1996/**49** 1997/**50**

• **FRED ROBERTS** Basketball. Milwaukee Bucks forward. Year/**Age:** 1995/**45** 1996/**46** 1997/**47**

• **NEAL ANDERSON** Football. (Graceville, FL) Running back with the Chicago Bears. Year/**Age:** 1995/**31** 1996/**32** 1997/**33**

• **BUDDY GRECO** Singer. (Philadelphia, PA) Best known song: "The Lady is a Tramp." Year/**Age:** 1995/**69** 1996/**70** 1997/**71**

• **ROBYN SMITH ASTAIRE** Former jockey. (San Francisco, CA) Married to Fred Astaire until his death in 1987. Year/**Age:** 1995/**51** 1996/**52** 1997/**53**

• **MARK "The Bird" FIDRYCH** Baseball. Former pitcher for Detroit. In 1976, the Tiger rookie was the American League All-Star starter and Rookie of the Year with a 19-9 record. Injuries ended his career as quickly as it started. Year/**Age:** 1995/**41** 1996/**42** 1997/**43**

• **EARVIN "MAGIC" JOHNSON** Basketball star. (East Lansing, MI) L.A. Lakers. On the 1992 Olympic Dream Team. Revealed he had AIDS in 1992. NBA's all-time leader in assists in regular season, Playoff and All-Star Game competition. Two-time All-Star Game MVP and led the Lakers to five NBA titles during the 1980s. He announced his comeback Sept. 29, 1992, but it never happened. He is on TV's "One On One." Year/**Age:** 1995/**36** 1996/**37** 1997/**38**

FACTS FROM THE PAST

1756   **DANIEL BOONE** married 16-year-old **REBECCA BRYAN**. The marriage lasted 56 years, and they had 10 children.

1901   To prove that **YELLOW FEVER** was spread by mosquitoes, nurse Clara Maass allowed herself to be bitten by one. She proved her point—and was dead within two weeks.

1935   President Franklin D. Roosevelt signed the **SOCIAL SECURITY ACT**, establishing a federal system of old-age insurance.

1941   The **LAST EXECUTION** in the **TOWER OF LONDON** took place. The victim was German spy **JOSEF JAKOBS**, who had been captured minutes after parachuting into England with a German sausage in his pocket.

1945   World War II ended with the surrender of Japan. This is **VICTORY DAY (V.J. DAY)**, celebrating the announcement by President Harry Truman that Japan had surrendered to the Allies, setting off celebrations across the nation. The official ratification of surrender occurred on the USS *Missouri* in Tokyo Bay, September 2, 1945.

1947   Golfer **BABE DIDRIKSON ZAHARIAS** turned professional, accepting $300,000 to do a series of golf movies.

1953   The **WHIFFLE BALL WAS INVENTED**. David Mullany, Sr., saw that his 13-year-old son was frustrated hitting tennis balls onto the school roof, breaking windows and trying to successfully throw a curve ball. He took a perfume carton shaped like a ball with holes on one-half and made holes in the other half. When the "ball" was thrown, it curved.

1971   Pop singer **ROD STEWART** released his first big hit: "Maggie Mae."

1982   Bill Neal became the **FIRST PERSON TO PADDLE A BATHTUB** across the **ENGLISH CHANNEL**. He made the 21-mile crossing from Dover to Cap Griz, France, in 13 hours and 29 minutes, using a single oar to paddle his steel bathtub. French authorities, annoyed by record-seeking adventurers, had earlier in the year threatened to arrest those arriving on their shores in "unconventional craft." Neal avoided arrest by having previously registered his "tub" with Lloyds of London as an ocean-going craft.

1986   13-year-old **DEANNA YOUNG** turned her parents in to the police for drug abuse. She brought cocaine, small amounts of marijuana and various pills into the Tustin, California, Police Station. Her parents were then arrested.

1991   Freed American hostage **EDWARD TRACY** returned to the U.S., arriving in Boston to be with his sister, Maria Lambert.

AUGUST 15

Can you put your foot behind your head?

BIRTHDAYS

- **JANICE RULE** Actress. (Norwood, OH) Her various television appearances include "McCloud." Year/**Age**: 1995/**64** 1996/**65** 1997/**66**

- **ABBY DALTON** Actress. (Las Vegas, NV) TV's "Falcon Crest." Year/**Age**: 1995/**63** 1996/**64** 1997/**65**

- **VERNON JORDAN** Civil Rights leader. (Atlanta, GA) Former Urban League Director. Year/**Age**: 1995/**60** 1996/**61** 1997/**62**

- **PETER YORK** Drummer. (England) With the SPENCER DAVIS GROUP. Year/**Age**: 1995/**52** 1996/**53** 1997/**54**

- **PHYLLIS SCHLAFLY** Anti-feminist. (St. Louis, MO) Wrote *A Choice, Not an Echo* in 1964. Year/**Age**: 1995/**71** 1996/**72** 1997/**73**

- **BOBBY HELMS** Singer. (Bloomington, IN) Biggest hit: "Jingle Bell Rock" on the Christmas charts from 1957 through 1962. He was the first to tie in Christmas with rock 'n' roll. His hit "Fraulein" was on the C&W charts for one year beginning March 20, 1957. Year/**Age**: 1995/**61** 1996/**62** 1997/**63**

- **MIKE CONNORS** Actor. (Born Krekor Ohanian in Fresno, CA) Starred in the TV series "Mannix" and "The FBI Story." Was spotted on the basketball court at UCLA by Director William Wellman who suggested that he might make a good Tarzan. Debuted in *Sudden Fear* with Joan Crawford. Year/**Age**: 1995/**70** 1996/**71** 1997/**72**

- **JIM DALE** Actor. (England) Pop singer, turned light comedian and star of the "Carry On" films: *Carry on Cowboy, Carry on Screaming, Carry on Cleo*, and *Barnum*. Year/**Age**: 1995/**60** 1996/**61** 1997/**62**

- **DAME WENDY HILLER** Actress. (England) Won Academy Award for *Separate Tables*, and appeared in *A Man for All Seasons* and *Making Love*. Year/**Age**: 1995/**83** 1996/**84** 1997/**85**

- **TESS HARPER** Actress. (Born Tessie Jean Washam in Mammoth Springs, AK)) In films *Tender Merices* and *Silkwood*. Year/**Age**: 1995/**45** 1996/**46** 1997/**47**

- **ROSE MARIE** Comedienne. (NYC) "Sally Rogers" on the hit TV series "The Dick Van Dyke Show." Appeared in the film *Family Man*. Year/**Age**: 1995/**70** 1996/**71** 1997/**72**

- **LINDA ELLERBEE** Author/newswoman. (Bryan, TX) Co-hosted "Our World" on ABC-TV. Did Maxwell House Coffee commercials. She has been fighting breast cancer. Year/**Age**: 1995/**51** 1996/**52** 1997/**53**

- **GENE UPSHAW** Football Hall of Famer. (Robstown, TX) Now a union executive. Year/**Age**: 1995/**50** 1996/**51** 1997/**52**

- **KATHRYN WHITMIRE** Politician. (Houston, TX) First woman mayor of Houston. Year/**Age**: 1995/**49** 1996/**50** 1997/**51**

- **JULIA CHILD** French chef. (Born Julia McWilliams in Pasadena, CA) Star of "Dinner With Julia." She debuted on Public TV in 1962. She ws the first woman to be inducted into the Culinary Institute of America's Hall of Fame. Year/**Age**: 1995/**83** 1996/**84** 1997/**85**

- **JIMMY WEBB** Songwriter. He wrote the 1967 Grammy winner, "Up Up & Away" and a lot of Glen Campbell songs, including "By the Time I Get to Phoenix." He also wrote "MacArthur Park." He used to meet his girlfriend at that park which is the edge of downtown Los Angeles. They would picnic under the trees and sometimes eat cake for lunch. He says it's "just about a love affair." Year/**Age**: 1995/**49** 1996/**50** 1997/**51**

- **HUGO WINTERHALTER** Musican (1909-1973 – Wilkes Barre, PA) Biggest hit: "Canadian Sunset" in 1956 with composer, pianist Eddie Heywood. (Died 9-17-73.)

- **NORMA SHEARER** Actress. (1904-1983 – Canada) Won an Oscar for *Divorcee* in 1929. (Died 6-12-83.)

- **ETHEL BARRYMORE** Actress. (1879-1959 – Philadelphia, PA) Won an Oscar for supporting actress in 1944 for *None But the Lonely Heart*. (Died 6-18-59.)

- **NAPOLEON BONAPARTE** French Emperor. (1769-1821) It's a public holiday at his birthplace, the Island of Corsica. (Died 5-5-1821.)

- **LAWRENCE OF ARABIA** Soldier/archeologist. (1888-1935 – Wales) Lawrence was born T.E. Lawrence. He died in England following a motorcycle crash. Peter O'Toole's acting career got a big boost when he played "Lawrence" in 1963, his first film. (Died 5-19-35.)

FACTS FROM THE PAST

1057   **MACBETH**, King of Scotland, was slain by the son of King Duncan. William Shakespeare did a little write-up about it later.

1877   Thomas Edison coined the telephone greeting "Hello." In a letter addressed this day to the president of the Telegraph Company in Pittsburgh, Edison suggested the use of "Hello" to answer the phone instead of "Ahoy" as suggested by Alexander Bell.

1939   The MGM movie musical **THE WIZARD OF OZ** premiered in Hollywood at Grauman's Chinese Threatre. It catapulted young child actress Judy Garland to overnight stardom. She used the song from the movie as her theme: "Somewhere Over the Rainbow." Shirley Temple was the first choice for the role of Dorothy, but after testing both stars, they felt Judy was better suited to the role. Frank Morgan played the Wizard because W.C. Fields held out for too much money.

1958   Singer **BUDDY HOLLY** married Maria Elena Santiago in a private ceremony in his parents' home in Lubbock, TX.

1969   The **WOODSTOCK FESTIVAL** opened in the fields near Bethel, NY. It attracted almost 400,000 people. Acts included: Janis Joplin, Creedence Clearwater Revival, Jimi Hendrix, Sly and the Family Stone, Jefferson Airplane, and Joe Cocker. The land belonged to farmer Max Yasgur.

1994   **CARLOS THE JACKAL**, (real name Ilich Ramirez Sanchez, nickname came from the title of Fredrick Forsyth's novel *The Day of the Jackal*.) the most wanted terrorist in 20 years, was arrested in Khartoum, Sudan. Among his crimes, he was convicted of killing two French couterintelligence agents and was also linked to the massacre of 11 Israeli athletes at the 1972 Munich Olympics.

How dark can you be and still be blond?

AUGUST 16

BIRTHDAYS

- **TIMOTHY HUTTON** Actor. (Malibu, CA) *Taps, Q&A, The Temp*, and *Ordinary People*. He played a dual role in the film *The Dark Half*. Year/**Age**: 1995/**35** 1996/**36** 1997/**37**

- **ROBERT CULP** Actor. (Berkeley, CA) Starred with Bill Cosby in the "I Spy" TV series and was in *Bob & Carol, Ted & Alice*, appeared as the US President in *The Pelican Brief* and in TV's "Greatest American Hero." Year/**Age**: 1995/**65** 1996/**66** 1997/**67**

- **FRANK GIFFORD** Sportscaster. (Santa Monica, CA) Played pro football for the NY Giants. He's part of the "Monday Night Football" broadcast. Also a member of the Football Hall of Fame. Married to Kathie Lee. In 1959 he appeared in the film *Up Periscope*. Year/**Age**: 1995/**65** 1996/**66** 1997/**67**

- **FESS PARKER** Actor. (Fort Worth, TX) Starred in the TV series "Davy Crockett." Year/**Age**: 1995/**70** 1996/**71** 1997/**72**

- **EYDIE GORME** Singer. (Born Edith Gormenzano in Bronx, NY) Biggest record: "Blame it on the Bossa Nova" in 1963. She and Steve Lawrence have one of entertainment's longest marriages. Year/**Age**: 1995/**63** 1996/**64** 1997/**65**

- **LESLEY ANN WARREN** Actress. (NYC) Played Dana Lambert on "Mission Impossible." In the film *Life Stinks*. Year/**Age**: 1995/**49** 1996/**50** 1997/**51**

- **BETSY VON FURSTENBERG** Actress. (Born Elizabeth Caroline Maria Agatha Felicitas Therese von Furstenberg-Hedringen in Germany) Films include: *Detective* with Frank Sinatra and *Oh Men, Oh Women*. During the latter, she was put on trial by Actors Equity after she kicked her co-star, Franchot Tone, in the shins. Year/**Age**: 1995/**63** 1996/**64** 1997/**65**

- **ANN BLYTH** Actress. (Mt. Kisco, NY) Movie star of the 1940's and 1950s. She got her break in Donald O'Connor's musicals. Later she appeared in *The Helen Morgan Story*, *Rose Marie*, *Kismet*, and Hostess Cupcake TV commercials. Year/**Age**: 1995/**67** 1996/**68** 1997/**69**

- **CHRISTIAN OKOYE** Football. (Nigeria) Running back for the Kansas City Chiefs. Year/**Age**: 1995/**34** 1996/**35** 1997/**36**

- **BEN HOGAN** Golfer. (Dublin, TX) He was named one of the greatest golfers in history. Won U.S. Open, two Masters and one British Open. Golfer of the Year four times. Year/**Age**: 1995/**83** 1996/**84** 1997/**85**

- **ANITA GILLETTE** Actress. Appeared as psychiatrist Dr. W. Emily Hanover on "Quincy." Year/**Age**: 1995/**59** 1996/**60** 1997/**61**

- **KATHIE LEE GIFFORD** TV talk show co-host. (Born Katherine Epstein in Paris, France) Wife of Frank Gifford. Co-star of TV's "Regis & Kathie Lee." Spokesperson for the "Carnival Cruise Lines." Year/**Age**: 1995/**42** 1996/**43** 1997/**44**

- **SEAN BONNIWELL** Leader singer/songwriter. (Los Angeles, CA) With rock quintet MUSIC MACHINE. Biggest hit: "Talk Talk" in 1966. Year/**Age**: 1995/**55** 1996/**56** 1997/**57**

- **MADONNA** Entertainer. (Born Madonna Louise Ciccone in Bay City, MI) In films: *Desperately Seeking Susan*, *Shanghai Surprise*, *Dick Tracy*, and *A League of Their Own* with Tom Hanks. Many top 10 hits including, "Like a Virgin." Pepsi paid her $5 million for one commercial. Time Warner signed her to a $60 million contract in 1992. Once she was the drummer for the group "The Breakfast Club." Year/**Age**: 1995/**37** 1996/**38** 1997/**39**

- **JULIE NEWMAR** Actress. (Born Julia Newmeyer in Los Angeles, CA) Appeared in movies *Maltese Bippy* with Rowan and Martin, *MacKenna's Gold*, and in the TV series, "The Living Doll" in 1963 as a robot. Best known as Cat Woman in the TV series "Batman." Year/**Age**: 1995/**60** 1996/**61** 1997/**62**

- **BARBARA GEORGE** Singer. (New Orleans, LA) Biggest hit: "I Know" in 1961. Year/**Age**: 1995/**53** 1996/**54** 1997/**55**

- **JAMES "J.T." TAYLOR** Singer. KOOL AND THE GANG. Hit: "Celebration" in 1980. Year/**Age**: 1995/**42** 1996/**43** 1997/**44**

- **MAE CLARKE** Actress. (1910-1992 – Philadelphia, PA) She was best known as the gun moll whose face was smashed with a grapefruit by James Cagney in the 1931 film *The Public Enemy*. (Died 4-29-92.)

FACTS FROM THE PAST

1829 The original **SIAMESE TWINS** Chang and Eng Bunker arrived in Boston on the ship *Sachem* to be exhibited to the western world.

1920 The one and only **FATALITY IN MAJOR LEAGUE BASEBALL** happened when Cleveland Indians shortstop **RAY CHAPMAN** was hit in the head by a fastball from Yankees pitcher Carl Mays.

1948 The "Sultan of Swat," **BABE RUTH** died in New York at age 53.

1975 **PETER GABRIEL** announced he was leaving **GENESIS**. The group auditioned more than 400 potential replacements before deciding that their drummer, Phil Collins, could be the lead singer.

1977 **ELVIS PRESLEY**, "The King of Rock 'n' Roll," died at his Graceland Mansion home in Memphis, TN. He was 42. His girlfriend Ginger Alden found him lying on the floor of the bathroom. He was pronounced dead at Memphis Baptist Memorial Hospital at 3:30 p.m. The death was the result of coronary arrhythmia.

1984 A federal court jury in Los Angeles acquitted former automaker **JOHN DELOREAN** on all 8 counts in a $24-billion cocaine conspiracy indictment, citing the government trapped him in a "sting" with a promise of money to save his failing auto company.

1985 **MADONNA** married **SEAN PENN**. Madonna filed for divorce in 1988.

1988 Vice President **GEORGE BUSH** announced that Indiana Senator **DAN QUAYLE** would be his running mate.

1994 **REBA MCENTIRE** was nominated for six Country Music Association awards, one more than either Alan Jackson and Vince Gill.

AUGUST 17

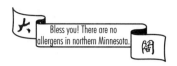
Bless you! There are no allergens in northern Minnesota.

BIRTHDAYS

• **ROBERT DeNIRO** Actor. (NYC) Won an Oscar for best supporting actor in *The Godfather, Part II* in 1974 and best actor in *Raging Bull*. Also starred in *Backdraft*, *Mad Dog and Glory*, and *This Boy's Life*. He made his directorial debut in *A Bronx Tale*. Was nominated for an Oscar in the films *Awakenings* and *Cape Fear*. He played the lead in the 1994 movie *Frankenstein*. He got his start on the soap "Search for Tomorrow." Year/**Age**: 1995/**52** 1996/**53** 1997/**54**

• **MAUREEN O'HARA** Actress. (Born Maureen Fitzsimmons in Ireland) She was in *The Hunchback of Notre Dame*, *Only The Lonely*, *The Shores of Tripoli*, *The Quiet Man*, and was the love interest of John Wayne in many old movies. Year/**Age**: 1995/**74** 1996/**75** 1997/**76**

• **SID HASHIAN** Drummer. With the group BOSTON. Their first album set a record for new LPs, selling 6 million copies. Year/**Age**: 1995/**46** 1996/**47** 1997/**48**

• **JIM COURIER** Tennis player. (Sanford, FL) In 1992 he became the first U.S. male to be ranked No. 1 since 1984, when John McEnroe held the spot. Year/**Age**: 1995/**25** 1996/**26** 1997/**27**

• **GUILLERMO VILAS** Tennis star. (Argentina) Became U.S. singles champ for the first time in 1977. Year/**Age**: 1995/**43** 1996/**44** 1997/**45**

• **CHRISTIAN LAETTNER** Basketball player. Pro player with Minnesota. Year/**Age**: 1995/**26** 1996/**27** 1997/**28**

• **SEAN PENN** Actor. (Santa Monica, CA) Controversial ex-husband of singer Madonna. Films include: *Shanghi Surprise*, *Colors*, *Carlito's Way*, *Casualties of War*, and *We're No Angels*. Year/**Age**: 1995/**35** 1996/**36** 1997/**37**

• **BELINDA CARLISLE** Singer. (Hollywood, CA) She started the GO-GO's group. Hist: "We Got the Beat" and "Heaven on Earth." Year/**Age**: 1995/**37** 1996/**38** 1997/**39**

• **BOOG POWELL** Former baseball star. When he came to bat, it always sounded like the fans were booing him, but they were yelling "Boog, Boog" which was the beginning of this type of cheering for stars with similar names. Year/**Age**: 1995/**54** 1996/**55** 1997/**56**

• **DONALD E. WAHLBERG, JR.** Singer/dancer. (Dorchester, MA) With NEW KIDS ON THE BLOCK (now known as NKOTB.) Hits include: "I'll Be Loving You (Forever)" and "Tonight." Donnie accidentally fell through a stage trapdoor during a concert June 24, 1990, in Saratoga, N.Y. Although injuries were minor, his two-night stay was in the intensive care unit making him less accessible to his many well-wishers. Year/**Age**: 1995/**26** 1996/**27** 1997/**28**

• **MAE WEST** Actress. (1892-1980 – Brooklyn, NY) Famous for sayings like, "Come up and see me sometime," "I've never met a man I didn't like," "I used to be snow white, but I drifted," and "It's not the men in my life, but the life in my men that counts." Once when she was in a nightclub checking her coat, the hat-check girl said, "Goodness, what beautiful diamonds." Mae said, "My dear, goodness had nothing to do with it." The lifesaving jacket was named in her honor. Her last movie was *Sextette* in 1978. (Died 11-22-80.)

• **SAMUEL GOLDWYN** Producer. (1882-1974 – Born Samuel Goldfish in Poland) Co-founded MGM. He won an Academy Award in 1946 for *The Best Years of Our Lives* and produced *All Quiet on the Western Front*. (Died 1-31-74.)

• **DAVID CROCKETT** American frontiersman. (1786-1836 – Hawkins County, Tennessee) Died a hero at the Battle of the Alamo on March 6, 1836. John Wayne portrayed "Crockett" in the 1960 film *The Alamo*. Davy wrote in his autobiography, "I leave this rule for others when I'm dead: Be always sure you're right, then go ahead." (Died 3-6-1836.)

FACTS FROM THE PAST

1807 **ROBERT FULTON**'s North River **STEAM BOAT** began chugging up New York's Hudson River on its successful round-trip journey to Albany. It took 32 hours.

1903 A donation of a million dollars was made to Columbia University by **JOSEPH PULITZER**, starting the Pulitzer Prizes in his name.

1933 **LOU GEHRIG** of the New York Yankees played his 1,308th game in St. Louis, breaking the consecutive record.

1938 **HENRY ARMSTRONG** became the lightweight boxing champion of the world. He already was the featherweight and welterweight champion. He was the only person in history to hold **THREE TITLES SIMULTANEOUSLY**.

1957 Richie Ashburn of the Phillies **ACCIDENTALLY HIT** spectator Alice Roth with a **FOUL BALL** and broke her nose. As Roth was being removed from the stands on a stretcher, Ashburn hit her with another foul ball.

1969 During the Woodstock Festival, the WHO's **PETE TOWNSHEND** knocked Yippie **ABBIE HOFFMAN** off the stage during the performance of "Tommy." Hoffman was trying to announce some propaganda to the audience.

1987 The last member of Adolf Hitler's inner circle, **RUDOLF HESS**, died in a Berlin hospital.

1992 Filmmaker **WOODY ALLEN** confirmed tabloid headlines that he was having an affair with actress Mia Farrow's 21-year-old adoped daughter, **SOON YI PREVIN**. Farrow was awarded custody of their children on June 7, 1993.

1992 Las Vegas entertainer **WAYNE NEWTON** filed bankruptcy, owing up to 200 creditors a total of $20 million. He blamed the recession.

1992 Well known Gulf War reporter **ARTHUR KENT**, known as the "Scud Stud,"was suspended by NBC for refusing an assignment in Croatia, implying that he was chicken. Kent flew to New York and staged a one-man protest outside the NBC studios at Rockefeller Center, saying he wouldn't stop until his name was cleared. An out of court settlement was reached in 1994.

1994 Actor **DAVID CARUSO** quit ABC-TV's "NYPD Blue" and was replaced by Jimmy Smits of 'L.A. Law." "NYPD Blue" was the highest-rated new drama of the 1993-94 season. Caruso left to sign a $2 million deal to star in the movie *Jade*.

Beware of falling rocks

AUGUST 18

BIRTHDAYS

- **ROBERT REDFORD** Actor/director. (Santa Monica, CA.) He was nominated for best actor in 1973 for *The Sting* and won an Oscar in 1981 for directing *Ordinary People.* Also appeared in *Butch Cassidy & the Sundance Kid, Out of Africa, Havana, Sneakers, Indecent Proposal,* and *Quiz Show.* Directed *A River Runs Through It.* He turned down the lead in *The Graduate.* Year/**Age:** 1995/**58** 1996/**59** 1997/**60**

- **RAFER JOHNSON** Actor. (Hillsboro, TX) A former Olympic decathalon champion. Year/**Age:** 1995/**60** 1996/**61** 1997/**62**

- **DENIS LEARY** Actor/comic. In the film *The Ref.* Year/**Age:** 1995/**38** 1996/**39** 1997/**40**

- **SHELLEY WINTERS** Actress. (Born Shirley Shrift in St. Louis, MO) Her mother, Rose Winters, was an opera singer. Shelley won an Oscar for supporting actress in *The Diary of Anne Frank* in 1959 and for *Patch of Blue* in 1965. Plays Roseanne's Grandma on the TV series. In 1993 film *The Pickle.* Year/**Age:** 1995/**73** 1996/**74** 1997/**75**

- **MARTIN MULL** Actor. (Chicago.) Appeared on "Mary Hartman, Mary Hartman" TV sitcom and "Roseanne." Year/**Age:** 1995/**52** 1996/**53** 1997/**54**

- **GAIL FISHER** Actress. (Orange, NJ) Won an Emmy for her work as "Mannix" secretary, Peggy Fair. Year/**Age:** 1995/**60** 1996/**61** 1997/**62**

- **MALCOLM-JAMAL WARNER** Actor. (Jersey City, NJ) Theo on TV's "The Cosby Show." Author of *Theo & Me.* Year/**Age:** 1995/**25** 1996/**26** 1997/**27**

- **DENNIS ELLIOTT** Drummer. (NYC) With FOREIGNER. Their biggest hit: "I Want to Know What Love Is" in '84. Year/**Age:** 1995/**45** 1996/**46** 1997/**47**

- **CHRISTIAN SLATER** Actor. *Robin Hood: Prince of Thieves, Jimmy Hollywood, Murder in the First, Untamed Heart,* and *True Romance.* Year/**Age:** 1995/**26** 1996/**27** 1997/**28**

- **MADELEINE STOWE** Actress.(Los Angeles, CA) Films: *Revenge, The Gangster Chronicles, Unlawful Entry, The Last of the Mohicans,* and *The Deerslayer.* Year/**Age:** 1995/**37** 1996/**38** 1997/**39**

- **PATRICK SWAYZE** Actor. (Houston, TX) *Dirty Dancing, Point Break, City of Joy, A Con Man's Paradise, Father Hood,* and *Ghost* with Demi Moore. Year/**Age:** 1995/**43** 1996/**44** 1997/**45**

- **ROMAN POLANSKI** Director. (Born to Polish parents in Paris, France) Directed *Rosemary's Baby* and *Pirates.* A former actor, he was the husband of actress Sharon Tate, one of Charles Manson's murder victims. Polanski calls himself a "student of fear." Year/**Age:** 1995/**62** 1996/**63** 1997/**64**

- **JOHNNY PRESTON** Singer. (Born John Preston Courville in Port Arthur, TX) Biggest hit: "Running Bear" in 1959. The song was written by J.P. Richardson "The Big Bopper." He and George Jones made the Indian noises. Year/**Age:** 1995/**56** 1996/**57** 1997/**58**

- **JACK PICKFORD** Actor. (1896-1933 – Canada) Mary Pickford's brother.

- **MERIWETHER LEWIS** U.S. explorer. (1774-1809) Leader of the Lewis & Clark Expedition. (Died 10-11-1809.)

- **ROBERTO CLEMENTE** Baseball. (1934-1972) Pittsburgh Pirates outfielder who won 4 batting titles and was MVP in 1966. He was killed in a plane crash on the way to help victims of an earthquake. (Died 12-31-72.)

FACTS FROM THE PAST

1859 French stuntman the **GREAT BLONDIN** crossed Niagara Falls on a tightrope, carrying another man on his shoulders.

1896 Carl Baker Neel and Samuel R. Neel won the United States Lawn Tennis Association's outdoor men's double championship by defeating Robert D. Wrenn and M.G. Chace in five sets. They were the **FIRST DOUBLES TEAM** consisting of two brothers to win a tennis championship.

1962 Richard Starkey (**RINGO STARR**) washed the grease from his hair, said good-bye to Rory Storme's Hurricanes, and signed on with **THE BEATLES,** making Pete Best very upset. Best had been the Beatles' drummer.

1963 **JAMES MEREDITH** became the first African-American to graduate from the University of Mississippi in its 115-year history.

1977 Eighteen white limousines and a white hearse rode through the streets of Memphis, TN, to take **ELVIS** to his burial. Elvis was buried in a mausoleum at a Memphis cemetery. The amount of flowers delivered by FTD to Graceland surpassed the number for any other event in the company's history. Two days after his death, following attempts to break into the mausoleum, Presley's body and that of his mother were re-buried in a plot on the grounds of Graceland.

1984 Democratic vice-presidential nominee **GERALDINE FERRARO,** faced with questions about her family's finances, announced that her husband, John Zaccaro, had changed his mind and would make his income tax returns public.

1987 American journalist **CHARLES GLASS** escaped from his kidnappers in Beirut after being abducted 62 days earlier.

1991 In an attempt to oust President **MIKHAIL GORBACHEV,** a coup was launched by Soviet hard-liners. A group arrived where Gorbachev was vacationing in Crimea demanding his resignation. When he refused, he and his family were kept imprisoned until the coup failed three days later.

1992 Boston Celtics star **LARRY BIRD** announced his retirement. In his 13 seasons he was MVP three times, played in 12 All-Star Games and hit double figures in points, rebounds and assists 69 times.

1994 Disturbed by the swelling tide of Cuban refugees in South Florida, **PRESIDENT CLINTON** shifted policy and ordered the refugees be taken to the U.S. Navy base at Guantanomo Bay, Cuba in stead of letting them merge into Florida's population.

AUGUST 19

BIRTHDAYS

• **JOHN STAMOS** Actor. (Born John Stamotopoulos in Cypress, CA) Uncle Jesse on TV's "Full House." He insisted his character be called Jesse Katsopolis to emphasize his Greek heritage. Also sings, plays guitar and has toured with the BEACH BOYS, playing drums. He was Blackie Parrish on "General Hospital." Year/**Age**: 1995/**32** 1996/**33** 1997/**34**

• **JONATHAN FRAKES** Actor. "STAR TREK: The Next Generation." Married to actress Genie Francis, "General Hospital's" Laura. Year/**Age**: 1995/**43** 1996/**44** 1997/**45**

• **JILL ST. JOHN** Actress. (Born Jill Oppenheim in Los Angeles, CA) She began acting at age 4. On TV's "Burke's Law." She appeared in *Tony Rome*, *Diamonds are Forever*, and *Come Blow Your Horn*. Year/**Age**: 1995/**55** 1996/**56** 1997/**57**

• **PETER GALLAGHER** Actor. Films: *Sex, Lies, and Videotape* and *Short Cuts*. Year/**Age**: 1995/**40** 1996/**41** 1997/**42**

• **JOHN DEACON** Bass player. With QUEEN. Their biggest hit: "Another One Bites the Dust" which many sports teams love to use after a victory. Year/**Age**: 1995/**44** 1996/**45** 1997/**46**

• **BILLY J. KRAMER** Singer. (England) His career was managed by Brian Epstein and produced by George Martin, who also managed and produced the Beatles. Billy and his group, THE DAKOTAS, scored their biggest hit in 1964: "Little Children." Year/**Age**: 1995/**52** 1996/**53** 1997/**54**

• **KEVIN DILLON** Actor. (New Rochelle, NY) In the film *Platoon*. Brother of Matt. Year/**Age**: 1995/**30** 1996/**31** 1997/**32**

• **TIPPER GORE** Second Lady. (Born Mary Elizabeth Aitcheson in Washington, DC) Married Vice President (then Tennessee Senator) Al Gore May 19, 1970. Author of *Raising PG Kids in an X-Rated Society*. She brought about the labeling of many albums which contained explicit lyrics. Year/**Age**: 1995/**47** 1996/**48** 1997/**49**

• **MORTEN ANDERSON** Football. (Denmark) Kicker for the New Orleans Saints. Year/**Age**: 1995/**35** 1996/**36** 1997/**37**

• **MARY JO FERNANDEZ** Tennis Pro. Year/**Age**: 1995/**24** 1996/**25** 1997/**26**

• **DIANA MULDAUR** Actress. TV's "L.A. Law." Year/**Age**: 1995/**57** 1996/**58** 1997/**59**

• **GINGER BAKER** Drummer. (England) With the '60s super group, CREAM. Their biggest hit was their first: "Sunshine of Your Love." Year/**Age**: 1995/**56** 1996/**57** 1997/**58**

• **BILL CLINTON** President. (Hope, AR) Won 1992 presidential election with running mate Al Gore, capturing 370 electoral votes. His inaugural speech was only 14 minutes long. Year/**Age**: 1995/**49** 1996/**50** 1997/**51**

• **WILLIE SHOEMAKER** Horse race jockey. (Fabens, TX) Willie called it quits in 1990 after 41 years of horseracing. He made 40,350 starts, winning 8,833 races— 1,009 state winners; four triumphs in the Kentucky Derby, including one at age 54; two Preakness victories and five wins in the Belmont Stakes. His mounts have earned $123,375,524. He was seriously injured in a car crash on April 8, 1991. Year/**Age**: 1995/**64** 1996/**65** 1997/**66**

• **JOHNNY NASH** Singer. (Houston, TX) Biggest hit: "I Can See Clearly Now" in 1972. Year/**Age**: 1995/**55** 1996/**56** 1997/**57**

• **GERALD McRANEY** Actor. (Collins, MI) Starred as Rick Simon, brother of A.J. on "Simon & Simon," and "Major Dad." Married to actress Delta Burke. Year/**Age**: 1995/**47** 1996/**48** 1997/**49**

• **RON DARLING** Baseball. (Worcester, MA) Major league pitcher. Year/**Age**: 1995/**35** 1996/**36** 1997/**37**

• **GENE RODDENBERRY** "Star Trek" TV creator/producer. (1921-1991) He was head writer for TV series "Have Gun Will Travel." He received a third of the profit from the "Star Trek" reruns. (Died 10-24-91.)

• **MALCOLM FORBES** Publisher. (1919-1990 – NYC) Publisher of the business magazine that bears his name and proponent of capitalism in all forms. On his 70th birthday, he spent $2 million to fly 584 of his closest friends to Tangiers, Morocco. (Died 2-24-90.)

• **ORVILLE WRIGHT** Aviation pioneer. (1871-1948 – Dayton, OH) (Died 1-30-48.)

• **GABRIELLE "COCO" CHANEL** Fashion designer. (1883-1971 – France) She was the subject of the Broadway show *Coco*. Created the perfume Chanel No. 5. (Died 1-10-71.)

FACTS FROM THE PAST

1917 The first baseball game to be played on New York's Polo Grounds resulted in the two team managers subsequently being arrested for violating the state's **BLUE LAW** prohibiting ball playing on Sunday. The managers were the legendary John McGraw and the equally legendary Christy Mathewson.

1929 The comedy program, **"AMOS & ANDY,"** with white actors Freeman Gosden and Charles Correll imitating stereotypes of African-American people, made its debut on NBC Radio. They got their start on WGN radio.

1934 **ADOLF HITLER** was made president of Germany by nearly 90% of the voters.

1951 St. Louis Browns owner Bill Veeck [vek] sent in 3' 7" midget **EDDIE GAEDEL** to pinch-hit in a game against Detroit. Gaedel, whose function was to draw walks, was later barred from play by American League President, Will Harridge. Eddie ware the number $1/_8$ on his jersey.

1960 U-2 pilot **FRANCIS GARY POWERS** was sentenced by a Moscow court to ten years in prison for spying. He was released in 19 months, an exchange for Russian spy Colonel Rudolph Abel. Powers was killed in a helicopter crash in 1977, while reporting traffic for a Los Angeles radio station.

1991 Soviet leader **MIKHAIL GORBACHEV WAS REMOVED** as president by Soviet Vice President Gennady Yanayev. Russian Federation President Boris Yeltsin, defying the coup, called for a general strike.

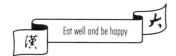 Eat well and be happy

AUGUST 20

BIRTHDAYS

- **JIMMY PANKOW** Trombonist. (Chicago, IL) With CHICAGO. He wrote many of their hits including "Make Me Smile" and "Colour My World." Year/**Age:** 1995/**48** 1996/**49** 1997/**50**

- **ROBERT PLANT** Singer. (Bromwich, England) Was lead singer with LED ZEPPLIN and The HONEYDRIPPERS before making some hit records on his own. Year/**Age:** 1995/**47** 1996/**48** 1997/**49**

- **ISAAC HAYES** Singer/actor. (Covington, TN) He had a #1 hit: "Theme from Shaft" in 1971. He composed the film score for the movie *Shaft*. He also teamed up with David Porter to write "Soul Man" and "Hold On I'm Coming." Year/**Age:** 1995/**53** 1996/**54** 1997/**55**

- **CONNIE CHUNG** Newswoman. (Born Constance Yu-Hwa in Washington, DC) Co-anchors "CBS Evening News" with Dan Rather. Host of CBS's "Saturday Night With Connie Chung" and "Eye to Eye." Married to Maury Povich. Year/**Age:** 1995/**49** 1996/**50** 1997/**51**

- **CARLA FRACCI** Dancer. (Italy) American Ballet Theatre. Year/**Age:** 1995/**59** 1996/**60** 1997/**61**

- **MARK LANGSTON** Baseball. (San Diego, CA) Year/**Age:** 1995/**35** 1996/**36** 1997/**37**

- **CRAIG NETTLES** Baseball veteran. (San Diego, CA) He was the American League home run leader in 1976. Year/**Age:** 1995/**51** 1996/**52** 1997/**53**

- **GEORGE MITCHELL** Senate Majority Leader. (Waterville, NE) (D/ME). Year/**Age:** 1995/**62** 1996/**63** 1997/**64**

- **AL LOPEZ** Baseball. (Tampa, FL) Year/**Age:** 1995/**86** 1996/**87** 1997/**88**

- **PETER HORTON** Actor. TV's "thirtysomething." Year/**Age:** 1995/**42** 1996/**43** 1997/**44**

- **RUDY GATLIN** Muscian. (Brentwood, TN) Hits include "All the Gold." Year/**Age:** 1995/**42** 1996/**43** 1997/**44**

- **KE HUY QUAN** Actor.. TV's "Together We Stand." Year/**Age:** 1995/**42** 1996/**43** 1997/**44**

- **SAM MELVILLE** Actor. (1936-1989) He played officer Mike Danko on the TV series "The Rookies."

- **H. P. LOVECRAFT** Author. (1890-1937 – Providence, RI) Wrote science fiction and horror stories. (Died 3-15-37.)

- **JIM REEVES** C&W singer. (1924-1964 – Galloway, TX) He died in a single-engine plane crash in fog, flying from Arkansas to Nashville. His biggest hit: "He'll Have to Go" in 1960. He was one of the first country singers to cross over into the pop field. (Died 7-31-64.)

- **RAJIV GANDHI** (1944-1991 – India) He was prime Minister from 8-4-89. He was killed in a bomb blast. (Died 5-21-91.)

- **EDGAR A. (ALBERT) GUEST** Poet/journalist. (1881-1959 – England) He was syndicated in many newspapers and published several poetry books. His son, Bud, hosted a radio show in Detroit, MI. (Died 8-5-59.)

- **JACQUELINE SUSANN** Author. (1921-1974 – Philadelphia, PA) She wrote *The Valley of the Dolls*. (Died 9-21-74.)

- **BENJAMIN HARRISON** 23rd U.S. President. (1833-1901 – North Bend, OH) He stood 5 feet, 6 inches, so they called him "Little Ben." He was the grandson of President William Henry Harrison, who signed the Declaration of Independence. (Died 3-13-01.)

- **OLIVER HAZARD PERRY** Navy Captain. (1785-1819 – South Kingston, RI) He claimed victory in the War of 1812 at the Battle of Lake Erie. He sent a message to his commander saying, "We have met the enemy, and they are ours." (Died 8-23-1819.)

FACTS FROM THE PAST

1741 Danish navigator, **VITUS BERING**, discovered Alaska. That's why they call the water around it the Bering Sea.

1882 **TCHAIKOVSKY**'s [chi-kof'-ski] *1812 Overture* had its premiere in Moscow. It was composed to be performed outdoors with the accompaniment of actual artillery and a battle theme.

1945 Brooklyn shortstop, **TOMMY BROWN**, age 17, became the youngest player to hit a home run in the major leagues. He got it off Pirate pitcher **PREACHER ROE**.

1960 **CONNIE FRANCIS** made her acting debut, when filming began on MGM's *Where the Boys Are* in Ft. Lauderdale, FL.

1968 **CYNTHIA LENNON** sued **JOHN LENNON** for divorce after she found out that Yoko Ono had been living in their home while Cynthia was on vacation. The grounds for divorce were listed as "adultery."

1974 **NOLAN RYAN** of the California Angels became the first major league pitcher to be **CLOCKED AT OVER 100 MPH.** On July 31, 1990, he pitched his 300th victory at age 43. He was the 20th pitcher to reach 300 wins. The other 19 are in the Baseball Hall of Fame.

1982 Gynecologist Dr. **HECTOR ZEVALLOS** and his wife, Rosalie, were freed eight days after they were kidnapped outside Edwardsville, IL, by an anti-abortion group called "Army of God."

1987 An argument by Lt. Col. **OLIVER NORTH** was rejected by a federal appeals court in Washington, DC. North stated that the independent counsel investigating the Iran-Contra affair was operating under an invalid Justice Department regulation.

1992 One-time White House hopeful **ROSS PEROT** released his book *United We Stand: How We Can Take Back Our Country*, on the final day of the Republican convention.

1994 Vice President **AL GORE** underwent surgery at Bethesda Naval Hospital to fuse an injured Achilles tendon, which he tore playing basketball with former congressional at the House gym.

AUGUST 21

The car honks twice

BIRTHDAYS

- **KENNY ROGERS** Entertainer. (Houston, TX) His biggest hits: "Lady," written by Lionel Richie and "Islands in the Stream" with Dolly Parton, written by the BEE GEES. Kenny was with the CHRISTY MINSTRELS and later the FIRST EDITION. Appears in Dole Pineapple TV commercials. Year/**Age:** 1995/**57** 1996/**58** 1997/**59**

- **JACKIE DeSHANNON** Singer. (Born Sharon Meyers in Hazel, KY.) She had her own radio show at age 6. Her biggest record: "Put a Little Love in Your Heart" in 1969. She was one of the warm-up acts for many of the BEATLES appearances in the U.S. during 1964. Year/**Age:** 1995/**51** 1996/**52** 1997/**53**

- **HAROLD REID** C&W singer. Sings bass with the STATLER BROTHERS. Biggest hit: "Flowers on the Wall" in 1966. They worked with Johnny Cash from 1963-71. Year/**Age:** 1995/**56** 1996/**57** 1997/**58**

- **HARRY SMITH** TV host. "CBS This Morning." Year/**Age:** 1995/**44** 1996/**45** 1997/**46**

- **JIM McMAHON** Quarterback. (Jersey City, NJ) With the Arizona Cardinals in 1994. Formerly with the Minnesota Vikings, Chicago Bears, and the Philadelphia Eagles. Year/**Age:** 1995/**36** 1996/**37** 1997/**38**

- **MELVIN VAN PEEBLES** Playwright. (Chicago, IL) Wrote and directed the 1971 play *Ain't Supposed to Die a Natural Death*. His son is actor/director Mario Van Peebles (Posse). Year/**Age:** 1995/**63** 1996/**64** 1997/**65**

- **CARL GIAMARESE** Guitarist. With the BUCKINGHAMS. Their #1 hit in 1966: "Kind of a Drag." Year/**Age:** 1995/**48** 1996/**49** 1997/**50**

- **DON KING** Boxing manager/promoter. (Cleveland, OH) Managed Mike Tyson. Year/**Age:** 1995/**64** 1996/**65** 1997/**66**

- **KIM CATTRALL** Actress. In films *Mannequin* and *Live Nude Girls*. Year/**Age:** 1995/**39** 1996/**40** 1997/**41**

- **ARCHIE GRIFFIN** Football. (Columbus, OH) Won the Heisman Trophy twice and started his pro career with Cincinnati in 1976. Year/**Age:** 1995/**41** 1996/**42** 1997/**43**

- **WILT "THE STILT" CHAMBERLAIN** Basketball star. (Born Wilton Norman Chamberlain in Philadelphia, PA) Played center and scored an NBA record of 31,419 points and was MVP four times. Appears in Nestles Crunch TV commercials. Year/**Age:** 1995/**59** 1996/**60** 1997/**61**

- **GERRY STALEY** Baseball. Pitched for the St. Louis Cardinals. Year/**Age:** 1995/**75** 1996/**76** 1997/**77**

- **CLARENCE WILLIAMS III** Actor. (NYC) Played Linc Hayes on "The Mod Squad." Film *Sugar Hill*. Year/**Age:** 1995/**56** 1996/**57** 1997/**58**

- **COUNT BASIE** Jazz great. (1904-1984 – Born William Basie in Red Bank, NJ) One of his first hits was "Open the Door, Richard" in 1947, but his most-played was "April in Paris." He wrote "One O'clock Jump" and "Jumpin' at the Woodside." (Died 4-26-84.)

FACTS FROM THE PAST

1614 Hungarian Countess Elizabeth Bathory, the **BLOOD-BATHING BEAUTY**, died in prison. Convinced that bathing in blood would preserve her complexion, the countess had kidnapped 610 girls over 10 years and hung them in chains in her castle as a source for her beauty baths. She was captured and tried and her henchmen were tortured, beheaded and burned for being her accomplices.

1831 Former slave **NAT TURNER** started an insurrection against slavery. He was later executed. There is an excellent, controversial book about him called *Confessions of Nat Turner* by William Styron.

1858 Illinois political contenders **ABRAHAM LINCOLN** and **STEPHEN DOUGLAS** began their 7 famous debates with slavery the main issue.

1887 Lefthanded pitcher **DAN CASEY** of the Phillies struck out in the 9th inning in a game with the New York Giants, inspiring **ERNEST L. THAYER** to write the poem *Casey at the Bat*.

1901 "Iron Man" **JOE McGINNITY WAS KICKED OUT** of the National League for abusing an umpire. The abuse included stepping on his toes, punching him and spitting in his face. McGinnity was so popular with his fans, he was later reinstated and heavily fined.

1945 The **LEND-LEASE PROGRAM** was ended by President Harry Truman. Under this plan, the U.S. had shipped $50 billion in aid to America's allies during World War II.

1950 22-year-old **ALTHEA GIBSON** became the first African-American tennis player to compete in the U.S. Open.

1980 President Jimmy **CARTER'S BROTHER, BILLY,** testified before a Senate Committee investigating his ties with Libya. Billy had received a personal loan for $200,000 from the Libyan government.

1983 The leader of the political opposition in the Philippines, **BENIGNO AQUINO,** was murdered in a conspiracy that involved high-level military officials. A million protestors marched in Manila on the first anniversary of the murder. Aquino's widow, Corazon, gained power when the late Ferdinand Marcos's regime crumbled in 1986.

1987 Sgt. Clayton Lonetree became the first Marine ever court-martialed for spying. The U.S. Embassy guard in Moscow was convicted in Quantico, VA, of passing secrets to the KGB while becoming romantically involved with a Soviet woman.

1991 A coup against Soviet President **MIKHAIL GORBACHEV** failed in the face of a popular uprising led by Russian federation President **BORIS YELTSIN.**

1994 Ruling party canidate **ERNESTO ZEDILLO PONCE de LEON** won the presidential election in Mexico.

Don't cross the road backwards

AUGUST 22

BIRTHDAYS

- **BILL PARCELL** Football coach. (Englewood, NY) He left coaching in January 1991, after leading the New York Giants to a Super Bowl victory. Then he decided later to come back. Coached Tampa Bay and the New England Patriots. Year/**Age**: 1995/**54** 1996/**55** 1997/**56**

- **NORMAN SCHWARZKOPF** U.S. General. (Trenton, NJ) In charge of U.S. Allied Forces in the Persian Gulf during the 1990-1991 conflict. He won a scholarship to West Point in 1952; became 2nd Lt., infantry in 1956 and General in 1988. He and wife Brenda, whom he met at an Army football game, have three children. Wrote book *It Doesn't Take a Hero.* Year/**Age**: 1995/**61** 1996/**62** 1997/**63**

- **VALERIE HARPER** Actress. (Suffern, NY) She played Rhoda on the "Mary Tyler Moore" TV series and repeated the character in her "Rhoda" TV series. Later on the sitcoms "Valerie" and "City." Year/**Age**: 1995/**55** 1996/**56** 1997/**57**

- **MATS WILANDER** Tennis star. Year/**Age**: 1995/**31** 1996/**32** 1997/**33**

- **MORTON DEAN** TV anchorman. (Fall River, MA) With CBS News since 1967. Year/**Age**: 1995/**60** 1996/**61** 1997/**62**

- **RAY BRADBURY** Science-fiction writer. (Waukegan, IL) He wrote *Martian Chronicles* and *Fahrenheit 451.* Year/**Age**: 1995/**75** 1996/**76** 1997/**77**

- **CINDY WILLIAMS** Actress. (Van Nuys, CA) Played Shirley Feeney on "Laverne & Shirley." She was Ron Howard's girl in *American Graffiti* and her first part was in the '50s with Steve McQueen. Appeared in *Rude Awakening, The Blob, Normal Life* and TV's "Getting By." Year/**Age**: 1995/**48** 1996/**49** 1997/**50**

- **TODD MARTIN** Tennis player. (Lansing, MI) Year/**Age**: 1995/**27** 1996/**28** 1997/**29**

- **IAN MITCHELL** Musician. (Scotland) Member of BAY CITY ROLLERS. They got their name by stabbing at a U.S. map and hit on Bay City, MI. Their biggest hit "Saturday Night" in 1975. Year/**Age**: 1995/**37** 1996/**38** 1997/**39**

- **ROLAND ORZABAL** Singer/musician. (England) With the duo TEARS FOR FEARS. Their biggest hit: "Shout" in 1985. Year/**Age**: 1995/**35** 1996/**36** 1997/**37**

- **SAM NEELY** C&W singer. (Corpus Christi, TX) Had a cross-over hit in 1972: "Loving You Just Crossed My Mind." Year/**Age**: 1995/**45** 1996/**46** 1997/**47**

- **JOHN LEE HOOKER** Blues singer. (Clarksdale, MS) He ran away to Detroit as a youngster to escape working on a farm, and has been singing the blues ever since. He was featured in the *Blues Brothers* film and his biggest hit was "Boom Boom" in 1962. Year/**Age**: 1995/**78** 1996/**79** 1997/**80**

- **DEBBI PETERSON** Drummer. (Los Angeles, CA) With the BANGLES. Biggest hit: "Walk Like An Egyptian." Year/**Age**: 1995/**35** 1996/**36** 1997/**37**

- **PAUL MOLITOR** Baseball. (St. Paul, MN) The only player to hit 5 for 5 in a World Series Game. World Series MVP in 1993. His 39-game hitting streak is the fifth longest in major league baseball. Set the designated hitter record for stolen bases (24) in 1992. Former Milwaukee Brewer, now with Toronto. Year/**Age**: 1995/**39** 1996/**40** 1997/**41**

- **CARL YASTRAZEMSKI** [yuh-strem'-ski] Former baseball star. (Southhampton, NY) "Yas," Boston Red Sox leftfielder won the batting crown in 1968 with the lowest average, .301, in big-league history for a titlist. Year/**Age**: 1995/**56** 1996/**57** 1997/**58**

- **TEX WILLIAMS** C&W singer. (1917-1985 – Ramsey, IL) Biggest hit: "Smoke, Smoke, Smoke (That Cigarette)" in 1947. #1 on the C&W charts for 16 weeks. (Died 10-11-85.)

- **CLAUDE DEBUSSY** Composer. (1862-1918 – France) Experimented with new harmonic techniques and combinations. His wife Lily, distraught over his womanizing, left a suicide note, then shot herself in the breast and groin. When Debussy found her seriously wounded, he left the house, leaving her to recover on her own. (Died 3-25-18.)

FACTS FROM THE PAST

1762 ANN FRANKLIN became the **FIRST FEMALE EDITOR** for an American newspaper, the *Newport (RI) Mercury.*

1770 Captain James Cook took possession of **AUSTRALIA** for the British crown.

1787 The first **EXPERIMENTAL STEAMBOAT WAS TESTED** on the Delaware River by John Fitch. Its top speed was 3 m.p.h.

1902 **THEODORE ROOSEVELT** became the first president to ride in an automobile (a Columbia Electric Victoria) in Hartford, CT.

1911 **LEONARDO Da VINCI**'s *Mona Lisa* was stolen from the Louvre museum sometime during the night. (The painting turned up two years later in Italy.)

1950 **ALTHEA GIBSON** became the first African-American tennis player to be accepted in competition for the National Championship.

1973 President Nixon named German born **HENRY KISSINGER** as Secretary of State. Kissinger served in that capacity until 1977. He won a **NOBEL PEACE PRIZE** in 1973 and was instrumental in the 1969 SALT Talks and opening U.S. ties with China.

1984 Republican National Convention in Dallas nominated **PRESIDENT REAGAN** and **VICE PRESIDENT BUSH** for second terms in office, breaking with tradition by approving both nominations with a single roll-call vote.

1989 **NOLAN RYAN** struck out his 5,000th batter becoming the first to reach that milestone when he fanned Oakland's Rickey Henderson in the fifth inning. It happened at 8:51 p.m. on a 3-2, 96-mph fastball.

1991 **MIKHAIL GORBACHEV** reclaimed power in the Soviet Union as his would-be successors fled, ending three days of mental terror throughout the world. Four people were killed during the coup attempt.

1992 Rock star **STING** married Trudie Styler in England, his long-time live-in love, after ten years and three children.

AUGUST 23
Astrological Sign of Virgo

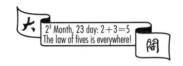

2³ Month, 23 day: 2 + 3 = 5
The law of fives is everywhere!

BIRTHDAYS

- **ANTONIA NOVELLO** Surgeon General. (Puerto Rico) She was the first woman and the first Hispanic in this post. Year/**Age:** 1995/**51** 1996/**52** 1997/**53**

- **BARBARA EDEN** Actress. (Born Barbara Huffman in Tucson, AZ) She starred as the 2,000-year-old genie on the "I Dream of Jeannie" TV sitcom with Larry Hagman and appeared on "Harper Valley PTA." Year/**Age:** 1995/**61** 1996/**62** 1997/**63**

- **SHELLEY LONG** Actress. (Fort Wayne, IN) Was Diane on TV's "Cheers" and in the films *Outrageous Fortune, Troop Beverly Hills, Good Advice, Don't Tell Her It's Me,* and Mom Brady in *The Brady Bunch.* In the 1993 TV sitcom "Good Advice." Year/**Age:** 1995/**46** 1996/**47** 1997/**48**

- **GENE KELLY** Actor/dancer. (Pittsburgh, PA) He received an Oscar nomination in 1945 for best actor in *Anchor's Away* with Frank Sinatra. His other films include: *Singing in the Rain, An American in Paris,* and *That's Dancing.* Year/**Age:** 1995/**83** 1996/**84** 1997/**85**

- **PETE WILSON** California Governor. (Lake Forest, IL) U.S. Senator 1983-91. Year/**Age:** 1995/**62** 1996/**63** 1997/**64**

- **PATRICIA McBRIDE** Ballet dancer. (Teaneck, NY) Year/**Age:** 1995/**53** 1996/**54** 1997/**55**

- **VERA MILES** Actress. (Born Vera Ralston in Boise City, OK) Appeared in *Psycho* in 1960 with Janet Leigh and Tony Perkins. Year/**Age:** 1995/**65** 1996/**66** 1997/**67**

- **RICK SPRINGFIELD** Actor/singer. (Born Richard Lewis Springthorpe in Australia) Biggest hit: "Jessie's Girl" in 1981. He played Noah Drake on the TV soap opera "General Hospital." Starred in the films *Hard to Hold* and *The Human Target.* Year/**Age:** 1995/**46** 1996/**47** 1997/**48**

- **RICHARD SANDERS** Actor. (Harrisburg, PA) Played Les Nesman, news, weather, and farm reporter for "WKRP in Cincinnati." Year/**Age:** 1995/**55** 1996/**56** 1997/**57**

- **CHRISTIAN "SONNY" JURGENSEN** Football. (Wilmington, NC) Three-time NFL leading passer with the Washington Redskins. Now a sports announcer. Year/**Age:** 1995/**61** 1996/**62** 1997/**63**

- **MARK RUSSELL** Political satirist. (Born Mark Ruslander in Buffalo, NY) Year/**Age:** 1995/**63** 1996/**64** 1997/**65**

- **MARK HUDSON** Singer. (Portland, OR) Of the HUDSON BROTHERS. Biggest hit: "So You Are a Star." Year/**Age:** 1995/**44** 1996/**45** 1997/**46**

- **QUEEN NOOR** of Jordan (Born Lisa Najeeb Halaby in Washington, DC) King Hussein's wife. Year/**Age:** 1995/**44** 1996/**45** 1997/**46**

- **BOB CROSBY** Bandleader. (1913-1993 – Spokane, WA) Bing's brother. Bob's biggest hit: "Big Noise from Winnetka" which was recorded at the Blackhawk Restaurant in Chicago, IL in 1938. (Died 3-9-93.)

- **JIMI JAMISON** Singer. With SURVIVOR, their biggest hit: "Eye of the Tiger" from *Rocky III.* Year/**Age:** 1995/**44** 1996/**45** 1997/**46**

- **RIVER PHOENIX** Actor. (1970-1993 – Madras, OR) Appeared in "Seven Brides for Seven Brothers" on TV and in the films *Stand By Me, This Thing Called Love,* and *Sneakers.* Received Academy Award nomination for supporting actor in *Running on Empty.* He died soon after collapsing in front of the viper Club on Sunset Strip in LA. (Died 10-31-93.)

- **KEITH MOON** Drummer. (1947-1978 – England) Original member of THE WHO. Biggest hit: "I Can See For Miles" in 1967. He died after overdosing on Hemenephrin, a prescription drug that was supposed to have helped him withdraw from alcohol on 9-7-78.

- **RUDY LEWIS** Singer. (1936-1964) With the DRIFTERS from 1961-63. Biggest hit: "Save the Last Dance for Me."

FACTS FROM THE PAST

1923 Radio's first comedians went on the air. **ERNIE HARE** and **BILLY JONES** were sponsored by the Happiness Candy Company and called themselves "The Happiness Boys."

1927 **BARTOLOMEO VANZETTI** and **NICOLA SACCO** were executed in Massachusetts for armed robbery and murder. In 1977 Massachusetts governor Michael Dukakis proclaimed them innocent.

1936 17-year-old Cleveland right hander **BOB FELLER** made his major league debut, striking out 17 St. Louis batters and allowing only six hits.

1947 An audience at the Hollywood Bowl heard **HARRY TRUMAN'S DAUGHTER** Margaret in her first public concert as a singer. The critics blasted her performance and Harry blasted the critics right from the White House.

1962 **JOHN LENNON** married **CYNTHIA POWELL** in a secret ceremony at the Mount Pleasant Registry Office in Liverpool, England. Cynthia was pregnant with Julian, who was born April 8, 1963.

1979 Soviet dancer **ALEXANDER GODUNOV** defected while the Bolshoi Ballet was on tour in New York, requesting and receiving political asylum in the United States.

1985 Martina Navratilova and Pam Shriver routed Bobby Riggs and Vitas Gerulatis in 3 straight sets at Atlantic City, in a much-ballyhooed **BATTLE OF THE SEXES.** There wasn't too much to keep the interest of the crowd of about 5,000, and many said that this would be the end of the "hustling" deals for Bobby Riggs.

1987 Robert Jarvik and Marilyn Mach vos Savant married. They called it a **UNION OF GREAT MINDS.** Savant has a 228 IQ and is in the *Guinness Book of World Records.* Jarvik invented the artificial heart. He designed the wedding ring from gold plated pyrolytic carbon used in his hearts. Sci-fi master Isaac Asimov gave away the bride and the best man was an ex-artificial heart patient.

1989 **VICTORIA BRUCKER** from San Pedro, CA, became the first U.S. girl to play in the Little League World Series.

Not only rain can fall
from the sky

AUGUST 24

BIRTHDAYS

• **CAL RIPKEN, JR.** Baltimore shortstop. (Havre de Grace, MD) Top All-Star vote-getter in 1992. His dad has been an Oriole coach and brother Billy, the second baseman. He's second to Lou Gehrig in playing the most consecutive games. In 1992 he signed a 5-year, $30.5-million contract with Baltimore, plus a $2-million, four-year deal to work for the Orioles after he retires from the playing field. Year/**Age**: 1995/**35** 1996/**36** 1997/**37**

• **DAVID FREIBURG** Bass guitarist. (Boston, MA) With QUICK-SILVER MESSENGER SERVICE and later JEFFERSON STARSHIP. Their biggest hit: "We Built This City" in 1985. JEFFERSON AIRPLANE evolved into STARSHIP in 1974. Mainstays of the group were Grace Slick, Paul Kantner, and Marty Balin. Year/**Age**: 1995/**57** 1996/**58** 1997/**59**

• **MARLEE MATLIN** Actress. (Chicago, IL) Won best actress Oscar for *Children of a Lesser God* and appears on TV's "Reasonable Doubts." In the film *Hear No Evil*. Year/**Age**: 1995/**30** 1996/**31** 1997/**32**

• **STEVE GUTTENBERG** Actor. (NYC) Starred in *Cocoon*, *Three Men and a Baby*, and *Three Men and a Little Lady*. Year/**Age**: 1995/**37** 1996/**38** 1997/**39**

• **MASON WILLIAMS** Guitarist. (Abilene, TX) Biggest hit: "Classical Gas" in 1968. He was also a song/comedy/sketch writer on the "Smothers Brothers Show" and "The Glenn Campbell Goodtime Hour." Year/**Age**: 1995/**57** 1996/**58** 1997/**59**

• **GERRY COONEY** Fighter. (Long Island, NY) Year/**Age**: 1995/**39** 1996/**40** 1997/**41**

• **JIM CAPALDI** Musician. (England) Drummer with TRAFFIC. Hit in 1983: "Living on the Edge." Year/**Age**: 1995/**51** 1996/**52** 1997/**53**

• **JOE REGALBUTO** Actor. He plays newsman Frank Fontana on TV's "Murphy Brown." and was in cast of "Knot's Landing" as Harry Fisher for one season. Year/**Age**: 1995/**46** 1996/**47** 1997/**48**

• **DURWARD KIRBY** TV personality. (Covington, KY) He was a regular on the "Garry Moore Show" on TV in the 1950s and 1960s. Year/**Age**: 1995/**83** 1996/**84** 1997/**85**

• **ERNEST WRIGHT** Singer. One of the original IMPERIALS. With the group since its start, with hits like: "Tears on My Pillow" and "Going Out of My Head." Year/**Age**: 1995/**56** 1996/**57** 1997/**58**

• **JAMES BRADY** Singer. Of the SANDPIPERS. Their biggest hit: "Guantanamera" in 1966. Year/**Age**: 1995/**51** 1996/**52** 1997/**53**

• **DENNIS JAMES** TV host. (Jersey City, NY) Hosted "Name That Tune" and did the Chesterfield commercials with the dancing cigarette boxes. Hosts UCP Telethon. Year/**Age**: 1995/**78** 1996/**79** 1997/**80**

• **LOUIS TEICHER** Pianist. (Wilkes-Barre, PA) Hits with Ferrante include "Exodus," "Tonight," and "Midnight Cowboy." Year/**Age**: 1995/**71** 1996/**72** 1997/**73**

FACTS FROM THE PAST

1814   During the **WAR OF 1812**, British troops easily fought their way into Washington, DC, and put the torch to most public buildings, including the White House. James Madison was the only president to ever face fire. He borrowed a couple of pistols and went into action, but when he saw that he was outnumbered, he left. Before evacuating the Executive Mansion, Dolley Madison rescued the silverware and her pet parrot.

1867   Railroad millionaire **JOHNS HOPKINS** died, leaving 7\frac{1}{2}$ million in his will for the purpose of founding a medical school in his name.

1932   **AMELIA EARHART** became the first woman to make a non-stop flight across the U.S., flying from Los Angeles to Newark, NJ, in 19 hours and 5 minutes.

1954   President Eisenhower signed a law to keep the **COMMUNIST PARTY** out of the United States. It never made it and was dropped.

1963   Stevie Wonder, at age 13, did what no one else had ever done. He reached #1 on the "Pop" and "R&B" charts the same week with his song "Fingertips, Part 2," and the same week had the #1 "Pop" album, *The 12-Year-Old Genius*.

1968   During the early morning hours **KEITH MOON** crowned his birthday bash by accidentally driving a Lincoln Continental into the Holiday Inn swimming pool in Flint, MI.

1983   **SHAWN MICHELLE STEPHENS**, the wife of Jerry Lee Louis, was found dead in their Herando, Mississippi, home.

1988   Minnesota's **DINO CICCARELLI** became the first hockey player to spend time in jail for a penalty on the ice. He was sentenced to 24 hours in jail and a $1,000 fine for hitting Toronto's **LUKE RICHARDSON** over the head twice with his hockey stick. He was released after two hours.

1989   **PETE ROSE** was suspended for betting on baseball games under a compromise reached with Commissioner A. Bartlett Giamatti. Rose denied charges against him. He's eligible for election to the Baseball Hall of Fame in 1993.

1990   **SINEAD O'CONNOR** banned the "Stars Spangled Banner" from her show in New Jersey.

1991   **MIKHAIL GORBACHEV** resigned as head of the Communist Party in the disintegrating Soviet Union.

1992   President Bush surveyed the ruins of South Miami after **HURRICANE ANDREW** struck early in the day. One of the worst natural disasters in the nation's history, it killed over 20 people, left 50,000 homeless and caused damage in the billions of dollars.

AUGUST 25

Listen for the sound of mice

BIRTHDAYS

- **MONTY HALL** Game show host. (Canada) Also developed and produced "Let's Make a Deal" on TV from 1963. During his 13 years on the show he received 20,000 kisses from people dressed as cucumbers, clowns, cold cuts, and the like. Year/**Age**: 1995/**72** 1996/**73** 1997/**74**

- **SEAN CONNERY** Actor. (Born Thomas Sean in Scotland) He was "007" in the *James Bond* movies and made his stage debut in 1953 in *South Pacific*. Won Oscar for supporting actor in *The Untouchables*. In the films *First Knight*, *Medicine Man*, and *Rising Sun*. Year/**Age**: 1995/**65** 1996/**66** 1997/**67**

- **MEL FERRER** Actor. (Born Melchior Gaston Ferrer in Elberon, NJ) His films include: *War and Peace*, *The Fall of the Roman Empire*, and *Sex and the Single Girl*. Year/**Age**: 1995/**78** 1996/**79** 1997/**80**

- **CLAUDIA SCHIFFER** Model. Engaged to magician David Copperfield. Year/**Age**: 1995/**25** 1996/**26** 1997/**27**

- **BILLY RAY CYRUS** C&W singer. (Flatwoods, KY) Hit: "Achy Breaky Heart" in 1993. Year/**Age**: 1995/**34** 1996/**35** 1997/**36**

- **MORGAN ENGLUND** Actor. (Nome, AK) Plays Dylan Lewis on the soap "Guiding Light." He's the son of Cloris Leachman. Year/**Age**: 1995/**31** 1996/**32** 1997/**33**

- **GEORGE C. (CORLEY) WALLACE**. Former Alabama Governor. (Clio, AL) Now wheelchair bound and suffers constant pain from the gunshot wounds inflicted by Arthur Bremer, in an attempted assassination during the 1972 presidential campaign. Year/**Age**: 1995/**76** 1996/**77** 1997/**78**

- **VAN JOHNSON** Actor. (Newport, RI) As an aspiring young actor, he wore red socks to an audition, got the part, and has worn red socks ever since. He appeared in *Caine Mutiny*, *Battleground*, *Miracle in the Rain*, and some 1940s musicals. Year/**Age**: 1995/**79** 1996/**80** 1997/**81**

- **GENE SIMMONS** Bassist. (Born Gene Klein in Israel) Of the group KISS. He got his stage name from the 1950's actress, Jean Simmons. He co-starred with Tom Selleck in the movie *Runaway*, and in *Wanted Dead or Alive* with Rutger Hauer. He had a 1990 hit "Forever." He claimed to have slept with 2,500 women. Year/**Age**: 1995/**46** 1996/**47** 1997/**48**

- **ROLLIE FINGERS** Baseball pitcher. The first to reach 300 saves in a career. He was inducted into the Baseball Hall of Fame in 1992. Cy Young and MVP winner in 1981. Year/**Age**: 1995/**49** 1996/**50** 1997/**51**

- **TOM SKERRITT** Actor. (Detroit, MI) *Steel Magnolias*, *A River Runs Through It*, Dr. Duke in *M*A*S*H* movie, and in TV's "Picket Fences." Year/**Age**: 1995/**62** 1996/**63** 1997/**64**

- **ALTHEA GIBSON** Tennis star. First African-American player to win a major tennis tournament. Year/**Age**: 1995/**66** 1996/**67** 1997/**68**

- **CORNELIUS BENNETT** Football. (Birmingham, AL) Buffalo Bills lineman. Year/**Age**: 1995/**29** 1996/**30** 1997/**31**

- **BLAIR UNDERWOOD** Actress. TV's "L.A. Law" and film *Posse*. Year/**Age**: 1995/**31** 1996/**32** 1997/**33**

- **ANNE ARCHER** Actress. (Los Angeles, CA) Daughter of actress Marjorie Lord. The suffering wife in *Fatal Attraction*. She did her own stunts in *Narrow Margin* with Gene Hackman. Also in *Patriot Games*, *Short Cuts*, and *Clear and Present Danger*. Year/**Age**: 1995/**48** 1996/**49** 1997/**50**

- **WALTER WILLIAMS** Singer. Of the O'JAYS. Biggest hit: "Love Train" in 1973. Year/**Age**: 1995/**53** 1996/**54** 1997/**55**

- **ELVIS COSTELLO** New wave singer/songwriter. (Born Declan McManus in London, England) His group was called THE ATTRACTIONS. They had a song in the top 40 in 1983 called "Every Day I Write the Book." Year/**Age**: 1995/**41** 1996/**42** 1997/**43**

- **RUBY KEELER** Actress/dancer. (1909-1993 – Born Ethel Hilda Keeler in Canada) Played a chorus girl in her 1933 film debut *42nd Street*. She was married to entertainer Al Jolson from 1928 to 1940, when they divorced. In 1971 she received rave reviews in the Broadway revival of *No, No, Nanette*. (Died 2-28-93.)

- **LEONARD BERNSTEIN** Composer/conductor. (1918-1990 – Lawrence, MA) Known for jumping up and down at moments of musical climax, this American maestro thrilled international audiences with his shows *On The Town* and *West Side Story*. Became conductor of the New York Philharmonic at age 40. (Died 10-14-90.)

- **ALLAN PINKERTON** First "super snooper." (1819-1884 – Scotland) In 1843, he was appointed Sheriff of Cook County in Chicago, IL. Created the first private detective agency. Not only was he the first "private eye," a term he created, but he was also the first Secret Service officer, hired by Abraham Lincoln. "The Pinkertons" were, of course, named for him. He foiled an earlier plot to kill Abraham Lincoln but turned goat when the Reno Brothers escaped him from on April Fools Day. (Died 7-1-1884.)

FACTS FROM THE PAST

1945 Baptist missionary and Army intelligence agent, **CAPTAIN JOHN BIRCH** was executed as a spy by Chinese Communists. The John Birch Society claims that he was the first American casualty in the global war against Communism.

1950 President Harry S. Truman ordered the Army to seize control of the **NATION'S RAILROADS** to avert a strike.

1970 **ELTON JOHN** played his first U.S. date at the Troubador Club in Los Angeles. He was unknown and had no hits at the time. Five years later (to the day), Elton returned to that club as a big star (1975) for a series of fundraisers for the U.C.L.A. eye clinic.

1982 The first U.S. Marines that President Reagan sent to Lebanon to supervise the **WITHDRAWAL OF PALESTINIAN AND SYRIAN FORCES FROM BEIRUT**, arrived in the Lebanese capital.

1986 **PAUL SIMON** released *Graceland*.

1991 **CARL LEWIS** ran a world-record 9.86 seconds in the 100-meter dash in Tokyo. That beat the previous record, 9.90, set by Leroy Burrell at the U.S. Championships two months earlier in New York City.

1994 **BILLY JOEL** and **CHRISTIE BRINKLEY** had their nine-year marriage dissolved by a New York Supreme Court Justice.

AUGUST 26
Women's Equality Day

BIRTHDAYS

- **MACAULAY CULKIN** Actor. (New York, NY) Star of *Home Alone* films, *My Girl*, *The Good Son*, *The Nutcracker*, and *Getting Even with Dad*. Year/**Age**: 1995/**15** 1996/**16** 1997/**17**

- **IRVING R. LEVINE** NBC financial correspondent. (Pawtucket, RI) He wrote *Main Street Italy*. Year/**Age**: 1995/**73** 1996/**74** 1997/**75**

- **GERALDINE ANNE FERRARO** V.P. nominee. (Newburgh, NY) The first woman nominated as candidate of a major political party for U.S. Vice President. Elected to Congress in 1978 and re-elected in 1980 and 1982. She is married to NY businessman John Zaccaro. Wrote *My Story*. Year/**Age**: 1995/**60** 1996/**61** 1997/**62**

- **VIC DANA** Singer. (Buffalo, NY) Biggest hit: "Red Roses for a Blue Lady" in 1965. Year/**Age**: 1995/**53** 1996/**54** 1997/**55**

- **BOB COWSILL** Singer. Of the COWSILLS. Their biggest hit: "The Rain, the Park and Other Things" in 1967. Year/**Age**: 1995/**46** 1996/**47** 1997/**48**

- **GEORGIA GIBBS** Singer. (Born Fredda Lipson in Worcester, MA) Known as "Her Nibs, Miss Georgia Gibbs." Early '50s recording star with hits: "Dance With Me, Henry" and "Tweedle-Dee." Year/**Age**: 1995/**69** 1996/**70** 1997/**71**

- **BENJAMIN (BEN) BRADLEE** *Washington Post* editor. (Boston, MA) He was Woodward and Bernstein's boss during the Watergate scandal investigation. Portrayed by Jason Robards in the film *All the President's Men*. He's married to writer Sally Quinn. Year/**Age**: 1995/**74** 1996/**75** 1997/**76**

- **VALERIE SIMPSON** Singer. (NYC) Half of ASHFORD & SIMPSON duo. Biggest hit: "Solid" in 1984. Year/**Age**: 1995/**49** 1996/**50** 1997/**51**

- **BRANFORD MARSALIS** Bandleader. (New Orleans, LA) TV's "Tonight Show." Year/**Age**: 1995/**35** 1996/**36** 1997/**37**

- **CHRIS BURKE** Actor with Downs Syndrome. TV's "Life Goes On." Year/**Age**: 1995/**30** 1996/**31** 1997/**32**

- **BEN WATTENBERG** Author. Year/**Age**: 1995/**62** 1996/**63** 1997/**64**

- **RONNY GRAHAM** Actor. (Philadelphia, PA) Played Reverend Bemis on the sitcom "Chico and the Man." Year/**Age**: 1995/**76** 1996/**77** 1997/**78**

- **DR. ALBERT SABIN** Polio pioneer. (1906-1993 – Poland) Discovered oral polio vaccine. His vaccine, along with one found earlier by Jonas Salk, helped to eliminate the frightening disease of polio from the U.S. (Died 3-3-93.)

- **JAN CLAYTON** Actress. (1925-1983 – Alamogordo, NM) Played Ellen Miller, Jeff's widowed mother on the "Lassie" TV series. (Died 8-28-83.)

- **LEE DeFOREST** Inventor. (1873-1961 – Council Bluffs, IA) He invented the triode, or three-element vacuum tube, which made radio and TV possible. (Died 6-30-61.)

- **CHRISTOPHER ISHERWOOD** Author. (1904-1986 – England.) Wrote novels, plays and short stories. *I Am a Camera* and *Cabaret* were based on his short story, "Sally Bowles." (Died 1-4-86.)

- **PRINCE ALBERT** (1819-1861) Consort of Queen Victoria, pictured on tobacco cans.

- **ROBERT WALPOLE** England's first prime minister. (1676) Very corrupt, he liked to accept bribes. He was the man who coined the phrase, "Every man has his price."

FACTS FROM THE PAST

1346 The cannon was used in battle for the first time when **EDWARD III** of England defeated **PHILIP VI** of France at the Battle of Crecy.

1907 With his hands tied to a 75-pound ball-and-chain, magician **HARRY HOUDINI** jumped off a bridge into San Francisco Bay. In less than 2 minutes, he swam to the surface, without the heavy attachments.

1939 WXBS **TELEVISED THE FIRST BASEBALL** games, a doubleheader between Cincinnati and Brooklyn. **RED BARBER** was the announcer. The Reds won the first game 5-2 and the Dodgers the second, 6-1.

1946 **NORMA JEAN BAKER** was signed to a contract with 20th Century Fox. Her name was changed to Marilyn after dancer Marilyn Miller and her mother's maiden name, Monroe. She only appeared in a bit scene in her first film, *Scudda-Hoo, Scudda-Hay*.

1947 The Brooklyn Dodger's **DON BANKHEAD** became the first African-American pitcher in the major leagues. He hit a home run, but allowed 10 hits in $3\frac{1}{2}$ innings. Pittsburgh beat the Dodgers 16-3.

1968 The **BEATLES** released the record "Hey, Jude," and it was #1 for 9 weeks—longer than any other **BEATLE** hit.

1970 **JIMI HENDRIX** made his last public appearance at England's Isle of Wight Pop Festival. Sharing top billing with Hendrix were Bob Dylan, Joni Mitchell, and Richie Havens.

1987 **SONNY BONO** decided to run for **MAYOR OF PALM SPRINGS, CA**. He was quoted as saying, "I've never been qualified for anything I've done."

1987 West German Chancellor **HELMUT KOHL** announced that his country would destroy 72 Pershing 1A rockets if the U.S. and Russia would scrap all intermediate-range nuclear weapons.

1989 *Playboy* founder **HUGH HEFNER** and **KIMBERLY CONRAD**, former Playmate, went honeymooning following their wedding, which was viewed by 157 million viewers around the world on Independent News coverage.

1992 Governor **EDWIN EDWARDS** declared a state of emergency after Hurricane Andrew hit Louisiana's southern parishes early in the morning, causing many injuries and extensive damage.

1994 President Clinton signed the **ANTI-CRIME BILL** into law following the Senate vote of 61-38 in favor.

AUGUST 27

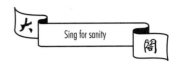

Sing for sanity

BIRTHDAYS

- **TUESDAY WELD** Actress. (Born Susan Kerr in NYC) Her first film was *Rock, Rock, Rock*, made when she was 14. She was nominated for an Oscar for supporting actress in *Looking for Mr. Goodbar* in 1977. Appeared with Al Pacino in *Author Author*. In *Falling Down* with Michael Douglas. Year/**Age:** 1995/**52** 1996/**53** 1997/**54**

- **MARTHA RAYE** Actress/comedienne. (Born Margaret Theresa Yvonne Reed in Butte, MT) She's affectionately known as "Moutha" Raye. Married at least 6 times, once to bandleader David Rose. She had her own TV show on NBC in the 1950s with Rocky Graziano and did denture cream commercials. Year/**Age:** 1995/**79** 1996/**80** 1997/**81**

- **TOMMY SANDS** Singer/actor. (Chicago, IL) At one time, married to Nancy Sinatra. Biggest hit: "Teenage Crush" in 1957. When he was 12 years old, he was a DJ in Houston, TX. He has been in five movies, including *The Longest Day* in 1962. Year/**Age:** 1995/**58** 1996/**59** 1997/**60**

- **BARBARA BACH** Actress. (Born Barbara Goldbach in NYC) Wife of Ringo Starr, they met during the filming of the prehistoric comedy *Caveman* in 1980. They have also appeared together in a short, *The Cooler*, TV miniseries *Princess Daisy*, and in Paul McCartney's *Give My Regards to Broadstreet*. Year/**Age:** 1995/**48** 1996/**49** 1997/**50**

- **DARYL DRAGON** Keyboardist. (Studio City, CA.) He's the Captain of CAPTAIN & TENNILLE. He's married to Toni Tennille. Their biggest hit: "Love Will Keep us Together" in 1975, written by Neil Sedaka. Year/**Age:** 1995/**53** 1996/**54** 1997/**55**

- **ALEX LIFESON** Singer. (Canada) Also bass player with RUSH. Year/**Age:** 1995/**42** 1996/**43** 1997/**44**

- **IRA LEVIN** Author. (NYC) He wrote the book and film *Rosemary's Baby* in 1968. Year/**Age:** 1995/**66** 1996/**67** 1997/**68**

- **PEE-WEE HERMAN** Comedian. (Born Paul Reubens in Peekskill, NY) Had his own popular Saturday morning children's show until he was arrested in an XXX-rated theater in July 1991. Films include: *Batman Returns* and *Pee Wee's Big Top*. Year/**Age:** 1995/**43** 1996/**44** 1997/**45**

- **MOTHER TERESA** Humanitarian. (Born Agnes Gonxha Bojaxhiu in Yugoslavia) Nobel Peace Prize winner. She founded the Missionaries of Charity in Calcutta, and opened facilities for the poor in New York and New Jersey. Year/**Age:** 1995/**85** 1996/**86** 1997/**87**

- **JEFF COOK** Musician (Fort Payne, AL) Member of ALABAMA and a cousin of two other members, Teddy Gentry & leader Randy Owen. Biggest hit: "Love in the First Degree" in 1981. Year/**Age:** 1995/**45** 1996/**46** 1997/**47**

- **LYNDON BAINES JOHNSON** 36th U.S. President. (1908-1973 – Stonewall, TX) Succeeded to the presidency after the assassination of John Kennedy. He was the youngest ever elected to the Senate at 41 years. LBJ was the first congressman to go on active duty and he gave JFK his break in politics. Today is a legal holiday in Texas. (Died 1-22-73.)

- **CHARLES DAWES** Politician. (1865-1951 – Marietta, OH) 30th vice president of the U.S. He wrote "Melody In A Major," which was later retitled "It's All In the Game," a hit in 1958 for singer Tommy Edwards. (Died 4-23-51.)

- **THEODORE DREISER** Author. (1871-1945 – Terre Haute, IN) He wrote *An American Tragedy* and *Sister Carrie*. (Died 12-28-45.)

FACTS FROM THE PAST

1859 Colonel Edwin Drake drilled the **FIRST SUCCESSFUL OIL WELL** in the U.S. near Titusville, PA., after drilling only 69 feet.

1912 **EDGAR RICE BURROUGHS** wrote the first magazine story about TARZAN, the abandoned son of an English nobleman raised by African apes, who became the "King of the Jungle." Rice continued to write jungle adventures for the next 15 years. Elmo Lincoln was the first Tarzan on film and Enid Markey, the first Jane. Tarzana, California, is named for Tarzan.

1965 **ELVIS PRESLEY** and the **BEATLES** met for 4 hours at Elvis's Beverly Hills mansion. In later years, Elvis was quoted as saying he never remembered the meeting. Presley was nervous and greeted them playing his guitar to the music on TV.

1966 **SIR FRANCIS CHICHESTER** made the first solo voyage around the world. He left England on this day and arrived home the following May.

1976 The U.S. Open Tennis Championship would not let **RENEE RICHARDS** compete because she used to be Dr. **RICHARD RASKIND**. The final decision was made after she refused to take chromosome test proving she was a woman.

1982 **RICKEY HENDERSON** of the Oakland A's stole his 119th base of the season in a game against the Brewers in Milwaukee, eclipsing Lou Brock's record of 118 steals in one season. He stole three more that day in the A's 5-4 loss.

1984 President Reagan announced that a schoolteacher would be chosen the **FIRST CITIZEN ASTRONAUT** to fly aboard the Space Shuttle. The chosen teacher was Sharon Christa (Christy) **McAULIFFE** of New Hampshire, one of the astronauts on the ill-fated *Challenger* in January 1986.

1990 Heavy fog that blanketed southeastern Wisconsin was a factor in the high-impact **HELICOPTER CRASH** that claimed the lives of all five people aboard, including blues guitarist **STEVIE RAY VAUGHAN** and members of rock star **ERIC CLAPTON**'s entourage. The Bell 206B JetRanger helicopter slammed into a ski hill at Alpine Valley, a ski resort and outdoor theater complex in East Troy, WI.

1992 **PRESIDENT BUSH** warned **SADDAM HUSSEIN** that as of this day any Iraqi aircraft entering a new no-fly zone, protecting 7 million Shiites from attack, would be shot down.

Even DJs get the blues

AUGUST 28

BIRTHDAYS

• **EMMA SAMMS** Actress. (England) Soap star on "General Hospital" as Holly Sutton. She left the show in 1993. Year/**Age**: 1995/**35** 1996/**36** 1997/**37**

• **SCOTT HAMILTON** Champion figure skater. (Haverford, PA) Appeared on "Stars on Ice." Year/**Age**: 1995/**37** 1996/**38** 1997/**39**

• **DONALD O'CONNOR** Entertainer. (Chicago, IL) He played Peter Sterling, Army private in *Francis, the Talking Mule.* In *Singing in the Rain* in 1952 with Debbie Reynolds and Gene Kelly. Year/**Age**: 1995/**70** 1996/**71** 1997/**72**

• **BEN GAZZARA** Actor. (NYC) In the 1950s, they called him the "most huggable heavy" since Bogart. His films included *Anatomy of a Murder,* and he appeared in the TV show "Run for Your Life." Year/**Age**: 1995/**65** 1996/**66** 1997/**67**

• **RON GUIDRY** Baseball. (Lafayette, LA) Yankee pitching ace and Cy Young award winner. Year/**Age**: 1995/**44** 1996/**45** 1997/**46**

• **WAYNE OSMOND** Singer. (Salt Lake City, UT) The OSMONDS' biggest hit: "One Bad Apple" in 1971. They started out as a barbershop quartet in 1959. Their first job was at Disneyland in 1962 and then the Andy Williams TV show as regulars for five years. Year/**Age**: 1995/**44** 1996/**45** 1997/**46**

• **BILLY GRAMMER** C&W. (Benton, IL) His biggest hits: "Gotta Travel On" and "Bonaparte's Retreat." Year/**Age**: 1995/**70** 1996/**71** 1997/**72**

• **DAVID SOUL** Actor/singer. (Born David Solberg in Chicago, IL) Had a hit in 1977: "Don't Give Up on Us" and appeared in the TV series "Starsky and Hutch." Year/**Age**: 1995/**52** 1996/**53** 1997/**54**

• **DANIEL STERN** Actor. Voice of adult Kevin Arnold on TV's "The Wonder Years." Year/**Age**: 1995/**38** 1996/**39** 1997/**40**

• **ROXIE ROKER** Actress. (Miami, FL)L She played Helen Willis, the upstairs neighbor, on "The Jeffersons" TV sitcom. Year/**Age**: 1995/**66** 1996/**67** 1997/**68**

• **DAVE HLUBEK** Musician. (Jacksonville, FL) Plays with the "Molly Hatchet" band. They've had a couple big albums, including *Flirting with Disaster.* Year/**Age**: 1995/**44** 1996/**45** 1997/**46**

• **LEE JANZEN** Golfer. (Austin, MN) In 1993, one of the youngest ever U.S. Open winners. Year/**Age**: 1995/**30** 1996/**31** 1997/**32**

• **JASON PRIESTLEY** Actor. Appears on TV's "Beverly Hills 90210." Films *Calendar Girl* and *Tombstone.* Year/**Age**: 1995/**26** 1996/**27** 1997/**28**

• **WILLIAM COHEN** Politician. (Bangor, ME) Republican Senator from Maine. Year/**Age**: 1995/**55** 1996/**56** 1997/**57**

• **LOU PINIELLA** Baseball manager. (Tampa, FL) Seattle Mariners. Year/**Age**: 1995/**52** 1996/**53** 1997/**54**

• **DANIEL SERIPHINE** Drummer. With CHICAGO. Their biggest hits: "If You Leave Me Now" and "Hard to Say I'm Sorry." Year/**Age**: 1995/**47** 1996/**48** 1997/**49**

• **NANCY KULP** Actress. (1921-1991 – Harrisburg, PA) She played Jane Hathaway on the TV series "Beverly Hillbillies" and also appeared on "Love That Bob" with Bob Cummings. She ran for Congress in 1984 as a Pennsylvania Democrat and lost. (Died 2-3-91.)

• **CHARLES BOYER** Actor. (1899-1978 – France) His films included *Algiers* in 1938. (Died 8-26-78.)

FACTS FROM THE PAST

1609 English navigator **HENRY HUDSON** discovered **DELAWARE BAY.**

1907 Two Seattle teenagers, Jim Casey and Claude Ryan, founded a local delivery service they called American Messenger Company. Some years later, when it had grown somewhat bigger, the name was changed to **UNITED PARCEL SERVICE.**

1909 Left-handed pitcher **DOLLY GRAY** walked seven straight hitters in one inning, giving the Washington rookie a major league record.

1938 **EDGAR BERGEN**'s ventriloquist dummy, Charlie McCarthy, was awarded an honorary degree from Northwestern University: "Master of Innuendo and Snappy Comeback."

1963 About 200,000 people joined in a **PEACEFUL CIVIL RIGHTS RALLY** in Washington, DC. The crowd heard **DR. MARTIN LUTHER KING, JR.,** declare, in front of the Lincoln Memorial, "I have a dream!" Peter, Paul, and Mary performed "Blowin' In the Wind."

1964 The **BEATLES** performed before 16,000 screaming fans at the first of two concerts at Forest Hills Tennis Stadium in New York. After the concert, the **BEATLES** met **BOB DYLAN,** who reportedly introduced them to marijuana. The **BEATLES** were paid $25,000. Former "Newlywed Game" show host Bob Eubanks brought them to Los Angeles.

1972 **MARK SPITZ** won the first of a **RECORD 7 GOLD MEDALS** at the 1972 Summer Olympics at Munich, West Germany, the 200-meter butterfly, beating the world record, which he himself had set several weeks before at the U.S. Olympic Trials in Chicago.

1982 A $14.1 billion **SUPPLEMENTAL APPROPRIATIONS BILL** designed to keep the government operating through September was vetoed by President Reagan. Congress overrode the veto.

1988 Winners in the **40TH ANNUAL EMMYS** in Pasadena, CA were: "The Wonder Years" and "thirtysomething." Individual awards to actresses Jane Seymour, Tyne Daly, Bea Arthur, and Estelle Getty. Also winning were Richard Kiley, John Larroquette (his 4th straight for "Night Court"), Michael J. Fox, and Larry Drake.

1994 **FIDEL CASTRO** and **PRESIDENT CLINTON** agreed to negotiate a stop to the high numbers of Cuban refugees coming to the U.S.

AUGUST 29

Stay organized

BIRTHDAYS

- **JAMES BRADY** Former Presidential Press Secretary. (Centralia, IL) Nicknamed "The Bear." Year/**Age**: 1995/**55** 1996/**56** 1997/**57**

- **MICHAEL JACKSON** Entertainer. (Gary, IN) He gave his first public performance in the fall of 1963, singing "Climb Every Mountain" in front of his kindergarten class at Garnett Elementary in Gary. He made over $70 million from the *Thriller* LP. His *Bad* LP was #1 in 23 countries. Michael spent nearly $50 million buying the rights to 251 BEATLES songs, outbidding Paul McCartney and Yoko Ono. He married Lisa Marie Presley on May 26, 1994 in the Dominican Republic. Year/**Age**: 1995/**37** 1996/**38** 1997/**39**

- **ELLIOTT GOULD** Actor. (Born Elliott Goldstein in Brooklyn, NY) He was nominated for supporting actor in 1969 for *Bob & Carol, Ted & Alice*. At one time, he was married to Barbra Streisand; they have a son, Jason. He also appeared in the movie *M*A*S*H*. Year/**Age**: 1995/**57** 1996/**58** 1997/**59**

- **ISABEL SANFORD** Actress. (NYC) An Emmy Award winner, she played Louise on "The Jeffersons." Year/**Age**: 1995/**62** 1996/**63** 1997/**64**

- **SIR RICHARD ATTENBOROUGH** Actor/director. (England) They call him "Dicky." He directed *Gandhi* and *Cry Freedom*. He played Santa Claus in the "Miracle On 34th Street" remake. Year/**Age**: 1995/**72** 1996/**73** 1997/**74**

- **WILLIAM FRIEDKIN** Film director. (Chicago, IL) He directed *The French Connection,* for which he won an Oscar in 1971. He also directed *The Exorcist, The Guardian*, and *Blue Chips*. He worked at WGN radio in Chicago when he was a young boy. Year/**Age**: 1995/**56** 1996/**57** 1997/**58**

- **REBECCA DeMORNAY** Actress. (Santa Rosa, CA) Her films include *Risky Business* in 1983, *Hand That Rocks the Cradle Guilty as Sin, Year*, and *The Three Musketeers*. **Age**: 1995/**33** 1996/**34** 1997/**35**

- **RICHARD GERE** Actor. (Philadelphia, PA) Appeared in *American Gigolo, And the Band Played On, First Knight, Officer & A Gentleman, Looking for Mr. Goodbar, Pretty Woman, Intersection*, and *Sommersby*. Married to model Cindy Crawford. Year/**Age**: 1995/**46** 1996/**47** 1997/**48**

- **GEORGE MONTGOMERY** Actor. (Born George Letz in Brady, MT) He and Dinah Shore were married at one time. Year/**Age**: 1995/**79** 1996/**80** 1997/**81**

- **CARL BANKS** Football. (Flint, MI) New York Giants lineman. Year/**Age**: 1995/**33** 1996/**34** 1997/**35**

- **WILLIAM PERDUE** Basketball. (Melbourne, FL) With the Chicago Bulls. Year/**Age**: 1995/**30** 1996/**31** 1997/**32**

- **ROBIN LEACH** TV host. (England) "Lifestyles of the Rich and Famous." Year/**Age**: 1995/**54** 1996/**55** 1997/**56**

- **OLIVER WENDELL HOLMES** Writer/physician. (1809-1894 – Cambridge, MA) Became famous at 21. Sir Arthur Conan Doyle was so impressed by him that he used the name Sherlock Holmes for his famous character. (Died 10-7-1894.)

- **NATHAN PRITIKIN** Nutritionist. (1915-1985 – Chicago, IL) On Feb. 21, 1985, he took his own life at the Albany Medical Center by slashing his wrists when his leukemia (which had been in remission for almost 30 years) reappeared. He had led a crusade to beat heart disease with a low-fat/low-cholesterol diet.

- **INGRID BERGMAN** Actress. (1915-1982 – Sweden) She won Oscars for best actress in *Gaslight* with Charles Boyer in 1944, *Anastasia* in 1956, and best supporting actress in *Murder on the Orient Express* in 1974. She is probably best remembered as Humphrey Bogart's love in *Casablanca* in 1943. Her last role was on TV as Prime Minister Golda Meir. (Died on her 67th birthday 8-29-82.)

- **CHARLIE PARKER** Alto saxophonist. (1920-1955 – Kansas City, KA) He started the "bebop" movement. A movie was made on his life: *Bird*, directed by Clint Eastwood. (Died 3-12-55.)

FACTS FROM THE PAST

1957   U.S. Senator Strom Thurmond set a Senate **FILIBUSTER RECORD** by talking for 24 hours and 18 minutes.

1958   George Harrison joined John Lennon's skiffle group, the **QUARRYMEN**. Paul McCartney was already a member. They performed at the Casbah Coffee Club with Ken Brown on drums. The program included Paul singing "Long Tall Sally" and John singing "Three Cool Cats."

1967   TV audiences watched the last episode of "**THE FUGITIVE,**" and learned that Fred Johnson, with his one good arm, killed **DAVID JANSSEN**'s wife. This was the largest TV audience in TV history, until the "Dallas" episode, "Who Killed J.R.?"

1971   **HANK AARON** of the Atlanta Braves knocked in his 100th run of the season, giving him the **NATIONAL LEAGUE RECORD** of 11 seasons with 100 or more RBIs.

1975   A young woman named **GLORIA MITCHELL** was playing a fifty-cent **SLOT MACHINE IN RENO**, Nevada. She had decided that she would stop when she had lost twenty dollars in the machine. Her 40th (and last) half dollar was inserted and bells started ringing – she won $41,964.

1977   **LOU BROCK** of the St. Louis Cardinals eclipsed the 49-year-old career **STOLEN-BASES RECORD** of Ty Cobb as he stole two bases during a game against the San Diego Padres, bringing his total to 893.

1982   British sailors **CHARLES BURTON** and **SIR RANULPH FIENNES** arrived in London after taking almost three years to sail around the world by way of both poles in their craft named *Benjamin Bowring*.

1994   The son of U.S. Surgeon General Joycclyn Elders, Kevin, was sentanced in Little Rock, AK to 10 years in prison for selling cocaine to an undercover police officer.

Today you will find money

AUGUST 30

BIRTHDAYS

- **TIMOTHY BOTTOMS** Actor. (Santa Barbara, CA) Brother of actors Joseph and Sam Bottoms. Made his film debut at age 19 in *The Last Picture Show*, followed by *Paper Chase*. He was also in *The Other Side of the Mountain, Part II, Texasville*, and *East of Eden* on TV. Year/**Age**: 1995/**44** 1996/**45** 1997/**46**

- **ELIZABETH ASHLEY** Actress. (Born Elizabeth Ann Cole in Ocala, FL) Married to George Peppard at one time and appeared in *The Carpetbaggers* with him in 1964. He wasn't pleased with the things she said about him in her book. She was also in *Ship of Fools*. Appears on TV's "Evening Shade." Year/**Age**: 1995/**56** 1996/**57** 1997/**58**

- **GARY LIOZZO** Singer. With the group AMERICAN BREED. Their biggest hit: "Bend Me, Shake Me" in 1967. Year/**Age**: 1995/**50** 1996/**51** 1997/**52**

- **JOHN PHILLIPS** Singer. Founded the MAMAS & PAPAS, along with Cass Elliott, Michelle Gilliam, and Dennis Doherty. Their biggest hit: "Monday Monday" in 1966. Year/**Age**: 1995/**60** 1996/**61** 1997/**62**

- **PEGGY LIPTON** Actress. She was in TV's "Mod Squad" and played Norma Jennings on "Twin Peaks."Year/**Age**: 1995/**48** 1996/**49** 1997/**50**

- **KITTY WELLS** C&W singer. (Born Muriel Deason in Nashville, TN) She was the first woman to have a #1 record on the C&W charts with "It Wasn't God Who Made Honky Tonk Angels" in 1952. Year/**Age**: 1995/**76** 1996/**77** 1997/**78**

- **MICHAEL CHIKLIS** Actor. Commissioner Tony Scali on TV's "The Commish." Year/**Age**: 1995/**32** 1996/**33** 1997/**34**

- **ROBERT PARISH** Basketball pro. (Shreveport, LA) Ended his 14-year career in 1994. Year/**Age**: 1995/**42** 1996/**43** 1997/**44**

- **FRANK "TUG" McGRAW** Baseball star. (Martinez, CA) He first pitched his way into the big leagues in 1969 with the NY Mets and later played for the Philadelphia Phillies. He said of his $75,000 salary "90% I'll spend on good times, women, and Irish whiskey. The other 10% I'll probably waste." His son is country singer Tim McGraw. Year/**Age**: 1995/**51** 1996/**52** 1997/**53**

- **JOHN McNALLY** Singer/guitarist. The SEARCHERS: "Love Potion Number Nine." Year/**Age**: 1995/**53** 1996/**54** 1997/**55**

- **JEAN-CLAUDE KILLY** Former Olympian. (France) A gold-medal skiing champion. Year/**Age**: 1995/**52** 1996/**53** 1997/**54**

- **GEOFFREY BEENE** Fashion designer. (Haynesville, LA) Year/**Age**: 1995/**69** 1996/**70** 1997/**71**

- **TED WILLIAMS** Baseball Hall of Fame star. (San Diego, CA) Ex-Boston Red Sox star. His lifetime batting average was .344. At age 42, he hit .316 with 29 home runs. Year/**Age**: 1995/**77** 1996/**78** 1997/**79**

- **SHIRLEY BOOTH** Actress. (1907-1992 – Born Thelma Booth Ford in NYC) Starred in "Hazel" TV series and won an Academy Award for *Come Back Little Sheba*. (Died 10-16-92.)

- **FRED MacMURRAY** Actor. (1908-1991 – Kankakee, IL) He starred as the father, Steve Douglas, in the TV series "My Three Sons." His films include *The Caine Mutiny*, *The Shaggy Dog*, and *The Absent Minded Professor*. (Died 11-5-91.)

- **MARY WOLLSTONECRAFT SHELLEY** Author. (1797-1851 – London) She created *Frankenstein*. (Died 2-1-1851.)

- **RAYMOND MASSEY** Actor. (1896-1983 – Canada) He won an Oscar for best actor in 1940 for *Abe Lincoln in Illinois*. He starred in more than 60 movies and portrayed Dr. Gillespie in the "Dr. Kildare" series on TV. (Died 7-29-83.)

FACTS FROM THE PAST

1893 **FRANCES CLEVELAND**, Mrs. Grover Cleveland, gave birth to a baby girl, Ester, the first baby ever born to a presidential wife in the White House.

1905 **TY COBB** made his major league batting debut, playing for the Detroit Tigers.

1918 **NIKOLAI LENIN** survived an attempted assassination in Moscow. It was 4 years before he was strong enough for an operation. The trauma eventually led to his death. Fanny Kaplan, a member of the Socialist-Revolutionary Party, fired the three shots at Lenin. She was executed September 3, 1918.

1945 The U.S. Marines sailed into Tokyo Bay, and **GENERAL DOUGLAS MacARTHUR** became the **FIRST FOREIGN CONQUEROR TO STEP ONTO JAPANESE SOIL** in more than 2,000 years. This was the beginning of the American occupation of Japan at the end of World War II.

1964 **MICKEY MANTLE** of the New York Yankees struck out for the 1,331st time to break Babe Ruth's record for the most strikeouts in a career.

1979 **ANN MEYERS** became the first woman to sign an NBA contract. She signed a one-year pact with the Indiana Pacers only to be cut from the team after two days.

1983 On its 3rd mission in space, the **CHALLENGER** carried the **FIRST AFRICAN-AMERICAN ASTRONAUT**, Air Force Lieutenant Col. **GUION BLUFORD, JR.** The crew also contained the oldest U.S. astronaut to date, Dr. William Thornton, 54. The mission was also the first launched in darkness.

1989 A federal jury in New York found "Hotel Queen" **LEONA HELMSLEY** guilty of income tax evasion, but acquitted her of extortion.

1991 **MIKE POWELL** jumped 29 feet, $4\frac{1}{2}$ inches in Tokyo, to break the previous long-jump record of 29 feet, $2\frac{1}{2}$ inches set by Bob Beamon at the 1968 Olympics.

1993 **DAVID LETTERMAN**'s CBS Late Night Show debuted with over 23 million viewers, double the size of the audience watching the Tonight Show with Jay Leno.

AUGUST 31

What ever you're thinking...
DON'T!

BIRTHDAYS

• **WARREN BERLINGER** Actor. (Brooklyn, NY) Appeared in *Love American Style*. Year/**Age**: 1995/**68** 1996/**69** 1997/**70**

• **BUDDY HACKETT** Comedian. (Born Leonard Hacker in Brooklyn, NY) Appeared in *The Music Man* with Robert Preston and regularly performs in Las Vegas and Atlantic City with a "very blue" routine. In *The Little Mermaid*. Year/**Age**: 1995/**71** 1996/**72** 1997/**73**

• **FRANK ROBINSON** Hall of Famer. (Beaumont, TX) First African-American manager in major league baseball, with the Baltimore Orioles. Year/**Age**: 1995/**60** 1996/**61** 1997/**62**

• **JAMES COBURN** Actor. (Laurel, NE) His first big movie role was in *The Great Escape* in 1963. In 1965, he starred in *Our Man Flint*. He once got paid $500,000 for uttering two words in a commercial: "Schlitz Light." Also appeared in *Hudson Hawk* and *The Saint of Fort Wahington*. Year/**Age**: 1995/**67** 1996/**68** 1997/**69**

• **VAN MORRISON** Singer. (Northern Ireland) Biggest hits: "Domino" and "Brown-Eyed Girl." For a while he was with the group THEM. Year/**Age**: 1995/**50** 1996/**51** 1997/**52**

• **JERRY ALLISON** Drummer. One of the original members of the CRICKETS. He quit the group just before Buddy Holly's fatal plane crash. Their biggest hit: "That'll be the Day" in 1957. Year/**Age**: 1995/**56** 1996/**57** 1997/**58**

• **DEBBIE GIBSON** Singer. (Brooklyn, NY) Hits include: "Only in My Dreams," "Lost In Your Eyes," and "Foolish Beat." Debbie has her own cologne, "Electric Youth" and published her first book in 1989, *Between the Lines*. She co-starred on Broadway in 1991 in *Les Miserables*. Year/**Age**: 1995/**25** 1996/**26** 1997/**27**

• **ANDY DILLARD** Pro golfer. (Tyler, TX) He turned pro in 1984. Year/**Age**: 1995/**34** 1996/**35** 1997/**36**

• **TONY De FRANCO** Singer. (Canada) Leader of the family group THE DEFRANCO FAMILY. Their biggest hit: "Heartbeat, It's A Lovebeat" in 1973. Year/**Age**: 1995/**35** 1996/**36** 1997/**37**

• **SIR BERNARD LOVELL** Astronomer. The force behind the world's first major radio telescope, in 1957. Year/**Age**: 1995/**81** 1996/**82** 1997/**83**

• **ALAN JAY LERNER** Playwright/lyricist. (1918-1986 – NYC) He wrote the words of the musicals *Brigadoon* and *Paint Your Wagon*, then teamed up with Frederick Loewe in 1956 to create *My Fair Lady*. His name is in the Songwriters Hall of Fame and he won Oscars for *Gigi* and *An American in Paris*. (Died 6-14-86.)

• **RICHARD BASEHART** Actor. (1914-1984 – Zanesville, OH) He played Admiral Harriman Nelson on TV's "Voyage to the Bottom of the Sea." (Died 9-17-84.)

• **FREDRIC MARCH** Actor. (1897-1975 – Born Earnest Frederick McIntyre Bickel in Racine, WI) He won Oscars in 1932 for best actor in *Dr. Jekyl & Mr. Hyde* and for *The Best Years of Our Lives* in 1975. His final film was *The Iceman Cometh* in 1975. (Died 4-14-75.)

• **ARTHUR GODFREY** Entertainer. (1903-1983 – NYC) One of TV's most successful personalities in the 1950s. In 1954, his combined broadcasts brought in 82 million viewers and 12% of CBS's total revenue. In 1959, he was responsible for $150 million in advertising billing for CBS. (Died 3-16-83.)

• **WILLIAM SAROYAN** Author. (1908-1981 – Fresno, CA) He wrote *The Human Comedy* and the Pulitzer Prize-winning play *The Time of Your Life*. He gave reporters this final statement a month before his death: "Everybody has got to die, but I have always believed an exception would be made in my case. Now what?" (Died 5-18-81.)

FACTS FROM THE PAST

1888 Mary Ann Nicholls was found murdered in London's East End in what's generally regarded as the first slaying committed by **JACK THE RIPPER.**

1940 **SIR LAWRENCE OLIVIER** married actress **VIVIEN LEIGH** at a friend's home. Katharine Hepburn and Garson Kanin were witnesses to the 3-minute ceremony. When the minister said, "I now pronounce you man and wife," Olivier said: "Bingo." Years later a knock-down, drag-out physical fight ended the 20-year marriage.

1955 **SIDNEY TURNER**, of London, England, was fined three pounds, ten shillings for a noise violation after telling his neighbors that he was going to drive them crazy. He played "Shake, Rattle and Roll" by Bill Haley and the Comets at top volume for 2½ hours straight.

1963 **WALTER CRONKITE** began his anchorman duties on the CBS Evening News. He retired in 1981.

1976 Carallyn Bowes became the **FIRST WOMAN TO RUN ACROSS CANADA**. She ran the 3,840 miles from Halifax, Nova Scotia, to Burnaby, British Columbia in 133 days.

1987 **MICHAEL JACKSON** released his *Bad* album.

1989 The **ROLLING STONES** opened their first concert tour in eight years before 50,000 fans in Philadelphia. Lead singer Mick Jagger strutted his stuff on a stage 110 feet high and 300 feet wide, showing a scene of industrial decay. During "Honky Tonk Woman," two balloon figures of scantily clad women, nearly as tall as the stage, were inflated.

1992 In a surprise move, the Oakland A's traded **JOSE CANSECO** to the Texas Rangers for outfielder Ruben Sierra, pitchers Jeff Russell and Bobby Witt and $400,000 cash. Canseco was the 1988 American League MVP and helped the A's to three consecutive American League pennants.

1994 IRA leader Jerry Adams announced that the Irish Republican Army would declare a cease-fire in their conflict with the British and Irish governments.

Emmy Award Winners

1948

Most Outstanding Live Personality:
Shirley Dinsdale and her puppet, Judy Splinters, KTLA
Technical Award:
Charles Mesak, Don Lee Television, for the phase-finder
Special Award:
Louis McManus, "for his original design of the Emmy."

1949

Most Outstanding Live Personality:
Ed Wynn
Most Outstanding Kinescope Personality:
Milton Berle

1950

Most Outstanding Personality:
Groucho Marx, KNBH (NBC)
Best Actor:
Alan Young, KTTV (CBS)
Best Actress:
Gertrude Berg, KTTV (CBS)

1951

Best Actor
Sid Caesar
Best Actress:
Imogene Coca
Best Comedian or Comedienne:
Red Skelton
Special Achievement Award:
Senator Estes Kefauver, "for outstanding public service on television."

1952

Most Outstanding Personality:
Bishop Fulton J. Sheen
Best Actor:
Thomas Mitchell
Best Actress:
Helen Hayes
Best Comedian:
Jimmy Durante
Best Comedienne:
Lucille Ball

1953

Most Outstanding Personality:
Edward R. Murrow
Best Male Star of Regular Series:
Donald O'Connor, "The Colgate Comedy Hour"
Best Female Star of Regular Series:
Eve Arden, "Our Miss Brooks"
Best Supporting Actor:
Art Carney, "The Jackie Gleason Show"
Best Series Supporting Actress:
Vivian Vance, "I Love Lucy"

1954

Most Outstanding New Personality:
George Gobel
Best Actor Starring in a Regular Series:
Danny Thomas, "Make Room for Daddy"
Best Actress Starring in a Regular Series:
Loretta Young, "The Loretta Young Show"
Best Supporting Actor in a Regular Series:
Art Carney, "The Jackie Gleason Show"
Best Supporting Actress in a Regular Series:

Audrey Meadows, "The Jackie Gleason Show"
Best Male Singer:
Perry Como
Best Female Singer:
Dinah Shore
Best News Reporter or Commentator:
John Daly

1955

Best Actor in a Continuing Performance:
Phil Silvers, "You'll Never Get Rich"
Best Actress in a Continuing Performance:
Lucille Ball, "I Love Lucy"
Best Actor in a Supporting Role:
Art Carney, "The Honeymooners"
Best Actress in a Supporting Role:
Nanette Fabray, "Caesar's Hour"
Best Emcee or Program Host:
Perry Como
Best Comedian:
Phil Silvers
Best Comedienne:
Nanette Fabray
Best Male Singer:
Perry Como
Best Female Singer:
Dinah Shore
Best News Commentator or Reporter:
Edward R. Murrow
Best Specialty Act:
Marcel Marceau

1956

Best Continuing Performance Dramatic Series (Actor):
Robert Young, "Father Knows Best"
Best Continuing Performance Dramatic Series (Actress):
Loretta Young, "The Loretta Young Show"
Best Male Personality (continuing performance):
Perry Como
Best Female Personality (continuing performance):
Dinah Shore
Best Continuing Performance by Comedian, Series:
Sid Caesar, "Caesar's Hour"
Best Continuing Performance by Comedienne, Series:
Nanette Fabray, "Caesar's Hour"
Best Supporting Performance (Actor):
Carl Reiner, "Caesar's Hour"
Best Supporting Performance (Actress):
Pat Carroll, "Caesar's Hour"
Best News Commentator:
Edward R. Murrow

1957

Best Continuing Performance by an Actor in a Leading Role in Dramatic or Comedy Series:
Robert Young, "Father Knows Best"
Best Continuing Performance by an Actress in a Leading Role in Dramatic or Comedy Series:
Jane Wyatt, "Father Knows Best"
Best Continuing Performance by Male Who Plays Himself:
Jack Benny, "The Jack Benny Show"
Best Continuing Performance by Female Who Plays Herself:
Dinah Shore, "The Dinah Shore Show"
Best Continuing Supporting Performance by an Actor in a Dramatic or Comedy Series:

Carl Reiner, "Caesar's Hour"
Best Continuing Supporting Performance by an Actress in a Dramatic or Comedy Series:
Ann B. Davis, "The Bob Cummings Show"
Best News Commentary:
Edward R. Murrow, "See It Now"

1958-1559

Best Actor in Leading Role - Dramatic Series:
Raymond Burr, "Perry Mason"
Best Actress in Leading Role - Dramatic Series:
Loretta Young, "The Loretta Young Show"
Best Actor in Leading Role - Comedy Series:
Jack Benny, "The Jack Benny Show"
Best Actress in Leading Role - Comedy Series:
Jane Wyatt, "Father Knows Best"
Best Performance by Actor in Musical or Variety Series:
Perry Como, "The Perry Como Show"
Best Performance by Actress in Musical or Variety Series:
Dinah Shore, "The Dinah Shore Chevy Show"
Best Supporting Actor in Dramatic Series:
Dennis Weaver, "Gunsmoke"
Best Supporting Actress in Dramatic Series:
Barbara Hale, "Perry Mason"
Best Supporting Actor in Comedy Series:
Tom Poston, "The Steve Allen Show"
Best Supporting Actress in Comedy Series:
Ann B. Davis, "The Bob Cumming Show"
Best News Commentator or Analyst:
Edward R. Murrow

1959-1960

Performance by Actor in Series:
Robert Stack, "The Untouchables"
Performance by Actress in Series:
Jane Wyatt, "Father Knows Best"
Performance in Variety or Musical Program or Series:
Harry Belafonte, "Tonight with Belafonte," on "The Revlon Revue"

1960-1961

Performance by Actor in Series:
Raymond Burr, "Perry Mason"
Performance by Actress in Series:
Barbara Stanwyck, "The Barbara Stanwyck Show"
Performance in Variety or Musical Program or Series:
Fred Astaire, "Astaire Time"
Performance in Supporting Role by an Actor or Actress in Single Program:
Don Knotts, "The Andy Griffith Show"
Performance in Supporting Role by an Actor or Actress in Single Program:
Roddy McDowall, "Not Without Honor," on "Our American Heritage"

1961-1962

Continued Performance by Actor in Series:
E. G. Marshall, "The Defenders"
Continued Performance by Actress in Series:
Shirley Booth, "Hazel"
Performance in Variety or Musical Program or Series:
Carol Burnett, "The Garry Moore Show"
Performance in Supporting Role by Actor:
Don Knotts, "The Andy Griffith Show"

Emmy Award Winners continued

Performance in Supporting Role by Actress:
Pamela Brown, "Victoria Regina," on "Hallmark Hall of Fame"

1962-1963
Continued Performance by Actor in Series:
E. G. Marshall, "The Defenders"
Continued Performance by Actress in Series:
Shirley Booth, "Hazel"
Performance in Variety or Musical Program or Series:
Carol Burnett, "Carol and Company"
Performance in Supporting Role by Actor:
Don Knotts, "The Andy Griffith Show"
Performance in Supporting Role by Actress:
Glenda Farrell, "A Cardinal Act of Mercy," on "Ben Casey"

1963-1964
Continued Performance by Actor in Series:
Dick Van Dyke, "The Dick Van Dyke Show"
Continued Performance by Actress in Series:
Mary Tyler Moore, "The Dick Van Dyke Show"
Performance in Variety Program or Series:
Danny Kaye, "The Danny Kaye Show"

1964-1965
Individual Achievements in Entertainment (Actors and Performers):
(1) **Dick Van Dyke**, "The Dick Van Dyke Show,"
(2) **Alfred Lunt**, "The Magnificent Yankee," on "Hallmark Hall of Fame,"
(3) **Lynn Fontanne**, "The Magnificent Yankee," on "Hallmark Hall of Fame,"
(4) **Barbra Streisand**, "My Name is Barbra,"
(5) **Leonard Bernstein**, "New York Philharmonic Young People's Concerts with Leonard Bernstein"

1965-1966
Continued Performance by an Actor in a Leading Role in Dramatic Series:
Bill Cosby, "I Spy"
Continued Performance by an Actress in Leading Role in Dramatic Series:
Barbara Stanwyck, "The Big Valley"
Continued Performance by an Actor in a Leading Role in Comedy Series:
Dick Van Dyke, "The Dick Van Dyke Show"
Continued Performance by an Actress in a Leading Role in Comedy Series:
Mary Tyler Moore, "The Dick Van Dyke Show"
Performance by an Actor in Supporting Role in Drama:
James Daly, "Eagle in a Cage," on "Hallmark Hall of Fame"
Performance by an Actress in a Supporting Role in Drama:
Lee Grant, "Peyton Place"
Performance by an Actor in a Supporting Role in Comedy:
Don Knotts, "The Return of Barney Fife," on "The Andy Griffith Show"
Performance by an Actress in a Supporting Role:
Alice Pearce, "Bewitched"
Achievement in Educational Television:
Julia Child, "The French Chef"

1966-1967
Continued Performance by an Actor in a Leading Role in Dramatic Series:

Bill Cosby, "I Spy"
Continued Performance by an Actress in a Leading Role in Dramatic Series:
Barbara Bain, "Mission: Impossible"
Continued Performance by an Actor in a Leading Role in Comedy Series:
Don Adams, "Get Smart"
Continued Performance by an Actress in a Leading Role in Comedy Series:
Lucille Ball, "The Lucy Show"
Performance by an Actor in a Supporting Role in Drama:
Eli Wallach, "The Poppy Is also a Flower"
Performance by an Actress in a Supporting Role in Drama:
Agnes Moorehead, "Night of the Vicious Valentine," on "The Wild, Wild West"
Performance by an Actor in a Supporting Role in Comedy:
Don Knotts, "Barney Comes to Mayberry" on "The Andy Griffith Show"
Performance by an Actress in a Supporting Role in Comedy:
Frances Bavier, "The Andy Griffith Show"

1967-1968
Continued Performance by Actor in Leading Role in Dramatic Series:
Bill Cosby, "I Spy"
Continued Performance by Actress in Leading Role in Dramatic Series:
Barbara Bain, "Mission: Impossible"
Continued Performance by Actor in Leading Role in Comedy Series:
Don Adams, "Get Smart"
Continued Performance by Actress in Leading Role in Comedy Series:
Lucille Ball, "The Lucy Show"
Performance by Actor in Supporting Role in Drama:
Milburn Stone, "Gunsmoke"
Performance by Actress in Supporting Role in Drama:
Barbara Anderson, "Ironside"
Performance by Actor in Supporting Role in Comedy:
Werner Klemperer, "Hogan's Heroes"
Performance by Actress in a Supporting Role in Comedy:
Marion Lorne, "Bewitched"
Special Classifications of Outstanding Individual Achievement:
(1) **Art Carney**, "The Jackie Gleason Show,"
(2) **Pat Paulsen**, "The Smothers Brothers Comedy Hour"
Continued Performance by Actor in Leading Role in Dramatic Series:
Carl Betz, "Judd for the Defense"
Continued Performance by Actress in Leading Role in Dramatic Series:
Barbara Bain, "Mission: Impossible"
Continued Performance by Actor in Leading Role in Comedy Series:
Don Adams, "Get Smart"
Continued Performance by Actress in Leading Role in Comedy Series:
Hope Lange, "The Ghost and Mrs. Muir"
Continued Performance by Actor in Supporting Role in Series:
Werner Klemperer, "Hogan's Heroes"
Continued Performance by Actress in Supporting Role in Series:
Susan Saint James "The Name of the Game"
Individual Achievement, Special

Classification:
(1) **Arte Johnson**, "Rowan and Martin's Laugh-In"
(2) **Harvey Korman**, "The Carol Burnett Show"

1969-1970
Continued Performance by Actor in Leading Role in Dramatic Series:
Robert Young, "Marcus Welby, M.D."
Continued Performance by Actress in Leading Role in Dramatic Series:
Susan Hampshire, "The Forsyte Saga"
Continued Performance by an Actor in a Leading Role in Comedy Series:
William Windom, "My World and Welcome to It"
Continued Performance by an Actress in a Leading Role in Comedy Series:
Hope Lange, "The Ghost and Mrs. Muir"
Performance by an Actor in a Supporting Role in a Drama:
James Brolin, "Marcus Welby, M.D."
Performance by an Actress in a Supporting Role in a Drama:
Gail Fisher, "Mannix"
Performance by an Actor in a Supporting Role in a Comedy:
Michael Constantine, "Room 222"
Performance by an Actress in a Supporting Role in a Comedy:
Karen Valentine, "Room 222"

1970-1971
Continued Performance by an Actor in a Leading Role in a Dramatic Series:
Hal Holbrook, "The Senator" on "The Bold Ones"
Continued Performance by an Actress in a Leading Role in a Dramatic Series:
Susan Hampshire, "The First Churchills"
Continued Performance by an Actor in a Leading Role in a Comedy Series:
Jack Klugman, "The Odd Couple"
Continued Performance by an Actress in a Leading Role in a Comedy Series:
Jean Stapleton, "All in the Family"
Performance by an Actor in a Supporting Role in a Drama
David Burns, "The Price," on "Hallmark Hall of Fame"
Performance by an Actress in a Supporting Role in a Drama:
Margaret Leighton, "Hamlet," on "Hallmark Hall of Fame"
Performance by an Actor in a Supporting Role in a Comedy:
Edward Asner, "The Mary Tyler Moore Show"
Performance by an Actress in a Supporting Role in a Comedy:
Valerie Harper, "The Mary Tyler Moore Show"

1971 - 1972
Continued Performance by An Actor in a Leading Role in a Dramatic Series:
Peter Falk, "Columbo"
Continued Performance by an Actress in a Leading Role in a Dramatic Series:
Glenda Jackson, "Elizabeth R.," on "Masterpiece Theatre"
Continued Performance by An Actor in a Leading Role in a Comedy Series:
Carroll O'Connor, "All in the Family"

Emmy Award Winners continued

Continued Performance by an Actress in a Leading Role in a Comedy Series:
Jean Stapleton, "All in the Family"
Achievement by a Performer in Music or Variety:
Harvey Korman, "The Carol Burnett Show"
Performance by an Actor in a Supporting Role in a Drama:
Jack Warden, "Brian's Song," on "ABC Movie of the Week"
Performance by an Actress in a Supporting Role in a Drama:
Jenny Agutter, "The Snow Goose," on "Hallmark Hall of Fame"
Performance by an Actor in a Supporting Role in a Comedy:
Edward Asner, "The Mary Tyler Moore Show"
Performance by an Actress in a Supporting Role in a Comedy:
Valerie Harper, "The Mary Tyler Moore Show" and
Sally Struthers, "All in the Family"

1972-1973

Performance by an Actor in a Leading Role in a Drama Series (continuing):
Richard Thomas, "The Waltons"
Performance by an Actress in a Leading Role in a Drama Series (continuing):
Michael Learned, "The Waltons"
Performance by an Actor in a Leading Role in a Drama or Comedy (limited episodes):
Anthony Murphy, "Tom Brown's Schooldays" on "Masterpiece Theatre"
Performance by an Actress in a Leading Role in a Drama or Comedy (limited episodes):
Susan Hampshire, "Vanity Fair" on "Masterpiece Theatre"
Continued Performance by an Actor in a Leading Role in a Comedy Series:
Jack Klugman, "The Odd Couple"
Continued Performance by an Actress in a Leading Role in a Comedy Series:
Mary Tyler Moore, "The Mary Tyler Moore Show"
Performance by Actor in a Supporting Role in Drama, a continuing or one-time appearance in a series, or for a special program:
Scott Jacoby, "That Certain Summer" on "Wednesday Movie of the Week"
Performance by an Actress in a supporting role in Drama, a continuing or one-time appearance in a series, or for a special program:
Ellen Corby, "The Waltons"
Performance by Actor in a Supporting Role in Comedy, a continuing or one-time appearance in a series, or for a special program:
Ted Knight, "The Mary Tyler Moore Show"
Performance by Actress in Supporting Role in Comedy, a continuing or one-time appearance in a series, or for a special program:
Valerie Harper, "The Mary Tyler Moore Show"
Performance by Actor in Supporting Role in Comedy, a continuing or one-time appearance in a series, or for a special program:
Tim Conway, "The Carol Burnett Show"

1973-1974

Actor of the Year (Series):
Alan Alda, "M*A*S*H"
Actress of the Year (Series):
Mary Tyler Moore, "The Mary Tyler

Moore Show"
Actor of the Year (Special):
Hal Holbrook, "Pueblo," on "ABC Theatre"
Actress of the Year (Special):
Cicely Tyson, "The Autobiography of Miss Jane Pittman"
Supporting Actor of the Year:
Michael Moriarty, "The Glass Menagerie"
Supporting Actress of the Year:
Joanna Miles, "The Glass Menagerie"
Best Lead Actor in Drama Series:
Telly Savalas, "Kojak"
Best Lead Actress in a Drama Series:
Michael Learned, "The Waltons"
Best Lead Actor in a Limited Series:
William Holden, "The Blue Knight"
Best Lead Actress in a Limited Series:
Mildred Natwick, "The Snoop Sisters"
Best Lead Actor in a Comdey Series:
Alan Alda, "M*A*S*H"
Best Lead Actress in a Comedy Series:
Mary Tyler Moore, "The Mary Tyler Moore Show"
Best Lead Actor in a Drama (special program or single appearance in a drama or comedy series):
Hal Holbrook, "Pueblo," on "ABC Theatre"
Best Lead Actress in a Drama (special program or single appearance in a drama or comedy series):
Cicely Tyson, "The Autobiography of Miss Jane Pittman"
Best Supporting Actor in Drama (special program, one-time appearance, of continuing role):
Michael Moriarty, "The Glass Menagerie"
Best Supporting Actress in Drama (special program, one-time appearance, or continuing role):
Joanna Miles, "The Glass Menagerie"
Best Supporting Actor in Comedy (special program, one-time appearance, or continuing role):
Rob Reiner, "All in the Family"
Best Supporting Actress in Comedy (special program, one-time appearance, or continuing role):
Cloris Leachman, "The Lars Affair" on "The Mary Tyler Moore Show"
Best Supporting Actor in Comedy-Variety, Variety or Music (special program, one-time appearance, or continuing Role):
Harvey Korman, "The Carol Burnett Show"
Best Supporting Actress in Comedy-Variety, Variety or Music (special program, one-time appearance, or continuing role):
Brenda Vaccaro, "The Shape of Things"
Television News Broadcaster:
(1) **Harry Reasoner**, "ABC News"
(2) **Bill Moyers**, "Essay on Watergate," on "Bill Moyers' Journal"

1974-1975

Lead Actor in a Drama Series:
Robert Blake, "Baretta"
Lead Actress in a Drama Series:
Jean Marsh, "Upstairs, Downstairs," on "Masterpiece Theatre"
Lead Actor in a Limited Series
Peter Falk, "Columbo"
Lead Actress in a Limited Series:
Jessica Walter, "Amy Prentiss"
Lead Actor in a Comedy Series:
Tony Randall, "The Odd Couple"
Lead Actress in a Comedy Series:
Valerie Harper, "Rhoda"
Lead Actor in a Special Program (Drama or Comedy):
Laurence Olivier, "Love Among the Ruins," on "ABC Theatre"

Lead Actress in a special Program (Drama or Comedy):
Katharine Hepburn, "Love Among the Ruins" on "ABC Theatre"
Continuing Performance by a Supporting Actor in a Drama Series:
Will Geer, "The Waltons"
Continuing Performance by a Supporting Actress in a Drama Series:
Ellen Corby, "The Waltons"
Continuing Performance by a Supporting Actor in a Comedy Series:
Ed Asner, "The Mary Tyler Moore Show"
Continuing Performance by a Supporting Actress in a Comedy Series:
Betty White, "The Mary Tyler Moore Show"
Continuing or Single Performance by a Supporting Actor in Variety or Music:
Jack Albertson, "Cher"
Continuing or Single Performance by a Supporting Actress in Variety or Music:
Cloris Leachman, "Cher"
Sports Broadcaster:
Jim McKay, "ABC's Wide World of Sports"

1975-1976

Lead Actor in a Drama Series:
Peter Falk, "Columbo"
Lead Actress in a Drama Series:
Michael Learned, "The Waltons"
Lead Actor in a Limited Series:
Hal Holbrook, "Sandburg's Lincoln"
Lead Actress in a Limited Series:
Rosemary Harris, "Notorious Woman" on "Masterpiece Theatre"
Lead Actor in a Comedy Series:
Jack Albertson, "Chico and the Man"
Lead Actress in a Comedy Series:
Mary Tyler Moore, "The Mary Tyler Moore Show"
Lead Actor in a Drama or Comedy Special:
Anthony Hopkins, "The Lindbergh Kidnapping Case," on "NBC World Premier Movie"
Lead Actress in a Drama or Comedy Special:
Susan Clark, "Babe"
Continuing Performance by Supporting Actor in a Drama Series (regular or limited):
Anthony Zerbe, "Harry O"
Continuing Performance by a Supporting Actress in a Drama Series (regular or limited):
Ellen Corby, "The Waltons"
Continuing Performance by a Supporting Actor in a Comedy Series (regular or limited):
Ted Knight, "The Mary Tyler Moore Show"
Continuing or Single Performance by a Supporting Actor in Variety or Music (continuing role, one-time appearance, or special):
Chevy Chase, "NBC's Saturday Night"
Continuing or Single Performance by a Supporting Actress in Variety or Music (continuing role, one-time appearance, special):
Vicki Lawrence, "The Carol Burnett Show"
Single Performance by a Supporting Actor in a Comedy or Drama Special:
Ed Flanders, "A Moon for the Misbegotten" on "ABC Theatre"
Single Performance by a Supporting Actress in a Comedy or Drama Special:
Rosemary Murphy, "Eleanor and Franklin" on "ABC Theatre"
Sports Personality:
Jim McKay, "ABC's Wide World of Sports" and "ABC's XII Winter Olympics"

Emmy Award Winners continued

1976-1977

Lead Actor in a Drama Series:
James Garner, "The Rockford Files"
Lead Actress in a Drama Series:
Lindsay Wagner, "The Bionic Woman"
Lead Actor in a Limited Series:
Christopher Plummer, "The Moneychangers," on "The Big Event"
Lead Actress in a Limited Series:
Patty Duke Astin, "Captains and the Kings," on "Best Sellers"
Lead Actor in a Comedy Series:
Caroll O'Connor, "All in the Family"
Lead Actress in a Comedy Series:
Beatrice Arthur, "Maude"
Lead Actor for a Single Appearance in a Drama or Comedy Series:
Louis Gossett, Jr., "Roots"
Lead Actress for a Single Appearance in a Drama or Comedy Series:
Beulah Bondi, "The Pony Cart" on "The Waltons"
Lead Actor in a Drama or Comedy Special:
Ed Flanders, "Harry S. Truman: Plain Speaking"
Lead Actress in a Drama or Comedy Special
Sally Field, "Sybil" on "The Big Event"
Lead Actress in a Drama or Comedy Special
Sally Field, "Sybil" on "The Big Event"
Continuing Performance by a Supporting Actor in a Drama Series:
Gary Frank, "Family"
Continuing Performance by a Supporting Actress in a Drama Series:
Kristy McNichol, "Family"
Continuing Performance by a Supporting Actor in a Comedy Series:
Gary Burghoff, "M*A*S*H"
Continuing Performance by a Supporting Actress in a Comedy Series:
Mary Kay Place, "Mary Hartman, Mary Hartman"
Continuing or Single Performance by a Supporting Actor in Variety or Music:
Tim Conway, "The Carol Burnett Show"
Continuing or Single Performance by a Supporting Actress in Variety or Music:
Rita Moreno, "The Muppet Show"
Single Performance by a Supporting Actor in a Comedy or Drama Series:
Edward Asner, "Roots"
Single Performance by a Supporting Actress in a Comedy or Drama Series:
Olivia Cole, "Roots"
Performance by a Supporting Actor in a Comedy or Drama Special
Burgess Meredith, "Tail Gunner Joe" on "The Big Event"
Performance by a Supporting Actress in a Comedy or Drama Special:
Diana Hyland, "The Boy in the Plastic Bubble" on "The ABC Friday Night Movie"

1977-1978

Lead Actor in a Drama Series:
Edward Asner, "Lou Grant"
Lead Actress in a Drama Series:
Sada Thompson, "Family"
Lead Actor in a Limited Series:
Michael Moriarty, "Holocaust"
Lead Actress in a Limited Series:
Meryl Streep, "Holocaust"
Lead Actor in a Comedy Series:
Carroll O'Connor, "All in the Family"
Lead Actress in a Comedy Series:

Jean Stapleton, "All in the Family"
Lead Actor for a Single Appearance in a Drama or Comedy Series:
Barnard Hughes, "Judge" on "Lou Grant"
Lead Actress for a Single Appearance in a Drama or Comedy Series:
Rita Moreno, "The Paper Palace" on "The Rockford Files"
Lead Actress in a Drama or Comedy Special:
Joanne Woodward, "See How She Runs" on "G.E. Theater"
Continuing Performance by a Supporting Actor in a Drama Series:
Robert Vaughn, "Washington: Behind Closed Doors"
Continuing Performance by a Supporting Actress in a Drama Series:
Nancy Marchand, "Lou Grant"
Continuing Performance by a Supporting Actor in a Comedy Series:
Rob Reiner, "All in the Family"
Continuing Performance by a Supporting Actress in a Comedy Series:
Julie Kavner, "Rhoda"
Continuing or Single Performance by a Supporting Actor in Variety or Music:
Tim Conway, "The Carol Burnet Show"
Continuing or Single performance by a Supporting Actress in Variety or Music:
Gilda Radner, "NBC's Saturday Night Live" Series:
Ricardo Montalban, "How the West Was Won"
Single Performance by a Supporting Actress in a Comedy or Drama Series:
Blanche Baker, "Holocaust"
Performance by a Supporting Actor in a Comedy or Drama Special:
Howard Da Silva, "Verna: USO Girl," on "Great Performances"
Performance by a Supporting Actress in a Comedy or Drama Special:
Eva La Gallienne, "The Royal Family"

1978-1979

Lead Actor in a Drama Series (Continuing or Single Performance):
Ron Leibman, "Kaz"
Lead Actress in a Drama Series (Continuing or Single Performance):
Mariette Hartley, "Married" on "The Incredible Hulk"
Lead Actor in a Comedy Series (Continuing or Single Performance):
Carroll O'Connor, "All in the Family"
Lead Actress in a Comedy Series (Continuing or Single Performance):
Ruth Gordon, "Sugar Mama," on "Taxi"
Lead Actor in a Limited Series or a Special (Continuing or Single Appearance):
Peter Strauss, "The Jericho Mile"
Lead Actress in a Limited Series or a Special (continuing or Single Appearance):
Bette Davis, "Strangers: The Story of a Mother and Daughter"
Supporting Actor in a Drama Series (Continuing or Single Performance):
Stuart Margolin, "The Rockford Files"
Supporting Actress in a Drama Series (Continuing or Single Performance):
Kristy McNichol, "Family"
Supporting Actor in a Comedy, Comedy-Variety or Music Series (Continuing or Single Performance):
Robert Guillaume, "Soap"

Supporting Actress in a Comedy, Comedy-Variety or Music Series (Continuing or Single Performance):
Sally Struthers, "California Her We Are," on "All in the Family"
Supporting Actor in a Limited Series or a Special (Continuing or Single Appearance):
Marlon Brando, "Roots: The Next Generations"
Supporting Actress in a Limited Series or a Special (continuing or single appearance):
Esther Rolle, "Summer of My German Soldier"

1979-1980

Lead Actor in a Drama Series:
Ed Asner, "Lou Grant"
Lead Actress in a Drama Series:
Barbara Bel Geddes, "Dallas"
Lead Actor in a Limited Series or a Special:
Powers Boothe, "Guyana Tragedy: The Story of Jim Jones"
Lead Actress in a Limited Series or a Special:
Patty Duke Astin, "The Miracle Worker"
Lead Actor in a Comedy Series:
Richard Mulligan, "Soap"
Lead Actress in a Comedy Series:
Cathryn Damon, "Soap"
Supporting Actor in a Drama Series:
Stuart Margolin, "The Rockford Files"
Supporting Actress in a Drama Series:
Nancy Marchand, "Lou Grant"
Supporting Actor in a Limited Series or Special:
George Grizzard, "The Oldest Living Graduate"
Supporting Actress in a Limited Series or a Special:
Mare Winningham, "Amber Waves"
Supporting Actor in a Comedy or Variety or Music Series:
Harry Morgan, "M*A*S*H"

1980-1981

Lead Actor in a Drama Series:
Daniel J. Travanti, "Hill Street Blues"
Lead Actress in a Drama Series:
Barbara Babcock, "Hill Street Blues"
Lead Actor in a Limited Series or a Special:
Anthony Hopkins, "The Bunker"
Lead Actress in a Limited Series or a Special:
Vanessa Redgrave, "Playing for Time"
Lead Actor in a Comedy Series:
Judd Hirsch, "Taxi"
Lead Actress in a Comedy Series:
Isabel Sanford, "The Jeffersons"
Supporting Actor in a Drama Series:
Michael Conrad, "Hill Street Blues"
Supporting Actress in a Drama Series:
Nancy Marchand, "Lou Grant"
Supporting Actor in a Limited Series or a Special:
David Warner, "Masada"
Supporting Actress in a Limited Series or a Special:
Jane Alexander, "Playing for Time"
Supporting Actor in a Comedy or Variety or Music Series:
Danny DeVito, "Taxi"
Supporting Actress in a Comedy or Variety or Music Series:
Eileen Brennan, "Private Benjamin"
Individual Achievement - special Class:
Sarah Vaughan, performer, "Rhapsody and Song—A Tribute to George Gershwin"

Emmy Award Winners continued

1981-1982
Lead Actor in a Drama Series:
Daniel J. Travanti, Hill Street Blues"
Lead Actress in a Drama Series:
Michael Learned, "Nurse"
Lead Actor in a Limited Series or a Special:
Mickey Rooney, "Bill"
Lead Actress in a Limited Series or a Special:
Ingrid Bergman, "A Woman Called Golda"
Lead Actor in a Comedy Series:
Alan Alda, "M*A*S*H"
Lead Actress in a Comedy Series:
Carol Kane, "Simka Returns," on "Taxi"
Supporting Actor in a Drama Series:
Michael Conrad, "Hill Street Blues"
Supporting Actress in a Drama Series:
Nancy Marchand, "Lou Grant"
Supporting Actor in a Limited Series or a Special:
Laurence Olivier, "Brideshead Revisited"
Supporting Actress in a Limited Series or a Special:
Penny Fuller, "The Elephant Man"
Supporting Actor in a Comedy or Variety or Music Series:
Christopher Lloyd, "Taxi"
Supporting Actress in a Comedy or Variety or Music Series:
Loretta Swit, "M*A*S*H"
Individual Achievement - Special Class:
(1) **Nell Carter** (performer), "Ain't Misbehavin'"
(2) **Andre De Shields** (performer), "Ain't Misbehavin'"

1982-1983
Lead Actor in a Drama Series:
Ed Flanders, "St. Elsewhere"
Lead Actress in a Drama Series:
Tyne Daly, "Cagney & Lacey"
Lead Actor in a Comedy Series:
Judd Hirsch, "Taxi"
Lead Actress in a Comedy Series:
Shelley Long, "Cheers"
Lead Actor in a Limited Series or a Special:
Tommy Lee Jones, "The Executioner's Song"
Lead Actress in a Limited Series or a Special:
Barbara Stanwyck, "The Thorn Birds"
Supporting Actor in a Drama Series:
James Coco, "Cora and Arnie," in "St. Elsewhere"
Supporting Actress in a Drama Series:
Doris Roberts, "Cora and Arnie," on "St. Elsewhere"
Supporting Actor in a Comedy, Variety or Music Series:
Christopher Lloyd, "Taxi"
Supporting Actress in a Comedy, Variety or Music Series:
Carol Kane, "Taxi"
Supporting Actor in a Limited Series or a Special:
Richard Kiley, "The Thorn Birds"
Supporting Actress in a Limited Series or a Special:
Jean Simmons, "The Thorn Birds"
Individual Performance in a Variety or Music Program:
Leontyne Price, "Live from Lincoln Center, Leontyne Price, Zubin Mehta and the New York Philharmonic"

1984
Lead Actor in a Comedy Series:
John Ritter, "Three's Company"

Lead Actress in a Comedy Series:
Jane Curtin, "Kate & Allie"
Lead Actor in a Drama Series:
Tom Selleck, "Magnum, P.I."
Lead Actress in a Drama Series:
Tyne Daly, "Cagney & Lacey"
Supporting Actor in a Drama Series:
Bruce Weitz, "Hill Street Blues"
Supporting Actress in a Drama Series:
Alfre Woodard, "Doris in Wonderland" on "Hill Street Blues,"

1985
Lead Actor in a Comedy Series:
Robert Guillaume, "Benson"
Lead Actress in a Comedy Series:
Jane Curtin, "Kate & Allie"
Lead Actor in a Drama Series:
William Daniels, "St. Elsewhere"
Lead Actress in a Drama Series:
Tyne Daly, "Cagney & Lacey"
Supporting Actor in a Drama Series:
Edward James Olmos, "Miami Vice"
Supporting Actress in a Drama Series:
Betty Thomas, "Hill Street Blues"

1986
Lead Actor in a Comedy Series:
Michael J. Fox, "Family Ties"
Lead Actress in a Comedy Series:
Betty White, "The Golden Girls"
Lead Actor in a Drama Series:
William Daniels, "St. Elsewhere"
Lead Actress in a Drama Series:
Sharon Gless, "Cagney & Lacey"
Supporting Actor in a Drama Series:
John Karlen, "Cagney & Lacey"
Supporting Actress in a Drama Series:
Bonnie Bartlett, "St. Elsewhere"

1987
Lead Actor in a Comedy Series:
Michael J. Fox, "Family Ties"
Lead Actress in a Comedy Series:
Rue McClanahan, "The Golden Girls"
Lead Actor in a Drama Series:
Bruce Willis, "Moonlighting"
Lead Actress in a Drama Series:
Sharon Gless, "Cagney & Lacey"
Supporting Actor in a Drama Series:
John Millerman, "Magnum P.I."
Supporting Actress in a Drama Series:
Bonnie Bartlett, "St. Elsewhere"

1988
Lead Actor in a Comedy Series:
Michael J. Fox, "Family Ties"
Lead Actress in a Comedy Series:
Beatrice Arthur, "The Golden Girls"
Lead Actor in a Drama Series:
Richard Kiley, "A Year in the Life"
Lead Actress in a Drama Series:
Tyne Daly, "Cagney & Lacey"
Supporting Actor in a Drama Series:
Larry Drake, "L.A. Law"
Supporting Actress in a Drama Series:
Patricia Wettig, "thirtysomething"

1989
Lead Actor in a Comedy Series:
Richard Mulligan, "Empty Nest"
Lead Actress in a Comedy Series:
Candice Bergen, "Murphy Brown"
Lead Actor in a Drama Series:
Carroll O'Connor, "In the Heat of the Night"

Lead Actress in a Drama Series:
Dana Delany, "China Beach"
Supporting Actor in a Drama Series:
Larry Drake, "L.A. Law"
Supporting Actress in a Drama Series:
Melanie Mayron, "thirtysomething"

1990
Lead Actor in a Comedy Series:
(1) **Ted Danson**, "Cheers"
(2) **Alex Rocco**, "The Famous Teddy Z"
Lead Actress in a Comedy Series:
Candice Bergen, "Murphy Brown"
Lead Actor in a Drama Series:
Peter Falk, "Columbo"
Lead Actress in a Drama Series:
Patricia Wettig, "thirtysomething"
Supporting Actor in a Drama Series:
Jimmy Smits, "L.A.Law"
Supporting Actress in a Drama Series:
Marg Helgenberger, "China Beach"

1991
Lead Actor in a Comedy Series:
Burt Reynolds, "Evening Shade"
Lead Actress in a Comedy Series:
Kristie Alley, "Cheers"
Lead Actor in a Drama Series:
James Earl Jones, "Gabriel's Fire"
Lead Actress in a Drama Series:
Patricia Wettig, "thirtysomething"
Supporting Actor in a Drama Series:
Timothy Busfield, "thirtysomething"
Supporting Actress in a Drama Series:
Madge Sinclair, "Gabriel's Fire"

1992
Lead Actor in a Drama Series:
Christopher Lloyd, "Avonlea"
Lead Actress in a Drama Series:
Dana Delany, "China Beach"
Supporting Actor in a Drama Series:
Richard Dysart, "L.A. Law"
Supporting Actress in a Drama Series:
Valerie Mahaffey, "Northern Exposure"
Lead Actor in a Comedy Series:
Craig T. Nelson, "Coach"
Lead Actress in a Comedy Series:
Candice Bergen, "Murphy Brown"
Supporting Actor in Comedy Series:
Michael Jeter, "Evening Shade
Supporting Actress in Comedy Series:
Laurie Metcalf, "Roseanne"

1993
Lead Actor in a Drama Series:
Tom Skerritt, "Picket Fences"
Lead Actress in a Drama Series:
Kathy Baker, "Picket Fences"
Supporting Actor in a Drama Series:
Chad Lowe, "Life Goes On"
Supporting Actress in a Drama Series:
Mary Alice, "I'll Fly Away"
Lead Actor in a Comedy Series:
Ted Danson, "Cheers"
Lead Actress in a Comedy Series:
Roseanne Arnold, "Roseanne"
Supporting Actor in a Comedy Series:
Michael Richards, "Seinfeld"
Supporting Actress in a Comedy Series:
Laurie Metcalf, "Roseanne"

SEPTEMBER MEMORIES

YEARS AGO

1985

POPULAR SONGS
"St. Elmo's Fire (Man in Motion)" by John Parr

"Money For Nothing" by Dire Straits

MOVIES
Insignificance
starring Gary Busey, Tony Curtis, Michael Emil, and Theresa Russell.

Scandal Sheet
starring Burt Lancaster as the editor of a gossip tabloid. Co-stars Lauren Hutton, Pamela Reed, and Robert Urich.

TV SHOWS
"Growing Pains"
sit-com about a family in suburban New York. Starring Kirk Cameron, Alan Thicke, Joanna Kerns, and Tracey Gold.

"Spenser: For Hire"
Robert Urich plays a Boston detective.

BOOKS
Foreign Affairs by Alison Lurie

1986

POPULAR SONGS
"Venus" by Bananarama

"Take My Breath Away" by Berlin

MOVIES
The Color of Money
Tom Cruise beomes a pool shark with the help of Paul Newman.

Star Trek IV: The Voyage Home
The Enerprise goes to San Francisco in the year 1986. Stars regulars William Shatner, Leonard Nimoy, and DeForest Kelley.

TV SHOWS
"Designing Women"
comedy about the Sugarbakers interior decorating business in the South."

"Our House"
A father, Wilford Brimley, takes in his daughter-in-law, Deidre Hall, and her children.

BOOKS
McMahon by Jim McMahon

1987

POPULAR SONGS
"I Just Can't Stop Loving You" by Michael Jackson

"Didn't We Almost Have It All" by Whitney Houston

MOVIES
Wall Street
starring Michael Douglas and Charlie Sheen. The world of Wall Street traders.

LaBamba
the life story of Ritchie Valens. Lou Diamond Phillips stars as the singer.

TV SHOWS
"My Two Dads"
starring Paul Reiser, Greg Evigan, Staci Keanan in the story of a girl with two dads.

"Thirtysomething"
a dramatic series following the lives of several yuppies.

BOOKS *Spycatcher* by Peter Wright with Paul Greengrass

SPECIAL DAYS

SEPTEMBER	1995	1996	1997
Labor Day	Sep. 4	Sep. 2	Sep. 1
Late For Something Day (*Les Waas, Procrasitnators Club*)	Sep. 4	Sep. 2	Sep. 1
Great Bathtub Race (*Nome, AK*)	Sep. 4	Sep. 2	Sep. 1
Bald Is Beautiful Convention (*Morehead City, NC*)	Sep. 8-10	Sep. 13-15	Sep. 12-14
Blame Someone Else Day		Sep. 13	
Turkey Day (*Worthington , MN*)	Sep. 8-10	Sep. 13-15	Sep. 12-14
Grandparents Day	Sep. 10	Sep. 8	Sep. 7
Pet Memorial Day	Sep. 10	Sep. 8	Sep. 14
Full Moon	Sep. 9	Sep. 27	Sep. 16
National Dog Week	Sep. 24-30	Sep. 22-28	Sep. 21-27
National Singles Week	Sep. 17-23	Sep. 15-21	Sep. 21-27
Autumn Begins	Sep. 23	Sep. 22	Sep. 22
Good Neighbor Day	Sep. 24	Sep. 22	Sep. 28

25 YEARS AGO

1970

POPULAR SONGS
"Ain't No Mountain High Enough" by Diana Ross

"Lookin' Out My Back Door" by Creedence Clearwater Revival

MOVIES
The Mind of Mr. Soames
a man in a coma, Terence Stamp, is brought back to life after 30 years.

A Boy Named Charlie Brown
the famous "Peanuts" comic strip comes to the big screen.

TV SHOWS
"Storefront Lawyers"
starring Robert Foxworth in this drama.

"The Partridge Family"
starring Shirley Jones, David Cassidy, Susan Dey, and Danny Bonaduce. A sitcom about a singing family.

BOOKS
Future Shock by Alvin Toffler

1971

POPULAR SONGS
"Go Away Little Girl" by Donny Osmond

"Maggie May" by Rod Stewart

MOVIES
McCabe and Mrs. Miller
starring Warren Beatty, Julie Christi, Shelley Duvall, and David Carradine. Under false pretenses, a gambler opens a bordello in the Northwest.

Carnal Knowledge
Jack Nicholson, Art Garfunkel, Ann-Margret, and Candice Bergen star in the story of two college students focusing on their sexual lives.

TV SHOWS
"Cade's County"
a police drama with Glenn Ford and Edgar Buchanan. The series takes place in Madrid County, CA.

BOOKS
The Drifters by James A. Michener

1972

POPULAR SONGS
"Black & White" by Three Dog Night

"Baby Don't Get Hooked On Me" by Mac Davis

MOVIES
Cabaret
starring Liza Minelli in the musical version of pre-WWII Berlin.

Napolean and Samantha
starring Jodie Foster, Michael Douglas, Will Greer, Johnny Whitaker, and Ellen Corby. The story of two children and a lion.

TV SHOWS
"M*A*S*H"
starring Alan Alda in the award winning sitcom about a surgical team in Korea.

"The New Bill Cosby Show"
variety show featuring the Quincy Jones Orchestra.

BOOKS *A World Beyond* by Ruth Montgomery

50 YEARS AGO

1945

POPULAR SONGS
"Boogie Woogie" by The Tommy Dorsey Orchestra

"Along the Navajo Trail" by Dinah Shore

MOVIES
The Spanish Main
starring Maureen O'Hara, Walter Slezak, and Paul Henreidin this pirate film which takes place on the high seas.

Blithe Spirit
based on the work of Noel Coward, featuring Constance Cummings, Rex Harrison, and Margaret Rutherford.

TV SHOWS
No regularly scheduled TV programming until May 1946.

BOOKS
The Age of Jackson by Arthur M. Schlesinger

1946

POPULAR SONGS
"Five Minutes More" by Frank Sinatra

"To Each His Own" by Freddy Martin

MOVIES
The Best Years of Our Life
starring Frederic March, Myrna Loy, and Dana Andrews. Three men return home after WWII.

Kitty
starring Paulette Goodard with Ray Milland. A girl from the wrong side of the tracks works her way up the royal ladder in London.

TV SHOWS
"Play The Game"
New York University professor Dr. H. Zorbaugh hosts charades.

"Geographically Speaking"
Mrs. Carveth Wells shares travel films.

BOOKS
The River Road by Frances Parkinson Keyes

1947

POPULAR SONGS
"I Wish I Didn't Love You So" by Vaughn Moore

"How Soon (Will I Be Seeing You)" by Jack Owens

MOVIES
Mother Wore Tights
starring Betty Grable and Dan Dailey in a 1940s musical of vaudeville.

The Paradise Case
an Alfred Hitchcock thriller starring Gregory Peck, Louis Jordan, Ethel Barrymore, and Charles Coburn.

TV SHOWS
"The Borden Show"
features a different program every week, such as variety shows, films, puppet shows, and dramas.

BOOKS
House Divided by Ben Ames Williams

SEPTEMBER 1

Can a disc jockey ride a horse?

BIRTHDAYS

- **RICHARD FARNSWORTH** Actor. (Los Angeles, CA) Film credits include *The Natural* and *Misery.* Year/**Age:** 1995/**75** 1996/**76** 1997/**77**

- **LILY TOMLIN** Actress/comedienne. (Detroit, MI) She became an overnight star as Ernestine, the mischievous telephone operator on "Laugh-In," and went on to appear in the films *9 to 5* with Jane Fonda and Dolly Parton, *Nashville, The Incredible Shrinking Woman, And the Band Played On, Shortcuts,* and *Beverly Hillbillies.* Won a Tony for her one-woman show. Year/**Age:** 1995/**56** 1996/**57** 1997/**58**

- **YVONNE de CARLO** Actress. (Born Peggy Middleton in Canada) She appeared in many westerns and *The Ten Commandments* in 1956, but is best known for the TV series "The Munsters" from 1964-1966. Year/**Age:** 1995/**73** 1996/**74** 1997/**75**

- **DEE DEE MYERS** White House Press Secretary. Year/**Age:** 1995/**34** 1996/**35** 1997/**36**

- **BARRY GIBB** Singer. (Isle of Man, England) One of the BEE GEES. Their biggest hit: "Night Fever" from the 1978 film *Saturday Night Fever.* He also recorded "What Kind of Fool" with Barbra Streisand and "Emotion" with Samantha Sang. Year/**Age:** 1995/**49** 1996/**50** 1997/**51**

- **SEIJI OZAWA** Conductor. (Japan) Leads the Boston Symphony. Year/**Age:** 1995/**60** 1996/**61** 1997/**62**

- **VITTORIO GASSMAN** Actor. (Italy) Films include *Anna* and *Bitter Rice.* He married Shelley Winters in 1952. Year/**Age:** 1995/**73** 1996/**74** 1997/**75**

- **ARCHIE BELL** Singer. (Houston, TX) His quartet, the DRELLS, biggest hit: "Tighten Up" in 1968. Year/**Age:** 1995/**51** 1996/**52** 1997/**53**

- **LEONARD SLATKIN** Conductor. (Los Angeles, CA) He leads the St. Louis Symphony. Year/**Age:** 1995/**51** 1996/**52** 1997/**53**

- **ANN RICHARDS** Texas Governor. She possesses a motorcycle drivers license. Year/**Age:** 1995/**62** 1996/**63** 1997/**64**

- **GLORIA ESTEFAN** [eh-steh'-fahn] Singer. (Born Gloria Fagardo in Havana, Cuba) One of her biggest hits: "Don't Want to Lose You" in 1989. He dad was bodyguard to President Batista. She is married to Emilio Estefan. Year/**Age:** 1995/**38** 1996/**39** 1997/**40**

- **"BOXCAR" WILLIE** C&W Muscian. (Born Lecil Travis Martin in Steratt, TX) He's nicknamed "the singing hobo." Year/**Age:** 1995/**64** 1996/**65** 1997/**66**

- **CONWAY TWITTY** Singer. (1933-1993 – Born Harold Lloyd Jenkins in Friars Point, MS) He took his stage name from a map showing Conway, AR, and Twitty, TX. His biggest hit: "It's Only Make Believe" in 1958. He owned "Twitty City," a tourist complex in Henderson, TN. In 1965 he switched from Rock 'n Roll to country music. (Died 6-5-93.)

- **RICHARD ARLEN** Actor. (1899-1976 – Born Richard Cornelius Van Mattimore in Charlottesville, VA) In films *The Virginian* and *Wings.* (Died 3-28-76.)

- **ROCKY MARCIANO** Boxer. (1924-1969 – Born Rocco Marchegiano in Brockton, MA) Heavyweight champ, undefeated, from 1952-56.

- **EDGAR RICE BURROUGHS** Author. (1875-1950 – Chicago, IL) Created Tarzan in 1912. His first published story was *Tarzan of the Apes.*

- **ENGELBERT HUMPERDINCK** Composer. (1854-1921 – Germany) Pop singer Engelbert took his name from him. Wrote "Hansel and Gretel" opera. (Died 9-27-21.)

FACTS FROM THE PAST

1682 **WILLIAM PENN** sailed with 100 British Quakers for the New World.

1864 Union General **WILLIAM SHERMAN** captured Atlanta.

1878 **EMMA NUTT** became the first woman telephone operator in the United States. She was hired by the Telephone Dispatch Co. of Boston. When the first phones were installed in Boston, being an operator was strictly a man's job. People liked the telephones, but didn't like the operators. They complained they were rude, so the company fired the men and hired Emma, who stayed for 33 years.

1910 **NANCY ASPINWALL** left San Francisco on horseback and headed for NYC. She rode 4,500 miles and arrived ten months later.

1932 New York City Mayor **JAMES** "Gentleman Jimmy" **WALKER** resigned after charges of graft and corruption in his administration.

1939 German planes and ground troops under the direction of **ADOLF HITLER** rumbled into Poland, marking the **beginning of World War II.**

1957 The **1958 EDSEL** automobile first appeared, with 27 features not available on other cars including a wrap-around windshield, 4 headlights, electric door locks and cruise control. It also had a grill that looked like a toilet seat. Ford sank $270 million into 3 model years, then retired it because of poor sales. The cost was approximately $2,700 per car.

1969 A coup in Libya brought **MOAMMAR GADHAFI** to power.

1972 American **BOBBY FISCHER** won the international chess crown in Reykjavik, Iceland, by defeating Soviet player Boris Spassky in their final match. Fischer repeated this feat in 1992 in Yugoslavia.

1976 **REPRESENTATIVE WAYNE HAYES** (D/OH) quit the House of Representatives in the wake of a scandal prompted by the discovery that Hayes had an affair with a comely but unskilled secretary, Elizabeth Ray, who was on his payroll.

1980 **RONALD REAGAN**, the Republican Presidential nominee, started a controversy when he criticized President **JIMMY CARTER** for opening his re-election campaign in Tuscumbia, AL. Reagan said, "It's the city that gave birth to the Ku Klux Klan." Later, Reagan apologized.

It's always good to
check your tires

SEPTEMBER 2

BIRTHDAYS

- **TONY THOMPSON** Singer. (Waco, TX) Number 1 hit with HI-FIVE: "I Like The Way (The Kissing Game)." Year/**Age**: 1995/**20** 1996/**21** 1997/**22**
- **JOE SIMON** Singer. (Simmesport, LA) Biggest hit: "Get Down, Get Down" in 1975. Year/**Age**: 1995/**52** 1996/**53** 1997/**54**
- **JIMMY CONNORS** Tennis star. (East St. Louis, IL) Became singles tennis champion and won at Wimbledon when he was 22. He is the only tennis player to win the U.S. Open on three different surfaces: clay, grass at Forest Hills, and hard court at Flushing Meadows. Year/**Age**: 1995/**43** 1996/**44** 1997/**45**
- **LINDA PURL** Actress. (Greenwich, CT) Appeared on "Happy Days" as Richie Cunningham's steady girlfriend. Eight years later, she came back to the show as a divorcee with whom Fonzie fell in love, but that didn't work out either. She also co-starred with Andy Griffith on "Matlock." Year/**Age**: 1995/**40** 1996/**41** 1997/**42**
- **MARK HARMON** Actor. (Burbank, CA) Played Dr. Bobby Caldwell, the womanizing plastic surgeon, on TV's "St. Elsewhere." Mark is married to Pam Dawber. He was named *People* magazine's "Sexiest Man Alive" in 1986. Stars on TV series "Reasonable Doubts." Year/**Age**: 1995/**44** 1996/**45** 1997/**46**
- **PETER UEBERROTH** Baseball. (Evanston, IL) Capitalist hero of the profitable 1984 Summer Olympics in LA. He turned a profit which many said would be impossible. He became Commissioner of Baseball (1984-89) and is credited with getting the players and owners together for a quick end to the 1985 baseball strike. Year/**Age**: 1995/**58** 1996/**59** 1997/**60**
- **ALLEN DRURY** Novelist. (Houston, TX) He wrote *Advise and Consent* in 1960. Year/**Age**: 1995/**77** 1996/**78** 1997/**79**

- **JOAN KENNEDY** Former wife of Senator Ted Kennedy. (Born Joan Bennett in Bronxville, NY) Year/**Age**: 1995/**59** 1996/**60** 1997/**61**
- **ROSALIND ASHFORD** Singer. (Detroit, MI) Part of the trio, MARTHA & THE VANDELLAS. Their biggest hit: "Dancing in the Street" in 1964. Year/**Age**: 1995/**52** 1996/**53** 1997/**54**
- **SAM GOODEN** Singer. (Chicago) With the group, the IMPRESSIONS. Their biggest hit: "It's All Right" in 1963. The group originally included Jerry Butler and Curtis Mayfield. Year/**Age**: 1995/**56** 1996/**57** 1997/**58**
- **JIMMY CLANTON** Singer. (Baton Rouge, LA) Biggest hit: "Just a Dream," which he wrote in 1958. Was a DJ in Lancaster, PA. Year/**Age**: 1995/**55** 1996/**56** 1997/**57**
- **MARGE CHAMPION** Dancer/choreographer. (Born Marjorie Belcher in Los Angeles, CA) In the film *Showboat*. At age 14, she was the model for the Disney animation of *Snow White*. She and then-husband Gower, choreographed many Broadway musicals and movies. Year/**Age**: 1995/**72** 1996/**73** 1997/**74**
- **TERRY BRADSHAW** Football. (Shreveport, LA) Pittsburgh Steelers QB who led them to 4 Super Bowl titles. He was in movies: *Smokey & the Bandit*, *Hooper*, and *Cannonball Run*. Terry had a country hit in 1976: "I'm So Lonesome I Could Cry." Is a Fox Network sports commentator. Year/**Age**: 1995/**47** 1996/**48** 1997/**49**
- **CHRISTA McAULIFFE** Astronaut. (1948-1986 – Born Sharon Christa Corrigan in Boston, MA) The New Hampshire schoolteacher and first ordinary citizen in space who perished with 6 crew members in the Jan. 28, 1986, *Challenger* explosion.

FACTS FROM THE PAST

1901 President Theodore Roosevelt gave his speech saying, American foreign policy should be to "Speak softly and carry a big stick."

1930 The **FIRST NON-STOP AIRPLANE FLIGHT FROM EUROPE** to the United States was completed as Captain Dieudonne Coste and Maurice Bellonte of France arrived in Valley Stream, New York, aboard *The Question Mark*.

1944 During World War II, Navy pilot **GEORGE BUSH WAS SHOT DOWN** by the Japanese as he completed a bombing run against an enemy radio communications center in the Bonin Islands. Bush was rescued by the U.S. submarine *Finback*. His two crew members perished.

1963 Alabama Governor **GEORGE C. WALLACE** prevented integration of Tuskegee High School by encircling the building with state troopers.

1963 **WALTER CRONKITE** became the first newsman to anchor a half-hour newscast on TV. His guest was President John F. Kennedy.

1964 **NORMAN MANLEY** hit two successive holes-in-one on the 7th and 8th holes at the Del Valle Country Club in Saugus, CA.

1970 **GENESIS** ran an ad in *Melody Maker* and Phil Collins answered the ad and joined the group.

1971 **JIMMY CONNORS** and **CHRIS EVERT** won their first U.S. Open singles matches. Evert went on to record 101 Open match victories in her career.

1978 **GEORGE HARRISON** married **OLIVIA TRINIDAD ARIAS**. George met Olivia in 1974 when she worked for Dark Horse Records in Los Angeles as a secretary. Olivia was born in Mexico in 1948 and educated in America. They have a son, Dhani.

1986 **CATHY EVELYN SMITH** was sentenced to three years in prison for involuntary manslaughter in connection with the 1982 drug overdose death of comedian **JOHN BELUSHI.**

1992 The long-awaited chess rematch between **BOBBY FISCHER** and **BORIS SPASSKY** began in Yugoslavia. It ended Nov. 5, 1992. Bobby Fischer defeated long-time opponent Boris Spassky, as he had done 20 years before. Fischer received $3.35 million and Spassky received $1.65 million.

SEPTEMBER 3

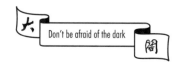
Don't be afraid of the dark

BIRTHDAYS

- **CHARLIE SHEEN** Actor. (Born Carlos Irwin Estevez in Los Angeles, CA) *Platoon, Wall Street, Hot Shots, Hot Shots! Part Deux, Navy Seals, The Three Musketeers, The Chase,* and *Men at Work.* Also in *Major League.* Son of actor Martin Sheen and brother of Emilio Estevez. Year/**Age**: 1995/**30** 1996/**31** 1997/**32**

- **DICK MOTTA** Basketball coach. The Washington Bullets coach popularized the phrase, "It's not over till the fat lady sings." Year/**Age**: 1995/**64** 1996/**65** 1997/**66**

- **EILEEN BRENNAN** Actress. (Los Angeles, CA) Appeared on the "Private Benjamin" TV series until she was seriously injured in an auto accident as she and Goldie Hawn were leaving a Los Angeles restaurant. She and Goldie starred together in the movie *Private Benjamin.* Year/**Age**: 1995/**60** 1996/**61** 1997/**62**

- **VALERIE PERRINE** Actress. (Galveston, TX) Appeared in *Superman* films, *Boiling Point,* and won best supporting actress Oscar in 1974 for *Lenny.* Year/**Age**: 1995/**52** 1996/**53** 1997/**54**

- **ANNE JACKSON** Actress. (Milvale, PA) She appeared in *Love & Other Strangers* and is married to actor Eli Wallach. She was on Broadway in *Lost in Yonkers.* Year/**Age**: 1995/**69** 1996/**70** 1997/**71**

- **IRENE PAPAS** Actress. (Greece) Appeared in *Attila, the Hun*; *The Guns of Navarone*; and *Zorba, the Greek.* Year/**Age**: 1995/**71** 1996/**72** 1997/**73**

- **AL JARDINE** Guitarist. With the BEACH BOYS. Their biggest hit: "I Get Around" in 1964. Year/**Age**: 1995/**53** 1996/**54** 1997/**55**

- **KITTY CARLISLE** Actress/singer. (Born Catherine Holzman in New Orleans, LA) She was married to composer Moss Hart until his death in 1961. Films include *A Night at the Opera*, the Marx Brothers classic. Year/**Age**: 1995/**81** 1996/**82** 1997/**83**

- **DIXIE LEE RAY** (1914-1994) Former chairwoman of the Atomic Energy Commission. At age 12 she bacame the youungest girl to climb Mt. Rainier, Washington's highest peak. (Died 1-2-94.)

- **GEORGE BIONDO** Musician. STEPPENWOLF. Biggest hit: "Born to be Wild." Year/**Age**: 1995/**50** 1996/**51** 1997/**52**

- **CHUCK & TOMPALL GLASER** C&W twins. (Spalding, NE) They debuted on the "Arthur Godfrey Talent Show" and sang back-up on Marty Robbins' "El Paso" hit. Their biggest hit was a male chauvinist song titled "Put Another Log on the Fire." Year/**Age**: 1995/**62** 1996/**63** 1997/**64**

- **EDDIE STANKY** Former baseball manager. Played for the Dodgers, and managed the Cardinals and White Sox. Year/**Age**: 1995/**79** 1996/**80** 1997/**81**

- **HANK THOMPSON** C&W. (Waco, TX) Has sold over 30 million records. Bob Dylan named Hank Thompson as one of the major influences in his career. Hank was the first country artist to record a "live" album in Las Vegas. His biggest hit, "The Wild Side of Life," was #1 on the C&W chart for 15 weeks in 1952. Year/**Age**: 1995/**70** 1996/**71** 1997/**72**

- **ALAN LADD, SR.** Actor. (1913-1964 – Hot Springs, AR) Only 5 ft. 6 in. tall and at times had to stand on a box or sit on a phone book while shooting scenes with leading ladies. His last movie was *The Carpetbaggers* in 1964. (Died 1-29-64.)

FACTS FROM THE PAST

1639 Attorney **THOMAS LECHFORD** of Massachusetts became the first American lawyer to be disbarred.

1833 The first successful **PENNY NEWSPAPER** in the U.S., the *New York Sun,* was started by **BENJAMIN DAY**.

1895 The **FIRST PRO FOOTBALL GAME** was played in Latrobe, PA, and was considered "professional" because quarterback **JOHN BROILER** was paid ten dollars plus expenses.

1935 At Utah's Bonneville Salt Flats, **SIR MALCOLM CAMPBELL** became the first person to drive a car 300 miles an hour.

1955 Because they were afraid to fly, **BILL HALEY** and the COMETS turned down their first invitation to tour outside the U.S. They were offered $2,000 a day for fifteen dates in Australia.

1967 The original version of the TV game show **"WHAT'S MY LINE?"** with John Charles Daly as host, broadcast its final episode after more than 17 years on CBS.

1970 **ARTHUR BROWN** (Biggest hit: "Fire" in 1968) was arrested and jailed for four days after he set fire to his helmet and stripped naked during his performance at the Palermo Pop Festival in Italy. He was told to get out of Italy and stay out.

1974 Former White House Counsel John Dean began serving a prison term for his involvement in **WATERGATE**.

1978 **EMILIO** and **GLORIA ESTEFAN** of the MIAMI SOUND MACHINE got married.

1984 Michael Wittowski from Chicago won the **$40 MILLION ILLINOIS LOTTERY,** becoming the largest single winner in U.S. history to that time.

1986 **ARNOLD PALMER** got a **SECOND HOLE-IN-ONE** for the second straight day. The ball went into the same hole using the same five iron.

1992 Pop music entertainer **PRINCE** signed a $100 million deal with Warner Brothers Records, $10 million per album, making him the highest paid rock star, surpassing previous big-buck leaders Madonna and Michael Jackson.

1992 Baseball owners voted to ask **FAY VINCENT** to resign as baseball commissioner. Vincent said he would not step down, but did so Sept. 7. Milwaukee Brewers' owner Bud Selig assumed the duties of commissioner.

It only takes a second . . .

SEPTEMBER 4

BIRTHDAYS

- **MERALD "BUBBA" KNIGHT** Singer. Brother of Gladys, member of PIPS. Biggest hit: "Midnight Train To Georgia." Year/**Age**: 1995/**53** 1996/**54** 1997/**55**
- **MARTIN CHAMBERS** Drummer. Biggest hit with PRETENDERS: "Back On The Chain Gang." Year/**Age**: 1995/**44** 1996/**45** 1997/**46**
- **JENNIFER SALT** Actress. (Los Angeles, CA) Played daughter Eunice on "Soap" comedy serial. Year/**Age**: 1995/**51** 1996/**52** 1997/**53**
- **TOM WATSON** Golfer. (Kansas City, MO) Won the British Open 5 times. He resigned from the K.C. Country Club in 1990, when they wouldn't approve a Jewish member. Year/**Age**: 1995/**46** 1996/**47** 1997/**48**
- **KEN HARRELSON** Former baseball player/pro golfer. He's a baseball executive today. Year/**Age**: 1995/**53** 1996/**54** 1997/**55**
- **LEONARD FREY** Actor. American character actor who appeared in *Fiddler on the Roof* in 1971. Year/**Age**: 1995/**56** 1996/**57** 1997/**58**
- **HOWARD MORRIS** Actor. (New York, NY) American TV comedian and writer. Appeared in *Boys Night Out* and *Splash,* and directed *With Six You Get Egg Roll.* Year/**Age**: 1995/**76** 1996/**77** 1997/**78**
- **JUDITH IVEY** Actress. (El Paso, TX) Played B.J. on the sitcom "Designing Women." Tony award winner for *Steaming* and *Hurly Burly.* Year/**Age**: 1995/**44** 1996/**45** 1997/**46**
- **MITZI GAYNOR** Entertainer. (Born Francesca Gerber in Chicago, IL) Her movie credits include: *Anything Goes, South Pacific*, and *No Business Like Show Business.* Year/**Age**: 1995/**64** 1996/**65** 1997/**66**
- **IONE SKYE** Actress. Starred in *Say Anything.* Year/**Age**: 1995/**22** 1996/**23** 1997/**24**
- **RONALD LaPREAD** Bassist. Hits with COMMODORES include "Still" and "Three Times A Lady." Year/**Age**: 1995/**45** 1996/**46** 1997/**47**
- **RAYMOND FLOYD** Pro-golfer. 1976 Masters Champion. Year/**Age**: 1995/**52** 1996/**53** 1997/**54**
- **RICHARD WRIGHT** Author. (1908-1960 – Natchez, MS) He was the first African-American writer to have a book reach No.1, *Black Boy*, April 29, 1945. (Died 11-28-60.)
- **RICHARD CASTELLANO** Actor. (1934-1988 – NYC) He played a mafia lieutenant in *The Godfather* and was nominated for an Oscar for his role in *Lovers and Other Strangers.* (Died 12-1-88.)
- **DICK YORK** Actor. (1927-1992 – Ft. Wayne, IN) He played Darrin Stevens, husband to Elizabeth Montgomery's Samantha, on the 1960s TV series "Bewitched" from 1964-69. Also in films, including *Going My Way* and *Inherit the Wind.* (Died 2-20-92.)
- **FRANCOIS RENE CHATEAUBRIAND** Poet/novelist/statesman/historian/explorer. (1776-1848 – France) He traveled the U.S., and the most famous way of cooking steak (the French way) was named for him. (Died 7-4-1848.)
- **HENRY FORD II** Auto-king. (1917-1987 – Detroit, MI) Headed the Ford Motor Co. from the 1940's until the early 1980's. (Died 9-29-87.)
- **IVAN, THE TERRIBLE** Russian czar. (1530-1584) As a young ruler, he tortured animals and threw dogs from rooftops. In 1570, he marched on Novgorod, killing thousands in a 5-week binge, many of them children who were thrown into an icy river. He even killed his son during a mad rage in 1580. (He died while playing a game of chess 3-18-1584.)

FACTS FROM THE PAST

1781 The city of **LOS ANGELES WAS FOUNDED** by **FELIPE DE NEVE**. It was originally called El Pueblo de Nuestra Senora La Reina de Los Angeles de Porciumcula.

1833 The *New York Sun* ran an ad: "To the unemployed: A number of steady men can find employment by vending the paper. A liberal discount is allowed to those who buy to sell again." Ten-year-old **BARNEY FLAHERTY** answered the ad, and even at his age, got the job to become the **FIRST NEWSBOY** in America. **TODAY IS NEWSPAPER CARRIER DAY**.

1882 **THOMAS EDISON** pulled the switch that turned on the first commercial electric lighting in history in Grand Central Station, NY.

1888 **GEORGE EASTMAN** patented the first roll film camera and registered his trademark: "Kodak." He made up the word because he thought "K" was a "strong, incisive sort of letter" and he wanted something "short, vigorous and incapable of being misspelled." The first hand-held camera took 100 exposures for each roll of film. The Eastman Museum is in Rochester, NY.

1951 The **FIRST LIVE, COAST-TO-COAST TELEVISION BROADCAST** took place when President Harry S. Truman spoke to the nation from the Japanese Peace Treaty Conference in San Francisco.

1959 WCBS radio in New York banned the song "Mack the Knife" due to some teenage stabbings.

1964 TV sitcom "**GILLIGAN'S ISLAND" PREMIERED** on CBS. The 98 episodes starred Bob Denver (Gilligan), Dawn Wells (Mary Ann), Tina Louise (Ginger), Russell Johnson (the Professor), Alan Hale (Skipper), Jim Backus (Mr. Howell), and Natalie Schafer (Mrs. Howell).

1972 **MARK SPITZ** from Sacramento, CA, won a record 7th gold medal in the 400-meter relay at the Munich, Germany, Olympics.

1987 West German teenager **MATHIAS RUST** was sentenced by a Soviet court to four years in a labor camp for flying a Cessna through Russian air defenses and into Red Square. He was released in 1988.

1993 Baseball pitcher **JIM ABBOTT**, born without a right hand, pitched a no-hitter. The New York Yankees beat the Cleveland Indians 4-0. This was the first no-hitter for the Yankees in 10 years.

SEPTEMBER 5

Always consider the past

BIRTHDAYS

- **RAQUEL WELCH** Actress. (Born Raquel Tejada in LaJolla, CA) She appeared in *Roust-About, Roustabout, Fantastic Voyage*, and *Our Man Flint*. Makes fitness tapes. Year/Age: 1995/**55** 1996/**56** 1997/**57**

- **CAROL LAWRENCE** Entertainer. (Born Carol Laria in Melrose Park, IL) She has two sons from her marriage to Robert Goulet. She appeared in the Broadway musical *West Side Story* in 1961. Appears on TV's "General Hospital." Year/Age: 1995/**61** 1996/**62** 1997/**63**

- **BOB NEWHART** Comedian. (Born George Robert Newhart in Oak Park, IL) Has had many different TV series. including "The Bob Newhart Show," "Newhart," and "Bob." His comedy album, *Button Down Mind*, has become one of the bestselling albums in history. Year/Age: 1995/**66** 1996/**67** 1997/**68**

- **JACK VALENTI** Film association president. (Houston, TX) He was a high-ranking government official under LBJ. He got out before LBJ left office and Johnson got him a job with the Motion Picture Association of America. He handles the ratings system. During the past year, the movie rating handed out most often has been "R." The rank of the other ratings, in order were PG, G, PG-13 and NC-17. Year/Age: 1995/**74** 1996/**75** 1997/**76**

- **WILLIAM DEVANE** Actor. (Albany, NY) "Knots Landing." He was first choice, but turned down the role of Sam Malone on "Cheers." Year/Age: 1995/**58** 1996/**59** 1997/**60**

- **JOHN STEWART** Singer. (San Diego, CA) Member of the KINGSTON TRIO from 1961-67. He wrote "Daydream Believer." His biggest hit: "Gold" in 1979. Year/Age: 1995/**56** 1996/**57** 1997/**58**

- **AL STEWART** Singer/guitarist. (Glasgow, Scotland) Biggest hits: "Time Passages" in 1978 and "Year of the Cat" in 1976. Year/Age: 1995/**50** 1996/**51** 1997/**52**

- **ARTHUR KOESTLER** Author. (1905-1983 – Hungary) He wrote the anti-Stalin novel *Darkness at Noon*. (Died 3-3-83.)

- **FLORENCE ELDRIDGE** Actress. (1901-1988 – New York, NY) In films *Les Miserables* and *Studio Murder Mystery* with her husband, Fredric March. (Died 8-1-88.)

- **FREDDIE MERCURY** Singer. (1946-1991 – Born Frederick Bulsara in Zanzibar) Lead vocalist for QUEEN. Biggest hits: "Another One Bites the Dust," "Crazy Little Thing Called Love," and "We Are The Champions." Solo hit: "I Was Born To Love You." He died of pneumonia brought on by AIDS. (11-24-91.)

- **DARRYL F. ZANUCK** Producer. (1902-1979 – Wahoo, NE) He was production chief for Warner's and co-founder of "20th Century Productions." Among his memorable films: *Grapes of Wrath*. (Died 12-22-79.)

- **JESSE JAMES** Outlaw. (1847-1882 – Clay City, MO) After many notorious crimes, he was betrayed and killed by a member of his own gang. (Died 4-3-1882.)

FACTS FROM THE PAST

1698   Russia's **PETER THE GREAT** imposed a tax on beards.

1882   The **FIRST LABOR DAY PARADE** in the U.S. was held as 10,000 Labor Union members paraded in New York City. The parade was organized by **PETER MCGUIRE**, a Carpenters and Joiners Union secretary.

1885   **JAKE GUMPER** of Fort Wayne, IN, bought the first gasoline pump to be manufactured in the United States.

1945   Iva Toguri D'Aquino, a Japanese-American suspected of being radio broadcaster **TOKYO ROSE**, was arrested in Yokohama. Convicted of treason in 1949, she served 6 years in prison and was pardoned in 1977.

1958   *Doctor Zhivago*, a novel by Russian author **BORIS PASTERNAK**, was published in the U.S. for the first time.

1960   **CASSIUS CLAY** won an Olympic gold medal in the light heavyweight division, scoring a unanimous decision over Zbigniew Pietrzykowski.

1969   **JAMES BROWN** announced that he was going to retire from live shows, saying he was a tired man. At the same time he was fighting a paternity suit in California brought on by a former president of the James Brown Fan Club.

1975   **PRESIDENT GERALD FORD** escaped an attempt on his life when Lynette "Squeaky" Fromme, a disciple of Charles Manson, attempted to shoot him in Sacramento, CA. The other woman who made an attempt on his life was Sara Jane Moore.

1978   The **CAMP DAVID SUMMIT** began with President Jimmy Carter, Israeli Prime Minister Menachem Begin and Egyptian President Anwar Sadat.

1979   An All-American from UCLA, **ANN MEYERS**, became the first female to sign a contract with an NBA team, the Indiana Pacers. She was cut after one week at training camp. Later she married baseball Hall of Fame pitcher Don Drysdale.

1987   After 30 years on TV **"AMERICAN BANDSTAND,"** hosted by **DICK CLARK** was cancelled.

1989   Tennis star **CHRIS EVERT** retired from professional play after a successful 19-year career. She stepped down after losing to Zina Garrison, 7-6, 6-2 in the U.S. Open.

1989   Calling **DRUGS** "the gravest domestic threat facing our nation today," President Bush announced what he called America's first integrated, comprehensive strategy for coping with the scourge. In his first televised address from the Oval Office as President, Bush set forth a $7.9 billion plan.

1990   The Hollywood Walk of Fame added a star for guitarist **B.B. KING**.

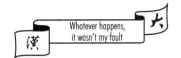

SEPTEMBER 6

BIRTHDAYS

- **DAVID ALLEN COE.** (Akron, OH) Biggest hit: "Mona Lisa Lost Her Smile." Appeared in the film *Take this Job and Shove It.* Year/**Age**: 1995/**56** 1996/**57** 1997/**58**

- **JOANNE WORLEY** Actress/comedienne. (Lowell, IN) One of the original cast members of TV's "Laugh-In."Appears on "Hollywood Squares." Year/**Age**: 1995/**58** 1996/**59** 1997/**60**

- **JANE CURTIN** Actress. (Cambridge, MS) Appeared on "Saturday Night Live" as Chevy Chase's cantankerous co-anchor. Later, on the "Weekend Update" with Dan Aykroyd and Bill Murray. Also starred on the CBS-TV sitcom "Kate & Allie" with Susan St. James. In the film *Coneheads.* Year/**Age**: 1995/**48** 1996/**49** 1997/**50**

- **MEL McDANIEL** C&W. (Cheeotah, OK) Biggest hit: "Baby's Got Her Blue Jeans On" in 1984. Year/**Age**: 1995/**53** 1996/**54** 1997/**55**

- **SWOOZIE KURTZ** Actress. (Omaha, NE) She played actress Laurie Morgan on the TV series "Love, Sidney" with Tony Randall. Now on TV's "Sisters." Her father manned her after a B-17 bomber he flew during WWII. The plane, nicknamed "The Swoose," stood for half swan, half goose. Year/**Age**: 1995/**51** 1996/**52** 1997/**53**

- **CE CE PENISTON** Singer. (Dayton, OH) She was crowned Miss Black Arizona in 1989. Biggest hit: "Finally" in 1991. Year/**Age**: 1995/**26** 1996/**27** 1997/**28**

- **JOHN DALTON** Teacher/physicist/chemist. (1766-1844 – England) Formulated the atomic theory. (Died 7-27-1844.)

- **KATHI WOLFGRAMM** Entertainer. (Minneapolis, MN) The JETS. Hit: "Crush on You" in 1986. Year/**Age**: 1995/**24** 1996/**25** 1997/**26**

- **ROGER WATERS** Bass player. (England) Founding member of PINK FLOYD but went solo in 1964. Biggest hit: "Another Brick in the Wall (Part II.)" Year/**Age**: 1995/**51** 1996/**52** 1997/**53**

- **JOSEPH PATRICK KENNEDY** American financier. (1888-1969 – Boston, MA) Made a fortune in real estate, movies and liquor. At one time had an affair with Gloria Swanson. He organized the U.S. Maritime Commission and was appointed Ambassador to Great Britain in 1938. He owned the Chicago Merchandise Mart and was the father of Joe,Jr., who was killed in World War II; John, who was murdered while president of the U.S.; Robert, who was killed while running for president, and Ted, whose chances at the presidency were dashed by scandal. (Died 11-18-69)

- **BILLY ROSE** Theatrical producer/songwriter/author. (1899-1966 – Born William Rosenberg in NYC) He was married to Fanny Brice. The songs he wrote include: "It's Only a Paper Moon," "That Old Gang of Mine," and "Me and My Shadow." (Died 2-10-66.)

- **JANE ADDAMS** American social worker. (1860-1935 – Cedarville, IL) Founded Hull House in Chicago. The first woman to win a Nobel Peace Prize. The original settlement of Hull House still stands at the University of Illinois. (Died 5-21-35.)

FACTS FROM THE PAST

1901 WILLIAM McKINLEY, 25th U.S. President, was shot twice in the chest by anarchist Leon Czolgosz in Buffalo, NY, while attending the Pan-American Exposition. He died eight days later. Czolgosz wanted to shoot a priest, but a friend told him, "There are so many priests."

1920 JACK DEMPSEY knocked out Billy Miske in the third round of a heavyweight title bout at Benton Harbor, Michigan.

1930 Blondie made her first appearance on the comic pages. "BLONDIE & DAGWOOD BUMSTEAD" became radio stars and were also in 28 movies and 2 television series. Blondie's maiden name was Boopadoop. (It was created by cartoonist CHIC YOUNG.)

1958 MARY ANN MOBLEY of Mississippi was crowned MISS AMERICA 1959 at the pageant in Atlantic City, New Jersey. She's married to talk show host Gary Collins.

1966 The Prime Minister of South Africa, HENDRIK VERWOERD, architect of the apartheid plan, was stabbed to death during a session of Parliament in Capetown. The assassin was a drifter who claimed the government was doing too much for the non-whites and not enough for the "poor whites."

1973 Former United Mine Workers president, W. A. (TONY) BOYLE, was arrested and charged with murder in connection with the 1969 murder of union rival, JOSEPH YABLONSKI, in Pennsylvania.

1975 Czechoslovakian tennis star MARTINA NAVRATILOVA, in New York for the U.S. Open, requested political asylum.

1978 JAMES WICKWIRE of Seattle and LOUIS REICHARDT of San Francisco became the FIRST AMERICANS to reach the summit of Pakistan's K2, the WORLD'S SECOND-HIGHEST MOUNTAIN.

1987 A 70-member medical team at Johns Hopkins Hospital in Baltimore succeeded in separating seven-month-old BENJAMIN and PATRICK BINDER, twin brothers from West Germany, who had been born joined at the head, after 22 HOURS OF SURGERY.

1991 The name of RUSSIA'S SECOND LARGEST CITY was changed from Leningrad back to St. Petersburg. The city was founded in 1703 by Peter the Great. It was changed to Petrograd in 1914 and, after Vladimir Lenin's death, to Leningrad in 1924.

SEPTEMBER 7

Don't ask, just listen

BIRTHDAYS

- **CHRISSIE HYNDE** Singer/guitarist. (Akron, OH) She was a journalist before becoming a rock star. Biggest hit with PRETENDERS: "Back on the Chain Gang" from the film *The King of Comedy*. Also sang "I Got You Babe" with UB40. Their name came from the code number on the British unemployment benefit card. Year/**Age**: 1995/**44** 1996/**45** 1997/**46**

- **SUSAN BLAKELY** Actress. (Germany) In films: *Towering Inferno* and *The Way We Were*. Year/**Age**: 1995/**47** 1996/**48** 1997/**49**

- **RICHARD ROUNDTREE** Actor. (New Rochelle, NY) He appeared in *Shaft* in 1971 and *Young Warriors*. Year/**Age**: 1995/**53** 1996/**54** 1997/**55**

- **GLORIA GAYNOR** Disco singer. (Newark, NJ) Her biggest hit: "I Will Survive" in 1979. Year/**Age**: 1995/**46** 1996/**47** 1997/**48**

- **AL McGUIRE** Basketball Hall of Famer. (Bronx, NY) He was the winningest coach ever at Marquette University in Milwaukee with a 295-80 record. He retired after Marquette beat North Carolina to win the 1977 NCAA title. Also did some college basketball color reporting for NBC. Year/**Age**: 1995/**67** 1996/**68** 1997/**69**

- **ELIA KAZAN** Producer/director. (Elia Kazanjoglous in Turkey) He directed *A Streetcar Named Desire*, *On the Waterfront*, and *Splendor in the Grass*. Year/**Age**: 1995/**86** 1996/**87** 1997/**88**

- **JULIE KAVNER** Actress. (Los Angeles, CA) Won an Emmy for playing Brenda, the younger sister, on "Rhoda." Appeared on the "Tracy Ullman Show," "This is my Life," and is the voice of Marge Simpson on "The Simpsons." Film *I'll Do Anything*. Year/**Age**: 1995/**44** 1996/**45** 1997/**46**

- **JOHN PHILLIP LAW** Actor. American leading man in *The Russians are Coming*, *Hurry Sundown*, and *Barbarella* with Jane Fonda. Year/**Age**: 1995/**58** 1996/**59** 1997/**60**

- **MICHAEL FEINSTEIN** Singer/pianist. (Hollywood, CA) Year/**Age**: 1995/**39** 1996/**40** 1997/**41**

- **JOHN BROCKINGTON** Football. (Brooklyn, NY) Rookie of the Year in 1971. In 1972 he led the Green Bay Packers to the Central Division title, rushing 1,027 yards and becoming the first player to rush for over 1,000 yards in the first two seasons. Year/**Age**: 1995/**47** 1996/**48** 1997/**49**

- **CORBIN BERNSEN** Actor. "L.A. Law" hunk. Son of actress Jeanne Cooper ("The Young and the Restless.") He married actress Amanda Pays. Films *Savage Land* and *Major League*. Year/**Age**: 1995/**40** 1996/**41** 1997/**42**

- **SONNY ROLLINS** Sax player. (New York, NY) Played sax on the movie soundtrack *Alfie*. Year/**Age**: 1995/**65** 1996/**66** 1997/**67**

- **ARTHUR FERRANTE** Pianist. (New York, NY) Duo piano hits with Teicher include: "Exodus" and Tonight." Year/**Age**: 1995/**73** 1996/**74** 1997/**75**

- **SIR ANTHONY QUAYLE** Actor/director. (1913-1989 – England) His film credits include Alfred Hitchcock's *The Wrong Man*, *Lawrence of Arabia*, and *Anne of a Thousand Days*, which brought him an Academy Award nomination for his role as Cardinal Wolsey. He built Stratford-upon-Avon into a center of British theater. (Died 11-20-89.)

- **PETER LAWFORD** Actor. (1923-1984 – England) Veteran of 60 movies, among them: *Mrs. Miniver*, *The Thin Man*, and *Oceans 11*. Ex-husband of Patricia Kennedy. (Died 12-24-84.)

- **BUDDY HOLLY** Entertainer. (1936-1959 – Born Charles Hardin Holley in Lubbock, TX) His last name was misspelled on his first recording contract, and he left it that way. He started the CRICKETS in high school, and they were unsuccessful playing country music and switched to rock 'n roll for their first hit in August 1957, "That'll Be the Day." He died in a plane crash with the "Big Bopper" and Richie Valens in Mason City, IA. They came up with the name Crickets after deciding against Beetles and Grasshoppers. The spelling was later changed by John Lennon and used by the BEATLES. (Died 2-3-59.)

FACTS FROM THE PAST

1813 A writer from Troy, NY, coined the nickname "**UNCLE SAM**" for the U.S., referring to Sam Wilson (Uncle Sam), owner of a meat packing firm which supplied provisions for soldiers. Barrels were stamped with a large "U.S." which an Irish watchman thought referred to "Uncle Sam Wilson." From then on, "U.S." meant "Uncle Sam," which became the nickname for the U.S. government.

1892 Fighter **JOHN L. SULLIVAN** was knocked out by **JIM CORBETT** in the 21st round of a New Orleans prizefight. It was the first major fight under Marquis of Queensberry rules, calling for the use of gloves.

1921 Miss Washington, DC, 16-year-old **MARGARET GORMAN**, won the **FIRST MISS AMERICA PAGEANT**. She won the qualifying title on the strength of a photo. Her prize was a golden statue of a mermaid. The merchants in Atlantic City, NJ, started the contest to keep the tourists in town after Labor Day. A local reporter coined the Miss America name.

1972 The Federal grand jury indicted **G. GORDON LIDDY**, **JAMES McCORD**, **E. HOWARD HUNT** and four others for the Watergate break-in.

1973 Porn star **LINDA LOVELACE** emceed a concert at the Hollywood Bowl and introduced the star with "Here he is, the biggest, largest, most gigantic and fantastic man, the costar of my next movie . . . **ELTON JOHN**."

1988 Republican **GEORGE BUSH** startled a friendly American Legion audience in Louisville, KY, by referring to September 7 as "Pearl Harbor Day," which is actually December 7. Realizing his mistake, Bush said, "Did I say September 7? Sorry about that."

1991 After making it to the semi-finals of the U.S. Open tennis tournament in New York City, 39-year old **JIMMY CONNORS** lost in the semi-finals to **JIM COURIER**, 6-3, 6-3, 6-2.

1992 Baseball commissioner **FAY VINCENT** resigned.

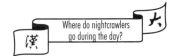

Where do nightcrawlers go during the day?

SEPTEMBER 8

BIRTHDAYS

- **DAVID STEELE** Bassist. (England) Hits with FINE YOUNG CANNIBALS include: "She Drives Me Crazy" and "Good Thing." In the film *Tin Men*. Year/**Age**: 1995/**35** 1996/**36** 1997/**37**
- **SID CAESAR** Comedian. (Yonkers, NY) He hosted the "Show of Shows" on TV with Imogene Coca from 1950 to 1954. Much of the show's success was due to its talented writers, such as Neil Simon, Mel Brooks, and Woody Allen. Year/**Age**: 1995/**73** 1996/**74** 1997/**75**
- **HENRY THOMAS** Actor. He starred in *E.T.* in 1982.
- **HEATHER THOMAS** Actress. (Greenwich, CT) She played stuntwoman Jody Banks in "The Fall Guy" with Lee Majors. Year/**Age**: 1995/**38** 1996/**39** 1997/**40**
- **SAL VALENTINO** Singer. (Born Sal Spaminato in San Francisco, CA) With BEAU BRUMMELS. Hits include: "Just a Little" and "Laugh, Laugh." Year/**Age**: 1995/**55** 1996/**56** 1997/**57**
- **HILLARY BROOKE** Actress. (Born Beatrice Peterson) She appeared in *The Admiral Was a Lady* and *Confidence Girl*. Year/**Age**: 1995/**81** 1996/**82** 1997/**83**
- **LEN BARNEY** Football Hall of Famer. (Gulfport, MS) Three-time All-Southwest Conference cornerback at Jackson State, MS. In 1967, Detroit Lions second-round draft pick. Played in seven Pro-Bowls. Year/**Age**: 1995/**50** 1996/**51** 1997/**52**
- **SAM NUNN** Senator. (Perryville, GA) D/GA. Chairman of the Senate Armed Forces Committee. Year/**Age**: 1995/**57** 1996/**58** 1997/**59**

- **JONATHAN TAYLOR THOMAS** Actor. He's on TV's "Home Improvement." Year/**Age**: 1995/**14** 1996/**15** 1997/**16**
- **MAURICE CHEEKS** Basketball. (Chicago, IL) Former Boston Celtic. Year/**Age**: 1995/**39** 1996/**40** 1997/**41**
- **BJ (BENJAMIN ROY) ARMSTRONG** Basketball. (Detroit, MI) With the Chicago Bulls. Year/**Age**: 1995/**28** 1996/**29** 1997/**30**
- **JIMMIE RODGERS** C&W singer. (1897-1933 – Meridian, MS) Often called the "Father of Country Music," he was the first country artist who appeared in a motion picture. The year was 1929, and it was a 10-minute film called *Singing Brakeman*. His name was added to Country Music Hall of Fame in 1961. (Died 5-26-33.)
- **PETER SELLERS** Actor. (1925-1980 – England) Nominated in 1964 for best actor in *Dr. Strangelove* but is probably best known for his "Inspector Clouseau" character in the *Pink Panther* films. Oscar nomination for playing the gardener in the movie *Being There*. (Died 7-24-80.)
- **PATSY CLINE** C&W singer. (1932-1963 – Born Virginia Patterson Hensley in Winchester, VA) Her biggest hit: "Crazy" in 1961. It is the second most popular juke box song of all time, behind "Hound Dog" and "Don't Be Cruel" by Elvis which are tied for first place. She died in a plane crash in Camden, TN. She was en route from St. Louis where she performed at a benefit concert for the widow of DJ Cactus Jack Call, who had died in a car crash. Actress Jessica Lange starred in a film about her life. She was the first woman elected to the Country Music Hall of Fame. (Died 3-5-63.)

FACTS FROM THE PAST

1858 **ABRAHAM LINCOLN** made a speech that produced the phrase: "You can fool all of the people some of the time, some of the people all of the time, but not all of the people all of the time."

1866 **SEXTUPLETS** were born to the **BUSHNELL** family from Chicago. This was the first recorded birth of sextuplets.

1883 The **NORTHERN PACIFIC RAILROAD** was joined between Garrison and Gold Creek, MT, linking St. Paul, MN, to Seattle, WA. **SITTING BULL** was invited to the ceremony. Only one officer could speak the Sioux language and he was horrified to hear the Indian say during his speech: "I hate all white people. You are thieves, liars and have taken away our land and made us outcasts." Not understanding a word Sitting Bull said, the white audience applauded. Afraid to give the true translation, the officer gave them a few friendly lines and the crowd applauded again.

1892 **FRANCIS BELLAMY**, a former Baptist preacher, wrote the "Pledge of Allegiance" in honor of the 400th anniversary of Columbus coming to America. It took him three hours to complete the original 23 words.

1962 Bobby Boris Picket's smash "**MONSTER MASH**" hit the charts.

1966 "STAR TREK" premiered on TV, starring **WILLIAM SHATNER** as Capt. Kirk and **LEONARD NIMOY** as Mr. Spock. It ran until September, 1969. The TV show inspired some films including *Wrath of Khan* and *Search for Spock*.

1971 **JOHN F. KENNEDY CENTER** for the Performing Arts opened in Washington with a performance of Leonard Bernstein's *Mass*.

1974 President Gerald Ford **PARDONED RICHARD NIXON** of all federal crimes he may have committed while in office.

1974 California's **NOLAN RYAN** threw a pitch 100.8 miles per hour against the Chicago White Sox, becoming the first player to break 100-mph.

1974 Stuntman **EVEL KNIEVEL** unsuccessfully tried to jump the Snake River Canyon, suffering only minor injuries. In a lawsuit against him for damages incurred by fans, he settled out of court for $2,478. His son has been trying to duplicate some of those stunts.

1982 **WILLIAM PALEY** announced his retirement as CBS board chairman. He founded the network in 1928.

1986 **DESMOND TUTU** became the first black to lead the Anglican Church in South Africa.

1988 **ELTON JOHN**'s costumes and concert pariphenalia grossed $6.2 million at a Sotheby's auction in London.

SEPTEMBER 9

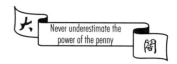

Never underestimate the power of the penny

BIRTHDAYS

- **INEZ FOXX** Singer. (Greensboro, NC) With her brother Charlie Fox, they reached #7 on the charts with "Mockingbird" in 1963. Year/Age: 1995/**52** 1996/**53** 1997/**54**

- **LUTHER SIMMONS** Singer. (NYC) With MAIN INGREDIENT. Biggest hit: "Everybody Plays the Fool." Year/Age: 1995/**53** 1996/**54** 1997/**55**

- **KRISTY McNICHOL** Actress. (Los Angeles, CA) She appeared in TV series "Family" as Letitia Lawrence, "Buddy," for which she won 2 Emmy Awards. Also in "Empty Nest," and in the movie *Little Darlings* with Tatum O'Neal. Year/**Age**: 1995/**33** 1996/**34** 1997/**35**

- **DOUG INGLE** Singer/keyboardist. (San Diego, CA) Leader of heavy-metal band IRON BUTTERFLY. 1968 hit: "In-A-Gadda-Da-Vida." Year/Age: 1995/**49** 1996/**50** 1997/**51**

- **BILLY PRESTON** Singer/musician. (Houston, TX) Biggest hit: "Will it Go Round in Circles" in 1973. Billy was the first non-BEATLE to be credited on a BEATLES record ("Get Back") for his musical contributions. While performing as a member of Little Richard's band during 1962 he first met the BEATLES in Germany. Year/Age: 1995/**49** 1996/**50** 1997/**51**

- **CLIFF ROBERTSON** Actor. (LaJolla, CA) He won an Oscar in 1968 for best actor in *Charly*. Appears in AT&T commercials. Year/Age: 1995/**70** 1996/**71** 1997/**72**

- **SYLVIA MILES** Actress. (NYC) Oscar nominee in 1969 for "Midnight Cowboy." Year/Age: 1995/**63** 1996/**64** 1997/**65**

- **FREDDY WELLER** C&W singer. (Atlanta, GA) He worked with Billy Jo Royal before joining PAUL REVERE & THE RAIDERS. He wrote "Dizzy" for Tommy Roe. Freddy's biggest hit: "Games People Play" in 1969, a pop hit for Joe South. Year/**Age**: 1995/**48** 1996/**49** 1997/**50**

- **SCOTT DeFREITAS** Actor. "As the World Turns." Year/**Age**: 1995/**26** 1996/**27** 1997/**28**

- **JIMMY "THE GREEK" SNYDER** Oddsmaker. (Born Demetrios George Synodinos in Steubenville, OH) Before he quit gambling, he would bet up to $250,000 on a football game. Year/Age: 1995/**76** 1996/**77** 1997/**78**

- **MICHAEL KEATON** Actor. (Born Michael Douglas, Pittsburgh, PA) *Batman* in the movies. Also *Beetlejuice, Mr. Mom, Dream Team, My Life, Much Ado About Nothing*, and *The Paper*. Year/Age: 1995/**44** 1996/**45** 1997/**46**

- **DAVID STEWART** Keyboardist/guitarist. (England) Half of the EURYTHMICS duo. Biggest hit: "Sweet Dreams" in 1983. Year/Age: 1995/**43** 1996/**44** 1997/**45**

- **JOE THEISMANN** Football star. (New Brunswick, NJ) Year/Age: 1995/**46** 1996/**47** 1997/**48**

- **ANGELA CARTWRIGHT** Actress. She was in the "Make Room for Daddy" TV series and played Penny on "Lost in Space" in the 1960s. Year/Age: 1995/**43** 1996/**44** 1997/**45**

- **TOM WOPAT** Actor. (Lodi, WI) "The Dukes of Hazzard." As a singer, his biggest hit: "The Rock and Roll of Love" in 1986. Year/Age: 1995/**44** 1996/**45** 1997/**46**

- **JOSEPH E. LEVINE** Movie producer. (1905-1987 – Boston, MA) His credits include: *The Graduate, Carnal Knowledge*, and *The Lion in Winter*. (Died 7-31-87)

- **COL. HARLAND SANDERS** Restauranteur. (1890-1980 – Henryville, IN) He was the originator of "Kentucky Fried Chicken." His first restaurant was in Corbin, KY. (Died 12-16-80.)

- **OTIS REDDING** Soulful blues singer. (1941-1967 – Dawson, GA) He was killed in a plane crash on Dec. 10, 1967, in Lake Monona, Madison, Wisconsin. At the time of his death, he'd been recording "Sittin' on the Dock of the Bay." A friend went back into the studio and finished the song, making it the first posthumous #1 record in history.

FACTS FROM THE PAST

1884 **ANTOINE FEUCHTWANGER**, a St. Louis frankfurter vender, decided that instead of giving away a white glove with each frank, he would place them in long buns, thereby inventing the hot dog.

1893 **A PRESIDENT'S CHILD** was born in the White House for the first time. President Cleveland's wife, Esther, gave birth to a daughter.

1950 The **FIRST TV SHOW** to feature a **RECORDED LAUGH TRACK** was "The Hank McCune Show," a situation comedy.

1956 **ELVIS PRESLEY** made the first of three appearances on the "Ed Sullivan Show" and pulled 82.6% of the total TV viewing audience. He performed "Don't Be Cruel" and "Ready Teddy." The guest-host for that first show was actor Charles Laughton. The *New York Times* said, "When Elvis executes his bumps and grinds, it should be remembered by CBS that even a 12-year-old's curiosity might be overstimulated." On his third appearance, Elvis was shot on camera only from the waist up.

1965 **SANDY KOUFAX** of the Los Angeles Dodgers pitched a perfect game against the Chicago Cubs, winning 1-0.

1982 **PATTI LABELLE** and **AL GREEN** made their Broadway debuts at the Alvin Theatre in New York City. They starred in a gospel-type musical *Your Arm's Too Short to Box With God*.

1984 **POPE JOHN PAUL** became the first pontiff to visit Canada as he began a 12-day tour of the country.

1990 **PRESIDENT BUSH** and **MIKHAIL GORBACHEV** both pledged their countries' support in actions against Iraq for its invasion of Kuwait.

1991 The former heavyweight boxing champion **MIKE TYSON** was indicted on rape charges in Indiana.

1992 Milwaukee Brewer outfielder, **ROBIN YOUNT**, singled off Cleveland pitcher, Jose Mesa, for the 3,000 hit of his career. He became the 17th player in major league history to reach that mark. He also got his 1,000th and 2,000th off the Cleveland Indians.

SEPTEMBER 10

BIRTHDAYS

- **SIOBHAN FAHEY** [shih-bohn] Singer. Of BANANARAMA. Biggest hit: "Venus" in 1986. Married to David Stewart. Year/**Age**: 1995/**38** 1996/**39** 1997/**40**

- **AMY IRVING** Actress. (Palo Alto, CA) Appeared in *Competition, Yentl, Benefit of a Doubt*, and *Crossing Delancey*. Ex-wife of Steven Spielberg. Year/**Age**: 1995/**42** 1996/**43** 1997/**44**

- **FAY WRAY** Actress. (Alberta, Canada) She played King Kong's girlfriend in the original *King Kong*. Year/**Age**: 1995/**88** 1996/**89** 1997/**90**

- **ROBERT WISE** Director (Winchester, IN) He won Oscars for *West Side Story* and *The Sound of Music*. Year/**Age**: 1995/**81** 1996/**82** 1997/**83**

- **CHARLES KURALT** Newsman. (Wilmington, NC) Host of "On the Road with Charles Kuralt" and "Sunday Morning" on CBS. After 35 years at CBS, he retired May 1, 1994. Year/**Age**: 1995/**61** 1996/**62** 1997/**63**

- **JOSÉ FELICIANO** Singer. (Puerto Rico) Biggest hit: "Light my Fire" in 1968. Also in 1968, he sang a controversial version of the "National Anthem" before the Detroit Tigers/St. Louis Cardinals game in Detroit which caused quite a stir at that time. Year/**Age**: 1995/**50** 1996/**51** 1997/**52**

- **ARNOLD PALMER** Pro golfer. (Latrobe, PA) He was golf's first million-dollar winner. He won 4 Masters and 2 British Open tournaments. Appears on Jiffy Lube commercials. Year/**Age**: 1995/**66** 1996/**67** 1997/**68**

- **JOE PERRY** Guitarist. Hits with AEROSMITH: "Dream On" and "Walk This Way." Year/**Age**: 1995/**45** 1996/**46** 1997/**47**

- **BOB LANIER** Basketball Hall of Famer. (Buffalo, NY) He was the Detroit Pistons number one NBA draft pick in 1970. An NBA All-Star eight times. He was traded to the Milwaukee Bucks in 1980. He now heads an advertising and promotion firm in Milwaukee, Bob Lanier Enterprises. Year/**Age**: 1995/**47** 1996/**48** 1997/**49**

- **TOMMY OVERSTREET** C&W singer. (Oklahoma City, OK) Biggest hit: "Ann, Don't Go Runnin" in 1972. Year/**Age**: 1995/**61** 1996/**62** 1997/**63**

- **MARGARET TRUDEAU** Former Canadian First Lady and disco dancer. She's now married to a millionaire furniture dealer. Wrote a book, *Beyond Reason*. Year/**Age**: 1995/**47** 1996/**48** 1997/**49**

- **ROGER MARIS** Baseball star (1934-1985 – Hibbing MN) He hit the most homeruns in a 162-game schedule: 61 with the NY Yankees in 1961. Tracy Stallard, a rookie Boston Red Sox pitcher, served up the 61st homer. He won back-to-back MVP Awards, but is not in the Baseball Hall of Fame. (Died 12-14-85)

- **EDMOND O'BRIEN** Actor. (1915-1985 – NYC) He won an Oscar as the Hollywood press agent in *The Barefoot Contessa* which starred Humphrey Bogart and Ava Gardner. He was also nominated for his role as Senator Raymond Clark in *Seven Days in May* and starred in "The Long Hot Summer" TV series. (Died 5-8-85.)

FACTS FROM THE PAST

1813   An American victory was claimed in the War of 1812 at the battle of Lake Erie. **LT. OLIVER HAZARD PERRY** sent a message to his commander saying, "We have met the enemy, and they are ours."

1846   Elias Howe of Spencer, MA, received a patent on his **SEWING MACHINE.**

1881   Roger Connor, first baseman for the Troy Trojans, got the **FIRST GRAND SLAM HOME RUN** in the major leagues. By hitting the homer with three men on base, he led his team to an 8-7 win over Worcester. He hit only one more home run that season.

1919   In New York City, a hero's welcome greeted **GENERAL JOHN PERSHING** and 25,000 soldiers who served in the U.S. 1st Division during WWI.

1955   One of the longest-running TV shows on CBS began when "**GUNSMOKE**" premiered. **BURT REYNOLDS** played the blacksmith from 1962 to 1965 with **JAMES ARNESS** as Marshall Dillon.

1963   **20 BLACK STUDENTS** entered public schools in Birmingham, Mobile and Tuskegee, AL after a standoff between Governor George Wallace and federal authorities.

1964   **ROD STEWART**'s first single, "Good Morning Little Schoolgirl" featured John Paul Jones (LED ZEPPELIN) on bass.

1965   A studio audience of one viewed the final broadcast of "**THE JACK PAAR SHOW.**" His only invited guest was his dog.

1966   **MUHAMMAD ALI** defended his heavyweight boxing title with a 12-round knockout of Carl Mildenberger in Frankfurt, Germany.

1982   **PRESIDENT REAGAN** felt his first major defeat on Capitol Hill when the Senate joined the House in overriding his veto of a $14.1 billion supplemental spending bill.

1987   **POPE JOHN PAUL II** was welcomed in Miami by President and Mrs. Reagan when he began a 10-day tour of the U.S.

1987   **MICHAEL JACKSON**'s **"Bad"** tour began at Tokyo's Korakuen Stadium.

1988   **STEFFI GRAF** of West Germany won the women's U.S. Open to become the first Grand Slam winner since Margaret Court in 1970.

1989   **DEION SANDERS** lived two **ALL-AMERICAN DREAMS** in the same week. First he hit a home run and went 3-for-4 with the New York Yankees (on 9-6-89) and on this day he scored a touchdown on a 68-yard punt return for the Atlanta Falcons.

1991   The Senate Judiciary Committee opened hearings on the nomination of **CLARENCE THOMAS** to the U.S. Supreme Court.

SEPTEMBER 11
No News is Good News Day

If you get lost, ask your wife for directions

BIRTHDAYS

- **CHARLES EVERS** Civil Rights leader. (Decatur, MS) He was the first African-American DJ in Mississippi. Year/**Age**: 1995/**72** 1996/**73** 1997/**74**

- **BOB PACKWOOD** Oregon Senator. (Portland, OR) Republican. Charged with 16 allegations of sexual harassment, Packwood apologized by saying "My actions were just plain wrong. I just didn't get it. I do now." Year/**Age**: 1995/**63** 1996/**64** 1997/**65**

- **LOLA FALANA** Entertainer. (Philadelphia, PA) She returned to the Las Vegas stage in 1989 after an 18-month battle with multiple sclerosis. Year/**Age**: 1995/**49** 1996/**50** 1997/**51**

- **BRIAN DePALMA** Movie director. (Newark, NJ) He directed *Obsession, Carrie, The Fury, Casualties of War, Cape Fear*, and *Raising Cain*. He directed the "Dancing in the Dark" video by Bruce Springstein. Year/**Age**: 1995/**55** 1996/**56** 1997/**57**

- **EARL HOLLIMAN** Actor. (Delhi, LA) He was Lt. Bill Crowley on "Police Woman," co-starring with Angie Dickinson. He was on "Delta." Year/**Age**: 1995/**67** 1996/**68** 1997/**69**

- **JIMMIE DAVIS** Composer/politician. (Quitman, LA) He co-wrote one of the great C&W standards: "You Are My Sunshine," and later became governor of Louisiana, in 1944; probably one of the first show biz people to go into politics. Year/**Age**: 1995/**93** 1996/**94** 1997/**95**

- **TOM LANDRY** Former Dallas Cowboys coach. (Mission, TX) The only coach the Dallas Cowboys had since being formed in 1960. He was fired in 1989 by new team owner Jerry Jones. Year/**Age**: 1995/**71** 1996/**72** 1997/**73**

- **WILLIAM XAVIER KIENZLE** Author/former priest. (Detroit, MI) Author of *The Rosary Murders*. Year/**Age**: 1995/**67** 1996/**68** 1997/**69**

- **JON MOSS** Drummer. (London, England) CULTURE CLUB. Hits include: "Karma Chameleon" in 1984. Year/**Age**: 1995/**37** 1996/**38** 1997/**39**

- **FERDINAND MARCOS** (1917-1989 – Born near Manila) In 1954 he married 26-year old Imelda. In 1966, he was elected president of the Philippines on an anti-corruption platform. In 1986, his opposition alleged widespread election fraud and soldiers announced they had broken with Marcos and declared Corazon Aquino the election winner. Marcos and his wife fled to Hawaii and the U.S. ordered them to remain there after a recording disclosed he tried to buy $25 million in weapons for a coup that involved kidnaping Aquino. (Died 9-28-89.)

- **ANNE SEYMOUR** Character actress. (1909-1988 – Born Anne Seymour Eckert in NYC) She was a Chicago radio performer in the 1930s and on many TV shows. She played Sara Delano Roosevelt in *Sunrise at Campobello*. She was in *Mirage* and in 1988 she was on the short-lived TV series "Empire."

- **PAUL "BEAR" BRYANT** Football. (1914-1983) He was football coach at the University of Alabama for 25 years and gained the title of "the winningest coach in college football." He won 323 games against 85 defeats and 17 ties.

- **D.H. LAWRENCE** English author. (1885-1930) Author of *Lady Chatterley's Lover.* (Died 3-2-30.)

FACTS FROM THE PAST

1609   **HENRY HUDSON** discovered the river called the Hudson.

1777   Forces under General George Washington were defeated by the British in the Battle of Brandywine near Wilmington, Delaware. The **STARS & STRIPES FLAG** was officially carried for the first time in that battle.

1789   **ALEXANDER HAMILTON** was appointed the first U.S. Secretary of the Treasury.

1847   **"OH, SUSANNAH"** was sung for the first time in public at the Eagle Saloon in Pittsburgh, PA. **STEPHEN FOSTER** sold the rights to the bartender for a bottle of whiskey.

1936   **THE BOULDER DAM** (now Hoover) was dedicated by FDR. He pressed a key in Washington which signaled the start of the dam's first hydroelectric generator in Nevada.

1969   What is said to be the **FIRST BOOTLEG RECORD ALBUM**, *Great White Wonder*, appeared in record stores in Los Angeles. The two-record set featured unreleased **BOB DYLAN** songs.

1974   **"LITTLE HOUSE ON THE PRAIRIE"** starring **MICHAEL LANDON** made its TV debut. It also made a star of Melissa Gilbert.

1975   **PRESIDENT GERALD FORD** began wearing a **BULLET-PROOF VEST** to campaign in his first public appearance since the assassination attempt on his life.

1981   U.S. First Lady **NANCY REAGAN** spent over $200,000 on a new china, saying, "The White House really badly, badly needs china."

1982   **CHRIS EVERT LLOYD** won her sixth U.S. Open by beating Hana Mandlikova 6-3, 6-1.

1982   California's **DEBRA SUE MAFFETT** was crowned Miss America at the Pageant in Atlantic City, NJ.

1984   **BARBARA MANDRELL** and two of her children were seriously injured in a car crash that killed the other driver. She spent a long time recuperating and firmly believes that seat belts saved their lives.

1985   **PETE ROSE** broke Ty Cobb's career hit record, hitting #4,192, on a line drive to left field on a 2-1 pitch from San Diego's Eric Show.

1987   CBS Anchorman **DAN RATHER** walked off the set of the "CBS Evening News" because a tennis tournament ran overtime. When tennis coverage ended and Rather was not there, the network went black for six minutes.

1991   In a move protested by the Havana government, Soviet President **MIKHAIL GORBACHEV** announced that the Kremlin would withdraw thousands of troops from Cuba.

SEPTEMBER 12

BIRTHDAYS

• **ELLA MAE MORSE** Singer. (Mansfield, TX) Biggest hit: "Shoo Shoo Baby" in 1943. She was Capitol Records' first artist. Year/**Age**: 1995/**70** 1996/**71** 1997/**72**

• **NEIL PEART** Drummer. (Canada) With RUSH. Hit: "New World Man" in 1982. Year/**Age**: 1995/**43** 1996/**44** 1997/**45**

• **GERRY BECKLEY** Singer/guitarist. With AMERICA. Hits include: "A Horse With No Name," "Sister Golden Hair," and "Tin Man." Year/**Age**: 1995/**43** 1996/**44** 1997/**45**

• **LINDA GRAY** Actress. (Santa Monica, CA) Was "JR's" long-suffering wife on "Dallas" and appeared in one of Kenny Rogers' *Gambler* movies on TV. Star of "Model's Inc." Year/**Age**: 1995/**55** 1996/**56** 1997/**57**

• **GEORGE JONES** C&W singer. (Saratoga, TX) Married to Tammy Wynette, 1969-75. Set the standard for duets in country music, with partners ranging from pop star Gene Pitney in the '60s to new-wave rocker Elvis Costello in the '70s. His first big hit came in 1955 with "Why, Baby, Why." His 1959 smash, "White Lightnin'," was written by rockabilly J. P. Richardson (the Big Bopper). Biggest hit: "Tender Years," #1 on C&W chart for 7 weeks in 1961. Year/**Age**: 1995/**64** 1996/**65** 1997/**66**

• **MARIA MULDAUR** Singer. Her biggest hit: "Midnight at the Oasis" in 1974. Year/**Age**: 1995/**52** 1996/**53** 1997/**54**

• **PETER SCOLARI** Actor. (New Rochelle, NY) Appeared in "Newhart." Year/**Age**: 1995/**41** 1996/**42** 1997/**43**

• **MICKEY LOLICH** Former baseball pitcher. (Portland, OR) Mickey was born right-handed but had a motorcycle accident as a child and became left-handed. He was a 1968 Detroit Tiger pennant race/World Series star. Year/**Age**: 1995/**55** 1996/**56** 1997/**57**

• **DERON CHERRY** Football. (Riverside, NJ) Kansas City Chiefs middle linebacker. Year/**Age**: 1995/**36** 1996/**37** 1997/**38**

• **DICKIE MOORE** Actor. (Los Angeles, CA) In the *Our Gang* films and with Shirley Temple in *Miss Annie Rooney*. Year/**Age**: 1995/**70** 1996/**71** 1997/**72**

• **IRENE DAILY** Actress. (NYC) "Another World." Year/**Age**: 1995/**75** 1996/**76** 1997/**77**

• **BARRY WHITE** Singer. (Galveston, TX) Biggest hit: "Can't Get Enough of Your Love, Babe" in 1974. Played piano on the song "Goodnight My Love" by Jesse Belvin when he was 11 years old. Year/**Age**: 1995/**51** 1996/**52** 1997/**53**

• **MAURICE CHEVALIER** Entertainer. (1888-1971 – Paris, France) Appeared in *GiGi*, *Fanny*, and *Can-Can*. (Died 1-1-71.)

• **MARGARET HAMILTON** Actress. (1902-1985) Was the wicked witch in the "Wizard of Oz." She also played Cora on Maxwell House TV commercials. (Died 5-16-85.)

• **JESSE OWENS** Olympic star. (1913-1980 – Oakville, AL) He won 4 gold medals at the 1936 Olympics in Berlin, Germany, and set 11 world records in track and field. On May 23, 1935, during a track meet at Ann Arbor, MI, Owens, of Ohio State University, broke five world records and tied a sixth in 45 minutes. (Died 3-31-80.)

• **RICHARD GATLING** Inventor. (1818-1903) Inventor of the Gatling gun. The U.S. still uses a variation of that gun on battle helicopters. They're called Vulcan miniguns. (Died 2-26-03.)

• **CHARLES DUDLEY WARNER** Author. (1829-1900.) Best remembered for his [not Mark Twain's] famous statement: "Everybody talks about the weather, but nobody does anything about it." (Died 10-20-1900.)

FACTS FROM THE PAST

1922 The word "**OBEY**" was removed from the bride's section of the wedding vows of the Episcopal Church. When Fergie married Prince Andrew of Britain, she used the word "obey," but Lady Di did not when she married Prince Charles.

1953 Massachusetts **SENATOR JOHN F. KENNEDY** married **JACQUELINE LEE BOUVIER** in Newport, RI. He was 36, she was 24.

1953 **NIKITA KHRUSHCHEV** was elected to power in Russia.

1959 "**BONANZA,**" the TV series starring Lorne Greene, Michael Landon, Dan Blocker, and Pernell Roberts, premiered on TV. Ended 1973.

1966 The **MONKEES' TV SERIES** premiered. The pre-fabricated musical group featured Mickey Dolenz, Peter Tork, Davey Jones, and Michael Nesmith; chosen not because they were good singers, musicians or actors, but because they looked right for the parts.

1976 Chicago White Sox designated hitter **MINNIE MINOSO** became the **OLDEST PLAYER** (53) to collect a hit in a regulation game.

1977 South African black student leader **STEVEN BIKO** died while in police custody, triggering an **INTERNATIONAL OUTCRY.**

1978 "**TAXI**" debuted. It made stars out of **DANNY DEVITO**, **MARILU HENNER**, **TONY DANZA**, **JUDD HIRSCH**, **CHRISTOPHER LLOYD**, and the late **ANDY KAUFMAN.**

1979 **PRESIDENT JIMMY CARTER** announced plans for a $2.4 million program to assist low-income families meet rising energy costs and help them get through the winter.

1980 "20/20" aired a **REPORT ON ELVIS PRESLEY'S DEATH**. The exposé raised so many questions, the official case was reopened.

1982 **JIMMY CONNORS** won his fourth U.S. Open, defeating Ivan Lendl.

1987 The press revealed that Democratic presidential candidate **JOSEPH BIDEN** borrowed, without credit, passages of a speech by British Labor party leader **NEIL KINNOCK** for a speech. This, among other damaging reports, forced Biden to drop out of the race.

1992 **JAN DAVIS** and **MARK LEE** became the first married couple in space during a shuttle mission.

1992 **MONICA SELES** won her sixth Grand Slam title, beating **ARANTXA SANCHEZ VICARIO** in the U.S. Open final.

SEPTEMBER 13

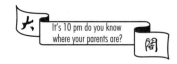

It's 10 pm do you know where your parents are?

BIRTHDAYS

- **JUDITH "MISS MANNERS" MARTIN** Etiquette expert. (Washington, DC) Her first job was with the *Washington Post* in 1958. She was a copy girl in the women's section. Most of her time was spent answering etiquette questions. In 1978, she started her own column, now in over 300 papers. Year/**Age:** 1995/**57** 1996/**58** 1997/**59**

- **CLAUDETTE COLBERT** Actress. (Born Lily Claudette Chauchoin in Paris, France) She won an Oscar for best actress in *It Happened One Night* in 1934. Year/**Age:** 1995/**92** 1996/**93** 1997/**94**

- **JACQUELINE BISSET** Actress. (England) She played Dean Martin's love interest in *Airport* and was also in *Bullitt, The Deep*, and *Wild Orchid*. Says her name rhymes with "kiss it." Year/**Age:** 1995/**51** 1996/**52** 1997/**53**

- **BARBARA BAIN** Actress. (Chicago, IL) She was in the "Mission Impossible" TV series from 1966 to 1973 and won 3 Emmys for that show. She was also in "Space 1999." Year/**Age:** 1995/**61** 1996/**62** 1997/**63**

- **MEL TORMÉ** Singer/composer. (Born Melvin Tormé in Chicago, IL) He wrote "The Christmas Song" which was a big hit for Nat "King" Cole. He composed it in 20 minutes on a hot July day in 1946, and it's been recorded by many artists. The "Velvet Fog" made his professional debut at age 4. Year/**Age:** 1995/**70** 1996/**71** 1997/**72**

- **DAVID CLAYTON-THOMAS** Singer. (Born David Thomsett) Formerly of BLOOD, SWEAT & TEARS. Their biggest hit: "Spinning Wheel" in 1969. He sang on the original "Bud Light" commercial, with the Clydesdale horse prancing through the snow. Year/**Age:** 1995/**54** 1996/**55** 1997/**56**

- **FRED SILVERMAN** Producer. (NYC) Was head of the NBC Network, 1978-81. Before that he ran the ABC and CBS Entertainment divisions. Year/**Age:** 1995/**58** 1996/**59** 1997/**60**

- **EILEEN FULTON** Actress. "As The World Turns." Year/**Age:** 1995/**62** 1996/**63** 1997/**64**

- **PETER CETERA** Singer. (Chicago, IL) Vocalist/bass player for the group, CHICAGO, and he's had some hits on his own, including "Glory of Love" in 1986. Year/**Age:** 1995/**51** 1996/**52** 1997/**53**

- **BILL MONROE** C&W singer. (Rosine, KY) He's called the father of modern bluegrass. His "Blue Moon of Kentucky" became a classic in country music. Year/**Age:** 1995/**83** 1996/**84** 1997/**85**

- **NELL CARTER** Actress. (Birmingham, AL) Starred in the TV sitcom "Gimme a Break" as Nell Harper and "Hangin' With Mr. Cooper." Year/**Age:** 1995/**47** 1996/**48** 1997/**49**

- **ROALD DAHL** Author. (1916-1990 – England) Wrote *Charlie and the Chocolate Factory* adapted for film as *Willy Wonka and the Chocolate Factory*. He also wrote the screenplay for the film *Chitty-Chitty-Bang-Bang*. He was married to actress Patricia Neal until their divorce in 1983. (Died 11-23-90.)

- **DICK HAYMES** Singer/actor. (1918-1980 – Buenos Aires, Argentina) Great ballad singer of the 1940s. Big hit: "Little White Lies." Movies: *State Fair* and and *All Ashore*. Rita Hayworth was one of his wives. (Died 3-28-80.)

- **MILTON S. HERSHEY** Tycoon. (1857) He built the first factory to mass produce milk chocolate. It made him a multi-millionaire.

FACTS FROM THE PAST

1814 **FRANCIS SCOTT KEY** wrote the words to the **"STAR SPANGLED BANNER."** In 1942 we first started singing our National Anthem at professional baseball games. The melody comes from "Anachreon In Heaven," an old English drinking song.

1899 Real estate broker **HENRY BLISS** was stepping down from a New York City streetcar at Central Park West and 74th Street, when he was struck by a car driven by Arthur Smith. Police rushed the man to nearby Roosevelt Hospital where he died a short time later, becoming the **FIRST AUTOMOBILE FATALITY.** Arthur Smith was arrested, held on $1,000 bail, and later released.

1939 The first helicopter flight was made by **IGOR SIKORSKY**.

1948 **MARGARET CHASE SMITH** (R/ME) was elected to the U.S. Senate; the first woman to serve in both Houses of Congress.

1949 The **LADIES PROFESSIONAL GOLF ASSOCIATION** of America was formed in NYC, with **PATTY BERG** as its first president.

1965 The song "Yesterday" was released as an American single, despite Mary Wells' plea to the **BEATLES** to give her the U.S. release. Paul McCartney recorded the song without the rest of the **BEATLES** in the studio. The song has become the most recorded in history.

1969 **JOHN LENNON, YOKO ONO** and the **PLASTIC ONO BAND** played their first concert at the Toronto Rock 'n' Roll Festival.

1969 "Suspicious Minds" became **ELVIS PRESLEY**'s first #1 single since "Good Luck Charm" in 1962. It turned out to be his last #1 hit.

1971 A 30-year-old Marine captain, **WAYNE ROLLINGS**, stationed at Kaneohe, HI, began doing **SIT-UPS**, and didn't stop until he had done a total of 17,000 in 7 hours, 27 minutes.

1989 In Chicago, IL, Jockey **PAT DAY** rode eight winners on **ARLINGTON INTERNATIONAL RACECOURSE**'s nine-race program to set a North American record. His total winning commissions were about $10,000 for the day.

1989 Francis T. "Fay" Vincent, Jr. became the **8TH COMMISSIONER OF BASEBALL**, succeeding A. Bartlett Giamatti who died of a heart attack two weeks earlier. His term was to run until 1994. He resigned under pressure from team owners September 7, 1992.

1993 Israeli Prime Minister Yitzhak Rabin and PLO Chairman Yasser Arafat signed an agreement at the White House in Washington D.C. in an attempt at peace between the **JEWS AND ARABS** following 45-years of war.

1993 **DAVID LETTERMAN** replacement **CONAN O'BRIEN**'s new late-night program on NBC-TV premiered.

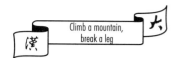

Climb a mountain,
break a leg

SEPTEMBER 14

BIRTHDAYS

- **JOE PENNY** Actor. (London, England) Played Sal on "Forever Fernwood." Starred on TV's "Jake and the Fatman." Year/**Age**: 1995/**39** 1996/**40** 1997/**41**

- **WALTER KOENIG** Actor. (Chicago, IL) Played Ensign Chekov on "Star Trek." Year/**Age**: 1995/**57** 1996/**58** 1997/**59**

- **MARY CROSBY** Actress. (Born Mary Frances Crosby in Los Angeles, CA) Daughter of Bing and Kathryn Crosby, she's probably best known as the person who shot J.R. on the "Dallas" TV series. Year/**Age**: 1995/**36** 1996/**37** 1997/**38**

- **KATE MILLETT** Feminist author. (St. Paul, MN) Wrote *Sexual Politics*. Year/**Age**: 1995/**61** 1996/**62** 1997/**63**

- **JOEY HEATHERTON** Entertainer. (Born Davenie Johanna Heatherton in Rockville Centre, NY) Year/**Age**: 1995/**51** 1996/**52** 1997/**53**

- **ZOE CALDWELL** Actress. (Australia) *Medea*. Year/**Age**: 1995/**62** 1996/**63** 1997/**64**

- **CLAYTON MOORE** Actor. (Chicago, IL) He portrayed "The Lone Ranger" for many years. He still makes personal appearances around the country and won the right to wear his mask again. Year/**Age**: 1995/**81** 1996/**82** 1997/**83**

- **JOHN LEHMAN** Former Navy Secretary. (Philadelphia, PA) He was the youngest Secretary of Navy when chosen by the Reagan administration to serve from 1981-87. Year/**Age**: 1995/**53** 1996/**54** 1997/**55**

- **FAITH FORD** Actress. (Alexandria, LA) Corky Sherwood Forrest on TV's "Murphy Brown." Year/**Age**: 1995/**31** 1996/**32** 1997/**33**

- **BARRY COWSILL** Singer. "The Rain, the Park & Other Things" in 1967 was the COWSILLS' biggest hit. Year/**Age**: 1995/**41** 1996/**42** 1997/**43**

- **JEAN SMART** Actress. "Designing Women." Year/**Age**: 1995/**36** 1996/**37** 1997/**38**

- **BUD PALMER** Sportscaster. Gravel-voiced ABC-TV correspondent. Year/**Age**: 1995/**71** 1996/**72** 1997/**73**

- **ALLAN BLOOM** Author. (1920-1992 – Indianapolis, IN) He wrote the bestseller *Closing of the American Mind*.

- **HUGHES RUDD** Newsman. (1921-1992 – Wichita, KS) He was a news correspondent with CBS for 20 years before going to ABC in 1979. He anchored the "CBS Morning News" from 1973-77. (Died 10-13-92.)

- **MARGARET SANGER** Feminist. (1883-1966 – Corning, NY.) Nurse/founder of the birth control movement in the U.S. in 1916 and first president of the International Planned Parenthood Foundation in 1953. (Died 9-6-66.)

- **CHARLES DANA GIBSON** Artist. (1867-1944 – Roxbury, MA) He created the famous "Gibson Girls," popular in the 1890s. They were elegant, athletic girls called the "perfect women."

FACTS FROM THE PAST

1741 Composer **GEORGE HANDEL** completed "**THE MESSIAH**" (best known for "The Hallelujah Chorus.") He worked day and night for 24 days, because he wanted it completed for an orphans' charity concert. He stayed in his room, drinking only coffee and when he finished a servant found him in tears. He thought he had seen God and heaven as he wrote.

1901 President William McKinley died of a gunshot wound. Vice President Theodore Roosevelt became president upon his death. At 42, he became the **YOUNGEST PRESIDENT IN U.S. HISTORY** to be sworn into office. (John Kennedy was 43.)

1927 Composer **GENE AUSTON** recorded his song, "My Blue Heaven." It sold 7 million copies. Auston received the first gold record.

1927 Dancer **ISADORA DUNCAN** was strangled to death when her long scarf got caught in the wheels of an open car in which she was riding.

1955 **LITTLE RICHARD**'s first recording session produced "Tutti Frutti." The title was taken from an ice cream flavor.

1963 **MARIANNE FISHER** of Aberdeen, South Dakota, gave birth to **AMERICA'S FIRST QUINTUPLETS**, 4 boys and a girl.

1965 "**MY MOTHER THE CAR**" debuted on NBC-TV, starring **JERRY VAN DYKE** as an attorney whose deceased mother was reincarnated as an automobile, a 1928 Porter. The car's voice was Ann Sothern.

1968 **DENNY McLAIN** of the Detroit Tigers became the first major league player in 34 years to **WIN 30 GAMES IN A SEASON**. The Tigers beat the Oakland Athletics.

1975 Pope Paul VI proclaimed **ELIZABETH ANN SETON** as America's **FIRST NATIVE-BORN SAINT**. Another first: women were allowed to participate in the canonization ceremony.

1982 **PRINCESS GRACE** of Monaco (formerly actress Grace Kelly) died at age 52 of injuries received after her car ran off a 45-foot embankment near Laturbe, France. She was the first movie actress to be pictured on a postage stamp.

1984 56-year-old balloonist **JOE KITTINGER** left Caribou, MA, in a 10-story-tall helium-filled balloon named "Rosie O'Grady's Balloon of Peace" and became the first person to solo across the Atlantic Ocean in a balloon, reaching the French coast near Cap Breton, in bad weather on SEPTEMBER 17th. He crash-landed in a wind and rain storm, suffering a broken ankle when he was thrown from the balloon's gondola during the landing. His 84-hour flight covered about 3,500 miles.

1985 "**THE GOLDEN GIRLS**" TV sitcom starring Bea Arthur, Estelle Getty, Betty White, and Rue McClanahan premiered on NBC.

1987 The *Guinness Book of World Records* recognized Dick Clark and "American Bandstand" for being the longest-running TV show.

1987 Tony Magnuson set the **SKATEBOARD HIGH-JUMP RECORD** by clearing nine-and-a-half feet above the top of a U-ramp.

SEPTEMBER 15

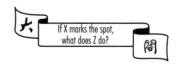

If X marks the spot,
what does Z do?

BIRTHDAYS

• **MERLIN OLSEN** Ex-football-player-turned actor. (Logan, UT) He was a member of the fearsome foursome of the LA Rams. He's a member of the Football Hall of Fame and a commentator for NBC. He was on "Little House on the Prairie" and "Father Murphy" TV series and is spokesman for F.T.D. florists. Year/Age: 1995/55 1996/56 1997/57

• **TOMMY LEE JONES** Actor. (San Saba, TX) Appeared in *House of Cards*, *The Client*, *The Fugitive*, *Natural Born Killers*, and *J.F.K.* He won an Emmy for his role in *The Executioner's Song* as convicted killer Gary Gilmore. Year/Age: 1995/49 1996/50 1997/51

• **JACKIE COOPER** Actor/director/producer. (Los Angeles, CA) Nominated for best actor in 1930 for the movie, *Skippy*. He was a child star in the *Our Gang* comedies, wrote a book and played Ensign Pulver in Mister Roberts on Broadway. Appeared in the Superman movies. Year/Age: 1995/73 1996/74 1997/75

• **GAYLORD PERRY** Baseball Hall of Fame pitcher. (Williamston, NC) He won 314 games. He has pitched for 6 teams and is the only man with Cy Young Awards in both leagues. He retired in 1983. Year/Age: 1995/57 1996/58 1997/59

• **JIMMY GILMER** Entertainer. (Amarillo, TX) Norman Petty produced the FIREBALLS after leaving Buddy Holly and the Crickets, and after the FIREBALLS split and re-grouped, they teamed up with Jimmy. His biggest hit: "Sugar Shack" in 1963. Year/Age: 1995/55 1996/56 1997/57

• **PRINCE HENRY of BRITAIN** Son of Prince Charles and Princess Diana, he is 3rd in line for the throne, behind his dad and brother Prince William. Year/Age: 1995/11 1996/12 1997/13

• **OLIVER STONE** Screenwriter & director. *Platoon, Born on the Fourth of July, Heaven and Earth, Natural Born Killers,* and *J.F.K.* Year/Age: 1995/49 1996/50 1997/51

• **ERNEST BYNER** Football. (Midgeville, GA) With the Redskins and Browns. Year/Age: 1995/33 1996/34 1997/35

• **BOBBY SHORT** Singer/pianist. (Danville, IL) His 1971 autobiography is titled *Black and White Baby*. Year/Age: 1995/69 1996/70 1997/71

• **DAN MARINO** Football quarterback. (Pittsburgh, PA) He threw 30 or more touchdown passes in 1984, '85 & '86, becoming the only NFL quarterback to accomplish this feat. He had a record 5,084 yards in 1984. Year/Age: 1995/34 1996/35 1997/36

• **JOE MORRIS** Football. (Ft. Bragg, NC) With the New York Giants. Year/Age: 1995/35 1996/36 1997/37

• **NORM CROSBY** Comedian. (Boston, MA) Year/Age: 1995/67 1996/68 1997/69

• **ROY ACUFF** C&W singer. (1903-1992 – Maynardsville, TN) Appeared on the Grand Ole Opry for the first time February 5, 1938. Elected to the Country Music Hall of Fame in 1962. His biggest hit: "The Wabash Cannonball." He was named the "King of Country Music" by baseball great Dizzy Dean. (Died 11-23-92.)

• **MARGARET LOCKWOOD** Actress. 1916-1990 – Born Margaret Day in Pakistan) Films include: *The Wicked Lady, Cast a Dark Shadow,* and the Alfred Hitchcock classic *The Lady Vanishes*. (Died 7-15-90.)

• **SHEILAH GRAHAM** Columnist. (1904-1988) One of Hollywood's most feared Hollywood gossip columnists. (Died 11-17-88.)

• **JULIAN "CANNONBALL" ADDERLEY** Saxophonist. (1928-1975 – Tampa, FL) His biggest hit with his quintet: "Mercy, Mercy, Mercy" in 1967. (Died 8-8-75.)

• **AGATHA CHRISTIE** Mystery writer. (1890-1976 – Torquay, England) She wrote 66 mystery novels, 13 short stories, one book of poetry, one volume of Christmas verse and stories, an autobiography and the world's longest running play, *The Mousetrap,* on stage continuously since Nov. 25, 1952. Her works appear in 103 languages and have sold over 500 million books. Many of her works have been turned into films, including *Murder on the Orient Express*. (Died 1-12-76.)

• **WILLIAM HOWARD TAFT** 27th U.S. President. (1857-1930 – Cincinnati, OH) First president to toss the baseball on opening day. Taft stood 6' 2" and weighed 325 pounds—the heaviest President in U.S. history. He got stuck in a bathtub once, so they had to order a custom tub. (Died 3-8-30.)

FACTS FROM THE PAST

1949 "THE LONE RANGER," based on the radio show of the same name, made its television debut on ABC with Clayton Moore as the masked hero and Jay Silverheels as Tonto.

1959 Soviet Premier **NIKITA KHRUSHCHEV** began a 13-day visit to the U.S. He was a former sheepherder. During his visit, the door to detente was pried open, but 7 months later, it was slammed shut by the shooting down of an American spy plane over Russia.

1969 **ED SULLIVAN** released "The Sulli-Gulli," his first and only rock record. He was hoping it would create a new dance.

1971 TV crime show "COLUMBO" debuted on NBC with star **PETER FALK**.

1972 The **WATERGATE** indictments began with charges against seven low-ranking perpetrators, including two former White House aides, G. Gordon Liddy and E. Howard Hunt. At that time, President Richard Milhous Nixon hadn't yet been publicly linked to the famous burglary and cover-up. He was reelected by a landslide over George McGovern less than two months later.

1978 Muhammad Ali defeated Leon Spinks in 15 rounds in New Orleans to win an unprecedented **4TH WORLD HEAVYWEIGHT BOXING TITLE.**

1982 The first issue of *USA Today* was published by **AL NEUHARTH**.

1992 Mississippi State coach **JACKIE SHERRILL** apologized for having castrated a bull calf at practice, which he had arranged as a motivational ploy before a game against Texas.

SEPTEMBER 16

BIRTHDAYS

- **RICHARD MARX** Singer. (Chicago, IL) Hits include "Satisfied" and "Right Here Waiting." Year/**Age**: 1995/**32** 1996/**33** 1997/**34**

- **DAVE BELLAMY** Singer/musician. (Darby, FL) He and his brother Howard make up the BELLAMY BROTHERS. Biggest hit: "Let Your Love Flow" in 1976. Dave wrote "Spiders and Snakes," a hit for Jim Stafford. Year/**Age**: 1995/**45** 1996/**46** 1997/**47**

- **ED BEGLEY, JR.** Actor. (Los Angeles, CA) On TV's "St. Elsewhere," and in films *Parenthood* and *Meet the Applegates*. Year/**Age**: 1995/**46** 1996/**47** 1997/**48**

- **BETTY KELLY** Singer. Hits with MARTHA & THE VANDELLAS: "Dancing in the Street" and "Heat Wave." Year/**Age**: 1995/**51** 1996/**52** 1997/**53**

- **LAUREN BACALL** Actress. (Born Betty Joan Perski in NYC) She was married to Humphrey Bogart from 1945 until his death in 1957. She made her film debut opposite him in *To Have & Have Not* in 1944 when she was 19. They met and fell in love during the filming. Year/**Age**: 1995/**71** 1996/**72** 1997/**73**

- **PETER FALK** Actor. (NYC) Nominated for supporting actor in 1960 for *Murder, Inc.* and in 1961 for *Pocketful of Miracles*. Probably best known for his portrayal of "Columbo" on TV which debuted on September 15, 1971, as part of the "NBC Mystery Movie." He made $125,000 per episode. Also TV soap "Love of Life." Year/**Age**: 1995/**68** 1996/**69** 1997/**70**

- **KENNY JONES** Drummer. (England) He was with the group SMALL FACES. Later, the group became just FACES and Rod Stewart became the leader. Their biggest hit: "Stay With Me" in 1972. Year/**Age**: 1995/**47** 1996/**48** 1997/**49**

- **B. B. KING** Singer/guitarist. (Born Riley B. King in Itta Bena, MS) He influenced many guitarists. His biggest hit: "The Thrill is Gone" in 1970. He started as a DJ, spinning R&B records on a radio station in West Memphis, AR. He recorded more than 50 albums. Year/**Age**: 1995/**70** 1996/**71** 1997/**72**

- **OREL HERSHISER** Baseball. (Buffalo, NY) Long-time Dodgers pitcher. In 1988 he threw 59 straight shut-out innings. Year/**Age**: 1995/**37** 1996/**38** 1997/**39**

- **ELGIN BAYLOR** Former basketball star. (Washington, DC) With the LA Lakers. Year/**Age**: 1995/**60** 1996/**61** 1997/**62**

- **DAVID COPPERFIELD** Magician. (Matuchen, NJ) Made the Statue of Liberty disappear in 1983. Year/**Age**: 1995/**38** 1996/**39** 1997/**40**

- **CHARLIE BYRD** Musician. (Chuckatuck, VA) Biggest hit: "Desafinado" with Stan Getz in 1962. Year/**Age**: 1995/**71** 1996/**72** 1997/**73**

- **ALLEN FUNT** TV producer. (NYC) He created and hosted "Candid Camera" for many years. He got the idea when he was in the army. He recorded servicemen's candid gripes and broadcast them on Armed Forces Radio. His first show was on radio called "Candid Microphone." Year/**Age**: 1995/**81** 1996/**82** 1997/**83**

- **ROBIN YOUNT** Former Milwaukee Brewer outfielder. (Danville, IL) American League MVP shortstop in 1982 and in centerfield in 1989. First AL player to capture this honor at two different positions since Hank Greenberg in 1940. Year/**Age**: 1995/**40** 1996/**41** 1997/**42**

- **GEORGE CHAKIRIS** Actor. An American dancer and leading man. He won an Oscar for *West Side Story*. Year/**Age**: 1995/**62** 1996/**63** 1997/**64**

- **ANN FRANCIS** Actress. (Ossining, NY) She appeared in *Blackboard Jungle*, *Funny Girl*, and *Laguna Heat*. Year/**Age**: 1995/**63** 1996/**64** 1997/**65**

- **JACK KELLY** Actor/game show host. (1927-1992 – Astoria, NY) He played Bart Maverick, brother to James Garner's Bret in the TV series "Maverick." Also appeared in films *To Hell and Back* and *She-Devil*. He was the former mayor of Huntington Beach, CA. (Died 11-7-92.)

- **JAMES CASH PENNEY** Tycoon. (1875-1971 – Hamilton, MO) Founded the J.C. PENNEY department stores. (Died 2-12-71.)

- **HENRY V** The "hero king." (1387-1422) In his youth he was wild, but after he assumed the British crown, he became virtuous. He married the French King's daughter, but shortly after the wedding, he caught dysentery and died. (Died 8-31-1422.)

FACTS FROM THE PAST

1782 The **GREAT SEAL OF THE UNITED STATES** was impressed on an official document for the first time, authorizing George Washington to negotiate a prisoner-of-war agreement. The design for the seal was developed by group led by Thomas Jefferson.

1840 The **TERM "O.K." WAS BORN**. A new Democratic political group was organized in New York City. It was called "The O.K. Club." The initials stood for the birthplace of U.S. President Martin Van Buren: Old Kinderhook, New York.

1908 **GENERAL MOTORS** was founded by entrepreneur William Crapo "Billy" Durant of Flint, MI.

1963 An independent label, Swan Records, released the **BEATLES'** "She Loves You" after Capitol rejected it. The single failed to click until the group dominated the charts in 1964.

1964 Producer **JACK GOOD** premiered his ABC-TV show "Shindig." It featured British and American rock entertainers, go-go-dancers and house band, the Shindogs. The first show starred **BOBBY SHERMAN**, the **EVERLY BROTHERS**, **SAM COOKE** and the **RIGHTEOUS BROTHERS**.

1968 The final **"ANDY GRIFFITH SHOW"** aired on network TV.

1992 **BARBRA STREISAND** ended her six-year absence from the stage to sing at a fund-raiser for presidential candidate **BILL CLINTON**. She sang "Happy Days Are Here Again," and "It Had to be You" and, she added, "Hillary too." The event raised $1.1 million in Beverly Hills, CA.

SEPTEMBER 17

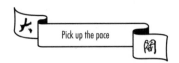
Pick up the pace

BIRTHDAYS

- **MARCUS SANDERS**. (Oklahoma City, OK) Number 1 hit with HI-FIVE: "I Like The Way (The Kissing Game)." Year/**Age**: 1995/**22** 1996/**23** 1997/**24**

- **JOHN RITTER** Actor. (Born Jonathan Ritter in Burbank, CA) Appeared on TV's "Three's Company," "Three's a Crowd," "Hooperman," "Hearts Afire," and in a film satirizing TV, *Stay Tuned*. His dad was the late cowboy and movie actor, Tex Ritter. Year/**Age**: 1995/**47** 1996/**48** 1997/**49**

- **FEE WAYBILL** Singer. (Born John Waldo in Omaha, NE) Leader of the TUBES. Hit in 1983, "She's A Beauty." The group appeared in the Olivia Newton-John film *Xanadu*. Year/**Age**: 1995/**45** 1996/**46** 1997/**47**

- **KYLE CHANDLER** Actor. Appeared on TV's "Homefront" as Jeff Metcalf and Pvt. Wiliam Griner on "Tour of Duty." Year/**Age**: 1995/**30** 1996/**31** 1997/**32**

- **ANNE BANCROFT** Actress. (Born Anna Marie Luisa Italiano in NYC) She won an Oscar in 1962 for *The Miracle Worker*, was nominated in 1967 for *The Graduate* and also appeared in *Agnes of God, Malice*, and *Point of No Return*. She and Mel Brooks have been married since 1964. Year/**Age**: 1995/**64** 1996/**65** 1997/**66**

- **RODDY McDOWALL** Actor. (London, England) He won a Tony Award for supporting actor in *The Fighting Cock* in 1960 and is known by early movie-goers for *Lassie, Come Home* in 1943, *How Green was My Valley* and *Planet of the Apes* in 1968. Also starred in *Fright Night* and *Overboard*. Year/**Age**: 1995/**67** 1996/**68** 1997/**69**

- **KEN KESEY** Author. (La Junta, CA) Author of *One Flew Over the Cuckoo's Nest*. Year/**Age**: 1995/**60** 1996/**61** 1997/**62**

- **RITA RUDNER** Comedian. Frequent guest on "Late Night with David Letterman." Year/**Age**: 1995/**40** 1996/**41** 1997/**42**

- **LAMONTE McLEMORE** Singer. (St. Louis, MO) With the 5TH DIMENSION. Biggest hit: "Aquarius" from the musical *Hair*. Year/**Age**: 1995/**56** 1996/**57** 1997/**58**

- **PAUL BENEDICT** Actor. (Silver City, NM) Played Harry Bentley on "The Jeffersons." Appeared in *The Freshmen* with Marlon Brando. Year/**Age**: 1995/**57** 1996/**58** 1997/**59**

- **GEORGE BLANDA** Football. Q.B. who spent 26 years as an active pro football player, scoring a record 2,002 points. At age 43, he won 4 games and tied one for the Raiders with last-minute passing and kicking heroics. Year/**Age**: 1995/**68** 1996/**69** 1997/**70**

- **ORLANDO CEPEDA** Baseball player. (Puerto Rico) Played for the Giants and St. Louis Cardinals. Year/**Age**: 1995/**58** 1996/**59** 1997/**60**

- **JOE RUDI** Baseball. Oakland A's World Series hero in 1972. Year/**Age**: 1995/**49** 1996/**50** 1997/**51**

- **PAT CROWLEY** Actress. Played Georgia Cameron, Joe's romantic interest on the cop show "Joe Forrester" and appeared in the TV series "Please Don't Eat the Daisies." Year/**Age**: 1995/**66** 1996/**67** 1997/**68**

- **BILL BLACK** Bassist. (1926-1965 – Memphis, TN) His combo's biggest hit: "White Silver Sands" in 1960. At one time, he was the bass player in Elvis Presley's band and backed Elvis on his early recordings. During the 1960s he was a warm-up act during the Beatles' U.S. tour. (Died 10-21-65.)

- **HANK WILLIAMS, SR.** C&W singer. (1923-1953 – Born Hiram Henry Williams in Georgiana, AL) He didn't read or write, but composed over 120 songs. Died in the back of a Cadillac enroute to a performance in Canton, OH. The cause was reported as a heart attack brought on by excessive drinking. (Died 1-1-53.)

FACTS FROM THE PAST

1787 The **U.S. CONSTITUTION** was completed and signed by a majority of delegates attending the Constitutional Convention in Philadelphia, PA., including George Washington. The original is displayed in the National Archives in Washington, DC, in a bulletproof display case filled with helium and water vapor to preserve it by maintaining proper humidity. Today is Citizenship Day.

1908 **ORVILLE WRIGHT** and Lieutenant **THOMAS SELFRIDGE** were demonstrating the Wright Brothers' latest plane for the army when a guy wire broke loose and fouled a propeller. Orville's left leg and hip were smashed. Selfridge had a fractured skull and died that night, becoming the **FIRST AIRPLANE FATALITY**.

1911 C.P. Rogers took off from New York City, landing 82 hours later in Pasadena, Ca, completing the **FIRST TRANSCONTINENTAL AIRPLANE FLIGHT.**

1955 Capitol Records released a **LES PAUL** single called "Magic Melody, Part Two," that it claims is the **SHORTEST SONG EVER RELEASED**. The tune consisted of only two notes — the last two notes of the musical phrase "Shave and a Haircut, Two Bits."

1957 Two male attorneys stood in as actress **SOPHIA LOREN** and producer **CARLO PONTI** were married by proxy in a ceremony in Juarez, Mexico. The Italian government did not consider the couple legally married until 1966.

1962 U.S. space officials announced the selection of **NINE NEW ASTRONAUTS**, including **NEIL A. ARMSTRONG**, who would become the first man to step onto the moon.

1967 The **DOORS** performed "Light My Fire" and "People Are Strange" on "The Ed Sullivan Show." **JIM MORRISON** promised to change or omit the line "Girl, we couldn't get much higher" in "Light My Fire" then sang it anyway.

1983 "Miss New York," **VANESSA WILLIAMS**, became the first African-American to be crowned Miss America. She resigned July 23, 1984, following a controversy surrounding the publication of explicit pictures.

1986 **WILLIAM H. REHNQUIST**, from Shorewood, WI, was confirmed by the Senate as the nation's 16th Chief Justice by a 65-33 vote.

Study to be a rocket scientist

SEPTEMBER 18

BIRTHDAYS

- **RYNE SANDBERG** Baseball player. (Spokane, WA) In 1992 he signed an extended contract with the Chicago Cubs for five years, at $30.5 million. The *Chicago Tribune* paid $20.5 million for the whole team in 1981. He retired in 1994 leaving behind a multi-million dollar contract. Year/**Age**: 1995/**36** 1996/**37** 1997/**38**

- **HOLLY ROBINSON** TV's "21 Jump Street" and "Hanging with Mr. Cooper." Year/**Age**: 1995/**31** 1996/**32** 1997/**33**

- **BILLY SIMS** Football. (St. Louis, MO) Year/**Age**: 1995/**40** 1996/**41** 1997/**42**

- **RICKY BELL** Musician. With the group BELL BIV DEVOE. Biggest hit: "Poison." Year/**Age**: 1995/**28** 1996/**29** 1997/**30**

- **JIMME RODGERS** Singer. (Camas, WA) His career was stopped from 1967 to 1969 after a suspicious assault on a freeway in Los Angeles, resulting in a skull fracture. Biggest hit: "Honeycomb" in 1957. Year/**Age**: 1995/**61** 1996/**62** 1997/**63**

- **JACK WARDEN** Actor. (Newark, NJ) TV/movie character actor, he was best supporting actor in *Shampoo*. Was also in *From Here to Eternity*, *All the President's Men*, and *Problem Child*. He also appeared on the TV series "Crazy Like a Fox." Year/**Age**: 1995/**75** 1996/**76** 1997/**77**

- **ROBERT BLAKE** Actor. (Born Michael Gubitosi in Nutley, NJ) He starred in *In Cold Blood* and in the "Baretta" TV series. As a child, he appeared in the "Our Gang," "Little Beaver," and "Red Ryder" series. Year/**Age**: 1995/**62** 1996/**63** 1997/**64**

- **ROSSANO BRAZZI** Italian actor. (Italy) He appeared in *Three Coins in a Fountain* and *South Pacific*. Year/**Age**: 1995/**79** 1996/**80** 1997/**81**

- **FRANKIE AVALON** Singer. (Born Francis Avallone in Philadelphia, PA) Biggest hit: "Venus" in 1959. He appeared in *Back to the Beach* with Annette Funicello. He now sells tanning products and a treatment for arthritis. Year/**Age**: 1995/**55** 1996/**56** 1997/**57**

- **JOHN RHODES** Former House Majority Leader. Year/**Age**: 1995/**79** 1996/**80** 1997/**81**

- **DEE DEE RAMONE** Bass player. (New York, NY) With the punk rock group RAMONES. They got their name from a pseudonym Paul McCartney used during a 1960 tour of Scotland. Year/**Age**: 1995/**43** 1996/**44** 1997/**45**

- **HARVEY HADDIX** Baseball pitcher. (1925-1994) Left-handed Pittsburgh pitcher who lost a historic 12-inning perfect game to the Milwaukee Braves in the 13th inning on May 26, 1959. (Died 1-8-94.)

- **FRED WILLARD** Actor. (Shaker Heights, OH) "Fernwood 2-Night." Year/**Age**: 1995/**56** 1996/**57** 1997/**58**

- **TEDDY KING** Singer. (1929-1977 – Boston, MA) Biggest hit: "Mr. Wonderful" in 1956.

- **GRETA GARBO** Actress. (1905-1990 – Born Greta Gustaffsson in Stockholm, Sweden) She was nominated four times for Oscars for best actress between 1929 and 1939. She could not speak a word of English when she was brought to Hollywood. Her first screen words were: "Gimme a whiskey with ginger ale and don't be stingy." Films include: *Camille*, *Grand Hotel*, and *Ninotchka*. (Died 4-15-90.)

- **SAMUEL JOHNSON** Writer. (1709-1784 – England) Known as the Hercules of Literature. One time he told a group of women, "Ladies, I am tame, you may stroke me." (Died 12-12-1784.)

FACTS FROM THE PAST

1769 The **FIRST SPINET PIANO** was built in the U.S. by John Harris. It had a 3 to 4 octave range.

1793 The cornerstone of the north wing of the Capitol building in Federal City (Washington, DC) was laid by **GEORGE WASHINGTON.** He was wearing a Mason's apron, especially embroidered for him by Madame LaFayette. In the cornerstone is a silver plaque with the details of the ceremony written on it. There were no streets, so one had to cross the stream to get there.

1895 The **FIRST CHIROPRACTIC TREATMENT** was given by **DANIEL DAVID PALMER,** who "adjusted" the back of Harvey Lillard in Davenport, IA.

1927 **CBS BEGAN** on this date with 16 stations. William Paley from Chicago put the Columbia Broadcasting System network together The cost was between $250,000 and $450,000 for controlling interest. Paley became president of CBS in 1928 at the age of 27.

1931 RCA Victor demonstrated the **FIRST 33$^1/_3$ (RPM) RECORD.** Nipper the dog was pictured on the label.

1947 Carnegie Hall had its first country show with **EARNEST TUBB** and **ROY ACUFF** as headliners.

1961 U.N. Secretary General **DAG HAMMARSKJOLD** was killed in a plane crash near Ndola, Northern Rhodesia creating a U.N. crisis.

1970 **JIMI HENDRIX,** one of the greatest rock guitarists ever, was found dead in a London apartment. He was 27. The coroner said Hendrix choked on vomit after taking barbiturates.

1975 The FBI captured newspaper heiress **PATRICIA HEARST** in San Francisco, along with William and Emily Harris, 19 months after Hearst was kidnapped, recruited into the Symbionese Liberation Army (SLA) and participated in terrorist activities as "Tanya."

1989 **HURRICANE HUGO** hit the U.S. Virgin Islands and Puerto Rico, damaging 80 percent of the buildings on St. Thomas and St. Croix. President Bush sent 1,000 military police to the Virgin Islands after two days of widespread looting.

1991 **PRESIDENT BUSH** said he was "fed up" and would send war planes to escort U.N. helicopters looking for hidden Iraqi weapons if **SADDAM HUSSEIN** continued to block work of weapon inspection teams.

1993 18-year-old Kimberly Clarice Aiken was chosen as the 1994 **MISS AMERICA**, pledging to use her reign to help the homeless.

SEPTEMBER 19

Use condominiums for safe sex

BIRTHDAYS

- **JOE MORGAN** Baseball. (Bonham, TX) Cincinnati second baseman. In the Baseball Hall of Fame. He won back to back MVP titles in 1975 and 1976. Year/Age: 1995/**52** 1996/**53** 1997/**54**

- **REX SMITH** Singer. (Jacksonville, FL.) Appeared in the TV movie *Sooner or Later* where he sang his hit, "You Take My Breath Away," and co-starred with Linda Ronstadt in *Pirates of Penzance* at the Uris Theatre in NYC. Year/Age: 1995/**39** 1996/**40** 1997/**41**

- **DAN HAMPTON** Football. Defensive tackle for the Chicago Bears. He had 10 knee operations, 5 on each leg. Year/Age: 1995/**37** 1996/**38** 1997/**39**

- **PAUL WILLIAMS** Singer/composer. (Omaha, NE) He has written many songs, plus themes for TV and movies, including: "Love Boat Theme" and songs for THE CARPENTERS. Won an Oscar for "Evergreen" in 1976. Year/Age: 1995/**55** 1996/**56** 1997/**57**

- **ADAM WEST** Actor. (Walla Walla, WA) Played Batman on TV. After the show was canceled, the only job he could get was being shot out of a cannon in a circus. In the film *The New Age*. The super-hero Batman was inspired by a Leonardo da Vinci painting. Year/Age: 1995/**67** 1996/**68** 1997/**69**

- **JIM ABBOTT** Baseball. (Flint, MI) The N.Y. Yankee pitcher was born without a right hand. He pitched a no-hitter September 4, 1993. Year/Age: 1995/**28** 1996/**29** 1997/**30**

- **TWIGGY** Actress/model. (Born Leslie Hornby in London, England) Fashion trendsetter in the 1960s with the "mini" skirt, she was much in demand as a model. She weighed 92 pounds and her figure was 31-23-31. She earned $2 million in royalties from her Twiggy doll and Yardley cosmetics. Films include: *The Boyfriend* and *Madame Sousatzka*. In 1991, appeared in TV series "The Princesses." Twiggy is now using the name of Lawson. Year/Age: 1995/**46** 1996/**47** 1997/**48**

- **DAVID McCALLUM** Actor. (Scotland) He played Illya Kuryakin in the TV series, "The Man from U.N.C.L.E." Year/Age: 1995/**62** 1996/**63** 1997/**64**

- **BILL MEDLEY** Singer. (Santa Anna, CA) With the RIGHTEOUS BROTHERS. Their biggest hit: "You're My Soul & Inspiration" in 1966. Bill and Jennifer Warnes recorded a hit song, "I've Had the Time of My Life" for the film *Dirty Dancing*. In 1990 "Unchained Melody" made a comeback when heard in the film *Ghost*. Year/Age: 1995/**55** 1996/**56** 1997/**57**

- **JEREMY IRONS** Actor. (England) Films include *House of Spirits, Die Hard 3, M. Butterfly, Damage* and *Dead Ringers*. Won Best Actor Oscar for *Reversal of Fortune*. Did voice of Scar in *The Lion King*. Year/Age: 1995/**47** 1996/**48** 1997/**49**

- **LARRY BROWN** Football. (Clairton, PA) In 1972 he became the third player in NFL history to rush for more than 4,000 years in his first four seasons. Named MVP and helped Washington go to the Super Bowl. Year/Age: 1995/**48** 1996/**49** 1997/**50**

- **JOAN LUNDEN** TV hostess. (Sacramento, CA) Joined ABC's "Good Morning, America" in 1980. Year/Age: 1995/**45** 1996/**46** 1997/**47**

- **KEVIN HOOKS** Actor. Played Morris Thorpe on "White Shadow." He directed *Passenger 57* with his father Roger in the cast. Year/Age: 1995/**37** 1996/**38** 1997/**39**

- **FREDA PAYNE** Singer. (Detroit, MI) She sang with DUKE ELLINGTON in the late '60s. Her biggest hit: "Band of Gold" in 1970. Year/Age: 1995/**50** 1996/**51** 1997/**52**

- **DUKE SNIDER** Baseball. (Born Edwin Snider in Los Angeles, CA) Brooklyn Dodger outfielder. Year/Age: 1995/**69** 1996/**70** 1997/**71**

- **NILE ROGERS** Musician. Member of HONEYDRIPPERS along with Robert Plant, Jeff Beck, and Jimmy Page. They had one hit: "Sea of Love" in 1984. Year/Age: 1995/**43** 1996/**44** 1997/**45**

- **SIR WILLIAM GERALD GOLDING** Author. (1911-1993 – Cornwall, England) Wrote *Lord of the Flies*. Nobel Prize winner in 1983. (Died 6-19-93.)

- **RAY DANTON** Actor. (1931-1992 – New York, NY) Films include: *The Longest Day, The George Raft Story*, and *I'll Cry Tomorrow* as Susan Hayward's love interest.

- **BROOK BENTON** Singer. (1931-1988 – Born Benjamin Peay in Camden, SC) Biggest hits: "Rainy Night in Georgia" in 1970 and "It's Just A Matter Of Time" in 1959. (Died 4-9-88.)

- **BRIAN EPSTEIN** The BEATLES only true manager. (1934-1967 – England) On November 9, 1961, Brian and his recordshop assistant Alistair Taylor went to a lunchtime session at the Cavern Club and saw the Beatles for the first time. He was enthusiastic about signing them and said the Beatles would become bigger than Elvis. (Died of accidental drug overdose 8-27-67.)

FACTS FROM THE PAST

1796 President **GEORGE WASHINGTON**'s farewell address was published. In it he said, "Observe good faith and justice toward all nations. Cultivate peace and harmony with all."

1819 Poet **JOHN KEATS** was so inspired that he wrote *Ode to Autumn*, one of the best-loved poems in the English language.

1959 Soviet leader **NIKITA KHRUSHCHEV** lost his temper when told that while in L.A. he could not visit Disneyland for security reasons. He did visit a movie set and an Iowa farm.

1981 Paul Simon and Art Garfunkel reunited for a free concert in New York's Central Park. More than 400,000 people turned out for **SIMON AND GARFUNKEL**'s first full concert in 11 years.

1985 Rock star **FRANK ZAPPA** testified before the Senate Commerce, Science and Transportation Committee, protesting the movement to rate the lyrics of rock music based on sexual and violent content.

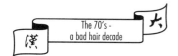

SEPTEMBER 20

BIRTHDAYS

• **GUNNAR & MATTHEW NELSON** Entertainers. Twin sons of the late Rick Nelson. Nelsons' biggest hit: "Love & Affection" in 1990. Year/Age: 1995/**26** 1996/**27** 1997/**28**

• **SOPHIA LOREN** Actress. (Born Sofi Villani Scicoloni in Naples, Italy) She won an Oscar for best actress in 1961 for *Two Women.* She lost her contract with Alitalia Airlines after executives found out she had spent time in prison. Year/Age: 1995/**61** 1996/**62** 1997/**63**

• **ANNE MEARA** Actress/comedienne. (NYC) Veronica Rooney on "Archie Bunker's Place" and appeared on "Alf." She and her husband, Jerry Stiller, have done comedy routines and commercials together. Year/Age: 1995/**66** 1996/**67** 1997/**68**

• **JAMES GALANOS** Fashion designer. Year/Age: 1995/**70** 1996/**71** 1997/**72**

• **RED AUERBACH** Basketball coach. (Brooklyn, NY) He coached the Boston Celtics to 9 NBA championships. In the Basketball Hall of Fame. Year/Age: 1995/**78** 1996/**79** 1997/**80**

• **PEG PHILLIPS** Actress. TV's "Northern Exposure." Year/Age: 1995/**77** 1996/**78** 1997/**79**

• **GOGI GRANT** Singer. (Born Audrey Brown) Her biggest hit: "The Wayward Wind" in 1956. Year/Age: 1995/**71** 1996/**72** 1997/**73**

• **JIM TAYLOR** Football. Former running back for the Green Bay Packers. Year/Age: 1995/**60** 1996/**61** 1997/**62**

• **CHARLIE DRESSEN** Baseball coach/manager. (Born 1898 in Decatur, IL) With the Dogers, Yankees, and Senators.

• **FERDINAND "JELLY ROLL" MORTON** American jazz pianist/singer/orchestra leader (1885-1941 – New Orleans) (Died 7-10-41.)

• **ALEXANDER, THE GREAT** King of Macedonia and military conqueror. (356-323 B.C.)

• **UPTON SINCLAIR** Politician/novelist. (1878-1968 – Baltimore, MD) Wrote novels of protest beginning with *The Jungle* in 1906 (see "Facts From The Past" below) He was awarded the Pulitzer Prize for *Dragon's Teeth* in 1942. (Died 11-25-68.)

FACTS FROM THE PAST

1519 Ferdinand Magellan set sail from Spain on a voyage that took one of his ships around the world. It was history's **FIRST GLOBAL CIRCUMNAVIGATION.** Magellan was killed en route.

1859 The **FIRST ELECTRIC COOKING RANGE**, called an "electro heater," was patented by George B. Simpson of Washington, DC.

1881 **CHESTER A. ARTHUR** was sworn in as the 21st president of the United States, succeeding James A. Garfield, who was assassinated.

1884 The **EQUAL RIGHTS PARTY** was formed in San Francisco, and Mrs. Belva Lockwood was nominated for President, with her running mate, Marietta Stowe.

1906 **UPTON SINCLAIR** (a cousin of Wallis Simpson, Duchess of Windsor) rocked the **MEAT-PACKING INDUSTRY** by publishing *The Jungle* at his own expense. It exposed the Chicago Stockyards and elsewhere. It told of how rats were swept into the sausage-making machinery. The exposé, repeatedly turned down by publishers, became a best seller and helped change the industry. Sinclair became a vegetarian.

1958 Civil Rights leader **MARTIN LUTHER KING, JR.,** was seriously wounded at a New York City department store when an apparently deranged African-American woman stabbed him in the chest.

1963 **PRESIDENT JOHN F. KENNEDY** proposed a joint U.S./Soviet expedition to the moon in a speech to the U.N. General Assembly.

1970 **JIM MORRISON** was found guilty of indecent exposure and profanity in connection with a concert in March 1969.

1971 A military jury at Fort McPherson, GA, found Army Captain **ERNEST MEDINA** innocent of all charges of involvement in the deaths of more than 100 Vietnamese civilians at MY LAI [mee-ly].

1973 In the "**BATTLE OF THE SEXES,**" tennis star **BILLIE JEAN KING** beat **BOBBY RIGGS** in straight sets, 6-4, 6-3, 6-3, at the Houston Astrodome. Howard Cosell was the announcer for the match.

1973 Singer **JIM CROCE** and five other people died when their plane hit a tree on takeoff, in route to a concert in Sherman, TX.

1973 Baseball great **WILLIE MAYS** announced his retirement. Mays played for the New York Giants, and later for the New York Mets.

1975 **BRUCE SPRINGSTEEN**'s album *Born To Run* was released.

1976 *Playboy* magazine released an interview with **JIMMY CARTER**, in which the Democratic presidential nominee admitted he had "looked on a lot of women with lust in his heart."

1980 **SPECTACULAR BID,** ridden by **BILL SHOEMAKER,** ran as the only entry in the Woodward Stakes at Belmont Park in New York after three potential challengers dropped out in horse racing's first walkover since 1949.

1984 "**THE COSBY SHOW**" premiered on NBC-TV.

1988 At the summer Olympics in Seoul, South Korea, Greg Louganis of the U.S. won the gold medal in springboard diving. The day before he had struck and injured his head on the diving board in a preliminary round.

1992 Philadelphia's **MICKEY MORANDINI** made the first unassisted triple play in the National League in 65 years. **JEFF KING,** who

SEPTEMBER 21

Never borrow your
boyfriends earrings

BIRTHDAYS

- **LARRY HAGMAN** Actor. (Fort Worth, TX) In "Staying Afloat." He played the vicious J.R. on TV's "Dallas" series. He played Captain (later Major) Tony Nelson on "I Dream of Jeannie" from 1965 to 1970. His mother is actress/singer Mary Martin. Year/**Age**: 1995/**64** 1996/**65** 1997/**66**

- **DICKEY LEE** Singer. (Born Dick Lipscomb in Memphis, TN) Biggest hit: "Patches" in 1962. Year/**Age**: 1995/**55** 1996/**56** 1997/**57**

- **DAVE COULIER** Actor. He plays Joey Gladstone on TV's "Full House." Year/**Age**: 1995/**36** 1996/**37** 1997/**38**

- **SIDNEY MONCRIEF** Basketball. (Little Rock, AK) With the Milwaukee Bucks and Atlanta Hawks. Year/**Age**: 1995/**38** 1996/**39** 1997/**40**

- **BILL MURRAY** Actor/comedian. (Evanston, IL) He appeared on "Saturday Night Live" and is now a star in the movies. He won an Emmy in 1977 for writing a "SNL" program. Films include: *Stripes, What About Bob?, Mad Dog and Glory*, and *Groundhog Day*. Year/**Age**: 1995/**45** 1996/**46** 1997/**47**

- **ARTIS GILMORE** Basketball star. (Chipley, FL) Former Chicago Bulls center. Year/**Age**: 1995/**46** 1996/**47** 1997/**48**

- **MARSHA NORMAN** Playwright. (Born Marsha Williams in Louisville, KY) Won a Pulitzer Prize for the *Play Nightt Mother* in 1983. Year/**Age**: 1995/**47** 1996/**48** 1997/**49**

- **CHUCK JONES** Cartoonist. (Spokane, WA) He was responsible for the Road Runner, Wiley Coyote and Pepe Le Pew. Year/**Age**: 1995/**83** 1996/**84** 1997/**85**

- **RICKI LAKE** Talk Show Hostess/Comic. Year/**Age**: 1995/**27** 1996/**28** 1997/**29**

- **ALFONSO RIBEIRO** Actor. TV's "Fresh Prince of Bel Air." Year/**Age**: 1995/**24** 1996/**25** 1997/**26**

- **CECIL FIELDER** Baseball. (Los Angeles, CA) Detroit Tiger first baseman. He has a five-year contract worth $36 million. Year/**Age**: 1995/**32** 1996/**33** 1997/**34**

- **ARIE LUYENDYK** [lion-dike] Racecar driver. (Holland) Won the Indy 500 in 1990. Was named to *People* magazine's "50 Most Beautiful People in the World" in 1992. Year/**Age**: 1995/**42** 1996/**43** 1997/**44**

- **HENRY GIBSON** Actor/comedian. (Germantown, PA) Probably best known for his poetry recitations on the "Laugh-in" TV series. Year/**Age**: 1995/**60** 1996/**61** 1997/**62**

- **STEPHEN KING** Author. (Portland, ME) Best-selling author of many horror novels, some of which have become movies. *Carrie*, and *Pet Sematary*. Before he wrote novels he was a janitor, baseball coach, library shelver and worked in an industrial laundry. Year/**Age**: 1995/**48** 1996/**49** 1997/**50**

- **DON FELDER** Guitarist. (Gainsville, FL) He was with the EAGLES in the 1970's. Their biggest hit: "One of These Nights" in 1975. Year/**Age**: 1995/**48** 1996/**49** 1997/**50**

- **H.G. (HERBERT GEORGE) WELLS** Author. (1866-1946 – England) Science/fiction author of *War of the Worlds*. Developed his taste for literature as a child because he had some injuries playing sports and so decided to become a writer. (Died 8-13-46.)

FACTS FROM THE PAST

1621 **CANADA** was given away by James of England to Sir Alexander Sterling, who later died bankrupt.

1893 The first successful **GASOLINE AUTOMOBILE** hit the streets of Springfield, MA. Brothers Charles and Frank Duryea created the first company in America to manufacture these cars. But Walter Chrysler and Henry Ford they were not. They never made it big in the auto business.

1897 The *New York Sun* newspaper ran an editorial in which **FRANCIS T. CHURCH** answered a question from 8-year-old Virginia O'Hanlon: "Is there a Santa Claus?" Church wrote: "Yes, Virginia, there is a Santa Claus…"

1937 *The Hobbit* was first published by **J.R.R. TOLKIEN**, who later created the *Lord of the Rings* series.

1948 **MILTON BERLE** made his debut as permanent host of "The Texaco Star Theater" on NBC-TV.

1955 After boxing champion **ROCKY MARCIANO** was knocked to the canvas, he got up and knocked out light heavyweight champ Archie Moore to retain his heavyweight title. Marciano became the only champion in history to retire with a 49-0 undefeated record.

1957 The famous TV series "**PERRY MASON**" starring Raymond Burr began.

1961 **ANTONIO ABERTONDO** swam the English Channel round trip. He swam the 44 miles without rest in 24 hours, 25 minutes.

1969 The NFL's longest punt came off the foot of **STEVE O'NEAL** of the New York Jets, 98 yards.

1977 **BERT LANCE** resigned as U.S. Budget Director after weeks of controversy over his past business and banking practices.

1981 A 99-0 vote hailed a turning point in U.S. political history when the Senate confirmed **SANDRA DAY O'CONNOR** to be the **FIRST FEMALE JUSTICE IN THE U.S. SUPREME COURT'S 191 YEARS.**

1983 Interior Secretary **JAMES WATT** apologized for saying he had a mixed advisory panel of "a black, a woman, two Jews and a cripple."

1992 250 million households tuned in to watch "**MURPHY BROWN**'s" (starring **CANDICE BERGEN**) rebuttal of Vice President **DAN QUAYLE**'s family values, single parents speech, May 19, 1992.

1992 "The Tonight Show" producer **HELEN KUSHNICK** was fired after allegedly banning guests from the show if they made appearances on competing late-night programs.

1993 Russian President **BORIS YELSIN** made a move for democratic reform by dissolving parliament and announcing new elections.

SEPTEMBER 22

BIRTHDAYS

- **TOMMY LASORDA** L.A. Dodgers baseball manager. (Norristown, PA) He used the Ultra Slim Fast Diet to drop a lot of pounds. He's spokesperson for Rolaids. Year/**Age**: 1995/**68** 1996/**69** 1997/**70**

- **DAVID COVERDALE** Singer. (England) With WHITE SNAKE. #1 hit: "Here I Go Again." Year/**Age**: 1995/**46** 1996/**47** 1997/**48**

- **SHARI BELAFONTE** Actress. Appeared in TV's "Hotel." Her dad is pop singer Harry Belafonte. Year/**Age**: 1995/**41** 1996/**42** 1997/**43**

- **CATHERINE OXENBERG** Actress. Year/**Age**: 1995/**34** 1996/**35** 1997/**36**

- **BONNIE HUNT** Actress. TV's "Grand." Year/**Age**: 1995/**31** 1996/**32** 1997/**33**

- **SCOTT BAIO** [bio] Actor. (Brooklyn, NY) He appeared as Chachi on TV's "Happy Days;" in the spinoff, "Joanie Loves Chachi," and later on "Charles in Charge." Year/**Age**: 1995/**34** 1996/**35** 1997/**36**

- **DEBBY BOONE** Singer. (Hackensack, NJ) Biggest hit: "You Light Up My Life" in 1977. Her parents are Pat and Shirley Boone, and her grandpa was Red Foley. She is married to Gabriel Ferrer, and they have 4 children. Year/**Age**: 1995/**39** 1996/**40** 1997/**41**

- **BOB LEMON** Baseball Hall of Famer. (San Bernardino, CA) Former White Sox and Yankee manager. Year/**Age**: 1995/**75** 1996/**76** 1997/**77**

- **INGEMAR JOHANSSON** Boxer. Briefly heavyweight champ in 1959. Year/**Age**: 1995/**63** 1996/**64** 1997/**65**

- **MARTHA SCOTT** Actress. (Jamesport, MO) Her films include: *Ben Hur*, *The Ten Commandments*, and *The Desperate Hours*. Year/**Age**: 1995/**81** 1996/**82** 1997/**83**

- **ROB STONE** Actor. Kevin on TV's "Mr. Belvedere." Year/**Age**: 1995/**33** 1996/**34** 1997/**35**

- **EUGENE ROACH** Actor. (Boston) He wrote the "Captain Kangaroo Show" before he became an actor and TV commercial spokesman. Year/**Age**: 1995/**67** 1996/**68** 1997/**69**

- **JOAN JETT** Singer/guitarist. (Philadelphia, PA) Formed her own band, THE BLACKHEARTS in 1980. Biggest hit: "I Love Rock 'N Roll." Starred in the film *Light of Day* as leader of the rock band called The Barbusters. Her co-star was Michael J. Fox. Year/**Age**: 1995/**35** 1996/**36** 1997/**37**

- **LYNN HERRING** Actress. (Enid, OK) Lucy Coe Jones on TV soap "General Hospital." Year/**Age**: 1995/**37** 1996/**38** 1997/**39**

- **PAUL MUNI** Actor. (1895-1967 – Born Muni Weisenfreund in Poland) In the films *The Last Angry Man* and *The Story of Louis Pasteur* for which he won an Oscar in 1936. (Died 8-25-67.)

- **ALLAN "ROCKY" LANE** Actor. (1901-1973 – Mishawaka, IN) He was the voice of the horse Mister Ed in the TV show of the same name. Also was Red Ryder on TV and films.

- **JACQUES HAUSSMANNE** Actor/producer/director/TV pitchman. (1902-1988 – Born Jacques Haussman in Bucharest, Romania) He appeared in *Paper Chase* and *Silver Spoons*. (Died 10-31-88.)

- **MICHAEL FARADAY** Scientist. (1791-1867 – England) Published pioneering papers that led to the practical use of electricity. (Died 8-25-1867.)

FACTS FROM THE PAST

1776 U.S. Captain **NATHAN HALE** became a hero (but a dead one) for being caught spying behind enemy lines on a mission for George Washington's Army. His last words were: "I only regret that I have but one life to lose for my country."

1789 Congress established the office of Postmaster General. **BENJAMIN FRANKLIN** was the first to hold the position.

1847 "OH SUSANNAH" was first introduced to the public in Pittsburgh. **STEPHEN FOSTER**'s hit song was sung at the Eagle Saloon.

1927 Attempting to regain the heavyweight boxing title, **JACK DEMPSEY** knocked champion **GENE TUNNEY** unconscious in the 7th round. The referee refused to start the count until Dempsey went to a neutral corner, giving Tunney an extra four seconds to recover. He did and went on to win the fight. Ten people died of heart attacks while listening to the fight on the radio.

1964 The musical *Fiddler on the Roof* starring **ZERO MOSTEL** opened on Broadway. It ran for a total of 3,242 performances.

1969 **WILLIE MAYS** of the San Francisco Giants hit his 600th career home run in a game against the San Diego Padres.

1973 **HENRY KISSINGER** was sworn in as U.S. Secretary of State, becoming the first **NATURALIZED CITIZEN** to hold the office.

1975 A 46-year-old political activist, **SARA JANE MOORE**, attempted to assassinate President Gerald Ford as he walked from a San Francisco hotel. The bullet she fired slightly wounded a man in the crowd. A bystander deflected the shot.

1985 Willie Nelson, Neil Young, and John Cougar hosted the first **FARM AID** in Champaign, Il. They raised $10 million for financially troubled farmers in the Midwest.

1991 A London newspaper, *The Mail*, revealed that former intelligence agent **JOHN CAIRNCROSS** admitted being the "fifth man" in the Soviet Union's British spy ring.

1992 **TONY BRADLEY** and **RICHARD ABRUZZO** from Albuquerque, NM, set a record, staying aloft in a hot-air-balloon gondola for 144 hours, 22 minutes. They became the first American balloonists to travel from the United States to Africa, leaving Bangor, ME, September 16 and landing near Casablanca September 22.

1993 In a 53-minute speech, President Clinton calls for **HEALTH REFORM** that would assure every American comprehensive medical benefits.

SEPTEMBER 23
Astrological Sign of Libra

Why isn't there athlete's hand, if there's athlete's foot?

BIRTHDAYS

• **MICKEY ROONEY** Actor. (Born Joseph Yule, Jr., in Brooklyn, NY) He's been nominated for Oscars 4 times, but has never won. His movie career began at age 2 in his parents' vaudeville act. He has appeared in *Boy's Town*, *Captains Courageous*, and the *Andy Hardy* series. He's in the Broadway production of "The Will Roger's Folllies." He was offered the role of Archie Bunker in TV's "All In The Family" before Carroll O'Connor. Year/Age: 1995/**75** 1996/**76** 1997/**77**

• **BRUCE SPRINGSTEEN** Singer. (Freehold, NJ) Referred to as "The Boss," he was one of the hottest entertainers of the '80s. One of his big hits: "Born in the U.S.A." In 1971, he was turned away trying to sneak into Graceland, Elvis Presley's Memphis home. In 1975 he appeared on the cover of "Time" and "Newsweek" simultaneously. "Streets of Piladelphia" is his most recent hit from the movie *Philadelphia*. Year/Age: 1995/**46** 1996/**47** 1997/**48**

• **RAY CHARLES** Singer. (Born Ray Charles Robinson in Albany, GA) Biggest hit: "I Can't Stop Loving You" in 1962. Frank Sinatra gave Ray his nickname, "The Genius," many years ago. Ray became blind at age 6 and was living in a home for the blind in Greenville, FL, where he discovered his love for music. Year/Age: 1995/**65** 1996/**66** 1997/**67**

• **MARY KAY PLACE** Actress/singer. She won an Emmy for supporting actress on "Mary Hartman, Mary Hartman" on TV and was on the follow-up show, "Forever Fernwood." She was also seen in *The Big Chill*. Biggest hit: "Baby Boy" in 1976. Year/Age: 1995/**48** 1996/**49** 1997/**50**

• **PAUL PETERSEN** Singer/actor. (Glendale, CA) Biggest hit: "My Dad" in 1963. He was one of the original Mouseketeers, caused a problem for the show and was fired. He wrote books including *It's A Wonderful Life*, a trivia book. From 1958-66 he appeared on the "Donna Reed Show." Year/Age: 1995/**51** 1996/**52** 1997/**53**

• **JULIO IGLESIAS** Singer. He and Willie Nelson had a giant hit: "To All the Girls I've Loved Before." At one time he was a pro soccer goalie in Madrid, Spain, until a car crash left him temporarily paralyzed. Year/Age: 1995/**52** 1996/**53** 1997/**54**

• **TONY MANDARICH** Football lineman. (Canada) Started his pro career with the Green Bay Packers, with whom he was a big disappointment. Year/Age: 1995/**29** 1996/**30** 1997/**31**

• **LARRY MIZE** Golfer. (Augusta, GA) Year/Age: 1995/**37** 1996/**38** 1997/**39**

• **ROMY SCHNEIDER** Actress. (1938-1982 – Born Rose Marie Albach-Retty in Vienna, Austria) She appeared in *What's New Pussycat?* in 1965 and in *The Cardinal*. (Died 5-29-82.)

• **WALTER PIDGEON** Actor. (1897-1984) A dignified romantic actor, he won an Oscar in 1942 for the film *Mrs. Miniver*. He appeared in over 100 films during his career. (Died 9-25-84.)

• **VICTORIA WOODHULL** American feminist/reformer. (1838-1927 – Homer, OH) First female candidate for the U.S. presidency, nominated by the Equal Rights Party. (Died 6-10-27.)

• **AUGUSTUS CAESAR** Roman Emperor. (63 B.C.-A.D 14)

FACTS FROM THE PAST

1779 The American warship, *Bonhomme Richard*, commanded by **JOHN PAUL JONES**, defeated the *HMS Serapis* during the Revolutionary War. During this battle Jones said: "I have not yet begun to fight."

1790 The "smoking gun" in the **BENEDICT ARNOLD** case was discovered when British spy John Andre was captured, along with papers outlining Arnold's plans to surrender West Point to the British.

1846 German astronomer **JOHANN GOTTFRIED GALLE** discovered the planet Neptune.

1879 **THE FIRST HEARING AID WAS PATENTED** by **RICHARD S. RHODES** of River Park, IL. The audiophone was a fan-like device held against the teeth.

1944 **PRESIDENT FRANKLIN ROOSEVELT** responded to charges that he left his dog Fala behind on an Aleutian Island and had sent a destroyer back to find him, at a high cost to the taxpayers.

1946 The quickest knockout in boxing history, eleven seconds, took place in Lewiston, ME. Ralph Walton was adjusting his mouthpiece. The bell sounded for the first round. His opponent, **AL COUTURE**, ran straight to Walton, landed a hard right, and knocked him out.

1952 Republican vice-presidential candidate **RICHARD M. NIXON** delivered what came to be known as the "Checkers" speech as he replied to allegations of improper campaign financing.

1957 President Eisenhower sent troops into Little Rock, AK to enforce a **FEDERAL DESEGREGATION** order.

1969 The ever-popular "**PAUL MCCARTNEY IS DEAD**" rumour was begun by *The London Daily Mirror*.

1976 **PRESIDENT GERALD FORD** and Democratic challenger **JIMMY CARTER** met in a nationally broadcast debate. During the debate, they were speechless for 27 minutes. (The sound system failed!)

1986 **JIM DESHAIES** of the **HOUSTON ASTROS** pitched a two-hit shutout against the Dodgers. He started the game by striking out the first eight batters he faced — setting a modern-day major-league record. He only got two more strikes during the game.

1992 Goaltender **MANOR RHEAUME** became the first woman to play in a major team sport. In 20 minutes on the ice, she gave up 2 goals in Tampa Bay's loss to St. Louis 6-4 in National Hockey League exhibition play.

1992 It was questionable as to whether or not there would be any **PRESIDENTIAL DEBATES** in this election when President Bush repeatedly objected to a single-moderator format proposed by a bipartisan commission.

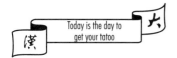

Today is the day to get your tatoo

SEPTEMBER 24

BIRTHDAYS

- **ANTHONY NEWLEY** British entertainer. (England) Appeared on Broadway in *Stop the World, I Want to Get Off* and *Roar of the Grease Paint*. Biggest hit: "What Kind of Fool am I?" At one time, he was married to Joan Collins. Year/**Age**: 1995/**64** 1996/**65** 1997/**66**

- **JOHN YOUNG** Astronaut. (San Francisco, CA) He worked with the space program until the *Challenger* disaster. Whenever there was a shuttle lift-off, Young flew over the area to make sure the cloud formations, fog, etc., would not hamper the lift-off, and if they had to make an emergency landing – he gave the final OK. Year/**Age**: 1995/**65** 1996/**66** 1997/**67**

- **JIM McKAY** Sportscaster. (Born James McManus in) Philadelphia, PA) He was the first court reporter on "The Verdict is Yours" and has won several Emmys for his work as host of "Wide World of Sports," especially for his on-the-spot coverage of the Munich crisis. He got his name when he was asked to host the show "The Real McKay" on CBS. Year/**Age**: 1995/**74** 1996/**75** 1997/**76**

- **"MEAN" JOE GREEN** Football star. (Temple, TX) Pittsburgh Steelers lineman, twice the NFL outstanding defensive player. He did the TV commercial with the little kid offering him a Coca-Cola. Year/**Age**: 1995/**49** 1996/**50** 1997/**51**

- **GERRY MARSDEN** Vocalist/guitarist. (Liverpool, England) With GERRY & THE PACEMAKERS. Biggest hit and their first recording: "Don't Let the Sun Catch You Crying." Year/**Age**: 1995/**53** 1996/**54** 1997/**55**

- **BARBARA ALLBUT** Singer. (Orange, NJ) Biggest hit with the ANGELS: "My Boyfriend's Back." Year/**Age**: 1995/**55** 1996/**56** 1997/**57**

- **RAFAEL PALMEIRO** Baseball. (Cuba) Baltimore Oriole first baseman. Year/**Age**: 1995/**31** 1996/**32** 1997/**33**

- **PHIL HARTMAN** Actor. (Canada) He is in the cast of "Saturday Night Live" and appears in films *Greedy* and *Houseguest*. Year/**Age**: 1995/**47** 1996/**48** 1997/**49**

- **SHEILA MacRAE** Actress. (Born Sheila Stephens in London, England) The "Jackie Gleason Show." She was married to singer Gordon MacRae. Year/**Age**: 1995/**71** 1996/**72** 1997/**73**

- **JOHN MACKEY** Football Hall of Famer. (New York, NY) 1963 Baltimore Colts' second round draft pick. Played nine years for the Colts and one with San Diego. He ran a deflected Johnny Unitas pass 75 yards for a touchdown and a Super Bowl V win over Dallas. Year/**Age**: 1995/**54** 1996/**55** 1997/**56**

- **LINDA McCARTNEY** Singer/photographer. (She was born Linda Eastman in NYC) Linda became a photographer for "Rolling Stone" magazine and married Paul following a divorce from her first husband. She has recorded with Paul and their ex-band, WINGS. Biggest hit: "Silly Love Songs" in 1976. In 1989 she had her first book published, *Linda McCartney's Home Cooking*. Year/**Age**: 1995/**54** 1996/**55** 1997/**56**

- **PHYLISS "JIGGS" ALLBUT** Singer. (Orange, NJ) Sister of Barbara. Also with THE ANGELS. Year/**Age**: 1995/**53** 1996/**54** 1997/**55**

- **JIM HENSON** Puppeteer. (1936-1990 – Greenville, MS) He created the Muppets in 1954 and had a couple of hit records, including Ernie's "Rubber Duckie" from "Sesame Street" and Kermit, the Frog's "The Rainbow Connection" from the *Muppet Movie*. He was the voice of Kermit and created Miss Piggy. (Died 5-16-90.)

- **F. SCOTT FITZGERALD** Author. (1896-1940 – St. Paul, MN) Wrote his first novel, *This Side of Paradise*, at age 24. His last novel was a total failure. His best-known book was *The Great Gatsby*. He also wrote *Tender is the Night*. (Died 12-21-40.)

FACTS FROM THE PAST

1869 The **BLACK FRIDAY PANIC** hit Wall Street after an attempt to corner the gold market was made by financiers **JAY GOULD** and **JAMES FISK**. Thousands of businessmen were ruined.

1929 **JAMES DOOLITTLE** flew the first instruments-only take-offs and landings. All commercial and military airplanes use the inventions.

1934 **BABE RUTH** made his farewell appearance as a regular player with the New York Yankees. The Boston Red Sox beat the Yanks 5-0.

1938 **DON BUDGE** won the American Tennis Championship at Forest Hills, NY., to become the first player to win all four major titles, American, Australian, French, and British.

1950 In a game against the Philadelphia Eagles, Jim Hardy of the Chicago Cardinals threw eight interceptions. It was the **MOST INTERCEPTIONS** against a professional quarterback in a single game.

1955 While in office, the 34th U.S. President, **DWIGHT EISENHOWER,** suffered a heart attack.

1957 The **BROOKLYN DODGERS** played their last game at Ebbets Field, beating the Pittsburgh Pirates 2-0.

1960 The last "**HOWDY DOODY**" program was broadcast. The famous children's TV show premiered in December of 1947 on NBC with host Buffalo Bob and his 4-foot-tall puppet, Howdy Doody.

1968 "**60 MINUTES**" made its TV debut with reporters Harry Reasoner and Mike Wallace.

1973 **TOM LANDRY** coached his 100th win. Dallas beat New Orleans 40-3 giving him an honor only a few pro coaches hold.

1988 In the Summer Olympics Canada's **BEN JOHNSON** won the fastest foot race in history as four men, including **CARL LEWIS**, went under ten seconds for 100 meters. (See Sept. 27, 1988)

1988 **JAMES BROWN** was arrested after a high-speed chase through Georgia and South Carolina. He was sentenced to six years in jail.

1988 The **EPISCOPAL CHURCH** elected its first female bishop, Rev. Barbara Harris, an African-American woman who had been a priest eight years.

SEPTEMBER 25

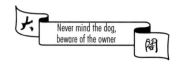
Never mind the dog, beware of the owner

BIRTHDAYS

- **WILL SMITH** Rapper/actor. (Born Willard Smith in West Philadelphia, PA) TV's "Fresh Prince of Bel Air." With DJ Jazzy Jeff and the Fresh Prince, hits include: "Nightmare on My Street," "Parents Just Don't Understand" and "Summertime." Films *Six Degrees of Seperation* and *Made in America.* Year/**Age:** 1995/**27** 1996/**28** 1997/**29**

- **JULIET PROWSE** Actress/dancer. (Bombay, India) She appeared in *Can-Can, G.I. Blues,* and the L'eggs hosiery commercials on TV. Year/**Age:** 1995/**59** 1996/**60** 1997/**61**

- **MICHAEL DOUGLAS** Actor/director. (New Brunswick, NJ) Son of Kirk Douglas, he appeared on TV in "Streets of San Francisco." Starred in *Cutthroat Island, Fatal Attraction, Basic Instinct,* and *Falling Down.* Won an Oscar for best actor in *Wall Street.* When he told his mother, Diana Douglas, that he hoped she wouldn't be embarrassed by his part in *Basic Instinct* she answered, "Why should I be embarrassed? It's not my bare ass out there." Year/**Age:** 1995/**51** 1996/**52** 1997/**53**

- **CHRISTOPHER REEVE** Actor. (NYC) *Superman.* Soap opera "Love of Life" and *The Remains of the Day.* Year/**Age:** 1995/**43** 1996/**44** 1997/**45**

- **ANSON WILLIAMS** Actor. Played Potsie on "Happy Days." Year/**Age:** 1995/**46** 1996/**47** 1997/**48**

- **ROBERT WALDEN** Actor. (NYC) Played Rossi on the "Lou Grant Show." Year/**Age:** 1995/**52** 1996/**53** 1997/**54**

- **SCOTTIE PIPPEN** Basketball pro. Plays forward for the Chicago Bulls. Member of the 1992 U.S. Gold Medal Olympic Dream Team. Played in two NBA All-Star Games. He helped lead the Bulls to three NBA championships in 1991, '92, and '93. Year/**Age:** 1995/**30** 1996/**31** 1997/**32**

- **ROYCE KENDALL** Singer. (St. Louis, MO) He and daughter Jeannie are the KENDALLS. Biggest hit: "Heaven's Just a Sin Away" in 1977. Year/**Age:** 1995/**61** 1996/**62** 1997/**63**

- **BARBARA WALTERS** TV personality. (Boston, MA) Appears on ABC's "20/20." She is one of the highest-paid journalists in America and opened the door for women to the big-money, high-profile TV jobs they hold today. Year/**Age:** 1995/**64** 1996/**65** 1997/**66**

- **JOHNNY SAIN** Baseball. Once a top Boston pitcher, he won 20 games in four seasons and won 24 in 1948. Year/**Age:** 1995/**78** 1996/**79** 1997/**80**

- **MARK HAMILL** Actor. (Oakland, CA) Star of *Star Wars* as Luke Skywalker. He got his start on the soap opera "General Hospital" playing Nurse Jessie Brewer's nephew. Year/**Age:** 1995/**43** 1996/**44** 1997/**45**

- **BURLEIGH DRUMMOND** Musician. With the group, AMBROSIA. Biggest hit: "How Much I Feel" in 1978. Year/**Age:** 1995/**44** 1996/**45** 1997/**46**

- **PHIL RIZZUTO** Baseball. (NYC) Former Yankee shortstop, now sportscaster. Year/**Age:** 1995/**77** 1996/**78** 1997/**79**

- **HEATHER LOCKLEAR** Actress. She played Krystle's niece, Sammy Jo, on "Dynasty," and Stacy Sheridan on "T.J. Hooker." She is in the TV series "Melrose Place." Married MOTLEY CRUE drummer, Tommy Lee, May 10, 1986. Year/**Age:** 1995/**34** 1996/**35** 1997/**36**

- **WILLIAM FAULKNER** Author. (1897-1962 – Born Falkner in New Albany, MS) Author of such classics as *The Sound and the Fury* and *As I Lay Dying.* 1949 Nobel Prize for Literature. (Died 7-6-62.)

FACTS FROM THE PAST

1493   **CHRISTOPHER COLUMBUS** set sail with 17 ships from Cadiz, Spain on his second trip to the Western Hemisphere.

1513   **VASCO NUNEZ DE BALBOA** of Spain became the first European to look upon the Pacific Ocean after crossing the Isthmus of Panama. He took possession of it in the name of **SPAIN.**

1888   **JACK THE RIPPER**'s first letter arrived at the Central News Agency in England, promising that in his next murder he would cut the woman's ear off because "I am down on whores." The body was found five days later just as he had advertised.

1953   Pianist **LIBERACE** made his Carnegie Hall debut before a capacity crowd.

1962   **SONNY LISTON** knocked out Floyd Patterson in round one to win the world heavyweight title at Comiskey Park in Chicago.

1964   The situation comedy **"GOMER PYLE, U.S.M.C."** made its debut on CBS-TV. It ran for five years.

1965   At 34, **WILLIE MAYS** became the oldest man to hit 50 home runs in a single season. Ten years earlier, he was the youngest to hit 50.

1975   **JACKIE WILSON** suffered a heart attack on stage at the Latin Casino in NJ as he was singing the line, "My heart is crying," from "Lonely Teardrops."

1978   **MELISSA LUDTKE**, a *Sports Illustrated* writer, filed suit in U.S. District Court and the judge ruled that major league baseball cannot bar women reporters from the locker room after the game.

1981   **SANDRA DAY O'CONNOR** was sworn in as the 102nd Justice of the Supreme Court. The oath was administered by Chief Justice Warren E. Burger. She was the **FIRST WOMAN** on the court.

1987   Debate topics for candidates Michael **DUKAKIS** and President George **BUSH** were drugs, the deficit and the Pledge of Allegiance.

1987   The nomination of Judge **WILLIAM SESSIONS** to be the new FBI director was unanimously approved by the Senate.

1987   Florence Griffith Joyner, **FLO-JO,** won a gold medal in the women's 100-meter dash at the Olympics in Seoul, Korea.

1992   **JIMMY CONNORS** beat **MARTINA NAVRATILOVA** in the $500,000 tennis Battle of Champions in Las Vegas, NV.

1993   A judge in Orlando, FL ruled that a 12-year-old boy, **GREGORY KINGSLEY** could legally divorce his biological parents.

Perform pleasantries
in pedal pushers

SEPTEMBER 26

BIRTHDAYS

- **CRAIG CHAQUICO** [chuck-ee-so] Guitar player. JEFFERSON STARSHIP. Biggest hit: "Nothing's Gonna Stop Us Now" from the film *Mannequin*. The group, later called STARSHIP, broke up in 1990. Year/**Age**: 1995/**41** 1996/**42** 1997/**43**

- **DONNA DOUGLAS** Actress. Elly May Clampett on TV's "The Beverly Hillbillies." She co-starred with Elvis in *Frankie and Johnny*. Year/**Age**: 1995/**56** 1996/**57** 1997/**58**

- **OLIVIA NEWTON-JOHN** Entertainer. (England) Her first hit: "I Honestly Love You," written by Peter Allen, who was going to record it until he heard her sing. A long time ago, Olivia won a Hayley Mills look-alike contest. Her biggest hit: "Physical" in 1981. Year/**Age**: 1995/**47** 1996/**48** 1997/**49**

- **LINDA HAMILTON** Actress. (Salisbury, MD) Movies: *The Terminator* and *Terminator II*. TV's "Beauty and the Beast" as Catherine Chandler. Year/**Age**: 1995/**39** 1996/**40** 1997/**41**

- **CARLENE CARTER** C & W Singer. (Madison, TN) Hits include "I Fell in Love," and "Every Little Thing." Her mother is June Carter, her dad is Carl Smith and stepfather is Johnny Cash. Year/**Age**: 1995/**40** 1996/**41** 1997/**42**

- **MELISSA SUE ANDERSON** Actress. (Berkeley, CA) She played Mary on TV's "Little House on the Prairie." Year/**Age**: 1995/**33** 1996/**34** 1997/**35**

- **JACK LaLANNE** Physical fitness pioneer. (San Francisco, CA) He had a popular TV fitness show in the '60s and '70s. Year/**Age**: 1995/**81** 1996/**82** 1997/**83**

- **KENT McCORD** Actor. He was on "Adam 12" as Jim Reed and was known as Kent McWhirter on the "Ozzie & Harriet" TV show. He changed his name later. He also has been the V.P. of the Screen Actors Guild under Ed Asner. Year/**Age**: 1995/**53** 1996/**54** 1997/**55**

- **PATRICK O'NEAL** Actor. (Ocala, FL) Appeared in *In Harm's Way*, *The Cardinal*, and *The Way We Were*. Year/**Age**: 1995/**68** 1996/**69** 1997/**70**

- **LUCIUS ALLEN** Basketball guard. Former UCLA and later pro player. Year/**Age**: 1995/**48** 1996/**49** 1997/**50**

- **LYNN ANDERSON** Singer. (Grand Forks, ND) Her biggest hit: "Rose Garden" in 1970. She was the Country Music Association Female Singer of the Year in 1970. Year/**Age**: 1995/**48** 1996/**49** 1997/**50**

- **BRYAN FERRY** Singer. (England) Lead singer of ROXY MUSIC. Recorded "Kiss and Tell" in 1988, from the movie *Bright Lights, Big City*. Year/**Age**: 1995/**50** 1996/**51** 1997/**52**

- **MARTY ROBBINS** Singer. (1925-1982 – Born Marin Robinson in Glendale, AZ) Biggest hit: "El Paso" in 1959. He survived a head-on crash while competing in the Daytona 500 in 1972 at a speed of 150 mph. Marty died just two months after being inducted into the Country Music Hall of Fame. (12-8-82.)

- **GEORGE GERSHWIN** Composer. (1898-1937 – Brooklyn, NY) He was 15 years old when he became a song plugger, and wrote "Swanee" on a bus when he was 21, at the time making $35 a week. He was 26 when he wrote "Rhapsody in Blue." His songs include: "Summertime," "American in Paris," and "Porgy & Bess." He died of a brain tumor. (7-11-37.)

- **GEORGE RAFT** Actor. (1895-1980, born George Ranft in NYC) Films included *Scarface, Boero, Around the World in Eighty Days,* and *Some Like it Hot*. He turned down the roll in *Casablanca*.

- **T.S. (THOMAS STERNS) ELIOT** Poet/dramatist/critic. (1888-1965 – St. Louis, MO) He wrote the poems *The Waste Land* and "The Love Song of J. Alfred Prufrock." He won the Nobel Prize for Literature in 1948. (Died 1-4-65.)

FACTS FROM THE PAST

1789 THOMAS JEFFERSON was appointed America's first Secretary of State; John Jay was named the first Chief Justice; Samuel Osgood began service as the first Postmaster General; and Edmund Jennings Randolph was named the first Attorney General.

1892 JOHN PHILIP SOUSA AND HIS BAND performed in public for the first time in Plainfield, NJ.

1908 ED REULBACH of the Chicago Cubs was the first player to pitch both games of a doubleheader and win both of them in shutouts.

1919 PRESIDENT WILSON suffered an incapacitating stroke while on a nationwide speaking tour.

1955 After word got out about PRESIDENT EISENHOWER's heart attack, the NEW YORK STOCK EXCHANGE suffered its worst decline since 1929.

1955 DEBBIE REYNOLDS and EDDIE FISHER were married. They divorced in 1959 after producing daughter Carrie.

1957 LEONARD BERNSTEIN's updated version of *Romeo & Juliet* opened on Broadway. It was called *West Side Story.*

1961 New York Yankee right fielder, ROGER MARIS hit his 60th home run off Baltimore's Jack Fisher, to tie Babe Ruth's all-time record for home runs in one season. On October 1st, he hit number 61 off Boston's Tracy Stallard to break the record. For many years Maris had the only asterisk in the record books behind his name because he had 162 games to set the record and Ruth had 154.

1962 The television comedy "THE BEVERLY HILLBILLIES" premiered on CBS. It ran for nine years.

1969 The album *Abbey Road* was released by the BEATLES. This was their last real album, recorded after *Let it Be*.

1975 THE ROCKY HORROR PICTURE SHOW premiered in Westwood, CA.

1983 CHALLENGER AUSTRALIA II won the America's Cup off Newport, RI. The victory ended the longest winning streak in sports: 132 years. The Americans were attempting to defend the cup for the 25th time.

1992 GLORIA ESTEFAN gave a benefit concert for Miami hurricane victims with PAUL SIMON and WHOOPI GOLDBERG.

SEPTEMBER 27

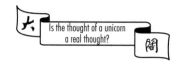
Is the thought of a unicorn a real thought?

BIRTHDAYS

• **MARK CALDERON** Singer. With COLOR ME BADD. Number 1 hit: "I Wanna Sex You Up," from the film, *New Jack City*. Year/Age: 1995/**25** 1996/**26** 1997/**27**

• **RANDY BACHMAN** Singer/guitarist. (Canada) With BACHMAN-TURNER OVERDRIVE. They were named for band members' last names and *Overdrive* magazine for truckers. Their biggest hit: "You Ain't Seen Nothing Yet" in 1974. Year/Age: 1995/**52** 1996/**53** 1997/**54**

• **WILFORD BRIMLEY** Actor. (Salt Lake City, UT) Among his films: *The Natural, Cocoon, The Electric Horseman, Tender Mercies*, and *The Firm*. Year/Age: 1995/**61** 1996/**62** 1997/**63**

• **JAYNE MEADOWS** Actress. (Born Jane Cotter in China) She and entertainer Steve Allen have been married since 1954. TV credits include: "Meeting of the Minds," "I've Got a Secret," and "The Steve Allen Show." Year/Age: 1995/**69** 1996/**70** 1997/**71**

• **ROBB WELLER** TV Host. "Entertainment Tonight" and "Home Show." Year/Age: 1995/**46** 1996/**47** 1997/**48**

• **GREG MORRIS** Actor. (Cleveland, OH) He played Barney Collier on the "Mission Impossible" TV series. Year/Age: 1995/**61** 1996/**62** 1997/**63**

• **MEAT LOAF** Rock singer. (Born Marvin Lee Aday) Biggest hit: "Two Outa Three Ain't Bad" in 1978. He also played Eddie in the film *The Rocky Horror Picture Show*. Year/Age: 1995/**48** 1996/**49** 1997/**50**

• **ARTHUR PENN** Director. (Philadelphia, PA) Films include: *Little Big Man, Bonnie and Clyde*, and *The Miracle Worker*. Year/Age: 1995/**73** 1996/**74** 1997/**75**

• **DICK SCHAAP** ABC sportscaster. Year/Age: 1995/**61** 1996/**62** 1997/**63**

• **SADA THOMPSON** Actress. (Des Moines, IA) She won an Emmy for her role as Kate Lawrence on "Family." In the 1993 mini-series "Queen." Year/Age: 1995/**66** 1996/**67** 1997/**68**

• **SHAUN CASSIDY** Singer. (Los Angeles, CA) Biggest hit: "Da Doo Ron Ron" in 1977. His mom is Shirley Jones and Jack Cassidy was his dad. He played Joe on the TV series "The Hardy Boys." He made his Broadway debut with David Cassidy in "Blood Brothers." Year/Age: 1995/**37** 1996/**38** 1997/**39**

• **WILLIAM CONRAD** Actor. (1920-1994, Louisville, KY) Started out in show biz announcing, writing and directing at KMPC radio in Los Angeles and was the radio voice of Marshal Dillon in "Gunsmoke" for 11 years. He's probably best known as TV's "Cannon." He appeared in *Killers* with Burt Lancaster and on the TV series "Jake and the Fat Man." He was narrator on "The Bulwinkle Show." (Died 2-11-94.)

• **KATHLEEN NOLAN** Actress. (St. Louis, MO) Former president of the Screen Actors Guild. She starred with Walter Brennan on the "Real McCoys" in the late 1950s and early 1960s. Year/Age: 1995/**62** 1996/**63** 1997/**64**

• **MIKE SCHMIDT** Baseball. (Dayton, OH) Philadelphia Phillies' home run champ. In 1980 it was Mike's game-winning homer that gave the Phillies the eastern title in a game against Montreal. Retired in 1989 with 548 home runs, ten gold gloves at third base, 12 all-star game selections, a World Series most valuable player award, 3 National League MVP honors and 7 seasons of leading the majors in home runs. Year/Age: 1995/**46** 1996/**47** 1997/**48**

• **CHERYL TIEGS** Model. (Alhambra, CA) She's married to photographer Peter Baird. Year/Age: 1995/**47** 1996/**48** 1997/**49**

FACTS FROM THE PAST

1825 **GEORGE STEPHENSON**'s Stockton & Darlington's line in England became the **FIRST LOCOMOTIVE TO HAUL A PASSENGER TRAIN.** One commentator warned that the railroad would make stay-at-home gad-abouts, honest men liars, and encourage intellectual decline.

1930 **BOBBY JONES** became the first player to win golf's **"GRAND SLAM"** (British Open, British Amatuer, U.S. Open and U.S. Amateur). Jones never turned pro and he retired at age 28.

1950 Fighter **EZZARD CHARLES DEFEATED JOE LOUIS** in 15 rounds in New York City for the heavyweight title.

1954 **"TONIGHT,"** hosted by **STEVE ALLEN,** made its debut on NBC-TV.

1964 The **BEACH BOYS** made their first appearance on "The Ed Sullivan Show." They sang "I Get Around."

1964 The Warren Commission issued a report concluding that **LEE HARVEY OSWALD** had acted alone in assassinating President John F. Kennedy in November 1963.

1973 **VICE PRESIDENT SPIRO AGNEW,** who had pleaded "no contest" to a tax evasion charge, said he would not resign. (But he did on October 10th.)

1983 **LARRY BIRD** signed a $15 million seven-year contract with Boston, making him the highest-paid player in Celtics history.

1987 **DOLLY PARTON**'s ABC variety show "Dolly" premiered. It was soon cancelled.

1988 The **BIGGEST DRUG BUST IN THE HISTORY OF SPORTS** took place at the Olympic Games in Seoul, South Korea. The 100-meter race which Canadian sprinter **BEN JOHNSON** won in 9.79 seconds; the fastest time ever recorded by man. On this day Johnson tested positive for steroids. 2nd place runner **CARL LEWIS** (USA) was awarded the gold.

1989 Two men, **JEFFREY PETKOVICH** and **PETER DEBERNARDI,** went over Niagara Falls in a barrel. They were the first pair ever to go over the 176-foot-high Horseshoe Falls and live. They said they did it to show kids there are better things to do than take drugs.

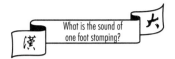

What is the sound of one foot stomping?

SEPTEMBER 28

BIRTHDAYS

- **NICK ST. NICHOLAS** Bass player. (Los Angeles, CA) With the group STEPPENWOLF. Biggest hit: "Born To Be Wild" in 1968. Year/**Age:** 1995/**52** 1996/**53** 1997/**54**

- **MARCELLO MASTROIANNI** Italian actor. (Italy) Nominated for an Oscar in 1962 for best actor in *Divorce, American Style,* and in 1977 for *A Special Day.* In the film *Used People* in 1992. Year/**Age:** 1995/**71** 1996/**72** 1997/**73**

- **JOHNNY DAWKINS** Basketball. Year/**Age:** 1995/**32** 1996/**33** 1997/**34**

- **BEN E. KING** Singer. (Henderson, NC) Biggest hit: "Stand By Me" in 1961. As the lead singer, he had a string of hits with The DRIFTERS, including his first, "There Goes My Baby," in the late '50s before moving on to a solo career. His career made a come-back in 1985 when a hit movie, named after his "Stand By Me" hit, also used the song as the theme for the film. Year/**Age:** 1995/**57** 1996/**58** 1997/**59**

- **ALANNAH CURRIE** Musician. (New Zealand) Handles the xylophone and percussion for the THOMPSON TWINS. Biggest hit: "Hold Me Now" in 1984. Year/**Age:** 1995/**38** 1996/**39** 1997/**40**

- **ARNOLD STANG** Actor. (Chelsea, MA) Seymour on "The Goldberg's" TV series in the '50s, and Francis, the stagehand on the "Milton Berle Show." He was the voice of cartoon character "Top Cat." Year/**Age:** 1995/**70** 1996/**71** 1997/**72**

- **WILLIAM WINDOM** Actor. (NYC) Appeared in "The Farmer's Daughter" with Inger Stevens and appears on "Murder, She Wrote." Year/**Age:** 1995/**72** 1996/**73** 1997/**74**

- **JERRY CLOWER** Country comedian. (Liberty, MS) Year/**Age:** 1995/**69** 1996/**70** 1997/**71**

- **BRIGITTE BARDOT** French actress. (Born Camille Javal Bardot in Paris, France) She's probably best known for the movie *And God Created Woman* in 1957. Year/**Age:** 1995/**61** 1996/**62** 1997/**63**

- **MOON ZAPPA** Actress. Daughter of Frank Zappa. Hit: *Valley Girl* in 1982. Year/**Age:** 1995/**28** 1996/**29** 1997/**30**

- **SYLVIA KRISTAL** Actress. (Netherlands) She appeared in the movie *Emmanuelle.* Year/**Age:** 1995/**43** 1996/**44** 1997/**45**

- **ELMER RICE** Writer. (1892-1967 – Born Elmer Reizenstein) Pulitzer Prize winner for *Street Scene.* (Died 5-8-67.)

- **WILLIAM S. PALEY** Founder of CBS. (1901-1990 – Chicago) A book about him details his love for the ladies. Responsible for Edward R, Murrow documentaries and "I Love Lucy." (Died 10-26-90.)

- **TOM HARMON** Football. (1919-1990) He was a University of Michigan football star in the 1940s. His son, Mark Harmon, is now a well-known actor. (Died 3-15-90.)

- **PETER FINCH** Actor. (1916-1977 – London, England) He was posthumously awarded an Oscar for the movie *Network.* (Died 1-14-77.)

- **ED SULLIVAN** TV host. (1902-1974 – Born Edward Vincent Sullivan in Manhattan, NY) Hosted "Toast of the Town" which later became the "Ed Sullivan Show." Prior to TV, he worked as a sportswriter. He caused a lot of talk when he appeared on the cover of *Esquire* magazine in a BEATLES wig in July of 1965. (Died 10-13-74.)

- **CONFUCIUS** Chinese philosopher/teacher. (551-479 B.C. – Shantung Province, China) Confucius is a Latinized name of K'ung Fu-tzu. He spent 40 years as a teacher.

FACTS FROM THE PAST

1066   **WILLIAM THE CONQUERER** invaded England and laid claim to the English throne.

1542   **CALIFORNIA** was discovered by Portuguese navigator **JOHN RODRIGUEZ CABRILLO**, who reached San Diego Bay on this date.

1920   Eight members of the Chicago White Sox were indicted for allegedly throwing the 1919 World Series against the Cincinnati Reds in what became known as the **BLACK SOX SCANDAL.** They claimed they were underpaid by Sox owner Charles Comiskey.

1941   Boston Red Sox outfielder **TED WILLIAMS** became the only player to hit over .400 in a single season. His average was .400 on the last day of the season when manager Joe Cronin gave Williams the opportunity to sit out the doubleheader and protect that record. Williams refused and hit 6 for 8 in the two games against the Philadelphia A's for a season batting average of .406. His salary was $18,000.

1960   Baseball immortal **TED WILLIAMS** went up to the plate one last time in a major league game and hit a 420-foot home run.

1961   The TV sitcom, **"HAZEL"** starring Shirley Booth, premiered. It ran for five years.

1974   First Lady **BETTY FORD** underwent a mastectomy at Bethesda Naval Medical Center in Maryland after discovering a cancerous lump on her breast.

1976   **GEORGE HARRISON** was sued by A&M Records over the non-delivery of his first contracted album, *Thirty-Three and a Third.* The album was released on Dark Horse in November of 1976.

1981   Stocks on the overseas market plunged, with a **BLUE MONDAY** prediction made by Joseph Granville.

1984   **PRESIDENT REAGAN** and Soviet Foreign Affairs Minister **ANDREI GROMYKO** had a meeting at the White House. Gromyko had met with all the U.S. presidents dating back to President Franklin D. Roosevelt.

1988   **JOHN DENVER**, not counting on the U.S. putting up another shuttle any time soon after the *Challenger* disaster**,** offered the Soviet Union $10 million to put him on the Soyuz Space Shuttle.

SEPTEMBER 29

Does M.D. mean
More Dinero?

BIRTHDAYS

- **LECH WALESA** [lek vah-len'-sah] Solidarity founder and Nobel Laureate. Year/**Age**: 1995/**52** 1996/**53** 1997/**54**

- **GENE AUTRY** Singer/actor/entrepreneur. (Born Orvon Autry in Tioga, TX) Biggest hit: "Rudolph, the Red-Nosed Reindeer" in 1949 for which he won the first platnum record for sales of over a million. From 1934 to 1954, he made 82 western movies in Hollywood. He owns the California Angels baseball team. Autry is the only person with five stars on the "Hollywood Walk of Fame," for radio, TV, movies, records and live performances. Elected to the Country Music Hall of Fame in 1969. Year/**Age**: 1995/**88** 1996/**89** 1997/**90**

- **ANITA EKBERG** Actress. (Sweden) She appeared in the movies *War & Peace* and *La Dolce Vita*. Year/**Age**: 1995/**64** 1996/**65** 1997/**66**

- **GREER GARSON** Actress. (Ireland) She won an Oscar in 1942 for best actress in *Mrs. Miniver*. Her acceptance speech was 10 minutes long. Year/**Age**: 1995/**87** 1996/**88** 1997/**89**

- **STANLEY KRAMER** Movie producer. (NYC) He has produced many films, including the multi-award winning *High Noon* in 1952. He now lives in Seattle, WA. Year/**Age**: 1995/**82** 1996/**83** 1997/**84**

- **MICHELANGELO ANTONIONI** Director. (Italy) Films include: *Zabriskie Point* and *Blow-Up*. Year/**Age**: 1995/**83** 1996/**84** 1997/**85**

- **MARK FARNER** Singer/guitarist. With GRAND FUNK RAILROAD. Biggest hit: "The Loco-Motion" in 1974. Year/**Age**: 1995/**47** 1996/**48** 1997/**49**

- **LARRY LINVILLE** Actor. Frank Burns on TV's "M*A*S*H." Year/**Age**: 1995/**56** 1996/**57** 1997/**58**

- **JOHN PAXSON** Basketball. (Dayton, OH) With the Chicago Bulls. In 1993, he scored a 3-point basket with 4 seconds remaining of game 6 to give the Bulls their 3rd NBA Championship. Year/**Age**: 1995/**35** 1996/**36** 1997/**37**

- **SEBASTIAN COE** Marathon runner. (England) Year/**Age**: 1995/**39** 1996/**40** 1997/**41**

- **HERSEY HAWKINS, JR.** Basketball. (Chicago, IL) With the Philadelphia 76ers. Year/**Age**: 1995/**30** 1996/**31** 1997/**32**

- **MADELINE KAHN** Actress. (Boston, MA) She starred as Madeline Wayne in the TV series "Oh, Madeline" in 1983-1984. She's in most of the Mel Brooks' films. Madeline got Lily Tomlin her first break in show business. Year/**Age**: 1995/**53** 1996/**54** 1997/**55**

- **JERRY LEE LEWIS** Singer. (Ferriday, LA) Biggest hit: "Great Balls of Fire" in 1958. His cousins are the Rev. Jimmy Swaggart, ex-TV evangelist; and C&W singer Mickey Gilley. He's been married 7 times. The 1989 film *Great Balls of Fire* about Jerry's life starred Dennis Quaid. Year/**Age**: 1995/**60** 1996/**61** 1997/**62**

- **BRYANT CHARLES GUMBEL** TV newscaster/host. (New Orleans, LA) Co-host of NBC's "Today Show." Year/**Age**: 1995/**47** 1996/**48** 1997/**49**

- **TREVOR HOWARD** Actor. (1916-1988 – England) Made more than 80 films including: *Mutiny on the Bounty*, *Ryan's Daughter*, *Superman*, and *Gandhi*. (Died 1-7-88.)

FACTS FROM THE PAST

1962   President John F. Kennedy nationalized the **MISSISSIPPI NATIONAL GUARD** as city officials defied federal court orders to enroll an African-American student, **JAMES MEREDITH**, at the University of Mississippi.

1964   **GLORIA SYKES** was injured in a **CABLE CAR ACCIDENT** in San Francisco. After 6 years, she was awarded $50,000 on a claim that the accident left her with insatiable sexual desires. Testifying on her behalf was a parade of psychiatrists and former lovers.

1976   While shooting at soda bottles, **JERRY LEE LEWIS** hit his bass player **NORMAN OWENS** twice in the chest with a .357 magnum. Lewis was charged with shooting a firearm in the city limits.

1977   **EVA SHAIN** became the first woman to officiate a heavyweight title boxing match—the Muhammad Ali-Ernie Shavers fight.

1977   **JAMES BROWN**'s band walked out on him during a tour in Florida, claiming they were underpaid and overworked.

1979   **POPE JOHN PAUL II** addressed a crowd of over one million people in Dublin to make an appeal for peace in Northern Ireland.

1987   New York Yankee **DON MATTINGLY** hit a grand-slam home run off Boston's Bruce Hurst, his sixth of the year. He hadn't even hit one in his first five seasons in the major leagues.

1988   The U.S. returned to the space race when the space shuttle **DISCOVERY** roared aloft from Kennedy Space Center, FL. Americans waited $2^1/_2$ years for this moment. More than 2,000 members of the press and more than a million people watched the spectacle. In a tribute to the **CHALLENGER** crew, who had perished in the shuttle explosion 32 months earlier, astronaut John Lounge said, "It's good to be back from where they wanted to go so badly."

1989   In Beverly Hills, CA, **ZSA ZSA GABOR** was convicted of slapping a police officer, driving without a valid driver's license and having an open intoxicant in her $215,000 Rolls Royce convertible. In response Gabor said, "I think Russia can't be worse than this."

1990   *Millie's Book* was the **BEST-SELLING NON-FICTION BOOK** in the United States. It was written for Millie, the President's dog, by First Lady Barbara Bush.

1992   **EARVIN "MAGIC" JOHNSON** announced that he would come out of retirement and again play basketball for the Los Angeles Lakers at over $14 million a season.

1993   Entertainer **SINEAD O'CONNOR** tore up a picture of the Pope on "Saturday Night Live." Two weeks later she was booed during a tribute to Bob Dylan at Madison Square Garden.

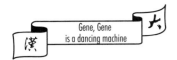

Gene, Gene is a dancing machine

SEPTEMBER 30

BIRTHDAYS

- **ROBIN ROBERTS** Baseball pitcher. (Philadelphia, PA.) He won 286 games in 19 seasons and never made more than $57,500 in a season. Year/**Age:** 1995/**69** 1996/**70** 1997/**71**

- **DEBORAH ALLEN** Singer. (Born Deborah Thurmond in Memphis, TN) Biggest hit: "Baby I Lied" in 1983. Year/**Age:** 1995/**42** 1996/**43** 1997/**44**

- **VICTORIA TENNANT** Actress. Wife of actor Steve Martin. Appeared in *Flowers In The Attic* and *L.A. Story*. Year/**Age:** 1995/**42** 1996/**43** 1997/**44**

- **ANGIE DICKINSON** Actress. (Born Angeline Brown in Kulm, ND) She starred in the TV series, "Police Woman" which premiered in 1974. In *Dressed to Kill* in 1980. She was once married to Burt Bacharach. She was voted Hollywood's Best Legs in 1962. Year/**Age:** 1995/**64** 1996/**65** 1997/**66**

- **DEBORAH KERR** [car] Actress. (Born Deborah Trimmer in Ireland) She has been nominated for Oscars for best actress in movies *From Here to Eternity* in 1953 and *The King & I* in 1956. Year/**Age:** 1995/**74** 1996/**75** 1997/**76**

- **BARRY WILLIAMS** Actor/singer. (Born Barry Blenkhorn) Greg on TV series "The Brady Bunch." Year/**Age:** 1995/**41** 1996/**42** 1997/**43**

- **MARILYN McCOO** Singer. (Jersey City, NJ) She and her husband, Billy, were members of the FIFTH DIMENSION. Their biggest hit: "Aquarius" from the musical *Hair* in 1969. Her biggest single: "You Don't Have to be a Star" in 1976. Year/**Age:** 1995/**52** 1996/**53** 1997/**54**

- **JILL COREY** Singer. (Born Norma Jean Speranza) Biggest hit: "Love Me to Pieces" in 1957. Year/**Age:** 1995/**60** 1996/**61** 1997/**62**

- **CRYSTAL BERNARD** Actress. TV's "Wings." Year/**Age:** 1995/**32** 1996/**33** 1997/**34**

- **JOHNNY MATHIS** Entertainer. (San Francisco, CA) He was a high school track star and set several track records in college. He was invited to try out for the 1956 Olympics, but chose a music career instead and became one of the first African-American millionaires. His biggest hit, and only #1 song: "Chances Are" in 1957. His album *Johnny Mathis' Greatest Hits* stayed on *BillBoard's* "top 100" charts for an unprecedented 7 years, surpassed only by PINK FLOYD's *Dark Side of the Moon*—on the charts for over 560 weeks. Year/**Age:** 1995/**60** 1996/**61** 1997/**62**

- **RULA LENSKA** Actress. (Born Roza-Maria Lubienska in England) Year/**Age:** 1995/**49** 1996/**50** 1997/**51**

- **WILLIAM WRIGLEY, JR.** Tycoon. (1861-1932 – Chicago, IL) He started the Wrigley chewing gum empire.

- **FRANKIE LYMON** Singer. (1942-1968 – NYC) At 14, he recorded the hit record "Why Do Fools Fall in Love?" He died of a heroin overdose at the age of 25 (2-28-68.)

- **TRUMAN CAPOTE** Author/playwright. (1924-1984 – Born Truman Streckfus Persons in Monroesville, AL) He became "Truman Capote" when his mother, Lilly May, married her second husband, Joe Capote. Two of his books *Breakfast at Tiffany's* and *In Cold Blood*, became movies. (Died 8-25-84.)

FACTS FROM THE PAST

1630 The **FIRST EXECUTION** in America took place. John Billington was hanged in Plymouth, MA, for fatally shooting John Newcomin.

1846 Surgeon **WILLIAM MORTON** of Charleston, MA, used an experimental anesthetic – **ETHER** – for the first time a patient.

1935 The famous musical **PORGY & BESS** by **GEORGE GERSHWIN** opened at the Colonial Theater in Boston.

1955 **JAMES DEAN** died in a car accident in California leaving behind a rebellious image that made him an idol for rock 'n' roll musicians and fans.

1960 The **"FLINTSTONES"** premiered on ABC-TV. It was the first cartoon for adults. Fred Flintstone worked for the Rock Head & Quarry Cave Construction Co. with the motto, "Own your own cave and be secure." Wilma's piano was called a "Stoneway."

1961 The bill for the **BOSTON TEA PARTY** was finally paid. Mayor Snyder of Oregon wrote a check for $1.96, the exact amount for all of the tea that was lost in that raid 188 years before this date.

1962 **JAMES MEREDITH** became the **FIRST AFRICAN-AMERICAN STUDENT** to enroll at the University of Mississippi.

1963 18-year old Houston rookie **JOHN PACIOREK** outfielder got three singles in his first at bat. He walked twice, scored four runs and had three RBIs. He then injured his back and never played in another pro game. He ended his career batting 1.00, the only player to do so.

1972 **ROBERTO CLEMENTE** got his 3,000th and last hit for Pittsburgh as the Pirates beat the New York Mets 5-0. He was killed in a plane crash December 31, 1972.

1980 Iran's spiritual leader, **AYATOLLAH KHOMEINI** [hoh-may'-nee], rejected a truce call from Iraqi President Saddam Hussein, saying war between the two countries would continue "to the end."

1987 **MIKHAIL GORBACHEV** shook up the Kremlin. when he retired President Andrei Gromyko and fired other long-time leaders.

1987 Campaign manager to Gov. **MICHAEL DUKAKIS**, **JOHN SASSO**, resigned after admitting he leaked an "attack" video tape to help bring down the candidacy of Delaware Senator **JOSEPH BIDEN**.

1988 **JOHN LENNON** was awarded a star on the Hollywood Walk of Fame.

1991 The Haitian President, **JEAN-BERTRAND ARISTIDE**, was ousted in a military coup.

1992 **GEORGE BRETT** of the Kansas City Royals got his 3,000th hit, the 18th player in major league history to do so.

OCTOBER MEMORIES

YEARS AGO

1985

POPULAR SONGS
"Saving All My Love For You" by Whitney Houston

"Part-Time Lover" by Stevie Wonder

MOVIES
A View To a Kill
starring Roger Moore as James Bond. Co-stars Grace Jones and Christopher Walken.

Desperately Seeking Susan
starring Rosanna Arquette, Madonna, and Aidan Quinn. A comedy about personal ads

TV SHOWS
"The Golden Girls"
sitcom about four roommates with Bea Arthur, Betty White, Estelle Getty, and Rue McClanahan.

"Oceanquest"
a documentary series with Shawn Weatherly and Al Giddings.

BOOKS
The Tree of Life by Hugh Nissenson

1986

POPULAR SONGS
"When I Think of You" by Janet Jackson

"True Colors" by Cyndi Lauper

MOVIES
Aliens
in this sequel Sigourney Weaver, Paul Reiser, and Michael Biehn star.

Hoosiers
starring Barbara Hershey and Dennis Hopper. The story of a coach, Gene Hackman, and his small town Indiana basketball team.

TV SHOWS
"My Sister Sam"
starring Pam Dawber and Rebecca Schaffer as sisters in this comedy series.

"Alf"
starring Anne Schedeen and Max Wright. A small furry alien from the planet Melmac lives with the Tanner family

BOOKS
Word For Word by Andy Rooney

1987

POPULAR SONGS
"Lost In Emotion" by Lisa Lisa & Cult Jam

"Bad" by Michael Jackson

MOVIES
Anna
starring Paulina Porizkova, Sally Kirkland, and Robby Fields. A Czech film star tries to make it in the U.S.

Three Men and a Baby
starring Tom Selleck, Ted Danson, and Steve Guttenberg as three bachelors who inherit a baby girl.

TV SHOWS
"Jake and the Fatman"
starring Joe Penny as Jake Styles and William Conrad as Jason Lochinvar.

"Tour of Duty"
starring Terrance Stamp as Sgt. Zeke Anderson. A drama about Vietnam in 1967.

BOOKS
The Bonfire of the Vanities by Tom Wolfe

SPECIAL DAYS

OCTOBER	1995	1996	1997
Fire Prevention Week	Oct. 8-14	Oct. 6-12	Oct. 5-11
Metric Week	Oct. 8-14	Oct. 13-19	Oct. 12-18
Newspaper Week	Oct. 8-14	Oct. 13-19	Oct. 12-18
Pet Peeve Week	Oct. 8-14	Oct. 13-19	Oct. 12-18
Columbus Day	Oct. 9	Oct. 14	Oct. 13
Candian Thanksgiving	Oct. 9	Oct. 14	Oct. 13
School Lunch Week	Oct. 8-14	Oct. 13-19	Oct. 12-18
Sweetest Day	Oct. 21	Oct. 19	Oct. 18
Full Moon	Oct. 8	Oct. 26	Oct. 16
Mother-In-Law Day	Oct. 22	Oct. 27	Oct. 26
Total Solar Eclipse	Oct. 24		

25 YEARS AGO

1970

POPULAR SONGS
"Cracklin' Rosie" by Neil Diamond

"Take On Me" by a-ha

MOVIES
Scrooge
the Charles Dickens classic becomes a musical starring Alec Guinness.

Joe
drama featuring Susan Sarandon and Peter Boyle.

TV SHOWS
"San Francisco International Airport" starring Lloyd Bridges as the airport manager in this action/suspense show.

"The Most Deadly Game"
starring Yvette Mimieux, George Maharis, and Ralph Bellamy. Criminologists deal with abnormal murders.

BOOKS
Islands In the Stream by Ernest Hemingway

1971

POPULAR SONGS
"Baby I'm-Want You" by Bread

"Have You Seen Her" by Chi-Lites

MOVIES
Mary, Queen of Scots
starring Vanessa Redgrave and Glenda Jackson as Queen Mary and Queen Elizabeth.

Fiddler on the Roof
the story of Tevye, a poor dairy farmer, his wife and three daughters.

TV SHOWS
"Cannon"
starring William Conrad as Detective Frank Cannon.

"Shirley's World"
starring Shirley MacLaine as a reporter/ photographer in this sitcom.

BOOKS
The Day of the Jackal by Frederick Forsyth

1972

POPULAR SONGS
"Ben" by Michael Jackson

"My Ding-A-Ling" by Chuck Berry

MOVIES
The Godfather
starring Marlon Brandon as Don Corleone. Also stars Al Pacino, James Caan, Talia Shire, and John Cazale. The story of the Corleone Mafia family.

Travels With My Aunt
an Aunt tries to liberate her nephew while dealing with an old lover.

TV SHOWS
"Maude"
sitcom starring Bea Arthur and Bill Macy. An "All In the Family" spin-off.

"The Waltons"
starring Will Gear, Michael Learned, and Richard Thomas. The story of an extended family during the depression.

BOOKS *Semi-Tough* by Dan Jenkins

50 YEARS AGO

1945

POPULAR SONGS
"Cottage For Sale" by Billy Eckstine

"June Is Bustin' Out All Over" by Hildegarde

MOVIES
Saratoga Trunk
the story of a Texas millionaire starring Gary Cooper and Ingrid Bergman.

Flame of the Barbary Coast
a melodrama starring John Wayne and Ann Dvorak.

TV SHOWS
No regularly scheduled TV programming until May 1946.

BOOKS
Atomic Energy for Military Purposes: the Smyth Report by Professor Henry deWolf Smyth

1946

POPULAR SONGS
"Rumors Are Flying" by Frankie Carle

"To Each His Own" by Ink Spots

MOVIES
Caesar and Cleopatra
starring Stewart Granger, Claude Rains, and Vivien Leigh in this film.

Canyon Passage
starring Dana Andrews, Brian Donlevy, and Susan Hayward in a western love triangle.

TV SHOWS
"Faraway Hill"
a romantic drama starring Flora Campbell.

"Television Screen Magazine"
Viewers see stamp collections, police chorus, and film segments of "White Berns Roams." Bill Berns hosts.

BOOKS
The Roosevelt I Knew by Frances Perkins

1947

POPULAR SONGS
"I Wish I Didn't Love You So" by Dick Haymes

"Golden Earrings" by Peggy Lee

MOVIES
Possessed
starring Joan Crawford as a schizophrenic in a story of madness and murder

Black Narcissus
starring Deborah Kerr, David Farrar, Sabu, Flora Robson, and Jean Simmons. The story of a stranger who enters a nun's convent in the Himalayas.

TV SHOWS
"Mary Kay and Johnny"
an early TV sitcom starring the Stearns as themselves.

BOOKS
East Side, West Side by Marcia Davenport

Country Music Association Award Winners

Entertainer of the Year
1967 - Eddy Arnold
1968 - Glen Campbell
1969 - Johnny Cash
1970 - Merle Haggard
1971 - Charley Pride
1972 - Loretta Lynn
1973 - Roy Clark
1974 - Charlie Rich
1975 - John Denver
1976 - Mel Tillis
1977 - Ronnie Milsap
1978 - Dolly Parton
1979 - Willie Nelson
1980 - Barbara Mandrell
1981 - Barbara Mandrell
1982 - Alabama
1983 - Alabama
1984 - Alabama
1985 - Ricky Skaggs
1986 - Reba McEntire
1987 - Hank Williams, Jr.
1988 - Hank Williams, Jr.
1989 - George Strait
1990 - George Strait
1991 - Garth Brooks
1992 - Garth Brooks
1993 - Vince Gill

Female Vocalist of the Year
1967 - Loretta Lynn
1968 - Tammy Wynette
1969 - Tammy Wynette
1970 - Tammy Wynette
1971 - Lynn Anderson
1972 - Loretta Lynn
1973 - Loretta Lynn
1974 - Olivia Newton-John
1975 - Dolly Parton
1976 - Dolly Parton
1977 - Crystal Gayle
1978 - Crystal Gayle
1979 - Barbara Mandrell
1980 - Emmylou Harris
1981 - Barbara Mandrell
1982 - Janie Frickie
1983 - Janie Frickie
1984 - Reba McEntire
1985 - Reba McEntire
1986 - Reba McEntire
1987 - Reba McEntire
1988 - K. T. Oslin
1989 - Kathy Mattea
1990 - Kathy Mattea
1991 - Tanya Tucker
1992 - Mary-Chapin Carpenter
1993 - Mary Chapin Carpenter

Male Vocalist of the Year
1967 - Jack Greene
1968 - Glenn Campbell
1969 - Johnny Cash
1970 - Merle Haggard
1971 - Charley Pride
1972 - Charley Pride
1973 - Charlie Rich
1974 - Ronnie Milsap
1975 - Waylon Jennings
1976 - Ronnie Milsap
1977 - Ronnie Milsap
1978 - Don Williams
1979 - Kenny Rogers
1980 - George Jones
1981 - George Jones
1982 - Ricky Skaggs
1983 - Lee Greenwood
1984 - Lee Greenwood
1985 - George Strait
1986 - George Strait
1987 - Randy Travis
1988 - Randy Travis
1989 - Ricky Van Shelton
1990 - Clint Black
1991 - Vince Gill
1992 - Vince Gill
1993 - Vince Gill

Album of the Year
1967 - *There Goes My Everything* by Jack Green/Decca
1968 - *Johnny Cash at Folsom Prison* by Johnny Cash/Columbia
1969 - *Johnny Cash at San Quentin Prison* by Johnny Cash/Columbia
1970 - *Okie from Muskogee* by Merle Haggard/Capitol
1971 - *I Won't Mention It Again* by Ray Price/Columbia
1972 - *Let Me Tell You about a Song* by Merle Haggard/Capitol
1973 - *Behind Closed Doors* by Charlie Rich/Epic
1974 - *A Very Special Love Song* by Charlie Rich/Epic
1975 - *A Legend in My Time* by Ronnie Milsap/RCA
1976 - *Wanted—The Outlaws* by Waylon Jennings, Willie Nelson, Tompall Glaser, Jessi Colter/RCA
1977 - *Ronnie Milsap Live* by Ronnie Milsap/RCA
1978 - *It Was Almost Like a Song* by Ronnie Milsap/RCA
1979 - *The Gambler* by Kenny Rogers/United Artist
1980 - *Coal Miner's Daughter*, original Motion Picture Soundtrack/MCA
1981 - *I Believe in You* by Don Williams/MCA
1982 - *Always on My Mind* by Willie Nelson/Columbia
1983 - *The Closer You Get* by Alabama/RCA
1984 - *A Little Good News* by Anne Murray/Capitol
1985 - *Does Fort Worth Ever Cross Your Mind* by George Strait/MCA
1986 - *Lost in the Fifties Tonight* by Ronnie Milsap/RCA
1987 - *Always and Forever* by Randy Travis/Warner Bros.
1988 - *Born to Boogie* by Hank Williams, Jr./Warner Bros.
1989 - *Will the Circle Be Unbroken Vol. II* by Nitty Gritty Dirt Band/Universal
1990 - *Pickin' on Nashville* by Kentucky HeadHunters/Murcury
1991 - *No Fences* by Garth Brooks/Capitol Nashville
1992 - *Ropin' the Wind* by Garth Brooks/Liberty
1993 - *I Still Believe In You* by Vince Gill/Tony Brown

Single of the Year
1967 - "There Goes My Everything" by Jack Greene/Decca
1968 - "Harper Valley P.T.A." by Jeannie C. Riley/Plantation
1969 - "A Boy Named Sue" by Johnny Cash/Columbia
1970 - "Okie from Muskogee" by Merle Haggard/Capitol
1971 - "Help Me Make It Through The Night" by Sammi Smith/Mega
1972 - "The Happiest Girl in the Whole U.S.A." by Donna Fargo/Dot
1973 - "Behind Closed Doors" by Charlie Rich/Epic
1974 - "Country Bumpkin" by Cal Smith/MCA
1975 - "Before the Next Teardrop Falls" by Freddy Fender/ABC-Dot
1976 - "Good Hearted Woman" by Waylon Jennings & Willie Nelson/RCA
1977 - "Lucille" by Kenny Rogers/United Artists
1978 - "Heaven's Just a Sin Away" by The Kendalls/Ovation
1979 - "The Devil Went Down to Georgia" by Charlie Daniels Band/Epic
1980 - "He Stopped Loving Her Today" by George Jones/Epic
1981 - "Elvira" by Oak Ridge Boys/MCA
1982 - "Always on My Mind" by Willie Nelson/Columbia
1983 - "Swingin'" by John Anderson/Warner Bros.
1984 - "A Little Good News" by Anne Murray/Capitol
1985 - "Why Not Me" by The Judds/RCA
1986 - "Bop" by Dan Seals/EMI-America
1987 - "Forever and Ever, Amen" by Randy Travis/Warner Bros.
1988 - "Eighteen Wheels and a Dozen Roses" by Kathy Mattea/PolyGram
1989 - "I'm No Stranger to the Rain" by Keith Whitley/RCA
1990 - "When I Call Your Name" by Vince Gill/MCA
1991 - "Friends in Low Places" by Garth Brooks/Capitol Nashville
1992 - "Achy Breaky Heart" by Billy Ray Cyrus/Mercury
1993 - "Chattahoochee" by Alan Jackson/Keith Stegall

Is ping-pong a contact sport?

OCTOBER 1

BIRTHDAYS

- **RANDY QUAID** Actor. (Houston, TX) Played the father on the TV sitcom "Davis Rules" with Jonathan Winters. In films *The Paper* and *Bye Bye Love*. Year/**Age**: 1995/**45** 1996/**46** 1997/**47**

- **CHRIS LOWE** Singer/keyboardist. (England) PET SHOP BOYS. Biggest hit: "West End Girls," in 1986. Year/**Age**: 1995/**36** 1996/**37** 1997/**38**

- **JIMMY CARTER** Former President. (Born James Earl Carter in Plains, GA) 39th U.S. President. He appeared on "What's My Line" four years before the election, and when he signed on, nobody knew who he was. He said: "I'm J. C., and I'm running for president." Year/**Age**: 1995/**71** 1996/**72** 1997/**73**

- **JULIE ANDREWS** Actress/singer. (Born Julia Wells in England) She won an Oscar for best actress in 1964 for *Mary Poppins*. At age 24, she appeared on Broadway in *My Fair Lady*. In the mid-'50s Julie appeared in a show in NY called *The Boyfriend*. She was unknown then, but everyone said after seeing the show that she would become a star. She is married to director Blake Edwards. Year/**Age**: 1995/**60** 1996/**61** 1997/**62**

- **HERB FAME** Singer. (Born Herbert Feemster in Washington, DC) Of PEACHES & HERB. "Peaches" was Francine Barker, later replaced by Linda Green. Biggest hit: "Reunited" in 1979. Year/**Age**: 1995/**52** 1996/**53** 1997/**54**

- **JAMES WHITMORE** Actor. (White Plains, NY) In 1975, he portrayed Harry Truman in *Give 'em Hell, Harry*. Year/**Age**: 1995/**74** 1996/**75** 1997/**76**

- **WALTER MATTHAU** Actor. (Born Walter Matuschanskayasky in NYC) He has appeared in many movies, including *The Odd Couple*, playing Oscar Madison, and played in *Dennis the Menace* as George Wilson, and *Grumpy Old Men*. He won an Oscar for *The Fortune Cookie* Year/**Age**: 1995/**75** 1996/**76** 1997/**77**

- **TOM BOSLEY** Actor. (Chicago, IL) Played Howard Cunningham on "Happy Days" and also starred in "Father Dowling." Year/**Age**: 1995/**68** 1996/**69** 1997/**70**

- **STELLA STEVENS** Actress. (Born Estelle Egglestone in Hot Coffee, MS) She appeared in *The Courtship of Eddie's Father* and *The Poseidon Adventure*. Year/**Age**: 1995/**59** 1996/**60** 1997/**61**

- **WILLIAM H. REHNQUIST** Chief Justice of the Supreme Court. (Shorewood, WI) A conservative, appointed to the court by President Nixon and sworn in January 7, 1972. Year/**Age**: 1995/**71** 1996/**72** 1997/**73**

- **ROD CAREW** Baseball Hall of Fame star. (Gatun, Panama) In 1972, he was the only baseball player in history to win a batting title and not hit one home run. He won the American League batting crown seven times. Year/**Age**: 1995/**50** 1996/**51** 1997/**52**

- **STEPHEN COLLINS** Actor. (Des Moines, IA) Appeared in *Star Trek* the movie. Year/**Age**: 1995/**48** 1996/**49** 1997/**50**

- **RICHARD HARRIS** Actor. (Limerick, Ireland) Films include: *Mutiny on the Bounty*, *A Man Called Horse*, *Camelot*, and *Unforgiven*. He had a hit record in 1968: "MacArthur Park." Year/**Age**: 1995/**65** 1996/**66** 1997/**67**

- **GEORGE PEPPARD** Actor. (1928-1994, Detroit, MI) He appeared in the movies *The Blue Max* and *The Carpetbaggers*. He starred on "The A-Team" on TV with Mr. T. He married Elizabeth Ashley twice. (Died of lung cancer 5-8-94.)

- **LAURENCE HARVEY** Actor. (1928-1973 – Born Larushke Skikne in Lithuania) Academy Award nomination for *Room at the Top*. (Died 11-25-73.)

- **DONNY HATHAWAY** Singer. (1945-1979 – Chicago, IL) Biggest hit: "The Closer I Get To You" in 1978 and with his college classmate Roberta Flack, "Where Is The Love" in 1972. He committed suicide by leaping to his death from the 15th floor of the Essex House Hotel in New York City. (Died 1-13-79.)

- **VLADIMIR HOROWITZ** Classical pianist. (1904-1989 – Russia) One of the 20th century's greatest musicians. In 1986, he received the highest civilian honor in the U.S., the Presidential Medal of Freedom. (Died 11-5-89.)

FACTS FROM THE PAST

1533 **BLOODY MARY** was crowned Queen of England. Henry VIII was her father. She wore a blue velvet gown trimmed with ermine. The crown was so massive, she had a hard time holding her head up.

1760 The first countess **KILLED BY COSMETICS** was Marie, Countess of Coventry, due to excess lead in the make-up. Some called her the original "dumb blonde."

1903 The **FIRST BASEBALL WORLD SERIES** began in Boston. The Pittsburgh Pirates beat the Boston Pilgrims (Red Sox) 7-3. Boston won the series, five games to three. Jim Sebring got the first series home run. **CY YOUNG** was the first losing pitcher.

1908 The Model T was introduced by Henry Ford at the cost of **$825 PER CAR.**

1946 For the **FIRST TIME IN MAJOR-LEAGUE HISTORY**, a playoff series to determine a league championship was played, between the St. Louis Cardinals and the Brooklyn Dodgers. The Cardinals won the first game, 4-2. Dodger Ralph Branca was the losing pitcher.

1962 **JOHNNY CARSON** first appeared on the "Tonight Show," which included Skitch Henderson's Orchestra, Ed McMahon announcing, guests Joan Crawford, Tony Bennett, Rudy Vallee, Mel Brooks, and Groucho Marx.

1980 **PAUL SIMON**'s semi-autobiographical film, *One Trick Pony,* was released. LOU REED, SAM & DAVE, LOVIN' SPOONFUL, and the B-52's made cameo appearances.

1992 **ROSS PEROT** announced that he was getting back into the 1992 presidential race. Perot told his supporters: "My decision in July hurt you. I apologize, I made a mistake."

OCTOBER 2

Death to all fanatics!

BIRTHDAYS

- **DON McLEAN** Singer. (New Rochelle, NY) His biggest hit: "American Pie" in 1971. In the song, he sings of "The day the music died," referring to the death of singer Buddy Holly. The song "Killing Me Softly" by Roberta Flack was written about Don McLean. Year/**Age**: 1995/**50** 1996/**51** 1997/**52**
- **GORDON "STING" SUMNER** Singer. (Newcastle, England) Bass guitarist for the POLICE. Biggest hit: "Every Breath You Take" in 1983. Nicknamed "Sting" because of a yellow and black jersey he liked to wear. Solo hits: "Set Them Free" and "Fortress Around Your Heart." Year/**Age**: 1995/**44** 1996/**45** 1997/**46**
- **REX REED** Columnist/critic. (Fort Worth, TX) He's a show biz critic who briefly flirted with an acting career when he made his disastrous movie debut as a would-be transsexual in *Myra Breckinridge*. Year/**Age**: 1995/**57** 1996/**58** 1997/**59**
- **ESAI MORALES** Actor. Year/**Age**: 1995/**63** 1996/**64** 1997/**65**
- **MAURY WILLS** Baseball star. (Washington, DC) In 1962, he stole 104 bases to set a new record. Year/**Age**: 1995/**63** 1996/**64** 1997/**65**
- **TIFFANY** Singer. (Born Tiffany Renee Darwisch in Oklahoma) Hits include: "I Think We're Alone Now," "Could've Been," and "I Saw Him Standing There." She was the voice of Judy Jetson in the "Jetsons" movie. Year/**Age**: 1995/**24** 1996/**25** 1997/**26**
- **LORRAINE BRACCO** Actress. (New York, NY) Hollywood Film star. Year/**Age**: 1995/**24** 1996/**25** 1997/**26**
- **MOSES GUNN** Actor. (1929-1993, St. Louis, MO) Appeared on "Father Murphy" and "Good Times." Appeared in films *Shaft* and *The Great White Hope*. (Died 12-16-93.)
- **CORDELL HULL** American statesman. (1871-1955) Served in both Houses of Congress and was U.S. Secretary of State. He worked on establishing the United Nations. (Died 7-23-55.)

- **WALLACE STEVENS** Author/poet. (1879-1955 – Reading, PA) Won a Pulitzer Prize in 1955 for *Collected Poems*. (Died 8-2-55.)
- **RICHARD III** (1452-1485 – England) 12th of 13 children, he married the wealthy widow of the Prince of Wales and then imprisoned his mother-in-law for life. His brother drowned in a cask of wine while he stood by and watched.
- **GROUCHO MARX** Actor/comedian. (1890-1977 – Born Julius Henry Marx in NYC) Probably most famous for his TV/radio quiz show, "You Bet Your Life," which began in 1947 and, of course, the "Marx Brothers" movies. He got his nickname because he was always so bitter. Groucho married three times. He always chased women in films. Later he said: "I only chased them if they ran downhill." He also said he would never join a club that would allow him to be a member. His trademark was a painted moustache, bushy eyebrows and a cigar. He wrote his own epitaph: "Here lies Groucho Marx, and lies and lies and lies. P.S. He never kissed an ugly girl." (Died 8-19-77.)
- **BUD ABBOTT** Actor/comedian. (1898-1974 – Born William Abbott in Asbury Park, NJ) He and Lou Costello made many comedy movies before they split up in 1957. One of their funniest routines was "Who's on First," seen in their first film *One Night in the Tropics*. (Died 4-24-74.)
- **MAHATMA GANDHI** Indian leader. (1869-1948 – Born Mohandas Gandhi in Porbandar, India) He was an atheist, took dancing lessons, smoked, took the vow of celibacy and would sleep next to young girls to test his chastity. He learned English from an Irish priest, so he spoke it with an Irish brogue for the rest of his life. He pioneered the tactic of non-violent civil disobedience, effectively utilized in the U.S. Civil Rights Movement in the 1960's. (Assassinated 1-30-48.)

FACTS FROM THE PAST

1872 The famous wager of **PHILEAS FOGG** that he would make it "around the world in 80 days" was made on this day. The bet was for 20 pounds, and he made it in 79 days, 23 hours, 59 minutes. Jules Verne wrote a book which was based on this bet.

1937 Warner Bros. released *Love Is on the Air* which featured the motion picture debut of then 26-year-old **ACTOR RONALD REAGAN.**

1950 **CHARLIE BROWN, SNOOPY & LUCY VAN PELT** were created on this date by cartoonist **CHARLES SCHULZ** in the comic strip "Peanuts," first published in nine newspapers in 1950 and now appearing in 2,000 papers in 68 countries.

1959 Rod Serling's **"TWILIGHT ZONE"** made its debut on CBS-TV.

1967 **THURGOOD MARSHALL** became the first African-American on the United States Supreme Court when he was sworn in as an associate justice.

1975 A bomb scare delayed a **BRUCE SPRINGSTEEN** show at Milwaukee's Uptown Theatre. Later, Bruce performed drunk after arriving on top of a writer's car. A journalist wrote: "I have seen the future of rock 'n roll, and he is on my windshield."

1984 **RICHARD W. MILLER** became the first FBI agent to be arrested and charged with espionage. (He was subsequently convicted, and is serving two life terms plus 50 years.)

1987 **PRESIDENT REAGAN**, in his weekly radio talk, said he would step up the war against drug traffickers and First Lady Nancy Reagan added that nothing frightened her more than "the drug epidemic among our children."

1988 The **SUMMER OLYMPIC GAMES** concluded in Seoul [sohl], South Korea, with the Soviet Union coming in first in the medals count, East Germany second, and the United States third.

1990 The Senate voted 90-9 to confirm **DAVID SOUTER** as the newest member of the Supreme Court. He was sworn in October 9, 1990. He's a moderate conservative.

Get real . . .
Is it as easy as it sounds.

OCTOBER 3

BIRTHDAYS

- **DAVE WINFIELD** Baseball. (St. Paul, MN) He played with the Blue Jays and Minnesota Twins. His two-run double in the 11th inning of game 6 clinched the 1992 World Series for Toronto. He was the 19th player to get 3,000 career hits. Year/**Age:** 1995/**44** 1996/**45** 1997/**46**

- **CHUBBY CHECKER** King of the "Twist." (Born Ernest Evans in Philadelphia, PA) Biggest hit: "The Twist" which was on the charts for 18 weeks in 1960 and 21 weeks in 1961. Dick Clark's wife gave him the name "Chubby Checker" after seeing him on "American Bandstand" in 1959. She thought, "We have a Fats Domino, let's call him a Chubby Checker." With the exception of "White Christmas," "The Twist" is the only record to become #1 again after being off the charts for over a year. Year/**Age:** 1995/**54** 1996/**55** 1997/**56**

- **LINDSEY BUCKINGHAM** Guitarist. (Palo Alto, CA) With FLEETWOOD MAC beginning in 1975. Their biggest hit: "Dreams" in 1977. He had two solo hits: "Go Insane" and "Trouble." Year/**Age:** 1995/**48** 1996/**49** 1997/**50**

- **MADLYN RHUE** Actress. (Washington, DC) Appeared as Daphne DiMera on "Days of Our Lives" soap opera and in the continuing TV drama "Executive Suite" in 1976. Year/**Age:** 1995/**61** 1996/**62** 1997/**63**

- **GORE VIDAL** Author. (West Point, NY) Wrote *Myra Breckenridge* in 1968 which was made into a movie in 1969—it was a dud. He played Senator Brickley Paiste in the film *Bob Roberts* in 1992. He and Norman Mailer have an on-going feud. He once said that babies should be born under license. National Book Award winner. Year/**Age:** 1995/**70** 1996/**71** 1997/**72**

- **DENNIS ECKERSLEY** Baseball. (Oakland, CA) Relief pitcher for the Oakland A's. Year/**Age:** 1995/**41** 1996/**42** 1997/**43**

- **ALAN O'DAY** Singer/songwriter/pianist. (Hollywood, CA) He wrote "Angie Baby" for Helen Reddy and "Rock & Roll Heaven" for the Righteous Brothers. His #2 hit in 1977: "Undercover Angel." Year/**Age:** 1995/**55** 1996/**56** 1997/**57**

- **JACK WAGNER** Actor/singer. His first TV appearance was on "Ozzie & Harriet" and appeared as rock singer Frisco Jones on "General Hospital." Year/**Age:** 1995/**36** 1996/**37** 1997/**38**

- **NEALE FRASER** Tennis star. (Australia) Won many doubles tourneys. Year/**Age:** 1995/**62** 1996/**63** 1997/**64**

- **FRED COUPLES** Golf pro. In 1992, he became the first American to win the Masters since Larry Mize in 1987. Year/**Age:** 1995/**36** 1996/**37** 1997/**38**

- **EMILY POST** American author/social arbiter. (1873-1960 – Baltimore, MD) (Died 9-25-60.)

- **STEVIE RAY VAUGHN** Blues guitarist. (1954-1990 – Dallas, TX) He overcame drug and alcohol problems and won 2 Grammy awards. He died in a helicopter crash at Alpine Valley in East Troy, WI on 8-27-90.

- **EDDIE COCHRAN** Singer (1939-1960 – Born in Oklahoma City, OK) Biggest hit: "Summertime Blues" in 1958. He was killed in a car crash. (Died 4-17-60)

- **THOMAS WOLFE** Novelist. (1900-1938 – Born in Asheville, NC) Considered by some to be one of the greatest prose writers in America. He wrote *Look Homeward Angel* and *You Can't Go Home Again.* (Died 9-15-38.)

FACTS FROM THE PAST

1863 President **ABRAHAM LINCOLN** issued a proclamation designating the last Thursday in November as **THANKSGIVING DAY**. It was moved to the 3rd Thursday in 1939 and then Congress placed Thanksgiving in its present location, the 4th Thursday in November.

1922 Democrat **MRS. REBECCA FELTON** became the **FIRST WOMAN** to be named to the **U.S. SENATE**, by the governor of Georgia.

1951 **BOBBY THOMPSON** hit a home run in the bottom of the 9th inning of a playoff game to win the National League pennant for the New York Giants, upsetting the Brooklyn Dodgers.

1955 **CAPTAIN KANGAROO** and the **"MICKEY MOUSE CLUB"** premiered on CBS and ABC, respectively.

1960 The **"ANDY GRIFFITH SHOW"** premiered.

1961 **HANK WILLIAMS, JIMMIE RODGERS** and **FRED ROSE** became the first members inducted into the Country Music Hall of Fame in Nashville.

1965 **MANFRED MANN** became the first western band to perform behind the Iron curtain.

1974 **FRANK ROBINSON** became the first African-American manager in baseball when he was named to manage the Cleveland Indians.

1988 The **JOHN LENNON** documentary, *Imagine,* premiered in Hollywood.

1989 **ART SHELL** became the first African-American head coach in modern NFL history, taking over the Los Angeles Raiders. It was 15 years to the day after the Cleveland Indians made Frank Robinson the first African-American manager in major-league baseball.

1990 **GERMANY CELEBRATED UNIFICATION** (officially at midnight). The new nation of 78 million took a holiday to celebrate the end of 45 years of division. The date was changed from November 9th because that date in 1938 was the onset of the Holocaust.

1991 Arkansas Governor **BILL CLINTON** announced that he was a candidate for the Democratic presidential nomination.

1992 Entertainer **SINEAD O'CONNOR** tore up a picture of the pope on TV's "Saturday Night Live." Two weeks later, during a Bob Dylan tribute at Madison Square Garden, she was booed off the stage.

1993 A U.S. helicopter was forced down over Somalia killing 18 and wounding 75. **PRESIDENT CLINTON** said that troops would be withdrawn by March 31, 1994.

OCTOBER 4

What is spam really made of?

BIRTHDAYS

- **ARMAND ASSANTE** Actor. (NYC) Films include: *Mambo Kings*, *Hoffa*, and *1492*. Plus numerous TV mini-series. Year/Age: 1995/**46** 1996/**47** 1997/**48**
- **BRENDAN GILL** Critic/author. (Hartford, CT) Writes for *New Yorker* magazine. Year/Age: 1995/**81** 1996/**82** 1997/**83**
- **JAMES FIELDER** Bass player. With BLOOD, SWEAT & TEARS. Hits include "You've Made Me So Very Happy" and "And When I Die." Year/Age: 1995/**48** 1996/**49** 1997/**50**
- **JIMMY WORKMAN** Actor. Film *Addams Family*. Year/Age: 1995/**15** 1996/**16** 1997/**17**
- **CHARLTON HESTON** Actor. (Evanston, IL) At one time he earned a living as a nude model. He won an Oscar in 1959 for best actor in *Ben Hur* and appeared as Moses in *The Ten Commandments*. He was also in *Khartoum*, *Planet of the Apes* and on TV's "Dynasty." Year/Age: 1995/**72** 1996/**73** 1997/**74**
- **JAN MURRAY** Comedian. (Born Murry Janofsky in NYC) Vaudevillian comic and original game show host of "Treasure Hunt." Year/Age: 1995/**78** 1996/**79** 1997/**80**
- **LeROY VAN DYKE** Singer. (Springfort, MO) Biggest hit: "Walk on By" in 1961. Year/Age: 1995/**66** 1996/**67** 1997/**68**
- **SUSAN SARANDON** Actress. (Born Susan Tomaling in NYC) Films: *Witches of Eastwick*, *Bull Durham*, *The Client*, *Thelma and Louise*, *Lorenzo's Oil*, and *Sleeper*. She got her start on "Search for Tomorrow." Year/Age: 1995/**49** 1996/**50** 1997/**51**
- **CLIFTON DAVIS** Actor/singer/composer. (Chicago, IL) He hosted a TV show with his wife Melba Moore in the early '70's. In "That's My Mama," he played Mama's bachelor son, Clifton Curtis, operator of a barber shop, and was Rev. Gregory in "Amen." Year/Age: 1995/**50** 1996/**51** 1997/**52**
- **LORI SAUNDERS** Actress. Played the daughter, Bobbie Jo, on "Petticoat Junction." Year/Age: 1995/**54** 1996/**55** 1997/**56**
- **ALVIN TOFFLER** Author. (NYC) Wrote *The Third Wave* and *Future Shock*. Year/Age: 1995/**67** 1996/**68** 1997/**69**

- **JACKIE COLLINS** Author. (London, England) Sister of actress Joan. Books include *Hollywood Wives*, *Hollywood Husbands*, *Rockstar*, *Lady Boss*, and *American Star*. Her books *Lucky* and *Chances* were made into a mini-series in 1990. Year/Age: 1995/**54** 1996/**55** 1997/**56**
- **MALCOLM BALDRIDGE** Industrialist. (1922-1987) Commerce Secretary at the time of his death – he was thrown from his horse while roping cattle. (Died 7-25-87.)
- **BUSTER KEATON** Silent film star. (1895-1966 – Born Joseph Francis Keaton in Piqua, KS) Always seen with bags under his eyes, he was known as the "great stone face." Magician Harry Houdini named him Buster after he was seen smiling after falling down a flight of stairs. He was in "A Funny Thing Happened on the Way to the Forum" (Died 2-1-66.)
- **DAMON RUNYON** Writer. (1884-1946 – Manhattan, KS) He wrote *Guys and Dolls* in 1932. He said "always try to rub up against money, for if you rub up against money long enough, some of it may rub off on you." He died of cancer and one of the earliest cancer fundraising campaigns was named for him. (Died 12-10-46.)
- **RUTHERFORD B. HAYES** 19th U.S. President. (1822-1893 – Delaware, OH) One of several presidents born in Ohio. He was the most mediocre person who ever ran for president and won. He was a general in the Civil War. Rutherford and his wife Lucy, the parents of eight children, celebrated their 25th wedding anniversary at the White House. The highlight of the evening was the couple's renewal of their marriage vows. Lucy Hayes wore the same dress in which she had been married. (Died 1-17-1893.)
- **EDWARD STRATEMEYER** Author. (1862-1930 – Elizabeth, NJ) Author of children's books, including *The Hardy Boys*, *Nancy Drew*, and *Tom Swift*. He used more than 60 pen names to write over 800 books. Over four million copies were in print in 1987. (Died 5-10-30.)

FACTS FROM THE PAST

1582 POPE GREGORY XIII issued a decree that the day following Tuesday, October 4, 1582, should be Friday, October 15, 1582, correcting the previously used **JULIAN CALENDAR** which was then 10 days out of date. This reform was in effect in most Catholic countries, but the Julian Calendar continued to be used in Britain and the American colonies until 1752.

1896 BEATRICE HOYT won the first U.S. Women's **GOLF CHAMPIONSHIP** in Morristown, NJ.

1923 New York Giants outfielder **CASEY STENGEL** hit an inside-the-park home run in the first World Series game played at the New Yankee Stadium. The Giants beat the Yanks 1-0.

1931 The comic strip **"DICK TRACY,"** created by **CHESTER GOULD**, made its debut.

1957 **"LEAVE IT TO BEAVER"** premiered on CBS-TV, starring **JERRY MATHERS** as "The Beaver."

1965 **JOHNNY CASH** was arrested at the Mexican border when 1,163 pills were found in his guitar case.

1976 Agriculture Secretary **EARL BUTZ** resigned in the wake of a controversy over a joke he had made about African-Americans.

1980 **CARLY SIMON** collapsed from exhaustion on stage in Pittsburgh, and the rest of her tour was cancelled.

1985 Just before Washington Redskin fullback **JOHN RIGGINS** passed out on the floor, he told Supreme Court Justice Sandra Day O'Connor, "Come on, Sandy, baby, loosen up."

1987 The **NATIONAL FOOTBALL LEAGUE** owners staged their first games since the players union went on strike, with non-striking and replacement personnel on the field. Dallas General Manager **TEX SCHRAMM** was behind the idea. The strike was over in 3 weeks.

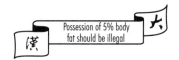

Possession of 5% body fat should be illegal

OCTOBER 5

BIRTHDAYS

- **BILL DANA** Actor/writer/comedian. (Quincy, MA) He had some very successful "José Jimenez" albums – *The Best of José* came out in 1985 with his most famous cut, "The Astronaut." Also, he was on "Make Room for Daddy" with Danny Thomas. Year/**Age**: 1995/**71** 1996/**72** 1997/**73**
- **JOHNNY DUNCAN** C&W. (Dublin, TX) Cousin of Jimmy and England Dan Seals. Duncan's biggest hit: "Thinkin' of a Rendezvous" in 1976. Year/**Age**: 1995/**57** 1996/**58** 1997/**59**
- **MARGIE SINGLETON** C&W. (Coushatta, LA) Biggest hit with Faron Young: "Keeping up with the Joneses" in 1964. Appeared on the "Louisiana Hayride" from 1957-59. Year/**Age**: 1995/**62** 1996/**63** 1997/**64**
- **JEFF CONAWAY** Actor. He played struggling actor Bobby Wheeler on "Taxi." Year/**Age**: 1995/**46** 1996/**47** 1997/**48**
- **STEVE MILLER** Singer/guitarist. (Dallas, TX) He was one of Les Paul's proteges and started playing for money when he was 12 with the Marksmen Combo. He got his first recording contract at age 24 after an appearance at the 1967 Monterey Pop Festival. The STEVE MILLER BAND had a big hit in 1974 called "The Joker." Year/**Age**: 1995/**52** 1996/**53** 1997/**54**
- **GLYNIS JOHNS** Actress. (South Africa) Nominated for an Oscar in 1960 for supporting actress in *The Sundowners*. Year/**Age**: 1995/**72** 1996/**73** 1997/**74**
- **KAREN ALLEN** Actress. (Carrollton, IL) Her films include *Ghost in the Machine, Raiders of the Lost Ark* and *Animal House*. Year/**Age**: 1995/**44** 1996/**45** 1997/**46**
- **DONALD PLEASENCE** Actor. (England) He appeared in *A Tale of Two Cities* and *Fantastic Voyage*. Star of the James Bond thriller *You Only Live Twice*, playing the villainous Blofeld with the nasty Persian cat—finally done in by 007. Year/**Age**: 1995/**76** 1996/**77** 1997/**78**

- **MARIO LEMIEUX** Hockey pro. (Canada) In 1987, he scored the winning goal in overtime to lead Canada to a 6-5 victory over Russia to win the Canada Cup. In 1992 he signed a $42 million contract. On January 12, 1993, it was announced that the Pittsburgh Penguin superstar had Hodgkin's disease, cancer of the lymph nodes. Year/**Age**: 1995/**30** 1996/**31** 1997/**32**
- **SIR BOB GELDOF** Singer/songwriter. (Ireland) With the BOOMTOWN RATS. Nominated for Nobel Peace Prize for organizing the superstar benefit group BAND AID. Year/**Age**: 1995/**41** 1996/**42** 1997/**43**
- **DIANE CILENTO** Actress. (Australia) Sean Connery's ex. Academy Award nomination for *Tom Jones*. Year/**Age**: 1995/**62** 1996/**63** 1997/**64**
- **ALLEN LUDDEN** TV host. (1918-1981 – Mineral Point, WI) Game show host of "Password," "The G.E. College Bowl" and "Liars' Club." Husband of Betty White. (Died 6-9-81.)
- **B. W. STEVENSON** Singer. (1949-1988 – Dallas, TX) Biggest hit: "My Maria" in 1973 and he wrote "Shambala," a hit for THREE DOG NIGHT.
- **CHESTER ALLAN ARTHUR** 21st U.S. President. (1830-1886 – Fairfield, VT) He refused to move into the White House in 1881 until the 81-year accumulation of old furniture and decorations was removed. Had Louis Tiffany do his interior decorating. (Died 11-18-1886.)
- **RAY KROC** McDonald's founder. (1902-1984) At one time, he was a piano player at WGN Radio in Chicago, IL. He started in the hamburger business by selling milkshake machines. He sold one to a McDonald's Drive-in in San Bernardino, CA. He noticed what they were doing in the fast-food business and bought them out, which was the beginning of the McDonald's restaurants. At one time, you could buy a franchise for $10,000.

FACTS FROM THE PAST

1925 **WSM RADIO** in Nashville started broadcasting. One of its first programs was "WSM Barn Dance" which was retitled **"GRAND OLE OPRY"** two years later. It became the longest running radio show in history.

1930 **LAURA INGALLS** made the first transcontinental airplane flight by a woman. She flew a Moth bi-plane from New York to California, arriving four days later. She logged 30 hours and 27 minutes of flying time, stopping nine times along the route.

1931 **CLYDE PANGBORN** and **HUGH HERNDON** completed the first non-stop flight across the Pacific Ocean, arriving in Washington state some 41 hours after leaving Japan.

1947 On the **FIRST TELEVISED WHITE HOUSE ADDRESS**, President Harry S. Truman asked Americans to refrain from eating meat on Tuesdays and poultry on Thursdays in order to help stockpile grain for starving people in Europe.

1969 The **"MONTY PYTHON'S FLYING CIRCUS"** premiered on TV. It completely baffled the British audiences. In 1975, U.S. censors cut the last two words of a very famous sketch. Two men sitting in a tub, with announcer **JOHN CLEESE** saying: "They washed their arms, they washed their legs, then they washed their **NAUGHTY BITS**."

1969 **DIANNE LINKLETTER** jumped to her death from her Hollywood apartment. Her father, TV star **ART LINKLETTER**, claimed at the time of her death Dianne was under the influence of LSD. He said it wasn't suicide, it was murder.

1983 **LECH WALESA**, the founder of Solidarity, Poland's free labor union, was named the winner of the **1983 NOBEL PEACE PRIZE**.

1986 **EUGENE HASENFUS**, ex-U.S. Marine of Marinette, WI, was shot down and captured by Nicaraguan government troops. He was flying a C-123 cargo plane ferrying supplies to the contra rebels. The **IRAN-CONTRA HEARINGS RESULTED** from the incident.

1988 The **DAN QUAYLE-LLOYD BENTSEN DEBATE** drew a TV audience of over 50 million people. Bentsen observed, "Mr. Quayle, you're no John F. Kennedy."

1989 Former **PTL EVANGELIST, JIM BAKKER**, was convicted by a jury in Charlotte, NC, of using his TV show to defraud his followers of over $158 million.

OCTOBER 6

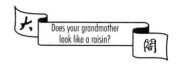

BIRTHDAYS

- **MILLIE SMALL** Singer. (Born Millicent Smith in Jamaica) Biggest hit: "My Boy Lollipop" in 1964. Year/**Age**: 1995/**49** 1996/**50** 1997/**51**

- **THOMAS McCLARY** Guitarist. (Tuskegee, AL) Original member of the COMMODORES with Lionel Richie. One of their biggest hits: "Three Times a Lady" in 1979. Year/**Age**: 1995/**46** 1996/**47** 1997/**48**

- **KEVIN CRONIN** Vocalist. (Champaign, IL) Leader of the group REO SPEEDWAGON. Their biggest hit: "Keep on Loving You" in 1980. Year/**Age**: 1995/**44** 1996/**45** 1997/**46**

- **THOR HEYERDAHL** Explorer/author. Has written several books, including his famed *Kon Tiki*, about a 1947 raft expedition. Year/**Age**: 1995/**81** 1996/**82** 1997/**83**

- **ANNA QUAYLE** Actress. (England) She won a Tony for *Stop the World, I Want to Get Off* in 1962. Year/**Age**: 1995/**59** 1996/**60** 1997/**61**

- **SHANA ALEXANDER** Author/journalist. (New York) Appeared on the "Count Counterpoint" segment of "60 Minutes." Year/**Age**: 1995/**70** 1996/**71** 1997/**72**

- **JERRY GROTE** Baseball. Played for the NY Mets. One of the best catchers of his time. Year/**Age**: 1995/**53** 1996/**54** 1997/**55**

- **RUBEN SIERRA** Baseball. (Puerto Rico) With the Oakland A's. Year/**Age**: 1995/**30** 1996/**31** 1997/**32**

- **DENNIS "OIL CAN" BOYD** Baseball. Year/**Age**: 1995/**36** 1996/**37** 1997/**38**

- **BRITT EKLAND** Actress. (Stockholm, Sweden) At one time, she was married to Peter Sellers and dated Rod Stewart. She was a leading lady in international films and also wrote a book. Year/**Age**: 1995/**53** 1996/**54** 1997/**55**

- **JACK SHARKEY** Boxer. (Born Joseph Cockoschay in Binghampton, NY 1902-1994) He won a June 1932 split decision against Max Schmeling motivating Schmeling's manager to say "We wuz robbed!" At one time, Sharkey said that journalism was "the lowest form of labor."

- **CAROLE LOMBARD** Actress. (1908-1942 – Born Jane Alice Peters in Fort Wayne, IN) She received an Oscar nomination in 1936 for best actress in *My Man Godfrey*. At the time of her death in a plane crash, she was married to actor Clark Gable, whom she married in 1939. (Died 1-16-42.)

- **JENNY LIND** Swedish opera star. (1820-1887 – Born Johanna Maria Lind in Sweden) She imitated a cat purring. Someone heard her and thought she had a great voice. (Died 11-2-1887.)

- **GEORGE WESTINGHOUSE** American inventor. (1846-1914) Invented railway braking systems. (Died 3-12-14.)

- **JANET GAYNOR** Actress. (1906-1984 – Philadelphia, PA) She was the first actress to win an Academy Award, for the movie, *Seventh Heaven* in 1927. (Died 9-14-84.)

FACTS FROM THE PAST

1866 The **RENO BROTHERS** pulled the **FIRST TRAIN ROBBERY** in America near Seymour, IN, robbing a train of $10,000.

1889 **THOMAS EDISON** first exhibited his moving picture machine, the **KINETOSCOPE,** which he patented in 1887.

1927 **TALKING MOVIES** with spoken dialogue and music were introduced in *The Jazz Singer* starring **AL JOLSON.** Georgie Jessel and Eddie Cantor both turned the part down. Warner Brothers made 53\frac{1}{2}$ million at a time when the company was on the verge of collapsing, and revolutionized the movie industry. Only one line was spoken in the film: "You ain't heard nothing yet," spoken by Al Jolson.

1943 **SMOKEY THE BEAR** was created to help prevent forest fires.

1946 The **FIRST SOAP OPERA ON NETWORK TV** was seen on DuMont in Washington, DC, and New York City. The soap "Faraway Hill," starring Flora Campbell, only lasted 12 weeks.

1954 E. L. **LYON** became the **FIRST MALE NURSE** for the U.S. Army.

1966 Baltimore Oriole **JIM PALMER** became the youngest pitcher to hurl a World Series shutout, beating the Dodgers 6-0. Losing pitcher **SANDY KOUFAX** retired after the series.

1968 The **"HEE-HAW"** TV series made its debut. The show was the brainchild of two Canadians and is taped in Nashville. It is best described as a country/western version of "Laugh-in." It was in syndication until 1992.

1969 For the first time, a **GEORGE HARRISON SONG** was put on the "A" side of a **BEATLES** 45. "Something" went on to hit #1.

1976 During **PRESIDENT FORD**'s second debate with Jimmy Carter, he said there was, "no Soviet domination of eastern Europe." He later retracted that statement.

1979 **POPE JOHN PAUL II** became the first pontiff to visit the White House, where he was received by President Jimmy Carter.

1981 **EGYPTIAN PRESIDENT ANWAR SADAT** was assassinated by Islamic fundamentalists in Cairo while he was reviewing a military parade commemorating the 1973 Egyptian/Israeli War. Eight others were killed in the attack.

1982 **PRESIDENT REAGAN**, while addressing a group of Republicans, was heckled for abandoning conservative principles.

1991 **ELIZABETH TAYLOR** married for the 8th time. She wed construction worker Larry Fortensky, whom she met in 1988 in the Betty Ford Center. A dozen helicopters, nine hot-air balloons and a photographer landing in a parachute converged on the Michael Jackson estate, attempting to get pictures for the tabloids.

1992 **ROSS PEROT**'s half-hour informercials drew a larger audience than NBC's "Seinfeld" and Fox's "The Simpsons."

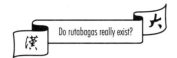

OCTOBER 7

BIRTHDAYS

• **ANN CURLESS** Singer. (Miami, FL) With EXPOSÉ, hits include "Season's Change" in 1987. Year/**Age:** 1995/**31** 1996/**32** 1997/**33**

• **AL MARTINO** Singer. (Born Alfred Cini in Philadelphia, PA) Biggest hit: "I Love You Because" in 1963. He won the Arthur Godfrey "Talent Scout" show in 1952. Appeared in *The Godfather* movie in 1972 as singer Johnny Fontane and *Godfather III* in 1990. Year/**Age:** 1995/**68** 1996/**69** 1997/**70**

• **DAVID HOPE** Bassist. (Topeka, KS) With KANSAS, biggest hit: "Dust in the Wind" in 1978. Year/**Age:** 1995/**46** 1996/**47** 1997/**48**

• **JUNE ALLYSON** Actress. (Born Ella Geisman in Lucerne, NY) American leading lady who could play a tomboy or a tease. She had her first big break in 1941 in *Best Foot Forward* which landed her at MGM in Hollywood where she made many movies including *The Glenn Miller Story* and *Little Women*. She was wed to Dick Powell from 1946 until his death in 1963. They had 2 children. Does the Depend TV commercials. Year/**Age:** 1995/**78** 1996/**79** 1997/**80**

• **TICO TORRES** Drummer. (New Jersey) With the group BON JOVI. One of their biggest hits: "You Give Love a Bad Name." Year/**Age:** 1995/**39** 1996/**40** 1997/**41**

• **DESMOND TUTU** Archbishop. (Klerksdrop, South Africa) Nobel Peace Prize winner in 1984. He was the first Black African-American Anglican bishop of Johannesburg, South Africa. Year/**Age:** 1995/**64** 1996/**65** 1997/**66**

• **OLIVER NORTH** U.S. Marine Corps Lt. Col. (San Antonio, TX) Iran-Contra affair. Year/**Age:** 1995/**52** 1996/**53** 1997/**54**

• **CHRISTOPHER NORRIS** Actress. Played Nurse Gloria 'Ripples' Brancusi on the "Trapper John" TV series. The nickname was dropped after the first couple of seasons. Year/**Age:** 1995/**42** 1996/**43** 1997/**44**

• **JOHN COUGAR MELLENCAMP** Entertainer. (Seymour, IN) Hits: "Jack & Diane," "Cherry Bomb," "Get a Leg Up." He didn't get into music until 1975. Year/**Age:** 1995/**44** 1996/**45** 1997/**46**

• **JUDY LANDERS** Actress. (Philadelphia, PA) Actress Audrey is her sister. Judy starred on TV in "B.J. and the Bear" and "Vegas." Year/**Age:** 1995/**34** 1996/**35** 1997/**36**

• **ALFRED DRAKE** Singer/actor. (1914-1992 – Born Alfred Capurro in NYC) He starred on broadway in *Kismet*, *Kiss Me Kate*, and as Curly in *Oklahoma*. (Died 7-25-92.)

• **ANDY DEVINE** Actor. (1905-1977 – Flagstaff, AZ) Recognized by his gravelly voice. He appeared on the TV series "Flipper" and in "Wild Bill Hickock" with Guy Madison. (Died 2-18-77.)

• **JAMES WHITCOMB RILEY** Poet. (1849-1916 – Greenfield, IN) The poet of the people said: "My work did itself, I'm only the willow bark through which the whistle comes." He started out as a house painter, sign writer and one of few who became popular by reciting his own poetry. His first work made him a profit of $166.40. Best known for "When the Frost is on the Punkin" and "Little Orphant Annie." (Died 7-22-16.)

• **DIANA LYNN** Actress. (1926-1971 – Born Dolores Loehr) She appeared in *Bedtime for Bonzo*, with then-actor Ronald Reagan. "The Tonight Show" producer Fred DeCordova directed the film. (Died 12-18-71.)

FACTS FROM THE PAST

1903 SCIENTIST SAMUEL LANGLEY tested a full-sized airplane over the Potomac River, but the plane nosed over and hit the water. He tried again and almost killed the pilot. A few days later, the **WRIGHT BROTHERS** did it right and Sam lost out on a big first.

1950 FRANK SINATRA made his debut on TV and signed a five-year contract at $250,000 per year.

1954 MARIAN ANDERSON became the first African-American singer hired by the **METROPOLITAN OPERA COMPANY** in New York.

1963 President John F. Kennedy signed a **NUCLEAR TEST BAN TREATY** involving the U.S., Britain and the Soviet Union.

1964 *See How They Run* became the **FIRST MADE-FOR-TV MOVIE** shown on television. It starred **JOHN FORSYTHE** and **SENTA BERGER**. The first movie that was made for TV in 1964 never got on the small screen. *The Killers* was considered too violent and was released to the theaters instead. That film starred Angie Dickinson, Lee Marvin, and Ronald Reagan.

1974 FANNE FOXE panicked after the speeding car she was riding in was stopped by police. She jumped out of the car and into the Tidal Basin in Washington, DC. After being rescued, she returned to the car where her embarrassed friend, the House Ways and Means Committee Chairman, **WILBUR MILLS** was waiting.

1975 JOHN LENNON won his fight with the U.S. Immigration Service when the New York State Supreme Court overturned an order to deport him. Lennon was given permanent resident status a year later.

1981 Vice President **HOSNI MUBARAK** was named by Egypt's parliament to succeed the assassinated Anwar Sadat.

1982 ANDREW LLOYD WEBBER's musical CATS, featuring the popular song "Memory," opened on Broadway.

1985 Palestinian gunmen hijacked the Italian **CRUISE SHIP, ACHILLE LAURO,** with more than 400 people aboard in the Mediterranean. 69-year-old **LEON KLINGHOFFER**, an American passenger, was killed while in his wheelchair and thrown overboard. The four terrorists surrendered on October 10th.

1985 LYNETTE WOODARD became the first female ever to play for the **HARLEM GLOBETROTTERS**.

OCTOBER 8

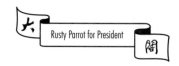

Rusty Parrot for President

BIRTHDAYS

- **SARAH PURCELL** TV hostess. (Richmond, IN) One of the original hosts of "Real People," a TV program featuring non-celebrities. Year/Age: 1995/**47** 1996/**48** 1997/**49**

- **STEPHANIE ZIMBALIST** Actress. (Encino, CA) Daughter of Efrem Zimbalist, Jr. She appeared on the "Remington Steele" TV series. Year/Age: 1995/**39** 1996/**40** 1997/**41**

- **DAVID CARRADINE** Actor. (Hollywood, CA) He's the son of actor John Carradine. In *The Long Riders* with his brothers Keith and Robert. Played Woodie Guthrie in *Bound for Glory*. In TV's "Kung Fu" and its sequel "Kung Fu: The Legend Continues." Year/Age: 1995/**55** 1996/**56** 1997/**57**

- **REV. JESSE JACKSON** Civil rights leader. (Greenville, NC) A Baptist preacher and Civil Rights leader, he was also a Democratic presidential candidate. Year/Age: 1995/**54** 1996/**55** 1997/**56**

- **PAUL HOGAN** Actor. (Australia) *Crocodile Dundee* films and *Lightening Jack* which was financed by local funds. Year/Age: 1995/**56** 1996/**57** 1997/**58**

- **SUSAN RAYE** C&W. (Eugene, OR) She was discovered by Buck Owens in Portland, OR. One of her hits: "I've got a Happy Heart" in 1971. Year/Age: 1995/**51** 1996/**52** 1997/**53**

- **CHEVY CHASE** Actor/comedian. (Born Cornelius Crane Chase in NYC) He won two Emmys on "Saturday Night Live" and was in the films *Cops and Robbersons*, *Caddyshack* and *National Lampoon's Vacation* and played opposite Goldie Hawn in *Foul Play*. His talk show was cancelled shortly after it started. Year/Age: 1995/**52** 1996/**53** 1997/**54**

- **RONA BARRETT** Columnist/novelist. (NYC) She has been a syndicated newspaper columnist since 1960 and has been featured on ABC's "Good Morning, America," NBC's "Today" and "Tomorrow" shows, and on ABC's "Entertainment Tonight." Year/Age: 1995/**59** 1996/**60** 1997/**61**

- **ROBERT "KOOL" BELL** Bass guitarist. (Youngstown, OH) KOOL & THE GANG. Hits include "Celebration" and "Hollywood Swinging." Year/Age: 1995/**45** 1996/**46** 1997/**47**

- **SIGOURNEY WEAVER** Actress. (Born Susan Weaver in Los Angeles, CA) Got the name Sigourney from a character in the book *The Great Gatsby*. Her films include: *Dave*, *Ghostbusters*, *Ghostbusters II*, and the *Alien* films. Oscar nominations for *Aliens*, *Working Girl* and *Gorillas in the Mist*. She charges $1 for autographs and donates it to AIDS research. Her dad. Sylvester Pat Weaver developed NBC's "Today Show" and he wrote the book *Best Seat in the House*. Year/Age: 1995/**46** 1996/**47** 1997/**48**

- **RAY HANDLEY** Football coach. Former Stanford University running back, 1963-65. Named head coach of the New York Giants May 15, 1991. Year/Age: 1995/**51** 1996/**52** 1997/**53**

- **EDDIE RICKENBACKER** Aviator/auto racer/war hero. (1890-1973 – Columbus, OH) Fought the Red Baron in WWI. His auto company made the first car with four-wheel brakes. He bought the Indy Speedway and was president of Eastern Airlines. He only had a third grade education. (Died 7-23-73.)

- **DANNY MURTAUGH** Baseball Manager. (1917-1976) He managed the Pittsburgh Pirates.

FACTS FROM THE PAST

1871 According to legend, Mrs. O'Leary's cow kicked over a kerosene lantern, touching off the 3-day **GREAT CHICAGO FIRE**. The fire killed about 300 people and destroyed more than 17,000 buildings. On this same day, but with less publicity, the worst fire in America's history was raging in the forests around Peshtigo, WI, killing about 1,500 people and scorching 1.28 million acres of timberland.

1918 A small group of soldiers were surrounded by Germans in the Argonne Forest of France. A young corporal, **ALVIN YORK**, had to take command for his wounded sergeant. He killed 20 enemy soldiers and then captured a hill, 132 enemy soldiers and 35 machine guns. The Germans, thinking they were outnumbered, surrendered. York was awarded the U.S. Medal of Honor and French Croix de Guerre.

1934 **BRUNO HAMPTON** was indicted for the muder of aviator Charles Linbergh's baby son.

1944 **"ADVENTURES OF OZZIE AND HARRIET"** made its debut on CBS radio… on the Nelsons' 9th wedding anniversary.

1945 **PRESIDENT TRUMAN** announced that atomic bob secrets would be shared only with Britain and Canada.

1956 **DON LARSEN** became the first pitcher to throw a no-hitter in a World Series game, in the 5th game between the Yankees and the Dodgers, winning the game 2-0, and the series 4 games to 3.

1980 Reggae singer **BOB MARLEY** collapsed on stage during a concert in Pittsburgh. He never performed again. It was discovered that Marley had brain and lung cancer. He died May 1, 1981, at the age of 36.

1981 One of the **MOST EXTRAORDINARY GATHERINGS OF AMERICAN PRESIDENTS** occurred when Richard Nixon, Gerald Ford, Jimmy Carter, and President Ronald Reagan met at the White House prior to their departure for Cairo, Egypt, to represent the United States at the funeral of Anwar Sadat. President Reagan remained at home because of concerns for his safety.

1984 **ANNE MURRAY** was the first woman to win the Country Music Association's album of the year award for *A Little Good News*.

1987 **CHUCK BERRY** was given a star on the Hollywood Walk of Fame.

1988 **ROBIN GIVENS** filed for divorce from heavyweight boxing champion **MIKE TYSON**, one week after she said on national TV that life with the fighter had become "pure hell." The petition cited irreconcilable differences as Robin's reason to end her eight-month marriage to Tyson, whose wealth was estimated at $40 million.

1993 **TED DANSON** appeared in blackface at the Friars Club roast of Whoopi Goldberg and told some off-color racial jokes. Montel Williams, Geraldo Rivera, and Larry King walked out.

You can't squeeze fruit in Europe

OCTOBER 9

Leif Erikson Day

BIRTHDAYS

- **MIKE SINGLETARY** Chicago Bears football star. (Houston, TX) Year/**Age**: 1995/**37** 1996/**38** 1997/**39**
- **ROBERT WUHL** Actor. Year/**Age**: 1995/**46** 1996/**47** 1997/**48**
- **JACKSON BROWNE** Singer. (Heidelberg, West Germany) He grew up in Los Angeles, CA. Member of the NITTY GRITTY DIRT BAND while still in high school, where he began writing songs. His biggest hit: "Doctor, My Eyes" in 1972. Year/**Age**: 1995/**45** 1996/**46** 1997/**47**
- **ZACHERY TY BRYAN** Actor. TV's "Home Improvement." Year/**Age**: 1995/**14** 1996/**15** 1997/**16**
- **SEAN ONO LENNON** (England) Only son of Yoko Ono and John Lennon, born on John's 35th birthday. Julian Lennon is John's son by his first wife, Cynthia. Year/**Age**: 1995/**20** 1996/**21** 1997/**22**
- **E. HOWARD HUNT** Former CIA employee/Watergate participant. He spent 33 months in prison for burglary, conspiracy and wire-tapping at Watergate. His wife Dorothy died (12-8-72) in a jet airplane crash. $10,000 in 100-dollar bills was found in her purse. Year/**Age**: 1995/**77** 1996/**78** 1997/**79**
- **JOE PEPITONE** Baseball. (Brooklyn, NY) Played first base on the 1963-64 Yankee pennant-winning team. He was the first major league player to use a hair dryer in the locker room. Today, major league locker rooms are equipped with outlets for blow dryers or have dryers as a standard feature. Year/**Age**: 1995/**55** 1996/**56** 1997/**57**

- **JOHN ENTWISTLE** Bassist. (London, England) With The WHO. Biggest hit: "I Can See for Miles" in 1967. Year/**Age**: 1995/**51** 1996/**52** 1997/**53**
- **BRIAN DOWNING** Baseball player. California Angels heavy hitter. Year/**Age**: 1995/**45** 1996/**46** 1997/**47**
- **KURT NEUMANN** Singer. With the BODEANS. Year/**Age**: 1995/**34** 1996/**35** 1997/**36**
- **JACQUES TATI** Film director. (1908-1982 – Born Jacques Tatischeff in France) Won an Academy Award for *Mon Oncle* in 1958. (Died 11-5-82.)
- **OTTO SCHNERING** Businessman. (1891 – Chicago, IL) He founded the Curtiss Candy Co. He developed the "Butterfinger" and "Baby Ruth" bars. Baby Ruth named for President Cleveland's daughter, often said to be named for Babe Ruth. Curtiss was his mother's maiden name.
- **JOHN LENNON** Musician/singer/composer. (1940-1980) (Born John Winston Lennon in Liverpool, England.) In 1956 he formed the QUARRY MEN, a skiffle group which changed its name and members; eventually becoming the most successful popular music group in history—the BEATLES. He and Paul McCartney composed most of the Beatles' hits. Biggest hit with Beatles: "Hey Jude." Biggest solo hit: "Just Like Starting Over" in 1980. John Lennon was fatally shot outside his New York City apartment. "Beetles" was a name Buddy Holly and the CRICKETS decided not to use. Lennon changed the spelling and said they used it as a tribute to Holly. (Died 12-8-80.)

FACTS FROM THE PAST

1002 **LEIF ERIKSON** landed in what is now North America.

1855 Joshua Stoddard of Worcester, MA, received a patent for the **FIRST CALLIOPE**. Like an organ with only an 8-note keyboard and powered by steam instead of cold air, it's louder than a jet plane at takeoff, which hits 100 decibels of sound. A calliope produces 135 decibels and could cause earaches.

1872 **AARON MONTGOMERY** started the mail-order business. He mailed out his first catalog, consisting of a single page. The firm became Montgomery Wards.

1905 Actress **SARAH BERNHARDT** had an accident while performing in an opera. A stage-hand forgot to put down a mattress and she landed on her right knee while jumping from a castle. There was a delay in treatment and the knee deteriorated and had to be amputated. She met Houdini one time and was so frustrated that she asked him to bring back her leg.

1929 **GENE AUTRY** began his first recording session.

1930 **LAURA INGALLS** became the first woman to fly across the U.S. as she completed a 9-stop flight from Roosevelt Field, NY, to Glendale, CA.

1973 **ELVIS AND PRISCILLA PRESLEY** were granted a divorce in Santa Monica Superior Court, ending their 6-year marriage. Priscilla received properties, shares in two music publishing companies, almost $1.5 million in cash and $4,200 a month in alimony for a year, plus half the sale price of a $750,000 home.

1975 **ANDRÉ SAKHAROV**, the "father of the hydrogen bomb," became the first Soviet citizen to win the coveted **NOBEL PEACE PRIZE**.

1983 The **OLDEST PERSON TO JOIN THE BROWNIES** was Helen Moss of Bicester, Oxfordshire, England, who joined on this day at the age of 86.

1985 **YOKO ONO** dedicated "Strawberry Fields," a 2$^1/_2$ acre garden memorial, to **JOHN LENNON** in New York City's Central Park.

1986 **ANDREW LLOYD WEBBER**'s musical *Phantom of the Opera* opened in London.

1986 The U.S. Senate convicted **U.S. DISTRICT JUDGE HARRY E. CLAIRBORNE** of "high crimes and misdemeanors," making him the fifth federal official to be removed from office through conviction after impeachment.

OCTOBER 10

Do you need packing tape to a rapper?

BIRTHDAYS

- **MIDGE URE** Singer. (Born James Ure in Scotland) Co-wrote "Do They Know it's Christmas?" Year/Age: 1995/**45** 1996/**46** 1997/**47**

- **BEN VEREEN** Entertainer. (Miami, FL) Broadway actor in the 1960's and 1970's. Probably best known for his portrayal of Chicken George in the TV miniseries "Roots" in 1977. He was hit by a car, June 9, 1992, and made a comeback from serious injuries in April, 1993, appearing with Gregory Hines in *Jelly's Last Jam* on Broadway. Character voice in *Once Upon a Forest.* Year/Age: 1995/**49** 1996/**50** 1997/**51**

- **ADLAI STEVENSON, JR.** Former Illinois Senator. Year/Age: 1995/**65** 1996/**66** 1997/**67**

- **DAVID LEE ROTH** Singer. (Bloomington, IN) He was first known as the lead singer of the VAN HALEN group. His biggest hit: "California Girls" in 1985. Year/Age: 1995/**40** 1996/**41** 1997/**42**

- **JOANNA SHIMKUS** Actress. (Canada) Leading lady in *Zita, The Virgin and the Gypsy,* and *A Time for Loving.* Year/Age: 1995/**51** 1996/**52** 1997/**53**

- **HAROLD PINTER** Playwright. (London) Wrote screenplay *The French Lieutenant's Woman* in 1981. Year/Age: 1995/**65** 1996/**66** 1997/**67**

- **JAMES CLAVELL** Author. (Australia) *Shogun, Noble House, Tai-pan,* and *Gai-Jin.* Year/Age: 1995/**71** 1996/**72** 1997/**73**

- **TANYA TUCKER** C&W. (Seminole, TX) She was in the movie *Jeremiah Johnson* and had her first hit, "Delta Dawn," at age 13. Year/Age: 1995/**37** 1996/**38** 1997/**39**

- **JOHN PRINE** Singer/songwriter. Year/Age: 1995/**49** 1996/**50** 1997/**51**

- **GENE TENACE** Baseball. Oakland A's catcher, who in the 1972 World Series hit 4 homers, drove in 9 runs and broke Joe Harris's record for the highest slugging average in a seven-game Series. Year/Age: 1995/**49** 1996/**50** 1997/**51**

- **BRETT FAVRE** Football. (Fenton, MS) Green Bay Packer quarterback. Year/Age: 1995/**25** 1996/**26** 1997/**27**

- **MICHAEL BIVENS** Singer. Hit with BELL BIV DeVOE, "Poison" in 1990. Year/Age: 1995/**27** 1996/**28** 1997/**29**

- **HELEN HAYES** Actress. (1900-1993 – Born Helen Hayes Brown in Washington, DC) She was an ambitious lady who often said "If you rest, you rust." She was one of TV's "Snoop Sisters" (Died 3-17-93.)

- **THELONIUS MONK** Jazz pianist. (1920-1982 – Rocky Mount, NC) (Died 2-17-82.)

- **JOHNNY GREEN** Composer. (1908-1989 – NYC) Won Oscars for *Easter Parade, West Side Story, Oliver,* and *An American in Paris.* (Died 5-15-89.)

- **IVORY JOE HUNTER** R&B singer/piano player. (1911-1974 – Kirbyville, TX) Biggest hit: "Since I Met You, Baby" in 1956. He wrote over 7,000 songs including "Ain't That Loving You Baby" for Elvis Presley. (Died 11-8-74.)

- **GIUSEPPE VERDI** Musician/composer. (1813-1901 – Italy) He performed his first opera when he was 26 years old. Prior to that, he was a farmer. He was attracted to music when he accidentally played a perfect "C" chord on a harpsichord. He was so angry when he couldn't do it again that he took a hammer and beat the instrument. He then took piano lessons. He composed several hit operas: *Aida, Rigoletto,* and *La Traviata.* (Died 1-27-01.)

FACTS FROM THE PAST

1886   Tobacco heir **GRISWOLD LORILLARD** shocked his contemporaries by showing up at the autumn ball in Tuxedo Park, NY, wearing a dress coat without "tails." The "tail-less" dinner jacket became known as the **TUXEDO.**

1911   Revolutionaries under **SUN YAT-SEN** overthrew China's Manchu Dynasty.

1935   The American opera *Porgy and Bess,* with music by **GEORGE GERSHWIN** and libretto by DuBose Hayward and Ira Gershwin, opened on Broadway.

1962   **BOBBY "BORIS" PICKETT**'s smash "**MONSTER MASH**" was banned by the BBC who felt it was offensive.

1965   The **SUPREMES** made their first appearance on the "Ed Sullivan Show."

1970   **FIJI** became independent after nearly a century of British rule in ceremonies attended by Prince Charles.

1973   V.P. **SPIRO AGNEW** resigned his office as part of a plea-bargain with the Justice Dept. on charges of income tax evasion, after being investigated for accepting bribes while serving as Governor of Maryland.

1978   At the Grand Ole Opry Country Music Awards, **DOLLY PARTON** was named "country entertainer of the year."

1978   President Carter signed a bill authorizing the **SUSAN B. ANTHONY DOLLAR COIN;** said to be one of the dumbest money ideas ever because it looked too much like a quarter.

1982   Pope John Paul II proclaimed the **REVEREND MAXIMILIAN KOLBE** [kohl'-bay], a Polish priest who died at the Nazi death camp Auschwitz [ow'-shvits], a saint of the Roman Catholic Church.

1987   Britain's **TOM McCLEAN** finished rowing across the Atlantic in 1987, setting a **RECORD** for a west-to-east crossing in 54 days, 18 hours.

1987   In Raleigh, NC, the Reverend **JESSE JACKSON** formally announced his bid for the Democratic presidential nomination.

1992   **MICHAEL JACKSON** got $20 million from HBO for the rights to broadcast his "Dangerous" concert from Bucharest. It was the most watched program in HBO's history.

Remember, you can sing as well as Milli Vanilli

OCTOBER 11

BIRTHDAYS

- **DARYL HALL** Singer. (Philadelphia, PA) Of HALL & OATES. Their biggest hit: "Maneater" in 1982. They met in a freight elevator while fleeing a gang fight at the Adelphi Ballroom in Philadelphia, PA. Year/**Age**: 1995/**47** 1996/**48** 1997/**49**

- **GENE WATSON** C&W. (Palestine, TX) One of his biggest hits: "Fourteen Carat Mind" in 1981. Year/**Age**: 1995/**52** 1996/**53** 1997/**54**

- **JEROME ROBBINS** Choreographer. (NYC) Dancer/ballet master who choreographed *West Side Story* for which he won an Oscar, and also *The King & I, Gypsy,* and *Fiddler on the Roof.* Year/**Age**: 1995/**77** 1996/**78** 1997/**79**

- **JOAN CUSACK** Actress. TV's "Saturday Night Live." Year/**Age**: 1995/**33** 1996/**34** 1997/**35**

- **STEVE YOUNG** Football. San Francisco 49er quarterback. He was named NFL MVP three times in four seasons. Year/**Age**: 1995/**34** 1996/**35** 1997/**36**

- **RON LEIBMAN** Actor. (NYC) Appeared as Martin Kazinski on the "Kaz" TV series in the late 1970's, for which he won an Emmy. Year/**Age**: 1995/**58** 1996/**59** 1997/**60**

- **LUKE PERRY** Actor. (Mansfield, OH) Stars in "Beverly Hills 90210." Appeared in *The Lane Frost Story*, about rodeos. Year/**Age**: 1995/**28** 1996/**29** 1997/**30**

- **ELMORE LEONARD** Author. (New Orleans, LA) Wrote *Glitz, LaBrava,* and *City Primeval.* Year/**Age**: 1995/**70** 1996/**71** 1997/**72**

- **DAVID MORSE** Actor. Appeared on "St. Elsewhere." Year/**Age**: 1995/**42** 1996/**43** 1997/**44**

- **DOTTIE WEST** C&W (1932-1991 – Born Dorothy Marsh in McMinnville, TN) She won country music's first Grammy for a female vocalist. Her best known hit was "Country Sunshine." Dottie died of injuries she suffered in a car accident on the way to the Grand Ole Opry (on 9-4-91).

- **HENRY HEINZ** Industrialist. (1884 – Pittsburgh) He was a baker and gardener who eventually started to can some of his harvest. He bottled pickles, beans, then soup and ketchup. He created "Heinz 57 Varieties."

- **ELEANOR ROOSEVELT** (1884-1962 – Born in NYC) Wife of Franklin Delano Roosevelt, 32nd U.S. President. She was the first president's wife to give a news conference in the White House [in 1933]. She was affectionately called "the first lady of the world." A prolific writer, she wrote, "This is my story . . . no one can make you feel inferior without your consent." (Died 11-7-62.)

- **PARSON MASON WEEMS** Pastor/Author. (1759-1825) Episcopal clergyman best remembered for fictitious stories that he presented as historical fact, such as the story describing George Washington cutting down his father's cherry tree with a hatchet. Readers accepted them as true, and they became bestsellers for many years. (Died 5-23-1825.)

FACTS FROM THE PAST

1868 **THOMAS EDISON** completed his first invention and filed for a patent on this day. He was 19 years old. The invention was an electric machine to count votes quickly for the U.S. Congress. It was successful but the Congress decided not to buy the machine. Edison's first was his first financial loss.

1881 The **FIRST ROLL FILM** for cameras was patented by **DAVID HENDERSON HOUSTON** of Cambria, WI.

1936 The **FIRST CASH AND PRIZES** were given away on a **RADIO** quiz program on CBS called "Professor Quiz."

1959 NFL Commissioner **BERT BELL** died of a heart attack while watching the Pittsburgh-Philadelphia football game. He owned both the Eagles and Steelers at different times of his life.

1968 **ASTRONAUTS** Wally Schirra, R. Walter Cunningam, and Donn Fulton Eisele were on board the first manned Apollo flight, Apollo VII.

1969 Near the windy city of Chicago, bluesman **MUDDY WATERS** was seriously injured and three other people were killed in a car crash.

1972 Michael Galen from Australia set a **WORLD RECORD, EATING 63 BANANAS** in 10 minutes, on a TV show.

1975 NBC-TV's **"SATURDAY NIGHT LIVE"** debuted, with guest host **GEORGE CARLIN** and the Not-Ready-for-Prime-Time Players, including John Belushi, Chevy Chase, Dan Aykroyd, Gilda Radner, and Jane Curtin.

1975 **BILL CLINTON** and **HILLARY RODHAM** were married in Fayetteville, AK one year before he was elected to his first public office, Attorney General of Arkansas.

1976 **WAYLON JENNINGS** won three Country Music Association Awards, including single of the year for "Good Hearted Woman."

1976 **JANE PAULEY** replaced Barbara Walters on the "Today Show," and went on to set a record for most years on a morning show.

1981 The Los Angeles Rams defensive back **LEROY IRVIN** ran 6 punts back for a total of 207 yards. L.A. beat Atlanta 37-35.

1984 Space Shuttle **ASTRONAUT KATHY SULLIVAN** became the first American woman to walk in space.

1991 In the first nationally broadcast **CLARENCE THOMAS HEARING**, Anita Hill testified that the Supreme Court nominee engaged in unwanted sexually explicit conversations on the job. Thomas denied the charges and told the Senate Committee, "No job is worth what I've been through."

1992 The Presidential candidates: **GEORGE BUSH, BILL CLINTON** and **ROSS PEROT**, held their first debate at Washington University in St. Louis, MO.

OCTOBER 12

Do the Royals eat pudding?

BIRTHDAYS

• **ADAM RICH** Actor. (NYC) Played the youngest of eight children on the 1970's comedy, "Eight Is Enough." In 1983, he was arrested for smoking pot and in 1988 he entered the Betty Ford Center for substance abuse. Year/Age: 1995/**27** 1996/**28** 1997/**29**

• **PAT ALAN DAY** Jockey. "Little Jesus." Voted the Eclipse Award as nation's best jockey three times. Year/Age: 1995/**42** 1996/**43** 1997/**44**

• **LUCIANO PAVAROTTI** Opera star. (Italy) In *Yes, Giorgio* in 1982. Year/Age: 1995/**60** 1996/**61** 1997/**62**

• **SUSAN ANTON** Entertainer. (Yucaipa, CA) A former Miss California, she starred in the movie *Golden Girl* and appears on stage in Las Vegas and Atlantic City. She was in "The Will Roger's Follies" on Broadway and TV's "Baywatch." Year/Age: 1995/**45** 1996/**46** 1997/**47**

• **SAM MOORE** Singer. (Miami, FL) Of "Sam and Dave." Biggest hit: "Soul Man" in 1967. They broke up in 1981. Year/Age: 1995/**60** 1996/**61** 1997/**62**

• **JAKE GARN** Senator. (R/UT) He was the first Congressional representative to go into space, aboard the *Discovery* shuttle on 4-12-85. He participated in medical experiments related to space sickness. He is chairman of the Senate subcommittee that oversees NASA spending. In 1986, he donated one of his kidneys to his daughter. Year/Age: 1995/**63** 1996/**64** 1997/**65**

• **TONY KUBEK** Sportscaster and former Yankee shortstop. (Milwaukee, WI) Year/Age: 1995/**58** 1996/**59** 1997/**50**

• **DICK GREGORY** Comedian/author/political activist. (St. Louis, MO) Year/Age: 1995/**63** 1996/**64** 1997/**65**

• **JEAN NIDETCH**. (Brooklyn, NY) Founded Weight Watchers. Year/Age: 1995/**72** 1996/**73** 1997/**74**

• **CHARLIE WARD** Football. (Thomasville, GA) He was the first black quarterback for Florida State U. and winner of the 1993 Heisman Trophy. He led his team to the National Championship with a win over Nebraska in the Orange Bowl in 1994. Year/Age: 1995/**25** 1996/**26** 1997/**27**

• **KIRK CAMERON** Actor.. (Panorama City, CA) Mike Seaver on "Growing Pains." His sister Candace appears on "Full House." Year/Age: 1995/**25** 1996/**26** 1997/**27**

• **RONALD McNAIR** Astronaut. (1950-1986) Physicist and second African-American astronaut in space, killed in the shuttle *Challenger* disaster. (Died 1-28-86.)

• **ELMER SPERRY** Inventor. (1860-1930) He held patents for more than 400 inventions including the Sperry Automatic Pilot, "Iron Mike," a tiny black box of intricate controls allowing the pilot to take his hands off the wheel and fly a plane in level flight for hours at a time, reducing pilot fatigue. Elmer founded Sperry-Rand Corp.

FACTS FROM THE PAST

1492 Around 2 a.m., while **CHRISTOPHER COLUMBUS** napped aboard the *Santa Maria*, Roderigo de Triano was up in the crow's nest of the *Pinta* and sighted the Bahamian Island of Guanahani, which Columbus renamed **EL SALVADOR**, claiming it in the name of Spain. The King and Queen of Spain had promised a reward to the first person who would spot land. Roderigo did and shouted "Land Ho," but Columbus collected the reward. It was the **1ST OF 4 VOYAGES** Columbus made.

1853 **JOHN C. MORRISSEY** beat **YANKEE SULLIVAN** for the heavyweight boxing championship. Sullivan was ahead after 36 rounds, but during a rest period he climbed out of the ring to shut up some of the hecklers. He failed to get back in the ring in time for the start of the next round and lost by default.

1933 Bank robber **JOHN DILLINGER** escaped from a jail in Allen County, OH, with the help of his gang who killed the sheriff. After this murder – the gang's first – they went on a rampage that earned Dillinger the FBI designation: **"PUBLIC ENEMY #1."**

1957 **LITTLE RICHARD** quit rock & roll for religion: "If you want to live for the Lord, you can't rock & roll." To prove his point, he tossed four diamond rings into the Hunter River in Sydney, Australia.

1960 **SOVIET PREMIER NIKITA KHRUSHCHEV** shattered decorum at the U.N. Assembly by pounding a desk with his shoe.

1962 Changing his mind about performing, **LITTLE RICHARD** played a Liverpool gig. The **BEATLES,** local and unknown at the time, opened for him.

1970 **LT. WILLIAM CALLEY** was court-martialled for the massacre of 102 civilians in My Lai during the Vietnam War.

1972 Pamela Ness of Kansas City, MO, set a new world's **RECORD FOR BELLY DANCING**. She shook her tummy for 27 continuous hours.

1973 President Richard Nixon nominated House Minority Leader **GERALD FORD** to succeed Vice President Spiro Agnew who resigned under pressure from an income tax evasion scandal on October 10th.

1978 British "punk" rock star, **SID VICIOUS**, was arrested in NY and charged with stabbing to death his American girlfriend, Nancy Spungen.

1979 **IAN ANDERSON** of JETHRO TULL was hit in the eye with a thorn from a rose, thrown at him by a fan at Madison Square Garden in New York City. Two shows had to be canceled.

1984 British **PRIME MINISTER MARGARET THATCHER** escaped an attempt on her life when a bomb planted by the Irish Republican Army exploded at a hotel in Brighton, England, killing five people and injuring 24.

Are you a loopy cultist?

OCTOBER 13

BIRTHDAYS

- **MARIE OSMOND** Entertainer. (Ogden, UT) She began her professional career in 1966 at age 7, the only girl in the performing Osmond family. Her biggest hit was "Paper Roses" in 1973. Her dad, George, was also born on this date. Year/**Age**: 1995/**36** 1996/**37** 1997/**38**

- **MARGARET THATCHER** Former British Prime Minister. (Born Margaret Hilda Roberts in England) She was Britain's only woman prime minister in 800 years of English parliamentary history. When Mr. Thatcher was asked who wears the pants in the family he quipped, "I do... and I also wash and iron them." Year/**Age**: 1995/**70** 1996/**71** 1997/**72**

- **DEMOND WILSON** Actor. (Valdosta, GA) He played Lamont on the "Sanford & Son" TV series with Redd Foxx. He gave up acting to become a preacher. Year/**Age**: 1995/**49** 1996/**50** 1997/**51**

- **LARAINE DAY** Actress. (Born Laraine Johnson in Roosevelt, UT) She appeared in *Young Dr. Kildare* in 1939 and *The High & the Mighty* in 1954. Year/**Age**: 1995/**75** 1996/**76** 1997/**77**

- **ROBERT LAMM** Singer. (Chicago, IL) He does keyboard and vocals for the group CHICAGO. Their biggest hit: "Hard to Say I'm Sorry" in 1982, with "If You Leave Me Now," in 1976, ranked closely behind. Year/**Age**: 1995/**51** 1996/**52** 1997/**53**

- **LACEY J. DALTON** C&W. (Born Jill Croston in Bloomsburg, PA) She co-starred as David Allen Coe's wife in the movie, *Take This Job and Shove It*. One of her biggest hits: "Takin' It Easy" in 1981. Year/**Age**: 1995/**49** 1996/**50** 1997/**51**

- **TISHA CAMPBELL** Actress. TV's "Rags to Riches." Year/**Age**: 1995/**25** 1996/**26** 1997/**27**

- **KELLY PRESTON** Actress. TV's "For Love and Honor." Married to John Travolta. Year/**Age**: 1995/**33** 1996/**34** 1997/**35**

- **JERRY RICE** Football. (Starkville, MS) San Francisco 49er wide receiver. Year/**Age**: 1995/**33** 1996/**34** 1997/**35**

- **ART GARFUNKEL** Entertainer. (Queens, NY) His biggest hit, with Paul Simon, was "Bridge Over Troubled Water" in 1970. Year/**Age**: 1995/**53** 1996/**54** 1997/**55**

- **JERRY JONES** NFL owner. (Los Angeles, CA) Owner of the Dallas Cowboys' winning Super Bowl XXVII team. Year/**Age**: 1995/**52** 1996/**53** 1997/**54**

- **NIPSY RUSSELL** Comedian. (Atlanta, GA) Co-hosted TV's "Les Crane Show." Year/**Age**: 1995/**71** 1996/**72** 1997/**73**

- **EDDIE MATTHEWS** Former baseball star. He played for the Milwaukee Braves at third base and hit 512 career home runs. He was pictured on the cover of the first *Sports Illustrated* in 1954 hitting a home run. His salary topped out at $70,000. He hit 47 home runs in 1953 and was asked to take a $5,000 cut. Year/**Age**: 1995/**64** 1996/**65** 1997/**66**

- **NANCY KERRIGAN** Skater. (Wobur, MA) U.S. Olympian was attacked with an iron bar after a practice session in Detroit. She still went on to capture a silver medal at the Norway Olympics (and to complain how "corney" Disney World seemed to her). Year/**Age**: 1995/**26** 1996/**27** 1997/**28**.

- **YVES MONTAND** Actor/singer. (1921-1991 – Born Ivo Livi in Italy) At one time, he was married to actress Simone Signoret. Starred in *On a Clear Day You Can See Forever* with Barbra Streisand. (Died 11-9-91.)

- **CORNEL WILDE** Actor. (1915-1989, NYC) Leading man in the 1940's and 1950's. Nominated for best actor in 1945 for his portrayal of composer Frederic Chopin in the film *A Song to Remember*. (Died 10-16-89.)

- **BURR TILLSTROM** Puppeteer. (1917-1985) He manipulated puppets on the "Kukla, Fran and Ollie" TV show, starring Fran Allison. (Died 10-6-85.)

- **LENNY BRUCE** Entertainer/comedian. (1925-1966) His life was portrayed in a movie starring Dustin Hoffman. (Died 8-3-66.)

FACTS FROM THE PAST

54 A.D. **ROMAN EMPEROR CLAUDIUS** was murdered by his wife. She fed him poisoned mushrooms, had the back of his throat tickled with a poisoned feather, had him given a poison enema and, finally, frustrated that he was still breathing, smothered him with a pillow.

1792 The White House cornerstone was laid. **JAMES HOBAN** designed the first family's home. John Adams was the first President to occupy the mansion, the oldest building in Washington, DC, with over 100 rooms on 3 floors.

1924 The celebrated husband-wife acting team of **ALFRED LUNT** and **LYNN FONTANNE** appeared together on film for the only time, in a play called *The Guardsman*. Lunt was ill on the day of the premiere, so Fontanne went to it alone. When she returned she was almost hysterical, saying, "Alfred, it was a total disaster. You come off great, except for a tendency to have thin lips, but I'm awful! I look like an ugly witch, my makeup is all wrong, my cheeks look cadaverous, my hair is a mess, and my voice sounds like half a squeak and half a groan!" Lunt thought for a moment and then said, "Thin lips, eh?"

1967 The first game of the new American Basketball Association was played between the Oakland Oaks and the Anaheim Amigos. The owner of the Oaks, **PAT BOONE**, sang the national anthem.

1983 The **INTERNATIONAL** Olympic Committee announced it would restore the two gold medals taken from **JIM THORPE** 70 years after he admitted having been paid to play baseball.

1989 **EVANGELIST BILLY GRAHAM** announced he'd appear in "Hollywood Boulevard's Sidewalk of Stars." His star was placed next to Wayne Newton's.

1992 The only vice presidential debate of the campaign was held at Georgia Tech University in Atlanta, GA. Hal Bruno of ABC News moderated the debate between **DAN QUAYLE, AL GORE,** and **JAMES STOCKDALE.**

1993 **TIFFANY TRUMP** was born to Marla Maples and Donald Trump.

OCTOBER 14

Do you have a silk screen?

BIRTHDAYS

- **BETH DANIEL** Golfer. (Charleston, SC) Has earned well over a million dollars playing golf on the pro circuit. Year/**Age**: 1995/**39** 1996/**40** 1997/**41**

- **ROGER MOORE** British actor. (Born George Roger Moore in London, England) He's been in several "James Bond" films. He made his first TV appearance in 1957 and until 1972, he starred in several American TV shows: "The Persuaders," "The Alaskans" in 1959, and "The Saint." He played Bo in the "Maverick" TV series. Year/**Age**: 1995/**68** 1996/**69** 1997/**70**

- **KARYN WHITE** Singer. (Los Angeles, CA) Hits include: "The Way You Love Me" and "Secret Rendezvous." 1995/**31** 1996/**32** 1997/**33**

- **GREG EVIGAN** Actor. (South Amboy, NJ) Appeared in TV's "B.J. and the Bear," "My Two Dads," and "Tek War." Year/**Age**: 1995/**42** 1996/**43** 1997/**44**

- **JIMMY JACKSON** Basketball. Year/**Age**: 1995/**25** 1996/**26** 1997/**27**

- **MELBA MONTGOMERY** Singer/actress. (Iron City, TN) She began her singing career after winning a Pet Milk singing contest in Nashville, TN, in 1958. Biggest hit: "No Charge" in 1974. Year/**Age**: 1995/**57** 1996/**58** 1997/**59**

- **JUSTIN HAYWARD** Singer/guitarist. (England) Of the MOODY BLUES. Biggest hit: "Nights in White Satin" in 1972. Year/**Age**: 1995/**49** 1996/**50** 1997/**51**

- **JOHN DEAN** Lawyer/Watergate whistleblower. (Akron, OH) He served 4 months in prison and wrote his memoir, *Blind Ambition*. He is now an investment banker. His wife Maureen is a novelist. Year/**Age**: 1995/**57** 1996/**58** 1997/**59**

- **RALPH LAUREN** Fashion designer. (NYC) Produced the perfume "Chaps." Year/**Age**: 1995/**56** 1996/**57** 1997/**58**

- **C. EVERETT KOOP** Former Surgeon General. (Brooklyn, NY) Former pediatric surgeon. Year/**Age**: 1995/**79** 1996/**80** 1997/**81**

- **HARRY ANDERSON** Actor. (Newport, RI) Judge Harry T. Stone on "Night Court" and Dave Barry in "Dave's World." Year/**Age**: 1995/**43** 1996/**44** 1997/**45**

- **ARLEEN SORKIN** Actress. Soap's "Days of Our Lives." Year/**Age**: 1995/**39** 1996/**40** 1997/**41**

- **CLIFF RICHARD** British rock 'n roll singer. (Born Harry Roger Webb in India) His first hit, "Living Doll," was from a 1950's movie. He worked with a group called THE SHADOWS for a while. Biggest U.S. hits: "Devil Woman" and "We Don't Talk Anymore." Year/**Age**: 1995/**55** 1996/**56** 1997/**57**

- **LILLIAN GISH** Actress. (1896-1993 – Springfield, OH) Her film career spanned 75 years, in films including *Birth of a Nation* in 1915. In *Orphans of the Storm* she co-starred with her sister Dorothy, played Alan Alda's mother in *Sweet Liberty* and most of her role in *A Wedding* was that of a corpse. Her last starring role was *The Whales of August* with Bette Davis in 1987. Gish never married, saying "Marriage is a 24-hour-a-day job, and I have always been much too busy to make a good wife." She left an estate of $10 million. (Died 2-27-93.)

- **ALLAN JONES** Actor/singer. (1908-1992 – Old Forge, PA) In the 1936 movie *Showboat* with Irene Dunne. He sang in the Marx Brothers movies *A Night at the Opera* and *A Day at the Races*. His biggest hit was "The Donkey Serenade" in 1938. He's the father of singer Jack Jones. (Died of lung cancer 6-92.)

- **BILL JUSTIS** Sax player. (1926-1982 – Birmingham, AL) Biggest hit: "Raunchy" in 1957. (Died 7-5-82.)

- **DWIGHT DAVID EISENHOWER** U.S. President. (1890-1969 – Denison, TX) 34th U.S. president, nicknamed "Ike," he held the rank of five-star general in the U.S. Army before becoming president. He even wore bright red pajamas with 5 stars on the lapels.He was the first native Texan to become President. During his 8 years as President, he played 800 rounds of golf, 221 of them at Augusta. (Died 3-28-69.)

FACTS FROM THE PAST

1912 While campaigning for the U.S. Presidency, **THEODORE ROOSEVELT** was shot by a man in Milwaukee, WI. He refused treatment until he made his speech, saying, "It may be the last speech I deliver, but I am going to deliver this one. It takes more than that to kill a bull moose." That's how he got the Bull Moose nickname.

1947 Test pilot **CHUCK YEAGER** flew the XS-1 rocket plane faster than the speed of sound over the desert of southern California, approximately 650 mph. He said, "I was just a lucky kid who caught the right ride." Yeager was portrayed by actor Sam Shephard in the movie, *The Right Stuff*.

1954 *The Ten Commandments* started filming in Egypt. **CECILE DeMILLE** assembled a cast of over 25,000 people in Egypt for the movie.

1971 Arco Industries sued songwriter **JOHN FOGERTY** and **CREEDENCE CLEARWATER REVIVAL** for a half million dollars. They claimed that Fogerty's "Travelin' Band" was copied from the song "Good Golly Miss Molly."

1972 **JOE COCKER** was arrested in a raid after a concert in Adelaide, Australia. Police said they found marijuana, heroin and hypodermic syringes. Cocker faced a fine of $2,000 and up to two years in jail. Instead, he was given an order to leave the country within four hours.

1972 Thirteen-year-old **MICHAEL JACKSON** had his first #1 solo hit, about a rat called "Ben."

1978 **CARDINAL KAROL WOJTYLA**'s had been praying at a mountaintop sanctuary near Palestrina, Italy about 25 miles southeast of Rome. When his car wouldn't start, he walked down the mountain to a small town, where he waved down a bus driver and told him he had to reach the Vatican in time for an important conclave. The driver told the Cardinal to climb aboard and raced the bus along the 12$\frac{1}{2}$ miles of winding mountain roads to Palestrina. Next, Cardinal Wojtyla caught a scheduled bus to Rome in time to join the procession of cardinals into the Sistine Chapel. Two days later, Karol Wojtyla was elected pope and changed his name to **JOHN PAUL II**.

1987 18-month-old **JESSICA McCLURE** fell 22 feet down an abandoned well in Midland, Texas. Hundreds of rescue workers succeeded in freeing Jessica 2$\frac{1}{2}$ days later. The story of the rescue was told in a TV movie.

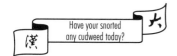

Have your snorted
any cudweed today?

OCTOBER 15
Grouch Day/Poet Laureate Contest Day

BIRTHDAYS

- **PENNY MARSHALL** Actress/director. (NYC) Of "Laverne & Shirley" fame. Directed *A League of Their Own*, Tom Hanks in *Big*, and and Robert DeNiro in *Awakenings*. Film *Renaissance Man*. Year/**Age**: 1995/**53** 1996/**54** 1997/**55**

- **JEAN PETERS** Actress. (Canton, OH) She married Howard Hughes in 1957, and they divorced in 1971. She received a hotel in the divorce settlement. She appeared in *Three Coins in a Fountain*. Year/**Age**: 1995/**69** 1996/**70** 1997/**71**

- **LINDA LAVIN** Actress. (Portland, ME) She was Alice in the "Alice" TV series. Year/**Age**: 1995/**58** 1996/**59** 1997/**60**

- **RICHARD CARPENTER** Entertainer. (NYC) He and his sister, Karen, were second only to the Everly Brothers as the all-time most successful duo. Karen died (2-4-83) at age 32 of anorexia. He wrote and produced many of their songs, and their biggest hit was "Close to You" in 1970. Year/**Age**: 1995/**49** 1996/**50** 1997/**51**

- **JIM PALMER** Baseball. (NYC) Baseball Hall of Fame pitcher and Jockey underwear model. In 19 years with Baltimore, his record was 268-152. Year/**Age**: 1995/**50** 1996/**51** 1997/**52**

- **TRACE ARMSTRONG** Football. (Bethesda, MD) With the Chicago Bears. Year/**Age**: 1995/**30** 1996/**31** 1997/**32**

- **BARRY McGUIRE** Singer. (Oklahoma City, OK) #1 hit in 1975: "Eve of Destruction." At one time, he was a member of the NEW CHRISTY MINSTRELS. Year/**Age**: 1995/**58** 1996/**59** 1997/**60**

- **ROSCOE TANNER** Tennis star. (Chattanooga, TN) Year/**Age**: 1995/**44** 1996/**45** 1997/**46**

- **MARIO PUZO** Author. (NYC) Author of *The Godfather*. Year/**Age**: 1995/**75** 1996/**76** 1997/**77**

- **LEE IACOCCA** Former Chrysler Chairman. (Born Lido Iacocca in Allentown, PA) The son of Italian immigrant parents, he went from engineer to president of the Ford Motor Co. He was fired by Henry Ford II. He took over the bankrupt Chrysler Corp. in 1979. His book *Iacocca* sold over 5 million copies. He retired in 1993. Year/**Age**: 1995/**71** 1996/**72** 1997/**73**

- **TORIANO "TITO" JACKSON** Singer. (Gary, IN) JACKSON FIVE. Biggest hit: "I'll Be There" in 1970. Year/**Age**: 1995/**42** 1996/**43** 1997/**44**

- **THE DUCHESS OF YORK, PRINCESS SARAH FERGUSON** Married to Prince Andrew of Britain. They separated in 1992. Year/**Age**: 1995/**36** 1996/**37** 1997/**38**

- **DAVID CARROLL** Arranger/conductor. (1913-1992– Chicago, IL) In 1954 he had a hit: "Melody of Love." He discovered the Smothers Brothers and produced records for THE DIAMONDS and THE PLATTERS. (Died of AIDS 3-11-92.)

- **MERVYN LeROY** Film producer. (1900-1987) Producer of *The Wizard of Oz*, *Thirty Seconds Over Tokyo*, and *Little Women*. He also directed *Gypsy* and *Mister Roberts*. Won an Oscar in 1942 for *Random Harvest*. It was LeRoy who introduced Ronald Reagan to Nancy Davis. (Died 9-13-87.)

- **ROBERT WALKER** Actor. (1918-1951 – Salt Lake City, UT) Handsome leading man married to Jennifer Jones. Father of Robert, Jr. Made 20 movies in 10 years. Died of a reaction to a sedative injection (8-28-51.)

FACTS FROM THE PAST

1860 Eleven-year-old Grace Bedell of Westfield, New York, wrote a letter to presidential candidate **ABRAHAM LINCOLN**, suggesting he would look better if he grew a beard.

1917 During World War I, Germany's famous woman spy, a Dutch dancer named **MATA HARI**, was shot by a firing squad outside Paris, France. Her real name was Gertrude Zelle.

1939 Washington's **FRANK FILCHOCK** became the first professional quarterback to throw a pass for a 99-yard touchdown.

1948 **GERALD FORD** married model/dancer Betty Bloomer. She had been married before and that was a problem. They dated for a year but put off the wedding until after the congressional race, for fear her divorce would affect his chances for winning. She once said she wished she'd married a plumber.

1951 The TV series, **"I LOVE LUCY" PREMIERED** on CBS-TV, starring Lucille Ball and Desi Arnaz. Lucy Ricardo's maiden name was MacGillicuddy. Before Ricky opened the The Ricky Ricardo Babaloo Club, he worked at the Tropicana. She missed only one out of the 20 years the series ran, taking a year off to star in *Damn Yankees*.

1955 **"GRAND OLE OPRY"** had its TV debut. Guests included Les Paul and Mary Ford.

1961 "Shop Around" by **THE MIRACLES** became Motown's first million seller (motherly advice on how to find the right girl).

1971 **RICK NELSON**, a teen idol of the fifties, wrote "Garden Party" in response to the negative respose he received trying to play his new material at Madison Square Garden. He was booed off stage.

1976 **IKE & TINA TURNER** split professionally.

1976 In the **FIRST VICE-PRESIDENTIAL DEBATE,** Democrat Walter F. Mondale and Republican Bob Dole faced off in Houston.

1976 **FLEETWOOD MAC'S** "Rumours" was released. It would go on to sell more than 15 million copies, a record for a rock group.

1985 President **DANIEL ORTEGA** suspended civil rights in Nicaragua, including free speech, public assemblies and privacy of mail, because of an alleged national emergency based on what he called brutal aggression of North America.

1990 **MIKHAIL GORBACHEV** won the **NOBEL PEACE PRIZE** for his part in ending the Cold War.

1991 In the closest vote ever for a nominee to the high court (52-48), Federal Appeals Court **JUDGE CLARENCE THOMAS** won Senate confirmation for the Supreme Court. He had to overcome last-minute accusations of sexual harassment.

OCTOBER 16
Boss's Day

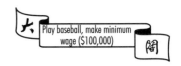
Play baseball, make minimum wage ($100,000)

BIRTHDAYS

- **ANGELA LANSBURY** Actress. (Born Angela Brigid Lansbury in London, England) A 3-time Oscar nominee, she has been active on Broadway since 1966 and has won 3 Tonys. She stars on and produces CBS-TV's "Murder, She Wrote." She was the voice of the tea pot in *Beauty and the Beast.* She has been married to agent Peter Shaw since 1949. Year/**Age**: 1995/**70** 1996/**71** 1997/**72**

- **TIM ROBBINS** Actor/director. (West Covina, CA) Films: *Bull Durham, Short Cuts, Hudsucker Proxy.* Married to Susan Sarandon. Year/**Age**: 1995/**37** 1996/**38** 1997/**39**

- **BARRY CORBIN** Actor. TV's "Northern Exposure." Year/**Age**: 1995/**55** 1996/**56** 1997/**57**

- **BOB WEIR** Guitarist. (San Francisco, CA) With the GRATEFUL DEAD group. Year/**Age**: 1995/**46** 1996/**47** 1997/**48**

- **TONY ANTHONY** Actor. Movies include *A Stranger in Town.* He mostly appeared in western films. Year/**Age**: 1995/**48** 1996/**49** 1997/**50**

- **TIM McCARVER** Baseball. Catcher for the St. Louis Cardinals, now a broadcaster. Year/**Age**: 1995/**54** 1996/**55** 1997/**56**

- **DAVE DeBUSSCHERE** Basketball. Burly New York Knicks forward. Year/**Age**: 1995/**55** 1996/**56** 1997/**57**

- **WENDY WILSON** Singer. (Los Angeles, CA) With the group WILSON PHILLIPS, two number one hits: "Hold On" and "Release Me." Her dad is Beach Boy Brian Wilson. The other two members of the group are her sister Carnie and Chynna Phillips. Their album *Wilson Phillips* sold 8 million copies. Year/**Age**: 1995/**26** 1996/**27** 1997/**28**

- **DAVID ZUCKER** Film producer. (Whitefish Bay, WI) Best known for movies *Airplane, My Life, Ruthless People,* and the *Naked Gun* films. He started Kentucky Fried Theater in Madison, WI, then moved it to Los Angeles. Year/**Age**: 1995/**48** 1996/**49** 1997/**50**

- **MANUTE BOL** Basketball. (Sudan) With the Philadelphia 76ers. Year/**Age**: 1995/**33** 1996/**34** 1997/**35**

- **SUZANNE SOMERS** Actress. (San Bruno, CA) She starred in "Three's Company" as Chrissy, "She's the Sheriff," and "Step by Step" TV series and is a published poet. Year/**Age**: 1995/**49** 1996/**50** 1997/**51**

- **EUGENE O'NEILL** Playwright. (1888-1953 – NYC) Won a Pulitzer Prize for *The Ice Man Cometh* in 1946. His *Long Day's Journey into Night* is autobiographical. (Died 11-27-53.)

- **NOAH WEBSTER** Publisher. (1758-1843 – West Hartford, CT) A teacher who didn't care for the textbooks, he published his own. Before he was 30, he wrote grammar and spelling books. They came out #2 and #3 behind the Bible in sales. His handwritten *American Dictionary of the English Language,* took 25 years and was published in 1828. (Died 5-28-1843.)

- **WILLIAM ORVILLE DOUGLAS** Supreme Court Justice. (1898-1980) He served longer as Justice of the U.S. Supreme Court than anyone else: 36 years. (Died 1-19-80.)

- **OSCAR WILDE** Poet/playwright. (1854-1900 – Ireland) At the height of his success he was arrested on a morals offense and was sent to prison for two years. Famous for *The Importance of Being Earnest* and *Picture of Dorian Gray.* His last words were, "This wallpaper is killing me, one of us has got to go." (Died 11-30-1900.)

FACTS FROM THE PAST

1793 **MARIE ANTOINETTE**, Queen of France, was beheaded. As she crossed the scaffold she stepped on the executioner's foot.

1859 Abolitionist **JOHN BROWN,** with 20 men, seized the U.S. arsenal at Harper's Ferry, WV. He was captured, the insurrection was put down, and he was hanged at Charleston, WV. He was trying to get the guns for a slave uprising that never happened.

1916 **MARGARET SANGER** opened the first birth control clinic, in New York City.

1933 **FRANKLIN ROOSEVELT** established diplomatic relations with the Soviet Union.

1957 **SAM COOKE'S** "You Send Me" was released. It would become Cooke's first million seller and hit number one on both the pop and R & B charts.

1962 In Washington, DC, the two-month tour **FIRST MOTOWN REVUE** premiered. It starred the Miracles, Supremes, Marvin Gaye, Mary Wells, and Little Stevie Wonder.

1968 **JIM DOREY** of the Toronto Maple Leafs set a record for garnering the most penalties in a single hockey game. While playing the Pittsburgh Penguins, Dorey was whistled down 9 times and spent a total of 48 minutes in the penalty box.

1968 **THE NEW YARDBIRDS** played their first concert at a club in London. The band was made up of Jimmy Page on guitar, John Paul Jones on bass, Robert Plant on vocals, and John Bonham on drums. They later changed their name to **LED ZEPPELIN.** WHO drummer Keith Moon came up with the name.

1970 **ANWAR SADAT** became President of Egypt, succeeding the late Gamal Abdul Nasser. He was assassinated in 1981.

1984 **BISHOP DESMOND TUTU** won the **NOBEL PEACE PRIZE** for his struggle for racial equality in South Africa.

1987 A 58$\frac{1}{2}$-hour drama in Midland, TX, ended happily as rescuers finally freed **JESSICA McCLURE**, an 18-month-old girl who had fallen 22 feet down an abandoned well.

1992 **GEORGE HARRISON, NEIL YOUNG, ERIC CLAPTON,** and others saluted **BOB DYLAN** at Madison Square Garden. The bald-headed girl, **SINEAD O'CONNOR,** disrupted the show when she was booed off stage for an earlier incident on "Saturday Night Live" when she tore up the Pope's picture.

Feel the fermentation

OCTOBER 17

BIRTHDAYS

- **JIMMY BRESLIN** Newspaper Columnist. (Jamaica, NY) Wrote *Table Money.* Year/Age: 1995/**65** 1996/**66** 1997/**67**

- **TOM POSTON** Actor/comedian. (Columbus, OH) He won an Emmy for best supporting actor in the comedy series, *Man on the Street.* Appeared on the "Steve Allen Show," "Mork and Mindy," "The Bob Newhart Show," and "Newhart" TV series. Year/Age: 1995/**68** 1996/**69** 1997/**70**

- **ALAN JACKSON** C & W Singer. (Newnan, GA) Hits include: "Chattahoochie" and "Don't Rock the Jukebox." Year/Age: 1995/**37** 1996/**38** 1997/**39**

- **ARTHUR MILLER** Dramatist/playwright. (NYC) Wrote *Death of a Salesman.* He was married to Marilyn Monroe from 1959 to 1961. Year/Age: 1995/**80** 1996/**81** 1997/**82**

- **EVEL KNIEVEL** Stuntman. (Born Robert Craig in Butte, MT) He tried to jump the Snake River Canyon on a motorcycle. Year/Age: 1995/**57** 1996/**58** 1997/**59**

- **JIM SEALS** Musician/singer. (Sidney, TX) Of SEALS & CROFTS. Biggest hit: "Get Closer" in 1976. Year/Age: 1995/**53** 1996/**54** 1997/**55**

- **VINCENT VAN PATTEN** Actor/tennisplayer. (Brooklyn, NY) Son of actor Dick Van Patten. Tennis film *The Break.* Year/Age: 1995/**38** 1996/**39** 1997/**40**

- **HOWARD ROLLINS** Actor. (Baltimore, MD) In film *Ragtime,* and detective Virgil Tibbs on TV's "In the Heat of the Night." Had been on leave from the series after being jailed for repeated traffic offenses in Georgia. Year/Age: 1995/**45** 1996/**46** 1997/**47**

- **BEVERLY GARLAND** Actress. (Born Beverly Fessenden in Santa Cruz, CA) Her films include: *DOA, The Desperate Hours,* and TV series "My Three Sons." Year/Age: 1995/**69** 1996/**70** 1997/**71**

- **GEORGE WENDT** Beefy actor. (Chicago, IL) The beer-guzzling regular Norm Peterson on "Cheers." The final show aired May 20, 1993. Year/Age: 1995/**47** 1996/**48** 1997/**49**

- **GARY PUCKETT** Singer. (Hibbing, MN) Leader of the group UNION GAP, named after the town of Union Gap, WA, and formed in San Diego, CA. Hits include: "Young Girl" and "Lady Willpower." Year/Age: 1995/**53** 1996/**54** 1997/**55**

- **MARGOT KIDDER** Actress. (Canada) She was Lois Lane in the *Superman* movies. Year/Age: 1995/**47** 1996/**48** 1997/**49**

- **CHARLES KRAFT** Industrialist. (Born in 1880 – Ontario, Canada) Builder with his brother James of Kraft Foods.

- **MONTGOMERY CLIFT** Actor. (1920-1966) His career was slowed by a car accident in 1957 which somewhat disfigured him. He appeared in *From Here to Eternity, Suddenly Last Summer* and *Judgment at Nuremberg.* (Died 7-23-66.)

- **RITA HAYWORTH** Actress. (1918-1987 – Born Margarita Carmen Cansino in NYC) One of the great film stars of the 1940's/50's. She was married 5 times, including her marriage to Orson Welles. She died of Alzheimer's disease. (Died 5-14-87.)

- **COZY COLE** Drummer. (1909-1981 – East Orange, NJ) Lead drummer for many big bands including CAB CALLOWAY and LOUIE ARMSTRONG. Cole's biggest hit: "Topsy II" in 1958. (Died 1-29-81.)

FACTS FROM THE PAST

1777 British forces surrendered to American troops in Saratoga, NY, in what was the turning point of the **REVOLUTIONARY WAR**.

1931 Mobster **AL CAPONE** was convicted of **INCOME TAX EVASION** and sentenced to 11 years in prison. He was paroled 8 years later and retired to Miami Beach where his mind deteriorated from advanced syphilis. He died in 1947 at age 48, heavily in debt. At one time he had a cash flow of $300,000 a week. He was suspected of having ordered up to 500 murders. His gang wars took an estimated 1,000 lives.

1933 Physicist **ALBERT EINSTEIN** arrived in the United States as a refugee from Nazi Germany.

1966 **"HOLLYWOOD SQUARES" PREMIERED** on NBC-TV with host Peter Marshall.

1967 The rock musical *HAIR* premiered off Broadway**.**

1968 **JOSÉ FELICIANO** released his controversial rendition of the national anthem on RCA records. He first performed it at a 1968 world series game between the Detroit Tigers and the St. Louis Cardinals—and was booed.

1969 The American Federation of Musicians allowed the **KINKS** to tour the U.S. after a three-year absence. The Federation had refused to let the British group perform in the U.S. after an unauthorized appearance on the TV show "Hullabaloo" in 1966.

1978 **FRANKIE VALLI** had a number-one hit with the title song from the movie *Grease.* It was the biggest hit of his solo career.

1979 **FLEETWOOD MAC** released *Tusk,* a highly experimental album that cost one million dollars to make.

1979 **MOTHER TERESA** of India was awarded the **NOBEL PEACE PRIZE** for her 30 years of work on behalf of the destitute in Calcutta.

1989 A powerful **EARTHQUAKE** rocked northern California, registering 6.9 on the Richter scale, killing 67 people and halting the World Series at Candlestick Park. Baseball commissioner Fay Vincent said, "there are more important things than our modest little sporting event." It was the first time a series was postponed due to an earthquake.

1990 Fugitive **LAWRENCIA BEMBENEK** was apprehended with her fiance as they were getting ready to flee their apartment in Thunder Bay, Ontario. The convicted killer had evaded police for over three months after she escaped from Taycheedah Correctional Institution.

1993 Houston Oiler's starting right tackle **DAVID WILLIAMS** was fined $125,000 for missing his teams win over the New England Patriots. During the game he was in a hospital delivery room with his wife Debi watching the birth of their son, Scot Cooper Williams.

OCTOBER 18

You never know...

BIRTHDAYS

- **WYNTON MARSALIS** Jazz trumpeter. (New Orleans, LA) He was the first artist to win Grammys for albums in both classical and jazz categories. He's the brother of Branford Marsalis. Year/**Age**: 1995/**34** 1996/**35** 1997/**36**

- **JESSE HELMS** Politician. (Monroe, NC) R/NC, U.S. Senator. Year/**Age**: 1995/**74** 1996/**75** 1997/**76**

- **MARTINA NAVRATILOVA** Tennis star. (Prague, Czechoslovakia) In 1992 she broke the record for career singles championships in professional tennis, with 158 tournament titles. Year/**Age**: 1995/**39** 1996/**40** 1997/**41**

- **GEORGE C. SCOTT** Actor. (Wise, VA) He's been married 5 times, twice to Colleen Dewhurst. He's been married to Trish Van Devere since 1972. He won an Oscar in 1970 for the film *Patton* but refused the award. The Patton role was turned down by Lee Marvin, John Wayne, Rod Steiger, and Robert Mitchum. Film *Malice*. Year/**Age**: 1995/**68** 1996/**69** 1997/**70**

- **JEAN CLAUDE VAN DAMME** Actor. (Brussels, Belgium) Played in action films *Kickboxer, Universal Soldier, Double Impact, Hard Target, Nowhere to Run,* and he was the alien in *Predator II*. Year/**Age**: 1995/**35** 1996/**36** 1997/**37**

- **MELINA MERCOURI** Actress. (1923-1994, Athens, Greece) *Never on Sunday*. She was the first woman to hold a senior bainet spot in Greece, "minister of Culture.". Shea was married to American director Jules Dassin whom she credits as the person who most influenced her life. (Died 3-6-94)

- **PAM DAWBER** Actress. (Detroit, MI) She co-starred with Robin Williams on TV's "Mork & Mindy." She is married to actor Mark Harmon. Year/**Age**: 1995/**44** 1996/**45** 1997/**46**

- **KEITH JACKSON** Sports announcer. (Philadelphia, PA) Year/**Age**: 1995/**67** 1996/**68** 1997/**69**

- **CHUCK BERRY**. Singer. (Born Charles Edward Anderson Berry in San Jose, CA; some sources say Jan. 15) Biggest hit: "My Ding-A-Ling" in 1972. Recording since 1953, it took him 19 years to get his first gold record. On the "Mike Douglas Show," John Lennon said, "If we had to give rock and roll another name, we'd probably call it Chuck Berry." Year/**Age**: 1995/**67** 1996/**68** 1997/**69**

- **ERIN MORAN** Actress. Played Joanie on the "Happy Days" TV series and later on "Joanie Loves Chachi." Year/**Age**: 1995/**34** 1996/**35** 1997/**36**

- **TOMMY HEARNS** Fighter. (Detroit, MI) Year/**Age**: 1995/**37** 1996/**38** 1997/**39**

- **MIKE DITKA**. Former Chicago Bears tightend/coach.. (Carnegie, PA) In NFL Hall of Fame. He had a 1986 Super Bowl Win. In 1987 he was accused of hitting a 49ers fan with a wad of gum during a 41-0 Monday night loss to San Francisco. Terry Ornelas of Napa, CA, filed a police complaint against Ditka but did not press criminal charges. Year/**Age**: 1995/**56** 1996/**57** 1997/**58**

- **PETER BOYLE** Actor. (Philadelphia, PA) In film *Taxi Driver*. Year/**Age**: 1995/**62** 1996/**63** 1997/**64**

- **LOTTE LENYA** Actress/singer. (1898-1981 – Vienna) Tony Award winner for *Threepenny Opera* in 1955. In the film *From Russia With Love* in 1963. (Died 11-27-81.)

- **LEE HARVEY OSWALD** Assassin. (1939-1963) Accused assassin of President John F. Kennedy, he was never formally charged with the crime. A government appointed agency, called the Warren Commission, claimed that Oswald, acting alone, assassinated JFK. Lee was shot to death two days after the assassination (on 11-24-63) by Jack Ruby while in Dallas police custody.

FACTS FROM THE PAST

1924 Illinois beat Michigan 39-14. Fighting Illini junior halfback **HAROLD "RED" GRANGE** scored four touchdowns in the first 12 minutes of the game, finishing with a total of five touchdowns, six completed passes, 402 yards on the ground and he also held for the kicker. At this game, sportswriter Grantland Rice, nicknamed Grange **"THE GALLOPING GHOST."**

1958 The **FIRST COMPUTER-ARRANGED MARRIAGE** took place. Shirley Sanders and Robert Kardell were matched by a computer and brought together on Art Linkletter's TV show. After a Hollywood wedding, they honeymooned in Honolulu, courtesy of the show.

1961 French painter **HENRI MATISSE**'s *Le Bateau* went on display at New York's Museum of Modern Art, attracting large crowds. Forty-six days later, someone discovered that it had been hanging upside down.

1962 **DR. JAMES D. WATSON** of the U.S., and **DR. FRANCIS CRICK** and **DR. MAURICE WILKINS** of Britain were named winners of the Nobel Prize for Medicine and Physiology for their work in determining the double-helix molecular structure of DNA (deoxyribonucleic acid).

1968 **JOHN LENNON** was arrested for pot possession in London. The arrest became the backbone of U.S. Immigration's multi-year battle to deny Lennon citizenship. The raid took place in **RINGO STARR**'s apartment.

1973 Allegheny Airlines was fined $50,000 for bumping consumer advocate **RALPH NADER** from an overbooked flight.

1974 **MARY WOODSON**, a girl friend of singer **AL GREEN**, threw a pot of boiling grits at Green as he was getting out of the bathtub in his home near Memphis, TN. Shortly after that incident, she shot herself to death. Green was hospitalized with second-degree burns on his back, neck and arms. He then turned to religion.

1977 **REGGIE JACKSON** of the New York Yankees tied **BABE RUTH**'s record of three home runs in one World Series game as New York beat the Los Angeles Dodgers 8-4 in the sixth game to win the fall classic.

1992 The **WORLD SERIES** opening ceremonies were botched when a U.S. Marine Corp color guard presented the Canadian flag upsidedown. President Bush, the Marines, and baseball officials all apologized. The Toronto Blue Jays defeated the Atlanta Braves 5-4.

If the phone rings after midnight, breathe heavy.

OCTOBER 19

BIRTHDAYS

- **WILLIAM HART** Singer. (Philadelphia, PA) Member of the DELFONICS. Biggest hit: "La-La-Means I Love You" in 1968. Year/Age: 1995/**48** 1996/**49** 1997/**50**

- **JOHN LITHGOW** Actor. (Rochester, NY) Received Oscar nominations for *The World According to Garp* (he did his part in drag) and appeared in *Terms of Endearment, Raising Cain, The Pelican Brief, Princess Caraboo,* and *Cliffhanger.* Won a Tony for *The Changing Room.* Year/Age: 1995/**50** 1996/**51** 1997/**52**

- **LAWANDA PAGE** TV actress. (Cleveland, OH) She played Aunt Ester, the butt of many of Fred's jokes, on "Sanford and Son." She had her own show also, but it didn't make it. Year/Age: 1995/**75** 1996/**76** 1997/**77**

- **JACK ANDERSON** Newspaper columnist. (Long Beach, CA) Column "Washington Merry-Go-Round." Year/Age: 1995/**73** 1996/**74** 1997/**75**

- **EVANDER HOLYFIELD** Boxer. Former heavyweight champion. Year/Age: 1995/**33** 1996/**34** 1997/**35**

- **PATRICIA IRELAND** President of the National Organization of Women (NOW). Year/Age: 1995/**50** 1996/**51** 1997/**52**

- **AMY LYNN CARTER** (Plains, GA) Daughter of former President Jimmy Carter. Year/Age: 1995/**28** 1996/**29** 1997/**30**

- **JEANNIE C. RILEY** Singer. (Born Jeannie Caralyn Riley in Anson, TX) Biggest hit: "Harper Valley P.T.A." in 1968. Year/Age: 1995/**50** 1996/**51** 1997/**52**

- **JOHN LE CARRE** Author. (Born David John Moore Cornwell in England) He has written many spy stories, including *The Spy Who Came in From the Cold* and *The Night Manager.* In 1993, after the British released photos of the real head of British Intelligence (a woman), Le Carre announced that he had been a real spy. Year/Age: 1995/**64** 1996/**65** 1997/**66**

- **KEITH REED** Composer. (England) Wrote some songs for PROCOL HARUM including "Whiter Shade of Pale." Year/Age: 1995/**50** 1996/**51** 1997/**52**

- **BRADLEY DAUGHERTY** Basketball. (Black Mountain, NC) With the Cleveland Cavaliers. Year/Age: 1995/**30** 1996/**31** 1997/**32**

- **LYNN DICKEY** Former Green Bay Packer Q.B. Year/Age: 1995/**45** 1996/**46** 1997/**47**

- **JENNIFER HOLLIDAY** Actress. (Riverside, TX) On Broadway in *Dream Girls.* Year/Age: 1995/**35** 1996/**36** 1997/**37**

- **PETER MAX** Artist. (Berlin, Germany) His first psychedelic poster sold nearly 3 million copies. He's won more than 60 awards for his art, designed a postage stamp commemorating "Expo '74," created a bicentennial book and was an official artist of the 1982 World's Fair. He and his former wife were so interested in astrology that they named their children Adam Cosmo and Libra Astro. Year/Age: 1995/**58** 1996/**59** 1997/**60**

- **ROBERT REED** Actor. (1932-1992 – Born John Robert Rietz in Highland Park, IL) Played architect Mike Brady on "The Brady Bunch." At the same time he headed the Brady family, he also appeared as the cranky police Lt. Adam Tobias on "Mannix." (Died 5-12-92.)

- **DAVE GUARD** Singer. (1934-1991 – San Francisco, CA) An original member of the KINGSTON TRIO. Their biggest hit: "Tom Dooley" in 1958. (Died 3-22-91.)

- **GEORGE McCRAE** Singer. (1944-1986 – West Palm Beach, FL) Biggest hit: "Rock Your Baby" in 1974.

- **CHARLES MERRILL** Businessman. (1885-1956 – Green Cove Springs, FL) Founded the Merrill-Lynch stock company in 1909.

FACTS FROM THE PAST

1781 Today is **YORKTOWN DAY**, marking the day when Lord Cornwallis surrendered to General George Washington at Yorktown, VA.

1874 The **FIRST WEDDING TO TAKE PLACE IN A BALLOON** occurred, as Mary Walsh and Charles Colon were hitched over Cincinnati, Ohio.

1936 An **AROUND-THE-WORLD AIRPLANE RACE** among 3 journalists ended at Lakehurst, New Jersey. **H.R. ELKINS** of the *New York World Telegraph* beat **DOROTHY KILGALLEN** of Hearst newspapers and **LEO KIERNAN** of the *New York Times* by completing the trip in 18 days, 11 hours, 14 minutes, and 33 seconds.

1951 President **HARRY S. TRUMAN** signed an act formally ending the state of war with Germany.

1953 **JULIUS LaROSA**, a regular on TV's "Arthur Godfrey Time," was fired on the air by Godfrey for not being "humble" enough.

1955 **JIM REEVES** joined the Grand Ole Opry on the recommendation of Ernest Tubb and Hank Snow.

1973 Former White House counsel, **JOHN DEAN**, pleaded guilty to a single count of conspiracy in the Watergate cover-up.

1982 Automaker **JOHN Z. DELOREAN** was arrested in Los Angeles and charged in a $24 million cocaine case. He was tried and acquitted.

1983 The Senate gave final Congressional approval to making the 3rd Monday of January a federal holiday honoring **DR. MARTIN LUTHER KING, JR**. President Reagan told a news conference the same day that he would sign the measure.

1987 **BILLY MARTIN** was named manager of the New York Yankees for the fifth time after Manager Lou Piniella, who had been expected to be fired, was promoted to general manager instead.

1989 Baseball announcer **JIM ROOKER** walked from Philadelphia to Pittsburgh. (Oct. 4-19, a distance of 315 miles) after telling his audience, with the Pirates leading the Phillies 10-0, on June 8, "If we lose, I'll walk back to Pittsburgh. Philadelphia did win 15-11.

OCTOBER 20

How does a fleck feel?

BIRTHDAYS

- **MELANIE MAYRON** Actress. Supporting actress Emmy winner for "thirtysomething." Year/Age: 1995/**43** 1996/**44** 1997/**45**

- **DR. JOYCE BROTHERS** Psychologist/author/wife/commentator/columnist. She first attracted national attention in 1955 when she memorized some 20 volumes of boxing trivia in less than 6 weeks, to score a total of $134,000 on TV's "$64,000 Question." Her column is syndicated in 350 papers. Year/Age: 1995/**67** 1996/**68** 1997/**69**

- **ART BUCHWALD** Columnist. (Mount Vernon, NY) He's one of the nation's best known satirists. His column appears in 550 newspapers around the world and he has published many collections of columns including *I Think I Don't Remember*. He won a suit against Paramount Pictures and Eddie Murphy concerning the script for the film *Coming To America*. He wrote the book *Leaving Home*. Year/Age: 1995/**70** 1996/**71** 1997/**72**

- **MICKEY MANTLE** Baseball star. (Spavinaw, OK) His home runs became a legend during his 18 years in the major leagues, which included 536 career home runs and a record 18 more in World Series play. He won the Triple Crown in 1956. He reached his salary top in 1968, $125,000. In recent years he has been charging $25,000 to appear at an autograph show. His autograph brings up to $60. Mantle said: "I never dreamed my name would be worth so much." Year/Age: 1995/**64** 1996/**65** 1997/**66**

- **KEITH HERNANDEZ** Baseball player. (San Francisco, CA) Year/Age: 1995/**42** 1996/**43** 1997/**44**

- **JERRY ORBACH** Actor. (NYC) He was the voice of the candelabra in *Beauty and the Beast*. In TV's "Law and Order." Won Tony for *Promises, Promises*. In film *Dirty Dancing*. Year/Age: 1995/**60** 1996/**61** 1997/**62**

- **WANDA JACKSON** C&W. (Maude, OK) She was the first country performer to be successful in Las Vegas. She traveled with Elvis Presley in 1955 and 1956. Her biggest hit: "In the Middle of a Heartache" in 1961. Year/Age: 1995/**58** 1996/**59** 1997/**60**

- **EARL HINDMAN** Actor. He plays the neighbor on "Home Improvement." Year/Age: 1995/**53** 1996/**54** 1997/**55**

- **TOM PETTY** Musician/singer/producer. (Jacksonville, FL) With HEART-BREAKERS: "Stop Draggin' My Heart Around" with Stevie Nicks. Member of TRAVELING WILBURYS. Year/Age: 1995/**43** 1996/**44** 1997/**45**

- **WILL ROGERS, JR.** Actor. (1911-1993 – NYC) Son of humorist Will Rogers. He served in Congress (D) as assistant to the U.S. Commissioner of Indian Affairs, owned a newspaper, appeared on the "Morning Show," CBS-TV and starred in films about his father. He died of a self-inflicted gunshot wound to the head (7-9-93.).

- **HERSCHEL BERNARDI** Actor. (1923-1986 – NYC) A singer and actor, he played Tevye on Broadway in *Fiddler on the Roof* and was the voice of Charlie Tuna on the TV commercials for over 20 years.

- **BELA LUGOSI** Actor. (1882-1956 – Born Bela Lugosi Blasko in Hungary.) He starred in many horror movies. Best known for his portrayals of Dracula. (Died 9-16-56.)

- **ELLERY QUEEN** Author. (1905-1982 – Born Frederic Dannay in Brooklyn, NY) He and his partner, Manfred B. Lee were known as Ellery Queen. They collaborated on over 30 mysteries, radio shows and magazines. Their first novel was *The Roman Hat Mystery* in 1929. (Died 9-3-82.)

FACTS FROM THE PAST

1910 The **FIRST CORK-CENTERED BASEBALL** was used in the World Series in Chicago. It was invented by Benjamin Shibe in 1909.

1922 Lieutenant Harold Harris became the **FIRST MEMBER OF THE CATERPILLAR CLUB** in Dayton, Ohio. The club is made up of persons who have escaped death by using a parachute. Harris bailed out of an airplane at McCook Field during a test flight.

1944 **GENERAL DOUGLAS MacARTHUR** returned to the Philippines $2^{1}/_{2}$ years after he said, "I shall return." He stepped ashore at Leyte, but because a Navy officer refused to let MacArthur's boat land on the dock being used to unload combat supplies, the General and his party had to wade ashore. MacArthur, his polished shoes and pressed khaki trousers soaking wet, was photographed glaring at the Navy man, and this legend has lived in statues and pictures ever since.

1947 **HOLLYWOOD** came under scrutiny when the **HOUSE UN-AMERICAN ACTIVITIES COMMITTEE** opened hearings in Washington, DC, into alleged Communist influence and infiltration in the movie industry.

1956 **HANNES LINDEMANN** became the first person to cross the Atlantic Ocean in a small boat (17-foot).

1968 **JACQUELINE KENNEDY** and Greek shipping magnate **ARISTOTLE (ARI) ONASSIS** were married on his island of Skorpios in the Ionian Sea. Teddy Kennedy looked after the business side of the deal. They had a 173-clause marriage agreement, providing for separate bedrooms and no children. Jackie was guaranteed $52,500 if she left Onassis in the first five years of the marriage. She only had to spend Catholic and summer holidays with him. Daughter Christine Onassis referred to Jackie as her father's "unfortunate compulsion." Ari's former lover Maria Callas used to say that Jackie gave a grandfather to her children.

1973 The so-called **SATURDAY NIGHT MASSACRE** took place. Special Watergate prosecutor, **ARCHIBALD COX**, was dismissed. Attorney General **ELLIOT RICHARDSON** and Deputy Att. Gen. **WILLIAM RUCKELSHAUS** resigned rather than carry out the order to fire Cox. Immediate demands for the impeachment of President Nixon ensued. He resigned on August 9, 1974.

1990 The Cincinnati Reds surprised the oddsmakers and beat the Oakland A's four straight to win the **WORLD SERIES**. Reds pitcher **JOSÉ RIJO** [rio] beat the A's twice and claimed the MVP Award. **BILLY HATCHER** had the best-ever series, batting average of .750. And José Canseco's wife Esther called Tony La Russa "a punk" for benching the Oakland star before Game 4.

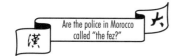

OCTOBER 21

BIRTHDAYS

- **LEE LOUGHNANE** Trumpeter. (Chicago, IL) Biggest hits with CHICAGO, "If You Leave Me Now" and "Hard To Say I'm Sorry." Year/**Age:** 1995/**49** 1996/**50** 1997/**51**

- **URSULA LeGUIN** Author (Berkley, CA) Wrote *Left Hand of Darkness*. Year/**Age:** 1995/**66** 1996/**67** 1997/**68**

- **STEVE LUKATHER** Guitarist. (Los Angeles, CA) Lead guitarist with TOTO (named for the dog in "Wizard of Oz"). Hits include: "Africa" and "Roseanna." Year/**Age:** 1995/**38** 1996/**39** 1997/**40**

- **CARRIE FISHER** Actress. (Beverly Hills, CA) The daughter of Eddie Fisher and Debbie Reynolds, she appeared in the *Star Wars* films as Princess Leia, and wrote an excellent book about her drug problems, *Postcards from the Edge* which became a hit movie. She was married to Paul Simon. Other books include: *Surrender the Pink* and *Delusions of Grandma*. Year/**Age:** 1995/**39** 1996/**40** 1997/**41**

- **ELVIN BISHOP** Guitarist. (Tulsa, OK) Former member of the PAUL BUTTERFIELD BLUES BAND. Biggest hit: "Fooled Around & Fell in Love" in 1976. Year/**Age:** 1995/**53** 1996/**54** 1997/**55**

- **EDWARD "WHITEY" FORD** Former Yankee pitcher and Hall of Famer. (NYC) He won a record 10 World Series games. This lefty had an overall record of 236-106. Among pitchers with over 200 wins, his percentage of .690 was an all-time high. Year/**Age:** 1995/**67** 1996/**68** 1997/**69**

- **JEREMY MILLER** Actor. Plays Ben on TV's "Growing Pains." Year/**Age:** 1995/**19** 1996/**20** 1997/**21**

- **GEORGE BELL** Baseball. (Dominican Republic) With the Chicago White Sox. Year/**Age:** 1995/**36** 1996/**37** 1997/**38**

- **RON ELLIOTT** Guitarist. (Haddsburg, CA) Member of BEAU BRUMMELS. Biggest Hit: "Just A Little" in 1965. Year/**Age:** 1995/**52** 1996/**53** 1997/**54**

- **MANFRED MANN** Singer. (England) Biggest hit: "Do Wah Diddy Diddy" in 1964. With EARTH BAND in 1976: "Blinded by the Light." Year/**Age:** 1995/**55** 1996/**56** 1997/**57**

- **STEVE CROPPER** Guitarist. (Ozark Mountains, MO) With BOOKER T & THE MG'S and the BLUES BROTHERS. Year/**Age:** 1995/**54** 1996/**55** 1997/**56**

- **GEORG SOLTI** [shol'-tee] Conductor. (Budapest, Hungary) Led the Chicago Symphony until 1992. He has won the most Grammy Awards of anyone - with 30. England dubbed him "Sir George." Year/**Age:** 1995/**83** 1996/**84** 1997/**85**

- **JIMMY BEAUMONT** Singer. (Pittsburgh, PA) Lead singer with the SKYLINERS. Their biggest hit: "Since I Don't Have You" in 1959. Year/**Age:** 1995/**55** 1996/**56** 1997/**57**

- **DIZZY GILLESPIE** Jazz trumpet player. (1917-1993 – Born John Birks Gillespie in Cheraw, SC) Known for the "Be-Bop" craze. He got his name from trumpeter Palmer Davis, because of all the dizzy, crazy things he would do. He was known for his bullfrog-cheek playing style. In 1953 an accident bent his horn and he continued to play it that way, claiming he could hear it better. (Died 1-6-93.)

- **GEORGIA BROWN** Actress/singer. (1933-1992 – England) Appeared as Nancy in stage production of *Oliver* in England and the U.S. On the "Ed Sullivan Show" February 9, 1964, with Davey Jones and the *Oliver* cast, the same night the Beatles first appeared on the program. Played Carla's psychic on TV's "Cheers." (Died 7-5-92.)

FACTS FROM THE PAST

1805 In the **BATTLE OF TRAFALGAR**, an English fleet under **ADMIRAL HORATIO NELSON** defeated a French and Spanish fleet, ending Napoleon's power on the seas. Lord Nelson signaled to his fleet, "England expects that every man will do his duty." Within 5 hours the entire French and Spanish fleet had been defeated. In the battle, a sniper's musket ball hit Nelson in the shoulder and he died at the precise moment of the enemy surrender. His body was preserved in rum.

1858 The **CAN-CAN** was performed for the first time in Paris. The idea behind the can-can, according to Mark Twain, was to expose yourself as much as possible.

1879 The first light bulb that really worked was turned on by **THOMAS EDISON** in Menlo Park, NJ, lasting 40 hours before burning out.

1918 **MARGARET OWEN** of New York City set a **TYPING SPEED RECORD** on a manual typewriter of 170 words per minute.

1958 **BUDDY HOLLY**'s last recording session took place in New York City. He cut three songs: "True Love Ways," "Raining in My Heart," and one started to make the charts when he was killed in a plane crash. It was written by Paul Anka and became #13 in the U.S. and #1 in England. Ironically, the title was "It Doesn't Matter Anymore."

1961 **BOB DYLAN** recorded his first album, called *Bob Dylan*. It cost $400 to produce and was finished in one day.

1972 **CHUCK BERRY** had many hits, but on this day, "My Ding-a-Ling" became his first #1 record.

1975 **ELTON JOHN** stepped onto the Hollywood Walk of Fame with a star in his name. Police were forced to block off streets because of the crowd.

1988 A federal grand jury in New York indicted former Philippines **PRESIDENT FERDINAND E. MARCOS** and his wife, Imelda, on charges of fraud and racketeering. He died before the trial and she was acquitted in 1990.

1989 Rescue workers in Oakland, California, pulled longshoreman **BUCK HELM** alive from the wreckage of the Nimitz freeway, part of which had collapsed during the October 17th **EARTHQUAKE**. (Although the rescue was hailed as miraculous, Helm died less than a month later of his injuries.)

1993 **MADONNA**'s *Sex* book went on sale for $49.95. It was covered in silver wrapping.

OCTOBER 22

Save ferrets and hedgehogs

BIRTHDAYS

- **ANNETTE FUNICELLO** Actress/singer/TV pitch woman. (Utica, NY) She was one of the original Mouseketeers. 1,000 kids tried for the part and 24 were chosen. Annette was one of the last because Disney wasn't sure of her talents. She did another beach movie in the '80's with Frankie Avalon called *Back to the Beach*. Walt Disney said Annette could do the film if she would follow 2 rules: (1) She could not wear a bikini and (2) she couldn't show her navel. She announced in summer 1992 that she had multiple sclerosis. Year/**Age**: 1995/**53** 1996/**54** 1997/**55**

- **CATHERINE DENEUVE** Actress. (Born Catherine Dorleac in Paris, France) She appeared in movies such as *The April Fools* and on TV commercials. She was nominated as best actress Oscar for *Indochine*. Has her own line of perfume. Year/**Age**: 1995/**52** 1996/**53** 1997/**54**

- **BRIAN BOITANO** Skater. (Mountain View, CA) Olympic Figure Skating Gold Medalist in 1988. Year/**Age**: 1995/**32** 1996/**33** 1997/**34**

- **DORY PREVIN** Composer/singer. She wrote the lyrics for the song "Come Saturday Morning." She was nominated for an Oscar for the film *The Sterile Cuckoo* with Liza Minnelli. At one time, she was married to André Previn. Year/**Age**: 1995/**65** 1996/**66** 1997/**67**

- **CHRISTOPHER LLOYD** Actor. He appeared on TV's "Taxi" series as Rev. Jim Ignatowski, a burned-out survivor of the psychedelic 1960's. Also in the *Back to the Future* movies. In 1975 he made his film debut in *One Flew Over the Cuckoo's Nest*. He was Uncle Fester in *Addams Family Values*, in *Star Trek III: the Search for Spock* and *Angels in the Outfield*. Year/**Age**: 1995/**57** 1996/**58** 1997/**59**

- **JOAN FONTAINE** Actress. (Born Joan de Havilland in Tokyo, Japan) Sister of Olivia de Havilland. She won an Oscar for best actress in 1941 in *Suspicion*. Year/**Age**: 1995/**78** 1996/**79** 1997/**80**

- **PATTI DAVIS** Author. Former first daughter. She wrote *House of Secrets* and *Bondage*. Year/**Age**: 1995/**42** 1996/**43** 1997/**44**

- **TONY ROBERTS** Actor. (NYC) On Broadway in *Play It Again Sam*. Appears on the soap opera "Edge of Night." Year/**Age**: 1995/**56** 1996/**57** 1997/**58**

- **DORIS LESSING** Novelist. (Persia) She wrote *Children of Violence* and *African Stories*. Year/**Age**: 1995/**76** 1996/**77** 1997/**78**

- **WILBUR WOOD** Baseball knuckleball pitcher. (Cambridge, MA) Played for Chicago Year/**Age**: 1995/**54** 1996/**55** 1997/**56**

- **ALAN LADD, JR.** Film producer. He was married at one time to Cheryl Ladd. In 1993 he was replaced as head of a major film studio. Year/**Age**: 1995/**58** 1996/**59** 1997/**60**

- **JEFF GOLDBLUM** Actor. (Pittsburgh, PA) In *The Fly, The Big Chill, Hideaway,*and *Jurassic Park*. Once married to Geena Davis. Year/**Age**: 1995/**43** 1996/**44** 1997/**45**

- **SARAH BERNHARDT** Actress. (1844-1923 – Paris) The illegitimate daughter of a Dutch prostitute, her mother told her she would die at an early age, and she kept a coffin with her at all times. She would serve tea on it, make love on it and sleep in it, too. She lived to an old age. (Died 3-26-23.)

- **BOBBY FULLER** Singer/guitarist. (1943-1966 – Baytown, TX) His group, BOBBY FULLER FOUR, biggest hit: "I Fought the Law" in 1966. (Died of asphyxiation in his car on 7-18-66.)

FACTS FROM THE PAST

1844 This is **WORLD'S END DAY** when William Miller, religious leader and creator of a movement known as "Millerism," said the world would come to an end. (He was born at Pittsfield, MA, 2-15-1782 and died 12-20-1849.)

1883 The original **METROPOLITAN OPERA HOUSE** in New York held its grand opening. The first opera performed at the Met was Gounod's *Faust*.

1934 Bank robber **PRETTY BOY FLOYD** was apprehended and shot to death by federal agents at an East Liverpool, Ohio, farm. He was handsome, so a madame who owned a bordello in Kansas City gave him the nickname, "Pretty Boy."

1938 **CHESTER CARLSON** invented the **XEROX PHOTOCOPIER**. His invention was turned down by IBM, RCA, Kodak, and many other companies who saw no use for a machine that only made copies. Carlson eventually made a fortune estimated at $100 million dollars. ("Xerox" comes from "xerography," which means "dry writing" and is a trademark.)

1939 NBC televised the **FIRST PROFESSIONAL FOOTBALL** game. The Brooklyn Dodgers played the Philadelphia Eagles at Ebbets Field in Brooklyn. Brooklyn won 23-14. The game was broadcast to a limited area – 500 TV sets picked up the transmission; the fans who saw the game at Ebbets outnumbered the TV audience.

1962 The **CUBAN MISSILE CRISIS** began when President **JOHN F. KENNEDY** ordered a naval quarantine until **FIDEL CASTRO** got Russian missiles off the island. In the following weeks, Russia backed down and removed the missiles and the missile-carrying aircraft.

1964 The **NOBEL PRIZE FOR LITERATURE** was awarded to **JEAN-PAUL SARTRE** who refused it, saying, "A writer must refuse to allow himself to be transformed into an institution."

1966 **THE BEACH BOYS'** "Good Vibrations" was released. It took six months and $4,000 to make—the most expensive single ever recorded up to that time.

1966 The **FIRST MOVIE IN THE U.S.** to earn a **MATURE AUDIENCE ONLY** rating, *Georgy Girl*, starring Lynn Redgrave and James Mason, opened. The hit song by **THE SEEKERS** came from the movie.

1978 **POPE JOHN PAUL II** was installed as Pontiff of the Roman Catholic Church. He was the first non-Italian Pope in 456 years.

Don't throw up on the bus

OCTOBER 23
Astrological Sign of Scorpio

BIRTHDAYS

- **ELLIE GREENWICH** Composer. She and husband Jeff Barry wrote "Leader of the Pack," "Be My Baby," "Chapel of Love," "Hanky Panky," and many other songs. Year/**Age**: 1995/**55** 1996/**56** 1997/**57**

- **DWIGHT YOAKAM** C & W. Year/**Age**: 1995/**39** 1996/**40** 1997/**41**

- **AL LEITER** Baseball. Pitcher for the Toronto Blue Jays. Year/**Age**: 1995/**30** 1996/**31** 1997/**32**

- **JOHNNY CARSON** The long-running host of the "Tonight Show," (Corning, IA) Began his broadcast career at KFAB in 1948 in Lincoln, NE. The first "Tonight Show" was aired October 1, 1962. Johnny, married several times, is now hitched to Alexis Maas. Today is "TV Talk Show Day," honoring those who bring out the best in the most difficult guests. By the way, Johnny is 9 years older than NBC. Year/**Age**: 1995/**70** 1996/**71** 1997/**73**

- **PELÉ** [pay-lay] Retired soccer star. (Born Edson Arantes do Nascimento in Brazil.) He was in the movie, *Escape to Victory* with John Huston, 1981. Year/**Age**: 1995/**55** 1996/**56** 1997/**57**

- **DOUG FLUTIE** Football player. (Manchester, MD) Was a Boston College Quarterback. He threw the "Hail Mary" pass to beat Miami in 1984. Was a Heisman trophy winner but was not successful in the Pros. He's in the Canadian Football League now. Year/**Age**: 1995/**33** 1996/**34** 1997/**35**

- **MIKE TOMCZAK** Football. (Calumet City, IL) Cleveland Browns backup quarterback. Former Chicago Bear. Year/**Age**: 1995/**33** 1996/**34** 1997/**35**

- **CHARLIE FOX** Singer. (Greensboro, NC) He and his sister, Inez, did the original "Mockingbird," #7 in 1963. James Taylor and Carly Simon made it to #5 in 1974 with their version. Year/**Age**: 1995/**56** 1996/**57** 1997/**58**

- **NED ROREM** Composer. (Richmond, IN) Won a Pulitzer Prize in 1976 for "Air Music" for the Bicentennial. Year/**Age**: 1995/**72** 1996/**73** 1997/**74**

- **FRED MARSDEN** Drummer. (England) Brother of Gerry Marsden from GERRY & THE PACEMAKERS. Biggest hit: "Don't Let the Sun Catch You Crying." Year/**Age**: 1995/**55** 1996/**56** 1997/**57**

- **JIM BUNNING** Baseball. (Southgate, KY) He pitched in the big leagues for 17 years. His record pitching for the Phillies, Pirates and Dodgers was 224-184. He's now a politician. Year/**Age**: 1995/**64** 1996/**65** 1997/**66**

- **CHI CHI RODRIQUEZ** Hall of Fame golfer. (Puerto Rico) Won 8 PGA events and 21 victories on the Senior Circuit in 6 years. He was inducted into the PGA World Golf Hall of Fame in 1992. Year/**Age**: 1995/**60** 1996/**61** 1997/**62**

- **MICHAEL CRICHTON** [kry' tuhn] Author. (Chicago, IL) Wrote *The Great Train Robbery, The Terminal Man, Rising Sun, Jurassic Park, Disclosure, The Great Imposter, The Secret of Canta Victoria,* and *Congo.* Also directed the films *Coma* and *Westworld.* Year/**Age**: 1995/**53** 1996/**54** 1997/**55**

- **"WEIRD AL" YANKOVIC** Parody singer. (Born Alfred Matthew Yankovic in Lynwood, CA) He records song parodies like: "Eat It" – a parody of Michael Jackson's "Beat It"– his biggest hit. He recorded his first single "My Bologne" in a men's room. More recently he did a parody of "Jurassic Park." Year/**Age**: 1995/**36** 1996/**37** 1997/**38**

- **GERTRUDE EDERLE** Swimmer. (1906 – NYC) The first woman to swim the English Channel, in 1926. To fight the cold water she covered her entire body with gallons of grease. She broke the men's record by 2 hours.

- **JAMES DALY** Actor. (1918-1978 – Wisconsin Rapids, WI) Played Dr. Lochner on TV's "Medical Center." Father of Tyne Daly. (Died 7-3-78.)

- **DIANA DORS** Actress. (1931-1984 – Born Diana Fluck in England) She was once married to TV host Richard Dawson. At one time, she was called England's answer to Marilyn Monroe. (Died 5-4-84.)

FACTS FROM THE PAST

1910 **BLANCHE SCOTT** was the first woman to make a solo airplane flight. She flew over a park in Fort Wayne, IN, at a height of 12 feet.

1933 Bank robber **JOHN DILLINGER** got his biggest haul, $75,346 from the Central National Bank in Greencastle, IN.

1947 Screen Actors Guild president **RONALD REAGAN** told the House Un-American Activities Committee the best way to combat Communist influence in Hollywood was "To make democracy work."

1958 Soviet poet and novelist **BORIS PASTERNAK**, author of *Doctor Zhivago,* was named winner of the **NOBEL PRIZE IN LITERATURE.** (However, Kremlin authorities succeeded in pressuring Pasternak into relinquishing the award.)

1962 Twelve-year-old **STEVIE WONDER** recorded his first record for Motown called "Thank You for Loving Me All the Way." It never made it, but a year later he had a #1 hit called "Fingertips II."

1973 In a surprising reversal, **PRESIDENT RICHARD NIXON** agreed to turn over White House tape recordings to Federal Judge John Sirica in the Watergate case.

1980 Members of the **SCREEN ACTORS GUILD** (SAG) and AFTRA ended a 95-day strike ratifying a 3-year contract with film and television producers.

1987 The U.S. Senate rejected, 58-to-42, the Supreme Court nomination of **ROBERT H. BORK.**

1989 In a case that inflamed racial tensions, Boston police received a call over a car phone from **CHARLES STUART**, who said he and his pregnant wife, Carol, had been shot by a African-American robber. Carol Stuart and their prematurely delivered baby died. Charles Stuart also died, an apparent suicide. It became clear that he had lied.

OCTOBER 24
United Nations Day

Today I feel like a fleck

BIRTHDAYS

- **BILL WYMAN** Bassist. (England) With the ROLLING STONES. Their biggest hit was "Honky Tonk Woman" in 1969. Year/**Age**: 1995/**59** 1996/**60** 1997/**61**
- **DAVID NELSON** Actor/TV executive. (Teaneck, NJ) Of "Ozzie & Harriet" fame. Brother of the late Rick Nelson. Year/**Age**: 1995/**59** 1996/**60** 1997/**61**
- **Y. A. TITTLE** Football Hall of Famer. (Born Yelberton Abraham Tittle in Marshall, TX) Q.B. for the 49er's, Giants and Colts, MVP in 1961 and 1963. Year/**Age**: 1995/**69** 1996/**70** 1997/**71**
- **KEVIN KLINE** Actor. (St. Louis, MO) Played Woody Reed on the "Search for Tomorrow" soap opera. It's TV's longest running serial and longest running daytime show of any kind. It began in 1951. Academy Award for supporting actor in *A Fish Called Wanda*. He was in the films *Grand Canyon* and *Dave*. He appeared in *Princess Caraboo* with his wife Phoebe Cates. Year/**Age**: 1995/**48** 1996/**49** 1997/**50**
- **JERRY EDMONTON** Drummer. (Los Angeles, CA) With the rock band STEPPENWOLF. Their biggest hit: "Born to Be Wild" in 1968. Year/**Age**: 1995/**49** 1996/**50** 1997/**51**
- **JIM BROSNAN** Baseball. Right-hander with the Cards, Reds, and Cubs from 1954-63. He wrote some books about his baseball experiences. Year/**Age**: 1995/**66** 1996/**67** 1997/**68**
- **IAN BAKER-FINCH** Golfer. (Australia) Year/**Age**: 1995/**35** 1996/**36** 1997/**37**

- **SANTO FARINA** Guitarist. (Brooklyn, NY) Of brothers SANTO & JOHNNY. Their biggest hit: "Sleepwalk." Year/**Age**: 1995/**58** 1996/**59** 1997/**60**
- **F. MURRAY ABRAHAM** Actor. (El Paso, TX) Appeared in *Amadeus* and *Last Action Hero*. Year/**Age**: 1995/**56** 1996/**57** 1997/**58**
- **MOSS HART** Playwright/director. (1904-1961 – NYC) Wrote *You Can't Take It With You* and *The Man Who Came to Dinner* with George S. Kaufman. Won a Tony for *My Fair Lady* in 1959. (Died 12-2-61.)
- **J. P. RICHARDSON** Entertainer. (1930-1959 – Born Jiles Perry Richardson in Sabine, TX) At one time he was a DJ at KTRM in Beaumont, TX, later a recording star known as the BIG BOPPER. Biggest hit: "Chantilly Lace." He died in a plane crash with Buddy Holly and Richie Valens on 2-3-59.
- **PRESTON FOSTER** Actor (1902-1970) He was in over 100 movies from 1930 to 1970 and also appeared in the TV series "Waterfront," from 1954 to 1956, and "Gunslinger" in 1960. (Died 7-14-70)
- **SARAH JOSEPHA HALE** Poet. (1788-1879 – Newport, NH) She was a magazine editor (first woman to hold such a position) who wrote the poem *Mary Had A Little Lamb,* which she claimed was a true story. After the nursery rhyme became popular, several other people claimed they had written it, including her son. She never made a penny from the poem. (Died 4-3-1879.)

FACTS FROM THE PAST

1836 The first matches were patented by **ALONZO DWIGHT PHILLIPS** of Springfield, Massachusetts.

1861 The first transcontinental telegraph message was sent when Justice Stephen J. Field of California telegraphed President **ABRAHAM LINCOLN.**

1901 A childless, widowed schoolteacher, **MRS. ANNA EDSON TAYLOR,** became the first person to survive going over Niagara Falls in a barrel equipped with a harness and cushions, a 160-foot drop. She was 43 years old, weighed 160 pounds and couldn't swim. Many people, before and since, have died trying this feat. It's now against the law. Anna thought she'd make a lot of money giving speeches, but she never did because she was a bad speaker. Forgotten, she died in poverty in 1921.

1939 **NYLON STOCKINGS** went on sale for the first time in Wilmington, Delaware.

1948 The term **"COLD WAR"** in regard to the Soviet/American relationships was first used by industrialist and statesman **BERNARD BARUCH.** He told the Senate War Investigating Committee, "Although the war is over, we are in the midst of a 'cold war' which is getting warmer."

1969 Actor **RICHARD BURTON** bought a million-dollar diamond for his wife **ELIZABETH TAYLOR**. The 69.42-carat diamond from Cartier in New York was then the world's most expensive diamond.

1970 **PRESIDENT NIXON** asked record companies to reduce the number of songs containing lyrics about sex and drugs.

1973 **KEITH RICHARDS** of the ROLLING STONES was fined $500 for four drug and three firearms offenses in London.

1980 The *Guinness Book of World Records* recognized **PAUL McCARTNEY** as history's biggest-selling songwriter and recording artist. He makes an estimated million dollars a day from all of his earnings and investments.

1987 The **MONKEES** drew over 100,000 during a benefit concert at Lowy's Park Zoo, Tampa, FL.

1989 A judge ordered **ZSA ZSA GABOR** to 72 hours behind bars, telling her, "If you slap a cop, you go to jail." On June 14, officer Paul Kramer stopped her Rolls Royce convertible, charging her with driving without a valid driver's license, having an open container of alcohol in her car and battery on a police officer.

1992 The Toronto (Canada) Blue Jays became the first team outside the U.S. to win the World Series. **DAVE WINFIELD**, the oldest player (41) on the team got the winning hit in the Blue Jays' 11th inning 4-3 victory in the 6th game. **CITO GASTON** became the first African-American manager to win the fall classic.

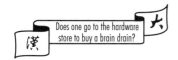
Does one go to the hardware store to buy a brain drain?

OCTOBER 25

BIRTHDAYS

- **JEANNE BLACK** Singer. (Born Gloria Jeanne Black in Pomona, CA) Her biggest hit: "He'll Have to Stay" in 1960, the answer to Jim Reeves' "He'll Have to Go." Year/**Age**: 1995/**58** 1996/**59** 1997/**60**
- **TRACY NELSON** Actress. On TV's "Father Dowling Mysteries." Year/**Age**: 1995/**32** 1996/**33** 1997/**34**
- **DAVE COWENS** Basketball star. Year/**Age**: 1995/**47** 1996/**48** 1997/**49**
- **HELEN REDDY** Singer. (Melbourne, Australia) She started her career when she won a plane ticket to the U.S. and a recording contract. Made her stage debut at age four and had her own TV show in the 1960's. Biggest hit: "I Am Woman" in 1972. Year/**Age**: 1995/**54** 1996/**55** 1997/**56**
- **MARION ROSS** Actress. (Albert Lea, MN) She was Mother Cunningham on the "Happy Days" TV series and is on "Brooklyn Bridge" as Grandma Sophie. Year/**Age**: 1995/**67** 1996/**68** 1997/**69**
- **MINNIE PEARL** C&W. (Born Sarah Ophelia Colley in Centerville, TN) Her biggest hit: "Giddyup Go-Answer" in 1966. Year/**Age**: 1995/**83** 1996/**84** 1997/**85**
- **ANTHONY FRANCIOSA** Actor. (Born Anthony Papeleo in NYC) He was nominated for best actor in 1957 for *A Hatful of Rain* and was married to actress Shelley Winters from 1957 to 1960. He also appeared in the TV series "Matt Helm" and "The Name of the Game." Year/**Age**: 1995/**67** 1996/**68** 1997/**69**
- **BILLY BARTY** Contemporary dwarf actor. Year/**Age**: 1995/**71** 1996/**72** 1997/**73**

- **BRIAN KERWIN** Actor. (Chicago, IL) On the soap "The Young and the Restless" in the 1970's and a spin-off from "BJ and the Bear" called "The Misadventures of Sheriff Lobo" and "Lobo." Year/**Age**: 1995/**46** 1996/**47** 1997/**48**
- **ANNE TYLER** Author. (Minneapolis, MN) Wrote *Morgan's Passing* and *Dinner at the Homesick Restaurant.* Year/**Age**: 1995/**54** 1996/**55** 1997/**56**
- **BOBBY THOMPSON** Former baseball star. In 1951, he hit the famous home run that won the pennant for the Giants, over the Dodgers. Year/**Age**: 1995/**72** 1996/**73** 1997/**74**
- **JOHN ANDERSON** Singer. (England) A vocalist with the group YES. Their biggest hit: "Owner of a Lonely Heart" in 1983. Year/**Age**: 1995/**51** 1996/**52** 1997/**53**
- **BOBBY KNIGHT** Indiana University basketball coach. (Massillon, OH) In 1984 he coached the Olympic team to a 97-82 victory over the NBA All Stars. The largest crowd to everwatch a basketball game, 67,596 packed the Hoosier Dome in Indiana. Year/**Age**: 1995/**55** 1996/**56** 1997/**57**
- **TAFFY DANOFF** Singer. (Born Kathy Nivert - Washington, DC) Wife of Bill Danoff. Their group STARLAND VOCAL BAND had a #1 hit: "Afternoon Delight" in 1976. Year/**Age**: 1995/**51** 1996/**52** 1997/**53**
- **PABLO PICASSO** Artist. (1881-1973 – Spain) Settled in Paris in 1903 and is known as the founder of "Cubism." He said: "I am only a public entertainer who has understood his time." His heirs paid $78 million in estate taxes when he died. They estimated his worth at $312 million, but the value of his artwork alone was much more than that. (Died 4-8-73.)

FACTS FROM THE PAST

2137 B.C. Ho and Hsi, Chinese **ROYAL ASTRONOMERS, WERE BEHEADED** after failing to accurately predict an eclipse of the sun, which caused panic in the streets of China.

1854 An English brigade of 600 men attacked the Russian army in a heavily fortified position during the **CRIMEAN WAR** and was wiped out. In "The Charge of the Light Brigade," poet **ALFRED LORD TENNYSON** wrote: "Theirs not to reason why, theirs but to do or die."

1962 Photographic evidence showed that there were Soviet **MISSLE BASES** in Cuba.

1964 The **ROLLING STONES** made one of an eventual two appearances on "The Ed Sullivan Show." Numerous complaint letters prompted Sullivan to promise they'd never appear on his show again, but they did in 1965.

1980 **PAUL KANTNER** of **JEFFERSON AIRPLANE** suffered a stroke, claiming it happened during sex. There was no permanent damage.

1983 1,900 American troops **INVADED THE TINY ISLAND OF GRENADA** at 5:30 in the morning. American reporters were not allowed to cover the invasion. The military blackout caused a lot of anger among American journalists. Nineteen Americans died in the fighting. A political coup a week before had made the island a Soviet-Cuban colony, according to President Reagan.

1987 The **MINNESOTA TWINS** beat the St. Louis Cardinals, 4-2 in Game 7 of the World Series. The Twins became the first team to do it without a road victory. It was Minnesota's first World Championship. The "indoor champs" were helped by the hanky-waving fans.

1987 The **NFL ENDED THEIR PLAYERS STRIKE.** Many teams kept some of the replacement players who performed well in the games.

1990 **EVANDER HOLYFIELD** knocked out James "Buster" Douglas in the third round of a scheduled 12-round bout in Las Vegas, Nevada, to become the undisputed **HEAVYWEIGHT BOXING CHAMPION.** Holyfield became the third champion in eight months, following Mike Tyson and Douglas.

1992 Presidential candidate **ROSS PEROT** told a "60 Minutes" TV audience that unidentified Republicans intended to "smear" his youngest daughter and disrupt her wedding using a photo of his daughter's head superimposed on another body. He said he had no proof, just three separate reports.

1994 A frightened **NICOLE BROWN SIMPSON** called 911 pleading for help, saying her ex-husband, O.J. Simpson had broken into her house and that she was afraid he would beat her up.

OCTOBER 26

How deep is your thought?

BIRTHDAYS

• **PAT SAJAK** TV host. (Chicago, IL) His career started when he was a newscaster for WEDC in Chicago in the mid-'60's. He was an armed forces DJ in Saigon during the Vietnam War. He started hosting "Wheel of Fortune" in 1981. Began his own talk show in 1989. It was canceled in the spring of 1990. "Love Connection" host Chuck Woolery was the first "Wheel of Fortune" host. Year/**Age**: 1995/**49** 1996/**50** 1997/**51**

• **JACLYN SMITH** Actress. (Houston, TX) She was one of the original cast of "Charlie's Angels" and is considered one of the most beautiful women in the world. Year/**Age**: 1995/**47** 1996/**48** 1997/**49**

• **BOB HOSKINS** Actor. (England) Films include: *Who Framed Roger Rabbit?*, *Heart Condition*, *Mermaids*, and *Hook* as Dustin Hoffman's first mate. Year/**Age**: 1995/**53** 1996/**54** 1997/**55**

• **MARLA MAPLES** Actress. She was on Broadway with "Will Roger's Follies." She is the wife of Donald Trump. Year/**Age**: 1995/**32** 1996/**33** 1997/**34**

• **KEITH HOPWOOD** Guitarist. (England) Hits with HERMAN'S HERMITS: "Mrs. Brown, You've Got A Lovely Daughter" and "I'm Henry VIII, I Am." Year/**Age**: 1995/**49** 1996/**50** 1997/**51**

• **CHUCK FORMAN** Football player. (Frederick, MO) Year/**Age**: 1995/**45** 1996/**46** 1997/**47**

• **LAUREN TEWES** Actress. Appeared as Julie McCoy on the "Love Boat" TV series. Year/**Age**: 1995/**41** 1996/**42** 1997/**43**

• **CARY ELWES** Actor. Year/**Age**: 1995/**33** 1996/**34** 1997/**35**

• **EDWARD BROOKE** Former Senator. (Washington, DC) R/MA. First African-American Senator in modern times. Year/**Age**: 1995/**75** 1996/**76** 1997/**77**

• **HILLARY RODHAM CLINTON** First Lady. (Park Ridge, IL) Year/**Age**: 1995/**47** 1996/**48** 1997/**49**

• **CHARLIE BARNET** Jazz sax player. (1913-1991 – NYC) (Died 9-4-91.)

• **CHARLES WILLIAM POST** First breakfast food millionaire.(1854-1914 – Springfield, IL) He invented "Grape Nuts," "Postum" and a cereal he called "Emmanuel's Manna" which he changed to "Post Toasties" after objections were made by the religious community.

• **JACKIE COOGAN** Actor. (1915-1984 – Los Angeles, CA) He was the first child star to appear in a full-length movie, *The Kid*, with Charlie Chaplin. He was also on the "Addams Family," minus hair and eyebrows as Morticia's kindly uncle Fester. Before he was out of short pants, he had made more than $4 million dollars, but when he was 21, he discovered his parents had spent it all, leaving him penniless. This resulted in the passage of the "Coogan Act," whereby parents are required to put into trust their children's earnings made while acting. (Died 3-1-84.)

• **MAHALIA JACKSON** Gospel singer. (1911-1972 – New Orleans, LA) Her first recording contract came in 1935 when a talent scout from Decca Records heard her sing at a funeral. Her later years she spent appearing with Billy Graham Crusades. (Died 1-27-72.)

FACTS FROM THE PAST

1785 The **FIRST IMPORTATION OF SPANISH MULES**—jackasses/donkeys—to the U.S. took place when King Charles III of Spain sent two to Boston as a gift. At the time, the exportation of full-blooded jacks from Spain was prohibited. George Washington's interest brought on the gift and George was responsible for having the first mules bred in America.

1858 Hamilton Smith of Philadelphia **INVENTED THE WASHING MACHINE,** which was called a "rotary motion machine."

1881 The **GUNFIGHT AT THE O.K. CORRAL** occurred in Tombstone, AZ. **WYATT EARP,** his two brothers, and **DOC HOLLIDAY** shot it out with the **IKE CLANTON** gang. Three members of Clanton's gang were killed and Earp's brothers were wounded. The "Boot Hill Cemetery," where they are buried, has become a popular Arizona tourist attraction.

1936 Country singer **ROY ACUFF AND HIS CRAZY TENNESSEANS** had their first recording session for the ARC Company, which later merged with Columbia. They recorded "Great Speckled Bird" and "Wabash Cannonball."

1949 President **HARRY S. TRUMAN** nearly doubled the minimum wage, from 40 to 75 cents an hour.

1965 The **BEATLES** were invested as Members of the British Empire by the Queen at Buckingham Palace. John Lennon later said the band shared a joint in a palace bathroom.

1966 **LIBERACE** played the parts of both good and evil pianists on "Batman" the TV series.

1970 **GARRY TRUDEAU**'s cartoon "Doonesbury" premiered.

1973 President Nixon released the first of the **WHITE HOUSE TAPES** concerning the Watergate affair.

1979 South Korean **PRESIDENT PARK CHUNG HEE** and five bodyguards were assassinated by the Director of the Korean CIA.

1984 Proctor & Gamble announced that after 28 years on the air, the daytime soap "**EDGE OF NIGHT**" was canceled due to poor ratings. December 28th was the final program. The show began in 1956.

1984 **BABY FAE**, a newborn with a severe heart defect, was given the heart of a baboon in an experimental transplant in Loma Linda, CA. Baby Fae lived 21 days with the animal heart.

1990 In his 12th pro hockey season **WAYNE GRETZKY** scored his 2,000th point.

1992 General Motors Chairman **ROBERT STEMPEL** resigned after he had failed to stop the Corporation's record financial losses.

Do you remember cummerbunds?

OCTOBER 27

BIRTHDAYS

• **NANETTE FABRAY** Entertainer. (Born Nanette Fabares in San Diego, CA) She made her vaudeville debut at age 4 as "Baby Nanette" and later appeared in the "Our Gang" comedies. Shelly Fabares's aunt. Year/**Age**: 1995/**75** 1996/**76** 1997/**77**

• **CARRIE SNODGRESS** Actress. (Park Ridge, IL) She was nominated for an Oscar in 1970 for best actress in *Diary of a Mad Housewife*. Carrie was married to Neil Young, had a son, got divorced and went to live on a farm. Film *8 Seconds*. Year/**Age**: 1995/**49** 1996/**50** 1997/**51**

• **PETE VUCKOVICH** Former pitcher. Appeared in movie *Major League*. Year/**Age**: 1995/**43** 1996/**44** 1997/**45**

• **RALPH KINER** Outfielder. Led or tied the National League in home runs for his first seven years in the majors with the Pittsburgh Pirates. Year/**Age**: 1995/**73** 1996/**74** 1997/**75**

• **FLOYD CRAMER** Pianist. (Shreveport, LA) Biggest hit: "Last Date" in 1960. Chet Atkins discovered him in 1955 and brought him to Nashville. He has played the piano on many hit records, including Brenda Lee's "I'm Sorry" in 1960. Year/**Age**: 1995/**62** 1996/**63** 1997/**64**

• **JOHN CLEESE** Comedian. (England) Part of the "Monty Python" crew. Films include: *Monty Python and the Holy Grail*, *Life of Brian*, *A Fish Called Wanda*, and *Splitting Heirs*. Year/**Age**: 1995/**56** 1996/**57** 1997/**58**

• **H. R. HALDEMAN** Former White House Chief of Staff. (1926-1993, Los Angeles, CA) His voice was the other one besides President Nixon's, lost in the much publicized $18^{1}/_{2}$ minute gap of an Oval Office taped conversation. For his part in Watergate, he served 18 months in prison for perjury, conspiracy and obstruction of justice. (Died 11-12-93)

• **FRAN LEBOWITZ** Author. Year/**Age**: 1995/**45** 1996/**46** 1997/**47**

• **KYLE ROTE** Football player. (San Antonia, TX) With NY Giants. Year/**Age**: 1995/**67** 1996/**68** 1997/**69**

• **SIMON LEBON** Singer. (England) Vocalist for DURAN DURAN. Biggest hit: "The Reflex" in 1984. The group provided the title track for the Bond film *A View to Kill*. He's married to model Yasmin. Year/**Age**: 1995/**37** 1996/**38** 1997/**39**

• **JAYNE OVERTON KENNEDY** Actress/sports commentator. (Washington, DC) First African American woman to do network sports, "NFL Today." Appeared on "Speak Up America." Year/**Age**: 1995/**44** 1996/**45** 1997/**46**

• **TERRY ANDERSON** News correspondent. (Lorain, OH) He was kidnapped March 16, 1985, in Beirut and was released in 1991. Year/**Age**: 1995/**48** 1996/**49** 1997/**50**

• **LEE GREENWOOD** C&W Singer. (Los Angeles, CA) His "God Bless the U.S.A." got a lot of play during the Persian Gulf War. Was a dealer in Las Vegas until 1981. His band is called TRICK. Year/**Age**: 1995/**53** 1996/**54** 1997/**55**

• **LEIF ERICKSON** Actor. (1911-1986) Best remembered for his role in the TV series, "The High Chaparral" as Big John Cannon. (Died 1-3-86.)

• **THEODORE "TEDDY" ROOSEVELT** U.S. President. (1858-1919 – NYC) 26th U.S. President. Two-time Republican president, the third time he ran on the "Bull Moose" ticket and lost. He was the first president to ride in an airplane, drive in a car and ride in a submarine. He was a leader in conservation and began the National Monument System, setting aside 18 protected areas, including the Grand Canyon. He also inspired the teddy bear. His best remembered words were "Speak softly and carry a big stick." (Died 1-6-19.)

• **DYLAN THOMAS** Poet/playwright. (1914-1953 – Wales) He often told lies for the fun of inventing them. Died after a 6-day coma brought on by drinking 18 straight whiskeys in a New York tavern on 11-9-53.

FACTS FROM THE PAST

1858 After failing 7 times in various business ventures, **ROLAND MACY** opened Macy's Department Store in NYC and became independently wealthy. Macy's became the world's biggest volume department store on 6th Avenue in New York City. It's now at Broadway and 34th St. It's the biggest store in the world, though it has been suffering financial trouble.

1947 The radio show "You Bet Your Life," starring **GROUCHO MARX**, premiered on ABC. A couple of years later it moved to NBC-TV.

1960 **BEN E. KING** recorded "Spanish Harlem" and "Stand By Me."

1964 **SONNY** and **CHER** got married. Cher wore bell-bottoms. They divorced February 20, 1974.

1975 **BRUCE SPRINGSTEEN**, landed cover shots on two magazines, giving his career a tremendous boost. Ironically, both *Time* and *Newsweek* were using the photos to illustrate the power of the media to create a star and critisizing that ability.

1978 Israel's **MENACHEM BEGIN** and Egypt's **ANWAR SADAT** jointly won the **NOBEL PEACE PRIZE** for progress in Middle East accord.

1980 **OPERA STAR BEVERLY SILLS** gave her last performance on an opera stage, appearing in a Lincoln Center production of *Die Fledermaus*. She moved into management.

1991 The **MINNESOTA TWINS** shut out the **ATLANTA BRAVES** 1-0 to win the world series. Jack Morris became the 2nd pitcher in World Series history to hurl 10 shutout innings. (Christy Mathewson did it in 1913.) It was the 4th of the seven game series to be decided on the last pitch.

1991 The **FIRST U.S. DEATH** from the thrill-sport, bungee-jumping, happened in Perris, CA. **HAL MARK IRISH**, jumping from a hot-air balloon, fell over 60 feet after coming off his bungee cord during a demonstration.

OCTOBER 28

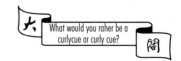
What would you rather be a curlycue or curly cue?

BIRTHDAYS

- **JULIA ROBERTS** Actress. (Smyrna, GA) Oscar nominations for *Pretty Woman* and *Steel Magnolias*. Other films include: *Dying Young, Hook, Mary Reilly, I Love Trouble,* and *The Pelican Brief.* She married singer Lyle Lovett 6-27-93. She was the first woman to appear on the cover of *G.Q.* Year/**Age:** 1995/**28** 1996/**29** 1997/**30**

- **BRUCE MORTON** Newsman. (Norwalk, CT) Washington, DC, news anchor for CBS since 1975. Year/**Age:** 1995/**65** 1996/**66** 1997/**67**

- **TELMA HOPKINS** Singer. (Louisville, KY) With DAWN, biggest hit: "Tie a Yellow Ribbon Round the Ole Oak Tree" in 1973. TV's "Getting By." Year/**Age:** 1995/**47** 1996/**48** 1997/**49**

- **BRUCE JENNER** Athlete. (Mt. Kisco, NY) He was Olympic Decathalon gold medalist in 1976; now a sportscaster. He's married to Linda Thompson, who was living with Elvis Presley at the time of his death. She was 3rd runner-up in the Miss U.S.A. Pageant and a regular on the TV series "Hee Haw." Year/**Age:** 1995/**46** 1996/**47** 1997/**48**

- **ERIK THORSTVEDT** Soccer. (Norway) He is one of the world's top goalkeepers. Plays for England's Tottenham Hotspurs. Year/**Age:** 1995/**33** 1996/**34** 1997/**35**

- **DENNIS FRANZ** Actor. Lt. Norman Buntz on "Hill Street Blues" and Sipowicz on "NYPD Blue." Year/**Age:** 1995/**51** 1996/**52** 1997/**53**

- **SUZY PARKER** Actress/model. She appeared on "Producer's Showcase" in 1957. Year/**Age:** 1995/**62** 1996/**63** 1997/**64**

- **DR. JONAS SALK** Researcher. (NYC) He developed the Salk polio vaccine. Year/**Age:** 1995/**81** 1996/**82** 1997/**83**

- **CHARLIE DANIELS** Country "rocker." (Wilmington, NC) Biggest hit: "The Devil Went Down to Georgia" in 1979. He was in the movie *Urban Cowboy.* Year/**Age:** 1995/**59** 1996/**60** 1997/**61**

- **CURTIS LEE** Singer. (Yuma, AZ) His biggest hit was "Pretty Little Angel Eyes" in 1961, produced by Phil Spector. Year/**Age:** 1995/**54** 1996/**55** 1997/**56**

- **JANE ALEXANDER** Actress. (Born Jan Quigley in Boston, MA) She received an Oscar nomination for *The Great White Hope* in 1970 and *All the President's Men* in 1976. She portrayed Eleanor Roosevelt on TV. She was named National Endowment for the Arts Chairwoman in 1993. Year/**Age:** 1995/**56** 1996/**57** 1997/**58**

- **MARK DERWIN** Actor. (Chicago, IL) Appeared on "The Young and The Restless." Plays A.C. Mallet on "Guiding Light." Year/**Age:** 1995/**35** 1996/**36** 1997/**37**

- **JAMIE GERTZ** Actress. She was in *The Lost Boys.* She made a guest appearance on "Seinfeld" and played on TV's "Square Pegs." Year/**Age:** 1995/**30** 1996/**31** 1997/**32**

- **PAUL WYLIE** Medal-winning Olympic figure skater. Year/**Age:** 1995/**31** 1996/**32** 1997/**33**

- **LEAF PHOENIX** Actor. He is the brother of the late River Phoenix. Year/**Age:** 1995/**21** 1996/**22** 1997/**23**

- **ANNIE POTTS** Actress. One of the four Atlanta interior decorators on TV's "Designing Women," last show May 24, 1993. "Love and War." Year/**Age:** 1995/**43** 1996/**44** 1997/**45**

- **DODY GOODMAN** Actress. (Columbus, OH) One of the regulars on the "Tonight Show" when it was hosted by Jack Paar from 1957-62. She played Martha Shumway on "Mary Hartman, Mary Hartman" and the follow-up, "Forever Fernwood." Year/**Age:** 1995/**66** 1996/**67** 1997/**68**

- **WAYNE FONTANA** Singer. (England) Biggest hit: "Game of Love" in 1965, with the MINDBENDERS. He left the group in late 1965. Year/**Age:** 1995/**50** 1996/**51** 1997/**52**

- **JOAN PLOWRIGHT** Actress. (England) In films *Avalon* and *Enchanted April.* Widow of Lord Lawrence Oliver. Year/**Age:** 1995/**66** 1996/**67** 1997/**68**

- **ELSA LANCHESTER** Actress. (1902-1986 – London, England) She received an Oscar nomination for *Come to the Stable* in 1949 and *Witness for the Prosecution* in 1957. She starred in *The Bride of Frankenstein* in 1935. She and actor Charles Laughton were married from 1929 until his death in 1962. (Died 12-26-86.)

FACTS FROM THE PAST

1886 The **STATUE OF LIBERTY WAS UNVEILED.** It was the work of sculptor **FREDERIC AUGUSTE BARTHOLDI,** and a gift from France, weighing 225 tons and 152 feet high. The statue was formally dedicated in New York Harbor 108 years ago today by President Grover Cleveland in the presence of its sculptor. The full name was "The Statue of Liberty Enlightening the World." On August 3, 1957, President Dwight Eisenhower changed the island's name to "Liberty" from "Bedloe."

1922 **FASCISM** came to Italy as Benito Mussolini took control.

1929 The **FIRST CHILD WAS BORN ON AN AIRPLANE** over Miami. The mom was **MRS. T. W. EVANS.**

1961 Record store owner **BRIAN EPSTEIN** set out to find an obscure new group called the Beatles upon the request by a customer for the release "My Bonnie."

1968 **CYNTHIA LENNON** sued her husband, John, for divorce, on grounds of adultery. John was living with a pregnant Yoko Ono.

1976 **JOHN EHRLICHMAN,** former top aide to President Nixon, entered a federal prison camp in Safford, AZ, to begin serving a sentence for **WATERGATE**-related convictions.

1986 **MARIE OSMOND** married for the second time, to Brian Blosil, a Provo, UT, record producer, at a private Mormon Church ceremony a year after her divorce from Steve Craig.

1986 **EVANGELIST PAT ROBERTSON** issued a statement that we should stop celebrating Halloween. He was quoted, "We ought to close Halloween down. Do you want your children dressing up like witches? They are acting out satanic rituals."

OCTOBER 29

BIRTHDAYS

- **WINONA RYDER** Actress. (Born Winona Horowitz in Winona, MN) Films include: Bram Stoker's *Dracula* as Mina, *Beetlejuice, Mermaids, The House of Spirits, Reality Bites, Edward Scissorhands, Boys, Ethan Hawke,* and *Age of Innocence.* Year/**Age:** 1995/**24** 1996/**25** 1997/**26**
- **PETER GREEN** Guitarist. (England) Ex-member of FLEETWOOD MAC. Biggest hit: "Dreams" in 1977. Year/**Age:** 1995/**49** 1996/**50** 1997/**51**
- **KATE JACKSON** Actress. (Birmingham, AL) She appeared as Sabrina on ABC's "Charlie's Angels" and with Bruce Boxleitner in "Scarecrow & Mrs. King." Also TV's short-lived "Baby Boom." She once considered a career as a professional tennis player. She appeared in the TV horror films *Killer Bees, Death Cruise,* and *Satin's School for Girls* in the 1970's. After a modified mastectomy in 1989, she said she's cured of her breast cancer. Year/**Age:** 1995/**47** 1996/**48** 1997/**49**
- **DENNIS POTVIN** Hockey. Year/**Age:** 1995/**42** 1996/**43** 1997/**44**
- **RICHARD DREYFUSS** Actor. (Brooklyn, NY) Won an Oscar in 1977 for best actor in *The Goodbye Girl.* He was seen in *Nuts* as Barbra Streisand's attorney, *Close Encounters of the Third Kind, Always, Lost in Yonkers, Stakeout,* and *Another Stakeout.* Year/**Age:** 1995/**48** 1996/**49** 1997/**50**
- **MELBA MOORE** Actress/singer. (NYC) She co-hosted a musical variety hour with her husband, Clifton Davis, in 1972 – a 5-week summer replacement for the "Carol Burnett Show." Year/**Age:** 1995/**50** 1996/**51** 1997/**52**
- **JESSE BARFIELD** Baseball. (Joliet, IL) Year/**Age:** 1995/**36** 1996/**37** 1997/**38**

- **BILL MAULDIN** World War II cartoonist. (Mountain Park, NM) Created GIs Willie and Joe. Year/**Age:** 1995/**74** 1996/**75** 1997/**76**
- **DENNY LAINE** Singer/guitarist. (England) With the MOODY BLUES and, later, Paul McCartney's WINGS. Year/**Age:** 1995/**51** 1996/**52** 1997/**53**
- **NEIL HEFTI** Composer/bandleader. (Hastings, NE) He composed TV themes such as "Batman." Year/**Age:** 1995/**73** 1996/**74** 1997/**75**
- **RANDY JACKSON**. (Gary, IN) Of the JACKSON FIVE. He replaced Jermaine in 1975. Their biggest hit: "I'll Be There" in 1970. Year/**Age:** 1995/**34** 1996/**35** 1997/**36**
- **ANDY RUSSELL** Former Pittsburgh Steeler linebacker. Year/**Age:** 1995/**54** 1996/**55** 1997/**56**
- **JON VICKERS** Tenor. (Canada) Made his New York Met debut in 1960. Year/**Age:** 1995/**69** 1996/**70** 1997/**71**
- **AKIM TAMIROFF** Actor. (1901-1972 – Russia) Academy Award nomination for *For Whom the Bell Tolls.* (Died 9-17-72.)
- **FANNY BRICE** Actress/comedienne. (1891-1951 – Born Fanny Borach in Brooklyn, NY) One of her best known films was *Ziegfeld Follies* in 1945, and Barbra Streisand portrayed her life in the musicals *Funny Girl* and *Funny Lady.* Near the end of her life she had a radio comedy, "Baby Snooks." (Died 5-29-51.)
- **DANIEL EMMETT** Composer. (1815-1904 – Clinton, OH) He created the words and music for "Dixie" which became the fighting song for the Confederate troops and the unofficial National Anthem of the South. (Died 6-28-04.)

FACTS FROM THE PAST

1618 SIR WALTER RALEIGH was accused of treason in a plot to oust King James I and was executed in London. He was in prison in the Tower of London for 15 years. He smoked a pipe before he was executed, then he felt the end of the axe and said, "This is sharp medicine, but it will cure all ills." Two strokes later, he lost his head.

1929 The **NEW YORK STOCK MARKET COLLAPSED**, wiping out thousands of investors, leading to the **GREAT DEPRESSION** of the 1930's. It was known as **BLACK TUESDAY**. Evangeline Adams predicted many things including Lindbergh's flight and how long it would take and she predicted the crash, but didn't believe it herself, and lost $100,000.

1936 Country singer **HANK SNOW** made his first recordings for the Victor label. They were "Lonesome Blue Yodel" and "Prisoned Cowboy."

1940 Secretary of War **HENRY L. STIMSON** drew the first number – 158 – in the first peacetime military draft in U.S. history.

1945 Gimbels Department Stores sold the first **BALLPOINT PEN**, for $12.95. Before that, inkwells caused problems for teachers all over the country.

1956 The "Chet Huntley/David Brinkley Report" replaced the "**CAMEL NEWS CARAVAN**" with John Cameron Swayze on NBC-TV. This top-rated news show ran for almost 14 years.

1960 **CASSIUS CLAY** made his professional fight debut. He beat the little known boxer Tunney Hunsaker in a 6-round decision. Three years later, he was the world heavyweight champion.

1969 *Rat Subterranean News* magazine published the "Paul is Dead" hoax. **PAUL McCARTNEY** stated, "I am alive and well, and concerned about the rumors of my death."

1972 President Richard Nixon declared there would be no amnesty for the American draft resisters after the **VIETNAM WAR.**

1976 **ELVIS PRESLEY** cut his last hit record, "Way Down," in his studio located in the basement of Graceland Mansion. In his last years, he did not like studio recording very much, so he had his own studio built. The raw, unedited version of "Way Down," which was done live in the studio before mixing, can be found on the album, *Our Memories of Elvis, Vol. II.*

OCTOBER 30

BIRTHDAYS

- **TIMOTHY B. SCHMIT** Bass guitarist. (Los Angeles, CA) POCO and the EAGLES. Year/**Age:** 1995/**48** 1996/**49** 1997/**50**

- **HENRY WINKLER** Actor. (NYC) His parents were refugees from Nazi Germany, and they wanted him to join the State Department. Instead, he ended up with a Master's Degree from Yale University School of Drama. He's most famous for his appearance as The Fonz on "Happy Days." He is 5'6" tall. He made his screen debut in *The Lords of the Flatbrush*. He produced "MacGyver" for seven seasons and directed the film *Cop and a Half*. Year/**Age:** 1995/**50** 1996/**51** 1997/**52**

- **GRACE SLICK** Entertainer. (Chicago, IL) With JEFFERSON STARSHIP which was originally JEFFERSON AIRPLANE. Her biggest hit was "Miracles" in 1975. She has a daughter, China, by guitarist Paul Kantner. Year/**Age:** 1995/**56** 1996/**57** 1997/**58**

- **OTIS WILLIAMS** Singer. Of the TEMPTATIONS. Their biggest hit: "I Can't Get Next to You" in 1969. Year/**Age:** 1995/**53** 1996/**54** 1997/**55**

- **EDDIE HOLLAND** Of the HOLLAND, DOZIER & HOLLAND production and songwriting team. He had one hit on his own in 1962 called "Jamie." Year/**Age:** 1995/**56** 1996/**57** 1997/**58**

- **DICK GAUTIER** Actor. (Los Angeles, CA) Played the robot, Hymie, in "Get Smart." Year/**Age:** 1995/**64** 1996/**65** 1997/**66**

- **LOUIS MALLE** Movie director. (France) Married to Candice Bergen. His U.S. films include *Goodbye Children* and *Pretty Baby*. Year/**Age:** 1995/**63** 1996/**64** 1997/**65**

- **RUTH HUSSEY** Actress. (Born Ruth Carol O'Rourke in Providence, RI) Year/**Age:** 1995/**81** 1996/**82** 1997/**83**

- **HARRY HAMLIN** Actor. "L.A. Law." Once married to actress Nicolette Sheridan. Year/**Age:** 1995/**44** 1996/**45** 1997/**46**

- **CLAUDE LELOUCH** Director. (France) He won Best Foreign Film Oscar for *A Man and a Woman* in 1966. Year/**Age:** 1995/**57** 1996/**58** 1997/**59**

- **EZRA POUND** Poet. (1885-1972 – Hailey, ID) He was indicted for treason, after being arrested by the U.S. Army in 1943 for his pro-Fascist radio broadcasts from Italy. He was held at St. Elizabeth's Hospital in Washington, DC, from 1946 to 1958. Being mentally unable to stand trial, he was never tried for treason. (Died 11-1-72.)

- **RICHARD SHERIDAN** Dramatist. (1751-1816 – Ireland) Known for his comedies: *The Critic*, *School for Scandal*, and *The Rivals*. (Died 7-7-1816.)

- **RUTH GORDON** Actress. (1896-1985 – Born Ruth Jones in Wollaston, MA) She won an Oscar for best supporting actress in 1968 for *Rosemary's Baby*. She and author Garson Kanin wrote the film *Adam's Rib*, which starred Spencer Tracy and Katharine Hepburn. (Died 8-28-85.)

- **JOHN ADAMS** 2nd U.S. president and the first vice president. (Born in Braintree, MA in 1735 – July 4, 1826) A confirmed hypochondriac, Adams complained about his ill health all his life…and lived to be 91. He had the distinction of being the longest-lived president and first president who was a college graduate. He was George Washington's V.P. and the father of John Quincy Adams, 6th U.S. President. (Died 7-4-1826.)

- **CHARLES ATLAS** Bodybuilder. (1894-1972 – Born Angelo Siciliano in Brooklyn, NY) He changed his name to "Charles Atlas" and began the world's most successful mail-order/muscle-building business. He was a 97-pound weakling and somebody kicked sand in his face. In his late teens he saw a statue of Atlas and changed his name. The world's most perfectly developed man was 79 when he died and was still in great condition. (Died 12-24-72.)

FACTS FROM THE PAST

1912   Vice-presidential candidate **JAMES SHERMAN** died a few days before the election, but still received 3.5 million votes.

1925   The first television transmission was seen in London, England. **JOHN BAIRD** built the transmitter in his attic from a tea chest, cardboard scanning discs, an empty biscuit box, old electric motors, darning needles, motorcycle lamp lenses, piano wire, glue, string and sealing wax.

1938   Actor **ORSON WELLES** made his famous **"WAR OF THE WORLDS" RADIO BROADCAST.** Near panic resulted when listeners believed the simulated news bulletins describing an invasion by Martians in New Jersey. Families rushed into the streets using wet towels as gas masks. A woman in Pittsburgh was found with a poison bottle saying she would rather die this way. $750,000 in lawsuits were filed against Welles.

1964   **ROY ORBISON** was awarded a gold record for "Oh Pretty Woman."

1967   Senator **EUGENE MCCARTHY** from Minnesota announced his candidacy for president, on an antiwar platform.

1972   **ELTON JOHN** appeared at a command performance benefit for the Queen of England.

1974   Kathy Silva filed for divorce less than six months after marrying Sylvester Stewart of **SLY AND THE FAMILY STONE** in New York City's Madison Square Garden.

1974   **MUHAMMAD ALI** regained his heavyweight boxing title, knocking out George Foreman in the 8th round of a scheduled 15-round bout in Zaire, Africa. Ringside seats were selling for $2,000.

1979   Birmingham, Alabama, elected its **FIRST AFRICAN-AMERICAN MAYOR**, former city councilman **RICHARD ARRINGTON**.

1985   Space shuttle **CHALLENGER** blasted off from Cape Canaveral. New Hampshire schoolteacher Christa McAuliffe, first civilian to go into space, witnessed the launch. She died in that same shuttle three months later, on 1-28-86.

Be good to broccoli

OCTOBER 31
Halloween/All Soul's Day

BIRTHDAYS

- **VANILLA ICE** Rapper. (Born Robert Van Winkle in Miami Lakes, FL) Hits include: "Ice Ice Baby" in 1990. First rapper to hit #1 on the Billboard singles chart. Year/**Age**: 1995/**28** 1996/**29** 1997/**30**

- **DEIDRE HALL** Actress. Won 3 Emmy nominations and a Soapie Award for "Days of Our Lives." Year/**Age**: 1995/**47** 1996/**48** 1997/**49**

- **LARRY MULLEN** Drummer. (Ireland) U-2 hit: "With or Without You" in 1987. Year/**Age**: 1995/**34** 1996/**35** 1997/**36**

- **LEE GRANT** Actress/director. (NYC) She won an Oscar for best supporting actress in *Shampoo* in 1976 and received a New York Drama Critics Award as the shoplifter in *Detective Story* on Broadway. For the film version, she received an Oscar nomination. Year/**Age**: 1995/**64** 1996/**65** 1997/**66**

- **DAVID OGDEN STIERS** Actor. (Peoria, IL) Played the pompous Winchester on "M*A*S*H." Year/**Age**: 1995/**53** 1996/**54** 1997/**55**

- **JANE PAULEY** Ex-"Today" show hostess. (Indianapolis, IN) "Real Life with Jane Pauley." Married to Garry Trudeau. Year/**Age**: 1995/**45** 1996/**46** 1997/**47**

- **DAN RATHER** CBS anchorman. (Wharton, TX) "48 Hours." Year/**Age**: 1995/**64** 1996/**65** 1997/**66**

- **DALE EVANS** Singer/actress. (Born Frances Smith in Uvale, TX) She was a successful singer/actress before and after she married Roy Rogers in 1947. She wrote the theme song for their TV show which first aired in Dec., 1951, called "Happy Trails to You." Year/**Age**: 1995/**83** 1996/**84** 1997/**85**

- **MICKEY RIVERS** Outfielder. Baltimore Orioles. Year/**Age**: 1995/**47** 1996/**48** 1997/**49**

- **DICK FRANCIS** Author. (Wales) Wrote *Decider, Break-In, Proof, Forfeit*, and the horse racing book *Whip Hand*. Year/**Age**: 1995/**75** 1996/**76** 1997/**77**

- **FRANK SHORTER** Runner. (Germany) Year/**Age**: 1995/**48** 1996/**49** 1997/**50**

- **MICHAEL COLLINS** Former astronaut. (Rome, Italy) He manned the command module of Apollo II while Neil Armstrong and Ed Aldrin walked on the moon July 21, 1969. His daughter Kate is an actress, who has played on "All My Children." Year/**Age**: 1995/**65** 1996/**66** 1997/**67**

- **JOHN CANDY** Actor/ comedian. (1950-1994). Films include *Trains, Planes and Automobiles*, *JFK*, *Home Alone*, *Stripes*, *Uncle Buck*, *Only the Lonely*, and *Cool Runnings* about the Jamaican bobsled team. (Died of a heart attack 3-4-94.)

- **MICHAEL LANDON** Actor/producer/director. (1937-1991 – Born Eugene Maurice Orowitz in Forest Hills, NY) He appeared in the 1957 film *I Was a Teenage Werewolf* and gained popularity in 1959 as Little Joe on the "Bonanza" TV series. He also wrote and produced, as well as acted in, many of the "Little House on the Prairie" and "Highway to Heaven" episodes. (Died of cancer 7-1-91.)

- **BRIAN PICCOLO** Football star. (1943-1970) His life was the subject of a made-for-TV movie, *Brian's Song*. The theme song by Michel LeGrand became popular in 1972 .

- **JOHN KEATS** Poet. (1795-1821 – Born in his father's livery stable in London, England) He died of consumption at age 25, soon after recovering from an attempted suicide by an overdose of opium. Keats was found drunk in a Baltimore tavern. He died four days later and is buried in Baltimore. He wrote: "I am a coward, I cannot bear the pain of being happy." (Died 2-23-1821.)

- **ETHEL WATERS** Actress/singer. (1900-1977 – Chester, PA) She was the first to sing W.C. Handy's "St. Louis Blues." She appeared as a regular on the Billy Graham Crusade. She appeared in films *Cabin in the Sky* and *Stage Door Canteen*. (Died 9-9-77.)

FACTS FROM THE PAST

1867 **CHARLES WELLER** coined the phrase, "Now is the time for all good men to come to the aid of the party," when he was testing a new typewriter invented by his friend, Christopher Sholes. Typists have been typing out that sentence ever since. Two of the first people to make regular use of the typewriter were quite famous in their respective fields: Mark Twain and Sigmund Freud. Twain bought his first typewriter, a Remington Model I, in 1874. His *Life On The Mississippi* was the first manuscript to be sent to a publisher in typewritten form.

1938 One day after his **"WAR OF THE WORLDS"** broadcast had panicked radio listeners, **ORSON WELLES** expressed "deep regret" but also bewilderment that anyone had thought the Martian invasion portrayed in the drama was real.

1956 Rear Admiral **G. J. DUFEK** became the first person to land an airplane at the South Pole.

1959 A former U.S. Marine from Fort Worth, TX, announced in Moscow that he would never return to the United States. His name: **LEE HARVEY OSWALD**. (He was posthumously found guilty of assassinating President John F. Kennedy on November 22, 1963.)

1964 **BOB DYLAN** brought **JOAN BAEZ** on stage for three duets during a concert in New York. Baez and Dylan were lovers. They broke up in 1965, the year Dylan married ex-model Shirley Noznisky.

1982 **POPE JOHN PAUL II** became the first Pontiff ever to step on Spanish soil. He was greeted by large crowds in predominately Roman Catholic Spain.

1984 Indian prime minister **INDIRA GANDHI** was assassinated near her residence by two Sikh [seek] security guards. Gandhi's son, Rajiv, was sworn in as prime minister.

1988 Instead of bobbing for apples at her Halloween party, **DEBBIE GIBSON** held a seance to contact **LIBERACE** and **SID VICIOUS**.

NOVEMBER MEMORIES

YEARS AGO

1985

POPULAR SONGS
"Separate Lives" by Phil Collins and Marilyn Martin

"We Built This City" by Starship

MOVIES
The Trip To Bountiful
starring Geraldine Page, in an Oscar winning performance, as an elderly lady going home to a house in ruins. Co-stars John Heard.

Silverado
starring Kevin Costner, Danny Glover, and others in a western.

TV SHOWS
"The Equalizer"
starring Edward Woodward as a retired secret agent, who now runs his own security firm.

"The Insiders"
starring Nicholas Campbell and Stoney Jacksonthe as two magazine reporters.

BOOKS
On Your Own by Brooke Shields

1986

POPULAR SONGS
"Amanda" by Boston

"You Give Love a Bad Name" by Bon Jovi

MOVIES
Hannah and Her Sisters
starring Woody Allen, Mia Farrow, and Barbara Hershey. Hannah's husband is involved in a love affair with her sister.

The Mission
starring Robert DeNiro, Liam Neeson, and Aidan Quinn in a story of missionary work of 18th-Century South American Indians.

TV SHOWS
"Matlock"
starring Andy Griffith and Linda Purl as lawyers who solve murders.

"Crime Story"
police drama starring Dennis Farina as Lt. Mike Torello.

BOOKS
Whirlwind by James Clavell

1987

POPULAR SONGS
"I Think We're Alone Now" by Tiffany

"Mony Mony 'Live' " by Billy Idol

MOVIES
The Last Emperor
starring Joan Chen and Peter O'Toole. The story of China's last emperor, Pu Yi.

Throw Mama From The Train
starring Danny DeVito and Billy Crystal in this comedy.

TV SHOWS
"Hooperman"
police drama featuring John Ritter as Detective Harry Hooperman.

"A Different World"
starring Lisa Bonet, Marisa Tomei, Jasmine Guy, and Sinbad in this "Cosby Show" spin-off, daughter Denise, attends college.

BOOKS *Man of the House: The Life and Political Memoirs of Speaker Tip O'Neill* with William Novak

SPECIAL DAYS

NOVEMBER	1995	1996	1997
Sadie Hawkins Day	Nov. 4	Nov. 2	Nov. 1
Great American Smokeout *(American Cancer Society)*	Nov. 16	Nov. 21	Nov. 20
Full Moon	Nov. 7	Nov. 25	Nov. 14
Live Turkey Olpymics *(New Prospect, CT)*	Nov. 19	Nov. 17	Nov. 23
World Championship Duck Calling Contest & Cook-Off *(Stuttgart, AK)*	Nov. 24-26	Nov. 22-24	Nov. 28-30
Thanksgiving Day	Nov. 23	Nov. 21	Nov. 27
Busiest Shopping Day of the Year	Nov. 24	Nov. 22	Nov. 28
1st Sunday of Advent	Nov. 26	Dec. 1	Nov. 30

YEARS AGO

1970

POPULAR SONGS

"I'll Be There" by The Jackson 5

"I Think I Love You" by The Partridge Family

MOVIES

Five Easy Pieces
starring Jack Nicholson and Karen Black. A drifter returns to his wealthy family, trying to resolve his differences.

Love Story
starring Ryan O'Neal and Ali McGraw as lovers who face her incurable disease.

TV SHOWS

"The Flip Wilson Show"
starring Flip Wilson as numerous different characters in this hour-long variety show.

"The Young Rebels"
starring Lou Gossett, Jr. and Rick Ely as rebels of the American Revolution.

BOOKS

Jonathan Livingston Seagull by Richard Bach

1971

POPULAR SONGS

"Gypsys, Tramps & Thieves" by Cher

"Theme From Shaft" by Isaac Hayes

MOVIES

The Last Picture Show
starring Jeff Bridges and Cybill Shepherd. A young man in Texas grows up in the 1950s.

Bednobs and Broomsticks
Disney fantasy starring Angela Lansbury. Mixes animation and live action.

TV SHOWS

"The Man and the City"
starring Anthony Quinn as Mayor Thomas Jefferson Alcala in Albuquerque, NM. Co-stars Mike Farrell.

"Longstreet"
starring James Franciscus as a blind New Orleans insurance investigator with Bruce Lee as his self-defense teacher.

BOOKS *Wheels* by Arthur Hailey

1972

POPULAR SONGS

"I Can See Clearly Now" by Johnny Nash

"Papa Was a Rolling Stone" by The Temptations

MOVIES

Play It Again Sam
starring Woody Allen as a Humphrey Bogart wanna-be. Susan Anspach plays his wife. Co-stars Diane Keaton and Tony Roberts.

The Candidate
starring Robert Redford as a man who campaigns for a seat on the U.S. Senate.

TV SHOWS

"The Streets of San Francisco"
starring Karl Malden and Michael Douglas as policeman in this action drama.

"The Brian Keith Show"
starring Brian Keith and Shelly Fabares in this comedy as father and daughter doctors.

BOOKS

August, 1914 by Alexander Solzhenitsyn

YEARS AGO

1945

POPULAR SONGS

"Till the End of Time" by Perry Como

"Symphony" by Freddy Martin Orchestra

MOVIES

The Lost Weekend
starring Ray Milland and Jane Wyman. The story of a frustrated writer who drinks to solve his problems.

Mildred Pierce
starring Joan Crawford as woman trapped in suburban glamour. Co-stars Eve Arden, Ann Blyth, Jack Carson, and Zachary Scott.

TV SHOWS

No regularly scheduled TV programming until May of 1946.

BOOKS

Brideshead Revistited by Evelyn Waugh

1946

POPULAR SONGS

"Guilty" by Margaret Whiting

"Ole Buttermilk Sky" by Mike Douglas with Kay Kyser's Orchestra

MOVIES

The Seventh Veil
starring James Mason, Herbert Lom, Ann Todd, and Hugh McDermott in this gothic romance.

The Harvey Girls
starring Angela Landbury, Judy Garland, John Hodiak, and Ray Bolger in the story of girls who go west to waitress.

TV SHOWS

"Boxing"
Rocky Marciano, Sugar Ray Robinson, etc. appear in this popular sport.

"You Are An Artist"
Artist Jon Gnagy teaches audience to draw.

BOOKS

Peace of Mind by Joshua L. Liebman

1947

POPULAR SONGS

"Too Fat Polka (I Don't Want Her, You Can Have Her, She's Too Fat For Me)" by Arthur Godfrey

"Civilization (Bongo, Bongo, Bongo)" by Danny Kaye with the Andrews Sisters

MOVIES

Miracle on 34th Street
starring Edmund Gwenn, Maureen O'Hara, Natalie Wood, and John Payne in the story of the real Kris Kringle playing Santa at Macy's Department Store.

The Farmer's Daughter
starring Ethel Barrymore and Loretta Young, A woman runs for congress.

TV SHOWS

"Eye Witness"
a televised guide of how TV works. host Ben Graver stars.

BOOKS

Together by Katharine T. Marshall

Television Hall of Fame

1984
Lucille Ball
Milton Berle

Rod Serling

Paddy Chayefsky
Norman Lear
Edward R. Murrow
William S. Paley
David Sarnoff

1985
Carol Burnett
Sid Caesar
Walter Cronkite
Joyce Hall
Rod Serling
Ed Sullivan
Sylvester (Pat) Weaver

1986
Steve Allen
Fred Coe

Walt Disney

Walt Disney
Jackie Gleason
Mary Tyler Moore
Frank Stanton
Burr Tillstrom

1987
Johnny Carson
Jacques-Yves Cousteau
Leonard Goldenson
Jim Henson
Bob Hope
Ernie Kovacs
Eric Sevareid

1988
Jack Benny
George Burns
Gracie Allen
Chet Huntley
David Brinkley

Ted Turner

Red Skelton
David Susskind
David Wolper
Lew Wasserman

1989
Roone Arledge
Fred Astaire
Perry Como
Joan Ganz Cooney
Don Hewitt
Carroll O'Connor
Barbara Walters

1990
James Garner
Desi Arnaz
Leonard Bernstein
Danny Thomas
Mike Wallace

I Love Lucy (The Show)

Lew Wasserman

1991-1992
Bill Cosby
Andy Griffith
Ted Koppel
Sheldon Leonard
Dinah Shore
R.E. (Ted) Turner

1993
Dick Clark
Bob Newhart
Phil Donahue
John Chancellor
Agnes Nixon
Jack Webb
Mark Goodson

1994
Alan Alda
Howard Cosell
Barry Diller
William Hanna/Joseph Barbera
Fred Friendly
Oprah Winfrey

Danny Thomas

Do atoms have sex?

NOVEMBER 1
Turkey Talk Line Opens

BIRTHDAYS

- **TED HENDRICKS** Football Hall of Famer. Played for the Colts, Packers and Raiders—215 straight games in 15 seasons. Year/**Age**: 1995/**48** 1996/**49** 1997/**50**
- **BARBARA BOSSON** Actress. (Charleroi, PA) Fay Furillo in "Hill Street Blues" and the corrupt mayor in "Cop Rock." Year/**Age**: 1995/**56** 1996/**57** 1997/**58**
- **LYLE LOVETT** C&W singer/actor. (Klein, TX) He won a Grammy in 1989 for Best Male Country Vocal. Biggest hit: "Cowboy Man" in 1986. He's married to actress Julia Roberts. Film *Short Cuts*. Year/**Age**: 1995/**39** 1996/**40** 1997/**41**
- **NARVEL FELTS** C&W. (Bernie, MO) Biggest hit: "Reconsider Me" in 1975. Year/**Age**: 1995/**56** 1996/**57** 1997/**58**
- **BETSY PALMER** Actress. (Born Patricia Bromek in East Chicago, IN) Once wrote for the *Chicago Tribune*. In *The Last Angry Man* and *It Could Happen to Jane*. On "I've Got a Secret" for 10 years. Year/**Age**: 1995/**69** 1996/**70** 1997/**71**
- **LARRY FLYNT** Magazine publisher. (Salyersville, KY) *Hustler*. Year/**Age**: 1995/**53** 1996/**54** 1997/**55**
- **MARCIA WALLACE** Actress. Carol on the "Bob Newhart Show" and Mrs Karbappel on "The Simpsons." Year/**Age**: 1995/**53** 1996/**54** 1997/**55**
- **RICK ALLEN** Musician. (England) With DEF LEPPARD. #1 albums include *Hysteria* and *Adrenalize*. He lost his left arm in a car accident on New Year's Eve, 1984. Year/**Age**: 1995/**33** 1996/**34** 1997/**35**
- **JEANNIE BERLIN** Actress. Appeared in *The Heartbreak Kid*. Year/**Age**: 1995/**45** 1996/**46** 1997/**47**
- **ROBERT FOXWORTH** Actor. (Houston, TX) Played Chase Gioberti on TV's "Falcon Crest." Year/**Age**: 1995/**54** 1996/**55** 1997/**56**
- **BILL ANDERSON** Singer. (Columbia, SC) Biggest hit: "Still" in 1963. "Whispering Bill" has been a member of the Grand Ole Opry since 1961. He has written several country hits and appeared in a few films. Year/**Age**: 1995/**58** 1996/**59** 1997/**60**
- **GARY PLAYER** Pro golfer. (South Africa) He won the Masters, U.S. Open, PGA, and the British Open twice. Year/**Age**: 1995/**60** 1996/**61** 1997/**62**
- **FERNANDO VALENZUELA** Los Angeles Dodger pitcher. (Mexico) In 1991, after 141 victories, in 10 seasons, the Dodgers released Valenzuela. In 1981, he was first to win the Cy Young and Rookie of Year honors in the same season. He also helped L.A. win the World Series that year. He tried a comeback with Baltimore in 1993. Year/**Age**: 1995/**35** 1996/**36** 1997/**37**
- **CHRIS MORRIS** Guitarist. (Nottingham, England) Biggest hit: "The Night Chicago Died" with PAPER LACE. Year/**Age**: 1995/**51** 1996/**52** 1997/**53**
- **STEPHEN CRANE** Writer. (1871-1900 – Newark, NJ) American journalist/novelist/short story writer, best known for his novel, *The Red Badge of Courage*. (Died 6-5-1900.)

FACTS FROM THE PAST

1512   After 4$\frac{1}{2}$ years of work, **MICHELANGELO'S** fresco on the ceiling of the **SISTINE CHAPEL** was unveiled.

1604   **WILLIAM SHAKESPEARE**'s tragedy, *Othello*, opened at Whitehall Palace in London. On this same day in 1611, his comedy, *The Tempest* debuted at the same place.

1848   The **FIRST MEDICAL SCHOOL FOR WOMEN** opened in Boston, MA. The Boston Female Medical School was founded by **SAMUEL GREGORY**.

1913   The **FORWARD PASS** was first used in football when Notre Dame team beat Army, 35 to 13 at West Point. **KNUTE ROCKNE** was the team captain.

1914   Before a party, New York debutante **MARY JACOB** decided she didn't want to put on her corset. She had her maid to put together two silk handkerchiefs with some ribbon to wear instead. Other young women at the dance asked where they could get similar underwear. Consumer demand proved the idea was worth money. Mary sold the patent for $15,000, unaware that the **MODERN LIGHT-WEIGHT BRA** would become a multi-million-dollar business. It wasn't until 1935 that bras came in a variety of cup sizes .

1950   Puerto Rican Nationalists tried to force their way into Blair House in Washington, DC, to **ASSASSINATE PRESIDENT HARRY S. TRUMAN**. They failed. Guards killed one, and the other was given a death sentence which was later changed to life imprisonment.

1955   **JACK GRAHAM**, 23 years old, kissed his mother goodbye and watched her board a doomed airliner at the Denver airport. While he, his wife, and baby son watched, the plane exploded above the airfield. His mother and 43 others died. He had taken out huge insurance policies on his mother's life and then planted a bomb in her suitcase. He was executed for the crime in 1957.

1964   AFL Houston Oilers quarterback **GEORGE BLANDA** completed 37 of 68 passes to set a couple of records against Buffalo.

1964   **JIM BROWN** of the Cleveland Browns became the first pro to rush for 10,000 yards.

1964   The **DAVE CLARK FIVE** made a guest appearance on the "Ed Sullivan Show." Sullivan pointed out that, "Unlike the Rolling Stones, they were nice, neat boys."

1987   **TOM WATSON** won the biggest payoff in golf to that date, earning $384,000 in the Nabisco Championship.

1987   **DENG XIAOPING RETIRED.** He was the leader of the Communist Party's Central Committee.

1992   Golfer **FRED COUPLES** clinched PGA Player of the Year honors, his second consecutive Vardon Trophy, for best scoring average and was first in winnings with $1,344,188.

NOVEMBER 2

Don't open your neighbor's mail

BIRTHDAYS

- **CHARLIE "STEELE" PENNACHIO** Singer. (NYC) With LINEAR. "Sending All My Love," in 1990. Year/**Age:** 1995/**28** 1996/**29** 1997/**30**

- **STEFANIE POWERS** Actress. (Born Stefanie Zofja Federkievicz in Hollywood, CA) She appeared with Robert Wagner in the TV series "Hart to Hart," playing Jennifer Hart. Year/**Age:** 1995/**53** 1996/**54** 1997/**55**

- **MAXINE NIGHTINGALE**. (England) In the musicals *Hair, Jesus Christ Superstar* and *Godspell*. Her biggest hit: "Lead Me On" in 1979. Year/**Age:** 1995/**42** 1996/**43** 1997/**44**

- **PATRICK BUCHANAN** Politician. (Washington, DC) President Reagan's director of communication. Ran unsuccessfully for the 1992 Republican nomination for president. Year/**Age:** 1995/**57** 1996/**58** 1997/**59**

- **ALFRE WOODARD** Actress. (Tulsa, OK) She played Dr. Turner on "St. Elsewhere," and has appeared on "Hill Street Blues" and "L.A. Law." On HBO, she appeared as Winnie Mandela, the wife of activist Nelson Mandela. She appeared in *Passion Fish, Bopha,* and *Heart and Souls.* Year/**Age:** 1995/**42** 1996/**43** 1997/**4**

- **BURT LANCASTER** Actor. (NYC) He got his start working as a circus acrobat. While in an elevator of the Palace Theater wearing a sergeant's uniform, he was asked by a Broadway producer if he were an actor. Burt said, "no," but read some lines and got the part in *The Sound of Hunting.* Burt won an Oscar in 1960 for *Elmer Gantry.* Year/**Age:** 1995/**82** 1996/**83** 1997/**84**

- **RAY WALSTON** Actor. (New Orleans, LA) He was the devil in *Damn Yankees,* appeared in *South Pacific,* and was in the TV series "My Favorite Martian" from 1963-65. Year/**Age:** 1995/**81** 1996/**82** 1997/**83**

- **ANN RUTHERFORD** Actress. (Canada) In *Andy Hardy* films and *The Secret Life of Walter Mitty.* Year/**Age:** 1995/**75** 1996/**76** 1997/**77**

- **BOBBY DALL** Bassist. (Harrisburg, PA) With POISON. Biggest hit: "Every Rose Has Its Thorn" in 1988. Year/**Age:** 1995/**34** 1996/**35** 1997/**36**

- **SHERE HITE** Author. (Born Shirley Gregory in Saint Joseph, MO) *Sexual Honesty: By Women For Women.* She also wrote *A Nationwide Study of Female Sexuality.* Shere is her nickname used to distinguish her from her mother. Year/**Age:** 1995/**53** 1996/**54** 1997/**55**

- **JAY BLACK** Singer. (Born David Blatt in NYC) Lead singer of Brooklyn group JAY & THE AMERICANS. Hits: "Come A Little Bit Closer," "Cara Mia," and "This Magic Moment." Year/**Age:** 1995/**54** 1996/**55** 1997/**56**

- **JIM BAKKEN** Football player. (Madison, WI) Star kicker for the St. Louis Cardinals. Year/**Age:** 1995/**55** 1996/**56** 1997/**57**

- **DANIEL BOONE** Explorer (1734-1820 – Reading, PA) American frontiersman and explorer, captured by Shawnee Indians at Blue Licks, KY, in 1778. He was adopted by Chief Blackfish, who nicknamed him "Big Turtle," but escaped 5 months later. Daniel died in Missouri at age 85 (9-26-1820).

- **JAMES K. POLK** 11th U.S. President. (1795-1849 – Micklenburg County, NC) He was the only president to serve as Speaker of the House. Polk declined to be a candidate for a second term. He died shortly after in Nashville, TN. (Died 6-15-1849.)

- **WARREN G. HARDING** 29th U.S. President. (1865-1923 – Corsica, OH) He was the first president to speak on radio. His administration was tainted by the "Teapot Dome" scandal. He died suddenly in office while on a speaking tour in San Francisco, CA. (Died 8-2-23.)

FACTS FROM THE PAST

1947 **HOWARD HUGHES** piloted his huge wooden flying boat, known as the Spruce Goose, on its only flight, which lasted about a minute over Long Beach Harbor in California. It had a wingspan of 319 feet, 11 inches—the widest plane ever built.

1948 **HARRY S. TRUMAN** was re-elected U.S. President against heavy odds. Polls showed him trailing Republican Thomas Dewey, and the *Chicago Tribune* newspaper printed a premature headline: **"DEWEY WINS!"**

1954 South Carolina Republican **STROM THURMOND** became the first person ever elected to the U.S. Senate as a write-in candidate. He's been there ever since.

1955 **TENNESSEE ERNIE FORD**'s "Sixteen Tons" first appeared on the *Billboard* music charts. It was one of the fastest-selling records in history. More than four million copies were sold.

1959 Game show contestant **CHARLES VAN DOREN** admitted to a House Sub-Committee that he had been given questions and answers in advance when he appeared on the **NBC-TV QUIZ SHOW** "Twenty-one."

1959 Montreal goalie **JACQUES PLANTE** put on a face mask and became the first NHL goalie to regularly use face protection.

1960 During a major trial in England, the D.H. Lawrence novel **LADY CHATTERLEY'S LOVER,** was found "not guilty" of obscenity.

1963 **DION,** distracted an disturbed by the go-go dancers walked out of a live taping of the British TV show "Ready, Steady, Go."

1974 **GEORGE HARRISON** began his first full-fledged solo tour.

1976 Former Georgia Governor **JIMMY CARTER** defeated Gerald Ford for the presidency. Carter was the first candidate from the Deep South since the Civil War to become President of the United States.

1986 The world record for **BATHTUB TRAVEL** was set by Greg Mutton. Powered by a 6 HP engine, the tub took Greg 36 miles in 87 minutes.

1992 **MAGIC JOHNSON** stepped down again after he was cut in an exhibition game. Other players feared his HIV infection.

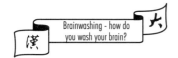
Brainwashing - how do you wash your brain?

NOVEMBER 3
Sandwich Day

BIRTHDAYS

- **PHIL SIMMS** Football quarterback. (Lebanon, KY) NY Giants. Year/**Age:** 1995/**39** 1996/**40** 1997/**41**

- **ROSEANNE** Actress. (Salt Lake City, UT) Her TV show, "Roseanne," was #1 for several seasons, beating "Cosby" and "Cheers." In the film *She-Devil*. Roseanne and former husband Tom Arnold own a restaurant in Eldon, Iowa. Wrote *My Life As A Woman* and *My Lives*. She wants to be known only as Roseanne. Year/**Age:** 1995/**43** 1996/**44** 1997/**45**

- **CHARLES BRONSON** Actor. (Born Charles Buchinsky in Scooptown, PA) He and the late actress Jill Ireland married in 1968 and had six children. Bronson said he changed his name when Senator Joe McCarthy made everything that sounded Russian "evil." He was in *The Magnificent Seven, Dirty Dozen,* and best known for *Death Wish* films. He got a part in his first film, *You're In The Army Now*, because he could belch on cue. Year/**Age:** 1995/**73** 1996/**74** 1997/**75**

- **LULU** Singer. (Born Marie McDonald McLaughlin Laurie in Scotland) In 1967, she had a #1 hit: "To Sir With Love" from the movie of the same name, starring Sidney Poitier. Formerly married to BEE GEE Barry Gibb, 1967-1973. Hit in 1981 "I Could Never Miss You." Year/**Age:** 1995/**47** 1996/**48** 1997/**49**

- **PHILIP M. CRANE** U.S. Representative (R/IL). (Chicago, IL) Year/**Age:** 1995/**65** 1996/**66** 1997/**67**

- **DENNIS MILLER** Comic. (Pittsburgh, PA) "Saturday Night Live" and talk show host. Started his own short-lived show Jan. 20, 1992, with guest Tom Hanks. His show was canceled a few months later. Year/**Age:** 1995/**42** 1996/**43** 1997/**44**

- **KEN BERRY** Actor/dancer. (Moline, IL) TV's "Mama" and "F Troop." Year/**Age:** 1995/**62** 1996/**63** 1997/**64**

- **TOM SHALES** TV critic. Year/**Age:** 1995/**47** 1996/**48** 1997/**49**

- **ADAM ANT** Singer. (Born Stewart Goddard in England) Formed ADAM & THE ANTS in 1976. Biggest hit: "Goody Two Shoes" in 1982. Year/**Age:** 1995/**41** 1996/**42** 1997/**43**

- **LARRY HOLMES** Heavyweight boxer. He won 48 straight fights before losing to Leon Spinks on Sept. 21, 1985. Year/**Age:** 1995/**46** 1996/**47** 1997/**48**

- **BOB FELLER** Baseball Hall of Famer. (Van Meter, IA) In 18 seasons for the Cleveland Indians, he won 266 games and lost only 162, pitched 3 no-hitters and 12 one-hitters, and finished with an ERA of 3.25. Year/**Age:** 1995/**77** 1996/**78** 1997/**79**

- **MICHAEL S. DUKAKIS** Former Massachusetts Governor. (Brookline, MA) Unsuccessful Democratic candidate for President in 1988. Year/**Age:** 1995/**62** 1996/**63** 1997/**64**

- **JOHN BARRY** Composer. (England) He has composed and conducted soundtracks for Oscar winners: *The Lion in Winter, Out of Africa*, and *Dances With Wolves*. One big hit was "Goldfinger" in 1965. Year/**Age:** 1995/**61** 1996/**62** 1997/**63**

- **BRONISLAU "BRONKO" NAGURSKI** Football Hall of Famer. (1908-1990 – Rainy River, Ontario, Canada) He played for the Chicago Bears and gained over 4,000 yards rushing. Charter member of the Pro Football Hall of Fame. (Died 1-7-90.)

- **JOHN MONTAGUE** (1718-1792) The 4th Earl of Sandwich. He is credited with inventing the sandwich as a timesaving nourishment while he was engaged in a 24-hr. gambling session in 1792.

- **STEPHEN AUSTIN** (1793-1836 – Wythe County, VA) A principal founder of Texas. Capital city was named after him. (Died 12-27-1836.)

FACTS FROM THE PAST

1507 Leonardo DaVinci was commissioned by the husband of **MONA LISA** (Lisa Gherardini) to paint her. One night while he was painting, she developed a toothache. Three of her teeth had to be pulled and the painting couldn't continue until she got some false teeth. But they didn't fit well and it's speculated that this is why Mona Lisa doesn't have a complete smile.

1796 **JOHN ADAMS** was elected the second U.S. President. Of the first 5 presidents, 3 died on the Fourth of July. Thomas Jefferson and John Adams died only a few hours apart on July 4, 1826. Five years later, James Monroe died.

1892 The **FIRST AUTOMATIC TELEPHONE** (which preceded today's dials, touchtones, etc.) went into service at La Porte, IN. The inventor was **ALMON STROWGER**, an undertaker in Kansas City, who created the device because he found out that one of the operators was the wife of his chief rival in the funeral business and was diverting calls for undertakers to her husband's establishment.

1936 **PRESIDENT FRANKLIN ROOSEVELT** was re-elected in a landslide over Republican Alf Landon. This same day, Republican Richard J. Daley won a seat in the Illinois House, beginning his career. He later became mayor of Chicago.

1952 The first frozen bread went on sale, made possible by earlier quick-freeze technology developed by **CLARENCE BIRDSEYE**. He was inspired by tasting naturally quick-frozen Arctic fish.

1957 **JERRY LEE LEWIS'** "Great Balls of Fire" was released. It hit number one on the pop, country, and R&B charts.

1961 **HANK WILLIAMS, SR.** and **JIMMIE RODGERS** were chosen as the first Country Music Hall of Famers.

1975 **"GOOD MORNING AMERICA"** was introduced to ABC-TV viewers with host David Hartman and co-host Nancy Dussault.

1977 **ELTON JOHN** announced at a London concert that he was retiring from live performances. There was speculation that his decision was prompted by flak he got for revealing he's bisexual. John didn't perform in public again until 1979.

1992 Arkansas Governor **BILL CLINTON** was elected the 42nd President of the United States, capturing 370 electoral votes in his victory over George Bush and Ross Perot. Five women won Senate seats including Democrate Carol Moseley-Braun, who became the first African-American woman senator.

NOVEMBER 4

Study to be a bouncer

BIRTHDAYS

- **JOE NIEKRO** Baseball pitcher. He and his brother Phil hold the major league record for wins by brothers. Year/Age: 1995/**51** 1996/**52** 1997/**53**
- **MARKIE POST** Actress. (Palo Alto, CA) Played Christine on TV's "Night Court." Was on "The Fall Guy" from 1982-1985. She is on TV's "Hearts Afire." Year/Age: 1995/**45** 1996/**46** 1997/**47**
- **WALTER CRONKITE** Newsman. (Born W. Leland Cronkite, Jr., in St. Joseph, MO) He was the host of CBS game show, "It's News to Me" in 1954 before he became CBS news anchor in 1962, succeeding Douglas Edwards. He retired in 1981 and was succeeded by Dan Rather. He was the longest-running TV news anchor ever. Year/Age: 1995/**79** 1996/**80** 1997/**81**
- **ART CARNEY** Actor. (Mt. Vernon, NY) He won an Oscar for best actor in 1974 for *Harry & Tonto*. He played Ed Norton, a city sewer worker, on "The Honeymooners" with Jackie Gleason, and in 1985, he and Jackie reunited for a TV movie, *Izzy and Moe*. Year/Age: 1995/**77** 1996/**78** 1997/**79**
- **DORIS ROBERTS** Actress. (St. Louis, MO) Played Mildred Krebs on TV's "Remington Steele." Year/Age: 1995/**65** 1996/**66** 1997/**67**
- **LORETTA SWIT** Actress. (Passaic, NJ) She portrayed "Hot Lips" Houlihan on TV's "M*A*S*H" series. She was the first one of that series to actually visit Korea. Year/Age: 1995/**58** 1996/**59** 1997/**60**
- **DELBERT McCLINTON** Singer. (St. Paul, MN) Biggest hit: "Giving It Up for Your Love" in 1980. He was the harmonica player on "Hey Baby," the hit for Bruce Channel. Year/Age: 1995/**47** 1996/**48** 1997/**49**

- **RALPH MACCHIO** Actor. (Long Island, NY) Appeared in *Karate Kid I, II, and III*. His first TV audition turned into a part in "Eight is Enough." Year/Age: 1995/**34** 1996/**35** 1997/**36**
- **KATE REID** Actress. (1931-1993, London, England) Played Linda Loman in *Death of a Salesman* on Broadway in 1984. Year/Age: 1995/**65** 1996/**66** 1997/**67**
- **CAMERON MITCHELL** Actor. (1918-1994, Dallastown, PA) He played Buck Cannon on TV's "High Chaparral." He also appeared in more than 90 films including *Carousel* in 1956. (Died 7-6-94.)
- **MARTIN BALSAM** Actor. (NYC) Character actor who has appeared in many movies. He won an Oscar for *A Thousand Clowns* in 1965. Year/Age: 1995/**76** 1996/**77** 1997/**78**
- **HARRY ELSTON** Musican. (Dallas, TX) Member of FRIENDS OF DISTINCTION. Biggest hit: "Grazing in the Grass" in 1969. Year/Age: 1995/**57** 1996/**58** 1997/**59**
- **ALFRED HEINEKEN** Brewery executive. (Amsterdam, Netherlands) Year/Age: 1995/**72** 1996/**73** 1997/**74**
- **WILL ROGERS** Actor/philosopher. (1879-1935 – Oolagah, OK) Died in a plane crash with pilot Wiley Post near Point Barrow, Alaska (8-15-35). He was in *The Wall Street Girl* on Broadway and film *A Connecticut Yankee in King Arthur's Court*. There is a Broadway show about him, the *Will Rogers Follies*.
- **GIG YOUNG** Actor. (1913-1978 – Born Byron Ellsworth Barr in St. Cloud, MN) He won an Oscar in 1969 as supporting actor in *They Shoot Horses, Don't They?*, co-starring Jane Fonda. He died in a bizarre murder/suicide, apparently shooting his young bride of 3 weeks and then killing himself. (Died 10-19-78.)

FACTS FROM THE PAST

1842 **MARY TODD** and **ABRAHAM LINCOLN** were married in her sister's home in Springfield, IL. Abraham was so depressed and worried about getting married that friends had to keep sharp objects away from him.

1879 The **CASH REGISTER** was invented by **J. RITTY** of Dayton, OH. He was a tavern owner and his bartenders were apparently raking off some incoming cash, so he decided he had to do something about it and invented the cash register.

1922 The entrance to **KING TUT'S TOMB** was discovered. The Egyptian child-king became pharaoh at age 9 and died when he was 19. The tomb was discovered more than 3,000 years after his death. Its priceless items are in Egypt's National Museum at Cairo. (See 11-25)

1924 **NELLIE TAYLOE ROSS** of Wyoming was the **FIRST FEMALE TO BE ELECTED GOVERNOR** in the U.S. She finished the term of her husband, William B. Ross. She was also the first woman director of the U.S. Mint.

1952 **DWIGHT D. EISENHOWER** was elected the 34th U.S. President, defeating Democrat Adlai Stevenson in the first Republican Presidential victory in 24 years.

1961 **BOB DYLAN** gave his first major concert performance at Carnegie Hall. About 50 people were in the audience. He earned $20.

1976 A false, phoned-in bomb threat, interrupted **BRUCE SPRINGSTEIN**'s NY Palladium Show. Springstein said the culprit might have been ex-manager and legal opponent Mike Appel.

1979 Revolutionaries in Iran stormed the U.S. **EMBASSY IN TEHRAN**. Some of the captives were freed several weeks later, but 52 of them remained in captivity for 444 days. The captors said they would keep the hostages until the former Shah, Mohammed Reza Pahlavi, was returned to Iran for trial. He was in the U.S. for medical treatment. The Shah died July 27, 1980. The hostages were released on President Reagan's inauguration day, January 20, 1981.

1980 **RONALD REAGAN** won the White House as he defeated Jimmy Carter. Republicans also won a majority of seats in the U.S. Senate.

1986 **TAMMY WYNETTE**, addicted to pain killers, checked into the Betty Ford Clinic.

1991 **THE RONALD REAGAN PRESIDENTIAL LIBRARY** opened in Simi Valley, CA. At the dedication ceremony with Reagan were President Bush, and former Presidents Carter, Ford, and Nixon.

Do groupers swim alone?

NOVEMBER 5

BIRTHDAYS

• **ROY ROGERS** Cowboy entertainer. (Born Leonard Sly in Duck Run, OH) The #1 box office Western star for 12 consecutive years. He starred in 87 westerns for Republic. The "Roy Rogers Show" was on TV from 1951-57. He married Arlene Wilkins in 1936. She died in 1946. He married Dale Evans in 1947. When he started in films in 1937, he earned $75 a week and the price of a movie ticket was a dime. Year/**Age**: 1995/**84** 1996/**85** 1997/**86**

• **ANDREA McARDLE** Singer/actress. (Philadelphia, PA) She was the original "Annie" on Broadway and toured as Dorothy in *The Wizard of Oz.* Year/**Age**: 1995/**32** 1996/**33** 1997/**34**

• **ELKE SOMMER** Actress. (Born Elkie Schletz in Berlin, Germany) Her father was a minister, and she was named "Miss Italy" in 1959. She appeared in *A Shot in the Dark, The Oscar* and *The Prize.* Year/**Age**: 1995/**54** 1996/**55** 1997/**56**

• **TATUM O'NEAL** Actress. (Los Angeles, CA) Ryan O'Neal's daughter. They appeared together in the 1973 film, *Paper Moon,* for which she won an Oscar – the youngest winner ever at 10 years old. Also in *Bad News Bears.* She starred in the TV miniseries "Woman on Trial: The Lawrencia Bembenek Story." She married tennis pro John McEnroe, and has since separated. Year/**Age**: 1995/**32** 1996/**33** 1997/**34**

• **IKE TURNER** Musician. (Clarksdale, MS) Of IKE & TINA TURNER fame. Biggest hit: "Proud Mary" in 1971. He and Tina divorced in 1976. In the Rock and Roll Hall of Fame. Year/**Age**: 1995/**64** 1996/**65** 1997/**66**

• **PAUL SIMON** Entertainer. (Born Paul Frederick Simon in Newark, NJ) Biggest hit—with Art Garfunkel—was "Bridge Over Troubled Water" in 1970, the 7th most-performed BMI song. "Mrs. Robinson" is 9th. He has turned out consistently interesting albums for over 20 years: *Loves Me Like a Rock, 50 Ways to Leave Your Lover,* and *Graceland.* He played the part of a record-industry promoter Tony Lacey in the 1977 Woody Allen film *Annie Hall.* Year/**Age**: 1995/**53** 1996/**54** 1997/**55**

• **ALFRED "GREASY" NEALE** Football Hall of Famer. (1891-1973) He created the five-man defensive line.

• **BRYAN ADAMS** Entertainer. (Canada) Singer, guitarist and songwriter. Hits include: "Heaven" in 1985 and "Everything I Do" from the film *Robin Hood: Prince of Thieves.* The song received 4 Grammy nominations in 1992. Year/**Age**: 1995/**36** 1996/**37** 1997/**38**

• **BILL WALTON** Basketball. He led the Portland Trail Blazers to an NBA championship basketball title in 1977. He was named MVP in 1978. Year/**Age**: 1995/**43** 1996/**44** 1997/**45**

• **SAM SHEPARD** Actor/playwright. (Born Samuel Shepard Rogers in Ft. Sheridan, IL) He was in *Days of Heaven* in 1978. The film won an Oscar for best cinematography. Also in *The Pelican Brief.* Year/**Age**: 1995/**52** 1996/**53** 1997/**54**

• **PETER NOONE** Singer. (England) Biggest hit with HERMAN'S HERMITS. "Mrs. Brown, You've Got a Lovely Daughter" in 1965. Starred on Broadway in *The Pirates of Penzance.* Year/**Age**: 1995/**48** 1996/**49** 1997/**50**

• **NATALIE SCHAFER** Actress. (1912-1991) The dizzy rich woman, Lovey, wife of Thurston Howell III, played by Jim Backus on "Gilligan's Island." (Died 4-10-91.)

• **JON-ERIK HEXUM** Actor. (1958-1984 – Tenafly, NJ.) Starred in children's show, "Voyager." He accidentally shot himself on the set of a TV show "Cover-up." (Died 10-19-84.)

• **BARRY SADLER** (1941-1989 – New Mexico) He recorded and wrote "Ballad of the Green Berets," which was #1 for five weeks in 1966. In 1978, he shot and killed the estranged boyfriend of a woman he was dating. He pleaded guilty and was sentenced to 30 days in prison and two years probation. In 1988 Sadler was critically wounded while training contra rebels in Guatemala. (Died 11-5-89.)

• **GRAM PARSONS** Singer/songwriter. (1946-1973 – Los Angeles, CA) With the BYRDS until he left to form the FLYING BURRITO BROTHERS. He died of a drug overdose in Joshua Tree, CA. See Nov. 6, 1973. (Died 9-19-73.)

FACTS FROM THE PAST

1782 Delegates from the 13 original colonies elected **JOHN HANSON** "President of the United States in Congress Assembled." Even George Washington called John "Mr. President." He held the job for one year and resigned when he became sick. Eight years and 6 successors later, with our new Constitution in effect in 1789, George Washington got the job. So technically, the first president was not George.

1831 England's **GEORGE OSBALDESTON**, a 155-pound jockey, rode horseback for 200 miles in eight hours and 42 minutes to win 1,000 guineas in a bet. He had to do it in less than 10 hours and if any of the horses failed to make the distance, he would lose.

1872 Suffragist **SUSAN B. ANTHONY** tried to vote in the presidential election, for Ulysses S. Grant (who won). She was later fined $100, which she never paid.

1883 America's first mailman, **RICHARD FAIRFIELD**, was appointed in Boston, MA. He received one penny for each letter.

1911 The **FIRST U.S. COAST-TO-COAST FLIGHT** ended. **GALBRAITH RODGERS**, 32, flew a Wright bi-plane. He didn't get the $50,000 prize money offered by William Randolph Hearst because he did it in 49 days instead of the required 30. It took so long because he crashed 19 times. He had a train following him with spare parts, and he, his wife and mother patched it up each time.

1955 The **FIRST FM-STEREO BROADCAST** was made. FM was invented by **EDWIN HOWARD ARMSTRONG** in 1933. The first broadcast was delayed because Armstrong had so many problems with lawsuits.

1970 At the "Whiske y" in Los Angeles, **BEACH BOY BRIAN WILSON** made a rare appearance with the group, but ended up falling several times and had to be helped off the stage.

NOVEMBER 6

Harden your hamstrings

BIRTHDAYS

- **MARIA SHRIVER** TV journalist. (Chicago, IL) On CBS-TV and married to Arnold Schwarzenegger. Year/**Age:** 1995/**40** 1996/**41** 1997/**42**

- **MIKE NICHOLS** Actor/film director. (Born Michael Igor Peschkowsky in Germany) He received an Oscar for *The Graduate.* His wife is TV newscaster Diane Sawyer. While Mike was taking drama lessons in the early 1950's, he was fired as a busboy at a Howard Johnson's restaurant in NYC when someone asked him the ice cream flavor of the week and he said "chicken." Year/**Age:** 1995/**64** 1996/**65** 1997/**66**

- **SALLY FIELD** Actress. (Pasadena, CA) She won an Oscar in 1979 for best actress in *Norma Rae* and, in 1984, as best actress in *Places in the Heart.* She won an Oscar for *Steel Magnolias.* In *Mrs. Doubtfire.* She starred in the TV series "The Flying Nun," and "Gidget." Year/**Age:** 1995/**49** 1996/**50** 1997/**51**

- **LORI SINGER** Actress. In the films *Footloose* and *Short Cuts.* Appeared on TV's "Fame." She was a concert cellist when she was a teenager. Year/**Age:** 1995/**34** 1996/**35** 1997/**36**

- **EUGENE PITT** Singer. (Brooklyn, NY) Lead singer of the "doo-wop" group, JIVE FIVE. Their biggest hit: "My True Story" in 1961. Year/**Age:** 1995/**58** 1996/**59** 1997/**60**

- **GLENN FREY** Guitarist. (Detroit, MI) Was with the EAGLES. Biggest hits: "The Heat is On" from the film *Beverly Hills Cop* in 1984 and "You Belong to the City" from TV's "Miami Vice" in 1985. TV's "South of Sunset." Toured with ex-Eagle Joe Walsh in 1993. Year/**Age:** 1995/**47** 1996/**48** 1997/**49**

- **NICOLE DUBUC** Actress. She was in TV's "Our House" and "Major Dad." Year/**Age:** 1995/**17** 1996/**18** 1997/**19**

- **LANCE KERWIN** Actor. (Newport Beach, CA) Starred in the TV series "James at Fifteen." Year/**Age:** 1995/**35** 1996/**36** 1997/**37**

- **PETER DeLUISE** Actor in TV's "21 Jump Street," Year/**Age:** 1995/**29** 1996/**30** 1997/**31**

- **DOUG SHAM** Entertainer. (San Antonio, TX) Leader of the SIR DOUGLAS QUINTET. Their biggest hit: "She's About a Mover" in 1965. Year/**Age:** 1995/**54** 1996/**55** 1997/**56**

- **STONEWALL JACKSON** C&W singer. (Tabor City, NC) He was named after the Confederate general of whom he is a descendent. Biggest hit: "Waterloo" in 1959. Year/**Age:** 1995/**63** 1996/**64** 1997/**65**

- **JAMES NAISMITH** Inventor. (1861-1939 – Canada) He invented the game of basketball in 1891. It became an Olympic sport in 1936. (Died 11-28-39.)

- **JOHN PHILIP SOUSA** Composer. (1854-1932 – Washington, DC) American composer/band conductor, remembered for his stirring marches, such as "Stars & Stripes Forever" and "Semper Fidelis." He was called the "King of American March Music." He hated modern dancing. He said it reminded him of eels. (Died 3-6-32.)

- **ADOLPHE SAX** Musician. (1814-1894) Belgian musician and inventor of the saxophone. He became very wealthy, but business mistakes led him to bankruptcy, and he died in poverty in Paris, France. (Died 2-7-1894.)

FACTS FROM THE PAST

1860 There was an 82% voter turnout when **ABRAHAM LINCOLN** was elected, beating out three other candidates. Even without TV/radio projections, Lincoln still had enough telegraph reports to know, before midnight, that he was the winner of the election.

1895 **GEORGE B. SELDEN** received the patent for the first gasoline-powered auto. But Henry Ford sued him and won six years later.

1913 **MOHANDAS GANDHI** was arrested while leading a march of Indian miners in South Africa.

1947 NBC began **"MEET THE PRESS,"** network television's oldest program. The show was created by **MARTHA ROUNTREE** who brought it to radio in 1945. The 28th anniversary of the program was commemorated by an appearance by President Gerald Ford, the first time an incumbent president had appeared on the show.

1961 One of the worst **BRUSH FIRES** flared on this day in Bel Air, CA. A bulldozer hit a rock and sparks set fire to the brush. Homes and valuables of Marlon Brando, Burt Lancaster, Fred MacMurray, and Kim Novak went up in flames. Luckily, MacMurray had loaned his art collection to a museum at the time. The only casualty was Kim Novak's cat.

1962 **RICHARD NIXON** held a press conference after losing the election for Governor of California to the incumbent, Pat Brown. He told the media bitterly, "…You won't have Nixon to kick around anymore."

1968 **RICHARD M. NIXON** defeated V.P. Hubert H. Humphrey and third-party candidate George C. Wallace for the presidency.

1969 For the first time a tie occurred in voting the Cy Young Baseball Award. Detroit's **DENNY McLAIN** and Baltimore's **MIKE CUELLAR** received an equal number of votes for best pitcher in the American League.

1973 Phil Kaufman and Michael Martin were fined $300 each for stealing the body of singer **GRAM PARSONS** from the Los Angeles International Airport. Parsons was cremated at the Joshua Tree Monument in accordance with his wishes on his *G.P.* album.

1974 **ELLA T. GRASSO** was elected governor of CT, the 1st woman to win a governorship without succeeding her husband.

1984 **MARVIN GAYE, SR.** got five years probation for shooting and killing his son, Marvin, in Los Angeles. He said his son provoked him.

1988 **RINGO STARR** and wife **BARBARA BACH** announced that they had both checked into an alcohol rehabilitation clinic.

1991 The last of the **OIL FIRES** ordered set in Kuwait by **SADDAM HUSSEIN** during the Gulf War were extinguished.

1993 **EVANDER HOLYFIELD** won back the heavyweight championship from Riddick Bowe. A parachutist crashed into ringside seats during the seventh round, delaying the fight for 20 minutes.

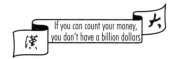

If you can count your money, you don't have a billion dollars

NOVEMBER 7

Election Day

BIRTHDAYS

- **AL HIRT** Trumpeter. (New Orleans, LA) Biggest hit: "Java" in 1964. He was once a member of country singer Don Gibson's band, and was also part owner of the New Orleans Saints football team. Year/**Age**: 1995/**73** 1996/**74** 1997/**75**
- **MARY TRAVERS** Singer. (Louisville, KY) Biggest hit for PETER, PAUL & MARY: "Leaving on a Jet Plane" in 1969, written by John Denver. Won a Grammy for "Blowin' in the Wind" in 1971. Year/**Age**: 1995/**58** 1996/**59** 1997/**60**
- **JONI MITCHELL** Singer. (Born Roberta Joan Anderson in Canada) Married to Chuck Mitchell from 1965 to 1966. Biggest hit: "Help Me" in 1974. Year/**Age**: 1995/**52** 1996/**53** 1997/**54**
- **JOAN SUTHERLAND** Opera star. (Sydney, Australia) This famous soprano retired in 1990. Year/**Age**: 1995/**69** 1996/**70** 1997/**71**
- **JOHNNY RIVERS** Singer. (Born John Ramistella in NYC) Biggest hit: "Poor Side of Town" in 1966. His records have sold over 30 million copies. Year/**Age**: 1995/**53** 1996/**54** 1997/**55**
- **WILLIAM F. "BILLY" GRAHAM** Evangelist REV. (Charlotte, NC) He was known as the fastest milker in his hometown in Mecklenberg County while working on his dad's dairy farm. He was one of the first evangelists to utilize television when he appeared on a 15-minute series, "Hour of Decision," which began Sept. 30, 1951. Since then, his crusades around the world have been widely telecast, usually as specials. Year/**Age**: 1995/**77** 1996/**78** 1997/**79**

- **DANA PLATO** Actress. (Maywood, CA) Was Philip Drummond's daughter, Kimberly, on "Diff'rent Strokes." Year/**Age**: 1995/**31** 1996/**32** 1997/**33**
- **NICK GILDER** Singer. (London, England) 1978 hit: "Hot Child in the City." Year/**Age**: 1995/**44** 1996/**45** 1997/**46**
- **BARRY NEWMAN** Actor. (Boston, MA) Starred in the crime TV show, "Petrocelli," in the 1970s. He also appeared on the soap opera, "The Edge of Night." Year/**Age**: 1995/**57** 1996/**58** 1997/**59**
- **JIM KAAT** Pitcher. Former Minnesota Twins lefty, he was 18-11 on the 1965 pennant-winning team. Year/**Age**: 1995/**57** 1996/**58** 1997/**59**
- **ARCHIE CAMPBELL** C & W. (1914-1987 – Bulls Gap, TN) Joined the Grand Ole Opry in 1968. (Died 8-29-87.)
- **ED DODD** Cartoonist. (1902-1991) Drew *Mark Trail*, the adventures of a conservation-minded outdoor writer, which made its debut in 1946. (Died 5-27-91.)
- **DEAN JAGGER** Actor. (1903-1991 – Columbus Grove, OH) He won an Oscar for supporting actor in the movie *Twelve O'Clock High* in 1949. One of Jagger's best known roles was as the general in *White Christmas*, the 1954 film starring Bing Crosby. He played Albert Vane, the principal, on "Mr. Novak." (Died 2-5-91.)
- **DEE CLARK** Singer. (1938-1990 – Born Delecta Clark in Blythsville, AK) His biggest hit: "Raindrops" in 1961. (Died 12-7-90.)

FACTS FROM THE PAST

1805 **LEWIS AND CLARK** sighted the Pacific Ocean at the mouth of the Columbia River in Oregon, mapping a region that had previously been only rumored to exist.

1874 The **ELEPHANT** was used as the symbol of the **REPUBLICAN PARTY** in a satirical cartoon by **THOMAS NAST**, depicting an elephant about to fall into a pit in reference to Grant's possible bid for a third term. Later, it was adopted as the GOP symbol.

1876 The **FIRST ANIMATED ELECTRIC SIGN** began operation. The sign encircled the Times building in New York City. Its first task was to deliver the returns of the presidential election between Hoover and Smith. It was nicknamed "The Zipper."

1916 Republican **JEANNETTE RANKIN** of Montana became the **FIRST WOMAN ELECTED TO CONGRESS**.

1967 **JOHN NANCE GARNER** died. He had been vice president under FDR. At 98 years old, he was the longest-lived vice president.

1967 **CARL STOKES** was elected first African-American mayor of a major city – Cleveland, Ohio.

1968 The **DOORS' JIM MORRISON** told a Phoenix audience to stand up. Local police – wary of Morrison's recent mooning incident – interpreted the act as an attempt to incite a riot and barred the group from future Phoenix appearances.

1969 The **ROLLING STONES** began their first American tour in three years. Their absence from U.S. stages was caused by repeated drug arrests, censorship, and alleged lewd activities.

1974 Entertainer **TED NUGENT** won the National Squirrel Shooting Archery Contest by hitting a squirrel at 150 yards. He also killed 27 more with a handgun.

1986 Entertainer formerly known as **PRINCE** crowned the homecoming queen during halftime of the football game at Hawthorne, CA high school.

1986 **FREED AMERICAN HOSTAGE DAVID JACOBSEN** was welcomed by President Reagan at the White House. Jacobsen warned that any U.S. military efforts to free the remaining captives held in Lebanon could result in their deaths.

1989 **KITTY DUKAKIS**, wife of Massachusetts Governor Michael Dukakis, was hospitalized after ingesting rubbing alcohol.

1991 **MAGIC JOHNSON** stunned the sports world by announcing that he had tested positive for the **HIV** virus. He said he would retire from basketball immediately (though he later changed his mind). Johnson had led the Los Angeles Lakers to five NBA championships.

NOVEMBER 8
Halfway thru Autumn

Today's disease: Green Sickness

BIRTHDAYS

- **KATHARINE HEPBURN** Actress. (Hartford, CT) She won an Oscar in 1932 for *Morning Glory*, in 1967 for *Guess Who's Coming to Dinner*, in 1968 for *Lion in Winter*, and in 1981 for *On Golden Pond* (with Henry Fonda). She's been acting for over 50 years and is the only actress who has won 4 Oscars from 12 nominations. (See May 12) Year/**Age**: 1995/**88** 1996/**89** 1997/**90**

- **MARY HART** TV personality. (Sioux Falls, SD) "Entertainment Tonight." Miss America runner-up 1971. Other TV talk shows: "PM Magazine" and "Regis Philbin Show." Married to movie and TV producer Burt Sugarman. Year/**Age**: 1995/**44** 1996/**45** 1997/**46**

- **MORLEY SAFER** Newsman. (Toronto, Canada) One of the hosts of "60 Minutes" on CBS-TV. Year/**Age**: 1995/**64** 1996/**65** 1997/**66**

- **BONNIE RAITT** Singer. (Los Angeles, CA) Daughter of musical comedy star John Raitt. She made her movie debut in 1980 in *Urban Cowboy* with John Travolta. She taught herself guitar at age 9. Winner of four Grammy Awards in 1990. Year/**Age**: 1995/**46** 1996/**47** 1997/**48**

- **PATTI PAGE** Singer. (Born Clara Ann Fowler in Claremore, OK) Her first #1 hit was "Tennessee Waltz" in 1950, one of the biggest selling records by a female singer. In her career, she sold over 60 million records. In the film *Elmer Gantry*. She got her name from the Page Milk Co. in Tulsa, OK. Year/**Age**: 1995/**68** 1996/**69** 1997/**70**

- **RICKIE LEE JONES** Singer. (Chicago, IL) Biggest hit: "Chuck E's In Love." Year/**Age**: 1995/**41** 1996/**42** 1997/**43**

- **NORMAN LLOYD** Actor. TV's "St. Elsewhere." Year/**Age**: 1995/**81** 1996/**82** 1997/**83**

- **IRA MAGAZINER** White House consultant. (Rhode Island) President Clinton's top adviser on health reform. Year/**Age**: 1995/**48** 1996/**49** 1997/**50**

- **CHRISTIE ANN HEFNER** Publisher. (Chicago, IL) President of *Playboy* magazine in Chicago, IL, and daughter of Hugh Hefner. Year/**Age**: 1995/**43** 1996/**44** 1997/**45**

- **ESTHER ROLLE** Actress. (Pompano Beach, FL) Played Florida Evans on "Maude" and "Good Times." Year/**Age**: 1995/**62** 1996/**63** 1997/**64**

- **LEIF GARRETT** Teen idol. (Hollywood, CA) Biggest hit: "I Was Made for Dancin' " in 1978. Year/**Age**: 1995/**34** 1996/**35** 1997/**36**

- **ANGEL CORDERO** Jockey. (Puerto Rico) This Hall of Famer won 7,076 races earning over $164 million. He won four Breeders' Cup races, three Kentucky Derbies, two Preaknesses and one Belmont. He retired in 1992. Year/**Age**: 1995/**53** 1996/**54** 1997/**55**

- **BRAM STOKER** Writer. (1847-1912 – Born Abraham Stoker in Dublin, Ireland) He created *Dracula* based on a dream he had. (Died 4-2-12.)

- **MINNIE RIPPERTON** Singer. (1948-1979 – Chicago, IL) She was a member of Stevie Wonder's backup group WONDERLOVE in 1973. "Lovin' You" written and produced by Stevie. It was her biggest hit in 1975. She died of cancer in Los Angeles on 7-12-79.

- **MARGARET MITCHELL** Author. (1900-1949) American author of her only novel, *Gone With the Wind*. The movie based on the novel was one of the most successful of all time and still is periodically brought back to theaters and TV. She died in a car accident 8-16-49.

FACTS FROM THE PAST

1887 Gambler/gunslinger **DOC HOLLIDAY** died from tuberculosis in a sanitarium in Glenwood Springs, CO. He was 35. The gunfighting dentist had once given odds of 8 to 5 that a bullet would kill him before consumption did.

1895 **WILLIAM ROENTGEN** [rent'-jin] of Bavaria, while experimenting with electricity, forgot to turn off a machine. The device overheated and began emitting rays. Within a few hours, Roentgen deduced the scientific principle involved and took the **FIRST X-RAY PICTURES**. He didn't patent the machine and received no money for the invention.

1935 United Mine Workers president **JOHN L. LEWIS** and several other labor leaders formed the Committee for Industrial Organization as part of the **AMERICAN FEDERATION OF LABOR**.

1950 The first jet-vs.-jet dogfight took place over Korea between a Soviet-built MIG-15 and an American Lockheed F-80. USAF Lt. **RUSSELL BROWN** destroyed the MIG. A few German jets had flown in WWII and were shot down by American prop airplanes.

1956 Turning down 18,000 names, the Ford Motor Co. decided to name their new car **"EDSEL,"** after Henry Ford's only son, Edsel Ford. Edsel shared control of the company from 1918 till his death in 1943.

1960 **JOHN F. KENNEDY** was elected the first Catholic U.S. President by defeating Republican Richard M. Nixon.

1966 Former movie actor **RONALD REAGAN** was elected governor of California.

1966 **EDWARD W. BROOKE** of Massachusetts became the first African-American to be elected to the U.S. Senate in the 20th century.

1968 **JEAN TERRELL** was named to replace Diana Ross in the **SUPREMES**.

1968 **JOHN LENNON** and his first wife, Cynthia, were divorced.

1983 Democrat **MARTHA COLLINS** elected the first female governor of Kentucky; **W. WILSON GOODE** elected the first black mayor of Philadelphia.

1988 **JERRY LEE LEWIS** filed for protection under the bankruptcy laws, declaring debts of more than $3,000,000.

 He was one cuboid

NOVEMBER 9

BIRTHDAYS

- **CHARLIE JONES** Sportscaster. Year/Age: 1995/**65** 1996/**66** 1997/**67**
- **ALAN GRATZER** Drummer. (Syracuse, NY) Hits with REO SPEEDWAGON: "Keep On Loving You" and "Take It On The Run." Year/Age: 1995/**47** 1996/**48** 1997/**49**
- **SPIRO AGNEW** Former vice president. (Baltimore, MD) Elected V.P. twice: in 1968 & 1972. On Oct. 10, 1973, he became the second to resign that office. The other was John C. Calhoun in 1832. Agnew entered a plea of "no contest" to a charge of income tax evasion on contract kickbacks received while he was governor of Maryland and after becoming V.P. He was the only convicted felon to get $^1/_2$ hour of free TV time on the major networks, declaring his innocence. Year/Age: 1995/**77** 1996/**78** 1997/**79**
- **DR. CARL SAGAN** Astronomer. (NYC) A Pulitzer Prize-winning writer, he is best-known for his ability to translate high science into simple talk. Wrote *Shadows of Forgotten Ancestors*. Year/Age: 1995/**61** 1996/**62** 1997/**63**
- **WHITEY HERZOG** Former baseball manager. (Omaha, NE) Former manager of the St. Louis Cardinals and the California Angels. Year/Age: 1995/**64** 1996/**65** 1997/**66**
- **BOB GIBSON** Baseball. (Omaha, NE) St. Louis Cardinal pitcher and the second pitcher in baseball history to reach 3,000 lifetime strike-outs. Year/Age: 1995/**60** 1996/**61** 1997/**62**
- **TOM WEISKOPF** Pro golfer. (Massillon, OH) Year/Age: 1995/**53** 1996/**54** 1997/**55**

- **LOU FERRIGNO** Actor. (Brooklyn, NY) Appeared in the TV series "The Incredible Hulk" as the hulk version of Bill Bixby. At the age of 21 he was the youngest Mr. Universe ever. Year/Age: 1995/**43** 1996/**44** 1997/**45**
- **HEDY LAMARR** Actress. (Born Hedwig Kiessler in Vienna, Austria) She appeared in *Algiers*, *White Cargo,* and *Samson & Delilah*. She turned down the part Ingrid Bergman became famous for in *Casablanca*. Year/Age: 1995/**82** 1996/**83** 1997/**84**
- **CLAUDE RAINS** Actor. (1889-1967 – England) In films *Casablanca* in 1942 and *The Invisible Man* in 1933. (Died 5-3-67.)
- **TOM FOGERTY** Rhythm guitarist. (1941-1990 – El Cerrito, CA) Co-founded CREEDENCE CLEARWATER REVIVAL. "Proud Mary" was their biggest hit in 1969. (Died 9-6-90.)
- **MARIE DRESSLER** Character actress. (1869-1934 – Born Leila Marie von Koerber in Canada) She won an Oscar in 1930 for *Min and Bill*. (Died 7-28-34.)
- **CLIFTON WEBB** Actor. (1891-1966 – Born Webb Parmalee Hollenbeck in Indianapolis, IN) Nominated twice for an Oscar in *Laura* and *Razor's Edge*. His last movie was *Satan Never Sleeps* in 1962. (Died 10-13-66.)
- **ED WYNN** Actor/comedian. (1886-1966) Father of actor Keenan Wynn. TV series "Ed Wynn Show" 1949-50, star of *Ziegfield Follies*, Emmy for "Requiem for a Heavyweight," and in film *Mary Poppins*. (Died 6-19-66.)

FACTS FROM THE PAST

1912 Carlisle beat Army 27-6 in one of the biggest upsets in college football history. **POP WARNER** coached Carlisle; **JIM THORPE** was the star player for Carlisle; and future U.S. President **DWIGHT EISENHOWER** was right halfback for Army.

1933 President **FRANKLIN D. ROOSEVELT** created the Civil Works Administration to provide jobs for more than 4 million people.

1961 Major **ROBERT WHITE** flew the X-15 rocket plane at a **WORLD RECORD SPEED** of 4,093 mph. The plane now hangs in the Smithsonian Institution in Washington, DC.

1962 **ROY ACUFF** was installed as the first living member of the Country Music Hall of Fame.

1965 A massive power failure blacked out northeastern America and parts of Canada. During the blackout **BOB DYLAN** and the band's **ROBBIE ROBERTSON** jammed with **BRIAN JONES** of the Rolling Stones in his NY Hilton suite.

1967 **ROLLING STONE** magazine began publication in San Francisco. John Lennon was on the cover. A free roach clip was included in the first issue.

1967 **ROGER McGUINN** fired David Crosby from the **BYRDS** after they argued over the group's musical director.

1980 In a nationally broadcast speech marking the start of the New Islamic Year, **IRAQI PRESIDENT SADDAM HUSSEIN** declared that his army was conducting a "holy war" against Iran in order to uphold the ideals of Islam.

1984 A bronze statue by **FREDERICK HART**, titled **"THREE SERVICEMEN,"** was unveiled on the site of the Vietnam Veterans Memorial in Washington DC. The statue, depicting a trio of battle-weary soldiers, was included in response to criticism that the memorial did not adequately represent Vietnam veterans.

1989 The **BERLIN WALL**, for 28 years the most potent symbol of a divided Europe, lost its meaning when East Germany opened its heavily guarded borders with the West. At 11:17 p.m. the gates swung open. Some celebrants danced on top of the wall, while others chipped away at the hated concrete barrier. Because this date is the anniversary of the 1938 "Crystal Night" when hundreds of Jewish businesses were destroyed, "Reunification Day" was set for October 3rd of each year.

1993 Actress **ANGIE DICKINSON** said, "Not on your life!" and walked out on a "This Is Your Life" TV tribute. She was the first to do so in 500 shows. Waiting to honor her were Burt Reynolds, Bob Hope, and Jackie Collins.

NOVEMBER 10

Grab some Grog

BIRTHDAYS

- **ROY SCHEIDER** Actor. (Orange, NJ) He was nominated for supporting actor in 1971 for *The French Connection* and in 1979 for *All That Jazz*. He appeared in *Jaws* in 1975, in *Jaws II, 2001, 2010*, and *52 Pickup* with Ann-Margret. Also TV's "Seaquest." Year/Age: 1995/**60** 1996/**61** 1997/**62**

- **GREG LAKE** Guitarist. (England) Of EMERSON, LAKE & PALMER. Their biggest hit: "From The Beginning" in 1972. Year/Age: 1995/**47** 1996/**48** 1997/**49**

- **JACK SCALIA** Actor. (Brooklyn,NY) TV's "High Performance," "Beringers," "Hollywood Beat," and "Long Island Lolita." Year/Age: 1995/**44** 1996/**45** 1997/**46**

- **SINBAD** Comic/Actor. (Benton Harbor, MI) TV's "A Different World" as Walter Oake. Host of "Showtime At the Apollo" and the "Redd Fox Show." Year/Age: 1995/**39** 1996/**40** 1997/**41**

- **DAVE LOGGINS** Singer. (Mountain City, TN) Cousin of Kenny Loggins. Biggest hit: "Please Come to Boston" in 1974. Year/Age: 1995/**48** 1996/**49** 1997/**50**

- **DONNA FARGO** Singer. (Born Yvonne Vaughn in Mt. Airy, NC) She took the name "Fargo" from the stuntman who drove the Batmobile in the "Batman" TV series. Her biggest hit was "Funny Face" in 1972. Year/Age: 1995/**50** 1996/**51** 1997/**52**

- **RONNIE HAMMOND** Singer. Of the ATLANTA RHYTHM SECTION. Biggest hit: "So in to You" in 1977. Year/Age: 1995/**45** 1996/**46** 1997/**47**

- **MacKENZIE PHILLIPS** Actress. (Alexandria, VA) Appeared on "One Day at a Time." She's the daughter of John Phillips of the MAMAS & PAPAS. Year/Age: 1995/**36** 1996/**37** 1997/**38**

- **RUSSELL MEANS** Activist. (Pine Ridge, SD) Native American rights supporter. Film *Wagons East*. Year/Age: 1995/**55** 1996/**56** 1997/**57**

- **BIRDIE TEBBETTS** Baseball. (Born George Tebbetts in Nashua, NH) Major league catcher who hit .310 in 1950. Later he managed the Cincinnati Reds, Braves, and Indians. Year/Age: 1995/**81** 1996/**82** 1997/**83**

- **ANN REINKING** Dancer/actress. (Seattle, WA) Tony nominee for *Pippin* in 1972. In films *Annie* and *Mickey and Maude*. Year/Age: 1995/**46** 1996/**47** 1997/**48**

- **JACK CLARK** Baseball. (New Brighton, PA) With San Francisco Giants. Year/Age: 1995/**39** 1996/**40** 1997/**41**

- **RICHARD BURTON** Actor. (1925-1984 – Born Richard Jenkins in Wales) He was nominated for an Oscar 7 times, but never won. His final appearance was with his daughter, Kate, in a 7-hour miniseries on TV called "Ellis Island" which was completed two weeks before his death. His alcoholism and two marriages to Liz Taylor overshadowed his talents as an actor. He was drinking up to 3 bottles a day at one time and was told he only had weeks to live, so he gave it up. One time he was visited in his dressing room by Winston Churchill who asked, "My Lord Hamlet, may I use your lavatory?" Burton is buried in the Lake Geneva village of Celigny, Switzerland. (Died 8-5-84.)

- **MARTIN LUTHER** Founder of Protestantism. (1483-1546 – Eisleben [ice-lay-bin], Germany) He believed the Bible to be the sole authority of the church and called for reformation of the Roman Catholic church, denying supremacy of the Pope. He was tried for heresy. He left the church and married a former nun with whom he had 6 children. (Died 2-18-1546.)

FACTS FROM THE PAST

1871 Journalist/explorer Henry Morton Stanley located missing Scottish missionary, David Livingstone, in Central Africa, and Stanley gave his famous greeting, **"DR. LIVINGSTONE, I PRESUME?"** The adventure was a newspaper promotion sponsored by the *New York Herald*. Stanley's companions died enroute. No white man had seen Livingstone in 6 years. Spencer Tracy made a movie about the incident in 1939. Stanley's real name was John Roland, a veteran of the Civil War.

1951 **DIRECT-DIAL** coast-to-coast **TELEPHONE SERVICE** began as Mayor M. Leslie Denning of Englewood, NJ, called the mayor of Alameda, CA.

1954 The **IWO JIMA MEMORIAL**—depicting a group of servicemen raising the American flag—was dedicated in Arlington, VA. The statue depicts the photo taken by **JOE ROSENTHAL** as the American flag was raised over Mt. Suribachi in February 1945.

1965 Bill Graham's first rock show at the Fillmore in San Francisco included the **JEFFERSON AIRPLANE** and the **GRATEFUL DEAD.**

1969 The children's educational program **"SESAME STREET"** made its debut on PBS. Big Bird and Kermit the Frog became mainstays of childhood.

1975 The ore carrier **EDMUND FITZGERALD** broke in two parts during a heavy storm on Lake Superior. There were no survivors of this worst Great Lakes ship disaster of the decade. 29 crew members died. **GORDON LIGHTFOOT** recorded a haunting ballad by the same name.

1980 In Chicago, CBS news anchor **DAN RATHER** claimed he was kidnapped in a speeding cab.

1982 Russian leader **LEONID BREZHNEV** died of heart failure.

1985 Given a 50/50 chance of survival, **JERRY LEE LEWIS** underwent successful ulcer surgery in Memphis.

1986 Fans stormed record stores to buy the new five-record album *Bruce Springsteen and the E Street Band Live, 1975-85*.

1992 Elizabeth Tamposi was fired by **PREDISDENT BUSH** for her role in a pre-election search for passport records of opponents.

1993 **JOHN WAYNE BOBBIT**, the man whose penis was cut off by his wife, was acquitted of a charge of marital sexual assault.

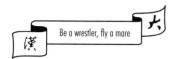

Be a wrestler, fly a mare

NOVEMBER 11
Veteran's Day

BIRTHDAYS

- **WYATT PAULEY** Guitarist. (Equador) With LINEAR, "Sending All My Love." Year/**Age**: 1995/**27** 1996/**28** 1997/**29**
- **MIC MICHAELI** Keyboardist. (Sweden) Hits with EUROPE include "The Final Countdown" in the film *Rocky IV* and *Carrie* in 1987. Year/**Age**: 1995/**33** 1996/**34** 1997/**35**
- **JIM PETERIK** Musician. Keyboard player for SURVIVOR. Hits include: "Eye of the Tiger" and "Burning Heart," both from *Rocky* films. Was lead singer with IDES OF MARCH. Year/**Age**: 1995/**45** 1996/**46** 1997/**47**
- **JONATHAN WINTERS** Comedian. (Dayton, OH) He was Mearth on "Mork and Mindy." He created a battery of mad characters from "Maude Frickert" to the "Hefty Trash Bag Garbageman." He is star of TV sitcom "Davis Rules." A reformed alcoholic, he carries a 6-pack of Diet Pepsi with him. Year/**Age**: 1995/**70** 1996/**71** 1997/**72**
- **JESSE COLIN YOUNG** Singer. (Born Peter Miller, NYC) Former lead singer of the YOUNGBLOODS. Biggest hit: "Get Together" in 1969. Year/**Age**: 1995/**51** 1996/**52** 1997/**53**
- **DENISE ALEXANDER** Actress. Dr. Leslie Williams on "General Hospital." Year/**Age**: 1995/**50** 1996/**51** 1997/**52**
- **STUBBY KAYE** Actor. Heavy comic actor who appeared in the films *Cat Ballou, Guys & Dolls,* and *Sweet Charity.* Year/**Age**: 1995/**77** 1996/**78** 1997/**79**
- **DEMI MOORE** Actress. (Born Demi Guynes in Roswell, NM) Played Jackie Templeton on TV's "General Hospital." In *The Seventh Sign.* She's married to Bruce Willis. She caused a stir in 1991 when she appeared nude and pregnant on the cover of two *Vanity Fair* magazines, with one hand across her breasts and the other under her stomach. Many stores banned the issues. Films include *About Last Night, The Scarlett Letter, Color of Night,Ghost, A Few Good Men,* and *Indecent Proposal.* Year/**Age**: 1995/**33** 1996/**34** 1997/**35**
- **KURT VONNEGUT, JR** American novelist. (Indianapolis, IN) *Slaughterhouse Five* and *Breakfast of Champions.* Year/**Age**: 1995/**73** 1996/**74** 1997/**75**
- **VINCE MARTELL** Guitarist. New York guitar player with VANILLA FUDGE. Their biggest hit: "You Keep Me Hanging On" in 1967. Year/**Age**: 1995/**50** 1996/**51** 1997/**52**
- **LEONARDO DICAPRIO** Actor. (Hollywood, CA) Credits include *Parenthood* and *Outsiders.* Year/**Age**: 1995/**21** 1996/**22** 1997/**23**
- **FRANK ZOELLER** Golfer. (New Albany, IN) Year/**Age**: 1995/**44** 1996/**45** 1997/**46**
- **PAT DAUGHERTY** Bass player. With the group BLACK OAK ARKANSAS. Their biggest hit: "Jim Dandy" in 1973. Year/**Age**: 1995/**48** 1996/**49** 1997/**50**
- **CHRIS DREJA** Guitarist. (England) Member of British rock band YARDBIRDS. Biggest hit: "For Your Love" in 1965. Year/**Age**: 1995/**49** 1996/**50** 1997/**51**
- **RONNIE DEVOE** Singer. (Boston, MA) Hit with BELL BIV DEVOE, "Poison" in 1990. Formerly with R&B quintet, NEW EDITION. Year/**Age**: 1995/**27** 1996/**28** 1997/**29**
- **GEORGE PATTON** General. (1885-1945 – San Gabriel CA) Military officer/graduate of West Point in 1909. They called him "old blood and guts" because he used to tell his recruits: "spill their blood, rip 'em up the belly or shoot 'em in the guts." He was a member of the 1912 U.S. Olympic Team in the modern pentathlon. Died of injuries in an auto accident on 12-21-45.
- **PAT O'BRIEN** Actor. (1899-1983 – Born William Joseph Patrick O'Brien in Milwaukee, WI) Made more than 110 films in 6 decades. Pat portrayed cops, priests and Knute Rockne to Ronald Reagan's "Gipper," in the movie *Knute Rockne, All-American* in 1941. His last movie was *Ragtime* in 1981. (Died 10-15-83.)

FACTS FROM THE PAST

1817 The **FIRST SWORD SWALLOWER** to perform in America appeared in New York City. Admission was $1 to see Senaa Samma.

1831 Former slave **NAT TURNER**, who had led a violent insurrection, was executed in Jerusalem, VA.

1918 In the 11th hour of the 11th day of the 11th month, **WORLD WAR I ENDED**. It was known as **ARMISTICE DAY**. General Irwin T. Parkleton called WWI "The war to end all wars." It wasn't.

1921 President **WARREN HARDING** dedicated the **TOMB OF THE UNKNOWN SOLDIER** at Arlington Cemetery in Arlington, VA. Today is Veteran's Day.

1938 **TYPHOID MARY DIED,** in New York City. Born Mary Mallon, she cooked in restaurants and private homes. She was the carrier of typhoid, and gave it to at least 53 people in America alone. Her brothers and boyfriend died of it even before she immigrated to America. She was tracked down but refused to cooperate. She attacked the doctor with a carving knife, so they put her in prison. She escaped twice and the second time she went to work in a maternity hospital where 20 people caught the disease.

1939 **KATE SMITH** first sang Irving Berlin's **"GOD BLESS AMERICA"** on network radio. **IRVING BERLIN** wrote the song at her request. All royalties were given to the Boy and Girl Scouts of America.

1958 **HANK BALLARD & THE MIDNIGHTERS** recorded "The Twist." Chubby Checker's version is not the original.

1981 L.A. Dodgers lefty **FERNANDO VALENZUELA**, became the first pitcher to win Rookie of the Year and the Cy Young award in the same season.

1983 **PRESIDENT REAGAN** became the first U.S. president to address the Diet, Japan's national legislature.

1992 U.S. senators received a letter from **BORIS YELTSIN** stating that Americans had been held in prison camps after WWII and some were executed though others lived willingly in his country.

NOVEMBER 12

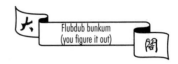
大 Flubdub bunkum (you figure it out) 閻

BIRTHDAYS

- **TEVIN CAMPBELL** Singer. (Akron, OH) Year/Age: 1995/**17** 1996/**18** 1997/**19**
- **NEIL YOUNG** Singer. (Canada) Song "Philadelphia" for the movie. His biggest hit: "Heart of Gold" in 1972. Received 1989 MTV Video of the Year award for "This Note's For You." Year/Age: 1995/**50** 1996/**51** 1997/**52**
- **NADIA COMANECI** [koh-muh-neech] Gymnast. (Romania) In the 1976 Olympics, she earned 7 perfect scores. She now lives in Canada. Year/Age: 1995/**34** 1996/**35** 1997/**36**
- **HARRY BLACKMUN** Supreme Court Justice. (Nashville, IL) A liberal, he was appointed to court June 9, 1970, by President Nixon. In Roe vs. Wade, he wrote the majority opinion, guaranteeing a woman's legal right to an abortion. Year/Age: 1995/**87** 1996/**88** 1997/**89**
- **JO STAFFORD** Singer. (Coalinga, CA) She sang with the PIED PIPERS in the 1950's with hits: "You Belong to Me" and "This Love of Mine." She married arranger/ conductor Paul Weston. They recorded a spoof album as "Darlene & Jonathan Edwards." Year/Age: 1995/**77** 1996/**78** 1997/**79**
- **BRIAN HYLAND** Singer. (Queens, NY) Biggest hit: "Itsy-Bitsy-Teenie-Weenie Yellow Polka-Dot Bikini" in 1960 when he was a sophomore in high school. Year/Age: 1995/**52** 1996/**53** 1997/**54**
- **TONYA HARDING** Former figure skater. She played a tough waitress in the direct-to-video release *Breakaway*. Year/Age: 1995/**25** 1996/**26** 1997/**27**
- **KIM HUNTER** Actress. (Born Janet Cole in Detroit, MI) She won an Oscar for best supporting actress in *A Streetcar Named Desire* in 1951. Year/Age: 1995/**73** 1996/**74** 1997/**75**

- **BOOKER T. JONES** Keyboardist. (Memphis, TN) Biggest hit with the M.G.'s: "Green Onions" in 1962. He married the sister of Rita Coolidge, Priscilla. Year/Age: 1995/**50** 1996/**51** 1997/**52**
- **ANN FLOOD** Actress. Appeared on TV's "Edge of Night." Year/Age: 1995/**63** 1996/**64** 1997/**65**
- **ELIZABETH CADY STANTON** Women's Rights activist. (1815-1902 – Johnstown, NY) Wrote a women's version of the Bible. (Died 10-26-02.)
- **RICHARD QUINE** Actor/director. (1920-1989) Directed *Solid Gold Cadillac*, *Bell, Book and Candle*, *How to Murder Your Wife*, and *Sex and the Single Girl*. Committed suicide 6-1-89.
- **INA BALIN** Actress. (1927-1990 – Born Ina Rosenberg) She appeared in *The Greatest Story Ever Told*, *From the Terrace* and *The Patsy*. (Died 6-20-90)
- **PRINCESS GRACE OF MONACO** (1929-1982 – Born Grace Kelly in Philadelphia, PA) She was a New York model/turned actress, and she won an Oscar for best actress in *The Country Girl* with Bing Crosby. In 1956, she and Bing had a top-10 record, "True Love," from the movie *High Society*. Her most famous line in the movie *To Catch a Thief* was spoken to Cary Grant when they were on a picnic. She said, "Would you like a leg or a breast?" meaning chicken, of course. On April 19, 1956, she married Prince Rainier of Monaco. She said her happiest moment was, "When my daughter Caroline took seven small steps toward me before throwing herself into my arms." She died of injuries received after her car ran off a 45-foot embankment near Laturbe, France on 9-14-82. Daughter Princess Stephanie, a passenger in the car, survived.

FACTS FROM THE PAST

1859 The **DARING YOUNG MAN ON THE FLYING TRAPEZE** made his debut in Paris. He was 21 years old and practiced for years swinging on trapeze over a swimming pool in his father's gymnasium. His name was Jules Leotard; best-remembered for designing the apparel called leotards.

1892 Guard **WILLIAM "PUDGE" HEFFELFINGER** received a $500 pro football first paycheck. His team, the Allegheny Athletic Association, beat the Pittsburgh Athletic Club 4-0 (touchdowns counted 4 points). The crowd numbered 5,000 and the profit for the game was $621.

1903 Tenor **ENRICO CARUSO** recorded the aria "On with the Motley" from Verdi's opera, *I Pagliacci*. It was number one for four weeks and became the first million-seller in recording history.

1920 Baseball got its first "Czar" as **JUDGE KENESAW MOUNTAIN LANDIS** was elected Commissioner of the American and National Leagues in response to the "Black Sox scandal."

1933 Hugh Gray, of the British Aluminum Company, was walking along the shore of **LOCH NESS** when the calm water erupted and a large body appeared in a cloud of spray. He took five pictures, but when the film was developed, four pictures were blank. The authorities knew there would be problems after all the publicity so they put up signs saying, "No molesting the monster."

1970 The **DOORS** played their last concert date together in New Orleans. They got their name from famous English writer Aldous Leonard Huxley who, in 1954, wrote *The Doors of Perception*.

1981 Astronauts **RICHARD TRULY** and **JOE ENGLE** rode *Columbia*, the first space shuttle, into Earth orbit.

1984 **MADONNA**'s biggest-selling album, *Like A Virgin*, was released.

1984 Space shuttle astronauts **DALE GARDNER** and **JOE ALLEN** snared a wandering satellite in history's first space salvage.

1987 **SLY STONE**'s comeback show in Los Angeles was disrupted when Stone arrived over an hour late and then was arrested for nonpayment of child support.

NOVEMBER 13

BIRTHDAYS

• **WHOOPI GOLDBERG** Actress/comedian. (NYC) Star of numerous films including *Corina,Corina, Boys on the Side, The Color Purple, Sister Act, Sarafina, National Lampoon's Loaded Weapon 1,* and *Made in America.* Won supporting actress Academy Award for *Ghost.* Regular guest on "Star Trek: The Next Generation." Year/Age: 1995/**46** 1996/**47** 1997/**48**

• **RICHARD MULLIGAN** Actor. (NYC) Appeared in *The Group, Little Big Man,* on the TV series, "The Hero," as the fidgety father on "Soap," and in "Empty Nest," for which he won an Emmy for lead actor in a comedy series. Year/Age: 1995/**63** 1996/**64** 1997/**65**

• **MADELEINE SHERWOOD** Actress. (Canada) Character actress who appeared in *Hurry Sundown,* was the mother in *Cat on a Hot Tin Roof,* and was in the TV series, "The Flying Nun." Year/Age: 1995/**73** 1996/**74** 1997/**75**

• **VINNY TESTAVERDE** Football. (Brooklyn, NY) Tampa Bay quarterback. Year/Age: 1995/**32** 1996/**32** 1997/**34**

• **JOE MANTEGNA** Actor. Movies: *Airheads, Queen's Logic.* Year/Age: 1995/**48** 1996/**49** 1997/**50**

• **JACK ELAM** Character actor. (Miami, AZ) Tall, thin, evil 'heavy' in most of his films, he appeared in *Support Your Local Sheriff, High Noon* and *Gunfight at the O.K. Corral.* Year/Age: 1995/**79** 1996/**80** 1997/**81**

• **DACK RAMBO** Actor. (Delano, CA) Appeared on the soap "All My Children" and "Dallas." Year/Age: 1995/**54** 1996/**55** 1997/**56**

• **CHARLIE TICKNER** Figure skater. (Oakland, CA) Year/**Age:** 1995/**42** 1996/**43** 1997/**44**

• **TRACY SCOGGINS** Actress (Galveston, TX) Plays gossip columnist "Cat"on the Superman series "Lois and Clark." Also on TV's "Dynasty" and "The Colbys." Year/Age: 1995/**36** 1996/**37** 1997/**38**

• **GARRY MARSHALL** Writer/producer. (NYC) A comedy writer, he worked on the "Dick Van Dyke Show" and "The Lucy Show." Later he produced "The Odd Couple," and "Mork & Mindy," created "Happy Days" and directed the films *Pretty Woman* and *A League of Their Own.* His sister is Penny Marshall, whom he cast in "Laverne and Shirley." Film *Exit to Eden.* Year/Age: 1995/**61** 1996/**62** 1997/**63**

• **OSKAR WERNER** Actor/director. (1922-1984 – Born Oskar Bachliessmayer in Vienna, Austria) He was nominated for an Oscar for best actor in *Ship of Fools* in 1965. He was also in *The Spy Who Came in from the Cold.* (Died 10-23-84.)

• **ROBERT LOUIS STEVENSON** Author. (1850-1894 – Scotland) His father forbade him to write. Author of *Kidnapped* and *Treasure Island,* which he wrote for his stepson. He wrote the entire book *Dr. Jekyl and Mr. Hyde* in 6 days. He got the idea from his association with low-life areas. (Died 11-13-1894.)

• **JEAN SEBERG** Actress. (1938-1979 – Marshalltown, IA) She was discovered by Otto Preminger and appeared in *The Mouse That Roared, Airport,* and *Joan of Arc.* (Died 8-31-79.)

FACTS FROM THE PAST

1805 **JOHANN GEORG LEHNER**, a Viennese butcher, invented a recipe for a new type of sausage and called it the frankfurter.

1921 **RUDOLPH VALENTINO** became the first male sex symbol in the U.S. when his film, *The Sheik*, was released.

1927 The **HOLLAND TUNNEL WAS OPENED** under the Hudson River, linking New York and New Jersey. The first underwater tunnel for vehicular traffic, it was named for **CLIFFORD MILBURN HOLLAND**, the engineer in charge of construction from 1910 until his death in 1924. Total cost to build was $48,400,000.

1937 NBC formed the first full-sized **SYMPHONY ORCHESTRA** exclusively for radio broadcasting. The conductor for its first 17 years was **ARTURO TOSCANINI**.

1939 The **"ROTOLACTOR"** was unveiled by its inventor, Henry Jeffers. The rotolactor was a **ROTATING MILKING MACHINE** that milked 240 cows per hour.

1940 **FANTASIA** was released. The idea came from a casual conversation between **WALT DISNEY** and orchestra leader Leopold Stokowski. They had been talking about a Mickey Mouse cartoon. It was a complete flop at first and, in 1967, it was re-released and became a hit.

1942 President Roosevelt lowered the **MINIMUM DRAFT AGE** from 21 to 18.

1946 **VINCENT SCHAEFFER** invented artificial snow, making skiers happy when he dropped ice pellets on Mount Greylock, MA.

1960 Famous author **NORMAN MAILER** received a suspended sentence for stabbing his wife.

1982 **RAY "BOOM BOOM" MANCINI** knocked out Duk Koo Kim in the 14th round to retain his WBA lightweight title. Kim, unconscious, was rushed to the hospital and died 4 days later.

1982 The **VIETNAM VETERANS MEMORIAL** was dedicated in Washington, DC, following three days of ceremonies and marches in the nation's capital. It was designed by **MAYA LIN**.

1985 New York Met **DWIGHT GOODEN**, 21 years old, became the youngest pitcher ever to win the Cy Young Award. In 1984 he was "Rookie of the Year."

1992 **RIDDICK BOWE** won his 32nd straight fight and became the new heavyweight champion, pounding Evander Holyfield for 12 rounds in Las Vegas.

NOVEMBER 14

Do you think birds invented migration?

BIRTHDAYS

- **STEPHEN BISHOP** Singer. (San Diego, CA) Wrote movie theme for *China Syndrome* and "It Might Be You" from film *Tootsie.* Year/**Age:** 1995/**44** 1996/**45** 1997/**46**

- **JEANETTE JURADO** Singer. (Los Angeles, CA) With EXPOSE, "Season's Change." Year/**Age:** 1995/**30** 1996/**31** 1997/**32**

- **DON STEWART** Actor. (Staten Island, NY) Year/**Age:** 1995/**60** 1996/**61** 1997/**62**

- **PRINCE CHARLES OF BRITAIN** His Royal Highness. (Born Charles Philip Arthur George Windsor, Knight of the Garter, Prince of Wales, Earl of Chester, Duke of Cornwall and Rothesay, Earl of Carrick, Baron Renfrew, Lord of the Isles and Great Steward of Scotland, at Buckingham Palace) He is an accomplished polo player, former husband of Princess Diana and father of two sons, William and Henry. Year/**Age:** 1995/**47** 1996/**48** 1997/**49**

- **WILLIE HERNANDEZ** Baseball. Year/**Age:** 1995/**41** 1996/**42** 1997/**43**

- **JACK SIKMA** Basketball. (Kankakee, IL) Played for the Milwaukee Bucks. Year/**Age:** 1995/**39** 1996/**40** 1997/**41**

- **McLEAN STEVENSON** Actor. (Bloomington, IL) He played Col. Henry Blake on "M*A*S*H" until 1975, when he was "killed off" when his plane was lost at sea. Since that success, he has made some poor career decisions and gotten himself into some terrible shows. He could have stayed with "M*A*S*H," gotten his royalties, and would never have had to work again. Year/**Age:** 1995/**66** 1996/**67** 1997/**68**

- **FRED GARRITY** Singer. (England) Leader of FREDDY AND THE DREAMERS. Biggest hit: "I'm Telling You Now" in 1965. Year/**Age:** 1995/**55** 1996/**56** 1997/**57**

- **BRYAN WATSON** Hockey. Year/**Age:** 1995/**53** 1996/**54** 1997/**55**

- **BRIAN KEITH** Actor. (Born Robert Keith, Jr., in Bayonne, NJ) On the TV series "Hardcastle & McCormick," "Family Affair," and "Heartland." Year/**Age:** 1995/**74** 1996/**75** 1997/**76**

- **JIMMY PIERSALL** Baseball player. He hit his 100th home run playing for the Mets in New York, June 23, 1963. He celebrated by running around the bases backward. Baseball commissioner Ford Frick was upset with his display. Year/**Age:** 1995/**66** 1996/**67** 1997/**68**

- **ROSEMARY DeCAMP** Actress. (Prescott, AZ) She specialized in active, motherly type roles and appeared in *Rhapsody in Blue, On Moonlight Bay,* and appeared on TV in the "Bob Cummings Show" and "That Girl." Year/**Age:** 1995/**85** 1996/**86** 1997/**87**

- **PHYLLIS AVERY** Actress. Played wife Peggy McNutley on the "Ray Milland" TV sitcom in the 1950s. Year/**Age:** 1995/**71** 1996/**72** 1997/**73**

- **AARON COPELAND** Classical composer. (1900-1990 – Brooklyn, NY) He wrote two operas, six ballets, and eight film scores, including Oscar-winning music for William Wyler's *The Heiress* in 1948. Also wrote music for *Billy the Kid.* (Died 12-2-90.)

- **HOWARD DUFF** Actor. (1917-1990 – Bremmerton, WA) He was in the TV series "Felony Squad" from 1966 to 1969 as Detective Sam Stone. Starred with wife Ida Lupino in TV's "Mr. Adams and Eve" in the 1950s based on situations from their lives. In TV's "Flamingo Road" in 1980s. (Died 7-9-90.)

- **JOHNNY DESMOND** Singer/entertainer. (1921-1985 – Detroit, MI) Biggest hit: "Yellow Rose of Texas" in 1955. (Died 9-6-85.)

- **ROBERT FULTON** Inventor. (1765-1815) Built the first steamboat, the *Clermont,* in 1807, referred to as "Fulton's Folly." (Died 2-24-1815.)

FACTS FROM THE PAST

1851 The novel *MOBY DICK* was first published in the U.S. It was written by Herman Melville.

1864 The city of Atlanta, GA, was burned, and General **WILLIAM T. SHERMAN** began his famous march to the sea.

1889 *New York World* reporter Nellie Bly [Elizabeth Cochrane] began her attempt to top the fictitious voyage of Jules Verne's Phileas Fogg by traveling **AROUND THE WORLD IN LESS THAN 80 DAYS.** She finished the trip in 72 days.

1943 The **FIRST PROFESSIONAL FOOTBALL PLAYER TO SCORE SIX TOUCHDOWNS** in a single game was Ernie Nevers of the St. Louis Cardinals. He scored all of his team's points as they beat the Bears, 40 to 6, at Chicago.

1947 Fighter **JAKE LaMOTTA**, "The Raging Bull," got knocked out for the first time in his career. Later he said he threw the fight to get a chance at the middleweight title, which he won in 1949.

1969 **APOLLO XII** blasted off for the second moon landing. It was struck by lightning but survived the hit without damage and completed the mission in which **CHARLES CONRAD** became the first man to fall down on the moon. He said, "It may have been a small step for Neil Armstrong, but it's a helluva big step for a little fellow like me."

1973 **PRINCESS ANNE** of Britain was married in London's Westminster Abbey to commoner **CAPTAIN MARK PHILLIPS**. The same afternoon, the Handicap Chase was won by a horse called "Royal Mark." The couple divorced in 1992.

1986 The Securities and Exchange Commission imposed a **RECORD $100 MILLION PENALTY** against inside-trader Ivan F. Boesky and barred him from working again in the securities industry.

1987 For the first time in ten years **SONNY AND CHER** reunited on "Late Night with David Letterman."

1993 PepsiCo Inc. ended its nine-year contract with **MICHAEL JACKSON** who had cancelled his "Dangerous" tour. He told the press that he was going to receive treatment for an addiction brought on by the stress of the molestation allegations.

Only small people can hide in a fob

NOVEMBER 15

BIRTHDAYS

- **CAROL BRUCE** Actress/singer. (Great Neck, NY) Mama Carlson in "WKRP." Year/**Age**: 1995/**76** 1996/**77** 1997/**78**

- **JOSEPH WAPNER** Judge. (Los Angeles, CA) TV's "People's Court." The autistic Raymond, portrayed by Dustin Hoffman in the film *Rainman*, referred to Judge Wapner throughout the movie. Year/**Age**: 1995/**76** 1996/**77** 1997/**78**

- **EDWARD (ED) ASNER** Actor. (Kansas City, MO) He won many Emmy awards while on the "Mary Tyler Show" from 1970-1977. He also won 3 Emmys for the "Lou Grant Show" and an Emmy for outstanding single performance for supporting actor in the 1977 mini-series, "Roots, Part I." He is now appearing on TV's "Heart's Afire." He's also been president of the Screen Actors Guild [SAG]. He holds the most Emmy awards of anyone. Year/**Age**: 1995/**66** 1996/**67** 1997/**68**

- **PETULA CLARK** Singer. (England) She received gold records for her songs sung in English, German & French in the 1950s/60s. She sold more than 25 million records and now lives and works in Switzerland. Hits include: "Downtown," "My Love," "I Know A Place," and "This Is My Song." Year/**Age**: 1995/**63** 1996/**64** 1997/**65**

- **C. W. McCALL** Singer. (Born William Fries in Audubon, IA) He had never written a song until 1974 when he wrote, "Old Home, Filler Up, Keep on Truckin' Cafe." His biggest hit was "Convoy" in 1976. Fries was an ad man who created the character C. W. McCALL for a bread company. Year/**Age**: 1995/**66** 1996/**67** 1997/**68**

- **JANET LENNON** of the LENNON SISTERS. Their biggest hit: "Tonight You Belong to Me" in 1956 with the Lawrence Welk Orchestra. Year/**Age**: 1995/**49** 1996/**50** 1997/**51**

- **JOANNA BARNES** Actress. (Boston, MA) She appeared in *Spartacus, Parent Trap* and *Goodbye Charlie.* Year/**Age**: 1995/**61** 1996/**62** 1997/**63**

- **MARI FERNANDEZ** Singer. (NYC) With SWEET SENSATION. Their biggest hit: "If Wishes Came True" in 1990. Year/**Age**: 1995/**28** 1996/**29** 1997/**30**

- **ANNI FRID LYNGSTAD** Vocalist. (Stockholm, Sweden) with ABBA. Biggest hits: "Dancing Queen" and "Take a Chance on Me." Year/**Age**: 1995/**50** 1996/**51** 1997/**52**

- **BEVERLY D'ANGELO** Actress/singer. (Columbus, OH) In films *Coal Miner's Daughter*, several National Lampoon films, *Paternity,* and *Hair.* Year/**Age**: 1995/**43** 1996/**44** 1997/**45**

- **SAM WATERSTON** Actor. (Cambridge, MA) Nominated for Academy Award in 1984 for *The Killing Fields.* TV's "Law & Order" and "I'll Fly Away." Film *Serial Mom.* Year/**Age**: 1995/**55** 1996/**56** 1997/**57**

- **LITTLE WILLIE JOHN** Singer. (1937-1968 – Born William Edgar John in Cullendale, AK) His biggest hit: "Sleep" in 1960. Died 5-26-68, while in Washington State Prison serving time for manslaughter.

- **CLYDE McPHATTER** Singer. (1931-1972) Lead singer of the DOMINOES from 1950 to 1953 and the DRIFTERS from 1953 to 1954. Biggest hit solo was "A Lover's Question" in 1959. (Died 6-13-72.)

FACTS FROM THE PAST

1492 **CHRISTOPHER COLUMBUS,** on his first trip to the New World, wrote in his journal that Indians were drying and smoking a native plant. This is believed to be the first reference to TOBACCO.

1806 Western explorer **ZEBULON PIKE** spotted the Colorado Mountains. One mountain was later named for him: **PIKE'S PEAK.**

1926 The **NATIONAL BROADCASTING COMPANY** went on the air "live" with a 4-hour program from the Waldorf Astoria Hotel in NYC. One of the NBC stars was Will Rogers.

1939 **PRESIDENT FRANKLIN D. ROOSEVELT** laid the cornerstone of the Jefferson Memorial in Washington, DC.

1956 **ELVIS PRESLEY** appeared in the movies for the first time in a premiere of *Love Me, Tender.*

1959 Four members of the Herbert Clutter family were murdered by **RICHARD HICKOCK** and **PERRY SMITH** in Holcomb, KS. The crime was the basis of Truman Capote's "documentary novel" **IN COLD BLOOD.**

1964 Kansas City quarterback **LEN DAWSON FUMBLED SEVEN TIMES** in a game against San Diego.

1969 The public requested the song "Ticket to Ride" off the CARPENTERS' *Offering* album and that launched their successful career.

1969 San Diego quarterback **DENNIS SHAW** set NCAA football records, throwing 7 touchdown passes in the first half, 4 of them in the second quarter, and a total of 9 in the game. San Diego beat New Mexico State 70-21.

1969 Hamburg's **STAR CLUB**, the **BEATLES'** early stomping ground, closed its doors for good.

1980 **POPE JOHN PAUL II** began a five-day visit to Germany, becoming the **FIRST PONTIFF IN 198 YEARS** to visit the birthplace of the Protestant Reformation.

1980 **DAVID BOWIE** opened on Broadway in the title role of the play *The Elephant Man.*

1984 **BABY FAE,** who made medical history and generated ethical questions as she fought for life for 3 weeks with the heart of a baboon, died after her kidneys began to fail.

1992 Race driver **RICHARD PETTY** drove the final race of his 35-year career in the Hooter's 500 at the Atlanta Motor Speedway. After a fiery crash put him out of contention, he commented, "I guess you're supposed to go out in a blaze of glory, but I didn't mean to do it this way."

NOVEMBER 16

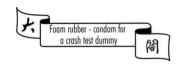

Foam rubber - condom for a crash test dummy

BIRTHDAYS

- **DAVID LEISURE** Actor. (San Diego, CA) Plays the pesky neighbor in "Empty Nest." Year/**Age:** 1995/**45** 1996/**46** 1997/**47**
- **MARTHA PLIMPTON** Actress. She was in *The Goonies*, and *Parenthood*. Year/**Age:** 1995/**25** 1996/**26** 1997/**27**
- **ELIZABETH DREW** Journalist. (Cincinnati, OH) Year/**Age:** 1995/**60** 1996/**61** 1997/**62**
- **BURGESS MEREDITH** Actor. (Cleveland, OH) He was nominated in 1975 for supporting actor in *Day of the Locust*, and in 1976 for the trainer in *Rocky*. He played "Penguin" on the original "Batman" TV series. He wrote *So Far, So Good A Memoir*. Year/**Age:** 1995/**87** 1996/**88** 1997/**89**
- **JOJO WHITE** Former pro basketball player. (St. Louis, MO) He was with the Boston Celtics. Year/**Age:** 1995/**49** 1996/**50** 1997/**51**
- **ROYAL DANO** Actor. He was one of the stars of *Omnibus* in the 1950s and starred as Abraham Lincoln in a continuing story, *Mr. Lincoln*. Year/**Age:** 1995/**73** 1996/**74** 1997/**75**
- **JOANNA PETTET** Actress. She was one of the huge cast of the TV show "Best Sellers" in 1976. Year/**Age:** 1995/**51** 1996/**52** 1997/**53**
- **GUY STOCKWELL** Actor. (Los Angeles, CA) Brother of Dean Stockwell. Films include *Airport* and *Please Don't Eat the Daisies*. Year/**Age:** 1995/**57** 1996/**58** 1997/**59**

- **MARTINE VAN HAMEL** Ballerina. (Brussels) American Ballet Theatre. Year/**Age:** 1995/**50** 1996/**51** 1997/**52**
- **DWIGHT GOODEN** Baseball. (Tampa, FL) NY Mets pitcher. He holds the record for the most strike-outs in a rookie season. Year/**Age:** 1995/**31** 1996/**32** 1997/**33**
- **LISA BONET** Actress. (San Francisco, CA) She played Denise Huxtable on "The Cosby Show." She was in the movies *Angel Heart* and *Bank Robber,* and had her own TV series, "Different World." Year/**Age:** 1995/**28** 1996/**29** 1997/**30**
- **HARVEY MARTIN** Football player. (Dallas, TX) Year/**Age:** 1995/**45** 1996/**46** 1997/**47**
- **ZINA GARRISON** Tennis star. (Houston, TX) Year/**Age:** 1995/**32** 1996/**33** 1997/**34**
- **GEORGE S. KAUFMAN** Writer. (1889-1961 – Pittsburgh, PA) Co-wrote the plays *The Man Who Came to Dinner* and *You Can't Take it With You* with Moss Hart. (Died 6-2-61.)
- **JIM JORDAN** Actor. (1896-1988 – Peoria, IL) Likable, bumbling character who was listened to by millions on the NBC radio network from 1935 to 1953. He and his wife, Marian, played "Fibber McGee and Molly." (Died 4-1-88.)
- **WILLIAM C. HANDY** American composer/bandleader. (1873-1958 – Florence, AL) Known as the "father of the blues." (Died 3-28-58.)

FACTS FROM THE PAST

1926 Ohio State University honored Maudine Ormsby as **HOMECOMING QUEEN**. She was five feet tall with big brown eyes, impressive milk glands and a moist nose—an award-winning **PUREBRED HOLSTEIN COW**.

1933 The U.S. and Soviet Union established **DIPLOMATIC RELATIONS**. President Roosevelt sent a telegram to Soviet leader **JOSEPH STALIN** expressing hope that U.S./Soviet relations would forever be normal and friendly. After the Communists seized power in the Russian Revolution in 1917, the U.S. had refused to establish relations.

1955 **JOHNNY CASH** made his first chart appearance with "Cry Cry Cry."

1957 It was discovered that a bachelor/handyman, who sometimes earned movie money as a babysitter, had **MURDERED SEVERAL WOMEN** and decorated his home with parts of their bodies. **ED GEIN** of Plainfield, WI, killed these women and robbed graves following the death of his mother. He was charged with first-degree murder, judged insane and died of cancer at the Mendota Mental Health Institute in Madison, WI in 1984.

1957 Boston's **BILL RUSSELL** established a new NBA record for rebounds with 32 in the first half, in a game against Philadelphia.

1959 **THE SOUND OF MUSIC** opened on Broadway. It would run for 1,453 performances. It starred **MARY MARTIN** and **THEODORE BIKEL**.

1966 Ohio doctor **SAMUEL SHEPPARD** was acquitted in his second trial on charges of **MURDERING HIS PREGNANT WIFE**, Marilyn, in 1954. The first trial was thrown out because of sensational pre-trial publicity in Cleveland, OH.

1969 President Nixon authorized the construction of the **ALASKA PIPELINE**, the **WORLD'S LARGEST CONSTRUCTION PROJECT**. It was hailed as the first step toward making the United States self-sufficient for energy supplies by 1980.

1978 **QUEEN** performed at **MADISON SQUARE GARDEN**. Several women in quite risque dress circled the stage on bicycles while the group sang "Fat Bottomed Girls."

1984 The **SPACE SHUTTLE DISCOVERY** landed at Cape Canaveral, FL, carrying on board the first two satellites ever salvaged from outer space. The astronauts who achieved this were Fred Hauck, David Walker, Dale Gardner, Anna Fisher, and Joseph Allen.

1988 Former **BEACH BOY MANAGER STEPHEN LOVE**, Mike's brother, was sentenced to five years' probation for embezzling more than $900,000 from the group.

1991 Democrat Edwin Edwards defeated former Ku Klux Klan leader **DAVID DUKE** in a landslide to reclaim the Louisiana governorship.

1993 **GEORGE BURNS** age 97 signed a contract to perform at Caesars of Las Vegas on his 100th birthday.

Show affection, fondle

NOVEMBER 17

BIRTHDAYS

- **LAUREN HUTTON** Model/actress. (Charleston, SC) She dropped out of college at 18 and worked as a waitress at the New York Playboy Club. By the time she was 30 she was the highest-paid model in history, with earnings over $300,000 a year. Films include *Once Bitten.* Year/**Age:** 1995/**52** 1996/**53** 1997/**54**

- **DANNY DeVITO** Actor. (Neptune, NJ) He was once a hairdresser know as Dr. Dan. He starred in the "Taxi" TV series and is married to Rhea Perlman of the "Cheers" TV series. Directed and co-starred in *The War of the Roses, Hoffa,* and *Jack the Bear.* Played the Penguin in *Batman Returns,* 1992. Year/**Age:** 1995/**51** 1996/**52** 1997/**53**

- **MARTIN SCORSESE** Movie director. (Born in Flushing, NY and raised in Manhattan's "Little Italy.") Some of his films include: *Alice Doesn't Live Here Anymore, Taxi Driver, New York, New York, The Color of Money, Raging Bull,* highly controversial *The Last Temptation of Christ, GoodFellas,* and *Cape Fear.* He directed the "Bad" video by Michael Jackson. Year/**Age:** 1995/**53** 1996/**54** 1997/**55**

- **BOB MATHIAS** Runner/congressman. (Tulane, CA) Two-time Olympic decathalon gold medalist and a Wheaties cover boy when Bruce Jenner was still in diapers. He also ran the stairs to light the torch at the L.A. Olympics in 1984. Year/**Age:** 1995/**65** 1996/**66** 1997/**67**

- **TOM SEAVER** Former baseball pitcher. (Born George Thomas Seaver in Fresno, CA) Inducted into the Baseball Hall of Fame with the highest percentage (98.8%) and second highest vote total ever (425), behind Johnny Bench (431). In 20 seasons, he won 311 games with 3,272 career strikeouts, 61 shutouts and five 20-win years. He pitched a no-hitter against St. Louis June 16, 1978. Year/**Age:** 1995/**51** 1996/**52** 1997/**53**

- **GORDON LIGHTFOOT** Singer. (Canada) His biggest hit: "Sundown" in 1974. He's been referred to as "Canada's answer to Bob Dylan." He also had the hit record "The Wreck of the Edmund Fitzgerald" in 1976. It was a true story of the ore ship that sank in Lake Superior on 11-10-75. Year/**Age:** 1995/**57** 1996/**58** 1997/**59**

- **MARY ELIZABETH MASTRANTONIO** Actress. (Lombard, IL) In films *The Abyss, The Color of Money, Robin Hood: Prince of Thieves, Class Action, Consenting Adults,* and *Scarface* with Al Pacino. Year/**Age:** 1995/**37** 1996/**38** 1997/**39**

- **MARTIN BARRE** Guitarist. (England) With JETHRO TULL. Hit: "Living in the Past." Year/**Age:** 1995/**49** 1996/**50** 1997/**51**

- **PETER COOK** Actor/Comedian. (England) At one time he worked a routine with Dudley Moore. Year/**Age:** 1995/**58** 1996/**59** 1997/**60**

- **ELVIN HAYES** Basketball. (Rayville, LA) He played in the first nationally televised basketball game. In it, his last-second free throws lifted the University of Houston over UCLA, breaking their 47-game winning streak. He later became an outstanding pro player. Year/**Age:** 1995/**50** 1996/**51** 1997/**52**

- **GENE CLARK** Guitarist. (1941-1991) With the BYRDS. Their biggest hit: "Turn, Turn, Turn" in 1965. They were the first group to play folk/rock music. They disbanded in 1973. Originally with the NEW CHRISTY MINSTRELS. (Died 5-24-91.)

- **MISCHA AUER** Actress. (1905-1967 – Russia) Academy Award nomination for *My Man Godfrey.* (Died 3-5-67.)

- **LEE STRASBERG** Actor/director. (1901-1982) He founded the Actors Studio. (Died 2-17-82.)

- **ROCK HUDSON** Actor. (1925-1985 – Born Roy Scherer, Jr., in Winnetka, IL) He received an Oscar nomination in 1956 for *Giant,* and starred in 62 films before turning to TV with the successful series "McMillan and Wife." Died of AIDS on 10-2-85.

- **DINO MARTIN** Tennis pro/sometime actor. (1951-1987 – Born Dean Paul Martin.) Son of singer Dean Martin. At one time, he was in the group DINO, DESI & BILLY with Desi Arnaz, Jr. and Billy, a friend of theirs. Their biggest hit: "I'm a Fool." He was a California Air National Guard captain, piloting a F-4C Phantom jet that crashed into snowy San Gorgonio Mountain in California. Married and divorced skater Dorothy Hamill and actress Olivia Hussey. (Died 3-21-87.)

FACTS FROM THE PAST

1934 **LYNDON BAINES JOHNSON** married Claudia Alta Taylor, better known as **LADY BIRD** which was a childhood nickname. He was the only president to get married in Texas. LBJ once said "I've learned that only two things are necessary to keep your wife happy. First, let her think she's having her own way and second, let her have it."

1956 **JIM BROWN** scored six touchdowns and kicked seven extra points for a total of 43 points, a NCAA record. He was playing for Syracuse against Colgate University.

1968 The **NETWORK PULLED THE PLUG** on the Jets/Raiders **FOOTBALL GAME** and went to the movie *Heidi.* Viewers missed seeing Oakland rally to beat the Jets, 43-32. In the remaining 65 seconds with the Jets leading 32-29, Raiders quarterback Daryle Lamonica led his team to 2 touchdowns.

1970 **ELTON JOHN** performed live over a New York radio station (WABC FM). The performance was released on the LP "17-11-70."

1977 **WYNNE ROBERTS** of England began playing the drums and continued for 564 hours, over 23 days, setting a new world record.

1973 President Nixon denied any wrongdoing in the **WATERGATE** scandal saying in a speech at Disneyland, "People have got to know whether or not their president is a crook. Well, I'm not a crook!"

1988 **PRESIDENT-ELECT BUSH** chose John Sununu as White House Chief of Staff.

1992 Three senators toured Vietnam and found no sign of any **U.S. PRISONERS** said to be sighted there after the War.

NOVEMBER 18

Make sure to button
your zipper

BIRTHDAYS

- **JAMESON PARKER** Actor. (Baltimore, MD) "Simon and Simon." He married actress Darleen Carr. He was shot in Oct. of 1992 during an argument with a neighbor. Year/**Age**: 1995/**45** 1996/**46** 1997/**47**

- **IMOGENE COCA** Actress/comedienne. (Philadelphia, PA) Appeared on "Show of Shows" with Sid Caesar from 1950 to 1954, for which she won an Emmy for best actress in 1951. Films include *National Lampoon's Vacation*. Year/**Age**: 1995/**87** 1996/**88** 1997/**89**

- **KEVIN NEALON** Actor. (Bridgeport, CT) "Saturday Night Live." Year/**Age**: 1995/**42** 1996/**43** 1997/**44**

- **GARY SHEFFIELD** Baseball. Year/**Age**: 1995/**27** 1996/**28** 1997/**29**

- **BRENDA VACCARO** Actress. (Brooklyn, NY) She used to live with Michael Douglas when she was in *Midnight Cowboy*, her first big film. Nominated for supporting actress in 1975 for Jacqueline Suzanne's *Once is not Enough*. Year/**Age**: 1995/**56** 1996/**57** 1997/**58**

- **GENE MAUCH** Baseball. He suffered through the longest losing streak of modern times: 23 straight losses as manager of the 1961 Phillies. In 1962, the Phillies improved to an 81-80 mark and finished in 7th place. Year/**Age**: 1995/**70** 1996/**71** 1997/**72**

- **SUSAN SULLIVAN** Actress. TV Tylenol spokesperson. She was "Maggie" on TV's "Falcon Crest" and in *Rich Man Poor Man Book II*. Year/**Age**: 1995/**51** 1996/**52** 1997/**53**

- **LINDA EVANS** Actress. (Born Linda Evanstad in Hartford, CT) Krystle on the "Dynasty" TV series. She produced a perfume called "Krystle." From 1965-1969 played Audra Barkley on "The Big Valley." Year/**Age**: 1995/**53** 1996/**54** 1997/**55**

- **HANK BALLARD** Singer. (Detroit, MI) Of the MIDNIGHTERS. He wrote and recorded the original "Twist," a song considered too dirty by many radio stations. It was the flip side of his first charted song, "Finger Poppin' Time." Year/**Age**: 1995/**59** 1996/**60** 1997/**61**

- **MICHAEL RAMOS** Entertainer. BO DEANS. Year/**Age**: 1995/**37** 1996/**38** 1997/**39**

- **GARY BETTENHAUSEN** Racecar driver. Year/**Age**: 1995/**54** 1996/**55** 1997/**56**

- **WARREN MOON** Football. (Los Angeles, CA) Quarterback for the Houston Oilers. Year/**Age**: 1995/**39** 1996/**40** 1997/**41**

- **ALAN B. SHEPARD** Astronaut. (East Derry, NH) America's first man in space, in 1961. That first space flight, in a 6 x 9 foot capsule, lasted 15 minutes, 22 seconds. Year/**Age**: 1995/**72** 1996/**73** 1997/**74**

- **DOROTHY COLLINS** Singer. (1926-1994 - Canada) Won a Tony nomination for "Follies" in 1971. Her biggest hit: "My Boy Flattop" in 1955. She was the featured singer on TV's "Your Hit Parade." (Died 7-21-94.)

- **JOHNNY MERCER** Songwriter. (1909-1976 – Savannah, GA) 3 of his Oscar-winning songs are: "On the Atchison, Topeka & Santa Fe," "Days of Wine & Roses," and "Moon River." He founded Capitol Records. (Died 6-25-76.)

- **GEORGE GALLUP** Pollster. (1901-1984 – Jefferson, IA) His son, George Gallup, Jr., is continuing the "Gallup Poll."

- **WILLIAM GILBERT** Lyricist. (1836-1911 – England) Collaborated with Arthur Sullivan to write a series of light operas, including *The Pirates of Penzance*. He wrote songs and plays in his spare time. (Died 5-29-11.)

FACTS FROM THE PAST

1307 **WILLIAM TELL** shot an apple from his son's head. Tell was a great marksman but refused to bow to Imperial rule. He was taken to prison, escaped and killed the local governor. That is what started the struggle for Swiss independence.

1820 U.S. Navy Capt. **NATHANIEL B. PALMER** discovered the continent of **ANTARCTICA**.

1865 **MARK TWAIN** published his first fiction, "The Celebrated Jumping Frog of Calaveras County" in the *New York Saturday Press*.

1902 A Brooklyn toymaker gave the **TEDDY BEAR** its name on this date, based on an incident in the life of **PRESIDENT THEODORE "TEDDY" ROOSEVELT**. The president had gone on a hunting trip and got a female bear with cubs in his gunsights and refused to pull the trigger. The incident inspired a political cartoon in the *Washington Evening Star* and toymaker Morris Michton saw it and created a fuzzy "Teddy Bear." It's still a commercial success.

1928 **MICKEY MOUSE** was first drawn by animator **UB IWERKS**, an associate of Walt Disney. The mouse was first called "Mortimer," but Mrs. Disney thought that was too stuffy so suggested "Mickey Mouse."

1948 **ALBEN W. BARKLEY** became the first vice president to marry in office. He married **ELIZABETH RUCKER** in St. Louis, MO.

1949 **JACKIE ROBINSON** of the Brooklyn Dodgers was named the National League's Most Valuable Player.

1954 The hit record "Mambo Italiano" by **ROSEMARY CLOONEY** was banned by ABC radio and TV for so-called "offensive lyrics."

1970 **JERRY LEE LEWIS** and wife Myra divorced after a rocky 13-years.

1988 President Ronald Reagan signed an executive order giving the Federal Emergency Management Agency broad new powers to carry out evacuation plans for **NUCLEAR POWER PLANTS.**

1988 Disney's **OLIVER & COMPANY**, featuring the voices of Billy Joel, Bette Midler, and Cheech Marin, opened nationally. Joel later said it was probably the hardest work he'd ever done.

1991 Shiite Muslim kidnapers released British envoy **TERRY WAITE** and American educator **THOMAS SUTHERLAND**. They had been held in Lebanon for over 6 years.

Do tastebuds bloom every year?

NOVEMBER 19

BIRTHDAYS

• **KATHLEEN QUINLAN** Actress. (Pasadena, CA) Her films include *The Promise, I Never Promised You a Rose Garden*, and *American Graffiti*. Year/**Age**: 1995/**41** 1996/**42** 1997/**43**

• **FRED LIPSIUS** Musician. Played piano and sax for BLOOD, SWEAT, & TEARS. Hits include: "You've Made Me So Very Happy" and "Spinning Wheel." Year/**Age**: 1995/**51** 1996/**52** 1997/**53**

• **DICK CAVETT** Talk show host. (Kearney, NE) He was a TV writer; first for Jack Paar and then for Johnny Carson. He was offered his own talk show on ABC in 1969, but the ratings slipped and the show was canceled, even though he won an Emmy and appeared on the covers of *Time* and *Life* Magazines. "Remember When" on cable TV. Year/**Age**: 1995/**59** 1996/**60** 1997/**61**

• **TED TURNER** CNN founder. (Cincinnati, OH) Atlanta Braves Baseball owner/cable TV entrepreneur/yachtsman. Married to Jane Fonda. He was *Time* magazine's "Man of the Year" in 1991. Year/**Age**: 1995/**57** 1996/**58** 1997/**59**

• **CALVIN KLEIN** Fashion designer. (Bronx, NY) He produced the perfumes "Eternity" and "Obsession." Year/**Age**: 1995/**53** 1996/**54** 1997/**55**

• **JODIE FOSTER** Actress. (Los Angeles, CA) She was in a topless Coppertone ad as a child. She started out on TV in "Mayberry R.F.D." and later the series "Paper Moon." At 12 years of age, she played a drug-addicted child prostitute in *Taxi Driver* for which she was nominated for an Oscar. Received the Academy Award for best actress in *The Accused* and *Silence of the Lambs*. She starred in *Sommersby* in 1993 and was in *Maverick*. She made her directing debut with *Little Man Tate* in 1991. Year/**Age**: 1995/**33** 1996/**34** 1997/**35**

• **JEANNE KILPATRICK** Former UN Ambassador. (Duncan, OK) Year/**Age**: 1995/**69** 1996/**70** 1997/**71**

• **GARRICK UTLEY** NBC newsman. (Chicago, IL) Year/**Age**: 1995/**56** 1996/**57** 1997/**58**

• **MEG RYAN** Actress. (CT) She turned down parts in *Pretty Woman, Ghost,* and *Silence of the Lambs*. Films include *When a Man Loves a Woman, When Harry Met Sally, D.O.A., Sleepless in Seattle,* and *Flesh and Bone* with husband Dennis Quaid. Year/**Age**: 1995/**34** 1996/**35** 1997/**36**

• **AHMAD RASHAD** Sportscaster. (Portland, OR) Married to actress Phylicia Rashad from "The Cosby Show." Year/**Age**: 1995/**46** 1996/**47** 1997/**48**

• **ALAN YOUNG** Actor. (England) Played Wilbur Post, Mr. Ed's pal. Mr. Ed was a talking horse on a TV sitcom of the same name. Year/**Age**: 1995/**76** 1996/**77** 1997/**78**

• **LARRY KING** Talk show host. (Born Larry Zeiger in Brooklyn, NY) "Larry King Live" was CNN's top-rated show in 1992. It was seen in 130 countries and heard on over 400 radio stations. His first job was a DJ at WAHR, a small station in Miami Beach. The station manager chose his name from an ad for "King" Wholesale Liquors. Year/**Age**: 1995/**62** 1996/**63** 1997/**64**

• **DAN HAGGERTY** Actor. (Hollywood, CA) Starred in "The Life & Times of Grizzly Adams" on TV in the late 1970s. Year/**Age**: 1995/**54** 1996/**55** 1997/**56**

• **TOMMY DORSEY** Bandleader. (1905-1956 – Mahoney Plane, PA) His hits include: "I'll Never Smile Again," "There are Such Things" and "Boogie Woogie." (Died 11-26-56.)

• **JAMES GARFIELD** 20th U.S. President. (1831-1881) The first left-handed president. After 17 years in Congress, he won the 1880 Presidential election by a narrow margin. In his first weeks in office he dismissed threats on his life, saying: "Assassination can no more be guarded against than death by lightning. It's best not to worry about either." Six months later, an assassin's bullet killed him. (Died 9-19-1881.)

• **ROY CAMPANELLA** Baseball Hall of Famer. (1921-1993) He was the National League's MVP in 1951, 1953 & 1955. Paralyzed in a car accident. (Died 6-26-93.)

FACTS FROM THE PAST

1861 **JULIA WARD HOWE** committed **"THE BATTLE HYMN OF THE REPUBLIC"** to paper. Some Union soldiers had adopted "John Brown's Body" as their marching song, using the tune of an old southern hymn. Mrs. Howe heard them singing this on the way to Washington and jotted down about five verses.

1863 President **ABRAHAM LINCOLN** delivered his **GETTYSBURG ADDRESS** as he dedicated a national cemetery at the site of the Civil War battlefield in Pennsylvania. He said, "We here highly resolve that these dead shall not have died in vain; that this nation, under God, shall have a new birth of freedom; and that government of the people, by the people, shall not perish from the earth."

1887 Emma Lazarus, known as **LADY LIBERTY'S POET**, died of lung cancer at the age of 38 in NYC. She composed: "Give me your tired, your poor, etc…" at the age of 34. The poem was called *New Colossus*. She wrote it to help raise money for the Statue of Liberty pedestal, but she never saw the statue.

1888 William Bundy invented the first **TIME-CARD CLOCK.**

1969 Apollo XII astronauts Alan Bean and Charles Conrad made man's **SECOND LANDING** on the moon.

1978 **REVEREND JIM JONES** from Indiana, leader of the People's Temple, directed the killing of more than 900 persons in a remote jungle location of Guyana. The religious cult members killed themselves by drinking Kool-Aid laced with cyanide.

1979 **CHUCK BERRY** was released from a California prison farm, after serving 100 days on a tax evasion charge. Just a month before his sentencing, he entertained at the White House.

1990 Rob Pilatus and Fabrice Morvan admitted they didn't sing on the **MILLI VANILLI HITS.** Their Grammy was revoked.

NOVEMBER 20
Alascattalo Day

Where in this blur is your station wagon?

BIRTHDAYS

- **DANNY McBRIDE** Musician. (NYC) From the group SHA NA NA. Year/**Age:** 1995/**50** 1996/**51** 1997/**52**

- **DICK SMOTHERS** Comedian. (NYC) He and brother Tom formed the comedy team "The Smothers Brothers." Dick is the more serious one. They appeared on CBS-TV in the 1970s and battled over program content for two years before they finally lost their show. They began singing together at San Jose State College. Appears on Magnavox commercials. Year/**Age:** 1995/**57** 1996/**58** 1997/**59**

- **ESTELLE PARSONS** Actress. (Lynn, MA) She won an Oscar for supporting actress in 1967 in *Bonnie & Clyde.* Appears as Roseanne's mom on TV's "Roseanne." Year/**Age:** 1995/**68** 1996/**69** 1997/**70**

- **ALISTAIR COOKE** Host. (England) He hosted "Omnibus," and retired in 1992 after 22 years on PBS as host of "Masterpiece Theater." Series "America." Year/**Age:** 1995/**87** 1996/**88** 1997/**89**

- **NORMAN GREENBAUM** Entertainer. Biggest hit: "Spirit in the Sky" in 1970. He's now a farmer in Ohio. Year/**Age:** 1995/**53** 1996/**54** 1997/**55**

- **RICHARD DAWSON** TV host. (England) Host of "Family Feud" which was the most popular TV game show until "Wheel of Fortune." He also appeared on some of the early "M*A*S*H" episodes and "Hogan's Heroes." He played a sleazy TV host with Arnold Schwarzenegger in *Running Man,* a very violent film. Year/**Age:** 1995/**63** 1996/**64** 1997/**65**

- **JOE WALSH** Rock guitarist. He was a member of the JAMES GANG and also the EAGLES. Toured with ex-Eagle Glenn Frey in 1993. Year/**Age:** 1995/**48** 1996/**49** 1997/**50**

- **JOSEPH BIDEN** U.S. Senator. (Scranton, PA) (D/DE) Senate Judiciary Committee Chairman. Year/**Age:** 1995/**53** 1996/**54** 1997/**55**

- **EVELYN KEYES** Actress. Her autobiography: *Scarlet O'Hara's Younger Sister.* Was the 8th wife of bandleader Artie Shaw. Year/**Age:** 1995/**76** 1996/**77** 1997/**78**

- **MARK GASTINEAU** Former football player. (Ardmore, OK) New York Jets. He has taken up boxing. Year/**Age:** 1995/**39** 1996/**40** 1997/**41**

- **BO DEREK** Actress. (Torrence, CA) Starred in *10, Ghosts Can't Do It,* and *Shattered Image.* She is married to producer John Derek. Year/**Age:** 1995/**39** 1996/**40** 1997/**41**

- **VERONICA HAMEL** Actress. (Philadelphia, PA) She was the public defender on "Hill Street Blues", appeared in "Secrets," and appeared in the miniseries "Kane & Abel." Year/**Age:** 1995/**52** 1996/**53** 1997/**54**

- **SEAN YOUNG** Actress. Films *Ace Ventura: Pet Detective, Fatal Instinct,* and *Cousins.* Year/**Age:** 1995/**36** 1996/**37** 1997/**38**

- **ROBERT BYRD** Senate Majority Leader. (North Wilkesboro, NC) Year/**Age:** 1995/**78** 1996/**79** 1997/**80**

- **JUNE CHRISTY** Jazz singer. (1925-1990 – Born Shirley Luster) She sang with the Stan Kenton band and had a hit in 1953: "My Heart Belongs to Only You." (Died 6-21-90.)

- **ROBERT F. KENNEDY** Politician. (1925-1968 – Brookline, MA) He was assassinated June 6, 1968, while campaigning for the U.S. Presidency in Los Angeles, CA. He was the seventh of nine children. He was the first to climb Mt. Kennedy in Canada.

- **DUANE ALLMAN** Rocker. (1946-1971 – Macon, GA) Former leader and guitarist with the ALLMAN BROTHERS BAND. Biggest hit: "Ramblin Man" in 1973. He died in a motorcycle crash near Macon, GA. (Died 10-29-71.)

- **CHESTER GOULD** Cartoonist. (1900-1985 – Pawnee, OK) He created the *Dick Tracy* comic strip which first appeared in the *Detroit Daily Mirror* October 4, 1931. Many inventions appeared in the strip before they were seen in real life: TV, two-way wrist radio, and closed-circuit TV. Dick's villains included Mole, Flyface, Pruneface and Flattop. (Died 5-16-85.)

- **EDWIN HUBBLE** Astronomer. (1889-1953 – Marshfield, MO) He discovered that the universe appears to be expanding. In 1924 he proved that there are other galaxies far from our own and in 1929, that all are moving away from us at speeds directly in proportion to their distance. The space telescope, deployed from the Space Shuttle Discovery April 25, 1990, was named in his honor. (Died 9-28-53.)

- **GENE TIERNEY** Actress (1920-1991 – Brooklyn, NY) Well known for the movie *Laura.* She received an Oscar nomination in 1945 for *Leave Her to Heaven.* (Died 11-6-91.)

FACTS FROM THE PAST

1620 Peregrine White, the son of William and Susanna White, was born aboard the **MAYFLOWER** in Massachusetts Bay. He was the **FIRST CHILD TO BE BORN** of English parents in **NEW ENGLAND**.

1947 Britain's future queen, **PRINCESS ELIZABETH**, married Philip Mountbatten, Duke of Edinburgh, in a ceremony broadcast worldwide from Westminster Abbey.

1954 In Hammond, IN, the bartenders union asked DJ **LEN ELLIS** at WJOB to stop playing the song "The Drunken Driver" by Ferlin Husky (about a drunken driver who kills two children) because it was hurting business.

1955 After promising he'd perform "16 Tons" on the "Ed Sullivan Show," **BO DIDDLEY** played "Bo Diddley" instead.

1973 Drummer **KEITH MOON** of **THE WHO** collapsed twice during a concert in San Francisco—jet lag was suspected. Pete Townshend called for a volunteer from the audience, and 19-year-old Scott Halpin finished the set with the band.

1977 The Chicago Bears' **WALTER PAYTON** rushed for a record 275 yards, 65 of those yards in the last 3 minutes of the Bears 10-7 win over Minnesota.

1992 Fire damaged a large part of Queen Elizabeth's weekend retreat, **WINDSOR CASTLE**. The queen, Prince Andrew, civilians, and troops managed to save most of the treasures.

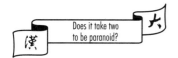

NOVEMBER 21
World Hello Day

BIRTHDAYS

• **DR. JOHN** Musician. (Born Malcolm John Rebennack in New Orleans, LA) Played organ on Aretha Franklin's "Spanish Harlem." His hits include "Right Place Wrong Time." Year/**Age**: 1995/**54** 1996/**55** 1997/**56**

• **TROY AIKMAN** Football. Super Bowl Champ Dallas Cowboys quarterback. Year/**Age**: 1995/**29** 1996/**30** 1997/**31**

• **GOLDIE HAWN** Actress/comedienne. (Washington, DC) She won an Oscar for supporting actress in 1969 for *Cactus Flower*. In 1992 she co-starred in *Housesitter* with Steve Martin and *Death Becomes Her* with Meryl Streep and Bruce Willis. She got her start as the dizzy blonde on the "Laugh-In" TV show. Year/**Age**: 1995/**50** 1996/**51** 1997/**52**

• **LIVINGSTON TAYLOR** Singer. (Boston, MA) He's the younger brother of James Taylor. His biggest hit: "I Will be in Love With You" in 1978. Year/**Age**: 1995/**45** 1996/**46** 1997/**47**

• **VIVIAN BLAINE** Actress. (Born Vivian Stapleton in Newark, NJ) She made films including *State Fair* and *Guys and Dolls*, but her greatest success was on Broadway. Year/**Age**: 1995/**74** 1996/**75** 1997/**76**

• **MARLO THOMAS** Actress. (Detroit, MI) She won an Emmy in 1974 for her children's special, "Marlo Thomas & Friends, Free to be You & Me." Starred in "Tribute to Women in Comedy." She and Phil Donahue have been married since 1980. Year/**Age**: 1995/**52** 1996/**53** 1997/**54**

• **JEAN SHEPHERD** C&W. (Paul's Valley, OK) She was married to Hawkshaw Hawkins at the time of his death. Her biggest hit was also her first: "A Dear John Letter" with Ferlin Husky in 1953. Year/**Age**: 1995/**62** 1996/**63** 1997/**64**

• **DAVID HEMMINGS** Actor. (England) Appeared in *Blow Up*, *The Charge of the Light Brigade,* and *Camelot.* Appears on TV's "L.A. Law." Year/**Age**: 1995/**54** 1996/**55** 1997/**56**

• **LAURENCE LUCKINBILL** Actor. (Fort Smith, AR) One-man show *Lyndon*, about President Johnson. Husband of Lucie Arnez. Year/**Age**: 1995/**61** 1996/**62** 1997/**63**

• **GEORGE "KEN" GRIFFEY, JR.** Baseball. (Donora, PA) Heavy hitter for the Seattle Mariners. Year/**Age**: 1995/**26** 1996/**27** 1997/**28**

• **NATALIA MAKAROVA** Ballet dancer. (Russia) Year/**Age**: 1995/**55** 1996/**56** 1997/**57**

• **STAN MUSIAL** Baseball Hall of Fame great. (Donora, PA) He won three MVP trophies, two home-run titles, two batting crowns and had a lifetime average of 331. One of his 6 All-Star game home runs ended the 1955 classic in the 12th inning in Milwaukee. Year/**Age**: 1995/**75** 1996/**76** 1997/**77**

• **LORNA LUFT** Singer. (Los Angeles, CA) Daughter of Judy Garland & Sid Luft and half-sister of Liza Minnelli. *Where the Boys Are*, 84. Year/**Age**: 1995/**43** 1996/**44** 1997/**45**

• **JULIET MILLS** Actress. (England) Daughter of John Mills and sister of Hayley. In films and TV series "Nanny and the Professor" in 1970. Year/**Age**: 1995/**54** 1996/**55** 1997/**56**

• **HARPO MARX** Comedian. (1893-1964 – Born Arthur Marx in NYC) He was the silent member of the Marx Brothers – the one who was mute. He really could talk but never would after he was told his tiny voice couldn't be heard well. He made his amateur debut when he visited a neighbor's house dressed as a hooker. Early in his career he played piano in a "house of ill repute." (Died 9-28-64.)

FACTS FROM THE PAST

1877 Inventor **THOMAS A. EDISON** announced the invention of his **PHONOGRAPH**, which he dubbed a "talking machine."

1922 **REBECCA L. FELTON** of Georgia was sworn in as the **FIRST WOMAN TO SERVE AS A MEMBER OF THE U.S. SENATE.**

1937 **THOMAS MORRIS** skipped rope 22,806 times in two hours in Sydney, Australia. This was faster than three skips a second and equivalent to walking about 12 miles.

1959 **ALAN FREED WAS FIRED** by WABC radio in New York for **REFUSING TO SIGN AN AFFIDAVIT** stating that he took bribes. Freed was the top DJ in the nation at the time and was blackballed by the radio industry after he was fired. He was the prime target of a congressional investigation into payola. Freed never worked again. He finally pleaded guilty to taking money from record promoters in 1962. He died 3 years later.

1963 **PRESIDENT JOHN F. KENNEDY** and his wife, Jacqueline, arrived in San Antonio to begin a two-day tour of Texas.

1973 President Nixon's attorney, J. Fred Buzhardt, revealed the presence of an $18^1/_2$ minute gap in one of the White House tape recordings relating to **WATERGATE.**

1975 **BOB ATHENEY** went bowling in St. Petersburg, FL, for 265 hours over 11 days — 1,976 games.

1980 An estimated 83 million TV viewers turned on the TV soap opera, "**DALLAS,**" to find out "**WHO SHOT J.R. EWING.**" A total of 41,470,000 households found out it was his sister-in-law, Kristin (his jilted mistress), played by **MARY CROSBY**.

1980 **DON HENLEY** of the Eagles was arrested and charged with unlawful possession of cocaine, quaaludes, marijuana and contributing to the delinquency of a minor, after a nude 16-year-old girl was treated for drug intoxication at Henley's home in Los Angeles.

1990 After being together for 12 years, **MICK JAGGER** and **JERRY HALL** were married on the Indonesian island of Bali. Their two children attended the wedding. They appeared together in the movie *Freejack*.

1990 Deposed junk bond king, **MICHAEL MILKEN**, sobbed as a judge sentenced him to 10 years in prison for his role in the **BIGGEST SCANDAL IN WALL STREET HISTORY**. He was released January 3, 1993, having served 22 months for his crime.

NOVEMBER 22

Thank-You-Ma'am
(its not what you think)

BIRTHDAYS

- **MICHAEL CALLAN** Actor. Numerous films include *Because They're Young*. In TV series "Love American Style" and "Occasional Wife." Year/**Age**: 1995/**60** 1996/**61** 1997/**62**

- **MARIEL HEMINGWAY** Actress. (Ketchum, ID) Star in TV's "Civil Wars." Woody Allen's young lover in *Manhattan*. She had her breasts enlarged for the role of a doomed Playboy Playmate in the 1983 film *Star 80*. She had her silicone breast implants removed and replaced with saline ones. Year/**Age**: 1995/**34** 1996/**35** 1997/**36**

- **TOM CONTI** Actor. (Scotland) "Masterpiece Theater," "Shirley Valentine." Year/**Age**: 1995/**54** 1996/**55** 1997/**56**

- **ROBERT VAUGHN** Actor. (NYC) He played Napoleon Solo in the TV series "The Man from U.N.C.L.E." Appeared in *The Big One*. Year/**Age**: 1995/**63** 1996/**64** 1997/**65**

- **BILLIE JEAN KING** Tennis star. (Long Beach, CA) She was U.S. Singles champ 4 times, Wimbledon champ 5 times and beat Bobby Riggs in a 1970s exhibition match. Covered Wimbledon for HBO. Year/**Age**: 1995/**52** 1996/**53** 1997/**54**

- **JAMIE LEE CURTIS** Actress. (Los Angeles, CA) Daughter of Janet Leigh and Tony Curtis. She won an Academy Award in 1983 for best supporting actress in *Trading Places* but is probably best known for the horror shows *Halloween I & II*, although she hates horror films. She was in the films *True Lies*, *Forever Young*, *My Girl*, and *Mother's Boys*. In TV's "Anything But Love." Year/**Age**: 1995/**37** 1996/**38** 1997/**39**

- **TERRY GILLIAM** Writer. (Minneapolis, MN) "Monty Python" writer/animator. Directed *The Fisher King*. Year/**Age**: 1995/**55** 1996/**56** 1997/**57**

- **HUGH MILLER** Football. Dallas Cowboys quarterback. Year/**Age**: 1995/**31** 1996/**32** 1997/**33**

- **GREG LUZINSKI** Baseball. Former White Sox power hitter, now coaching a high school team in New Jersey. Year/**Age**: 1995/**45** 1996/**46** 1997/**47**

- **RODNEY DANGERFIELD** Comedian. (Born Jacob Cohen in Babylon, NY) The man who "can't get no respect" appeared in the movies *Caddy Shack*, *Back to School*, and *Ladybug*. Year/**Age**: 1995/**74** 1996/**75** 1997/**76**

- **BORIS BECKER** Tennis star. (Germany) Started tennis training intensively at age 9. Year/**Age**: 1995/**28** 1996/**29** 1997/**30**

- **TINA WEYMOUTH** Bass player. TALKING HEADS and TOM TOM CLUB. Year/**Age**: 1995/**45** 1996/**46** 1997/**47**

- **GUION S. BLUFORD, JR.** First African-American astronaut. (Philadelphia, PA) Flew three space shuttle missions. Retired in 1993 to work for an aerospace firm. Year/**Age**: 1995/**53** 1996/**54** 1997/**55**

- **GERALDINE PAGE** Actress. (1924-1987 – Kirksville, MO) She received 8 Oscar nominations before winning in 1986 for best actress in *A Trip to Bountiful*. (Died 6-13-87.)

- **HOAGY CARMICHAEL** Singer/composer. (1899-1981 – Born Hoagland Howard Carmichael in Bloomington, IN) He gave up the practice of law to become an actor/composer. His most recorded song is "Stardust." He wrote "Georgia on My Mind," Ray Charles's first #1 hit in 1960. He sang his Oscar-nominated "Ole Buttermilk Sky" in the 1946 western *Canyon Passage*, starring Lloyd Bridges and Brian Donlevy. (Died 12-27-81.)

FACTS FROM THE PAST

1718 **BLACKBEARD, THE PIRATE**, was killed when British soldiers cornered him aboard his small ship and shot and stabbed him more than 25 times. Then they flew his beard from the ship's bow.

1917 The **NATIONAL HOCKEY LEAGUE** started with teams from Toronto, Montreal, Quebec, and Ontario. They didn't wear protective face masks until 1929. Clint Benedict was the first to wear one after a puck hit him, breaking his nose. The first U.S. team, the Boston Bruins, didn't join the NHL until 1924.

1955 **ELVIS PRESLEY** was signed by RCA Victor after the company purchased his contract from Sam Phillips of Sun Records for $40,000. The deal was signed by Elvis and RCA's Steve Sholes at the Warwick Hotel in NYC. With the money, Elvis bought his mom a pink Cadillac.

1961 *Blue Hawaii*, **ELVIS**'s biggest moneymaker movie, premiered and grossed $4.7 million.

1963 **PRESIDENT JOHN F. KENNEDY WAS ASSASSINATED** as he rode in a motorcade in Dallas, TX. Lyndon Johnson became the 36th U.S. President immediately thereafter. Two days later, Lee Harvey Oswald, the accused assassin, was murdered by nightclub owner Jack Ruby, as millions watched on TV.

1965 **BOB DYLAN** married ex-model Sara Lowndes after his love affair with Joan Baez ended. The marriage was not made public until the following February.

1967 **"ALICE'S RESTAURANT,"** Arlo Guthrie's **22-MINUTE SONG**, was released on Reprise Records soon after he performed it at the Newport Folk Festival. Guthrie starred in the 1970 movie based on the song.

1972 **PRESIDENT RICHARD NIXON** lifted a 22-year ban on American **TRAVEL TO MAINLAND CHINA.**

1990 British Prime Minister **MARGARET THATCHER** resigned. Elected in 1979, she was the only prime minister in 160 years to win 3 consecutive elections.

1992 **MICHAEL PLANT**'s boat *Coyote* was found floating upside down 460 miles north of the Azores. The solo, around-the-world sailor left New York for France October 16. On November 25 the Coast Guard gave up the search and announced that Plant was presumed dead.

NOVEMBER 23
Astrological Sign of Sagittarius

BIRTHDAYS

• **BETTY EVERETT** Singer. (Greenwood, MS) Biggest hit: "Shoop Shoop Song" in 1964. Year/**Age**: 1995/**55** 1996/**56** 1997/**57**

• **SUSAN ANSPACH** Actress. (Southern CA) She appeared in *Five Easy Pieces* and *Play it Again, Sam.* Year/**Age**: 1995/**50** 1996/**51** 1997/**52**

• **VIN BAKER** Basketball. Year/**Age**: 1995/**24** 1996/**25** 1997/**26**

• **LUIS TIANT** Baseball pitcher. He was one of the reasons that the Boston Red Sox won the American League pennant in 1975, racking up 18 victories. Year/**Age**: 1995/**55** 1996/**56** 1997/**57**

• **JERRY BOCK** Broadway composer. (New Haven, CT) *Fiddler on the Roof* and *Fiorello.* Year/**Age**: 1995/**67** 1996/**68** 1997/**69**

• **BRUCE HORNSBY** Singer/pianist. (Williamsburg, VA) With his group THE RANGE, biggest hit: "The Way It Is" in 1986. Year/**Age**: 1995/**40** 1996/**41** 1997/**42**

• **GLORIA LYNNE** Singer. (NYC) Biggest hit: "I Wish You Love" in 1964. Year/**Age**: 1995/**64** 1996/**65** 1997/**66**

• **MAXWELL CAULFIELD** Actor. (England) Played Miles Colby on TV's "The Colbys." Year/**Age**: 1995/**36** 1996/**37** 1997/**38**

• **KRSYSZTOF PENDERECKI** Composer. (Poland) Controversial Grammy winner, wrote opera *Devils of Loudan.* Year/**Age**: 1995/**62** 1996/**63** 1997/**64**

• **STEVE LANDESBERG** Actor. (Bronx, NY) Played Arthur Dietrich in "Barney Miller." Year/**Age**: 1995/**50** 1996/**51** 1997/**52**

• **VICTOR JORY** Actor. (1902-1982 – Alaska) Films include *Gone With the Wind* in 1939. (Died 2-2-82.)

• **WILLIAM H. BONNEY** Outlaw a/k/a "Billy, The Kid.." (1859-1881 – Born Henry McCarty in NYC) Legendary outlaw. His first brush with the law came when he was caught stealing a bag of laundry. The sheriff locked him in a cell and he escaped up the jail's chimney. (Died 7-14-1881.)

• **FRANKLIN PIERCE** 14th U.S. President. (1804-1869 – Hillsboro, NH) He was inaugurated on Friday, March 4, 1853 and was the only president who did not "swear" in the presidential oath. He said instead, "I do solemnly affirm." (Died 10-8-1869.)

• **BORIS KARLOFF** Actor. (1887-1969 – Born William Henry Pratt in London, England) In films, he usually played villains. He starred in *Frankenstein*, and Boris said the monster was the best friend he ever had. He narrated *The Grinch Who Stole Christmas.* He also appeared in the TV series "Mystery Playhouse" in 1949 and "Thriller," in 1960-62 and was a regular panelist on the quiz show "Down You Go" in 1954-55. (Died 2-2-69.)

• **DAVID RAPPAPORT** Actor. (1951-1990 – London, England) Dwarf who played devious lawyer known as Mighty Mouth on "L.A. Law." Died of self-inflicted gunshot wound. (5-2-90.)

FACTS FROM THE PAST

1899 The **FIRST JUKE BOX** was installed in the Palais Royal Hotel in San Francisco. Devised by **LOUIS GLASS**, it consisted of an Edison tinfoil phonograph with four listening tubes and a coin slot for each tube. A nickel purchased a couple of minutes of music. "Juke" was slang for disorderly house or brothel. "Juke Organ" was the original name. The box made $1,000 in six months.

1903 Italian opera star **ENRICO CARUSO** made his American debut at the Metropolitan Opera in New York City in *Rigoletto*. Caruso's popularity was crucial in transforming the phonograph from a novelty to a medium for home entertainment. He was the first artist to have a million-selling record, "Vesti La Giubba (On with the Money)" from *Pagliacci*.

1936 The **FIRST ISSUE OF LIFE MAGAZINE** hit the stands. This picture magazine was created by Henry Luce.

1942 Seaman Poon Lim's merchant ship S.S. *Lomond* was torpedoed and sank. He set the **WORLD'S SURVIVAL-AT-SEA RECORD** by living aboard a life raft for more than four months, 133 days. He had only 60 days worth of rations. He fished for food with a hook he made from a flashlight spring, and he kept fit by swimming. After his rescue by Brazilian fishermen, he was congratulated on his record and he said, "I hope no one ever has to break it."

1959 A spokesman for RCA Victor denied that **ELVIS PRESLEY** would change his musical style upon leaving the army. But, after his military service ended in March of 1960, he basically became a middle-of-the-road singer, spending more time as a "movie star" instead of as a rock 'n' roller.

1964 The **ROLLING STONES** arrived late for the BBC radio shows "Top Gear" and "Saturday Club." The BBC banned them after that.

1967 Reports of a death greatly exaggerated: **ALBUM ROCK** format pioneer **TOM DONAHUE** told Rolling Stone, "Top 40 radio as we know it is dead, and its corpse is rotting up the airwaves."

1976 **JERRY LEE LEWIS** was arrested outside Graceland Mansion for brandishing a pistol and demanding to see Elvis. Lewis was charged with public intoxication and possession of a weapon.

1983 Actress **MARY TYLER MOORE** married 30-year-old cardiologist **DR. ROBERT LEVINE** in NYC. She was 45, and this was her third marriage, his first.

1985 **LARRY WU-TAI**, retired CIA analyst was convicted for spying for China. He committed suicide a year later.

1989 **PAUL McCARTNEY** began his first North American tour in 13 years, playing the first of five dates in the Los Angeles suburb of Inglewood. Scalpers got as much as $600 for tickets.

NOVEMBER 24

Rap and thunderclap, man

BIRTHDAYS

- **MARLIN FITZWATER** Press secretary. (Salinas, KS) Under President George Bush. Year/Age: 1995/**53** 1996/**54** 1997/**55**

- **BEV BEVANS** Drummer. (England) Hits with "ELO," "Don't Bring Me Down," and "Telephone Line." Year/Age: 1995/**49** 1996/**50** 1997/**51**

- **JOHNNY CARVER** C&W. (Jackson, MS) His biggest hit: "Tie a Yellow Ribbon" in 1973, a C&W cover version of the hit by TONY ORLANDO & DAWN. Year/Age: 1995/**55** 1996/**56** 1997/**57**

- **OSCAR ROBERTSON** Former basketball star. He played guard position, averaging 25.7 points per game. He was MVP in 1964. The 1976 Oscar Robertson Federal Court decision is credited with boosting free agency and causing player salaries to soar in the NBA. Year/Age: 1995/**57** 1996/**58** 1997/**59**

- **WILLIAM BUCKLEY, JR.** Columnist/TV commentator/author. (NYC) Host of "Firing Line" on PBS Television and founded the National Review in 1955. Blackford Oakes novels. Year/Age: 1995/**70** 1996/**71** 1997/**72**

- **STANLEY LIVINGSTON** Actor is. (Los Angeles, CA) Co-starred as Chip on "My Three Sons" TV comedy with Fred MacMurray. Year/Age: 1995/**45** 1996/**46** 1997/**47**

- **PETE BEST** Drummer. (Randolph Peter Best - Madras, India) The QUARRYMEN (The BEATLES) performed at Pete's mother's club, The Casbah. The group had a dispute with their drummer and Pete sat in with them. In August 1960 he became a Beatle. When the Beatles were on the verge of success following their first EMI recording session Pete was told that he was being replaced by Ringo Starr. The evening Ringo made his first "Cavern" appearance, a Pete Best fan gave George Harrison a black eye. Year/Age: 1995/**54** 1996/**55** 1997/**56**

- **LEE MICHAELS** Singer. (Los Angeles, CA) His biggest hit: "Do You Know What I Mean?" in 1971. Year/Age: 1995/**49** 1996/**50** 1997/**51**

- **DAVE BING** Basketball. (Washington, DC) Played for the Detroit Pistons. Year/Age: 1995/**52** 1996/**53** 1997/**54**

- **RON DELLUMS** House Armed Services Chairman. Year/Age: 1995/**60** 1996/**61** 1997/**62**

- **STEVE YEAGER** Baseball catcher. Year/Age: 1995/**47** 1996/**48** 1997/**49**

- **DWIGHT SCHULTZ** Actor. Played H.M. "Howlin' Mad" Murdock on "The A-Team." Once worked for the New York Pest Control Bureau. Year/Age: 1995/**48** 1996/**49** 1997/**50**

- **SCOTT JOPLIN** Ragtime musician. (1868-1917 – Texarkana, TX) By the time he was 7 years old, he had taught himself to play the guitar, piano and bugle. 56 years after his death, his ragtime song, "The Entertainer," was featured in the movie *The Sting* in 1973. Ragtime got its name from its syncopated rhythms – ragged time. (Died 4-4-17.)

- **DALE CARNEGIE** Author. (1888-1955 – Maryville, MO) Author of *How to Win Friends & Influence People*, which was translated into 29 languages. (Died 11-1-55.)

- **ZACHARY TAYLOR** 12th U.S. President. (1784-1850 – Montebello, VA) He was an Indian fighter who became a general, accused of chewing, spitting and cussing his way through the Mexican War. He had never voted in a presidential election, until he voted for himself. He had no political experience at all. Tests performed on his exhumed remains in 1991 showed he died of natural causes and not .)

FACTS FROM THE PAST

1615   **FRENCH KING LOUIS XIII** married Anne of Austria. They were both 14 years old at the time. Louis was very nervous about the marriage and his mother had to escort him to his wife's bedroom.

1789   **LUCY HANKS** was charged with fornication, which was a criminal offense in the state of Kentucky, where she lived. The charges were dropped after Lucy became engaged to the man she was accused of consorting with—Henry Sparrow, whom she eventually married. Lucy had given birth to a child out of wedlock five years earlier – a daughter she named Nancy. But later, Nancy Hanks' eldest son always felt that his mother's "illegitimacy" and his family's poverty were obstacles to his winning what he referred to as "the race of life." Later on, Nancy married a man named Thomas Lincoln. They gave birth to **ABRAHAM LINCOLN**.

1859   **CHARLES DARWIN** published **ORIGIN OF THE SPECIES** and the Christian community accused him of heresy. It was a paper in which Darwin explained his theory of evolution through the process of natural selection. He had labored for years to complete the paper. Others were involved, but Darwin got most of the credit and criticism. Many fundamentalists, to this day, fight the idea.

1930   **RUTH NICHOLS** became the first woman to fly an airplane coast to coast. She took off from Long Island, NY, and landed, after several stops, in California on December 1st.

1963   **LEE HARVEY OSWALD,** accused killer of President Kennedy, was shot to death in Dallas, TX, by nightclub owner Jack Ruby, as millions watched on live nationwide television.

1971   A man who called himself **D. B. COOPER** parachuted from a Northwest Airlines 727 with $200,000 he collected from the airline as ransom. He jumped out over a Seattle wilderness area and was never caught, though money has been found spread over a wide area.

1972   "In Concert," which later becomes "**DON KIRSHNER'S ROCK CONCERT,**" premiered on ABC-TV. First-night guests included Alice Cooper, the Allmans, Chuck Berry, Poco, and Seals & Crofts.

1992   On the 40th anniversary of her accession to the throne, **QUEEN ELIZABETH** called 1992 a "horrible year" (in Latin). Her troubles included her children's marital problems and a major fire at Windsor Castle.

1993   Congress passed the **BRADY BILL** requiring a five-day waiting period for handgun buyers.

Timeshare with a friend.

NOVEMBER 25

BIRTHDAYS

- **STACEY LATTISAW** Singer. (Washington, DC) She made her first album at age 12. Hits include: "Let Me Be Your Angel" in 1980. Year/**Age:** 1995/**29** 1996/**30** 1997/**31**

- **KATHRYN CROSBY** (Houston,TX) Actress and widow of Bing Crosby. Year/**Age:** 1995/**62** 1996/**63** 1997/**64**

- **JOHN F. KENNEDY, JR.** Attorney. (Washington, DC) Son of Jacqueline and President John Kennedy. Year/**Age:** 1995/**35** 1996/**36** 1997/**37**

- **RICARDO MONTALBAN** Actor. (Mexico City, Mexico) He has one of entertainment's longest successful marriages to Georgianna Young [since 1944], sister of Loretta Young. He received four-star reviews for his part in the 1982 *Star Trek II: The Wrath of Kahn* and an Emmy for the TV miniseries *How the West was Won*. He appeared as Mr. Roarke on TV's "Fantasy Island" and has done Chrysler commercials. Year/**Age:** 1995/**75** 1996/**76** 1997/**77**

- **JOE DiMAGGIO** Baseball. (Martinez, CA) Baseball Hall of Famer. His batting average was .325 (over a 15-yr. career), and he has the distinction of becoming the first American League player to earn over $100,000 a year. He holds the hitting-streak record of 56 straight games. He was married to actress Marilyn Monroe for a short time. Year/**Age:** 1995/**81** 1996/**82** 1997/**83**

- **ERNEST HARDEN, JR.** Actor. He played Ralph Hart on "The Jeffersons." Year/**Age:** 1995/**35** 1996/**36** 1997/**37**

- **RUSSELL "BUCKY" DENT** Baseball. (Savannah, GA) NY Yankee shortstop. Year/**Age:** 1995/**44** 1996/**45** 1997/**46**

- **BERNIE KOSAR** Football. (Boardman, OH) Former Cleveland Browns quarterback. Holds Brown passing record, 489 yards in one game. Set AFC Championship game record completing 28 out of 41 passes for 356 yards. Year/**Age:** 1995/**32** 1996/**33** 1997/**34**

- **CHRISTINA APPLEGATE** Actress. (Hollywood, CA) Kelly Bundy on "Married . . . with Children." Year/**Age:** 1995/**24** 1996/**25** 1997/**26**

- **MARTIN FELDSTEIN** Economist. (NYC) Presidential economic advisor. Year/**Age:** 1995/**56** 1996/**57** 1997/**58**

- **LENNY WILKENS** Basketball. Played for the Detroit Pistons. Coach for Seattle, Portland, Cleveland, and the Atlanta Hawks. Year/**Age:** 1995/**57** 1996/**58** 1997/**59**

- **AMY GRANT** Singer. (Augusta, GA) 1991 hit: "Baby Baby." Year/**Age:** 1995/**35** 1996/**36** 1997/**37**

- **BOB LIND** Singer. (Baltimore, MD) 1966 hit "Elusive Butterfly." Year/**Age:** 1995/**51** 1996/**52** 1997/**53**

- **JOHN LARROQUETTE** Actor. (New Orleans, LA) Record four straight Emmy winner. Assistant D.A. Daniel Fielding on "Night Court" andand "John Larroquette Show." Year/**Age:** 1995/**48** 1996/**49** 1997/**50**

- **VIRGIL THOMSON** Composer. (1896-1989 – NYC) Won an Academy Award for scoring *Louisiana Story*. (Died 9-3-89.)

- **RENE ENRIQUEZ** Actor. (1933-1990) He played Lt. Ray Calletano on "Hill Street Blues." (Died 3-23-90.)

- **POPE JOHN XXIII** (1881-1963 – Italy) Fourth son of a family of 14. Not a very good student, he only got into the local seminary by the skin of his teeth. But once he was ordained, he had a brilliant career. He became Pope in 1958. He was asked how many people work in the Vatican. He replied "About half." He had a sense of humor! (Died 6-3-63.)

- **ANDREW CARNEGIE** Tycoon. (1835-1919 – Scotland) American financier, philanthropist and benefactor of more than 2500 libraries, as well as Carnegie Hall. He said, "The man who dies rich, dies disgraced." He gave away $300 million in his career. He came to America when he was 12, making $1.20 a week in his first job. Founder of U.S. Steel, he gave pensions to former presidents' wives. His mother believed no girl was good enough for him and he promised not to marry. A year after she died he got married and his wife had to sign an agreement waiving her rights as his heiress – an early prenuptial agreement. (Died 8-11-19.)

FACTS FROM THE PAST

1715 **SYBILLA MASTERS** became the first female inventor when her husband filed and was granted (women could not file) a patent for Sybilla's invention of a machine that cleaned and cured Indian corn.

1867 **ALFRED NOBEL** patented the **FIRST DYNAMITE**, which made him a rich man. His will established a fund for the **NOBEL PRIZES** in the amount of $9.2 million, first awarded in 1901.

1920 Radio station WTAW of College Station, TX, broadcast the **FIRST PLAY-BY-PLAY DESCRIPTION OF A FOOTBALL GAME,** between the University of Texas and Texas A&M.

1922 **KING TUT'S TOMB** was opened. It was infested by cobras. Archeologists dug for 6 months when the temperature was above 120 degrees and found nothing. Finally the water boy was playing outside the digging area and found a step.

1949 Tap dancer **BILL "BOJANGLES" ROBINSON** died. He was 71. His life inspired the song "Mr. Bojangles" by the NITTY GRITTY DIRT BAND.

1952 Agatha Christie's mystery *Mousetrap* opened in London...and it's still going strong. It is the **WORLD'S LONGEST-RUNNING PLAY**. The producer/director thought it would last one year. By its 25th anniversary, 4 million people had seen it.

1955 Bill Haley's **"ROCK AROUND THE CLOCK"** hit #1 on the British charts, $4^1/_2$ months after it topped the charts in the U.S.

1968 The **BEATLES'** *White Album* was released. The double LP had more songs than anyone had put on an album until then.

1982 Comic **BILL COSBY** was best man, as jazz trumpet player **MILES DAVIS** married for the third time, to actress **CICELY TYSON** in NYC.

NOVEMBER 26

Have a tollgate party today.

BIRTHDAYS

- **ROBERT GOULET** Singer/actor. (Lawrence, MA) Hit: "My Love, Forgive Me" in 1964. Father of actress Nicolett Goulet. In recent months, toured as King Arthur with the revival of the stage presentation of *Camelot*. Films include *Naked Gun 2½*. Recorded over 40 albums. Divorced from entertainer Carol Lawrence. Year/**Age**: 1995/**62** 1996/**63** 1997/**64**

- **JOHN McVIE** Guitarist. (England) Bass guitarist for FLEETWOOD MAC. Their biggest hit: "Dreams" in 1977. Year/**Age**: 1995/**49** 1996/**50** 1997/**51**

- **SHAWN KEMP** Basketball. Year/**Age**: 1995/**26** 1996/**27** 1997/**28**

- **CHARLES M. SCHULZ** Cartoonist. (Minneapolis, MN) He's the creator of "Peanuts" and the Snoopy gang. In 1950, he started out in 8 papers and now his income is estimated at $5 million a year. Year/**Age**: 1995/**73** 1996/**74** 1997/**75**

- **RICH LITTLE** Impressionist. (Ottawa, Canada) He does over 150 impressions. Year/**Age**: 1995/**57** 1996/**58** 1997/**59**

- **JAN STENERUD** Pro football kicker. During his 19-year NFL career, he became the all-time leader in field goals with 373 and 1,699 points. He was second leading scorer to George Blanda with 2,002 points. He invented a kicking tee that is now used by almost every kicker in the league. Spending most of his career with the Kansas City Chiefs, he became the first full-time place kicker to be enshrined in the Pro Football Hall of Fame in 1991. Year/**Age**: 1995/**52** 1996/**53** 1997/**54**

- **JAMIE ROSE** Actress. Played Chase's daughter Victoria on "Falcon Crest." Year/**Age**: 1995/**36** 1996/**37** 1997/**38**

- **WENDY TURNBULL** Tennis star. Year/**Age**: 1995/**43** 1996/**44** 1997/**45**

- **MARIAN MERCER** Actress. (Akron, OH) She was on the "Dean Martin Show," "Jonathan Winters Show," "Mary Hartman, Mary Hartman," and "Home Free." Year/**Age**: 1995/**60** 1996/**61** 1997/**62**

- **TINA TURNER** Entertainer. (Born Annie Mae Bullock in Nutbush, TN) (Her name is posted on the city limits sign.) She has a song called "Nutbush City Limits." Ike & Tina Turner were a husband/wife singing duo until they separated in 1976. Their biggest hit was "Proud Mary" in 1971. The violent breakup left Tina on welfare before her giant comeback. Her biggest recording: "What's Love Got to Do With It?" in 1984 which also became the title of a hit movie about her life in 1993. Year/**Age**: 1995/**57** 1996/**58** 1997/**59**

- **FRANCIS DEE** Actress. (Los Angeles, CA) In films: *Blood Money* and *I Walked with a Zombie*, now considered cult movies. Year/**Age**: 1995/**87** 1996/**88** 1997/**89**

- **ERIC SEVAREID** TV newsman. (1912-1992 – Velva, ND) With CBS for 38 years. In the movie *The Right Stuff*. (Died 7-9-92.)

- **JOHN HARVARD** Clergyman. (1607-1638 – London) His name was given to America's first college. (Died 9-24-1638.)

FACTS FROM THE PAST

1789 President George Washington proclaimed the **FIRST U.S. HOLIDAY** to be **THANKSGIVING DAY**. However, it was not an official holiday until President Lincoln signed a proclamation.

1964 **LITTLE RICHARD** made his first U.S. TV appearance on the "Judy Garland Show."

1966 The **MONKEES'** "I'm A Believer" went gold, making believers out of many of the band's skeptics.

1968 The blues-rock power trio CREAM played its farewell concert at the Royal Albert Hall in London. CREAM had sold 15 million albums in a little over three years. Guitarist **ERIC CLAPTON** and drummer **GINGER BAKER** went on to form the short-lived group BLIND FAITH, while bass player **JACK BRUCE** began a solo career.

1973 President Nixon's personal secretary, **ROSEMARY WOODS**, told a Washington court she had mistakenly **PRESSED THE WRONG BUTTON** and caused an 18½ minute gap in a key **WATERGATE TAPE**.

1973 The **BOSTON STRANGLER** was murdered by another inmate in his cell at Walpole State Prison in Massachusetts. Despite his confession and an eye-witness description of him, it was never conclusively proven that **ALBERT DESALVO** was the "strangler" who sexually assaulted and murdered 13 women.

1975 Charles Boykin of Tallahassee, FL, and his congregation **BURNED $2,000 WORTH OF ROCK RECORDS**. The minister said that 984 out of 1,000 unwed mothers were impregnated with rock music playing in the background.

1975 A federal jury in Sacramento, CA, found Manson follower **LYNETTE "SQUEAKY" FROMME** guilty of trying to **ASSASSINATE PRESIDENT GERALD FORD**.

1988 **PLO CHAIRMAN YASSER ARAFAT** was denied an entry visa into America. He wanted to tour New York and address the U.N. General Assembly.

1988 Members of **PINK FLOYD** watched the launch of a joint Soviet-French space mission from Soviet Central Asia. One of the cosmonauts had requested an advance copy of Pink Floyd's live album, *The Delicate Sound of Thunder*, to play during the flight.

1989 A city councilman, **OTIS LYONS**, in Pittsburgh, PA, stirred up the city fathers when he said "I **REFUSE TO SUPPORT ABORTION** in cases of incest. Some of the great leaders in the Bible married their sisters."

1992 Britain's **QUEEN ELIZABETH**, purportedly the world's richest woman, volunteered to pay income tax. Her total wealth has been estimated at over $8 billion. She also declared that she would take her children off the public payroll.

NOVEMBER 27

BIRTHDAYS

- **CAROLINE KENNEDY** (New York, NY) Daughter of the 35th U.S. President John F. Kennedy and Jackie. She is married to Edwin Schlossberg. Year/**Age**: 1995/**38** 1996/**39** 1997/**40**

- **EDDIE RABBIT** Singer. (Born Edward Thomas in Brooklyn, NY) He once worked in a mental hospital. Biggest hit: "I Love a Rainy Night" in 1980. He wrote "Kentucky Rain," a hit for Elvis Presley. Year/**Age**: 1995/**54** 1996/**55** 1997/**56**

- **GAIL SHEEHY** Author. [she'-he] (Mamaroneck, NY) Author of *Passages*. Year/**Age**: 1995/**58** 1996/**59** 1997/**60**

- **"BUFFALO" BOB SMITH** Puppeteer. (Buffalo, NY) He was responsible for the "Howdy Doody Show," the first popular TV show for kids, which premiered in 1947. The "Howdy Doody Show" was the first Tuesday-through-Friday program in 1948 and the first show in color in 1955. Year/**Age**: 1995/**78** 1996/**79** 1997/**80**

- **LEVI STRAUSS** Businessman. (1809-1902) He went to California to get rich making canvas tents for the Gold Rush prospectors, but ended up using the canvas to make durable pants, which he called "waist-high overalls." Eventually, they became "Levis." The Levi Strauss Company is now the largest apparel company in the world. (Died 9-26-1902.)

- **ROBIN GIVENS** Actress. (New York, NY) She was in the film *Boomerang* and on TV's "Head of the Class" and "Angel Street." Her "ex" is former heavyweight champion Mike Tyson. Year/**Age**: 1995/**31** 1996/**32** 1997/**33**

- **DAVID MERRICK** Broadway producer. (St. Louis, MO) He produced *Beckett; Oliver; Hello, Dolly*; and *42nd Street*. Year/**Age**: 1995/**83** 1996/**84** 1997/**85**

- **JALEEL WHITE** Actor. Plays Steve Urkel on "Family Matters." Year/**Age**: 1995/**19** 1996/**20** 1997/**21**

- **MONA WASHBOURNE** Actress. (1903-1984 – England) Appeared in *My Fair Lady*, *Night Must Fall* and *Mrs. Brown, You've Got a Lovely Daughter*.

- **BRUCE LEE** Actor. (1940-1973 – Born Li Jun Fan in San Francisco, CA) Ironically, his last movie before he died was *The Game of Death* in 1973. He played Kato on the "Green Hornet" TV show before his martial arts movie days. *Dragon*, a movie of his life, was released in 1993. His son Brandon Lee died of abdominal wounds after being shot by a gun supposedly rigged with blanks. He was filming a scene for a film *The Crow*, March 31, 1993. (Died 7-20-73.)

- **JIMI HENDRIX** Singer. (1942-1970 – Seattle, WA) His biggest hit: "All Along the Watch Tower" in 1968. He was known for violent on-stage activity like smashing his guitar. In a flight from New York to London for his first appearance in Europe, he changed the spelling of his name from Jimmy to Jimi. He died of an overdose of sleeping pills at the Cumberland Hotel in London on 9-18-70.

- **JOE MACK** Inventor. (1870 – Brooklyn, NY) He and his brothers were in the silk business but weren't satisfied with their horse-drawn wagon delivery system. So, in 1899, they began making their own delivery wagons with gasoline engines. In 1900, they created the world's first successful passenger bus and, in 1911, they gave up the silk business and formed the Mack Truck Company, just in time for the huge market created by World War

FACTS FROM THE PAST

1889   **CURTIS BRADY** of New York, after promising not to frighten horses, was given the first permit to operate a motor vehicle in Central Park.

1934   **"BABY FACE" NELSON** died in a hail of bullets fired by G-men in Barrington, Illinois.

1947   **JOE DiMAGGIO** won a third MVP award by one vote over Ted Williams. Williams led the league in 6 categories, DiMaggio in one.

1954   **ALGER HISS** was released from a Pennsylvania Federal Penitentiary after serving 44 months of a 5-year perjury sentence. He continued to deny charges that he had **PROVIDED SECRET STATE DEPT. DOCUMENTS** for transmission to the Soviet Union.

1957   *The Chirping Crickets*, the **ONLY BUDDY HOLLY ALBUM ISSUED DURING HIS LIFETIME**, was released. It contained "That'll Be The Day," "Not Fade Away," and "Maybe Baby."

1966   The Washington Redskins beat the NY Giants in a game in which **16 TOUCHDOWNS** were scored: 10 by Washington, 6 by the Giants. The kickers were brothers Charley (Washington) and Pete (New York) Gogolak. They both missed extra points in Washington's 72-41 win.

1967   The **BEATLES'** album *Magical Mystery Tour* was released.

1970   **POPE PAUL THE VI** was stabbed in the chest during a visit to the Philippines by a Bolivian painter disguised as a priest.

1978   Actor **MARLON BRANDO** made his **TV DEBUT** in the TV mini-series **"ROOTS."**

1978   San Francisco supervisor **Dan White shot and KILLED GEORGE MOSCONE AND HARVEY MILK**, a fellow supervisor and leader of the city's gay population, in the City Hall.

1984   William Schroeder spoke for the first time after receiving the **JARVIK-7** permanent **ARTIFICIAL HEART** on November 25th. He asked for a can of beer. He was the second human recipient of the artificial heart. He died August 6, 1986, after living a record 620 days.

1989   **PAUL McCARTNEY SUGGESTED** the three **SURVIVING BEATLES MIGHT REUNITE**, but George Harrison quickly threw cold water on that idea, telling AP Network News that, "There won't be a Beatles reunion as long as John Lennon remains dead."

NOVEMBER 28

You're twisted. Buy a torque!

BIRTHDAYS

- **SUSAN SPENCER** CBS news correspondent. Year/**Age:** 1995/**49** 1996/**50** 1997/**51**
- **R. B. GREAVES** Singer. (Born Ronald Bertram Greaves at the U.S. Air Base in Georgetown, British Guyana) He is the late Sam Cooke's nephew. Biggest hit: "Take A Letter Maria" in 1969. Year/**Age:** 1995/**50** 1996/**51** 1997/**52**
- **HOPE LANGE** Actress. (Redding Ridge, CT) She was nominated for an Oscar for best supporting actress in *Peyton Place* and has been on the screen since 1956. Year/**Age:** 1995/**62** 1996/**63** 1997/**64**
- **BERRY GORDY, JR.** Record producer. (Detroit, MI) Motown Records executive. At one time, he was married to Diana Ross. Year/**Age:** 1995/**66** 1996/**67** 1997/**68**
- **MICHAEL RITCHIE** Film director. (Waukesha, WI) Directed *The Candidate* and others. Year/**Age:** 1995/**57** 1996/**58** 1997/**59**
- **RANDY NEWMAN** Singer/songwriter. (Los Angeles, CA) His biggest hit: "Short People" in 1978. He also wrote: "Mama Told Me Not to Come." Scored the film *Parenthood*. Year/**Age:** 1995/**52** 1996/**53** 1997/**54**
- **JUDD NELSON** Actor. (Portland, ME) Appeared in *Breakfast Club* and *Blindfold*. Year/**Age:** 1995/**36** 1996/**37** 1997/**37**
- **PAUL SHAFFER** Orchestra leader/comedian. (Canada) "Late Night with David Letterman." Year/**Age:** 1995/**46** 1996/**47** 1997/**48**

- **GARY HART** Colorado Senator. (Born Gary Hartpence in Ottawa, KS) He ran for the presidency in 1984, and after an adultery scandal, dropped out of the 1988 presidential race. Year/**Age:** 1995/**59** 1996/**60** 1997/**61**
- **ED HARRIS** Actor. (Englewood, NJ) Appeared in *Glengarry Glen Ross*. Year/**Age:** 1995/**45** 1996/**46** 1997/**47**
- **PAUL WARFIELD** Football. Miami Dolphins. In Pro Hall of Fame. Year/**Age:** 1995/**53** 1996/**54** 1997/**55**
- **ALEXANDER GODUNOV** Ballet dancer/actor. (Russia) Appeared in *Die Hard*. Year/**Age:** 1995/**45** 1996/**46** 1997/**47**
- **BRUCE CHANNEL** Singer. (Jacksonville, TX) Biggest hit: "Hey! Baby" in 1962, featuring harmonica player Delbert McClinton. Year/**Age:** 1995/**55** 1996/**56** 1997/**57**
- **ROY TARPLEY** Basketball. (NYC) Played college ball at Michigan. Had drug problems in NBA. Year/**Age:** 1995/**31** 1996/**32** 1997/**33**
- **GLORIA GRAHAME** Actress. (1925-1981 – Los Angeles, CA) Won an Academy Award for *The Bad and the Beautiful* in 1952. (Died 10-5-81.)
- **JEAN BAPTISTE LULLY** Composer. (1632-1687 – Italy) He had a bad temper. He died from blood poisoning when he stuck his own foot with a baton while in a rage of anger. (Died 3-22-1687.)
- **JOHN BUNYAN** English cleric/author. (1628-1688) While in prison, he wrote *Pilgrim's Progress*. (Died 8-31-1688.)

FACTS FROM THE PAST

1520 Portugese navigator Ferdinand Magellan entered the Pacific Ocean on his way **AROUND THE WORLD**. He was the first European to sail the Pacific from the east.

1678 **KING CHARLES II** of England accused his wife, **CATHERINE OF BRAGANZA**, of treason. She didn't bear him any children.

1895 America's **FIRST AUTOMOBILE RACE** got under way: 6 cars began a 55-mile round-trip from Chicago's Jackson Park to Evanston, IL. J. Frank Duryea won it in a gasoline-powered auto invented by his brother, Charles, with an average speed of 7 mph. It took 7 hrs., 5 min., and his prize was $2,000.

1919 American-born **LADY ASTOR** was elected the first female member of the British Parliament.

1922 Communication via **SMOKE SIGNAL** was modernized when the first skywriting was created over New York City. Captain Cyril Turner of the Royal Air Force wrote "Hello U.S.A., Call Vanderbilt 7200." More than 47,000 people did!

1925 The first **WSM BARN DANCE** was held in Nashville, TN. The show was renamed **"GRAND OLE OPRY"** in 1927.

1943 President Franklin Roosevelt, British Prime Minister Winston Churchill, and Soviet Premier Joseph Stalin met at **TEHERAN, IRAN**, to discuss and determine a plan for an Allied assault. The meeting concluded December 1st, resulting in a plan called **OPERATION OVERLORD**, which commenced with the landing on Normandy's beaches June 6, 1944, known as **D-DAY**.

1963 **CAPE CANAVERAL** was renamed **CAPE KENNEDY,** in honor of President John F. Kennedy. The change was initiated by President Lyndon Johnson.

1964 **WILLIE NELSON** made his **DEBUT** at the Grand Ole Opry.

1964 "Leader of the Pack" by the **SHANGRI-LAS** reached number one on *Billboard's* pop chart.

1974 **JOHN LENNON** made his last concert appearance, a Thanksgiving concert starring **ELTON JOHN**, at New York's Madison Square Garden. It turned into a special event when Elton was joined on stage by his close friend, Lennon. They did 3 numbers together.

1979 President **JIMMY CARTER** said he was grimly resolved to win the release of the **AMERICAN HOSTAGES IN IRAN,** but pledged the U.S. would not yield to blackmail. At the same time, Iran's Bani-Sadr, Foreign Minister, was removed, dashing hopes for negotiations to release the hostages.

1989 **ROMANIAN GYMNAST NADIA COMANECI,** arrived in New York after escaping her homeland by way of Hungary.

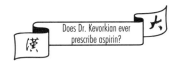

NOVEMBER 29

BIRTHDAYS

- **DR. DAVID RUBEN** Author. He wrote *Everything You Wanted To Know About Sex But Were Afraid To Ask.* Year/**Age**: 1995/**62** 1996/**63** 1997/**64**
- **GARRY SHANDLING** Comedian. (Tucson, AZ) Appears on HBO's "The Larry Sanders Show." Year/**Age**: 1995/**46** 1996/**47** 1997/**48**
- **ANDREW McCARTHY** Actor. (New York, NY) *Mannequin, Weekend At Bernies.* Year/**Age**: 1995/**33** 1996/**34** 1997/**35**.
- **JOEL WHITBURN** Music historian. (Menomonee Falls, WI) He has every hit that ever made the Hot 100. "The world's foremost chart researcher," he has published over 30 books detailing the history and development of charted music from 1890 to the present. Year/**Age**: 1995/**56** 1996/**57** 1997/**58**
- **DIANE LADD** Actress. (Born Diane Ladnier, Meridian, MS) She was nominated for best supporting actress in *Alice Doesn't Live Here Anymore.* She also appeared in *Chinatown, Father Hood, The Gift, The Cemetery Club, Fatherhood,* and *Hold Me, Thrill Me, Kiss Me.* Actress Laura Dern is her daughter. Year/**Age**: 1995/**63** 1996/**64** 1997/**65**
- **DENNY DOHERTY** Singer. (Canada) Formerly of the MAMAS & PAPAS. Biggest hit: "Monday, Monday" in 1966. Year/**Age**: 1995/**55** 1996/**56** 1997/**57**
- **JODY MILLER** C&W. (Phoenix, AZ) Biggest hit: "Queen of the House" in 1965. Year/**Age**: 1995/**54** 1996/**55** 1997/**56**
- **CHUCK MANGIONE** Flugelhorn player. (Rochester, NY) Biggest hit: "Feels so Good" in 1978. Wrote "Give It All You Got," the song for the 1980 Winter Olympics. Year/**Age**: 1995/**55** 1996/**56** 1997/**57**
- **MINNIE MINOSO** Former baseball great. He was with the Chicago White Sox from 1949-64, with a .298 lifetime average. Year/**Age**: 1995/**72** 1996/**73** 1997/**74**
- **CATHY MORIARTY** Actress. (Bronx, NY) In the film *Raging Bull, Soapdish, Me and the Kid,* and *Matinee.* She owns The Beverly Hills Pizzaria. She loves to cook! Year/**Age**: 1995/**35** 1996/**36** 1997/**37**

- **FELIX CAVALIERE** Singer/organist. (NYC) With the RASCALS. Their biggest hit: "People Gotta Be Free" in 1968. Year/**Age**: 1995/**51** 1996/**52** 1997/**53**
- **VINCE SCULLY** Baseball broadcaster. (Bronx, NY) Year/**Age**: 1995/**68** 1996/**69** 1997/**70**
- **HOWIE MANDELL** Comedian. (Canada) Played Dr. Wayne Fiscus on "St. Elsewhere" TV series and does stand-up comedy. TV cartoon character Bobby in "Bobby's World." Year/**Age**: 1995/**40** 1996/**41** 1997/**42**
- **MECO MONARDO** Musician. (Johnsonburg, PA) Biggest hit: "Star Wars Theme" in 1977. He produced Gloria Gaynor's hit, "Never Can Say Goodbye." Year/**Age**: 1995/**56** 1996/**57** 1997/**58**
- **FUZZY THURSTON** Former Green Bay Packer star. Year/**Age**: 1995/**62** 1996/**63** 1997/**64**.
- **SUZY CHAFFEE** Skier. "Suzy 'Chapstick'" commercials. Year/**Age**: 1995/**49** 1996/**50** 1997/**51**
- **PAUL SIMON** Unsuccessful 1988 presidential candidate. (D/IL) (Eugene, OR) In 1990 he said he wouldn't run for president again. Year/**Age**: 1995/**67** 1996/**68** 1997/**69**
- **JONATHAN RASHLEIGH KNIGHT** Singer/dancer. (Worcester, MA) With the group NEW KIDS ON THE BLOCK. Hits include: "You Got It (The Right Stuff)" and "This One's for the Children." Brother Jordan is also a member of the group. Year/**Age**: 1995/**27** 1996/**28** 1997/**29**
- **MERLE TRAVIS** C&W songwriter. (1917-1983 – Tahleguah, OK) Wrote "16 Tons" and "Smoke, Smoke, Smoke That Cigarette." His biggest hit: "Divorce Me C.O.D." (Died 10-2-83)
- **LOUISA MAY ALCOTT** Author. (1832-1888 – Germantown, PA) She intensely disliked little girls. Her publisher persuaded her to write a book about little girls. She did, even though she said the book bored her to tears, and that's how she came to write *Little Women.* She was told by an editor at a publishing house she would never write anything that had popular appeal. (Died 3-6-1888.)

FACTS FROM THE PAST

1872 HORACE GREELEY died insane, just three weeks after losing the presidency to U.S. Grant.

1929 U.S. Navy Lt. Commander Richard Byrd radioed that he had made the **FIRST FLIGHT OVER THE SOUTH POLE**.

1953 Printers were working on the first **PLAYBOY** magazine which included the famous Marilyn Monroe nude calendar photo, now worth a few hundred dollars. **HUGH HEFNER**'s first issue, out in December of 1953, sold over 70,000 copies. In the first couple of years *Playboy* sold 500,000 copies a month. At its peak, monthly circulation was at 7 million copies.

1959 **BOBBY DARIN'S "MACK THE KNIFE"** won the Grammy for record of the year. Darin was also named best new artist.

1961 **ENOS, THE CHIMP**, was launched from Cape Canaveral aboard the Mercury-Atlas V spacecraft, the **FIRST ASTRONAUT TO ORBIT EARTH**.

1963 President Lyndon Johnson named **CHIEF JUSTICE EARL WARREN** to head a committee to investigate **PRESIDENT JOHN F. KENNEDY'S ASSASSINATION.**

1981 **NATALIE WOOD DROWNED** in a boating accident off Santa Catalin Island, CA at age 43. Robert Wagner and Christopher Walken were on board the yacht when the tragedy occurred.

1990 The **U.N. SECURITY COUNCIL**, in a **HISTORIC ACTION** that marked a major diplomatic triumph for the Bush administration, authorized the use of force **AGAINST IRAQ**, should it not withdraw from Kuwait by January 15.

1992 New York Jet defensive end **DENNIS BYRD** received a neck injury during a game with the Kansas City Chiefs. The damage resulted in paralysis of his legs and partial paralysis of his upper body.

NOVEMBER 30

When did you first notice lint in your belly bouton?

BIRTHDAYS

• **MANDY PATINKIN** Actor/singer. (Chicago, IL) Won Tony Award in Broadway debut, *Evita*. Films include: *Alien Nation*, *Dick Tracy,* and *Yentl*. Year/**Age**: 1995/**43** 1996/**44** 1997/**45**

• **BILLY IDOL** Entertainer. (Born William Broad in London, England) "Speed,""Cradle of Love," and "Mony Mony." Year/**Age**: 1995/**40** 1996/**41** 1997/**42**

• **DICK CLARK** Entertainer. (Mt. Vernon, NY) He started "Bandstand" in 1956 as a local TV show in Philadelphia. It later went national and became a number one program. He has hosted "Bloopers" and game shows such as "$10,000 Pyramid." He began his career as a radio DJ. Year/**Age**: 1995/**66** 1996/**67** 1997/**68**

• **RICHARD CRENNA** Actor. (Los Angeles, CA) Appeared on TV shows "Our Miss Brooks" & "The Real McCoys." Film *Hot Shots! Part Deux*. Year/**Age**: 1995/**69** 1996/**70** 1997/**71**

• **EFREM ZIMBALIST, JR.** Actor. (NYC) He appeared on the TV series "FBI" from 1965 to 1974 and played Stuart Bailey on "77 Sunset Strip" from 1958 to 1964. He's the son of a famous concert violinist and opera singer and the father of actress Stephanie Zimbalist. He may have been fighting for the truth in "The FBI," but he may be lying about his age. (He claims to be 72/73/74, but a picture has been found of Zimbalist being held by his parents as a baby in early 1919, meaning his birthday today makes him 76/77/78.) Year/**Age**: 1995/**72** 1996/**73** 1997/**74**

• **JUNE POINTER** Singer. (Oakland, CA) With THE POINTER SISTERS. Their biggest hit: "Fire" in 1978 and "The Slow Hand" in 1981. Year/**Age**: 1995/**41** 1996/**42** 1997/**43**

• **GEORGE McARDLE** Bass guitarist. (Australia) Of THE LITTLE RIVER BAND. Their biggest hit: "Reminiscing" in 1978. Year/**Age**: 1995/**41** 1996/**42** 1997/**43**

• **ROBERT GUILLAUME** Actor. (St. Louis, MO) Star of "Soap" and "Benson" TV series. Film *The Meteor Man*. Year/**Age**: 1995/**58** 1996/**59** 1997/**60**

• **DAVID MAMET** Playwright. (Chicago, IL) Won awards for *Glengarry Glen Ross*, *Edmond*, and *American Buffalo*. Year/**Age**: 1995/**48** 1996/**49** 1997/**50**

• **PAUL STOOKEY** Singer. (Baltimore, MD) Of PETER, PAUL & MARY. Their biggest hit: "Leaving on a Jet Plane" in 1969. His hit: "The Wedding Song" in 1971. Year/**Age**: 1995/**58** 1996/**59** 1997/**60**

• **THURMAN "TEDDY" WILBURN** C&W singer. (Hardy, MO) He and the late Virgil Doyle made up the WILBURN BROTHERS. They were members of the Grand Ole Opry and had their own TV show with Loretta Lynn. Year/**Age**: 1995/**64** 1996/**65** 1997/**66**

• **BO JACKSON** Pro baseball player. (Bessemer, AL) Also played pro football. Chicago White Sox and California Angels. Year/**Age**: 1995/**33** 1996/**34** 1997/**35**

• **G. GORDON LIDDY** Watergate. (NYC) A former FBI agent and lawyer; he was a "plumber" in the Watergate break-in, 1972. He served the most time for the crime, 52 months. He has since been lecturing and hosting a radio talk show in Washington, DC. Year/**Age**: 1995/**65** 1996/**66** 1997/**67**

• **VIRGINIA MAYO** Actress. (Born Virginia Jones in St. Louis, MO) She gave up her film career in 1967 but continued to act on stage in stock and dinner theaters. Year/**Age**: 1995/**75** 1996/**76** 1997/**77**

• **ABBIE HOFFMAN** Political activist. (Abbott Hoffman - 1936-1989 – Worcester, MA) One of the Chicago 7, a group of radicals who stood trial on charges of conspiring to disrupt the bloody 1968 Democratic National Convention in Chicago. The others were Thomas Hayden, Jerry Rubin, David Dellinger, Rennie Davis, Lee Weiner, and John Froines. Hoffman started the loosely organized Yippie movement, or Youth International Party, in 1968 to bring together radicals to protest the government and the Vietnam War. He wrote *Revolution for the Hell of It* and *Steal This Book*. He committed suicide with an overdose of drugs and alcohol. on 4-13-89.

• **SIR WINSTON CHURCHILL** (1874-1965 – Oxfordshire, England) He was the only man to be made an honorary U.S. citizen by an Act of Congress in 1963. During WWII he had a special vault at the Dunhill shop in London, where he kept his cigars. During the Blitz a German bomb landed on Dunhill's and blew the building to bits, but Winston's cigars survived the blast. He reportedly smoked more than 300,000 cigars in his lifetime. He flunked the sixth grade. (Died 1-24-65.)

• **MARK TWAIN** Author. (1835-1910 – Born Samuel Clemens in Florida, MO) He loved writing in bed, where he penned *Tom Sawyer* and *Huckleberry Finn*. In 1909 Twain said: "I came in with Halley's Comet, it's coming again next year, and I expect to go out with it." He died one day after the comet showed, on 4-21-10.

FACTS FROM THE PAST

1946 **DOC BLANCHARD** and **GLENN DAVIS** played their last game for Army, beating Navy 21-18. Davis averaged over 8 yards per carry and held a NCAA record with 59 touchdowns. The Army teams that Davis and Blanchard were on were undefeated.

1954 **ELIZABETH HODGES** of Sylacauga, AL, was taking a nap on her couch when she was hit on the arm by an **$8\frac{1}{2}$-LB. METEORITE** that crashed through her roof. She and her landlady argued over who owned it and went to court. Mrs. Hodges won and was offered hundreds of dollars for the rock, but decided to donate it to Alabama University.

1967 **DAVID EISENHOWER AND JULIE NIXON** announced their engagement.

1969 **SIMON AND GARFUNKEL**'s first TV special was broadcast. AT&T cancelled its sponsorship of the special because it included footage from Vietnam and Robert Kennedy's funeral.

1977 **DAVID BOWIE** sang a duet with Bing Crosby on his Christmas Special. The sang the "Little Drummer Boy."

1988 **KOHLBERG KRAVIS ROBERTS AND CO.** won the corporate takeover of **RJR NABISCO** with a $24.53 billion bid.

MTV Video Music Award Winners

1984 Video Music Awards
Video of the Year: Cars, "You Might Think"
Male: David Bowie, "China Girl"
Female: Cyndi Lauper, "Girls Just Want To Have Fun"
Group: ZZ Top, "Legs"
New Artist: Eurythmics, "Sweet Dreams"
Video Vanguard: The Beatles, David Bowie, Richard Lester
Viewer's Choice Award: Michael Jackson, "Thriller"

1985 Video Music Awards
Video of the Year: Don Henley, "Boys of Summer"
Male: Bruce Springsteen, "I'm On Fire"
Female: Tina Turner, "What's Love Got To Do With It"
Group: USA For Africa, "We Are The World"
New Artist: til' tuesday, "Voices Carry"
Video Vanguard: Lol Creme & Kevin Godley, David Byrne, Russell Mulcahy
Viewer's Choice Award: USA For Africa, "We Are The World"

1986 Video Music Awards
Video of the Year: Dire Straits, "Money For Nothing"
Male: Robert Palmer, "Addicted To Love"
Female: Whitney Houston, "How Will I Know"
Group: Dire Straits, "Money For Nothing"
New Artist: a-Ha, "Take On Me"
Video Vanguard Award: Madonna, Zbigniew Rybeznski
Viewer's Choice Award: a-Ha, "Take On Me"

1987 Video Music Awards
Video of the Year: Peter Gabriel, "Sledgehammer"
Male: Peter Gabriel, "Sledgehammer"
Female: Madonna, "Papa Don't Preach"

Group: Talking Heads, "Wild Wild Life"
New Artist: Crowded House, "Don't Dream It's Over"
Film Video: Talking Heads, "Wild Wild Life"
Video Vanguard Award: Peter Gabriel, Julien Temple
Viewer's Choice Award: U2, "With Or Without You"

1988 Video Music Awards
Video of the Year: INXS, "Need You Tonight/Mediate"
Male: Prince, "You Got The Look"
Female: Suzanne Vega, "Luka"
Group: INXS, "Need You Tonight/Mediate"
New Artist: Guns N' Roses, "Welcome To The Jungle"
Film Video: Los Lobos, "La Bamba"
Breakthrough Video: INXS, "Need You Tonight/Mediate"
Video Vanguard Award: Michael Jackson
Viewer's Choice Award: INXS, "Need You Tonight/Mediate"

1989 Video Music Awards
Video of the Year: Neil Young, "This Note's For You"
Male: Elvis Costello, "Veronica"
Female: Paula Abdul, "Straight Up"
Group: Living Colour, "Cult of Personality"
New Artist: Living Colour, "Cult of Personality"
Rap: DJ Jazzy Jeff & The Fresh Prince, "Parents Just Don't Understand"
Dance: Paula Abdul, "Straight Up"
Metal/Hard Rock: Guns N' Roses, "Sweet Child O' Mine"
Film Video: U2 with BB King, "When Love Comes To Town"
Breakthrough Video: Art of Noise featuring Tom Jones, "Kiss"

Video Vanguard Award: George Michael
Viewer's Choice Award: Madonna, "Like A Prayer"

1990 Video Music Awards
Video of the Year: Sinead O'Connor, "Nothing Compares 2 U"
Male: Don Henley, "The End of The Innocence"
Female: Sinead O'Connor, "Nothing Compares 2 U"
Group: B 52s, "Love Shack"
New Artist: Michael Penn, "No Myth"
Rap: M.C. Hammer, "U Can't Touch This"
Dance: M.C. Hammer, "U Can't Tough This"
Metal/Hard Rock: Aerosmith, "Janie's Got A Gun"
Film Video: Billy Idol, "Cradle of Love" From *Ford Fairlaine*
Breakthrough Video: Tears For Fears, "Sowing The Seeds Of Love"
Video Vanguard Award: Janet Jackson
Viewer's Choice Award: Aerosmith, "Janie's Got A Gun"

1991 Video Music Awards
Video of the Year: R.E.M., "Losing My Religion"
Male: Chris Isaak, "Wicked Game"
Female: Janet Jackson, "Love Will Never Do Without You"
Group: R.E.M., "Losing My Religion"
New Artist: Jesus Jones, "Right Here, Right Now"
Rap: LL Cool J., "Mama Said Knock You Out"
Dance: C&C Music Factory, "Gonna Make You Sweat (Everybody Dance Now)"
Metal/Hard Rock: Aerosmith, "The Other Side"
Alternative: Jane's Addiction, "Been Caught Stealing"
Film Video: Chris Isaak, "Wicked Game" From *Wild At Heart*
Breakthrough Video: R.E.M.,

"Losing My Religion"
Michael Jackson's Video Vanguard Award: Bon Jovi, Wayne Isham

1992 Video Music Awards
Video of the Year: Van Halen, "Right Now"
Male: Eric Clapton, "Tears In Heaven"
Female: Annie Lenox, "Why"
Group: U2, "Even Better Than The Real Thing"
New Artist: Nirvana, "Smells Like Teen Spirit"
Rap: Arrested Development, "Tennessee"
Dance: Prince & The New Power Generation, "Cream"
Metal/Hard Rock: Metallica, "Enter Sandman"
Alternative: Nirvana, "Smells Like Teen Spirit"
Film Video: Queen, "Bohemian Rhapsody" From *Wayne's World*
Breakthrough Video: Red Hot Chili Peppers, "Give It Away"
Michael Jackson's Video Vanguard Award: Guns N' Roses

1993 Video Music Awards
Video of the Year: Pearl Jam, "Jeremy"
Male: Lenny Kravitz, "Are You Gonna Go My Way"
Female: k.d. lang, "Constant Craving"
Group: Pearl Jam, "Jeremy"
New Artist: Stone Temple Pilots, "Plush"
Rap: Arrested Development, "People Everyday"
Dance: En Vogue, "Free Your Mind"
Metal/Hard Rock: Pearl Jam, "Jeremy"
Alternative: Nirvana, "In Bloom"
Film Video: Alice In Chains, "Would?" From *Singles*
Breakthrough Video: Los Lobos, "Kiko & The Lavender Moon"
Viewer's Choice: Aerosmith, "Livin' On The Edge"

DECEMBER MEMORIES

YEARS AGO

1985

POPULAR SONGS
"Broken Wings" by Mr. Mister

"Say You, Say Me" by Lionel Richie

MOVIES
Out of Africa
starring Meryl Streep as a Danish woman. Robert Redford plays a plantation owner.

White Nights
starring Mikhail Baryshnikov as a defected Russian ballet star who finds himself back in that country after a plane crash. Gregory Hines also plays a dancer.

TV SHOWS
"Teh Colbys"
a "Dynasty" spin-off starring Charlton Heston and Katherine Ross.

"Stir Crazy"
starring Larry Riley and Joe Guzaldo. Based on the movie of the same name.

BOOKS
Inside, Outside by Herman Wouk

1986

POPULAR SONGS
"The Next Time I Fall" by Peter Cetera and Amy Grant

"Walk Like An Egyptian" by Bangles

MOVIES
An American Tail
animated classic about Feivel the mouse.

The Mosquito Coast
starring Harrison Ford, Helen Mirren, and River Phoenix. A story of an inventor's life over in the jungle.

TV SHOWS
"L.A. Law"
starring Corbin Bersen, Susan Dey, Harry Hamlin, Jimmy Smits, Richard Dysart, Jill Eikenberry, and others. A dramatic series based on the life of L.A. attorneys.

"Head of the Class"
starring Howard Hessman as a teacher.

BOOKS
Yeager by Chuck Yaeger and Leo Janos

1987

POPULAR SONGS
"Heaven is a Place on Earth" by Belinda Carlisle (formerly of the Go-Gos)

"Faith" by George Michael

MOVIES
Harry and the Hendersons
starring John Lithgow and Melinda Dillon. A Seattle family adopts Bigfoot.

Raising Arizona
starring Nicholas Cage, Holly Hunter, Trey Wilson, and John Goodman in a comedy about stealing a baby.

TV SHOWS
"Wiseguy"
starring Ken Wahl in this drama as an under-cover agent for a crime bureau.

"Full House"
starring Bob Saget, John Stamos, and David Coulier. A comedy about the Tanner family.

BOOKS *Windmill of the Gods*
by Sidney Sheldon

SPECIAL DAYS

DECEMBER	1995	1996	1997
Full Moon	Dec. 7	Dec. 24	Dec. 14
Winter Begins	Dec. 22	Dec. 21	Dec. 21
1994 Dubious New Stories *(Maplewood, NJ)*	Dec. 29		
1995 Dubious New Stories *(Maplewood, NJ)*		Dec. 27	
1996 Dubious New Stories *(Maplewood, NJ)*			Dec. 26

YEARS AGO

1970

POPULAR SONGS

"I Think I Love You" by The Partridge Family

"My Sweet Lord" by George Harrison

MOVIES

Airport
starring Dean Martin, George Kennedy, and Burt Lancaster. A mad passenger carries a bomb aboard a plane.

Little Big Man
starring Dustin Hoffman as Jack Crabb, a 121-year old survivor of Custer's Last Stand.

TV SHOWS

"The Mary Tyler Moore Show"
Mary Richards (Tyler Moore) works for WJM-TV news in Minneapolis. Also stars Ed Asner, Ted Knight, and Valerie Harper.

"The Senator"
starring Hal Holbrook as Senator Stowe.

BOOKS

Up the Organization by Robert Townsend

1971

POPULAR SONGS

"Family Affair" by Sly & the Family Stone

"Day After Day" by Bad Finger

MOVIES

Nicholas and Alexandra
starring Laurence Olivier, Jack Hawkins, Michael Jayston and Janet Suzman. The story of the Royal Family 14 years before the Russian Revolution.

Bless the Beasts and Children
problem children try to free captive buffalo.

TV SHOWS

"Owen Marshall, Counselor At Law"
starring Arthur Hill as attorney Owen Marshall. Also stars Lee Majors and David Soul.

"The Partners"
Starring Don Adams and Rupert Crosse. A comedy about a pair of goofy detectives.

BOOKS

Honor Thy Father by Gay Talese

1972

POPULAR SONGS

"I Am Woman" by Helen Reddy

"Me and Mrs. Jones" by Billy Paul

MOVIES

Pete 'N' Tillie
starring Walter Matthau, Rene Auberjonois, and Geraldine Page. The story of a middle-aged couple with a dying son.

Man of La Mancha
starring Sophia Loren and Peter O'Toole. Musical version of the Don Quixote story.

TV SHOWS

"Bridget Loves Bernie"
starring David Birney and Meredith Baxter. A Jewish writer marries an Catholic teacher.

"The Bob Newhart Show"
starring Newhart as a psychologist in this sitcom. Co-stars Suzanne Pleshette, Marcia Wallace, Peter Bonerz, and Bill Daily.

BOOKS

The Living Bible by Kenneth Taylor

YEARS AGO

1945

POPULAR SONGS

"It's Been a Long, Long Time" by Kitty Kallen with Harry James Orch

"Chickery Chick" by Sammy Kaye

MOVIES

The Bells of St. Mary's
the sequel to *Going My Way* with Bing Crosby and Ingrid Bergman. This time the priest and Mother Superior talk a man into building a new parish.

Leave Her To Heaven
starring Jeanne Crain, Cornel Wilde, Vincent Price, and Gene Tierney. A neurotic woman goes to great lengths to keep her husband.

TV SHOWS

No regularly scheduled TV programming until May of 1946.

BOOKS

Stuart Little by E.B. White

1946

POPULAR SONGS

"The Old Lamp-Lighter" by Sammy Kaye

"(I Love You) For Sentimental Reasons" by Nat "King" Cole Trio

MOVIES

Its a Wonderful Life
staring James Stewart as George Bailey, a man in crisis during the Christmas season. Co-stars Donna Reed and Lionel Barrymore.

Road To Utopia
three people, Bob Hope, Dorothy Lamour, and Bing Crosby, search for gold in Alaska.

TV SHOWS

"Let's Rumba"
viewers are taught to do the "Ranchero" by host D'Avalos.

"Campus Hoopla"
Bob Stanton hosts this teen show with quizzes, songs, dances, and sports.

BOOKS

The Miracle of the Bells by Russell Janney

1947

POPULAR SONGS

"Ballerina" by Vaughn Monroe

"Here Comes Santa Claus (Down Santa Claus Lane)" by Gene Autry

MOVIES

The Egg and I
a comedy story about running a chicken farm with Fred MacMurray and Claudette Colbert. Co-star Ma & Pa Kettle.

Life With Father
starring William Powell as Father and Irene Dunne is his wife.

TV SHOWS

"Americana"
a quiz show on American history hosted by John Mason Brown.

"Charade Quiz"
charades are played with host Bill Slater.

BOOKS

The American Past by Roger Butterfield

DECEMBER 1
World AIDS Day

Poor outies!

BIRTHDAYS

• **CHARLENE TILTON** Actress. She played Lucy on the "Dallas" TV series. Year/**Age:** 1995/**37** 1996/**38** 1997/**39**

• **RICHARD PRYOR** Comedian. (Peoria, IL) Raised in his grandmother's house of prostitution, where his mother worked. He nearly died in 1980, freebasing cocaine. Films include: *See No Evil, Hear No Evil.* Year/**Age:** 1995/**55** 1996/**56** 1997/**57**

• **DAVID DOYLE** Actor. (Omaha, NE) Played Bosley on TV's "Charlies Angels." Year/**Age:** 1995/**70** 1996/**71** 1997/**72**

• **BETTE MIDLER** Actress/singer. (Patterson, NJ) Her mother named her after Bette Davis and pronounced it "Bet" because she thought that's the way Davis said it. She got her start on the soap opera "The Edge of Night." Biggest hits: "The Rose" from the film of the same name, in 1980, and her first #1 hit, "Wind Beneath My Wings" from the film *Beaches* in 1989, which won Grammy Awards for Best Song and Best Record of the Year. Films *For the Boys* in 1991 and *Hocus Pocus.* Year/**Age:** 1995/**50** 1996/**51** 1997/**52**

• **LEE TREVINO** Pro golfer. (Dallas, TX) He has won the U.S. Open and the British Open twice. Year/**Age:** 1995/**56** 1996/**57** 1997/**58**

• **LOU RAWLS** Singer. (Chicago, IL) Got his first break when he replaced Sam Cooke in the group SOUL STIRRERS. Biggest hit: "You'll Never Find Another Love Like Mine" in 1976. Year/**Age:** 1995/**60** 1996/**61** 1997/**62**

• **DIANNE LENNON** Singer. (Los Angeles, CA) One of the famous LENNON SISTERS who gained fame on the "Lawrence Welk Show." Their biggest hit: "Tonight You Belong to Me" in 1956. Year/**Age:** 1995/**56** 1996/**57** 1997/**58**

• **CAROL ALT** Model. (Queens, NY) Magazine cover girl. A photographer discovered her while she was waitressing at a Long Island restaurant. Year/**Age:** 1995/**35** 1996/**36** 1997/**37**

• **JOHN DENSMORE** Drummer. With the DOORS. Biggest hit: "Light My Fire" in 1967. Year/**Age:** 1995/**51** 1996/**52** 1997/**53**

• **GILBERT O'SULLIVAN** Singer. His biggest hit: "Alone Again, Naturally," in 1972. Year/**Age:** 1995/**49** 1996/**50** 1997/**51**

• **BILLY PAUL** Singer. (Born Paul Williams in Philadelphia, PA) Biggest record: "Me and Mrs. Jones." Year/**Age:** 1995/**61** 1996/**62** 1997/**63**

• **WOODY ALLEN** Actor/producer. (Born Allen Stewart Konigsberg in Brooklyn, NY) Started out as a nightclub comic, nominated for best actor in 1977 for *Annie Hall*, and he won an Oscar for best director of the same movie. Gained notoriety in 1992 for having an affair with his ex-companion, Mia Farrow's, adopted daughter. Nominated for original screenplay Oscar for *Husbands and Wives*. In film *Manhattan Murder Mystery*. Year/**Age:** 1995/**60** 1996/**61** 1997/**62**

• **DENNIS WILSON** Entertainer/drummer. (1941-1983 – Hawthorne, CA) With the BEACH BOYS. Biggest hit: "I Get Around" in 1964. He died in a drowning accident. on 12-28-83.

• **CYRIC RITCHARD** Actor. (1897-1977 – Australia) Won a Tony in 1954 as Captain Hook in Broadway's *Peter Pan*. (Died 12-18-77.)

• **WALTER ALSTON** Baseball manager. (1911-1984 – Butler City, OH) Led the Dodgers to 7 pennants and 4 World Series victories.

• **MARY MARTIN** Entertainer. (1913-1990 – Weatherford, TX) On Broadway she originated the role of Nurse Nellie Forbush in *South Pacific*. Played opposite Robert Preston in *I Do! I Do!* She was the young postulant nun, Maria, in *Sound of Music* and *Peter Pan* on Broadway and TV. Her son is actor Larry Hagman, "Dallas." (Died 11-3-90.)

FACTS FROM THE PAST

1917 The **BOYS TOWN ORPHANAGE** in Nebraska was opened by Father Flanagan. They now even admit girls. The Boys Town poster inspired the hit recording, "He Ain't Heavy, He's My Brother."

1921 The game of **BINGO MADE ITS DEBUT.** It is now over a $6-billion-a-year industry. 67% of the players are under 45 years of age.

1935 The world's largest seller of houses and hotels began business, but those buildings were on a **BOARD GAME** called **MONOPOLY.** The space on which a player has the greatest statistical chance of landing is Illinois Avenue, followed by B & O Railroad, Free Parking, Tennessee Avenue, New York Avenue and the Reading Railroad. The place names are in Atlantic City.

1937 Jolly Irene of the **RINGLING BROS. CIRCUS** fell out of bed. It took 5 policemen to get her back in. She weighed almost half a ton.

1955 African-American seamstress **ROSA PARKS** defied the law by refusing to give up her seat on a Montgomery, Alabama, city bus to a white man. Parks was arrested, causing a year-long boycott of the buses by African-Americans. Later, the law requiring African-Americans to sit in the **BACK OF THE BUS** was eliminated by the Supreme Court.

1957 The **"ED SULLIVAN SHOW"** featured three "new" acts. They were Buddy Holly, Sam Cooke and the Silhouettes.

1958 RCA Records signed **NEIL SEDAKA**.

1976 **SEX PISTOL, JOHNNY ROTTEN,** used profanity live on BBC-TV. The press branded the band "rotten punks," making them the symbol for "punk rock."

1982 **MICHAEL JACKSON'S** *Thriller* album was released, becoming the all-time best-selling album. The Epic album included hits "Billie Jean" and "The Girl is Mine," a duet with Paul McCartney. Actor Vincent Price is on the title track.

1988 Soviet President **MIKHAIL GORBACHEV** won nearly unanimous approval of a dynamic political structure from the Supreme Soviet.

1992 **AMY FISHER** was sentenced to five to fifteen years for shooting and seriously wounding Mary Jo Buttafuoco. Three TV movies about the case aired in January 1993.

Kudos for karrots

DECEMBER 2
Pan American Health Day

BIRTHDAYS

- **JULIE HARRIS** Actress. (Grosse Pointe, MI) She was nominated for best actress in 1952 for *Member of the Wedding.* Appeared on TV's "Secrets" and "Knots Landing." Film: *The Dark Half.* Year/**Age**: 1995/**70** 1996/**71** 1997/**72**

- **LEO GORDON** Tough-guy actor. Appeared in *The St. Valentine's Day Massacre* and *Beau Geste.* Year/**Age**: 1995/**73** 1996/**74** 1997/**75**

- **ROBERT PAIGE** Actor. (1910-1987, Born John Arthur Page) Former radio announcer who appeared in many films including: *Bye Bye Birdie, Hellzapoppin,* and *Son of Dracula.* (Died 12-21-87.)

- **RICK SAVAGE** Guitarist. (England) Bass player with DEF LEPPARD. Year/**Age**: 1995/**35** 1996/**36** 1997/**37**

- **JOHN WESLEY RYLES** C&W. (Bastrop, LA) His first hit was "Kay" in 1969. Year/**Age**: 1995/**45** 1996/**46** 1997/**47**

- **MILTON DeLUGG** Bandleader. Year/**Age**: 1995/**77** 1996/**78** 1997/**79**

- **K.D. LANG** Singer. (Born Kathryn Dawn Lang in Canada) LP "Ingenue." Year/**Age**:1995/**34** 1996/**35** 1997/**36**

- **MONICA SELES** Tennis player. (Serbia) Her career suffered a setback when she was stabbed at the "Citizen Cup" tournament in Hamburg, Germany, in 1993. She won 18 pro singles titles before she was 18. She became a US citizen in 1994. Year/**Age**: 1995/**22** 1996/**23** 1997/**24**

- **STONE PHILLIPS** TV journalist and newsmagazine anchor. Year/**Age**: 1995/**41** 1996/**42** 1997/**43**

- **RANDY GARDNER** Figure skater. (Marina del Rey, CA) Works with Tai Babylonia. Year/**Age**: 1995/**37** 1996/**38** 1997/**39**

- **ALEXANDER HAIG, JR.** General. (Balay-Cynwyd, PA) Vietnam general and former Secretary of State under President Reagan. He was one of the 1988 presidential hopefuls. Year/**Age**: 1995/**71** 1996/**72** 1997/**73**

- **ADOLPH GREEN** Playwright/composer. (NYC) In the Songwriters Hall of Fame and Tony winner for *Applause, Hallelujah,* and *On the Twentieth Century.* Wrote with Betty Comden. Year/**Age**: 1995/**80** 1996/**81** 1997/**82**

- **EZRA STONE** Actor/producer. (1917-1994, New Bedford, MA) Played Henry Aldrich on "The Aldrich Family" radio show. Know for his high-pitched voice responding "Coming Mother" to the command, "Hen-Ree!" (Died 3-3-94.)

- **MARIA CALLAS** Opera star. (1923-1977 – NYC) Died 9-16-77 in Paris, France.

- **SABU** Actor. (1924-1963 – Born Sabu Dastagir in India) A boyish Indian actor, in *The Elephant Boy.* (Died 12-2-63.)

- **CHARLES RINGLING** Circus entrepreneur. (1862-1926) Started his first circus in the 1880s. (Died 12-3-26.)

- **CHARLIE VENTURA** Tenor sax player from the big-band era. (1916-1992 – Philadelphia, PA) Played with Gene Krupa, Stan Kenton, Charlie Parker, and Count Basie. Later had his own band and played sax on several of Jackie Gleason's albums. (Died 1-17-92.)

FACTS FROM THE PAST

1804 **NAPOLEON BONAPARTE** formally became Emperor of France. Just as the Pope was about to place the crown on the emperor's head, Napoleon grabbed it and crowned himself. The "clunk" could be heard throughout the Cathedral of Notre Dame, and the crowd of onlookers laughed uneasily at Napoleon's impatience.

1823 In his annual message to Congress, President **JAMES MONROE** warned all European nations that America would tolerate no further colonization in the New World. His warning would become known as the Monroe Doctrine.

1859 **JOHN BROWN**, militant abolitionist, was hanged for his raid on Harper's Ferry the previous October.

1933 *Dancing Lady*, **FRED ASTAIRE**'s first film, was released. His dancing partner for this movie was Joan Crawford.

1942 **DR. ENRICO FERMI** and staff at the University of Chicago produced the first controlled atomic chain reaction, and their breakthrough led directly to the **ATOMIC BOMB**, 3 years later in 1945. This chain reaction took place under the football stands at the University of Chicago.

1949 Gene Autry's song, **"RUDOLPH, THE RED-NOSED REINDEER,"** hit the record charts. A Montgomery Ward ad man, Robert L. May, came up with a "Red-Nosed Reindeer" promotion in 1939, and they chose the name "Rudolph."

1954 The U.S. Senate voted to condemn **SEN. JOSEPH R. McCARTHY** (R/WI), for what it called "conduct that tends to bring the Senate into dishonor and disrepute."

1973 **The WHO** spent the night in a **MONTREAL JAIL** after causing $6,000 worth of damage to a hotel room. The experience inspired John Entwistle to write "Cell Block Number Seven."

1982 The first successful **ARTIFICIAL HEART IMPLANT OPERATION** was performed by a surgical team at the University of Utah Medical Center. The patient was 61-year-old retired dentist, Dr. Barney Clark, from Seattle. Dr. Clark lived 112 days. The heart was originally invented by ventriloquist Paul Winchell. (Clark died on 3-23-83.)

1991 **PAUL McCARTNEY'S** *The Liverpool Oratorio*, hit No. 1 on the *Billboard* classical charts. McCartney was commissioned by the Liverpool Royal Philharmonic to write the piece to celebrate the orchestra's 150th anniversary.

1991 American hostage **JOSEPH CICIPPIO** was released by Lebanese kidnappers after being held for over five years. The remaining U.S. hostages, **ALANN STEEN** and **TERRY ANDERSON** were released in the next couple days.

DECEMBER 3

Dare to deviate

BIRTHDAYS

- **BOBBY ALLISON** Racecar driver. (Hueytown, AL) He's in the International Motorsports Hall of Fame in Birmingham, AL. Year/**Age**: 1995/**58** 1996/**59** 1997/**60**

- **ANDY WILLIAMS** Singer. (Wall Lake, IA) His biggest hit: "Butterfly" in 1957. He was married to French actress/singer Claudine Longet from 1962-1970, and they have 3 children. Owns 17 gold records for "Moon River," "Born Free," and others. He now owns an $11 million Moon River Theatre complex in Branson, MO. Year/**Age**: 1995/**67** 1996/**68** 1997/**69**

- **ANNA CHLUMSKY** Actress. She portrayed "Vada Sultenfuss" oposite McCauley Culkin in the film *My Girl* in 1991. Year/**Age**: 1995/**15** 1996/**16** 1997/**17**

- **KATARINA WITT** Skater. (Germany) Two-time Olympic gold medalist. With Brian Boitano, their *Carmen on Ice* show received a 1990 TV Emmy. Year/**Age**: 1995/**30** 1996/**31** 1997/**32**

- **FERLIN HUSKY** C&W. (Flat River, MO) He also recorded under the name Simon Crum. His biggest hit: "Gone" in 1957; one of the great rock-a-billy songs of the 50's. He originally recorded the song in 1952 under the name Terry Preston. He's been married 6 times and has 7 children. Year/**Age**: 1995/**68** 1996/**69** 1997/**70**

- **RICK MEARS** Indy-winning racecar driver. (Wichita, KS) Won the Indy 500 four times. Survived a 213-mph crash while qualifying in 1992. A top moncy winner at over $4 million. Year/**Age**: 1995/**44** 1996/**45** 1997/**46**

- **JAYE P. MORGAN** Singer. (Born Mary Margaret Morgan in Mancos, CO) Her biggest record was "That's All I Want from You" in 1954. Year/**Age**: 1995/**64** 1996/**65** 1997/**66**

- **MICKEY THOMAS** Entertainer. JEFFERSON STARSHIP. Their biggest hit was "Miracles" in 1975. Year/**Age**: 1995/**47** 1996/**48** 1997/**49**

- **OZZY OSBOURNE** Rock guitarist. (Birmingham, England) He once worked in a slaughter house. Now a "heavy metal" hero. Year/**Age**: 1995/**47** 1996/**48** 1997/**49**

- **JEAN-LUC GODARD** Writer/director of the "New Wave." (France) Films include *Breathless* and *Hail Mary*. Year/**Age**: 1995/**65** 1996/**66** 1997/**67**

- **HARRY "SUITCASE" SIMPSON** Baseball. He got his nickname from packing and unpacking so much. In the '50s, he played for the Indians, Athletics, Yanks, Athletics again, White Sox, and Pirates. He hit the most triples in the American League in 1956 and 1957. Year/**Age**: 1995/**70** 1996/**71** 1997/**72**

- **CLEVELAND ABBE** Father of the U.S. Weather Bureau. (1838-1926 – NYC) He was the first Weather Bureau Meteorologist. He created daily weather bulletins and forecasts by telegraph in 1869.

- **GILBERT STUART** American portrait painter. (1755-1828 – North Kingstown, RI) His most famous painting was of George Washington. He also did portraits of Monroe, Jefferson and Madison. He sold his paintings for prices so low, he couldn't even buy a meal with the money. (Died 7-9-1828.)

FACTS FROM THE PAST

1639 The **FIRST ANNULMENT** by court decree was passed. James Luxford of Boston was found to have two wives and his second marriage was deemed void. James was sent back to England.

1922 The **FIRST** successful **TECHNICOLOR PICTURE** was *The Toll of the Sea*, shown at the Rialto Theater in NYC. You could see the green of the ocean and of the faces of people on board a ship.

1947 The **TENNESSEE WILLIAMS** play *A Streetcar Named Desire*, starring Jessica Tandy as Blanche Dubois and Marlon Brando as Stanley Kowalski, opened on Broadway.

1948 The **"PUMPKIN PAPERS"** came to light as the House Un-American Activities Committee announced that former communist spy Whittaker Chambers had produced microfilm of secret documents hidden inside a pumpkin on his Maryland farm.

1966 **LEW ALCINDOR** (later Kareen Abdul-Jabbar) made his college debut with UCLA. In this first game, he scored 56 points.

1967 **DR. CHRISTIAAN BARNARD**, a South African surgeon, performed the world's first successful heart transplant in Capetown, South Africa. The patient was Louis Washkansky. He lived 18 days with the new heart.

1976 Gunmen fired shots into the home of reggae entertainer **BOB MARLEY** in Kingston, Jamaica, hitting his wife Rita, his manager Don Taylor and a friend. None were seriously hurt. He performed at the "Smile Jamaica" festival two nights later.

1979 Eleven people died when thousands of rock **FANS JAMMED THE ENTRANCES** to get to open seating at Riverfront Colosseum in Cincinnati, Ohio, for the performance by the British group, **THE WHO**. This tragedy caused many concert promoters to have reserved seating only and most cities banned first-come, first-served seating.

1984 Dr. Ruth's book **FIRST LOVE! A YOUNG PEOPLE'S GUIDE TO SEXUAL INFORMATION** arrived in the nation's bookstores. It mistakenly advised readers that the safest time to have sex is during a woman's most fertile period.

1990 **IBEN BROWNING** caused a commotion by predicting that a **MAJOR QUAKE** would hit the New Madrid Fault on this day. He based his prediction on tidal forces. Many schools and businesses closed in the region for the day. Nothing happened.

1991 **JOHN SUNUNU** resigned as White House Chief of Staff. He said he had become "a political burden" on President Bush.

1991 Baseball star **BOBBY BONILLA** signed a five-year contract with the New York Mets for $29 million.

Horray for hulahoops

DECEMBER 4

BIRTHDAYS

- **BERNARD KING** Basketball star. (Brooklyn, NY) NBA Rookie Team 1977-1978. Played pro for Utah, New Jersey, New York, Golden State, and Washington. In the movie *Fast Break*. Also, TV's "Miami Vice" and "Ryan's Hope." Year/Age: 1995/**39** 1996/**40** 1997/**41**

- **FREDDY "BOOM BOOM" CANNON** Singer. (Born Fred Picariello – Lynn, MA) His biggest hit was "Palisades Park" in 1962, written by Chuck Barris of the "Gong Show." He got his nickname from the big bass drum sounds on his records. Year/Age: 1995/**55** 1996/**56** 1997/**57**

- **GARY ROSSINGTON** Guitarist. (Jacksonville, FL) Former guitarist with LYNYRD SKYNYRD. Biggest hit: "Sweet Home Alabama" in 1974. Year/**Age**: 1995/**44** 1996/**45** 1997/**46**

- **DEANNA DURBIN** Former movie star/singer. (Canada) She's been living in France for many years. She appeared on the "Eddie Cantor Radio Show" at age 13. Year/**Age**: 1995/**75** 1996/**76** 1997/**77**

- **JEFF BRIDGES** Actor. (Los Angeles, CA) Son of actor Lloyd Bridges and brother of Beau. His films include: *Fearless*, *Blown Away*, *The Last Picture Show* in 1971, and *Thunderbolt & Lightfoot* in 1974 for which he received an Oscar nomination for best supporting actor, and *American Heart*. Year/Age: 1995/**46** 1996/**47** 1997/**48**

- **WINK MARTINDALE** TV game-show host. (Born Winston Martindale in Jackson, TN) He had a hit record: "Deck of Cards" in 1959. He started out as DJ, later a game-show host of "Tic Tac Dough." Year/Age: 1995/**61** 1996/**62** 1997/**63**

- **PATRICIA WETTIG** Actress. "Nancy Weston" of "thirtysomething." Year/Age: 1995/**44** 1996/**45** 1997/**46**

- **MARISA TOMEI** Actress. (Brooklyn, NY) She was Lisa Bonet's roommmate on "A Different World." Won an Oscar for *My Cousin Vinny*. In films *Chaplin*, *Oscar, The Paper,* and *Untamed Heart*. Year/Age: 1995/**31** 1996/**32** 1997/**33**

- **MAX BAER, JR.** Actor. (Oakland, CA) He appeared on the "Beverly Hillbillies" TV series as Jethro and Jethrine Bodine. His dad was Max Baer, Sr., the famous boxer. Year/**Age**: 1995/**58** 1996/**59** 1997/**60**

- **CHRIS HILLMAN** Bass guitarist. (Los Angeles, CA) Biggest hit with the BYRDS: "Turn! Turn! Turn!" in 1965. Year/Age: 1995/**53** 1996/**54** 1997/**55**

- **HARVEY KUEHN** Baseball. (1930-1988 – Milwaukee, WI) Former baseball star with the Detroit Tigers and manager of the 1982 Milwaukee Brewers, American League Champions. That year, he was named American League "Manager of the Year."

- **VICTOR FRENCH** Actor. (1934-1989 - Santa Barbara, CA) Appeared as Isaiah Edwards on "Little House on the Prairie."

- **CHESTER GREENWOOD** Inventor. (1858-1937) At the age of 16, during a cold 1874 Massachusetts winter, he invented "Ear Muffs" and went on to become a millionaire.

- **LILLIAN RUSSELL** Actress. (1861-1922 – Born Helen Louise Leonard in Clinton, IA) She was an American singer/actress who gained fame in the comic opera *The Great Mogul* in 1881. She made only one movie: *Wildfire* in 1915. (Died 6-6-22.)

- **SAMUEL BUTLER** Author, painter, philosopher, composer. (1612-1680 – England) Liked to poke fun at people. He once said: "Cleanliness is almost next to godliness;" "Invention is the mother of necessity;" and "All animals, except man, know that the principal business of life is to enjoy it." (Died 9-25-1680.)

FACTS FROM THE PAST

1950 Polish track star Stella Walsh died, an innocent bystander, during an armed robbery. She won the 1932 Olympic gold medal in the 100-yard dash. After the autopsy the Cleveland, OH, coroner announced that "she" was a man.

1956 **ELVIS PRESLEY**, **CARL PERKINS**, **JOHNNY CASH** and **JERRY LEE LEWIS** made a series of impromptu recordings at Sun Records in Memphis. They were released 25 years later under the title **THE MILLION DOLLAR QUARTET.**

1958 A little Cessna 172 took off from Las Vegas, NV, and didn't land until 2-7-59, the **WORLD'S LONGEST AIRPLANE FLIGHT**. Bob Timm and John Cook, with continual mid-air refueling, stayed up for 64 days.

1960 **CAMELOT** opened on Broadway. The original stars were Julie Andrews, Richard Burton, Robert Goulet, and Roddy McDowell.

1965 **KEITH RICHARDS** was knocked unconscious when his guitar touched an ungrounded microphone during a ROLLING STONES concert in Sacramento, CA. He recovered and finished the show.

1965 The United States launched **GEMINI SEVEN** with air force Lieutenant Colonel Frank Borman and Navy Commander James A. Lovell aboard.

1978 **SAN FRANCISCO** got its **FIRST FEMALE MAYOR** as city supervisor Dianne Feinstein was named to replace the assassinated George Moscone (mahs-koh'-nee).

1984 A **HIJACK DRAMA** began as four armed men seized a Kuwaiti airliner en route to Pakistan and forced it to land in Tehran, where the hijackers killed American passenger **CHARLES HEGNA**.

1991 **TERRY ANDERSON**, the last American hostage, was released after 6$^1/_2$ years in captivity.

1991 The **JUDDS**, Naomi and Wynonna, gave their last concert. Naomi retired because of hepatitis. They recorded 4, million-seller albums and 11, No. 1 country hits since their first hit in 1984, "Mama He's Crazy."

1992 **PRESIDENT BUSH** ordered Marines and Army soldiers to Somalia to protect humanitarian relief convoys attempting to feed thousands of starving people.

DECEMBER 5

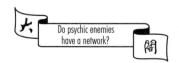

Do psychic enemies
have a network?

BIRTHDAYS

- **JIM MESSINA** Singer. (Maywood, CA) Of LOGGINS & MESSINA. Their biggest hit: "Your Mama Won't Dance" in 1973. At one time, Jim was a member of BUFFALO SPRINGFIELD and POCO. Year/**Age**: 1995/**48** 1996/**49** 1997/**50**

- **LITTLE RICHARD** Entertainer. (Born Richard Penniman in Macon, GA) Biggest hit: "Long Tall Sally" in 1956. Also recorded "Tutti Frutti" with the now-famous line "A wop bop a loo bop, a lop bam boom." He wrote a book about his life and is now an ordained minister. Year/**Age**: 1995/**63** 1996/**64** 1997/**65**

- **MORGAN BRITTANY** Actress. (Born Suzanne Cupito in Hollywood, CA) Appeared on "Dallas" and is married to stuntman Jack Gill. Year/**Age**: 1995/**45** 1996/**46** 1997/**47**

- **PABLO MORALES** Swimmer. (Santa Clara, CA) Gold medalist in the 1984 and 1992 Olympics. His victories in '92 came after he quit swimming when he failed to make the 1988 team. Year/**Age**: 1995/**31** 1996/**32** 1997/**33**

- **JIM PLUNKETT** Football. (San Jose, CA) Heisman Trophy winner from Stanford University. Played pro for the New England Patriots. Year/**Age**: 1995/**48** 1996/**49** 1997/**50**

- **LANNY WADKINS** Golfer. (Richmond, VA) He was the 1985 PGA Player of the Year. Year/**Age**: 1995/**45** 1996/**46** 1997/**47**

- **JOAN DIDION** Author. (Sacramento, CA) Wrote *Democracy* and *A Star is Born.* Year/**Age**: 1995/**61** 1996/**62** 1997/**63**

- **JOSE CARRERAS** Tenor. (Spain) He made his debut with the New York Met in 1974. Year/**Age**: 1995/**49** 1996/**50** 1997/**51**

- **CARRIE HAMILTON** Actress. (NYC) In the film *Tokyo Pop* and TV movie "Hostage" with her mother Carol Burnett, 1988. Year/**Age**: 1995/**32** 1996/**33** 1997/**34**

- **CALVIN TRILLIN** Author. (Kansas City, MO) *New Yorker* magazine. Books: *If You Can't Say Something Nice, Uncivil Liberties,* and *Remembering Denny.* Year/**Age**: 1995/**60** 1996/**61** 1997/**62**

- **PHILIP WRIGLEY** Gum mogul. (1894-1977 – Chicago, IL) Died in Elkhorn, WI (4-12-77).

- **MARTIN VAN BUREN** 8th U.S. President. (1782-1862 – Kinderhook, NY) He has the distinction of being the 1st U.S. President born a U.S. citizen. He was the last sitting vice president before George Bush to be elected President. (Died 7-24-1862.)

- **WALT DISNEY** Animator/special effects genius. (1901-1966 – Chicago, IL) Created Mickey Mouse in 1928 and won numerous Oscars for his films. Disney's first job was lettering theater slides that said "no smoking" or "coming soon to this theater." At 27, he created his first cartoon with sound, which was also the first Mickey Mouse cartoon in 1928. He was fired by a newspaper editor who said he had "no good ideas." (Died 12-15-66.)

- **GEORGE ARMSTRONG CUSTER** General. (1839-1876 – New Rumley, OH) The only thing that survived that last battle at "Custer's Last Stand" was a horse. The horse belonged to one of his officers, and it is stuffed and on display at Stanford University. Larry Verne made a record called "Mr. Custer," which was #1 in 1960. (Died 6-25-1876.)

FACTS FROM THE PAST

1791 Composer **WOLFGANG AMADEUS MOZART** died at age 35 under mysterious circumstances that would later be explored in the movie *Amadeus.* He had written symphonies and operas before he was 10 years old, but became a "has-been" in his twenties. When he died, no one bothered to record where he was buried.

1848 President **JAMES POLK** verified to Congress reports of gold discovered in California. The big **GOLD RUSH** began in 1849.

1893 The **FIRST ELECTRIC CAR** hit the streets, built by a Toronto firm. It could go fifteen miles between charges.

1917 This was the year they almost didn't have Christmas. The U.S. Council for National Defense, during WWI, proposed an **EMBARGO ON BUYING AND SELLING HOLIDAY GIFTS** to conserve the nation's resources. **A.C. GILBERT**, inventor of the Erector Set, was president of the Toy Association. He and a group went to Washington, confronted the Council, and brought toys with them. Mr. Gilbert told how important the toys were in modeling patriotic character in youth. Then he passed the toys around. From that moment on, according to the newspaper, the men of the U.S. Council for Defense were boys again. They said, "You're right, toys appeal to the hearts of everyone of us," and reversed their decision.

1929 The **FIRST NUDIST ORGANIZATION** in America was established: The American League for Physical Culture in New York City. It was organized by 3 men who soon decided it would be more educational if it were co-educational. At first they stayed indoors huddling around steam pipes in a Lexington Avenue basement. Then, the first nudist summer camp at Central Valley, NY, opened.

1955 The American Federation of Labor and the Congress of Industrial Organizations formed the **AFL/CIO. GEORGE MEANY**, a plumber, was elected the labor federation's first president.

1968 **GRAHAM NASH** quit THE HOLLIES because he disagreed with the group's plans to record an album of Bob Dylan songs.

1968 The release of "Beggar's Banquet" caused a feast of celebration. **THE ROLLING STONES** celebrated with a custard pie fight at London's Elizabethan Rooms Hotel.

1984 A federal grand jury in North Carolina indicted PTL founder **JIM BAKKER** and former aide Richard Dortch on fraud and conspiracy charges. (Bakker was convicted of all counts; Dortch pleaded guilty to four counts and cooperated with prosecutors in exchange for a lighter sentence.)

1992 **ICE CUBE**'s album made a debut at #1, making him the first hard-core rap artist to accomplish that feat.

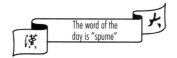

The word of the day is "spume"

DECEMBER 6

St. Nicholas Day

BIRTHDAYS

- **JONATHAN KING** Singer. (Born Kenneth King in England) 1966 hit: "Everyone's Gone to the Moon." He discovered and named "Genesis" and "10cc." Year/**Age**: 1995/**51** 1996/**52** 1997/**53**
- **PETER BUCK** Guitarist. (Athens, GA) Guitarist for R.E.M. Hit: "Stand" in 1989. Year/**Age**: 1995/**3** 1996/**40** 1997/**41**
- **DAVE BRUBECK** Jazz musician. (Concord, CA) Biggest hit: "Take Five" in 1961. Year/**Age**: 1995/**75** 1996/**76** 1997/**77**
- **LARRY BOWA** Baseball star. Former team captain of the Chicago Cubs. Year/**Age**: 1995/**49** 1996/**50** 1997/**51**
- **KIN SHRINER** Actor and comedian/talk show host **WIL SHRINER** [twins]. (Toledo, OH) Their dad was TV entertainer/comedian Herb Shriner. "Why Didn't I Think of That?" Year/**Age**: 1995/**42** 1996/**43** 1997/**44**
- **HELEN CORNELIUS** C&W singer. (Hannibal, MO) She won the "Ted Mack Amateur Hour" in her younger days. Biggest record with Jim Ed Brown: "I Don't Want to Have to Marry You" in 1976. Year/**Age**: 1995/**54** 1996/**55** 1997/**56**
- **JANINE TURNER** Actress. TV's "Northern Exposure." Year/**Age**: 1995/**33** 1996/**34** 1997/**35**.
- **LEN BARRY** Singer. (Born Leonard Borisoff in Philadelphia, PA) He was the lead singer for the DOVELLS. Len's biggest hit: "1-2-3" in 1965. The DOVELLS biggest hit: "Bristol Stomp" in 1961. Bristol is a town in Pennsylvania. Year/**Age**: 1995/**53** 1996/**54** 1997/**55**
- **THOMAS HULCE** Actor. (Whitewater, WI) Star of the film *Amadeus* as Mozart. Other films include *Frankenstein*, *Parenthood*, and HBO's *Eugene & Dominick*. Year/**Age**: 1995/**42** 1996/**43** 1997/**44**

- **STEVE WRIGHT** Comedian. (NYC) In *Desperately Seeking Susan*. Year/**Age**: 1995/**40** 1996/**41** 1997/**42**
- **EVE CURIE** Author. (France) Wrote the bestseller *Madame Curie*, about her mother. Year/**Age**: 1995/**91** 1996/**92** 1997/**93**
- **WALLY COX** Actor. (1924-1973 – Detroit, MI) Voice of cartoon character on TV's "Mr. Peepers" and appeared often on "Hollywood Squares." (Died 2-15-73.)
- **JOCKO CONLAN** Baseball umpire. (1899-1989 – Born John Bertrand Conlan in Chicago, IL) National League umpire for 24 years. He was the fifth umpire inducted into the Baseball Hall of Fame in 1974. (Died 4-16-89.)
- **AGNES MOOREHEAD** Actress. (1906-1974 – Reedsburg, WI) She appeared in many movies and played Endora, Samantha's (Elizabeth Montgomery) meddlesome mother, on the TV series "Bewitched."
- **LYNN FONTANNE** Actress. (1887-1983 – London, England) One of Broadway's premier actresses. Her husband was actor Alfred Lunt. Died at her home in Genesee Depot, WI. (Died 7-3-83.)
- **GEORGE "BABY FACE" NELSON** Criminal. (1908-1934 – Chicago, IL) Mickey Rooney played him in the 1957 film, *Baby Face Nelson*. He was a member of the Dillinger gang. (Died 11-27-34.)
- **IRA GERSHWIN** Lyricist/author. (1896-1983 – NYC) Pulitzer Prize winner who collaborated with his brother, George, and many other composers. For Broadway they wrote: *Lady Be Good*, *Funny Face* and *Strike Up the Band*. His songs included "I Got Rhythm," "The Man I Love," and many others. (Died 8-17-83.)

FACTS FROM THE PAST

342 A.D. The real **JOLLY OLD ST. NICHOLAS** died on this date. He became associated with gift-giving because he secretly provided dowries to poor brides-to-be. He also established the first known homes for the aged. *A Visit from St. Nicholas,* or *Twas the Night Before Christmas,* is the most famous Christmas poem, written by Dr. Clement Clarke Moore, a New York minister for his children in 1822. Today is **ST. NICHOLAS DAY** when the kids hang up their stockings.

1898 **FRANCES BIRD-LOUGHTON**, dressed in her brother's clothes, stuck false whiskers on her face and a pipe in her mouth and bluffed her way past the porters at the all-male Sparrow's Club in London, England. Then she locked herself in the "loo," staying there for the next 18 hours, pushing women's suffrage flyers under the door. Finally, four constables dismantled the restroom door and escorted Frances to the police station. Her husband was fined 25 pounds for her offense!

1923 A presidential address was broadcast on radio for the first time as **PRESIDENT CALVIN COOLIDGE** spoke to a joint session of Congress.

1941 President Franklin D. Roosevelt made a personal appeal for peace to Emperor Hirohito of Japan. **PEARL HARBOR** was attacked the next day.

1955 New York psychologist **DR. JOYCE BROTHERS** won the top prize on the TV quiz show, "The $64,000 Question," by correctly answering questions about boxing.

1969 A **ROLLING STONES** concert at Altamonte Speedway in Livermore, CA, was attended by 300,000 fans. "Honky Tonk Woman" was their #1 song at the time. Four people died, including Meredith Hunter who was stabbed to death by a Hell's Angel who was providing concert security.

1973 House Minority leader **GERALD R. FORD** was sworn in as U.S. Vice-President, succeeding Spiro T. Agnew, who resigned.

1984 **HIJACKERS** aboard a Kuwaiti jetliner on the ground in Tehran killed a second hostage, U.S. official William L. Stanford.

1992 **JERRY RICE**, San Francisco wide receiver, caught his 101st touchdown pass, wiping out the NFL record of 100 held by former Seattle star **STEVE LARGENT**. It took Rice 8 seasons and Largent 14.

DECEMBER 7

Square dancing, sport of the future

BIRTHDAYS

• **C. THOMAS HOWELL** Actor. Appeared in *Breaking the Rules, ET, The Outsiders,* and *Soul Man.* He was a cowboy star in the Junio Rodeo Association. Year/**Age**: 1995/**29** 1996/**30** 1997/**31**

• **LARRY BIRD** Basketball star. (French Lick, IN) Boston Celtics forward, retired in 1992. He was one of three players to win the NBA MVP award three years in a row, 1984-86. He scored over 20,000 points. He played with the US Dream Team on Aug. 8, 1992. Year/**Age**: 1995/**39** 1996/**40** 1997/**41**

• **ELLEN BURSTYN** Actress. (Born Edna Rae Gillooly in Detroit, MI) She won an Oscar in 1974 for *Alice Doesn't Live Here Anymore* as best actress. Other films include *Clamity Jane, The Exorcist* and *The Cemetery Club.* She appeared on the TV soap opera "The Doctors," using the name Ellen McRae. Year/**Age**: 1995/**63** 1996/**64** 1997/**65**

• **ELI WALLACH** Actor. (Brooklyn, NY) Appeared in *Magnificent Seven, How the West Was Won, Godfather III, Mistress,* etc. He's married to actress Anne Jackson. Year/**Age**: 1995/**80** 1996/**81** 1997/**82**

• **TOM WAITS** Singer/songwriter/self-styled derelict. (Pomona, CA) He was Frank Zappa's opening act in the 70's. In the films *Paradise Alley* and *Bram Stoker's Dracula.* Limo driver in the film *Short Cuts.* Year/**Age**: 1995/**46** 1996/**47** 1997/**48**

• **VICTOR KERMIT KIAM II** Author/businessman. (New Orleans, LA) Owns and sells Remington shavers. Year/**Age**: 1995/**69** 1996/**70** 1997/**71**

• **MARTHA COLLINS** Former Kentucky Governor. (Shelbyville, KY) Year/**Age**: 1995/**59** 1996/**60** 1997/**61**

• **JOHNNY BENCH** Baseball. (Oklahoma City, OK) Catcher for the Cincinnati Reds and is part Choctaw Indian. He was NL Rookie in 1968 and NL MVP in 1970. Year/**Age**: 1995/**48** 1996/**49** 1997/**50**

• **PRISCILLA BARNES** Actress. (Ft. Dix, NJ) Appeared in *License to Kill.* Year/**Age**: 1995/**40** 1996/**41** 1997/**42**

• **TED KNIGHT** Actor. (1923-1986 – Born Tadewurz Wladzui Knopka in Terryville, CT) He won a 1972-73 Emmy as best supporting actor on the "Mary Tyler Moore Show" as newscaster Ted Baxter. At the time of his death, he was in production on "Too Close for Comfort." (Died 8-26-86.)

• **ROD CAMERON** Actor. (1912-1982) Born in Canada, he appeared in *Northwest Mounted Police* in 1940, *Wake Island* in 1942, and others. He appeared on TV in "State Trooper" from 1956 to 1959. (Died 12-21-82.)

• **HARRY CHAPIN** Singer/songwriter. (1942-1981) Hits include: "Cat's in the Cradle," "Taxi," and a DJ favorite, "WOLD." He was killed in a traffic accident on the Long Island Expressway in New York on 7-16-81.

• **LOUIE PRIMA** Singer/bandleader. (1911-1978 – New Orleans, LA) Married to Keely Smith 1952-1961. Their biggest hit: "That Old Black Magic" in 1958. He was the voice of King Louis in the Disney film *Jungle Book.* (Died 8-24-78.)

FACTS FROM THE PAST

1784   **DAVID WILKINSON** of Rhode Island, patented the first screw.

1803   The Electoral College chose **JAMES MADISON** as the 4th U.S. President. He has the dubious distinction of being the shortest president in history.

1908   The **WATCH & WARD SOCIETY** of Boston successfully prosecuted a book salesman who had offered copies of Elinor Glyn's spicy book *Three Weeks.* This was the beginning of the phrase, "banned in Boston," which came to mean more to the impoverished author than the Pulitzer Prize, because it sold more books.

1941   American radar showed some 200 planes approaching **PEARL HARBOR**, Hawaii, but the radar was too unsophisticated to differentiate between friend and foe. Death toll was 2,400 lives lost, along with 6 major U.S. war planes. Oddly enough, on December 6th, Dorothy Edgers, a naval employee, had intercepted a Japanese message about the plan, but a supervisor at the Office of Naval Intelligence decided it could wait until Monday morning. Pearl Harbor was attacked on Sunday and on Monday, December 8th, America declared war on Japan. The photo of one ship, the USS *Shaw,* exploding is one of the most famous combat photographs of any war.

1963   Fifteen days after the assassination of President John F. Kennedy, his widow, Jacqueline, vacated the White House, and the Lyndon Johnson family moved in.

1964   **BRIAN WILSON**'s nervous breakdown midflight between LA and Houston eventually caused him to stop touring with the Beach Boys.

1968   **ERIC BURDON** announced that the **ANIMALS** would break up later in the month. This was the second version of the group. The first version split in 1966. Their hits were "Sky Pilot" and "San Franciscan Nights."

1972   America's last moon mission was launched when **APOLLO 17** blasted off from Cape Canaveral. Flight Commander Eugene Cernan was the last man on the moon.

1987   Soviet leader **MIKHAIL S. GORBACHEV** set foot on American soil for the first time, arriving for a Washington summit with President Ronald Reagan. They signed a treaty agreeing to eliminate medium-range nuclear missiles. Gorbachev also said he would reduce the number of Soviet military troops by half a million.

1988   **MIKHAIL GORBACHEV** addressed the United Nations and called for new world order. At the same time, a massive earthquake killed 25,000 people in Armenia.

Gift of the day: breath mints

DECEMBER 8

BIRTHDAYS

• **KIM BASINGER** Actress. (Athens, GA) Films include: *Batman, The Real McCoy, The Getaway, Wayne's World II, The Marrying Man, Final Analysis,* and partly animated *Cool World.* She married Alec Baldwin Aug. 19, 1993. She went into bankruptcy after court found her guilty of failing to keep a verbal contract. Year/Age: 1995/**42** 1996/**43** 1997/**44**

• **TERI HATCHER** Actress. (Sunnyvale, CA) Lois Lane on TV's "Lois and Clark: the New Adventures of Superman." In films *Soap Dish, Tango and Cash,* and *Straight Talk.* Year/Age: 1995/**31** 1996/**32** 1997/**33**.

• **GREGG ALLMAN** Entertainer. (Nashville, TN) His biggest hit: "Ramblin' Man" in 1973, with the ALLMAN BROTHERS BAND. In the film *Rush.* He was mariied to Cher for a short time. Year/Age: 1995/**48** 1996/**49** 1997/**50**

• **JERRY BUTLER** Singer. (Sunflower, MS) His biggest hit: "Only the Strong Survive" in 1969. Lead singer with IMPRESSIONS. Year/Age: 1995/**55** 1996/**56** 1997/**57**

• **FLIP WILSON** Entertainer. (Born Clerow Wilson in Jersey City, NJ) While in the U.S. Air Force, he entertained his fellow enlisted men with his audacious sense of humor and was so successful, he was sent on a tour to the Pacific to boost morale. He got his big break on the "Tonight Show." His most famous character is "Geraldine." Year/Age: 1995/**62** 1996/**63** 1997/**64**

• **JAMES MacARTHUR** Actor. (Los Angeles, CA) Best known as Dano in "Hawaii Five-O" TV series. Son of actress Helen Hayes. Year/Age: 1995/**58** 1996/**59** 1997/**60**

• **SINEAD O'CONNOR** Singer. "Nothing Compares to You." Year/Age: 1995/**28** 1996/**29** 1997/**30**

• **JOHN RUBINSTEIN** Actor/composer. (Beverly Hills, CA) He was the youngest child of pianist Arthur Rubinstein. His scored films include *The Candidate.* Won a Tony for *Children of a Lesser God* and in the film *Crazy Like a Fox.* Year/Age: 1995/**49** 1996/**50** 1997/**51**

• **MAXIMILIAN SCHELL** Actor/producer. (Vienna, Austria) In 1961, he won an Oscar for *Judgment at Nuremburg.* Appeared in *The Freshman.* Year/Age: 1995/**65** 1996/**66** 1997/**67**

• **JIM MORRISON** Singer. (1943-1971) Former lead singer of the DOORS. Their biggest hit: "Light My Fire" in 1967. Died (7-3-71) of a heart attack in the bath of his Paris home. There was no announcement of his death for 6 days. He was already buried. He quit music a few months earlier to become a poet. He is buried in a Paris cemetery with the epitaph "James Morrison, Poet."

• **WILLIAM CRAPO DURANT** Automobile executive.(1861-1947 – Boston) Co-founded Chevrolet, organized General Motors Corp., lost it, regained and again lost control. He started his own car company and went bankrupt in the De-pression. He ended up running a bowling alley. (Died 3-18-47.)

• **JAMES THURBER** Humorist/artist. (1894-1961 – Columbus, OH) *New Yorker* magazine. Wrote *The Secret Life of Walter Mitty.* His book *My World – and Welcome to It* was the basis of a 1969 TV show starring William Windom. (Died 11-2-61.)

• **SAMMY DAVIS, JR.** Entertainer. (1925-1990 – NYC) His biggest hit: "Candy Man" in 1972. He got his start in show biz dancing with his dad and uncle in the WILL MASTIN TRIO. Author of *Why Me?* (Died of cancer 5-16-90.)

FACTS FROM THE PAST

1776 **GENERAL GEORGE WASHINGTON** and his forces made their historic crossing of the Delaware River, near Trenton, NJ, and landed on Pennsylvania soil.

1886 The **AMERICAN FEDERATION OF LABOR** was founded in Columbus, OH. It was headed by Samuel Gompers.

1941 The U.S. entered World War II, 33 minutes after President Roosevelt asked a joint session of Congress for the declaration of war against Japan. Immediately, the **DEFENSE DEPARTMENT** ordered, among other things, 476,628 bazookas, 57,027 tanks, 4 billion rounds of .45-caliber ammunition, 23 million gas masks, 57 million wool undershirts, and 116 million pounds of peanut butter.

1961 The **BEACH BOYS** first single, "Surfin'" was released.

1963 **FRANK SINATRA, JR.** was kidnapped from Harrah's South Lodge in Lake Tahoe. The ransom was $240,000. The ransom money was "bugged" and two ex-classmates of his sister were arrested.

1968 **GRAHAM NASH** announced he would form a group with ex-Byrd David Crosby and ex-Buffalo Springfield member Stephen Stills.

1980 **JOHN LENNON**, 40, former Beatle, was shot to death in New York City as he and his wife, Yoko Ono, were entering the Dakota, their residence. A 25-year-old former mental patient and Beatles fan, **MARK DAVID CHAPMAN**, was arrested for the slaying. He is serving a 20-year sentence at Attica Prison. **HOWARD COSELL** made the announcement of the shooting during the broadcast of the "Monday Night Football" game on ABC-TV. Two people committed suicide after hearing of the death.

1982 **NORMAN MAYER WAS SHOT TO DEATH** by police after holding the Washington Monument hostage for 10 hours. He threatened to blow it up if the U.S. didn't stop building nuclear weapons. He claimed he had the explosives inside a van. There were none.

1984 A jury in Roanoke, VA, found *Hustler* magazine publisher **LARRY FLYNT** innocent of libeling the Reverend Jerry Falwell with a parody advertisement, but awarded Falwell $200,000 for emotional distress. (However, the award later was overturned by the U.S. Supreme Court.)

1984 Ex-**COASTERS MANAGER PATRICK CAVANAUGH** was found guilty of murdering group member Buster Wilson.

1992 **BARRY BONDS** signed a contract with the San Francisco Giants for $43.7 million over 6 years, the largest contract in baseball history.

DECEMBER 9

Play pog!

BIRTHDAYS

- **JACK HUES** Singer. With British group, Wang Chung. Biggest hit: "Everybody Have Fun Tonight," 1986. Year/**Age**: 1995/**41** 1996/**42** 1997/**43**

- **TOM KITE** Golfer. (Austin, TX) Ended the 1980's as the all-time leading money winner on tour with more than $5.6 million in career earnings. He is now at over $8 million. Year/**Age**: 1995/**46** 1996/**47** 1997/**48**

- **KIRK DOUGLAS** Actor. (Born Issur Danielovitch Demsky in New Amsterdam, NY) He received an Oscar nomination in 1949 for *Champion*, *The Bad & the Beautiful* in 1952, and *Lust for Life* in 1956. He is the father of Michael. He has appeared in over 75 films including *Tough Guys* and *Greedy*. Year/**Age**: 1995/**79** 1996/**80** 1997/**81**

- **BEAU BRIDGES** Actor. (Los Angeles, CA) The son of actor Lloyd Bridges and brother of actor Jeff Bridges. Appeared in the film *Married To It*, *Sidekicks*, TV's "Harts of the West" with his dad, and on HBO's "James Brady Story." Year/**Age**: 1995/**54** 1996/**55** 1997/**56**

- **DONNY OSMOND** Singer. (Ogden, UT) Biggest hits: "Go Away, Little Girl" in 1971 with sister, Marie, and "I'm Leaving it All Up to You" in 1974. With the OSMOND BROTHERS, "One Bad Apple" in 1971. Owns 23 gold records. Year/**Age**: 1995/**38** 1996/**39** 1997/**40**

- **DICK VAN PATTEN** Actor. (NYC) Early in his career he played Nels on TV's "I Remember Mama" and later was Tom Bradford on "Eight is Enough." Year/**Age**: 1995/**67** 1996/**68** 1997/**69**

- **DINA MERRILL** Actress. (Born Nedenia Hutton Rumbough in NYC) She is an heiress to the Post Cereal fortune. Wife of actor Cliff Robertson. Year/**Age**: 1995/**70** 1996/**71** 1997/**72**

- **DAVID HOUSTON** C&W. (1935-1993, Shreveport, LA) He's a descendant of Sam Houston and Robert E. Lee. Biggest hit: "Almost Persuaded" – #1 on the C&W chart for 9 weeks in 1966 and won a Grammy. (Died 11-30-93.)

- **JOHN MALKOVICH** Actor. (Christopher, IL) Oscar nomination for *Places in the Heart*. Also in *The Killing Fields*, *Of Mice and Men*, *Dangerous Liaisons*, and *In the Line of Fire* where he plays the assassin. Year/**Age**: 1995/**42** 1996/**43** 1997/**44**

- **SYLVIA** C&W. (Born Sylvia Allen in Kokomo, IN) Biggest hit: "Nobody" in 1982. Year/**Age**: 1995/**39** 1996/**40** 1997/**41**

- **MICHAEL NOURI** Actor. (Washington, DC) TV's "The Gangster Chronicles." Year/**Age**: 1995/**50** 1996/**51** 1997/**52**

- **JOAN ARMATRADING** Singer. Year/**Age**: 1995/**44** 1996/**45** 1997/**46**

- **DEACON JONES** Football. (Born David Jones in Eatonville, FL) Year/**Age**: 1995/**57** 1996/**58** 1997/**59**

- **DOUGLAS FAIRBANKS, JR.** Actor. (Born Douglas Elton Ulman, Jr., in NYC) His father was Douglas Fairbanks, Sr., and his stepmother was actress Mary Pickford. Year/**Age**: 1995/**86** 1996/**87** 1997/**88**

- **DICK BUTKUS** Former Chicago Bear. (Chicago, IL) He's now a TV commercial star, actor, and sports announcer. "First & Ten." Year/**Age**: 1995/**53** 1996/**54** 1997/**55**

- **REDD FOXX** Actor/comedian. (1923-1991 – Born John Elroy Sanford in St. Louis, MO) He starred in the TV series, "Sanford & Son" from 1972-1977. He died after suffering a heart attack on the set of his new TV show, "The Royal Family." (Died 10-11-91.)

- **JOHN CASSAVETES** Actor/producer. (1929-1989 – NYC) He has directed films and teamed up with Sidney Poitier for his finest performance, *Edge of the City*, in 1957. He also starred in *The Dirty Dozen* and *Rosemary's Baby*. (Died 2-3-89.)

- **BRODERICK CRAWFORD** Actor. (1911-1986 – Born William Pendergast in Philadelphia, PA) Won an Oscar in 1969 for *All the King's Men* and played Capt. Dan Matthews on TV's "Highway Patrol" from 1955-1959. (Died 4-26-86.)

FACTS FROM THE PAST

1843 Henry Cole procrastinated too long in sending the usual notes, so he hired an artist, engaged a printer and created the **FIRST CHRISTMAS CARDS.**

1951 **BOB WATERFIELD** of the **LOS ANGELES RAMS** became the first professional football player to kick five field goals in one game. He made 5 of 5, including one for 40 yards against the Detroit Lions.

1967 President Lyndon **JOHNSON'S DAUGHTER, LINDA**, married Charles Robb, in the first wedding at the White House since 1914.

1975 President Gerald Ford signed a $2.3 billion seasonal **LOAN AUTHORIZATION** that officials of New York City and State said would prevent a city default.

1978 John Belushi and Dan Aykroyd recorded "Soul Man" and released it under the title **THE BLUES BROTHERS.**

1979 **LARRY BIRD** and **MAGIC JOHNSON** first met as professionals at the Forum in Los Angeles. The Lakers won 123-105 with Magic's 23 points, 8 rebounds and 6 assists against Bird's 16-3-3.

1990 Political and labor union leader **LECH WALESA** won Poland's runoff presidential election,

1992 Former Playboy Club bunny, cop and prison fugitive, **LAWRENCIA "BAMBI" BEMBENEK** was freed in Milwaukee 11¹/₂ years after being arrested for murder.

1992 British Prime Minister **JOHN MAJOR** announced that the Prince and Princess of Wales officially separated.

1992 **RUSSIAN CONGRESS** rejected Boris Yelton's reform-minded nominee for prime minister.

1993 The CIA's head of Spy Operation, **CLAIR GEORGE**, was convicted of lying to Congress about the Iran-Contra affair. He was later pardonned by President Bush.

DECEMBER 10

BIRTHDAYS

- **TORIANO EASLEY** Number 1 hit: "I Like The Way (The Kissing Game)." Year/**Age**: 1995/**21** 1996/**22** 1997/**23**

- **RAVEN-SYMONE PEERMAN** Actress. Played Lisa Bonet's stepdaughter on "The Cosby Show." Year/**Age**: 1995/**10** 1996/**11** 1997/**12**

- **CHAD STUART** Singer. (England) 1964 hit with CHAD & JEREMY: "Yesterday's Gone." Year/**Age**: 1995/**52** 1996/**53** 1997/**54**

- **JOHN RODRIGUEZ** C&W. (Born Raul Davis Rodriguez – Sabinal, TX) Biggest hit: "Ridin' My Thumb to Mexico" in 1973. Year/**Age**: 1995/**44** 1996/**45** 1997/**46**

- **WALTER CLYDE ORANGE** Drummer. (Tuskegee, AL) Of the COMMODORES. Biggest hit: "Three Times a Lady" in 1978. Year/**Age**: 1995/**48** 1996/**49** 1997/**50**

- **SUSAN DEY** Actress. (Pekin, IL) Played Laurie on the "Partridge Family" in the '70s, "L.A. Law" in the '80s, and "Love and War" in 1992. Year/**Age**: 1995/**43** 1996/**44** 1997/**45**

- **GLORIA LORING** Actress/singer. (NYC) Starred in the soap opera "Days of Our Lives" and had a hit record with Carl Anderson called "Friends & Lovers." At one time, she was married to Alan Thicke. Year/**Age**: 1995/**49** 1996/**50** 1997/**51**

- **HAROLD GOULD** Actor. (Schenectady, NY) Father on TV's "Rhoda" and appears on "Golden Palace." Year/**Age**: 1995/**72** 1996/**73** 1997/**74**

- **MARK AGUIRRE** Basketball player. (Chicago, IL) DePaul University star, later NBA Dallas, then Detroit where he was a member of two straight championship teams. Year/**Age**: 1995/**35** 1996/**36** 1997/**37**

- **TOMMY RETTIG** Actor. (Jackson Heights, NY) He was the little boy, Jeff in "Lassie." Year/**Age**: 1995/**54** 1996/**55** 1997/**56**

- **JESSICA CLEAVES** Singer. (Los Angeles, CA) With the group FRIENDS OF DISTINCTION, biggest hit: "Grazing in the Grass" in 1969. Year/**Age**: 1995/**47** 1996/**48** 1997/**49**

- **KENNETH BRANAGH** Actor/director. Year/**Age**: 1995/**35** 1996/**36** 1997/**37**

- **DOROTHY LAMOUR** Actress. (Born Mary Leta Dorothy Stanton in New Orleans, LA) She was "Miss New Orleans of 1931" and starred in all the *Road* films with Bing Crosby and Bob Hope, including the first one, in 1940, *Road to Singapore*. Year/**Age**: 1995/**81** 1996/**82** 1997/**83**

- **DENNIS MORGAN** Actor/singer. (Born Stanley Morner in Prentice, WI) Some sources say he's really 84/85/86 today. He appeared in *The Great Ziegfeld*, *Two Guys from Milwaukee* with Jack Carson, *Desert Song*, *Kitty Foyle*, and *My Wild Irish Rose*. Year/**Age**: 1995/**84** 1996/**85** 1997/**86**

- **FIONNULA FLANAGAN** Actress. She appeared in *How the West was Won* and won an Emmy for her appearance in "Rich Man, Poor Man" in 1976. Year/**Age**: 1995/**54** 1996/**55** 1997/**56**

- **MELVIL DEWEY** (1851-1931 – Adams Center, NY) Invented the Dewey Decimal System used in libraries. (Died 12-26-31.)

- **CHET HUNTLEY** Newscaster. (1911-1974 – Cardwell, MT) He and David Brinkley anchored "NBC Nightly News" together for 15 years. (Died 3-2-74.)

- **EMILY DICKINSON** American poet. (1830-1886 – Amherst, MA) She wrote more than 1,500 poems, but only 3 were published before her death, not because of rejection, but because she was a recluse and mysterious. Her sister, Lavinia, found nearly 2,000 of Emily's poems written on scraps of paper, locked in a drawer. They were published beginning in 1890. After her death, she was recognized as one of the most original poets in the English language. (Died 5-15-1886.)

FACTS FROM THE PAST

1871 **WILD BILL HICKOK** lost his job as the marshal of Abilene, Kansas. He was fired for committing two honest mistakes: While investigating a shooting, he shot and killed an innocent bystander. Then when he heard someone come running up behind him, he turned and shot that man, too, discovering he had shot his own deputy. After being fired, Wild Bill joined Buffalo Bill's Wild West Show.

1896 Swedish chemist **ALFRED BERNHARD NOBEL** died. He invented dynamite (which he called safety powder). He never married, but had a platonic relationship with his secretary, Bertha. His will established the Nobel Prize. The **FIRST NOBEL PRIZE** was awarded in 1901, on the 5th anniversary of his death.

1906 **PRESIDENT THEODORE ROOSEVELT** was awarded the **NOBEL PEACE PRIZE** for helping to mediate the end of the Russo/Japanese War. He was the first American so honored.

1927 The WSM Barn Dance was renamed the **GRAND OLE OPRY.**

1950 Ralph C. Bunche was presented the **NOBEL PEACE PRIZE**, the **FIRST AFRICAN-AMERICAN** to receive this award.

1953 The first issue of **PLAYBOY** magazine went on sale. It featured the famous nude calendar shot of Marilyn Monroe. Publisher Hugh Hefner wasn't at all sure he'd ever print other issues, so it didn't even have an issue date!

1967 **OTIS REDDING AND THE BAR-KAYS** were killed when their plane crashed into Lake Monona in Madison, WI.

1971 **FRANK ZAPPA** broke his leg and ankle when a jealous fan pulled him into an orchestra pit, shouting, "I love Zappa."

1983 **DANUTA WALESA,** wife of the Polish labor leader Lech, accepted the Nobel Peace Prize on his behalf.

1983 **RAUL ALFONSIN** was inaugurated as Argentina's first civilian president after nearly eight years of military rule.

1992 Senator **BOB PACKWOOD** (R/OR) apologized for "plain wrong" sexual advances toward female employees, but refused to resign. He told the conference at the Capitol "I just didn't get it. I do now."

DECEMBER 11

Bring back boomerangs

BIRTHDAYS

- **SUSAN SEIDELMAN** Movie director. (Philadelphia, PA) *Desperately Seeking Susan* and *She-Devil*. Year/**Age**: 1995/**43** 1996/**44** 1997/**45**

- **NIKKI SIXX** Bass player. (Born Frank Ferranno in Los Angeles, CA) Member of MOTLEY CRUE. Year/**Age**: 1995/**37** 1996/**38** 1997/**39**

- **RITA MORENO** Entertainer. (Born Rosita Dolores Alverio in Puerto Rico.) She won an Oscar for best supporting actress in *West Side Story* in 1961. Appears on "The Electric Company." Emmy, Tony, and Grammy winner. Year/**Age**: 1995/**64** 1996/**65** 1997/**66**

- **DAVID GATES** Singer. (Tulsa, OK) Biggest hit: "Goodbye Girl" in 1978. He was the lead singer of the group BREAD, and their biggest hit was "Make It With You" in 1970. Year/**Age**: 1995/**55** 1996/**56** 1997/**57**

- **BRENDA LEE** Singer. (Born Brenda Mae Tarpley in Atlanta, GA) Biggest hit: "I'm Sorry" in 1960. Year/**Age**: 1995/**51** 1996/**52** 1997/**53**

- **JERMAINE JACKSON** Singer. (Gary, IN) His biggest hit was "Daddy's Home" in 1973. With the JACKSON FIVE, his biggest hit was "I'll Be There" in 1970. He married Berry Gordy's daughter, Hazel, in 1973. Year/**Age**: 1995/**41** 1996/**42** 1997/**43**

- **CARLO PONTI** Producer/director. (Italy) Married to actress Sophia Loren, and they have 2 sons. He is 21 years older then Sophia and 6 inches shorter. One of his most successful movies was *Marriage, Italian Style*, in 1965. Year/**Age**: 1995/**82** 1996/**83** 1997/**84**

- **TERI GARR** Actress. (Lakewood, OH) Appeared in *Tootsie* in 1982 and *Mr. Mom* in 1983. Year/**Age**: 1995/**46** 1996/**47** 1997/**48**

- **DONNA MILLS** Actress. (Chicago, IL) Appeared on "Knot's Landing" as Abby Ewing. Year/**Age**: 1995/**52** 1996/**53** 1997/**54**

- **ROBERT COCHRAN** Skier. (Claremont, NH) Year/**Age**: 1995/**44** 1996/**45** 1997/**46**

- **RON CAREY** Actor. (Newark, NJ) Year/**Age**: 1995/**60** 1996/**61** 1997/**62**

- **BESS ARMSTRONG**. Actress in *Four Seasons* with Alan Alda. Year/**Age**: 1995/**41** 1996/**42** 1997/**43**

- **GILBERT ROLAND** Actor. (1905-1994, Born Antonio Damasco in Mexico) At one time married to Constanse Bennett. He was in 11 Cisco Kid films. He made over 100 movies including the silent film Camille in 1936. (Died of prostate cancer 5-15-94.)

- **JEAN-LOUIS TRINTIGNANT** Actor. (France) Films include: *And God Created Woman* and *A Man and a Woman*. Year/**Age**: 1995/**65** 1996/**66** 1997/**67**

- **CHRISTINA ONASSIS** Greek shipping heiress. (1950-1988)

- **PEREZ PRADO** King of the Mambo. (1918-1983 – Matangas, Cuba) Biggest hits, "Patricia" and "Cherry Pink and Apple Blossom White." (Died 12-4-83.)

- **WILLIE MAE "Big Mama" THORNTON** Singer. (1926-1984 – Montgomery, AL) The blues singer was the first to record "Hound Dog," an R&B hit, later a pop hit for Elvis Presley. (Died 7-25-84.)

FACTS FROM THE PAST

1844 In Hartford, CT, **DR. HORACE WELLS** convinced Dr. John Riggs to pull Wells's tooth after administering nitrous oxide (**LAUGHING GAS**). The operation was a complete success, even though Wells' tooth was perfectly healthy and didn't need to be removed in the first place. It was the first demonstration of anesthesia in dentistry.

1892 The **FIRST PUBLIC GAME OF BASKETBALL** was played at the School for Christian Workers in Springfield, MA. The students beat the teachers 5-1. Each time a goal was scored, a ladder was used to retrieve the (soccer) ball from the closed-bottomed peach basket. (Specially designed laced basketballs appeared in 1894, but the basket bottoms weren't opened until 1906.)

1928 The police in Buenos Aires stopped an attempt on the life of President-Elect **HERBERT HOOVER**.

1936 Britain's **KING EDWARD VIII ABDICATED** to marry an American divorcee, Wallis Warfield Simpson. In a radio address, he said he found it impossible to carry out his duties as king "without the help and support of the woman I love." Edward became the Duke of Windsor. A TV movie in the 1970s told the story, starring Richard Chamberlain and Faye Dunaway.

1946 **JOHN D. ROCKEFELLER, JR.** offered to donate a 6-block plot of Manhattan real estate for headquarters of the United Nations.

1961 Two U.S. helicopter companies arrived in **SAIGON** on an aircraft carrier. This was the first direct U.S. military support for South Vietnam's battle against the VietCong. President John Kennedy signed the order.

1964 Singer **SAM COOKE** died. He was married to Barbara Campbell when he picked up a 22-year-old woman, Elisa Boyer, and took her to an L.A. motel. She claimed he forced her into the room and ripped off her clothes. She escaped while he was in the bathroom. Cooke ran after her and, thinking she hid in the motel manager's office, he broke down the door and assaulted the manager Bertha Franklin. Franklin then shot Cooke.

1983 **POPE JOHN PAUL II** made a historic visit to a Lutheran church in Rome, the first visit by a Roman Catholic pontiff to a Protestant church in his own diocese.

1991 **WILLIAM KENNEDY SMITH** was found not guilty by a jury in West Palm Beach, FL. In the most publicized rape case in U.S. history, Patricia Bowman accused Smith of raping her on the Kennedy estate lawn on March 30, 1991. **SENATOR TED KENNEDY** testified in court.

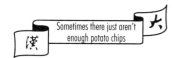

Sometimes there just aren't enough potato chips

DECEMBER 12

BIRTHDAYS

- **FRANK SINATRA** Entertainer. (Born Francis Albert Sinatra in Hoboken, NJ) He was the teenage rave in the 1940s. He received an Oscar for best supporting actor in *From Here to Eternity* in 1953 and starred in 51 films from 1941 to 1979. One of his biggest hits was with his daughter, Nancy, in 1967: "Somethin' Stupid." He has recorded over a hundred albums. Year/**Age**: 1995/**80** 1996/**81** 1997/**82**

- **TRACY AUSTIN** Tennis star. (Rolling Hills, CA) At age 17, she became the all-time youngest U.S. tennis champion. She was inducted into the Hall of fame with 23 pro singles titles under her belt before the age of 18. Year/**Age**: 1995/**33** 1996/**34** 1997/**35**

- **JOHN OSBORNE** Playwright. (England) He wrote the Oscar-winning screenplay for *Tom Jones*. Won a Tony for *Luther*. Year/**Age**: 1995/**66** 1996/**67** 1997/**68**

- **ED KOCH** Film critic. (New York) Ex-NYC Mayor. Year/**Age**: 1995/**71** 1996/**72** 1997/**73**

- **CONNIE FRANCIS** Singer. (Born Concetta Franconcero in Newark, NJ.) Biggest hit: "Everybody's Somebody's Fool" in 1960. In films: *Where the Boys Are* and *Follow the Boys*. She was raped in a hotel room November 8, 1974, and received $3 million in damages. Year/**Age**: 1995/**57** 1996/**58** 1997/**59**

- **CATHY RIGBY** Gymnast/actress. (Long Beach, CA) Year/**Age**: 1995/**43** 1996/**44** 1997/**45**

- **DICKY BETTS** Guitarist. (Macon, GA) With the ALLMAN BROTHERS BAND. He was the leader of the band after Duane Allman died in a cycle accident in 1971. Their biggest hit: "Ramblin' Man" in 1973. Year/**Age**: 1995/**52** 1996/**53** 1997/**54**

- **DIONNE WARWICK** Singer. (East Orange, NJ) She won Grammy Awards for Best Female Pop Vocalist with "Do You Know the Way to San Jose" in 1968, for "I'll Never Fall in Love Again" in 1970, and "I'll Never Love This Way Again" in 1979. She recorded a big hit with THE SPINNERS in 1974, "Then Came You." Year/**Age**: 1995/**54** 1996/**55** 1997/**56**

- **SHIRLEY ENGLEHORN** Former pro golfer. Year/**Age**: 1995/**55** 1996/**56** 1997/**57**

- **GROVER WASHINGTON, JR**. Singer. (Buffalo, NY) Biggest hit: "Just the Two of Us," with Bill Withers in 1981. Year/**Age**: 1995/**52** 1996/**53** 1997/**54**

- **MAYIM HOYA BIALIK** Actress. (San Diego, CA) TV's "Blossom." Year/**Age**: 1995/**20** 1996/**21** 1997/**22**

- **ANA ALICIA** Actress. On "Falcon Crest." Year/**Age**: 1995/**38** 1996/**39** 1997/**40**

- **BOB PETTIT** Basketball star. (Baton Rouge, LA) He was the first NBA player to score 20,000 points. He was the NBA scoring leader twice. Year/**Age**: 1995/**63** 1996/**64** 1997/**65**

- **JOE WILLIAMS** Singer. (Cordele, GA) Sang with the Count Basie Orchestra. Year/**Age**: 1995/**77** 1996/**78** 1997/**79**.

- **BOB BARKER** Game show host. (Darrington, WA) "The Price Is Right." He has devoted his life to saving wild animals. Year/**Age**: 1995/**72** 1996/**73** 1997/**74**

- **SHELIA E.** Instrumentalist/composer/singer. (Born Shelia Escovedo in San Francisco, CA) Biggest hit: "The Glamorous Life" in 1984. Year/**Age**: 1995/**36** 1996/**37** 1997/**38**

- **CURT JURGENS** Actor. (1915-1982 – Germany) Among his 150-plus films: *The Spy Who Loved Me* and *The Enemy Below*. (Died 6-18-82.)

FACTS FROM THE PAST

1792 In Vienna, Austria, **LUDWIG VON BEETHOVEN**, 22, paid 19 cents for his first music lesson from Franz Joseph Haydn. (Haydn said he showed a lot of promise!)

1851 U.S. Cabinet member **JOEL POINSETT** died. He was a member of Congress and Secretary of War from 1837-40. His name was given to the Christmas plant Poinsettia after he introduced the Central American flower.

1897 **"THE KATZENJAMMER KIDS"** first appeared in the *New York Journal*. The comic strip was created by cartoonist **RUDOLPH DIRKS**. It featured Hans and Fritz, who constantly annoyed *der Captain, der Inspector,* and *Momma.*

1899 The **WOODEN GOLF TEE** was patented by George Bryant of Boston. Before that, golfers mounded a pile of dirt (which they called a "tee") and placed the ball on top of it.

1901 The **FIRST RADIO SIGNAL** to cross the Atlantic was picked up near St. Johns, Newfoundland, by inventor **GUGLIELMO MARCONI**.

1946 A United Nations committee voted to accept a six-block tract of Manhattan offered as a gift by John D. Rockefeller, Jr., for the site of the **UNITED NATIONS HEADQUARTERS**.

1957 Rock singer **JERRY LEE LEWIS** secretly married his 13-year-old cousin, Myra. When it became public, Lewis was denounced by moralists across the U.S. and the scandal nearly ended his career.

1974 The **ROLLING STONES** announced that guitarist Mick Taylor was leaving the group. He was eventually replaced by Ron Wood.

1975 **SARA JANE MOORE** pleaded guilty to a charge of trying to kill President Ford in San Francisco the previous September.

1989 "Hotel Queen" **LEONA HELMSLEY** broke into tears in federal court after being sentenced to four years in prison for tax evasion. The 69/70/71-year-old owner of 26 hotels, convicted of **EVADING $1.2 MILLION IN TAXES**, remained free until 1992. She was released from prison 1-26-94.

1992 Miami quarterback **GINO TORRETTA** won the Heisman Trophy.

DECEMBER 13
2 Days to Mail Packages/1 Week for Cards

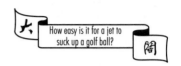

How easy is it for a jet to suck up a golf ball?

BIRTHDAYS

- **JOHN ANDERSON** C&W singer. (Apopka, FL) Won a gold record in 1983 for "Swingin'." Year/**Age**: 1995/**41** 1996/**42** 1997/**43**

- **JOHN DAVIDSON** Entertainer. (Pittsburgh, PA) In 1977, he narrowly escaped death when his musical director was killed, along with 163 others, in a fire at the Beverly Hills Supper Club in Kentucky. He bravely assisted with the rescues. Appeared in *Cosmo* Magazine in 1974 wearing only a towel. Year/**Age**: 1995/**54** 1996/**55** 1997/**56**

- **DICK VAN DYKE** Actor. (West Plains, MO) He won 3 successive Emmys for the "Dick Van Dyke Show" which was funded by Danny Thomas and produced by Carl Reiner. Mary Tyler Moore played his wife, Laura Petrie. Dick was also the chimney sweep in *Mary Poppins*. Year/**Age**: 1995/**70** 1996/**71** 1997/**72**

- **CHRISTOPHER PLUMMER** Actor. (Toronto, CA) Appeared in *Sound of Music* in 1966 and in *Waterloo* in 1970. Year/**Age**: 1995/**68** 1996/**69** 1997/**70**

- **RICHARD ZANUCK** Producer. (Los Angeles, CA) Produced *The Sting* and *Jaws* and won an Oscar for *Driving Miss Daisy*. He's the son of film exec./producer Darryl Zanuck.

- **FERGUSON JENKINS** Baseball Hall of Fame star. (Canada) The former Chicago Cubs star pitcher struck out 3,192 players. Year/**Age**: 1995/**52** 1996/**53** 1997/**54**

- **LEMAR PARRISH** Football. Year/**Age**: 1995/**48** 1996/**49** 1997/**50**

- **CHELSEA HERFORD** Actress. Casey Cooper on TV's "Major Dad." Year/**Age**: 1995/**14** 1996/**15** 1997/**16**

- **ARCHIE MOORE** Boxer. (Benoit, MS) He held the light heavyweight boxing championship until he was 48 years old. Year/**Age**: 1995/**79** 1996/**80** 1997/**81**

- **TED NUGENT** Singer. (Detroit) Heavy metal rock guitarist. He was the lead singer for the AMBOY DUKES and remembered as the lead vocalist on the classic rock song, "Journey to the Center of Your Mind." Ted had only one hit: "Cat Scratch Fever" in 1977. Year/**Age**: 1995/**47** 1996/**48** 1997/**49**

- **JEFF "SKUNK" BAXTER** Guitarist. Played with STEELY DAN. Their biggest hit: "Do it Again" in 1972. He also was with the DOOBIE BROTHERS, "What a Fool Believes." Year/**Age**: 1995/**47** 1996/**48** 1997/**49**

- **JOHNNY WHITAKER** Actor. He was Jody on "Family Affair," 1966 to 1971 and was also featured on several Walt Disney productions. Year/**Age**: 1995/**36** 1996/**37** 1997/**38**

- **RANDY OWEN** Singer. (Ft. Payne, AL) Vocals and guitarist for ALABAMA. Their biggest hit: "Love in the First Degree" in 1981. Year/**Age**: 1995/**46** 1996/**47** 1997/**48**

- **CARLOS MONTOYA** Guitarist/composer. (1903-1933 – Madrid, Spain) He transformed the flamenco guitar from Spanish folk music to a sound accepted internationally. Known for his "Flamenca" suite. (Died 3-3-93.)

- **VAN HEFLIN** Actor. (1910-1971 – Walters, OK) Won an Academy award for *Johnny Eager* in 1942. Also in *Shane* in 1953. (Died 7-23-71.)

- **ANISSA JONES** Actress. (1958-1976) Played Buffy on "Family Affair." Died of a cocaine overdose.

FACTS FROM THE PAST

304   **ST. LUCY DIED.** She devoted so much of her life to religion that she didn't have any time to devote to men. When she refused to marry a certain young nobleman, he kept trying to change her mind, explaining he was haunted by her beautiful eyes. Lucy responded by cutting out her eyes and sending them to the young man.

1809   Jane Todd Crawford became the **FIRST WOMAN** in history to have a **TUMOR SUCCESSFULLY REMOVED** from an ovary. **DR. EPHRAIM MCDOWELL** performed the surgery in Danville, Kentucky. No anesthesia was used.

1915   San Diego, CA, hired **RAINMAKER CHARLES HATFIELD** for $10,000 to bring rain to the city's half-empty reservoirs. He did his work so well that by the end of January, 44 inches of rain had fallen, causing major flooding. When he came down from the mountain to collect, they chased him out of town. His secret died with him.

1918   **WOODROW WILSON** became the first U.S. President to visit European countries while in office, arriving in Brest, France.

1928   **GEORGE GERSHWIN**'s *An American in Paris* made its debut at N.Y.'s Carnegie Hall.

1964   In a ceremony in El Paso, TX, President Lyndon B. Johnson and Mexican President Gustavo Diaz Ordaz set off an explosion that diverted the Rio Grande, reshaping the **U.S.-MEXICAN** border and ending a century-old dispute.

1974   **GEORGE HARRISON** became the first rock 'n' roll artist to be invited to the **WHITE HOUSE**. He had lunch with President Gerald Ford and was given a "WIN" button. ("WIN" meant "Whip inflation now!")

1978   The Philadelphia mint began stamping the **SUSAN B. ANTHONY** dollar, which went into circulation the following July. (And out of circulation very quicky because it was too easy to mistake for a quarter.)

1979   Spectators who gathered to watch the lighting of the **NATIONAL CHRISTMAS TREE** in Washington were surprised when only the star blazed to life; President Jimmy Carter explained the tree would remain dark until the American hostages in Iran were freed.

1983   **MARTHA LAYNE COLLINS** was inaugurated as Kentucky's first female governor, saying, "This first for Kentucky will be ever dedicated to putting Kentucky first."

1985   **PHIL COLLINS** entered the acting field as a sleazy TV game show host on an episode of "Miami Vice."

DECEMBER 14
Audubon X-Mas Bird Count Begins

BIRTHDAYS

- **GEORGE FURTH** Actor/director. (Chicago, IL) Film *The Good Guys*. Year/**Age**: 1995/**64** 1996/**65** 1997/**66**

- **PATTY DUKE** Actress. (Born Annamarie Duke in NYC) She won an Oscar for supporting actress in *The Miracle Worker* in 1962. She produced a movie based on her autobiography, *Call Me Anna*, which was shown on TV in 1990. When Patty was 12 years old she won $32,000 on TV's "$64,000 Challenge," but later admitted she was given the answers in advance. She played identical cousins on her TV series and was the youngest actress (16) to have a show named after her. She was married to John Astin. Year/**Age**: 1995/**49** 1996/**50** 1997/**51**

- **MICHAEL OVITZ** Businessman. Heads up the Disney Corporation. Year/**Age**: 1995/**49** 1996/**50** 1997/**51**.

- **CHARLIE RICH** Entertainer. (Forest City, AR) Affectionately known as the "Silver Fox," because he turned prematurely white. He took easily to drinking, but before his hit, "Behind Closed Doors," he checked himself into a sanitarium to dry out. Another of his many hits: "The Most Beautiful Girl" in 1973. Year/**Age**: 1995/**63** 1996/**64** 1997/**65**

- **MOREY AMSTERDAM** Actor/comedian. (Chicago, IL) He was the first host of the nightly "Broadway Open House" which was the forerunner of the "Tonight Show." Probably best known for the "Dick Van Dyke Show." Year/**Age**: 1995/**81** 1996/**82** 1997/**83**

- **ABBE LANE** Singer/actress. (Brooklyn, NY) At one time married to Xavier Cugat, and starred on his TV show in the 1950s. Year/**Age**: 1995/**63** 1996/**64** 1997/**65**

- **STAN SMITH** Tennis player. (Pasadena, CA) Year/**Age**: 1995/**49** 1996/**50** 1997/**51**

- **JOYCE VINCENT** Singer. (Detroit, MI) From the trio DAWN, which included Tony Orlando and Telma Hopkins. Biggest hit: "Tie a Yellow Ribbon Round the Ole Oak Tree." Year/**Age**: 1995/**49** 1996/**50** 1997/**51**

- **DON HEWITT** Producer. (NYC) Producer of "60 Minutes." He produced the first Kennedy-Nixon debate. Year/**Age**: 1995/**73** 1996/**74** 1997/**75**

- **ALAN KULWICKI** Racecar driver. (1954-1993 – Milwaukee, WI) He won the 1992 Winston Cup Championship in his Hooters Ford. Died in a plane crash on his way to defend his title in the NASCAR Food City 500 in Bristol, TN. (Died 4-1-93.)

- **DAN DAILEY** Actor. (1915-1978 – NYC) On Broadway in *Babes in Arms*. (Died 10-17-78.)

- **LEE REMICK** Actress. (1935-1991 – Born Ann Remick in Boston, MA) She received an Oscar nomination for best actress as an alcoholic in *Days of Wine & Roses* with Jack Lemmon in 1962. In her final public appearance on April 29, 1991, she received a star on the Hollywood Walk Of Fame. (Died 7-2-91.)

- **NOSTRADAMUS** "Profit." (1503-1566 – Born Michel de Nostredame in France) Best remembered for his astrological rhymes, which many believed predicted the future. He accurately prophesied the 1666 Great Fire of London, the Civil War in Spain and that Hitler would lead Germany into war. He predicted he would die on July 2, 1566, and he did!

FACTS FROM THE PAST

1799 First U.S. president **GEORGE WASHINGTON** died at Mt. Vernon, VA, at age 67, probably from a combination of pneumonia and ignorant medical attention. His doctors followed the accepted 1799 medical procedures and drained a significant quantity of blood from him, probably contributing to his rapid demise. He and Martha are buried on the grounds of Mt. Vernon.

1911 The **SOUTH POLE** was located and visited by **ROALD AMUNDSEN**, 4 companions and 52 sled dogs. They all returned safely to camp. Early in the next year, Captain Robert Scott and a party of 5 all perished during a return trip to the pole. Their frozen bodies were found 11 months later.

1953 The **BROOKLYN DODGERS** signed pitcher **SANDY KOUFAX**. At the time he had a very wild pitching style. At times, he even threw it over the backstop. He later developed into one of the best major league pitchers ever.

1961 **JIMMY DEAN**'s "Big Bad John" became the first country song to get an official gold record from the Recording Industry Association of America. The association has been certifying gold records since 1958.

1964 **MICHAEL BROWN** of the **LEFT BANKE** met Renee Fladen at a New York studio. She rejected him and in despair he wrote "Pretty Ballerina" and "Walk Away Renee."

1972 **ALICE COOPER** wanted to do some Christmas shopping without being bothered by fans, so Alexander's department store in New York City stayed open late. He wore his silver pants with a "Paul Lives" button.

1973 Italian police found **J. PAUL GETTY III**, grandson of the American oil tycoon, who had been kidnapped 5 months earlier. The kidnappers cut off part of his ear and sent it to the family to show they were holding him captive.

1979 Stuntman **STAN BARRETT** became the first person to break the sound barrier on land. He reached more than 739 miles per hour in a 60,000 horsepower rocket vehicle at Rogers Dry Lake, CA.

1984 **MADONNA** scored her first number-one hit, "Like A Virgin."

1986 The experimental aircraft **VOYAGER**, piloted by **DICK RUTAN** and **JEANA YEAGER**, took off from Edwards Air Force Base in California on the first non-stop, non-refueled flight around the world. The trip took nine days.

1992 President-elect **CLINTON**'s economic conference opened in Little Rock, AK. The two-day meeting was attended by 326 people from all walks of life.

DECEMBER 15

Spit for the health of it

BIRTHDAYS

- **CARMINE APPICE** Drummer. (NYC) Biggest hit with VANILLA FUDGE "You Keep Me Hangin' On" in 1968. Year/**Age**: 1995/**49** 1996/**50** 1997/**51**

- **DON JOHNSON** Actor. (Galena, MO) Star of "Miami Vice." He's had a hit album in video, "Heartbeat." Married to actress Melanie Griffith. Films include *Paradise*, a remake of *Born Yesterday*, and *Guilty As Sin*. Year/**Age**: 1995/**46** 1996/**47** 1997/**48**

- **ERNEST ASHWORTH** C&W. (Huntsville, AL) Biggest hit: "Talk Back Trembling Lips" in 1963. Year/**Age**: 1995/**67** 1996/**68** 1997/**69**

- **TIM CONWAY** Comedian. (Chagrin Falls, OH) His first TV break was on "McHale's Navy" in 1962. He won 3 Emmys for his appearance on "The Carol Burnett Show." Tim also stars in the very funny *Dorf* golf instruction videos. Year/**Age**: 1995/**62** 1996/**63** 1997/**64**

- **DAVE CLARK** Drummer. (England) Leader of the DAVE CLARK FIVE in the 1960s. Their biggest hit: "Over & Over" in 1965. He produced a big musical in London called *Time*, starring Cliff Richard. Host of 1990s "Ready Steady Go" reruns. He also pioneered the first music video. Year/**Age**: 1995/**53** 1996/**54** 1997/**55**

- **CINDY BIRDSONG** Singer. (Philadelphia, PA) She replaced Florence Ballard with the SUPREMES in 1967. Before that, Cindy had been with PATTI LABELLE & THE BLUEBELLES. Year/**Age**: 1995/**56** 1996/**57** 1997/**58**

- **PAUL SIMENON** Bass player. (England) With the group CLASH; their biggest hit "Rock the Casbah" in 1982. Year/**Age**: 1995/**40** 1996/**41** 1997/**42**

- **MAXWELL ANDERSON** Dramatist. (1888-1959 – Atlantic, PA) His plays include *Key Largo*. Won a Pulitzer for *Both Your Houses*. (Died 2-28-59.)

- **ALAN FREED** Disc jockey. (1922-1965) He was a DJ who coined the term "rock 'n roll" in 1950. Payola charges in 1960 caused his career to decline. He died broke. (Died 1-2-65.)

- **J. PAUL GETTY** Oil tycoon. (1892-1976 – Minneapolis, MN) One of the world's richest men. Joined his dad's oil company in 1914 vowing he'd make a million dollars in 2 years and he did. He later invested in barren land in Kuwait, pumping 16 million barrels of oil a year, within 4 years.

- **ALEXANDRE EIFFEL** Engineer. (1832-1923) He was the French engineer who designed the 1000-foot-high million-dollar steel Eiffel Tower and who helped in the design of the Statue of Liberty. The Eiffel Tower, weighing over 7000 tons, was built for the Paris International Exposition in 1889. The total cost of more than $1 million was recovered from .sightseers within one year! (Died 12-23-23)

- **JESSE BELVIN** Singer. (1932-1960 – San Antonio, TX) He had two hits in 1953: "Dream Girl" and "Goodnite My Love" with 11-year-old Barry White. He wrote "Earth Angel" for the PENGUINS in 1954. He and his wife were killed in an auto accident on 2-6-60.

FACTS FROM THE PAST

1874 The first Society for the **PREVENTION OF CRUELTY TO CHILDREN** was founded in NY. The Society for the Prevention of Cruelty to Animals received a severely abused child. They were then inundated with child abuse cases. **ELBRIDGE GERRY** then set up a society to deal with child abuse, but he was criticized for interfering.

1890 The legendary Sioux Indian leader, **SITTING BULL**, who was about 60 years old, was shot to death by federal troops, on a reservation in South Dakota. He had led the massacre of General Custer at Little Big Horn.

1938 Ground-breaking ceremonies for the **JEFFERSON MEMORIAL** took place in Washington, DC, presided over by President Franklin D. Roosevelt.

1939 The film of Margaret Mitchell's **GONE WITH THE WIND** starring Vivian Leigh and Clark Gable, premiered at Loew's Grand Theater in Atlanta, GA.

1944 Major **GLENN MILLER** disappeared on a flight over the English Channel. His famous Army Air Force band had been entertaining American troops in Europe, with such songs "In the Mood" and "Moonlight Serenade."

1961 Former Nazi official **ADOLF EICHMANN** was sentenced to death in Israel.

1965 Two **GEMINI SPACECRAFT** rendezvoused to within six feet of one another, proving that America could haul parts into orbit and assemble structures in space.

1968 **GRACE SLICK** and the JEFFERSON AIRPLANE appeared on the "Smothers Brothers Comedy Hour." Grace was in blackface and raised a black leather-gloved fist in a black power salute after singing "Crown of Creation." The incident was one of the reasons that the show was canceled in 1969.

1973 **JERMAINE JACKSON** said "I Do" to Hazel Gordy.

1986 The movie **RAISING THE TITANIC** cost $32 million to make. This budget was three times the cost of building the ship.

1988 **JAMES BROWN** was sentenced to six years in prison for failing to stop for police during a two-state car chase. He was released in 1990 on probation to perform community service.

1989 **PRESIDENT BUSH** sent U.S. troops into Panama to battle Panamanian forces supporting General **MANUEL NORIEGA**. Panama named Noriega head of government and declared a state of war with the United States.

DECEMBER 16

BIRTHDAYS

- **STEVEN BOCHCO** Writer/producer. (NYC) Created TV show "Hill St. Blues" and "NYPD Blue." Year/Age: 1995/**52** 1996/**53** 1997/**54**

- **BENNY ANDERSON** Keyboardist. (Stockholm, Sweden) Biggest hit with ABBA, "Dancing Queen." Year/Age: 1995/**49** 1996/**50** 1997/**51**

- **GEORGE SCHAEFFER** TV producer. Produced "Hallmark Hall of Fame," one of TV's best-known dramatic anthology series. Year/Age: 1995/**75** 1996/**76** 1997/**77**

- **BILLY RIPKEN** Second Baseman for the Texas Rangers. Year/Age: 1995/**31** 1996/**32** 1997/**33**.

- **LESLEY STAHL** CBS news correspondent. (Lynn, MA) On "Face the Nation." She joined TV's "60 Minurtes" in March of 1991. Year/Age: 1995/**54** 1996/**55** 1997/**56**

- **BEN CROSS** Actor. (Born Bernard Cross in England) Played runner Harold Abrahams in *Chariots of Fire*. On TV in "Dark Shadows." Year/Age: 1995/**48** 1996/**49** 1997/**50**

- **WILLIAM "REFRIGERATOR" PERRY** Football. (Aiken, SC) He played college ball at Clemson. The defensive tackle for the Chicago Bears in Super Bowl XX scored a TD on a one-yard dive. Year/Age: 1995/**33** 1996/**34** 1997/**35**

- **LIV ULMAN** Actress. (Tokyo, Japan) She received two Oscar nominations for best actress in *The Emigrants* in 1972 and *Face to Face* in 1976. Starred in *Scenes from a Marriage*. Year/Age: 1995/**56** 1996/**57** 1997/**58**

- **BILLY GIBBONS** Singer. (Houston, TX) Vocals/guitar for ZZ TOP. Their biggest hit: "Legs" in 1984. Year/Age: 1995/**45** 1996/**46** 1997/**47**

- **ALISON LaPLACA** Actress. "TV's "Duet." Year/Age: 1995/**36** 1996/**37** 1997/**38**

- **TONY HICKS** Guitar player. (England) With the HOLLIES. Biggest hit was "Long Cool Woman" in 1972. Year/Age: 1995/**50** 1996/**51** 1997/**52**

- **NOEL COWARD** Actor/composer. (1899-1973) His writing career started slowly. He built a reputation as an actor first. He wrote some of the wittiest songs and plays ever. He wrote 27 plays including *Blithe Spirit*. (Died 3-26-73.)

- **LUDWIG von BEETHOVEN** Composer. (1770-1827 – Bonn, Germany) His music teacher said, "As a composer, he is hopeless." He was totally deaf by age 30, but his impairment didn't halt his composing and conducting, even though he was unable to hear the orchestra or applause. When his deafness increased, he became a social outcast, refusing parties. He taught himself to hear through his teeth. He would bite on a long piece of wood and touch it to the piano so he could feel the vibrations. He always bathed in cold water before he composed because he said it helped him concentrate. Ludwig was often in love, but he never married. (Died 3-26-1827.)

- **MARGARET MEAD** American anthropologist/author. (1901-1978 – Philadelphia, PA) Known for studying primitive peoples of the southwest Pacific Ocean area. (Died 11-15-78.)

FACTS FROM THE PAST

1811 Before Charles Richter came along with his scale, **SEISMOLOGISTS** rated earthquakes on a 1 to 12 scale. The only 12 to ever hit America shook Missouri on this day in 1811.

1905 **VARIETY** magazine came out for the first time.

1951 The radio show "Dragnet" made its TV debut on NBC, starring **JACK WEBB** as Sergeant Joe Friday.

1960 **STEPHEN BALTZ**, 11, survived a **MID-AIR COLLISION OVER NYC**, between a United DC-8 and a TWA Super Constellation. He later died, bringing the total dead to 134 (6 died on the ground). Sir Edmund Hillary was to have flown in the jet, but missed the flight.

1966 **JIMI HENDRIX**'s first single, "Hey Joe," was released in the United Kingdom.

1968 **CREEDENCE CLEARWATER REVIVAL**'s debut album went **GOLD**.

1977 The film **SATURDAY NIGHT FEVER,** starring John Travolta, premiered, starting the disco craze. The movie and the soundtrack by the Bee Gees broke records and became huge money makers.

1979 Quarterback **ROGER STAUBACH** played in his last regular season game with the Dallas Cowboys. Trailing Washington 34-21 in the 4th quarter, Staubach drove the Cowboys to victory with under 5 minutes left in the game.

1985 **SYLVESTER STALLONE** married Brigitte Nielsen. At the time, they were working on the movie *Cobra*.

1986 **MIKHAIL GORBACHEV** released Andrei Sakharov, the father of the dissident movement and Nobel Peace Prize winner, from exile.

1987 **GARY HART** told the press "Let the people decide" as he got back into the presidential race following the Donna Rice incident.

1987 Businessman John Hudson, trying to recoup his losses on his unsold **OLIVER NORTH** dolls, put more stuffing in them, added a birthmark and sold them as **GORBACHEV DOLLS**.

1987 For the second time, **MADONNA FILED FOR DIVORCE** from Sean Penn. This time she followed through.

1989 A pipe bomb explosion killed Judge **ROBERT VANCE** of the U.S. Circuit Court of Appeals in Birmingham, AL. White supremacists were angry about recent court rulings.

1990 **JEAN-BERTRAND ARSTIDE** was elected president of Haiti. He was later overthrown in a military coup.

DECEMBER 17
Wright Brother's Day

Train to two-step

BIRTHDAYS

- **MIKE MILLS** Guitarist. (Athens, GA) With R.E.M. Biggest hit: "Losing My Religion" in 1991. Year/Age: 1995/**39** 1996/**40** 1997/**41**

- **TOMMY STEELE** Singer/actor. (London, England) He appeared in *The Happiest Millionaire, Finian's Rainbow*, and *Half a Sixpence*. Year/Age: 1995/**59** 1996/**60** 1997/**61**

- **ROBERT GUICCIONE** *Penthouse* publisher. (Born Robert Sabatini in Brooklyn, NY) Year/**Age**: 1995/**65** 1996/**66** 1997/**67**

- **EARNIE HUDSON** Actor. TV's "Broken Badges," "Highcliffe Manor," and "The Last Precinct." Year/Age: 1995/**50** 1996/**51** 1997/**52**

- **SARAH DALLIN** Singer. (England) With the group BANANARAMA. Their biggest hit: "Venus" in 1986. Year/Age: 1995/**34** 1996/**35** 1997/**36**

- **WANDA HUTCHINSON** Singer. Part of a sisters group the EMOTIONS from Chicago, IL. Biggest record: "Best of My Love" in 1977. Year/Age: 1995/**44** 1996/**45** 1997/**46**

- **MARILYN BECK** Hollywood columnist. (Chicago, IL) Wrote *Marilyn Beck's Hollywood*. Year/**Age**: 1995/**67** 1996/**68** 1997/**69**

- **WILLIAM SAFIRE** Journalist. (NYC) Pulitzer Prize winner with the *N.Y. Times*. Year/Age: 1995/**66** 1996/**67** 1997/**68**

- **GENE RAYBURN** Game-show host. (Christopher, IL) Announcer on "Steve Allen's Tonight Show," and game shows "Match Game," and "Tic Tac Dough." Year/Age: 1995/**78** 1996/**79** 1997/**80**

- **EUGENE LEVY** Actor/comedian. (Canada) "Look Who's Talking" and "Splash." Year/Age: 1995/**49** 1996/**50** 1997/**51**

- **ERSKINE CALDWELL** Author. (1903-1987) His depictions of rural poverty in *Tobacco Road* and *God's Little Acre* outraged many. (Died 4-11-87.)

- **EDDIE KENDRICKS** Singer. (1939-1992 – Union Springs, AL) With the TEMPTATIONS, he sang lead on "The Way You Do the Things You Do," "Just My Imagination," "Get Ready," and others from 1960-71. (Died 10-6-92.)

- **NAT STUCKEY** C&W songwriter. (1934-1988 – Cass County, TX) He wrote and recorded "Sweet Thang." He was a radio announcer in Shreveport, LA, when he wrote his first #1 hit, "Waiting in Your Welfare Line," recorded by Buck Owens and also wrote "Pop a Top" for Jim Ed Brown. (Died 8-24-88.)

- **PAUL BUTTERFIELD** Guitarist. (1942-1987 – Chicago, IL) He spearheaded a white "blues" revival in the U.S. in the 1960's, introducing a blues "rock" outfit in 1965, the all-electrified PAUL BUTTERFIELD BLUES BAND with Mike Bloomfield on guitar and Elvin Bishop on guitar. (Died 5-4-87.)

FACTS FROM THE PAST

1791 The **ONE-WAY STREET** came into being in traffic regulations established in New York City on this day.

1903 **WILBUR AND ORVILLE WRIGHT** flew their 12 h.p. airplane at Kitty Hawk, NC, on its first 12-second flight. Locals thought they were crazy and yelled "kill devil" and their dad said, "It's given only to God and angels to fly." Orville piloted while Wilbur ran alongside holding a wing tip to keep it steady. "Flyer One" is at the National Air and Space Museum, Washington, DC.

1933 In the **FIRST WORLD CHAMPIONSHIP FOOTBALL GAME,** the Chicago Bears defeated the New York Giants, 23 to 21. Bears quarterback Bronko Nagurski and his teammates each received $210.34. The Giants players got $140.22.

1955 **CARL PERKINS** couldn't sleep, so he got up and started to write a song on a paper bag. Sam Phillips changed a few lines and the song became the **FIRST, EVER, TO BE #1** in the **R&B, COUNTRY & TOP 40 FIELDS**: "Blue Suede Shoes."

1965 The Houston **ASTRODOME OPENED.** The headliners were the **SUPREMES** and **JUDY GARLAND.**

1969 An estimated 50 million TV viewers watched as singer **TINY TIM** married Miss Vicki during the "Tonight Show" on NBC-TV. She was 17 years old. They were divorced a few years later.

1975 **LYNETTE FROMME** was sentenced in federal court in Sacramento, CA, to life in prison for her attempt on the life of President Gerald R. Ford on September 5, 1975.

1977 Last minute replacement **ELVIS COSTELLO** fooled the producers of "Saturday Night Live." He promised not to play "Radio Radio" but reneged on his promise after the cast and crew taunted him.

1982 **KAREN CARPENTER** made her last public appearance, at Buckley School in Sherman Oaks. Her godchildren attended the school.

1986 The **SANDINISTA GOVERNMENT** pardoned American mercenary **EUGENE HASENFUS**, and he left the country after saying "A day that I will surely remember in my heart forever."

1986 **JOHN DELOREAN** was found "not guilty" of embezzling $8.5 million.

1986 A Las Vegas jury found that **NBC** had defamed **WAYNE NEWTON** by linking him to organized crime.

1987 **JIMMY "THE GREEK" SNYDER** was censured by CBS for commenting that "the black is a better athlete to begin with because he has been bred to be that way since the days of slavery and if more blacks become coaches, there's not going to be anything left for white people."

1989 **"THE SIMPSONS"** debuted on FOX Network.

1992 U.S., Canada, and Mexico sign the **NORTH AMERICAN FREE TRADE AGREEMENT** in separate ceremonies.

Music is needed on Mondays

DECEMBER 18

BIRTHDAYS

• **KIEFER SUTHERLAND** Actor. Son of Actor Donald. *Flatliners, Article 99, The Three Musketeers, The Cowboy Way, A Few Good Men*, and *The Vanishing*. Year/**Age:** 1995/**28** 1996/**29** 1997/**30**

• **BRYAN "CHAS" CHANDLER** Guitarist. (England) He played bass for the ANIMALS, then went on to manage JIMI HENDRIX. Animals' biggest hit: "House of the Rising Sun" in 1964. Year/**Age:** 1995/**56** 1996/**57** 1997/**58**

• **RAY LIOTTA** Actor. (Newark, NJ) TV's "Casablanca." Films include *Corrina, Corrina, No Escape,* and *Goodfellas.* Year/**Age:** 1994/**41** 1996/**42** 1997/**43**.

• **KEITH RICHARDS** Guitarist of the ROLLING STONES. (Kent, England) He plays lead guitar for the group. Their biggest hits were "Satisfaction" in 1965 and "Honky Tonk Women" in 1969. Keith's only single was "Run, Rudolph, Run," Chuck Berry's Christmas song, in 1982. Year/**Age:** 1995/**52** 1996/**53** 1997/**54**

• **BRAD PITT** Actor. (Missouri) Films: *A River Runs Through It, Kalifornia.* TV's "Glory Days," and "Legends of the Fall." Year/**Age:** 1995/**30** 1996/**31** 1997/**32**

• **OSSIE DAVIS** Actor. (Cogdell, GA) Appeared in films: *Joe Louis Story, No Way Out, The Scalphunters,* and *Malcolm X.* Year/**Age:** 1995/**78** 1996/**79** 1997/**80**

• **ELLIOT EASTON** Guitarist. (Boston, MA) With the group CARS. Their biggest hit: "Drive" in 1984. Year/**Age:** 1995/**42** 1996/**43** 1997/**44**

• **ANITA O'DAY** Singer. (Chicago, IL) She did "Opus One" with Gene Krupa's orchestra, and trumpet player Roy Eldridge did a duet with her called "Let Me Off Uptown." Year/**Age:** 1995/**75** 1996/**76** 1997/**77**

• **LEONARD MALTIN** Movie reviewer/author. (NYC) "Entertainment Tonight." Year/**Age:** 1995/**45** 1996/**46** 1997/**47**

• **STEVEN SPIELBERG** Film producer. (Cincinnati, OH) His name is now a household word, due to *Jaws, Close Encounters, Raiders of the Lost Ark, Schindler's List,* and *Jurassic Park.* Was married to actress Amy Irving; they have a son. Married actress Kate Capshaw (star of *The Black Tie Affair*) in 1991. Year/**Age:** 1995/**48** 1996/**49** 1997/**50**

• **CHARLES OAKLEY** Basketball. (Cleveland, OH) With the New York Knicks. Year/**Age:** 1995/**32** 1996/**33** 1997/**34**

• **JANIE FRICKIE** C&W singer. (South Whitney, IN) Biggest hit: "Your Heart's Not in It" in 1984. Year/**Age:** 1995/**48** 1996/**49** 1997/**50**

• **GEORGE STEVENS** Film director. (1904-1975 – Oakland, CA) Won an Oscar in 1951 for *A Place in the Sun* starring Elizabeth Taylor. Also directed *It's a Mad, Mad, Mad, Mad World* and *The Greatest Story Ever Told.* (Died 3-8-75.)

• **EDWIN HOWARD ARMSTRONG** Inventor. (1890-1954 – New York) He was the inventor of wide-band FM radio broadcasting. "FM" stands for frequency modulation.

• **BETTY GRABLE** Actress/singer. (1916-1973 – St. Louis, MO) She was married to actor Jackie Coogan from 1937-1940 and to bandleader Harry James from 1943-1965. She was probably the #1 pin-up girl of World War II and appeared in many films. (Died 7-3-73.)

• **TY COBB** Baseball great. (1886-1961 – Born Tyrus Raymond Cobb in Narrows, GA) Played over 3,000 baseball games. At the age of 40 he hit .357 with 22 stolen bases and 93 RBI. (Died 7-17-61.)

FACTS FROM THE PAST

1719 *Mother Goose's Melodies for Children,* the **FIRST MOTHER GOOSE ENGLISH LANGUAGE BOOK,** appeared in the U.S., published by Thomas Fleet of Boston. His mother-in-law had read stories to her grandchildren and Tom had them printed. The name for the books came from her married name, **ELIZABETH FOSTER GOOSE.**

1737 Famous violin-maker Antonio Stradivari died. There are several ways to determine if a violin is a genuine **STRADIVARIUS:** one is to drop it on a hard surface, like cement, and then listen carefully to the sound . . . another is to bite it. If it has a date on it after 1737, you should be suspicious.

1796 *The Monitor* became the **FIRST SUNDAY NEWSPAPER** to be published in North America, by **PHILLIP EDWARDS** of Baltimore.

1892 British scientist **SIR RICHARD OWEN** died. He created the word **DINOSAUR,** meaning "terrible reptile." Dinosaurs were dominant until about 65 million years ago when, mysteriously, they were all killed off within a short period of time.

1899 **GEORGE GRANT** patents the golf tee.

1918 **AL CAPONE** married Mae Coughlin. He was 19 and she 21. Being underage, he lied and said he was 20 years old.

1930 **ADOLPH RUPP** coached his first Kentucky Wildcat game, winning over Georgetown 67-19. His 41-year career record was 880-190 with four NCAA and one NIT championship.

1975 **ROD STEWART** quit the group **FACES** and started a solo career.

1982 Fullback **BO JACKSON** played in his first Bowl game (Tangerine), picking up 75 yards rushing and receiving, scoring twice. He was MVP in his Auburn team's win over Boston College 33-26.

1983 Mick Jaggar stood as best man when **KEITH RICHARDS** married model **PATTI HANSEN.**

1992 Former UNLV star coach **JERRY TARKANIAN** was fired after coaching only 20 regular season games for the San Antonio Spurs.

1992 **KIM YOUNG-SAM** was elected South Korea's first civilian president in three decades.

DECEMBER 19

Tuesdays are terrible!

BIRTHDAYS

• **ALYSSA MILANO** Actress. (Brooklyn, NY) She played Tony's daughter Samantha on "Who's The Boss." Film *Double Dragon.* Year/**Age:** 1995/**23** 1996/**24** 1997/**25**

• **JOHN McEUEN** Muscian. (Long Beach, CA) NITTY GRITTY DIRT BAND. Played the banjo and mandolin. Year/**Age:** 1995/**49** 1996/**50** 1997/**51**

• **CHARLIE RYAN** Singer. (Graceville, MN) Biggest hit: "Hot Rod Lincoln" in 1960. Year/**Age:** 1995/**80** 1996/**81** 1997/**82**

• **CICELY TYSON** Actress. (NYC) She received an Oscar nomination as best actress in *Sounder* in 1972. In 1974, she received "Actress of the Year" award for the TV special, "Autobiography of Miss Jane Pittman." Also in "The Marva Collins Story." She was married to jazz musician Miles Davis. Year/**Age:** 1995/**56** 1996/**57** 1997/**58**

• **ROBERT URICH** Actor. (Toronto, Canada) Played on the TV series "Vegas" as Dan Tanna, "Spencer for Hire," "Crossroads," and "It Had to be You." At one time, he was a TV account executive at WGN-TV in Chicago, IL. Burt Reynolds helped him get started. Year/**Age:** 1995/**49** 1996/**50** 1997/**51**

• **TIM REID** Actor. (Harvey, IL) Appeared on "WKRP in Cincinnati" and on "Frank's Place" on TV. He and Tom Dressen as "Salt & Pepper" started out in Chicago at Mr. Kelly's. Year/**Age:** 1995/**51** 1996/**52** 1997/**53**

• **ZAL YANOVSKY** Guitarist/singer. (NYC) From the LOVIN' SPOONFUL. Their biggest hit: "Summer in the City" in 1966. Year/**Age:** 1995/**51** 1996/**52** 1997/**53**

• **EDMUND PURDOM** Actor. (England) Appeared in the films *Titanic, Student Prince,* and *The Egyptian.* Year/**Age:** 1995/**71** 1996/**72** 1997/**73**

• **JENNIFER BEALS** Actress. (Chicago, IL) *Flashdance* in 1983. In TV film "Indecency" in 1992. Year/**Age:** 1995/**32** 1996/**33** 1997/**34**

• **KEVIN McHALE** Basketball. (Hibbing, MN) Boston Celtics. Was often seen on the TV sitcom "Cheers." Year/**Age:** 1995/**38** 1996/**39** 1997/**40**

• **REGGIE WHITE** Football. (Tennessee) Green Bay Packer's left defensive end. Signed a 4-year, $17-million contract in 1993. Year/**Age:** 1995/**33** 1996/**34** 1997/**35**

• **GORDON JACKSON** Author. (1923-1990 – Scotland) Emmy winner, playing Hudson the butler in PBS series "Upstairs, Downstairs."

• **MAURICE WHITE** Singer. (Chicago, IL) EARTH, WIND & FIRE singer. Biggest hit: "Shining Star" in 1975. Year/**Age:** 1995/**53** 1996/**54** 1997/**55**

• **AL KALINE** Baseball Hall of Famer. He was an outfielder with the Detroit Tigers and had a lifetime batting average of .297, over 3,000 hits and 399 home runs. Year/**Age:** 1995/**60** 1996/**61** 1997/**62**

• **"LITTLE" JIMMY DICKENS** C&W singer. (Bolt, WV) He's 4 feet, 1 inch tall and his biggest hit was "May the Bird of Paradise Fly Up Your Nose" in 1965. His nickname is "Tater." He's in the Country Music Hall of Fame. Year/**Age:** 1995/**69** 1996/**70** 1997/**71**

• **DAVID SUSSKIND** TV producer/talk show host. (1920-1987 – NYC) He was responsible for many of the top TV plays of the 1950's, including the "Kraft Television Theater." He won an Emmy in 1966 for producing "The Ages of Man" and in 1967 for outstanding dramatic program: *The Death of a Salesman.* (Died 2-22-87.)

FACTS FROM THE PAST

1686 Alexander Selkirk, a Scottish sailor, was rescued from an island where he was stranded for 52 months. His experience was the basis for Daniel DeFoe's novel, **ROBINSON CRUSOE.**

1732 Benjamin Franklin began publication of **POOR RICHARD'S ALMANAC** in Philadelphia, PA. Some of his famous sayings are still widely quoted: "Time is money" and "A penny saved is a penny earned." His pen name was Richard Saunders.

1950 **GEN. DWIGHT EISENHOWER** was named Commander of the NATO forces.

1955 **CARL PERKINS** recorded "Blue Suede Shoes," a song widely associated with Elvis though it was a bigger hit for Perkins.

1957 **MEREDITH WILLSON**'s *Music Man,* starring Robert Preston, opened on Broadway.

1958 The **FIRST KNOWN RADIO BROADCAST FROM OUTER SPACE** was transmitted when Pres. Eisenhower's recorded voice issued a Christmas greeting for the whole world from the Atlas satellite which was launched the previous day. The message said: "To all mankind, America's wish for Peace on Earth and Good Will to men everywhere."

1980 **DOLLY PARTON**'s first movie, *Nine to Five,* premiered. She won two Grammy Awards for the title song.

1985 Country singer **JOHNNY PAYCHECK** was accused of shooting a man in a bar-room brawl in Hillsboro, OH. He was released from jail in 1991.

1988 **JOHNNY CASH** and friend **WAYLON JENNINGS** met up in the recovery room. Both had undergone heart bypass surgery though 6 days apart.

1989 American troops prepared for "Operation Just Cause" in Panama with intent to oust General **MANUEL NORIEGA** after he declared war on the U.S.

1993 **DONALD TRUMP AND MARLA MAPLES** exchanged vows in a 15-minute ceremony at Trump's Plaza Hotel in NYC. Guest DJ Howard Stern said the marriage would last 4 or 5 months.

DECEMBER 20

BIRTHDAYS

- **MALA POWERS** Actress. She appeared on one of the few successful TV series based on a comic strip, *Hazel*, which came to TV in 1961. The cartoons, created by Ted Key, appeared in the *Saturday Evening Post* magazine. Year/**Age:** 1995/**64** 1996/**65** 1997/**66**

- **ANN RICHARDS** Actress/Poet. (Australia) Films include *Sorry, Wrong Number, An American Romance,* and *Love Letters.* Year./**Age:** 1995/**77** 1996/**78** 1997/**79**.

- **NADINE GORDIMER** Novelist. (Africa) Wrote *The Conservationist* in 1975. Year/**Age:** 1995/**72** 1996/**73** 1997/**74**

- **MAX LERNER** Journalist/author. (Russia) Columnist for *NY Post.* Wrote the book *Ted and the Kennedy Legion.* Year/**Age:** 1995/**93** 1996/**94** 1997/**95**

- **ANITA WARD** R&B singer. (Memphis, TN) Biggest hit: "Ring My Bell" in 1979. Year/**Age:** 1995/**40** 1996/**41** 1997/**42**

- **DAVID LEVINE** Author/artist. (Brooklyn, NY) Won awards for his books *Fables of Aesop* and *The Heart of Stone.* Year/**Age:** 1995/**69** 1996/**70** 1997/**71**

- **JENNY AGUTTER** Actress. (London, England) Won an Emmy Award for her role in *The Snow Goose* on the "Hallmark Hall of Fame." Year/**Age:** 1995/**43** 1996/**44** 1997/**45**

- **PETER CRISS** Musician. (NYC) Drummer for KISS. Biggest hit was "Beth" in 1976. Year/**Age:** 1995/**50** 1996/**51** 1997/**52**

- **GEORGE ROY HILL** Film director. (Minneapolis, MN) He was nominated for best director Oscar for *Butch Cassidy and the Sundance Kid* in 1969, and won the director Oscar for *The Sting* in 1973. Year/**Age:** 1995/**73** 1996/**74** 1997/**75**

- **LUKE HOBBS** Inventor. (Born 1896 – Carbon, WI) He developed the J-57 split-compressor turbojet aircraft engine; the first with 10,000 pounds of thrust.

- **DR. SAMUEL MUDD** Doctor. (1833-1883) Today is "Mudd Day" at his birthplace in Bryantown, MD. Sentenced to life imprisonment for giving medical aid to John Wilkes Booth, assassin of President Lincoln. He was pardoned after 4 years by President Andrew Johnson. His descendants are still trying to clear his name. (Died 1-1-1883.)

- **HARVEY FIRESTONE** American industrialist/businessman. (1868-1938 – Columbiana, OH) Founder of the Firestone Tire and Rubber Co. He was also the author of two books about rubber and a close friend of Henry Ford and Thomas Edison. (Died 2-7-38.)

- **IRENE DUNNE** Actress. (1904-1990 – Louisville, KY) She received 5 Oscar nominations for best actress, but never won. She starred in *Showboat* and *Cimarron* and appeared in many films including *I Remember Mama* and *Magnificent Obsession.* Cary Grant co-starred with Dunne in the comedies *The Awful Truth* and *My Favorite Wife.* (Died 9-4-90.)

FACTS FROM THE PAST

1606 Captain **CHRISTOPHER NEWPORT** commanded three ships sailing from England with over 100 people on board, heading for North America. They arrived the following May and set up the first permanent English settlement at Jamestown, VA.

1812 An Indian woman named **SACAGAWEA** died. As a young Shoshone Indian woman, with her two-month-old boy strapped to her back, she traveled with the **LEWIS & CLARK** Expedition, serving as an interpreter. It was said the expedition could not have succeeded without her aid.

1879 **INVENTOR THOMAS EDISON** demonstrated another one of his bright ideas . . . the **INCANDESCENT LAMP.**

1892 The **PNEUMATIC AUTOMOBILE TIRE** was invented by Alexander Brown and George F. Stillman of Syracuse, NY. Before the pneumatic, tires were made of metal, wood or solid rubber, and punctures and blowouts were unheard of, but the ride was rough.

1967 Singer **JIMMY RODGERS** was severely beaten in a roadside attack in Los Angeles. He underwent three brain operations and ended up with a steel plate in his skull. Rodgers is best known for the songs "Honeycomb" and "Kisses Sweeter Than Wine."

1975 Bernie Leadon of the **EAGLES** was replaced by Joe Walsh.

1981 *Dreamgirls* opened on Broadway. Michael Bennett had imposed a press blackout until the opening. The show was based on the story of **DIANA ROSS AND THE SUPREMES**. It ran for more than 1,500 performances and picked up six Tony Awards in 1982.

1985 **HOWARD COSELL** retired from television sports at the age of 68, after 20 years with ABC-TV.

1986 **TWO LAWSUITS** resulted from concerts on this day. A woman in St. Petersburg claimed her 15-year-old suffered hearing dysfunction and mental anguish after hearing **MOTLEY CRUE** and a 24-year-old woman said she suffered acoustic trauma following a **DAVID LEE ROTH** concert at the L.A. Forum.

1988 Lavon Muhammed, AKA **"BILLIE JEAN JACKSON,"** pleaded guilty of violating a restraining order to stay away from Michael Jackson's home. She falsely claimed to be Jackson's wife and the mother of his children.

1989 **MANUEL NORIEGA** found sanctuary in the Vatican Embassy in Panama City and later gave himself up to U.S. authorities and was flown to Miami, Florida, for trial.

1992 After not being able to see his family for over a year, **ORESTES LORENZO PEREZ**, in the cover of darkness, flew to Cuba. He landed on a road, barely missing a bus, truck, car, street light and rock, quickly picked up his wife and two sons and brought them to the U.S. where they were able to celebrate Christmas (it's outlawed in Cuba).

1993 Long time rocker, sometimes politician, **FRANK ZAPPA**, died on this date. Zappa's well known strangeness was surpassed only by the quality of the music he created.

DECEMBER 21
Humbug Day

Think thick thoughts
on Thursdays

BIRTHDAYS

- **FLORENCE GRIFFITH JOYNER** Runner. (Los Angeles, CA) Olympic gold medalist. Played Terry Halloway, a celebrity photographer on daytime soap "Santa Barbara." She replaced Arnold Schwarzenegger as head of the President's Council on Physical Fitness and Sports. Year/**Age**: 1995/**36** 1996/**37** 1997/**38**

- **JANE FONDA** Actress. (Born Jayne Seymour Fonda in NYC) Film *Cop Gives Waitress $2 Million Tip.* She won an Oscar for *Klute* in 1971, *Coming Home* in 1979, and Best Supporting Actress for *On Golden Pond.* Also famous for her exercise videos. Jane never knew that her mother committed suicide in an asylum until she read about it in a movie magazine. She was 12 years old when it happened and she was told that her mother died of a heart attack. Jane rejected the role Faye Dunaway played in *Bonnie & Clyde.* Married Ted Turner on her 54th birthday. Year/**Age**: 1995/**58** 1996/**59** 1997/**60**

- **CHRIS EVERT** Tennis star/sportscaster. (Ft. Lauderdale, FL) When she was 19 years old she won Wimbledon and was chosen Female Athlete of the Year. Year/**Age**: 1995/**41** 1996/**42** 1997/**43**

- **PHIL DONAHUE** TV host. (Cleveland, OH) He failed his first audition as a radio broadcaster because of what he calls his "nasal Midwest accent." He's married to actress Marlo Thomas and moved his show from Chicago to New York City, so he could spend more time with her. Year/**Age**: 1995/**60** 1996/**61** 1997/**62**

- **KHRYSTYNE HAJE** Actress. "Head of the Class." Year/**Age**: 1995/**27** 1996/**28** 1997/**29**

- **RAY HILDEBRAND** Singer. (Joshua, TX) Paul of PAUL AND PAULA duo. Biggest hit was "Hey, Paula" in 1963. Year/**Age**: 1995/**55** 1996/**56** 1997/**57**

- **CARL WILSON** Guitarist. (Hawthorne, CA) BEACH BOYS. He was only 14 years old when they started out. One of their biggest hits: "I Get Around" in 1964. Year/**Age**: 1995/**49** 1996/**50** 1997/**51**

- **ANDY VAN SLYKE** Baseball. (Utica, NY) Pittsburgh Pirate Centerfielder. Year/**Age**: 1995/**35** 1996/**36** 1997/**37**

- **BETTY WRIGHT** Singer. (Miami, FL) Biggest hit: "Clean-up Woman" in 1972. Year/**Age**: 1995/**51** 1996/**52** 1997/**53**

- **FREDDIE HART** C&W. (Born Fred Segest in Lochapoka, AL) "Easy Loving" in 1971 was CMA song of the year. Year/**Age**: 1995/**62** 1996/**63** 1997/**64**

- **ED NELSON** Actor. He played Senator Mark Denning on the soap "Capitol," and Dr. Michael Rossi on "Peyton Place" and "Return to Peyton Place." Year/**Age**: 1995/**67** 1996/**68** 1997/**69**

- **PAUL WINCHELL** Ventriloquist and co-inventor of the artificial heart. (NYC) Won "Major Bowes Radio Amateur Hour" at 13. Does Smurf voices. Year/**Age**: 1995/**73** 1996/**74** 1997/**75**

- **FRANK ZAPPA** Singer. (1940-1993 Baltimore, MD) Leader of the MOTHERS OF INVENTION. Hits "Don't Eat the Yellow Snow," "Valley Girl," and "Shake Your Booty" with daughter Moon Unit. Film *Head* in 1968. He fought to keep warnings off of record labels.

FACTS FROM THE PAST

1914 The **FIRST FEATURE-LENGTH SILENT FILM** comedy, *Tillie's Punctured Romance,* was released. It starred Marie Dressler, Mabel Normand, Charlie Chaplin, and Mack Swain.

1937 **WALT DISNEY**'s movie, *Snow White and the Seven Dwarfs,* opened in L.A. as the first feature-length animated cartoon in color.

1959 **TOM LANDRY** accepted the coaching job with the Dallas Cowboys. He led his team to 22 consecutive winning seasons in 29 years.

1968 **JANIS JOPLIN** made her first appearance after leaving "Big Brother and the Holding Company." She performed in Memphis on a bill with Booker-T-and-the-M-G's, Rufus and Carla Thomas and the Bar-Kays.

1968 **DAVID CROSBY, STEPHEN STILLS, AND GRAHAM NASH** premiered together in California. Nash had announced his departure from the HOLLIES earlier in the month. Crosby had been with the BYRDS and Stills with BUFFALO SPRINGFIELD. Neil Young, also from Buffalo Springfield, joined Crosby, Stills and Nash in 1969.

1968 **JAMES LOVELL, JR., FRANK BORMAN**, and **WILLIAMS ANDERS** lifted off in the Apollo 8 spacecraft from Cape Canaveral on man's first trip to the vicinity of the moon.

1969 **VINCE LOMBARDI** coached his last football game as his team, the Washington Redskins, lost to the Dallas Cowboys, 20-10.

1969 **DIANA ROSS AND THE SUPREMES** made their last appearance together. They sang "Someday We'll Be Together" on "The Ed Sullivan Show."

1970 **ELVIS PRESLEY** paid a visit to President Richard Nixon at the **WHITE HOUSE,** asking to be named "Federal-agent-at-large," helping to combat the drug problem.

1978 Police in Des Plaines, IL **ARRESTED JOHN GACY** and began unearthing the remains of 33 men and boys that Gacy was later convicted of mudering.

1980 **HEIRESS MARTHA "SUNNY" VON BULOW** sank into a second and irreversible coma at her mansion in Newport, RI. Her husband Claus was accused of causing the comas by injecting her with insulin. He was acquitted after two trials.

1984 **GEORGEANN WELLS**, 6'7", became the first woman to slam-dunk a basketball, in a game which her Virginia team dominated, beating the University of Charleston 110-82.

Fridays are for friends

DECEMBER 22
Astrological Sign of Capricorn

BIRTHDAYS

- **CLAUDIA ALTA "LADYBIRD" TAYLOR JOHNSON** (Karnack, TX) Widow of the 36th U.S. President Lyndon B. Johnson. When she was a little girl, her mother died and left her $67,000. She built up a great communication center in Austin, TX. Year/**Age:** 1995/**83** 1996/**84** 1997/**85**
- **MAURICE & ROBIN GIBB** Singers. (The BEE GEE twins – Born in Manchester, England) Their #1 hit: "Stayin' Alive" in 1978. The group's LP *Saturday Night Fever* was recorded in two weeks and sold over 27 million copies. Year/**Age:** 1995/**46** 1996/**47** 1997/**48**
- **LAURALEE BELL** Actress. Cricket Blair, the bosses daughter, on TV's "The Young and the Restless." Year/**Age:** 1995/**27** 1996/**28** 1997/**29**
- **STEVE CARLTON** Baseball Hall of Famer. (Miami, FL) He won 20 games 5 times and won the Cy Young award 4 times. His pitching helped the Philadelphia Phillies to a World Series victory over Kansas City in 1980, their first world championship in 97 years. Year/**Age:** 1995/**51** 1996/**52** 1997/**53**
- **DIANE SAWYER** TV journalist. (Glasgow, KY) First woman to co-host "60 Minutes" on CBS-TV Sunday nights. Was national "Junior Miss" in 1962, did some weather work on TV and was a press aide for President Nixon before the "CBS Morning News" in 1981, which she co-anchored with Charles Kuralt. Anchors on ABC's "Prime Time." Year/**Age:** 1995/**50** 1996/**51** 1997/**52**
- **HECTOR ELIZONDO** Actor. (NYC) In the film *American Gigolo* in 1980. Year/**Age:** 1995/**59** 1996/**60** 1997/**61**
- **MATTY ALOU** Baseball. Outfielder for the San Francisco Giants. Year/**Age:** 1995/**57** 1996/**58** 1997/**59**
- **JAN STEPHENSON** Golfer. (Australia) Year/**Age:** 1995/**44** 1996/**45** 1997/**46**

- **PAUL MARTIN** C&W lead singer. (Winchester, KY) Biggest hit was "Yet" with the group EXILE. Year/**Age:** 1995/**32** 1996/**33** 1997/**34**
- **BARBARA BILLINGSLEY** Actress. (Los Angeles, CA) Commercials for Phillips Milk of Magnesia. Beaver's mom in "Leave It To Beaver." Year/**Age:** 1995/**73** 1996/**74** 1997/**75**
- **BILLY BRUTON** Baseball. He hit the game-winning home run when the Braves first moved to Milwaukee from Boston in 1953. He led the league in stolen bases his first 3 years in the league and topped all batters in the 1958 World Series, going 7 for 17. He's been a Chrysler executive in Pontiac, MI. Year/**Age:** 1995/**66** 1996/**67** 1997/**68**
- **STEVE GARVEY** Former All-Star first baseman. (Tampa, FL) He was the National League MVP with the Dodgers in 1974. Year/**Age:** 1995/**47** 1996/**48** 1997/**49**
- **DAVID PEARSON** Auto racer. (Spartanburg, SC) Won the NASCAR three times and the Daytona once. Year/**Age:** 1995/**61** 1996/**62** 1997/**63**
- **DAME PEGGY ASHCROFT** Actress. (1907-1991– England) Won the Oscar for best supporting actress in 1984 for the film *A Passage to India.* (Died 6-14-91.)
- **GIACOMO PUCCINI** Composer. (1858-1924 – Born 12 miles northeast of the Leaning Tower of Pisa in Italy) The composer of *La Boheme* and *Madame Butterfly*. He hated music as a child and whenever he hit a wrong note his teacher would kick him in the shin-bone. For the rest of his life when he hit a wrong note his foot would jerk up in the air, a habit that was hard to kick. (Died 12-22-24.)
- **"HAWKSHAW" HAWKINS** C&W singer. (1921-1963 – Huntington, AL) He died in a plane crash with Patsy Cline and Cowboy Copas (on 3-5-63). He was married to Jean Shepard. Biggest hit: "Slow Poke" in 1951.

FACTS FROM THE PAST

1864 Union **GENERAL WILLIAM T. SHERMAN** sent a message to President Abraham Lincoln from Georgia saying: "I beg to present you, as a Christmas gift, the city of Savannah." The day before, Sherman captured the city, forcing Confederate General Hardee's troops to retreat.

1882 The **FIRST STRINGS OF CHRISTMAS TREE LIGHTS** were shown off by wealthy Easterners when Thomas Edison's invention to replace candles were first made available.

1943 President **FRANKLIN ROOSEVELT**, British Prime Minister **WINSTON CHURCHILL** and Chinese leader **CHIANG KAI-CHEK** agreed at a Cairo meeting on measures to **DEFEAT JAPAN** in World War II.

1944 **GENERAL ANTHONY McAULIFFE**, Commander of the 101st Airborne Division, replied to the German demand for his surrender at Bastogne with the celebrated speech: "Nuts!" It is the **SHORTEST ENTRY** in Bartlett's *Familiar Quotations.*

1963 An official 30-day mourning period ended for assassinated **PRESIDENT JOHN F. KENNEDY.**

1968 Commander **LLOYD BUCHER** and 81 crew members of the USS *Pueblo* were released by the North Koreans after almost a year of captivity.

1978 **KENNEY JONES** became **The WHO'S NEW DRUMMER**, replacing Keith Moon, who had died four months earlier.

1984 **BERNARD GOETZ** shot four teenagers in a New York subway, after one asked him for $5.00. He was convicted of illegal possession of a weapon and given 6 months in prison, a $5,000 fine, probation for 5 years, and ordered to perform 280 hours of community service at New York University Medical Center.

1987 Musician **NIKKI SIXX** of Motley Crue died of a heroin overdose.

1993 **MICHAEL JACKSON DENIED** allegations that he sexually molested a 13-year-old boy.

DECEMBER 23

Sit around on Saturdays

BIRTHDAYS

- **PAUL HORNUNG** Football. (Louisville, KY) Former Notre Dame All-American and Green Bay Packer star, known as the Golden Boy. A TV sports announcer. Year/Age: 1995/**60** 1996/**61** 1997/**62**
- **COREY HAIM** Actor. (Toronto, CA) In films *Murphy's Romance* and *Dream a Little Dream.* Year/Age: 1995/**24** 1996/**25** 1997/**26**
- **JERRY KOOSMAN** Major league pitcher. (Appleton, MN) He and 4 other NY Met starters in 1969 did not give up a home run for a period of more than one month. Year/Age: 1995/**52** 1996/**53** 1997/**54**
- **JOSÉ GRECO** Flamenco dancer. (Italy) Year/Age: 1995/**77** 1996/**78** 1997/**79**
- **RUTH ROMAN** Actress. (Boston, MA) Leading lady of the 1950s, she appeared in many movies and on the TV series "The Long, Hot Summer" in 1964. Often seen on "Murder She Wrote." Year/Age: 1995/**72** 1996/**73** 1997/**74**
- **HARRY SHEARER** Actor. Saturday Night Live. Year/Age: 1995/**52** 1996/**53** 1997/**54**
- **SLASH** (Saul Hudson, Los Angeles, CA) Guitarist with Gun's-n-Roses. Hit "Sweet Child O' Mine." in 1988.
- **HARRY GUARDINO** Actor. (NYC) He was in *King of Kings, Dirty Harry*, and a couple of TV series. Year/Age: 1995/**70** 1996/**71** 1997/**72**
- **JAMES GREGORY** Actor. (NYC) Appeared in *The Manchurian Candidate, The Silencers* and *P.T. 109.* Inspector Luger on the "Barney Miller" TV sitcom. Year/Age: 1995/**84** 1996/**85** 1997/**86**
- **ROBERT BLY** Author. (Madison, MN) National Book Award winner for *The Light Around the Body.* Year/Age: 1995/**69** 1996/**70** 1997/**71**
- **JIM HARBAUGH** Football. (Toledo, OH) Former Chicago Bears quarterback. Year/Age: 1995/**32** 1996/**33** 1997/**34**

- **SUSAN LUCCI** Actress. (Westchester, NY) In the soap opera "All My Children." She came up a loser at the Daytime Emmy Awards a record 13 times. Year/Age: 1995/**46** 1996/**47** 1997/**48**
- **GERALD O'LAUGHLIN** Actor. (NYC) *Our House.* Year/Age: 1995/**74** 1996/**75** 1997/**76**
- **JAMES STOCKDALE** War hero. (Galesburg, IL) He was a vice admiral in the Navy, shot down on his second combat tour of North Vietnam and was a POW for eight years, four in solitary confinement. He was awarded the Medal of Honor and 26 combat decorations. He was Ross Perot's choice for a running mate in the 1992 presidential election. Year/Age: 1995/**72** 1996/**73** 1997/**74**
- **JOHNNY CONTARDO** Singer. (NYC) Of SHA NA NA. Their biggest hit: "Just Like Romeo & Juliet" in 1975. Year/Age: 1995/**44** 1996/**45** 1997/**46**
- **DON McNEILL** Was host of radio's "The Breakfast Club." He would tell listeners to "march around the breakfast table." He has been on a campaign to raise money to fight Alzheimer's disease. His wife died from it. Year/Age: 1995/**88** 1996/**89** 1997/**90**
- **ELIZABETH HARTMAN** Actress. (1941-1987 – Boardman, OH) Academy Award nomination for *A Patch of Blue* in 1965. Committed suicide. (Died 6-11-87.)
- **TIM HARDIN** Singer/songwriter. (1941-1980 – Eugene, OR) He was found dead of a heroin overdose in his Hollywood apartment. He had one hit in the top 100: "Simple Song of Freedom" in 1969. He wrote "If I Were a Carpenter," a hit for Bobby Darin. (Died 12-29-80.)
- **CONNIE MACK** Former baseball catcher. (1862-1956 – Born Cornelius McGillicuddy in East Brookfield, MA) He was manager of the Philadelphia A's for 50 years, winning 9 pennants. His best year, as catcher for Washington, was in 1889 when he batted .293 and earned $2,750.

FACTS FROM THE PAST

1783 **GEORGE WASHINGTON** resigned as Commander-in-Chief of the U.S. Army and retired to his home at Mount Vernon, VA, with no inkling that he would be drafted to be President 6 years later.

1823 The poem, *A Visit from St. Nicholas*, by **CLEMENT CLARKE MOORE**, was published anonymously in the Troy, NY, *Sentinel.* The poem is also called *Twas the Night Before Christmas.*

1888 Gifted artist **VINCENT VAN GOGH**, living in France, became angry with Rachel, a prostitute, and hacked off part of his left ear with a very rusty razor. He then wrapped the ear in a package and sent it to her with a note to "keep this object carefully." The girl opened the package, thinking it was a gift, and when she saw the bloody mess, she fainted. From then on, Van Gogh deteriorated, and two years later he committed suicide.

1947 The **TRANSISTOR WAS INVENTED** by **JOHN BARDEEN, WILLIAM SHOCKLEY**, and **WALTER BRATTAIN** of Bell Laboratories. It replaced the bulkier vacuum tube and led the way for more compact integrated circuits.

1969 After meeting through an A&R executive, **ELTON JOHN AND BERNIE TAUPIN** began writing together. Their union was a result of both failing to find work after answering the same ad looking for writers.

1972 The **WORLD RECORD** for consecutive push-ups was set by **RICHARD KNECHT**. He did 25,222 on a hard surface without pinned feet. It took the 8 year old 11 hours and 14 minutes.

1986 Baseball players started **SELLING THEIR AUTOGRAPHS** to admiring fans who also paid to get into baseball card shows.

1986 Weary and battered from 9 days of hazardous flight, the **VOYAGER AIRCRAFT** touched down at Edwards Air Force Base, CA, with pilots **DICK RUTAN** and **JEANA YEAGER** becoming the first ever to circle the globe without refueling.

DECEMBER 24

Christmas Eve

BIRTHDAYS

- **LULUBELLE** C&W. (Born Myrtle Cooper in Bonne, NC) Of "Lulubelle & Scotty" fame. Year/**Age:** 1995/**82** 1996/**83** 1997/**84**

- **MIKE CURB** Corporate Head/Policitan. Biggest hit: "Burning Bridges" in 1971. He was president of MGM Records and Warner Records and was elected Lt. Governor of CA in 1978. Remember when Gov. Jerry Brown was afraid to leave the state for fear of what Mike might do wrong while he was away? Year/**Age:** 1995/**51** 1996/**52** 1997/**53**

- **ANTHONY S. FAUCI** Federal Health Administrator. (Brooklyn, NY) Year/**Age:** 1995/**55** 1996/**56** 1997/**57**.

- **BILL ROGERS** Marathon runner. Year/**Age:** 1995/**48** 1996/**49** 1997/**50**

- **HENRY VESTINE** Guitarist. (Los Angeles, CA) With CANNED HEAT. Hit: "Going Up the Country" in 1968. Year/**Age:** 1995/**50** 1996/**51** 1997/**52**

- **MARY HIGGINS CLARK** Author of suspense novels including *Remember Me* and *All Around the Town.* Year/**Age:** 1995/**64** 1996/**65** 1997/**66**

- **JOHN "TOOZ" MATUSZAK** Football star/actor. (1950-1989 – Milwaukee, WI) Defensive lineman during late 1970s for then-Oakland Raiders. Film appearances included *North Dallas Forty, Caveman, Ice Pirates,* and *One Man Force.* Wrote his autobiography *Cruisin with the Tooz,* in 1987.

- **LEE DORSEY** Singer. (1924-1986 – Born Irving Lee Dorsey in New Orleans, LA) He was a fighter under the name "Kid Chocolate" in the 1950's. Biggest hit: "Ya Ya" in 1961. (Died 12-1-86.)

- **NICHOLAS MEYER** Director/novelist. (New York, NY) *Star Trek II.* Author and screenwriter for *Seven Per-Cent Solution.* Year/**Age:** 1995/**50** 1996/**51** 1997/**52**

- **CAROL HANEY** Actress. (1924-1964) American dancer and choreographer to Gene Kelly. She appeared in *Kiss Me Kate* and *Pajama Game.* (Died 5-1-64.)

- **ROBERT JOFFREY** Choreographer. (1930-1988 – Seattle, WA) Built the Joffrey Ballet into one of the nation's top companies, today ranking with the NYC Ballet and American Ballet Theater. (Died 3-25-88.)

- **AVA GARDNER** Actress. (1922-1990 – Born Lucy Johnson in Smithfield, NC) She was nominated for best actress in 1953 for *Mogambo.* She starred in more than 60 films, including *The Barefoot Contessa, Night of the Iguana,* and *On the Beach.* She was just as famous for her three husbands, Mickey Rooney, band leader Artie Shaw, and Frank Sinatra. Died of pneumonia in London on 1-25-90.

- **HOWARD ROBARD HUGHES** Aviator/billionaire. (1905-1976 – Houston, TX) He backed actress Katharine Hepburn in *The Philadelphia Story* in 1941. His "Spruce Goose" (largest plane ever built) has been on display next to the Queen Mary in Long Beach, CA.; it was moved to Oregon in 1992. He had a Chrysler with a pure air filtering system (he refused to be in a room or a car without clean air, which kept him a recluse throughout most of his life). When his father died, Howard bought out all the shareholders in his father's drill company. Eventual profits from that company totaled $746 million. He died enroute on a chartered plane from Acapulco, Mexico, to a Houston hospital, leaving no will (4-5-76).

FACTS FROM THE PAST

1814 The **WAR OF 1812 ENDED** when the U.S. and Britain signed the **TREATY OF GHENT** in Belgium. Word of the treaty failed to reach British forces, which attacked New Orleans on January 8, 1815, an attack that was repulsed by the Americans and inspired the song "The Battle of New Orleans" by Johnny Horton.

1865 The **KU KLUX KLAN** was founded in a cellar of a ruined mansion in Tennessee. Six of the founding members were high-ranking Confederates who had a defeated air about them. They claimed it was a social club designed to cheer up mothers and girls. The first Grand Wizard was General Nathan B. Forrest, a slave trader.

1871 **GIUSEPPE VERDI**'s opera *Aida* had its world premiere in Cairo, Egypt, to celebrate the opening of the Suez Canal.

1906 Canadian-born physicist **REGINALD FESSENDEN** became the first person to broadcast a music program over radio, from Brant Rock, MA.

1908 The Mayor of New York City **REVOKED THE LICENSES OF 550 MOVIE HOUSES,** forcing them to agree not to give Sunday performances or show "immoral" films.

1920 Opera star **ENRICO CARUSO** gave what was to be his last public performance at the Metropolitan Opera in New York City.

1943 Pres. Franklin D. Roosevelt announced that Gen. **DWIGHT D. EISENHOWER** would command the Allied invasion of Europe.

1955 The **LENNON SISTERS** were guest vocalists on "The Lawrence Welk Show." The response was so great that they became regulars on the show for 13 years.

1961 "The Lion Sleeps Tonight" by the **TOKENS** became the first African song to reach #1 on the American pop charts. It was first heard in the U.S. by **THE WEAVERS** under the title "Winoweh" (wihn'-oh-way) in 1951. Robert John also had a top-ten version in 1972.

1967 Joe Namath became the first quarterback to pass for 4,000 yards. He threw for 343 yards in the Jets' 42-31 win over San Diego.

1968 The 3-man crew of **APOLLO 8** sent back a prayer for "Peace on Earth" from outer space. **BILL ANDERS** read from the *Bible.*

1972 **MANFRED MANN**'s University of Miami concert was cut short by police, who pulled the plug at curfew. Angry students rioted for over two hours.

DECEMBER 25
Christmas Day

Ho ho ho. Imagine Santa Claus using Grecian Formula.

BIRTHDAYS

- **RICKEY HENDERSON** Baseball star. (Chicago, IL) Oakland A's power hitter. American League MVP in 1990. Traded to the Toronto Blue Jays in 1993. Year/Age: 1995/**37** 1996/**38** 1997/**39**

- **ROBIN CAMPBELL** Singer. (England) UB40. Biggest hit: "Red Red Wine." They got the group name from a British unemployment form. Year/Age: 1995/**41** 1996/**42** 1997/**43**

- **BARBARA MANDRELL** Entertainer. (Houston, TX) Her biggest pop hit was "If Loving You is Wrong" in 1979. Year/Age: 1995/**47** 1996/**48** 1997/**49**

- **NOEL REDDING** Bass guitarist. (England) With the JIMI HENDRIX EXPERIENCE, "All Along the Watch Tower." Year/Age: 1995/**50** 1996/**51** 1997/**52**

- **SISSY SPACEK** Actress. (Born Mary Elizabeth Spacek in Quitman, TX) She was a baton twirler and homecoming queen in high school. Sissy was nominated for best actress in *Carrie*, *Missing*, *Crimes of the Heart,* and *The River* and won an Oscar for *Coalminer's Daughter*, based on Loretta Lynn's life. Was in the film *J.F.K*, *The Long Walk Home*, *Trading Mom,* and also, voice of the brain in the Steve Martin film, *The Man with Two Brains*. Year/Age: 1995/**46** 1996/**47** 1997/**48**

- **GARY SANDY** Actor. (Dayton, OH) He played Stacy Reddin on the soap opera "Secret Storm" and Andy Travis, P.D. on "WKRP in Cincinnati." Year/Age: 1995/**50** 1996/**51** 1997/**52**

- **ANNIE LENNOX** Singer. (Scotland) Also composer, keyboard and flute player for the EURYTHMICS. The name comes from a dance form that taught children music through movement. Their biggest hit: "Sweet Dreams Are Made of This" in 1983. She was in the film *Revolution* with Al Pacino. Year/Age: 1995/**41** 1996/**42** 1997/**43**

- **JIMMY BUFFET** Singer. (Mobile, AL) Biggest hit: "Margaritaville" in 1977. He owns a store, selling a line of his own tropical clothing. He has written two books and had a bit part in the film *Cobb*. Year/Age: 1995/**49** 1996/**50** 1997/**51**

- **KEN STABLER** Football. (Foley, AL) With the Oakland Raiders. Year/Age: 1995/**50** 1996/**51** 1997/**52**

- **LARRY CSONKA** Football star. (Stow, OH) Played for the Miami Dolphins and NY Giants and rushed for over 7,000 yards in his career. Year/Age: 1995/**49** 1996/**50** 1997/**51**

- **TONY MARTIN** Singer. (Born Alfred Morris in San Francisco, CA) He and actress/dancer Cyd Charisse have one of Hollywood's longest marriages. His biggest hit was "There's No Tomorrow" in 1949. Year/Age: 1995/**82** 1996/**83** 1997/**84**

- **CAB CALLOWAY** Entertainer. (Born Cabell Calloway in Rochester, NY) Appears in Janet Jackson video, "Alright." Known for his "hi-de-ho" scat singing. His theme: "Minnie the Moocher." Year/Age: 1995/**88** 1996/**89** 1997/**90**

- **MIKE MAZURKI** Actor. (1909-1990 – Born Mikhail Mazurwski of Ukrainian descent in Tarnopal, Austria) A character actor and former heavyweight wrestler. He appeared in *Davy Crockett*, *Donavan's Reef* and many others. (Died 12-9-90.)

- **ANWAR SADAT** Leader. (1918-1981 – Egypt) Nobel Prize winner. Assassinated (10-6-81.).

- **ROBERT RIPLEY** (1893-1949, Born Leroy Ripley– Santa Rose, CA) Creator of *Ripley's Believe It or Not* in 1918. His favorite "Believe It Or Not" was: Neils Paulson from Sweden, who died in 1907 at the age of 160, left two sons . . . one nine years old and the other 103 years old. (Died 5-27-49.)

- **CHRIS KENNER** Singer. (1929-1976 – Kenner, LA) His biggest hit: "I Like it Like That" in 1961. (Died 1-28-76.)

- **ROD SERLING** Screenwriter. (1924-1975 – Syracuse, NY) Creator of "Twilight Zone." (Died 6-28-75.)

- **CLARA BARTON** American nurse and philanthropist. (1821-1912 – Born Clarissa Harlowe Barton in Oxford, MA) Founder of the American Red Cross. (Died 4-12-12.)

- **ISAAC NEWTON** Inventor. (1642-1727 – England) He got the idea of universal gravity after seeing an apple fall in his garden in 1665. (Died 3-20-1727.)

FACTS FROM THE PAST

1066 **WILLIAM THE CONQUEROR** was crowned King of England. He was the last person ever to invade the British Isles successfully. He made French the language of the court and educated classes, changing forever the way English is spoken.

1776 **GEORGE WASHINGTON'S TROOPS** began to cross the Delaware River for a surprise attack against Hessian forces encamped at Trenton, NJ, leading to the turning point of the American Revolution.

1818 The most popular Christmas carol ever, **"SILENT NIGHT, HOLY NIGHT,"** was sung for the first time in Oberndorf, Austria, composed the day before by obscure Austrian composer **FRANZ GRUBER**. The song was originally composed for the guitar.

1868 Three years after the Civil War ended, President Johnson pardoned all **CONFEDERATE SOLDIERS** and granted them amnesty.

1931 **OPERA** was **BROADCAST OVER THE RADIO** for the first time from the Metropolitan Opera House in New York City. Listeners throughout the U.S. and overseas heard *Hansel & Gretel* by Engelbert Humperdinck, a German composer who died in 1921.

1959 **RINGO STARR** got his wish: a set of drums for Christmas. It was his first.

1968 At 1:10 a.m. EST, after **APOLLO 8** circled the moon for 20 hours, the spacecraft's service propulsion system engine was fired to achieve the velocity required to "escape" from the lunar orbit. Shortly afterwards, Jim Lovell told the world: "Hello, Houston… there is a Santa Claus … we're coming home!"

1977 Israeli Prime Minister Menachem Begin and Egyptian President Anwar Sadat held **PEACE TALKS IN EGYPT**.

1991 **MIKHAIL GORBACHEV** resigned. **BORIS YELTSIN** took control of nuclear weapons and other facets of the former Soviet government.

Tell a bedtime story to someone you love.

DECEMBER 26

National Whiner's Day/IRS Forms Arrive

BIRTHDAYS

- **STEVE ALLEN** Entertainer. (NYC) TV host/composer/author/entertainer. He had a record in the top 40 in 1955 called "Autumn Leaves." He was the host of his own variety show from 1956 to 1961 and was the host of the first "Tonight Show" from 1954 to 1956. He played lead in *The Benny Goodman Story*, but did not play the clarinet in the film, that was Goodman. Allen is an excellent piano player. He writes mysteries with himself as the detective. He is married to actress Jayne Meadows. Year/**Age**: 1995/**74** 1996/**75** 1997/**76**

- **CARLETON FISK** Baseball. (Bellows Falls, VT) In 1990, he became all-time home-run leader among catchers. In the 1991 All-Star Game, he became the oldest to catch and to get a hit in the history of the annual classic. He holds the record for catching in the most games – 2,226 – set in 1993. He was released by the Chicago White Sox 6-28-93. Year/**Age**: 1995/**48** 1996/**49** 1997/**50**

- **OZZIE SMITH** Baseball. (Mobile, AL) In 1992 he made his 10th consecutive All-Star start as shortstop. Year/**Age**: 1995/**41** 1996/**42** 1997/**43**

- **BERNHARD LANGER** Golfer. (Anhausen, Germany) He won his second Masters tournament in 1993. Year/**Age**: 1995/**38** 1996/**39** 1997/**40**

- **ALAN KING** Comedian. (Brooklyn, NY) He appeared regularly on the "Kraft Music Hall," a musical variety show on TV, from 1967 to 1971. In the film *Bonfire of the Vanities*. Year/**Age**: 1995/**68** 1996/**69** 1997/**70**

- **CHRIS CHAMBLISS** Former baseball player. Played first base for the Yankees. Year/Age: 1995/**47** 1996/**48** 1997/**49**

- **JANE LAPOTAIRE** Actress. (England) Tony winner in *Piaf*. Year/Age: 1995/**51** 1996/**52** 1997/**53**

- **RICHARD WIDMARK** Actor. (Sunrise, MN) Widmark was nominated for supporting actor in 1947 for *Kiss of Death*. Starred on TV's "Madigan." Sandy Koufax, former pro baseball pitcher, is his son-in-law. Year/Age: 1995/**81** 1996/**82** 1997/**83**

- **PHIL SPECTOR** Song producer. (NYC) Record producer and member of the TEDDY BEARS when they had a #1 record, "To Know Him is to Love Him" in 1958. Best known for his "Wall of Sound." He produced the big hits for DARLENE LOVE, The PARIS SISTERS, CRYSTALS, RONETTES, and The RIGHTEOUS BROTHERS. Year/Age: 1995/**55** 1996/**56** 1997/**57**

- **HENRY MILLER** Novelist. (1891–1980 – NYC) Controversial American novelist.

- **NORMAN ANGELL** Author. (1874-1967 – England) He wrote *The Great Illusion* in 1910. Nobel Peace Prize winner in 1933. (Died 10-7-67.)

- **MAO TSE TUNG** (1893-1976) Founding father of the People's Republic of China. (Died 9-9-76.)

FACTS FROM THE PAST

1492 The **FIRST SPANISH SETTLEMENT** in the Western Hemisphere was founded at La Navidad, in what is now Haiti, by Christopher Columbus; it was later destroyed by native "Indians."

1776 **GEORGE WASHINGTON'S TROOPS** captured 1,000 Hessians in an American Revolutionary War battle at Trenton, NJ. A famous painting, *George Washington Crossing the Delaware,* was inspired by this battle.

1799 The late **GEORGE WASHINGTON WAS EULOGIZED** by Colonel Henry Lee as "First in war, first in peace and first in the hearts of his countrymen."

1865 **JAMES NASON** of Franklin, MA, **INVENTED THE COFFEE PERCOLATOR.**

1908 **JACK JOHNSON** became the first African-American heavyweight champion when he knocked out Tommy Burns in the 14th round in Rushcutter Bat, Australia.

1924 **JUDY GARLAND**, $2^1/_2$ years old, then billed as Baby Frances, made her debut as part of the family's vaudeville act on the New Grand Theatre stage, managed by her father.

1941 **BOBBY RIGGS** won his first pro tennis game. He beat world champion **FREDERICK PERRY**.

1963 The **BEATLES'**, "I Want To Hold Your Hand," was released. It became their first U.S. smash.

1967 The **BEATLES'** first self-directed film, **MAGICAL MYSTERY TOUR,** premiered on the BBC in black and white.

1968 **LED ZEPPELIN** begin their first U.S. tour.

1972 **HARRY S. TRUMAN,** 33rd U.S. President, died at the age of 88.

1972 The **BIGGEST-RECORDED INDIVIDUAL MONEY LOSS** took place when **ARTHUR DECIO** of Elkhart, IN, lost $25 MILLION DOLLARS due to a drop in the stock market.

1989 The U.S. ordered loud **ROCK AND ROLL MUSIC** to be played outside the Vatican Embassy in Panama **IN HOPES OF DRIVING GENERAL MANUEL NORIEGA** out of the Embassy. The U.S. Justice Department asked that all nations freeze the bank accounts of Noriega. It was reported that Noriega had eluded American pursuers for days by driving around in cars and hiding in six private homes before arranging to meet a Vatican representative at a local Dairy Queen.

DECEMBER 27

Question Authority!

BIRTHDAYS

- **KARLA BONOFF** Singer/songwriter. (Los Angeles, CA) Biggest hit: "Personally" in 1982. Year/**Age**: 1995/**43** 1996/**44** 1997/**45**
- **TOVAH FELDSHUH** Actress. (NYC) *Fiddler on the Roof* and *Cheaper to Keep Her*. Year/**Age**: 1995/**43** 1996/**44** 1997/**45**
- **COKIE ROBERTS** (Born Corinne Boggs in Washington, D.C.) ABC news correspondent, panelist on "this Week With David Brinkley" and senior political analyst for National Public Radio. Year/**Age**: 1995/**52** 1996/**53** 1997/**54**
- **SCOTTY MOORE** Guitarist. Guitarist for Elvis. Year/**Age**: 1995/**62** 1996/**63** 1997/**64**
- **JOHN AMOS** Actor. (Newark, NJ) He appeared in TV's "Good Times," and miniseries "Roots." Also appeared in *Die Hard II*. Year/**Age**: 1995/**54** 1996/**55** 1997/**56**
- **MICK JONES** Guitarist. From the group FOREIGNER. Biggest hit: "I Want To Know What Love Is," 1984. Year/**Age**: 1995/**51** 1996/**52** 1997/**53**
- **PETER QUAIFE** Bassist. (England) KINKS' biggest hit: "Come Dancing" in 1983. Year/**Age**: 1995/**52** 1996/**53** 1997/**54**
- **MIKE PINDER** Singer. (England) Keyboard and vocalist from the group MOODY BLUES. Their biggest hit: "Nights in White Satin" in 1972. Year/**Age**: 1995/**54** 1996/**55** 1997/**56**
- **ANNA RUSSELL** Singer/comedienne. (England) She satirized opera singing. Wrote *The Power of Being a Positive Stinker*. Year/**Age**: 1995/**84** 1996/**85** 1997/**86**

- **ARTHUR KENT** TV journalist. (Canada) Known for his Gulf War reports during the missile attacks, when he was nicknamed the "Scud Stud." Fired by NBC for refusing an assignment in Croatia. Year/**Age**: 1995/**42** 1996/**43** 1997/**44**
- **GERARD DEPARDIEU** Actor. (France) Films include *Green Card* and *1492*. Year/**Age**: 1995/**47** 1996/**48** 1997/**49**
- **ROY WHITE** Ex-Yankee outfielder. Year/**Age**: 1995/**52** 1996/**53** 1997/**54**
- **WILLIAM MASTERS** Sex researcher. (Cleveland, OH) Of "Masters and Johnson." Year/**Age**: 1995/**80** 1996/**81** 1997/**82**
- **OSCAR LEVANT** Pianist/composer. (1906-1972 – Pittsburgh, PA) Films *Rhapsody in Blue* and *American in Paris*. (Died 8-14-72.)
- **MARLENE DIETRICH** Veteran entertainer. (1901 – 1992) (Born Maria Magdelena von Losch in Berlin, Germany) She debuted as tuxedo-clad Lola-Lola in *The Blue Angel*. She was nominated for an Oscar for best actress in *Morocco* in 1930. (Died 5-6-92.)
- **SIDNEY GREENSTREET** Actor. (1879-1954 – England) He received an Oscar nomination in 1941 for supporting actor in *The Maltese Falcon*. (Died 1-19-54.)
- **LOUIS PASTEUR** Chemist and bacteriologist. (1822-1895 – Dole, France) Responsible for the pasteurization process of milk. Father of microbiology and the first to prove that diseases are caused by germs. His professors rated him as a mediocre student destined for routine work. (Died 9-28-1895.)

FACTS FROM THE PAST

1831 CHARLES DARWIN and the H.M.S. *Beagle* embarked on a trip that revolutionized people's thinking and **LED TO THE THEORY CALLED EVOLUTION.**

1845 ETHER was first administered for childbirth by Dr. Crawford Long in Jefferson, GA, who gave it to his wife, and she successfully gave birth to a baby girl.

1900 CARRY NATION, a militant prohibitionist, busted up the Carey Hotel bar in Wichita, KS, shouting "Peace on earth, good will to men." She used a cane and an iron rod to break bottles and furnishings and generally wreak havoc.

1908 THE WORLD DIDN'T END, even though followers of "prophet" Lee J. Spangler had been assured it would. They all had purchased special white gowns and sat atop a mountain, waiting for God to carry them home.

1932 New York City welcomed the grand opening of **RADIO CITY MUSIC HALL.**

1947 "HOWDY DOODY TIME" debuted on network television. It was originally called the "Puppet Television Theater," and was one of the first TV shows for children. The character "Fluba Dub" from the show was a combination of eight animals: hair from the raccoon; whiskers from a cat; neck from a giraffe; flippers from the seal; ears of a cocker spaniel; tail of a pig; memory of an elephant; and, the body of a dachshund. The show's host was Buffalo Bob.

1971 SONNY & CHER nabbed a variety show on CBS-TV after a successful summer replacement series.

1975 While TED NUGENT was performing in Spokane, a man with a .44 Magnum pointed a gun at him. The man was immobilized by fans and police before he could shoot.

1983 POPE JOHN PAUL met with the man who had shot him, Mehmet Ali Agca, and forgave him.

1985 American naturalist, DIAN FOSSEY, who had studied gorillas in the wild, was found hacked to death at a research station in Rwanda. The film **GORILLAS IN THE MIST** told her story.

1987 Sportscaster GAYLE STERENS broadcast the **FIRST FEMALE PLAY-BY-PLAY OF AN NFL GAME** on NBC. The score was Kansas City 41, Seattle 20.

1992 Entertainer HARRY CONNICK, JR., was arrested at Kennedy Airport in New York City after telling authorities he had an unloaded 9mm pistol in his luggage. He said his sister gave it to him and he forgot he had it.

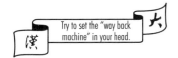

DECEMBER 28

BIRTHDAYS

- **DENZEL WASHINGTON** Actor. (Mt. Vernon, NY) TV's "St. Elsewhere." He won an Oscar for the film *Glory* and was nominated for an Oscar for *Malcolm X*. Also appeared in , *Much Ado About Nothing*, *The Pelican Brief*, and *Philadelphia* Year/**Age**: 1995/**41** 1996/**42** 1997/**43**

- **ROEBUCK STAPLES** Guitarist. (Winoma, MS) With his sons and daughters, he formed the STAPLE SINGERS in 1970. Biggest hits: "I'll Take You There" and "Let's Do It Again." Year/**Age**: 1995/**80** 1996/**81** 1997/**82**

- **MAGGIE SMITH** Actress. (England) She won an Oscar in 1969 for best actress in *The Prime of Miss Jean Brodie*. Also in *Room With A View*, in *Sister Act* as Mother Superior, and *The Secret Garden*. Year/**Age**: 1995/**61** 1996/**62** 1997/**63**

- **EDGAR WINTER** Entertainer. (Beaumont, TX) Biggest hit: "Frankenstein" in 1973. Year/**Age**: 1995/**49** 1996/**50** 1997/**51**

- **JOHNNY OTIS** Singer. (Born Johnny Veliotes in Berkeley, CA) His biggest hit: "Willie & the Hand Jive" in 1958. Year/**Age**: 1995/**74** 1996/**75** 1997/**76**

- **LEW AYRES** Comedian/actor. (Minneapolis, MN) American leading man of the 1930's and 1940's, although his career suffered during WWII when he declared himself a "conscientious objector." He was in the *Dr. Kildare* movies, *Johnny Belinda*, and *Advise and Consent*. Year/**Age**: 1995/**87** 1996/**88** 1997/**89**

- **MARTIN MILNER** Actor. (Detroit, MI) He appeared in some movies and on TV in "Life of Riley," "Route 66," and "Adam 12." Year/**Age**: 1995/**68** 1996/**69** 1997/**70**

- **LOU JACOBI** Actor. (Canada) He was on the "Dean Martin Show" and "Somerset," the first serial spin-off from another serial, "Another World." In the 1990 film *Avalon*. Year/**Age**: 1995/**82** 1996/**83** 1997/**84**

- **JOE DIFFIE** C&W singer. (Tulsa, OK) Year/**Age**: 1995/**37** 1996/**38** 1997/**39**

- **LEE BOWMAN** Actor. (1914-1979, Cincinnati, OH) Films include *Smash-Up* in 1947 co-starring Susan Hayward. (Died 12-25-79.)

- **HUBIE GREEN** Pro golfer. (Born Hubert Green in Birmingham, AL) Year/**Age**: 1995/**49** 1996/**50** 1997/**51**

- **SAM LEVENSON** Author. (1911-1980 – NYC) TV's "Sam Levenson Show." Wrote the best seller *Sex and the Single Child*. (Died 8-27-80.)

- **MANUEL PUIG** Author. (1932-1990 – Argentina) 1979 novel *Kiss of the Spider Woman*. (Died 7-22-90.)

- **DORSEY BURNETT** Singer. (1932-1979 – Memphis, TN) Biggest hit: "Tall Oak Tree" in 1960. He was part of the JOHNNY BURNETTE TRIO before going on his own in 1960. (Died 8-17-79.)

- **CHARLIE WEAVER** Comic. (1905-1974 – Real name was Cliff Arquette) He was a frequent "Tonight Show" guest when Jack Paar was host and on "Hollywood Squares."

- **THOMAS WOODROW WILSON** 28th U.S. President. (1856-1924 – Born in Staunton, PA) Twice elected to the U.S. Presidency. He suffered a paralytic stroke in 1919 and never regained his health. There was speculation that his wife was running the government during his illness. (Died 2-3-24.)

- **EARL "FATHA" HINES** Pianist. (1905-1983 – Duquesne, PA) He was a jazz pianist who influenced generations of musicians with his innovative "trumpet-style" right-hand notes played atop strong octaves. A Chicago DJ called him "Fatha" in the 1930's and the nickname stayed with him. Bill Eckstine sang with his band from 1939-43 and Earl taught Stan Kenton to play the piano. (Died 4-22-83.)

FACTS FROM THE PAST

1732 The *Pennsylvania Gazette* carried the first-known advertisement from the first issue of *Poor Richard's Almanac* by Richard Saunders, a.k.a. **BENJAMIN FRANKLIN**. It was published through the year 1758 and has been imitated many times since.

1832 Vice President **JOHN CALHOUN**, having serious disagreements with President Andrew Jackson, resigned his office. He was the **FIRST TO RESIGN FROM THE VICE PRESIDENCY.**

1869 **CHEWING GUM WAS PATENTED** by Dr. **WILLIAM SEMPLE**, a dentist in Mount Vernon, OH. (History didn't record the flavor!) The patent, which was strictly honest, referred to "a combination of rubber with other articles."

1949 "That Wonderful Guy" debuted on ABC television. It was a situation comedy about a young would-be actor who gets a job as valet to a pompous, overbearing theatre critic. The show wasn't a hit, but the young actor who played the part of Harold, the valet—**JACK LEMMON**—went on to become one of the top motion picture stars ever, winning two Academy Awards.

1962 **PRESIDENT JOHN F. KENNEDY** flew to Miami to greet the first Cuban prisoners released by Fidel Castro in exchange for American ransom after the Bay of Pigs fiasco.

1973 Alexander Solzhenitsyn published **GULAG ARCHIPELAGO**, an expose of the Soviet prison system, which led to his expulsion from the Soviet Union. He's been living in Vermont.

1979 **PRESIDENT JIMMY CARTER** accused the Soviet Union of "gross intervention" in Afghanistan's internal affairs following the Russians' large scale military airlift into the nation. Carter used the emergency Hotline, telling Soviet Leader Brezhnev that, if not corrected, the Soviet takeover of Afghanistan would have serious consequences in U.S./Soviet relations.

1981 Elizabeth Jordan Carr, the **FIRST AMERICAN TEST-TUBE BABY**, was born in Norfolk, VA. **LOUISE BROWN**, the **WORLD'S FIRST TEST-TUBE BABY** was born in Oldham, England, in 1978.

1992 Somalia's two main warlords, Mohamed Farrah **AIDID** and Ale Mahdi **MOHAMED** promised to end their hostilities.

DECEMBER 29

How much wood could you chuck?

BIRTHDAYS

- **MARY TYLER MOORE** Actress. (Brooklyn, NY) She once played an elf in a TV commercial. She started out as the "legs" on the "Richard Diamond" series in the 1950's; her face was never seen. She wound up 20 years later as a multi-million-dollar TV tycoon. She won an Emmy in 1966 for "The Dick Van Dyke Show" and many others for the "Mary Tyler Moore Show," including "actress of the year" in 1974. Year/**Age**: 1995/**59** 1996/**60** 1997/**61**

- **JON VOIGHT** Actor. (Yonkers, NY) He received an Oscar nomination for best actor in 1969 for *Midnight Cowboy* for which he received $17,000, and one in 1978 for *Coming Home*. Year/**Age**: 1995/**57** 1996/**58** 1997/**59**

- **RAY NITCHKE** Former Green Bay Packer. Year/**Age**: 1995/**59** 1996/**60** 1997/**61**

- **GELSEY KIRKLAND** Prima ballerina. (Bethlehem, PA) Wrote the book *Dancing On My Grave*. Acting debut on "L.A. Law" in 1994. Year/**Age**: 1995/**43** 1996/**44** 1997/**45**

- **ED FLANDERS** Actor. (Minneapolis, MN) He won an Emmy in 1976 for *A Moon for the Misbegotten* and, in 1977 for playing Harry Truman in *Plain Speaking* on PBS. Starred on TV's "St. Elsewhere." Year/**Age**: 1995/**61** 1996/**62** 1997/**63**

- **TED DANSON** Emmy winner. (San Diego, CA) Played Sam Malone on TV's "Cheers." Ted was not the original choice for the role. William DeVane of "Knots Landing" was asked first. Films include: *Pontiac Moon, Three Men and A Baby, Cousins, Dad, Three Men and A Little Lady, Made in America,* and *Getting Even With Dad*. Year/**Age**: 1995/**48** 1996/**49** 1997/**50**

- **TOM JARRIEL** ABC news correspondent. Year/**Age**: 1995/**60** 1996/**61** 1997/**62**

- **INGA SWENSON** Actress. (Omaha, NE) Played Gretchen Kraus on TV's "Benson." Year/**Age**: 1995/**63** 1996/**64** 1997/**65**

- **WILLIAM G. BADDIS** Author. (NYC) His novels include *Carpenters Gothic* and *The Recognitions*. Year/**Age**: 1995/**73** 1996/**74** 1997/**75**

- **RAY THOMAS** Singer. From the MOODY BLUES. (England) Their biggest hit: "Nights in White Satin" in 1972. Year/**Age**: 1995/**54** 1996/**55** 1997/**56**

- **MARIANNE FAITHFUL** Entertainer. (England) Her biggest hit was "As Tears Go By" in 1964. Mick Jagger was her boyfriend at the time and gave her the song to record. Later, the ROLLING STONES recorded it and had a bigger hit. Year/**Age**: 1995/**49** 1996/**50** 1997/**51**

- **YVONNE ELLIMAN** Singer. (Honolulu, HI) Played Mary Magdalene on stage in rock opera *Jesus Christ, Superstar*. Sang backing vocals on Eric Clapton's "I Shot the Sheriff." Biggest hit: "If I Can't Have You." Year/**Age**: 1995/**42** 1996/**43** 1997/**44**

- **PABLO CASALS** Cellist. (1876-1973 – Spain) (Died 10-22-73.)

- **ANDREW JOHNSON** 17th U.S. President. (1808-1875 – Raleigh, NC) He became president upon Abraham Lincoln's assassination and was the only U.S. president to be impeached and acquitted. He was a tailor by trade and made all his own clothes. (Died 7-31-1875.)

FACTS FROM THE PAST

1890 The **WOUNDED KNEE MASSACRE** took place in South Dakota, and more than 200 American Indians (men, women, and children) were massacred by the U.S. 7th Cavalry. Government efforts to suppress ceremonial religious practice had resulted in the death of Chief Sitting Bull on December 15, 1890, which further inflamed the unhappy Indians and culminated in this slaughter.

1903 The **FIRST MOVIE SERIAL SHORT FEATURE**, *Adventures of Kathlyn*, appeared in a Chicago theater (part 1 of 13 parts).

1903 Joseph Karwowski in Herimer, NY, filed a patent for a **"METHOD OF PRESERVING THE DEAD."** He first surrounded the corpse with a thick layer of sodium silicate. After the corpse was enclosed, he allowed it to remain for a short time within a chamber having a dry heat temperature, evaporating the water from the encasing layer. Then he applied molten glass to a desired thickness. The body would be kept in this visible state indefinitely. He added that the same method could be used to preserve only the head.

1930 **FRED NEWTON** became the first and only person to **SWIM THE LENGTH OF THE MISSISSIPPI RIVER**. It took him about six months to cover the 1,826 miles from Minnesota to New Orleans. He was in the water for 742 hours and was protected from the cold water by a layer of axle grease on his body.

1980 **BETTY CASH** and **VICKIE LANDRUM** got **BURNED BY A UFO**, near Houston, Texas. The two women had been driving along a country road when they saw "an extremely bright, luminous object" in the night sky. They stopped the car and, although it was only 40 degrees outside, inside the car it became so hot that they had to turn on the air conditioning . . . and still they felt the heat. After the incident, Cash developed boils on her neck and head, and her hair started to fall out. Both of them suffered burns. Cash's doctor reported that "she had all the signs of radiation poisoning."

1982 Coach **PAUL "BEAR" BRYANT** ended his career with an Alabama win over Illinois 21-15. His 323rd victory in his 38 years of coaching. He died the following month.

1983 **PRINCESS CAROLINE** of Monaco married Italian Stefano Casiraghi (while still awaiting an annulment of her first marriage).

1987 Cosmonaut Yuri Romanenko ended his **RECORD 326-DAY SPACE FLIGHT**.

1992 Governor **MARIO CUOMO** released **JEAN HARRIS**. In 1981 she was convicted of murdering Scarsdale Diet doctor Herman Tarnower.

1992 **DAVID** and **SHARON SCHOO** were arrested as they left the plane at O'Hare International Airport in Chicago, accused of leaving their two young daughters home alone while vacationing in Mexico. The children were put up for adoption.

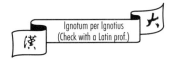

DECEMBER 30

BIRTHDAYS

- **BEN JOHNSON** Sprinter. (Jamaica) Lost his Olympic gold medal when it was found out that the runner for Canada was using steroids. Year/**Age:** 1995/**34** 1996/**35** 1997/**36**
- **TRACEY ULLMAN** Actress. (Slough, England) *I'll Do Anything, Household Saints,* and *Give My Regards To Broad Street,* and "Tracey Ullman Show" on FOX TV. Year/**Age:** 1995/**36** 1996/**37** 1997/**38**
- **DAVY JONES** Singer. (England) The MONKEES. TV series 1966-1968. Group's biggest hit: "I'm a Believer." Davy was in the London cast of *Oliver* broadcast on "Ed Sullivan" Feb. 9, 1964 (the "Beatles" debut). He joined fellow Monkees Peter and Mickey for a comeback in 1987. At one time he was a jockey. Year/**Age:** 1995/**50** 1996/**51** 1997/**52**
- **BARRY ALVAREZ** Football Coach. (Burgettstown, PA) He lead the University of Wisconsin to a Rose Bowl victory over UCLA in 1994. He was then asked to sign a 15-year contract. Year/**Age:** 1995/**49** 1996/**50** 1997/**51**.
- **NOEL STOOKEY** Singer. (Baltimore, MD) He changed his name to "Paul" because "Peter, Noel & Mary" didn't sound right. Their biggest hit was "Leaving on a Jet Plane" in 1969. Year/**Age:** 1995/**58** 1996/**59** 1997/**60**
- **SANDY KOUFAX** L.A. Dodger pitcher. (Brooklyn, NY) At age 36, he became the youngest player ever elected to the Baseball Hall of Fame. He is married to actor Richard Widmark's daughter. Year/**Age:** 1995/**60** 1996/**61** 1997/**62**
- **BO DIDDLEY** Singer. (Born Otha Elias McDaniel in McComb, MS) He's one of the most influential blues artists in recording history. Biggest hit was "Bo Diddley" in 1955. Year/**Age:** 1995/**67** 1996/**68** 1997/**69**
- **JO VAN FLEET** Actress. (Oakland, CA) Won Academy Award for *East of Eden* in 1955. Year/**Age:** 1995/**76** 1996/**77** 1997/**78**

- **JEFF LYNNE** Entertainer/producer. (England) With ELO. Their biggest hit: "Don't Bring Me Down" in 1979. A member of the TRAVELING WILBURYS. Year/**Age:** 1995/**48** 1996/**49** 1997/**50**
- **JOHN HILLERMAN** Actor. (Denison, TX) Higgins on TV's "Magnum, P.I." Year/**Age:** 1995/**63** 1996/**64** 1997/**65**
- **JACK LORD** Actor. (NYC) Best known for the "Hawaii Five-O" TV series. Year/**Age:** 1995/**65** 1996/**66** 1997/**67**
- **SKEETER DAVIS** C&W. (Born Mary Frances Penick in Dry Ridge, KY) Her biggest hit: "The End of The World" in 1963. She once appeared on a Rolling Stones Tour. Year/**Age:** 1995/**64** 1996/**65** 1997/**66**
- **MIKE NESMITH** Video producer. (Houston, TX) Hits with the MONKEES include: "Daydream Believer" and "Last Train to Clarksville." Hit with the FIRST NATIONAL BAND: "Joanne," in 1970. When the song "Valerie" was played on the Monkees TV show, a DJ taped it and played it on his radio show. Fans forced the Monkees to record it. Nesmith refused to be on the record. He said it was the worst song of all time. It hit #3 and was the group's last hit. His mother invented Liquid Paper. Year/**Age:** 1995/**53** 1996/**54** 1997/**55**
- **BERT PARKS** TV host. (1914-1992 – Born Bert Jacobson in Atlanta, GA) For many years, the host of the "Miss America Pageant." His song, "There she is, Miss America," was heard at the pageant for 25 years. He was fired in 1980 when the producers wanted a younger look. He returned in 1990, but had problems lip-syncing the song. (Died 2-2-92.)
- **DEL SHANNON** Singer. (1939-1990 – Born Charles Westover in Coppersville, MI) Biggest hit "Runaway" in 1961, used as the theme on TV's "Crime Story." First artist to cover a Beatle song - "From Me To You." He wrote "I Go To Pieces." Died by a self-inflicted gunshot wound to the head on 2-8-90.

FACTS FROM THE PAST

1853 The U.S. bought 45,000 square miles of land from Mexico in a deal that was called the **GADSDEN PURCHASE** after the man who engineered it, **JAMES GADSDEN**. The area became the southern part of Arizona and New Mexico.

1894 **AMELIA BLOOMER** died at age 76. Born Amelia Jenks, in her marriage to Dexter Bloomer, the young bride vowed to love and honor, but the word "obey" went unsaid. She is best remembered for the type of trouser/dress she promoted, called **BLOOMERS**.

1941 **WINSTON CHURCHILL** arrived in Ottawa, Canada, after his talks with President Roosevelt, over strategy to win the war with Germany. In a speech, he said, "Hitler thought that England would have her neck wrung like a chicken… some chicken… some neck."

1951 The **"ROY ROGERS SHOW"** debuted on NBC-TV. Every week on his Double R Bar Ranch you'd find his horse Trigger, his dog Bullet, and Pat Brady's jeep, Nellybelle.

1954 The 24-minute shot clock was used in professional basketball for the first time in a game between Rochester and a Boston team.

1962 Singer **BRENDA LEE** was injured when she ran into her burning Nashville home to rescue her poodle, Cee Cee. The dog died and the home was destroyed.

1963 The **JOHN F. KENNEDY HALF-DOLLAR** was authorized by Congress.

1965 **FERDINAND MARCOS** was **INAUGURATED** as president of the Philippines.

1972 **PRESIDENT NIXON** ordered a halt in the **BOMBING OF HANOI AND HAIPHONG** and announced that the secret North Vietnamese peace talks would resume in Paris on January 8, 1973.

1978 **WOODY HAYES** was fired as Ohio State's football coach, after punching a player from Clemson University during the Gator Bowl game. The player, Charlie Bauman, had intercepted an Ohio State pass.

1993 **PRESIDENT BUSH** made his final foreign trip in office. He stopped in Somalia to visit U.S. troops aiding famine victims.

DECEMBER 31
New Year's Eve/Leap Second Day/Make Up Your Mind Day

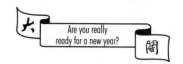
Are you really ready for a new year?

BIRTHDAYS

- **PATTI SMITH** Singer. (Chicago, IL) Her biggest record: "Because the Night," written with Bruce Springsteen. Year/**Age**: 1995/**49** 1996/**50** 1997/**51**

- **REX ALLEN** C&W singer. (Wilcox, AZ) One-time rodeo rider and on the "Barn Dance Show" from WLS in Chicago in the 1940s. He made 32 western films in the 1950s and several hit records, including "Crying in the Chapel." He's in the Cowboy Hall of Fame. Year/**Age**: 1995/**75** 1996/**76** 1997/**77**

- **JOHN DENVER** Singer/composer. (Born Henry John Deutschendorf in Roswell, NM) He changed his name to his favorite city in Colorado while he was a member of the CHAD MITCHELL TRIO. His biggest hit was "Annie's Song" in 1974. Annie was his wife; they broke up in 1982. He was in the movie "Oh God" in 1978. A space buff. Year/**Age**: 1995/**52** 1996/**53** 1997/**54**

- **BEN KINGSLEY** Actor. (England) He won an Oscar in 1982 as best actor in *Gandhi*, and a nomination for *Bugsy*. Also in the films *Sneakers*, *Dave*, and *Schindler's List*. Year/**Age**: 1995/**52** 1996/**53** 1997/**54**

- **JOSEPH MULREY McINTYRE** Singer/dancer. (Needham, MA) NEW KIDS ON THE BLOCK: "I'll Be Loving You (Forever)," "Hangin' Tough," "Step By Step," and "If You Go Away." Year/**Age**: 1995/**23** 1996/**24** 1997/**25**

- **SARAH MILES** Actress. (England) She received an Oscar nomination for best actress in *Ryan's Daughter* in 1970. Year/**Age**: 1995/**52** 1996/**53** 1997/**54**

- **TOM HAMILTON** Bass player. (New Hampshire) AEROSMITH. Year/**Age**: 1995/**44** 1996/**45** 1997/**46**

- **DIANE VON FURSTENBERG** Fashion designer. (Belgium) Year/**Age**: 1995/**49** 1996/**50** 1997/**51**

- **SIR ANTHONY HOPKINS** Actor. (Wales) He appeared in many movies including *The Silence of The Lambs*, for which he won an Oscar. Won an Emmy in 1976 for an NBC world premier movie, *The Lindbergh Kidnapping Case*. He was Van Helsing in Bram Stoker's *Dracula*. Other films: *Legends of the Fall*, *The Innocent*, *August*, *Howard's End*, and *The Remains of the Day*. Year/**Age**: 1995/**58** 1996/**59** 1997/**60**

- **VAL KILMER** Actor. Films *Top Gun*, *The Doors*, *Tombstone*, *Batman Forever*, and *The Real McCoy*. Year/**Age**: 1995/**35** 1996/**36** 1997/**37**

- **TIM MATHESON** Actor. (Los Angeles, CA) TV's "Bonanza," "The Virginian," and "Tucker's Witch." In the movie *Animal House*. Year/**Age**: 1995/**48** 1996/**49** 1997/**50**

- **BURTON CUMMINGS** Lead singer. (Canada) From the group GUESS WHO. Their biggest hit: "American Woman" in 1970. Year/**Age**: 1995/**48** 1996/**49** 1997/**50**

- **DONNA SUMMER** Singer. (Born LaDonna Andrea Gaines in Boston, MA) She hit it big in the German production of *Hair*. Her biggest hit: "Bad Girls" in 1979. She was the only other person, besides Dick Clark, to host the "American Bandstand" which she did in 1979. Year/**Age**: 1995/**47** 1996/**48** 1997/**49**

- **ANDY SUMMERS** Guitarist. (England) Guitarist for the POLICE. Biggest hit: "Every Breath You Take" in 1983. Year/**Age**: 1995/**54** 1996/**55** 1997/**56**

- **JULE STYNE** [joo'-lee styn] Broadway composer/producer. (Born Stein in England) Wrote the scores for *Peter Pan*, *Bells are Ringing*, *Funny Girl*. Year/**Age**: 1995/**90** 1996/**91** 1997/**92**

- **PAT BRADY** Actor. (1915-1972) Roy Rogers jeep-driving sidekick. The jeep's name was "Nellybelle." (Died 2-27-72.)

FACTS FROM THE PAST

1879 Inventor Thomas Edison first demonstrated the **ELECTRIC INCANDESCENT LIGHT** to a New Year's crowd in Menlo Park, NJ.

1929 **GUY LOMBARDO** and his Royal Canadians made their **FIRST ANNUAL NEW YEAR'S EVE BROADCAST** over the CBS radio network from the Roosevelt Grill in New York City.

1943 There was a near-riot of bobbysoxers in New York's Times Square, as **FRANK SINATRA** opened a singing engagement at the Paramount Theater. George Evans handled publicity for Sinatra, and it was his idea to have teenage girls sit in the front row to scream when Frankie came out on the stage.

1946 The **END OF WORLD WAR II** was officially proclaimed by President Harry S. Truman.

1947 **LEONARD SLYE** married **FRANCES SMITH** in Oklahoma. They are better known as **ROY ROGERS AND DALE EVANS.**

1953 **WILLIE SHOEMAKER** set a record for the **MOST RACES WON BY A JOCKEY** in a year – 485.

1961 The **BEACH BOYS** played their **FIRST CONCERT** under that name in Long Beach, CA. The band was previously known as the **PENDLETONES, KENNY AND THE CADETS** and **CARL AND THE PASSIONS.**

1970 **PAUL McCARTNEY SUED** the other three Beatles to dissolve their partnership. The action sparked a bitter feud between McCartney and John Lennon.

1972 **ROBERTO CLEMENTE** of the Pittsburgh Pirates and 4 other people were **KILLED IN A CRASH** of a chartered cargo plane on mission to assist earthquake-devastated Nicaragua.

1985 Singer **RICK NELSON**, his fiancee and five members of his band were **KILLED** when their private plane crashed in Texas.

1986 **DONNA RICE** met **U.S. SENATOR GARY HART** at a New Year's Eve party hosted by Don Henley. This friendship later proved to be a downfall in his presidential bid.

1991 **LEE IACOCCA** stepped down as **CHAIRMAN OF THE CHRYSLER CORPORATION** and Robert Eaton, General Motors Corp. top executive in Europe, was named his successor. Iacocca had held the position for 14 years.

INDEX

Bold type = birthday
Page number references follow date references

B

G

O

PHILLIPS, Mackenzie **Nov. 10**
PHILLIPS, Michelle **April. 6**, Jun. 4
PHILLIPS, Peg Sept 20
PHILLIPS, Phil **Mar. 14**
PHILLIPS, Sam Nov. 22, Dec. 17; 10
PHILLIPS, Stone **Dec. 2**; 113
PHILLIPS, Wade **Jun. 21**
PHILLIPS, Wally **Jul. 7**
PHILLIPS, Wilson Apr. 29, Oct. 16
PHOENIX, Leaf **Oct. 28**
PHOENIX, River **Aug. 23**
PIAZZA, Marguerite **May 6**
PICASSO, Pablo **Oct. 25**
PICCARD, Auguste **Jan. 28**, May 27
PICCARD, Jean Felix **Jan. 28**
PICCARD, Jeanette **Jan. 5**
PICCOLO, Brian **Oct. 31**
PICKENS, Slim **Jun. 29**
PICKETT, Bobby "Boris" **Feb. 10**, Sep. 8, Oct. 10
PICKETT, Wilson Mar. 4, **Mar. 18**; 10
PICKFORD, Jack **Aug. 18**
PICKFORD, Mary **Apr. 8**, Apr. 15, Aug. 13, Aug. 18, Oct. 14, Dec. 9; 78
PIDGEON, Walter **Sep. 23**; 77
PIED PIPERS Nov. 12; 359
PIERCE, Franklin **Nov. 23**
PIERCE, Webb **Aug. 8**
PIERSALL, Jimmy Apr. 14, **Nov. 14**
PIERSON, Kate **Apr. 27**
PIETRO, George Feb. 18
PIHOS, Pete 220
PIKE, Zebulon **Jan. 5**, Nov. 15
PILATUS, Rob **Jun. 8**, Nov. 19
PINA, Ezio 182
PINCAY, Laffit May 5
PINCHOT, Bronson **May 20**
PINCUS, Gregory **Apr. 9**
PINDER, Mike May 4, **Dec. 27**
PINIELLA, Lou **Aug. 28**
PINK FLOYD Jan. 18, Jan. 27, Feb. 17, Mar. 6, Apr. 17, May 2, Jul. 28, Sep. 6, Sep. 30, Nov. 26
PINKERTON, Allan **Aug. 25**
PINKINS, Tonya 186
PINTAURO, Danny **Jan. 6**
PINTER, Harold **Oct. 10**
PINZA, Ezio Apr. 7; 182
PIPP, Wally Jun. 2
PIPPEN, Scottie **Sep. 25**
PIPS May 28, Jun. 2, Sep. 4
PISCOPO, Joe **Jun. 17**
PITNEY, Gene **Feb. 17**, Sep. 12
PITT, Eugene **Nov. 6**
PLACE, Martha M. Mar. 20
PLACE, Mary Kay **Sep. 23**; 291
PLANK, Ed 148
PLANT, Michael Nov. 22
PLANT, Robert Jan. 2, Feb. 2, **Aug. 20**, Sep. 19, Oct. 16
PLANTE, Jacques Nov. 2
PLASMATICS Jan. 18
PLATO, Dana **Nov. 7**
PLATOV, Evgeny Feb. 21
PLATTERS Jan. 17, Apr. 5, Jun. 6, Aug. 10, Oct. 15; 10
PLAYER, Gary **Nov. 1**
PLEASANCE, Donald **Oct. 5**
PLESHETTE, Suzanne **Jan. 31**
PLIMPTON, George **Mar. 18**
PLIMPTON, Martha **Nov. 16**
PLOWHATAN, Chief Apr. 5
PLOWRIGHT, Joan **Oct. 28**; 183
PLUMB, Eve **Apr. 29**
PLUMMER, Amanda **Mar. 23**; 185
PLUMMER, Christopher Mar. 23, **Dec. 13**; 184, 290
PLUNKETT, Jim **Dec. 5**
PLUNKETT, Maryann 186
POCO Jan. 7, Feb. 23, Feb. 28, Mar. 8, Oct. 30, Nov. 24, Dec. 5
PODBORSKI, Steve **Jul. 25**
PODOLOFF, Maurice 148
POE, Edgar Allan **Jan. 19**, Mar. 6, May 16

POGUE, Lt. Feb. 8
POINDEXTER, Buster **Jan. 9**
POINDEXTER, John Jul. 15
POINSETT, Joel Dec. 12
POINTER SISTERS Jan. 23, Mar. 19, Jul. 11, Nov. 30
POINTER, Anita **Jan. 23**
POINTER, Bonnie **Jul. 11**
POINTER, Jun. **Nov. 30**
POINTER, Ruth **Mar. 19**
POITIER, Sidney **Feb. 20**, Mar. 10, Apr. 13, Nov. 3, Dec. 9; 80
POLANSKI, Roman Aug. 9, **Aug. 18**
POLHEMUS, Gretchen Feb. 28
POLHILL, Robert Apr. 22
POLICE Jul. 16, Oct. 2, Dec. 31
POLK, James **Nov. 2**, Dec. 5
POLLACK, Sydney **Jul. 1**; 81
POLLAN, Tracy Jun. 9, **Jun. 22**
POLLARD, Jim 148
POLLARD, Jonathan Jay Jun. 4
POLLARD, Michael **May 30**, Jul. 30
POMUS, Doc 10
PONTI, Carlo Sep. 17, **Dec. 11**
POP, Iggy **Apr. 21**
POPE, Alexander **May 21**
POQUELLOS Jun. 10
PORIZKOVA, Paulina **Apr. 9**
PORTER, Chuck May 9
PORTER, Cole **Jun. 9**
PORTER, Darrel **Jan. 17**
PORTER, David Aug. 20
PORTER, H.V. 148
PORTER, Katherine Anne 287
PORTER, Sylvia **Jun. 18**
PORTER, Terry **Apr. 8**
PORTER, William S. Apr. 25
POST, Charles William **Oct. 26**
POST, Emily **Oct. 3**
POST, Markie **Nov. 4**
POST, Wiley Jun. 23, Jul. 15, Jul. 22, Nov. 4
POSTON, Tom **Oct. 17**; 288
POTTS, Annie **Oct. 28**
POTVIN, Dennis Oct. 29
POUND, Ezra **Oct. 30**
POVICH, Maury **Jan. 17**, Aug. 20
POWELL, Boog **Aug. 17**
POWELL, Colin **Apr. 5**
POWELL, Cynthia Aug. 23
POWELL, Dick Oct. 7
POWELL, Jane **Apr. 1**
POWELL, Laurence Apr. 17, Aug. 4
POWELL, Mike Aug. 30
POWELL, William Aug. 2
POWER, Tyrone Nov. 13
POWERS, Francis Gary May 1, Aug. 19
POWERS, John May 1
POWERS, Mala **Dec. 20**
POWERS, Stefanie Jan. 3, Feb. 10, **Nov. 12**
POWERS, Stephanie Nov. 2 (Correct Date)
POZO-SECO SINGERS May 27
PRADO, Perez Apr. 7, **Dec. 11**
PREMINGER, Otto Nov. 13
PRENTISS, Paula May 22
PRESCOTT, Sam Apr. 18
PRESCOTT, William **Feb. 20**, Jun. 17
PRESLEY, Elvis Jan. 4, Jan. 5, **Jan. 8**, Jan. 10, Jan. 19, Jan. 23, Jan. 28, Feb. 3, Feb. 6, Feb. 10, Feb. 16, Feb. 17, Feb. 22, Feb. 25, Mar. 3, Mar. 5, Mar. 17, Mar. 19, Mar. 21, Mar. 24, Mar. 25, Apr. 3, Apr. 6, Apr. 23, May 1, May 12, May 13, May 16, May 31, Jun. 1, Jun. 5, Jun. 20, Jun. 21, Jun. 26, Jun. 27, Jun. 29, Jul. 1, Jul. 6, Jul. 18, Jul. 20, Aug. 11, Aug. 13, Aug. 16, Aug. 18, Aug. 19, Aug. 27, Sep. 9, Sep. 12, Sep. 13, Sep. 17, Oct. 10, Oct. 20, Oct. 29, Nov. 15, Nov. 22, Nov. 23, Nov. 27, Dec. 4, Dec. 21; 10, 359
PRESLEY, Lisa Marie **Feb. 1**, Aug. 6, Aug. 29
PRESLEY, Priscilla Ann Beaulieu May 1. **May 24**, Aug. 11, Oct. 9
PRESLEY, Reg **Jun. 12**
PRESTON, Billy May 8, Jun. 17, Jul. 23, **Sep. 9**

PRESTON, Johnny **Aug. 18**
PRESTON, Robert **Jun. 8**, Dec. 1, Dec. 19; 183, 184
PRESTON, Kelly **Oct. 13**
PRETENDERS Sep. 4, Sep. 7
PREVIN, Andre Feb. 26, **Apr. 6**, Oct. 22,
PREVIN, Dory **Oct. 22**
PREVIN, Matthew Phineas Feb. 26
PREVIN, Sacha Villiers Feb. 26
PREVIN, Soon Yi Aug. 17
PRICE, Alan **Apr. 19**
PRICE, Leontyne **Feb. 10**; 292
PRICE, Marc **Feb. 23**
PRICE, Mark **Feb. 16**
PRICE, Nicholas **Jan. 28**
PRICE, Ray **Jan. 12**; 326
PRICE, Vincent Dec. 1, Apr. 10, **May 27**, Jul. 23; 181
PRICE, William W. Apr. 24
PRIDE, Charlie **Mar. 18**; 326
PRIEST, Judas Oct. 25
PRIESTLEY, Jason **Aug. 28**; 113
PRIESTLEY, Joseph **Mar. 13**, Jul. 14, Aug. 1
PRIMA, Louie Mar. 9, **Dec. 7**
PRINCE Mar. 23, **Jun. 7**, Jul. 27, Sep. 3, Nov. 7; 77, 219, 325
PRINCE, Faith 186
PRINCE, Harold **Jan. 30**
PRINCIP, Gavrilo Jun. 28
PRINCIPAL, Victoria **Jan. 3**, Mar. 5
PRINE, John **Oct. 10**
PRINZE, Freddie May 23, Jun. 16, **Jun. 22**
PRITCHARD, Charles **Feb. 29**
PRITIKIN, Nathan **Aug. 29**
PROCTER, Harley Apr. 15, Aug. 9
PROFESSOR LONGHAIR 10
PROVOST, Jon **Mar. 12**
PROWSE, Juliet **Sep. 25**
PRUETT, Jeanne **Jan. 30**
PRYCE, Jonathan 185, 186
PRYOR, Rain **Jul. 16**
PRYOR, Richard Jun. 9, Jul. 16, **Dec. 1**
PUCCINI, Giacomo Feb. 17, **Dec. 22**
PUCKETT, Gary **Oct. 17**
PUCKETT, Kirby **Mar. 14**
PUENTO, Tito **Apr. 2**
PUERTA, Joe **Jul. 2**
PUETT, Tommy **Jan. 12**
PUIG, Manuel Dec. 28
PULITZER, Joseph **Apr. 10**, Aug. 17
PULITZER, Peter Feb. 10
PULITZER, Roxanne **Feb. 10**
PULLIAM, Keshia Knight **Apr. 9**
PULLMAN, George **Mar. 3**
PURCELL, Sarah **Oct. 8**
PURDOM, Edmund **Dec. 19**
PURIFY, Bobby **May 12**
PURIFY, James **May 12**
PURL, Linda **Sep. 2**
PUZO, Mario **Oct. 15**; 325
PYLE, Ernie 9, 359

Q

QUAID, Dennis **Apr. 9**, Sep. 29, Nov. 19
QUAID, Randy **Oct. 1**
QUAIFE, Peter **Dec. 27**
QUAN, Ke Huy **Aug. 20**
QUARRY MEN Jun. 15, Oct. 9, Nov. 24
QUATRO, Suzi **Jun. 3**
QUAYLE, Anna **Oct. 6**; 183
QUAYLE, Anthony **Sep. 7**
QUAYLE, Dan Jan. 20, **Feb. 4**, Feb. 11, Mar. 11, May 9, May 19, Jun. 15, Jul. 14, Jul. 29, Aug. 16, Sep. 21, Oct. 5, Oct. 13
QUAYLE, Marilyn **Jul. 29**
QUEEN Jul. 19, Aug. 19, Sep. 5, Nov. 16
QUEEN, Ellery **Oct. 20**
QUEEN, Richard Jul. 11
QUESTION MARK AND THE MYSTERIANS Oct. 7
QUIGLEY, Ernest 148
QUINE, Richard **Nov. 12**
QUINLAN, Karen Anne **Mar. 29**
QUINLAN, Kathleen **Nov. 19**

SLANY, Mary Decker **Aug. 4**
SLASH **Dec. 23**
SLATER, Christian **Aug. 19**
SLATKIN, Leonard Sep. 1
SLAUGHTER, Enos **Apr. 27**
SLAYTON, Donald "Deke" **Mar.** 1, Apr. 9
SLEDGE, Debbie **Jul. 9**
SLEZAK, Erika **Aug. 5**
SLEZAK, Walter 147, 182
SLICK, Grace Jan. 25, Mar. 5, Mar. 19, Apr. 24, May 13, **Oct. 30**, Dec. 15
SLY AND THE FAMILY STONE Mar. 15, Jun. 5, Aug. 14, Aug. 15; 10, 77
SMALL FACES Jan. 30, Apr. 1, Sep. 16
SMALL, Millie **Oct. 6**
SMALLEY, Dave **Jul. 10**
SMALLEY, Roy Sr. **Jun. 9**
SMART, Jean **Sep. 14**
SMIRNOFF, Yakov **Jan. 24**
SMITH, "Buffalo" Bob **Nov. 27**
SMITH, Adam 43, 77
SMITH, Alexis 184
SMITH, Arthur Sep. 13
SMITH, Bessie 10
SMITH, Betty 253
SMITH, Bubba **Feb. 28**
SMITH, Cal **Apr. 7**; 326
SMITH, Carl **Mar. 15**, Sep. 26
SMITH, Cathy Evelyn Sep. 2
SMITH, Connie **Aug. 14**
SMITH, Curt **Jun. 24**
SMITH, Dean 148
SMITH, Dr. Robert Jun. 10
SMITH, Dr. S.F. Jul. 4
SMITH, Ed May 15
SMITH, Emmitt Jan. 30
SMITH, Gen. E. Kirby Jul. 21
SMITH, Hamilton Oct. 26
SMITH, Harry **Aug. 21**
SMITH, Huey "Piano" **Jan. 26**, Aug. 4
SMITH, Hyrum Jun. 27
SMITH, Jaclyn **Oct. 26**
SMITH, John Apr. 26, May 12, May 14
SMITH, Jonathon 115
SMITH, Joseph Aug. 8
SMITH, Kate **May 1**, May 11, May 19, Nov. 11
SMITH, Keeley **Mar. 9**, Dec. 7
SMITH, Lillian 77
SMITH, Liz **Feb. 2**
SMITH, Maggie **Dec. 28**; 80, 81, 186, 393
SMITH, Mandy Jun. 2
SMITH, Margaret Chase Sep. 13
SMITH, Margo **Apr. 9**
SMITH, Michael J. Jan. 28, Jul. 28
SMITH, O.C. **Jun. 21**
SMITH, Ozzie **Dec. 26**
SMITH, Patti **Dec. 31**
SMITH, Perry Nov. 15
SMITH, Randy Feb. 18
SMITH, Rex Jan. 10, Jan. 21, Aug. 21, **Sep. 19**
SMITH, Robyn May 10, **Aug. 14**
SMITH, Roger Apr. 28, Jul. 12
SMITH, Samantha Apr. 25
SMITH, Sammi **Aug. 5**; 326
SMITH, Stan **Dec. 14**
SMITH, Taran Noah **Apr. 8**
SMITH, Will **Sep. 25**
SMITH, William Kennedy Mar. 30, Dec. 11
SMITH, Willie Donnell **Feb. 29**
SMITHERS, Jan **Jul. 3**
SMITHSON, Hugh Jun. 27
SMITHSON, James Jun. 27
SMITHSON, Joseph Aug. 10
SMITS, Jimmy **Jul. 9**; 292
SMOKEY THE BEAR Oct. 6
SMOTHERS BROTHERS Oct. 15, Nov. 20
SMOTHERS, Dick **Nov. 20**
SMOTHERS, Tommy **Feb. 2**
SMYTH, Patty **Jun. 26**
SMYTHE, J. Anthony Apr. 29
SNEAD, Sam Mar. 18, **May 27**
SNEVA, Tom **Jun. 1**
SNIDER, Dee **Mar. 15**
SNIDER, Duke **Sep. 19**

SNIPES, Wesley Aug. 4, Jul. 31
SNODGRASS, Carrie **Oct. 27**
SNODGRASS, W.D. (William Dewitt) **Jan. 5**
SNOW, Hank **May 9**, Oct. 19, Oct. 29
SNOW, Phoebe **Jul. 17**
SNOWDON, Lord (Anthony Armstrong Jones) **Mar. 7**, Mar. 19, May 10 Jul. 6
SNYDER, Jimmy "The Greek" Jan. 15, **Sep. 9**, Dec. 17
SOCRATES **May 12**
SOLTI, Sir Georg Mar. 14, Apr. 16, **Oct. 21**
SOLZHENITSYN, Alexander May 27, Dec. 28
SOMERS, Suzanne Jun. 20, **Oct. 16**
SOMMER, Elke **Nov. 5**
SONDERGUARD, Gale 78
SONDHEIM, Stephen **Mar. 22**; 45
SONNY AND CHER Nov. 14
SONS OF THE PIONEERS Jul. 2
SONTAG, Susan **Jan. 28**
SONY Jun. 21
SONY, Philips And Polygram Mar. 2
SOPWITH, Tom Jun. 28
SORKIN, Arleen **Oct. 14**
SOTHERN, Ann **Jan. 22**, Sep. 14
SOTO, Mario May 17
SOUL STIRRERS Jan. 22, May 5, Dec. 1; 10
SOUL ASYLUM Jan. 20
SOUL, David **Aug. 28**; 77
SOULE, John Feb. 3
SOULJAH, Sister Jun. 13
SOUSA, John Philip Sep. 26, **Nov. 6**
SOUTER, David Oct. 2
SOUTH, Joe **Feb. 28**, Sep. 9; 44
SOVINE, Red Mar. 18, **Jul. 17**
SPACEK, Sissy Feb. 6, **Dec. 25**; 81
SPACEY, Kevin 186
SPAHN, Warren **Apr. 23**, Aug. 11; 254
SPALDING, Al Apr. 25
SPALDING, Albert Feb. 3; 254
SPANGLER, Lee J. Dec. 27
SPANKY & OUR GANG Jun. 19
SPANO, Joe **Jul. 7**
SPARROW, Henry Nov. 24
SPASSKY, Boris **Jan. 30**, Mar. 4, Sep. 1, Sep. 2
SPEAKER, Tris 254
SPEARS, Billy Jo **Jan. 14**
SPECTER, Arlen **Feb. 12**
SPECTOR, Phil Jan. 18, Jul. 22, Aug. 10, **Dec. 26**; 10
SPECTOR, Ronnie Mar. 2, **Aug. 10**
SPELLING, Aaron **Apr. 22**, May 16; 115
SPELLING, Tori **May 16**
SPELTERINA, Signorina Maria Jul. 12
SPENCER DAVIS GROUP **Apr. 3**, May 12, Jun. 14, Aug. 15
SPENCER, Brenda Jan. 29
SPENCER, Jeremy Jun. 15
SPENCER, Lt. Winfield Apr. 7
SPENCER, Susan **Nov. 28**
SPENCER, Tracie **Jul. 12**
SPERRY, Elmer **Oct. 12**
SPIELBERG, Steven Jun. 11, Sep. 10, **Dec. 18**
SPILLANE, Mickey **Mar. 9**; 287
SPINER, Brent **Feb. 2**
SPINETTI, Victor 183
SPINKS, Leon Feb. 15, **Jul. 11**, Sep. 15, Nov. 3
SPINKS, Michael Jun. 27
SPINNERS Aug. 9, Dec. 12
SPIRA, Howard Jul. 4, Jul. 30
SPIRIT Feb. 20
SPITZ, Mark **Feb. 10**, Aug. 28, Sep. 4
SPIVAK, Lawrence **Jun. 11**
SPOCK, Dr. Benjamin Jan. 15, **May 2**, Jul. 11, Jul. 14
SPOOKY TOOTH Apr. 26
SPRINGER, Richard Paul Apr. 13
SPRINGFIELD, Dusty **Apr. 16**
SPRINGFIELD, Rick **Aug. 23**
SPRINGFIELD, Tom **Jul. 2**
SPRINGFIELDS Jul. 2
SPRINGSTEIN, Bruce Jan. 19, Jan. 20, Jan. 28, Feb. 25, Apr. 15, May 13, May 22, Jun. 12, Jun. 18, Jul. 29, Sep. 11, Sep. 20, **Sep. 23**, Oct. 2, Oct. 27, Nov. 4, Dec. 31

SQUIRE, Chris **Mar. 4**
ST. CLAIR, Bob 220
ST. JAMES, Lyn May 24
ST. JAMES, Susan **Aug. 14**, Sep. 6; 77, 289
ST. JOHN, Jill **Aug. 19**
ST. JOHN, Lynn 148
ST. NICHOLAS, Nick **Sep. 28**
STABLER, Ken **Dec. 25**
STACK, Robert **Jan. 13**, Jan. 30, Feb. 18; 288
STACY, Hollis **Mar. 16**
STAFFORD, Jim Sep. 16
STAFFORD, Jo **Nov. 12**
STAFFORD, Susan Feb. 18
STAFFORD, Thomas May 22
STAGG, Amos Alonzo 148
STAHL, Lesley **Dec. 16**
STALEY, Gerry **Aug. 21**
STALIN, Joseph Feb. 4, Mar. 5, Mar. 6, Jul. 17, Nov. 16, Nov. 28
STALLARD, Tracy Sep. 10, Sep. 26
STALLONE, Sylvester Jun. 22, **Jul. 6**, Dec. 16
STAMOS, John **Aug. 19**
STAMP, Terrence **Jul. 22**
STAMPLEY, Joe **Jun. 6**
STANDELLS Feb. 5, May 24, Sep. 18, Oct. 25
STANFORD, William L. Dec. 6
STANG, Arnold Mar. 31, **Sep. 28**
STANKY, Eddie Jan. 7, **Sep. 3**
STANLEY, Henry Morton **Jan. 28**, Mar. 21, Nov. 10
STANLEY, Kim **Feb. 11**
STANLEY, Pat 183
STANLEY, Paul **Jan. 20**
STANTON, Edwin M. Jun. 15
STANTON, Elizabeth Cady Jul. 19, **Nov. 12**
STANTON, Frank 360
STANTON, Harry Dean **Jul. 14**
STANWYCK, Barbara **Jul. 16**; 9, 288, 289, 292
STAPLE SINGERS Dec. 28
STAPLES, Peter **May 3**
STAPLES, Roebuck **Dec. 28**
STAPLETON, Jean **Jan. 19**; 289, 290, 291
STAPLETON, Maureen **Jun. 21**; 81, 182, 184
STARGELL, Willie **Mar. 6**
STARLAND VOCAL BAND May 7, Oct. 25; 45
STARR, Bart **Jan. 9**, Jan. 15; 220
STARR, Kay **Jul. 21**
STARR, Ringo Jan. 11, Jan. 20, Apr. 27, Jun. 17, Jun. 21, Jul. 5, **Jul. 7**, Jul. 23, Aug. 1, Aug. 4, Aug. 18, Aug. 27, Oct. 18, Nov. 6, Nov. 24, Dec. 25
STATLER BROTHERS Jan. 23, Mar. 8, Jun. 5, Aug. 8, Aug. 21
STAUB, Rusty **Apr. 4**
STAUBACH, Roger **Feb. 5**, Dec. 16; 220
STAUTNER, Ernie 220
STEAGALL, Red Mar. 28
STEAM 393
STEEL, Danielle **Aug. 14**; 181
STEELE, David **Sep. 8**
STEELE, Michael **Jun. 2**
STEELE, Tommy **Dec. 17**
STEELY DAN Jan. 10, Feb. 20, Dec. 13
STEEN, Alann Dec. 2
STEENBURGEN, Mary **Feb. 8**; 81
STEIGER, Rod **Apr. 14**, Oct. 18; 80
STEIN, Chris **Jan. 5**
STEIN, Gertrude **Feb. 3**
STEINBECK, John **Feb. 27**
STEINBERG, David **Aug. 9**
STEINBRENNER, George Jan. 3, Jan. 11, Feb. 25, Apr. 28, **Jul. 4**, Jul. 30
STEINEM, Gloria Jan. 29, **Mar. 25**
STEINMETZ, Christian 148
STEINWAY, Henry **Feb. 15**
STEITZ, Edward 148
STEMPEL, Robert Oct. 26
STENERUD, Jan Mar. 9, **Nov. 26**; 220
STENGEL, Casey **Jul. 30**, Oct. 4; 254
STENNIS, John **Aug. 3**
STEPHANIE, Princess Of Monaco **Feb. 1**, Nov. 12
STEPHANOPOULOS, George **Feb. 10**

About Bob Barry

Daily Celebrity Almanac

Author/Researcher

Bill Cosby, Paul McCartney, Burt Reynolds, Ann-Margret, Gregory Peck, Caroline Kennedy, and on and on, ad infinitum. Drop a name . . . almost any famous name, and it will belong to a personality Bob Barry has interviewed in person or by telephone on one of his radio programs. This is just one of the reasons Barry was selected as America's number one radio personality by *Billboard* magazine.

Barry has been involved in all facets of radio and television. He has been acclaimed in countless publications and has received more lines of print in the Milwaukee morning and evening newspapers than any other radio personality in the history of Milwaukee radio.

He has received many awards, including "Outstanding Radio Performer" and "Regional Radio Personality of the Year" (four times). Up against extremely tough competition, he won the much-coveted *Billboard* magazine "International Personality of the Year" award.

Now most of Barry's time is spent gathering information and updates for the *Daily Celebrity Almanac*, used by countless radio and TV personalities throughout the world. Barry also makes announcements for a "Commercial On Hold" company and is one of the voices heard on tape at business establishments across the country. These telephone commercials are designed to inform and entertain clients and prospects while they are on hold. He is also seen and heard in radio and TV commercials around the Midwest area. In 1994, Bob began hosting a weekly half hour TV Infomercial Program seen in Milwaukee and Chicago.

Barry emceed hundreds of concerts throughout the year, including such groups as the Beatles, Dave Clark Five, and the Rolling Stones. Barry is still much in demand for personal appearances before audiences of all ages numerous times each year and is active in many fund-raising events for charity. Some of the proceeds from the *Daily Celebrity Almanac* go to Cystic Fibrosis, where he holds a seat on the Board of Directors. Barry has also been advisor to the annual *Billboard* magazine International Radio Programming Forum in New York City. In his spare time, he hosts celebrity cruises to warm, sunny destinations.